THE BIRDWATCHER'S YEARBOOK 2026

edited by Neil Stratton

www.thebirdwatchersyearbook.co.uk

Published in 2025 by
Neil Stratton
Heiton Mains, Heiton, Scottish Borders TD5 8JR
United Kingdom

01573 450 695 / 07949 132 990
neildstratton@btinternet.com / Neil@thebirdwatchersyearbook.co.uk
www.thebirdwatchersyearbook.co.uk

© Neil Stratton, 2025

ISBN: 978-1-9192312-0-4

Front and back cover illustrations: Sylvie Soudan
Male [formerly Common] Redpoll
Instagram: Sylvie.Soudan

Colour illustrations for *News from the World of Birds*:
  Dan Powell
  01329 668 465
  danpowell11@btinternet.com
  www.powellwildheart.com

Printed and bound in the United Kingdom by
Henry Ling Ltd, The Dorset Press, Dorchester, DT1 1HD

CONTENTS

CONTENTS

In order to help readers find their way around **The Yearbook,** *the various national regions are colour coded and a region's colour is used for the names of its reserves and the margins of its pages.*

PREFACE

Neil Stratton
Editor,
The Birdwatcher's Yearbook

*After starting out as a birdwatcher in the YOC, I went on to study Zoology and Developmental Genetics at university before metamorphosing into a translator, as one does, whilst maintainng a lifelong interest in birds.
Besides editing **The Yearbook**, I do the occasional bird survey and participate in the activities of my local bird club.
Don't hesitate to e-mail me at: neildstratton@btinternet.com.*

Following on from Neil Gartshore's ten years at the helm and his own move to Northumberland, **The Yearbook** has migrated a few miles further north and settled in the Scottish Borders. Although, as chance would have it, it has ended up in the hands of another Neil, me, Neil Stratton, with the invaluable support of my wife Jane.

Before turning to what you can expect to find in the 2026 edition, I would first like to thank t'other Neil for all his work over the last decade and for passing **The Yearbook** on to me in such good shape; and I am sure the many loyal readers who buy it every year would like to join me in doing so—I only hope they will not be disappointed as I take it forward.

Without more ado, what is staying the same and what is changing?

Much will stay the same. Once again, James Lowen offers a look back at the past year and Gordon Hamlett reviews recent bird books. There is a diary, a checklist based on the official British List, a county by county directory of key office holders, clubs and organizations, as well national organizations, plus an extensive selection of bird reserves.

However, although much of the content is the same, much of it is arranged in a different way.

The directory of services and suppliers has been broken up and various elements of it interspersed with relevant articles or sections of **The Yearbook.** The Directory of Lecturers and Photographers, for example, now follows James Lowen's look back on the last year; the listing of publishers and booksellers is placed immediately after Gordon Hamlett's review of recent bird books, and so on.

The *Diary* has been doubled in length and combined with the tide tables and the sunrise/sunset times; the aim here being to bring everything that relates to any given day together in one part of the book.

The *Checklist* is still based on the official British List, but not as you know it. The work that has been going on to produce a single sequence of bird species that all can adopt has now been completed and the resulting list published as AviList v25. The British Ornithologist's Union, who maintain the official British List, have announced that the underlying taxonomy for future editions of the British List will be that of AviList v25 (and subsequent updates). However, the BOU has not yet issued such a list and the current version of the British List is still based on the pre-AviList v25 IOC sequence. Since this edition of **The Yearbook** is designed for use throughout 2026 and since the BOU has already announced its intention to switch from the IOC sequence to that of AviList v25 or subsequent updates, **The Yearbook** has decided to jump the gun. The checklist in this edition contains all the species admitted to categories A to C of the British List, up to the announcement of 12 August '25; but these have been arranged in the AviList v25 sequence, not as in the current but soon to be discarded British List.

This year, so as to offer readers an idea of how common or rare at least some of the species they are looking at are, the checklist also features the APEP-4 population estimates first published in *British Birds* in February 2020. APEP-5, with more up to date estimates, is in the pipeline and it had been hoped that it would be released in time to be included in this year's edition of **The Yearbook**. Alas it is still grinding through the review and approvals process and will not be published until 2026. So, for the time being, we will have to content ourselves with the 2020 iteration of APEP, whilst looking forward to the APEP-5 estimates in the 2027 edition..

In another change, the county by county listing of *Reserves* and the *County Directory* of office holders and organizations have been combined. There is now just a single *County Directory* and all the information relating to a county, be it name of bird recorder or details of this or that reserve, is all presented together in one unbroken sequence.

As in previous years, the counties are grouped in regions, but these regions are no longer arranged alphabetically but in a geographical sequence, as are the counties wthin the regions, and the individual reserves within the counties (see the main contents pages and the contents pages for the *County Directory* for more details about this reorganization). The aim of doing this is not some abstract love of fractals but to place reserves that are close to each other geographically, close to each other in the book; so that if, having visited one reserve, you feel like going on to another one nearby, you will find it nearby in the book. To help readers find their way around the book, the regions are now colour-coded and the maps have been provided with keys. Rather than me going on endlessly here trying explain the new system go and try it out for yourself.

The single directory of national organizations has also been broken up. If an organization is primarily concerned with birds in the UK or in one of its constituent member nations, its entry is now placed in a section at the the start of that nation's *County Directory*. In the case of organizations that are UK-wide in their activities, the entry is placed in the organization section for the nation where it headquarters are based Usually, but not always, this is England. Those organizations that have national offices as well as a central headquarters, have their headquarters listed in the relevant national section and their national offices in the corresponding national sections. There is then also a section for wildlife organizations that are not primarily focused on birds or that are primarily concerned with birds outside the UK.

So far as reserves are concerned, as you can see from the thickness of the book, a considerable number of additional reserves have been added. This has been done for two reasons. Firstly, there were a number of regions that, although their office-holders and organizations were listed in the *County Directory,* had no reserves featured. These included, the *Isles of Scilly,* the *Isle of Man*, the *Channel Islands*, *Herefordshire* and *Northern Ireland.* This edition now features reserves from all of these regions. The second reason is that the number reserves featured for each Scottish or Welsh county was, on average, lower than for an English county. An attempt has been made to redress this imbalance. It's for you to judge if I have succeeded.

Finally, for this edition I have commissioned a series of paintings of a *Bird of the Year* from Sylvie Soudan and you will see these on the covers of this edition and throughout the book. For 2026, the *Bird of the Year* is the Redpoll, chosen because Artic, Common and Lesser have recently been lumped. Sylvie, working from a mix of photographs and specimens in the collection of the National Museum of Scotland, has produced images of all three of these former species.

Scanning this QR code, which is printed in various places throughout the book, with your mobile phone's camera will take you to **The Yearbook** *website.*

*There you will find an **Updates** section listing information that has changed since the edition went to press and a **Contact Form** to use if you wish to alert the editor to an error, details that have changed or to make a suggestion for future content.*

NEWS FROM THE WORLD OF BIRDS

*James Lowen offers a selection of the past year's
interesting stories about wild birds from across the UK,
with illustrations by Dan Powell*

*James Lowen is a naturalist, author
and editor from Norfolk. Although
his 17 books cover subjects as
diverse as Iberian mammals and
Neotropical butterflies, at heart he
remains a British birdwatcher.'*

*Firecrest have been doing well,
especially in southern England.*

Bird populations: bad news and good

Official government data released confirms that UK birds declined by
2% overall between 2018 and 2023 (7% in England) due to a panoply of
pressures including habitat loss, pesticide use and the climate crisis. Farmland birds have particularly suffered, decreasing by 9% (2018–23) or 61%
(1970–2023): notable population crashes from 2018 to 2023 have been
recorded for Turtle Dove (54%) and Tree Sparrow (25%). Woodland bird
populations have also ebbed, by 10% between 2018 and 2023.

Now totalling 7 million records of 217 species since 1995, data from the
BTO/JNCC/RSPB Breeding Bird Survey unsurprisingly echo these formal findings, identifying marked declines for species such as Turtle Dove
(98% since 1995), Yellow Wagtail (20% in five years), Willow Tit (90%
since 1995), Chaffinch (40% in 10 years), Bullfinch (24% in five years)
and Yellowhammer (33% since 1995). Swift, the species championed by
campaigner Hannah Bourne-Taylor, is down 69% since 1995, and 47%
in the decade to 2023. Even Blackbird is suffering in England, at least,
numbers dropping by a tenth in the past 10 years, partly as a result of
the mosquito-borne Usutu virus, which arrived in the UK during 2020
and which has been linked to mass die-offs of the species in Europe. In
Scotland, upland birds have shown the largest declines (20% since 1994),
notably in Curlew (60%).

On the plus side, Little Egret numbers have rocketed 2,726% since
1995 (when the species was still a national rarity), with other notable
increases for Red Kite (2,464%) and, perhaps less pleasingly, Ring-necked
Parakeet (2,406%). Firecrest increased by 240% during 2013–23, particularly in southern England. Since 1995, Cuckoo has declined by a third in
the UK overall: the species is moving north, with England losing 71% but
Scotland gaining 67%. There are also promising signs of recoveries over a
10-year period for Skylark (up 18%) and Corn Bunting (up 38%), although
numbers are still well down on 1994.

Scarce breeders and winterers

There was some positive news for a number of rare breeding birds. Osprey recolonization in England took another bold step in 2025, when a
pair bred successfully in Norfolk after a 250-year absence. In the Scottish Borders, a media-dubbed 'love triangle' between two female and
one male Osprey during 2025 resulted in four chicks hatching. Sadly, the
youngsters succumbed after the male abandoned the nest and failed to
provide food. Goshawk figures suggest a 24% increase from 2021–22,
and the species seems to have spread further since, colonizing many new
woodlands: might we one day see this impressive raptor in urban parks,
as in several European countries?

Corncrake is showing positive signs, with 2024 seeing 12–14 males on
Canna (Inner Hebrides, where 5,000 acres of suitable breeding habitat
has been created), up from just one or two previously, plus record counts

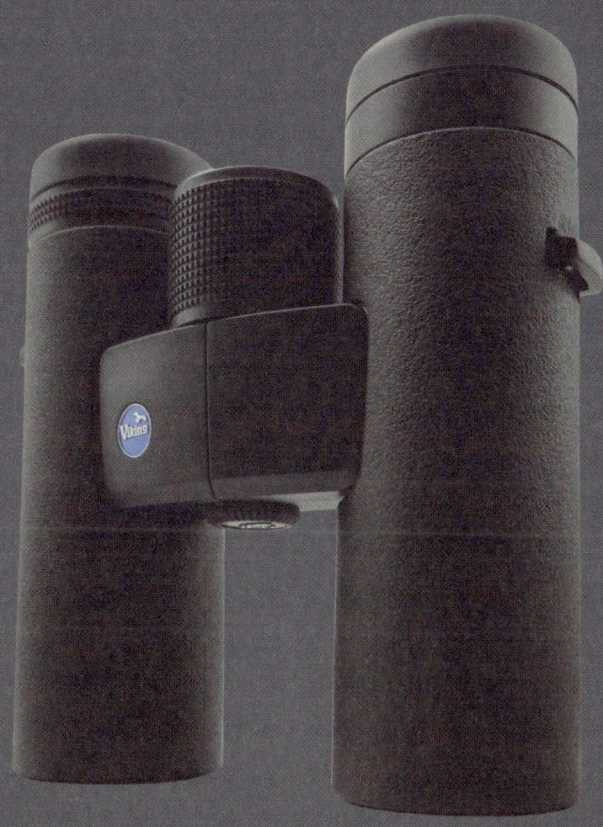

Bittern are booming and spreading their wings.

of three on Bardsey (Gwynedd), six on Rathlin (Northern Ireland) and nine in the Cambridgeshire/Norfolk washes (following a reintroduction project). In 2025, Lesser Spotted Woodpecker had its most successful breeding season for decades, with 24 monitored nests fledging an average of 3.8 chicks (2024 equivalents: nine nests producing an average of 1.3 chicks). Woodlark is doing well in the New Forest, with the 260 breeding pairs counted in 2024 representing a 50% increase in just five years. Bittern continued its spread, with 283 booming males counted in 2024 (up 20% on 2023, the biggest annual jump since monitoring started in 1990), including at 12 new sites.

Although long predicted to be a future British breeding bird, Zitting Cisticola has stubbornly remained a rare vagrant. Until 2025, that is, when a pair raised four young at Walberswick (Suffolk). A sign of things to come?

The RSPB announced record years for several species across its reserve network, including 30 pairs of Common Crane (those at Lakenheath being helped by 'runways' cut through reedbeds), 120 pairs of Bearded Reedling at Blacktoft Sands alone, 38 pairs of Spoonbill (including the first nesting attempt in Cambridgeshire since the 17th century), 211 churring male Nightjars (including 93 in Dorset's Purbeck, where conservation grazing across 1,300 hectares has helped improve habitat). On the charity's Fairburn Ings reserve, three pairs of Cattle Egret bred in 2024—the first to ever nest in Yorkshire.

On the downside, the latest report of the Rare Breeding Birds Panel (covering 2022) reveals that Slavonian Grebe reached a nadir of 20 pairs, which raised just seven young, Montagu's Harrier failed to breed for the third consecutive year, and avian flu was found to impact the productivity of White-tailed Eagle and Golden Eagle.

An awful winter for Bewick's Swan saw just 87 birds return to Slimbridge, where numbers have declined 86% in 50 years. The decline (echoed in Ireland, where no birds at all wintered for the first time ever) is partly due to milder temperatures permitting 'short-stopping', with birds wintering farther east; but breeding productivity might also be an issue, given that the meagre Slimbridge total lacked juveniles and just 1% of the Nene/Ouse Washes wintering population were youngsters. The Wetlands Birds Survey 2023/24 also revealed worrying wildfowl declines, with record lows for Eider (down 20% in 10 years) and Mallard (down 34% in 25 years), plus major 10-year declines for Red-breasted Merganser (25%), Goldeneye (21%), Tufted Duck (19%) and Scaup (52%). Only Shoveler bucked the trend, increasing 71% since 1998 to yet another record high.

Seabirds

Skomer saw its record Puffin total in 2025, with 43,626 individuals topping the previous record by over a thousand. The English mainland's final colony of Puffin, however, looks doomed; in 2025, no chicks were raised in Purbeck for the 11th consecutive year. In Northern Ireland, Fulmar numbers in 2024 were down more than half on the turn of the century. Overall Scottish seabird numbers remain poor, with populations roughly half that of 1986. Arctic Skua has suffered particularly harshly, with an 83% decline thought to be due to food shortages and increased predation by Great Skua.

The Bass Rock Gannet colony continues to decline, with 46,045 nests in 2024 representing a 6.7% decrease on 2023. Numbers appear not to have recovered after the 2022 avian flu outbreak. The situation is unlikely to be helped by the Scottish Government's approval of the Berwick Banks windfarm, which, it is planned, will consist of over 300 wind turbines and cover some 390 square miles. Great Skua is faring slightly better, with Shetland numbers creeping back up (but still as much as 83% down on pre-pandemic figures). Another hint of resurgence came from Coquet Island, where Roseate Tern hatched a record 191 chicks in 2024. In further promising news, an international legal challenge to the UK ban on commercial fishing for sandeels in the North Sea, in place since early 2024, has been rejected. Species likely to continue to benefit include Puffin and Kittiwake.

A rosy future for Roseates?

Wader fortunes

The 2024 update of the Red List of globally threatened birds provided sorry reading for shore-bird enthusiasts, with Grey Plover, Dunlin, Ruddy Turnstone and Curlew Sandpiper all moved to higher threat categories. Otherwise, there are signs of good news. Although Curlew remains globally Near Threatened, five years of removing 7,000 non-native Stoats from Orkney (where they arrived in 2010) appears to be paying dividends, with nest-survival rates in 2024 the highest recorded and breeding densities up from 31 pairs per square kilometre to 37.5. More than a hundred Curlews have now been reintroduced to Dartmoor (Devon), with some colour-ringed individuals spotted wintering in Iberia. Elmley reserve (Kent) continues to 'headstart' Curlews, releasing into the wild fledged birds originating from northern England. Forty years of Stone-curlew conservation, led by the RSPB, have helped more than double the national population, with nearly 350 pairs now breeding. Meanwhile, countrywide surveys showed that Avocet and Black-tailed Godwit reached their highest recorded wintering numbers in 2023/24, with respective 10-year increases of 37% and 18%.

but grey one for others?

News of places

Wild- and human-started fires during the dry spring of 2025 affected a number of important sites in western Britain. By mid-April, Welsh firefighters had already battled 1,400 fires, with the total UK land area burnt by then being larger than Birmingham. Sites affected included the Poole Harbour heaths in Dorset (sites for Nightjar and Dartford Warbler), Kincorth Hill (Aberdeenshire), Gentleshaw Common (Staffordshire), Rosenannon Downs (Cornwall), Elmley (Kent) and Abergeswyn Commons in Powys (a key Golden Plover breeding site). Arson and/or vandalism also damaged hides at nature reserves in Cambridgeshire, Northamptonshire and Nottinghamshire, while vandals have repeatedly destroyed fencing designed to protect beach-nesting Ringed Plovers in north-west Norfolk.

Landscape restoration was a prominent theme this year. Former farmland at Martlesham Wilds (Suffolk) is helping wildfowl and waders, and has been colonized by Woodlark. This species, plus Nightjar, will be among those helped by a £1.2-million project to remove invasive pine trees from Avon Heath (Dorset). In Leicestershire, the Market Harborough Rewilding Project will return farmland to semi-natural habitats. A Norfolk farm near Methwold is being converted into a wetland, funded by the not-uncontroversial approach of selling units of biodiversity net gain; Lapwing is among species expected to benefit. In Dorset, the National Trust is funding its tenant farmers to restore wood pasture in Purbeck. In Cambridgeshire, land has been bought for a new wetland as part of the Great Fen project, which celebrated its 25th anniversary in 2025.

A 445-acre segment of the Castle Howard estate (Yorkshire) aims to reinvigorate land for nature, with Turtle Dove being a particular target species. In the same county, a former arable farm near Doncaster is being transformed into a mosaic of habitats. In Wiltshire, Roundbarrow Farm will be converted into chalk downland. In Essex, the RSPB has purchased more land at its Wallasea Island reserve, which will be converted into natural grassland and a coastal lagoon to help Avocet, Lapwing and Redshank. The Wildfowl and Wetlands Trust, inspired by its success at Steart Marshes, will turn farmland on Somerset's Awre Peninsula into saltmarsh. In Sussex, the marine environment and river systems from Chichester to Camber Sands will be rejuvenated thanks to £1 million worth of funding while 15 wetlands, including Pevensey Levels and Pulborough Brooks, will be restored to benefit wildfowl and waders.

Moving beyond landscape restoration, in Kent, Elmley reserve received funding to improve accessibility, which will include free transfers from the nearest railway station. In Northumberland, the Wildlife Trusts have agreed a two-phase agreement to buy the 9,390-acre Rothbury Estate, where birdlife includes Curlew and Red Grouse. In Dumfries and Galloway, the first recipient of the National Lottery Heritage Fund's £150-million Landscape Connections programme was the Solway Firth. The £1.5-million grant aims to support nature recovery and sustainable tourism. In Yorkshire, the county wildlife trust has expanded North Cave Wetlands, which is already home to 3% of UK breeding Avocets. In Shetland, Fair Isle Bird Observatory reopened for business in May 2025, after the previous building burned down in 2019.

Finally, the RSPB came under criticism for closing visitor centres, shops and/or cafés at five reserves, namely Dungeness, Fairhaven Lake, Loch Garten, Newport Wetlands and Rainham Marshes. Although its income continues to increase, the charity argued that its costs have been rising quicker. It is retaining retail operations at Minsmere, where the government's decision to proceed with a new nuclear reactor at adjacent Sizewell is sparking alarm. On the plus side the RSPB expanded its Geltsdale reserve, which is expected to benefit Black Grouse, Osprey, Hen Harrier and Curlew, and rebuilt the oldest hide at its famous Leighton Moss reserve.

Bird persecution

Raptors continue to be the target of crime. In the past year alone, two male Hen Harriers disappeared in euphemistically termed 'mysterious circumstances' from RSPB Geltsdale and Peregrine Falcon eggs were smashed at St Albans Cathedral. The latest Birdcrime report from the RSPB reveals that at least 1,344 birds of prey were illegally killed from 2009–23. Most incidents are associated with land managed for gamebird shooting, Despite lobbying from the RSPB and Wild Justice, the government has no plans to ban driven grouse shooting. In better news, the Westminster government has upped funding for England's National Wildlife Crime Unit as part of its new Rural and Wildlife Crime Strategy, Wild Justice appointed its first Chief Executive, and the RSPB launched an interactive map showing the whereabouts of two hundred satellite-tagged Hen Harriers.

NEWS FROM THE WORLD OF BIRDS

Splits, lumps and shuffles

Birdwatchers have long been confused by which of several global author-ities to follow for avian taxonomy. Should one choose BirdLife taxonomy, or that of the International Ornithological Committee, or perhaps the eBird/Clements checklist? After several years of discussions and nego-tiations, a new chapter in bird listing commenced in June 2025 with the publication of 'AviList v2025'. This new, globally unified checklist replaces those of the three bodies listed above—and the British Ornithologists' Union has already announced its adoption as the basis for the British List. The outcome reduces the global species total by about 1%, and involves numerous lumps, splits, genus changes and reclassifications. The most pertinent changes from a UK perspective are the lumping of five species: Green-winged Teal is lumped with Eurasian, Cabot's Tern with Sandwich, Yelkouan Shearwater with Balearic, Hooded Crow with Carrion, and Amur (Stejneger's) Stonechat with Siberian. AviList will be updated annu-ally, so expect plenty more changes…

Scientific titbits

Our obsession with pets, notably dogs and cats, is increasingly being fingered as causing direct disturbance and mortality to birds. But new research also reveals more insidious routes for Rover and Felix to cause birds harm. One study has linked both raised levels of unhatched eggs and an increased mortality in unfledged chicks to chemical treatments used on pets, because adults line their nests with 'contaminated' animal hair. All 103 nests studied contained chemicals, including two banned for agri-cultural uses in the EU, prompting researchers to call for a reassessment of the environmental risk of pesticides used in flea and tick treatments.

As urbanization expands, understanding how birds adapt to noisy en-vironments is increasingly important. Non-breeding Robins have been found to adapt their winter songs in urban areas—cutting through the noise by singing fewer, longer syllables at higher pitch. Further research could reveal whether these adjusted song traits are linked to winter ter-ritory quality, predator avoidance or overall survival.

Spending plenty of time outdoors, birdwatchers are probably more exposed to tick-borne Lyme disease—a severe bacterial disease that is seemingly on the rise in the UK—than many sectors of the human population. Now it transpires that ticks in woodlands where non-native Pheasants are released are nearly 2.5 times more likely to carry *Borrelia* bacteria than those at nearby sites without pheasant releases. Given that 47 million Pheasants are shunted annually into the UK landscape, this adds health concerns to existing environmental issues problems caused by the shooting industry.

Finally, sleep is vital for all animals, but renders them vulnerable to predation. Many birds have evolved a solution, sleeping with half of the brain only, while the other remains alert. But new research on Jackdaws shows that when the pressure to recover rises after a long period of wakefulness, birds prioritize deep sleep over defence. And with that, it's time for a nap…

which Swifts can do on the wing.

TALKING ABOUT BIRDS:
LECTURERS AND PHOTOGRAPHERS

This section offers a selection of lecturers who give talks and/or offer photographic services. If you are interested in their services, please contact the individuals directly via the details at the end of their listing—mentioning *The Birdwatcher's Yearbook* when making an enquiry.

- (**L**) indicates Letcturer; (**P**) indicates Photographic services.
- *Lectures* offers a selection of the talks that are available but not necessarily a full list.
- *Distance* gives an idea of how far lecturers are willing to travel and any restrictions.
- *Time* is when lecturers are available, plus any restrictions.
- *Online talks* indicates if these are offered
- *Fee:* this is for guidance. It may vary for a number of reasons, such as the distance travelled.

ALIBONE, Mike (L)

Northamptonshire-based, Optics Editor for *Birdwatch* magazine, producing equipment reviews and providing purchasing advice for readers whilst writing other ad hoc features. Also qualified ecologist and experienced tour organizer, having undertaken numerous birding trips to the four corners of the Western Palearctic, with Israel as a speciality destination, as well as to Africa, south-east Asia, South America and the USA.

Lectures: Birding Israel—north to south, migration and conservation; Birds of Colombia—a neotropical nirvana; Birding Northamptonshire—key sites and population dynamics; An Insight into Birding Optics—budget bins to top tier 'scopes: are leading-edge optics really the best value? Top testing tips and an overview of latest technology.
Distance: Any considered. *Time:* Flexible. *Online talks:* yes. *Fee:* Standard £100 (negotiable for small groups) plus travel, charged at 25p per mile.

Contact:
07955 755 244;
alibone.mike@gmail.com;
www.northantsbirds.com; **X**: @bonxie

BUCKINGHAM, John (L, P)

Long-standing and popular lecturer, worldwide bird and wildlife photographer, tour leader and bird ringer.

Lectures: 60+ titles covering birds, wildlife, botany, ecology and habitats in UK, Europe, Africa, Australia, Indian sub-continent, North-South and Central America. Includes favourites such as How Birds Work; The Natural History of Birds; Wonders of Bird Migration; and two new titles: Birds of Armenia—Eastern Gem of the Caucasus; Birds of Morocco—From the High Atlas Snow to The Sahara Sands.
Distance: Any. *Time:* Any. *Online talks:* yes. *Fee:* £100 plus expenses, online and zoom talks at £75 inclusive.
Photography: Huge range of birds, botany and wildlife from UK, Europe, Africa, Americas, Australia, Asia and worldwide. Products and services: Digital images available for publication and purchase plus original slides for lectures and personal use.

Contact:
10 Courtlands, Kingsdown Road, Kingsdown, Walmer, Kent CT14 8BW.
01304 364 231 & 07971 230 842;
john.birdtalk@btinternet.com

COLLINS, Chris (L)

Wildwings and Limosa Holidays Managing Director, experienced lecturer, guide and wildlife photographer.

Lectures: Birds of the Russian Far East/In search of the Spoon-billed Sandpiper; Arctic Russia: Realm of the Ice Bear; Birds of Guyana; Unknown Antarctica: Birds of the Ross Sea and New Zealand Subantarctic Islands; Around the World in 80 minutes; Amazing Birds; Pacific Odyssey: New Zealand to Japan.
Distance: Four hours from Surrey/London or overnight accommodation. *Time:* Any by prior agreement.
Online talks: yes. *Fee:* £120 + travel expenses.

Contact:
9 Pound Close, Long Ditton, Surbiton, Surrey KT6 5JW.
020 8398 1742;
chris@birdsandwildlife.com;
www.birdsandwildlife.com/lectures

DAVIES, Martin (L)

Located in Cambridgeshire. An RSPB staff member for more than 40 years, based in various Regional Offices then the International Division. Together with Tim Appleton, was co-founder and co-organizer of the Birdfair at Rutland Water for 27 years. Now runs own consultancy company. A zoologist by training, and all-round naturalist and photographer—as well as butterflies, moths and birds, the talks feature many mammals, reptiles, amphibians, dragonflies and flowers, along with landscapes and people. Most feature strong conservation and evolutionary themes.
Lectures: Current titles offered include: Butterflies of the Atlantic Islands; How many Butterflies are there in Europe and the Western Palaearctic; Only Found Here —endemism in Butterflies across Europe and the Eu-

ropean Red List, All the UK Butterflies in a Year—by Cheating, Moths and Butterflies in UK, Wild Arctic Europe, Wild Canadian Rockies, Wild Turkey, Wild Cuba, Wild Ethiopia, Lines in Nature.

Distance: Anywhere in the UK but longer distances will normally involve travel by train. Offer of overnight accommodation appreciated if more than 120 miles from home. Overseas bookings are also considered. *Time:* Most evenings during the week; will consider daytime or weekend talks. Can normally provide own equipment (except if travelling by train when this would largely need to be provided at the venue). Will consider online talks but prefer in-person. *Fees:* Standard fee £100 (but negotiable depending on group size and localness) plus petrol costs or train fare. All payments made through Parides Ecological and Training Consultancy and invoice provided.
Contact:
5 Winchfield, Great Gransden,
Sandy, Bedfordshire SG19 3AN
07786 514004;
mdavies854@btinternet.com

GALVIN, Chris (L, P)

A birding photographer with passion for wildlife for more than 30 years.
Lectures: Northwest Year; Around the World in 80 Birds; Bee-eaters & Kingfishers: an intro to the Birds of Goa; Birding by Camera; Birding on the Doorstep; Just Add Water; Kenya—More than just Birds.
Distance: 150 miles radius from home. *Time:* Any. *Online talks:* no. *Fee:* £90 to £150 depending on distance travelled.
Photography: Birds. Products and services: Images for publication, prints, mounted prints, commissions considered.
Contact:
17 Henley Rd, Allerton, Liverpool, Merseyside L18 2DN.
0151 729 0123 or 07802 428 385;
chris@chrisgalvinphoto.com;
www.chrisgalvin.co.uk

WILDLIFE LECTURERS AND PHOTOGRAPHERS

GARTSHORE, Neil (L)

Previously spent 23 years working with National Trust; The Percy FitzPatrick Institute of African Ornithology/ Cape Town, South Africa; RSPB. Self-employed since 2006: runs 'Calluna Books', specializing in buying/selling natural history books, past publisher of *The Birdwatcher's Yearbook*. Tour guides for Dorset-based Birdfinders (to Spain/Lesvos), is the author of *Best Birdwatching Sites in Dorset* and is able to offer a variety of talks.

Lectures: Dorset's Best Birdwatching Sites; Poole Harbour and its Birds; Birding in Spain—marshes, mountain and migration; Lesvos—Jewel in the Aegean; A Sub-Antarctic Experience: the Prince Edward Islands; Japan— birding in the land of the rising sun; The Farne Islands (in the 1980's)—Northumberland's seabird city; Wildlife Wanderings in South Africa; Birding Cuba.
Ask for a list/further details.
Distance: Any considered. *Time:* Flexible—sometimes available at short notice. *Online talks:* yes. *Fee:* Variable, depending on distance travelled. Online talks at £50.

Contact:
07986 434 375;
enquiries@callunabooks.co.uk;
www.callunabooks.co.uk

GINNAW, Simon (L)

Birder and naturalist since childhood, worked with the RSPB, as a Country Park Ranger, and Forestry Commission in South-east England. Now Warden at the Elmley National Nature Reserve and freelance tour leader.

Lectures: Kent's Wild Year; A Woodland Year; Secret Lives Of Our Woodland Birds; Secret Lives Of Our Coastal Birds; Hungary: Spring Birding in Hungary: the heart of Europe; A Year on my Local Patch; Spring Birding in Hauts-de-France; Ask for a list/details.
Distance: Any considered. *Time:* Evenings—sometimes available at short notice. *Online talks:* yes. *Fee:* £75 plus fuel expenses.

Contact:
Kingshill Farm, Elmley, Minster on Sea, Sheerness ME12 3RW
07783 354 337;
simon@elmleynaturereserve.co.uk;

LOVELL, Stephen (L)

All-round naturalist with interests in all aspects of natural history. RSPB and RHS listed speaker. Guest speaker for the British Wildlife Watching Club in Scotland. Photographer and Adult Education Tutor. Lectures given to RSPB, Wildlife Trust, Natural History societies, U3A, Probus and a host of other groups. Specialist Nature Guide for Lincolnshire.
Now running Greenspaces which specializes in small group day trips and short breaks. Also organizes workshops covering a variety of topics. Check our wildlife blog on the website.

Lectures: Available on a wide range of European destinations including Lesvos, Majorca, Menorca, Extremadura. A wide range of talks on various areas of Britain with many covering Scotland. Other talks available on a wide variety of destinations around the world including

WILDLIFE LECTURERS AND PHOTOGRAPHERS

Costa Rica, Trinidad and Tobago, Cuba, Nepal, Sri Lanka, India, Tanzania, Borneo, Iceland and whale watching in Mexico. I have a wide variety of talks covering garden related topics such as Encouraging Wildlife into the Garden. There are also talks on The Miracle of Migration. Iberian Lynx, and The State of Nature in the UK. More talks are constantly being added.
Distance: Any considered. *Time:* Any. *Online talks:* yes.
Fee: £100 plus travel (which will be reduced if two or more talks are given in close proximity).

Contact:
6 Abingdon Close, Doddington Park,
Lincoln, LN6 3UH.
01522 689 456 or 07957 618 684;
stephenlovell58@btinternet.com;
www.stevelovellgreenspaces.co.uk

LOWEN, James (L, P)

A multi-award-winning author and photographer specializing in natural history, conservation and travel who offers value-for-money online talks as well as in-person lectures. He has written 17 books, winning Travel Guidebook of the Year 2016 (for *A Summer of British Wildlife*), Travel Guidebook of the Year 2018 (for *52 European Wildlife Weekends*) and the Nautilus Silver Award (for *A Butterfly Pavilion*). Additionally his travel narrative *Much Ado About Mothing* was longlisted for the Wainwright Prize for Nature Writing and two of his wildlife guidebooks were Travel Guidebook of the Year runners-up. An experienced naturalist based in Norfolk, James writes regularly for *Bird Watching*, *BirdLife*, *The Countryman*, *BBC Wildlife* and *The Telegraph*. He also edits *Neotropical Birding* and *Birding Asia* magazines and is the deputy editor of the journal *Cotinga*. With his photography represented FLPA and Alamy.
Lectures: Full brochure and client praise available on

'Lecturer' page of website (see below), but popular talks include: Much ado about mothing; Antarctic wildlife – exploring the great white continent; Wildlife of the Pantanal, South America's Serengeti; Europe's best

wildlife weekends; A pavilion of butterflies; Tango birding in Argentina; Japan—the world's best winter birding?; The best of Britain's summer wildlife; Britain's top wildlife weekends; and Britain's top birding weekends.
Distance: Negotiable, overnight accommodation may be needed. *Time:* Any. *Fees:* (online) £75 or (in-person events within 2 hours of Norwich) £100 plus 45p per mile plus £10 per hour travel time.
Photography: All wildlife, from UK, Argentina, Brazil, Antarctica, Japan, various European countries.
Products and services: digital images, prints, lectures, commissioned photography.
Contact:
Norwich, Norfolk.
07523 000 490;
lowen.james@gmail.com;
http://jameslowen.com;
X @JLowenWildlife
BlueSky: @JamesLowenWild

MAYER, Edward (L)

Founder of Swift Conservation advice service.

Lectures: Swifts, Their Lives and Conservation, also supporting and enhancing Urban Biodiversity—talks and training sessions for enthusiasts, ornithologists, architects, developers, planners, biodiversity and facilities staff. Talks from 30 minutes to two hours, training from one hour to one day.
Distance: UK/Europe. *Time:* Any. *Online talks:* yes. *Fee:* From £110, depending on type and length of talk, or collection/donation, plus travel expenses.
Contact:
52 Cholmley Gardens, London NW6 1AH.
020 7794 2098 & 07941 038 788;
mail@swift-conservation.org;
www.swift-conservation.org

MILES, John (L)

Former warden for RSPB, tour guide [Nature Scotland], consultant, journalist and author of: *Best Birdwatching Sites: The Solway*; [co-author] *Best Birdwatching Sites: Yorkshire*; *Hadrian's Birds*; *Exploring Lakeland Wildlife*; *Where to Watch Birds in Cumbria*; *Pharoah's Birds*; *Hadrian's Wildlife*;

and a series of children's books [Fifteen titles, growing every year with Chickbooks. Check the web site to see which of these books are now on YouTube].

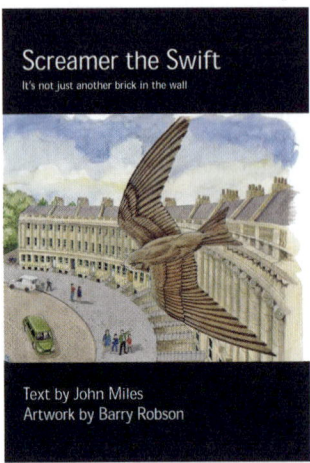

Lectures: The Solway—the whole of Cumbria and Dumfries and Galloway; Where to watch birds in Cumbria; Hadrian's Wildlife—History of birds back to Roman times plus many present day locations to visit; Death on the Nile—looks at the history of birds from Ancient Egypt to present time birds while cruising the Nile; Mull: Not just Eagles!—year round look at this island; Go Birding—follows John around Britain in search of articles in 'Go Birding' in *Bird Watching* magazine; British Bee-eaters—Will they ever BEE Every Year!; Caithness—the forgotten part of Scotland!; Islay—Not just Geese!; Yorkshire—Not just a White Rose!; My Norfolk—looks at John's many trips from 'up north' to this part of the country; Islay—Not just Geese— An island full of surprises; Owls of the Fellfoot Forward—A look at 6 species of owl in East Cumbria; Speyside—From Osprey warden in 1980 to tours and talks at the Grant Arms Hotel; Aberdeenshire—From marrying a local lass to many visits to see the mother-in-law! [well the local area!]; more coming in 2027
Distance: Anywhere in UK. *Time:* Evenings best.
Online talks: yes. *Fee:* Prices on request.
Contact:
Jockey Shield, Castle Carrock, Carlisle,
Cumbria CA4 9NF.
01228 670 205;
john@chickbooks.co.uk;
chickbooks.co.uk

OFFORD, Keith (L, P)

Raptor specialist. Coordinator of North-east Wales Raptor Study group. Photographer, lecturer, course & workshop tutor, tour leader, conservationist.
Lectures: 16 talks covering raptors—biology, iden-tification, harriers, merlins, bird flight, British uplands, gardens, migration, woodland wildlife, Texas, Spain, Sri Lanka, Estonia, Morocco, Iceland, Costa Rica, Namibia, Kruger National Park, Western Cape.

Distance: Any. *Time:* Sept to Apr. *Online talks:* yes. *Fee:* £100 (pro-rota to travel distance per mile after 100 miles) plus travel costs.
Contact:
Yew Tree Farmhouse, Craignant, Selattyn,
Nr Oswestry, Shropshire SY10 7NP.
01691 718 740;
keith@keithofford.co.uk;
www.keithofford.co.uk

ROTHERHAM, Prof Ian (L)

Former local authority ecologist, environmental cam-paigner, researcher, lecturer, writer, broadcaster.
Lectures: Numerous illustrated talks on all aspects of conservation inc.: Rewilding Nature; Rewilding Your Garden; Rewilding the River Don; Wild Deer of the Peak District; the Lost Fens; Yorkshire's Forgotten Fen-lands; Shadow Woods—a search for lost landscapes; Wild woods and woodland heritage; Wildlife and histo-ry of moors, heaths and bogs; The Heritage of the Peak District Moors and Bogs; Urban Wildlife; Gardening for Wildlife; Alien and invasive species; Wild Peak District; Eco-history; Wilder Visions—re-constructing nature for the 21st century; Wilding Nature; Eco-fusion—our hybrid future; Loving the aliens?; Understanding the ancient woods; Sherwood Forest—wildlife, history and heritage; Sherwood Forest's Ancient Trees; Wildlife and Heritage—Yorkshire's Viking Coast; Dereliction to Tourism Hub—the story of RSPB Dearne Valley; A Murky History of Peat and Peatlands; Taking Action for

Nature; Climate Change, Biodiversity Extinction and the rest—time for despair or trigger to action; Wilder Hedgerows for Nature & History; Woodland Ghosts & Shadows in the Landscape.

Distance: Prepared to travel if expenses are covered. *Time:* Any by arrangement. *Online talks:* yes. *Fee:* £95, plus petrol 50p per mile.
Contact:
42 School Lane, Norton, Sheffield, S8 8BL.
07751 089 499;
ianrotherham36@gmail.com;
www.ukeconet.org;
Blog: http://ianswalkonthewildside.wordpress.com/

TODD, Ralph (L)

Wildlife photographer and lecturer, former tour leader and course tutor.

Lectures: On the Trail of the Crane—parts 1 and 2; Polar Odyssey; Return of the Osprey; Natural Won-

ders and Wildlife of Iceland; Birds and People—Travels Through Time; Where Yeehaa meets Ole; Springtime in Lesvos; Antarctic Adventure.
Distance: Any. *Time:* Any—also short notice. *Online talks:* yes (at a reduced rate). *Fee:* £75 plus expenses.

Contact:
9 Horsham Road, Bexleyheath, Kent DA6 7HU.
01322 528 335;
rbtodd@btinternet.com

van GROUW, Katrina (L)

Katrina van Grouw, author of *The Unfeathered Bird* and *Unnatural Selection*, is an experienced and highly qualified artist, a writer, and ornithologist. A former curator of ornithology collections at the British Natural History Museum, Katrina is now studying for a PhD in palaeo-ornithology at the University of Cambridge—while working on an extended new version of *The Unfeathered Bird*.

Katrina offers two talks about her books:
From Art to Zoology: A story of evolution. An entertaining and inspiring talk on the making of *The Unfeathered Bird* and the transition from fine artist to science author.
Unnatural Selection: Evolution at the Hand of Man. About Darwin, evolution, and why domesticated animals deserve a second look.
"Katrina is a dazzling speaker. Her talk will enthral anyone interested in birds."
"One of the most interesting and entertaining talks we had heard for a long time. This talk is really not to be missed!
Distance: Any. *Time:* Flexible—sometimes available at short notice. *Online talks:* yes. *Fee:* £100 plus travel expenses.

Contact:
36 Northern Road, Aylesbury,
Buckinghamshire HP19 9QY.
01296 398 571 & 07503 038 687;
katrinavangrouw@aol.co.uk

WHITE, Mick LRPS (L, P)

Professional wildlife photographer and Lecturer

Lectures: I offer a selection of talks covering a range of wildlife subjects and destinations, along with some practical guidance on taking wildlife Images both in the UK and abroad. A full list can be found on my regularly updated website (see below).

Photography: I also offer a range of photographic workshops for small groups and individuals covering a wide range of wildlife subjects, full details of which can be found on my website along with booking information. *Distance:* Any. *Time:* Anytime. *Online talks:* yes. *Fee: Lectures:* £75 + travel @ 40p per mile + any accommodation costs incurred. *Workshops:* max group size 6 is £70pp or Individual tuition is £150 per day.

Contact:
230 The Glade, Shirley, Croydon, Surrey CR0 7UG.
07765 131 588;
mickwhite870@gmail.com;
www.mickwhitephotography.com

YOUNG, Glyn Dr (L)

Conservation expert and Lecturer

Threatened Waterfowl Specialist Group
IUCN Species Survival Commission

Formerly Curator Birds at Jersey's Durrell Wildlife Conservation Trust, I have spent more than 50 years searching for obscure and rare birds and devising conservation strategies for them. My primary, but not ex-clusive, focus has been on wildfowl. Besides managing projects on Madagascar, Galápagos and Jersey, I have undertaken field trips to India, the Mascarene Islands, Comoros, Samoa, St Lucia, New Zealand and South Africa. I currently chair the IUCN Threatened Waterfowl Specialist Group.

Lectures: Talks include: Saving the Madagascar Pochard; Reintroduction: what is it and when to use it; The future of Galápagos Islands' landbirds; The world's threatened wildfowl and what is being done to save them. *Distance:* Any. *Time:* Any time. *Online talks:* yes. *Fee:* £75 + any travel and accommodation expenses incurred.

Contact:
I, Bridgend, Yarrow Terrace,
Selkirk RD7 5AS.
07475 683 410;
fotsimaso@protonmail.com

If you are a lecturer or a photographer and would like to have a listing in this directory (a small charge applies)—Contact us for details:

Neil@thebirdwatchersyearbook.co.uk

or scan this QR code

BTO SPEAKERS

The BTO recognizes the important role that bird clubs and natural history societies play and encourages its members to support their local club. It also offers the Bird Club Partnership, which is open to any club.

To help clubs and similar organizations to find speakers for their indoor meetings or to organize regional events, the BTO has compiled a directory of staff speakers who are able to give talks. The talks vary in their subject matter but the majority of them focus on the work carried out by the BTO and its network of volunteers.

Contact:
Ieuan Evans
01842 750 050;
ieuan.evans@bto.org
www.bto.org/community/bird-club-partners

opticron

MM4 77 VHD Fieldscope
MM4 77 GA VHD & VHD/45
SDLv4 18-54x, HR3 20-60x
Fieldscope + Eyepiece from £868

MM3 80 Fieldscope
MM3 80 GA ED & ED/45
HR3 20-60x, MM3 20-60x
Fieldscope + Eyepiece from £588

Imagic IS Image Stabilised
10x30, 12x30, 14x30, 16x42
Prices from £569

Traveller BGA ED
8x32, 10x32
Prices from £379

Natura WA ED
8x42, 10x42
Prices from £329

Optics Events

Optics Events are a great opportunity to test and compare equipment under field conditions. Working with our retail partners we run events across the UK throughout the year where staff are on hand to offer expert advice to help you make the best choice based on budget and application.

See latest dates: **www.opticron.co.uk/dealers-and-events**

BEST BIRD BOOKS
OF THE PAST YEAR

*Gordon Hamlett offers a selection of the past year's
best bird books.*

*Gordon Hamlett is the author of the
best-selling* Best Birdwatching Sites
in the Scottish Highlands. *He has
written for* Birdwatching Magazine,
*and edited the UK Bird Sightings
section of that magazine, for over 30
years, as well as writing for assorted
other bird magazines. He reckons that
he holds the unofficial world record
for the number of bird books reviewed.
Outside of birdwatching, he owns over
30,000 classical CDs, and is an avid
Manchester City fan.*

Introduction

Normally, when I am writing this round-up, a theme suggests itself that
I can hang the article on. This year, absolutely nothing suggested itself.
Until, that is, I looked at the titles of the books in front of me. The word
'wild' appeared all over the place. Not just in terms such as 'wildlife', or
're-wilding', but also the word 'wild' itself, a term I can't recall seeing in
previous reviews.

And this sums up this year's miscellany; they are all over the place. The
traditional days of field guides, monographs and where-to-watch guides
seems to be disappearing rapidly.

I could have included some titles in three different categories and argued a good case for each of them. There is something here for everyone.
It might just not be in the place you expected it. So, start dropping hints
for Santa straight away, and, as usual, suggest that Father Christmas does
his shopping in independent bookshops. They really do need your help.

Identification Guides

Do not be put off by the words 'North' and 'America' in *The Gull Guide—
North America* (Ayyash, Princeton University Press, £35). Covering 36
species, plus seven hybrids in over 1,800 photos, you can see that this
a comprehensive guide to a range of species, regularly recorded on this
side of The Pond, as well birds only seen here as the occasional vagrant,
where plumage detail is scant. A must for larophiles.

Continuing the American theme, *A Field Guide to the Birds of North
America* (McMullan et al, Pelagic Publishing, £29.99) comes as something
of a surprise. The birds are all painted, whereas we have become accus-
tomed to top of the range photographic guides recently. The book covers
1,100 species via 6,000 pictures and fits comfortably into the pocket.
The downside of this, is that everything feels cramped, with the text
being particularly tiny. I must confess too, that I don't particularly like
the illustrations, so it might be worth comparing this with the National
Geographic or Sibley guides to see which you prefer.

Stretching from the Virgin Isles to Barbados, *Wildlife of the Eastern Caribbean* (S&G Holliday, Princeton University Press, £25) is a photographic
guide covering mammals, reptiles, butterflies etc. as well as birds—420
species in total. Just about fitting in a big pocket, I would be happy to take
this one book on my holiday, covering all wildlife needs.

Americans might think that *A Wildlife Guide to Georgia* (De Meulenaer,
Pelagic Publishing, £25) was about them too, but no, this is the country
rather than the state. The best birdwatching sites are featured, with additional identification tips to key species such as all the raptors flying
through the migration hotspot of Batumi. A must-have if you are visiting
the country.

Two books that will definitely fit in your pocket are *Birds of Australia*
(Ingwersen, John Beaufoy, £12.99) and *Birds of Vietnam* (Bao et al, John

Beaufoy, £12.99). The photographic guides both cover 280 species, though usually with just one picture per species. Probably only of great help if you are really travelling light.

Wild Malaysia (Davison et al, John Beaufoy, (£29.99) and *Wild Singapore* (Davison et al, John Beaufoy, £29.99) both look at the wildlife across all the various habitat types. Illustrated in full colour, they are fine, basic research material, prior to a visit.

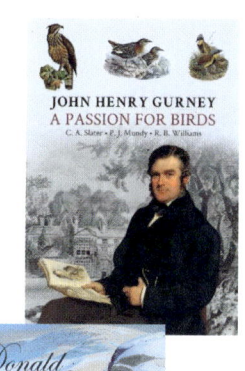

Biography

My knowledge of Gurney stretched as far as Gurney's Pitta, so I was intrigued to see what else he had done in his birding life to justify a 480-page blockbuster. Well, quite a lot as it turns out. *John Henry Gurney—A Passion for Birds* (Slater, Mundy and Williams, John Beaufoy Publishing, (£39.99) covers his passions for birding in Norfolk, and southern Africa, and his life-long study of raptors. Profusely illustrated throughout, this is a fascinating study of an ornithologist who deserves to be much better known. My only slight criticism is the title. There are already at least eight other books on the shelves with 'A Passion for Birds' in the title.

Donald Watson—Bird Artist and Writer (ed. Crofts, Whittles Publishing, £17.99) is a collection of six essays celebrating the life of this wonderful artist and field ornithologist. Best known for his work on Hen Harriers, including a first-rate Poyser monograph, I was delighted to see several of his limpid watercolours of one of my all-time favourite birds included here. That alone was worth the price of the book for me; the rest of this delightful set of reminiscences is simply a magnificent bonus.

Birdwatching in Britain

I once took a birdwatching friend, new to the area, to Holme Fen. There, there are two posts, which were hammered flat into the ground in 1848. As water was drained from the area, so the posts started to appear and now stand some 13 feet proud of the ground. My friend's flabber was well and truly gasted.

Fenland Nature (Poyser and Stirrup, Pelagic Publishing, £35) looks at the geology, geography and wildlife of the area over the last 14,000 years, reflecting on how the landscape has been changed by man, culminating with current restoration of The Great Fen. Illustrated in full colour throughout, this book makes you want to immediately go out and explore this forgotten area of East Anglia.

It is unusual to find one Scottish book that covers an area away from the Highlands and Islands, so to find two in the same year is something special. Just because you live in a city, doesn't mean that you can't go out watching wildlife. *Wild Places, Wild Encounters* (Cousquer, Whittles Publishing, £18.99) explores Edinburgh, through a series of walks in and around the city, looking at the birds etc., that you can find en route. There are full details for people using public transport, as well as suggested cafés along the route.

Ian Carter is no stranger to these pages, and his latest book, *Wild Galloway* (Whittles Publishing £17.99) is a departure from his usual titles on Red Kite conservation. As his career winds down, he has moved to Galloway and considers how the wildlife, from Golden Eagles to Scaup, benefits from having so few people around to mess it up.

If you live in Whisby, or Castor Hanglands, or Wallasea, then *The Cuckoo's Lea* (Warren, Bloomsbury, £20) is the book for you. Michael Warren explores the links between birds and ancient place names, not always immediately obvious as can be seen from the examples above. If you love words and birds, this is a total joy from beginning to end.

Lincolnshire doesn't often get a look-in in these pages, so I enjoyed reading about a rewilding attempt in the county. *A Wilding Year* (Dale, Batsford, £14.99) watches the wildlife return as the author's farm gets sympathetically redeveloped. Illustrated with charming watercolours throughout. On a somewhat larger scale, the beautifully written *Across a Waking Land* (Morgan-Grenville, Icon Books, £11.99) details a 1,000 mile walk in spring, covering every habitat type between Lymington and Cape Wrath.

Many of us have birded the odd island group, Scilly or Skomer perhaps, or one of the many Scottish island groups. But what if your job took you, not only to these islands, but many more, right around the world. Michael Brooke is a seabird researcher and in *No Island Too Far* (Pelagic Publishing, £30), he recounts his travels to the likes of Pitcairn, Galápagos, Easter Island, Hawaii and beyond. A witty mix of birds and travelogue, this is guaranteed to invoke a very deep shade-of-green envy. My only complaint is that the size of the text is too small for my aging eyes.

Monographs and science

At the time of writing, there are various plans to bring the likes of mammoths, Dodos and Great Auks back from extinction. In the meantime, you will have to make do with *The Great Auk* (Birkhead, Bloomsbury Sigma, £20), which covers history of this species over the previous 20,000 years. As I would read a shopping list written by Tim Birkhead, this superb account is self-recommending.

You might wonder what a book entitled *The Highland Cow and the Horse of the Woods* (Dennis, Whittles Publishing, £20) is doing in a bird book review, until you realise that Horse of the Woods is a translation of the Gaelic word, Capercaillie. Roy Dennis, responsible for reintroducing White-tailed Eagles into Britain, and Ospreys to Rutland Water among his many achievements, argues that Highland cows can do the job of aurochs in helping to improve the lot of this now, much endangered mega-grouse. An excellent, easy to read, well-argued book, I still think that 'Capers and Coos' would have been a better title!

A Merlin chasing a Meadow Pipit always reminds me of a World War 1 dogfight, with both predator and prey twisting and turning, this way and that, in the struggle between capture and escape. If you want to discover more about our smallest bird of prey, then *The Merling* (Rennie, Pelagic Publishing, £30) will increase your knowledge base considerably, starting with the fossil history of falcons.

Crossbills and Conifers (Benkman, Pelagic Publishing, £65) is an evolutionary study of the many races (mostly American) and species of Crossbills. It is at the top end of monographs, i.e. not an easy bedtime read, and let down by a poor index. I was hoping to see what the author thought about Scottish Crossbills, and though they are mentioned in the text, there is no easy way of finding the references.

Everyone loves owls, and *Owls of Europe* (Scherzinger and Mebs, Helm, £60) is a definite step up from the usual collection of pretty pictures. As well as identification tips, there sections on the biology, behaviour, and conservation of each species. I thought that the level of the text was pitched just right—intelligent and interesting, without being too heavy (see above). If owls are your thing, there is much here to be recommended.

Little Terns are one our most charismatic species, 'squeakers' as they are known in our house. *Clinging to the Edge* (Boon, Pelagic Publishing, £27.99) is a witty, personal account of the problems associated with protecting the breeding colony at Spurn Point in East Yorkshire.

It's a question I have probably been asked more than any other—'Why is that bird standing/sleeping on one leg?' Well, here's your answer. *Birds at Rest* (Pasquier, Princeton, £30) examines an area of bird behaviour I haven't seen written about before; what happens when birds roost. Why, when, how, with whom etc.? It's fascinating stuff.

I last studied physics at A-level over 50 years ago, so I wondered how I was going to get on with *The Physics of Birds and Birding* (Hurben, Pelagic Publishing, £30). I need not have worried. Yes, there are graphs, and charts, and equations, but nothing too taxing, as questions about flight, magnetism and migration, colour, sounds, and even binocular optics are explained.

Remote camera systems are becoming increasingly widespread from scientists trying to discover previously unseen bits of behaviour, to amateurs simply wanting to set up a trail camera. *Night Vision and Daylight Camera Systems for Wildlife* (Young, Pelagic Publishing, £35) takes you through various options, showing you how to set up your system, and get the most from your equipment.

Art and Photography

If you are about to visit, or have just returned from a trip, then you are going to want a copy of *Birds of the Tropical Andes* (Deutsch and Parr, Princeton University Press, £30). In order to relive your memories or whet your appetite. This large format coffee table book is full of close-ups of all the key species.

Of rather more interest, *Color in Nature* (Marshall et al, Princeton University Press, £30) features loads of stunning photos. The pictures are put into context though, examining how creatures see things, and use colour themselves, from a neuroscience and evolutionary biology point of view. Camouflage and sexual attraction feature prominently, and there are many departures into spectral shifts such as creatures seeing in ultraviolet rather than 'our' visible light spectrum. There is even a bit about why girls like pink!

I don't know if Angela Harding has got any compromising pictures of her publisher, but she has managed to get three books of her prints published this year. I detect a theme in the two small format titles—*Spring Unfurled* and *Falling into Autumn* (Little Brown, £12.99 each), which are simply annotated prints. The larger format book, *Still Waters and Wild Waves* (Little Brown, £25) goes into much greater detail about her methods, with pictures of her sketchbooks and photographic inspirations. As with all artists, I suggest that you google them before buying, to see if you like their style.

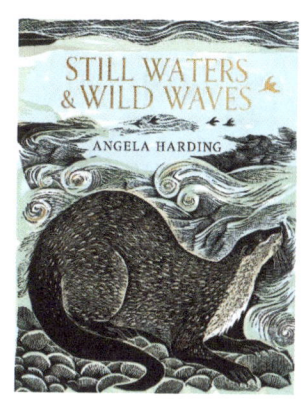

There is nothing harder than trying to describe to someone where a raptor is, when you only have your binoculars full of sky as a reference point. You hear silly things like 'can you see that cloud that looks a bit like a map of Australia upside down'. They never work. I know; that was one of mine. There have been several books on cloud identification recently including an absolute belter that featured in last year's article.

BEST BIRD BOOKS OF THE PAST YEAR

Clouds—How to Identify Nature's Most Fleeting Forms (Graham, Princeton University Press, £25) takes a somewhat different approach in so much that it uses clouds from paintings by the great masters as your reference point. If you want to know about Seiche sloshing, it appears that JMW Turner is your man.

Miscellaneous titles

These next two titles both feature Swifts on their cover and look at the importance of birds in our lives, albeit from two totally different viewpoints. You must be pretty dedicated to your cause, to walk down Whitehall, completely naked save for some body paint. Hannah Bourne-Taylor loves Swifts and wants all new houses to come complete with Swift-bricks to provide more nesting spaces for them.

Nothing too controversial you would have thought, and at a cost of about £30 each, not too expensive either. Don't you believe it. In *Nature Needs You*, (Eliott and Thompson, £16.99), she comes up against the full force of the British political system. It's not a pretty battle.

The *Life-affirming Magic of Birds* (Bingham, Aurum, £16.99) is the sort of book that should be available on prescription. Using her own problems as an example, Charlie takes us through her journey of reconnecting with nature, and discovering that no matter how bad things seem, they are always a lot better when you are watching birds. But we sort of knew that anyway, didn't we?

Two books linked by birdsong. *Whistling in the Dark* (Mabey, Aurum, £12.99) is all about the Nightingale, as seen through poetry, prose, myth and music. From one of our great nature writers, what more could you possibly want. A total joy.

About as far away from a Nightingale as you can possibly get, *A Year of Tropical Birdsong* (Couzens, Batsford, £20) tells the story of 52 species, as diverse as the Indian Peafowl to the Hawaiian I'iwi, through the medium of their songs. The unique selling point here is that for every species, there is a QR code that you can scan with your phone, and listen to the song being discussed.

'Shake a tree, and a bird will fall out', one of my mentors used to say to me, 'except for coal tits, which have to be prised out of yew trees with a crowbar.' The relationship between birds and trees has been around for millions of years, ever since they have co-existed on the planet. *Of the Trees and the Birds* (Parsons, Whittles Publishing, £18.99) looks at some aspects of the relationship that you might not have considered before, such as the tree using the ultraviolet spectrum, to signify the ripest berries. New theories include whether birds can 'talk' to the trees.

My final three books are not about birds per se, but of species likely to be of great interest to birdwatchers. All three of these photographic guides are from the always superb WILDGuides series (Princeton University Press) and are strongly recommended.

We've all been there, when everyone else can see the rare warbler, and you can't. 'It's in the third hornbeam from the left' goes the shout. That's great, but what's a hornbeam? 'There it is, in the tree', goes another call. As we are in the middle of a wood, that's highly probable, but still no help whatsoever.

Trees of Britain and Ireland (Stokes, £19.99) has 3,000 photos and 270 illustrations of all 113 native trees, and 190 of the commonest non-native species. There are separate identification keys to leaves, flowers, cones, fruits, and twigs, as well as a section on tree biology.

The second book is the third edition of *The Hoverflies of Britain and Ireland* (Ball and Morris, £25). The fact that this edition is being published just a couple of years after the previous one illustrates the fast-moving changes to taxonomy and knowledge. I've seen a couple of species in our garden but didn't have a clue that there were 177 species, illustrated with over 1,000 photos.

The book I have found most useful is *Dragonflies of Britain and Ireland* (Smallshire and Swash, fifth edition, £18.99). Whereas with birds, I have a good idea of what field marks I should be looking for, I just don't know where to start with dragonflies. Should I be looking at the head, or thorax, or wings? As they zip past so quickly, I don't have the time to examine everything before it has gone. How do I separate ruddy darters from common darters, migrant hawkers from common hawkers? Fortunately, this book tells me, with plenty of observation tips and even mnemonics to point me in the right direction. With 600 photos and 550 illustrations covering 58 species, that works out at about 20 pictures per species. As a birdwatcher, this is probably the book I shall refer to most!

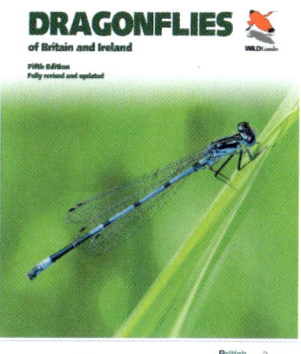

WILDGuides

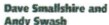

Dave Smallshire and
Andy Swash

The paintings of Redpolls, like these two formerly Common Redpolls, reproduced on the front and back covers of this edition and elsewhere in the book are the work of Sylvie Soudan and have been prepared from photographs and specimens in the collection of the National Museums of Scotland.

The publishers of **The Yearbook** *and Sylvie would like to thank Martin Stervander, the Museums's Senior Curator of Birds, for access to the collections and for advice during preparation of the paintings.*

If you woukd like to order high quality giclé prints of these paintings of Redpolls you can do so by going to www.thebirdwatchersyearbook.co.uk If you would like to see other examples of Sylvie's work, go to her Instagram account: Sylvie.Soudan.

BIRD & WILDLIFE PUBLICATIONS

BBC Wildlife
Subscriptions: BBC Wildlife Magazine, Our Media Ltd 3 Queensbridge, Northampton, NN4 7BF; 03330 162 121; via website; www.discoverwildlife.com/subscribe-utm_term-main-menu

Birdwatch
Subscriptions: Warners Group Publications, The Maltings, West Street, Bourne, Lincs, PE10 9PH. 01778 392 498;
birdwatchsubs@warnersgroup.co.uk;
www.birdguides.com/store/subscriptions/birdwatch/

Bird Watching
Subscriptions: Bauer Media, Media House, Lynch Wood, Peterborough PR23 6EA; 01733 468 000;
birdwatching@bauermedia.co.uk;
www.birdwatching.co.uk

British Birds
Subscriptions: 4 Harlequin Gardens, St Leonards- on-Sea, East Sussex TN37 7PF; 01424 755 155;
subscriptions@britishbirds.co.uk;
W: www.britishbirds.co.uk

British Wildlife Publishing (part of NHBS Ltd)
Subscriptions: 1-6 The Stables, Ford Road, Totnes, Devon TQ9 5LE; 01803 467 166;
subs@britishwildlife.com; www.britishwildlife.com

BOOK PUBLISHERS

Aurum
The Quarto Group, Inc. 1 Triptych Place, Second Floor London SE1 9SH; 0207 700 900
Publisher Richard Green: richard.green@quarto.com
https://www.quarto.com/Aurum

Bloomsbury Publishing (inc Helm, Poyser)
50 Bedford Square, London WC1B 3DP;
0207 631 5600; contact@bloomsbury.com;
www.bloomsbury.com/uk/non-fiction/natural-history/

Batsford Books
43 Great Ormond Street, London WC1N 3AZ;
0207 462 1500;
www.batsfordbooks.com

Bradt Travel Guides Ltd
31a High Street, Chesham, Bucks HP5 1BW; 01753 893 444; info@bradtguides.com; www.bradtguides.com

Brambleby Books
Orchard Cottage, Heasley Mill, South Moulton, Devon EX36 3LE; 07531 015 379; info@bramblebybooks.co.uk; www.bramblebybooks.co.uk

HarperCollins Publishers
103 Westerhill Road, Bishopbriggs, Glasgow, G64 2QT; 0141 306 3100; enquiries@harpercollins.co.uk; www.harpercollins.co.uk

Icon Books
Omnibus Business Centre, 39-41 North Road, London N7 9DP;
0207 697 9695; info@iconbooks.com;
www.iconbooks.com

John Beaufoy
11 Blenheim Court, 316 Woodstock Road Oxford OX2 7NS, UK: 01865 510920;
johnb@johnbeaufoy.com; www.johnbeaufoy.com

Liverpool University Press
4 Cambridge Street, Liverpool L69 7ZU;
lup@liverpool.ac.uk;
www.liverpooluniversitypress.co.uk

Pelagic Publishing
via website; www.pelagicpublishing.com

Princeton University Press (inc Wildguides)
99 Banbury Road, Oxford OX2 6JX;
01993 814 500; sales@press.princeton.edu;
www.press.princeton.edu/wildguides

(The) Sound Approach
Carey House, Carey, Wareham, Dorset BH20 7PG;
01202 641 004; enquiries@soundapproach.co.uk;
www.soundapproach.co.uk

Whittles Publishing
Dunbeath Mill, Dunbeath, Caithness, KW6 6EG;
01593 731 333 info@whittlespublishing.com;
www.whittlespublishing.com

BOOKSELLERS

Atropos Books
The Boat House, Church Cove, Lizard, Nr Helston, Cornwall TR12 7PH; 01326 290 287;
books@atropos.info; www.atroposbooks.info

Calluna Books
11 Cheviot Close, Ellington, Morpeth, Northumberland NE61 5HZ; 07986 434 375 & 01670 641 199;
enquiries@callunabooks.co.uk;
www.callunabooks.co.uk

Ken Mullins Books
2 Wroxham Close, Upton, Birkenhead, CH49 0UY;
07866 479 010; kendonago@hotmail.com

READING ABOUT BIRDS

NHBS (Natural History Book Service + equipment)
1-6 The Stables, Ford Road, Totnes, Devon TQ9 5XN;
01803 865 913; customer.services@nhbs.com;
www.nhbs.com

Pandion Books
23 Wickham Close, Bideford, Devon 01237 459 731;
pandionbks@aol.com

Picture Book
6 Stanley Street, Leek, Staffs ST13 5HG; 01538 399 033;
info@leekbooks.co.uk; www.leekbooks.co.uk

Steve Holliday (Bird Reports/Journals)
2 Larriston Place, Cramlington, Northumberland
NE23 8ER: 01670 731 963 (eves/w.ends);
birdreports@hotmail.co.uk

Wildside Books
29 Kings Avenue, Eastbourne, East Sussex BN21 2PE;
01323 416 211; wildsidebooks@hotmail.com

Wild Sounds & Books (+ equipment)
Roses Pightle, Cross Street, Salthouse, Norfolk
NR25 7XH; 01263 741 100; isales@wildsounds.com;
www.wildsounds.com

OTHER PRODUCTS

Bird Journal (Bluebird Technology)
1 Turnbridge Court, Swavesey, Cambridge, CB24 4GH;
mail@birdjournal.com; www.birdjournal.com

Easybirder Dvds
Dave Gosney, Valley View Cottage, 15 Low Rd, Sheffield,
S6 5FY; 0114 285 3712; dave@easybirder.co.uk;
www.easybirder.co.uk

BIRD INFORMATION SERVICES & BIRDLINE NUMBERS

Bird Forum
Free to join, online forum. www.birdforum.net

BirdGuides
Offers subscription bird news services online and via
e-mail, text message and apps for Apple and Android
devices: 01778 392 027; via website; www.birdguides.
com

Flightline
Northern Ireland's daily bird news service: 028
91467408; nibirds@live.co.uk; http://nibirds.blogspot.
co.uk

Rare Bird Alert
Offers subscription instant bird news service—available online, by pager or phone app: 01603 457 016;
admin@rarebirdalert.co.uk; www.rarebirdalert.co.uk

Birdlines
Scotland 09068 700 234 www.the-soc.org.uk/content/
bird-recording/birdline-scotland
East Anglia 09068 700 245;
www.birdlineeastanglia.co.uk
Midlands 09068 700 247
Note:
*09068 Birdline numbers are charged at premium line
rates (65p per minute from landline or mobile + any
connection charges your mobile provider may charge).*

*Female [Lesser] Redpoll, Sylvie Soudan
Instagram: Sylvie.Soudan*

THE PITFALLS OF THE INTERNET

Formerly Curator of Birds at the Durrell Wildlife Conservation Trust, Dr Glyn Young has managed numerous species rescue projects, primarily, but not exclusively, focused on ducks, in various parts of the world.

Dr Glyn Young offers some personal reflections on the dangers of over-reliance on the Internet

Once upon a time we didn't know where birds were. This was an era before increasing numbers of us travelled the world to see all the birds we could dream of and to develop lengthy life lists. This was an age before the widespread use of social media and birding apps that tell us where to go to find any bird we could ever wish to see. This was a time before the advent of eBird. It is strange then that for all our increased knowledge we have perhaps forgotten how to really find some birds and are losing the opportunity to learn about them.

Back in the days of the 'heroic' pioneering ornithologists, our first ideas about what bird lived where started to form from their expedition reports and the specimens with details tagged on they sent home, in many cases after shooting them. Gradually, as the expeditions ventured further and further afield and the reports piled up, we built up a more detailed idea of the range of this or that species or the kind of habitats in which it was found.

Once, for example, we had established that the only records for a species from Finland were from pine forests, we might then have investigated whether it was found throughout such forests or whether there were further constraints such as climate—was it there all year, was it found in the north and in the south of that forest? Nowadays, understanding such restrictions on a species's distribution can then be used in combination with remote sensing technologies to predict its potential range. If we believe that it is only found in littoral mangrove forest, we can use existing maps or satellite imagery to extrapolate to other locations where it might be found. Having done so, we would then aim to carry out a 'ground truthing' exercise and to visit points in that potential range to see if our predictions were correct and then, if the bird wasn't there, to try to learn why; further refining our understanding of its habitat requirements.

Knowledge of such habitat requirements and whether or not the range of a species is restricted to a particular biome, vegetation type or geological feature helps in turn to build a picture of its ecology.

Madagascan endemics

So much for theory and principles. On a personal level, I have long been interested in some of the rarest and least known birds on the planet. Birds whose distributions are very unclear.

I first began to research Madagascar's four endemic ducks (one subspecies and three species)—Madagascar White-backed Duck *Thalassornis leuconotus insularis*, Meller's Duck *Anas melleri*, Madagascar (or Bernier's) Teal *A. bernieri* and Madagascar Pochard *Aythya innotata*—back in the 1980s. They were, to say the least, poorly known. Indeed, Madagascar Teal, described in 1860, unseen by Jean Delacour's extensive surveys in 1929-1931 (although two were 'collected'), was only 'rediscovered' in 1969;

1 Young, H.G., Razafindrajao, F. & Lewis, R.E. (2013). *Madagascar's wildfowl (Anatidae) in the new millennium.* Wildfowl 63: 5–23.

THE PITFALLS OF THE INTERNET

whilst there was just a single reliable report of the Pochard (a fishermen caught one) between 1960 and 2006. In fact, by 2006, the Pochard was on the verge of being officially declared extinct. There was much to find out[1].

While very few ornithologists had ever seen all four of Madagascar's endemic ducks, there were a small number who had seen one or two of them in the past and recorded the fact in published expedition reports. Fortunately for me, Tim Dee[2] had written a book reviewing the historical records of all Madagascar's endemic birds, and this gave me a picture of what had happened up until the 1980s, although, just to be sure, I double-checked these records.

At the same time, as birdwatchers became braver and wanted to travel more, a small number had started to visit Madagascar and some even came across ducks; although typically only Meller's Duck, which could be found at some well-known and visited rain forest sites, as well as at a refuge in the capital city, Antananarivo. A trait of travelling birdwatchers has always been their desire to let others know where they went, what they saw, what it cost and, often, what they ate during the trip. Soon lists of trip reports were circulated by mail and you could pay for what were often badly photocopied notes. Then the Internet kicked off, making it easier to find these unpublished reports and they even became free to download!

Up close and personal with the Madagascar Pochard, one of the world's rarest ducks.

A little while earlier, In 1973, Dafila Scott (now to be found in *Wildlife Art* p.164) and Jo Lubbock[3] had mounted an expedition to study the Madagascar Teal, which had then recently been 'rediscovered' on some lakes around Antsalova on the west coast. With no roads in the area and broad rivers, it was quite a feat. Even when I visited some 20 years later, in 1992, 1993 and 1994, it was still a challenge to get to the lakes. My 1994 visit involved three days of walking behind an ox cart before we reached the Teal. These visits did, however, give me a good idea of Teal ecology and habitat requirements. Meanwhile, friends and colleagues had begun to see Teal elsewhere, even in the very north-east of the country (this team documented the first ever nest in 1997), albeit in habitat normally described as 'western'; that is in seasonal mangrove, which is where all the west coast sightings were from. Birdwatchers began to ask me for advice on seeing the Teal and, if they ever reached suitable habitat, records started to come in.

Sailing on by

Then, one day in 1995 it started to come crashing down. A survey that year of the Betsiboka River found numbers of Teal on the mudflats in the estuary, and at the mouth of the river in particular. Not long afterwards, an enterprising birdwatcher looking for mangrove specialists hired a local boat at the large coastal town of Mahajanga and ventured out into the estuary. There he found some Teal roosting in the mangrove trees at high tide. We were very excited and received some excellent new photos and behavioural notes. However, the new Teal site, Bombetoka Bay, was relatively easy to get to from a town that was visited when travelling around Madagascar. Now birders could guarantee a Teal sighting; and none were going to spend days on foot trying to find one elsewhere but without any guarantee that they would succeed. Reports on the Internet now came

2 Dee, T.J. 1986. *The Endemic Birds of Madagascar*. International Council for Bird Preservation, Cambridge, UK.
3 Scott, D. & Lubbock, J. (1974): *Preliminary observations on waterfowl in Western Madagascar*. Wildfowl 25: 117-120.

almost exclusively from this one site, Bombetoka Bay. Fortunately, our team continued to look for them at otherwise unvisited sites, confirming their requirements and devising conservation strategies.

We had gone from no sightings of the Madagascar Teal prior to 1970 to lots but all, apart from our own team's sightings, were from the same spot. This was great for the individuals seeking to build their lists but it didn't tell us much about the overall distribution of the Teal, the range of habitats in which it lived or where else it might be found.

The Madagascar Pochard was 'rediscovered' in 2006 by a scientist who was looking for something else. What's more, it was found at a site far removed from its last known location and in habitat very different from that in which it was expected to live. In short, as we then understood things, it shouldn't have been where it was—but there it was. Conversely; anyone setting out to find the Madagascar Pochard at its known old haunts and in habitat it was thought to favour, would have failed.

Madagascar Pochard, sans author

When, in 2006, I saw my first Madagascar Pochard I became the first living person who had seen all four of Madagascar's endemic ducks. Sadly, since then, the declining White-backed Duck has probably been the least seen and, even now, White-backeds are not on many people's lists. One reason might be that the Madagascar White-backed Duck is 'merely' a subspecies of a better-known African species that is not hard to find on the mainland—I once saw them amongst ladies doing their washing in a Nairobi suburb. Given that it was just a subspecies, would birders visiting Madagascar be prepared to put in the effort needed to find it?

Different island, same story

In 2007, I helped survey birds for two months on the Caribbean island of St Lucia. During this survey we failed to record the native Forest Thrush *Turdus lherminieri*, a species that is found on four of the Lesser Antilles (St Lucia, Guadeloupe, Montserrat and Dominica). This is a group of islands that hosts some very exciting single or multiple island endemics, including several parrots and orioles, that are much sought after by travelling birders. Naturally, all of these birders will visit each of the islands to complete their lists. And they'll write up their travels and post the news online. Are they seeing Forest Thrush? Indeed they are on one or several of these islands; but not, it seems, as eBird has confirmed just now, on St Lucia. After seeing one elsewhere, do they scour St Lucia for a Forest Thrush? I doubt it. Is the Forest Thrush extinct or close to extinction on St Lucia? Quite possibly; but unless we put the effort in to look for it where it might not be rather than concentrating on where we know it to be present, we will not know for certain.

Twitching Forest Thrushes can be dangerous work. The team kitted out in full Fer-de-Lance garb. Yes, those are snake guards they are wearing.

Not seeing the wood for the trees

In the 1980s, some friends and I went on a birdwatching trip to Morocco and visited an area where Dunn's Lark *Eremalauda dunni* had been recorded in a published report. The entire area for miles around was uniform in its habitat but the report in question had specified a numbered telegraph pole at a particular site. We heard of visiting birdwatchers stopping at this one pole, failing to see the lark, and moving on for the next species on their list rather than scouring the wider area. Personally, I wasn't too fussed that no lark had shown up on that pole (they're not ducks after all) and we were only passing through; but how many opportunities were missed because someone told birders which particular pole they'd got lucky at in the past?

Similarly, a friend told me that, when surveying an area of forest in Thailand, one of the highlights was a very charismatic species of terrestrial babbler. Said babbler was a much sought after species and a widely circulated report identified the path to go to if you wanted to see them. My friend told me that he regularly encountered frustrated birders who had failed to find the babbler on that path and who, despite my friend telling them that he'd seen the bird at several other spots, kept on going back to the path identified in the report before departing for home disappointed.

The Internet has its uses

The Internet does, however, have its uses. Some years ago, we realized that the Galápagos Martin *Progne modesta* was very rarely seen and its true distribution and numbers were unknown. It is not unique in this because, although Galápagos might be a well-known place to visit and sees many travelling birdwatchers, terrestrial habitats in the archipelago can be inhospitable and some of its birds remain poorly understood. Perhaps therefore it might just be that while scientists were only rarely seeing the Martin, the much larger number of visiting birdwatchers were recording it. So, we went through the bird lists and trip reports, and what they revealed was that actually very few people ever saw a Martin and that its status might really not be good. Alarm bells rang and alerted local scientists. Historical documents were examined and an expedition mounted in 2017[4]. What this found was that the status of the Martin was indeed poor and new and serious threats were uncovered.

Some Galápagos endemics are easier to spot than others.

None of the above means that I do not use eBird to look for reports away from the expected sites and it does indeed have records of all the above birds; but there's nothing like going out and finding a bird for yourself.

Spot the Martin.

4 Anchundia, D.; Fessl, B. 2020. *The conservation status of the Galápagos Martin* Progne modesta: *Assessment of historical records and results of recent surveys.* Bird Conservation International.

TRAVEL

Aigas Field Centre
Beauly, Inverness-shire IV4 7AD: 01463 782 443; info@aigas.co.uk; www.aigas.co.uk

Art Safari
Harbourmaster's Office, Ferry Quay, Woodbridge, Suffolk IP12 1BW: 01394 382 235; via website; www.artsafari.co.uk

Avian Adventures
49 Sandy Road, Norton, Stourbridge, Worcs DY8 3AJ; 01384 372 013; avianadventures@btinternet.com; www.avianadventures.co.uk

(The) Bird ID Company
01263 861 892 or 07785 534 734; info@birdtour.co.uk; www.birdtour.co.uk

Bird Watching & Wildlife Club
Grant Arms Hotel, 25 The Square, Grantown-on-Spey, Highlands PH26 3HF; 01479 872 526; bookings@grantarmshotel.com; birdwatchingandwildlifeclub.co.uk

Birdfinders
Westbank, Cheselbourne, Dorset DT2 7NW; 01258 839 066; birdfinders@aol.co.uk; www.birdfinders.co.uk

Birdquest Ltd
Two Jays, Kemple End, Stonyhurst, Clitheroe, Lancashire BB7 9QY; 01254 826 317; birders@birdquest-tours.com; www.birdquest-tours.com

Birdwatching Breaks
Cygnus House, Gordon's Mill, Balblair, Ross-shire IV7 8LQ; 01381 610 495; via website; www.birdwatchingbreaks.com

Birdwatching Trips
Alan Davies & Ruth Miller, 12 Ormeside Court, 19 Church Walks, Llandudno, LL30 2HG; 01492 872 407; info@birdwatchingtrips.co.uk; www.birdwatchingtrips.co.uk

British-Bulgarian Society
www.b-bs.co.uk
Balkania Travel, c/o Ognian Avgarski, 63 Alphabet Square, London E3 3RT; 020 7536 9400; ognian@balkaniatravel.com

Dungeness Bird Tours
Paul Trodd, Plovers, 1 Toby Road, Lydd-on-Sea, Romney Marsh, Kent TN29 9PG; 01797 366 935; troddy@plovers.co.uk; http://ploversblog.blogspot.com/p/bird-tours.html

Experience Nature
Wildlife Watching & Photography Holidays
Ashley Grove: 07704 189 835; experiencenature-tours@gmail.com;
www.experiencenature.co.uk

Greenspaces Nature
Small group birdwatching and natural history tours in the UK/specialist guide for Lincolnshire.
Steve Lovell: 07957 618 684;
stephenlovell58@btinternet.com;
www.stevelovellgreenspaces.co.uk

Greentours Natural History Holidays
2 The Grendons, Witheridge, Tiverton, Devon, EX16 8QB; 01298 83563; enquiries@greentours.co.uk;
www.greentours.co.uk

Heatherlea (Scotland) Ltd
The Mountview Hotel, Nethy Bridge, Inverness-shire PH25 3EB; 01479 821 248; via website;
www.heatherlea.co.uk

Limosa Holidays
9 Pound Close, Long Ditton, Surbiton, Surrey KT6 5JW; 01692 580 623; tours@limosaholidays.co.uk;
www.limosaholidays.co.uk

Natures Images
4 Deer Park Drive, Newport, Shropshire TF10 7HB; 01952 411 436; via website; www.natures-images.co.uk

Naturetrek
Mingledown Barn, Wolf's Lane, Chawton, Alton, Hampshire GU34 3HJ; 01962 733 051; info@naturetrek.co.uk;
www.naturetrek.co.uk

Orcadian Wildlife
Gerraquoy, St. Margaret's Hope, South Ronaldsay, Orkney KW17 2TH; 01856 831 240;
enquiries@orcadianwildlife.co.uk;
www.orcadianwildlife.co.uk

Oriole Birding
The Manor House, 9 Station Road, Great Ryburgh, Norfolk NR21 0DX; 0800 999 3036;
info@oriolebirding.com; www.oriolebirding.com

Sarus Bird Tours
12 Walton Drive, Bury, Lancashire BL9 5JU; 0161 761 7279; sarus@sarusbirdtours.co.uk;
www.sarusbirdtours.co.uk

Shetland Nature
Susannah Parnaby, Admin & Bookings, c/o Shirva, Fair Isle, Shetland ZE2 9JU;
info@shetlandnature.net; day trip enquiries: daytrips@shetlandnature.net
www.shetlandnature.net

Shetland Wildlife
Windy Stacks, Quendale, Shetland ZE2 9JD; 01950 460 939; info@shetlandwildlife.co.uk;
www.shetlandwildlife.co.uk

Shrike Birding Tours

Bespoke and small group birding and wildlife tours in the UK/specialist guide for the East Midlands. John Hague: 07766 113 346; john.hague17@gmail.com; www.shrikebirdingtours.com

Speyside Wildlife

Wester Camerorie, Ballieward, Grantown-on-Spey, Highlands PH26 3PR; 01479 812 498; enquiries@speysidewildlife.co.uk; www.speysidewildlife.co.uk

Think Galapagos

34 Woodlands, Beverley HU17 8BX; 01482 887 453; info@thinkgalapagos.com; www.thinkgalapagos.com

(The) Travelling Naturalist

Long Barn South, Sutton Manor Farm, Bishop's Sutton, Alresford, Hampshire SO24 0AA; 01305 267 994; sales@thetravellingnaturalist.com; www.naturalist.co.uk

Wildfoot Travel

133 Gravel Lane, Wilmslow, Cheshire SK9 6EG; 0800 195 3385; via website; www.wildfoottravel.com

Wildlife Travel

The Manor House, Broad St, Great Cambourne, Cambridge, CB23 6DH; 01954 713 575; wildlifetravel@wildlifebcn.org; www.wildlife-travel.co.uk

Wildlife Worldwide

Long Barn South, Sutton Manor Farm, Bishop's Sutton, Alresford, Hampshire SO24 0AA; 01962 302 086; reservations@wildlifeworldwide.com; www.wildlifeworldwide.com

Wildwings

9 Pound Close, Long Ditton, Surbiton, Surrey KT6 5JW; 0117 965 8333; tours@wildwings.co.uk; www.wildwings.co.uk

Wingspan Bird Tours

1 Yeo Valley, Stoford, Yeovil. Somerset. BA22 9UX 07968 188 998; info@wingspanbirdtours.com

Wise Birding Holidays Ltd

3 Moormead, Budleigh Salterton, Devon EX9 6QA; 07973 483 227; chris@wisebirding.co.uk; www.wisebirding.co.uk

Yorkshire Coast Nature

07747 753 260; richard.baines@yorkshirecoastnature.co.uk; www.yorkshirecoastnature.co.uk

OPTICAL DEALERS

Ace Optics

8 Belmont, Lansdown Road, Bath, BA1 5DZ; 01225 466 364; sales@aceoptics.co.uk; www.aceoptics.co.uk

Birdnet Optics Ltd

5 Trenchard Drive, Harpur Hill, Buxton, Derbyshire SK17 9JY; 01298 71844; paulflint@birdnet.co.uk; www.birdnet.co.uk

Bresser UK

Suite 3G, Eden House, Enterprise Way, Edenbridge, Kent TN8 6HF; 01342 837 098; sales@bresseruk.com; www.bresseruk.com

Cley Spy

Manor Farm Barns, Glandford, Holt, Norfolk NR25 7JP; 01263 740 088; via website; www.cleyspy.co.uk

Clifton Cameras

Staverton Technology Park, Herrick Way, Cheltenham, Gloucs GL51 6TQ; 01453 548 128; sales@cliftoncameras.co.uk; www.cliftoncameras.co.uk

Focalpoint Optics

Sevenoaks Saw Mill, Antrobus, Cheshire CW9 6JB; 01925 730 399; sales@focalpointopticsltd.com; www.focalpointopticsltd.com

In Focus

01727 827 799; enquiries@infocusoptics.co.uk; www.at-infocus.co.uk
Cotswolds: Unit 11, Toghill House Farm, Freezinghill Lane, Wick, Bristol BS30 5RT; 01225 891 352
Hertfordshire: Willows Farm, Coursers Road, Colney Heath, Hertfordshire AL4 0PF; 01727 827 799
Lancashire: Brockholes, Preston New Road, Samlesbury, Preston, Lancashire PR5 0AG; 01704 897 020
Rutland: Anglian Water Birdwatching Centre, Egleton Reserve, Rutland Water, Rutland LE15 8BT; 01572 770 656
Yorkshire: Westleigh House, Wakefield Road, Denby Dale, West Yorkshire HD8 8QJ; 01484 864 729

London Camera Exchange

shops via website; www.lcegroup.co.uk Online orders: 01962 670 007
Bath: 13 Cheap Street, Bath, Avon BA1 1NB; 01225 462 234
Bristol: 42 Park Street, Bristol, BS1 5JG; 0117 927 6185
Chester: 9 Bridge Street Row, Chester, CH1 1NW; 01244 326 531
Chichester: 17 Eastgate Square, Chichester, PO19 1JL; 01243 531 536
Colchester: 12 Eld Lane, Colchester, Essex CO1 1LS; 01206 573 444
Derby: 17 Sadler Gate, Derby, Derbyshire DE1 3NH; 01332 348 644
Exeter: 174 Fore Street, Exeter, Devon EX4 3AX;

01392 279 024

Gloucester: 12 Southgate Street, Gloucester, GL1 2DH; 01452 304 513

Guildford: 202 High Street,, Guildford, Surrey GU1 3HZ; 01483 504 040

Hereford: 16 Widemarsh Street, Hereford, HR4 9EW; 01432 272 655

Leamington: 4C Lunn Poly House, Clarendon Avenue, Royal Leamington Spa, CV32 5PP; 01926 886 166

Lincoln: 6 Silver Street, Lincoln, LN2 1DY; 01522 514 131

London (Strand): 98 Strand, London WC2R 0EW; 0207 379 0200

Manchester: 16 Cross Street, Manchester, M2 7AE; 0161 834 7500

Newcastle: 76 High Street, Gosforth, Newcastle Upon Tyne, NE3 1HB; 0191 213 0060

Norwich: 12 Timber Hill, Norwich, Norfolk NR1 3LB; 01603 612 537

Nottingham: 7 Pelham Street, Nottingham, NG1 2EH; 0115 941 7486

Oxford: 3 New Inn Hall Street, Oxford OX1 2DH; 01865 410 456

Plymouth: 56 Cornwall Street, Plymouth, Devon PL1 1LR; 01752 664 894

Portsmouth: Kingswell Path, Cascades Shopping Centre, Portsmouth, PO1 4RR; 023 9283 9933

Reading: 7 Station Road, Reading, Berkshire RG1 1LG; 0118 959 2149

Southampton (Civic Centre): 11 Civic Centre Road, Southampton, Hants SO14 7FJ; 023 8033 1720

Southampton (High Street): 10 High Street, Southampton, Hants SO14 2DH; 023 8022 1597

Taunton: 6 North Street, Taunton, Somerset TA1 1LH; 01823 259 955

Winchester: 15 The Square, Winchester, Hampshire SO23 9ES; 01962 866 203

Worcester: 8 Pump Street, Worcester WR1 2QT; 01905 22314

Park Cameras

01444 237 070; sales@parkcameras.com; www.parkcameras.com

Burgess Hill: York Road, Burgess Hill, West Sussex RH15 9TT

London: 34 Rathbone Place, London W1T 1JN

Sherwoods

The Arden Centre, Little Alne, Wootton Wawen, Henley-in-Arden, Warwickshire B95 6HW; 01789 488 880; sales@sherwoods-photo.com; www.sherwoods-photo.com

South West Optics

Riviera House, Nicholson Road, Torquay, Devon, TQ2 7TD 01872 263 444; sales@swoptics.co.uk; www.swoptics.co.uk

Stealth Birding Ltd

63-66 Hatton Garden, 5th Floor, Suite 23 London EC1N 8LE; 07706 427 618; sales@stealthbirding.com; www.stealthbirding.co.uk

Uttings Ltd

Norwich, Norfolk NR2 1NR; via website; www.uttings.co.uk

Wex Photographic

Customer Service Team: 01603 486 413; via website; www.wexphotographic.com

Belfast: Unit 2 Boucher Plaza, 4-6 Boucher Road, Belfast, BT12 6HR; 028 9077 7770

Birmingham: Retail Unit 1, 100 Hagley Road, Birmingham, B16 8LT; 0121 326 7636

Bristol: Unit 7 Montpelier Central, Station Road, Montpelier, Bristol, BS6 5EE; 0117 942 2000

Cambridge: 11 Green Street, Cambridge, CB2 3JU; 01223 650 287

Edinburgh: Unit 4, 39 Haddington Place, Edinburgh, EH7 4AG; 0131 553 9979

Glasgow: 240a Bath Street, Glasgow, G2 4JW; 0141 353 0875

Leeds: Units F&G, Moor Allerton District Centre, Leeds, LS17 5NY; 0113 521 0025

London: 37-39 Commercial Road, London, E1 1LF; 020 7380 1144

Manchester: Unit 4, Downing Street Industrial Estate, Charlton Place, Manchester, M12 6HH; 0161 274 4455

Milton Keynes: Unit 14 Lloyds Court, Silbury Boulevard, Milton Keynes, MK9 3EH; 01908 843 000

Newcastle: Unit 1 Mill House, Haddricks, Mill Rd, Newcastle-upon-Tyne NE3 1QL; 0191 814 1617

Norwich: Unit B Frenbury Estate; Drayton High Road, Norwich, NR6 5DP; 01603 481 933

Nottingham: 103-107 Carrington Street, Nottingham, NG1 7FE; 0115 773 3647

Wilkinson Cameras

Online Sales & Customer Service; 01772 252 188; sales@wilkinson.co.uk; www.wilkinson.co.uk

Store addresses:

Carlisle: 14-16 English Street, Carlisle, Cumbria CA3 8HX

Chester: 18 Frodsham Street, Chester, CH1 3JL;

Kendal: 5 Highgate, Kendal, Cumbria LA9 4DA;

Liverpool: 4 Bold Street, Liverpool, L1 6DS;

Preston: 27 Friargate, St George's Centre, Preston, Lancs PR1 2NQ

Southport: 38 Eastbank Street, Southport, Merseyside PR8 1ET

Warrington: 10 The Mall, The Golden Square, Warrington, WA1 1QE

OPTICAL IMPORTERS AND MANUFACTURERS

Alpha Optical Distribution Ltd (inc Kite Optics)
Unity Business Centre, 26 Roundhay Road, Leeds, LS7 1AB; 07725 081 436; kite@alphaodl.co.uk: www.alphaodl.co.uk; www.kiteoptics.com

Canon UK Ltd
4 Roundwood Avenue, Stocley Park, Uxbridge, Middlesex UB11 1AF
Online Store & Support: 0207 660 0186; store.uk@cc.canon-europe.com; www.canon.co.uk

Carl Zeiss Ltd
ZEISS House, Building 1030, Cambourne Business Park, Cambourne, CB23 6DW; 01223 401 500; customercare.uk@zeiss.com; www.zeiss.co.uk

Hawke
Avocet House, Wilford Bridge Rd, Melton, Woodbridge, Suffolk IP12 1RB; 0345 345 5555; uk@hawkeoptics.com; www.hawkeoptics.com

Holdan (*Steiner binos, Velbon & Slik tripods & more*)
Brookfield House, Peakdale Road, Glossop SK13 6LQ; 01457 851 000; sales@holdan.co.uk; www.holdan.co.uk

Kowa Optimed
via website; www.kowaproducts.com

Leica Camera Ltd
64-66 Duke Street, Mayfair, London W1J 6JD; 0207 629 1351; onlinestore.uk@leica-camera.com; www.leica-camera.com

NatureRAY Ltd
20-22 Wenlock Road, Lonson N1 7GU; 020 3576 3570; info@natureray.com; https://natureray.com/

Newpro UK Ltd (*Vortex Optics, PhoneSkope*)
3 Radcot Estate, Park Rd, Faringdon, Oxfordshire SN7 7BP; 01367 242 411; sales@newprouk.co.uk; www.newprouk.co.uk

Nikon UK Ltd
Customer Service Team: 0330 123 0932; via website; www.nikon.co.uk

Optical Vision Ltd
(*Barr & Stoud, Helios, Acuter Optics*)
Unit 3, Woolpit Business Park, Woolpit, Bury St Edmunds, Suffolk IP30 9UP; info:opticalvision.co.uk; www.opticalvision.co.uk

Opticron
Unit 21, Titan Court, Laporte Way, Luton, Bedfordshire LU4 8EF; 01582 726 522; sales@opticron.co.uk; www.opticron.co.uk

Swarovski Optik UK & Ireland
Suite 6G, Gatwick House, Peeks Brook Lane, Horley, Surrey RH6 9ST; 056 0109 2600
info-uk@swarovskioptik.com;
Customer Service (Austria): 00800 3242 5056; www.swarovskioptik.com

Transcontinenta UK Ltd
(*Bushnell binos, Velbon tripods & more*)
896 Plymouth Road, Slough Trading Estate, Slough, Berkshire SL1 4LP: 020 3966 5947; info@transcontinenta.co.uk; www.transcontinenta.co.uk/en/brands

Vanguard World Uk Ltd
01202 651 281; info@vanguardworld.co.uk; www.vanguardworld.co.uk

Videndum Media Distribution UK (*inc. Manfrotto*)
Resolution Rd, Ashby-de-la-Zouch, Leicestershire LE65 1DW; 01530 566 090; via website; www.manfrotto.co.uk-en

Viking Optical Ltd
Blyth Road, Halesworth, Suffolk IP19 8EN; 01986 875 315; sales@vikingoptical.co.uk; www.vikingoptical.com

OPTICAL REPAIRS AND SERVICING

East Coast Binocular Repairs
Stable Yard, Ryston Hall, Ryston Norfolk PE38 0AA: 01366 387 581; admin@binocular-repair.co.uk; www.binocular-repair.co.uk

Fixation UK Ltd (*Nikon/Canon repairs & servicing*)
Unit C, 250 Kennington Lane, Lambeth, London SE11 5RD; 0207 582 3294; admin@fixationuk.com; www.fixationuk.com

Optrep Optical Repairs
16 Wheatfield Rd, Selsey, W. Sussex PO20 0NY; 01243 601 365; info@opticalrepairs.com; www.opticalrepairs.com

Viking Optical Repair Centre
Blyth Road, Halesworth, Suffolk IP19 8EN; 01986 875 315 (option 2); repairs@vikingoptical.co.uk; www.vikingoptical.com

CLOTHING SUPPLIERS

Freet (shoes & boots)
16 High Garth, Richmond, North Yorkshire DL10 4DG; 01748 883 365; freet@freetbarefoot.com; www.freetbarefoot.com

Paramo Directional Clothing Systems
Durgates Industrial Estate, Wadhurst, East Sussex TN5 6DF: 01892 786 444; via website; www.paramo-clothing.com

Rohan
Brunleys, Kiln Farm, Milton Keynes, MK11 3HR; 0800 840 1411; post@rohan.co.uk; www.rohan.co.uk

Tilley Endurables
01326 574 402; info@tilley-uk.com; https://uk.tilley.com/

EQUIPMENT SUPPLIERS

Lowepro
Videndum Media Distribution UK, Resolution Road, Ashby-de-la-Zouch, Leicestershire LE65 1DW; 01530 566 090; via website; www.lowepro.com/uk-en/

(The) Birders Store
Unit 4a King Charles Place, St Johns, Worcester, WR2 5AJ; 01905 312 877; sales@birders-store.co.uk; www.birders-store.co.uk

(The) One Stop Nature Shop
Dalegate Market, Burnham Deepdale, King's Lynn, Norfolk PE31 8FB: 01485 211 223; sales@onestopnature.co.uk; www.onestopnature.co.uk

Outdoor Photography Gear
c/o Armadillo Storage, 73 Manchester Road, Warrington, Cheshire WA1 4AE; 01925 555 727; sales@outdoorphotographygear.co.uk; www.outdoorphotographygear.co.uk

Scopac
07810 560 916; scopac6@gmail.com; www.scopac.co.uk

Wildlife Watching Supplies
The Workshop, Town Living Farmhouse, Puddington, Tiverton, Devon EX16 8LW: 01884 860 692; sales@wildlifewatchingsupplies.co.uk; www.wildlifewatchingsupplies.co.uk

Male [Lesser] Redpoll, Sylvie Soudan
Instagram: Sylvie.Soudan

2026 EVENTS DIARY

The **Events Diary** lists a selection of events from the UK, Europe and further afield.

At the time of going to press, the dates for some of these events had not yet been confirmed. These are marked 'tbc' and are listed under the month when they are usually held.

Visit the relevant website/contact the organizers to check progress and for further details.

The **Updates** section of www.thebirdwatchersyearbook.co.uk will also post details as these are finalized.

If you are organizing or know of an event in 2027 that you would like to see featured in this section of *The Birdwatcher's Yearbook 2027*, please e-mail Neil@thebirdwatchersyearbook.co.uk by the end of September 2026.

JANUARY

6 Jan-13 Feb: Big Schools' Birdwatch (RSPB)
UK-wide event to get children interested in wild birds (first half of Spring Term).
Register at: https://action.rspb.org.uk/page/133476/subscribe/1?ea.tracking.id=rspb_web

23-25: Big Garden Birdwatch (RSPB)
UK-wide survey of garden birds, registration opens December 2025..
https://www.rspb.org.uk/whats-happening/big-garden-birdwatch

FEBRUARY

2: World Wetlands Day
Wetlands and traditional knowledge: celebrating cultural heritage
Various events around the globe celebrating the importance of wetland environments.
https://www.ramsar.org/our-work/activities/world-wetlands-day

14-21: National Nest Box Week
A BTO initiative to encourage more people to erect nest boxes.
Various events—see website for details.
https://www.nestboxweek.com/

23-27: Pacific Seabird Group
2026 annual meeting.
Seabirds: Connecting Oceans, Islands, and people; online
https://psg.wildapricot.org/annual-meeting/

28: BTO Annual Conference
Mercure Hotel, Northampton

MARCH

14: Joint SOC/BTO
Scottish Birdwatchers' Spring Conference
organized by Tayside branch of SOC/BTO
Invercarse Hotel, Dundee

www.the-soc.org.uk/support-us/events

22-36: Eilat Bird Festival (Israel)
https://eventbuzz.co.il/lp/event/eilat2026

31-02/04: BOU Annual Conference
Birds and people: challenges and opportunities of coexistence. Nottingham University, UK.
https://bou.org.uk/event/birds-and-people-bou2026/

APRIL

MAY

26-29: 8th International Swift Conference.
Catlebar, Mayo, Ireland:
Hosted by Swift Conservation Ireland
https://swiftsmayo2026.ie

30 May-1 June: NZ Bird Conference
Wanaka, New Zealand.
https://www.birdsnz.org.nz/nz-bird-conference-2026/

JUNE

tbc: OSME (Ornithological Society of the Middle East, Caucasus & Central Asia)
Summer Meeting & 46th AGM.
https://osme.org/

JULY

7-9: AFO-WOS Joint Annual Meeting
Newport, Rhode Island, USA
Association of Field Ornithologists- Wilson Ornithological Society
https://afowos2026.org

10-12: Global Bird Fair
Lyndon Top, Rutland, LE15 8RN https://globalbirdfair.org/

Neotropical Birding and Conservation AGM
To be held at Global Bird Fair (provisional)

2026 EVENTS DIARY

https://www.neotropicalbirdingandconservation.org

AUGUST
3-7: 144th American Ornithology Conference
University of Massachusetts, Amherst
American Ornithological Society (AOS)
www.americanornithology.org/meetings

SEPTEMBER
7-11: 4th World Seabird Conference
Hobart, Tasmania, Australia
World Seabird Union
https://worldseabirdunion.org/world-seabird-conference-home/

11-13: Spurn Migration Festival
https://www.spurnmigfest.com/

12-13: Festival of Bird Art
inc National Bird Carving Championships.
The Agricultural Business Centre, Agricultural Way,
Bakewell, Derbys DE45 1AH.
https://www.bdwca.org.uk/

tbc: (Sep/Oct) International Wader Study Group Annual Conference
https://www.waderstudygroup.org/

tbc: Oriental Bird Club Autumn Meeting & AGM
https://www.orientalbirdclub.org/

29: BOU Autumn Conference.
Avian futures: predicting and preparing for the future of avian biodiversity
York UK, Zoom & Bluesky
https://bou.org.uk/event/avian-futures-bouasm26/

OCTOBER
2-5: Bird Watching & Nature Activities Festival in Sagres, Portugal.
https://www.birdwatchingsagres.com/

03: RSPB Members' Day & AGM
https://www.rspb.org.uk/reserves-and-events/events-dates-and-inspiration/events/agm/

5-11: 29th International Ornithological Congress
Campeche, Mexico.

15-24 (provisional): Society of Wildlife Artists,
check dates before travelling:
www.mallgalleries.org.uk
The Natural Eye, Annual Exhibition Mall Galleries, Pall Mall, London SW1Y 5BD.
https://swla.co.uk/

17-18: North West Bird Watching Festival
WWT Martin Mere, Fish Lane, Burscough, Lancashire L40 0TAL 01704 895 181.
https://www.wwt.org.uk/wetland-centres/ martin-mere/north-west-bird-watching-festival

25-30: Raptor Research Foundation
Duluth, Minnesota, USA
https://raptorresearchfoundation.org/events/

26-29: 50th Annual Meeting of The Waterbird Society
Cape May, New Jersey, USA
https://waterbirds.org/annual-meeting/

tbc: African Bird Club
AGM plus programme of talks on research & conservation work in Africa.
https://www.africanbirdclub.org/

tbc: Welsh Ornithological Society National Conference
https://birdsin.wales/

NOVEMBER
2-6: 8th International Sea Duck Conference
Cape Cod, Massachusetts, USA
Dates and venue provisional
https://seaduckvj/org...

tbc: Scottish Ornithologists' Club AGM & Annual Conference
https://www.the-soc.org.uk/support-us/events

DECEMBER
~~~~~~~~~~

VARIOUS DATES THROUGH THE YEAR (BTO)
BTO Garden BirdWatch Talks: these are given by a number of speakers to a wide variety of groups across the country.

BTO Training Courses: one day courses/residential courses —subjects include identifying birds; bird survey techniques; breeding bird survey; & bird identification/wetland bird survey.

Local Bird Club Conferences: the BTO encourage & support local bird clubs through their 'Bird Club Partnership'.

Regional Bird Ringer's Conferences: usually one-day conferences held in the different regions of the UK.

Check out the BTO's website: www.bto.org or phone: 01842 750 050 for more information on BTO-related talks, courses or conferences in 2026.

			SMS	LN	Ler	St Mary's Scilly: 49° 55' N; 06° 18' W Lowestoft Ness: 52° 28' N; 01° 45' E Lerwick: 60° 09' N; 01° 09' W
1	Th		08:23	08:04	09:08	UK: New Year's Day
			16:34	15:50	15:08	
2	Fri		08:23	08:03	09:08	S
			16:35	15:51	15:10	
3	Sat	Full	08:23	08:03	09:07	
			16:37	15:52	15:11	
4	Sun		08:23	08:03	09:06	
			16:38	15:53	15:13	
5	Mon		08:23	08:03	09:06	
			16:39	15:55	15:15	
6	Tues		08:22	08:02	09:05	
			16:40	15:56	15:17	
7	Wed		08:22	08:02	09:04	
			16:41	15:57	15:18	
8	Th		08:22	08:01	09:03	
			16:42	15:58	15:20	
9	Fri		08:21	08:01	09:02	
			16:44	16:00	15:22	
10	Sat	Third	08:21	08:00	09:00	
			16:45	16:01	15:24	
11	Sun		08:20	07:59	08:59	
			16:46	16:03	15:26	
12	Mon		08:20	07:59	08:58	
			16:48	16:04	15:29	
13	Tues		08:19	07:58	08:56	
			16:49	16:06	15:31	
14	Wed		08:18	07:57	08:55	
			16:51	16:07	15:33	
15	Th		08:17	07:56	08:53	
			16:52	16:09	15:35	
16	Fri		08:17	07:55	08:52	
			16:54	16:11	15:37	

Bank Holidays: **UK**; England, Wales, Scotland, Northern Ireland

Dover 51° 07' N; 01° 19' E		
L	H	
03:24	08:44	1
16:01	21:21	
04:31	09:44	2
17:09	22:16	
05:35	10:40	3
18:12	23:07	
06:33	11:32	4
19:08	23:54	
07:28	12:19	5
19:57		
08:18	00:38	6
20:41	13:03	
09:03	01:21	7
21:20	13:48	
09:43	02:05	8
21:56	14:32	
10:21	02:49	9
22:29	15:17	
10:58	03:34	10
23:05	16:06	
11:39	04:23	11
23:50	17:02	
12:31	05:20	12
	18:06	
00:53	06:28	13
13:33	19:15	
02:06	07:39	14
14:37	20:20	
03:13	08:42	15
15:36	21:15	
04:09	09:34	16
16:28	22:00	

To make an *approximate estimate* of the state of the tide at a range of locations around the coast of Great Britain, add or substract the tidal differences printed on page 91 to the state of the tide at Dover shown on this and following pages. Remember, the actual state of the tide is subject to short-term influences and the tidal differences listed on page 91 are empirical observations and not official UKHO predictions..

			SMS	LN	Ler	St Mary's Scilly: 49° 55' N; 06° 18' W Lowestoft Ness: 52° 28' N; 01° 45' E Lerwick: 60° 09' N; 01° 09' W
17	Sat		08:16	07:54	08.50	Int. Swan Census
			16:55	16:12	15:40	
18	Sun	New	08:15	07:53	08:48	WeBS core count Int. Swan Census
			16:57	16:14	15:42	
19	Mon		08:14	07:52	08:47	
			16:58	16:16	15:45	
20	Tues		08:13	07:51	08:45	
			17:00	16:17	15:47	
21	Wed		08:12	07:50	08:43	
			17:01	16:19	15:50	
22	Th		08:11	07:49	08:41	
			17:03	16:21	15:52	
23	Fri		08:10	07:48	08:39	
			17:05	16:23	15:55	
24	Sat		08:09	07:46	08:37	
			17:06	16:24	15:57	
25	Sun		08:08	07:45	08:35	S: Burns Night
			17:08	16:26	16:00	
26	Mon	First	08:06	07:44	08:33	
			17:10	16:28	16:02	
27	Tues		08:05	07:42	08:31	
			17:11	16:30	16:05	
28	Wed		08:04	07:41	08:28	
			17:13	16:32	16:07	
29	Th		08:03	07:39	08:26	
			17:15	16:34	16:10	
30	Fri		08:01	07:38	08:24	
			17:16	16:35	16:13	
31	Sat		08:00	07:36	08:22	
			17:18	16:37	16:15	

Dover 51° 07' N; 01° 19' E		
L	H	
04:57	10:16	17
17:14	22:38	
05:39	10:52	18
17:57	23:12	
06:20	11:26	19
18:38	23:45	
07:01	12:00	20
19:17		
07:41	00:16	21
19:56	12:32	
08:19	00:49	22
20:31	13:05	
08:55	01:24	23
21:05	13:40	
09:31	02:02	24
21:41	14:20	
10:09	02:45	25
22:22	15:05	
10:54	03:33	26
23:12	16:00	
11:53	04:32	27
	17:11	
00:20	05:52	28
13:08	18:51	
01:43	07:26	29
14:29	20:15	
03:05	08:47	30
15:53	21:24	
04:25	09:53	31
17:14	22:20	

The Sunrise/Sunset times printed in the diary section are adjusted for British Summer Time.
The Dover tidal predictions are **NOT**. **All Dover tide times are GMT**.

DIARY—FEBRUARY 2026

			SMS	LN	Ler	St Mary's Scilly: 49° 55' N; 06° 18' W Lowestoft Ness: 52° 28' N; 01° 45' E Lerwick: 60° 09' N; 01° 09' W
I	Sun	Full	07:59	07:35	08.19	
			17:20	16:39	16:18	
2	Mon		07:57	07:33	08:17	
			17:21	16:41	16:21	
3	Tues		07:56	07:31	08:14	
			17:23	16:43	16:23	
4	Wed		07:54	07:30	08:12	
			17:25	16:45	16:26	
5	Th		07:53	07:28	08:10	
			17:26	16:47	16:29	
6	Fri		07:51	07:26	08:07	
			17:28	16:49	16:31	
7	Sat		07:49	07:24	08:04	
			17:30	16:51	16:34	
8	Sun		07:48	07:23	08:02	
			17:32	16:52	16:37	
9	Mon	Third	07:46	07:21	07:59	
			17:33	16:54	16:39	
10	Tues		07:44	07:19	07:57	
			17:35	16:56	16:42	
11	Wed		07:43	07:17	07:54	
			17:37	16:58	16:44	
12	Th		07:41	07:15	07:51	
			17:39	17:00	16:47	
13	Fri		07:39	07:13	07:49	
			17:40	17:02	16:50	
14	Sat		07:36	07:11	07:46	
			17:44	17:04	16:52	

Why St Mary's Scilly, Lowestoft Ness and Lerwick, rather than London, Manchester and Edinburgh, as previously?
1. The sunrise/sunset locations chosen for this edition are closer to significant birdwatching sites than the ones for which times were previously provided.
2. The three sites span almost the entire spread of UK latitude and longitude, allowing users to make approximate estimates for themselves for sites other than those for which times are printed here.
Both **Latitude** and **Longitude** affect the time of sunrise/sunset. See pages 48 and 49 for further details.

Dover 51° 07' N; 01° 19' E		
L	H	
05:37	10:48	1
18:15	23:07	
06:35	11:34	2
19:06	23:48	
07:24	12:14	3
19:48		
08:07	00:26	4
20:25	12:50	
08:44	01:04	5
20:56	13:26	
09:15	01:41	6
21:22	14:01	
09:42	02:17	7
21:44	14:37	
10:07	02:52	8
22:08	15:15	
10:35	03:29	9
22:41	15:59	
11:15	04:17	10
23:31	17:04	
12:23	05:29	11
	18:23	
01:03	06:52	12
13:53	19:40	
02:33	08:09	13
15:04	20:46	
03:39	09:10	14
16:03	21:36	

The Dover tidal predictions, although 'official', are nevertheless predictions and subject to variation over time.
So, for example, the first high tide at Dover on 1 January 2026 was predicted to be at 08:33 in the tide table reproduced in **The Birdwatcher's Yearbook 2025**. One year on, the prediction for that same tide, is 08:44—a difference of 11 minutes—even though both predictioms were made by the same authority, the UK Hydrographic Office, albeit a year apart. Therefore, although the tidal predictions reproduced here are offered in good faith and believed to be as accurate a forecast as it is possible to make, readers are advised to check tide times locally shortly before any intended coastal visit where the state of the tide matters.

			SMS	LN	Ler	St Mary's Scilly: 49° 55' N; 06° 18' W Lowestoft Ness: 52° 28' N; 01° 45' E Lerwick: 60° 09' N; 01° 09' W
15	Sun		07:36	07:09	07:43	
			17:44	17:06	16:55	
16	Mon		07:34	07:07	07:41	
			17:45	17:08	16:58	
17	Tues	New	07:32	07:05	07:38	
			17:47	17:10	17:00	
18	Wed		07:30	07:03	07:35	
			17:49	17:11	17:03	
19	Th		07:28	07:01	07:32	
			17:51	17:13	17:06	
20	Fri		07:26	06:59	07:29	
			17:52	17:15	17:08	
21	Sat		07:24	06:57	07:27	
			17:54	17:17	17:11	
22	Sun		07:22	06:55	07:24	WeBS core count
			17:56	17:19	17:13	
23	Mon		07:21	06:53	07:21	
			17:57	17:21	17:16	
24	Tues	First	07:19	06:50	07:18	
			17:59	17:23	17:19	
25	Wed		07:17	06:48	07:15	
			18:01	17:25	17:21	
26	Th		07:15	06:46	07:12	
			18:02	17:26	17:24	
27	Fri		07:13	06:44	07:09	
			18:04	17:28	17:26	
28	Sat		07:11	06:42	07:06	
			18:06	17:30	17:29	

The effect of Longitude on Sunrise/Sunset times
The sun rises or sets one hour earlier/later for every 15 degrees of longitude east/west of a site at the same latitude for which the time or sunrise/sunset is known. Therefore, if you know the longitude for a site for which you wish to work out the sunrise/sunset time, subtract 4 minutes for every degree that your site is east of a site for which the time is known and add 4 minutes for every degree west. For fractions of a degree, remember that there are 60 minutes in a degree, so a difference of one minute of longitude is the equivalent of 4 seconds of time.

Dover 51° 07' N; 01° 19' E		
L	H	
04:33	09:54	15
16:54	22:14	
05:20	10:30	16
17:40	22:48	
06:03	11:04	17
18:23	23.22	
06:46	11:38	18
19:02	23:55	
07:25	12:11	19
19:39		
08:03	00:28	20
20:13	12:43	
08:37	01:02	21
20:46	13:18	
09:10	01:39	22
21:21	13:57	
09:46	02:20	23
22:00	14:40	
10:29	03:06	24
22:49	15:33	
11:25	04:05	25
23:57	16:48	
12:48	05:36	26
	18:42	
01:28	07:30	27
14:22	20:14	
03:02	08:55	28
16:05	21:23	

The effect of Latitude of Sunrise/Sunset
The effect of latitude on sunrise/sunset times is not so straightforward and varies over the course of the year. A precise calculation requires the use of trigonometry. For **The Birdwatcher's Yearbook 2027** I am planning to prepare a table of factors that would allow you to calculate the time of sunrise/sunset on any day for any location whose latitude and longitude is known; but for 2026 I suggest you first calculate the effect of longitude, as explained opposite, using whichever of the three reference sites is closest in latitude to the site you are interested in and then adjust for latitude using the three sites given here as a guide.

			SMS	LN	Ler	St Mary's Scilly: 49° 55' N; 06° 18' W Lowestoft Ness: 52° 28' N; 01° 45' E Lerwick: 60° 09' N; 01° 09' W
1	Sun		07:09	06:40	07:03	
			18:07	17:32	17:32	
2	Mon		07:06	06:37	07:01	
			17:09	17:34	17:34	
3	Tues	Full	07:04	06:35	06:58	
			18:11	17:36	17:37	
4	Wed		07:02	06:33	06:55	
			18:12	17:37	17:39	
5	Th		07:00	06:31	06:52	
			18:14	17:39	17:42	
6	Fri		06:58	06:28	06:49	
			18:16	17:41	17:44	
7	Sat		06:56	06:26	06:46	
			18:17	17:43	17:47	
8	Sun		06:54	06:24	06:43	
			18:19	17:45	17:49	
9	Mon		06:52	06:21	06:40	
			18:20	17:47	17:52	
10	Tues		06:50	06:19	06:37	
			18:22	17:48	17:54	
11	Wed	Third	06:48	06:17	06:34	
			18:24	17:50	17:57	
12	Th		06:45	06:15	06:31	
			18:25	17:52	17:59	
13	Fri		06:43	06:12	06:28	
			18:27	17:54	18:02	
14	Sat		06:41	06:10	06:25	
			18:28	17:55	18:04	
15	Sun		06:39	06:08	06:22	
			18:30	17:57	18:07	
16	Mon		06:37	06:05	06:19	
			18:32	17:59	18:09	

	Dover 51° 07' N; 01° 19' E		
	L	H	
04:33	09:58		1
17:16	22:14		
05:36	10:45		2
18:07	22:56		
06:26	11:23		3
18:50	22:33		
07:09	11:57		4
19:27			
07:45	00:07		5
19:58	12:28		
08:16	00:42		6
20:23	12:59		
08:40	01:14		7
20:43	13:30		
09:00	01:44		8
21:02	13:59		
09:19	02:10		9
21:26	14:24		
09:46	02:35		10
21:59	14:52		
10:23	03:10		11
22:42	15:35		
11:17	04:29		12
23:56	17:36		
13:08	06:14		13
	18:59		
01:55	07:33		14
14:33	20:09		
03:07	08:37		15
21:01	21:01		
04:03	09:23		16
16:27	21:41		

			SMS	LN	Ler	St Mary's Scilly: 49° 55' N; 06° 18' W Lowestoft Ness: 52° 28' N; 01° 45' E Lerwick: 60° 09' N; 01° 09' W
17	Tues		06:35	06:03	06:16	NI: St Patrick's Day
			18:33	18:01	18:12	
18	Wed		06:33	06:01	06:12	
			18:35	18:03	18:14	
19	Th	New	06:30	05:58	06:09	
			18:36	18:04	18:17	
20	Fri		06:28	05:56	06:06	
			18:38	18:06	18:19	
21	Sat		06:26	05:53	06:03	
			18:40	18:08	18:22	
22	Sun		06:24	05:51	06:00	WeBS core count
			18:41	18:10	18:24	
23	Mon		06:22	05:49	05:57	
			18:43	18:11	18:26	
24	Tues		06:19	05:46	05:54	
			18:44	18:13	18:29	
25	Wed	First	06:17	05:44	05:51	
			18:46	18:15	18:31	
26	Th		06:15	05:42	05:48	
			18:48	18:17	18:34	
27	Fri		06:13	05:39	05:45	
			18:49	18:18	18:36	
28	Sat		06:11	05:37	05:42	
			18:51	18:20	18:39	
29	Sun		07:09	06:35	06:39	British Summer Time starts: 1:00 am
			19:52	19:22	19:41	
30	Mon		07:06	06:32	06:36	
			19:54	19:24	19:44	
31	Tues		07:07	06:30	06:33	
			19:55	19:25	19:46	

Dover 51° 07' N; 01° 19' E		
L	H	
04:52	17:14	17
10:01	22:18	
05:38	10:37	18
17:58	22:53	
06:22	11:11	19
18:38	23:28	
07:02	11:45	20
19:52		
07:40	00:02	21
19:51	12:19	
08:15	00:39	22
20:26	12:56	
08:50	01:17	23
21:03	13:37	
09:27	02:00	24
21:45	14:24	
10:12	02:50	25
22:37	15:23	
11:13	03:58	26
23:50	16:46	
12:43	05:40	27
	18:31	
01:26	07:32	28
14:25	20:04	
03:05	08:51	29
15:57	21:08	
04:23	09:44	30
16:56	21:54	
05:18	10:25	31
17:42	22:33	

			SMS	LN	Ler	*St Mary's Scilly:* 49° 55' N; 06° 18' W *Lowestoft Ness:* 52° 28' N; 01° 45' E *Lerwick:* 60° 09' N; 01° 09' W
1	Wed		07:02	06:28	06:30	
			19:57	19:27	19:49	
2	Th	Full	07:00	06:25	06:27	
			19:58	19:29	19:51	
3	Fri		06:58	06:23	06:24	**UK**: Good Friday
			20:00	19:31	19:53	
4	Sat		06:56	06:21	06:21	
			20:02	19:32	19:56	
5	Sun		06:54	06:18	06:18	Easter Sunday
			20:03	19:34	19:58	
6	Mon		06:51	06:16	06:15	**E, W, NI**: Easter Monday
			20:05	19:36	20:01	
7	Tues		06:49	06:14	06:12	
			20:06	19:38	20:03	
8	Wed		06:47	06:11	06:09	
			20:08	19:39	20:06	
9	Th		06:45	06:09	06:06	
			20:09	19:41	20:08	
10	Fri	Third	06:43	06:07	06:03	
			20:11	19:43	20:11	
11	Sat		06:41	06:05	06:00	
			20:13	19:45	20:13	
12	Sun		06:39	06:02	05:57	
			20:14	19:46	20:16	
13	Mon		06:37	06:00	05:54	
			20:16	19:48	20:18	
14	Tues		06:35	05:58	05:51	
			20:17	19:50	20:21	
15	Wed		06:33	05:56	05:48	
			20:19	19:52	20:23	

Dover 51° 07' N; 01° 19' E		
L	H	
06:03	10:59	1
18:22	23:09	
06:42	11:31	2
18:56	23:44	
07:14	12:02	3
19:24		
07:41	00:16	4
19:47	12:32	
08:02	00:47	5
20:07	13:01	
08:21	01:13	6
20:28	13:26	
08:43	01:33	7
20:56	13:47	
09:13	01:57	8
21:31	14:14	
09:51	02:32	9
22:14	14:56	
10:41	03:32	10
23:17	16;48	
12:09	05:39	11
	18:15	
01:11	06:54	12
13:54	19:24	
02:26	07:56	13
14:58	20:18	
03:24	08:44	14
15:50	21.02	
04:15	09:26	15
16:39	21:41	

			SMS	LN	Ler	St Mary's Scilly: 49° 55' N; 06° 18' W Lowestoft Ness: 52° 28' N; 01° 45' E Lerwick: 60° 09' N; 01° 09' W
16	Th		06:31	05:53	05:45	
			20:20	19:53	20:26	
17	Fri	New	06:29	05:51	05:42	
			20:22	19:55	20:28	
18	Sat		06:27	05:49	05:39	
			20:23	19:57	20:31	
19	Sun		06:25	05:47	05:36	WeBS core count
			20:25	19:59	20:33	
20	Mon		06:23	05:45	05:33	
			20:27	20:00	20:36	
21	Tues		06:21	05:42	05:30	
			20:28	20:02	20:38	
22	Wed		06:19	05:40	05:27	
			20:30	20:04	20:41	
23	Th		06:17	05:38	05:24	
			20:31	20:06	20:43	
24	Fri	First	06:15	05:36	05:22	
			20:33	20:07	20:46	
25	Sat		06:13	05:34	05:19	
			20:34	20:09	20:48	
26	Sun		06:11	05:32	05:16	
			20:36	20:11	20:51	
27	Mon		06:09	05:30	05:13	
			20:37	20:12	20:53	
28	Tues		06:07	05:28	05:10	
			20:39	20:14	20:56	
29	Wed		06:06	05:26	05:07	
			20:41	20:16	20:58	
30	Th		06:04	05:24	05:05	
			20:42	20:18	21:01	

Dover 51° 07' N; 01° 19' E		
L	H	
05:04	10:04	16
17:25	22:20	
05:51	10:41	17
18:08	22:58	
06:35	11:19	18
18:50	23:27	
07:16	11:58	19
19:30		
07:56	00:17	20
20:10	12:39	
08:35	01:01	21
20:53	13:26	
09:18	01:50	22
21:40	14:19	
10:08	02:48	23
22:37	15:23	
11:15	04:02	24
23:54	16:38	
12;41	05:34	25
	18:05	
01:20	07:14	26
14:06	19:34	
02:42	08:24	27
15:20	20:36	
03:50	09:14	28
16:18	21:23	
04:45	09:54	29
17:05	22:04	
05:29	10:29	30
17:45	22:41	

			SMS	LN	Ler	St Mary's Scilly: 49° 55' N; 06° 18' W Lowestoft Ness: 52° 28' N; 01° 45' E Lerwick: 60° 09' N; 01° 09' W
1	Fri	Full	06:02	05:22	05:02	
			20:44	20:19	21:03	
2	Sat		06:00	05:20	04:59	
			20:45	20:21	21:06	
3	Sun		05:58	05:18	04:56	
			20:47	20:23	21:08	
4	Mon		05:57	05:16	04:54	UK: Early May Bank Holiday
			20:48	20:24	21:11	
5	Tues		05:55	05:14	04:51	
			20:50	20:26	21:13	
6	Wed		05:53	05:13	04:48	
			20:51	20:28	21:16	
7	Th		05:52	05:11	04:46	
			20:53	20:29	21:18	
8	Fri		05:50	05:09	04:43	
			20:54	20:31	21:21	
9	Sat	Third	05:49	05:07	04:41	
			20:56	20:33	21:23	
10	Sun		05:47	05:05	04:38	
			20:57	20:34	21:26	
11	Mon		05:45	05:04	04:36	
			20:59	20:36	21:28	
12	Tues		05:41	05:02	04:33	
			21:00	20:38	21:30	
13	Wed		05:43	05:00	04:31	
			21:01	20:39	21:33	
14	Th		05:41	04:59	04:28	
			21:03	20:41	21:35	
15	Fri		05:40	04:57	04:26	
			21:04	20:42	21:38	

Dover 51° 07' N; 01° 19' E		
L	H	
06:07	11:01	1
18:19	23:17	
06:38	11:34	2
18:48	23:61	
07:03	12:07	3
19:13		
07:27	00:22	4
19:38	12:38	
07:51	00:49	5
20:05	13:05	
08:20	01:12	6
20:37	13:28	
08:53	01:38	7
21:14	13:59	
09:32	02:16	8
21:58	14:44	
10:20	03:16	9
22:56	15:55	
11:25	04:54	10
	17:20	
00:20	06:09	11
12:59	18:30	
01:38	07:10	12
14:09	19:28	
02:38	08:02	13
15:05	20:18	
03:33	08:47	14
15:58	21:03	
04:26	09:30	15
16:50	21:47	

			SMS	LN	Ler	St Mary's Scilly: 49° 55' N; 06° 18' W Lowestoft Ness: 52° 28' N; 01° 45' E Lerwick: 60° 09' N; 01° 09' W
16	Sat	New	05:38	04:56	04:24	
			21:06	20:44	21:40	
17	Sun		05:37	04:54	04:21	WeBS core count
			21:07	20:46	21:42	
18	Mon		05:36	04:53	04:19	
			21:08	20:47	21:45	
19	Tues		05:34	04:51	04:17	
			21:10	20:49	21:47	
20	Wed		05:55	04:50	04:15	
			21:11	20:50	21:49	
21	Th		05:32	04:49	04:13	
			21:12	20:52	21:51	
22	Fri		05:31	04:47	04:10	
			21:14	20:53	21:54	
23	Sat	First	05:30	04:46	04:08	
			21:15	20:54	21:56	
24	Sun		05:29	04:45	04:06	
			21:16	20:56	21:58	
25	Mon		05:28	04:44	04:04	UK: Spring Bank Holiday
			21:17	20:57	22:00	
26	Tues		05:27	04:42	04:03	
			21:19	20:58	22:02	
27	Wed		05:26	04:41	04:01	
			21:20	21:00	22:04	
28	Th		05:25	04:40	03:59	
			21:21	21:01	22:06	
29	Fri		05:24	04:39	03:57	
			21:22	21:02	22:08	
30	Sat		05:23	04:38	03:56	
			21:23	21:04	22:10	
31	Sun	Full	05:22	04:37	03:54	
			21:24	21:05	22:12	

Dover 51° 07' N; 01° 19' E		
L	H	
05:19	10:13	16
17:40	22:32	
06:10	10:57	17
18:28	23:17	
06:58	11:42	18
19:15		
07:45	00:04	19
12:30	12:30	
08:32	00:54	20
20:52	13:22	
09:21	01:49	21
21:45	14:17	
10:14	02:49	22
22:43	15:15	
11:14	03:55	23
23:47	16:17	
12:20	05:09	24
	17:26	
00:54	06:31	25
13:26	18:44	
01:58	07:39	26
14:28	19:51	
02:59	08:32	27
15:26	20:45	
03:56	09:16	28
16:19	21:31	
04:44	09:56	29
17:04	22:13	
05:24	10:33	30
17:42	22:52	
05:59	11:10	31
18:16	23:28	

DIARY—JUNE 2026

			SMS	LN	Ler	St Mary's Scilly: 49° 55' N; 06° 18' W Lowestoft Ness: 52° 28' N; 01° 45' E Lerwick: 60° 09' N; 01° 09' W
1	Mon		05:21	04:37	03:52	
			21:25	21:06	22:14	
2	Tues		05:21	04:36	03:51	
			21:26	21:07	22:15	
3	Wed		05:20	04:35	03:50	
			21:27	21:08	22:17	
4	Th		05:20	04:34	03:48	
			21:28	21:09	22:19	
5	Fri		05:19	04:34	03:47	
			21:29	21:10	22:20	
6	Sat		05:18	04:33	03:46	
			21:30	21:11	22:22	
7	Sun		05:18	04:32	03:45	
			21:31	21:12	22:23	
8	Mon	Third	05:18	04:32	03:44	
			21:31	21:13	22:24	
9	Tues		05:17	04:31	03:43	
			21:32	21:14	22:26	
10	Wed		05:17	04:31	03:42	
			21:33	21:14	22:27	
11	Th		05:17	04:31	03:41	
			21:34	21:15	22:28	
12	Fri		05:16	04:30	03:41	
			21:34	21:16	22:29	
13	Sat		05:16	04:30	03:40	
			21:35	21:16	22:30	
14	Sun		05:16	04:30	03:40	WeBS core count
			21:35	21:17	22:31	
15	Mon	New	05:16	04:30	03:39	
			21:36	21:18	22:32	

Dover 51° 07' N; 01° 19' E		
L	H	
06:30	11:45	1
18:46		
07:01	00:01	2
19:18	12:19	
07:32	00:32	3
19:51	12:50	
08:06	01:02	4
20:27	13:19	
08:42	01:32	5
21:05	13:51	
09:21	02:08	6
21:48	14:31	
10:04	02:53	7
22:36	15:20	
10:55	03:51	8
23:35	16:20	
11:58	05:01	9
	17:26	
00:43	06:12	10
13:10	18:33	
01:49	07:14	11
14:17	19:33	
02:50	08:10	12
15:19	20:29	
03:51	09:03	13
16:19	21:23	
04:52	09:55	14
17:17	22:16	
05:53	10:47	15
18:14	23:09	

			SMS	LN	Ler	St Mary's Scilly: 49° 55' N; 06° 18' W Lowestoft Ness: 52° 28' N; 01° 45' E Lerwick: 60° 09' N; 01° 09' W
16	Tues		05:16	04:30	03:39	
			21:36	21:18	22:32	
17	Wed		05:16	04:30	03:39	
			21:37	21:18	22:33	
18	Th		05:16	04:30	03:38	
			21:37	21:19	22:33	
19	Fri		05:16	04:30	03:38	
			21:37	21:19	22:34	
20	Sat		05:16	04:30	03:38	
			21:38	21:19	22:34	
21	Sun	First	05:16	04:30	03:39	
			21:38	21:20	22:34	
22	Mon		05:17	04:30	03:39	
			21:38	21:20	22:34	
23	Tues		05:17	04:31	03:39	
			21:38	21:20	22:34	
24	Wed		05:17	04:31	03:40	
			21:38	21:20	22:34	
25	Th		05:17	04:31	03:40	
			21:38	21:20	22:34	
26	Fri		05:18	04:32	03:41	
			21:38	21:20	22:34	
27	Sat		05:18	04:32	03:41	
			21:38	21:20	22:34	
28	Sun		05:19	04:33	03:42	
			21:38	21:20	22:33	
29	Mon	Full	05:19	04:33	03:43	
			21:38	21:19	22:33	
30	Tues		05:20	04:34	03:44	
			21:38	21:19	22:32	

Dover 51° 07' N; 01° 19' E		
L	H	
06:50	11:37	16
19:10		
07:45	00:02	17
20:05	12:27	
08:36	00:54	18
20:56	113:17	
09:23	01:47	19
21:46	14:07	
10:09	02:40	20
22:34	14:57	
10:54	03:34	21
23:32	15:49	
11:42	04:30	22
	16:44	
00:12	05:31	23
12:35	17:46	
01:07	06:36	24
13:32	18:53	
02:03	07:39	25
14:32	19:59	
03:00	08:35	26
15:31	20:58	
03:55	09:25	27
16:24	21:48	
04:43	10:10	28
17:10	22:32	
05:26	10:50	29
17:49	23:09	
06:04	11:26	30
18:26	23:43	

			SMS	LN	Ler	*St Mary's Scilly:* 49° 55' N; 06° 18' W *Lowestoft Ness:* 52° 28' N; 01° 45' E *Lerwick:* 60° 09' N; 01° 09' W
1	Wed		05:21	04:35	03:45	**The Birdwatcher's Yearbook 2027** available to order
			21:37	21:19	22:31	
2	Th		05:21	04:35	03:46	
			21:37	21:18	22:30	
3	Fri		05:22	04:36	03:47	
			21:37	21:18	22:30	
4	Sat		05:23	04:37	03:49	
			21:36	21:17	22:29	
5	Sun		05:23	04:38	03:50	
			21:36	21:17	22:28	
6	Mon		05:24	04:39	03:51	
			21:35	21:16	22:26	
7	Tues	Third	05:25	04:40	03:53	
			21:35	21:16	22:25	
8	Wed		05:26	04:41	03:54	
			21:34	21:15	22:24	
9	Th		05:27	04:42	03:56	
			21:33	21:14	22:23	
10	Fri		05:28	04:43	03:58	
			21:33	21:13	22:21	
11	Sat		05:29	04:44	03:59	
			21:32	21:13	22:20	
12	Sun		05:30	04:45	04:01	
			21:31	21:12	22:18	
13	Mon		05:31	04:46	04:03	NI: Orangemen's Day
			21:30	21:11	22:17	
14	Tues	New	05:32	04:47	04:05	
			21:30	21:10	22:15	
15	Wed		05:33	04:49	04:07	
			21:29	21:09	22:13	
16	Th		05:34	04:50	04:09	
			21:28	21:08	22:11	

	Dover 51° 07' N; 01° 19' E		
	L	H	
	06:42	12:00	1
	19:03		
	07:19	00:15	2
	19:41	12:32	
	07:56	00:46	3
	20:19	13:02	
	08:32	01:16	4
	20:56	13:33	
	09:08	01:48	5
	21:33	14:09	
	09:45	02:25	6
	22:13	14:50	
	10:25	03:10	7
	22:57	15:38	
	11:14	04:03	8
	23:53	16:34	
	12:17	05:08	9
		17:42	
	01:02	06:29	10
	13:33	18:58	
	02:15	07:46	11
	14:48	20:11	
	03:26	08:52	12
	15:58	21:17	
	04:38	09:53	13
	17:06	22:19	
	05:48	10:47	14
	18:11	23:14	
	06:49	11:36	15
	19:09		
	07:43	00:04	16
	20:03	12:21	

			SMS	LN	Ler	St Mary's Scilly: 49° 55' N; 06° 18' W Lowestoft Ness: 52° 28' N; 01° 45' E Lerwick: 60° 09' N; 01° 09' W
17	Fri		05:35	04:51	04:11	
			21:27	21:07	22:09	
18	Sat		05:37	04:52	04:13	
			21:26	21:05	22:08	
19	Sun		05:38	04:54	04:15	WeBS core count
			21:25	21:04	22:06	
20	Mon		05:39	04:55	04:17	
			21:24	21:03	22:04	
21	Tues	First	05:40	04:56	04:19	
			21:20	21:02	22:02	
22	Wed		05:41	04:58	04:21	
			21:21	21:00	21:59	
23	Th		05:43	04:59	04:23	
			21:20	20:59	21:57	
24	Fri		05:44	05:01	04:26	
			21:29	20:57	21:55	
25	Sat		05:45	05:02	04:28	
			21:17	20:56	21:53	
26	Sun		05:47	05:04	04:30	
			21:16	20:55	21:51	
27	Mon		05:48	05:05	04:32	
			21:15	20:53	21:48	
28	Tues		05:49	05:07	04:35	
			21:13	20:51	21:46	
29	Wed	Full	05:51	05:08	04:37	
			21:12	20:50	21:43	
30	Th		05:52	05:10	04:39	
			21:10	20:48	21:41	
31	Fri		05:53	05:11	04:42	
			21:09	20:47	21:39	

Dover 51° 07' N; 01° 19' E L	H	
08:30	00:50	17
20:49	13:15	
09:!0	01:35	18
21:30	13:49	
09:46	02:18	19
22:08	14:32	
10:20	03:01	20
22:44	15:16	
10:54	03:46	21
23:23	16:02	
11:35	04:36	22
	16:54	
00:09	05:36	23
12:30	17:57	
01:08	07:56	24
13:41	19:10	
02:14	07:56	25
14:51	20:26	
03:17	08:59	26
15:52	21:29	
04:13	09:50	27
16:44	22:15	
05:01	10:30	28
17:28	22:50	
05:44	11:05	29
18:08	23:21	
06:25	11:37	30
18:47	23:52	
07:04	12:08	31
19:26		

			SMS	LN	Ler	St Mary's Scilly: 49° 55' N; 06° 18' W Lowestoft Ness: 52° 28' N; 01° 45' E Lerwick: 60° 09' N; 01° 09' W
1	Sat		05:55	05:13	04:44	
			21:07	20:45	21:36	
2	Sun		05:56	05:14	04:47	
			21:06	20:43	21:34	
3	Mon		05:58	05:16	04:49	S: Summer Bank Holiday
			21:04	20:41	21:31	
4	Tues		05:59	05:18	04:51	
			21:03	20:40	21:28	
5	Wed		06:00	05:19	04:54	
			21:01	20:38	21:26	
6	Th	Third	06:02	05:21	04:56	
			20:59	20:36	21:23	
7	Fri		06:03	05:22	04:59	
			20:58	20:34	21:21	
8	Sat		06:05	05:24	05:01	
			20:56	20:32	21:18	
9	Sun		06:06	05:26	05:03	
			20:54	20:30	21:15	
10	Mon		06:08	05:27	05:06	
			20:53	20:28	21:12	
11	Tues		06:09	05:29	05:08	
			20:51	20:26	21:10	
12	Wed	New	06:11	05:31	05:11	
			20:49	20:24	21:07	
13	Th		06:12	05:32	05:13	
			20:47	20:22	21:04	
14	Fri		06:14	05:34	05:16	
			20:45	20:20	21:01	
15	Sat		06:15	05:36	05:18	
			20:43	20:18	20:59	
16	Sun		06:17	05:37	05:20	WeBS core count
			20:42	20:16	20:56	

Dover 51° 07' N; 01° 19' E		
L	H	
07:41	00:22	1
20:04	12:38	
08:16	00:52	2
20:39	13:09	
08:48	01:22	3
21:12	13:42	
09:21	01:57	4
21:45	14:20	
09:57	02:37	5
22:25	15:04	
10:42	03:26	6
23:15	15:57	
11:40	04:28	7
	17:07	
00:25	06:05	8
13:03	18:46	
01:54	07:42	9
14:31	20:14	
03:18	08:54	10
15:51	21:26	
04:40	09:54	11
17:06	22:25	
05:48	10:44	12
18:09	23:14	
06:43	11:27	13
19:02	23:56	
07:29	12:07	14
19:48		
08:09	00:34	15
20:28	12:46	
08:43	01:10	16
21:02	13:24	

			SMS	LN	Ler	St Mary's Scilly: 49° 55' N; 06° 18' W Lowestoft Ness: 52° 28' N; 01° 45' E Lerwick: 60° 09' N; 01° 09' W
17	Mon		06:18	05:39	05.23	
			20:40	20:14	20:53	
18	Tues		06:19	05:41	05:25	
			20:38	20:12	20:50	
19	Wed		06:21	05:42	05:28	
			20:36	20:10	20:47	
20	Th	First	06:22	05:44	05:30	
			20:34	20:08	20:44	
21	Fri		06:24	05:46	05:33	
			20:32	20:06	20:41	
22	Sat		06:25	05:47	05:35	
			20:30	20:04	20:38	
23	Sun		06:27	05:49	05:37	
			20:28	20:01	20:35	
24	Mon		06:28	05:51	05:40	
			20:36	19:59	20:33	
25	Tues		06:30	05:52	05:42	
			20:24	19:57	20:30	
26	Wed		06:31	05:54	05:45	
			20:22	19:55	20:27	
27	Th		06:33	05:56	05:47	
			20:20	19:52	20:24	
28	Fri	Full	06:34	05:57	05:49	
			20:18	19:50	20:21	
29	Sat		06:36	05:59	05:52	
			20:15	19:48	20:18	
30	Sun		06:37	06:01	05:54	
			20:13	19:46	20:15	
31	Mon		06:39	06:02	05:57	E, W, NI: Summer Bank Holiday
			20:11	19:43	20:12	

Dover 51° 07' N; 01° 19' E		
L	H	
09:12	01:46	17
21:31	14:02	
09:12	02:23	18
21:31	14:40	
10:01	03:03	19
22:25	15:20	
10:30	03:49	20
23:00	16:08	
11:14	04:48	21
	17:12	
00:02	06:01	22
12:44	18:29	
01:35	07:19	23
14:17	19:55	
02:49	08:33	24
15:26	21:09	
03:49	09:26	25
16:20	21:51	
04:39	10:04	26
17:05	22:22	
05:24	10:36	27
17:46	22:52	
06:04	11:07	28
18:26	23:23	
06:42	11:38	29
19:04	23:54	
07:17	12:10	30
19:40		
07:51	00:23	31
20:14	12:41	

			SMS	LN	Ler	St Mary's Scilly: 49° 55' N; 06° 18' W Lowestoft Ness: 52° 28' N; 01° 45' E Lerwick: 60° 09' N; 01° 09' W
1	Tues		06:40	06:04	05:59	
			20:09	19:41	20:09	
2	Wed		06:42	06:05	06:01	
			20:07	19:39	20:06	
3	Th		06:43	06:07	06:04	
			20:05	19:36	20:03	
4	Fri	Third	06:45	06:09	06:06	
			20:03	19:34	20:00	
5	Sat		06:46	06:10	06:08	
			20:01	19:32	19:57	
6	Sun		06:48	06:12	06:11	
			19:58	19:29	19:54	
7	Mon		06:49	06:14	06:13	
			19:56	19:27	19:50	
8	Tues		06:51	06:15	06:16	
			19:54	19:25	19:47	
9	Wed		06:52	06:17	06:18	
			19:52	19:22	19:44	
10	Th		06:54	06:19	06:20	
			19:50	19:20	19:41	
11	Fri	New	06:55	06:20	06:23	
			19:48	19:18	19:38	
12	Sat		06:57	06:22	06:25	
			19:45	19:15	19:35	
13	Sun		06:58	06:24	06:27	WeBS core count
			19:43	19:13	19:32	
14	Mon		07:00	06:25	06:30	
			19:41	19:11	19:29	
15	Tues		07:01	06:27	06:32	
			19:39	19:08	19:26	

Dover 51° 07' N; 01° 19' E		
L	H	
08:24	00:55	1
20:46	13:15	
08:57	01:30	2
21:19	13:52	
09:33	02:11	3
21:59	14:36	
10:18	03:00	4
22:49	15:30	
11:19	04:08	5
	16:55	
00:04	06:06	6
12:49	18:53	
01:49	07:40	7
14:29	20:20	
03:27	08:51	8
15:56	21:27	
04:41	09:45	9
17:03	22:18	
05:37	10:29	10
17:57	22:59	
06:24	11:09	11
18:43	23:35	
07:04	11:46	12
19:23		
07:39	00:08	13
19:57	12:21	
08:08	00:40	14
20:25	12:56	
08:32	01:13	15
20:49	13:30	

			SMS	LN	Ler	St Mary's Scilly: 49° 55' N; 06° 18' W _Lowestoft Ness_: 52° 28' N; 01° 45' E _Lerwick_: 60° 09' N; 01° 09' W
16	Wed		07:03	06:29	06:35	
			19:37	19:06	19:23	
17	Th		07:04	06:30	06:37	
			19:34	19:04	19:20	
18	Fri	First	07:05	06:32	06:39	
			19:32	19:01	19:17	
19	Sat		07:07	06:34	06:42	
			19:30	18:59	19:14	
20	Sun		07:08	06:35	06:44	
			19:28	18:56	19:11	
21	Mon		07:10	06:37	06:46	
			19:26	18:54	19:08	
22	Tues		07:11	06:39	06:49	
			19:23	18:52	19:05	
23	Wed		07:13	06:40	06:51	
			19:21	18:49	19:02	
24	Th		07:14	06:42	06:53	
			19:19	18:47	18:59	
25	Fri		07:16	06:44	06:56	
			19:17	18:45	18:55	
26	Sat	Full	07:17	06:46	06:58	
			19:15	18:42	18:52	
27	Sun		07:19	06:47	07:01	
			19:12	18:40	18:49	
28	Mon		07:20	06:49	07:03	
			19:10	18:37	18:46	
29	Tues		07:22	06:51	07:05	
			19:08	18:35	18:43	
30	Wed		07:24	06:52	07:08	
			19:06	18:33	18:40	

Dover 51° 07' N; 01° 19' E		
L	H	
08:52	01:47	16
21:09	14:02	
09:14	02:20	17
21:32	14:35	
10:25	02:58	18
22:05	15:19	
10:25	04:01	19
22:55	16:35	
11:34	05:22	20
	17:56	
00:48	06:41	21
13:40	19:17	
02:19	07:54	22
14:54	20:28	
03:21	08:47	23
15:48	21:11	
04:11	09:26	24
16:34	21:45	
04:55	10:00	25
17:16	22:18	
05:35	10:33	26
17:57	22:51	
06:13	11:06	27
18:36	23:23	
06:50	11:39	28
19:13	23:55	
07:25	12:14	29
19:47		
08:00	00:30	30
20:22	12:50	

			SMS	LN	Ler	St Mary's Scilly: 49° 55' N; 06° 18' W Lowestoft Ness: 52° 28' N; 01° 45' E Lerwick: 60° 09' N; 01° 09' W
1	Th		07:25	06:54	07:10	
			19:04	18:30	18:37	
2	Fri		07:27	06:56	07:12	
			19:02	18:28	18:34	
3	Sat	Third	07:28	06:57	07:15	
			18:59	18:26	18:31	
4	Sun		07:30	06:59	07:17	
			18:57	18:23	18:28	
5	Mon		07:31	07:01	07:20	
			18:55	18:21	18:20	
6	Tues		07:33	07:03	07:22	
			18:53	18:19	18:22	
7	Wed		07:34	07:04	07:25	
			18:51	18:16	18:19	
8	Th		07:36	07:06	07:27	
			18:49	18:14	18:16	
9	Fri		07:37	07:08	07:29	
			18:47	18:12	18:13	
10	Sat	New	07:39	07:09	07:32	
			18:45	18:10	18:10	
11	Sun		07:41	07:11	07:34	WeBS core count
			18:43	18:07	18:07	
12	Mon		07:42	07:13	07:37	
			18:40	18:05	18:04	
13	Tues		07:44	07:15	07:39	
			18:38	18:03	18:01	
14	Wed		07:45	07:17	07:42	
			18:36	18:01	17:58	
15	Th		07:47	07:18	07:44	
			18:34	17:58	17:55	
16	Fri		07:48	07:20	07:47	
			18:32	17:56	17:53	

Dover 51° 07' N; 01° 19' E		
L	H	
08:36	01:08	1
20:58	13:30	
09:17	01:53	2
21:41	14:18	
10:06	02:48	3
22:36	15:23	
11:12	04:11	4
	17:07	
00:00	05:57	5
12:50	18:52	
01:51	07:26	6
14:29	20:14	
03:20	08:34	7
15:47	21:12	
04:22	09:24	8
16:45	21:57	
05:12	10:06	9
17:34	22:35	
05:54	10:44	10
18:15	23:08	
06:31	11:20	11
18:51	23:40	
07:03	11:55	12
19:21		
07:31	00:11	13
19:46	12:28	
07:54	00:44	14
20:07	12:59	
08:15	01:15	15
20:28	13:28	
08:41	14:44	16
20:56	13:55	

DIARY—OCTOBER 2026

			SMS	LN	Ler	St Mary's Scilly: 49° 55' N; 06° 18' W Lowestoft Ness: 52° 28' N; 01° 45' E Lerwick: 60° 09' N; 01° 09' W
17	Sat		07:50	07:22	07:49	
			18:30	17:54	17:50	
18	Sun	First	07:52	07:24	07:52	
			18:28	17:52	17:47	
19	Mon		07:53	07:25	07:54	
			18:26	17:50	17:44	
20	Tues		07:55	07:27	07:57	
			18:24	17:48	17:41	
21	Wed		07:57	07:29	07:59	
			18:22	17:45	17:38	
22	Th		07:58	07:31	08:02	
			18:20	17:43	17:35	
23	Fri		08:00	07:33	08:04	
			18:19	17:41	17:33	
24	Sat		08:01	07:34	08:07	
			18:17	17:39	17:30	
25	Sun		07:03	06:36	07:09	British Summer Time ends: 2:00 am
			17:15	16:37	16:27	
26	Mon	Full	07:05	06:38	07:12	
			17:30	16:35	16:24	
27	Tues		07:06	06:40	07:14	
			17:11	16:33	16:21	
28	Wed		07:08	06:42	07:17	
			17:09	16:31	16:19	
29	Th		07:10	06:44	07:20	
			17:08	16:29	16:16	
30	Fri		07:11	06:45	07:22	
			17:06	16:27	16:13	
31	Sat		07:13	06:47	07:25	
			17:04	16:25	16:11	

Dover 51° 07' N; 01° 19' E		
L	H	
09:14	02:13	17
21:33	14:33	
09:57	03:01	18
22:20	16:00	
10:56	04:39	19
23:36	17:22	
12:47	05:55	20
	18:35	
01:33	07:04	21
14:08	19:38	
02:40	07:58	22
15:05	20:26	
03:32	08:41	23
15:54	21:06	
04:18	09:19	24
16:40	21:42	
05:01	09:56	25
17:24	22:17	
05:42	10:33	26
18:06	22:53	
06:23	11:10	27
18:47	23:30	
07:02	11:50	28
19:25		
07:42	00:11	29
20:05	12:31	
08:24	00:55	30
20:47	13:18	
09:11	01:47	31
21:35	14:15	

			SMS	LN	Ler	St Mary's Scilly: 49° 55' N; 06° 18' W Lowestoft Ness: 52° 28' N; 01° 45' E Lerwick: 60° 09' N; 01° 09' W
1	Sun	Third	07:15	06:49	07:27	
			17:02	16:23	16:08	
2	Mon		07:16	06:51	07:30	
			17:01	16:22	16:05	
3	Tues		07:18	06:53	07:33	
			16:59	16:20	16:03	
4	Wed		07:20	06:55	07:35	
			16:57	16:18	16:00	
5	Th		07:21	06:56	07:38	
			16:56	16:16	15:58	
6	Fri		07:23	06:58	07:40	
			16:54	16:14	15:55	
7	Sat		07:25	07:00	07:43	
			16:53	16:13	15:53	
8	Sun		07:26	07:02	07:45	
			16:51	16:11	15:50	
9	Mon	New	07:28	07:04	07:48	
			16:50	16:09	15:48	
10	Tues		07:29	07:06	07:51	
			16:48	16:08	15:46	
11	Wed		07:31	07:07	07:53	
			16:47	16:06	15:43	
12	Th		07:33	07:09	07:56	
			16:45	16:05	15:41	
13	Fri		07:34	07:11	07:58	
			16:44	16:03	15:39	
14	Sat		07:36	07:13	08:01	
			16:43	16:02	15:36	
15	Sun		07:38	07:15	08:03	
			16:41	16:00	15:34	

Dover 51° 07' N; 01° 19' E		
L	H	
10:05	02:50	1
22:36	15:30	
11:17	04:06	2
	17:01	
00:01	05:31	3
12:43	18:33	
00:01	05:31	4
12:43	18:33	
02:46	08:02	5
15:16	20:43	
03:46	08:53	6
16:13	21:27	
04:37	09:37	7
17:01	22:05	
05:20	10:16	8
17:42	22:39	
05:57	10:54	9
18:16	23:13	
06:30	11:30	10
18:45	23:47	
06:58	12:04	11
19:10		
07:24	00:21	12
19:35	12:36	
07:50	00:53	13
20:02	13:05	
08:21	01:22	14
20:35	13:35	
08:57	01:52	15
21:13	14:10	

			SMS	LN	Ler	St Mary's Scilly: 49° 55' N; 06° 18' W Lowestoft Ness: 52° 28' N; 01° 45' E Lerwick: 60° 09' N; 01° 09' W
16	Mon		07:39	07:16	08.06	
			16:40	15:59	15:32	
17	Tues	First	07:41	07:18	08:08	
			16:39	15:57	15:30	
18	Wed		07:42	07:20	08:11	
			16:38	15:56	15:28	
19	Th		07:44	07:22	08:13	
			16:37	15:55	15:26	
20	Fri		07:46	07:23	08:16	
			16:36	15:53	15:24	
21	Sat		07:47	07:25	08:18	
			16:35	15:52	15:22	
22	Sun		07:49	07:27	08:21	WeBS core count
			16:34	15:51	15:20	
23	Mon		07:50	07:28	08:23	
			16:33	15:50	15:18	
24	Tues	Full	07:52	07:30	08:25	
			16:32	15:49	15:17	
25	Wed		07:53	07:32	08:28	
			16:31	15:48	15:15	
26	Th		07:55	07:33	08:30	
			16:30	15:47	15:13	
27	Fri		07:56	07:35	08:32	
			16:29	15:46	15:12	
28	Sat		07:57	07:36	08:34	
			16:29	15:45	15:10	
29	Sun		07:59	07:38	08:37	
			16:28	15:44	15:09	
30	Mon		08:00	07:39	08:39	S: St Andrew's Day
			16:27	15:44	15:07	

	Dover 51° 07' N; 01° 19' E		
	L	H	
	09:40	02:31	16
	21:58	15:07	
	10:33	03:34	17
	22:55	16:32	
	11:46	04:53	18
		17:44	
	00:20	06:04	19
	13:08	18:47	
	01:41	07:03	20
	14:13	19:39	
	02:42	07:53	21
	15:08	20:24	
	03:35	08:38	22
	16:01	21:06	
	04:25	09:21	23
	16:51	21:47	
	05:14	10:05	24
	18:27	23:15	
	06:01	10:49	25
	18:27	23:15	
	06:47	11:35	26
	19:13		
	07:35	00:01	27
	20:00	12:24	
	07:35	00:51	28
	20:29	13:16	
	09:16	01:45	29
	21:41	14:15	
	10:12	02:43	30
	22:38	15:22	

			SMS	LN	Ler	St Mary's Scilly: 49° 55' N; 06° 18' W
						Lowestoft Ness: 52° 28' N; 01° 45' E
						Lerwick: 60° 09' N; 01° 09' W
1	Tues	Third	08:01	07:41	08.41	
			16:27	15:43	15:06	
2	Wed		08:03	07:42	08:43	
			16:26	15:42	15:05	
3	Th		08:04	07:44	08:45	
			16:26	15:42	15:04	
4	Fri		08:05	07:45	08:47	
			16:25	15:41	15:03	
5	Sat		08:07	07:46	08:48	
			16:25	15:41	15:03	
6	Sun		08:08	07:48	08:50	
			16:24	15:40	15:01	
7	Mon		08:09	07:49	08:52	
			16:24	15:40	15:00	
8	Tues		08:10	07:50	08:54	
			16:24	15:40	14:59	
9	Wed	New	08:11	07:51	08:55	
			16:24	15:39	14:58	
10	Th		08:12	07:52	08:57	
			16:24	15:39	14:58	
11	Fri		08:13	07:53	08:58	
			16:24	15:39	14:57	
12	Sat		08:14	07:54	09:00	
			16:24	15:39	14:57	
13	Sun		08:15	07:55	09:01	WeBS core count
			16:24	15:39	14:57	
14	Mon		08:16	07:56	09:02	
			16:24	15:39	14:56	
15	Tues		08:17	07:57	09:03	
			16:24	15:39	14:56	

Dover 51° 07' N; 01° 19' E		
L	H	
11:13	03:45	1
23:41	16:34	
12:18	04:52	2
	17:51	
00:47	06:06	3
13:22	19:02	
01:53	07:16	4
14:26	20:01	
02:56	08:15	5
15:26	20:51	
03:53	09:05	6
16:20	21:34	
04:43	09:51	7
17:04	22:14	
05:25	10:32	8
17:42	22:52	
06:01	11:10	9
18:15	23:29	
06:34	11:46	10
18:45		
07:05	00:04	11
19:16	12:19	
07:37	00:37	12
19:49	12:50	
08:11	01:07	13
20:23	13:20	
08:48	01:36	14
21:00	13:51	
09:27	02:08	15
21:40	14:28	

			SMS	LN	Ler	St Mary's Scilly: 49° 55' N; 06° 18' W Lowestoft Ness: 52° 28' N; 01° 45' E Lerwick: 60° 09' N; 01° 09' W
16	Wed		08:17	07:58	09:04	
			16:24	15:39	14:56	
17	Th	First	08:18	07:59	09:05	
			16:24	15:39	14:56	
18	Fri		08:19	07:59	09:06	
			16:25	15:40	14:56	
19	Sat		08:20	08:00	09:07	
			16:25	15:40	14:57	
20	Sun		08:20	08:01	09:07	
			16:25	15:40	14:57	
21	Mon		08:21	08:01	09:08	
			16:26	15:41	14:57	
22	Tues		08:21	08:02	09:09	
			16:26	15:41	14:58	
23	Wed		08:22	08:02	09:09	
			16:27	15:42	14:58	
24	Th	Full	08:22	08:03	09:09	
			16:28	15:43	14:59	
25	Fri		08:22	08:03	09:09	**UK:** Christmas Day
			16:28	15:43	15:00	
26	Sat		08:23	08:03	09:10	
			16:29	15:44	15:01	
27	Sun		08:23	08:03	09:10	
			16:30	15:45	15:02	
28	Mon		08:23	08:04	09:10	**UK:** Boxing Day Bank Holiday
			16:30	15:46	15:03	
29	Tues		08:23	08:04	09:09	
			16:31	15:47	15:04	
30	Wed	Third	08:23	08:04	09:09	
			16:32	15:48	15:05	
31	Th		08:23	08:04	09:09	
			16:33	15:49	15:07	

Dover 51° 07' N; 01° 19' E		
L	H	
10:10	02:50	16
22:25	15:14	
11:01	03:41	17
23:18	16:14	
12:02	04:44	18
	17:31	
00:26	05:56	19
13:13	18:43	
01:42	07:03	20
14:20	19:43	
02:51	08:02	21
15:23	20:38	
03:53	08:57	22
16:24	21:30	
04:51	09:50	23
17:22	22:21	
05:47	10:42	24
18:19	23:11	
06:42	11:33	25
19:14		
07:37	00:00	26
20:06	12:24	
08:29	00:48	27
20:54	13:14	
09:19	01:37	28
21:39	14:06	
10:05	02:27	29
22:22	14:59	
10:51	03:18	30
23:07	15:53	
11:39	04:11	31
23:57	16:52	

2027 YEAR PLANNER

JANUARY

FEBRUARY

MARCH

APRIL

MAY

JUNE

JULY

AUGUST

SEPTEMBER

OCTOBER

NOVEMBER

DECEMBER

No	Name	+/-h:m
I	Dover	0:0
2	Dungeness	-0:12
3	Selsey Bill	-0:09
4	Swanage	-2:36
5	Portland	-4:23
5	Exmouth	-4:48
7	Salcombe	-5:23
8	Newlyn	+5:59
9	Padstow	-5:47
10	Bideford	-5:17
11	Bridgwater	-4:23
12	Sharpness Dock	-3:19
13	Cardiff (Penarth)	-4:16
14	Swansea	-4:52
15	Skomer Island	-5:00
16	Fishguard	-3:48
17	Barmouth	-2:45
18	Bardsey Island	-3:07
19	Caernavon	-1:07
20	Amlwch	-0:22
21	Connah's Key	+0:20
22	Hilbre Island	-0:05
23	Morecambe	+0:20
24	Silloth	+0:51
25	Girvan	+0:54
26	Lossiemoutb	+0:48
27	Fraserburgh	+1:20
28	Aberdeen	+2:30
29	Montrose	+3:30
30	Dunbar	+3:42
31	Holy Island	+3:58
32	Sunderland	+4:38
33	Whitby	+5:12
34	Bridlington	+5:53
35	Grimsby	-5:20
36	Skegness	-5:00
37	Blakeney	-4:07
38	Gorleston	-2:08

TIDAL DIFFERENCES

The difference in hours and minutes between High/Low Tide at Dover and the locations listed in the table on this page.

Shetland 42, 43

Orkney 44, 45

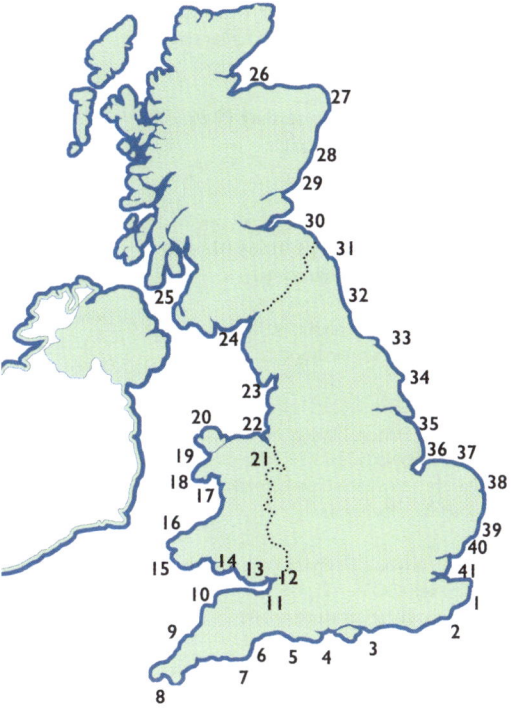

To estimate the state of the tide at any of these locations add or substract (in the case of negative differences shown in magenta) the hours and minutes indicated to the time of the high or low tide at Dover printed in the diary section.

Remember, the Dover tide times printed in the diary section are in all cases given in GMT. Adjust for BST (see diary for dates) if necessary.

No	Name	+/-h:m
39	Aldeburgh	-0:13
40	Bradwell Waterside	+1:11
41	Herne Bay	+1:28
42	Sullom Voe	-1:34
43	Lerwick	+0:01
44	Kirkwall	-0:26
45	Widewall Bay	-1:30

CAUTION

The tidal differences printed here are based on empirical observations. They are NOT issued by or official predictions of the UK Hydrographic Office. They are provided as an approximate guide, not a guarantee.

BIRD/GARDEN SUPPLIERS

Ark Wildlife Ltd
Dog Kennel Farm, Charlton Road, Nr Hitchin, Hertfordshire SG5 2AB; 0800 085 4865; office@arkwildlife.co.uk; www.arkwildlife.co.uk

Bamfords
Globe Mill, Midge Hall, Leyland, Lancashire PR26 6TN; 01772 456 300; sales@bamfords.co.uk; www.bamfords.co.uk

Brinvale Bird Foods
Brinvale Farm, Broughton Lane, Long Clawson, Melton Mowbray, Leicestershire LE14 4NB; 01664 823 230; info@brinvale.com; www.brinvale.com

CJ Wildbird Foods Ltd
The Rea, Upton Magna, Shrewsbury, Shropshire SY4 4UR; 0800 731 2820; sales@birdfood.co.uk; www.birdfood.co.uk

Eyebrook Wild Bird Feeds
Rectory Farm, Great Easton, Market Harborough, Leicestershire LE16 8SN; 01536 770 771; rectoryfarm@eyebrookwildbirdfeeds.co.uk; www.eyebrookwildbirdfeeds.co.uk

Gardenature
8-9 Baker Close, Oakwood Business Park North, Clacton on Sea, Essex CO15 4TL; 01255 429 931; hello@gardenature.co.uk; www.gardenature.co.uk

Garden Wildlife Direct
Unit 1 Industrial, Millennium City Park, Millennium Road, Preston, Lancashire PR2 5BL: 01772 440 242; help@gardenwildlifedirect.co.uk; www.gardenwildlifedirect.co.uk

Impeckable (nestboxes)
25 High St, Brymbo, Wrexham, LL11 5BL; 07554 385 878; info@impeckable.co.uk; www.impeckable.co.uk

Jacobi Jayne & Co
Wealden Forest Park, Herne Common, Herne Bay, Kent CT6 7LQ; 0800 072 0130; help@livingwithbirds.com; www.livingwithbirds.com

Kennedy Wild Bird Foods Ltd
The Warehouse, 74 Station Rd, Deeping St James, Peterborough, PE6 8RQ; 01778 342 665; info@kennedywildbirdfood.co.uk; www.kennedywildbirdfood.co.uk

(The) Nestbox Company
Eastcote House, Barston Lane, Eastcote, Solihull, West Midlands B92 0HS; 01675 442 299; mail@nestbox.co.uk; www.nestbox.co.uk

New Forest Bird Foods
Unit 1E(N), Flux, Hamilton Business Park, Gore Road, New Milton, Hampshire BH25 6TL; 07952 393 183; questions@newforestbirdfoods.co.uk; www.newforestbirdfoods.co.uk

(The) Owl Box
Tyddyn Waen, Nr Llangaffo, Isle of Anglesey, North Wales LL60 6LP; 01248 421 091; info@theowlbox.co.uk; www.theowlbox.co.uk

Soar Mill Seeds
Globe Mill, Midge Hall Lane, Leyland, Lancashire PR26 6TN: 01772 456 317; sales@soarmillseeds.co.uk; www.soarmillseeds.co.uk

Vine House Farm Bird Foods
Vine House Farm, Main Rd, Deeping St Nicholas, Spalding, Lincolnshire PE11 3DG; 01775 630 208; birdseed@vinehousefarm.co.uk; www.vinehousefarm.co.uk

Walter Harrison's
Pedigree House, Ambleside, Gamston, Nottingham, NG2 6NQ: 0115 982 3900; via website; www.walterharrisons.com

WILDLIFE WELFARE

A number of organizations work towards the care and rehabilitation of injured, sick and abandoned birds/wildlife across the UK, and individual wildlife hospitals carry out the same role on a local basis—a selection of these are listed below. The RSPCA (England & Wales), SSPCA (Scotland) and USPCA (Northern Ireland) are the national charities that help and advise on injured wildlife (**NOT** the RSPB). You can also find independent local rescue centres on www.helpwildlife.co.uk

ORGANIZATIONS

BRITISH WILDLIFE REHABILITATION COUNCIL (1987)
Promotes the care and welfare of sick, injured and abandoned wild animals, while supporting and educating workers active in this field. Organizes symposia and regional workshops. Periodically issues a newsletter, *The Rehabilitator*. Website includes a list of rehabilitators.

Contact: BWRC, PO Box 8686, Grantham, Lincolnshire NG31 0AG: secretary@bwrc.org.uk (general correspondence); www.bwrc.org.uk

CARING FOR BIRDS: Welfare Organizations

HELPWILDLIFE.CO.UK (2005)

A web-based group who utilize the Internet to help the public know what to do when faced with a wild bird/animal that may need help—their aim is to provide informed, unbiased advice about caring for sick or injured animals.

Volunteers trawl the Internet for details of those who might be able to help so that assistance can be offered quickly in an emergency. Their directory lists over 700 wildlife rescue organizations and independent rehabilitators. Visitors to the site are invited to provide feedback on the listings to ensure they are kept as up to date as possible.

Contact: The site itself DOES NOT offer wildlife rescue facilities. For general enquiries contact via their website— www.helpwildlife.co.uk

INTERNATIONAL CENTRE FOR BIRDS OF PREY (1967)

The ICBP works for the conservation of birds of prey through breeding programmes, habitat conservation and education. The Centre is not open to the public but does depend on donations to fund its work.

Contact: ICBP, Boulsdon House, Newent, Gloucs GL18 1JJ: 01531 820 286; jpj@icbp.org; www.icbp.org

PEOPLE'S DISPENSARY FOR SICK ANIMALS (1917)

Provides free veterinary treatment for sick/injured animals whose owners qualify for this charitable service, and also promotes responsible pet ownership.

Contact: PDSA, Whitechapel Way, Priorslee, Telford, Shropshire TF2 9PQ: 0300 3737 223; www.pdsa.org.uk

RAPTOR FOUNDATION (1989)

Provides medical care for injured raptors and returns rehabilitated birds back to the wild or provides a sanctuary for un-releasable birds. Researches into environmental and conservation matters. The centres assists in breed & release schemes to rebuild populations across Europe. An advice/rescue service is available for injured raptors and owls. Centre is open daily, 10am-5pm (4pm mid Oct-mid-Feb), closed 1 Jan 1 & 25/26 Dec.

Contact: The Raptor Foundation, The Heath, St Ives Road, Woodhurst, Cambs PE28 3BT: 01487 741 140; via website; www.raptorfoundation.org.uk

RAPTOR RESCUE (1978)

Raptor Rescue has evolved into one of the UK's foremost organizations dedicated to ensuring all sick and injured birds of prey are cared for by suitably qualified people and, wherever possible, released back into the wild.

Contact: Raptor Rescue: 07462 463 722 (national help and advice line, *and the preferred means of contact for the quickest response*); secretary@raptorrescue.org.uk; www.raptorrescue.org.uk

ROYAL SOCIETY FOR THE PREVENTION OF CRUELTY TO ANIMALS (1824): RSPCA

The oldest welfare charity looking out for the needs of animals on farms, in research labs, in the wild, in paddocks and in our homes. The RSPCA operate four wildilfe centres providing specialist care for the rehabilitation of wildlife throughout England and Wales. In cases of animal cruelty, inspectors are contacted through their National Contact Centre, which can be reached via the Society's national cruelty and advice line: 0300 1234 999 (between 8am-8pm).

Contact: RSPCA Headquarters, Willberforce Way, Southwater, Horsham, West Sussex RH13 9RS: via website; www.rspca.org.uk

SCOTTISH SOCIETY FOR THE PREVENTION OF CRUELTY TO ANIMALS (1839): SSPCA

Represents animal welfare interests to Government, local authorities and others. Educates young people to realize their responsibilities. Maintains an inspectorate to patrol and investigate and to advise owners about the welfare of animals in their care.

Maintains a National Wildlife Rescue Centre. Birds, including birds of prey, are rehabilitated and where possible released back into the wild: 03000 999 999 (animal helpline 7:30am-9pm).

Contact: SSPCA, Kingseat Road, Halbeath, Dunfermline, Fife KY11 8RY: via website; www.scottishspca.org

ULSTER SOCIETY FOR THE PREVENTION OF CRUELTY TO ANIMALS (1836): USPCA

Represents animal welfare in Northern Ireland with the purpose of preventing cruelty and relieving suffering to all animals, both pets and wildlife.

Contact: USPCA, Unit 5-6, Carnbane East Industrial Estate, Newry, Co Down BT35 6HQ: 028 3025 1000; enquiries@uspca.co.uk; www.uspca.co.uk

WILDLIFE HOSPITALS

All of the organizations and wildlife hospitals that look after the health and welfare of our wildlife rely on funding from memberships and/or donations.

In an emergency, **DO NOT** *send an e-mail, use the emergency phone numbers.*

England

ANIMAL HOUSE BIRDS OF PREY

Specializes in the rescue and rehabilitation of birds of prey.
Contact: 58 Dale Edge, Eastfield, Scarborough, **North Yorkshire** YO11 3EP: 07807 038 553; animalhouse1059674@hotmail.co.uk; www.facebook.com/AnimalHouseBirdsofPrey/

BERWICK SWAN & WILDLIFE TRUST

All categories of wildlife. Pools for swans, other waterfowl. Veterinary support. Memberships.
Contact: Windmill Way East, Ramparts Business Park, Berwick-upon-Tweed, **Northumberland** TD15 1TU: 01289 302 882; swan-trust@hotmail.co.uk; www.swan-trust.org

BRENT LODGE WILDLIFE HOSPITAL

All species of wild birds and small mammals.
Contact: Brent Lodge Bird & Wildlife Trust, Cow Lane, Sidlesham, Chichester, **West Sussex** PO20 7LN: 01243 641 672 (also emergency number); enquiries@brentlodge.org; www.brentlodge.org

BRITISH WILDLIFE RESCUE CENTRE

All species, including imprints and permanently injured. Hospital, large aviaries and caging. Veterinary support.
Contact: Wildlife Barn, London Road, Weston, **Staffordshire** ST18 0JS: 01889 271 308; admin@thebwrc.com; www.thebwrc.com

GENTLESHAW BIRD OF PREY & WILDLIFE CENTRE

All birds of prey (inc. owls). Hospital cages and aviaries; release sites. Veterinary support. Open to the public.
Contact: Fletcher's Garden Centre, Stone Road, Eccleshall, **Staffordshire** ST21 6JY: 01785 850 379; gentleshaw1@btconnect.com; www.gentleshawwildlife.co.uk

HAWK CONSERVANCY TRUST

The HCT is an important centre for receiving injured birds of prey and has one of the few specialist birds of prey hospitals in the UK. Open to the public.
Contact; Visitor Centre, Sarson Lane, Weyhill, Andover, **Hampshire** SP11 8DY: 01264 773 850; info@hawkconservancy.org; www.hawk-conservancy.org

RSPCA WILDLIFE CENTRES (not 24-hours)

East Winch, Gayton Rd, East Winch, **Norfolk** PE32 1LG: 0300 123 0709 (8am-8pm).
Mallydams Wood, Peter James Lane, Hastings, **East Sussex** TN35 4AH: 0300 123 0723 (8am-7pm).
Stapley Grange, London Road, Stapeley, Nantwich, **Cheshire** CW5 7JW: 0300 123 0722 (8am-8pm); Stapeley@rspca.org.uk
West Hatch, Cold Road, Taunton **Somerset** TA3 5RT: 0300 123 0721 (8:30am-9pm).
0300 1234 999 (national cruelty line 8am-8pm); www.rspca.org.uk/whatwedo/care/wildlifecentres & www.rspca.org.uk/whatwedo/yourlocal

SWAN LIFELINE

Thames Valley 24-hour swan rescue and treatment service. Veterinary support and hospital unit. Membership available.
Contact: Swan Rescue HQ & Treatment Centre, Cuckoo Weir Island, South Meadow Lane, Eton, **Berkshire** SL4 6SS: 01753 859 397 (24hr emergency line); enquiries@swanlifeline.uk (non-emergency); www.swanlifeline.uk

SWAN SANCTUARY (1980s)

Founded by Dorothy Beeson, this is the largest and only completely self-contained swan hospital in the UK. It has several nursing ponds and rehabilitation lakes. 24-hr rescue service, with volunteers on hand to recover swans (and other animals).
Contact: The Swan Sanctuary, Felix Lane, Shepperton, **Middlesex** TW17 8NN: 01932 240 790 (emergency); via website; www.theswansanctuary.org.uk

TIGGYWINKLES, THE WILDLIFE HOSPITAL TRUST

All British species. Veterinary referrals and helpline for vets and others on wild bird treatments. Full veterinary unit and staff. Membership available.
Contact: Tiggywinkles, Aston Road, Haddenham, Aylesbury, **Buckinghamshire** HP17 8AF: 01844 292 292 (24hr emergency helpline): via website (non-emergency); www.sttiggywinkles.org.uk

THE WILDLIFE AID FOUNDATION

Wildlife hospital and rehabilitation centre helping all native British species. Special housing for birds of prey. Membership scheme and fund raising activities. Veterinary support.
Contact: Randalls Farmhouse, Randalls Road, Leather-

head, **Surrey** KT22 0AL: 01372 360 404 (24-hr emergency helpline); via website; www.wildlifeaid.org.uk

VALE WILDLIFE HOSPITAL AND REHABILITATION CENTRE

All wildlife. Intensive care. Veterinary support. Phone manned 7am-5pm; hospital open for admissions 7am-10pm.
Contact: Station Road, Beckford, Tewkesbury, **Gloucestershire** GL20 7AN: 01386 882 288; info@valewildlife.org.uk; www.valewildlife.org.uk

Scotland

HESSILHEAD WILDLIFE RESCUE CENTRE

All species. Releasing aviaries. Veterinary support. Visits on open days. Membership available.
If you have an injured animal contact via telephone, not e-mail.
Contact: Hessilhead Wildlife Rescue Trust, Gateside, Beith, **Ayrshire** KA15 1HT: 01505 502 415; via website; www.hessilheadwildlife.org.uk

NATIONAL WILDLIFE RESCUE CENTRE

Six rescue and rehoming centres around the country—no visiting, but casualties accepted at any time—in addition to National Wildlife Rescue Centre.
Contact: SSPCA, National Wildlife Rescue Centre, Fishcross, Clackmannanshire FK10 3AN: 03000 999 999

(7am-9pm): via website; www.scottishspca.org/our-work/our-centres

Wales

GOWER BIRD HOSPITAL

All species of wild birds, also small mammals. Cares for sick, injured and orphaned wild animals with the sole intention of returning them to the wild.
Contact: Sandy Lane, Pennard, **Swansea**, SA3 2EW: 01792 371 630; info@gowerbirdhospital.org.uk; www.gowerbirdhospital.org.uk

Channel Islands

GSPCA ANIMAL SHELTER

All species. 24-hour emergency service. Veterinary support. Wildlife hospital undergoing a major rebuilding programme.
Contact: Les Fiers Moutons, St Andrews, **Guernsey** GY6 8UD: 01481 257 261; (07781 104 082 emergency); admin@gspca.org.gg; www.gspca.org.gg

JSPCA ANIMAL SHELTER

All species. 24-hour emergency service. Veterinary support. Educational Centre.
Contact: 89 St Saviour's Road, St Helier, **Jersey** JE2 4GJ: 01534 724 331; (07797 720 331 emergency); info@jspca.org.je; www.jspca.org.je

CHECKLIST OF BRITISH BIRDS

The rationale underlying all checklists is that the species should be arranged in a sequence that reflects their phylogenetic relationships. Unfortunately, in recent years there have been a number of different lists in which the species are arranged in different sequences, reflecting differing and changing views on how they are related. In the case of the British List, issued by the British Ornithologists' Union (**BOU**) and its Records Committee (**BOURC**), the sequence used has been that of the International Ornithological Committee (**IOC**).

For some time, efforts have been being made to try and unify the various different lists and to produce a single list that all could agree on. In June 2025 these labours bore fruit in the form of a new unified list known as AviList; or **AviList v25** in its current version, because it too is likely to change over time as our understanding of avian phylogeny evolves.

In July 2025, the BOU announced that, after a final IOC-based update, it will adopt AviList as the sequence for future editions of the official British List. However, as of the date this edition of **The Yearbook** went to press (October 2025), it had not yet issued such a list, with the current British List being the IOC-based 10th edition, as published in June 2022 (*Ibis* 164: 860-910), with subsequent updates up until 7th January 2025 and changes up until 12th August 2025.

Since this edition of **The Yearbook** will be used throughout 2026 and the BOU has already announced its intention to switch to the AviList sequence for future British Lists—the fact that it has not yet published such a British List notwithstanding—the checklist published in this edition takes the British List, incorporating changes up until 12th August 2025, but arranges the species in the AviList v25 sequence. The checklist published here is, in essence, **The Yearbook's** prediction of what a future British List will look like, when it is eventually issued.

Since checklists are intended to reflect the phylogenetic relationships of their constituent species, **The Yearbook's** checklist now has headings showing where a new order (suffix *-iformes*) or family (suffix *-idae*) starts. Each individual species entry is has the following elements.

Species Categories

The British Ornithologists' Union assigns species to one or more of the following categories.

A—Species recorded in an apparently natural state at least once since 1st January 1950.

B—Species recorded in an apparently natural state at least once between 1st January 1800 and 31st December 1949, but not subsequently.

C—Species that derive from translocation(s) (i.e. human-mediated movement and release) resulting in the establishment of self-sustaining populations within Britain, and vagrants from self-sustaining populations from outside Britain that have derived from translocation(s).

C1 *Naturalized translocated species*
Species that have occurred only as a result of translocation(s), e.g. Red-legged Partridge.

C2 *Naturalized established species*
Species with established populations resulting from translocation(s), but which also occur in an apparently natural state, e.g. Greylag Goose.

C3 *Naturalized re-established species*
Species successfully re-established in areas of former occurrence following a conservation translocation(s), e.g. Red Kite.

C4 *Naturalized feral species*
Species which have been domesticated and which now have populations established in the wild, e.g.

Rock Pigeon (Dove)/Feral Pigeon.

C5 *Vagrant naturalized species*
Vagrant species from populations outside Britain which derive from translocation(s).

C6 *Former naturalized species:*
Species formerly placed in C1 whose naturalized populations are either no longer self-sustaining or are considered extinct, e.g. Lady Amherst's Pheasant.

The official British List includes all species in categories A, B and C, and it is this list that forms the basis for *The Yearbook's* checklist. Species that *only* appear in the following categories do not form part of the British List.

D—Species that would otherwise appear in Category A but there is reasonable doubt that they have ever occurred in a natural state.

E—Species that have been recorded as introductions, human-assisted transportees or escapes from captivity, and whose breeding populations (if any) are thought not to be self-sustaining. Species in Category E that have bred in the wild in Britain are designated as E*.

F—Records of bird species recorded between c.16 000 BP (before present) to 1800.

Vagrants that are not on the British List, but which may have occurred in other parts of the British Isles, are not included. Readers who wish to record such species may use the extra rows provided. It should be noted that separate lists exist for Northern Ireland (kept by the Northern Ireland Rare Birds Committee) and the Isle of Man (kept by the Manx Ornithological Society); and that Irish records are assessed by the Irish Rare Birds Committee.

Vernacular names

Just as for many years there have been multiple different lists, so there have been multiple English names for any given species. The current British List, as published by the BOU, gives both a recommended British English name and, where it differs, an 'international' English variant, as used by the IOC. AviList not only proposes its own 'international' English name but also lists the English names used by the various lists it has unified; as well giving the various national and local arbiters of lists based on AviList the freedom to adopt local variants if they see fit—thank heavens for scientific names! The result is that many species have a multitude of English names. The names followed in **The Yearbook's** checklist will largely be the 'British' variants used by the BOU for the current British list unless very different from the names adopted by the widely used guidebooks. Where there is more than one frequently used English name, the alternative is given in the spare line in the relevant species entry. Where variants of a name differ in the addition or omission of one of more qualifying adjectives these are sometimes placed in square brackets, which are also used to indicate that although part of the recommended British English name of a species, some of these additional adjectives might be felt to be 'over the top' for a checklist primarily designed to be used in the UK—how many Alpine Choughs have you seen recently on your local patch?

Scientific names

Binomial scientific names are supposedly immutable and the same the world over whatever vernacular name is used for a species. This, however, is not quite true. The generic name (the first word in the binomial) can change if the underlying science warrants the creation of a new genus, the elimination of an existing one or the move of a species from one genus to another. Likewise, the specific name (the second word in the binomial) can change if a species is split or lumped.

Talking of lumping, a small number of species have been lumped as a result of the adoption of AviList. The name of the former species that has been lumped wih another is given in line below the entry for the species whose vernacular name has been retained.

BTO species codes (BTO)

Almost all species on the British List have been assigned a standard five-letter code by the BTO, which is primarily used in ringing. Many of the more commonly encountered species have also been assigned a two-letter code, which is mainly used in field surveys. For reasons of space, where it exists, the two-letter code is given but remember that every species with a two-letter code also has a five-letter one, should you need it. Typically, a five-letter BTO code consists of the first three letters of the first word in its English name and then the first two letters of the second word in the name, with variations on this pattern when the English name does not follow the two word norm. A dash indicates that no code has been set.

EURING species numbers (EUR)

EURING databases collate recovery records from ringing schemes throughout Europe species have been assigned numerical codes. Since these codes cover the full Holarctic bird list there are many apparent gaps in the British List. It is important that these are not filled arbitrarily by observers wishing to record species not listed in the charts, as this would compromise the integrity of the scheme.

Similarly, the addition of a further digit to indicate subspecies is to be avoided, since EURING has already assigned numbers for this purpose. The numbering follows the Voous species sequence so some species are now out of sequence following the re-ordering of the British List.

For full details, visit: www.euring.org

How common is what you are seeing?

Where available/relevant, the status of a species as assessed by one or more of the following three bodies is shown.

Rare Breeding Birds Panel (RBBP)

The species monitored by the Rare Breeding Birds Panel (see **UK Organizations**) are those with a sustained population of fewer than 2,000 breeding pairs (based on the most recent 5-year mean). For non-native species the threshold is 300 breeding pairs.

The following codes in the RBBP column reflect the status of each species considered by the RBBP in its most recent report, covering 2022

A—Regular Rare Breeding Birds

B—Occasional Rare Breeding Birds

B*—As B but breeding has only occurred in a hybrid pair

C—Potential Rare Breeding Birds

D—Regular Rare Non-native Breeding Birds

E—Occasional Rare Non-native Breeding Birds

F—Potential Rare Non-native Breeding Birds

*—Colonizing Breeding Species

**—Former Breeding Species

For full details: 49th Report of the Rare Breeding Birds Panel covering 107 scarce native and 14 non-native taxa

that bred or attempted to breed in 2022.
Published November 2024 in *British Birds* 117: 586-656:
Mark Eaton and the Rare Breeding Birds Panel;
or visit: www.rbbp.org.uk

British Birds Rarities Committee (BBRC)

Species ranked as rarities by the BBRC are indicated by an 'R' (and subspecies rarities by an asterisk *) in the column headed BBRC. The BBRC revises the list of rarities from time to time and the most recent list dates from May 2020. Since there have been changes to the British List since then, some species that would warrant being treated as rarities may not be marked as such For full details visit: www.bbrc.org.uk

APEP-4

From time to time, the Avian Population Estimates Panel produces a report estimating the breeding and/or wintering population of the commoner species found in the UK.

The fourth such report, **APEP-4**, was published in February 2020 in *British Birds* 113: 69-104: Population estimates of birds in Great Britain and the United Kingdom. Woodward, I, Aebischer, N, Burnell, D, Eaton, M, Frost, T, Hall, C, Stroud, D A, Noble, D.

Where available, estimates of breeding (B) and/or wintering (W) populations are shown to the right of the species names and codes.

APEP-5 is in preparation but the data is still being reviewed. It is expected that it will be published in the early part of 2026. Fingers crossed, it will be available in time for inclusion in **The Birdwatcher's Yearbook 2027.**

CHECKLIST OF BRITISH BIRDS

The *Checklist* begins on page 100 but before the list proper begins with species on the British List arranged in AviList v 25 order, a blank table, formatted like the Checklist, is printed on the facing page. Should you be fortunate enough to record species not on the British List, you can use the blank rows in the table opposite for this purpose.

A note on layout

Although each page of the *Checklist* appears at first sight to be formatted in a uniform way, there are in fact numerous minor differences in positioning between one page and another. These are not accidental but deliberate and have been adopted to accommodate the possibility of species being included in multiple BOU categories, having vernacular names with several qualifying adjectives, long scientific names and a 5-letter BTO code. Fortunately for the layout, there are relatively few nightmare species that bust the boundaries of every column. Most species content themselves with breaking the bounds of just one or two rather than all, so it is possible to accommodate every species by shifting one or two column boudaries left or right.

I apologize for these minor shifts in positioning from one page to the next of the checklist but I felt that it was worth departing from rigid uniformity of layout for the sake of content.

CHECKLIST OF BRITISH BIRDS

F	E	D	C	B	A	Dec	Nov	Oct	Sep	Aug	Jul	Jun	May	Apr	Mar	Feb	Jan	2026	Life

BBRC
RBBP
EUR
BTO

ANSERIFORMES: Duck, Swans and Geese
Anatidae: Ducks, Swans and Geese

Code	Common name	Scientific name	BTO	EUR	RBBP	BBRC	Life
C1E*	Ruddy Duck	Oxyura jamaicensis	RY	02250	D		B: 2-3 pairs, 2017. W: 23 individuals, 2016
AC2F	Mute Swan	Cygnus olor	MS	01520			B: 7,000 (6,300-7,600) pairs, 2016. W: 52,500 individuals, 2012/13-2016/17
AEF	Bewick's Swan	Cygnus columbianus	BS	01530		*	W: 4,350 individuals, 2015.
	Tundra Swan						
AE*F	Whooper Swan	Cygnus cygnus	WS	01540	A		B: 28 pairs, 2013-17. W: 19,500 individuals, 2015.
AEF	Brent Goose	Branta bernicla	BG	01680			W: 105,000 individuals, 2012/13-2016/17
AE*F	Red-breasted Goose	Branta ruficollis	EB	01690	E	R	
AC2E*	Canada Goose	Branta canadensis	CG	01660		*	B: 54,000 pairs, 2013-17. W: 160,000 individuals, 2012/13-2016/17
AC2E*F	Barnacle Goose	Branta leucopsis	BY	01670			B: 1,450 pairs, 2021-15. W: 105,000. -
AE	Cackling Goose	Branta hutchinsii	LQ	16640	E	R	
AE*	Ross's Goose	Anser rossii	RJ	16400		R	
AC2E*	Snow Goose	Anser caerulescens	SJ	01630	D		B: 2+ pairs, 2010-14. W: 75 individuals, 2011/12-2015/16
AC2C4E*F	Greylag Goose	Anser anser	GJ	01610			B: 47,000 pairs, 2013-17. W: 230,000 individuals, 2012/13-2016/17

ANSERIFORMES: Duck, Swans and Geese
Anatidae: Ducks, Swans and Geese

			BTO	EU	RBBP	BBRC	Life / 2026 notes
AE*F	Lesser White-fronted Goose	Anser erythropus	LC	01600	F	R	
AE£F	White-fronted Goose	Anser albifrons	WG	01590	E		B: 0-1 pairs, 2013-17. W: 14,000 individuals, -
AE	Tundra Bean Goose	Anser serrirostris	XR	01574			W: 300 individuals, 2011/12-2014/15
AE*F	Pink-footed Goose	Anser brachyrhynchus	PG	01580	B		W: 510,000 individuals, 2015/16
AE*F	Taiga Bean Goose	Anser fabalis	XF	01571	E		W: 230 individuals, 2016/17-2017/18
CIE*	Mandarin Duck	Aix galericulata	MN	01780			B: 4,400+ pairs, 2007-11. W: 13,500 individuals, 2007-11
CIC5E*	Egyptian Goose	Alopochen aegyptiaca	EG	01700			B: 1,850 pairs, 2013-17. W: 5,600 individuals, 2012/13-2016/17
AF	[Common] Shelduck	Tadorna tadorna	SU	01730			B: 7,850+ pairs, 2016. W: 51,000 individuals, 2021/13-2016/17
BDE*F	Ruddy Shelduck	Tadorna ferruginea	UD	01710	D	R	
AF	Long-tailed Duck	Clangula hyemalis	LN	02120	B		W: 13,500+ individuals, 2011/12-2014/15
A	Steller's Eider	Polysticta stelleri	ES	02090		R	
A	King Eider	Somateria spectabilis	KE	02070	B*	R	

Sub-total

Monthly columns (Jan, Feb, Mar, Apr, May, Jun, Jul, Aug, Sep, Oct, Nov, Dec) and columns A, B, C, D, E, F are blank.

ANSERIFORMES: Duck, Swans and Geese
Anatidae: Ducks, Swans and Geese

	Common name	Scientific name	BTO	EUR	RBBP	BBRC	Life	2026	Jan	Feb	Mar	Apr	May	Jun	Jul	Aug	Sep	Oct	Nov	Dec	A	B	C	D	E	F
AF	[Common] Eider	Somateria mollissima	E	02060			B: 37,000 pairs, 2012-15. W: 86,000 individuals, 2011/12-2014/15																			
A	Harlequin Duck	Histrionicus histrionicus	HQ	02110		R																				
AF	Common Scoter	Melanitta nigra	CX	12131	A		B: 52 pairs, 2007. W: 135,000+ individuals, 2011/12-2014/15																			
A	Black Scoter	Melanitta americana	DX	02132		R																				
AF	Surf Scoter	Melanitta perspicillata	FS	02140		R	W: 24 individuals, 2012/13-2016/17																			
AF	Velvet Scoter	Melanitta fusca	VS	02151	C		W: 3,350+ individuals, 2011/12-2014/15																			
A	White-winged Scoter	Melanitta deglandi	VD	02152		R																				
A	Stejneger's Scoter	Melanitta stejnegeri	-	02153																						
AE	Bufflehead	Bucephala albeola	VH	02160		R																				
AE	Barrow's Goldeneye	Bucephala islandica	VG	02170		R																				
AE*F	[Common] Goldeneye	Bucephala clangula	GN	12180	A		B: 200 females, 2006-10. W: 21,000, 2012/13-2016/17																			
AF	Smew	Mergellus albellus	SY	02200	C		W: 125 individuals, 2012/13-2016/17																			
AE	Hooded Merganser	Lophodytes cucullatus	HO	02190		R																				

ANSERIFORMES: Duck, Swans and Geese
Anatidae: Ducks, Swans and Geese

			BTO	EUR	RBBP	BBRC	Life	2026	Jan	Feb	Mar	Apr	May	Jun	Jul	Aug	Sep	Oct	Nov	Dec	A	B	C	D	E	F
AF	Red-breasted Merganser	*Mergus serrator*	RM	02210	A		B: 1,650+ pairs, 2008-11. W: 11,000 individuals, 2012/13-2016/17																			
AF [Common Merganser]	Goosander	*Mergus merganser*	GD	02230			B: 4,800 (4,250-5,250)+, 2016. W: 14,500, 2012/13-2016/17																			
AC2E*F	Red-crested Pochard	*Netta rufina*	RQ	01960	D		B: 39 (20-47)+ pairs, 2010-14. W: 570 individuals, 2012/13-2016/17																			
AE	Ferruginous Duck	*Aythya nyroca*	FD	02020	B	R	W: 9 individuals,, 2012/13-2016/17																			
AE*F	[Common] Pochard	*Aythya ferina*	PO	01980	A																					
AE	Canvasback	*Aythya valisineria*	VB	01970		R																				
AE	Ring-necked Duck	*Aythya collata*	NG	02000	B*		W: 18 individuals, 2012/13-2016/17																			
AE	Redhead	*Aythya americana*	AZ	01990		R																				
AF	Tufted Duck	*Aythya fuligula*	TU	02030			B: 16,500-19,000, 2016. W: 140,000 individuals, 2012/13-2016/17																			
A	Lesser Scaup	*Aythya affinis*	AY	02050	C	R																				
AF	[Greater] Scaup	*Aythya marila*	SP	02040	B		B: 0-1 pairs, 2013-17. W: 6,400+ individuals, 2011/12-2014/15																			
AE	Baikal Teal	*Sibirionetta formosa*	IK	18300	R																					
	Sub-total																									

103

ANSERIFORMES: Duck, Swans and Geese
Anatidae: Ducks, Swans and Geese

	English	Scientific	BTO	EUR	RBBP	BBRC	Life	2026	Jan	Feb	Mar	Apr	May	Jun	Jul	Aug	Sep	Oct	Nov	Dec	A	B	C	D	E	F
AF	Garganey	Spatula querquedula	GY	01910	A		B: 105 pairs, 2013-17																			
AE*	Blue-winged Teal	Spatula discors	TB	01920	B*	R																				
AF	[Northern] Shoveler	Spatula clypeata	SV	01940	A		B: 1,100 pairs, 2013-17. W: 19,500 individuals 2012/13-2016/17																			
AE	Falcated Duck	Mareca falcata	FT	01810		R																				
AC2E*F	Gadwall	Mareca strepera	GA	01820			B: 1,250-3,200 pairs, 2016. W: 31,000 Individuals, 2012/13-2016/17																			
AE*F	[Eurasian] Wigeon	Mareca penelope	WN	01790	A		B: 200+ pairs, 2013-17. W: 450,000 individuals, 2012/13-2016/17																			
AE	American Wigeon	Mareca americana	AW	01800			W: 18 individuals, 2012/13-2016/17																			
AC2C4E*F	Mallard	Anas platyrhynchos	MA	01860	A		B: (61,000-145,000)+ pairs, 2012/13-2016/17. W: 675,000 individuals, 2012/13-2016/17																			
A	[American] Black Duck	Anas rubripes	BD	01870	B*	R																				
AEF	[Northern] Pintail	Anas acuta	PT	01890	A		B: 27 pairs, 2013-17. W: 20,000 individuals, 2012/13-2016/17																			
AF	[Eurasian] Teal	Anas crecca	T.	01840			B: (2,700-4,750) pairs, 2016. W: 435,000 individuals,2012/13-2016/17																			

Now synonymous with Green-winged Teal

GALLIFORMES: Grouse, Pheasants & Allies
Phasianidae: Grouse, Pheasants & Allies

	English name	Scientific name	BTO	EUR	RBBP	BBRC	Life	2026	Jan	Feb	Mar	Apr	May	Jun	Jul	Aug	Sep	Oct	Nov	Dec	A	B	C	D	E	F
AF	[Rock] Ptarmigan	Lagopus muta	PM	03300			B: 2,000-15,000 pairs, 2007																			
AF	Red Grouse	Lagopus scotica	RG	03290			B: 265,000 pairs, 2016																			
C3E*F	[Western] Capercaillie	Tetrao urogallus	CP	03350	A		W: 1,100 individuals, 2015/16																			
AEF	Black Grouse	Lyrurus tetrix	BK	03320			B: 4,850 males, 2016																			
AC2E*F	Grey Partridge	Perdix perdix	P.	03670			B: 37,000 territories, 2016																			
C6E*	Golden Pheasant	Chrysolophus pictus	GF	03960	D		B: 15 males, 2010-14																			
C6E*	Lady Amherst's Pheasant	Chrysolophus amherstiae	LM	03970	D		B: 0 males, 2016																			
C1E*F	[Common] Pheasant	Phasianus colchicus	PH	03940			B: 2,300,000 females, 2016																			
	Indian Peafowl	Pavio cristatus	FT	35670	E																					
(not on British List but included because you may encounter)																										
AE*F	[Common] Quail	Coturnix coturnix	Q.	03700	A		B: 350 males, 2013-17																			
C1E*F	Red-legged Partridge	Alectoris rufa	RL	03580			B: 72,500 territories, 2016																			
	Sub-total																									

PODICEPEDIFORMES: Grebes
Podicepedidae: Grebes

			BTO	EUR	RBBP	BBRC	Life	2026	Jan	Feb	Mar	Apr	May	Jun	Jul	Aug	Sep	Oct	Nov	Dec	A	B	C	D	E	F
AF	Little Grebe	Tachybaptus ruficollis	LG	00070			B: (3,650-7,300) pairs, 2016. W: 15,500 individuals, 2012/13-2016/17																			
A	Pied-billed Grebe	Podilymbus podiceps	PJ	00060	B*	R																				
AF	Slavonian Grebe	Podiceps auritus	SZ	00110	A		B: 28 pairs, 2013-17. W: 995 individuals, 2011/12-2014/15																			
AF	Red-necked Grebe	Podiceps grisegena	RX	00100	B	*	B: (0-1) pairs, 2013-17. W: 60 individuals, 2011/12-2014/15																			
	P.g. holbolli 1 record																									
AF	Great Crested Grebe	Podiceps cristatus	GG	00090			B: 4,900+ pairs, 2016. W: 18,000 individuals, 2012/13-2016/17																			
A	Black-necked Grebe	Podiceps nigricollis	BN	00120	A		B: 55 pairs, 2013-17. W: 115 individuals, 2011/12-2014/15																			

OTIDIFORMES: Bustards
Otidae: Bustards

			BTO	EUR	RBBP	BBRC	Life	2026	Jan	Feb	Mar	Apr	May	Jun	Jul	Aug	Sep	Oct	Nov	Dec	A	B	C	D	E	F
AE*F	Great Bustard	Otis tarda	US	04460	A	R	B: 4 pairs, 2013-17																			
A	Asian Houbara	Chlamydotis macqueenii	HOUBU	04440		R																				
	Macqueen's Bustard																									
AF	Little Bustard	Tetrax tetrax	LITBS	04420	A	R																				

CUCULIFORMES: Cuckoos
Cuculidae: Cuckoos

			BTO	EUR	RBBP	BBRC	Life	2026	Jan	Feb	Mar	Apr	May	Jun	Jul	Aug	Sep	Oct	Nov	Dec	A	B	C	D	E	F
A	Great Spotted Cuckoo	Clamator glandarius	UK	07160		R																				
A	Yellow-billed Cuckoo	Coccyzus americanus	YEBCU	07280		R																				

CUCULIFORMES: Cuckoos
Cuculidae: Cuckoos

	English name	Scientific name	BTO	EUR	RBBP	BBRC	Life	2026	Jan	Feb	Mar	Apr	May	Jun	Jul	Aug	Sep	Oct	Nov	Dec	A	B	C	D	E	F
A	Black-billed Cuckoo	Coccyzus erythropthalmus	BLBCU	0727		R																				
AF	[Common] Cuckoo	Cuculus canorus	CK	0724			B: 18,000 (9,800-26,000)+ pairs, 2016																			

PTEROCLIFORMES: Sandgrouse
Pteroclidae: Sandgrouse

	English name	Scientific name	BTO	EUR	RBBP	BBRC	Life	2026	Jan	Feb	Mar	Apr	May	Jun	Jul	Aug	Sep	Oct	Nov	Dec	A	B	C	D	E	F
A	Pallas's Sandgrouse	Syrrhaptes paradoxus	PALSA	0663		R																				

COLUMBIFORMES: Pigeons & Doves
Columbidae: Pigeons & Doves

	English name	Scientific name	BTO	EUR	RBBP	BBRC	Life	2026	Jan	Feb	Mar	Apr	May	Jun	Jul	Aug	Sep	Oct	Nov	Dec	A	B	C	D	E	F
A	Mourning Dove	Zenaida macroura	-	0695		R																				
A	Oriental Turtle Dove	Streptopelia orientalis	RUTDO	0689		R																				
AF	Turtle Dove [European]	Streptopelia turtur	TD	0687	A		B: 3,600 territories, 2016																			
A	Collared Dove [Eurasian]	Streptopelia decaocto	CD	0684			B: 810,000 (730,000-890,000) pairs, 2016																			
AF	Woodpigeon [Common]	Columba palumbus	WP	0670			B: 5,150,000 (4,850,000-5,450,000) pairs, 2016																			
AC4E*F	Rock Dove also Feral Pigeon	Columba livia	DV/FP	0665			B: 465,000 (380,000-550,000) pairs, 2016																			
AF	Stock Dove	Columba oenas	SD	0668			B: 320,000 territories, 2016																			

Sub-total

GRUIFORMES: Rails, Cranes
Gruidae: Cranes

Status	English name	Scientific name	BTO	EUR	RBBP	BBRC	Life	2026	Jan	Feb	Mar	Apr	May	Jun	Jul	Aug	Sep	Oct	Nov	Dec	A	B	C	D	E	F
A	Sandhill Crane	*Antigone canadensis*	SANCR	04360		R																				
AE*F	[Common] Crane	*Grus grus*	AN	04330	A																					

Rallidae: Rails

Status	English name	Scientific name	BTO	EUR	RBBP	BBRC	Life	2026	Jan	Feb	Mar	Apr	May	Jun	Jul	Aug	Sep	Oct	Nov	Dec	A	B	C	D	E	F
AF	Water Rail	*Rallus aquaticus*	WA	04070			B: 3,900+ territories, 2016-17																			
AE*F	Corncrake	*Crex crex*	CE	04210	A		B: 1,100 males, 2016-17																			
A	Sora	*Porzana carolina*	JR	04090		R																				
AF	Spotted Crake	*Porzana porzana*	AK	04080	A		B: 27 males, 2012-17																			
AF	[Common] Moorhen	*Gallinula chloropus*	MH	04240			B: 210,000 territories, 2016. W: 305,000 individuals, 2012/13-2016/17																			
AF	[Eurasian] Coot	*Fulica atra*	CO	04290			B: 26,000+ pairs, 2016. W: 205,000 individuals, 2012/13-2016/17																			
A	American Coot	*Fulica americana*	AO	04300		R																				
A	Allen's Gallinule	*Porphyrio alleni*	ALLGA	04250		R																				
A	American Purple Gallinule	*Porphyrio martinica*	AMPGA	04260		R																				
AE	Purple/Western Swamphen	*Porphyrio porphyrio*	PURSW	04270		R																				

(Western on list but Purple used in field guides)

GRUIFORMES: Rails, Cranes
Rallidae: Rails

	Common name	Scientific name	BTO	EUR	RBBP	BBRC	Life	2026	Jan	Feb	Mar	Apr	May	Jun	Jul	Aug	Sep	Oct	Nov	Dec	A	B	C	D	E	F
A	Little Crake	*Zapornia parva*	JC	04100	C	R																				
A	Baillon's Crake	*Zapornia pusilla*	VC	04110	C	R	B: (0-6) males, 2016																			

CHARADRIFORMES: Waders, Gulls & Relatives
Burhinidae: Stone-Curlews

	Common name	Scientific name	BTO	EUR	RBBP	BBRC	Life	2026	Jan	Feb	Mar	Apr	May	Jun	Jul	Aug	Sep	Oct	Nov	Dec	A	B	C	D	E	F
AF	[Eurasian] Stone-curlew	*Burhinus oedicnemus*	TN	04590	A		B: 365+ pairs. 2013-17																			

Recurvirostridae: Stilts, Avocets

	Common name	Scientific name	BTO	EUR	RBBP	BBRC	Life	2026	Jan	Feb	Mar	Apr	May	Jun	Jul	Aug	Sep	Oct	Nov	Dec	A	B	C	D	E	F
AEF	[Pied] Avocet	*Recurvirostra avosetta*	AV	04560	A		B: 1,950 pairs, 2013-17. W: 8,700 individuals, 2012/13-2016/17																			
A	Black-winged Stilt	*Himantopus himantopus*	IT	04550	*		B: 3 (0-6) pairs, 2013-17																			

Haematopodidae: Oystercatchers

	Common name	Scientific name	BTO	EUR	RBBP	BBRC	Life	2026	Jan	Feb	Mar	Apr	May	Jun	Jul	Aug	Sep	Oct	Nov	Dec	A	B	C	D	E	F
AF	[Eurasian] Oystercatcher	*Haematopus ostralegus*	OC	04500			B: 95,500 pairs, 2016. W: 305,000 individuals, 2012/13-2016/17																			

Charadriidae: Plovers

	Common name	Scientific name	BTO	EUR	RBBP	BBRC	Life	2026	Jan	Feb	Mar	Apr	May	Jun	Jul	Aug	Sep	Oct	Nov	Dec	A	B	C	D	E	F
AF	Grey Plover	*Pluvialis squatarola*	GV	04860			W: 33,500 individuals, 2012/13-2016/17																			
AF	[European] Golden Plover	*Pluvialis apricaria*	GP	04850			B: (32,500-50,500) pairs, 2016. W: 410,000 individuals, 2006/7																			
A	American Golden Plover	*Pluvialis dominica*	ID	04840																						

Sub-total

CHARADRIFORMES: Waders, Gulls & Relatives
Charadriidae: Plovers

	English name	Scientific name	BTO	EUR	RBBP	BBRC	Life	2026	Jan	Feb	Mar	Apr	May	Jun	Jul	Aug	Sep	Oct	Nov	Dec	A	B	C	D	E	F
A	Pacific Golden Plover	*Pluvialis fulva*	IF	04842		R																				
A	[Eurasian] Dotterel	*Eudromius morinellus*	DO	04820	A		B: 425 (280-645) males, 2011																			
A	Killdeer	*Charadrius vociferus*	KL	04740	C	R																				
AF	[Common] Ringed Plover	*Charadrius hiaticula*	RP	04700			B: 5,450 (5,250-5,600) pairs, 2016. W: 42,500 individuals, 2012.13-2016/17																			
A	Semipalmated Plover	*Charadrius semipalmatus*	TV	04710		R																				
A	Little Ringed Plover	*Thinornis dubius*	LP	04690	A		B: 1,250 (1,200-1,399) pairs, 2007																			
AF	[Northern] Lapwing	*Vanellus vanellus*	L.	04930			B: 97,500 pairs, 2016. W: 635,000 individuals, 2006/7																			
A	Grey-headed Lapwing	*Vanellus cinereus*	-			R																				
A	Sociable Lapwing	*Vanellus gregarius*	IP	04910		R																				
A	White-tailed Lapwing	*Vanellus leucurus*	WHTPL	04920		R																				
A	Caspian Plover	*Anarhychus asiaticus*	CASPLL	04800		R																				
A	Tibetan Sand Plover	*Anarhychus atrifrons*	-	042780		R*																				

110

CHARADRIFORMES: Waders, Gulls & Relatives

Charadriidae: Plovers

	English Name	Scientific Name	BTO	EUR	RBBP	BBRC	Life	2026	Jan	Feb	Mar	Apr	May	Jun	Jul	Aug	Sep	Oct	Nov	Dec	A	B	C	D	E	F
A	Siberian Sand Plover	*Anarhychus mongolus*	DQ	04780		R*																				
A	Greater Sand Plover	*Anarhychus leschenaultii*	DP	04790		R																				
A	Kentish Plover	*Anarhychus alexandrinus*	KP	04770	**	R																				

Scolopacidae: Sandpipers, Snipe

	English Name	Scientific Name	BTO	EUR	RBBP	BBRC	Life	2026	Jan	Feb	Mar	Apr	May	Jun	Jul	Aug	Sep	Oct	Nov	Dec	A	B	C	D	E	F
A	Upland Sandpiper	*Bartramia longicauda*	UP	05440		R																				
B	Eskimo Curlew	*Numenius borealis*	ESKCU	05370		R																				
A	Little Whimbrel/Curlew	*Numenius minutus*	LITWH	05360		R																				
A	Hudsonian Whimbrel	*Numenius hudsonicus*	NU	05381		R																				
AF	[Eurasian] Whimbrel	*Numenius phaeopus*	WM	05380	A	*	B; 310 pairs, 2009. W: 41 individuals, 2012/13-2016/17																			
AF	[Eurasian] Curlew	*Numenius arquata*	CU	05410	C		B: 58,500 pairs, 2016. W: 125,000 individuals, 2012/13-2016/17																			
AF	Bar-tailed Godwit	*Limosa lapponica*	BA	05430			W: 53,500 individuals, 2012/13-2016/17																			
AF	Black-tailed Godwit	*Limosa limosa*	BW	05320	A		B: 53 pais, 2013-17. W: 41,000 individuals, 2012/13-2016/17																			
	Sub-total																									

CHARADRIFORMES: Waders, Gulls & Relatives
Scolopacidae: Sandpipers, Snipe

	Species	Scientific name	BTO	EUR	RBBP	BBRC	Life	2026	Jan	Feb	Mar	Apr	May	Jun	Jul	Aug	Sep	Oct	Nov	Dec	A	B	C	D	E	F
A	Hudsonian Godwit	Limosa haemastica	HU	05330		R																				
A	Long-billed Dowitcher	Limnodromus scolopaceus	LD	05270		R																				
A	Short-billed Dowitcher	Limnodromus griseus	SHBDO	05260		R																				
AF	Jack Snipe	Lymnocryptes minimus	JS	05180	C		W: 110,000 individuals, 2004/05																			
AF	[Eurasian] Woodcock	Scolopax rusticola	WK	05290			B: 57,000 (43,000-71,000) males, 2016. W: 1,400,000 individuals, 2003/04																			
AF	Great Snipe	Gallinago media	DS	05200	C	R																				
A	Wilson's Snipe	Gallinago delicata	WILSN	05192		R																				
AF	[Common] Snipe	Gallinago gallinago	SN	05190			B: 66,500 pairs. W: 1,100,000 individuals 2004/05																			
A	Terek Sandpiper	Xenus cinereus	TK	05550		R																				
A	Common Sandpiper	Actitis hypoleucos	CS	05560			B: 13,000 pairs, 2016. W: 52 individuals, 2012/13-2016/17																			
A	Spotted Sandpiper	Actitis macularius	PQ	05570	B	R																				
A	Wilson's Phalarope	Phalaropus tricolor	VF	05630		R																				
AF	Grey Phalarope	Phalaropus fulicarius	PL	05650																						

CHARADRIIFORMES: Waders, Gulls & Relatives
Scolopacidae: Sandpipers, Snipe

	Common name	Scientific name	BTO	EUR	RBBP	BBRC	Life	2026	Jan	Feb	Mar	Apr	May	Jun	Jul	Aug	Sep	Oct	Nov	Dec	A	B	C	D	E	F
AF	Red-necked Phalarope or Red Phalarope	*Phalaropus lobatus*	NK	05640	A		B: 64 males, 2013-17																			
AF	Green Sandpiper	*Tringa ochropus*	GE	05530	A		B: 2 pairs, 2013-17. W: 290, 2011/12-2014/15																			
A	Solitary Sandpiper	*Tringa solitaria*	I.	05520		R																				
A	Grey-tailed Tattler	*Tringa brevipes*	YT	05580		R																				
A	Marsh Sandpiper	*Tringa stagnatilis*	MD	05470		R																				
A	Wood Sandpiper	*Tringa glareola*	OD	05540	A		B: 30 pairs, 2012-17																			
AF	[Common] Redshank	*Tringa totanus*	RK	05460			B: 22,000 pairs, 2016. W: 100,000 individuals, 2012/13-2016/17																			
A	Lesser Yellowlegs	*Tringa flavipes*	LY	05510																						
A	Spotted Redshank	*Tringa erythropus*	DR	05450			W: 68 individuals, 2012/13-2016/17																			
A	[Common] Greenshank	*Tringa nebularia*	GK	05480	A		B: 1,100+ pairs, 1995. W: 920 individuals, 2012/13-2016/17																			
A	Greater Yellowlegs	*Tringa melanoleuca*	LZ	05500		R																				
AF	[Ruddy] Turnstone	*Arenaria interpres*	TT	05610	C		W: 43,000 individials, 2012/13-2016/17																			
	Sub-total																									

CHARADRIFORMES: Waders, Gulls & Relatives
Scolopacidae: Sandpipers, Snipe

	Common name	Scientific name	BTO	EUR	RBBP	BBRC	Life	2026	Jan	Feb	Mar	Apr	May	Jun	Jul	Aug	Sep	Oct	Nov	Dec	A	B	C	D	E	F
AF	[Red] Knot	*Calidris canutus*	KN	04960			W: 265,000 individuals, 2012/13-2016/17																			
A	[Great] Knot	*Calidris tenuirstris*	KO	04950		R																				
AF	Ruff	*Calidris pugnax*	RU	05170	A		B: 13 females, 2013-17. W: 920 individuals, 2012/13-2016/17																			
A	Sharp-tailed Sandpiper	*Calidris acuminata*	VV	05080		R																				
A	Broad-billed Sandpiper	*Calidris falcinellus*	OA	05140	C	R																				
A	Curlew Sandpiper	*Calidris ferruginea*	CV	05090																						
A	Stilt Sandpiper	*Calidris himantopus*	MI	05150		R																				
A	Red-necked Stint	*Calidris ruficollis*	-	05000		R																				
A	Temminck's Stint	*Calidris temminckii*	TR	05020	**		B: 0 pairs, 2013-17.																			
A	Long-toed Stint	*Calidris subminuta*	LOTST	05030		R																				
A	Buff-breasted Sandpiper	*Calidris subruficollis*	BQ	05160	C																					
AF	Sanderling	*Calidris alba*	0497	04970	C		W: 20,500 individuals, 2012/13-2016/17																			

CHARADRIFORMES: Waders, Gulls & Relatives
Scolopacidae: Sandpipers, Snipe

AF			BTO	EUR	RBBP	BBRC	Life	2026	Jan	Feb	Mar	Apr	May	Jun	Jul	Aug	Sep	Oct	Nov	Dec	A	B	C	D	E	F
AF	Dunlin	*Calidris alpina*	DN	05120		*	B: (8,600-10,500) pairs, 2005-07. W: 350,000 individuals, 2012/13-2016/17																			
A	Purple Sandpiper	*Calidris maritima*	PS	05100	A		B: 1 pair, 2013-17. W: 9,500 individuals, 2012/13-2016/17																			
A	Baird's Sandpiper	*Calidris bairdii*	BP	05060		R																				
A	Pectoral Sandpiper	*Calidris melanotos*	PP	05160	C																					
A	Semipalmated Sandpiper	*Calidris pusilla*	PZ	04980		R																				
A	Western Sandpiper	*Calidris mauri*	ER	04990		R																				
A	Little Stint	*Calidris minuta*	LX	05010			W: 8 individuals, 2012/13-2016/27																			
A	Least Sandpiper	*Calidris minutilla*	EP	05040		R																				
A	White-rumped Sandpiper	*Calidris fuscicollis*	WU	05050																						

Glareolidae: Coursers, Pratincoles

AF			BTO	EUR	RBBP	BBRC	Life	2026	Jan	Feb	Mar	Apr	May	Jun	Jul	Aug	Sep	Oct	Nov	Dec	A	B	C	D	E	F
A	Cream-coloured Courser	*Cursorius cursor*	CRCCO	04640		R																				
A	Oriental Pratincole	*Glareola maldivarum*	GM	04660		R																				

Sub-total

CHARADRIFORMES: Waders, Gulls & Relatives
Glareoliidae: Coursers, Pratincoles

			BTO	EUR	RBBP	BBRC	Life	2026	Jan	Feb	Mar	Apr	May	Jun	Jul	Aug	Sep	Oct	Nov	Dec	A	B	C	D	E	F
A	Black-winged Pratincole	*Glareola nordmanni*	KW	04670		R																				
A	Collared Pratincole	*Glareola pratincola*	KM	04650		R																				
Stercorariidae: Skuas																										
AF	Arctic Skua / Parasitic Jaeger	*Stercorarius parasiticus*	AC	05670			B: 785 (535-1550), 2015																			
AF	Long-tailed Skua / Long-tailed Jaeger	*Stercorarius longicaudus*	OG	05680	B																					
AF	Pomarine Skua / Pomarine Jaeger	*Stercorarius pomarinus*	PK	05660																						
AF	Great Skua	*Stercorarius skua*	NX	05690			B: 9,650 pairs, 1998-2002.																			
A	South Polar Skua	*Stercorarius maccormicki*	SOPSK	05700		R																				
Alcidae: Auks																										
A	Tufted Puffin	*Fratercula cirrhata*	-	06560		R																				
AF	[Atlantic] Puffin	*Fratercula arctica*	PU	06540			B: 580,000 pairs, 1998-2002																			
A	Ancient Murrelet	*Synthliboramphus antiquus*	-	06450		R																				
A	Long-billed Murrelet	*Brachyramphus perdix*	IM	06412																							
AF	Black Guillemot	*Cepphus grylle*	TY	06380		*	B: 19,500 pairs, 1998-2003																			

CHARADRIFORMES: Waders, Gulls & Relatives

Alcidae: Auks

			BTO	EUR	RBBP	BBRC	Life	2026	Jan	Feb	Mar	Apr	May	Jun	Jul	Aug	Sep	Oct	Nov	Dec	A	B	C	D	E	F
A	Razorbill	*Alca torda*	RA	06360			B: 165,00 (100,000–250,000) pairs, 2015.																			
BF	Great Auk	*Pinguinus impennis*	-	06370			Your Jurassic Park moment																			
AF	Little Auk	*Alle alle*	LK	06470		*																				
AF	Brünnich's Guillemot	*Uria lomvia*	TZ	06350		R																				
	Thick-billed Murre																									
A	[Common] Guillemot	*Uria aalge*	GU	06340			B: 950,000 pairs, 1998-2002																			
	Common Murre																									

Laridae: Gulls, Terns

			BTO	EUR	RBBP	BBRC	Life	2026	Jan	Feb	Mar	Apr	May	Jun	Jul	Aug	Sep	Oct	Nov	Dec	A	B	C	D	E	F
A	Aleutian Tern	*Onychoprion aleuticus*	ALETE	06170		R																				
A	Sooty Tern	*Onychoprion fuscatus*	SOOTE	06220		R																				
A	Bridled Tern	*Onychoprion anaethetus*	BRITE	06230		R																				
A	Little Tern	*Sternula albifrons*	AF	06240			B: 1,450 pairs, 2013-17.																			
A	Least Tern	*Sternula antillarum*	-	06242	C	R																				
A	Caspian Tern	*Hydroprogne Caspia*	CJ	06060		R																				
	Sub-total																									

CHARADRIFORMES: Waders, Gulls & Relatives
Laridae: Terns,

	English name	Scientific name	BTO	EUR	RBBP	BBRC	Life	2026	Jan	Feb	Mar	Apr	May	Jun	Jul	Aug	Sep	Oct	Nov	Dec	A	B	C	D	E	F
A	Gull-billed Tern	*Geochelidon nilotica*	TG	05910		R																				
A	Whiskered Tern	*Chlidonias hybrida*	WD	06260		R																				
A	White-winged Black Tern or White-winged Tern	*Chlidonias leucopterus*	WJ	06280	C																					
A	Black Tern	*Chlidonias niger*	BJ	06270	**	*																				
AF	Sandwich Tern	*Thalasseus sandvicensis*	TE	06110		R	**B:** 14,000 (13,000-15,000) pairs, 2015. **W:** 65 individuals, 2011/12-2014/15																			
	Now synonymous with Cabot's Tern																									
A	Elegant Tern	*Thalasseus elegans*	ELETE	06120		R																				
A	Royal Tern	*Thalasseus maximus*	QT	06070		R																				
A	Lesser Crested Tern	*Thalasseus bengalensis*	TF	06090	B*	R																				
A	Forster's Tern	*Sterna forsteri*	FO	06180		R																				
A	Arctic Tern	*Sterna paradisaea*	AE	06160			**B:** 53,500 pairs, 2000.																			
AF	Common Tern	*Sterna hirundo*	CN	06150		*	**B:** 11,000 (8,900-13,500) pairs, 2015																			
A	Roseate Tern	*Sterna dougallii*	RS	06140	A		**B:** 100 pairs, 2013-17																			

CHARADRIFORMES: Waders, Gulls & Relatives
Laridae: Gulls

	English name	Scientific name	BTO	EUR	RBBP	BBRC	Life
AF	Little Gull	Hydrocoloeus minutus	LU	05780	B		
A	Ross's Gull	Rhodostethia rosea	QG	06010		R	
AF	[Black-legged] Kittiwake	Rissa tridactyla	KI	06020			B: 205,000 (175,000-255,000) pairs, 2015.
A	Sabine's Gull	Xema sabini	AB	05790			
A	Ivory Gull	Pagophila eburnea	IV	06040		R	
A	Slender-billed Gull	Chroicocephalus genei	EI	05850	C	R	
A	Bonaparte's Gull	Chroicocephalus philadelphia	ON	05810		R	
AF	Black-headed Gull	Chroicocephalus ridibundus	BH	58200			B: 140,000+, 1998-2002 pairs. W: 2,200,000 (2,100,000-2,300,000)+ indivs, 2003/04-2005/06
A	Laughing Gull	Leucophaeus atricilla	LF	05760		R	
A	Franklin's Gull	Leucophaeus pipixcan	FG	05770		R	
B	Great Black-headed Gull	Ichthyaetus ichthyaetus	GBHGU	05730		R	
	Pallas's Gull						
A	Audouin's Gull	Ichthyaetus audouinii	AUDGU	05880		R	

Sub-total

Columns across the recording grid: 2026, Jan, Feb, Mar, Apr, May, Jun, Jul, Aug, Sep, Oct, Nov, Dec, A, B, C, D, E, F

	CHARADRIFORMES: Waders, Gulls & Relatives **Laridae:** Gulls		BTO	EUR	RBBP	BBRC	Life	2026	Jan	Feb	Mar	Apr	May	Jun	Jul	Aug	Sep	Oct	Nov	Dec	A	B	C	D	E	F
A	**Mediterranean Gull**	*Ichthyaetus melanocephalus*	MU	05750	A		B: 1,200+ pairs, 2013-17. W: 4,000 individuals, 2011/12-2014/15																			
A	**Ring-billed Gull**	*Larus delawarensis*	IN	05880	B*		W: 21 individuals, 2012/13-2016/17																			
AF	**Common Gull**	*Larus canus*	CM	05900		*	B: 48,500 pairs, 1998-2002. W: 710,000 (680,000-730,000) individuals. 2003/04-2005/06																			
A	**Caspian Gull**	*Larus cachinnans*	YC	59270			W: 125 individuals, 2011/12-2014/15																			
A	**Kelp Gull**	*Larus dominicanus*	-	-		R																				
A	**American Herring Gull**	*Larus smithsonianus*	AH	26560		R																				
AF	**[European] Herring Gull**	*Larus argentatus*	HG	05920			B: 130,000 pairs, 1998-2002. W: 740,000 (710,000-780,000)+ individuals																			
A	**Yellow-legged Gull**	*Larus michahellis*	YG	59360	A	*	B: 2 pairs, 2013-17. W: 840 individuals, 2011/12-2014/15																			
AF	**Great Black-backed Gull**	*Larus marinus*	GB	06000			B: 15,000 (7,200-19,000)+ individuals, 2015. W: 77,000 (72,000-82,000)+, 2003/04-2005/06																			
AF	**Glaucous Gull**	*Larus hyperboreus*	GZ	05998	B*		W: 165+ individuals, 2011/12-2015/16.																			
AF	**Lesser Black-backed Gull**	*Larus fuscus*	LB	05910		*	B: 110,000 pairs, 1998-2002. W: 130,000 (120,000-130,000)+ individuals, 2003/04-2005/06.																			
L.f. fuscus Baltic Gull																										
A	**Glaucous-winged Gull**	*Larus glaucescens*	GLWGU	05960		R																				

CHARADRIFORMES: Waders, Gulls & Relatives
Laridae: Gulls

			BTO	EU	RBBP	BBRC	Life	2026	Jan	Feb	Mar	Apr	May	Jun	Jul	Aug	Sep	Oct	Nov	Dec	A	B	C	D	E	F
A	Slaty-backed Gull	*Larus schistisagus*	-	5950		R																				
A	Iceland Gull	*Larus glucoides*	IG	05980		*																				

PHAETHONTIFORMES: Tropicbirds
Phaethontidae: Tropicbirds

			BTO	EU	RBBP	BBRC	Life
AE	Red-billed Tropicbird	*Phaethon aethereus*	RTTBI	00640		R	

GAVIFORMES: Divers
Gavidae: Divers

			BTO	EU	RBBP	BBRC	Life
AF	Red-throated Diver	*Gavia stellata*	RH	00020	A		B: 1,250 (1,000-1,550) pairs, 2006. W: 21,500 individuals, 2011/12-2014/15
	Red-throated Loon						
AF	Great Northern Diver	*Gavia immer*	ND	00040	B*		W: 4,400+ individuals, 2015/16
	Common Loon						
A	White-billed Diver	*Gavia adamsii*	VW	00050			W: 80+ individuals, 2010-12
	Yellow-billed Loon						
A	Pacific Diver	*Gavia pacifica*	KD	00033		R	
	Pacific Loon						
AF	Black-throated Diver	*Gavia arctica*	RV	00030	A		B: 215 (190-215) pairs, 2006. W: 560+ individuals, 2004/05-2009/09
	Black-throated Loon						
	Sub-total						

PROCELLARIIFORMES: Tube noses
Diomedeidae: Albatrosses

	English name	Scientific name	BTO	EUR	RBBP	BBRC	Notes
A	Yellow-nosed Albatross [Atlantic]	Thalassarche chlororhynchos	YENAL	00151		R	
A	Black-browed Albatross	Thalassarche melanophris	AA	00140	C	R	

Oceanitidae: Southern Storm Petrels

	English name	Scientific name	BTO	EUR	RBBP	BBRC	Notes
A	Wilson's Storm Petrel	Oceanites oceanicus	WILPE	00500			
B	White-faced Storm Petrel	Pelagodroma marina	WHFPE	00510		R	

Hydrobatidae: Northern Storm Petrels

	English name	Scientific name	BTO	EUR	RBBP	BBRC	Notes
AF	European Storm-petrel or European Storm Petrel	Hydrobates pelagicus	TM	00520			B: 25,500 (21,000-33,500) AOS, 1998-2002.
A	Band-rumped Storm-petrel or Band-rumped Storm Petrel	Hydrobates castro	BRSPE	00580		R	
A	Swinhoe's Storm-petrel or Swinhoe's Storm Petrel	Hydrobates monorhis	SWSPE	00560		R	
AF	Leach's Storm-petrel or Leach's Storm Petrel	Hydrobates leucorhous	TL	00550			B: 48,000 (36,500-65,000) pairs, 1998-2002.

Procellariidae: Petrels, Diving Petrels, Shearwaters

	English name	Scientific name	BTO	EUR	RBBP	BBRC	Notes
AF	[Northern] Fulmar	Fulmarus glacialis	F.	00220			B: 350,000 (195,000-680,000) pairs, 2015.
A	White-chinned Petrel	Procellaria aequinoctialis	WHCPE	27800			
A	Scopoli's Shearwater	Calonectris diomedea	SCOSH	00360		R	

PROCELLARIIFORMES: Tube noses
Procellariidae: Petrels, Diving Petrels, Shearwaters

			BTO	EUR	RBBP	BBRC	Life	2026	Jan	Feb	Mar	Apr	May	Jun	Jul	Aug	Sep	Oct	Nov	Dec	A	B	C	D	E	F
AF	Cory's Shearwater	*Calonectris borealis*	CQ	00361																						
AF	Sooty Shearwater	*Ardenna grisea*	OT	00430																						
A	Great Shearwater	*Ardenna gravis*	GQ	00400																						
AF	Manx Shearwater	*Puffinus puffinus*	MX	00460			B: 300,000 (280,000-320,000) pairs, 1998-2002.																			
A	Yelkouan Shearwater	*Puffinus yelkouan*	YELSH	00462		R																				
	Now synonymous with Mediterranean/Balearic Shearwater																									
A	Barolo Shearwater	*Puffinus baroli*	MV	00482	C	R																				
A	Soft-plumaged Petrel	*Pterodroma mollis*	-	00261																						
A	Black-capped Petrel	*Pterodroma hasitata*	BLCPE	00290		R																				
A	Zino's Petrel	*Pterodroma madeira*	ZINPE	00263		R																				

CICONIIFORMES: Storks
Ciconiidae: Storks

			BTO	EUR	RBBP	BBRC	Life	2026	Jan	Feb	Mar	Apr	May	Jun	Jul	Aug	Sep	Oct	Nov	Dec	A	B	C	D	E	F
AEF	Black Stork	*Ciconia nigra*	OS	01310		R																				
AEF	White Stork	*Ciconia ciconia*	OR	01340	*																					

Sub-total

123

SULIFORMES: Totipalmate water and diving birds
Fregatidae: Frigatebirds

	Common name	Scientific name	BTO	EUR	RBBP	BBRC	Life	2026	Jan	Feb	Mar	Apr	May	Jun	Jul	Aug	Sep	Oct	Nov	Dec	A	B	C	D	E	F
A	Ascension Frigatebird	*Fregata aquila*	-	99030		R																				
A	Magnificent Frigatebird	*Fregata magnificens*	MAGFR	930		R																				

Sulidae: Gannets, Boobies

	Common name	Scientific name	BTO	EUR	RBBP	BBRC	Life	2026	Jan	Feb	Mar	Apr	May	Jun	Jul	Aug	Sep	Oct	Nov	Dec	A	B	C	D	E	F
AF	[Northern] Gannet	*Morus bassanus*	GX	00710			B: 295,000 nests, 2013-14																			
A	Red-footed Booby	*Sula sula*	-	00670		R																				
A	Brown Booby	*Sula leucogaster*	BROBO	00700		R																				

Phalacrocoracidae: Cormorants, Shags

	Common name	Scientific name	BTO	EUR	RBBP	BBRC	Life	2026	Jan	Feb	Mar	Apr	May	Jun	Jul	Aug	Sep	Oct	Nov	Dec	A	B	C	D	E	F
AF	[European] Shag	*Gulosus aristotelis*	SA	00800		*	B: 17,500 (13,500-20,500) pairs, 2015. W: 110,000+ individuals, 1998-2002																			
AE	Double-crested Cormorant	*Nannopterum auritum*	-	00780		R																				
AF	[Great] Cormorant	*Phalacrocorax carbo*	CA	00720		*	B: 8,900 pairs, 1998-2002. W: 64,500+ individuals, 2012/13-2016/17																			

PELECANIFORMES: Ibis, Herons, Pelicans
Threskiornithidae: Ibis, Spoonbill

	Common name	Scientific name	BTO	EUR	RBBP	BBRC	Life	2026	Jan	Feb	Mar	Apr	May	Jun	Jul	Aug	Sep	Oct	Nov	Dec	A	B	C	D	E	F
AE	Glossy Ibis	*Plegadis falcinellus*	IB	01360	C		W: 27 individuals, 2011/12-2014/15																			
AEF	[Eurasian] Spoonbill	*Platalea leucorodia*	NB	01440	A		B: 29 pairs, 2017. W: 105 individuals, 2011/12-2014/15																			

PELECANIFORMES: Ibises, Herons, Pelicans

Pelecanidae: Pelicans

	English name	Scientific name	BTO	EUR	RBBP	BBRC	Life
AF	Dalmatian Pelican	Pelecanus crispus	DE	00890		R	

Ardeidae: Herons

	English name	Scientific name	BTO	EUR	RBBP	BBRC	Life
A	Least Bittern	Botaurus exilis	-	00970		R	
AF	[Eurasian] Bittern	Botaurus stellaris	BI	00950	A	R	B: 191+ males, 2017. W: 795 individuals, 2017/18.
A	American Bittern	Botaurus lentiginosus	AM	00960	C	R	
A	Little Bittern	Botaurus minutus	LL	00980	A	R	B: 5 males, 2013-17.
A	Snowy Egret	Egretta thula	NY	01150		R	
AF	Little Egret	Egretta garzetta	ET	01190	A		B: 1,100+ pairs, 2013-17. W: 11,500, individuals, 2012/13-2016/17
AE*F	Night-heron [Black-crowned]	Nycticorax nycticorax	NT	01040	B		B: (0-1) pairs, 2013-17
A	Green Heron	Butorides virescens	HR	01070		R	
A	Chinese Pond Heron	Ardeola bacchus	-	01100		R	
A	Squacco Heron	Ardeola ralloides	QH	01080		R	
A	Great [White] Egret	Ardea alba	HW	01210	A		B: (8-12) pairs, 2017. W: 72 individuals, 2011/12-2014/15

Sub-total

Column headers: BTO · EUR · RBBP · BBRC · Life · 2026 · Jan · Feb · Mar · Apr · May · Jun · Jul · Aug · Sep · Oct · Nov · Dec · A · B · C · D · E · F

PELECANIFORMES: Ibises, Herons, Pelicans
Ardeidae: Herons

	English name	Scientific name	BTO	EUR	RBBP	BBRC	Life	2026	Jan	Feb	Mar	Apr	May	Jun	Jul	Aug	Sep	Oct	Nov	Dec	A	B	C	D	E	F
AE	[Western] Cattle Egret	*Ardea ibis*	EC	01110	*		B: (10-15) pairs, 2017. W: 66 individuals, 2011/12-2014/15																			
A	Purple Heron	*Ardea purpurea*	UR	01240	B		B: 0 pairs, 2013-17																			
AF	Grey Heron	*Ardea cinerea*	H.	01220			B: 10,500 (10,000-11,000) pairs, 2013-17. W: 45,500 individuals, 2012/13-2016/17																			
A	Great Blue Heron	*Ardea herodias*	-	01230		R																				

CAPRIMULGIFORMES: Nightjars, Nighthawks
Caprimulgidae: Nightjars, Nighthawks

	English name	Scientific name	BTO	EUR	RBBP	BBRC	Life	2026	Jan	Feb	Mar	Apr	May	Jun	Jul	Aug	Sep	Oct	Nov	Dec	A	B	C	D	E	F
A	Common Nighthawk	*Chordeiles minor*	COMNI	07860		R																				
B	Red-necked Nightjar	*Caprimulgus ruficollis*	RENNI	07790		R																				
AF	[European] Nightjar	*Caprimulgus europaeus*	NJ	07780			B: 4,600 (3,700-5,500) males, 2004.																			
	Egyptian Nightjar	*Caprimulgus aegyptius*	EGYNI	07810		R																				

APODIFORMES: Swifts
Apodidae: Swifts

	English name	Scientific name	BTO	EUR	RBBP	BBRC	Life	2026	Jan	Feb	Mar	Apr	May	Jun	Jul	Aug	Sep	Oct	Nov	Dec	A	B	C	D	E	F
A	White-throated Needletail	*Hirundapus caudacutus*	NI	07920		R																				
A	Chimney Swift	*Chaetura pelagica*	CHISW	07900		R																				
AF	Alpine Swift	*Tachymarptis melba*	AI	07980		R																				

APODIFORMES: Swifts
Apodidae: Swifts

			BTO	EUR	RBBP	BBRC	Life	2026	Jan	Feb	Mar	Apr	May	Jun	Jul	Aug	Sep	Oct	Nov	Dec	A	B	C	D	E	F
A	Pacific Swift	*Apus pacificus*	PACSW	07970		R																				
	Fork-tailed Swift																									
A	White-rumped Swift	*Apus caffer*	WHRSW	07990		R																				
A	Little Swift	*Apus affinis*	LITSW	08000		R																				
AF	[Common] Swift	*Apus apus*	SI	07950		*	B: 59,000 (43,000-75,000)+ pairs, 2016																			
A	Pallid Swift	*Apus pallidus*	II	07960	C	R																				

STRIGIFORMES: Owls
Tytonidae: Barn Owls

			BTO	EUR	RBBP	BBRC	Life	2026	Jan	Feb	Mar	Apr	May	Jun	Jul	Aug	Sep	Oct	Nov	Dec	A	B	C	D	E	F
AE*F	[Western] Barn Owl	*Tyto alba*	BO	07350		*	B: (4,000-14,000) pairs, 2016																			
	Dark-breasted subspecies occasional breeder																									

Strigidae: Owls

			BTO	EUR	RBBP	BBRC	Life	2026	Jan	Feb	Mar	Apr	May	Jun	Jul	Aug	Sep	Oct	Nov	Dec	A	B	C	D	E	F
AF	Tengmalm's Owl	*Aegolius funereus*	TENOW	07700		R																				
	Boreal Owl																									
C I E*F	Little Owl	*Athene noctua*	LO	07570			B: 3,600 (2,350-4,900) pairs, 2016.																			
AF	[Northern] Hawk Owl	*Surnia ulula*	HAWOW	07500		R																				
A	[Eurasian] Scops Owl	*Otus scops*	IQ	07390	C	R																				
AF	Short-eared Owl	*Asio flammeus*	SE	07580	A		B: (620-2,200) pairs, 2007-11																			
	Sub-total																									

STRIGIFORMES: Owls
Strigidae: Owls

	Common name	Scientific name	BTO	EUR	RBBP	Life	2026	Jan	Feb	Mar	Apr	May	Jun	Jul	Aug	Sep	Oct	Nov	Dec	A	B	C	D	E	F
AF	Long-eared Owl	Asio otus	LE	07670	A	B: (1,800-6,000) pairs, 2007-11.																			
AEF	Snowy Owl	Bubo scandiacus	SO	07490 **	R																				
AF	Tawny Owl	Strix aluco	TO	07610	A	B: 50,000 pairs, 2005																			

ACCIPITRIFORMES: Osprey, Kites, Hawks, Eagles, Harriers, Buzzards
Pandionidae: Osprey

	Common name	Scientific name	BTO	EUR	RBBP	Life	2026	Jan	Feb	Mar	Apr	May	Jun	Jul	Aug	Sep	Oct	Nov	Dec	A	B	C	D	E	F
AE*F	Osprey	Pandion haliaetus	OP	03010	A	B: 240+, 2013-17																			

Accipitridae: Kites, Hawks, Eagles, Harriers, Buzzards

	Common name	Scientific name	BTO	EUR	RBBP	Life	2026	Jan	Feb	Mar	Apr	May	Jun	Jul	Aug	Sep	Oct	Nov	Dec	A	B	C	D	E	F
A	Black-winged Kite	Elanus caeruleus	BLSKI	23500																					
AE	Egyptian Vulture	Neophron percnopterus	EGYVU	02470	R																				
A	[Euroepan] Honey Buzzard	Pernis apivoris	HZ	02310	A	B: (33-59) pairs, 2000																			
A	Short-toed [Snake] Eagle	Circaetus gallicus	SHTEA	02560	R																				
B	[Greater] Spotted Eagle	Clanga clanga	SPOEA	02930	R																				
AE	Booted Eagle	Hieraaetus pennatus	-	02980	R																				
AEF	Golden Eagle	Aquila chrysaetos	EA	02960	A	B: 510 pairs, 2015																			
AF	[Eurasian] Sparrowhawk	Accipiter nisus	SH	02690		B: 30,500 pairs, 2016																			

ACCIPITRIFORMES: Hawks et al (see above)
Accipitridae: Kites, Hawks, Eagles, Harriers, Buzzards

			BTO	EUR	RBBP	BBRC	Life	2026	Jan	Feb	Mar	Apr	May	Jun	Jul	Aug	Sep	Oct	Nov	Dec	A	B	C	D	E	F
AC3E*F	[Eurasian] Goshawk	*Astur gentilis*	GH	02670	A		B: 620+ pairs, 2013-17																			
A	Pallid Harrier	*Circus macrourus*	PALHA	02620	B*	R																				
AF	Hen Harrier	*Circus cyaneus*	HH	02610	A		B: 545 pairs, 2016																			
A	Northern Harrier	*Circus hudsonius*	-	02612	B*	R																				
AF	Montagu's Harrier	*Circus pygargus*	MO	02630	A		B: 8 pairs, 2013-17																			
AF	Marsh Harrier	*Circus aeruginosus*	MR	02600	A		B: (590-695) pairs, 2016																			
[Western]																										
AC3E*F	Red Kite	*Milvus milvus*	KT	02390	A		B: 4,400 pairs, 2016																			
AE	Black Kite	*Milvus migrans*	KB	02380	B*																					
AC3E*F	White-tailed Eagle	*Haliaeetus albicilla*	WE	02430	A		B: 123+pairs, 2013																			
AEF	Rough-legged Buzzard	*Buteo lagopus*	RF	02900	C	*	W: 29 individuals, 2012/13-2016/17																			
A	[Common] Buzzard	*Buteo buteo*	BZ	02870		*	B: (63,000-87,500) pairs, 2016.																			
AE*F	Long-legged Buzzard	*Buteo rufinus*	LOLBU	02880																						
	Sub-total																									

BUCEROTIFORMES: Hornbills, Hoopoes, Wood Hoopoes
Upupidae: Hoopoes

			BTO	EUR	RBBP	BBRC	Life
AE	[Eurasian] Hoopoe	Upupa epops	HP	08460	B		

CORACIIFORMES: Kingfishers & Allies
Coraciidae: Rollers

			BTO	EUR	RBBP	BBRC	Life
A	[European] Roller	Coracias garrulus	ROLLE	08410		R	

Meropidae: Bee-eaters

			BTO	EUR	RBBP	BBRC	Life
A	[European] Bee-eater	Merops apiaster	MZ	08400	B		B: 1 (0-3), 2013-17
A	Blue-cheeked Bee-eater	Merops persicus	BLCBE	08390		R	

Alcedinidae: Kingfishers

			BTO	EUR	RBBP	BBRC	Life
AF	[Common] Kingfisher	Alcedo atthis	KF	08310			B: (3,850-6,400) pairs, 2016
A	Belted Kingfisher	Megaceryle alcyon	BELKI	08340		R	

PICIFORMES: Woodpeckers & Allies
Picidae: Woodpeckers

			BTO	EUR	RBBP	BBRC	Life
AF	[Eurasian] Wryneck	Jynx torquilla	WY	08480	**		B: 0 pairs, 2013-17
AF	Green Woodpecker [European]	Picus viridis	G.	08560			B: 45,500 (40,500-50,500) pairs, 2016
A	Yellow-bellied Sapsucker	Sphyrapicus varius	YEBSA	08720		R	
AF	Great Spotted Woodpecker	Dendrocopos major	GS	08760			B: 130,000 (120,000-145,000) pairs, 2016
AF	Lesser Spotted Woodpecker	Dryobates minor	LS	08870	A	*	B: (600-1,000) pairs, 2015

FALCONIFORMES: Caracaras, Falcons
Falconidae: Falcons

			BTO	EUR	RBBP	BBRC	Life	2026	Jan	Feb	Mar	Apr	May	Jun	Jul	Aug	Sep	Oct	Nov	Dec	A	B	C	D	E	F
A	Lesser Kestrel	*Falco naumanni*	LESKE	03030		R																				
AF	[Common] Kestrel	*Falco tinnunculus*	K.	03040			B: 31,000 pairs, 2016																			
AE	American Kestrel	*Falco sparverius*	AMEKE	03050		R																				
A	Red-footed Falcon	*Falco vespertinus*	FV	03070																						
AE	Amur Falcon	*Falco amurensis*	-	03080		R																				
AF	Merlin	*Falco columbarius*	ML	03090	A	*	B: 1,150 (890-1,450) pairs, 2008																			
AF	Eleonora's Falcon	*Falco eleonorae*	ELEFA	03110		R																				
AF	[Eurasian] Hobby	*Falco subbuteo*	HY	03100	A		B: 2,050 pairs, 2016																			
AEF	Peregrine [Falcon]	*Falco peregrinus*	PE	03200	A	*	B: 1,750 (1,600-1,900), 2014.																			
AEF	Gyr Falcon or Gyrfalcon	*Falco rusticolus*	YF	03180		R																				

PSITTACIFORMES: Parrots
Psittaculidae: Old World Parrots

			BTO	EUR	RBBP	BBRC	Life	2026	Jan	Feb	Mar	Apr	May	Jun	Jul	Aug	Sep	Oct	Nov	Dec	A	B	C	D	E	F
C!E*	Ring-necked Parakeet or Rose-ringed Parakeet	*Psittacula krameri*	RI	07120			B: 12,000 pairs, 2016																			

Sub-total

131

Status	English name	Scientific name	BTO	EUR	RBBP	BBRC	Life	2026	Jan	Feb	Mar	Apr	May	Jun	Jul	Aug	Sep	Oct	Nov	Dec	A	B	C	D	E	F
PASSERIFORMES: Passerines—perching birds																										
Tyrannidae: Tyrant Flycatchers																										
A	Eastern Kingbird	*Tyrannus tyrannus*	-	09480		R																				
A	Eastern Phoebe	*Sayornis phoebe*	-	09090		R																				
A	Acadian Flycatcher	*Empidonax virescens*	-	09140		R																				
A	Alder Flycatcher	*Empidonax alnorum*	ALDFL	09230		R																				
A	Yellow-bellied Flycatcher	*Empidonax flaviventris*	-	09130		R																				
Vireonidae: Vireos																										
A	Philadelphia Vireo	*Vireo philadelphicus*	PHIVI	16310		R																				
A	Red-eyed Vireo	*Vireo olivaceous*	EV	16330		R																				
A	Yellow-throated Vireo	*Vireo flavifrons*	-	16280		R																				
Oriolidae: Orioles																										
A	[Eurasian] Golden Oriole	*Oriolus oriolus*	OL	15080	**						B: 0 (0-2), males, 2013-17														
Laniidae: Shrikes																										
AEF	Great Grey Shrike	*Lanius excubitor*	SR	15200	C	*								W: 98 individuals, 2012/13-2016/17											
A	Masked Shrike	*Lanius nubicus*	MASSH	15240		R																				

PASSERIFORMES: Passerines—perching birds
Laniidae: Shrikes

	Species	Scientific name	BTO	EUR	RBBP	BBRC	Life	2026	Jan	Feb	Mar	Apr	May	Jun	Jul	Aug	Sep	Oct	Nov	Dec	A	B	C	D	E	F
A	Lesser Grey Shrike	Lanius minor	LEGSH	15190		R																				
A	Woodchat Shrike	Lanius senator	OO	15230	C	*																				
A	Daurian Shrike	Lanius isabellinus	IL	15140		R																				
	Isabelline Shrike																									
AF	Red-backed Shrike	Lanius collurio	ED	15150	A	R	B: 3 pairs, 2013-17																			
A	Turkestan Shrike	Lanius phoenicuroides	TURSH	15152		R																				
	Red-tailed Shrike																									
A	Long-tailed Shrike	Lanius schach	LOTSH	15170		R																				
A	Brown Shrike	Lanius cristatus	-	15130		R																				
	Corvidae: Crows, Jays																									
AE*F	[Red-billed] Chough	Pyrrhocorax pyrrhocorax	CF	15590	A	R	B: 355 pairs, 2014-15. W: 1,250, 2014/15																			
AF	[Eurasian] Jay	Garrulus glandarius	J.	15390	A		B: 170,000 territories, 2016																			
AF	[Eurasian] Magpie	Pica pica	MG	15490	A		B: 610,000 territories, 2016																			
AF	[Northern] Nutcracker	Nucifraga caryocatactes	NC	15570		R																				
AF	[Western] Jackdaw	Coloeus monedula	JD	15600		*	B: 1,550,000 (1,350,000-1,750,000), 2016.																			
	Sub-total																									

133

PASSERIFORMES: Passerines—perching birds
Corvidae: Crows

Cat	Common name	Scientific name	BTO	EUR	RBBP	BBRC	Life	2026	Jan	Feb	Mar	Apr	May	Jun	Jul	Aug	Sep	Oct	Nov	Dec	A	B	C	D	E	F
AF	Rook	*Corvus frugilegus*	RO	15630			B: 980,000 (865,000–1,100,000) pairs, 2016																			
AF	[Northern] Raven	*Corvus corax*	RN	15720			B: 10,000+ pairs, 2016																			
AF	Carrion Crow	*Corvus corone*	C.	15670			B: 1,335,000 territories, 2016.																			

Now synonymous with Hooded Crow

Remizidae: Penduline Tits

Cat	Common name	Scientific name	BTO	EUR	RBBP	BBRC	Life	2026	Jan	Feb	Mar	Apr	May	Jun	Jul	Aug	Sep	Oct	Nov	Dec	A	B	C	D	E	F
A	[Eurasian] Penduline Tit	*Remiz pendulinus*	DT	14900	C																					

Paridae: Tits

Cat	Common name	Scientific name	BTO	EUR	RBBP	BBRC	Life	2026	Jan	Feb	Mar	Apr	May	Jun	Jul	Aug	Sep	Oct	Nov	Dec	A	B	C	D	E	F
AF	[Eurasian] Blue Tit	*Cyanistes caeruleus*	BT	14620			B: 3,400,000 territories, 2016																			
AF	Great Tit	*Parus major*	GT	14640			B: 2,350,000 territories, 2016																			
AF	Coal Tit	*Periparus ater*	CT	14610		*	B: 660,000 territories, 2016																			
A	Crested Tit	*Lophophanes cristatus*	CI	14540	A		B: (1,000–2,000) pairs, 2007																			
A	Marsh Tit	*Poecile palustris*	MT	14400			B: 28,500 territories, 2016																			
A	Willow Tit	*Poecile montanus*	WT	14420	A	*	B: 2,750 pairs, 2016																			

Panuridae: Bearded Tit/Reedling

Cat	Common name	Scientific name	BTO	EUR	RBBP	BBRC	Life	2026	Jan	Feb	Mar	Apr	May	Jun	Jul	Aug	Sep	Oct	Nov	Dec	A	B	C	D	E	F
A	Bearded Tit/Reedling	*Panurus biarmicus*	BR	13640	A		B: 695 pairs, 2013-17																			

PASSERIFORMES: Passerines—perching birds

Alaudidae: Larks

	English name	Scientific name	BTO	EUR	RBBP	BBRC	Life	2026	Jan	Feb	Mar	Apr	May	Jun	Jul	Aug	Sep	Oct	Nov	Dec	A	B	C	D	E	F
AF	Woodlark	*Lullula arborea*	WL	09740	A		B: 2,300 (1,850-2,750) pairs, 2016																			
A	White-winged Lark	*Alauda leucoptera*	WHWLA	09650		R																				
AF	[Eurasian] Skylark	*Alauda arvensis*	S.	09760			B: 1,550,000 territories, 2016																			
AEF	Crested Lark	*Galerida cristata*	CRELA	09720		R																				
AF	Shore Lark or Horned	*Eremophila alpestris*	SX	09780	B	*	W: 110 individuals, 2012/13-2016/17																			
A	Short-toed Lark [Greater]	*Calandrella brachydactyla*	VL	09680	C	R																				
A	Bimaculated Lark	*Melanocorypha bimaculata*	BIMLA	09620		R																				
A	Black Lark	*Melanocorypha yeltoniensis*	BLALA	09660		R																				
A	Calandra Lark	*Melanocorypha calandra*	CALLA	09610		R																				

Cisticolidae: Cisticolas & Allies

A	Zitting Cisticola	*Cisticola juncidis*	FZ	12260	B	R																				

Acrocephalidae: Reed Warblers & Allies

A	Icterine Warbler	*Hippolais icterina*	IC	12590	B		B: (0-2) pairs, 2013-17																			

Sub-total

PASSERIFORMES: Passerines—perching birds
Acrocephalidae: Reed Warblers & Allies

			BTO	EUR	RBBP	BBRC	Life	2026	Jan	Feb	Mar	Apr	May	Jun	Jul	Aug	Sep	Oct	Nov	Dec	A	B	C	D	E	F
A	Melodious Warbler	Hippolais polyglotta	ME	12600	C																					
A	Olive-tree Warbler	Hippolais olivetorum	OLTWA	12580		R																				
A	Thick-billed Warbler	Arundinax aedon	THBWA	12540		R																				
A	Booted Warbler	Iduna caligata	DM	12561	C	R																				
A	Sykes's Warbler	Iduna rama	SYKWA	12562		R																				
A	E. Olivaceous Warbler	Iduna pallida	EAOWA	12550		R																				
	Eastern																									
A	W. Olivaceous Warbler	Iduna opaca	WEOWA	12552																						
	Western																									
A	Sedge Warbler	Acrocephalus schoenobaenus	SW	12430			B: 240,000 territories, 2016																			
A	Aquatic Warbler	Acrocephalus paludicola	AQ	12420		R	Autumn: 3+, 2013-17																			
A	Paddyfield Warbler	Acrocephalus agricola	PY	12470		R																				
A	Blyth's Reed Warbler	Acrocephalus dumetorum	BLRWA	12480	C																					
A	Marsh Warbler	Acrocephalus palustris	MW	12500	A		B: 8 pairs, 2013-17																			
A	Common Reed Warbler	Acrocephalus scirpaceus	RW	12510		*	B: 130,000 (100,000-155,000)+, 2016																			

PASSERIFORMES: Passerines—perching birds
Acrocephalidae: Reed Warblers & Allies

	English name	Scientific name	BTO	EUR	RBBP	BBRC	Life	2026	Jan	Feb	Mar	Apr	May	Jun	Jul	Aug	Sep	Oct	Nov	Dec	A	B	C	D	E	F
A	Great Reed Warbler	*Acrocephalus arundinaceus*	QW	12530	C	R																				

Locustellidae: Grasshopper Warblers & Allies

	English name	Scientific name	BTO	EUR	RBBP	BBRC	Life	2026	Jan	Feb	Mar	Apr	May	Jun	Jul	Aug	Sep	Oct	Nov	Dec	A	B	C	D	E	F
A	Pallas's Grasshopper W	*Helopsaltes certhiola*	PAGWA	12330		R																				
	Pallas's Grasshopper Warbler																									
A	Lanceolated Warbler	*Locustella lanceolata*	LANWA	12350		R																				
A	River Warbler	*Locustella fluviatilis*	VW	12370	C	R																				
A	Savi's Warbler	*Locustella luscinioides*	VI	12380	A	R	**B:** 5 pairs, 2013-17																			
A	Grasshopper Warbler	*Locustella naevia*	GH	12360	*	*	**B:** 12,000 territories, 2016																			
	Common Grasshopper Warbler																									

Hirundinidae: Swallows

	English name	Scientific name	BTO	EUR	RBBP	BBRC	Life	2026	Jan	Feb	Mar	Apr	May	Jun	Jul	Aug	Sep	Oct	Nov	Dec	A	B	C	D	E	F
AF	Sand Martin	*Riparia riparia*	SM	09810			**B:** (70,000-225,000) nests, 2016																			
A	Tree Swallow	*Tachycineta bicolor*		09830		R																				
A	Purple Martin	*Progne subis*		09890		R																				
AF	[Eurasian] Crag Martin	*Ptyonoprogne rupestris*	CRAMA	09910		R																				

Sub-total

PASSERIFORMES: Passerines—perching birds
Hirundinidae: Swallows

			BTO	EUR	RBBP	BRRC	Life	2026	Jan	Feb	Mar	Apr	May	Jun	Jul	Aug	Sep	Oct	Nov	Dec	A	B	C	D	E	F
AEF	[Barn] Swallow	*Hirundo rustica*	SL	09920		*	B: 705,000 territories, 2016																			
AF	[Western] House Martin	*Delichon urbicum*	HM	10010		*	B: 480,000 (335,000-620,000) pairs, 2016																			
A	Red-rumped Swallow [European]	*Cecropis rufula*	VR	09950	C	R																				
A	Red-rumped Swallow [Eastern]	*Cecropis daurica*	-	-																						
A	American Cliff Swallow	*Petrochelidon pyrrhonota*	CLISW	09980		R																				

Aegithalidae: Bushtits

			BTO	EUR	RBBP	BRRC	Life	2026	Jan	Feb	Mar	Apr	May	Jun	Jul	Aug	Sep	Oct	Nov	Dec	A	B	C	D	E	F
AF	Long-tailed Tit	*Aegithalos caudatus*	LT	14370		*	B: 380,000 territories, 2016																			

Cettiidae: Bush Warblers & Allies

			BTO	EUR	RBBP	BRRC	Life	2026	Jan	Feb	Mar	Apr	May	Jun	Jul	Aug	Sep	Oct	Nov	Dec	A	B	C	D	E	F
A	Cetti's Warbler	*Cettia cetti*	CW	12200			B: 3,450+ males, 2016																			

Phylloscopidae: Leaf Warblers & Allies

			BTO	EUR	RBBP	BRRC	Life	2026	Jan	Feb	Mar	Apr	May	Jun	Jul	Aug	Sep	Oct	Nov	Dec	A	B	C	D	E	F
A	Wood Warbler	*Phylloscopus sybilatrix*	WO	13080			B: 6,500 (6,000-7,050) males, 2016																			
A	Western Bonelli's Warbler	*Phylloscopus bonelli*	IW	13071	C	R																				
A	Eastern Bonelli's Warbler	*Phylloscopus orientalis*	EABWA	13072		R																				
A	Yellow-browed Warbler	*Phylloscopus inornatus*	YB	13000	C		W: 25 individuals, 2012/13-206/17																			

PASSERIFORMES: Passerines—perching birds
Phylloscopidae: Leaf Warblers & Allies

			BTO	EUR	RBBP	BBRC	Life	2026	Jan	Feb	Mar	Apr	May	Jun	Jul	Aug	Sep	Oct	Nov	Dec	A	B	C	D	E	F
A	**Hume's [Leaf] Warbler**	*Phylloscopus humei*	HULWA	13002		R																				
A	**Pallas's [Leaf] Warbler**	*Phylloscopus proregulus*	PA	12980	C																					
A	**Radde's Warbler**	*Phylloscopus schwarzi*	RADWA	13010																						
A	**Sulphur-bellied Warbler**	*Phylloscopus griseolus*	-	13050																						
A	**Dusky Warbler**	*Phylloscopus fuscatus*	UY	13030																						
A	**Willow Warbler**	*Phylloscopus trochilus*	WW	13120		*	B: 2,300,000 territories, 2016																			
A	**Iberian Chiffchaff**	*Phylloscopus ibericus*	IR	13115	B	R	B: (0-1) pairs, 2013-17																			
A	**[Common] Chiffchaff**	*Phylloscopus collybita*	CC	13110			B: 1,750,000 territories, 2016																			
A	**E. Crowned Warbler**	*Phylloscopus coronatus*	-	12860		R																				
	Eastern																									
A	**Green Warbler**	*Phylloscopus nitidus*	GRNWA	12910		R																				
A	**Two-barred Warbler**	*Phylloscopus plumbeitarsus*	TWBGW	12920		R																				
	Two-barred Greenish Warbler																									
A	**Greenish Warbler**	*Phylloscopus trochiloides*	NP	12930	C																					
	Sub-total																									

PASSERIFORMES: Passerines—perching birds
Phylloscopidae: Leaf Warblers & Allies

Status	English name	Scientific name	BTO	EUR	RBBP	BBRC	Life
A	Pale-legged Leaf Warbler	*Phylloscopus tenellipes*	-	12880		R	
A	Arctic Warbler	*Phylloscopus borealis*	AP	12950			

Sylviidae: Sylvid Warblers & Allies

Status	English name	Scientific name	BTO	EUR	RBBP	BBRC	Life
AF	Garden Warbler	*Sylvia borin*	GW	1276			B: 145,000 territories, 2016
AF	[Eurasian] Blackcap	*Sylvia atricapilla*	BC	1277			B: 1,650,000 territories, 2016
A	Barred Warbler	*Curruca nisoria*	RR	1273			
AF	Lesser Whitethroat	*Curruca curruca*	LW	1274		*	B: 79,000 territories, 2016
	C. c. halimondendri, Central Asian Lesser Whitethroat						
A	W. Orphean Warbler	*Curruca hortensis*	ORPWA	1272		R	
	Western						
A	E. Orphean Warbler	*Curruca crassirostris*	EAOWA	12722		R	
	Eastern						
A	Asian Desert Warbler	*Curruca nana*	DESWA	12700	C	R	
AF	[Common] Whitethroat	*Curruca communis*	WH	12750		*	B: 1,100,000 territories, 2016
A	Spectacled Warbler	*Curruca conspicillata*	VY	12640	C	R	
A	Marmora's Warbler	*Curruca sarda*	MAMWA	12610	C	R	
A	Dartford Warbler	*Curruca undata*	DW	12620	A		B: 2,200 pairs, 2017

Tracking columns (all blank): 2026, Jan, Feb, Mar, Apr, May, Jun, Jul, Aug, Sep, Oct, Nov, Dec, A, B, C, D, E, F

PASSERIFORMES: Passerines—perching birds
Sylviidae: Sylvid Warblers & Allies

	Common name	Scientific name	BTO	EUR	RBBP	BBRC	Life	2026	Jan	Feb	Mar	Apr	May	Jun	Jul	Aug	Sep	Oct	Nov	Dec	A	B	C	D	E	F
A	Rüppell's Warbler	*Curruca ruppeli*	RUPWA	12690		R																				
A	Sardinian Warbler	*Curruca melanocephala*	VX	12670	C	R																				
A	Moltoni's Warbler	*Curruca subalpina*	MOLWA	12652		R																				
A	W. Subalpine Warbler	*Curruca iberiae*	VZ	12654	C	R																				
A	E. Subalpine Warbler	*Curruca cantillans*	EASWA	12651	C	R																				

Western

Eastern

Bombycillidae: Waxwings

	Common name	Scientific name	BTO	EUR	RBBP	BBRC	Life	2026	Jan	Feb	Mar	Apr	May	Jun	Jul	Aug	Sep	Oct	Nov	Dec	A	B	C	D	E	F
AE	Cedar Waxwing	*Bombycilla cedrorum*	-	10460		R																				
AEF	[Bohemian] Waxwing	*Bombycilla garrulus*	WX	10480	C		W: 10,000 individuals, 2012/13-2016/17																			

Regulidae: Goldcrests, Kinglets

	Common name	Scientific name	BTO	EUR	RBBP	BBRC	Life	2026	Jan	Feb	Mar	Apr	May	Jun	Jul	Aug	Sep	Oct	Nov	Dec	A	B	C	D	E	F
A	Ruby-crowned Kinglet	*Corthylio calendula*	RUCKI	13130																						
A	[Common] Firecrest	*Regulus ignicapilla*	FC	13150			B: 2,000+ territories, 2017																			
AF	Goldcrest	*Regulus regulus*	GC	13140			B: 790,000 territories, 2016																			

Tichodromidae: Wallcreeper

	Common name	Scientific name	BTO	EUR	RBBP	BBRC	Life	2026	Jan	Feb	Mar	Apr	May	Jun	Jul	Aug	Sep	Oct	Nov	Dec	A	B	C	D	E	F
A	Wallcreeper	*Tichodroma muraria*	WALLC	14820		R																				

Sub-total

PASSERIFORMES: Passerines—perching birds

Sittidae: Nuthatches

			BTO	EUR	RBBP	BBRC	Life
A	Red-breasted Nuthatch	*Sitta canadensis*	-	14720			
AF	[Eurasian] Nuthatch	*Sitta europaea*	NH	14790			B: 250,000 territories, 2016

Certhidae: Treecreepers

			BTO	EUR	RBBP	BBRC	Life
AF	[Eurasian] Treecreeper	*Certhia familiaris*	TC	14860		*	B: 225,000 territories, 2016

C. f. familiaris, Northern Treecreeper

			BTO	EUR	RBBP	BBRC	Life
A	Short-toed Treecreeper	*Certhia brachydactyla*	TH	14870	A		

Troglodytidae: Wrens

			BTO	EUR	RBBP	BBRC	Life
AF	[Eurasian] Wren	*Troglodytes troglodytes*	WR	10660			B: 11,000,000 territories, 2016

Mimidae: Mockingbirds

			BTO	EUR	RBBP	BBRC	Life
A	Grey Catbird	*Dumetella carolinensis*	-	10800		R	
A	Brown Thrasher	*Toxostoma rufum*	BROTH	10690		R	
AE	Northern Mockingbird	*Mimus polyglottos*	-	10670		R	

Sturnidae: Starlings

			BTO	EUR	RBBP	BBRC	Life
AF	[Common] Starling	*Sturnus vulgaris*	SG	15820			B: 1,750,000 (1,550,000-1,950,000) pairs, 2016
AE	Rose-coloured Starling	*Pastor roseus*	OE	15940			

Rosy Starling

Column headers (month/period tracking columns, all blank): 2026, Jan, Feb, Mar, Apr, May, Jun, Jul, Aug, Sep, Oct, Nov, Dec, A, B, C, D, E, F

PASSERIFORMES: Passerines—perching birds
Cinclidae: Dippers

	English name	Scientific name	BTO	EUR	RBBP	BBRC	Life / notes
AF	**[White-throated] Dipper**	**Cinclus cinclus**	DI	10500		*	B: (6,900-20,500) pairs, 2016

C. c cinclus, Black-bellied Dipper

Turdidae: Thrushes & Allies

	English name	Scientific name	BTO	EUR	RBBP	BBRC	Life / notes
A	White's Thrush	Zoothera aurea	WHITH	11700		R	
A	Varied Thrush	Ixoreus naevius	VT	11720		R	
A	Wood Thrush	Hylocichla mustelina	-	11750		R	
A	Swainson's Thrush	Catharus ustulatus	SWATH	11770		R	
A	Veery	Catharus fuscescens	VEERY	11790		R	
A	Grey-cheeked Thrush	Catharus minimus	GRATH	11780		R	
A	Hermit Thrush	Catharus guttatus	HERTH	11760		R	
A	Siberian Thrush	Geokichla sibirica	SIBTH	11710		A	
AF	Mistle Thrush	Turdus viscivorus	M.	12020			B: 165,000 territories, 2016
AF	Song Thrush	Turdus philomelos	ST	12000			B: 1,300,000 territories, 2016
AF	Redwing	Turdus iliacus	RE	12010	A		B: 24 pairs, 2013-17. W: 690,000 individuals, 1981-84

Sub-total

Column headers: Life · 2026 · Jan · Feb · Mar · Apr · May · Jun · Jul · Aug · Sep · Oct · Nov · Dec · A · B · C · D · E · F

PASSERIFORMES: Passerines—perching birds
Turdidae: Thrushes

			BTO	EUR	RBBP	BBRC	Life	2026	Jan	Feb	Mar	Apr	May	Jun	Jul	Aug	Sep	Oct	Nov	Dec	A	B	C	D	E	F
AF	[Common] Blackbird	*Turdus merula*	B.	11870			B: 5,050,000 (4,800,000-5,250,000) pairs, 2016																			
AF	Fieldfare	*Turdus pilaris*	FF	11980	A		B: (0-1) pairs, 2013-17. W: 720,000 individuals, 1981-84																			
AF	Ring Ouzel	*Turdus torquatus*	RZ	11860		*	B: 7,300 (5,550-9,400) pairs, 2016																			
A	Red-throated Thrush	*Turdus ruficollis*	RETTH	11970		R																				
A	Black-throated Thrush	*Turdus atrogularis*	BLTTH	11972		R																				
A	Naumann's Thrush	*Turdus naumanni*	NAUTH	11961		R																				
A	Dusky Thrush	*Turdus eunomus*	DUSTH	11962		R																				
A	Eyebrowed Thrush	*Turdus obscurus*	EYBTH	11950		R																				
AE	American Robin	*Turdus migratorius*	AR	12030		R																				

Muscicapidae: Old World Flycatchers

			BTO	EUR	RBBP	BBRC	Life	2026	Jan	Feb	Mar	Apr	May	Jun	Jul	Aug	Sep	Oct	Nov	Dec	A	B	C	D	E	F
A	Rufous-tailed Scrub Robin	*Cercotrichas galactotes*	RUBRO	10950		R																				
A	Asian Brown Flycatcher	*Muscicapa dauurica*	-	99014		R																				
AF	Spotted Flycatcher	*Muscicapa striata*	SF	13350			B: 41,500 territories, 2016																			

144

PASSERIFORMES: Passerines—perching birds
Muscicapidae: Old World Flycatchers

	English name	Scientific name	BTO	EUR	RBBP	BBRC	Life	2026	Jan	Feb	Mar	Apr	May	Jun	Jul	Aug	Sep	Oct	Nov	Dec	A	B	C	D	E	F
AF	[European] Robin	Erithacus rubecula	R.	10990			B: 7,350,000 territories, 2016																			
A	White-throated Robin	Irania gutturalis	WHTRO	11170		R																				
AF	Thrush Nightingale	Luscinia luscinia	FN	11030	C	R																				
A	[Common] Nightingale	Luscinia megarhynchos	N	11040		*	B: 5,500 (5,100-6,000) males, 2012																			
A	Bluethroat	Luscinia svecica	BU	11060	B	R	B: (0-1) pairs, 2013-17																			
A	Siberian Rubythroat	Calliope calliope	SIBRU	11050		R																				
A	Siberian Blue Robin	Larvivora cyane	-	11120		R																				
A	Rufous-tailed Robin	Larvivora sibilans	RUTRO	11020																						
A	Red-breasted Flycatcher	Ficedula parva	FY	13430																						
A	Taiga Flycatcher	Ficedula albicilla	TAIFL	13430		R																				
A	Collared Flycatcher	Ficedula albicollis	COLFL	13480		R																				
A	Pied Flycatcher	Ficedula hypoleuca	PF	13490		*	B: (22,000-25,000) pairs, 2016																			

[European]

Sub-total

PASSERIFORMES: Passerines—perching birds
Muscicapidae: Old World Flycatchers

			BTO	EUR	RBBP	BBRC	Life	2026	Jan	Feb	Mar	Apr	May	Jun	Jul	Aug	Sep	Oct	Nov	Dec	A	B	C	D	E	F
AE	Red-flanked Bluetail	*Tarsiger cyanurus*	REFBL	11130																						
AF	Black Redstart	*Phoenicurus ochruros*	BX	11210	A	*	B: 58 pairs, 2013-17. W: 400 individuals, 1981-84																			
A	Moussier's Redstart	*Phoenicurus moussieri*	MOURE	11270		R																				
AF	[Common] Redstart	*Phoenicurus phoenicurus*	RT	11220		*	B: 135,000 (97,000-170,000) pairs, 2016.																			
A	[Common] Rock Thrush	*Monticola saxatilis*	OH	11620		R																				
AE	Blue Rock Thrush	*Monticola solitarius*	BLRTH	11660		R																				
AF	Whinchat	*Saxicola rubetra*	WC	11370		R	B: 49,500 (18,500-79,000) pairs, 2016																			
A	Siberian Stonechat	*Saxicola maurus*	-	11394		R																				
	Now synonymous with Amur Stonechat																									
A	[European] Stonechat	*Saxicola rubicola*	SC	11390		R	B: 65,000 (43,000-87,000) pairs, 2016																			
A	Desert Wheatear	*Oenanthe deserti*	DESWH	11490		R																				
A	W. Black-eared Wheatear	*Oenanthe hispanica*	BLEWH	11481		R																				
	Western																									
A	Pied Wheatear	*Oenanthe pleschanka*	PI	11147		R																				

PASSERIFORMES: Passerines—perching birds
Muscicapidae: Old World Flycatchers

	English name	Scientific name	BTO	EUR	RBBP	BBRC	Life	2026	Jan	Feb	Mar	Apr	May	Jun	Jul	Aug	Sep	Oct	Nov	Dec	A	B	C	D	E	F
A	Eastern Black-eared Wheatear	*Oenanthe melanoleuca*		11482		R	BTO Code: EBEWH																			
AF	[Northern] Wheatear	*Oenanthe oenanthe*	W.	11460			B: 170,000 (120,000–220,000) pairs, 2016																			
A	Isabelline Wheatear	*Oenanthe isabellina*	ISAWH	11440		R																				
A	White-crowned Black Wheatear	*Oenanthe leucopyga*	WHCBL	11570		R																				

Prunellidae: Accentors

	English name	Scientific name	BTO	EUR	RBBP	BBRC	Life	2026	Jan	Feb	Mar	Apr	May	Jun	Jul	Aug	Sep	Oct	Nov	Dec	A	B	C	D	E	F
A	Alpine Accentor	*Prunella collaris*	ALPAC	10940		R																				
AF	Dunnock	*Prunella modularis*	D.	10840			B: 2,500,000 territories, 2016																			
A	Siberian Accentor	*Prunella montanella*	SIBAC	10860		R																				

Passeridae: Old World Sparrows

	English name	Scientific name	BTO	EUR	RBBP	BBRC	Life	2026	Jan	Feb	Mar	Apr	May	Jun	Jul	Aug	Sep	Oct	Nov	Dec	A	B	C	D	E	F
A	Rock Sparrow	*Petronia petronia*	ROCSP	16040		R																				
AF	[Eurasian] Tree Sparrow	*Passer montanus*	TS	15980			B: 245,000 territories, 2016																			
A	Spanish Sparrow	*Passer hispaniolensis*	SPASP	15920		R																				
AF	House Sparrow	*Passer domesticus*	HS	15910			B: 5,300,000 (4,800,000–5,750,000) pairs, 2016																			

Sub-total

PASSERIFORMES: Passerines—perching birds
Motacillidae: Wagtails, Pipits

			BTO	EUR	RBBP	BBRC	Life	2026	Jan	Feb	Mar	Apr	May	Jun	Jul	Aug	Sep	Oct	Nov	Dec	A	B	C	D	E	F
AF	Grey Wagtail	*Motacilla cinerea*	GL	10190			B: 37,000 pairs, 2016																			
AF	[Western] Yellow Wagtail	*Motacilla flava*	YW	10170		*	B: 19,500 territories, 2016																			
	Blue-headed (*M. f. flava*) occasional breeder.																									
A	Citrine Wagtail	*Motacilla citreola*	IZ	10180	B*	R																				
A	Eastern Yellow Wagtail	*Motacilla tschutschensis*	-	26643		R																				
AF	Pied Wagtail	*Motacilla alba*	PW	10200		*	B: 505,000 (445,000-570,000) pairs, 2016																			
	White Wagtail (*M. a. alba* rare but regular breeder)																									
A	Blyth's Pipit	*Anthus godlewskii*	BLYPI	10040		R																				
A	Tawny Pipit	*Anthus campestris*	TI	10050		R																				
AF	Richard's Pipit	*Anthus richardi*	PR	10020																						
A	Pechora Pipit	*Anthus gustavi*	PECPI	10100		R																				
A	Tree Pipit	*Anthus trivialis*	TP	10090			B: 105,000 (66,000-145,000) pairs, 2016																			
A	Olive-backed Pipit	*Anthus hodgsoni*	OV	10080																						
A	Red-throated Pipit	*Anthus cervinus*	VP	10120		R																				
A	American Pipit	*Anthus rubescens*	VP	10120		R																				
	Buff-bellied Pipit																									

PASSERIFORMES: Passerines—perching birds

Motacillidae: Wagtails, Pipits

	Common name	Scientific name	BTO	EUR	RBBP	BBRC	Life	2026	Jan	Feb	Mar	Apr	May	Jun	Jul	Aug	Sep	Oct	Nov	Dec	A	B	C	D	E	F
AF	Meadow Pipit	*Anthus pratensis*	MP	10110			B: 2,450,000 (2,100,000- 2,750,000) pairs, 2016																			
AF	[European] Rock Pipit	*Anthus petrosus*	RC	10142			B: 36,000 pairs, 1988-91																			
	Scandinavian (subspecies) Rock Pipit: Occasional																									
AF	Water Pipit	*Anthus spinoletta*	WI	10141			W: 205 individuals, 2012/13-2016/17																			

Fringillidae: Finches

	Common name	Scientific name	BTO	EUR	RBBP	BBRC	Life	2026	Jan	Feb	Mar	Apr	May	Jun	Jul	Aug	Sep	Oct	Nov	Dec	A	B	C	D	E	F
AF	Brambling	*Fringilla montifringilla*	BL	16380	B		B: (0-1) pairs, 2013-17. W: (45,000-1,800,000) individuals, 1981-84																			
AEF	[Eurasian] Chaffinch	*Fringilla coelebs*	CH	16360		*	B: 5,050,000 territories, 2016																			
A	Evening Grosbeak	*Hesperiphona vespertina*	EVEGR	17180		R																				
AF	Hawfinch	*Coccothraustes coccothraustes*	HF	17170	A		B: (500-1,000) pairs, 2011.																			
A	Common Rosefinch	*Carpodacus erythrinus*	SQ	16790	B																					
AEF	Pine Grosbeak	*Pinicola enucleator*	PINGR	16990		R																				
AF	[Eurasian] Bullfinch	*Pyrrhula pyrrhula*	BF	17100			B: 265,000 territories, 2016																			
AE	Trumpeter Finch	*Bucanetes githagineus*	TRUFI	16760		R																				
AEF	[European] Greenfinch	*Chloris chloris*	GR	16490			B: 785,000 (735,000-835,000) pairs, 2016																			
	Sub-total																									

PASSERIFORMES: Passerines—perching birds
Fringillidae: Finches

			BTO	EUR	RBBP	BBRC	Life / 2026	Jan	Feb	Mar	Apr	May	Jun	Jul	Aug	Sep	Oct	Nov	Dec	A	B	C	D	E	F
AF	Twite	*Linaria flavirostris*	TW	16620			B: 7,850 (5,850-10,000) pairs, 2013																		
AF	[Common] Linnet	*Linaria cannabina*	LI	16600			B: 560,000 territories, 2016																		
AF	Redpoll	*Acanthis flammea*	FR	16630		*	B: 260,000 pairs, 2016																		
	Encompasses the former Arctic, Common and Lesser Redpolls																								
A	Two-barred Crossbill	*Loxia leucoptera*	PD	16650		R																			
A	Parrot Crossbill	*Loxia pytyopsittacus*	PC	16680	A		B: 65 pairs, 2008																		
A	Scottish Crossbill	*Loxia scotica*	CY	16670			B: 6,800 (4,050-11,500) pairs, 2008																		
AF	[Red] Crossbill	*Loxia curvirostra*	CR	16660			B: 26,000 (19,500-34,000), pairs, 2016																		
A	Citril Finch	*Carduelis citrinella*	CITFI	16440		R																			
AF	[European] Goldfinch	*Carduelis carduelis*	GO	16530			B: 1,650,000 (1,450,000-1,800,000) paors, 2016																		
AF	[European] Serin	*Serinus serinus*	NS	16400	B		B: 0 pairs, 2013-17																		
A	[Eurasian] Siskin	*Spinus spinus*	SK	16540			B: 445,000, pairs, 2016																		

Calcariidae: Longspurs and Snow Buntings

			BTO	EUR	RBBP	BBRC	Life / 2026																		
AF	Snow Bunting	*Plectrophenax nivalis*	SB	18500	A	*	B: 60 (48-83) territories, 2011. W: (10,000-15,000) individuals, 1981-84																		

PASSERIFORMES: Passerines—perching birds
Calcariidae: Longspurs and Snow Buntings

			BTO	EUR	RBBP	BBRC	Life	2026	Jan	Feb	Mar	Apr	May	Jun	Jul	Aug	Sep	Oct	Nov	Dec	A	B	C	D	E	F
AF	Lapland Bunting	*Calcarius lapponicus*	LA	18470	B		**B:** (0-1) pairs, 2013-17. **W:** 310 individuals, 2912/13-2016/17																			
	Lapland Longspur																									

Emberizidae: Old World Buntings

			BTO	EUR	RBBP	BBRC	Life	2026	Jan	Feb	Mar	Apr	May	Jun	Jul	Aug	Sep	Oct	Nov	Dec	A	B	C	D	E	F
A	Pallas's Reed Bunting	*Emberiza pallasi*	PARBU	18780		R																				
AF	[Common] Reed Bunting	*Emberiza schoeniclus*	RB	18770			**B:** 275,000 territories, 2016																			
A	Yellow-browed Bunting	*Emberiza chrysophrys*	YEBBU	18710		R																				
A	Chestnut Bunting	*Emberiza rutila*	CHEBU	18750		R																				
AE	Yellow-breasted Bunting	*Emberiza aureola*	YO	18760	C	R																				
A	Little Bunting	*Emberiza pusilla*	LJ	18740		R																				
A	Rustic Bunting	*Emberiza rustica*	RUSBU	18730		R																				
AE	Black-faced Bunting	*Emberiza spodocephala*	-	18530		R																				
AE	Black-headed Bunting	*Emberiza melanocephala*	BLHBU	18810		R																				
A	Red-headed Bunting	*Emberiza bruniceps*	REHBU	18800		R																				
AF	Corn Bunting	*Emberiza calandra*	CB	18820			**B:** 11000 (9,050-13,000) territories, 2016																			
	Sub-total																									

PASSERIFORMES: Passerines—perching birds
Emberizidae: Buntings

			BTO	EUR	RBBP	BBRC	Life	2026	Jan	Feb	Mar	Apr	May	Jun	Jul	Aug	Sep	Oct	Nov	Dec	A	B	C	D	E	F
A	Chestnut-eared Bunting	*Emberiza fucata*	CHABU	18690		R																				
A	Rock Bunting	*Emberiza cia*	ROCBU	18600		R																				
AE	Ortolan Bunting	*Emberiza hortulana*	OB	18660																						
A	Cretzschmar's Bunting	*Emberiza caesia*	CREBU	18680		R																				
A	Cirl Bunting	*Emberiza cirlus*	CL	19580	A		B: 1,100 territories, 2016																			
A	Pine Bunting	*Emberiza leucocephalos*	EL	18560		R																				
AF	Yellowhammer	*Emberiza citrinella*	Y.	18570			B: 700,000 territories, 2016																			

Passerellidae: New World Sparrows

			BTO	EUR	RBBP	BBRC	Life	2026	Jan	Feb	Mar	Apr	May	Jun	Jul	Aug	Sep	Oct	Nov	Dec	A	B	C	D	E	F
A	Lark Sparrow	*Chondestes grammacus*	LARSP	18240		R																				
AE	Dark-eyed Junco	*Junco hyemalis*	JU	18420		R																				
AE	White-throated Sparrow	*Zonotrichia albicollis*	WHTSP	18400		R																				
AE	White-crowned Sparrow	*Zonotrichia leucophrys*	WHCSP	18390		R																				
A	Savannah Sparrow	*Passerculus sandwichensis*	SAVSP	18260		R																				

PASSERIFORMES: Passerines—perching birds

Passerellidae: New World Sparrows

	Species	Scientific name	BTO	EUR	RBBP	BBRC	Life	2026	Jan	Feb	Mar	Apr	May	Jun	Jul	Aug	Sep	Oct	Nov	Dec	A	B	C	D	E	F
AE	Song Sparrow	Melospiza melodia	SONSP	18350		R																				
A	Eastern Towhee	Pipilo erythrophthalmus	RUSTO	17980		R																				

Icteridae: New World Blackbirds, Orioles

	Species	Scientific name	BTO	EUR	RBBP	BBRC	Life	2026	Jan	Feb	Mar	Apr	May	Jun	Jul	Aug	Sep	Oct	Nov	Dec	A	B	C	D	E	F
A	Bobolink	Dolichonyx oryzivorus	BOBOL	18970		R																				
AE	Baltimore Oriole	Icterus galbula	NOROR	19180		R																				
A	Red-winged Blackbird	Agelaius phoeniceus	-	19090		R																				
A	Brown-headed Cowbird	Molothrus ater	-	18990		R																				

Parulidae: New World Warblers

	Species	Scientific name	BTO	EUR	RBBP	BBRC	Life	2026	Jan	Feb	Mar	Apr	May	Jun	Jul	Aug	Sep	Oct	Nov	Dec	A	B	C	D	E	F
A	Ovenbird	Seiurus aurocapilla	OVENB	17560		R																				
A	Northern Waterthrush	Parkesia noveboracensis	NORWA	17570		R																				
A	Black-and-white Warbler	Mniotilta varia	BAWWA	17200		R																				
A	Golden-winged Warbler	Vermivora chrysoptera	-	17220		R																				
A	Tennessee Warbler	Leiothlypis peregrina	TENWA	17240		R																				

Sub-total

PASSERIFORMES: Passerines—perching birds
Parulidae: New World Warblers

	Common Name	Scientific Name	BTO	EUR	RBBP	BBRC	Life	2026	Jan	Feb	Mar	Apr	May	Jun	Jul	Aug	Sep	Oct	Nov	Dec	A	B	C	D	E	F
A	Common Yellowthroat	Geothlypis trichas	COMYE	17620		R																				
AE	American Redstart	Setophaga ruticilla	AD	17550		R																				
A	Hooded Warbler	Setophaga citrina	HOOWA	17710		R																				
AE	Northern Parula	Setophaga americana	NORPA	17320		R																				
AE	Magnolia Warbler	Setophaga magnolia	MAGWA	17500		R																				
A	Blackburnian Warbler	Setophaga fusca	-	17470		R																				
AE	Blackpoll Warbler	Setophaga striata	BLAWA	17530		R																				
A	Bay-breasted Warbler	Setophaga castanea	-	17540		R																				
A	Chestnut-sided Warbler	Setophaga pensylvanica	-	17340		R																				
A	[American] Yellow Warbler	Setophaga aestiva	YLWWA	17330		R																				
A	Cape May Warbler	Setophaga tigrina	CAMWA	17490		R																				
A	Yellow-rumped Warbler aka Myrtle Warbler	Setophaga coronata	YERWA	17510		R																				
A	Canada Warbler	Cardellina canadensis	-	17730																						

PASSERIFORMES: Passerines—perching birds
Parulidae: New World Warblers

			BTO	EUR	RBBP	BBRC	Life	2026	Jan	Feb	Mar	Apr	May	Jun	Jul	Aug	Sep	Oct	Nov	Dec	A	B	C	D	E	F
A	Wilson's Warbler	*Cardellina pusilla*	-	17720																						
Cardinalidae: Cardinals & Allies																										
A	Rose-breasted Grosbeak	*Pheucticus ludovicianus*	ROBGR	18870		R																				
AE	Indigo Bunting	*Passerina cyanea*	INDBU	18920		R																				
A	Summer Tanager	*Piranga rubra*	SUMTA	17860		R																				
A	Scarlet Tanager	*Piranga olivacea*	SCATA	17880		R																				
	Sub-total																									

Checklist: Based on the 10th edition of the British Ornithologists' Union 'Official British List'. Published 2022 in Ibis 164: 860-910, with subsequent updates to 12th August 2025, rearranged in AviList v25 sequence.

APEP-4: Based on the 4th report of the Avian Population Estimates Panel Published February 2020 in British Birds 113: 69-104: Population estimates of birds in Great Britain and the United Kingdom. Woodward, I, Aebischer, N, Burnell, D, Eaton, M, Frost, T, Hall, C, Stroud, D A, Noble, D.

RBBP: 49th Report of the Rare Breeding Birds Panel covering 107 scarce native and 14 non-native taxa that bred or attempted to breed in 2022. Published November 2024 in British Birds 117: 586-656: Mark Eaton and the Rare Breeding Birds Panel

BBRC: Go to https://brtishbirds.co.uk/rarities-committee. The list of species/subspecies the committee assesses as rarities was last updated in May 2020. Species added to the British List or splits since then are not therfore marked with an R even if their frequency might justify it.

BIRDS OF CONSERVATION CONCERN (BOCC) 5

The fifth list of the BOCC was published in December 2021 in *British Birds* 114, 723-747: Stanbury, A, Eaton, M, Aebischer, N, Balmer, D, Brown, A, Douse, A, Lindley, P, McCulloch, N, Noble, D, and Win I. *The status of our bird populations: the fifth Birds of Conservation Concern in the United Kingdom, Channel Islands and Isle of Man and second IUCN Red List assessment of extinction risk for Great Britain.*
In September 2024 an addendum to this list relating to seabirds was published in *British Birds* 117, 471-487: Stanbury A, Burns, F, Aebischer N, Baker H, Balmer D, Brown A, Dunn T, Lindley P, Murphy M, Noble D, Owens R and Quinn L *The status of the UK's breeding seabirds: an addendum to the fifth Birds of Conservation Concern in the United Kingdom, Channel Islands and Isle of Man and second IUCN Red List assessment of extinction risk for Great Britain.* The following lists incorporate the changes introduced by the 2024 addendum relating to seabirds but the species sequence has *not* been updated on the basis of AviList v25.

RED LIST [73]

Grey Partridge
Ptarmigan
Capercaillie
Black Grouse
Bewick's Swan
White-fronted Goose
Long-tailed Duck
Velvet Scoter
Common Scoter
Common Goldeneye
Smew
Common Pochard
Greater Scaup
Red-necked Grebe
Slavonian Grebe
Turtle Dove
Common Swift
Common Cuckoo
Corncrake
Leach's Storm-petrel
Balearic Shearwater
Dotterel
Ringed Plover
Northern Lapwing
Whimbrel
Eurasian Curlew
Black-tailed Godwit
Ruff
Dunlin
Purple Sandpiper
Woodcock
Red-necked Phalarope
Kittiwake
Common Gull
Great Black-backed Gull
Herring Gull
Arctic Tern
Roseate Tern
Arctic Skua
Great Skua
Puffin
Hen Harrier

Montagu's Harrier
Lesser Spotted
  Woodpecker
Merlin
Red-backed Shrike
Marsh Tit
Willow Tit
Skylark
Marsh Warbler
Savi's Warbler
Grasshopper Warbler
House Martin
Wood Warbler
Starling
Mistle Thrush
Fieldfare
Ring Ouzel
Spotted Flycatcher
Common Nightingale
Whinchat
House Sparrow
Tree Sparrow
Tree Pipit
Yellow Wagtail
Hawfinch
Greenfinch
Twite
Linnet
Redpoll
Corn Bunting
Cirl Bunting
Yellowhammer

AMBER LIST [99]

Common Quail
Whooper Swan
Brent Goose
Barnacle Goose
Greylag Goose
'Bean' Goose
Pink-footed Goose
Common Eider

Red-breasted
  Merganser
Common Shelduck
Garganey
Shoveler
Gadwall
Eurasian Wigeon
Mallard
Pintail
Eurasian Teal
Black-necked Grebe
Stock Dove
Woodpigeon
European Nightjar
Spotted Crake
Moorhen
Common Crane
Black-throated Diver
Great Northern Diver
European Storm-petrel
Fulmar
Manx Shearwater
Eurasian Spoonbill
Eurasian Bittern
Little Bittern
Cattle Egret
Great White Egret
Shag
Northern Gannet
Stone-curlew
Oystercatcher
Avocet
Black-winged Stilt
Grey Plover
Bar-tailed Godwit
Turnstone
Red Knot
Curlew Sandpiper
Sanderling
Common Snipe
Common Sandpiper
Green Sandpiper
Spotted Redshank

Greenshank
Common Redshank
Wood Sandpiper
Black-headed Gull
Mediterranean Gull
Lesser Black-backed
  Gull
Yellow-legged Gull
Caspian Gull
Iceland Gull
Glaucous Gull
Little Tern
Common Tern
Sandwich Tern
Razorbill
Common Guillemot
Short-eared Owl
Tawny Owl
Osprey
Honey-buzzard
Marsh Harrier
Eurasian Sparrowhawk
White-tailed Eagle
Common Kestrel
Rook
Shore Lark
Sedge Warbler
Yellow-browed Warbler
Willow Warbler
Common Whitethroat
Dartford Warbler
Short-toed Treecreeper
Wren
Dipper
Song Thrush
Redwing
Pied Flycatcher
Black Redstart
Common Redstart
Northern Wheatear
Dunnock
Meadow Pipit
Water Pipit

BIRDS OF CONSERVATION CONCERN (BOCC) 5

Grey Wagtail
Bullfinch
Parrot Crossbill
Scottish Crossbill
Lapland Bunting
Snow Bunting
Reed Bunting

GREEN LIST [73]

Red Grouse
Mute Swan
Goosander
Tufted Duck
Little Grebe
Great Crested Grebe
Rock Dove/Feral
   Pigeon
Collared Dove
Water Rail
Common Coot
Red-throated Diver
Sooty Shearwater

Great Shearwater
Grey Heron
Little Egret
Great Cormorant
European Golden
   Plover
Little Ringed Plover
Little Stint
Jack Snipe
Little Gull
Black Tern
Long-tailed Skua
Pomarine Skua
Black Guillemot
Little Auk
Barn Owl
Long-eared Owl
Golden Eagle
Northern Goshawk
Red Kite
Common Buzzard
Common Kingfisher

Green Woodpecker
Great Spotted
   Woodpecker
Hobby
Peregrine Falcon
Red-billed Chough
Eurasian Jay
Magpie
Jackdaw
Common Raven
'Carrion/Hooded Crow'
Coal Tit
Crested Tit
Blue Tit
Great Tit
   Woodlark
Bearded Tit
Reed Warbler
Barn Swallow
Sand Martin
Common Chiffchaff
Cetti's Warbler

Long-tailed Tit
Blackcap
Garden Warbler
Lesser Whitethroat
Eurasian Treecreeper
Eurasian Nuthatch
Blackbird
Robin
European Stonechat
Goldcrest
Firecrest
Waxwing
Rock Pipit
White/Pied Wagtail
Common Chaffinch
Brambling
Common Crossbill
Goldfinch
Siskin

SCHEDULE 1 SPECIES

Under the provisions of the Wildlife and Countryside Act 1981, the following bird species (listed in Schedule 1—Part I of the Act) are protected by special penalties at all times.

Avocet
Bee-eater
Bittern
Bittern, Little
Bluethroat
Brambling
Bunting, Cirl
Bunting, Lapland
Bunting, Snow
Buzzard, Honey
Chough
Corncrake
Crake, Spotted
Crossbills (all species)
Divers (all species)
Dotterel
Duck, Long-tailed
Eagle, Golden
Eagle, White-tailed
Falcon, Gyr
Fieldfare
Firecrest
Garganey

Godwit, Black-tailed
Goshawk
Grebe, Black-necked
Grebe, Slavonian
Greenshank
Gull, Little
Gull, Mediterranean
Harriers (all species)
Heron, Purple
Hobby
Hoopoe
Kingfisher
Kite, Red
Merlin
Oriole, Golden
Osprey
Owl, Barn
Owl, Snowy
Peregrine
Petrel, Leach's
Phalarope, Red-necked
Plover, Kentish
Plover, Little Ringed

Quail, Common
Redstart, Black
Redwing
Rosefinch, Scarlet
Ruff
Sandpiper, Green
Sandpiper, Purple
Sandpiper, Wood
Scaup
Scoter, Common
Scoter, Velvet
Serin
Shorelark
Shrike, Red-backed
Spoonbill
Stilt, Black-winged
Stint, Temminck's
Stone-curlew
Swan, Bewick's
Swan, Whooper
Tern, Black
Tern, Little
Tern, Roseate

Tit, Bearded
Tit, Crested
Treecreeper, Short-toed
Warbler, Cetti's
Warbler, Dartford
Warbler, Marsh
Warbler, Savi's
Whimbrel
Woodlark
Wryneck

The following birds and their eggs (listed in Schedule 1—Part II of the Act) are protected by special penalties during the close season, which is Feb 1 to Aug 31 (Feb 21 to Aug 31 below high water mark), but may be killed outside this period—Goldeneye, Greylag Goose (in Outer Hebrides, Caithness, Sutherland, and Wester Ross only), Pintail.

BRITISH BUTTERFLY CHECKLIST

Species	2026	Life	Species	2026	Life
Chequered Skipper			Painted Lady		
Small Skipper			Small Tortoiseshell		
Essex Skipper			Peacock		
Lulworth Argus			Comma		
Silver-spotted Skipper			Small Pearl-bordered Fritillary		
Large Skipper			Pearl-bordered Fritillary		
Dingy Skipper			High Brown Fritillary		
Grizzled Skipper			Dark Green Fritillary		
Swallowtail			Silver-washed Fritillary		
Wood White			Marsh Fritillary		
Real's Wood White			Glanville Fritillary		
Clouded Yellow			Heath Fritillary		
Brimstone			Speckled Brown		
Large White			Wall		
Small White			Mountain Ringlet		
Green-veined White			Scotch Argus		
Orange-tip			Marbled White		
Green Hairstreak			Grayling		
Brown Hairstreak			Gatekeeper		
Purple Hairstreak			Meadow Brown		
White-letter Hairstreak			Ringlet		
Black Hairstreak			Small Heath		
Small Copper			Large Heath		
Small Blue					
Silver-studded Blue			**Additional species**		
Brown Argus					
Northern Brown Argus					
Common Blue					
Chalkhill Blue					
Adonis Blue					
Holly Blue					
Duke of Burgundy					
White Admiral					
Purple Emperor					
Red Admiral			**Total**		

BRITISH DRAGONFLY CHECKLIST

Species	2026	Life	Species	2026	Life
Banded Demoiselle			Northern Emerald		
Beautiful Demoiselle			Brilliant Emerald		
Small Red Damselfly			Common Club-tail		
Northern Damselfly			Scarlet Darter		
Irish Damselfly			White-faced Darter		
Southern Damselfly			Broad-bodied Chaser		
Azure Damselfly			Scarce Chaser		
Variable Damselfly			Four-spotted Chaser		
Dainty Damselfly			Black-tailed Skimmer		
Common Blue Damselfly			Keeled Skimmer		
Red-eyed Damselfly			Wandering Glider		
Small Red-eyed Damselfly			Black Darter		
Blue-tailed Damselfly			Yellow-winged Darter		
Scarce Blue-tailed Damselfly			Red-veined Darter		
Southern Emerald Damselfly			Banded Darter		
Scarce Emerald Damselfly			Ruddy Darter		
Emerald Damselfly			Common Darter		
Willow Emerald Damselfly					
Winter Damselfly			**Additional species**		
White-legged Damselfly					
Small Red Damselfly					
Southern Migrant Hawker					
Azure Hawker					
Southern Hawker					
Brown Hawker					
Norfolk Hawker					
Common Hawker					
Migrant Hawker					
Vagrant Emperor					
Emperor Dragonfly					
Lesser Emperor					
Hairy Dragonfly					
Golden-ringed Dragonfly					

WILDLIFE ART GALLERY

A number of the UK's talented wildlife artists are showing an example of their work here.

Allen, Richard

07842 213 244; richardallenart@btinternet.com;
instagram/X: @richardallenart
www.richardallenillustrator.com

Cook, Robert

07905 394 099; info@robcookart.com;
www.robcookart.com

Nigel Artingstall

07890 561 329; nigel@nigelartingstall.com;
www.nigelartingstall.com

Day, Nick

07763 109 020; birdmanday@yahoo.com;
instagram: @nickdayart
www.wildlife-art-prints-and-posters.com

Finney, David
dave@davidfinney.com; www.davidfinney.co.uk

Lewington, Ian

01235 819 792: lewbirder@btinternet.com;
www.ian-lewington.co.uk

Hatton, John

01524 262 234; jhattonart@gmail.com;
www.johnhattonart.co.uk

McCallum, James

email@jamesmccallum.co.uk;
www.jamesmccallum.co.uk

Parry, David
01672 563 708;
davidparryart@gmail.com;
www.davidparryart.com

Paul, Jeremy

01624 832 980; jpaul@manx.net;
www.jeremypaulwildlifeartist.co.uk

Sinden, Chris

01594 829 903; chrissinden@btinternet.com;
www.sindencox-art.co.uk/chris.html

Warren, Michael

07770 772 450; mikewarren.artist@gmail.com;
www.mikewarren.co.uk

Whittlestone, Richard

01246 582 720; art@richardwhittlestone.co.uk;
www.richardwhittlestone.com

Not all wildlife has feathers

Powell, Dan & Rosemary

Dan Powell is the artist who produced the paintings for James Lowens's 'News from the world of birds' article.
01329 668 465; danpowell11@btinternet.com; www.powellwildlifeart.com

Soudan, Sylvie

Sylvie Soudan, who has a diploma in botanical illustration from the Royal Botanic Garden Edinburgh, painted the now lumped Redpolls on the covers and elsewhere in this edition of **The Yearbook**. Instagram: Sylvie.Soudan

Or you might like to take a look at the work of...

Akroyd, Carry
via website; www.carryakroyd.co.uk

Angus, Max
07766 277 915; studioenquiry@maxangus.co.uk; www.maxangus.co.uk

Bartlett, Paul
01382 698 346; pauljbartlett@hotmail.com; www.naturalselectiongallery.co.uk

Bennett, David
via website; www.davidbennettwildlifeart.com

Bowers, Niki
via website; www.nikibowers.co.uk

Bowles, Ian
01732 810 637; ianbowles.wildlifeart@btinternet.com; www.ianbowleswildlifeartist.co.uk

Brockie, Keith
01887 830 609; kbrockie@btinternet.com; www.keithbrockie.co.uk

Cox, Jackie
07780 877 300; jcox953@btinternet.com; www.sindencox-art.co.uk/jackie.html

Daly, David
via website; www.davedalyartist.com

Derry, Nick
nickderry@yahoo.co.uk; https://nickderry.com

Durnell, Aimee & Pete
07851 387 542; aimeegrug@hotmail.co.uk; www.fb.com/Durnellart

Edwards, Brin
via website; www.brin-edwards.com

Foker, John
jffoker@googlemail.com; www.bearparkartists.co.uk

Forkner, Andrew
01993 776 322; info@andrewforkner.co.uk; www.andrewforkner.co.uk

Fuller, Robert
01759 368 355; mail@robertefuller.com; www.robertefuller.com

Gale, John
johngaleartist@outlook.com; www.galleryofbirds.co.uk

Garner, Jackie
01453 847 420; artist@jackiegarner.co.uk; www.jackiegarner.co.uk

Greenhalf, Robert
via website; www.robertgreenhalf.co.uk

Griffiths, Ian
07971 678 464; mail@artbygriff.com; www.artbygriff.com

Haslen, Andrew
wildlifeartgallery@btinternet.com; www.andrewhaslen.com

Heselden, Russ
01953 850 145; heselden860@btinternet.com;
www.russheselden.co.uk

Hodges, Gary
01273 047 897; gary@garyhodges-wildlife-art.com;
www.garyhodges-wildlife-art.com

Hooper, Lisa
01988 700 392; mail@hoopoeprints.co.uk;
www.hoopoeprints.co.uk

Howey, Paul
via website; www.paulhowey.co.uk

Hunt, Alan
via website; www.alanmhunt.com

Ingram, Alison
01403 263 179; alison@alisoningram.co.uk;
www.alisoningram.co.uk

Johnson, Richard
via website; www.richardjohnsonart.bigcartel.com/

Jones, Kittie
via website; www.kittiejones.com

Kemp, Carolyn
via website; www.carolynkemp.co.uk

Langman, Mike
07833 178 855; via website; www.mikelangman.co.uk

Lewington, Richard
01235 848 451: rewington@btopenworld.com
www.richardlewington.co.uk

Lockwood, Rachel
01263 740 947; rachel@rachellockwoodartist.com;
www.rachellockwoodartist.co.uk

Lodge, Chris
greenbroadbill@hotmail.com; www.chrislodgeart.com

Mackay, Andrew
via website; www.ajm-wildlife-art.co.uk

Manning, Julia
01458 223 025; julia@juliamanning.co.uk;
www.juliamanning.co.uk

Message, Stephen
07909 585 988; messagewildlifeart@btinternet.com;
www.message-wildlife-art.co.uk

Miller, David
01646 682 907; david@davidmillerart.co.uk;
www.davidmillerart.co.uk

Neill, William
bill_neill@hotmail.com

Newell, Kerry
07752 325 031; kerrynewell1@gmail.com;
www.kerrynewell.com

Pearson, Bruce
via website; www.brucepearson.net

Pendleton, Chris
07895 058 431; chris@pendleton.co.uk;
www.pendleton.co.uk

Phillips, Antonia
01308 420 423; via website; www.antoniaphillips.co.uk

Pollard, Nick
info@nikpollard.co.uk; www.nikpollard.co.uk

Pomroy, Jonathan
01439 788 014; pomroyjonathan@gmail.com;
www.jonathanpomroy.co.uk

Poole, Greg
via website; www.gregpoole.co.uk

Pound, Adele
via website; www.adelepound.co.uk

Proud, Alastair
via website; www.alastairproud.co.uk

Rees, Darren
07803 921 989; darrenreesart@btinternet.com;
www.darrenrees.com

Ridley, Martin
07925 549 002; art@martinridley.com;
www.martinridley.com

Rose, Chris
07913 290 742; chris@chrisrose-artist.co.uk;
www.chrisrose-artist.co.uk

Scott, Dafila
via website; www.dafilascott.co.uk

Small, Brian
via website; www.briansmallbirdillustration.com

Stock, Andrew
andrew@andrewstock.co.uk;
www.andrewstock.co.uk

Threlfall, John
john@johnthrelfall.co.uk;
www.johnthrelfall.co.uk

Tratt, Richard
rtratt@btinternet.com; www.richardtratt.co.uk

Truss, Jonathan
07765 003 309; jon@jonathantruss.com;
www.jonathantruss.com

Watling, Gareth
via website; www.garethwatling.com

White, Vicky
mail@vicky-white.co.uk; www.vicky-white.co.uk

Wilson, Eric
07546 802 577; via website; www.ericwilsonsart.com

Woodhead, Darren
01620 823 213; via website; www.darrenwoodhead.com

Wootton, Tim
01856 831 336; tim.wootton@tiscali.co.uk;
http://tim-wootton.blogspot.co.uk

Woolf, Colin
07909 920 181; sales@wildart.co.uk;
www.wildlifewatercolourpaintings.co.uk

Wildlife Art

Besides individual artists, there is

THE SOCIETY OF WILDLIFE ARTISTS (founded 1964) This registered charity seeks to generate an appreciation of the natural world through all forms of fine art inspired by wildlife. The Natural Eye exhibition is held annually in Oct/Nov at the Mall Galleries, London. Through bursary schemes, the Society has been able to help young artists (18 or over) with awards of up to £750 towards travel, education or the cost of materials. *Contact:* The Federation of British Artists, 17 Carlton House Terrace, London SW1Y 5BD: 020 7930 6844; info@mallgalleries.com; www.swla.co.uk

Various galleries regularly show wildlife art, they include

Birdscapes Gallery
Manor Farm Barns, Glandford, Holt, Norfolk NR25 7JP; 01263 741 742; art@birdscapes.co.uk; www.birdscapesgallery.co.uk
Opening times: All year, daily 11am to 5pm, may close for part of the day before a new exhibition.

David Shepherd Wildlife Foundation
7 Kings Road, Shalford, Guildford, Surrey GU4 8JU. 01483 272 323; dswf@davidshepherd.org; www.davidshepherd.org

Cheng Kim Loke Gallery, Slimbridge
Wildfowl & Wetland Trust,
Slimbridge, Gloucestershire GL2 7BT;
01453 891 900; info.slimbridge@wwt.org.uk;
www.wwt.org.uk
Opening times: All year, daily except Dec 25, 9.:0am to 5.30pm (to 5.00pm Feb/Mar & to 4:30pm Nov/Jan)— last entry one hour before closing time. Admission charge for non-WWT members.

Gordale (host of *Exhibition Of Wildlife Art*)
Gordale Garden and Home Centre, Chester High Road, Burton, South Wirral, Cheshire CH64 8TF; 0151 336 2116; admin@gordale.co.uk; www.gordale.co.uk & www.ewa-uk.com
Opening times: Stages an annual Exhibition of Wildlife Art in late July. Free admission.

House Of Bruar (includes *Wildlife Art Gallery*)
By Blair Atholl, Perthshire PH18 5TW;
0345 136 0111; mailorder@houseofbruar.com;
www.houseofbruar.com/gallery/
Opening times: All year, daily (not Dec 25 & Jan 1). 9:30am to 5:30pm. Free admission.

Mall Galleries
The Mall, London SW1;
0207 930 6844; info@mallgalleries.com;
www.mallgalleries.org.uk
Opening times: Stages the Society of Wildlife Artists' annual exhibition (date varies year to year, usually around Sep-Nov (10am to 5pm). Admission charge.

Nature in Art
Wallsworth Hall, Main A38, Twigworth, Gloucester GL2 9PA;
01452 731 422 (admin); via website;
www.natureinart.org.uk
Opening times: Closed Mondays (exc. Bank Holidays) and Dec 24 to 26 otherwise open daily 10am to 5pm. Admission charge.

Pinkfoot Gallery
High Street, Cley-next-the-Sea, Norfolk NR25 7RB; 01263 740 947; info@pinkfootgallery.co.uk; www.pinkfootgallery.co.uk
Opening times: All year, daily (not Christmas), Mon closed out of school holidays otherwise 10am-5pm (Mon to Sat), 11am-4pm (Sun). Free admission.

Waterston House
Donald Watson Art Gallery, housed in the headquarters of the Scottish Ornithologists Club, Waterston House, Aberlady, East Lothian EH32 0PY; 01875 871 330; via website; www.the-soc.org.uk
One of the
Opening times: Wed-Sun (10am-5pm summer/4pm winter - not Dec 25/26 & Jan 1). Free entry.

The Wildlife Art Gallery
Online Art Gallery: wildlifeartgallery@btinternet.com; www.wildlifeartgallery.com

COUNTY DIRECTORY: CONTENTS

COUNTY DIRECTORY: CONTENTS/INDEX

RESERVES INDEX

RESERVES INDEX

RESERVES INDEX

RESERVES INDEX

RESERVES INDEX

INTRODUCTION TO THE COUNTY DIRECTORY

In a change from previous editions, all the information relating to an individual county is now grouped together in one place, beginning with details of the local publications and organizations, followed by its map, and concluding with a selection of its reserves. For some counties, since the primary purpose of the map is to give you an overall idea of where the featured reserves are, the map is not placed precisely between the list of contacts and the featured reserves but on the first full spread of reserves.

As in previous editions, the counties are grouped together in regions but *unlike previous editions* these regions are no longer arranged alphabetically but geographically in sequences that very roughly follows sinuous lines snaking around each of the four nations. Likewise, within a region, the counties are no longer arranged alphabetically but geographically, so that neighbouring counties follow each other in **The Yearbook**. Finally—think of **The Yearbook** as a fractal—the reserves within each county are arranged geographically in a sequence that one might follow if taking a tour of all of a county's reserves. The rationale behind the switch from alphabet to geography as the organizing principle is to place sites that are close to each other in the field, close to each other in the book. Furthermore, some Wildlife Trusts cover more than one county. Arranging the counties geographically makes it easier to place counties that share a Wildlife Trust next to each other. For those of you who prefer alphabet to geography, there is a *Contents* page for the *County Directory,* a *Reserves Index* and alphabetically arranged keys for each of the maps, so that you can go straight to any desired reserve rather than follow my tortuous routes.

Between reserve entries, you will find passages set in italic type. These are brief directions designed to take you from one reserve to the next one on my Grand Tour. Of course, you do not have to follow the sequence I have mapped out. As in previous editons, simply go to the *Directions* section of the reserve you wish to visit and follow the route to it from the nearest large town or major road.

Another change from previous editions, introduced with the aim of cutting down on repetitious abbreviations, is that if an item of information such an e-mail address does not exist or could not be found, it is simply not listed rather than marked as n/a. For much the same reason, telephone numbers are no longer marked as 'T', e-mail addresses as 'E' and websites as 'W', since it should be self-evident if a piece of information is a phone number or a website address.

As before, each county entry begins with a short introductory paragraph, which is then followed by

Bird Atlas/Avifauna
The titles, authors, publishers and dates of publication of recent[ish] county publications, if any, are listed here. Some of these titles are still available to buy new but if out of print try the second hand market—check out the booksellers listed in *Reading About Birds.*

Bird Recorder
The name of and contact details of the County Bird Recorder.

Bird Report
The annual county bird report is usually, but not always, published by the county bird club. In some counties, annual reports are also published for smaller recording areas.

The (date-) refers to the start of the current title or, in some cases, its predecessor. In the first instance, contact the relevant person/club for the current report (and back issues). Check out the booksellers listed in *Reading About Birds* when searching for 'out of print' reports.

BTO Regional Representative[s]
The local BTO Representative is the first point of contact if you wish to help with national bird surveys in your county—get involved, make a difference!

In a change this year, rather than give out personal e-mails and telephone numbers, this QR code is printed alongside the person's name. Scan the code with your phone's camera and you will be taken to the Regional Network Directory page on the BTO website. You can then select the county you want. If scanning QR codes is not for you, go to
www.bto.org
and follow the links to the Directory

Wetland Bird Survey (WeBS) Local Organizer[s]
This section lists the WeBS Local Organizers for a county's wetlands. For details of how to help, contact your local organizer or the WeBS Office, BTO, The Nunnery, Thetford, Norfolk IP24 2PU:
01842 750 050; webs@bto.org

Club

Many counties have their own county-wide bird/natural history clubs; some have smaller clubs based in particular areas of the county. Contact details are provided along with the date the club was founded, its approximate membership and where and when it holds indoor meetings. See the *Introduction to Scotland* (p. 354) for the slightly different arrangement in Scotland.

Ringing Group/Bird Observatory

For more information about becoming a licensed ringer, contact the BTO (see UK Bird Organizations).

To contact a Ringing Group go to its website (if there is one) or contact the BTO to forward your enquiry.

Bird Observatories are a great place to see birds at close quarters—many of them run events and offer accommodation.

If you find a ringed bird, contact the BTO/relevant other organization—details will be on the ring.

RSPB Local Group[s]

Contact details for RSPB Local Groups in the area, along with information about meetings.

Wildlife Trust

There are 46 independent Wildlife Trusts in the national network. Each organizes activities and manages a number of nature reserves. A selection of these will be listed in the Reserves section, but the local Wildlife Trust will have many more up its sleeve. See the *Introduction to Scotland* (p. 355) for the slightly different arrangement in Scotland.

Map

The county map shows the locations of the featured reserves in relation to the county's main towns, roads and rivers. It is intended to provide general guidance to help you get your bearings. It is *not* a substitute for a road atlas, OS map or sat nav.

As previously mentioned, within each county, sites are arranged in a sequence that one might (but do not have to) follow if visiting each site, one after the other. Passages in italic type at the end of an entry provide brief directions from one site to the next.

Of course many/most readers will not visit the reserves of any single county in such a way, and the *Directions* section of each entry will continue to provide a guide to reaching a reserve from a nearby major town or road.

Each reserve entry is structured as follows:

SITE NAME (colour-keyed to its region) and number on the map.

The organization that owns and/or manages it.

Habitats: The main habitats for each reserve.

Birds: A reserve's highlight birds, along with the best time of year to see them. Remember, these are just the 'stars'. Over time, the species found at a reserve may change. Please do not hesitate to let the editor know if you feel the species list needs attention.

Other: Although most of the reserves in *The Yearbook* have been selected because they are 'good' for birds, many offer far more than just birds. This heading flags up interesting flora and/or fanua, other than birds

Directions: A post code (if available) and six-figure Ordnance Survey grid reference are given along with a short description of how to find the reserves—use these in conjunction with a road atlas or sat nav. Rememeber, very roughly, the further north and west you go and the higher you climb, the larger the area a post code covers and the less precise your sat nav becomes. You should also remember that there are still large areas with poor mobile signal.

Public transport: Details are given if it's reasonably feasible to get to a reserve using public transport. You are strongly advised to check with the listed transport providers (or via *Traveline*—see below) before travelling, as services and timetables can change. Many services do not run on a Sunday.

Traveline is a partnership of transport companies, local authorities and passenger groups providing information by phone or online to help you plan your journey. Call: 0871 200 22 33 (charges apply). Go to: www.traveline.info

Visiting: This is a catch-all section which includes information about access/opening times and facilities. Contact the reserve directly if you have any special requirements or you wish to check the available facilities in detail.

Many reserves place restrictions on dogs. These will be listed, if known. Any dog mess should be picked up and disposed of in the bins provided... or taken offsite. Do not leave dogs unattended in cars.

Contact: If available, a telephone number and an e-mail address are listed and, in a few cases, a website address.

UK/England
ORGANIZATIONS

These pages briefly describe a number of organizations and projects, some of which may also have local contact details listed in the **County Directory,** *that specifically focus on wild birds or on the places where birds live in England. Contact details are provided here for their English headquarters. In the event that an organization's English headquarters are not also its UK headquarters, contact details for the UK headquarters are provided in the introductory section to the nation where those headquarters are located.*

The figure in brackets after the name of the organization is the year in which it was founded.

UK wildlife organizations that are not specifically focused on birds or their habitats in the UK are listed in a separate section after the **County Directory.**

ARMY ORNITHOLOGICAL SOCIETY (1960)

Open to serving and ex-Army personnel, other services and their families, MOD civil servants and members of the Commonwealth Forces who have a casual or a more in depth interest in bird life. Activities include field meetings, expeditions, assistance with bird surveys and ringing projects, and a long term survey of seabirds on Ascension Island. AOS newsletter and annual journal *Adjutant.*
Contact: The Army Ornithological Society, Prince Consort's Library, Knollys Road, South Camp, Aldershot, Hampshire GU11 1PS: via website; www.armybirding.org.uk

ASSOCIATION OF COUNTY RECORDERS AND EDITORS (1993)

ACRE's basic aim is to promote best practice in the work of County Recorders, providing a forum for discussions on producing county bird reports and in problems arising in assessing records, managing county databases, systems and archives. Provides a discussion medium for interactions of the County Recorders and Report Editors with the British Birds Rarities Committee (BBRC), the Rare Breeding Bird Panel (RBBP) and the British Trust for Ornithology (BTO).
Contact: Hugh Pulsford (ACRE Secretary): 01565 880 171; ahugh.pulsford@btinternet.com

BARN OWL TRUST (1988)

The Trust is dedicated to conserving Barn Owls and their environment and is the main source of Barn Owl information in the UK. The Trust, and its members, erect nestboxes and are closely involved in habitat creation both on its own land and through farm visits. Also offers practical guidance to developers and planners—advising on Barn Owl mitigation measures, undertakes research and provides care for injured owls. Produces a number of publications inc. *The Barn Owl Conservation Handbook.* Events held.
Contact: Barn Owl Trust, Waterleat, Ashburton, Devon

TQ13 7HU: 01364 653 026; info@barnowltrust.org.uk; www.barnowltrust.org.uk

BIRDING FOR ALL (2000)

Formerly The Disabled Birder's Association, BFA (2010) is a charity and international movement that aims to promote access to reserves/other birdwatching places and to a range of services so that people with different needs can birdwatch as freely as the able-bodied. Membership is free (donations welcomed) and is open to everyone. New members are needed to help send a stronger message to those who own/manage nature reserves to improve access when they are planning and improving facilities. BFA also seeks to influence those who provide birdwatching services and equipment.
Contact: Bo Beolens (Chair), Birding For All, 18 St Mildreds Road, Cliftonville, Margate, Kent CT9 2LT: fatbirder@gmail.com; www.birdingforall.com

BIRD OBSERVATORIES COUNCIL (BOC)

See Wales

BRITISH BIRDS RARITIES COMMITTEE (1959)

The BBRC is the official adjudicator of rare bird records in Britain and the Channel Islands with a panel of ten voting on the records—its annual report is published in *British Birds.* In the case of rarities trapped for ringing, records should be sent to the Ringing Office of the BTO, who will forward them to the BBRC.
Contact: Paul French (Sec), BBRC, 1, Greenfield Bungalows, Easington, East Riding of Yorkshire, HU12 0TZ: secretary@bbrc.org.uk; www.bbrc.org.uk

BRITISH ORNITHOLOGISTS' CLUB (1892)

The BOC promotes scientific discussion between members and others interested in ornithology and facilitates the publication of scientific information in connection with ornithology with a particular interest in avian systematics, taxonomy and distribution. Publishes the *Bulletin of the British Ornithologists' Club* quarterly (online only), as well as a continuing series of publications including the BOC checklist series. It also holds a number of evening meetings each year (contact/see website for details).

Contact: British Ornithologists' Club, c/o Natural History Museum at Tring, Akeman Street, Tring, Herts HP23 6AP: 0220 8876 4728 & 07919 174 898; info@boc-online.org; www.boc-online.org

BRITISH ORNITHOLOGISTS' UNION (1858)
See Wales

BRITISH ORNITHOLOGISTS' UNION RECORDS COMMITTEE
See Wales

BRITISH TRUST FOR ORNITHOLOGY (1933)
An independent charitable research institute that combines professional and citizen science aimed at using evidence of change in wildlife populations, particularly birds, to inform the public, opinion-formers and environmental policy/decision makers. The BTO collects high quality monitoring data on birds and other wildlife from fieldwork by 60,000 volunteer birdwatchers in partnership with professional research scientists. Surveys include the national Bird Ringing Scheme, the Nest Record Scheme, the Breeding Bird Survey (with the JNCC/RSPB), the Wetland Bird Survey, in particular Low Tide Counts (with the RSPB/JNCC), which all contribute to an integrated programme of population monitoring. The BirdTrack recording system is an important resource for recording bird data and all birdwatchers are encouraged to use it to log their bird sightings.

The BTO has a network of voluntary regional representatives (see County entries), who organize fieldworkers for the programme of national surveys in which members and supporters participate. The results of these co-operative efforts are communicated to government departments, local authorities, industry and conservation bodies for effective action (see National Projects p180 for details of some of the current activities). Members receive the magazine *BTO News* four times a year and have the option of subscribing to the peer-reviewed journals *Bird Study* (four times yearly) and *Ringing and Migration* (twice a year). Local meetings are held in conjunction with bird clubs and societies, there are regional and national birdwatchers' conferences, and specialist courses in bird identification and modern censusing techniques.

Grants are made for research, and members have the use of a lending and reference library at Thetford.

Contact: British Trust for Ornithology, The Nunnery, Thetford, Norfolk IP24 2PU: 01842 750 050; info@bto;org; www.bto.org

BRITISH WATERFOWL ASSOCIATION
The BWA is dedicated to education about waterfowl, their conservation, and raising the standards of keeping and breeding ducks, geese and swans in captivity. It publishes *Waterfowl* members magazine three times a year.

Contact: BWA Secretary, Holme House, Dale, Ainstable, Carlisle, CA4 9RH: 07514 601 167; secretary@waterfowl.org.uk; www.waterfowl.org.uk

CAMPAIGN TO PROTECT RURAL ENGLAND CPRE (1926)
The CPRE, now styling itself *'The countryside charity'*, campaigns at all levels for a beautiful and living countryside by working to protect, promote and enhance our towns and countryside, to make them better places to live, work and enjoy, and to ensure the countryside is protected now and for future generations.

Contact: CPRE, 15-21 Provost Street, London N1 7NH: 020 7981 2800; info@cpre.org.uk; www.cpre.org.uk

COUNTRY LAND & BUSINESS ASSOCIATION CLA (1907)
The CLA is at the heart of rural life and is the voice of the countryside for England and Wales, campaigning on issues which directly affect those who live and work in rural communities. Anyone who owns rural land or runs a rural business will benefit from joining the CLA, and its members range from some of the largest landowners, with interests in forest, moorland, water and farming, to some with little more than a paddock or garden.

Contact: Country Land and Business Association Ltd, 16 Belgrave Square, London SW1X 8PQ: 020 7235 0511; mail@cla.org.uk; www.cla.org.uk

EDWARD GREY INSTITUTE OF FIELD ORNITHOLOGY (1937)
The EGI takes its name from Edward Grey, first Viscount Grey of Fallodon, a life-long lover of birds and former Chancellor of the University of Oxford.

The Institute now has a permanent staff of research students, senior visitors and post-doctoral research workers. The Institute houses the Alexander Library of Ornithology, one of the largest collections of 19th-20th-21st century material on birds in the world. The Library is open for reference use only to all holders of a university card or valid Bodleian Library card. External visitors are welcome on a day pass by arrangement by contacting: Sophie Wilcox, Alexander (and Sherardian) Library, South Parks Road, Oxford OX1 3RB: 01865 275 025; sophie.wilcocx@bodleian.ox.ac.uk

Contact: The Edward Grey Institute: egi@biology.ox.ac.uk

The EGI, Department of Biology, University of Oxford, The Life and Mind Building, South Parks Road, Oxford, OX1 3RB: https://egioxford.web.ox.ac.uk

ENVIRONMENT AGENCY (1996)

A non-departmental body that aims to protect and improve the environment and to contribute towards the delivery of sustainable development through the integrated management of air, land and water.

Functions include pollution prevention and control, waste minimization, management of water resources, flood defence, improvement of salmon and freshwater fisheries, conservation of aquatic species, navigation and use of inland and coastal waters for recreation.

Contact: Environment Agency, National Customer Contact Centre, PO Box 544, Rotherham, S60 1BY. General enquiries: 03708 506 506 (Mon-Fri, 8am-6pm) Environment incident hotline (24hr): 0800 80 70 60; Floodline (24 hrs): 0345 988 1188; enquiries@environment-agency.gov.uk; www.gov.uk/government/organisations/ environment-agency

FORESTRY COMMISSION (1919)

The FC supports the delivery of English forestry operations inc. grants for forestry activities and felling licences.

Contact: Forestry Commission, 620 Bristol Business Park, Coldharbour Lane, Bristol, BS16 1EJ 0300 067 4321; nationalenquiries@forestrycommission.gov.uk; www.gov.uk/government/organisations/forestry-commission

FORESTRY ENGLAND (2019)

FE looks after England's public forests, managing them for people, wildlife and for the economy.
Contact: Forestry Commission—as above.
info@forestryengland.uk; www.forestryengland.uk

GAME AND WILDLIFE CONSERVATION TRUST (1931)

The GWCT uses science to promote game and wildlife management as an essential part of nature conservation and supports best practice for field sports that contribute to improving the biodiversity of the countryside. 100+ staff, inc many scientists, run over 60 research projects. The results are used to advise government, landowners, farmers and conservationists on practical management techniques which will benefit game species, their habitats and other wildlife. In June the *Annual Review* lists papers published in the peer-reviewed scientific press.
Members receive *Gamewise* magazine.
Contact: Game and Wildlife Conservation Trust, Burgate Manor, Fordingbridge, Hampshire SP6 1EF: 01425 652 381; info@gwct.org.uk; www.gwct.org.uk

Scottish office: *see Scotland*

GAY BIRDERS CLUB (1994)

A club for gay, lesbian, bisexual and transgender birdwatchers over the age of consent and their friends and supporters, in the UK and worldwide. The club has a network of regional contacts and organizes day trips, weekends and longer events at notable birdwatching locations in the UK and abroad. Members receive a quarterly newsletter *Out Birding* with details of all events. A 'Grand Get Together' is held every two years.
Contact: GBC contact@gbc-online.org.uk; www.gbc-online.org.uk

HAWK AND OWL TRUST (1969)

The Trust is dedicated to the conservation and appreciation of wild birds of prey and their habitats. It achieves its major aim of creating and enhancing nesting, roosting and feeding habitats for birds of prey through projects which involve practical research, creative conservation and education—on its own reserves and in partnership with landowners, farmers and others. Members are invited to take part in fieldwork, population studies, surveys, etc. Publishes a members' magazine (*Peregrine*) and educational materials for all ages. The Trust manages two reserves: Sculthorpe Moor in Norfolk and Shapwick Moor on the Somerset Levels.
Contact: Hawk and Owl Trust, Turf Moor Road, Sculthorpe, Fakenham, Norfolk NR21 9GN: 01328 856 788;
via website; www.hawkandowltrust.org

NATIONAL TRUST (1895)

With a membership of over 5.7 million, the Trust works for the preservation of places of historic interest or natural beauty in England, Wales and Northern Ireland. In addition to historic houses, castles, ancient monuments, parks and gardens, the Trust protects some 620,000 acres of land and 780 miles of coastline Its nature reserves include many SSSIs/ASSIs, NNRs, SPAs and Ramsar sites.
Contact: The National Trust (membership), Heelis Kemble Drive, Swindon, Wiltshire SN2 2NA; 0344 800 1895; enquiries@nationaltrust.org.uk; www.nationaltrust.org.uk

NATURAL ENGLAND (2006)

NE is the government's adviser for the natural environment in England, helping to protect England's nature and landscape for people to enjoy and for the services they provide. Responsibilities include helping land managers and farmers to protect wildlife and landscapes; improving public access to the coastline; managing about two thirds of the 221 National Nature Reserves; managing programmes that help restore and create wildlife habitats; and providing evidence to help make decisions affecting the natural environment. There are 12 area teams.

Contact: Natural England, Foss House, Kings Pool, 1-2 Peasholme Green, York, YO1 7PX:
0300 060 3900 (enquiries);
enquiries@naturalengland.org.uk;
www.gov.uk/government/organisations/natural-england

RARE BREEDING BIRDS PANEL (1972)
With representatives from the BTO, JNCC, RSPB, three independent members and a Secretary, the RBBP collects all information on rare breeding birds in the UK, so that changes in status can be monitored as an aid to conservation as well as being stored for posterity.
Bespoke recording forms are used (obtainable from the website). Records should be submitted via county and regional recorders. The RBBP also monitors breeding by scarcer non-native species and seeks records of these in the same way. An annual report is published in *British Birds.*
Contact: RBBP, Mark Eaton (Secretary):
secretary@rbbp.org.uk; www.rbbp.org.uk

ROYAL AIR FORCE
ORNITHOLOGICAL SOCIETY (1965)
Open to any serving and ex-RAF personnel, other Services, MOD civil servants and their families. Organizes field meetings and expeditions at home and abroad and undertakes surveys and ringing operations. Publishes a newsletter and a journal.
Contact: RAFOS, Jan Knight (Gen Sec):
rafos_secretary@hotmail.com;
www.rafornithology.org.uk

ROYAL NAVAL BIRDWATCHING SOCIETY (1946)
RNBWS is open to anyone with a common interest in birds at sea. Maintains an extensive seabird database with records received from most sea areas of the world. Publishes *The Sea Swallow* (annual report).
Contact: RNBWS: secretary@rnbws.org.uk;
www.rnbws.org.uk

ROYAL SOCIETY FOR
THE PROTECTION OF BIRDS (1889)
The RSPB is the UK partner of BirdLife International, and is Europe's largest voluntary wildlife conservation body with 1.2 million members (inc youth members). As a registered charity, it is governed by an elected body and its work covers five areas: science, species, places, people and policy. The RSPB manages over 220 nature reserves in the UK, covering *c.*395,000 acres that are home to over 18,500 species. The aim is to maintain a countrywide network of reserves with examples of all the main bird communities and having due regard to the conservation of plants and other animals.

There is an active network of local groups (see **County Directory**), which hold regular indoor and outdoor meetings. There are extensive volunteering opportunities, including working on the RSPB's nature reserves.
The RSPB's International Department works closely with Birdlife International and its partners in other countries and is involved with numerous projects overseas, especially in Europe and Asia.
Contact: RSPB: The Lodge, Potton Road, Sandy, Bedfordshire SG19 2DL: 01767 680 551;
firstname.surname@rspb.org.uk;
Support Services Team: 01767 693 680 (9am-5pm, Mon-Fri); membership@rspb.org.uk
Wildlife Team: 01767 693 690 (9:30am-4:30pm, Mon-Fri); wildlife@rspb.org.uk www.rspb.org.uk
England Headquarters
1st Floor, One Cornwall Street, Birmingham B3 2JN.
The contact details of the RSPB's other national offices are listed in the Organization sections of the relevant countries.

SEABIRD GROUP (1966)
The group promotes and helps to coordinate the study and conservation of seabirds. It maintains close links with other national/international ornithological bodies and organizes regular conferences on seabird biology and conservation topics. Small grants available to assist with research/survey work on seabirds.
Publishes regular newsletters and *Seabird* (journal).
Contact: Antoine Grissot (Membership Sec):
membership@seabirdgroup.org.uk;
www.seabirdgroup.org.uk

SWIFT CONSERVATION (2009)
An advice service aiming to reverse the decline in the UK's Swift population. Swift Conservation runs a website providing extensive information on Swifts, and on how to preserve existing/to set up new Swift nesting sites. It runs a lecture and training service, providing guidance for the general public, planners, developers and architects and supplies advice and help both directly and via volunteers. Has links to similar assistance across Europe, the Middle East, Central Asia and North America and campaigns for better protection of Swifts and other birds that rely on nesting places in, or on, buildings.
Contact: Swift Conservation:
mail@swift-conservation.org;
www.swift-conservation.org

WADER QUEST (2012)
A voluntary charity dedicated to supporting wader conservation through fundraising and increasing awareness about the acute problems facing wader populations around the world. Specializes in supporting community wader conservation projects by purchasing equipment

and materials from the charity's Grants Fund. Quarterly online newsletter and merchandising available. Talks and events are undertaken throughout the year in partnership with other organizations.
Contact: Wader Quest, 3rd Floor, 86-90 Paul Street, London EC2A 4NEJ: via website; www.waderquest.net

WWT, the charity for wetlands and wildlife (1946)
Founded by Sir Peter Scott to conserve wetlands and their biodiversity, WWT has 10 wetland centres across the UK, which have entries in the relevant counties. The centres are nationally, or internationally, important for wintering wildfowl. Walks, talks and events are available for visitors, and resources and programmes are provided for school groups. Most of the centres have collections of wildfowl from around the world, including many endangered species.
WWT's conservation programmes focus on the science and processes that underpin conservation action, threats to wetlands and their wildlife and conserving threatened species, as well as restoring wetlands at scale around the world.. WWT also leads Wetland Link International, a project with 350 members over six continents that promotes the role of wetland centres for education and public awareness.
Contact: WWT, Slimbridge, Gloucestershire GL2 7BT: 01453 891198; supporter@wwt.org.uk or via website; www.wwt.org.uk

WILDLIFE TRUSTS (1995)
Founded in 1912 (as The Society for Promotion of Nature Reserves) the Trusts are the largest UK charity dedicated to conserving all habitats and species. Has a membership of 900,000 through 46 individual county trusts (see *County Directory*). Collectively, they manage over 2,600 nature reserves and lobby for better protection of the UK's natural heritage. Members receive their local Trust magazine, which includes a UK News section.
Contact: The Wildlife Trusts, The Kiln, Waterside, Mather Road, Newark, NG24 1WT: 01636 677 711; via website; www.wildlifetrusts.org

WILDLIFE WATCH (1977)
Junior branch of the Wildlife Trusts with 150,000 members. There are 50+ Wildlife Watch groups across the UK where children can join in a wide range of activities. Membership is through a local Trust as a junior member.
Contact: Wildlife Trusts—as above.
watch@wildlifetrusts.org; www.wildlifewatch.org.uk

WOODLAND TRUST (1972)
The UK's largest woodland conservation charity works to protect and campaign on behalf of the country's woods by managing over 1,000 sites, creating new native woodlands and restoring ancient woodland for the benefit of wildlife and people.
Contact: Woodland Trust, general enquiries: 0330 333 3300; enquiries@woodlandtrust.org.uk; www.woodlandtrust.org.uk
England: Kempton Way, Grantham, Lincolnshire NG31 6LL: 0330 333 3300; england@woodlandtrust.org.uk
The contact details of the Woodland Trust's other national offices are listed in the Organization sections of the relevant countries.

UK Projects

National ornithological projects depend for their success on the active participation of amateur birdwatchers. In return they provide birdwatchers with an excellent opportunity to contribute in a positive and worthwhile way to the scientific study of birds and their habitats—the vital foundation of all conservation programmes. The following entries present a number of ongoing projects and who to contact for further information.

BIG GARDEN BIRDWATCH
RSPB
The Big Garden Birdwatch was first launched in 1979 and has grown into fun for all the family. All you need to do is count the birds in your garden, or a local park, for one hour during (usually) the last weekend of January (in 2026, 23-25 January). The long-term trends of birds coming into gardens can be monitored. In 2025, over 590,000 people participated in the event, counting just over 9.1 million birds. 80 species were recorded with House Sparrow, Blue Tit and Starling in the top three places.
Contact: RSPB.

BIRDS IN GREENSPACES
Purpose: Birds in Greenspaces is a new citizen science project which will take place in 2026, and aims to find out the importance of greenspaces for UK bird populations. By creating an accessible project, we want to get as many people as possible to engage with and record the birds that use the parks, playing fields, and other public-access sites in our cities, towns, and villages. The findings will then be used to create guidance for those who manage these spaces, to ensure they are the best they can be for both birds and people.
Location/s: UK-wide
Time commitment: No minimum time requirement
Required knowledge: No minimum experience required
Additional information: Binoculars not required
Contact: greenspaces@bto.org; bto.org/greenspaces

BIRDTRACK
Purpose: BirdTrack is an exciting project that looks at

the migration and distribution of birds throughout Britain and Ireland. BirdTrack allows volunteers to store and manage their own personal bird records via either the web version of BirdTrack or the BirdTrack smartphone app, and uses these to support species conservation at local, regional, national and international scales. The project is a free and convenient way of storing your bird records online, and lets you keep up to date with what others are seeing, view the latest trends, and contribute your data to BTO science.

Location/s: Records can be entered for anywhere in the world

Time commitment: No time commitment required.

Required knowledge: Suitable for anyone from beginners to expert birdwatchers.

Project partners: BTO, RSPB, BirdWatch Ireland, Scottish Ornithologists' Club and Welsh Ornithological Society

Contact: birdtrack@bto.org; www.birdtrack.net

Social Media: X @birdtrack Bluesky @birdtrack.bsky.social

BREEDING BIRD SURVEY (BBS)

Purpose: Population change of the UK's widespread breeding bird species, providing an indicator of the health of the countryside. Changes are reported for the UK and its four constituent countries, as well as smaller geographical areas.

Location/s: UK-wide. Surveys are conducted on randomly selected OS 1km squares.

Time commitment: Two survey visits annually per square (early-Apr/mid-May and mid-May/late-Jun), with an optional pre-season recce visit to check access and record habitat. A single square is equivalent to around seven hours per year, including data entry.

Required knowledge: Surveyors should be able to identify all the bird species likely to be present in a given square by sight and sound, given sufficient views/vocalizations.

Additional information: Since its inception, BBS has been a great success—now around 3,000 volunteers cover nearly 4,000 squares and record over 200 species annually. BBS is particularly keen to attract more volunteers in our under-recorded upland habitats, but also across the UK, where increasing coverage enables the calculation of trends at smaller spatial scales. Alongside BBS is the Waterways Breeding Bird Survey (WBBS), which operates a very similar method along rivers and canals, measuring population change in waterways specialists.

Project partners: BTO, JNCC & RSPB

Contact: bbs@bto.org or your local BTO Regional Representative (see County entries).

Websites:
BBS. www.bto.org/bbs
WBBS. www.bto.org/wbbs.

Find a square: https://app.bto.org/bbs/public/request-square.jsp.

Social media: Bsky: @bbs-birds.bsky.social

GARDEN BIRDWATCH (GBW)
BTO

Purpose: To monitor birds and other wildlife that visit garden habitats. Data collected are used to produce long-term trends to monitor regional, seasonal and year-to-year changes in garden populations of our commoner birds, mammals, reptiles, amphibians and selected insects.

Location/s: Your garden!

Time commitment: Flexible. Recommend a minimum of 20 minutes a week, but consistency is more important (same effort every week)

Required knowledge: To identify birds (and other wildlife if desired) visiting your garden

Additional information: Participation is free, with the opportunity for participants to help fund the survey through an annual subscription to Bird Table, a quarterly magazine.

GOOSE AND SWAN MONITORING PROGRAMME (GSMP)

Purpose: The UK supports 13 internationally important native goose and migratory swan populations. The GSMP aims to record population sizes and distributions as well as breeding success. Species surveyed include Pink-footed, Barnacle, Bean, Brent, Greater White-fronted and Greylag Geese, plus the scheme also includes a sexennial International Swan Census, which focuses on Whooper and Bewick's Swans.

Location/s: UK-wide

Time commitment: Two or three monthly visits in winter on set weekends.

Required knowledge: Participants will need to be confident in your identification of the relevant goose or swan species for the census that you are carrying out.

Project partners: JNCC & NatureScot

Contact: gsmp@bto.org; www.bto.org/gsmp

Social Media: @webs-gsmp.bsky.social

HERONRIES CENSUS
BTO

Purpose: Started in 1928, this census represents the longest continuous series of population data for any European breeding bird, the Grey Heron! Herons may be hit hard during periods of severe weather and are vulnerable to pesticides and pollution. Each year, counts of apparently occupied nests (AONs) are made at as many of the UK heronries as possible. Counts of Cormorant nests at heronries are encouraged and Little Egret and other incoming species of colonial waterbirds are included, whether nesting with Herons or on their own - these include Great White Egret, Cattle Egret and Spoonbill.

Location/s: UK-wide but contributions from under-recorded areas and notifications of new colonies are particularly welcomed.

Time commitment: Up to 3 site visits annually, in March, April and May. Each visit requires 10 minutes to 1 hour of survey time.

Required knowledge: No specialized ornithological knowledge or experience is required.

Contact: herons@bto.org

or your local BTO Regional Organizer (see County entries) https://www.bto.org/get-involved/volunteer/projects/heronries-census

NEST RECORD SCHEME

BTO

Purpose: The Nest Record Scheme asks participants to locate nests and monitor their progress over several visits, making counts of the number of eggs and/or chicks on each occasion and recording whether they are successful in their chicks fledging. Information from NRS complements demographic information collected by other BTO surveys and feeds into the BTO's Integrated Population Monitoring, highlighting the causes of changes in bird populations. Guidance on how to become a BTO nest recorder, including best practice guidelines on minimizing disturbance while visiting nests, is available online. You can participate by following the progress of a few nests in your local area, erecting and monitoring boxes or becoming a highly skilled nest finder.

Location/s: UK-wide

Time commitment: No minimum time requirement

Project partners: JNCC

Contact: nrs@bto.org

www.bto.org/get-involved/volunteer/projects/nrs

RINGING SCHEME

Project Partners: BTO, JNCC, The National Parks & Wildlife Service (Ireland) & ringers

Marking birds with individually numbered metal rings allows the study of survival, productivity and movements of British and Irish birds. Over 2,600 trained and licensed ringers mark nearly a million birds annually in Britain and Ireland. Training for a 'C-permit' licence can take at least a year, but more often two or more years, depending on the aptitude of the trainee and the amount of ringing they can do. A 'restricted permit' can usually be obtained more quickly (*c.*6 months). To find out more about ringing/to find a trainer visit:

https://www.bto.org/ our-science/projects/bird-ringing-scheme/taking-part

Anyone can contribute to the scheme by reporting seen or found ringed or colour-marked birds:

http://blx1.bto.org/euring/main/index.jsp

or contact BTO HQ. Anyone finding a ringed bird

should note the ring number, species, when and where found and, if possible, what happened to it. If the bird is dead, it may also be possible to remove the ring, which should be kept in case there is a query. Anyone reporting a ringed bird will be sent details of where and when the bird was originally ringed.

Check out the 'Demog Blog' (no longer updated) for news and stories: http://btoringing.blogspot.co.uk

Contact: BTO. E: ringing@bto.org

CONSTANT EFFORT SITES (CES) SCHEME

Project Partners: BTO, JNCC The National Parks & Wildlife Service (Ireland) & ringers

Started in 1983, the CES scheme coordinates standardized mist-netting at around 120 sites across Britain and Ireland (with 12 standard visits between May-August). The scheme allows the BTO to monitor trends on the abundance of adults and juveniles, productivity and adult survival rates for 24 species of common songbirds. Information from CES complements demographic information collected by other BTO surveys and feeds into the BTO's Integrated Population Monitoring programme which highlights the causes of changes in bird populations. Results are updated annually and published on-line as part of the BirdTrends Report.

Contact: BTO. E: ces@bto.org

RETRAPPING ADULTS FOR SURVIVAL (RAS) SCHEME

Project Partners: BTO, JNCC The National Parks & Wildlife Service (Ireland) & ringers

Under the RAS scheme, started in 1998, ringers aim to catch or re-sight adult birds of a single species in a study area during the breeding season. This data allows the BTO to monitor survival rates in adult birds and is particularly useful for those species not widely covered by CES scheme. and forms part of the BTO's Integrated Population Monitoring framework.

Contact: BTO: ras@bto.org

UK BEACHED BIRD SURVEY

RSPB

The UKBBS has been running, in its current format, since 1991. The results of the annual survey (carried out in February) are used in conjunction with those from other European countries and aim to contribute to international monitoring efforts to document trends in chronic marine oil pollution and to promote adequate methods of controlling illegal oil discharge to help reduce seabird mortality.

Contact: RSPB.

WETLAND BIRD SURVEY (WeBS)

Purpose: The Wetland Bird Survey (WeBS) is the monitoring scheme for non-breeding waterbirds in the UK. The principal aims of the scheme are to identify population sizes of waterbirds, determine trends in numbers and distribution and, crucially, identify important sites for waterbirds.

Location/s: WeBS Core Counts are made annually at around 3,400 wetland sites of all habitats, although estuaries and large still waters predominate. Monthly coordinated counts are made mostly by over 3,000 volunteers (making over 40,000 visits), principally between September and March, with fewer summer counts.

Time commitment: Counts are relatively straightforward and may take from a few minutes up to a few hours, depending on the size of the site—numbers of all target species in the count area are recorded. Counts are monthly. See **Diary** for 2026 Core Count dates.

Required knowledge: Varies depending on complexity / diversity at the site but a good ID of common water-birds is highly advantageous.

Additional information: The WeBS data is used to designate important waterbird sites and protect them against adverse development, for research into the causes of declines, for establishing conservation priorities and strategies, and to formulate management plans for wetland sites and waterbirds. WeBS participants receive an annual newsletter and a comprehensive annual report.

Project partners: BTO, JNCC & RSPB

Contact: Gillian Birtles (General WeBS enquiries) WeBS Office, BTO: webs@bto.org; https://www.bto.org/get-involved/volunteer/projects/wetland-bird-survey

Social Media: @webs-gsmp.bsky.social

Arctic Redpoll, Finland
Sylvie Soudan
Instagram: Sylvie.Soudan

Isles of Scilly

An archipelago of granite islands, which may be the high points of what was once a larger island or group of islands drowned by post-glaciation sea-level rises and isostatic readjustment. Lying in the Atlantic 25 miles WSW of Land's End, the islands have a total land area of 6.2 sq miles and a highest elevation of 167 ft. The five inhabited ones—St Mary's, St Martin's, Tresco, Bryher, St Agnes—are arranged around a central sound in the form of an inverted Y and are fringed by a large number of islets and rocks. Windswept, with mild winters and cool but sunny summers, they are a magnet for birdwatchers because of their various overlapping bird assemblages.

Bird Atlases/Avifauna
The Essential Guide to Birds of The Isles of Scilly
Bob L Flood, N Hudson & B Thomas
(privately published, 2007).
The Birds of the Isles of Scilly
Peter Robinson (Christopher Helm, 2003).
The Birds of Cornwall and the Isles of Scilly
RD Penhallurick (Browsers Bookshop, 1978).

Bird Recorder
James Lidster, Oldenhof 3, Driel 6665DP
The Netherlands
+31 (0)626861824; recorder@scilly-birding.co.uk

Bird Report
Isles of Scilly Bird Report and Natural History Review
(1969-), from ISBG—Carole Cilia, Hivemia, Jackson's Hill, St Mary's, Isles of Scilly TR21 0JZ.
01720 423 540; membership@scilly-birding.co.uk

11	Annet
4	Chapel Down
10	Gugh
2	Lower Moors
1	Peninnis Head
7	Pentle Bay
8	Pool of Bryher
9	Shipman Head
6	Tresco
3	Upper Moors
5	White Island

BTO Regional Representative
Will Wagstaff.

Clubs
Isles of Scilly Bird Group (2000; 375).
Carole Cilia, (Membership Sec), Hivernia, Jackson's Hill, St Mary's, Isles of Scilly TR21 0JZ 01720 423 540; membership@scilly-birding.co.uk; www.scilly-birding.co.uk

RSPB Local Group
None

Wildlife Trusts
The Isles of Scilly Wildlife Trust (1984).
Trenoweth, St Marys, Isles of Scilly TR21 0NS.
01720 422 153; hello@ios-wildlifetrust.org.uk; www.ios-wildlifetrust.org.uk

Approximately 75% of the land area of the Isles of Scilly is owned by the Duchy of Cornwall.
Habitats: Windswept maritime heath, farmland (especially spring flowers), rocky shores and sandy beaches, with, in the main, rock on the outer, seaward facing shores and sand on the inner, sheltered ones. Small areas of woodland and freshwater pools.
Birds: The location of the islands means that they offer several distinct but overalpping bird assemblages.
1: Summer/winter residents
The species you would expect given the islands' location at the SW tip of the UK, mild climate and limited range of habitats.

2: Passage migrants and vagrants
Located 20 to 30 miles out into the Atlantic on the W edge of the UK and at the S entrance to the Irish Sea, the islands lie on the 'normal' spring and autumn migration routes for a wide variety of species and offer them a place to rest and feed. In addition, their position to the W of the UK and W tip of France but S of Ireland makes them a first landfall for migrants that are off-course, such as Nearctic warblers caught by storms and blown out to sea during their autumn migration S along the E coast of the USA. Whilst migrants pass through the islands in both spring and autumn, the peak season for rarities is the autumn because of the combination of inexperienced young birds navigating poorly and birds being caught in autumn storms and blown across the Atlantic.

3: Seabirds and pelagics
As a group of oceanic islands with many uninhabited and predator-free islets, they host numerous seabird breeding colonies, as well as also lying on the edge of the foraging areas of seabirds breeding elsewhere or the oceanic migration routes of S Hemisphere tubenoses. The peak period for this group is mid to late summer.
Other: Lying at the extreme SW point of the UK in the Atlantic, they experience mild winters and cool summers. Subtropical plants in the Abbey Gardens on Tresco; Scilly Shrew, introduced Red Squirrel. Grey Seal. Pelagic boat trips, see below, frequently encounter sharks and cetaceans.
Directions: The main town (Hugh Town) is 38 miles WSW of Penzance and can be reached from the mainland by passenger ferry, fixed wing aircraft or helicopter. There is no vehicle ferry.
The Isles of Scilly Steamship Group (01736 334220; sales@islesofscilly-travel.co.uk; www.islesofscilly-travel.co.uk) operates a frequent but not daily passenger ferry service (2hr 45 min) between Penzance and Hugh Town on St Mary's. No service between 10 Nov 25 and 16 Mar 26. Current ferry, Scillonian III, due to be replaced by bigger and faster Scillonian IV in 2026. There is a park & ride car park in Penzance at TR20 8TH, with a shuttle bus service to the ferry terminal. For day trips park in town car parks. Penzance train station is 600 yards from the quay for the ferry.
The same company operates Skybus flights between Exeter, Newquay and Land's End airports and the airport on St Mary's. Bus transfer service between Penzance train station and Land's End airport
Penzance Helicopters (01736 780828; info@penzance-helicopters.co.uk; https://penzancehelicopters.co.uk) operates a helicopter service between Penzance heliport and St Mary's and Tresco.
Public transport: Various boat companies offer inter-island transfers and sightseeing trips/wildlife safaris. Consult the quayside blackboards on the various islands and, in particular:

St Mary's Boatmen Association Ticket Kiosk
Open 9:30-10:15am & 1:30-2pm & 01720 423999
www.scillyboating.co.uk
Tresco Boat Services
01720 423373
www.tresco.co.uk/arriving/tresco-boats
St Agnes Boating
01720 422704
www.stagnesboating.co.uk
A community bus service (017810 435 417; stevesims99@gmail.com) operates a scheduled, hop-on/hop-off bus service around St Mary's during the main season. There are no buses on any of the other islands.
Visiting: A substantial portion of the Duchy's landholding is let, rent-free, to the Isles of Scilly Wildlife Trust, which, in turn, manages the land for nature conservation purposes and sets aside some of the areas it looks after as defined wildlife reserves. These include:

ST MARY'S
1 PENINNIS HEAD
Habitats: 40 acres, cliff, gorse, heath.
Birds: *Breeding:* Stonechat, Meadow Pipit. *Passage:* Wryneck, Ring Ouzel, Wheatear.
Other: *Winter:* Humpback & Fin Whales, Common Dolphin. Early Meadow Grass, Western Clover.
Directions: SV 908 102. Immediately S of Hugh Town, several points of acces. King Edward's Road, off Church Road/Old Town Road, runs down middle of headland.
Visiting: Open all hours, free. No facilities but close to Hugh Town. Several paths, uneven in places, leading to S tip of St Mary's. Conservation grazing by Red Ruby cattle in spring and autumn. Dogs on lead

2 LOWER MOORS
Habitats: 25 acres, two main pools plus smaller ones, reeds, willow carr. Trust has a programme to restore wetland.
Birds: *Winter:* Water Rail, Snipe, Jack Snipe. Occasional Corncrake, Spotted Crake. Good for vagrants, in recent years: Yellow-billed Cuckoo, Great Blue Heron, Purple Heron, Little Bittern, Red-flanked Bluetail, Bluethroat.
Other: Restoration programme leading to increase in wetland plants.
Directions: TR21 0JY; SV 911 107. Path runs across reserve from Telegraph Road to Trench Road and then Old Town Road; both to E of Hugh Town.
Visiting: Open all hours, free, no facilities. Viewing screen at smaller pool, 2 hides at larger. Paths can be wet in winter, grazed occasionally, dogs on lead.

3 UPPER MOORS & PORTH HELLICK POOL
Habitats: 40 acres, largest pool on St Mary's, reed fringed, stream, wet woodland, farmland, shingle and beach
Birds: Gadwall, Coot, Water Rail, Sedge Warbler, Ringed

Plover (declining). *Passage:* Pied & Spotted Flycatchers. Vagrants: Belted Kingfisher recorded in 2018, Red-rumped Swallow.

Other: Cetaceans offshore.

Directions: TR21 0NZ; SV 921 110. From Lower Moors continue along Telegraph Road or Old Town Road and at the junction of either of them with the A3110, turn R. 600 yards from where Old Town Road joins the A3110 take path on R, which runs through reserve, past pool, to Porth Hellick.

Visiting: Open all hours, free, no facilities. 2 hides overlooking pool. Trail includes boardwalk. Grazed occasionally, dogs on lead.

NE of St Mary's and SE of St Martin's

The uninhabited **Eastern Islands,** some closed to landing all year, some during the breeding season. Breeding Fulmar, Razorbill, Puffin, Cormorant, Grey Seal

ST MARTIN'S

There is but one road, with a couple of dead ends branching off, on St Martin's, which runs from the quay of Higher Town (toilets) in the E to that of Lower Town (pub) in the W. By road, the two quays are 1.5 miles apart. Otherwise there is dense network of paths.

4 CHAPEL DOWN

Habitats: 85 acres, waved maritime heath.

Birds: Breeding: Fulmar, Manx Shearwater, Lesser Black-backed Gull. Stonechat, Meadow Pipit.

Other: Red-barbed Ant. Orange Bird's-foot.

Directions: TR25 0QL; SV 941 157. Land at Higher Town quay, (toilets) then paths towards E end of island (head for red and white Daymark beacon).

Visiting: Open all hours, free, no facilities.

One path runs the length of the N coast from Chapel Down to White Island. In doing so it passes Great Bay, a sandy bay on the N coast, which is the exception that proves the rule: it is sandy yet outward facing because it is sheltered by the projecting White Island.

5 WHITE ISLAND

Habitats: 40 acres: 'waved' heath.

Birds: Breeding: Lesser & Great Black-backed & Herring Gulls, Fulmar

Other: Nationally rare lichens on N slope.

Directions: TR25 0QN; SV 923 176. Tidal island off NW tip of St Martin's. If you don't plan to walk from Chapel Down, land at Lower Town and head N.

Visiting: Open all hours (check tides, cut off at high tide). Paths rocky and uneven. Dogs on lead.

Between St Martin's and Tresco

Teän and **St Helen's,** uninhabited islands. Landing permitted but some areas restricted during breeding season. **Teän:** breeding Great & Lesser Black-backed & Herring Gulls. Rare flora. Dogs on lead. **St Helen's:**

Fulmar, Manx Shearwater, Puffin, Razorbill, Guillemot, Great & Lesser Black-backed Gulls. Rats still present on St Helen's but Seabird Recovery Project now attempting to remove them.

6 TRESCO

The island of Tresco—oriented NW-SE, 2 miles long—is let long term in its entirety by the Duchy to a single family.

Habitats: Heathland in N, bulb fields, woods, pools and dunes to S. Rocky shores, dunes and beaches. Formal gardens planted with sub-tropical plants.

Birds: Passage migrants such as Golden Plover and Dotterel on heathland in N. Woods along the shore of the Great Pool good for vagrants: Black-and-White Warbler and Hermit Thrush in recent years. Great Pool good for wintering wildfowl, autumn waders—recent Lesser Yellowlegs.

Other: Sub-tropical plants from the Abbey Gardens have now spread into the dunes at the S end.

Directions: TR24 0QQ; SV 893 141 (Abbey Gardens Visitor Centre). Two main settlements and quays, roughly mid-way along the island: Norrard on the E coast and, further S, New Grimsby on the W coast. Abbey Gardens and pools to S of New Grimsby. Another quay, Carn Near, beyond gardens at S tip. Walk from quays.

There is also a heliport to the S of the Abbey Gardens with flights from Penzance heliport.

Visiting: Island open all hours, free. Toilets, pub, bicycle hire in New Grimsby. Charge for entry to Abbey Gardens (free if staying on Tresco), open 10am-4pm. Also has a shop and cafe (closed in winter).

As a birdwatcher, you are probably more interested in the exotics to be found on or around the Great Pool than in the Abbey Gardens. The Great Pool is 0.5 mile long and runs NW-SE from just SE of New Grimsby to just short of **Pentle Bay** on the island's SE coast and to the N of the Abbey Gardens complex. The Pool has wooded margins and Pool Road (good for migrant passerines) runs along its NE side, where there are 2 hides. A second pool, Abbey Pool, lies to the S, with the formal Abbey Gardens to its W and dunes to the S.

Contact for Tresco: 01720 422 849

7 PENTLE BAY, MERRICK & ROUND ISLANDS

Habitats: Sandy bay, rocky islands. SSSI

Birds: Storm Petrel breed on Round Island. Common Tern also breed on offshore islets and heathland on Tresco. Recent steep declines in Common Tern. Roseate Tern used to breed but now lost.

Directions: TR24 0QQ; SV 907 142. Pentle Bay, on SE coast of Tresco, close to SE end of Great Pool. Round Island lies st the N end pf the channel between St Martin's and Tresco; Merrick Island lies in the channel between Tresco and Bryher.

Visiting: Pentle Bay managed by Tresco Estate, the islands by the IoSWT. Islands can be viewed from boats, arrange with boatmen, do not disturb during breeding season.

BRYHER
To the W of Tresco, main settlement, The Town (quay, toilets, pub) on E side, facing Tresco.

8 POOL OF BRYHER & POPPLESTONE BANK
Habitats: 15 acres, brackish pool separated from sea by beach and mobile dunes.
Birds: Pool good for migrants, including rarities. Great White Egret and Great Blue Heron have been recorded.
Other: Brackish water flora, Early Meadow-grass in dunes.
Directions: TR23 0PR; SV 874 149. Hell Bay Hotel, 0.5 mile due W of The Town, terrace overlooks Pool.
Visiting: Open all hours, free, no facilities but nearby hotel. Grazed spring and late summer. Dogs on lead.

9 SHIPMAN HEAD & SHIPMAN HEAD DOWN
Habitats: 100 acres, rocky shore waved martitime heath.
Birds: Seabird colony on Head: breeding Great & Lesser Black-backed & Herring Gulls, Razorbill, Fulmar, Shag and Manx Shearwater. Occasional breeding Ringed Plover and Oystercatcher on heath. *Passage:* Dotterel, Wryneck, Ring Ouzel, Wheatear.
Other: Lichens normally associated with ancient woodland: *Lobaria pulmonaria, L. scrobiculata, Sticta sylvatica.*
Directions: TR23 0PR; SV 874 162. Walk N through Town, past pub, for just over 0.5 mile. When road ends continue on paths N across Down to Head for another 0.6 mile.
Visiting: Open, all hours, free, no facilities after leaving The Town. Stay on paths, which can be steep, rocky and uneven. Winter grazing, dogs on lead.
To the S of Bryher
Samson, uninhabited, may be landed on, though some areas closed during breeding season. Lesser Black-backed Gull breeding colony
And to the W of Samson
Norrad Rocks, a group of uninhabited islets. Closed to landing at all times. Breeding seabirds: Puffin, Razorbill, Guillemot, Fulmar, Storm Petrel, Cormorant. 4 gull spp, Grey Seals

ST AGNES & GUGH
To the SW of St Mary's (20 minutes by boat). Gugh is an uninhabited tidal Island to the E of St Agnes that is connected to it by a sandy tombolo, 'The Bar'.

10 GUGH
Habitats: 91 acres, rocky tidal island, maritime waved heath, areas of grassland and bracken.

Birds: Largest Herring Gull colony and only remaining Kittiwake colony in archipelago. Since rats eradicated from St Agnes and Gugh, Manx Shearwater and Storm Petrel are breeding again.
Other: No rats. Orange Bird's-Foot.
Directions: SV 887 083. Land at quay on St Agnes, then a 500 yard walk S to The Bar. Can only be crossed at low tide.
Visiting: Open all hours (but only accessible at low tide, before crossing check what time you need to leave by), free, no facilities but pub and toilets by quay.
W & SW of St Agnes:

11 ANNET
is a low, 60 acre island 0.5 mile W of St Agnes. Closed to landing, it hosts the archipelego's largest and most diverse seabird colony: 6,000 pairs, 10 species inc Great & Lesser Black-backed Gulls, Puffin, Razorbill, Fulmar, Max Shearwater, Storm Petrel. Also Grey Seal and Lesser White-toothed (Scilly) Shrew, endemic to the Isles of Scilly.
2 miles further to SW a series of islets form the **Western Rocks.** Closed to landing, beeding seabirds inc: Fulmar, Storm Petrel, Puffin, Razorbill, Guillemot, Cormorant, Shag, Great & Lesser Black-backed Gulls.

Generic IoSWT contact: 01720 422 153; hello@ios-wildlife-trust.org.uk

SCILLY PELAGICS
Not a reserve but a tour/boat company run by Bob Flood and Joe Pender that offers trips to view seabirds, either at breeding colonies or foraging grounds, combined with shark tagging. Chum is distributed to attract sharks and seabirds, paticularly tubenoses.
Offering:
Single-evening, mid-week trips, and weekend packages consiting of a mix of 3 or 4 day-long or evening trips watching birds returning to colonies or foraging in Scillonian waters. Run Jun-early Sep, possibly later depending on weather and demand.
Besides commoner seabirds, species that may be encountered include: Wilson's & European Storm Petrels; Cory's, Great, Sooty & Manx Shearwaters; Arctic, Long-tailed, Pomarine & Great Skuas, Sabine's Gull, Grey Phalarope. Rarities that have been recorded: Zino's Petrel, Desertas Petrels, Scopoli's Shearwater, Swinhoe's Storm Petrel, Band-rumped Storm-Petrel, South Polar Skua, Red-footed & Brown Boobies.
Cetaceans include: Short-beaked Common Dolphin (regular), Fin, Humpback Whale & Minke Whales, Bottlenose & Risso's Dolphins possible.
Contact: Bob Flood; live2seabird@gmail.com
Joe Pender: 0777 620 4631; joesapphire@aol.com; board on St Mary's Quay

Cornwall

Many migrants pass through the county in the spring and, particularly, autumn; and these birds (including rarities) can turn up anywhere. Migrant hot-spots near Land's End include Cot and Nanquidno Valleys. Choughs have recolonized the Lizard and Cirl Buntings are spreading as the result of a reintroduction programme. For the seawatching enthusiast, an autumn visit to a Cornish headland, such as St Ives or Porthgwarra, is a must with a good chance of Cory's, Great and Sooty Shearwaters, skuas, terns and gulls …or even something much rarer.

Bird Atlases/Avifauna
Peter Robinson (Christopher Helm, 2003).
The Birds of Cornwall and the Isles of Scilly
RD Penhallurick (Browsers Bookshop, 1978).

Bird Recorder
Cornwall
Bob Bosisto, Prospect House, Gluvian,
St Columb Major, TR9 6DA.
07909 934 906; recorder@cbwps.org.uk

Bird Report
Birds in Cornwall (1931-), from CBWPS,
secretary@cbwps.org.uk

BTO Regional Representatives
Simon Taylor
Assistant Representative:
Samantha Haley
Wetland Bird Survey (WeBS)
Local Organizer: webs@bto.org
Cornwall (excl. Tamar complex)
Derek Julian
Tamar complex
Charles Nodder:

Ringing Groups
Devon & Cornwall Wader RG
Memb. sec.: join@dcwrg.org.uk; www.dcwrg.org.uk
West Cornwall RG
westcornwallringinggroup@gmail.com
www.cornishringing.blogspot.com

RSPB Local Group
Kernow (1972, relaunched 2023 -).
Valeria Ochoa Galvis; rspbkernowgroup@gmail.com;
https://group.rspb.org.uk/kernow/
Meetings: Contact/see website for details.

Wildlife Trusts
Cornwall Wildlife Trust (1962; 18,500).
Five Acres, Allet, Truro TR4 9DJ.
01872 273 939;
info@cornwallwildlifetrust.org.uk;
www.cornwallwildlifetrust.org.uk

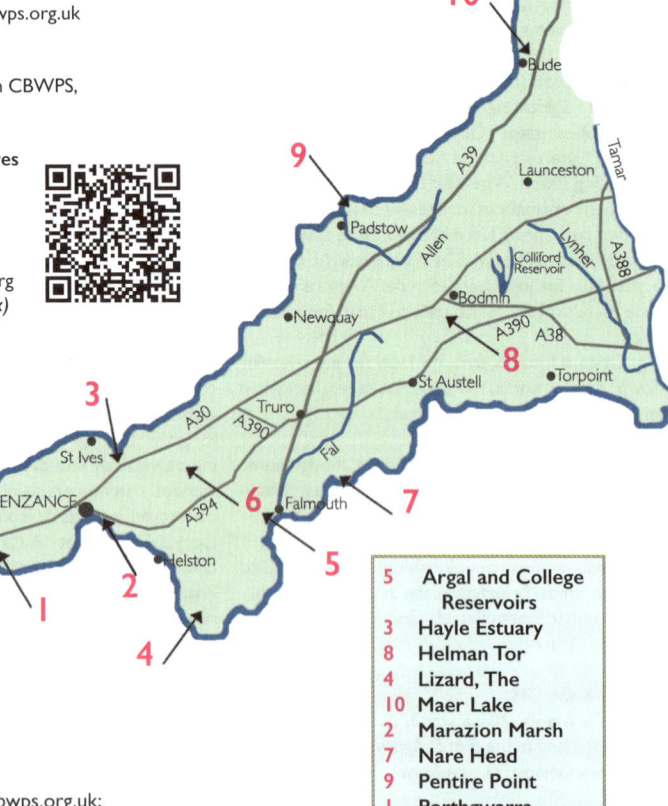

Clubs
Cornwall Bird Watching
and Preservation Society
(1931; 1,000).
Dan Bloomfield (Hon. Sec):
07986 511883; secretary@cbwps.org.uk;
https://cbwps.org.uk
Meetings: Contact/see website for details.

5	Argal and College Reservoirs
3	Hayle Estuary
8	Helman Tor
4	Lizard, The
10	Maer Lake
2	Marazion Marsh
7	Nare Head
9	Pentire Point
1	Porthgwarra
6	Stithians

Cornwall

Start as you mean to go on. Land's End airport, with flights to the Isles of Scilly and car parks by the terminal, is 1.25 miles N of the A30 on the B3306, just over 2 miles E of the turning for Porthgwarra.

1 PORTHGWARRA
St Aubyn Estate

Habitats: A steep-sided valley running down to a SE facing cove with a headland to W sheltering it from the Atlantic. Small woods in valley botom, grass and moorland on headland rising to 217 ft.

Birds: Resident: Raven, Chough, Rock Pipit. *Spring:* Migrants inc. overshoots. *Summer:* Seawatching, esp common and scarce tubenoses, skuas. *Autumn:* Common and scarce migrants, inc American rarities. Lapland Bunting regular.

Other: Common, Bottlenose, Risso's Dolphin, Harbour Porpoise, Basking Shark.

Directions: TR19 6JP; SW 371 218. (car park). At W tip of Cornwall, just S of Land's End. Take the A30 from Penzance for Land's End. Just before land's End turn sharp L on to B3315 for Polgigga. In Polgigga, do not follow B3315 when it turns sharp L but take minor road straight ahead (after dog leg) for Porthgwarra (1.75 miles).

Public transport: Bus: 1/1A, Penzance-Land's End, open top, stops in Porthcurno, c.1 mile E along South West Coast Path. Land's End Coaster. Scenic Buses (say-hello@scenicbuses.co.uk).

Visiting: Pay & display car park, toilets, café. Circular trail (steep and rough in places) from valley up to headland. South West Coast Path passes through cove and Land's End is a walk of just over 3 miles.

Contact:

Head round Penzance on A30 and exit for

2 MARAZION MARSH
RSPB

Habitats: Wet and dry reedbed, willow carr, meadow, fen.

Birds: 250+ spp. *Spring/summer:* Breeding swans, herons inc Little Egret, Little Grebe, Reed, Sedge & Cetti's Warblers, Stonechat, Reed Bunting. *Autumn:* Large roost of Swallows & martins in reedbeds, migrant warblers (inc regular Aquatic, difficult to see), Water Rail, waders inc Green Sandpiper. *Winter:* Wildfowl, Snipe, Bittern; former large Starling flock now smaller and arrive later in year (large murmuration on Bodmin Moor. Buzzard, Marsh Harrier and Sparrowhawk.

Other: 22 spp dragonflies, 500 spp vascular plants, inc Lawn Camomile & Yellow Flag.

Directions: TR17 0AA; SW 510 312. One mile E of Penzance, 500 yards W of Marazion off seafront road.

Public transport: Bus: 2, 2A, 15 and U4 from Penzance bus station to Marazion. Most buses going E stop here but check with Cornwall Transport. Alight Longrock

Station House (opp Cornwall Council car park). First Group.

Visiting: Open all hours, not suitable for wheelchair users. Park in car parks within walking distance. No coaches. Viewing bay on seafront pavement overlooks pools and reedbeds of sanctuary area. Dogs on leads. Nearest toilets in Marazion & seafront car park.

Contact: RSPB, 01736 360 624; cornwall@rspb.org.uk

Or continue for

3 HAYLE ESTUARY
RSPB

Habitats: Intertidal mudflats, saltmarsh, lagoon & islands (access to Ryan's Field, Lelant Water, Carnsew Pool, Copperhouse Pool).

Birds: Spring/summer: Migrant waders, breeding Shelduck. *Autumn:* Rare, often Nearctic waders, terns, gulls inc Mediterranean. *Winter:* Large numbers of wildfowl and waders. Top UK site for Ring-billed Gull, but not annual. Other gull spp, Kingfisher, Great Northern Diver.

Directions: TR27 6JF; SW 551 364. Follow signs to Hayle from A30. Take B3301 through Hayle past Tempest factory, turn L into Chenalls Road signposted **St Erth & Hayle Estuary NR**, turn R after 200 yards into Ryans Field car park.

Other parking in Hayle & Lelant.

Public transport: Bus—services to Hayle. Train—Hayle (limited stops) & St Erth (one mile).

Visiting: Open all hours. Ryan's Field: no coaches. Eric Grace Memorial Hide (information board) overlooks Ryan's Field but birds here only at high tide. Not suitable for wheelchair users. Circular walk around Ryan's Field. Public footpath around Carnsew Pool. Wheelchair access along Copperhouse Pool (King George Memorial Path).

Dogs on leads restricted to public footpaths.

Contact: RSPB: 01736 360 624; cornwall@rspb.org.uk

Head back on A30 to junction with A394.

4 LIZARD, THE NNR
Natural England/National Trust/Cornwall Wildlife Trust.

Habitats: Heathland, coastal grassland, cliffs & coves, puddles & ponds.

Birds: All year: Chough, Raven, Gannet, Barn Owl, Dartford Warbler. *Spring/autumn passage:* migrants, seabirds often inc scarce/rare spp. *Summer:* Wheatear, warblers, Puffin (offshore). *Winter:* Divers, Razorbill, Guillemot, Hen Harrier, Merlin, Peregrine, Short-eared Owl, Purple Sandpiper, winter thrushes.

Other: 250 spp of national/international importance esp coastal flora, Cornish Heath. Adder, Common Lizard.

Directions: Main route to The Lizard is by heading S on A3083/B3293 from A394 at Helston. NNR (6,175

acres) is scattered across area. *Places of interest* inc. Goonhilly Downs TR12 6RW (SW 736 201); Kynance Cove TR12 7PJ (SW 687 132); Lizard Village TR12 7NU (SW 701 116); Windmill Farm TR12 7LH (SW 694 152); but birds can turn up anywhere!

Public transport: Bus: 34 Helston-Lizard village (not Sun). Plymouth Citibus (01752 662 271).

Visiting: Open all year. Car parks, most with toilets, spread around area. Cafe/refreshments in Lizard Village —Chough watch point to S of village.

Contact: Natural England, 07789 745 657; Richard.glasson@naturalengland.org.uk; National Trust: 01326 222 170; lizard@nationaltrust.org.uk; Cornwall WT: 01872 273 939; info@cornwallwildlifetrust.org.uk

Continue on A394 to its junction with A39.

5 ARGAL & COLLEGE RESERVOIRS
South West Lakes Trust
Habitats: Reservoir, woodland.

Birds: All year: Great Crested Grebe, Buzzard, Sparrowhawk, Kingfisher, Grey Wagtail, common wildfowl, common scrub spp.

Summer: Cuckoo, hirundines, warblers, Marsh Tit. *Spring/autumn passage:* Common & Green Sandpipers, scarer species possible, depending on water levels, terns (inc Black). *Winter:* Wildfowl inc Wigeon, Teal, Goldeneye, Goosander—scarcer spp possibly inc Bittern and Greater Scaup, winter thrushes.

Directions: TR10 9JG; SW 762 328. SW of Penryn. From A39 take turn to Mabe Burnthouse then at roundabout turn L on to Church Road and continue to Argal Reservoir car park (0.8 mile on R).

Public transport: None.

Visiting: Open all year. Car park (charge), toilets at Argal. Circular walks around both reservoirs—walk over dam at Argal to road, walk L to end of lay-by—track to College over road (care when crossing).

Contact: South West Lakes Trust: 01566 771 930; info@swlakestrust.org.uk; www.swlakestrust.org.uk

Head N on A30, then A393 for Redruth. On outskirst, take B3300 to join B3297.

6 STITHIANS RESERVOIR
South West Lakes Trust
Habitats: Open water, marshland, meadows, wet woodland, heathland.

Birds: Passage: Good for waders inc Common, Green & Wood Sandpipers. Osprey, Great White Egret, Garganey. *Winter:* Diving ducks inc Scaup and Goldeneye. Raptors inc Merlin and Short-eared Owl. Winter gull flocks inc Mediterranean. Reservoir has good track record for rarities: inc Pied-billed Grebe, Pectoral, White-rumped & Semipalmated Sandpipers, Lesser Yellowlegs, Wilson's Phalarope, Caspian Tern and Black Kite.

Directions: TR16 6NW; SS 709 369. Signposted from B3297 S of Redruth.

Public transport: None.

Visiting: Good viewing from causeway. Hide near main centre (opposite Golden Lion Inn), open to all. Two other hides for members of CBWPS. Toilets, cafe (9am-4pm). Footpath around reservoir.

Contact: Stithians Activity Centre: 01209 860 301; South West Lakes Trust: 01566 771 930; info@swlakestrust.org.uk; www.swlakestrust.org.uk

Instead of leaving A30, continue to Truro and A390.

7 NARE HEAD
National Trust
Habitats: Coastal headland, open sea.

Birds: Spring/summer: Razorbill, Guillemot, Shag, Sandwich, Common & Arctic Terns, possible Whimbrel, Fulmar, occasional Chough. *Passage:* Migrants. *Winter:* Great Northern, Black & Red-throated Divers, Slavonian, Black-necked & Red-necked Grebes, Common & Velvet Scoters.

Directions: TR2 5PQ; SW 919 378 (Nare Head car park). Parking also in Carne. Part of NT's Roseland estate. Approx ten miles SE of Truro. From A390 head S on A3078 to two miles S of Tregony just past garage. Follow signs to Veryan then L signposted to Carne. Go straight over at crossroad, following Carne & Pendower. Turn L on a bend following NT signs for **Nare Head.** Bearing R, cross over a cattle grid to car park (Nare Head is about four miles from garage).

Public transport: None.

Visiting: Open daily. Car Park. Unstable cliff edges approach with care.

Contact: National Trust: 01872 501 062; roseland@nationaltrust.org.uk

Head N from Truro on A39 to junction with A30.

8 HELMAN TOR NATURE RESERVE
Cornwall Wildlife Trust
Habitats: 734 acre, inc wetland, grassland, heath & scrub.

Birds: Cuckoo, Curlew (occasional, passage), Sparrowhawk, Nightjar (very occasional, no longer confirmed breeding), Tree Pipit, Grasshopper Warbler, Lesser Whitethroat, Willow Tit.

Other: Butterflies (inc. Marsh & Small Pearl-bordered Fritillaries, Silver-studded Blue). Royal Fern, sundews & other bog plants.

Directions: PL30 5DF; SX 062 615 (Tor car park). Large wetland complex spreading from slopes of Helman Tor inc Breney Common & Red Moor Memorial Reserve. 2.5 miles S of Bodmin and 2 miles NW of Lostwithiel. From A30/A391 (Innis Downs) roundabout south of Bodmin, turn N to Lanivet and take first R under A30 bridge. Shortly after the bridge take 1st L up hill. After c.0.5 mile, turn R at Reperry Cross then immediately fork L for Trebell Green. Keep R past grass triangle and, shortly after a sharp R bend, take narrow L turn, with granite posts either side. Helman Tor car park (SX 062 615) is at the top of this road.

Public transport: None.

Visiting: Open all hours, keep to paths. Small car park at Helman Tor, Wilderness trail from here can be very muddy after heavy rain—only boardwalk sections offer suitable surface for wheelchairs (can be slippery when wet).

Contact: Cornwall WT: 01872 273 939;
info@cornwallwildlifetrust.org.uk
Return to A30.

9 PENTIRE POINT

National Trust.

Habitats: Coastal headland, open sea.

Birds: All year: Fulmar, Peregrine Falcon, Kestrel, Raven. Chough, Stonechat *Spring/summer:* Razorbill, Guilemot, Puffin (few), Gannet, Skylark, Whitethroat Wheatear. *Spring Passage:* Manx Shearwater, Arctic & Great Skua. *Autumn passage:* Storm & Leach's Petrels, terns.

Directions: PL27 6Q Y; SW 942 799 (Pentireglaze car park) or PL27 6QZ. SW 953 796 (Lundy Bay car park). Also car park in New Polzeath (not NT). Leave A30 at Bodmin & join A389 to Wadebridge then B3314 signed Polzeath,—follow local signs to your destination.

Public transport: Bus: 96 Wadebridge to Launceston (stops at Polzeath, Mon-Sat). Take SW Coast Path around Pentire Point. Go Cornwall Bus (0808 196 2632).

Visiting: Open all hours. Car parks (pay & display for non-members). Pentireglaze car park: cafe & toilet (in winter, check for opening hours).

Contact: National Trust: 01208 863 046;
pentire@nationaltrust.org.uk
Return to A389, the take A39 N to Bude.

10 MAER LAKE

Cornwall Wildlife Trust/
Cornwall Bird Watching & Preservation Society

Habitats: Wetland meadows, open water.

Birds: Passage & overwintering site for wildfowl & waders inc Golden Plover, Black-tailed Godwit. Scarce/rare species have occurred.

Directions: EX23 8SP; SS 205 074. Viewable from roadside of Maer Lane, between N side of Bude & village of Maer.

Public transport: Bus: 128/219 from town centre stop at Flexbury Buffalo Bills (by car park) Go Cornwall Bus (0808 196 2632).

Visiting: Bird hide. Use Crooklets Car Park (pay & display, 500 m away). Walk E inland from car park for 120 metres, turn L into Maer Down Road, then R into Maer Lane. *Caution:* narrow and no footpath. Pedestrian access to hide through coded gate on R. Check CWT

website for access details.

Contact: Cornwall WT: 01872 273 939;
info@cornwallwildlifetrust.org.uk

Devon

The county offers a wide variety of habitats, including the marshes of the Exe estuary (wildfowl & waders), the pebblebed heathlands (Dartford Warbler) in the east and the moorlands of Exmoor, which extend into west Somerset, and Dartmoor. The south coast holds localized, but increasing, pockets of Cirl Buntings. The island of Lundy in the Bristol Channel attracts spring & autumn migrants, often turning up rarities.

Bird Atlases/Avifauna

Devon Bird Atlas 2007-2013
Stella D Beavan & Mike Lock
(Devon Birdwatching & Preservation Society, 2016).
The Birds of Devon
Michael Tyler
(Devon Birdwatching & Preservation Society, 2010).
The Birds of Lundy
Tim Davis & Tim Jones
(Harpers Mill Publishing, 2007).
The Birds of Dartmoor
Roger Smaldon
(Isabelline Books, 2005).

Bird Recorder

Vacant. Email monitored by *Devon Birds*
recorder@devonbirds.org

Bird Reports

Devon Birds (1929-), from DB - Tony Utting (Sec), 17 Camomile Way, Newton Abbot, Devon, TQ12 1US; 07484 832 566; shop@devonbirds.org
or form on www.devonbirds.org
Lundy Field Society Annual Report (1947-) from LFS - Michael Williams (Hon Sec), 10 Nutholt Lane, Ely, CB7 4PL: secretary@lundy.org.uk. Digital versions of all editions available from www.lundy.org.uk.

BTO Regional Representative

Ocea Weir
Wetland Bird Survey (WeBS)
Local Organizers: webs@bto.org
Devon (other sites)
Peter Reay
Exe estuary
Martin Overy
Tamar complex
See **Cornwall.**
Taw & Torridge
Chris Dee

Clubs

Devon Birds (1928; 1,200)
Tony Utting (Sec, Devon Birds), 17 Camomile Way, Newton Abbot, Devon, TQ12 1US; 07484 832 566; secretary@devonbirds.org; www.devonbirds.org

Branches
Check programme of events under each branch.

East Devon
Alex Parsons: 01392 669 842; apar67819@gmail.com
www.devonbirds.org/branch/east-devon
Meetings: No indoor meetings.

Mid Devon
Tom Misselbrook: tom.misselbrook@devonbirds.org;
www.devonbirds.org/branch/mid-devon
Meetings: No indoor meetings.

Plymouth
Liz Harris: 01752 789 594;
liz.harris@devonbirds.org
www.devonbirds.org/branch/plymouth
Meetings: Indoor occasional 7:30pm Mutley Baptist Church, Plymouth, PL4 6LB. Outdoor throughout the year.

South Devon
Jeff Hacon: Jeff.hacon@devonbirds.org
www.devonbirds.org/branch/south-devon
Meetings: 7.30pm, 3rd Monday of the month (Sep-Apr, exc. Dec). The Courtenay Centre in Newton Abbot, TQ12 2QA.

Taw & Torridge
Ray Turner (Branch Rep.): 01598 710 609;
ray.turner@devonbirds.org
www.devonbirds.org/branch/taw-torridge
Meetings: 7:30pm, 2nd Wednesday of the month (Oct-Apr). Contact/see website for details.

Kingsbridge Natural History Society (1989; 50)
Mike Hitch (Membership Sec): 01548 581 442;
mikejhitch@btinternet.com;
www.knhs.org.uk
Meetings: 7:30pm, 4th Monday of the month (Sep-Apr). West Charleton Village Hall, West Charleton, Kingsbridge, TQ7 2AG.

Lundy Field Society (1946; 640)
Michael Williams (Hon Sec), 10 Nutholt Lane, Ely, CB7 4PL: secretary@lundy.org.uk; www.lundy.org.uk
Meetings: AGM, 2nd Saturday of Mar in Crediton. Exceptonally, the AGM will be held on Lundy in May in 2026.

Topsham Birdwatching & Naturalist Society (1969; 100)
Gordon Davis (Hon Sec), 12 Brent Close, Woodbury, Exeter EX5 1JH: 01395 232 305;
contact@topshambns.org.uk;
www.topshambns.org.uk
Meetings: 7:30pm, 1st or 2nd Friday of the month (Sep-Apr). Matthews Hall, Fore Street, Topsham, Exeter, EX3 0HF.

Ringing Groups/Bird Observatories

Axe Estuary RG
stan@thestanbridges.com;
https://axeestuaryringinggroup.blogspot.co.uk

Devon & Cornwall Wader RG
Memb. sec.: join@dcwrg.org.uk; www.dcwrg.org.uk

Slapton Bird Observatory RG

Lundy Bird Observatory
Re-established 2023. Joe Parker, Warden, Lundy RO, Lundy, via Bideford EX39 2LY:
birdobs@lundyisland.co.uk www.lundybirdobs.org.uk

RSPB Local Groups

Exeter & District (1974; 220).
Steve Manktelow, acting leader:
RSPBexetergroup@gmail.com;
https://group.rspb.org.uk/exeter/
Meetings: 7:30 pm, 3rd Wednesday of most months, (Sep-Apr). St Thomas Church Hall, Church Rd, St Thomas, Exeter, EX2 9BQ.

Plymouth (1974; 75).
Vince Bedford: vincebedford@live.co.uk;
https://group.rspb.org.uk/plymouth/
Meetings: 7:30pm, Wednesdays in Sep, Nov, Jan & Mar. Quaker House, Trinity United Reformed Church, 74 Mutley Plain, Plymouth, PL4 6LF.
Contact/see website for details.

Wildlife Trust

Devon Wildlife Trust (1962; 37,500).
Cricklepit Mill, Commercial Road, Exeter, EX2 4AB.
01392 279 244; contactus@devonwildlifetrust.org;
www.devonwildlifetrust.org

1 LUNDY

Owned by National Trust/managed by Landmark Trust.
Habitats: Island (3.5 miles long, 0.5 miles wide), 12 miles N of Hartland Point in Bristol Channel. Farmed area in S, moorland to N. Island is a Marine Protected Area.
Birds: 160 spp annually. *Breeding:* Seabirds, inc. Manx Shearwater (12,600 pr) and Puffin (1,300 ind)—both recovering after rat eradication. Fulmar, Shag, Gannet (offshore), Storm Petrel (breeds, occasionally offshore), Razorbill, Guillemot, Kittiwake. *Spring/autumn passage:* Regular common migrants pass through, always a chance of scarce or rare spp. Occasional large 'falls'.
Other: Endemic Lundy Cabbage & Bronze Lundy Cabbage Flea Beetle.
Directions: EX39 2EY (Bideford Office). EX34 9EQ (Ilfracombe Office). Parking in both towns.
Public transport: None.
Visiting: Lundy's own passenger ferry/supply ship *MS Oldenburg* sails at least three times p/w from either Bideford or Ilfracombe (crossing takes c.2 hours each way).
Day trips. Boat runs from Apr-Oct, onshore time limited

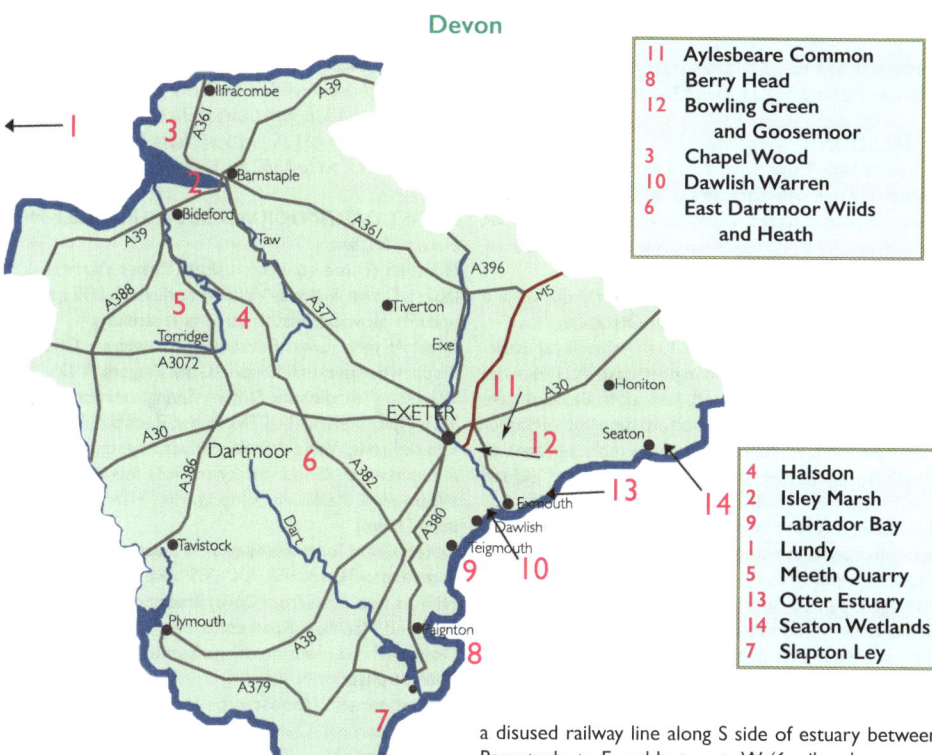

11	Aylesbeare Common
8	Berry Head
12	Bowling Green and Goosemoor
3	Chapel Wood
10	Dawlish Warren
6	East Dartmoor Wiids and Heath

4	Halsdon
2	Isley Marsh
9	Labrador Bay
1	Lundy
5	Meeth Quarry
13	Otter Estuary
14	Seaton Wetlands
7	Slapton Ley

to four/eight hours depending on sailing.

Residential trips (accommodation available). Sailing (Tue/Thur/Sat) Apr-Oct & helicopter service (Fri/Mon) late Jan to Mar & Nov to early Jan. Contact/see website for sailing/flight dates, times, costs and accommodation options. Crossings may be cancelled due to bad weather.

Contact: Booking Office: 01271 863 636; info@lundyisland.co.uk; www.landmarktrust.org.uk/Lundyisland Lundy Field Society: secretary@lundy.org.uk; www.lundy.org.uk

Head E on A39 towards Barnstaple.

2 ISLEY MARSH
RSPB

Habitats: Intertidal mudflat and saltmarsh, tidal estuary.
Birds: Canada Goose, Common Sandpiper, Little Egret. *Winter:* Brent Goose, Shelduck, Curlew, Spoonbill, Dunlin, Knot, Bar-tailed Godwit, Redshank, Greenshank, Little Egret, Stonechat.
Other:
Directions: EX31 3EN; SS 487 324. The reserve lies to the N of Yelland, on the S side of the Taw estuary. The B3233 runs through Yelland from Barnstaple in the E to Instow in the W. There is a path (700 yards) from the road to the S edge of the reserve (on-street parking in residential area). Otherwise, the Tarka Trail follows

a disused railway line along S side of estuary between Barnstaple, to E, and Instow, to W (6 miles, the reserve is c.1.5 miles from Instow).

Public transport: Bus: 21/21A Barnstaple to Westward Ho! stops in Yelland.

Visiting: Open all hours, free, no facilities. No paths across reserve but footpath along disused railway all along S edge. Dogs allowed on Tarka Trail, compact surface but rough in places.

Contact: 01392 833311; exe.estuary@rspb.org.uk
Take A361 from Barnstaple towards Ifracombe.

3 CHAPEL WOOD
RSPB

Habitats: Iron Age hill fort and ruined 13C chapel, broadleaved wood on steep hillside. Stream along edge of reserve.

Birds: Buzzard, Raven. Common woodland sp inc Tawny Owl, Green & Great Spotted Woodpeckers, Mistle Thrush, Nuthatch, Redpoll.

Other: Red Deer, Brown Hare, Badger. Bluebells
Directions: EX33 1JA; SS 482 414.1.25 miles N of Knowle take L off A361 for Spreacombe and Georgeham. Fork L after 0.75 miles over bridge. Park in lay-by.

Public transport: Bus: 3 Barnstaple to Ifracombe, stops in Heddon Mills (Mon-Sat). First Bus. 1.5 mile walk.

Visiting: Open all hours, free, no facilities. Park in lane. follow footpath to reserve. 1 mile circular trail. Steep unsurfaced paths, not wheelchair accessible. Dogs on lead.

Contact: 01392 833 311; exe.estuary@rspb.org.uk
Return to Bideford on A39, then A386 to Great Torrington.

4 HALSDON
Devon Wildlife Trust
Habitats: River, woodland, floodplain meadow.
Birds: All year: Buzzard, Tawny Owl, Kingfisher, Dipper, Grey Wagtail, Marsh Tit, common woodland spp. *Summer:* Sand Martin, warblers. *Winter:* Goosander.
Other: Butterflies & dragonflies. Devon Whitebeam and Wild Service trees. Bluebells. Fungi. Otter.
Directions: EX19 8ND; SS 553 131 (Ashwell car park). 5.5 miles SE of Great Torrington. Take A3124 from Great Torrington to Beaford. Just after Beaford take minor road on R towards Dolton, then turn R again. Continue for 0.85 miles (along very narrow lane) to Trust's Ashwell car park on R. Another car park (Quarry entrance—EX18 8RL. SS 560 116) is one mile further along this road on R. Level track to river, most of woodland paths are steep/unsurfaced.
Public transport: None.
Visiting: Open all hours. Two small car parks at Ashwell & Quarry entrances. Walks through woodland and alongside River Torridge. Hide by river. Dogs on lead.
Contact: Devon WT: 01392 279 244;
contactus@devonwildlife trust.org
A minor road heading S from Halsdon joins West Lane from Dalton at a crossroads. Turn R. After 0.6 mile turn R and road then crosses Torridge and joins A386.

5 MEETH QUARRY
Devon Wildlife Trust
Habitats: Lakes (flooded quarry), ponds, woodland, grassland. Adjoins DWT Ash Moor reserve.
Birds: All Year: Great Crested & Little Grebes, Barn Owl, Kingfisher, Yellowhammer. *Summer:* Hobby, hirundines, warblers. *Winter:* Wildfowl inc Goosander, Pochard, Tufted Duck, Woodcock, Snipe.
Other: Roe Deer, Brown Hare, 14 spp dragonflies, butterflies, Otter.
Directions: EX20 3ER; SS 546 078. Eight miles NW Okehampton. From A386 Hatherleigh-Great Torrington road at Meeth look for sign to **Tarka Trail & Meeth Quarry NR**. Enter service road here & drive for c.1 mile to reach reserve/car park.
Public transport: Bus: 75A Okehamption-Great Torrington passes through Meeth—alight at Meeth Village stop and walk down service road to reserve entrance (c1 mile).
Visiting: Open all year. Car park at reserve entrance open 8am-8pm weekends, 9am-5pm weekdays. Toilet (disabled), picnic area, hide. Colour-coded trails (pushchair friendly)—red trail suitable for wheelchairs/mobility scooters. 3 mile 'Meeth Quarry Wild Walk' good introduction to area. 'Tarka Trail' cycle route starts/ends in Meeth, cuts through reserve. Dogs on lead.

Contact: Devon WT: 01392 279 244;
contactus@devonwildlife trust.org
Continue S on A386, turn L on to A3072 at Lamerton Cross and then R on to A3124 just S of North Tawton. After crossing A30, turn R on to A382 for Bovey Tracey.

6 EAST DARTMOOR WOODS & HEATHS NNR
Natural England
Habitats: Three connected sites (Yarner Wood, Trendlebere Down & Bovey Valley Woodlands), 900 acres of upland oakwood, heathland, bogs & streams.
Birds: All year: Raven, Buzzard, Sparrowhawk, Goshawk, 3 spp woodpeckers, Dipper, Grey Wagtail & Dartford Warbler (Trendlebere Down). *Spring/summer:* Cuckoo, Tree Pipit, Skylark, Pied Flycatcher, Redstart, Stonechat, Whitethroat, Wood Warbler, Linnet. Nightjar on heaths. *Autumn/winter:* Good variety of birds feeding at Yarner Wood hide, inc Siskin, Redpoll. Hen Harrier (Trendlebere Down).
Other: Good for butterflies inc fritillaries & Grayling.
Directions: TQ13 9LJ; SX 785 788 (Yarner Wood). NNR is two miles from Bovey Tracey on road to Becky Falls and Manaton. Road continues across Trendlebere Down—three roadside car parks and adjacent paths.
Public transport: None.
Visiting: Yarner Wood car park open 7:30am-7:30pm (dusk if earlier). Outside these hours, access on foot from Trendlebere Down. Information/interpretation display and self-guided trails available in Yarner Wood car park & hide with feeding station (Nov-Mar). Dogs under close control.
Contact: Natural England, Yarner Wood, 01626 832 330.
Continue S on A382, taking A381 at Newton Abbot, then A3122 to Dartmouth, whence take A379.

7 SLAPTON LEY NNR
Field Studies Council/Natural England
(Devon, Cornwall & Isles of Scilly Team).
Habitats: Freshwater lake, reedbeds, marsh & woodland.
Birds: All year: Cirl Bunting, Cetti's Warbler. Most south-westerly population of Great Crested Grebe. *Spring/summer:* Migrant warblers. Good seawatching in favourable conditions in spring & autumn, migrants on passage. Large gathering of Swallows in autumn roosts. *Winter:* Divers & grebes on sea, Bittern at Higher Ley. Diving ducks and grebes on Lower Ley.
Other: UK's only site for Strapwort. Otter, Dormouse.
Directions: TQ7 2QP; SX 825 448 (Field Centre). Largest freshwater lake in SW England, lying S of Dartmouth on south coast, is separated from Start Bay by a shingle bank which carries A379.
Public transport: Bus: 3 from Plymouth/Kingsbridge to Dartmouth stops at Slapton (outside field centre—limited on Sun). Stagecoach South West.
Visiting: Pay & display car parks off A379 at Torcross

and Slapton Sands. Higher Ley is closed to public, but can be viewed from public footpath. Hides overlooking Torcross & Stokely Bay areas of lagoon & surrounding backdrops. Field Centre offers variety of residential courses.
Contact: Slapton Ley Field Centre: 01548 580 466; enquiries.sl@field-studies-council.org; www.slnnr.org.uk
Head back N along A379 for Brixham.

8 BERRY HEAD NNR
Torbay Coast & Countryside Trust
Habitats: Limestone cliffs (200 ft), grassland, quarry.
Birds: All year: Cirl Bunting (in flocks in winter), Peregrine Falcon (hunting in quarry area), Fulmar. *Spring/summer:* Up to 1,200 nesting Guillemots on cliffs below Southern Fort. *Passage:* Well known for migrants.
Other: Limestone flora inc eight spp orchid, Small Hare's-ear. Harbour Porpoise, Common Dolphin, Greater & Lesser Horseshoe Bats (walks arranged), Bloody Nose Beetle and variety of butterflies.
Directions: TQ5 9AP. SX 940 561 (Berry Head car park). Signposted from Brixham on minor roads from A3022 & A379. Located at end of Gillard Road, past Landscove Holiday Village.
Public transport: Bus: 17 from Brixham to Victoria Road (0.5 mile walk to Berry Head: some steep sections). Stagecoach South West.
Visiting: Open all year. Pay & display car park. Guardhouse visitor centre open Easter-Oct 10am-4pm Tues-Sun/1pm-4pm Mon & Oct-Easter 10am-4pm Sat/Sun only. CCTV images of nesting seabirds, cafe & toilets. Wheelchair-friendly 300 yard path from car park to visitor centre & cafe. Two mobility vehicles for hire (prebook). Bird hide overlooking cliffs.
Contact: Berry Head NNR, 01803 882 619; berry-head@countryside-trust.org.uk; www.countryside-trust.org.uk/explore/berry-head/
Continue along A379.

9 LABRADOR BAY
RSPB
Habitats: Reserve covers 1.25 miles of coastline. Part of a working farm grazed by cattle in summer, sheep in winter with coastal cliff top, woodland, scrub, arable & semi-improved grassland.
Birds: Purchased to help secure future of Cirl Buntings, which can be seen all year round—breeding pairs in spring/summer and in flocks during autumn/winter, when they feed on stubble with other farmland birds inc Skylark, Chaffinch and Yellowhammer. Peregrine and Buzzard also regular.
Other: Offshore—Dolphins, Basking Shark.
Directions: TQ1 4TP; SX 931 705. The bay lies 2.7 miles S of Teignmouth on the A379 coast road between Shaldon & Maidencombe.

Public transport: Bus: 22 Dawlish to Torquay, Stagecoach South West, Alight at Deane Lane, enter reserve via footpath opposite. Do not walk along A379 to car park. Train—Teignmouth is two miles away, then use SW Coast Path.
Visiting: Open all hours. Pay & display car park (not RSPB), nearest toilets one mile (Maidencombe, summer only). Several walks around the site, longest inc three miles of South West Coast Path.
Contact: RSPB, 01392 833 311; exe.estuary@rspb.org.uk
Further along A379.

10 DAWLISH WARREN NNR
Teignbridge District Council.
Habitats: High tide roost site for Exe estuary wildfowl and waders on mudflats and shore. Dunes, dune grassland, woodland, scrub, ponds.
Birds: Excellent variety of birds all year, esp on migration. Cirl Bunting breeding, regular all year. *Summer:* Particularly good for terns. *Winter:* Waders and wildfowl in large numbers. Also good for divers offshore (Slavonian Grebe now very rare).
Directions: EX7 0NF; SX 983 788. On S side of Exe estuary mouth. Turn off A379 just N of Dawlish (signposted to Dawlish Warren). At mini-roundabout, just after Welcome Inn, turn R. Pass under tunnel (by train station) then turn L (away from amusements), park at far end of car park and walk through gates.
Public transport: Bus: 11 Torquay/Paignton to DW. Stagecoach South West. Train: Dawlish Warren.
Visiting: Open public access, but the roosting waders are monitored by the rangers on some high tides and visitors may be asked to alter their walk or avoid sensitive areas to avoid bird disturbance. Pay & display car park. Visitor centre open Apr-Aug 2pm-5pm/Sat-Sun, 2pm-4pm/Wed-Fri (closed Mon-Tues) Sep-Mar 1pm-4pm/Sat-Sun (may be closed if in use by groups or wardens out on site). Toilets at entrance tunnel and in resort area. There is no longer a bird hide (access paths eroded by storms). Access to the end of Warren Point (for viewing estuary) is tide and weather dependent, relying on a walk along the beach in soft sand. Risk of being cut off at high tide, consult tide times and weather forecast. No dogs on beach or dunes beyond ninth groyne at any time.
Contact: Teignbridge District Council: 01626 215 751; greenspaces@teignbridge.gov.uk; www.dawlishwarren.co.uk (DW Recording Group)
Continue on A379 into Exeter, cross Exe and then M5 at J5, exiting on A376 and then A3052.

11 AYLESBEARE COMMON
RSPB
Habitats: Heathland, wood fringes, streams and ponds.
Birds: All year: Buzzard, Dartford Warbler, Yellowham-

mer. *Spring/summer:* Hobby, Nightjar, Tree Pipit, Stonechat. *Winter:* Possible Hen Harrier.

Other: Good variety of dragonflies (inc Southern Damselfly) and butterflies.

Directions: EX5 2JS; SY 057 897. Five miles E of J 30 of M5 at Exeter, 0.5 mile past Halfway Inn on B3052. Turn R to Hawkerland, car park is on L. Reserve is on opposite side of main road.

Public transport: Bus: 9 & 9A Exeter to Seaton/Honiton request stop at Joneys Cross (reserve entrance). Stagecoach South West.

Visiting: Open all year. Car park, two trails, picnic area, group bookings, guided walks, special events. One track suitable for wheelchairs/pushchairs, disabled access via metalled track to private farm. Dogs on lead.

Contact: RSPB 01395 233 655;
aylesbeare.common@rspb.org.uk
Alternatively, do not take A3052, exit A376 at roundabout for Dart's Farm Shopping Village, cross the Clyst and park in Topsham.

12 BOWLING GREEN AND GOOSEMOOR

RSPB

Habitats: Coastal grassland, open water/marsh.

Birds: *Spring:* Shelduck, passage waders inc Little Stint, Ringed Plover, Ruff and sandpipers, Whimbrel. *Passage:* Garganey and Yellow Wagtail. *Summer:* Gull/tern roosts, high tide wader roosts contain many passage birds. *Autumn:* Wildfowl, Peregrine Falcon, wader roosts. *Winter:* Large numbers of Wigeon, Shoveler, Teal, Black-tailed Godwit, Curlew, Golden Plover. Avocet and Brent Geese.

Other: Hairy Dragonfly, Wasp Spider.

Directions: EX3 0EN. SX 683 825 (Holman Way car park). On E side of River Exe, four miles SE of Exeter in Bowling Green Road, Topsham.

Public transport: Bus: 57 Exeter to Topsham, alight at Elm Grove Road (0.6 mile from reserve). Also stops at Darts Farm Shopping Village (inc RSPB shop). Stagecoach.

Train: Exeter to Exmouth stops at Topsham (reserve—one mile).

Visiting: Open all hours. Park at Holman Way or The Quay public car parks in Topsham, not in lane by reserve. Lookout Hide (wheelchair accessible) located on Bowling Green Road—short walk from parking areas (Blue Badge bay outside). Nearest RADAR toilets at The Quay car park. Viewing platform. RSPB shop at Darts Farm (EX3 0QH, 01392 879 438), one mile from reserve, E of Topsham across River Clyst.

Contact: RSPB, 01392 833 311;
exe.estuary@rspb.org.uk
Take B3179 from previous roundabout on A376, then B3178 for Budleigh Salterton. Just past cricket ground on L, turn L. T junction almost immediately. Turn L for South Farm,
or R on to Granary Road, which leads to S car park.

13 OTTER ESTUARY NATURE RESERVE

Pebblebed Heaths Conservation Trust

Habitats: Major restoration works were completed in Dec 2023 and the site forms an extension to the Pebblebed Heaths NNR. Tidal estuary: saltmarsh, mudflats, foreshore, woodland, scrub, reedbed.

Birds: *All year:* Shelduck, Little Egret, Grey Heron, Goosander, gulls, Barn Owl, Kestrel, Cetti's Warbler, Stonechat. *Spring/autumn passage:* Osprey, Whimbrel, Common Sandpiper, Bar-tailed Godwit, Spotted Redshank, Wheatear. *Winter:* Wildfowl inc Wigeon, Teal, Dark-bellied Brent Goose and waders inc Black-tailed Godwit, Curlew, Snipe, Redshank, Greenshank, Dunlin, Ringed Plover, Water Rail, winter thrushes. *Offshore:* Divers & grebes, Common Scoter, Shag and auks. Common woodland/scrub spp.

Other: Beaver, Otter.

Directions: EX9 6BG; SY 072 820 (Lime Kiln car park); EX9 7AB (SY 070 829 (Otter Estuary Nature Reserve car park, South Farm Road). Lies immediately to E of Budleigh Salterton.

Public transport: Bus: 157/357 Exmouth to Sidmouth (daily) stop in Budleigh Salterton at Granary Lane, close to South Farm car park for N & S circular walks.

Visiting: Car parks (pay & display): EDDC Lime Kiln for S end of estuary; South Farm Road central for N or S end (funds from SFR car park directly support the management of the Nature Reserve). Footpaths inc circular walks (from both car parks) to W of estuary; footpath to E of estuary is out and back. Viewing areas, information boards. Nearest toilets on the seafront.

Contact: Pebblebed Heaths Conservation Trust 01395 443 881; mail@pebblebedheaths.org.uk www.pebblebedheaths.org.uk
Head N on B3178 to junction with A3052 at Newton Poppleford. Turn R for Seaton.

14 SEATON WETLANDS

East Devon District Council

Habitats: Intertidal lagoon, estuary (Axe), reedbeds, freshwater grazing marsh, scrapes, ditches.

Birds: *All year:* Little Egret, Shelduck, Peregrine, Water Rail, Oystercatcher, Kingfisher, Cetti's Warbler. *Spring/summer:* Osprey (also autumn), passage waders, hirundines, Wheatear, Reed & Sedge Warblers. *Autumn/Winter:* Wildfowl inc Wigeon, Teal & waders inc Lapwing, Black-tailed Godwit, Ringed Plover, Dunlin, Curlew, Snipe and scarcer spp, Water Pipit, Redwing, Fieldfare.

Other: Dragonflies, butterflies, Otter, Water Vole.

Directions: EX12 2XA; SY 248 914 (main car park: Black Hole Marsh, Colyford Common & Stafford Marsh). EX12 2LF; SY 247 907 (Seaton Marshes). Eight miles E of Sidmouth. From A3052 in Colyford take Seaton Road (brown signs **Seaton Wetlands**). After 0.5 mile turn L

into Seaton Cemetery, continue through to car park.
Public transport: Both access points can be reached easily on foot from Seaton sea front.
Visiting: Open all hours. Seaton Wetlands—main car park (free/donation welcomed), toilets inc disabled, Discovery Hut (Sat-Mon, 10am-4pm, subject to available volunteers) for information, refreshments. Five hides, pond dipping. Easy access paths, mobility scooter for hire. Events. Seaton Marshes car park (free), hide, part of site accessible to wheelchairs/pushchairs. No dogs (except assistance dogs) at either site.
Contact: East Devon DC: 01395 517 557;

Dorset

The county holds internationally important habitats and the Isle of Portland is a migration hot-spot, making this one of the UK's top birdwatching destinations. The heathlands hold Hobby, Nightjar, Dartford Warbler and Woodlark. Poole Harbour attracts internationally important numbers of wintering waders & wildfowl and Osprey have now been successfully reintroduced. White-tailed Eagles from the nearby I.o.W. reintroduction programme are also regular visitors. Two RSPB reserves in Weymouth (Lodmoor & Radipole) are probably the best urban birdwatching sites in the country and the Portland Bird Observatory is the place to be at migration time.

Bird Atlas/Avifauna
The Birds of Dorset
George Green
(Christopher Helm, 2004)

Bird Recorders
Recorder (Rarities)
Ian Stanley: recorder@dorsetbirds.co.uk
Assistant Recorder
Geoff Upton, 25, Monmouth Road, Dorchester DT1 2DE; dorsetbirdclub@hotmail.com
Recorder (Rare Breeding Birds)
Shaun Robson: shaun.narwhal@btinternet.com

Bird Reports
Dorset Birds (1977-), from DBC - Richard Charman, 24 Widworthy Drive, Broadstone, BH18 9BD: sales@dorsetbirds.co.uk
Portland Bird Observatory Report (1963-), from PBO - Martin Cade, The Old Lower Light, Portland Bill, DT5 2JT: 01305 820 553; obs@btinternet.com
The Birds of Christchurch Harbour (1956-), print and/ or digital from CHOG—Charles Stubbs (Report Editor): editor@chog.org.uk

BTO Regional Representative
Pete Cadogan
Wetland Bird Survey (WeBS)
Local Organizer; webs@bto.org
Dorset (excl. estuaries)
Nicola Hoar
Poole Harbour
Paul Morton
Radipole & Lodmoor
Stephen Hales
The Fleet & Portland Harbour
Stephen Groves

Clubs
Christchurch Harbour Ornithological Group (1956; 700)
David Taylor (Gen Sec),
Dairy Cottage, Sopley, BH23 7AZ;
secretary@chog.org.uk;
www.chog.org.uk
Meetings: 7:30pm, 2nd Wednesday of the month (Oct-Mar).
Venue—contact/see website for details.

Dorset Bird Club (1987; 525)
Richard Charman (Membership Sec), 24 Widworthy Drive, Broadstone, BH18 9BD: membership@dorsetbirds.co.uk; www.dorsetbirds.co.uk
Meetings: Irregular indoor meetings—contact/see website for details.

Ringing Groups/Bird Observatory
Christchurch Harbour Ringing Station
Radipole RG
Stour RG
Wessex RG
Portland Bird Observatory
Martin Cade (Warden), The Old Lower Light, Portland Bill, DT5 2JT: 01305 820 553; obs@btinternet.com; www.portlandbirdobs.com

RSPB Local Groups
South Dorset (1976; 120).
Chris Wyeth: chriswyeth@hotmail.com; https://group.rspb.org.uk/southdorset/
Meetings: 7:30pm, 4th Thursday of the month (Sep-Nov; Jan-Apr). The 'Quiet Space', Woodlands Crescent, Poundbury, Dorchester, DT1 3SE (behind the garden centre).

Wildlife Trust
Dorset Wildlife Trust (1961; 27,000)
Brooklands Farm, Forston, Dorchester, DT2 7AA: 01305 264 620; enquiries@dorsetwildlifetrust.org.uk; www.dorsetwildlifetrust.org.uk

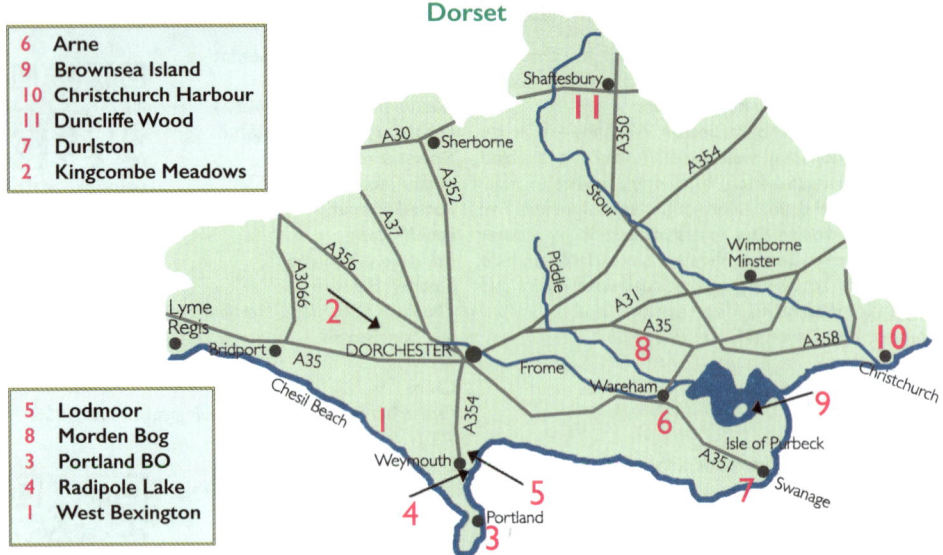

Dorset

6	**Arne**
9	**Brownsea Island**
10	**Christchurch Harbour**
11	**Duncliffe Wood**
7	**Durlston**
2	**Kingcombe Meadows**

5	**Lodmoor**
8	**Morden Bog**
3	**Portland BO**
4	**Radipole Lake**
1	**West Bexington**

Entering Dorset from Devon, head to Bridport on A35 At roundabout at S end of Bridport, take B3157 E along coast to

1 WEST BEXINGTON

Dorset Wildlife Trust

Habitats: Shingle, coastal scrub, grazing marsh, reedbed.
Birds: All year: Common scrub spp, Stonechat, Cetti's Warbler, Reed Bunting, Yellowhammer. *Spring/autumn passage:* Good for migrants inc scarce & rare spp, wildfowl and waders. Seabird passage, esp. Apr/May & Aug-Nov—shearwaters, skuas, terns, gulls. *Winter:* Divers & grebes offshore. Merlin.

Other: Adder, Dormouse, Water Vole. Dragonflies.
Directions: DT2 9DG; SY528 866. 10 miles NW of Weymouth. Take B3157 from Weymouth (Chickerell)—10 miles or B3157 off A35 at Bothenhampton—five miles, heading to village of Swyre. Here take small road S to West Bexington—beach car park at end of this road (1.2 miles).
Public transport: Buses: X52/X53 Jurassic Coaster route from Weymouth to Bridport goes through Swyre (Lemon Tree stop). First Bus. Take footpath down to coast (0.75 mile)—entrance next to bus stop.
Visiting: Open all hours. Public pay & display at West Bexington next to reserve. Circular walk around reserve through open areas. No dogs on reserve but permitted on adjacent areas. From West Bexington explore W towards Cogden Beach (bus stop & NT car park here on B3157—pay & display, NT members free).
Contact: Dorset Wildlife Trust: 01305 264 620;
info@dorsetwildlifetrust.org.uk
*Either, head back to Bridport, and then A35 and A3066 N to Beaminster. At Beaminster take B3163, which joins A356 and approach **Kingcombe Meadows** from the NW.*

2 KINGCOMBE MEADOWS NNR

Dorset Wildlife Trust
Habitats: Unimproved grass, hedgerows, fields, river.
Birds: All year: Common woodland spp (inc Marsh Tit), Buzzard, Raven, Yellowhammer, possible Dipper and Kingfisher on river. *Summer:* Cuckoo, warblers. *Winter:* Woodcock, Snipe, winter thrushes, Redpoll, Siskin.
Other: Flora inc orchids, butterflies, fungi (inc 27 spp of wax-caps), Otter, Dormouse.
Directions: DT2 0EQ; SY 554 990. A37 from Dorchester towards Yeovil, turn L on to A356 after Grimstone. One mile past Maiden Newton turn L to Toller Porcorum (Toller Lane) then R in village to Lower Kingcombe (Kingcombe Road). Info Centre/car park 1st on R, Kingcombe Visitor Centre 2nd on R.
Public transport: Train: Maiden Newton (3.5 miles)
Visiting: Reserve open all hours. Car park. Info centre and toilets open 10am-4pm, two circular marked trails. Dogs on leads. Kingcombe Visitor Centre: cafe & shop open 10am-4pm (Mar-Dec). Visitor Centre runs workshops, courses and events, accommodation available.
Contact: Dorset WT: 01305 264 620;
info@dorsetwildlifetrust.org.uk
Kingcombe Visitor Centre: 01300 320 684;
kingcombe@dorsetwildlifetrust.org.uk;
www.kingcombe.org
Or continue along coast on B3157 to junction with A354 in Weymouth. Take A354 S to Portland

3 PORTLAND BIRD OBSERVATORY

Portland Bird Observatory
Habitats: Portland—cliffs, scrub, quarries, open fields. Migration watch point, seawatching.
Birds: 355+ spp on Portland. *All year:* Little Owl. *Spring/ autumn:* Most regular common and scarce migrants

recorded annually, national rarities frequently turn up. Good selection of offshore passage inc divers, Common Scoter, shearwaters (inc Balearic), skuas inc Pomarine & occasional Long- tailed, terns inc Arctic & Black. *Summer:* Breeding Razorbill, Guillemot, Fulmar, Shag, Little Tern (Ferrybridge). Puffin (occasionally at the Bill).*Winter:* Purple Sandpiper, Short-eared Owl, Black Redstart, Mediterranean Gull (large numbers at Ferrybridge), divers, grebes, Red-breasted Merganser (Portland Harbour).

Directions: DT5 2JT; SY 681 690. Six miles S of Weymouth, Observatory on road to Portland Bill.

Public transport: Bus: 1 Weymouth to The Bill. First Wessex, Dorset & Somerset.

Visiting: Open all hours. Parking only for Portland Bird Obs members. Self-catering accommodation available—take own towels, sheets, sleeping bags. Information, toilets, natural history bookshop. Large pay & display car park and toilets at The Bill.

Contact: Martin Cade (Warden PBO): 01305 820 553; obs@btinternet.com;
http://portlandbirdobs.blogspot.co.uk/
The next two reserves are in or close to Weymouth.

4 RADIPOLE LAKE
RSPB

Habitats: Lake, reedbeds.

Birds: Excellent for rare/scarce gulls, regular rarities. *All year:* Marsh Harrier, Bearded Tit, Cetti's Warbler. *Spring/ summer/autumn:* Hirundines, Reed & Sedge Warblers, passage waders & other migrants. Garganey regular in spring. *Winter:* Bittern, wildfowl, Water Rail, pre-roost gatherings of gulls and Pied Wagtail.

Directions: DT4 7TZ; SY 675 795. In Radipole Park Drive, Weymouth (signposted with brown signs). Enter footpaths from Swannery car park.

Public transport: Train—station 400 yards from reserve, serving London & Bristol.

Visiting: Public footpaths open all hours. Public pay & display car park. Discovery Centre open daily (not 24-26 Dec) 9:30am-5pm (4pm Nov-Jan). Centre has small cafe and disabled toilets. Network of wheelchair friendly paths, two signposted trails, one viewing shelter, viewpoints. Dogs on leads.

Contact: RSPB: 01929 553 360;
weymouth.reserves@rspb.org.uk

5 LODMOOR NATURE RESERVE
RSPB

Habitats: Marsh, shallow pools, large reedbed and scrub, remnant saltmarsh.

Birds: All year: Little Egret, Marsh Harrier (breeding), Water Rail, Kingfisher, Cetti's Warbler, Bearded Tit. *Spring/summer:* Hobby, Common Tern colony, common warblers inc Reed, Sedge, Lesser Whitethroat, occasionally Grasshopper, hirundines. *Passage:* Waders (inc Common, Green & Wood Sandpipers). Other migrants and rarities regularly turn up. *Winter:* Bittern. Wildfowl, waders inc Black-tailed Godwit, Snipe, Lapwing and gulls inc Mediterranean, occasional Iceland and Glaucous. Great White Egret regularly seen.

Directions: DT3 6HS; SY 688 809. One mile NE of Weymouth town centre, adjacent to A3155 (Preston Road).

Public transport: Bus—frequent local service to Overcombe Corner, Lodmoor Country Park from Weymouth seafront. Train—Weymouth, bus or easy walk along seafront to reserve (one mile).

Visiting: Open all hours. Pay & display car parks nearby, street parking on N side (Southdown Ave). One viewing shelter, trails mostly accessible to wheelchairs.

Contact: RSPB: 01929 553 360;
weymouth.reserves@rspb.org.uk
Head E from Weymouth on A353, then A352 to Wareham.

6 ARNE
RSPB

Habitats: Lowland heath, woodland, reedbed and saltmarsh, extensive mudflats of Poole Harbour.

Birds: All year: Little Egret, Spoonbill, Marsh Harrier (breed in harbour), Barn Owl, Dartford Warbler, Stonechat. *Summer:* Sandwich & Common Terns, Hobby, Nightjar, hirundines, warblers. *Passage:* Osprey, Spotted Redshank, Whimbrel, Greenshank. *Winter:* 30,000 waders/wildfowl use Poole Harbour, many seen from Arne inc grebes, divers, Brent Goose, Black-tailed Godwit, Avocet, plus occasional Eider, Scaup and Long-tailed Duck. Hen Harrier, winter thrushes and finches. Osprey reintroduction programme in Poole Harbour since 2017, now breeding.

Other: Sika Deer, all six spp UK reptiles, 32 spp butterflies inc Silver-studded Blue, 850 spp Moths, 23 spp Dragonflies and 500 spp flowering plants.

Directions: BH20 5BJ;SY 971 876. Head S from Wareham over causeway, turn L at Stoborough to Ridge continue to Arne.

Public transport: None to reserve. Train—nearest station is Wareham (four miles).

Visiting: Trails open all hours. Entrance fee per person or car park charge if out of hours (RSPB members free). Car park open 8.30am-dusk, coaches and escorted parties by prior arrangement. Shop & cafe (opposite car park) and welcome area, toilets open daily (not 25/26 Dec) 9:30am-4:30pm (4pm Nov-Mar)—toilets in car park/cafe. Eight signposted trails, limited wheelchair access on trails. Two hides, one viewpoint and two viewing screens. Dogs on leads/no dogs on new Hyde Heath extension, take dog waste away.

Contact: RSPB: 01929 553 360; arne@rspb.org.uk
Continue on A351 to Swanage.

7 DURLSTON NNR AND COUNTRY PARK

Dorset County Council

Habitats: 280 acre, sea cliffs, woodland, grassland, hedges, cliff, meadows and downland.

Birds: All year: Peregrine, Kestrel, Raven, woodland species. *Spring/autumn passage:* migrants (esp important site for visible migration in autumn). *Summer:* Cliff-nesting seabird colonies inc Fulmar, Guillemot, Razorbill and Shag, good variety of scrub and woodland breeding spp. Can be good for seabird passage—esp Apr/May and Aug/Nov.

Other: 34 spp butterflies inc. Lulworth Skipper, 800 spp moths & 500+ spp flowering plants, inc nine spp orchid. Bottlenose Dolphin.

Directions: BH19 2JL; SZ 032 773. Lighthouse Road, Swanage, one mile S of town centre (signposted).

Public transport: None

Visiting: Open dawn-dusk. Pay as you leave parking (ANPR). Durlston Castle: visitor centre open daily (not Dec 25/26) 10am-5pm Apr-Oct, 10am-4pm Nov-Mar. Cafe (in Castle) open daily (not Dec 25/26) 9:30am-5pm & Fri/Sat evenings Apr-mid Oct. Toilets, exhibitions, art displays & shop. Dolphin watch point hide, way-marked trails. Walks & events.

Contact: Durlston CP: 01929 424 443; info@durlston.co.uk; www.durlston.co.uk

Instead of heading SE for Swanage on A351, head NE for Poole.

8 MORDEN BOG NNR (WAREHAM FOREST)

Natural England (Wessex Team)

Habitats: NNR—mainly lowland heath (dry and wet heath, bog and valley mire), large decoy pond with surrounding coniferous forest & lowland heath.

Birds: All year: Buzzard, Dartford Warbler, Meadow Pipit, Stonechat, Siskin, Lesser Spotted Woodpecker (by Sherford Bridge—best in spring). *Spring/summer:* Osprey, Hobby, Nightjar, Woodlark, Tree Pipit, Spotted Flycatcher, Redstart. *Winter:* Great Grey Shrike (almost annual).

Other: Butterflies, inc Silver-studded Blue, Grayling, dragonflies, and all six British reptile spp.

Directions: BH20 7ES; SY 919 926 (parking area). N of Wareham, part of a wider Wareham Forest site. From Wareham take A351 to Sandford then turn L on to B3075 towards Morden. Drive through forest until reaching lay-by (on R) at Sherford Bridge. Park & cross road through metal gate.

Public transport: Can access forest from Wareham train station follow blue signs (bus stop here as well).

Visiting: Open all hours, many footpaths.

Contact: Natural England (main enquiries): 0300 060 3900; enquiries@naturalengland.org.uk

Continue on A351 to Poole.

9 BROWNSEA ISLAND NATURE RESERVE

Dorset Wildlife Trust/National Trust

Habitats: 250 acre, saline lagoon, reedbed, lakes, coniferous & mixed woodland.

Birds: All year: Spoonbill, Little Egret. *Summer:* Little Grebe, Common & Sandwich Terns, Mediterranean Gull. *Autumn:* Returning wildfowl/waders. Curlew Sandpiper, Little Stint and rarities often turn up on DWT Lagoon. *Winter:* Water Rail, Kingfisher. Avocet, Black-tailed & Bar-tailed Godwits, Spotted Redshank, Greenshank. Other waders, gulls and wildfowl.

Other: Red Squirrel (up to 250 on island), Water Vole, Bechstein's Bat. Good variety of butterflies and dragonflies.

Directions: BH15 1HJ; SZ 010 902 (Poole Quay). Brownsea Island Ferries (01929 462 383): half hourly crossings from Poole Quay. Greenslade Pleasure Boats (01202 669 955): half hourly crossings from Poole Quay. Boat charges apply in addition to landing fee.

Public transport: Poole—bus & train stations are short walk from Poole Quay/boats (mainly down pedestrian shopping area to the Old Town).

Visiting: Island open late-Mar to end-Oct, 10am-5pm. Landing fee (free for NT members). Free admission to northern area that Doreset Wildlife Trust manages for DWT members (show card to NT staff) but landing fee must be paid if visiting rest of island. Toilets, information centre, cafe, gift shop, five hides, nature trail. Assistance dogs only.

Contact: Dorset WT: info@dorsetwildlifetrust.org.uk; National Trust: 01202 707 744; brownseaisland@nationaltrust.org.uk

Head E through Poole and Bournemouth to

10 CHRISTCHURCH HARBOUR

Bournemouth, Christchurch and Poole Council.

Habitats: Estuary of the rivers Avon and Stour. 870 acre SSSI, mudflat, saltmarsh, wet meadow, grassland, heath, dunes, woodland and scrub. A tidal lagoon (a double high tide: two peaks with a slight ebb in between) to the SE of the confluence of the Avon and Stour. Aligned roughly W-E with a narrow opening to the English Channel at the E end. Poole-Bournemouth conurbation to the W; Christchurch to the N. Hengistbury Head, a sandy spit of land separating the Harbour from the English Channel on S and E sides. Within the Harbour as a whole, two areas designated as nature reserves: **Stanpit Marsh** and **Hengistbury Head.**

Birds: c.330 spp recorded; 220 spp possible in any one year. Primarily of interest for wide range of passage migrants due to diversity of habitats; also seawatching from headland. The Christchurch Harbour Ornithological Group publishes a daily list on its website: www.chog.org.uk

Other: 34 spp butterflies, 1,000 spp moths, 33 spp of dragon/damselflies and 98 spp of solitary bees recorded.

Directions: A35 runs from Bournemouth to the N of Christchurch.

For **Stanpit Marsh** BH23 3ND; SZ 172 925, leave A35/Christchurch bypass at Purewell Cross roundabout and take B3059 Purewell Cross Road into Christchurch. After 0.5 mile go straight across roundabout (2nd exit). Car park after 600 yards on R.

For **Hengistbury Head Nature Reserve** BH6 4EW; SZ 162 911. Leave the A35 between the Bailey and Fountain roundabouts and take Stour Road (B3059) S. Go straight across roundabout (2nd exit) after crossing Stour. After another 200 yards, turn L into Broadway. Visitor Centre 1.25 miles at end of road.

Public transport: Bus: Beach Breezer 70 Rockley Park to Hoburne Park (Apr-Oct) stops at Hengistbury Head and by car park for Stanpit Marsh, morebus (01202 338 420). Train—Christchurch station, to N of A35.

Visiting: **Stanpit Marsh Nature Reserve** (Christchurch Borough Council) car park (free) open all hours, 500 yard track to Visitor Centre (10am-4pm every day). 160 acre nature reserve to the N of the lagoon. Salt and freshwater marsh, reedbeds, creeks and mudflat Circular trail, gravel, some raised bridges. Can be muddy and inaccessible on highest tides. Grazing ponies and cattle. Dogs on lead.

Hengistbury Head Nature Reserve pay & display car park open all hours. Visitor Centre (10am-4pm, every day; 01202 128 444) fully accessible for disabled, cafe, shop, toilets (inc disabled). Smooth flat trails, slope up to headland. Land Train (Easter-Oct) adapted for disabled runs to headland, where further toilets.

Stour Valley Way follows river, along S side of Harbour and ends at headland. Other nature reserves nearby.

Contact: robin.harley@bcpcouncil.gov.uk

Head back to W side of Poole, then take A350 to Blandford Forum and then Shaftesbury.

11 DUNCLIFFE WOOD

Woodland Trust

Habitats: Semi-natural woodland.

Birds: All year: Buzzard, Raven, common woodland spp inc Tawny Owl, Treecreeper, Marsh Tit, Bullfinch. *Spring/summer:* Common warblers. *Winter:* Redwing, Fieldfare. *Other:* Woodland flora inc Bluebells. Butterflies, 6 spp. bats, Glow Worm.

Public Transport: None.

Directions: SP8 5LZ; ST 816 223. Three miles W of Shaftesbury. Take A30 from Shaftesbury towards Sherborne. One mile before East Stour turn L on to unclassified road towards Stour Row. Continue 0.5 mile until reach junction on R (by New Gate Farm) and continue on another 60 yards to car park on L (height barrier). Footpath sign points to wood.

Visiting: Open all hours. Car park. Criss-crossed by series of paths & tracks inc. waymarked walk—unsuitable for wheelchairs/pushchairs.

Contact: Woodland Trust: 0330 333 3300; england@woodlandtrust.org.uk

Channel Islands

Crown Dependencies rather than a part of the UK but included here, in South West England, because of their geographical location. A group of six small, mainly granite, inhabited islands and a number of uninhabited islets spread over an area measuring 40 miles N-S and 30 miles E-W to the W of the Cotentin peninsula. Highest point Les Platons (Jersey): 469 ft. Second highest tidal range in the world and strong currents. Popultion density of humans is high compared with UK.

There are vehicle ferry links to the islands from Poole and Portsmouth, various French ports; and also vehicle and passenger ferry services, some seasonal, between the islands. Jersey, Guernsey and Alderney have airports.

ALDERNEY

Northernmost and third largest of the inhabited islands, with a land area of 3.1 sq miles. Aligned roughly E-W, it is some 3 miles long. Around a seventh of the island is set aside as nature reserve and its position to the south of mainland UK means it has species such as Zitting Cisticola, as well as seabird colonies on offshore islets and stacks.

Atlas/Avifauna
The Birds of Alderney
Jeremy G Sanders
(privately published, 2007).

Bird Recorder
Matt Scragg, c/o Alderney Bird Observatory—see below.

Ringing Group/Bird Observatory
Alderney Bird Observatory
Matt Scragg, Warden, Alderney Bird Observatory,
Postal address: La Rocquaine, Vert Courtil, Alderney, GY9 3UZ
07966119618; warden@alderneybirdobservatory.org;
www.alderneybirdobservatory.org

RSPB Local Group
No Groups.

BTO Regional Representative
Chris Mourant
Wetland Bird Survey (WeBS)
Local Organizer: webs@bto.org
Roland Gauvain

Wildlife Trust

Alderney Wildlife Trust (2002)
Slades, 48 Victoria Street, St Anne, Alderney GY9 3TA:
01481 822 935; info@alderneywildlife.org;
www.alderneywildlife.org

A1 ALDERNEY BIRD OBSERVATORY

Alderney Bird Observatory Ltd
Habitats:
Birds: Spring and autum migration, seabirds.
Other:
Directions: Formerly based in the Nunnery, its current HQ is Telegraph House, near Essex Castle. Take the Rue de Longis NE out of St Anne (the main town of Alderney. Essex castle is on the S coast, just to the W of Longis Nature Reserve.
Public transport: There are no buses on Alderney, which is only 3 miles long, but it is possible to hire a car.
Visiting: The Observatory does not offer overnight accommodation but accommodation can be booked on the island.
Contact; Matt Scragg, Warden. Postal address: La Rocquaine, Vert Courtil, Alderney, GY9 3UZ; 07966 119 618;
warden@alderneybirdobservatory.org
www.alderneybirdobservatory.org

A2 LONGIS NATURE RESERVE

Alderney Wildlife Trust
Habitats: Rocky, 260 acre headland at E end of island occupying an eighth of its land area. Grass, heath and woodland with two reed-fringed pools.
Birds: Little Grebe, Shoveler, Teal, Shelduck, Snipe, Common Sandpiper, Whimbrel, Sanderling,Common Tern, Buzzard, Little Egret, Water Rail, Barn Owl, Zitting Cisticola, Dartford Warbler, Reed Warbler, Stonechat, Wheatear, Grey Heron
Other: Glanville Fritillary, Clouded Yellow, Small Copper. Small Hare's-ear, Sand Crocus, Bastard Toadflax, Orange Bird's-foot. Endemic Alderney Sea Lavender on rocky shore
Directions: GY9 3XL;
Public transport: None
Visiting: Park on road, at the Nunnery or lighthouse. Open all hours, free. Toilets (accessible), picnic area. Keep dogs under control, part of reserve grazed by Guernsey cattle. Each of the pools has a wheelchair-accessible hide and access path but most other trails through reserve not suitable for wheel/pushchairs. 1.5 mile coastal path around headland.
Contact: AWT: 01481 822 935;
admin@alderneywildlife.org

A3 ALDERNEY COMMUNITY WOODLAND

Alderney Wildlife Trust
Habitats: 42 acres, mainly deciduous developing woodland habitat at the centre of the island, some coniferous plantings. Also orchard and glade to E of the site; grassland and scrub in areas not yet planted.
Birds: Common woodland spp inc Firecrest and Goldcrest, Cuckoo. *Winter:* Redwing, Fieldfare.
Other: Ash, Hazel, Oak, Hornbeam, Common Blue, Speckled Wood, Painted Lady, Ivy Bee
Directions: GY9 3YB
Public transport: None
Visiting: Parking by the cemetery, short walk into woodland. Open all hours, free. 2 miles of woodland and meadow trails some steep. Several different types of bunker; inc a two-storey observation bunker, with ladder access to the top offering panoramic views of the island.
Contact: AWT: 01481 822 935
admin@alderneywildlife.org

A4 VAU DU SAOU NATURE RESERVE

Alderney Wildlife Trust
Habitats: 17 acres, coastal valley, with stream, and clifftop, on S side of island. Heather, scrub and wood.
Birds: Woodcock, Fulmar, Gannet, Shag, Buzzard, Kestrel, Sparrowhawk, Peregrine Falcon, Raven, Fulmar, Blackcap.
Other: Elm, Hazel, Goat Willow, Alder, Bluebells, Foxglove, Wood sage, Holly blue, Speckled wood, Slow worm.
Directions: GY9 3TT
Public transport: None
Visiting: Parking by the standing stone along the Airport perimeter track. Open all hours, free. Access along coastal path, steps and steep slopes into the valley. Wildlife Bunker (Countryside Interpretation Centre) housed in a converted WW2 German bunker, displaying information on the island's military and wildlife history—seabird observation point, wildlife displays and shelter from the elements. Open 24/7 and powered by a solar lighting system. Over half a mile of coastal and woodland walks.
Contact: AWT: 01481 822 935
admin@alderneywildlife.org

A5 BONNE TERRE VALLEY

Alderney Wildlife Trust
Habitats: 2.4 acres, sheltered, wet wooded valley on W side. Historic watermill with damned stream. Wet meadow, grassland and scrub.
Birds: Common woodland and scrub spp inc Cetti's Warbler. Woodcock, Water Rail, Kingfisher.
Other: Hawthorn, Blackthorn, Elder, Bluebells, Greater Tussock Sedge, Water Mint, Great Willow Herb, Primrose, Red Campion, Speckled Wood

Channel Islands

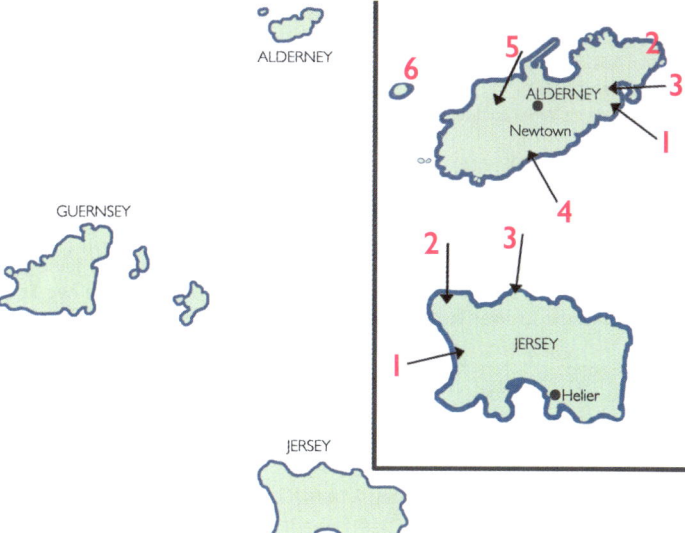

Directions: GY9 3UT
Public transport: None
Visiting: Parking on road along Tourgis Hill, by Fort Tourgis or on Petit Val. Open all hours, free. 1.5 miles of woodland paths; steep, uneven and with steps in places. Historic watermill at the foot of the valley, restored by the Alderney Society. 1.5 miles of woodland paths.
Contact: AWT: 01481 822 935
admin@alderneywildlife.org

A6 BURHOU ISLET
Alderney Wildlife Trust
Habitats: Uninhabited sandstone island, exposed rock, bracken. Part of W Alderney Ramsar site.
Birds: Breeding colonies of Storm Petrel, Puffin, Lesser Black-backed Gull. Also Great Black-backed Gull
Other: No rats.
Directions: Two miles to NW of Alderney. Several organizations run Boat Tours from Alderney. All offer round island tours,
Alderney Wildlife Trust: 01481 822 935;
admin@alderneywildlife.org
Avante II: 01481 823 307/07781 115 132;
davevenn4@gmail.com
Lady Maris II: 07781 100 829;
ladymaris2alderney@gmail.com
Public transport: None
Visiting: Island closed to visitors Mar-Jul. Round island boat tours also pass gannetries on Ortac and Les Etacs (17,000 individuals) but do not land on Burhou. However, the boats of all the companies can be chartered for landings outside the close season. No jetty. Getting ashore requires a degree of agility and my not be possible in bad weather. Alderney Bird Observatory Organizes annual ringing trip to Burhou.
Contact: AWT: 01481 822 935;
admin@alderneywildlife.org

GUERNSEY
Mid-way between and somewhat to the west of Alderney and Jersey, Guernsey is the second largest and most densely populated of the islands. The Société Guernesiaise has a number of mainly small wildlife reserves scattered across the island.

Bird Atlas/Avifauna
Birds of the Bailiwick: Guernsey, Alderney, Sark & Herm
Duncan Spencer & Paul Hillion
(Jill Vaudin Publishing 2011).

Bird Recorder
Mark Lawlor, St Etienne, Les Effards, St Sampsons, Guernsey GY2 4YN: 07781 122 313; mplawlor@cwgsy.net

Bird Report
Guernsey Rare Bird Report (1992-), download from website: www.guernseybirds.org.gg

BTO Regional Representative
Chris Mourant
Wetland Bird Survey (WeBS)
Local Organizer: webs@bto.org
Guernsey Coast
Mary Simmons

Club

La Société Guernesiaise (1882)
Secretary, La Société Guernesiaise, Candie Gardens, St Peter Port, Guernsey GY1 1UG: 01481 725 093; info@societe.org.gg; www.societe.org.gg

Ornithology Section (c.1890; 115).
Julie Davis (Sec) c/o Candie Gardens, see above: 07781 432 129; ornithology@societe.org.gg; www.societe.org.gg/wp/ornithology/
Meetings: (Ornithology Section). Quarterly—7:30pm, first Thursday in Mar, Jun, Sep and 1st Wednesday in Dec. Frossard Theatre, Candie Gardens, see above.

RSPB Local Group

Guernsey Bailiwick (1975; 200)
Ian Le Page: rspbguernsey@gmail.com; https://group.rspb.org.uk/guernsey/
Meetings: Autumn/winter—contact/see website for details. La Villette Hotel, St Martins, Guernsey GY4 6QG.

The National Trust of Guernsey

26 Cornet Street, St. Peter Port, GY1 1LF: 07781 106 461; emc@nationaltrust.gg; www.nationaltrust.gg

JERSEY

The southernmost and largest of the three main islands.

Bird Recorder

Romano da Costa, 27 Nomond Avenue, La Pouquelaye, St Helier JE2 3FW: 07797 823 233; ornithology@societe.je

Bird Report

Jersey Bird Report (1991-2024)
from Ornithology Section, La Société Jersiaise—see below.

BTO Regional Representative

Tony Paintin
Wetland Bird Survey (WeBS)
Local Organizers: webs@bto.org
Jersey Coast
Vacant
Jersey Inland
Vacant
webs@bto.org

Club

Natural History Museum: Sociétié Jersiaise (1873)
La Société Jersiaise, 7 Pier Road, St Helier, Jersey JE2 4XW: 01534 758 314; hello@societe.je; www.societe.je

Ornithology Section:

Romano da Costa: ornithology@societe.je
www.societe.je/our-sections/ornithology/
Meetings: Ornithology Section, 8pm, 1st and 3rd Thursdays of the month. Arthur Mourant Room—address as above.

RSPB Local Group

No Group.

National Trust for Jersey

The Elms, La Chève Rue, St Mary, Jersey, JE3 3EN: 01534 483 193; cris@nationaltrust.je; www.nationaltrust.je

Three coastal sites located around W half of the island. Starting in the S on the W coast

J1   LA MARE AU SEIGNEUR (ST OUEN'S POND)

National Trust for Jersey
Habitats: Originating from fish ponds dating back to 1309. Acquired in 1975, the reserve covers 120 acres of reeds, pools, fen, grazed meadows, dune grassland and a wader scrape.
Birds: 200 spp in last 10 years. Marsh Harrier first bred in Jersey at this site in 2002 and it still holds half of Jersey's estimated population (20-22 prs). Winter roost in the reeds for local and visiting Harriers, with up to 50 being counted in an evening. *Breeding:* Water Rail, Lapwing, Cetti's, Reed & Sedge Warbler, Stonechat, Meadow Pipit. *Winter:* Bittern, wildfowl and waders inc Ruff, Green Sandpiper.
Other: Jersey Bank Vole, White-toothed Shrew. Grass Snake, Slow Worm, Green Lizard. Southern Marsh Orchid, Pyramidal Orchid, Common Spotted-orchid, Heat Spotted-orchid, Jersey Orchid (endemic to Jersey and Guernsey).
Directions: JE3 7FN. Immediately to E of La Grande Route des Mielles (B25), which runs N-S along the coast of St Ouen's Bay on the island's W coast between Les Mielles Golf Course and the Chemin de l'Ouziere.
Public transport: Bus: 22/X22 Liberation Station in St Helier to L'Etacq.
Visiting: Open 9am-5pm every day, free. Jersey Wetland Centre built into WWII bunker under a sand bank overlooking the main pond. Entrance immediately off La Grande Route des Mielles, with free car park across the road at Sands cafe. Eddie's Hide, S of main pond overlooking wader scrape, accessed by short footpath from parking area across road at Watersplash eatery.
Contact: Jon Parkes: 01534 483 193; Jon.Parkes@nationaltrust.je
Head to the N end of the Bay and

J2 PLEMONT
& PLEMONT SEABIRD SANCTUARY

National Trust for Jersey

Habitats: 28-acre former holiday camp on rocky headland acquired in 2014 and being returned to nature. 2 ponds created, gorse planted, ongoing restoration of coastal grassland. Cliffs below in early stages of seabird restoration project. Area surrounded by hedgerow and fields with annual winter bird crops.

Birds: Fulmar, Puffin, Razorbill, Gannet, Shag, Swift, Dartford Warbler, Chough, Raven, Peregrine Falcon, Marsh Harrier, Buzzard, Kestrel, Wheatear, Stonechat, farmland birds.

Other: Jersey Bank Vole, Bottlenose Dolphin, Porpoise, Grey Seal, Green Lizard, Slow Worm, Swallowtail butterfly, Wild Carrot, Evening Primrose.

Directions: NW Jersey. Take the Route de Plemont (C105N) towards the giant puffin sculptures. Before reaching them, park on the right-hand side car park to access the area.

Public transport: Bus route 8 from bus station in St Helier to Portinfer junction, then walk along Route de Plemont towards the giant puffin sculptures.

Visiting: Free, open all year round. An information board to the NW of the giant puffins.

Contact: Cristina Sellares: 01534 483 193; cris@nationaltrust.je

*There are plans to instal an anti-predator fence along the headland to protect nesting seabirds. This is still subject to planning approval. There is no public footpath at present and the headland can be dangerous in high winds. **Do not attempt to walk clifftop until the project is further advanced.***

Then head E on B13 to

J3 LE DON PATON SOREL

National Trust for Jersey

Habitats: 35-acre coastal headland acquired by the National Trust for Jersey. Managed since 2009 to remove bracken, and grazed with Manx Loaghtan sheep to restore coastal grassland and heathland. A Red-billed Chough re-introduction project started in 2013, establishing a population that breeds in the wild (63 individuals in 2025). The release aviary is still on site. Agricultural fields surrounding the area. **Sorel Point**, to the E, is a spring migration viewing point.

Birds: Marsh Harrier, Buzzard, Peregrine Falcon, Kestrel, Chough, Raven, Dartford Warbler, Stonechat, farmland birds. *Passage:* Hen Harrier, Wryneck, Ring Ouzel.

Other: Green Lizard, Slow Worm, Jersey Bank Vole, a variety of butterflies and pollinators.

Directions: Route du Nord W (C100) then Rue de Sorel, car park on the left, where the footpath starts. Walk 270 yards to a small gate into the Trust land. Alternatively park at the Priory Inn by Devil's Hole, at the end of La Grande Rue (C103), and walk the footpath E towards Sorel through the bottom of Mourier Valley.

Public transport: Bus route 7 to Devil's Hole.

Visiting: Free, accessible all year round. There are Chough re-introduction project information boards by the Sorel car park and near the project aviary.

Contact: Cristina Sellares: 01534 483 193; cris@nationaltrust.je

[Arctic] Redpoll
Sylvie Soudan
Instagram: Sylvie.Soudan

Somerset,
inc. Bristol & Avon

Habitat restoration over many years on the old peat workings of the Somerset Levels has changed the area dramatically. Common Cranes (successfully reintroduced) and breeding Bitterns have been boosted by this work and a variety of herons & egrets, including Little Bittern, Great White & Cattle Egrets, are also colonizing the area. In winter the Levels hold large numbers of wildfowl and are worth a visit to witness a spectacular Starling murmuration. Coastal sites attract wintering wildfowl and waders.

Bird Atlases/Avifauna
The Birds of Exmoor and the Quantocks
David Ballance, Brian Gibbs & Roger Butcher
(privately published, 2nd ed 2016).
Somerset Atlas of Breeding and
*   Wintering Birds 2007-2012*
David Ballance, Rob Grimmond, Julian Thomas & Eve Tigwell (Somerset OS, 2014).
Avon Atlas 2007-11
Richard L Bland & M Dadds
(Bristol Naturalists' Society, 2012).
A History of the Birds of Somerset
DK Ballance
(Isabelline Books, 2006).

Bird Recorders
Avon
Rupert Higgins, 28 Egerton Road, Bishopston, Bristol, BS7 8HL: avonbirdrecorder@outlook.com
Somerset
Brian Gibbs, 23 Lyngford Road, Taunton, TA2 7EE: 01823 274 887; brian.gibbs@somersetbirding.org.uk

Bird Reports
Avon Bird Report (1977-), from Harvey Rose, Arncliffe, Coast Road, Walton Bay, Clevedon, BS21 7AS: bktlgodwit@gmail.com
Somerset Birds (1912-), from the Somerset Bird Recorder—see above.

BTO Regional Representatives
Avon
Jonathan Angell
Somerset
Eve Tigwell
Wetland Bird Survey
(WeBS) Local Organizers: webs@bto.org
Avon (other sites)
Rupert Higgins
Severn Estuary (Somerset & Avon)
Harvey Rose

Somerset Levels & Somerset (other sites)
Eve Tigwell

Clubs
Bristol Naturalists' Society (1862; 490)
Melanie Parker (Hin Sec of Society & Ornithology Section): info@bristolnats.org.uk; www.bristolnats.org.uk
Meetings: Contact/see website for details.
Bristol Ornithological Club (1966; 600)
Gareth Roberts (Secretary): 07785 573 064; bocsecretary@hotmail.com; www.bristolornithologicalclub.co.uk
Meetings: 7:30pm, 3rd Thursday of the month (Sep-Mar). Newman Hall, Grange Court Road, Westbury-on-Trym, BS9 4DR (not Jan, via Zoom).
Exmoor Natural History Society (1974; 480)
Caroline Giddens (Sec), 12 King George Road, Minehead, TA24 5JD: 01643 707 624; carol.enhs@talktalk.net; www.enhs.org.uk
Meetings: 7:30pm, 1st Wednesday of the month (Oct-Mar). Methodist Church Hall, The Avenue, Minehead, TA24 5AY—contact/see website for details.
10am, 2nd Tuesday of the month at Luckbarrow, West Luccombe, TA24 8HX.
Somerset Ornithological Society (1974; 475)
Dick Best (Membership Sec), Quantock View Farm, Steart, TA5 2PXP: 01278 651 063; jr.best@hotmail.co.uk; www.somersetbirding.org.uk
Meetings: Contact/see website for details.

Ringing Groups/Bird Observatory
Chew Valley RG: cvrs.contact@gmail.com
www.chewvalleyringingstation.co.uk
Gordano Valley RG

RSPB Local Groups
Bath and District (1969; 186)
David Butterworth: leader.rspbbath@gmail.com; https://group.rspb.org.uk/bath/
Meetings: 7:30pm, 3rd Wednesday of the month (Sep-Apr, via zoom Jan-Feb). St Andrew's Community Church, Hawthorn Grove, Combe Down, Bath, BA2 5QA. Contact/see website for details.
Bristol (2021; n/a)
bristolgroupRSPB@gmail.com; https://group.rspb.org.uk/bristol/
Meetings: Contact/see website for details.
South Somerset (1979; 150)
Denise Chamings: denisechamings99@outlook.com; https://group.rspb.org.uk/southsomerset/
Meetings: 7:30pm, 3rd Thursday of the month (Sep-May). The Millennium Hall, Seavington St. Mary, Ilminster, TA19 0QH.

Wildlife Trusts

Avon Wildlife Trust (1980; 17,000)
17 Great George Street, Bristol, BS1 5QT.
0117 917 7270;
mail@avonwildlifetrust.org.uk;
www.avonwildlifetrust.org.uk

Somerset Wildlife Trust (1964; 23,000)
34 Wellington Road, Taunton, Somerset TA1 5AW:
01823 652 400;
enquiries@somersetwildlife.org;
www.somersetwildlife.org

1 SUTTON BINGHAM RESERVOIR

Wessex Water.

Habitats: Reservoir, hay meadow, surrounding farmland, mature hedgerows. Southern tip of reservoir is in Dorset.

Birds: All year: Great Crested Grebe, Buzzard, Peregrine, Sparrowhawk, Grey Heron, Little Egret, Kingfisher. *Spring/autumn passage:* Hirundines, waders (esp when water levels low) inc Green & Common Sandpipers, Redshank), Osprey. *Summer:* Hobby, warblers. *Winter:* Wildfowl, gulls (worth checking through), Snipe, winter thrushes, Siskin and Redpoll. Has turned up interesting birds in past.

Other: Bats, butterflies, meadow flora.

Directions: BA22 9QL; ST 548 111. Two miles S of Yeovil. Head S from Yeovil (for *c.1* mile) or N from Dorchester on A37. Take turn signed to Sutton Bingham/East Coker. Follow minor road SW for 2 miles to car park (just beyond causeway).

Public transport: None.

Visiting: Car park (height restriction), toilets, nature trail, picnic area. Parts of reservoir viewable from road (care when stopping). No dogs.

Contact: Wessex Water: 01935 872 389

Head W to Taunton and Wellington on A358, then A38.

2 LANGFORD HEATH

Somerset Wildlife Trust

Habitats: Semi-natural ancient woodland, scrub, heathy grassland.

Birds: All year: Buzzard, Sparrowhawk, common woodland/scrub spp, inc 3 spp woodpeckers. *Spring/summer:* Cuckoo, Tree Pipit, common warblers inc Garden, Spotted Flycatcher. Occasional Wood Warbler, Redstart and Pied Flycatcher (former breeders). *Winter:* Woodcock, Siskin, Redpoll.

Other: Butterflies inc Purple Hairstreak and Silverwashed Fritillary. Moths, reptiles, bats. Woodland flora inc. Bluebells.

Directions: TA21 0SD; ST 106 227. Three miles NW of Wellington. Turn W off B3187 to Milverton, follow signs to Langford Budville. From here take road signed to Wiveliscombe—this road runs along E edge of re-

serve—park in lay-by (has a 'Jubilee' seat here) at S edge near information board.

For N end of reserve continue along road, turn L (to Polshill, narrow road) and park in another lay-by (information board).

Public transport: None.

Visiting: Two waymarked trails (starting/finishing at main access point at 'Jubilee' seat lay-by)—two miles and 0.6 mile (some boardwalk sections). Dogs on lead.

Contact: Somerset WT: 01823 652 400;
enquiries@somersetwildlife.org

Continue W to Minehead on A358 and A39.

3 DUNKERY & HORNER WOOD NNR

National Trust

Habitats: 3,950 acre, ancient oak woodland, moorland, part of 11,980 acre NT Holnicote Estate in Exmoor National Park.

Birds: All year: Dipper, Grey Wagtail, woodpeckers, Buzzard, Sparrowhawk. *Spring/summer:* Redstart, Stonechat, Whinchat, Tree Pipit, Pied Flycatcher, Wood Warbler. Dartford Warbler possible.

Other: Holnicote estate holds 15 of UK's bat spp. Silver-washed & Heath Fritillary butterflies. Red Deer.

Directions: TA24 8HY; SS 898 455 (Horner). 4.5 miles W of Minehead. Take A39 W to minor road 0.5 mile E of Porlock signposted to Horner. Park in village.

Public transport: Bus: 10 (not Sun) between Minehead and Porlock. Operated by various companies—First Buses of Somerset, Atwest and W Ridler & Sons.

Visiting: Open all year. Pay & display car parks at Bossington (SS 898 480) and Horner (SS 898 455), inc toilets. Free small car parks at Allerford, Selworthy (overflow only), Selworthy Beacon, Webbers Post, 150 miles of footpaths. Webber's Post circular walk suitable for wheelchairs. Rugged terrain to Dunkery Beacon.

Contact: National Trust: 01643 862 452;
holnicote@nationaltrust.org.uk

Head back E on A39, then

4 WWT BRIDGWATER BAY NNR/
   STEART MARSHES

WWT

Habitats: 6,320 acre Parrett estuary, intertidal mudflats, saltmarsh.

Birds: 200 spp. *All year:* Curlew, Oystercatcher, Avocet. Shelduck (Europe's second largest moulting ground with up to 7,000 birds in Jul). *Spring/autumn:* Passage migrants, inc occasional vagrants. Waders inc internationally important numbers of Whimbrel and Black-tailed Godwit. *Winter:* Raptors inc Peregrine, Merlin, harriers and Short-eared Owl. Waders and wildfowl inc nationally important numbers of Teal and Avocet..

Other: Saltmarsh flora. Rare invertebrates inc Great Silver Water Beetle, Aquatic Snail & Hairy Dragonfly.

Directions: TA5 2PL; ST 257 408. 3.25 miles N of Bridg-

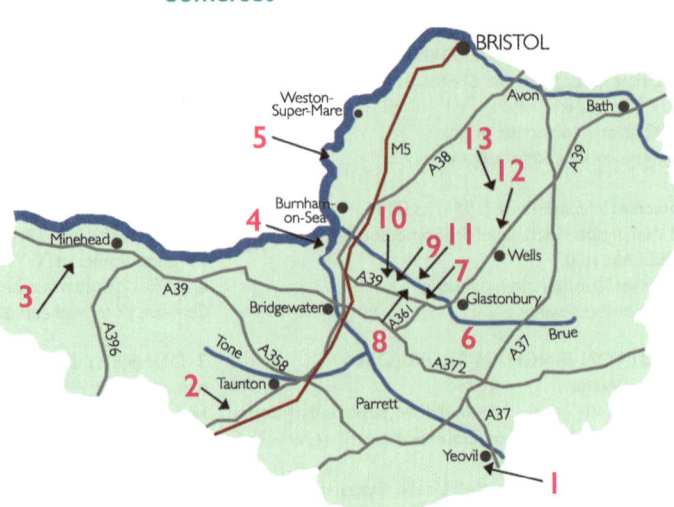

water extending to Burnham-on-Sea. Take J23 or 24 off M5. Turn N off A39 at Cannington and take minor roads to car park at Steart.

Public transport: None.

Visiting: Car park, interpretive panels—follow footpath c.0.5 mile to tower hide. Hides open daily. Permits needed for Steart Island (by boat only). Dogs on leads.

Steart Marshes

TA4 2PU; ST 252 442.

Open all year. Parking two miles before Bridgewater Bay NNR parking area. Hides and toilets open 9am-4:30pm (not 25 Dec). Viewing screens, trails.

Contact: 01278 651 090; info.steart@wwt.org.uk
Either head N from Burnham-on-Sea on minor coast road.

5 BREAN DOWN

National Trust

Habitats: Extension of Mendips hard limestone, featuring calcareous grassland, scrub and steep cliffs.

Birds: All year: Peregrine, Raven. *Summer:* Blackcap, Garden Warbler, Whitethroat, Stonechat. *Passage:* Gannet, divers, shearwaters, waders, skuas, gulls and passerines. *Winter:* Shelduck, Curlew, Dunlin on mudflats.

Other: Chalkhill Blue, Marbled White and other butterflies. Three rare plants—White Rock Rose, Somerset Hair Grass, Dwarf Sedge.

Directions: TA8 2RS; ST 296 586. 300 ft high promontory jutting into Bristol Channel, five miles N of Burnham-on-Sea. From J22 of M5, head for Weston-super-Mare on A38/A370. Turn off at Lympsham & head for Brean. At Brean, head N to car park at bottom of Brean Down.

Public transport: Bus: 20 Burnham-on-Sea to West-on-super-Mare, alight at Brean—1.75 miles to reserve). First Bristol, Bath & the West.

Visiting: Open all year. Pay & display car park opens with shop & cafe (9am-5pm), NT members free. Toilet (inc.

disabled) at bottom of Brean Down. Steep slope not recommended for wheelchair users. Dogs on lead.

Contact: National Trust: 01278 751 874; breandown@nationaltrust.org.uk
or head S from Burnham-on-Sea on A38, then take A372.

6 GREYLAKE

RSPB

Habitats: Reedbed, wet grassland, formerly arable farmland.

Birds: Spring/summer: Kingfisher, Grey Heron, Little Egret and breeding Garganey, Snipe, Lapwing, Redshank, Skylark, Meadow Pipit, Yellow Wagtail. *Autumn:* Green Sandpiper, waders on passage. *Winter:* Waders and wildfowl inc Lapwing, Golden Plover, Teal, Pintail, Shoveler and Wigeon. Peregrine Falcon, Merlin, Hen Harrier. Cranes reintroduced in area sometimes seen.

Other: Roe Deer, Water Vole, Stoat, Otter, dragonflies inc Four-spotted Chaser.

Directions: TA7 9PB; ST 399 346. Off A361 Taunton to Glastonbury road, between Othery and Greinton.

Public transport: Bus: 29 (not Sun) Taunton to Glastonbury stops in Greinton (by phone box) or Othery (by London Inn)—driver may stop at reserve on request otherwise two mile walk along A361 (*not advisable*—fast road, no path). First Buses of Somerset.

Visiting: Open all year, dawn-dusk. Two circular trails interpretive signs, two hides, one viewing platform, easy-access trail suitable for wheelchairs. Assistance dogs only, on leads.

Contact: RSPB: 01458 252 805; greylake@rspb.org.uk
There follows a cluster of separately managed but adjacent reserves in the Avalon Marshes to the W of Glastonbury and N of the A39 totalling around 2,500 acres.

7 HAM WALL

RSPB

Habitats: 655 acre, wetland, inc SW's largest reedbed.

Birds: All year: Bittern, Great White & Little Egrets, Marsh Harrier, Cetti's Warbler, Water Rail, Barn Owl. *Spring/summer:* Migrant warblers, hirundines, Hobby, sandpipers, cranes. Possible rare herons. *Autumn:* Migrant thrushes, Redpoll, Siskin, Kingfisher, Bearded Tit. *Winter:* Wildfowl, Starling roost, Peregrine, Merlin, Short-eared Owl.

Other: Otter, Water Vole, Grass Snake. Dragonflies, butterflies.

Directions: BA6 9SX; ST 449 397. W of Glastonbury. From A39 turn N in Ashcott and follow road on to moor (towards Meare). After three miles pass Church Farm Horticultural building. Shortly after, at metal bridge, reserve is opposite side of road to **Shapwick Heath NNR** (also has car park).

Public transport: Bus: 75 (not Sun) Wells to Bridgwater stops in Ashcott—two miles to reserve. First Buses Somerset. 688 (Mon-Fri) Glastonbury to Meare—1.5 miles to reserve. Libra Travel (01373 812 255).

Visiting: Open all year. Car park open 5am-6:30pm (Nov-Jan), 5am-8pm (Feb-Mar & Sep-Oct), 5am-10pm (Apr-Aug), parking charge for non-RSPB members). Alternative Natural England car park available outside of Ham Wall opening times. Coach parking Mar-Oct—book with reserve. Coaches not permitted Nov-Feb. Catering kiosk serving hot & cold drinks/light snacks and ice creams open weekends 10am-4pm, weekdays when volunteers available. Toilets. Two viewing platforms, five viewing screens, two hides, four trails. Wheelchair users can access viewing areas from main track (use RADAR key/borrow from Info Point when open). Assistance dogs welcome, other dogs (short lead) on main path/public footpath (Ham Wall loop) only—take waste away.

Contact: RSPB: 01458 860 494; ham.wall@rspb.org.uk
On the other side of Ashcott Road

8 SHAPWICK HEATH NNR

Natural England

Habitats: 1,240 acres fen, reedbed, open water (peat extraction in past), wet woodland. Immediately to the NW of **Ham Wall**.

Birds: Breeding: 60+ spp, essentially as for **Ham Wall**.

Other: White Admiral

Directions: E entrance: BA6 9SX; ST 449 396, as for **Ham Wall**. For W end, exit the A39 for Shapwick, pass through it and head N on what becomes Station Road. This runs S-N through the W end of the reserve with Hawk and Owl Trust car park for **Shapwick Moor** at the S boundary. 400 yards beyond the N boundary it passes the **Avalon Marshes Centre**, with large car park at BA6 9TT (approximate); ST 425 414, cafe, craft centre, toilets. Open 10am-5pm every day.

Public transport: Bus: 75 (see **Ham Wall**) stops in Shapwick, then walk along Station Road.

Visiting: Car park, voluntary donation. Open all hours. Nearest facilities at **Avalon Marshes Centre** and **Ham Wall**. Foot/cycle path through centre of reserve. 7 hides, inc one tower, some with ramps, Two disabled trails, some smaller paths not wheelchair suitable. No dogs except assistance dogs.

Contact: 01458 860120; somersetnnrs@naturalengland.org.uk
Just to the W of the above.

9 CATCOTT LOWS AND HEATH

Somerset Wildlife Trust

Habitats: 225 acres

Birds: Essentially as for **Ham Wall** but SWT flag up wintering duck—Mallard, Gadwall, Wigeon, Teal, Shelduck, Pintail, Shoveler—and waders—Lapwing, Snipe, Black-tailed Godwit.

Other: Great-crested Newt

Directions: TA7 8NG; ST 400 417 (car park). Exit A39 for Catcott then take minor road N to Burtle. Reserve car park off this road.

Public transport: Bus: 75 (see **Ham Wall**) stops in Catcott, then walk towards Burtle.

Visiting: Open all hours, free, no facilities (but see nearby reserves). Hide at car park wheelchair acessible. Tower hide not wheelchair accessible and path uneven and muddy. Hides, droves and footpaths open at all times. Other parts of reserve by permit only. Dogs on short lead on public footpaths, otherwise assistance dogs only.

Contact: 01823 652400; enquiries@somersetwildlife.org
Adjacent to Shapwick Heath and linked by public footpaths to Shapwick Heath and Catcott.

10 SHAPWICK MOOR

Hawk and Owl Conservancy Trust

Habitats: 138 acres of arable farmland acquired in 2007. Return to traditional farming: late-cut hay meadows, broad grass margins, no artificial fetilizer, water levels raised and controlled with ditches and native hedgerows planted.

Birds: Snipe, Lapwing, Buzzard, Sparrowhawk, Barn Owl, Kestrel, Kingfisher, Reed Bunting. *Spring/Summer:* Hobby, Reed & Sedge Warblers. *Winter:* Stonechat, finch flocks.

Other: Vole and Field Mouse populations boosted by changed management regime providing food sources for raptors.

Directions: TA7 9NW (to S of car park); ST 417 398. As for W end of **Shapwick Heath** NNR, take Station Road N out of Shapwick. Car park at SE corner of reserve

Public transport: Bus: 75 (see **Ham Wall**) stops in Shapwick, then walk along Station Road.

Visiting: Open all hours, free. Car park with height barrier. level stone paths to 2 hides with ramped access, one on high ground also overlooks Shapwick Heath. Nearest facilities at **Avalon Marshes Centre** 1.5 miles N. Station Road runs along E edge to **AMC**. Dogs under close control.

Contact: 0844 984 2824; enquiries@hawkandowl.org; www.shapwick. hawkandowl.org

To the N of Shapwick Heath NNR and on the other side of the village of Westhay.

11 WESTHAY MOOR NNR

Somerset Wildlife Trust

Habitats: 260 acres of restored peat workings. Open water, reedbed, lowland acid mire, scrub, grassland.

Birds: Much the same assembly as **Ham Wall** but SWT flags up that it has 7 of the UK's 9 breeding herons. Occasional Hen Harrier in winter.

Other: Emperor Dragonfly, Sundew.

Directions: BA6 9TX; ST 456 437. Either continue along Station Road from the reserves to the S past the **Avalon Marshes Centre** to the village of Westhay, where it joins the B3151 from Glastonbury, or take the latter from Glastonbury. Then continue along the B3151 out of Westhay, taking 1st R for Upper and Lower Godney. Reserve car park just over 1 mile along this minor road on L.

Public transport: Rather than walking up from the villages along the A39, the 75 stops in Glastonbury, thence walk along minor roads to the Godneys and then the reserve.

Visiting: Open all hours, free (charge for car park), no faciliities. 2 trails from car park (1 or 2 miles), 6 hides (1 tower), some with ramps for wheelchairs. Access restricted to public rigfs of way and permissive paths. Some paths can be wet and muddy. Grazed by livestock. Assistance dogs only except on public rights of way, when should be on leads.

Contact: 01823 652400; enquiries@somersetwildlife.org

Return to A39 and head for Wells.

12 STOCKHILL WOOD AND PRIDDY POOLS

Forestry England.

Habitats: Coniferous woodland, marsh, pools.

Birds: All year: Buzzard, Red Kite, Sparrowhawk, Tawny Owl, Green & Great Spotted Woodpeckers, Skylark, Stonechat, Treecreeper, Cetti's Warbler, Siskin, Reed Bunting, common woodland spp. *Spring/ summer:* Nightjar, Cuckoo, Raven, Spotted Flycatcher, Redstart, warblers—Blackcap, Whitethroat, Reed, Sedge, Garden & Willow Warblers, Chiffchaff.

Autumn/winter: Snipe, Crossbill.

Other: Butterflies.

Directions: BA5 3AS; ST 551 513. Three miles N of Wells. From A39 just before leaving Wells turn L on to Old Bristol Road, then immediately R to continue on Old Bristol Road. Stay on this road for 3.5 miles. At Hunter's Lodge Inn, cross over junction, and continue on to car park on R.

Public transport: None.

Visiting: Open all hours. Stockhill Wood is to R of the road. Priddy Pools (not owned by Forestry England) to L. Car park (height barrier), picnic benches. Has circular easy access trail and other paths.

Contact: Forestry England: 0300 067 4800; westengland@forestryengland.uk

Continue N on Old Bristol Road for 5.5 miles to

13 CHEW VALLEY LAKE

Avon Wildlife Trust/Bristol Water Plc

Habitats: Largest artificial lake in SW England with important reedbed.

Birds: 270+ spp—often attracts rarities. *Summer:* Breeding Great Crested & Little Grebes, Gadwall, Tufted Duck, Shoveler, Pochard, Reed Warbler. Hobby hunt in late summer. When mud exposed can attract waders inc Dunlin, Ringed Plover and Green Sandpiper. *Winter & passage:* Wildfowl inc important numbers of Shoveler, Gadwall, Teal and Tufted Duck. Large numbers of Goosander, Great Crested Grebe and Cormorant. Bewick's Swan, Goldeneye, Smew. Large winter gull roost (up to 50,000+), mostly Black-headed, Common & Mediterranean.

Other: Ruddy Darter and Migrant Hawker dragonflies.

Directions: BS40 6HN; ST 570 581. (Avon WT reserve at Herriotts Bridge). Nine miles S of Bristol. Take B3114 south from Chew Stoke, bear L for West Harptree and head NE on A368. View reserve from causeway at Herriots Bridge, where there is car parking.

Public transport: None.

Visiting: Permit (fee) required to enter reservoir enclosure and to use access road, paths and five hides—available to members of recognized ornithological/naturalist societies—contact Bristol Water. Roadside viewing at Herons Green Bay (parking for coaches) and Herriots Bridge.

Public trails/hide (Hollow Brook), E shore: Grebe Trail (0.75 mile long), hard surface for wheelchairs, dogs on leads. Unsurfaced Bittern Trail (one mile) leads to hide—can be muddy. No dogs.

Contact: Avon WT: 0117 917 7270; hello@avonwildlifetrust.org.uk; Bristol Water, Woodford Lodge, Chew Stoke, BS18 8SH. 01275 332 339.

Gloucestershire

The Forest of Dean/Wye Valley, between the River Severn and the Welsh border, is a good place to find Goshawk, Wood Warbler, Pied Flycatcher and Hawfinch. The Symonds Yat Peregrine Falcon watch point is worth a visit. On the east bank of the river, the iconic wetlands of Slimbridge are well-known for wintering geese and Bewick's Swans whilst the sand and gravel pits of the Cotswold Water Park, one of the largest man-made wetland complexes in the UK, attracts wintering waterfowl and passage waders.

Bird Atlases/Avifauna
The Birds of Gloucestershire
Gordon Kirk & John Phillips
(Liverpool University Press, 2013).
Available as a free electronic version:
www.glosnats.org/publications-birds
Birds of The Cotswolds: A New Breeding Atlas
Iain Main, Dave Pearce & Tim Hutton
(Liverpool University Press 2009).

Bird Recorder
Richard Baatsen: 07879 850 196;
glos.bird.recorder@gmail.com (excl. S.Gloucs = Avon)

Bird Report
Gloucestershire Bird Report (1948-), from GNS,
50 Kingsmead, Abbymead, Gloucester, GL4 5DY:
gnsmembership@btinternet.com

BTO Regional Representative
Gordon Kirk
Wetland Bird Survey (WeBS)
Local Organizers: webs@bto.org
Cotswold Water Park (Gloucs/Wilts)
Claire Carpenter
Gloucestershire
(inc. Severn Estuary, excl. CWP)
Michael Smart

Clubs
Gloucestershire Naturalists' Society (1948; 450)
Andrew Bluett (Membership Sec), c/o 50 Kingsmead, Abbymead, Gloucester, GL4 5DY: 07584 689 090 or 01452 610 085; gnsmembership@btinternet.com
www.glosnats.org
Meetings: Contact/see website for details.
Cheltenham Bird Club (1976; 100)
contact@cheltenhambirdclub.org.uk;
www.cheltenhambirdclub.org.uk
Meetings: 7:15pm, most Mondays (Oct-Mar), Belmont School, Warden Hill Road, Cheltenham, GL51 3AT. Monthly field meetings throughout year to local and more distant sites. Contact/see website for details.

Dursley Birdwatching & Preservation Society (1953; 150) dursleybirders@gmail.com; www.dbwps.org.uk
Meetings: 7:45pm, last Monday of the month (Sep-Apr). Dursley Community Centre, Rednock Drive, Dursley, GL11 4BX. Field Trips twice monthly throughout the year, both locally and further afield.
We also run a small grant scheme for local charities with conservation aims.

Ringing Groups/Bird Observatory
Cotswold Water Park RG
Severn Estuary Gull Group

RSPB Local Group
Gloucestershire (1973; 200)
Rachel Hickley: racheleditor@btinternet.com;
https://group.rspb.org.uk/gloucestershire/
Meetings: 7:30pm, 3rd Tuesday of the month (Sep & Mar in person; Oct-Nov/Jan-Feb via zoom). Also field meeting. All meeting free for members; £3 for non-members. Contact/see website for details.

Wildlife Trust
Gloucestershire Wildlife Trust (1961; 27,000)
Conservation Centre, Robinswood Hill Country Park, Reservoir Road, Gloucester, GL4 6SX: 01452 383 333; info@gloucestershirewildlifetrust.co.uk;
www.gloucestershirewildlifetrust.co.uk

I BAN-Y-GOR & LANCAUT
Gloucestershire Wildlife Trust
Habitats: Two reserves (140 acres in total both SSSI) sharing same car park. **Ban-y-Gor** occupies the N slopes, **Lancaut** the S slopes of the narrow neck of land formed by a loop of the River Wye. Damp ancient coppiced and pollarded woodland on N-facing slopes down to the Wye (**Ban-y-Gor**) and ancient woodland in disused quarries on S facing slopes at **Lancaut**, with cliffs, scree and saltmarsh (Wye is still tidal). See Gwent for **Piercefield Woods** on other side of Wye.
Birds: Breeding Peregrine Falcon and Raven on the cliffs, as well as Goshawk, Sparrowhawk and Kestrel. Cormorant, Grey Heron on the Wye.
Other: Ancient coppiced woodland on N-facing slopes of **Ban-y-Gor** with ferns and mosses; and ancient gorge woodland (Whitebeam, Wild Service, Small-leaved Lime, Wayfaring, amidst Yew, Oak and Beech) in disused limestone quarries on S-facing slopea at **Lancaut**.
Directions: NP 16 7JB; ST 536 967, car park (permissive) for both sites. Head NE out of Chepstow on A48 then take B4228 in Tutshill and head N. After 1.65 mile, take Lancaut Lane on L to car park.
Public transport:
Visiting: Open all hours, free, no facilities. Slopes steep. Follow waymarked trails, can be muddy, not climbers'

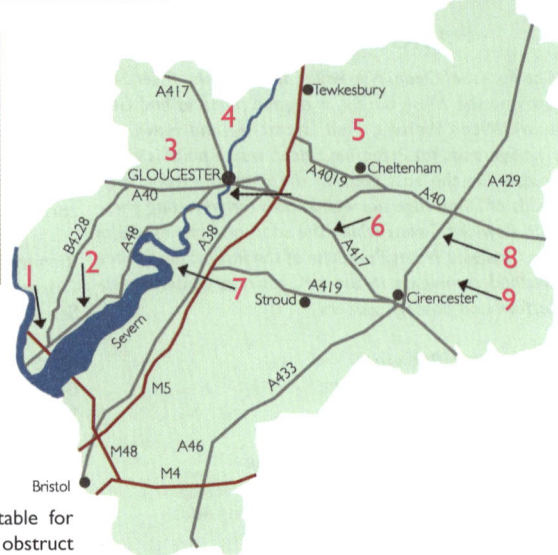

1 Ban-y-Gor/Lancaut
8 Chedworth & Withington Woods
5 Coombe Hill Canal & Meadows
6 Crickley Hill
4 Highnam Woods
3 Nagshead
2 Park, The & Poor's Allotment
7 Slimbridge
9 Whelford Pools

trails to bottom of cliffs. Benches. Not suitable for wheelchairs. Dogs under control. Do not obstruct lanes for farm traffic.
Contact: Gloucestershire WT: 01452 383 333; info@gloucestershirewildlifetrust.co.uk
Continue N on B4228 for just over 2 miles.

2 PARK, THE & POOR'S ALLOTMENT
Gloucestershire Wildlife Trust
Habitats: Heathland, grassland/scrub, ponds, woodland.
Birds: All year: Common scrub/woodland spp, Linnet, Stonechat, Yellowhammer, *Spring/summer:* Common warblers, Nightjar, Woodcock. *Winter:* Jack Snipe.
Other: Slow Worm, Common Lizard, Dormouse. Butterflies, orchids.
Directions: GL15 6PT; ST 558 992. 3.5 miles NE of Chepstow. Follow B4228 from Chepstow towards Coleford. Tidenham Chase car park is on L after passing turning to Boughspring. Sites either side of B4228.
Public transport: None.
Visiting: Open all hours. Car park (Tidenham Chase). 1.6 mile circular walk taking in both areas & easy access to the adjoining Tidenham Chase (Forestry England). Wider countryside walks, inc Offa's Dyke.
Contact: Gloucestershire WT: 01452 383 333; info@gloucestershirewildlifetrust.co.uk
Return to B4228 and continue N Coleford whence take B4431 E to Parkend, car park on L just before Parkend.

3 NAGSHEAD
RSPB
Habitats: Much of reserve is 200-year-old oak plantations, grazed in some areas by sheep, with a mixture of open areas, conifer/mixed woodland.
Birds: All year: Buzzard, Goshawk, Woodcock, 3 spp. woodpeckers, Raven, Hawfinch, Crossbill, good numbers all year. *Spring/Summer:* Pied & Spotted Flycatchers,

Wood Warbler and common warblers, Redstart, Tree Pipit. *Winter:* Mandarin, Siskin, other finches.
Other: Golden-ringed Dragonfly seen annually. White Admiral, Silver-washed and Small Pearl-bordered Fritillary butterflies present. Wild Boar in wider area.
Directions: GL15 4LA; SO 606 085. In Forest of Dean, N of Lydney. Signposted immediately W of Parkend village on B4431 road to Coleford.
Public transport: Bus: 27 (not Sun) Lydney to Parkend. Stagecoach.
Visiting: Free, opening times vary through year, check website as manned by volunteers. Coach/minibus access, advise in advance. Visitor centre (with toilets) open 11am-3pm at weekends, 1st week Apr-last week Sep plus Bank Holidays and Wed in school holidays. Two circular waymarked nature trails (one mile and 2.25 miles)—trails hilly but there is limited wheelchair access.
Two woodland hides not accessible to wheelchairs. Keep dogs on leads during bird nesting season.
Contact: RSPB: 01594 562 852; nagshead@rspb.org.uk; preferably use e-mail; www.rspb.org.uk/nagshead
Head NE from Coleford on A4136, then A40

4 HIGHNAM WOODS
RSPB
Habitats: Ancient woodland in Severn Vale with areas of coppice, scrub.
Birds: All year: Buzzard, Sparrowhawk, 3 spp woodpecker, Marsh Tit, Raven. Hawfinch possible but elusive.
Spring/summer: Nightingale still breeding but declining, Spotted Flycatcher and common migrant warblers. *Winter:* Feeding site near car park good for woodland birds.

Other: Tintern Spurge in Jun-Aug. White Admiral, Wood White and White-letter Hairstreak butterflies.

Directions: GL2 8AA; SO 778 190. Signposted on A40, three miles W of Gloucester.

Public transport: Bus: 24 (Mon-Sun) and 33 (Sun) Gloucester to Cinderford stops near Highnam Woods. Stagecoach.

Visiting: Open all hours. Car park now closed for the foreseeable future but access on foot still possible. One nature trail (1.5 miles)—can be very muddy, some limited wheelchair access. One open-backed hide, 150 yards from car park. Dogs allowed on leads.

Contact: RSPB 01594 562 852; highnam.woods@rspb.org.uk; preferably use e-mail.
Continue into Gloucester, then NE on A38.

5 COOMBE HILL CANAL AND MEADOWS

Gloucestershire Wildlife Trust.

Habitats: Wet grassland/flood meadow, ditches, canal, scrub.

Birds: Spring/summer: Little, Great White & Cattle Egrets. Breeding waders inc Avocet, Oystercatcher, Lapwing, Little Ringed Plover, Redshank. Yellow Wagtail, warblers. *Passage:* Garganey, waders inc Whimbrel, Ruff, Black-tailed Godwit, Common Sandpiper. *Winter:* Peregrine Falcon, wildfowl (inc Pintail, Teal, Wigeon, Whooper Swans), Bittern (rarely), Water Rail, Snipe, winter thrushes. Kingfisher.

Other: 17 spp dragonflies inc Hairy, Emperor & Scarce Chaser. Scarce plants inc Common Meadow-rue, Fine-leaved Water-dropwort, Golden Dock, True Fox Sedge, Greater Dodder.

Directions: GL19 4BB; SO 886 272. Midway between Gloucester and Tewkesbury off A38 at Coombe Hill. At crossroads in Coombe Hill take small no through road (The Wharf, by the Swan Inn) to car park. 0.5 mile walk from car park along canal towpath to entrance.

Public transport: Bus: 71 Gloucester to Tewkesbury—stops near Swan Inn, Coombe Hill, Stagecoach (01452 418 630).

Visiting: Open all hours. Small car park. Hide, paths level but can get rutted/muddy. Floods in Winter months. Dogs on a lead/not allowed on permissive paths.

Contact: Gloucestershire WT: 01452 383 333; info@gloucestershirewildlifetrust.co.uk
Return to Gloucester and either head E to

6 CRICKLEY HILL

Gloucestershire Wildlife Trust.

Habitats: Limestone grassland, scrub, woodland.

Birds: All year: Red Kite, Buzzard, Kestrel, common woodland spp. *Summer:* Cuckoo, common warblers, hirundines.

Other: Butterflies, limestone grassland flora.

Directions: GL4 8JY; SO 928 162. Near Birdlip (between Gloucester & Cheltenham). From Gloucester take A417 to Air Balloon roundabout, then first exit on to A436 and an immediate L on to Leckhampton Hill. Crickley Hill is on L.

Public transport: None.

Visiting: All year. Gate at entrance to Crickley Hill open 6am-6pm (Oct-Mar); 6am-9pm (Apr-Sep). Pay & display car park (not suitable for coaches/minibuses). Visitor centre, toilets, shop, cafe—open 9:30am-4:30pm (4pm in winter). Various trails, some accessible for wheelchairs/pushchairs, picnic area. Dogs welcome, on leads when stock on site.

Contact: Gloucestershire WT: 01452 383 333; info@gloucestershirewildlifetrust.co.uk
Or S to

7 WWT SLIMBRIDGE WETLAND CENTRE

The Wildfowl & Wetlands Trust

Habitats: Reedbed, freshwater pools, wet grassland, saltmarsh, mudflats. Captive waterfowl ponds.

Birds: 200+ spp annually, good list of rarities. *Breeding:* Garganey, Gadwall, Tufted Duck, Shelduck, Lapwing, Avocet, Oystercatcher, Redshank, Little Ringed Plover, Water Rail, Cranes, Marsh Harrier, Common Tern, Kingfisher, Cuckoo, Reed Bunting and a good range of warblers. *Passage:* Wind-blown seabirds, waders, terns (inc Arctic, a few Little, Black & Sandwich) and gulls (inc Little, Mediterranean & Yellow-legged). Osprey, Yellow Wagtail, Whinchat and Wheatear and large passerine movements. Hobbies now reach double figures in summer. *Winter:* 10,000 wildfowl esp Bewick's Swan (declining), White-fronted Goose, Wigeon, Teal, Pintail, Tufted Duck and Pochard. Bittern. Waders inc Lapwing, Black-tailed Godwit, Golden Plover, Spotted Redshank and Little Stint. Large roosts of up to 25,000 gulls, Peregrine Falcon and Goshawk.

Other: Brown Hare, Roe Deer, Otter, Polecat and Water Vole. Grass Snake. 27 spp dragonflies inc Scarce Chaser, Hairy Dragonfly and Willow Emerald.

Directions: GL2 7BT; SO 723 048. On banks of River Severn, S of Gloucester. Signposted from M5 (exit J13 or 14). Into Slimbridge from A38.

Public transport: Local buses stop on A38. Pre-bookable Robin bus service drops at Slimbridge. Train—stations at Cam and Dursley (4 miles).

Visiting: Open daily (not 25 Dec), 9:30am-5:30pm (5pm Feb & Mar), last entry one hour before closing. Large car park with toilets. Admission charges for non-WWT members. Restaurant, shop, toilets, Changing Places Toilet, Scott House Museum, gallery, cinema, soft play. Outdoor facilities inc a wildfowl collection of spp from around world, an observatory and observation tower, 13 hides including Estuary Tower with lift and roof terrace. Plenty of family attractions inc a pond zone, aviary, Living Wetland Theatre, bird demonstrations, commentated swan feeds in winter, 4x4 safaris and a canoe safari trail. All paths wheelchair accessible (wheelchair and mobility scooter hire available, book in advance). Binoculars for hire. Assistance dogs only. *Contact:* WWT Slimbridge Wetland Centre: 01453 891 900; info.slimbridge@wwt.org.uk *Or head E on A40. 8.5 miles E of Cheltenham take minor road S for Compton Abdale. Continue S for another 1.25 miles, then fork L Car park on R after 1 mile.*

8 CHEDWORTH AND WITHINGTON WOODS

National Trust (Chedworth)
Habitats: Semi-natural woodland, surrounding grassland, farmland.
Birds: *All year:* common woodland spp (inc. Marsh Tit), possible Lesser Spotted Woodpecker, Red Kite, Buzzard, Sparrowhawk, Little Owl (adjacent farmland with suitable trees/old buildings), Raven, Yellowhammer. Mandarin (adjacent fields where River Coln passes close to woodland). *Summer:* Swift/House Martin breed around villa. Common warblers inc Garden and Lesser Whitethroat. *Winter:* Woodcock, Siskin, Redpoll, Brambling, occasional Hawfinch.
Other: Roman Snail. Roe, Fallow and Muntjac Deer. Butterflies.
Directions: GL54 3LJ (Chedworth Roman Villa); SP 056 135. Lies between Cheltenham & Cirencester, 1.5 miles E of Yanworth. Follow the Roman Villa brown sign from A429 at Fossbridge.
Public transport: None.
Visiting: Woodlands can be accessed from Roman Villa car park, open daily. There is an entrance fee if you want to visit the villa. Visitor centre/cafe/shop/toilets etc. open 10am-5pm. A number of public footpaths start from car park, inc a disused railway line providing limited access to centre of wood.
Contact: National Trust: 01242 890 256; chedworth@nationaltrust.org.uk
Continue S on A429 and minor road to A417, then head E.

9 WHELFORD POOLS

Gloucestershire Wildlife Trust
Habitats: Former gravel pit workings—two large lakes, three smaller dragonfly pools.
Birds: *Spring/summer:* Common Tern, Kingfisher, Nightingale, plus breeding Great Crested Grebe, Sedge Warbler and Reed Bunting. Artificial nesting bank for Sand Martins. *Passage:* Waders. *Winter:* Wildfowl inc Wigeon, Pochard and Tufted Ducks, occasional Bittern sightings.
Other: County's only site for Pea Mussel. Emperor, Migrant Hawker, Black-tailed Skimmer and Red-eyed Damselfly all breed.
Directions: GL7 4DY; SU 172 995. Lakes lie in eastern section of Cotswold Water Park between Fairford and Lechlade, from minor road S of A417.
Public transport: Cycle path from Lechlade.

Visiting: Open all hours. Car park for 12 vehicles (one disabled bay). Two bird hides. Dogs must be on leads. *Contact:* Gloucestershire WT: 01452 383 333; info@gloucestershirewildlifetrust.co.uk

Wiltshire

The chalk Marlborough Downs and the extensive Salisbury Plain are internationally threatened habitats and occupy most of the county. The Plain is largely used as a training ground by the Army and there is limited public access, so the birds, including breeding Quail, Stone Curlew and the reintroduced Great Bustard, are subject to less disturbance than those on the Downs. The Wildlife Trust manages nearly 40 reserves across a range of habitats.

Bird Atlas/Avifauna
Birds of Wiltshire
J Ferguson-Lees, P Castle & P Cranswick (Wiltshire Ornithological Society, 2007).

Bird Recorder
Paul Castle, Wiltshire & Swindon Biological Records Centre, Elm Tree Court, Long Street, Devizes, SN10 1NJ:
recorderwiltsbirds@gmail.com

Bird Report
Wiltshire Bird Report (Hobby) (1975-), from WOS—Sales Manager: sales@wiltshirebirds.co.uk

BTO Regional Representative
North
Robin Smith
South
Robin Smith
Wetland Birds Survey (WeBS)
Local Organizers: webs@bto.org
Avon Valley
See **Hampshire.**
Cotswold Water Park
See **Gloucestershire**
Wiltshire
Jennifer Stunell

Clubs
Wiltshire Ornithological Society (1974; 508).
David Little (Chair): chair@wiltshirebirds.co.uk; www.wiltshirebirds.co.uk
Contact/see website for details.
Salisbury & District Natural History Society (1952; 110).
John Pitman (Ornithology Section): 01722 327 395; jacpitman@btinternet.com;

Wiltshire

www.salisburynaturalhistory.com
Meetings: 7:30pm, 3rd Thursday of the month (Sep-Apr). The Meeting Room, Salisbury Baptist Church, Brown Street, Salisbury, SP1 2AS.

Ringing Groups/Bird Observatory
Cotswold Waterpark RG
North Wilts RG
Wessex RG
West Wilts RG
www.westwiltsringinggroup.wordpress.com

RSPB Local Group
South Wiltshire (1986; 500+).
Tony Goddard: goddard543@hotmail.com; https://group.rspb.org.uk/southwiltshire/
Meetings: 7.30pm, 2nd Tuesday of the month (Sep-Oct & Mar-Apr). Salisbury Methodist Church, St Edmund's Church Street, Salisbury SP1 1EF. Also Zoom talks (Nov-Feb).
Contact/see website for details.

Wildlife Trust
Wiltshire Wildlife Trust (1962; 23,000).
Elm Tree Court, Long Street, Devizes, SN10 1NJ. 01380 725 670; info@wiltshirewildlife.org; www.wiltshirewildlife.org

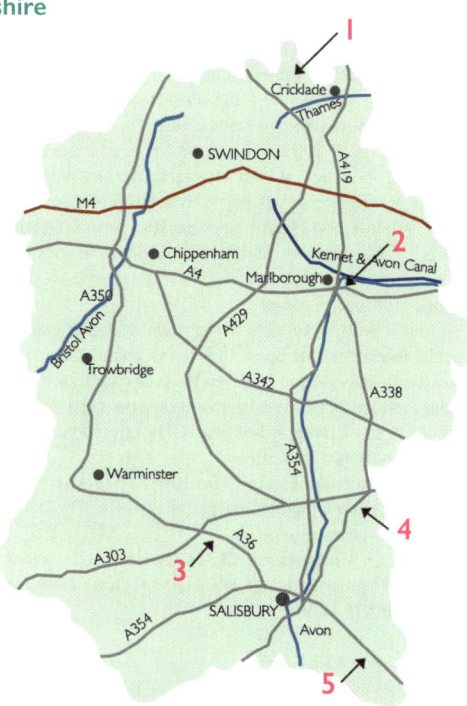

1	Cleveland Lakes
3	Langford Lakes
5	Langley Wood
2	Savernake Forest
4	Winterbourne Down

Instead of heading E to Whelford Pools in Gloucestershire, join A419 at Cirencester.

1 CLEVELAND LAKES
Cotswold Lakes Trust
Habitats: Lakes with islands, scrapes, lagoons, reedbed, marsh, ditches, loafing areas. [Part of Cotswold Lakes, formerly known as Cotswold Water Park, covering 42 sq. miles/180 lakes, across Wilts, Gloucs & W Oxfordshire]
Birds: Summer: Breeding ducks, Great Crested Grebe, Hobby, Sand Martin, warblers, Reed Bunting, Little Egret, Grey Heron. *Winter:* Large numbers wildfowl spp, plus Bittern, Water Rail, Stonechat. These and passage waders also viewable from "Twitchers' Gate" on the lane to N of Lake 74 (SU 065 946).
Other: Otter, Water Vole, several spp of dragonfly and butterfly.
Directions: SN6 6QW; SU 059 933 (Waterhay Car Park). Lakes 68A/B and 74 of Cotswold Water Park. From A419 Cirencester to Swindon road, take B4696 towards Cotswold Water Park West (passing Gateway Centre). After 1.5 miles turn L on to Fridays Ham Lane. Follow road to Ashton Keynes village and turn L to Cricklade/Leigh road. Waterhay Car Park is on L next

to River Thames. Take bridleway north to kissing gate on R. Permissive path follows southern edge of Lake 68A/B before turning N towards hide.
Public transport: Bus: 51—Swindon-Cheltenham-Cirencester stops at Gateway Centre. Stagecoach West.
Visiting: Open all hours. Car park, most paths firm and flat but subject to severe flooding in winter. Dogs on short leads at all times. Toilets, refreshments and information available at Gateway Centre next to A419.
Contact: Cotswold Lakes Trust: 01793 752 413; info@cotswoldlakestrust.org; www.cotswoldlakestrust.org
Continue S on A419, then A346 from Swindon to Marlborough.

2 SAVERNAKE FOREST
Savernake Estate.
Habitats: Chalk grassland, woodland.
Birds: All year: Sparrowhawk, Buzzard, Red Kite, Woodcock, owls, 3 spp woodpeckers, Marsh & Willow Tits, Jay, other woodland birds. *Spring/summer:* Garden Warbler, Blackcap, Willow Warbler, Chiffchaff, Wood Warbler, Redstart, occasional Nightingale, Tree Pipit, Spot-

ted Flycatcher. *Winter:* Finch flocks possibly inc Siskin, Redpoll, Brambling and Hawfinch.

Other: Rare lichens and fungi, all main deer spp apart from Red. Badger, Fox. Ancient trees.

Directions: SN8 3HN; SU 210 683 E of Marlborough. From Marlborough, A4 to Hungerford runs along N side of forest. Two pillars mark Forest Hill entrance on A4, 1.5 mile E of A346/A4 junction. The 'Grand Avenue' leads straight through middle of woodland to join minor road from Stibb.

Public transport: None.

Visiting: Privately owned—no vehicular rights of way or public footpaths but open all year to public. Car park, picnic site at NW end by A346. Visitors can drive along main avenues, but all roads closed on one day a year—usually first working day of year. Only enter fenced-off areas if there is a footpath.

Contact: Savernake Estate Office: 01672 512 161; savernakeestate1@gmail.com; www.savernakeestate.co.uk

Head S from Marlborough on A346 towards Salisbury then W on A303, passing to the S of Parsomage Down NNR. The A303 joins A36 to W of

3 LANGFORD LAKES

Wiltshire Wildlife Trust.

Habitats: Four former gravel pits, with islands and reed fringes. 78 acres, with 39 acres of open water, also wet meadow and woodland, scrub, chalk river.

Birds: 150+ spp. Visiting Marsh Harrier, Barn Owl and Peregrine Falcon. *Summer:* Breeding Coot, Moorhen, Tufted Duck, Pochard, Gadwall, Little & Great Crested Grebe. Hobby, Kingfisher, Common Sandpiper, Grey Wagtail, warblers (eight spp). *Passage:* Sand Martin, Green Sandpiper and other waders, Black Tern. *Winter:* Common wildfowl—Wigeon, Shoveler, Teal, Water Rail, Little Egret, occasionally Bittern.

Other: Otter, Water Vole, Water Shrew. Spawning Salmon and Trout in river.

Directions: SP3 4NH; SU 037 370. Nr Steeple Langford, S of A36, approx eight miles W of Salisbury. In centre of village, turn S into Duck Street, signposted Hanging Langford. Langford Lakes is first L just after small bridge.

Public transport: Bus: 265 (not Sun) Salisbury to Bath stops in Steeple Langford (0.3 mile from reserve). First West of England.

Visiting: Reserve open 24/7 unless winds dangerously high. Advance notice required for coaches. Visitor centre, cafe, toilets, education centre. Trails and five hides, accessible to wheelchairs. Cycle racks (reserve 250 yards from Wiltshire Cycleway between Great Wishford and Hanging Langford). No dogs.

Contact: Wiltshire WT: 01380 725 670; info@wiltshirewildlife.org

Continue E on A303.

4 WINTERBOURNE DOWNS

RSPB

Habitats: Flower-rich chalk grassland, woodland, cultivated plots with wild bird seed margins.

Birds: All year: Buzzard, Red Kite, Grey Partridge, Skylark, Linnet, Corn Bunting (now regular), Yellowhammer (declining). *Spring/summer:* Stone Curlew, Lapwing, Whitethroat. *Winter:* Redwing, Fieldfare, finches and buntings.

Other: Butterflies, chalkland flora. Brown Hare, Roe Deer.

Directions: SP4 0HE; SU 214 401. NE of Salisbury. From A303, follow directions to Newton Tony. Drive through village & turn R at Allington sign into Station Hill. Car park on R at brow of hill. From Salisbury, take A338 N to Allington. Turn R at Newton Tony sign, follow the road through Allington and along single track road towards Newton Tony. Car park on L at top of hill.

Public transport: Bus: 67/67X (not Sun) Salisbury to Tidworth, alight at Newton Tony primary school and walk up Station Road to reserve car park on R. Stagecoach South (0345 241 8000).

Visiting: Open all hours (not 20-21 Jun/summer solstice). Car park (10 spaces, one Blue Badge space, cycle rack, height restriction). Two marked circular trails, two viewing screens (for Stone-curlew). Picnic area.

Contact: RSPB: 01980 629 215; info.wiltshirereserves@rspb.org.uk

Stay on A346 to Salisbury, then take A36 heading SE.

5 LANGLEY WOOD NNR

Natural England.

Habitats: Ancient oak woodland (marks northern tip of New Forest).

Birds: All Year: Buzzard, Sparrowhawk, common woodland spp, 3 spp. woodpeckers, Hawfinch, Crossbill, Siskin. *Summer:* Hobby (open areas), Woodcock, Cuckoo, Nightjar, Tree Pipit, Redstart, warblers (inc Wood), Spotted Flycatcher, Firecrest. *Winter:* Redpoll.

Other: 600 spp fungi, flora (inc Bluebell spectacle, Yellow Bird's Nest), butterflies (inc Silver-washed & Pearl-bordered Fritillaries), 5 spp deer, Dormouse, bats.

Directions: SP5 2PB; SU 219 203. Ten miles SE Salisbury. From A36 between Salisbury and Southampton take B3079 at Landford. Take 1st R (Hamptworth Road) and follow to reserve entrance—2.5 miles along this road.

Public transport: Bus: 44 Salisbury–Woodfalls (not Sun/bank hols) stops at Lover (Redlynch Church stop, 0.6 mile from reserve gate—*CARE* no pavement). Salisbury Reds: 01202 338 420.

Visiting: Open all hours. Small parking area by gate (noticeboard showing paths). Paths can be muddy when wet.

Contact: Natural England: 07771 944 557.

*For **Hampshire**, head back to Salisbury.*

Hampshire
and Isle of Wight

This huge county includes the New Forest, which holds such scarce breeding birds as Honey Buzzard, Goshawk, Firecrest, Hawfinch, Dartford Warbler and Nightjar, together with regular Great Grey Shrike in winter. The marshes at Keyhaven, Farlington and elsewhere around the Solent are the best sites for migrants and for wintering wildfowl and waders. Blashford Lakes has a good selection of waterbirds including wintering Bittern. White-tailed reintroduction to Isle of Wight.

Bird Atlases/Avifauna
Rare Birds of Hampshire
John Clark
(Hampshire Ornithological Society, 2022).
Hampshire Bird Atlas 2007-2012
John Eyre (ed)
(Hampshire Ornithological Society, 2015).
Birds of Hampshire
JM Clark & JA Eyre,
(Hampshire Ornithological Society, 1993).

Bird Recorders
Hampshire
Martin Pitt: 07926 841 139; mjpitt35clere@hotmail.com
Isle of Wight
Robin Attrill, 17 Waterhouse Moor, Harlow, Essex CM18 6BA. 07487 557 103; robinpattrill@gmail.com

Bird Reports
Hampshire
Hampshire Bird Report (1978-), from HOS—Nicola Whitmarsh.: 01489 853 116; hos.nwhitmarsh@yahoo.com
Isle of Wight
Isle of Wight Bird Report (1996-), from IOWOG.
Dave Hunnybun, 40 Church Hill Road, Cowes, IoW PO31 8HH davehunnybun@hotmail.com

BTO Regional Representatives
Hampshire
George Batho
Isle of Wight
Drew Lyness
Wetland Bird Survey (WeBS)
Local Organizer: webs@bto.org
Avon Valley
John Clark
Hampshire (Estuaries/Coastal)
Geoff Butler
Hampshire (Inland—excl. Avon Valley)
Keith Wills
Isle of Wight: Vacant

Clubs
Hampshire Ornithological Society (1979; 2,250).
Dave Palmer (Sec), 2 Dunmow Hill, Fleet, Hants, GU51 3AN: 07399 903 499; dave.palmer64@btinternet.com; www.hos.org.uk
Meetings: Members' Day at the end of March—contact/see website for details.
Isle of Wight Natural History & Archaeological Society (1919; 350).
Jackie Hart (Sec), Unit 16, Prospect Business Centre, West Cowes, IoW PO31 7HD: 01983 282 596; iwnhas@btconnect.com; www.iwnhas.org
Meetings: Includes a Bird Group—contact/see website for details.
Isle Of Wight Ornithological Group (1986; 148).
Dave Hunnybun (Sec), 40 Churchill Road, Cowes, IoW PO31 8HH: 01983 292 880; davehunnybun@hotmail.com; https://iwogroup.org.uk
Meetings: Monthly outdoor meetings & AGM.

Ringing Groups/Bird Observatory
Farlington RG
Fishlake Meadows RG
Isle of Wight RG.
Itchen RG
New Forest RG
https://mobile.twitter.com/nf_ringinggroup
Titchfield Haven RG
Wessex RG

RSPB Local Groups
Basingstoke (1979; 55).
Peter E. Hutchins: RSPBbasingstoke@gmail.com; https://group.rspb.org.uk/basingstoke/
Meetings: 7:45pm, 3rd Monday of the month (Sep-May). Church Cottage, St Michael's Church, Church Square, Basingstoke, RG21 7QW.
New Forest (2000; 165).
Keith Partridge: 01425 652864; newforestgroup@rspb.org.uk; https://group.rspb.org.uk/newforest/
Meetings: 7:30pm, 2nd Wednesday of the month (Sep-Jun).
Lyndhurst Community Centre, off High Street, Lyndhurst, SO43 7NY.
Field trips detailed on website.
North East Hants (1976; 145).
Sue Radbourn: nehantsRSPB@gmail.com; https://group.rspb.org.uk/northeasthants/
Meetings: 7:30pm, (Sep-Apr)—contact/see website for details. At either Memorial Hall, Sandy Lane, Church Crookham, GU52 8LD or St Phillip and St James Church Hall, Kings Road, Fleet, GU51 3AR.
Portsmouth (1974; 177).
Matt Coumbe: portsmouthRSPB@gmail.com; https://group.rspb.org.uk/portsmouth/

Hampshire

Meetings: 7:30pm, 4th Wednesday of the month (Sep-Jun). St Wilfrid's Church Hall, Padnell Road, Waterlooville, PO8 8DZ.

Winchester & District (1974; 80).
Martin Keys: WinchRSPB1974@gmail.com;
https://group.rspb.org.uk/winchester/
Meetings: 7.30pm, 1st Wednesday of the month (not Jan or Aug). Shawford Parish Hall, Pearson Lane, Shawford, Winchester, SO21 2AA.

Wildlife Trust
Hampshire & Isle Of Wight Wildlife Trust (1960; 29,000)
Beechcroft, Vicarage Lane, Curdridge, SO32 2DP.
01489 774 400; reception@hiwwt.org.uk;
www.hiwwt.org.uk

New Forest National Park Authority
Lymington Town Hall, Avenue Road,
Lymington, SO41 9ZG
01590 648 600 (general enquiries);
via website;
www.newforestnpa.gov.uk

If entering from Wiltshire, take A354 from Salisbury

1 MARTIN DOWN NNR
Natural England/Hampshire County Council
Habitats: 842 acres, unimproved chalk downland, scrub, woodland/hazel coppice.
Birds: All year: Yellowhammer, Skylark. *Spring/summer:* Grey Partridge, Turtle Dove, Nightingale (all now scarce), Cuckoo, plus warblers inc Lesser Whitethroat. *Winter:* Occasional Merlin, Hen Harrier.
Other: 20+ spp butterflies. Species-rich chalk downland with variety of orchids, Pasqueflower and Milkwort.
Directions: SP5 5RH; SU 036 200 (main car park). Fourteen miles SW of Salisbury, 0.6 mile W of Martin village. N part of site is crossed by the A354. Main car park is on A354 and another at end of Sillens Lane, a minor road from Martin village.
Public transport: Bus: 20 (Mon-Fri) Salisbury to Blandford. Damory (01202 338 420).
Visiting: Open access, but organized groups of 10+ should book in advance. Two car parks, interpretive boards. Main car park height barrier (7ft 6 in), coaches by prior arrangement. Hard flat track from A354 car park suitable for wheelchairs.
Contact: Hampshire County Council: 01590 674 656; centralcountrysidesites@hants.gov.uk

Head SE on minor roads from Martin for Fordingbridge.

2 BLASHFORD LAKES
Hampshire & Isle of Wight Wildlife Trust/
Wessex Water/Bournemouth Water
Habitats: Flooded gravel pits, areas of wet ancient woodland, also dry grassland and lichen heath.
Birds: Spring/summer: Breeding birds inc Common Tern, Sand Martin (in artificial bank), Lapwing, Redshank, Oystercatcher, Little Ringed Plover. Kingfisher, Reed Warbler. *Autumn:* Waders on migration inc Green & Common Sandpipers and Greenshank, also Hobby, Black Tern and passerines. *Winter:* Up to 5,000 wintering wildfowl, inc internationally important numbers of Shoveler, Gadwall and Coot. Grey Heron, Little Egret and Bittern. Up to 9,000 gulls roost on Ibsley Water.
Other: 25 spp dragonflies inc Brown Hawker, Scarce Chaser, Large and Small Red-eyed damselflies. Roe Deer, Badger, Otter, Fox, reptiles inc Adder and Grass Snake.

Directions: BH24 3PJ; SU 151 083. From Ringwood take A338 for two miles towards Fordingbridge/Salisbury, pass Ivy Lane on R & take next R at Ellingham Cross, into Ellingham Drove. The main car park for hides is first L after 400 yards.

Public transport: Bus: X3 Bournemouth-Salisbury at Ellingham Cross, 500 yards W of main entrance. More Bus (01202 338 420).

Visiting: Car parks (coaches/groups by arrangement). Education centre/toilets, six hides open daily (not 25 Dec) 9am-4:30pm. Paths open outside these hours but no vehicle access. RADAR keys needed to open kissing gates for wheelchairs. Viewing screens, recent sightings board, webcams. No dogs.

Contact: Hampshire & Isle of Wight WT: BlashfordLakes@hiwwt.org.uk
Head S from Ringwood on B3347, then A35 for Lyndhurst.

3 ACRES DOWN

Within New Forest National Park.

Habitats: Woodland, heathland.

Birds: All year: Common woodland spp inc 3 spp Woodpeckers, Stonechat, Marsh Tit, Hawfinch. *Early spring/summer:* Goshawk and Honey Buzzard from raptor watch point. Hobby, Nightjar, Cuckoo, Woodlark, Redstart, warblers inc Dartford & Wood, Firecrest, Crossbill. *Winter:* Occasional Great Grey Shrike.

Other: Butterflies, dragonflies, reptiles.

Directions: SO43 7GE; SU 267 097 (car park). Head SW from Lyndhurst on A35, turn R after the Swan pub towards Emery Down, then bear R at the New Forest Inn towards Minstead. After 1.5 miles turn L to Acres Down—car park is beyond Acres Down Farm (take R fork).

Public transport: None.

Visiting: Open access. Small shop/refreshments at Acres Down Farm on lane just before car park. Dogs on lead Mar-July & under control at all other times.

Contact: New Forest National Park Authority: 01590 646 600 (general enquiries line); via website; www.newforestnpa.gov.uk.
B3056 SE from Lyndhurst for Beaulieu joins B3054.

4 NORTH SOLENT NNR/
NEEDS ORE

Natural England/Beaulieu Estate/
Game & Wildlife Conservation Trust

Habitats: 2,025 acres but fragmented and quite widely scattered. N shore of Solent and upstream along Beaulieu River. Tidal mudflat, lagoons, shingle, saltmarsh, also areas of heath and woodland.

Needs Ore, at the mouth of the Beaulieu River, occupying point of land between W bank of river and N shore of the Solent, is one area of the NNR. It consists of an island, shingle, mudflats, lagoons, saltmarsh and scrub.

Birds: 277 spp recorded at **Needs Ore.** Trials currently being undertaken in support of breeding Ringed Plover and Oystercatcher (main Hampshire breeding site for these species) and to encourage the return of breeding Terns (Common, Artic, Little & Sandwich). Measures include shingle covered rafts and islands, raised shingle platforms and the transformation of scrub and grassland into new areas of shingle higher up the shore, combined with predator exclusion.

Besides the above, the 277 include wintering waders (declining), passage migrants, scarce and common, vagrant Hoopoe and Bee-eater spp, and you might even glimpse a White-tailed Eagle.

Other:

Directions: SO42 7XJ; SZ 427 977 (Beaulieu River Sailing Club at Needs Ore). Gated access restricted to permit holders (see below). Leave the B3054 W of Beaulieu and take the minor road for Buckler's Hard. After 1.7 miles, before you reach Buckler's Hard, turn R for St Leonard's. After sharp R bend at St Leonard's, gated access track is on L.

Public transport: None.

Visiting: Areas quite widely scattered on both sides of the Beaulieu River and accessed separately. **Needs Ore,** which has a history of wardened access and protection for ground-nesting birds dating back to 1962, requires a permit to visit (see below) and access is restricted during the breeding season. A shore hide and one overlooking Black Water

Contact: Permits for Needs Ore: Beaulieu Estate office (01590 614 621; estate@beaulieu.co.uk).
NNR: Adam Wells, Natural England: 01590 616 236
GWCT: Mike Short: mshort@gwct.org.uk
Return to Lyndhurst, then M27 and M271

5 TESTWOOD LAKES NATURE RESERVE

Southern Water/Hampshire & Isle of Wight Wildlife Trust *Habitats:* Flooded gravel pits, scrapes, wet and dry grasslands, woodland and hedgerows.

Birds: Spring: Shelduck, Little Ringed Plover, Lapwing, Sand Martin, Willow Warbler. *Summer:* Swift, Swallow, Blackcap, Whitethroat. *Autumn:* Wheatear, Yellow Wagtail, Goldfinch. *Winter:* Wildfowl inc. Tufted Duck, Wigeon, Pochard, Teal, Gadwall, Goosander, Common & Green Sandpipers, Meadow Pipit, Redwing, Fieldfare, Siskin, Hawfinch.

Other: Variety of butterflies and dragonflies inc Emperor, Migrant Hawker and Golden-ringed.

Directions: SO40 3YD; SU 347 155. Take M271 West J2 towards Totton. L at first roundabout, then L on to A36. L at next roundabout onto Brunel Rd. Entrance on L after 0.25 mile.

Public transport: Bus: 12/X7 (not Sun) from Southampton stop at Testwood Crescent (0.5 mile from reserve)—Bluestar (01202 338421) / Salisbury Reds. Train—Totton is 1.5 miles from reserve.

Visiting: Car parks open 8am-5pm (4pm winter)—height restriction. Two hides (open 10am-4pm daily), two screens. Surfaced paths around lakes and to hides relatively flat—RADAR key (available at Centre) needed for wheelchair users to get through gates. Testwood Lakes Centre only open when staff at Centre for organized groups. Not open at weekends. Disabled toilet in Education Centre. All terrain wheelchair available to hire (book in advance). No dogs in conservation and education areas.

Contact: Hampshire & Isle of Wight Wildlife Trust: TestwoodLakes@hiwwt.org.uk

Return to M271, M27 and M3, take A272 for Petersfield, at J10, then R on to A32.

6 OLD WINCHESTER HILL NNR

Natural England

Habitats: Chalk grassland, scrub, woodland. Iron Age hill-fort. In South Downs National Park.

Birds: All year: Red Kite, Buzzard, Raven, Grey Partridge, Yellowhammer. *Summer/breeding:* Hobby, Turtle Dove, Whitethroat and other regular 'scrub' spp. *Passage:* Migrants inc Wheatear, Redstart, Whinchat, Ring Ouzel. Rarities have turned up from time to time. *Winter:* Raptors inc Hen Harrier (occasional), Peregrine Falcon, Merlin, winter thrushes.

Other: Species-rich chalk downland with variety of orchids, scarcities inc Round-headed Rampion & Field Fleawort, butterflies (37 spp recorded) inc Chalkhill Blue & Silver-spotted Skipper.

Directions: GU32 1HW; SU 646 214. Mid-way between Winchester and Petersfield. Approach off A32 Fareham to Alton road at Warnford. Just E of George & Falcon pub take Hayden Lane towards Clanfield. Small car park after 1.8 miles on R.

Public transport: Bus: 67 Winchester-Petersfield (not Sun)—stops at West Meon (two miles from reserve). Stagecoach in Hampshire (0345 121 0190).

Visiting: Open all hours. Car park (height barrier), picnic area and interpretation, well-marked footpaths. Fully accessible trail (towards hill-fort) at southern side of reserve with allocated disabled parking (RADAR key holders)—further along the lane from main car park. Dogs under close control (grazing stock).

Contact: Natural England: 0300 060 6000; enquiries@naturalengland.org.uk

S on A32, crossing M27, to A27, then head W.

7 TITCHFIELD HAVEN NNR

Hampshire County Council

Habitats: 370 acres, in Lower Meon valley. Shoreline, reedbeds, freshwater scrapes, wet grazing meadows.

Birds: 200+ spp. *Spring/summer:* Waders inc Avocet and Black-tailed Godwit, wildfowl, Common Tern, breeding Cetti's Warbler, Water Rail. *Autumn/winter:* Bittern, Kingfisher, Bearded Tit, Brent Geese, Wigeon, Teal, Shoveler

and Snipe. Occasional rarities at any time.

Other: Six spp nationally rare plants, Roe Deer, Badger and Pipistrelle Bat. Water Voles released in 2013. 19 spp dragonflies and 30+ spp butterflies.

Directions: PO14 3JT: SU 532 022. Located on Cliff Road, Hill Head in Fareham. Reach from A27 & B3334 W of Fareham. Council car park adjacent to Hill Head Sailing Club.

Public transport: Bus: 21 (not Sun) Stubbington to Fareham stops in Solent Road, 200 yards from reserve. First Bus.

Visiting: Charge for reserve. Open daily 9am-4pm (closed 24-26 Dec). Ticket kiosk. 7 hides (wheelchair access). Guided walks. Public footpath follows derelict canal along W side of reserve and road skirts S edge. Guide dogs only.

Contact: Titchfield Haven: 01329 662 145; titchfield.enquiries@hants.gov.uk

Return to A27, head E.

8 FARLINGTON MARSHES

Hampshire & Isle of Wight Wildlife Trust.

Habitats: Coastal grazing marsh with pools and reedbeds. Views over saltmarsh/intertidal mudflats of Langstone Harbour/ Langstone Harbour immediately W of **Chichester Harbour** in W Sussex.

Birds: Spring/summer: Passage waders. Breeding waders and wildfowl inc Shelduck, Lapwing, Redshank, Cetti's, Sedge & Reed Warblers, Bearded Tit. *Late summer:* Passage migrants—Yellow Wagtail, Whinchat, Wheatear etc. and returning waders, always a chance of rarities/less common spp inc Spotted Crake, Curlew Sandpiper, stints. *Autumn/winter:* Waders and wildfowl, good numbers of Teal, Wigeon, Pintail, Marsh Harrier, Short-eared Owl regular visitors. Internationally-important numbers of Dark-bellied Brent Goose and Bar-tailed Godwit. Important high tide roost site, best viewed over high spring tides.

Other: Corky Fruited Waterdropwort, Slender Hares-ear, Southern Marsh & Early Marsh Orchids. Water Vole.

Directions: PO6 1RN; SU 685 045. N of Langstone Harbour. Main entrance off roundabout junction A2030/A27—take small lane between the A27 westbound and A2030 Portsmouth road—height restriction barrier, three parking areas available.

Public transport: Bus: 21 Portsmouth to Havant stops by Farlington Sainsbury's (north of A27), 20 min walk to reserve. Stagecoach South (0345 121 0190). Train—Hilsea is 1.5 miles from reserve.

Visiting: Open all hours. 2.5 mile circular walk around sea wall, plenty of benches—exposed to wind and sea spray. Information at entrance and shelter. Paths mostly level but main track along sea wall uneven in places, muddy when wet. Short slopes up to sea wall. Wheelchair access via RADAR gates. Dogs on leads at all times.

Contact: Hampshire & Isle of Wight Wildlife Trust: feedback@hiwwt.org.uk
N on A2(M), A3, then A325 towards Farnham

9 ALICE HOLT FOREST
Forestry England.
Habitats: Mixed woodland, ponds.
Site made up of a series of inclosures.
Birds: Breeding: Woodcock, Nightjar, Tree Pipit, Spotted Flycatcher, Garden Warbler, Firecrest, Siskin. Common woodland spp inc Marsh Tit, Woodlark and Crossbill occasionally seen (may breed). *Winter:* Mandarin Duck (best seen in Straits Inclosure), Redwing, Fieldfare.
Other: Butterflies.
Directions: GU10 4LS; SU 812 417 (main centre). SW of Farnham. Take A325 from Farnham to Bucks Horn Oak and follow signs to Alice Holt.
Public transport: Bus:18 Aldershot, via Farnham, to Bordon—alight at stop after petrol station in Bucks Horn Oak.
Stagecoach (0345 241 8000). Train: Bentley & Farnham.
Visiting: Car park inc disabled bays open 8am-9pm (May-Sep, closing time earlier for rest of year)—charges apply/cashless payments only, membership available for regular visitors. Visitor Centre, cafe for take-away food & drinks, toilets inc. disabled. Various trails, many accessible for wheelchairs. Cycle hire.
There are also three small car parks (charge at Abbots Wood) to access some of the inclosures but all areas are accessible from the main car park. Abbotts Wood Inclosure SU 811 410 (on Dockenfield Street) and Straits Inclosure SU 802 434 (on Frith End Road) may be closed at certain times of year. Lodge & Holt Pond Inclosure SU 805 400 (on Gravel Hill Road).
Contact: Forestry England: 0300 067 4448; enquiries.aliceholt@forestryengland.uk
N from Farnham on A331, cross M3 and join A30.

10 YATELEY COMMON
Hampshire County Council/MOD
Habitats: Heathland, scrub, woodland, ponds.
Birds: All year: Woodcock, Woodlark, Dartford Warbler. Common woodland spp inc Green & Great Spotted Woodpeckers. *Spring/summer:* Little Grebe, Hobby, Nightjar, Tree Pipit, Linnet. *Winter:* Siskin, Redpoll.
Other: Fungi. Butterflies (inc Silver-studded Blue) and dragonflies. Adder, Grass Snake, Common Lizard.
Directions: Lies to W of Blackwater, bisected by A30 (HCC to N, MOD to S).
Various access points.
North:
(1) GU46 6BB; SU 821 598 (Wyndham's Pool Car Park, off Cricket Hill car park)
  Take Cricket Hill Lane, off A30 towards Yateley, car park (signposted) 0.5 mile on R.
(2) GU17 0AW; SU 833 591 (Stroud Pond Car Park)

Off A30, eastbound 0.9 mile from A327/Cricket Hill roundabout.
(3) GU17 0AS; SU 838 594 (Gravel Pit Car Park)
Off A30, eastbound 1.25 miles from A327/Cricket Hill roundabout.
South:
GU17 9LJ; SU 827 590
  Lay-by on A30, 1.2 miles westbound from A30/B3272 roundabout.
Public transport: Bus: 3 Aldershot to Yateley via Camberley. Alight at Potley Hill roundabout, walk 0.6 mile along Cricket Hill Lane to Wyndham's Pool car park entrance—west side of common or alight at Darby Green Chapel Corner for access to east Side of common. Stagecoach (0345 241 8000). Train—Blackwater, 0.6 mile E of east side of common.
Visiting: Open all year. Three car parks and lay-by parking. Network of paths & bridleways. Self-guided trail from Wyndham's Pool car park, Cricket Hill (1).
Contact: Hampshire County Council: 01252 870 425; northern.sites@hants.gov.uk
Return to A331 and then N on A321 for Berkshire.

The final two Hampshire reserves are on the Isle of Wight, reached by ferry services from various Hampshire ports. Newtown Harbour lies at the W end of the island.

11 NEWTOWN HARBOUR NNR
& OLD TOWN HALL
National Trust
Habitats: A tidal estuary with a narrow opening to the sea almost closed by sand spits fed by rivers that form 3 'lakes' at high tide, with a central tidal salt marsh. Mud flats and fringing woodland.
Birds: Primarily of interest for wintering wader and wildfowl: Dark-bellied Brent Goose, Wigeon, Teal, Pintail, Goldeneye, Red-breasted Merganser, Spoonbill, Golden, Grey & Ringed Plovers, Knot, Dunlin, Black-tailed Godwit, Greenshank. *Spring/autumn:* Osprey, a variety of other raptors, passage waders, Yellow Wagtail, Redstart, Wheatear, Whinchat, Spotted Flycatcher.
Other: Red Squirrel.
Directions: PO30 4PA; SZ 424 926). Visitor Point and car park at Old Town Hall, to S of confluence of rivers. Take minor road to N from A3054 at Winchester Corner, just before Shalfleet. Follow brown signs for car park for just over 1 mile.
Public transport: Bus: 7, Newport to Yarmouth, stops 1 mile from reserve at Shalfleet. See www.islandbuses.info
Visiting: Reserve dawn-dusk, car park (pay & display, NT members free), Old Town Hall currently closed for restoration but toilets (inc accessible) and cafe at Visitor Point (10am-5pm). Paths flat but can be muddy, 2 hides, one public, one two storey, best at low tide. Dogs on lead, clean up mess.

Newtown Harbout lies almost due S across Solent from **4 N Solent NNR**.

Contact: 01983 531 785; oldtownhall@nationaltrust.org.uk

Take A3054 E to Ryde, Brading Marshes lie at the E end of the island.

12 BRADING MARSHES
RSPB

Habitats: Low-lying grazing marsh and pasture re-claimed from the sea in 19C on either side of canalized River Yar, pools, woods on hills to S.

Birds: Water Rail, Little Egret, Marsh Harrier, Green Woodpecker, Cetti's Warbler. *Summer:* Cuckoo, Lapwing, Hobby, Blackcap, Chiffchaff, Reed & Sedge Warblers. *Passage:* Little Ringed, Plover, Green, Common & Wood Sandpipers, Ruff, Whimbrel. *Winter:* Dark-bellied Brent, Teal, Shoveler, Wigeon, Snipe, Black-tailed Godwit. Occasional Bittern, Hen Harrier and Short-eared Owl. Fieldfare, Redwing.

Other: Red Squirrel. Wild Daffodil.

Directions: PO36 0DY; SZ 610 869 (Brading Station). Lies at E end of island between Brading to SW and Bembridge Harbour to NE. A3055 runs from N coast to S through Brading. No car parks at reserve. Park at Brading station (400 yards along Station Road to E of A3055) for E end of reserve (there is also another car park at N end of Brading, charge, with toilets). For W end turn off A3055 to N of Brading and take the B3330/ Carpenters Road for St Helens. Once there park in NT Duver car park (SZ 637 892, charge for non-NT members, toilets) on the sandy spit at mouth of harbour. For S of reserve take B3395 E at S end of Brading. Then take 2nd R along minor road past Bembridge Fort to Culver Down car park (SZ 636 856, charge).

Public transport: Bus: 2 & 3 serve Brading, Southern Vectis. Train—Brading.

Visiting: Open all hours, free, no facilities on reserve but in nearby towns. Miles of footpath, some across NT or private farmland. No hides but 4 viewpoints. Paths can be muddy, not suitable for wheelchairs. It is 2.25 miles as the crow flies between Brading station and the Duver car park.

Contact: 01983 873 681

Berkshire

Despite being bisected by the M4 and its proximity to London, the county has a decent range of habitats. Wildfowl are well provided for by the county's many gravel pits, which also attract a good selection of other species. The heaths and downs add yet more species and Red Kites are now a common sight.

Bird Atlas/Avifauna
The Birds of Berkshire
Neil Bucknell, Brian Clews, Renton Righelato & Chris Robinson
(Birds of Berkshire Atlas Group, 2nd ed. 2013).

Bird Recorder
Marek Walford: records@berksoc.org.uk

Bird Report
The Birds of Berkshire (1974-), from BOC: secretary@berksoc.org.uk
Newbury District Bird Report: covers a 10-mile radius from Newbury Museum inc.parts of N Hants, S Oxon (1960-), from NDOC, enquiries@newburybirders.co.uk

BTO Regional Representative
Sean Murphy:
Wetland Bird Survey (WeBS)
Local Organizer: webs@bto.org
Sean Murphy

Clubs
Berkshire Ornithological Club (1947; 270).
Angela Gunn (Membership Sec), 17 Bideford Close, Woodley, Reading, Berks RG5 3SE: membership@berksoc.org.uk; www.berksoc.org.uk
Meetings: 7:30pm, alternate Wednesdays (Oct-Apr, except Christmas) University of Reading, RG6 6UR—see website for details.
Newbury District Ornithological Club (1959; 100).
Lesley Staves (Sec): 01488 682 301; via website; www.newburybirders.co.uk
Meetings: 7:30pm, monthly on a Thursday (Oct-Mar). Greenham Church Hall, New Road, Greenham, Newbury, RG19 8RZ.
Theale Area Bird Conservation Group (1988; 45).
Catherine McEwan (Club Sec): 0118 941 5792; tabcgsec@yahoo.com;
www.facebook.com/ThealeAreaBirdConservationGroup
Meetings: 8pm, 1st Tuesday of the month (all year). The Fox and Hounds Public House, Deans Copse Road, Reading, RG7 4BE.

Ringing Groups/Bird Observatory
Berkshire Downs RG
Middle Thames Bird Conservation Trust
https://middlethames.wordpress.com/: via website
Newbury RG:
www.newburyrg.blogspot.com
Runnymede RG:
https://runnymederinging.blogspot.com

RSPB Local Groups
Reading (1986; 100).

George Noble: readingrspb@gmail.com; https://group.rspb.org.uk/reading/
Meetings: 8.00 pm, 2nd Tuesday of the month (Sep-Jun). Pangbourne Village Hall, Station Road, Pangbourne, Reading, RG8 7AN.
Wokingham & Bracknell (1979; 152).
Alan Moore: RSPBWandb@gmail.com; https://group.rspb.org.uk/wokinghamandbracknell/
Meetings: 8:00pm, 2nd Thursday of the month (Sep-Jun). Finchampstead Memorial Hall, The Village, Finchampstead, Wokingham, RG40 4JU.

Wildlife Trust
Berkshire, Bucks. & Oxon Wildlife Trust (1959; 29,000). The Lodge, 1 Armstrong Road, Littlemore, Oxford, OX4 4XT: 01865 775 476; info@bbowt.org.uk; www.bbowt.org.uk

hurst, from High Street turn L along Lower Church Road. At T-junction turn L for Mill Road car park or R for Lower Sandhurst Road car park.
Public transport: Train—nearest stations, Crowthorne and Sandhurst—both a one mile walk .
Visiting: No access to lakes, view from footpaths bordering E, S & W sides—paths can be used by wheelchairs though surface not particularly suitable. Southern path forms part of Blackwater Valley long distance footpath. Two bird hides open to MGLG members, two public viewing screens. Feeding station viewable from bench on W path.
Contacts: Moor Green Lakes Group: via website; www.mglg.org.uk
Blackwater Valley Countryside Partnership: 01252 331 353; blackwater.valley@hants.gov.uk;

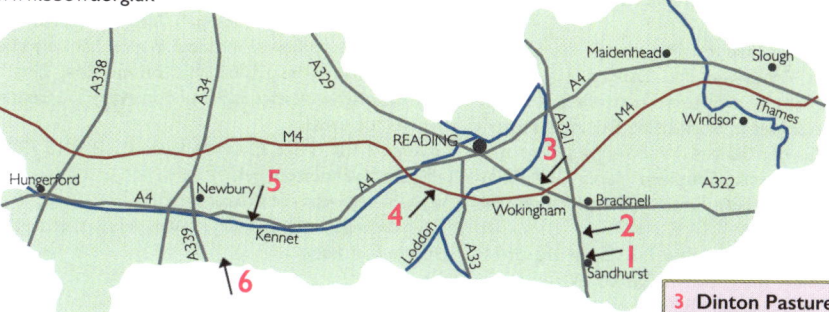

Entering on the A331 from Hampshire, two reserves just N of Sandhurst.

3	Dinton Pastures
6	Greenham and Cookham Commons
1	Moor Green Lakes
5	Thatcham Reedbeds
4	Theale Gravel Pits
2	Wildmoor Heath

1 MOOR GREEN LAKES

Moor Green Lakes Group/Blackwater Valley Countryside Partnership.
Habitats: 90 acres, three lakes with gravel islands, beaches and scrapes. River Blackwater, grassland, surrounded by willow, ash, hazel and thorn hedgerows.
Birds: 200+ spp, 60 spp regularly breeding. *Spring/summer:* Little Ringed Plover, Hobby, Reed Warbler, Whitethroat, Sedge Warbler, Common Sandpiper. Mandarin Duck, Common Tern and Barn Owl breed on site. Dunlin and Green Sandpiper on passage. *Winter:* Wigeon, Teal, Gadwall and of particular interest, a roost of Goosander on Grove Lake. Little Egret regular, Snipe, Lapwing and Green Sandpiper. Gull roost on adjacent Manor Farm workings inc up to 1,000 Lesser Black-backed.
Other: 31 spp butterflies and 15 spp dragonflies.
Directions: RG40 3TF; SU 805 628 (free car park in Lower Sandhurst Road, Finchampstead (open 8am-dusk). Alternatively use Horseshoe Lakes free car park in Mill Lane, Sandhurst (GU47 8JW; SU 820 620). Lies *c.* one mile NW of Sandhurst—take A321 N from Sand-

On other side of A321.

2 WILDMOOR HEATH

Berks, Bucks & Oxon Wildlife Trust
Habitats: 225 acres, wet & dry lowland heath, bog, mixed woodland and mature Scots pine plantation.
Birds: Year round: Firecrest. *Spring/summer:* 55 spp inc Hobby, Nightjar, Woodlark, Tree Pipit, Stonechat, Dartford Warbler, Reed Bunting.
Other: 20 spp dragonflies, Silver-studded Blue butterfly, Slow Worm, Adder, Grass Snake, Common Lizard, Roe Deer. Bog plants inc sundews.
Directions: RG45 7PW; SU 838 630. Between Bracknell and Sandhurst. From Sandhurst shopping area, take A321 NW towards Wokingham. Turn R at mini-roundabout on to Crowthorne Road. Continue for about one mile through one set of traffic lights. Car park is on R at bottom of hill.
Public transport: Bus: 194 Bracknell-Camberley runs past reserve car park (Crowthorne Road/Sandhurst Road). Courtney Buses (0118 973 3486). Train—Sandhurst station, one mile S of reserve.

Visiting: Open all year. Car park. No access to woodland N of Rackstraw Road at Broadmoor Bottom. Not suitable for wheelchairs due to slope of site and muddy, uneven terrain. Dogs on a lead.

Contact: BBOWT: 01628 829 574; info@bbowt.org.uk

Continue N on A321, then A329 at Wokingham.

3 DINTON PASTURES

Wokingham Borough Council

Habitats: 333 acres, woodland, meadow and lakes on banks of River Loddon. Sandford Lake managed for wildfowl, Lavell's Lake best for waders & scrub species.

Birds: All year: Kingfisher, Water Rail, Barn Owl. *Spring/summer:* Hobby, Little Ringed Plover, Common Tern, Nightingale (not for last couple of years), common warblers. *Winter:* Bittern, wildfowl inc Goldeneye, Wigeon, Teal, Gadwall, thrushes. Waders inc Green & Common Sandpipers, Snipe, Redshank.

Other: Water Vole, Harvest Mouse, Great Crested Newt, Loddon Pondweed and Loddon Lily. Purple Emperor and Purple Hairstreak butterflies. 20+ spp dragonflies inc Emperor, Black-tailed Skimmer, Migrant Hawker and Golden Ringed. White-legged Damselfly and Banded Demoiselle. Southern Marsh, Bee, Common Spotted & Pyramidal Orchids, Broad-leaved Helleborine.

Directions: RG10 0TH; SU 784 718. From J10 of M4 head for Reading, then follow sign to Winnersh on A329. Park is signposted off B3030 between Hurst and Winnersh.

Public transport: Bus:127/128/129 between Reading and Wokingham stop near main entrance, Courtney Bus (0118 973 3486). Train—Winnersh station is 15 mins walk.

Visiting: Open all year, dawn-dusk. Car park charges apply 6am-10pm daily. Information centre, cafe open daily 8:30am-5pm (4pm in winter), toilets (suitable for wheelchairs). Various trails between one and three miles, one hide overlooking Sandford Lake and two hides overlooking Lavells Lake. Electric buggies for hire, walks leaflet. Dogs allowed.

Contact: Dinton Pastures Country Park: 0118 974 2016;

countryside@wokingham.gov.uk;

www.dinton-pastures.co.uk

Return to J10 of M4, then exit at J11 or J12.

4 THEALE GRAVEL PITS

Theale Area Bird Conservation Group

Hosehill Lake LNR managed by BBOWT on behalf of Berkshire Council

Habitats: Three complexes of various sized gravel pits spread out across Theale flood plain.

Birds: Spring/summer: Migrant warblers, breeding Nightingale and Common Tern, passage Arctic & Black Terns, large number of hirundines (Martin bank at Hosehill),

resident Peregrine Falcon favours pylon area. *Autumn:* Dunlin, Common Sandpiper and other passage waders. Little Gull, Osprey, along with terns on passage. *Winter:* Large numbers of wildfowl, inc Goldeneye and Goosander. Thousands of gulls on nearby Moatlands pit. Bittern sometimes recorded in Hosehill Lake LNR reedbed.

Other: Good variety of dragonflies and butterflies. Grass Vetchling worthy of note.

Directions: RG7 4GB; SU 646 699 (lay-by parking). Group of pits, S of Reading, situated between J11 & 12 of M4, immediately S of Theale town centre. From Theale town centre head S on Station Road/Hanger Road and park in lay-bys in Dean Copse Road, by Fox & Hounds Pub—main pit and Hosehill Lake LNR.

Public transport: Train—Theale station, short walk to nearest pits.

Visiting: Open all hours. Parking for a few vehicles in lay-bys near Fox & Hounds pub. Tern rafts, Sand Martin bank and wild flower meadow in Hosehill Lake LNR, with information boards/benches on mile-long circular walk. Regular work parties 9am-noon every Sat. Contact TABCG for details.

Contact: TABCG Sec, Cathy McEwan: 0118 9415 792; tabcgsec@yahoo.com;

https://tabcg.webs.com/thealesites.htm

Either continue W on M4 to J13, then A339 S; or take A4 direct to Thatcham.

5 NATURE DISCOVERY CENTRE AND
THATCHAM REEDBEDS

Berks, Bucks & Oxon Wildlife Trust

Habitats: Lakes, reedbeds, scrub.

Birds: All year: Red Kite, Egyptian Goose, common wildfowl, Grey Heron, Great Crested & Little Grebe, Water Rail, Kingfisher, Cetti's Warbler, Reed Bunting. *Spring/summer:* Cuckoo, Common Tern, hirundines, Reed & Sedge Warblers. *Winter:* Wildfowl inc Pochard, occasional Bittern.

Other: Moths inc. Garden Tiger, butterflies, and dragonflies inc demoiselles, Desmoulin's Snail.

Directions: RG19 3FU; SU 506 672. E of Newbury: from A339, take A4 towards Thatcham. Turn R after 1.2 miles (signposted **Lower Way & Centre**) then R after 0.8 miles into Centre.

Public transport: Bus: 1c Newbury-Thatcham circular, alight Derwent Road stop (Lower Way, Thatcham)—short walk to Centre. Newbury & District (01635 33855) Train—Newbury and Thatcham stations—short walks to bus stops on route 1c.

Visiting: Visitor centre, shop, cafe open 10:30am-3:30pm (closed Mon). Car park, toilets, waymarked trails (flat/level), picnic and play areas. Dogs under close control—keep out of lake. Small car park beyond centre for reedbeds.

Contact: Discovery Centre: 01635 874 381; ndc@bbowt.org.uk

Head back to A339, then S.

6 GREENHAM & CROOKHAM COMMONS

Berks, Bucks & Oxon Wildlife Trust.

Habitats: 1,100 acres, heathland, grassland, woodland. Restored from former airfield.

Birds: All year: Sparrowhawk, Woodcock, Woodlark, Stonechat, Dartford Warbler, Firecrest, common scrub and woodland spp. *Summer:* Hobby, Nightjar, Nightingale, hirundines, common warblers. Little Ringed Plover. *Passage:* Wheatear, Ring Ouzel and Yellow Wagtail. *Winter:* Snipe, Green Sandpiper, thrushes, Siskin, Redpoll. *Other:* Butterflies, dragonflies. Autumn Lady's-tresses.

Directions: RG19 8DB; SU 499 650. Two miles SE of Newbury. From A339 take Pinchington Lane (signposted to Greenham Common, passing retail park). Turn R at roundabout (Pyle Hill car park here) on to Burys Bank Road following brown signs one mile to Control Tower (main car park).

Public transport: Bus: 2 & 8 Newbury services (Mon-Sat) stop at Marchant Close, very short walk to Pyle Hill entrance. Newbury & District (01635 33855). Train:—Newbury.

Visiting: Open all hours. Main car park opens 8am, closing time varies (free, donation, height barrier), other car parks open 24/7 at Crookham (RG19 8EJ; SU 524 645, height barrier) and Pyle Hill (RG19 3BX; SU 484 652). Cafe (not open every day). Variety of routes, some colour-coded. Main tracks level and accessible. Dogs on lead (Mar-Jul).

Contact: BBOWT: 01635 35157; info@bbowt.org.uk

Head N on A339 and then A34 to Oxfordshire.

Oxfordshire

Red Kites, first reintroduced to the Chilterns, are now commonplace over this largely agricultural county. Farmoor Reservoir, near Oxford can be excellent for passage migrants, wintering wildfowl and rarities. The wet meadows and reedbeds on the RSPB reserve at Otmoor continue to develop to benefit breeding waders (Redshank, Snipe and Lapwing) and Marsh Harrier, whilst wildfowl numbers increase during winter with Short-eared Owl, Hen Harrier, Merlin and Peregrine often present. The Downs in the south can be good for other raptors, particularly in winter.

Bird Atlases/Avifauna

Birds of the Heart of England (Banbury area)
TG Easterbrook
(Liverpool University Press, 2013).
Birds of Oxfordshire
JW Brucker, AG Gosler & AR Heryet
(Pisces Publications, 1992).

Bird Recorder

Ian Lewington, 119 Brasenose Road, Didcot, OX11 7BP: 01235 819 792; recorder@oos.org.uk

Bird Reports

Birds Of Oxfordshire (1915-), from OOS—Barry Hudson (Sec), Pinfold, 4 Bushey Row, Bampton, Witney, OX18 2JU: secretary@oos.org.uk

Banbury Ornithological Society Annual Report (1966-), from BOS: treasurer@banburyos.org

BTO Regional Representatives

North
Frances Buckel
South
John Melling

Wetland Bird Survey (WeBS)

Local Organizers: webs@bto.org
Oxfordshire (North)
Sandra Bletchly
Oxfordshire (South)
Ben Carpenter

Clubs

Oxford Ornithological Society (1921; 330).
Barry Hudson (Sec), Pinfold, 4 Bushey Row, Bampton, Witney, OX18 2JU: 01993 200 790 & 07788 496 847; secretary@oos.org.uk; www.oos.org.uk
Meetings: 7:45pm, 2nd Wednesday of the month (Sep-May). Exeter Hall, Oxford Road, Kidlington, OX5 1AB.

Banbury Ornithological Society (inc parts of Northants/Oxon/Warwick). (1952; 100).
Frances Buckel (Sec): 07935 026 820; secretary@banburyos.org;
www.banburyornithologicalsociety.org.uk
Meetings: 7:30pm, 2nd Monday of the month (Sep-May). The Banbury Cricket Club, White Post Road, Bodicote, OX15 4BN. Jan & Feb to be held by zoom, Outdoor meetings: Jun-Aug. Contact/see website for details.

RSPB Local Groups

Oxford (1977; 100).
Roy Grant: roy.otters@hotmail.co.uk;
https://group.rspb.org.uk/oxford/
Meetings: 7:45pm, 1st Thursday of the month (Sep-May) except 2nd Thursday Sep & Jan).
Sandhills Primary School, Terrett Avenue, Sandhills, Oxford, OX3 8FN.

Vale of White Horse (1977; 100).
Bob Knight: leader@rspb-vwh.org.uk;
www.rspb-vwh.org.uk/
Meetings: A mixture of zoom and in person meetings. 7:45pm, 3rd Monday of the month (Sep-May). The River Room, All Saints Church, Sutton Courtenay, Abingdon, OX14 4AE.

Oxfordshire

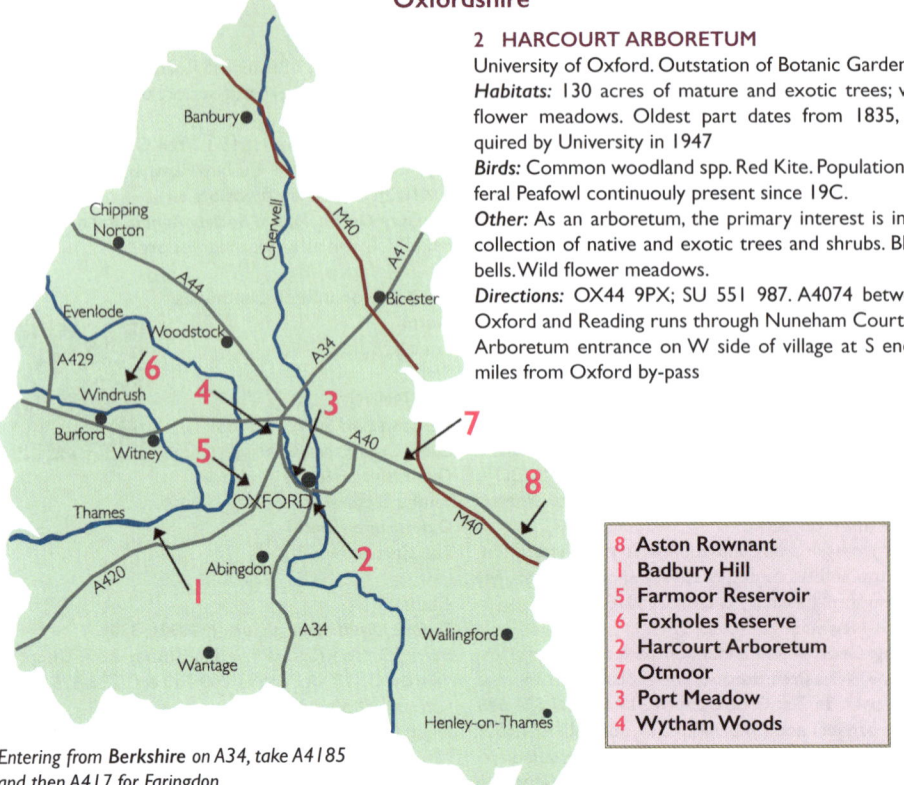

2 HARCOURT ARBORETUM

University of Oxford. Outstation of Botanic Garden
Habitats: 130 acres of mature and exotic trees; wild flower meadows. Oldest part dates from 1835, acquired by University in 1947
Birds: Common woodland spp. Red Kite. Population of-feral Peafowl continuouly present since 19C.
Other: As an arboretum, the primary interest is in its collection of native and exotic trees and shrubs. Bluebells. Wild flower meadows.
Directions: OX44 9PX; SU 551 987. A4074 between Oxford and Reading runs through Nuneham Courtney. Arboretum entrance on W side of village at S end, 3 miles from Oxford by-pass

8	Aston Rownant
1	Badbury Hill
5	Farmoor Reservoir
6	Foxholes Reserve
2	Harcourt Arboretum
7	Otmoor
3	Port Meadow
4	Wytham Woods

*Entering from **Berkshire** on A34, take A4185 and then A417 for Faringdon.*

1 BADBURY HILL

National Trust
Habitats: Ancient woodland, Iron Age hill fort.
Birds: All year: Red Kite, Buzzard, Sparrowhawk, common woodland spp inc Treecreeper, Nuthatch, Tawny Owl. *Spring/summer:* Cuckoo, common warblers, occ Firecrest. *Surrounding fields:* Red-legged Partridge, Skylark, Whitethroat, Linnet, Yellowhammer. *Winter:* Fieldfare, Redwing, finches, occasional Redpoll, Crossbill.
Other: Spring Bluebells (Badbury Clump area) and other woodland flora. Butterflies.
Directions: SN7 7NL; SU 261 945. 1.2 miles W of Faringdon on the B4019 to Highworth. From A420 take A417 into Faringdon, turn L at roundabout onto B4019 (to Highworth), then R staying on B4019 (to Coleshill/Highworth)—car park 1.5 mile on R.
Public transport: None.
Visiting: Open dawn-dusk, all year. Pay-&-display car park (National Trust members free). No toilets. Woodland paths and trails. Dogs under close control.
Contact: National Trust: 01793 762 209; badburyclump@nationaltrust.org.uk
Take A420 from Faringdon for Oxford, then A415 for Abingdon. At junction with A4074 turn L for Oxford and approach from S.

Public transport: Bus: X40 Oxford-Reading stops in Nuneham Courtenay. Arboretum entrance in village on W side.
Visiting: Entrance charge includes parking in on-site car park. Open 10am-5pm (last entry 4pm). Accessible toilets and baby changing facilities. Coffee kiosk at weekends. Some paths easy but many grass or wood chip. Assistance dogs only. All-terrain wheelchair available, book in advance.
Contact: 01865 610 300; admin@obg.ox.ac.uk
Continue N on A4074 to Oxford ring road and A34, which forms W by-pass. Oxford has a complex one-way system and restrictive parking. Probably easiest to use one of the park-and-ride car parks on ring road and then walk to

3 PORT MEADOW

Oxford City Council
Habitats: Common land, on east bank of River Thames (adjacent to Thames Towpath and Burgess Field).
Birds: All year: Sparrowhawk, Little Owl, Reed Bunting. *Spring/summer/passage:* Waders, hirundines, chats, warblers. *Winter:* When the area is wet, wildfowl and waders inc Wigeon, Teal, Gadwall, Snipe, Lapwing, plus occasional Goosander, Golden Plover, Water Rail.
Other: Butterflies, dragonflies, meadow plant spp.

Oxfordshire

Directions: OX2 6ED; SP 512 073 (S car park). Lies on the NW outskirts of Oxford, accessed via Walton Well Road and Aristotle Lane in south or Wolvercote in north.

Public transport: Bus: 6 from Oxford city centre (Magdalen Street, stop C3) to Wolvercote (also stops at Plantation Road—short walk to south access). Oxford Bus Co.

Visiting: Open all year. Car parks off Godstow Road (north end) OX2 8PU and Walton Well Road (south end) OX2 6ED. Dogs under control. Nature Park to E between Meadow proper and canal.

Contact: Cutteslowe Park Offices, Harboard Road, Oxford, OX2 8ES.

Also off the A34.

4 WYTHAM WOODS
University of Oxford

Habitats: 1,000 acres of semi-natural ancient woodland, 17C secondary woodland, mid-20C plantations, limestone grassland, mire and ponds.

Birds: Besides common woodland spp, the Woods have been used for ecological reasearch by the University of Oxford since the 1940s. One of the long-running research programmes (75 years and still going strong) is the Wytham Tit Project, a population study of Great & Blue Tits, as well as Coal & Marsh Tits. Willow Tit no longer present in Wytham.

Other: 500+ spp plants and 800+ spp butterflies and moths.

Directions: OX2 8QJ; SP 473 096 (main car park). Take the exit for Wytham from the A34 western Oxford Bypass. Drive through the village to main car park. No access from B4044. Secure bike racks in car park, cycle path from Botley but no bicycles in the woods

Public transport: Bus: Hourly ST2 Science Transit Shuttle between Oxford and Wytham.; 6 Oxford to Wolvercote, then 25 min walk, Oxford Bus Company

Visiting: Open every day, Mon-Fri 10am-dusk; weekends and bank holidays: dawn-dusk. Free but must apply in advance for a walking permit (https://www.wythamwoods.ox.ac/permit). Free car park. Wheelchair users e-mail: wytham.woods@admin.ox.co.uk in advance for gate code. Extensive network of paths. Assistance dogs only

Contact: 01865 614 460;
wytham.woods@admin.oc.ac.uk

Take A40 from A34, then B4044 on L for Eynsham and (toll bridge) Farmoor.

5 FARMOOR RESERVOIR
Thames Water

Habitats: County's largest body of freshwater contained in two concrete basins separated by a causeway. Shallow pools in Pinkhill Reserve. Reedbed, wet grassland, pools in Shrike Meadow and Buckthorne Meadow reserves.

Birds: Summer: Ringed Plover, Common Tern and Black-headed Gull. Large numbers of hirundines. Warblers such as Cetti's Grasshopper, Willow & Sedge. Hobby, Cuckoo. *Passage:* migrants such as White & Yellow Wagtails, Wheatear, Black Tern, Little Gull, Dunlin and Little Stint. *Winter:* Wildfowl, grebes, divers and gulls. Snipe and Water Rail at Pinkhill. A long history of rarities.

Other: Dragonflies, aquatic life-forms.

Directions: OX2 9NS; SP 452 061. Lies W of Oxford between A 40 & A420. Widely signposted by brown tourist signs. At mini-roundabout in Farmoor village (on B4044), turn L & look for car park at Gate 3.

Public transport: Bus: S1 between Oxford and Witney stop in Farmoor village (0.5 mile walk to Gate 3). Stagecoach.

Visiting: Free car parking at Gate 3. Car park off B4017. Bird hides at Pinkhill Reserve, W of reservoir, along the Causeway, on the W bank of the reservoir and at Shrike Nature Reserve. All hides open access. Dogs are not allowed on the reservoir site but permitted along the countryside walk.

Contact: hanna.jenkins@thameswater.co.uk
Return to A420 and leave on A424 at Burford.

6 FOXHOLES RESERVE
Berks, Bucks & Oxon Wildlife Trust

Habitats: Broadleaved ancient woodland, grassland.

Birds: All year: Raven, Tawny Owl, Little Owl, Green & Great Spotted Woodpeckers, Marsh Tit, common woodland spp. *Spring/summer:* Spotted Flycatcher and warblers. *Winter:* Redwing, Fieldfare, Woodcock.

Other: Fantastic show of Bluebells from mid-Apr and into May. Autumn fungi (200+ spp). Silver-washed Fritillary among 23 spp butterflies, 7 spp bats.

Directions: OX7 6QD; SP 255 207. Travelling N on A424 from Burford, take R turn to Bruern. Continue past staggered crossroads towards Bruern for two miles then past R turn to Shipton-under-Wychwood. Park in lay-by after 200 yards and walk 600 yards down pot-holed track to reserve entrance—no parking along this track.

Public transport: None.

Visiting: Open all year. Car park, 1.75 mile circular wildlife walk—keep to paths (can be very muddy).

Contact: BBOWT: 01865 775 476; info@bbowt.org.uk.
Return on A40 to Oxford and then A34 for Bicester from ring road. Turn R on to B4027 from A34.

7 OTMOOR NATURE RESERVE
RSPB

Habitats: Wet grassland, reedbed, open water, hedgerows.

Birds: Spring/autumn passage: Greenshank, Green & Common Sandpipers, Spotted Redshank, Short-eared

Owl and occasional Black Tern. *Summer:* Breeding birds inc. Bittern, Marsh Harrier, Cetti's & Grasshopper Warblers, Lapwing, Redshank, Curlew, Snipe, Yellow Wagtail, Shoveler, Gadwall, Pochard, Tufted Duck, Little & Great Crested Grebes. Hobby breeds locally. *Winter:* Wigeon, Teal, Shoveler, Pintail, Gadwall, Pochard, Tufted Duck, Lapwing, Golden Plover, Hen Harrier, Peregrine, Merlin.
Directions: OX3 9TD (Otmoor Lane); SP 570 126. Car park seven miles NE of Oxford city centre. From J8 of M40, take A40 W to Wheatley, then B4027. Take turn to Horton-cum-Studley, then first L to Beckley. After 0.7 mile turn R (before the Abingdon Arms public house). After 200 yards, turn L into Otmoor Lane. Car park at the end of lane (approx one mile)—if full, do not park along Otmoor Lane (emergency access).
Public transport: None.
Visiting: Open dawn-dusk, no entry fee. Small car park (charge, cash only, for non-members) with cycle racks, visitor trail (three mile round trip) and two screened viewpoints. Not accessible by coach and is unsuitable for large groups. No dogs allowed on reserve visitor trail (except public rights of way). In wet conditions, visitor route can be muddy and wellingtons are essential.
Contact: RSPB: 01865 351 163; otmoor.admin@rspb.org.uk
Follow directions above back to M40, then follow directions below.

8 ASTON ROWANT NNR
Natural England
Habitats: Chalk grassland, chalk scrub, beech woodland.
Birds: All year: Red Kite, Buzzard, Sparrowhawk, Woodcock, Tawny Owl, Green & Great Spotted Woodpeckers, Skylark, Meadow Pipit, Marsh Tit. *Spring/summer:* Blackcap, other warblers, Turtle Dove. *Passage:* inc Ring Ouzel, Wheatear and Stonechat. *Winter:* Brambling, Siskin, winter thrushes.
Other: Rich chalk grassland flora, inc Chiltern Gentian, Clustered Bellflower and Frog, Bee, Pyramidal & Fragrant Orchids. Less common butterflies inc Silver-spotted, Dingy and Grizzled Skippers, Chalkhill Blue, Adonis Blue, Green Hairstreak and Dark Green Fritillary.
Directions: HP14 3YL; SU 731 966 for Beacon Hill car park. From the M40 Lewknor interchange at J6, travel NE for a short distance and turn R on to A40. After 1.5 miles at the top of hill, turn R and R again into a narrow, metalled lane. Car park is signposted from A40. OX49 5HX; SU 726 958 for Cowleaze Wood car park.
Public transport: Bus: 275 High Wycombe to Oxford stops at Stokenchurch and Aston Rowant. Red Rose Travel (01296 747 926) and Link40 High Wycombe to Thame, stops at Lewknor village. Carousel Buses (01494 450 151). Short walks to reserve.
Visiting: Open all year. On-site parking at Beacon Hill and Cowleaze Wood—viewpoint, seats, interpretation panels. Some wheelchair access at Cowleaze Wood

(contact for details).
Contact: Natural England, Aston Rowant NNR: 01844 351 833; michael.venters@naturalengland.org.uk
Return to M40 and head N for **Buckinghamshire**.

Buckinghamshire

Sandwiched between the River Ouse to the north and the River Thames to the south, the county offers a good mixture of woodlands, lakes & gravel pits. The higher ground of the Chiltern escarpment is an excellent area for Red Kites. Some interesting species breed in the county, including Little Ringed Plover, Firecrest and Hawfinch.

Bird Atlas/Avifauna
The Birds of Buckinghamshire
David Ferguson
(Buckingham Bird Club, 2nd ed 2012).

Bird Recorder
Mike Wallen, 15 Bennetts Lane, Rowsham, HP22 4QU; 07976 560 040; mwallen0987@gmail.com

Bird Report
Buckinghamshire Bird Report (1980-), from Mike Wallen, as above.

BTO Regional Representative
Drew Lyness
Wetland Bird Survey (WeBS)
Local Organizer: webs@bto.org
Buckinghamshire (North)
Martin Routledge
Buckinghamshire (South)
Vacant

Clubs
Buckinghamshire Bird Club (1981; 30).
Neil Manthorpe (Membership Sec): 07423 671 528; contactbucksbirdclub@gmail.com; www.bucksbirdclub.co.uk
Meetings: Contact/see website for details.
Amersham Birdwatching Club (n/a; 60).
Alistair McKenzie: 07958 792 488; abcsecretaryamersham@gmail.com www.amershambirdwatchingclub.co.uk
Meetings: 7:45pm, 3rd Friday of the month (Sep-May).
Barn Hall Community Centre, Chiltern Avenue, Amersham, HP6 5AH.

Ringing Groups/Bird Observatory
Colne Valley RG

Buckinghamshire

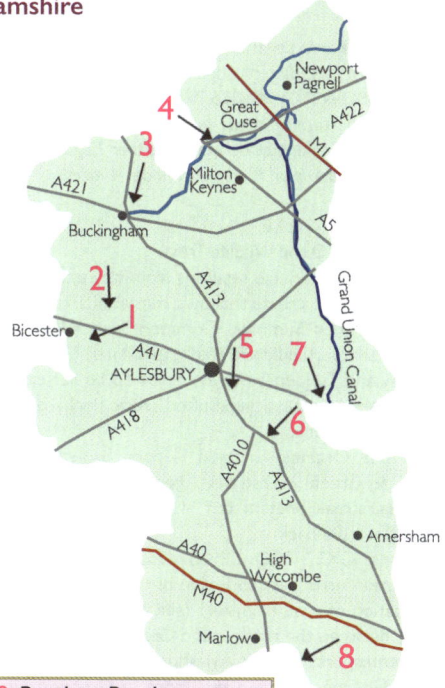

Hughenden RG
Runnymede RG:
https://runnymederinging.blogspot.com
RSPB Local Groups
Aylesbury (1981; 80).
Susie Haybrook: seheybrook@gmail.com;
https://group.rspb.org.uk/aylesbury/
Meetings: 7:30pm, 3rd Monday of the month (Sep-Apr).
Prebendal Farm Community Centre, Fowler Road, Aylesbury, HP19 7QW.
North Bucks (1976; 180 households):
rspbnorthbucks@gmail.com;
https://group.rspb.org.uk/northbucks/
Meetings: 7.45pm, 2nd Thursday of the month (Sep-May, by zoom in Jan/Feb). The Cruck Barn, Alston Drive, Bradwell Abbey, Milton Keynes, MK13 9AP. Contact/see website for details.

If entering on M40 from **Oxfordshire**, *take A34 for Bicester at J9, then A41 for Aylesbury and a cluster of reserves straddling the A41.*

1 UPPER RAY MEADOWS
Berks, Bucks & Oxon Wildlife Trust
Habitats: A cluster of separate wet meadows totalling 546 acres on the floodplain of the upper River Ray, spread over an area measuring 4 miles from NE to SW (roughly the line of the River Ray) and 1.5 miles SE to NW. Pools, ditches and hedgerows. SSSI.
Birds: Kingfisher, Short-eared Owl, Peregrine Falcon. *Breeding:* Curlew, Lapwing. Skylark, Yellow Wagtail, Reed Bunting, Yellowhammer, Corn Bunting. *Winter:* Wigeon, Teal, Snipe (large numbers winter but do not breed), Jack Snipe, Golden Plover, Fieldfare, Redwing, Meadow Pipit, mixed flocks of finches/buntings.
Other: Flora typical of traditonally managed hay meadows and floodplain.
Directions & Visiting: The area of the meadows is centred on the point where the A41 crosses the Ray at Heath Bridge, just under 4 miles SE of the junction of the A34 and A41 on the S side of Bicester. From SW to NE, going upstream along the Ray, the meadows are:
Arncott Bridge Meadow: Turn R off A41 at sign to Ambrosden and Arncott. Park on roadside in Ambrosden, walk 0.75 mile S beyond village to bridge over Ray. Access off Ploughley Road. Access only in Aug & Sep.
Meadow Farm: Turn R off A41 on to B4011 for Blackthorn. Entrance to Meadow Farm after village on L. Park beyond farmhouse. No public access. Pre-booked groups only.
Cow Leys: Turn R off A41 for Piddington after railway bridge. Reserve immediately on L, park on verge on L. Open all year
Dorothy Bolton Meadow: Take L for Marsh Gibbon after A41 crosses Ray. After 100 yards park on verge on

Map no.	Reserve
8	Burnham Beeches
2	Calvert Jubilee
7	College Lake
4	Floodplain Forest
3	Foxcote Reservoir
1	Upper Ray Meadows
6	Wendover Woods
5	Weston Turville Reservoir

R. Access Jul-Sep.
Long Herdon & Grange Meadows: Continue along road for Marsh Gibbon for 0.75 miles park on verge. Reserve 500 yards S. Access all year. Flower-rich hay meadows
Leaches Farm: Stay on A41. Park in lay-by on L after Leaches Farm Business Centre. Cross A41. Follow footpath after stile. Access all year. Flower-rich hay meadows.
Ludgershall Meadow: Recent acquisition. Walk across **Leaches Farm**. Enter through gate in SE corner. Do not park in Ludgershall village. Access all year.
Gallows Bridge Farm: Continue on A41 for 1.5 miles. Take L for Grendon Underwood. After 100 yards turn L park at end of track. No access except to bird hides. Access is free. No facilities. Paths flat but uneven, can be soft. Floods in winter. Gates. Hides at **Gallow Bridge Farm** accessible for a robust wheelchair. Grazing animals. Dogs allowed on footpaths, otherwise assistance dogs only.
Public transport: Bus: 17 Aylesbury to Bicester runs along A41. Stops at Kingswood Crossroads to E of **Gal-**

lows Bridge Farm several times a day, Red Rose Travel (0333 188 7811; Office@redrosetravel.com) *Contact:* BBOWT: 01442 826 774; info@bbowt.org.uk *Continue along turning taken for Gallows Bridge Farm (see above) to Grendon Underwood and then Edgcott. Gawcott Road car park is on R after just under 4 miles.*

2 CALVERT JUBILEE
Berks, Bucks & Oxon Wildlife Trust
Habitats: 54 acres. Lake resulting from clay extraction, banks sculpted to create shallows, raft islands, reedbed.
Birds: Kingfisher. *Summer:* Common Tern, Willow & Cetti's Warblers, Chiffchaff, Blackcap. *Winter:* Goosander, Smew and Goldeneye have ceased to be regular in recent years. Mallard, Scaup, Tufted Duck, Pochard. Bittern. Glaucous Gull.
Other: Bee Orchids. Grizzled Skipper, Brown Argus, Brown & Green Hairstreaks. Pepper Saxifrage and Black Hairstreak present but in areas closed due to HS2 and ash die back.
Directions: OX27 0BQ; SP 682 252. Extensive HS2 works mean no access to E side but Gawcott Road, a continuation of road from A41 (see above), runs along W side between the reserve and Grebe Lake (sailing).
Public transport: Bus: 17 Aylesbury to Bicester runs along A41. One service a day stops in Grendon Underwood and Edgcott (1.5 mile walk). Red Rose Travel (0333 188 7811; Office@redrosetravel.com)
Visiting: Open all hours, free. No facilities. Small car park on Gawcott Road, opposite Greatmoor Sailing Club. Bridleway and boardwalk, two hides. Grazing livestock. Assistance dogs only. Path to hides flat but other sections bumpy and with steps and bridges. Section of reserve lost to HS2 in 2020.
Contact: BBOWT: info@bbowt.org.uk
Continue N on Gawcott Road (HS2 permitting) to Buckingham.

3 FOXCOTE RESERVOIR
Berks, Bucks & Oxon Wildlife Trust
Habitats: Reservoir, meadow & pasture.
Birds: All year: Great Created Grebe, Kingfisher, Grey Wagtail, Cetti's Warbler, Reed Bunting. *Summer:* Hobby, Reed & Sedge Warblers. *Passage:* Common & Green Sandpipers, occasional Osprey. *Winter:* Wildfowl (inc. Wigeon, Pochard, Goldeneye, Goosander), Water Rail, Lapwing, Golden Plover, gulls. Occasional Bittern.
Other: Dragonflies, Otter.
Directions: MK18 5EY; SP 713 361. Two miles NE of Buckingham. Take A413 N from Buckingham, after one mile turn R on to Main Street in Maids Moreton. Continue until T-junction & turn L on to Foxcote Road, reserve entrance after one mile on L—limited parking in lay-by opposite gate.
Public transport: None.
Visiting: Open all year. Hides. No dogs. Can also be

viewed from road (E side)—telescope essential. Public footpath runs E side to (private) Foxcote Wood (through farm, lay-by parking opposite entrance).
Contact: BBOWT: 01865 775 476; info@bbowt.org.uk
Return to Buckingham and then take A422 for Stony Stratford. 4th exit (Towcester/London Road) from roundabout at junction with A5. Bear L on to Queen Eleanor Street (passing Stony Stratford Nature Reserve on L. Turn L on to Stratford Road and pass under A5, the L on to Old Wolverton Road. This will take you first to Manor Farm Court and then Haversham Road.

4 FLOODPLAIN FOREST NATURE RESERVE
The Parks Trust
Habitats: River Great Ouse floodplain—grassland, woodland, open water.
Birds: All year: Red Kite, Little Egret, Barn & Little Owls, Kingfisher, Reed Bunting. *Spring/summer:* Lapwing, Redshank, Little Ringed Plover, Common Tern, Sand Martin, common warblers. *Winter:* Wildfowl inc Goosander, Pintail, Snipe, Winter thrushes.
Other: Otter, Grass Snake. Bats, dragonflies.
Directions: NW of Milton Keynes (Wolverton). Free car parks at MK12 5NN; SP 809 415 (Manor Farm Court) & MK19 7AU; SP 817 421 (Haversham Road), height restriction).
Public transport: Bus: 4/6/33/33A/X33 regular services Milton Keynes to Wolverton. Arriva. Train—Wolverton 0.5 mile walk to Haversham Road entrance.
Visiting: Site floods, so not always accessible. Open all hours. Surfaced footpaths lead from car parks to accessible circular route and three hides. Benches along path by river. Dogs on lead.
Numerous other flooded workings in vicinity on flood plain. Some have fishing, some sailing and others are nature reserves
Contact: the Parks Trust: 01908 233 600; info@theparkstrust.com
Take A4146 S from Milton Keynes and then A418 to Aylesbury.

5 WESTON TURVILLE RESERVOIR
Berks, Bucks & Oxon Wildlife Trust
Habitats: 50 acre, reservoir, reedbed, woodland.
Birds: All year: Red Kite, Great Crested & Little Grebes, Water Rail, Kingfisher, Grey Wagtail, Reed Bunting, common woodland spp inc Green & Great Spotted Woodpeckers, Treecreeper) *Spring/summer:* Cuckoo, hirundines, warblers inc Reed, Sedge, Whitethroat. *Passage:* Hobby, Common Tern, Common & Green Sandpipers. Occasional Osprey and Black Tern. *Winter:* Bittern (occasional), wildfowl inc Shoveler, Pochard, Gadwall, Snipe, winter thrushes, Redpoll, Siskin.
Other: Flora.
Directions: HP22 5PS; SP 859 097. 0.5 mile SE of Ayles-

bury. From Aylesbury leave A413 on B4009 to Wendover. 0.25 mile after roundabout, turn L on to World's End Lane opposite The Village Gate pub—park in lay-by on R after 0.3 mile.

Public transport: Bus: 50 (not Sun) Aylesbury to Halton Camp stops in Weston Turville (opp Church Lane)—short walk S along World's End Lane to reserve on L. Red Rose Travel (01296 747 926).

Visiting: Open all hours. Access by 1.25 mile perimeter footpath (part of walk along minor roads). Sailing on reservoir.

Contact: BBOWT: 01442 826 774; info@bbowt.org.uk
Continue on B4009.

6 WENDOVER WOODS

Forestry England

Habitats: Large mixed woodland, largely coniferous with some broad-leaved & scrub.

Birds: Firecrest, Sparrowhawk, Buzzard, Goshawk, Red Kite, Woodcock, 3 spp woodpeckers, Hawfinch (rare), Crossbill, common woodland spp. *Summer:* Cuckoo, Tree Pipit, warblers. *Spring/autumn:* Passage migrants. *Winter:* Siskin, Redpoll, Brambling, winter thrushes.

Other: Badgers, butterlies and Bluebell display. .

Directions: HP22 5NQ; SP 890 090. From Wendover (A413) take B4009 for Tring, turn R c.1 mile N of RAF Halton, signposted **Wendover Woods** & St Leonards.

Public transport: Bus: 8/8A Aylesbury bus station to RAF Halton (c.1.3 miles from visitor centre). Arriva (Mon-Sat: 0344 800 4411), Redline (Sun: 01296 426 786). Train—Wendover.

Visiting: Open daily (not 25 Dec) 8am to dusk. Large car park—charges apply. Toilets, play area, cafe, walking and cycling trails, picnic area, wildlife hides, Firecrest Trail.

Contact: Forestry England: 01296 696 184: wendoverwoods@forestryengland.uk
www.theparkstrust.com
Continue on B4009. *Cross A41 and continue on B488 for 2.5 miles along NW edge of Tring.*

7 COLLEGE LAKE

Berks, Bucks & Oxon Wildlife Trust

Habitats: Deep lake in former chalk pit, shallow pools, chalk and rough grasslands, woodlands, scrub.

Birds: Spring/summer: Breeding Lapwing, Redshank and Little Ringed Plover. Sand Martin, Hobby, Common Tern, Skylark and Shelduck. *Winter:* Wildfowl (Wigeon, Shoveler, Teal, Gadwall), waders inc Snipe, Peregrine. Scarcer birds turn up regularly.

Other: Chalk grassland flowers. Arable Weed Project inc displays of cornfield flowers in Jun/Jul. Butterflies inc Small Blue and Green Hairstreak. 16 spp dragonflies. Brown Hare.

Directions: HP23 5QG; SP 935 139. Two miles N of Tring on B488, 0.25 mile N of canal (Grand Union)

bridge at Bulbourne turn L into gated entrance. Marked with brown tourist signs.

Public transport: Train—Tring, two mile walk, mostly on canal towpath.

Visiting: Tue-Sun 10am-5pm, last entry 4pm. (Cafe: 10am-4pm). Also open Bank Holiday Mondays. Large car park, coach park. Visitor centre/shop, toilets inc disabled. Interactive interpretation, 10 hides (some with wheelchair access). Network of wheelchair-friendly trails. Electric tramper available, phone to book.

Tring Reservoirs, a few hundred yards to SW, are just over the county bounndary in **Hertfordshire**.

Contact: BBOWT: 01442 826 774; collegelake@bbowt.org.uk
Take A41 from Tring to M25, the S to M40 or M4. Then as below.

8 BURNHAM BEECHES NNR

City of London Corporation.

Habitats: Ancient woodland, streams, pools, heathland (Stoke Common), grassland, scrub.

Birds: All year: Mandarin (good numbers), Sparrowhawk, Tawny Owl, 3 spp woodpeckers, Treecreeper. *Spring/summer:* Cuckoo, Stock Dove, possible Turtle Dove. *Winter:* Siskin, Crossbill, Brambling. Flocks of Redwing. Red Kite and Buzzard, possible Woodcock. Marsh Tit.

Other: Ancient Beech and Oak pollards with associated wildlife. Rich array of fungi.

Directions: SL2 3PS; SU 958 850. 2.5 miles N of Slough and on W side of A355, running between J2 of M40 and J6 of M4. Entry from A355 via Beeches Road. Also smaller parking areas in Hawthorn Lane and Pumpkin Hill to the S and Park Lane to the W.

Public transport: Bus: X74 Slough to Farnham Common.
First Berkshire & Thames Valley. Train—Slough.

Visiting: Open all year (not Dec 25). Main Lord Mayor's Drive open 8am-dusk. Coach parking. Visitor centre, Beeches Cafe, public toilets and information point open 10am-5pm. Network of wheelchair accessible roads and paths, most start at Victory Cross. Motorized buggy available for hire.

Contact: Burnham Beeches Office, Hawthorn Lane, Farnham Common, SL2 3TE: 01753 647 358; burnham.beeches@cityoflondon.gov.uk; www.cityoflondon.gov.uk
Return to M25

London
(Greater)

The London Natural History Society, publishers of the London Bird Report, base their recording area on a 20-mile radius from St Paul's Cathedral (which overlaps with some of the surrounding counties). Despite being a busy, sprawling city, the capital offers a number of green spaces and purpose-built reservoirs that attract a wide variety of birds, including the occasional oddity.

For public transport visit: Transport for London, 0343 222 1234; www.tfl.gov.uk

Bird Atlas/Avifauna
The London Bird Atlas
Ian Woodward, Richard Arnold & Neil Smith (John Beaufoy Books, 2017).
The Birds of London
Andrew Self
(Christopher Helm, 2014).

Bird Recorder
Roger Payne: 07930 608005; rogerwpayne@gmail.com

Bird Report
London Bird Report
20-mile radius of St Paul's Cathedral. (1936-), from LNHS: publicationsales@lnhs.org.uk

BTO Regional Representatives
London, North
Ben Hillier
London, South
Richard Arnold
Wetland Bird Survey (WeBS)
Local Organizers: webs@bto.org
Greater London (excl. Thames Estuary—see *Essex*)
Ben Hillier
Lee Valley
See *Hertfordshire*
South West London
See *Surrey*

Clubs
The London Bird Club (1858; 1,000 LNHS members). (Ornithology Section of London NHS).
Gehan de Silva Wijeyeratne (Chair): lbcchair@lnhs.org.uk; www.lnhs.org.uk/index.php/sections/london-bird-club
Meetings: 7:00pm zoom talks (all year)—contact/see website for details.
Marylebone Birdwatching Society (1981; 160).
Steve Ripley (Chair), 29 Berriman Road, Holloway, London N7 7PN: 07929 966 705; birdsmbs@yahoo.com; www.birdsmbs.org.uk

Meetings: Zoom talks (members only), local outings and coach trips—contact/see website for details.
Ringing Groups/Bird Observatory
Runnymede RG.
https://runnymedeiringing.blogspot.com
Southern Colour RG:
Barry Williams (Chair): baz_williams@hotmail.com
www.southern-colour-ringing-group.org.uk
Walthamstowe Wetlands RG:
www.wildlondon.org.uk/walthamstow-wetlands-ringing-group

RSPB Local Groups
Bexley (1979; all local RSPB members are welcome).
Cath Bradshaw (Sec.): bexleylocalRSPBgroup@gmail.com; https://group.rspb.org.uk/bexley/
Meetings: 7:15pm, 2nd Friday of the month (Sep-May). John Fisher Church Hall, 48 Thanet Road, Bexley, DA5 1AP. e-mail for details.
Bromley (1972; 200).
Ian Micklewright: bromleyRSPB@gmail.com; https://group.rspb.org.uk/bromley/
Meetings: 7.00pm, 2nd Wednesday of the month (Sep-Jun). United Reformed Church (Verrall Hall), Widmore Road, Bromley, BR1 1RY.
Central London (1975; 200)
Alison Gibson: rspb.cllg.contact@gmail.com; https://group.rspb.org.uk/centrallondon/
Meetings: Monthly online talks (days/dates vary, not Aug). Local walks, coach trips, occasional in-person events—see website for details, all events open to non-members, book via Eventbrite.
Croydon (1973; 545).
John Davis: johndaviswine1@gmail.com; https://group.rspb.org.uk/croydon/
Meetings: 7:30pm, 2nd Monday of the month (not Jun). Croham Road Baptist Church, 52 Croham Road, South Croydon, Surrey, CR2 7BA.
North East London (2009; 200)
Ray Watson: nelondonRSPB@yahoo.co.uk; https://group.rspb.org.uk/nelondon/
Meetings: 8:00pm, 2nd Tuesday of the month (Sep-Jun). Gwinnell Room, St Mary's Church, 207 High Road, South Woodford, London E18 2PA.
North West London (1983; n/a)
Bob Husband: rspb.nwlondon@gmail.com; https://group.rspb.org.uk/nwlondon/
Meetings: Currently not holding indoor meetings—contact/see website for further details.
Pinner & District (1972; 60).
Ian Jackson: imjpinRSPB@gmail.com; https://group.rspb.org.uk/pinner/
Meetings: 8:00pm, 2nd Thursday of the month (Sep-May). St John The Baptist Church Hall, Church Lane, Pinner, Middx HA5 3AA.

Richmond & Twickenham (1979; 255).
Clare Million: richmondRSPB@yahoo.co.uk;
https://group.rspb.org.uk/richmond/
Meetings: 7:30pm, 1st Tuesday of the month & 2:00pm, on the following Tuesday (Sep-Apr). The Hyde Room, York House, Richmond Road, Twickenham, TW1 3AA.

Wildlife Trust

London Wildlife Trust (1981; 11,000).
Fivefields, 8-10 Grosvenor Gardens, Victoria, London SW1W 0DH: 020 7261 0447;
enquiries@wildlondon.org.uk;
www.wildlondon.org.uk

No attempt will be made to navigate the reader around London from one site to the next. The sites have been arranged, very roughly, in a circle, starting with Staines in the W, proceeding E around the N of London and then returning W through the S of London to Kew. To reach the individual sites, see the Directions sections.

1 STAINES MOOR, RESERVOIRS & GEORGE VI RESERVOIR

Thames Water/Spelthorne Borough Council
Habitats: 1,270 acres, two large, raised reservoirs, concrete banks one divided by causeway, on either side of A3044 (reservoirs total 765 acres), grazed neutral grassland to W (Staines Moor), rivers (Colne), ponds, marsh, scrub. SSSI
Birds: Staines Reservoirs (George VI inaccessible but more of the same) SSSI because of numbers and variety of wintering duck. Gulls, terns on passage and breeding Common Tern on artifical islands. Grebes. Numbers and variety of waders highest when water levels low. Every few years one basin drained, exposing more mud and attracting more waders. Passage waders also on Moor, especially when wet. Redshank and Lapwing have bred in past. Blackcap, Whitethroat & Lesser Whithroat, Reed & Grasshopper Warblers breed on Moor. Sparrowhawk, Kestrel. Hobby in summer.
Other: Unusual flora due to chalk deposited by Colne when it floods.
Directions: TW19 7UE; TQ 056 734 car park on B378 just N of path up to Staines Reservoirs causeway. Leave M25 at J14, take A3113 E for Heathrow. Take 3rd exit (A3044) at next roundabout for Staines. Turn L at traffic lights on to B378, then R at mini roundabout. Car park for Staines Reservoirs after 500 yards on R.
Public transport: Bus: 116, 203, 216, 400, 416 & 555/6/7 all stop on A30, which along S side of Moor and the reservoirs. Train—Staines, to S of Moor and Reservoirs on other side of A30.
Visiting: Small, free, unsurpervised car park to E of Staines Reservoirs. Walk 50 yards S then footpath up embankment to causeway splitting Staines Reservoirs into N & S basins. Causeway a public footpath, open all hours, free. No facilities. Lay-by parking at other end of causeway on A3044 at TW18 4HY; TQ 046 729. Access to George VI on other side of A3044 restricted to permit holders. Staines Moor between George VI and M25 can be accessed from A30 to S with lay-bys at TQ 037 723 (E-bound) and TQ 040 722 (W-bound) or from the residential streets of Stanwell Moor to the N just off J14 of the M25. Footpaths across Moor including one along base of George VI embankment and the Colne Valley Way, which parallels the River Colne.
Wraysbury Reservoir immediately to W on other side of M25.
Contact:

2 BRENT RESERVOIR (WELSH HARP)

Canal & River Trust.
Habitats: Reservoir surrounded by marshland, woodland, unimproved grassland and playing fields.
Birds: 250+ spp. *Spring/summer:* Breeding Great Crested Grebe, Gadwall, Shoveler, Pochard, Common Tern, woodland species and up to eight spp warbler. Long history of rare birds inc London's first Great White Egret in 1997 and UK's first Iberian Chiffchaff in 1972. *Winter:* Good variety of wildfowl and gull spp.
Other: 28 spp butterflies, inc Marbled White and Ringlet, 15 spp dragonflies. A notable site for bats.
Directions: NW9 8SE; TQ 208 870 (Birchen Grove). NW London close to J1 of M1—take A406 (N Circular Rd) towards Neasden, then 2nd slip road on L on to A4088 (brown sign to reservoir), continue to next brown sign, turn R into Birchen Grove continue to car park.
Public transport: Train—Hendon station (Thameslink) and Neasdon (Underground) at opposite ends of the reservoir.
Visiting: Open access at all times. Park in Birchen Grove to access Welsh Harp Open Space nature reserve. Raised viewing platform and permanently open public hide overlooks northern marsh. Circular walk.
Contact: Welsh Harp Conservation Group: via website; https://brentres.wordpress.com/ (see website for other access arrangements).

3 WALTHAMSTOW WETLANDS

London Wildlife Trust.
Habitats: Wetlands—10 reservoirs providing drinking water for London, spread over 521 acres.
Birds: *All year:* Great Crested Grebe, Cormorant (breeding colony), Grey Heron (heronry), Tufted Duck, Peregrine Falcon, Kingfisher, Grey Wagtail. *Summer:* Common Tern, Hobby, hirundines, Reed & Sedge Warblers. *Spring/autumn passage:* Common Sandpiper, Redshank, Greenshank, waders, terns, migrant passerines. *Winter:* Wildfowl inc Teal, Shoveler, Goldeneye, Goosander. Water Rail, occasional scarce grebes and divers.
Other: Dragonflies, Bank Vole, bats, amphibians.

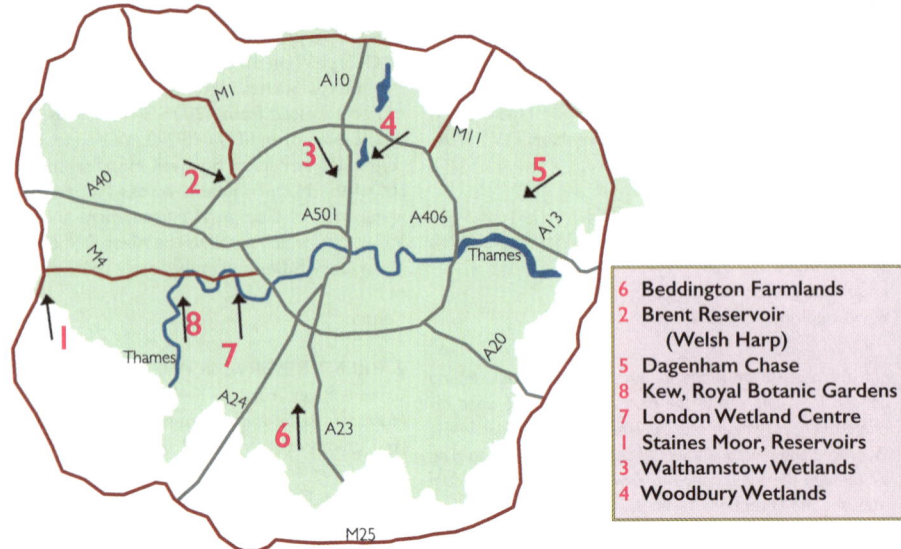

6 Beddington Farmlands
2 Brent Reservoir
  (Welsh Harp)
5 Dagenham Chase
8 Kew, Royal Botanic Gardens
7 London Wetland Centre
1 Staines Moor, Reservoirs
3 Walthamstow Wetlands
4 Woodbury Wetlands

Directions: N17 9NH; TQ 351 889. Close to central London. Entrance on A503 (Ferry Lane).
Public transport: Bus: 123 Wood Green to Ilford and 230 Wood Green to Walthamstow alight at Walthamstow Wetlands/Ferry Boat Inn stop, by reserve entrance. Underground (Victoria) to Blackhorse Road, walk W along Forest Road or Tottenham Hale (Victoria), walk E along Ferry Lane.
Visiting: Open daily 9:30am 5pm, Oct-Mar closes 4pm. The Engine House Visitor Centre, cafe (closes 4:45pm), shop, toilets. Hide, information trail. Activities and events. No dogs (except assistance dogs).
Contact: London WT: 020 3989 7448;
walthamstow@wildlondon.org.uk

4 WOODBERRY WETLANDS
London Wildlife Trust
Habitats: A working Reservoir, reedbeds.
Birds: All year: Great Crested Grebe, Sparrowhawk, Peregrine Falcon, Kestrel, Kingfisher, Reed Bunting. *Summer:* Hobby, Reed, Sedge & Cetti's Warblers. *Passage:* Common Sandpiper, occasionally other waders, terns. Hirundines. *Winter:* Wildfowl, gulls, Bittern.
Other: Bats, Fox, amphibians.
Directions: N16 5HQ; TQ 326 873. Off A503 (Seven Sisters Road), Woodberry Down—turn S into Woodburry Grove/Lordship Road. Two entrances on to New River Path—one from Lordship Road and one from Newton Close.
Public transport: Bus: 253, 254, 259 & 279 stop in nearby Seven Sisters Road. Train—Manor House Underground (Piccadilly line) five min walk from W entrance and Stamford Hill station five min walk from N entrance.

Visiting: Open daily 9:30am 5pm, Oct-Mar closes 4pm. Visitor centre, toilets (inc disabled, baby changing facilities), shop, cafe/refreshments, picnic area. Guide dogs only. Wheelchair accessible path, seating.
Contact: London WT: 020 7261 0447;
enquiries@wildlondon.org.uk

5 DAGENHAM CHASE LNR
London Borough of Barking & Dagenham.
Habitats: Shallow wetlands, reedbeds, horse-grazed pasture, scrub and wetland.
Birds: 190 spp. *Summer:* Breeding Lapwing, Water Rail, Little Ringed Plover, Kingfisher, Reed Warbler, Lesser Whitethroat, Reed Bunting. *Spring/autumn passage:* Yellow Wagtail, Wheatear, Ruff, Wood Sandpiper, Sand Martin, Ring Ouzel, Black Redstart and Hobby regular. *Winter:* Good numbers of Shoveler, Teal, Snipe, Redwing and Fieldfare.
Other: 140 plant spp, the nationally rare Black Poplar tree. Wasp Spider, butterflies and dragonflies.
Directions: RM7 0SS; TQ 509 860 (Millennium Centre). Lies in Dagenham Corridor S of A124 between A1112 & A125, an area of green belt between the London Boroughs of Barking, Dagenham & Havering.
Public transport: Bus: 174 from Romford or Dagenham, five mins walk. Underground—Dagenham East (District Line), 15 mins walk.
Visiting: Open all hours, not suitable for wheelchairs. Eastbrookend and Beam Valley Country Parks border site—surfaced footpaths suitable for wheelchairs. Millennium Centre (0208 595 4155) in Eastbrookend CP, toilets, car parking, Timberland Trail walk.
Contact: LBB&D 020 8227 2332;
parksandcountryside@lbbd.gov.uk

6 BEDDINGTON FARMLANDS

Valencia Waste Management/Thames Water
Beddington Farm Bird Group

Habitats: 400 acres, former and current sewage works and waste site (and, before that, farmland) now being restored for wildlife. Two main lakes, ponds, reedbed, several areas of wet grassland, scrub.

Birds: 258 spp (pre-AviList) recorded. *Summer:* Gadwall, Pochard, Lapwing, Little Ringed Plover, Cetti's, Reed & Sedge Warblers. *Passage:* A stopover for a wide variety of migrants, depending on weather conditions. Good for but not restricted to warblers, chats and wagtails. *Winter:* Gull numbers well down since end of landfill; variety of duck, Snipe, Jack Snipe, Water Rail, Water Pipit, Stonechat. Firecrest now overwinter and Dartford Warbler has been recorded.

Other: Brown Hairstreak, Mullein Moth. Red-veined Darter.

Directions: SM6 7BY; TQ 287 651 free Beddington Car Park West in Beddington Park, within walking distance of S gate. Immediately to E of A237, which runs N-S close to W side of Farmlands between Mitcham and Wallington. Other nearby parking options. Not all free.

Public transport: Bus: 151, 127, 407, 410, 463, 612 & 633 all stop close to one or more of the entrances to the permissive path, Train—Hackbridge, Mitcham Junction. Tram: Wimbledon to Beckenham Junction or Elmers End stop within walking distance.

Visiting: Public (i.e. non-members of Beddington Farm Bird Group) access restricted to permissive path running N-S along W side of reserve from Mitcham Common to Beddington Park. Entrances to this path: through gate at N end from Mitcham Park/Golf Course (TQ 287 673); from Beddington Lane tram stop or Carshalton Road (A237) by crossing railway via bridge from Hackbridge, opposite Sainsburys Local at (TQ 286 666); and gate at S end (TQ 287 657) from Beddingon Park, opposite Elmwood Close. Path closed one day a year, otherwise open all hours. Three public hides (no seats) overlooking farmlands. Reserve itself fenced off. Cafe (9am-4:30pm) toilets in Beddington Park. Path flat but can be muddy. Dogs allowed. Occasional public walks, plans to increase the number of hides.

Contact: Beddington Farm Bird Group:
beddingtonfarmlands.sightings@gmail.com
Warden: charlie.owens@sutton.gov.uk

7 LONDON WETLAND CENTRE

The Wildfowl & Wetlands Trust.

Habitats: Main lake, reedbeds, wader scrape, open water lakes, wet woodland, grazing marsh.

Birds: All year: Cetti's Warbler. *Summer:* Important numbers of wetland breeding spp inc grebes, swans, variety of duck (inc Pochard), Lapwing, Little Ringed Plover, Redshank, warblers, Reed Bunting. Artificial nesting bank for Sand Martins and rafts for nesting terns. Peregrine Falcons, which nest on Charing Cross Hospital, sighted regularly. *Winter:* Nationally important numbers of waterfowl, inc Gadwall and Shoveler. Bittern, Jack Snipe, Water Pipit.

Other: Water Voles, Slow Worm, Grass Snake, Common Lizard. Seven spp bat, 22 spp dragonflies and 25 spp butterflies. Notable plants inc Snake's Head Fritillaries, Cowslip, Pyramidal and Bee Orchids.

Directions: SW13 9WT; TQ 226 768. Less than one mile N of South Circular Road (A205), take A306 N, signposted into Queen Elizabeth's Walk, Barnes. In London Zone 2/3, one mile from Hammersmith.

Public transport: Bus: 485 (not Sun/bank hol) comes into centre. *Others:* 33 from Richmond. Train—Barnes.

Visiting: Coaches by arrangement. Open 9:30am-5:30pm Mar-Oct, 9:30am-4:30pm Nov-Feb (10am-3pm 24 Dec, closed 25 Dec), last admission one hour before closing. Admission charge for non-WWT members. Visitor centre, discovery centre and children's adventure area, restaurant (hot/cold food), shop, observatory building, 6 hides (all wheelchair accessible), sustainable gardens, pond zone, nature trails. Events. Assistance dogs only.

Contact: London Wetland Centre: 020 8409 4400; info.london@wwt.org.uk

8 ROYAL BOTANIC GARDENS, KEW

Habitats: 500 acre botanic garden woodland, meadow, lakes, specimen plants. Other side of Thames Path from tidal stretch of Thames. Syon Park on opposite bank of Thames.

Birds: Common woodland spp but also Great Crested & Little Grebes, various duck, gulls. Tree-top walkway offers opportunity for close-up views of birds in canopy.

Other: It's a botanic garden! Areas of grass left uncut to encourage insects.

Directions: Four entrances. Car park (pay & display) next to Brentford Gate (TW9 3AF; TQ 183 774. Limited parking on Kew Green and some nearby residential roads. Kew Green to W of A205 just S of Kew Bridge. Brentford Gate car park reach via lane on N side of Kew Green.

Public transport: Bus: 65 (connects 3 gates and Ealing Broadway and Richmond stations); 110 (Richmond station and close to gate on Kew Green and Kew Gardens underground; 237 & 267 stop at Kew Bridge Station. Train—Kew Bridge, Richmond stations. Underground—Kew Gardens, Ealing Broadway and Richmond stations.

Visiting: Four entrances: one by car park, one on Kew Green, two on A205. Charge, Gardens open 10am (8am for members), closing time varies between 4pm and 8pm depending on season. Array of cafes and restaurants, opening times vary. Toilets, inc accessible, glasshouses, not all parts wheelchair accessible, network of

paths inc tree-top walkway 60 ft above ground through crowns of Horse & Sweet Chestnut, Beech and various Oak spp, 37 acre natural area of native woodland.
Contact: 020 8332 5655; info@kew.org
Take A316 SW and then M3 into Surrey.

Surrey

London's urban sprawl continues to spread into much of the north of the county, but the heathlands at Chobham, Farnham, Frensham and Thursley have not yet been overwhelmed and still hold the habitat's specislists: Hobby, Nightjar, Woodlark and Dartford Warbler.

Bird Atlases/Avifauna
Birds of Surrey Bird Atlas 2007-2012
Surrey Bird Club
(Surrey Bird Club, 2018).
Birds of Surrey
Jeffery J Wheatley
(Surrey Bird Club, 2007).

Bird Recorder
Kevin Duncan (Recorder):
recorder@surreybirdclub.org.uk

Ed Stubbs (Assistant Recorder):
acr@surreybirdclub.org.uk

Bird Reports
Surrey Bird Report (1953-), from SBC—Penny Williams: 07771 804357; membership@surreybirdclub.org.uk
Surbiton and District Bird Watching Society Annual Bird Report (1970-), from SDBWS—Thelma Caine, 21 More Lane, Esher, KT10 8AJ: thelmacaine512@btinternet.com

BTO Regional Representatives
Penny Williams
Wetland Bird Survey (WeBS)
Local Organizer: webs@bto.org
Surrey & SW London
Penny Williams

Clubs
Surrey Bird Club (1957; 400)
Penny Williams (Gen Sec), Bournbrook House, Sandpit Hall Lane, Chobham, GU24 8HA: 01276 857 736; membership@surreybirdclub.org.uk; www.surreybirdclub.org.uk
Meetings: Contact/see website for details.
Surbiton & District Birdwatching Society (1954; 130)

Alice Laird (Membership enquiries): alicesdbws@martinhwatson.co.uk; surbitonbirds.org
Meetings: 7:30pm 3rd Tuesday of the month (not Aug). St Matthews C of E Primary School, Langley Road, Surbiton, KT6 6LW.

Ringing Groups/Bird Observatory
Hersham RG
Runnymede RG: https://runnymederinging.blogspot.com

RSPB Local Groups
Dorking & District (1984; 110)
Glenn Carmichael: RSPBdorking@gmail.com; https://group.rspb.org.uk/dorkinganddistrict/
Meetings: Online and in person meetings (in Dorking); programme of walks. Contact/see website for details.
East Surrey (1984; 150)
John Lawrence: jfjlawrence@gmail.com; https://group.rspb.org.uk/eastsurrey/
Meetings: 7:30pm, 2nd Wednesday of the month (not Aug). White Hart Barn, High Street, Godstone, RH9 8DU.
Guildford & District (1974; 350)
Tony Cummins: info@RSPBguildford.org.uk; https://wp.rspbguildford.org.uk/
Meetings: 2:00pm, 1st Thursday of the month (Sep-Mar). Shalford Village Hall, Kings Road, Shalford, GU4 8JU and 7:30pm, 4th Wednesday of the month (Sep-May/note: Nov, Jan, Feb will be via zoom). Onslow Village Hall, The Square, Wilderness Road, Guildford, GU2 7QR.
North West Surrey (1974; 92)
Alan Sharps: nwsleader@yahoo.co.uk; https://group.rspb.org.uk/nwsurrey/
Meetings: 7:45pm, 4th Thursday of the month (Sep-Nov, Jan-Jun). St Charles Borromeo School, Portmore Way, Weybridge, KT13 8JD.

Wildlife Trust
Surrey Wildlife Trust (1959; 15,000)
School Lane, Pirbright, Woking, GU24 0JN: 01483 795 440; info@surreywt.org.uk; www.surreywildlifetrust.org

If entering along M3, leave at J3.

1 CHOBHAM COMMON NNR
Surrey Wildlife Trust.
Habitats: Largest NNR in south-east England (1,420 acres). Lowland wet and dry heath, with pools, mixed broadleaved and pine woodlands.
Birds: 115+ spp inc Hobby, Nightjar, Woodlark and Dartford Warbler. Also Cuckoo, Lesser Spotted Woodpecker, Skylark, Stonechat, Linnet and Yellowhammer.

Surrey

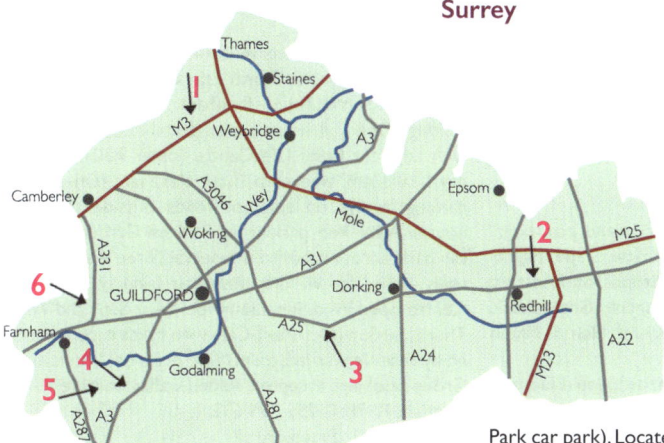

Other: 350+ spp. flowering plants, 25 spp mammal, 29 spp.butterflies inc Silver-studded Blue and 22 spp dragonflies, Raft Spider.

Directions: KT16 0ED; SU 973 648 (Staple Hill car park). From J3 of M3 head N on A322 and A30 in direction of Sunningdale. From Broomhall turn R into Chobham Road (B383) then L at roundabout (B386) & R at next roundabout over M3—R into Staple Hill Road. Other car parks in area.

Public transport: Buses: 73, Woking to Chobham, Falcon Buses (01932 787 752). 37A (Mon-Fri, limited). Stagecoach. Both stop in Bowling Green Road, S of Common. Services to Sunningdale from Ascot, Windsor, Camberley and Staines. Train—Sunningdale, 0.5 mile from NW corner of Common.

Visiting: Open all hours. Six car parks with information boards (parking charges apply), three self-guided trails. Site leaflet available from rangers.

Contact: Surrey WT: 01483 795 440; info@surreywt.org.uk

Take M3 back to M25 and head E.

2 NUTFIELD MARSHES
Surrey Wildlife Trust

Habitats: Flooded sand pits, scrub, grassland.

Birds: All year: Little & Great Crested Grebes, Kingfisher, Ring-necked Parakeet, Grey Wagtail, Reed Bunting. *Summer:* Common Tern, hirundines, warblers inc Garden and Lesser Whitethroat. *Passage:* Waders inc. Common Sandpiper, possible godwits, Whimbrel and Spotted Redshank. *Winter:* Wildfowl inc Goldeneye, Pochard, occasional Scaup, Smew and divers, Red-necked & Black-necked Grebes. Gulls, Green Sandpiper, Lapwing, Snipe, occasional Jack Snipe, Golden Plover, Fieldfare, Redwing, Brambling.

Other: Dragonflies and butterflies, Grass Snake.

Directions: RH1 4EU; TQ 299 517 (Mercer's Country Park car park). Located between M25 & M23. From A25 take Nutfield Marsh Road, after one mile turn R into Mercer's CP (walk from here).

Public transport: Bus: 430/435 Redhill to Merstham, alight at Watercolour. Metrobus (01293 449 191). Train—Redhill and Merstham.

Visiting: Open all hours, three sites—The Moors, Spynes Mere and Holmethorpe Lagoons—part of a complex with Mercer's Country Park. Car park, toilets, cafe at Mercer's CP.

Contact: Surrey WT: 01483 795 440: info@surreywt.org.uk

Take A25 W to Dorking.

3 LEITH HILL
National Trust

Habitats: Woodland, grassy escarpment, heathland. Much of site an SSSI.

Birds: All year: Buzzard, Sparrowhawk, Woodcock, Little Owl, common woodland spp. *Summer:* Nightjar and Woodlark (follow 1.75 mile heathland trail from tower), common warblers. Redstart and Wood Warblers (occasionally now). *Winter:* Thrushes and finches, inc Crossbill.

Other: Woodland flora, butterflies, dragonflies, bats.

Directions: RH5 6LX; TQ 139 429 (Windy Gap car park), RH5 6HG; TQ 146 432 (Landslip car park)—both due S of Leith Hill Tower on Abinger Road. SW of Dorking. Signposted from A25 at Wotton & from A29 at Ockley.

Public transport: None.

Visiting: Open all hours. A folly tower standing on the highest point in Surrey. Refreshments by tower (not NT). Self-guided trails around the area—leaflet available (some trails steep and uneven). Nearby Leith Hill Place open 1 Apr–30 Oct on Fri/Sat/Sun and bank hols, 11am-4:30pm (entrance fee), refreshments 11am-4:30am. 0.5 mile W of Windy Gap car park, follow brown sign off Abinger Road/Leith Hill Road. Park in Rhododendron Wood car park (charge) or walk there on trails from other car parks.

Contact: National Trust: leithhill@nationaltrust.org.uk
Continue on A25 towards Guildford, then bear S on A248. At junction with A3100 head S towards Goldalming and then Milford. Cross A3 and join B3001 as below.

4 THURSLEY NNR

Natural England

Habitats: Wet and dry heathland, woodland, peat bog.
Birds: Summer: Hobby, Lapwing, Curlew, Snipe, Nightjar, Woodlark, Spotted Flycatcher, Stonechat, Redstart, Crossbill. *Passage:* Waders inc Redshank, Greenshank, Wood & Common Sandpipers. *Winter:* Hen & Marsh Harriers, Great Grey Shrike.
Other: Large populations of Silver-studded Blue and Grayling butterflies but Purple Emperor have not been seen recently. 26 spp dragonflies. Sandier sites on reserve provide habitat for many spp of solitary bees and wasps and tiger beetles. Damp areas support carnivorous sundews and large population (1,000s) of Early Marsh Orchid. All six native reptiles.
Directions: GU8 6LW; SU 898 417 (The Moat car park). From Guildford, take A3 SW to B3001 (Elstead/Churt road). Moat car park, S of Elstead village. Alternative parking on recreation ground in Thursley.
Public transport: Bus: 46 (not Sun) Guildford/Godalming to Farnham stops in Elstead. Stagecoach.
Visiting: Open access. Boardwalk in wetter areas along the Heath Trail (2.25 miles in length). Parties must obtain prior permission. Keep dogs on a lead/under control, especially during breeding season and out of nesting habitat.
Contact: Natural England: 01428 685 675;
james.giles@naturalengland.org.uk
Continue on B3001 towads Farnham.

5 FARNHAM HEATH

RSPB

Habitats: Heathland, acid grassland, mixed woodland and chestnut coppice. Pine plantation being thinned to encourage mixed woodland and scrub.
Birds: Spring/Summer: Woodcock, Nightjar, Woodlark, Tree Pipit, Dartford Warbler, woodland birds, inc Stock Dove, Green & Great Spotted Woodpeckers, Blackcap, Spotted Flycatcher and Redstart. *Winter:* Crossbills in pine woods, winter finches and thrushes, inc. Brambling around feeders.
Other: 150+ spp fungi. Bats in summer. Sand Lizard, plus variety of butterflies inc Grayling & Silver-studded Blue. Field Cricket.
Directions: GU10 2DL; SU 859 433. Take B3001 SE from Farnham. Take R hand fork, signposted Tilford, immediately past level crossing. Keep to that road. Just outside Tilford village look for sign to **Rural Life Centre**. Entrance is on R after 0.5 mile.
Public transport: Bus: 19 Farnham to Hindhead (not Sun) stops in Millbridge village, outside entrance to

Pierrepont House. Reserve is a mile away, along Reeds Road (follow signs to **Rural Life Centre**). Stagecoach in Hants & Surrey. Train—Farnham.
Visiting: Open all hours. Large grass car park, shared with adjacent Rural Life Centre (open 9:30am weekdays, 10:30am weekends, may close at 4pm—some parking lay-bys on adjacent roads outside of these hours). Also, free parking in Squires Garden Centre car park, across road from reserve. Three way-marked trails—good for walking, pushchair friendly. Rural Life Centre open Wed-Sun 11am-4pm (Apr-Sep) and Wed, Thurs and Sun (Oct-Mar). Cafe with cakes recommended by reserve warden, toilets (inc. disabled), picnic area. Group bookings accepted, guided walks available.
Contact: RSPB: 01252 795 632;
farnham.heath@rspb.org.uk
Continue into Farnham on B3001 then as below.

6 TICE'S MEADOW NATURE RESERVE

Surrey County Council/Tice's Meadow Bird Group
Habitats: Open water with islands and scrapes, ponds, reedbed, woodland, scrub, wet and dry grassland.
Birds: 201 spp recorded. *All year:* Common wildfowl, Egyptian Goose, Little Egret, Red Kite, Lapwing, Barn Owl, Kingfisher, Stonechat. *Spring/summer:* Little Ringed Plover, Common Tern, Hobby, hirundines, warblers inc Reed & Sedge. *Passage:* Waders, passerines. *Winter:* Water Rail, Snipe, Jack Snipe, winter thrushes.
Other: 30 spp dragonflies, 34 spp butterflies.
Directions: GU9 9LY; SU 867 489 (main entrance on Badshot Lea Road, B3028). Lies between Farnham and Aldershot.
Public transport: Buses: 15 Tice's Meadow to Aldershot (daily); 16 Farnham to Aldershot (not Sun). Stagecoach South. Train—Aldershot, Farnham.
Visiting: Open all hours, nearby roadside parking. Network of paths inc part of Blackwater Valley Path (N section of site) and one mile circular biodiversity trail. Gates with RADAR locks on main entrance and from housing estate (Overton Close, SU 872 488). Hide, viewpoints, benches. Dogs under control, on lead during breeding season.
Contact: Surrey County Council: 0300 200 1003;
countryside.estate@surreycc.gov.uk
Tice's Meadow Bird Group:
ticesmeadow@hotmail.co.uk; www.ticesmeadow.org
Return to Milford via B3001, then A283 S for W Sussex.

Sussex

Divided, for administrative purposes into 'East' & 'West' Sussex, the county is dominated by the chalk hills of the South Downs. Coastal sites from Chichester Harbour in the west through to Rye Harbour in the east guarantee a good day's birdwatching with an interesting mix of wildfowl, waders, raptors, terns and Bittern, depending on the season. Selsey Bill (west) is a good spot for a seawatching, with a noticeable skua passage in the spring and, together with Beachy Head (east), it attracts spring and autumn migrants. Ashdown Forest offers a fine mix of woodland and heathland birds while RSPB Pulborough Brooks holds important numbers of wintering wildfowl, with a chance of Bewick's Swans.

Bird Atlas/Avifauna
The Birds of Sussex
Sussex Ornithological Society/ Adrian LR Thomas (BTO, 2014).

Bird Recorder
David Thorns: recorder@sos.org.uk.

Bird Report
Sussex Bird Report (1948-). Most recent editions (2023-24) from Val Bentley, Lanacre, Blackgate Lane, Henfield, BN5 9HA: mandpcommittee@sos.org.uk. New members receive a copy of the latest Report. Earlier editions (1948-2021) can be downloaded from: https://www.sos.org.uk/sos-downloadable-publications

BTO Regional Representatives
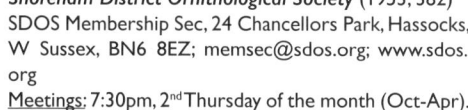
Helen Crabtree
Wetland Bird Survey (WeBS)
Local Organizers: webs@bto.org
Chichester Harbour
Peter Hughes
Sussex (Other Sites—Coastal)
Dave Boddington
Sussex (Other Sites—Inland).
Helen Crabtree

Clubs
Sussex Ornithological Society (1962; 2,000+).
Alan Swetman (Sec): 10 Hills Road, Steyning, W Sussex, BN44 3QG; 07472 139 927; secretary@sos.org.uk; www.sos.org.uk
Meetings: Annual conference Haywards Heath, occasional other meetings—contact/see website for details.
Friends of Rye Harbour Nature Reserve (1973; 2,000+).
Discovery Centre, Harbour Road, Rye Harbour, TN31 7FW; ryeharbourfriends@gmail.com; www.ryeharbourfriends.net & www.sussexwildlifetrust.org.uk/ryeharbour
Meetings: Special events, including monthly walks and talks, held for Friends. Contact/see website for details.
Henfield Birdwatch (1998; 300+)
Mike Russell, Tor-Est-In, Lower Station Road, Henfield, West Sussex BN5 9UG: 07931 444947;
mikerussell51@yahoo.co.uk;
www.henfieldbirdwatch.co.uk

Shoreham District Ornithological Society (1953; 382)
SDOS Membership Sec, 24 Chancellors Park, Hassocks, W Sussex, BN6 8EZ; memsec@sdos.org; www.sdos.org
Meetings: 7:30pm, 2nd Thursday of the month (Oct-Apr). St Nicolas and St Mary Primary School, Eastern Road, Shoreham-by-Sea, BN43 6PE.

Ringing Group/Bird Observatory
Beachy Head Ringing Station.
Cuckmere RG
Rye Bay RG
Steyning RG

RSPB Local Groups
Brighton & District (1974; 100+)
Mark Weston: markrweston1964@gmail.com ;
https://group.rspb.org.uk/brighton/
Meetings: 7:30pm, 4th Thursday of the month (Sep-Nov,/ Jan-May). Woodingdean Community Centre, Warren Road, Woodingdean, Brighton, BN2 6BA.
Chichester (1979; 120)
Stuart Malcolm: chichesterbirds@gmail.com;
https://group.rspb.org.uk/chichester/
Meetings: 7:30pm, 4th Thursday of the month (Sep-May) The Masonic Hall, 7 South Pallant, Chichester, West Sussex PO19 1SY. Zoom and hall meetings are held. Contact/see website for details.
Crawley & Horsham (relaunched 2022; -)
Paul Stillman: crawley.horsham.rspb@gmail.com;
https://group.rspb.org.uk/crawleyandhorsham/
Meetings: Contact/see website for details.
East Grinstead (1998; 60)
Sue Dennis: eastgrinsteadrspb@gmail.com;
https://group.rspb.org.uk/egrinstead/
Meetings: 8:00pm, last Wednesday of the month (Sep-Nov/Jan-Jun). Main Hall, East Court, College Lane, East Grinstead, West Sussex RH19 3LT.
Eastbourne & District (1994; 100)
Tony Vass: eastbourneRSPB@gmail.com;
https://group.rspb.org.uk/eastbourne/
Meetings: 2:15pm & 7pm, 1st Wednesday of the month (Sep-Dec & Feb-Jun). St. Wilfrid's Church Hall, Eastbourne Rd, Pevensey Bay, East Sussex BN24 6HL.
Hastings & St Leonards (1983; 65)
Sue Neighbour: RSPB.HStL@gmail.com;
https://group.rspb.org.uk/hastings/
Meetings: 7:30pm, 3rd Friday of the month. The Taplin Centre, Upper Maze Hill, St Leonards-on-Sea, East Sussex TN38 0LQ.

Wildlife Trust
Sussex Wildlife Trust (1961; 38,000)
1st Floor, The Keep, Woollards Way, Brighton BN1 9BT; 01273 492 630; enquiries@sussexwt.org.uk; www.sussexwt.org.uk

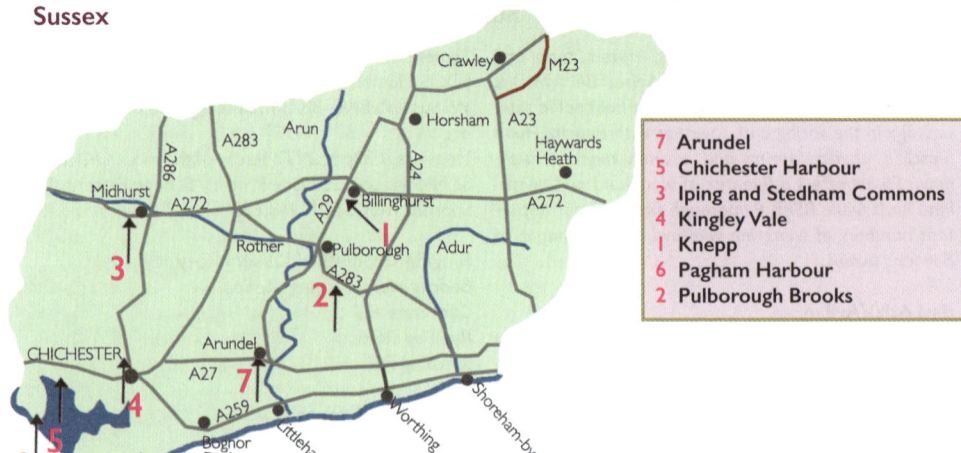

7	**Arundel**
5	**Chichester Harbour**
3	**Iping and Stedham Commons**
4	**Kingley Vale**
I	**Knepp**
6	**Pagham Harbour**
2	**Pulborough Brooks**

West

*If entering W Sussex on A283 from **Surrey**, take the A272 at Petworth and head E.*

I KNEPP

Knepp Estate/Knepp Rewilding Project
Habitats: 3,500 acres, woodland, scrub, grassland, lake, wetland, wood pasture
Birds: White Stork reintroduction programme. *All year:* Common woodland spp, Great Crested Grebe, Red Kite, Tawny & Barn Owls, Kingfisher, Raven. *Spring/summer:* Cuckoo, Turtle Dove, Hobby, Nightingale, Garden Warbler, Whitethroat, Lesser Whitethroat, Blackcap, Spotted Flycatcher. *Winter:* Redwing, Fieldfare, Hawfinch (large winter roost in '24), Snipe, Siskin, Wigeon, Teal, Shoveler, Gadwall. Green Sandpiper on autumn passage.
Other: Fallow & Red Deer, grazing stock includes Old English Longhorn Cattle, Tamworth Pigs & Exmoor Ponies. Purple Emperor butterfly.
Directions: RH13 8NQ; TQ 157 198 (Walkers' car park, at Dial Post off A24), five miles SE of Billinghurst.
Public transport: None.
Visiting: Use Walkers' car park (free, donation suggested). Keep to public footpaths: 16 miles of walks within rewilding project, with five tree viewing platforms and hide overlooking Knepp Lake (map downloadable at www.knepp.co.uk/footpath-maps or available in car park). Keep dogs under close control, preferably on lead at all times.
Other facilities: Knepp Wilding Kitchen with toilets (9am-4pm, open for dinner Saturday), also shop (9am-5pm). Knepp Wildland Safaris. Calendar of events—booking required, limited places. Luxury glamping and pitch your own camping available Easter-end Oct, plus two self-contained cabins available year-round.
Contact: Knepp Estate: www.knepp.co.uk

Take the A24 S and then A283 W at Storrington

2 PULBOROUGH BROOKS

RSPB
Habitats: Lowland wet grassland (wet meadows/ditches). Restored heathland, hedgerows, scrub and woodland.
Birds: Spring/summer: Breeding waders and songbirds (inc Lapwing, Avocet and Nightingale), Hobby, Firecrest, Spotted Flycatcher, Nightjar, Woodlark, Barn Owl. *Autumn:* Passage waders, Redstart, Whinchat, Yellow Wagtail, incoming wildfowl spp. *Winter:* Thousands of wildfowl and waders, Peregrine Falcon, Marsh Harrier and White-tailed Eagle hunt regularly. Hen Harrier, Merlin and Short-eared Owl are possible.
Other: Good variety of butterflies inc Brown & Purple Hairstreak and dragonflies inc Emperor, Four-spotted Chaser and Downy Emerald.
Directions: RH20 2EL; TQ 058 164. Part of South Downs National Park, signposted on A283 between Pulborough (via A29) & Storrington (via A24). Two miles SE of Pulborough.
Public transport: Train—Pulborough (two miles) with connecting 100 bus (Burgess Hill to Horsham, not Sun)—request stop, ask driver to stop outside reserve entrance. Compass Travel (01903 690 025).
Visiting: Two trails, four hides, two viewpoints open dawn-dusk (not 24-26 Dec). Large car park inc coach area, cycle stands. Parking fee for visitor centre and heathland trail. Admission fee for wetland nature trail (RSPB members free parking and entry). Visitor centre open daily (not 24-26 Dec) 10am-4pm (inc shop, cafe), displays, toilets. Play and picnic areas. Electric buggy available for hire—book in advance, only wetland trail suitable. Assistance dogs only on wetland trail, access on lead to parts of wooded heathland trail/public footpaths.

Contact: RSPB: 01798 875 851;
pulborough.brooks@rspb.org.uk
Continue W on A283 to Petworth, then A272 to Midhurst.

3 IPING & STEDHAM COMMONS NATURE RESERVE

Sussex Wildlife Trust
Habitats: 313-acre heathland, woodland, scrub.
Birds: All year: Sparrowhawk, Woodlark, Dartford Warbler, Stonechat, common woodland and scrub spp inc Great Spotted & Green Woodpeckers. *Summer:* Hobby, Cuckoo, Nightjar, Tree Pipit, warblers inc Garden, Willow, Whitetroat, Linnet. *Passage:* Hirundines. *Winter:* Fieldfare, Redwing, Siskin, Redpoll, Crossbill.
Other: Butterflies inc Silver-studded Blue and dragonflies. Adder, Common Lizard. Heath Sand Wasp, Minotaur Beetle.
Directions: GU29 0PB; SU 852 219. Two miles W of Midhurst, car park on Elsted Road, 250 yards off A272.
Public transport: Bus: 92 Midhurst to Petersfield, alight at Iping Lane & walk 250 yards down Elsted Road to car park (cars, no path). Stagecoach South (0345 241 8000).
Visiting: Open all year. Car park (height barrier). Dogs under close control on paths/on lead.
Contact: Sussex WT: 01273 492 630;
enquiries@sussexwt.org.uk
Head S on A286, take B2141 on R before Chichester.

4 KINGLEY VALE NNR

Natural England
Habitats: Largest yew forest in W Europe (30,000+ yew trees). Chalk grassland, mixed oak/ash woodland and scrub. Chalk heath. Part of South Downs National Park.
Birds: All year: Common woodland spp inc Green Woodpecker, Treecreeper, Nuthatch, Goldcrest, Firecrest, Bullfinch. Woodcock, Buzzard, Red Kite, Barn & Tawny Owls, Hawfinch, Raven. *Spring/summer:* Nightingale, Grasshopper Warbler, Whitethroat, Lesser Whitethroat, Blackcap. *Autumn passage:* Osprey, Hen Harrier and Hobby. *Winter:* Redwing, Fieldfare, other thrushes (attracted to Yew berries).
Other: Ancient Yew trees, Yellow Meadow Ant, 39 spp butterflies inc Brown Argus and Chalkhill Blue, 11 spp orchid, Brown Hare, Dormouse, Fallow & Roe Deer, bats.
Directions: PO18 9BE; SU 825 087 (West Stoke car park). Approx five miles NW of Chichester town centre. N from Chichester on A286 to Mid Lavant, then turn L by church on to Downs Road, follow to West Stoke. Turn R at junction after church to West Stoke car park—0.6 mile from reserve entrance.
Public transport: Train—Chichester (three miles).
Visiting: Via footpath from car park, bridleway access via Woodend. No disabled access. Nature trail and an unmanned information centre, leaflets and nature trail

guides. Dogs on lead.
Contact: Natural England: 0300 060 6000;
enquiries@naturalengland.org.uk;
South Downs National Park Authority: 01730 814 810;
info@southdowns.gov.uk
Continue S to Chichester.

5 CHICHESTER HARBOUR

Chichester Harbour Conservancy
Habitats: Deep saltwater channels, mud banks, sand dunes and shingle.
Birds: Internationally important for birds, with an estimated 55,000 birds residing or passing through each year. *Spring/summer:* Little, Sandwich & Common Terns breed. Dartford Warbler breeds at Sandy Point NR. *Autumn/winter:* Waders inc Lapwing, Golden Plover, Curlew, Whimbrel, Black & Bar-tailed Godwits, Oystercatcher, Turnstone, Snipe, Dunlin and Sanderling. Up to 10,000 Brent Geese, Red-breasted Merganser and common wildfowl species. Kingfisher, Short-eared Owl, Hen Harrier, Skylark.
Other: Common Seal, Water Vole, Stoat, Marsh Samphire, Sea Purslane, Sea Lavender and Sea Aster.
Directions: West of Chichester, with various viewing points along 47 miles of coastline to Hayling Island. East Head/West Wittering good for birdwatching—from A27 S of Chichester, follow brown signs for West Wittering Beach. Sandy Point NR in SE corner of Hayling Island can only be visited on guided walks.
Public transport: Various Stagecoach services in area.
Visiting: Five paths suitable for wheelchairs: Cobnor Point/ Itchenor/ Prinsted/ North Common, Northney/ Sandy Point, Hayling Island. Wheelchair-accessible viewing platform and toilet at Itchenor. RADAR-key toilet at Dell Quay.
Langstone Harbour with **Farlington Marshes** in **Hampshire** is immediately to W.
Contact: Harbour Office (inc Friends of Chichester Hbr), Itchenor, PO20 7AW: 01243 512 301;
info@conservancy.co.uk; www.conservancy.co.uk;
info@friendsch.org; www.friendsch.org
To the SE.

6 PAGHAM HARBOUR

West Sussex County Council/RSPB
Habitats: Mudflats, intertidal saltmarsh, shingle beaches, lagoons, reedbed, grassland and farmland.
Birds: All year: Little Egret, Marsh Harrier, Stonechat, Yellowhammer, Reed Bunting. *Spring:* Passage migrants (warblers, hirundines, Wheatear). *Summer:* Breeding Sandwich, Little & Common Terns, Black-headed Gull, Ringed Plover, Oystercatcher, Cattle Egret. *Autumn:* Passage waders inc Curlew Sandpiper, Whimbrel, Ruff and Little Stint, wildfowl, migrants, inc Osprey, Pied & Spotted Flycatchers. *Winter:* 20,000 wildfowl and waders inc Brent Goose, Pintail, Golden Plover, Lapwing. Merlin,

241

Slavonian Grebe.
Other: Common & Grey Seals (winter). Wide variety of grasses, butterflies and dragonflies inc Emperor, Broad-bodied Chaser and Hairy Dragonfly, Common Darter, Blue & Azure Damselflies.
Directions: PO20 7NE; SZ 856 966. Five miles S of Chichester on B2145 towards Selsey. After 0.5 mile turn R at first roundabout still following Selsey. Look for entrance just after leaving Sidlesham after speed limit increases to 50 mph.
Public transport: Bus: 51 (Chichester-Selsey) stops by visitor centre. Stagecoach. Train—Chichester.
Visiting: Sidlesham Ferry (visitor centre) and Church Norton car parks open all hours (free for RSPB members, no overnight parking). Groups and coach parties must book in advance. Visitor centre, with hot drinks/light snacks, toilets (inc disabled) open daily (not 24-26 Dec), 10am-4pm. Two hides, several viewpoints, three trails. Dogs under close control and staying on footpaths. No cycling on footpaths.
Contact: RSPB: 01243 641 508;
pagham.harbour@rspb.org.uk
Return N on B2145 and at junction with A27 head E on it to Arundel.

7 WWT ARUNDEL
WWT
Habitats: 65 acres, pools, scrapes, reedbed (one of largest in Sussex, SSSI), wet grassland beside tidal river Arun.
Birds: Lapwing, Kingfisher, Cetti's Warbler, Firecrest. *Spring/summer:* Cattle Egret (breeding), Reed & Sedge Warbler, Sand Martin (nest bank). *Autumn:* Gadwall, Teal, Water Rail, Snipe, Redpoll and Goldfinch flocks. *Winter:* Marsh Harrier, Little Egret and Pied Wagtail roosts, increasing numbers of raptors inc Peregrine Falcon and Red Kite. Bewick's Swans possible in cold weather.
Other: Water Vole. Grass Snake. Dragonflies.
Directions: BN18 9BP; TQ 021 082. Leave the A27 at either of two roundabouts to S of Arundel, take minor roads into Arundel, then follow brown duck signs and take Mill Road, which runs round S & E sides of Castle. WWT car park after just under a mile on R.
Public transport: Bus 9, Littlehampton to Arundel, Stagecoach; 85, Chichester to Arundel (not Sun), Compass. Then walk from town centre. Train—Arundel.
Visiting: Free car park, charge for centre (members free). Open 10am-4:30pm (2pm on 24 Dec, closed 25 Dec), cafe (closes 4pm), shop. Accessible car parking, toilets. Most paths level and surfaced and hides with lower windows for wheelchairs, wheelchairs available to borrow. Boat safaris. Captive Dalmatian Pelicans and Red-breasted Geese. 8 hides. assistance dogs only.
Contact: 01903 883 355; info.arundel@wwt.org.uk
Continue E on A27 into

East

Take minor road R off A27 for Alfriston, just before cross River Cuckmere.

8 LULLINGTON HEATH NNR
Natural England
Habitats: Grazed chalk downland/heath, scrub/gorse.
Birds: Summer: Breeding Nightingale, Turtle Dove, Cuckoo, Garden Warbler, Yellowhammer. *Passage:* Migrants inc Wheatear, Redstart, Ring Ouzel. *Winter:* Woodcock, Brambling (adjacent forest).
Other: Bell Heather, Ling, gorse on chalk heath, orchids.
Directions: BN26 5QJ; TQ 562 013 (Jevington). Five miles NW of Eastbourne, between Jevington & Litlington, on N edge of Friston Forest. Turn off A259 at Friston and head to Jevington—park here. Walk past church (on South Downs Way), after c.0.5 mile, once out of trees, continue straight on (SDW goes off to R) for 0.25 mile to reserve. Alternative parking around Friston Forest, inc Seven Sisters CP visitor centre on A259.
Public transport: Bus: 12/12X Brighton to Eastbourne stop at Friston/Seven Sisters CP. Brighton & Hove Buses (01273 886 200).
Visiting: Access on foot via footpaths & bridleways (some steep). Nearest toilets/refreshments at pubs in Jevington, Litlington or Seven Sisters CP, 1.25 miles to S.
Contact: Natural England: 01323 423 962
Return to A27 and then A259, heading E for

9 RYE HARBOUR
Sussex Wildlife Trust/Environment Agency/
East Sussex County Council/Rother District Council—
main partners of management agreement.
Includes Castle Water (217 acres), owned by Sussex Wildlife Trust.
Habitats: 1,150 acres, sea, sand, shingle, saline lagoons, saltmarsh, coastal grazing marsh, ditches, freshwater gravel pits and reedbeds.
Birds: c.280 spp, c.70 spp have bred. *Spring:* Passage waders, especially roosting Whimbrel. *Summer:* Turtle Dove, breeding terns (three spp), waders (seven spp. inc Avocet), gulls (six spp inc Mediterranean), Garganey, Shoveler, Cetti's Warbler, Bearded Tit, Wheatear. *Winter:* Wildfowl and waders, inc nationally important numbers of Shoveler and Sanderling. Smew, Water Rail, Bittern, Barn & Short-eared Owls.
Other: Good shingle flora inc endangered Least Lettuce and Stinging Hawksbeard. Saltmarsh supports unusual plants inc Marsh Mallow and Sea-heath and specialist insects inc Saltmarsh Bee and Star-wort Moth. Dragonflies inc Red-veined Darter and Scarce Emerald Damselfly.
Directions: TN31 7TT; TQ 942 189. Main access (large car park) is 1.5 miles SE of Rye, off A259 along Harbour

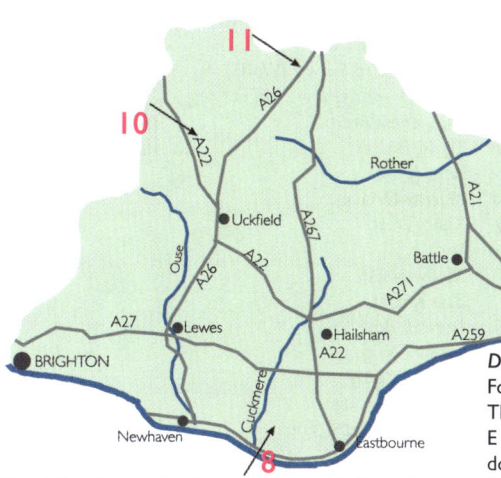

Directions: The Forest lies between Crowborough, Forest Row and Maresfield—crossed by A22 and A275. The Forest Centre (RH18 5JP; TQ 432 323) is one mile E of Wych Cross traffic lights on A22, opposite Ashdown Park Hotel.

Public transport: Bus—various services run through Forest. Stagecoach 54; Metrobus 270 and 291; Sussex Bus 31; Brighton & Hove Buses (Regency) 29; Compass Travel 261.

Visiting: Open all year, over 40 signposted car parks, many walks throughout Forest (various maps available—downloadable for small donation). Dogs should be under control at all times—grazing stock present. Forest Centre—information barn, toilets.

Contact: The Ashdown Forest Centre, Coleman's Hatch Road, Wych Cross, Forest Row, East Sussex, RH18 5JP:

01342 823 583; conservators@ashdownforest.org; www.ashdownforest.org;

Friends of Ashdown Forest

www.friendsofashdownforest.co.uk/

The Ashdown Forest Foundation

www.ashdownforestfdn.org

Take A26 from Crowborough for Tunbridge Wells.

Road (to the end)—signposted Rye Harbour. Access also from Winchelsea (SW of site).

Public transport: Bus: 313 Rye (train station) to Rye Harbour. Stagecoach in Hastings. Train—Rye & Winchelsea.

Visiting: Open all hours—public footpaths, three circular trails: (2, 4.3 & 6 miles long) and tarmac path between Rye Harbour and Winchelsea car parks. Main car park in Rye Harbour village close to local facilities inc shop, pubs, toilets and disabled facilities. Reserve's own Discovery Centre has shop, cafe, toilets (inc disabled) and events spaces. Site is flat with some wheelchair access to four hides on eastern side, although there are stiles where stock is grazing. One hide and viewpoint on Castle Water side. Organized groups should book in advance.

Contact: Sussex WT: 01797 360960;

via website; https://rye.sussexwildlifetrust.org.uk

Friends of Rye Harbour: www.ryeharbourfriends.co.uk

Take A268 NW from Rye. At junction with A21, go straight over and take B2099 and then, just past Wadhurst, the B2100 for Crowborough.

10 ASHDOWN FOREST

The Conservators of Ashdown Forest are responsible for its management.

Habitats: 6,175 acres, heathland (60%), woodland (40%).

Birds: All year: Buzzard, Sparrowhawk, Red Kite, Raven, Dartford Warbler, Stonechat, Crossbill, woodland species inc Marsh Tit and Siskin. *Spring/summer:* Hobby, Woodcock, Cuckoo, Nightjar, Woodlark, Redstart, Tree Pipit, Spotted Flycatcher, migratory warblers. *Winter:* Hen Harrier, Great Grey Shrike, winter thrushes, Brambling, Redpoll, Siskin.

Other: Deer (Fallow, Roe, Muntjac), Dormouse, bats. Dragonflies, Raft Spider. 34 spp butterflies inc Purple Emperor, Silver-studded Blue, White Admiral.

11 BROADWATER WARREN
NATURE RESERVE
RSPB

Habitats: Heathland, woodland (Sussex/Kent border).

Birds: All year: Common woodland/scrub spp inc 3 spp woodpeckers, Marsh Tit. Kingfisher, Stonechat, Linnet, Yellowhammer. Dartford Warbler (15 territories in '25, up from zero in 2018). *Summer:* Nightjar, Cuckoo, Woodlark, Grey Wagtail, Spotted Flycatcher, common warblers. *Winter:* Crossbill, Redwing, Fieldfare, Siskin, Redpoll.

Other: Butterflies, dragonflies, fungi, Adder, Dormouse.

Directions: TN3 9JP; TQ 554 372. SW of Tunbridge Wells. A26 S from Tunbridge Wells towards Crowborough. After 2.1 miles, turn R into Broadwater Forest Lane—continue 0.8 miles to car park on L.

Public transport: Bus: 228/229, Tunbridge Wells to Crowborough, Arriva; 28/29/29A/29B, Tunbridge Wells

to Brighton, Brighton and Hove (01273 886 200). Alight on A26 at Eridge Green Church stop. Walk down Warren Farm Lane (next to Church) to Sussex WT Eridge Rocks NR and through reserve N into Broadwater Warren. Train—Eridge. Walk NE along Eridge Road. After 1.2 miles turn R down Park Corner Lane and at end of lane turn R along Broadwater Forest Lane, gate into reserve 0.2 miles on R. *Take care—no pavements.* *Visiting:* Car park open daily 9am-5pm (10am Tues). Cycle racks, information boards, Two viewing points, two nature trails, guided walks.
Contact: RSPB: 01892 752 430; broadwater.warren@rspb.org.uk.

Kent

The Dungeness area offers excellent birdwatching with an RSPB reserve and a bird observatory ensuring that it is well watched—seawatching from the shingle spit here will pick up divers, sea duck, shearwaters, skuas and terns as they move through the Channel. There is another observatory at Sandwich Bay, a series of marshes along the north coast (with a good selection of birds of prey wintering on the Isle of Sheppey), reedbeds at Stodmarsh, plus a number of woodlands holding Nightingales.

Bird Atlases/Avifauna
Kent Breeding Bird Atlas 2008-13
Rob Clements, Murray Orchard, Norman McCanch & Stephen Wood
(Kent Ornithological Society, 2015)
The Birds of Kent: A Review of Their Status and Distribution
DW Taylor
(Meresborough Books, 2nd ed 1984)

Bird Recorder
Barry Wright, 6 Hatton Close, Northfleet, DA11 8SD: umbrellabirds66@gmail.com

Bird Reports
Kent Bird Report (1952-), from KOS—Chris Roome, Rowland House, Station Road, Staplehurst, TN12 0PY. chris.roome@kentos.org.uk.
Dungeness Bird Observatory Report (1989-), from DBO—David Walker, Dungeness BO, 11 RNSSS Cottages, Dungeness, Romney Marsh, TN29 9NA: 01797 321 309; dungenessobs@vfast.co.uk
Sandwich Bay Bird Observatory Report (1962-), from SBBOT, Guilford Road, Sandwich Bay, Sandwich, CT13 9PF: 01304 617 341; info@sbbot.org.uk

BTO Regional Representative
Murray Orchard:
Wetland Bird Survey (WeBS)
Local Organizers: webs@bto.org
Dungeness Area
David Walker
Kent (East)
Murray Orchard
Kent (West)
Vacant
Medway Estuary
Bob Knight
Pegwell Bay
Steffan Walton
Swale Estuary
Brian Watmough
Thames Estuary (Foulness)
See *Essex*
Thames Estuary (Hoo)
Murray Orchard

Club
Kent Ornithological Society (1952; 700).
Chris Roome, Rowland House, Station Road, Staplehurst, TN12 0PY: membership@kentos.org.uk; www.kentos.org.uk
Meetings: Contact/see website for details.

Ringing Groups/Bird Observatories
Dartford RG
East Kent Wildlife Group
Reculver RG.
Swale Wader Group:
via website; www.swalewaders.co.uk
Dungeness Bird Observatory
David Walker (Warden), Dungeness Bird Observatory, 11 RNSSS Cottages, Dungeness, Romney Marsh, TN29 9NA: 01797 321 309; dungenessobs@vfast.co.uk; www.dungenessbirdobs.org.uk
Sandwich Bay Bird Observatory
Steffan Walton (Warden), Sandwich Bay Bird Observatory, Guilford Road, Sandwich, CT13 9PF: 01304 617 341; info@sbbot.org.uk; www.sbbot.org.uk

RSPB Local Groups
Canterbury (1973; 90)
Andre Farrar: andre.farrar57@gmail.com; https://group.rspb.org.uk/canterbury/
Meetings: 7:30pm 2nd Friday of the month (Sep-May). Blean Village Hall, 2 School Lane, Blean, Canterbury CT2 9JA.
Gravesend (1977; 170)
Steve Cullum: groupleader@rspbgravesend.org.uk; https://group.rspb.org.uk/gravesend/
Meetings: 7:30pm, 2nd Thursday of the month (Sep-May).

Northfleet School for Girls, Hall Road, Northfleet, Gravesend, DA11 8AQ & 2:00pm, 4th Tuesday of the month. Masonic Hall, 25 Wrotham Road, Gravesend, DA11 0PA.

Maidstone (1974; 250)

Kevin Willis: maidstoneRSPB@gmail.com; https://group.rspb.org.uk/maidstone/

Meetings: 7:30pm, 3rd Thursday of the month (not Aug). Grove Green Community Hall, Penhurst Close, Grove Green, Bearsted, Maidstone, ME14 5BT.

Medway (1974; 150)

Group Secretary: info.rspbmedway@gmail.com; https://group.rspb.org.uk/medway/

Meetings: 7.30pm, 3rd Tuesday of the month (not Aug). Parkwood Community Centre, Parkwood Green, Gillingham, ME8 9PN.

Sevenoaks (1974; 140)

Nigel Meachem: 7oaksrspb@gmail.com; https://group.rspb.org.uk/sevenoaks/

Meetings: 7:45pm, 1st Thursday of the month (Sep-May). Otford Memorial Hall, High Street, Otford, Sevenoaks, TN14 5PQ.

Thanet (1975; 180)

Kerry Sabin-Dawson: ksd.rspbthanet@gmail.com; https://group.rspb.org.uk/thanet/

Meetings: 7.30pm, 2nd Monday of the month (Sep-May). St Peter's Church Hall, Hopeville Avenue, Broadstairs, CT10 2TR.

Tonbridge (1975; no formal membership)

rspb.tonbridge@gmail.com; https://group.rspb.org.uk/tonbridge/

Meetings: 7:30pm, (usually) 3rd Wednesday of the month (Sep-Apr). St Philip's Church, Salisbury Road, Tonbridge, TN10 4PA—contact/see website for details.

Wildlife Trust

Kent Wildlife Trust (1958; 32,000)

Tyland Barn, Sandling, Maidstone, ME14 3BD: 01622 662 012: info@kentwildlifetrust.org.uk; www.kentwildlifetrust.org.uk

If entering from East Sussex on the A26, continue on A26 to junction with A25 N of Sevenoaks.

1 SEVENOAKS WILDLIFE RESERVE

Kent Wildlife Trust

Habitats: 182 acres. Former gravel pit. 5 lakes surrounded by woodland, reedbed, river.

Birds: All year: Great Crested Grebe, Tufted Duck, Kingfisher, 3 spp woodpeckers, Grey Wagtail. *Spring passage:* Hirundines, Yellow Wagtail. *Summer:* Little Ringed Plover and Lapwing (both breed), Sand Martin, common warblers. *Autumn:* Green & Common Sandpipers, other waders possible. Hirundines, Spotted Flycatcher, Wheatear. *Winter:* Wildfowl numbers much higher than summer, may inc Goldeneye, Goosander and rarer grebes in hard weather. Little Egret roost, Snipe, Water Rail,

gulls, Redwing, Fieldfare, Siskin, Redpoll. Rarities occasionally seen.

Other: Over 2,000 spp have been recorded on reserve. Glow-worm, bats, dragonflies, fungi.

Directions: TN13 3DH; TQ 521 563. N of Sevenoaks. Entrance on A25, c.1 mile W of Bat & Ball junction with A225.

Public transport: Train—Bat & Ball, one mile walk to reserve entrance; also Sevenoaks station, slightly further.

Visiting: Open dawn-dusk. Car park (charge). Refurbished Visitor Centre opening January 2026 (open 10am-4pm from 1 Apr.) with cafe, shop, toilets. Picnic area. Wheelchair access to visitor centre, 3 hides and most of trails. No dogs (except assistance dogs) but allowed in car park/picnic area on lead. Picnic only in designated area. Cycle racks, no cycles on reserve. Deep water in places, under-16s must be accompanied by an adult

Contact: Kent WT: 01732 741 673; sevenoaks.vc@kentwildlife.org.uk

Return to Tonbridge on A21.

2 TUDELEY WOODS & PEMBURY HEATH

Hadlow Estate

Habitats: Ancient, semi-natural mixed woodland, heathland. Formerly, but no longer, an RSPB reserve.

Birds: All year: Common woodland species, 3 spp woodpeckers, Marsh Tit. *Spring/summer:* Turtle Dove, Spotted Flycatcher, common warblers, inc Garden. Nightjar and Tree Pipit on heath. *Winter:* Woodcock, winter thrushes and finches, Crossbill.

Other: Butterflies, inc White Admiral and Silver-washed Fritillary. Golden-ringed Dragonfly, 1,000+ spp fungi. Bluebells, orchids and other woodland plants. Dormouse.

Directions: TN11 0PT; TQ 617 433. 0.5 mile SW Tonbridge. Take A21 from Tonbridge towards Tunbridge Wells. Take L turn (signposted to Capel) into Half Moon Lane—also known as Dislingbury Road—(immediately before petrol station). Parking area 0.3 mile on L. Pembury Heath can be accessed from here, footpath to S of the road links to trail.

Public transport: None.

Visiting: Open during daylight hours. Limited on road parking available. Three trails of 1, 1.5 and 3 miles. Access by Public Footpath and limited Bridleway, also by Permissive Footpath. No commercial activities inc professional dog walking allowed on Permissive paths. Dogs must be kept on leads on all Permissive paths at all times as this is a wildlife conservation area.

Contact: via website; www.hadlow.com

Continue S on A21 and then A262 for Cranbrook.

3 HEMSTED FOREST

Forestry England

Habitats: Coniferous and broad-leaved woodland.

Birds: All year: Usual woodland suspects inc 3 spp

11	Capel Fleet
5	Dungeness NNR
6	Dungeness BO
10	Elmley Marshes
4	Ham Street Woods
3	Hemstead Forest
12	Northward Hill
9	Oare Marshes
2	Sandwich Bay BO
1	Sevenoaks Wildlife Reserve
7	Stodmarsh
2	Tudeley Woods and Pembury Heath

woodpeckers, Buzzard, Sparrowhawk, Goshawk, (possible). Barn, Tawny & Little Owls, Marsh Tit, Redpoll, Siskin, *Spring/summer:* Cuckoo, Turtle Dove, warblers inc Garden, Lesser Whitethroat. *Winter:* Woodcock, Crossbill, Brambling, winter thrushes.

Other: Dormouse.

Directions: TN17 4AN; TQ 811 343. Two miles SE of Cranbrook. From A229 S of Cranbrook turn L on to B2086 to Beneden then turn L for Sissinghurst. After 0.7 miles turn R (Goddards Green Road)—car park entrance is 500 yards on L.

Public transport: None.

Visiting: Open all hours. Height restriction at car park. Around five miles of hard surfaced road and network of unsurfaced tracks.

Contact: Forestry England: 0300 067 4500; enquiries.eastfd@forestryengland.uk

Continue on A262 and then A28 to Ashford. Thence S on A2070.

4 HAM STREET WOODS NNR

Natural England

Habitats: Ancient woodland.

Birds: All year: Common woodland spp inc 3 spp woodpeckers, Marsh Tit. Sparrowhawk, Tawny Owl. *Spring/summer:* Hobby, Turtle Dove, Tree Pipit, Nightingale, warblers inc Garden and Whitethroat, Spotted Flycatcher. *Winter:* Brambling, Siskin, Redpoll, winter thrushes.

Other: Dormouse, Great Crested Newt, butterflies inc White Admiral and Purple Emperor, ancient woodland flora, fungi.

Directions: TN26 2HH; TR 003 337. Six miles S Ashford. Car park off B2067 at end of Bourne Lane in Hamstreet village.

Public transport: Bus 11 Assford-Lydd (not Sun), alight at Hamstreet railway station. Stagecoach. Train:—Ham Street—0.3 miles from reserve.

Visiting: Open all hours. Three waymarked trails through reserve—rough paths, unsuitable for wheelchairs. Both Saxon Shore Way and Greensand Way

trails pass through.

Contact: Natural England: 0300 060 3900; enquiries@naturalengland.org.uk

Continue S on A2070 then B2075 for Lydd.

5 DUNGENESS NNR

RSPB

Habitats: Shingle, 90 flooded gravel pits, sallow scrub, newly-extended reedbed on Denge Marsh, wet grassland.

Birds: All year: Bittern, Marsh Harrier, Bearded Tit, Cetti's Warbler. *Spring:* Garganey, Little Ringed Plover among a wide variety of waders, Wheatear, Yellow Wagtail, Lesser Whitethroat, Black Redstart. *Autumn:* Migrant waders and passerines, inc large flocks of hirundines. *Winter:* Smew, Goldeneye, Black-necked & Slavonian Grebes, Wigeon, Goosander, Bewick's Swan, Marsh & Hen Harriers, other raptors.

Other: Jersey Cudweed, Nottingham Catchfly, endemic leafhopper.

Directions: TN29 9PN; TR 062 197. One mile out of Lydd on Dungeness Road, turn R for main site. Visitor centre and car park are one mile along entrance track. Entrance to Hanson ARC site and car park is opposite main reserve entrance on L of Dungeness Road.

Public transport: Bus: 11 (not Sun) from Ashford via Lydd stops at reserve entrance on request. Stagecoach.

Visiting: Open daily (not 25/26 Dec) 9am-9pm/sunset when earlier. Coach parking available. Visitor centre open 10am-5pm (4pm Nov-Feb). Parties 12+ by prior arrangement. Entry fee for non-RSPB members. Visitor centre, fully equipped classroom/meeting room, toilets (inc disabled access). Six hides (wheelchair accessible), viewing screen, two nature trails. Assistance dogs only. Hide and viewing screen at Hanson ARC site.

Contact: RSPB: 01797 320 588; dungeness@rspb.org.uk

6 DUNGENESS BIRD OBSERVATORY

Dungeness Bird Observatory Trust

Habitats: Shingle promontory with scrub and gravel pits.

Birds: Summer: Breeding spp inc Raven, Wheatear and Black Redstart. *Passage:* Important migration site, regular overshoots inc Bee-eater, Hoopoe, Purple Heron and Red-rumped Swallow. Excellent seawatching when weather conditions suitable.

Other: Long Pits are excellent for dragonflies, inc Small Red-eyed damselfly. Moth trapping throughout year.

Directions: TN29 9NA; TR 085 173. Three miles SE of Lydd. Turn S off main Dungeness Road just before Pilot Inn—continue to end of road, past two lighthouses.

Public transport: Bus—see **Dungeness NNR**—alight at Pilot Inn, 1.75 miles from Observatory.

Visiting: Observatory open throughout year. Wardens on site between Mar and Nov. Accommodation for up to nine people (reduced charges for Friends). Apply in writing to the warden or by phone. No wheelchair access. Bring own sleeping bag/sheets and toiletries. Shared facilities inc a fully-equipped kitchen. Coach parking available at mini-railway station.

Contact: Dungeness Bird Observatory, 11 RNSSS Cottages, Dungeness, Romney Marsh, Kent TN29 9NA: 01797 321 309; dungenessobs@vfast.co.uk; www.dungenessbirdobs.org.uk

Take A2070 back to Ashford, then A28 to Canterbury and on to

7 STODMARSH NNR

Natural England

Habitats: 617 acres, largest area of reedbed in SE England, marsh, open water, woodland. Lies between the Great Stour, to the N, and the Little Stour, to the S, close to their confluence, with further areas of wetland to the W extending almost to Canterbury.

Birds: Bittern (breeding and also winter visitor), Snipe, Marsh Harrier, Kingfisher, Great Crested Grebe, Coot, Moorhen, Reed Bunting, Bearded Tit. *Autumn:* Passage waders. *Winter:* Starling roost.

Other: Water Vole, Beaver. Shining Ramshorn Snail, Sharp-leaved Pondweed.

Directions: CT3 4BB; TR 221 610. Mid way between Canterbury and Margate immediately to S of A28 but separated from it by railway line and Great Stour. Turn S off A28 on to Grove Ferry Road at the E end of Upstreet, Cross Great Stour at Grove Ferry (pay & display car park, toilets and pub at NE end of reserve) and follow Grove Road. 2.25 miles after crossing Great Stour take lane on R, then 1st R and 1st R again. Follow the lane round a sharp L turn and enter Stodmarsh from the SE. The turning for the car park will be on your R.

Public transport: Bus: 8, Sturry to Upstreet along A28, Stagecoach East Kent. Enter the reserve from Grove Ferry at NE end. Train—Sturry (outskirts of Canterbury) 3 miles.

Visiting: Reserve car park, voluntary donation, to NE of Stodmarsh village, turning between Red Lion pub and church. Accessible toilets. Open all hours. The Stour Valley Walk traverses the reserve from Stodmarsh in the S to the Great Stour in the N and then follows the river. 5 hides, several trails, some wheelchair accessible.

Contact: Natural England: 0300 060 3900; enquiries@naturalengland.org.uk

or, at Canterbury, take A257 for

8 SANDWICH BAY BIRD OBSERVATORY

Sandwich Bay Bird Observatory Trust

Habitats: Coastal, dune land, farmland, marsh, handful of small scrapes.

Birds: All year: Breeding residents inc Avocet, Grey Partridge, Stonechat, Stock Dove, Little Owl, Corn Bunting. *Spring/autumn passage:* Good variety of migrants and waders. Annual Golden Oriole. Firecrest and Yellow-browed Warbler occur in The Elms. *Summer:* Little Ringed Plover, Garganey, Hobby. *Winter:* White-fronted Goose, waders, Short-eared & Long-eared Owl. Water Pipit.

Other: Sand dune plants inc Lizard Orchid, Sand Catchfly and Sand Sedge. Bright Wave butterfly, Red-veined Darter and Dainty Damselfly

Directions: CT13 9PF; TR 355 575. 2.5 miles from Sandwich, five miles from Deal. A256 to Sandwich from Dover or Ramsgate. From Sandwich follow signs to Golf Courses, continue on into Sandwich Bay Estate, turn R after 0.25 mile. There is small fee at Tollgate for non-members visiting Obs.

Public transport: Train—Sandwich two miles from Observatory.

Visiting: Aim to open daily 10am-4pm (summer), disabled access. Field Study Centre—toilets, refreshments, hostel-type accommodation and self-contained flat, mobility scooter (to book).

Contact: Sandwich Bay Bird Obs, Guilford Road, Sandwich, CT13 9PF: 01304 617 341; info@sbbot.org.uk; www.sbbot.org.uk

Return to Canterbury and then join A2 heading W.

9 OARE MARSHES LNR

Kent Wildlife Trust

Habitats: 200 acres. Grazing marsh, freshwater dykes, open water scrapes, reedbed, mudflats/Swale Sea Channel.

Birds: All year: Waders and wildfowl, Little Egret, Marsh Harrier, Water Rail, Barn & Little Owls. *Spring/summer:* Avocet, Garganey, Green, Wood & Curlew Sandpipers, Little Stint, Black-tailed Godwit, Little Tern. *Winter:* Brent Goose, Red-breasted Merganser, Hen Harrier, Merlin, Peregrine Falson, Short-eared Owl, Bittern, Stonechat. Divers, grebes and seaducks on Swale. Good record for attracting rarities.

Other: Dragonflies, Common Seal on sandbank.

Directions: ME13 0QD; TR 013 647 (car park). Off Church Road, Oare, two miles N of Faversham. From

Kent

A2 follow signs to Oare and Harty Ferry.

Public transport: Bus: 3 (not Sun) Sittingbourne-Canterbury stops in Oare, I mile from reserve. Stagecoach in East Kent. Train—Faversham (3 miles).

Visiting: Open all hours. Car park (charge). 2 hides. Seasonally accessible for wheelchairs (in wet weather not possible to complete circuit to E hide). RADAR gates, path to sea hide level, surfaced with compacted roadstone. All visitors should stay on paths. Dogs on leads.

Contact: Kent WT: 01622 662 012;

nadia.ward@kentwildlife.org.uk

Continue W on A2 to intersection with A249

10 ELMLEY MARSHES NNR

Privately owned/managed

Habitats: 3,300 acre estate—coastal grazing marsh, ditches and pools alongside Swale Estuary with extensive intertidal mudflats and saltmarsh.

Birds: Spring/summer: Breeding waders—Redshank, Lapwing, Avocet plus passage waders. Common Tern colonies. Hobby, Cuckoo, Yellow Wagtail. *Autumn:* Passage waders and raptors. *Winter:* Spectacular numbers of wildfowl, especially Wigeon and Brent & White-fronted Geese. Waders. Hunting raptors—Peregrine Falcom, Merlin, Marsh & Hen Harrier. Owls: Barn, Little Long-eared & Short-eared.

Other: Water Vole, Brown Hare. High densities of common butterflies, and rare bumblebees, flies and beetles.

Directions: ME12 3RW; TQ 937 680. From J5 of M2, follow A249 towards Sheerness. Reserve signposted from exit for Iwade and Ridham Dock, immediately before Sheppey bridge. At roundabout, take second exit on to old road bridge. On Isle of Sheppey, after 1.25 miles, turn R following reserve sign. Follow rough track for *c.*2 miles to car park at Kingshill Farm. **Do not** leave car on entrance track.

Public transport: Train—Swale nearest station. On Sittingbourne-Sheerness line, 3 miles to reserve. Alighting at Sittingbourne involves fewer changes and better chance of a taxi to reserve.

Visiting: Opening days/times vary—contact/check website—tickets should be purchased for day of visit. Groups by appointment. Toilets in car park. Activities, tours. Accommodation available on site. Four hides, nearest I mile from car park. Swale viewing screen 200 yards from car park. Paths pushchair friendly. Guide dogs only.

Contact: 07930 847 520;

info@elmleynaturereserve.co.uk;

www.elmleynaturereserve.co.uk

Continue on A249.

11 CAPEL FLEET RAPTOR WATCHPOINT

RSPB

Habitats: purpose-built 360° vantage point, overlooking farmland and marshland.

Birds: Raptors/owls (species vary with seasons)—Buzzard, Sparrowhawk, Marsh Harrier, Hen Harrier, Montagu's Harrier, Kestrel, Hobby, Peregrine, Merlin, Short-eared Owl, Barn Owl. Rough-legged Buzzard are occasionally seen in winter. *Winter:* Wildfowl inc White-fronted Goose.

Directions: ME12 4BG; TR 022 681. From A2/M2, take A249 N on to Isle of Sheppey, then A2500 E towards Leysdown-on-Sea. A2500 becomes B2231 at Eastchurch. After 1.7 miles turn R onto Harty Ferry Road (road is narrow), continue for *c.*2 miles, car park entrance on L. Can continue along road to Ferry House Inn for views across Swale (**Oare Marshes** on opposite bank).

Public transport: None.

Visiting: Open all hours. Car park (free), benches and info panel. Advisable to check for any unexopected closures at:

www.rspb.org.uk/days-out/reserves/capel-fleet

Contact: RSPB: 01634 222 480;

northkentmarshes@rspb.org.uk

Continue W on A2 to intersection with A228.

12 NORTHWARD HILL

RSPB

Habitats: Ancient and scrub woodland overlooking grazing marsh.

Birds: Spring/summer: Wood holds UK's largest heronry, with *c.*150 pairs of Grey Heron and *c.*50 pairs of Little Egret. Breeding Nightingale (*c.*20 pairs), Turtle Dove, scrub warblers and woodpeckers. Marshes—breeding Lapwing, Redshank, Avocet, Marsh Harrier, Shoveler, Pochard. *Winter:* Wigeon, Teal, Shoveler. Passage waders, inc Black-tailed Godwit, raptors, Corn Bunting. Long-eared Owl.

Other: Good variety of dragonflies over marsh, White-letter Hairstreak butterfly in woods.

Directions: ME3 8DS; TQ 768 765. Four miles NE of Rochester. Leave M2 at J1 and join A228, signposted Grain. Turn off A228 for High Halstow then L in village into Cooling Road—reserve signposted *c.*I mile on R.

Public transport: Difficult, contact reserve for more info.

Visiting: Open all hours. Car park (dawn-dusk), toilets. Trails in public area of wood joining Saxon Shoreway link to grazing marsh. Three trails, from 0.7 to 2.3 miles, often steep, not suitable for wheelchairs. Four viewpoints with benches. Dogs only allowed on Saxon Shoreway.

Contact: RSPB: 01634 222480;

northkentmarshes@rspb.org.uk

Return to A2 and junction with M25. Then round M25 to begin exploration of Bedfordshire.

Apologies to Kent for removing spaces between reserve entries—take it as a compliment, there's just so much good stuff to cram in.

Bedfordshire

One of England's smallest counties is home to the RSPB's HQ at The Lodge near Sandy. Unsurprisingly, this is one of the best watched sites in the county, with a series of excellent records, inc Nightjars breeding on restored heathland. There are several country parks, which attract a good range of species, although they can be busy. Blows Down, near Luton, is one of the best southern sites to see Ring Ouzel on spring passage.

Bird Atlases/Avifauna
An Atlas of the Breeding Birds of Bedfordshire 1988-92
RA Dazley & P Trodd
(Bedfordshire Natural History Society, 1994).
The Birds of Bedfordshire
P Trodd & D Kramer
(Castlemead Publications, 1991).

Bird Recorder
Peter Nash, 5 Coopers Close, Sandy, SG19 1NQ:
07753 411 786; recorder@bedsbirdclub.org.uk

Bird Report
Bedfordshire Bird Report (1946-), from BBC:
chairbbc@bnhs.org.uk

BTO Regional Representative
Phil Cannings
Wetland Bird Survey (WeBS)
Local Organizer: webs@bto.org
Bedfordshire
Richard Bashford

Club
Bedfordshire Bird Club (1992; 357)
Sheila Alliez (Hon Sec), Flat 61 Adamson Court, Adamson Walk, Kempston, Bedford, MK42 8QZ:
01234 855 227; secretary@bedsbirdclub.org.uk;
www.bedsbirdclub.org.uk
Meetings: A mixture of zoom and in person meetings. 8:00pm, last Tuesday of the month (Sep-Mar). Maulden Village Hall, junction of Ampthill and Flitwick Road, Maulden, MK45 2DN. Contact/see website for details.

RSPB Local Group
Bedford (1970; 70)
Caroline Brown: BedfordRSPBlocalgroup@gmail.com; https://group.rspb.org.uk/bedford/
Meetings: 7.30pm, 3rd Thursday of the month (Sep-May, not Jan). Biddenham Village Hall, Nodders Way, Biddenham, Bedford MK40 4BJ.

Wildlife Trust
The Wildlife Trust for Bedfordshire, Cambridgeshire and Northamptonshire (1994; 36,000)
The Manor House, Broad Street, Great Cambourne, Cambridge CB23 6DH: 01954 713 500;

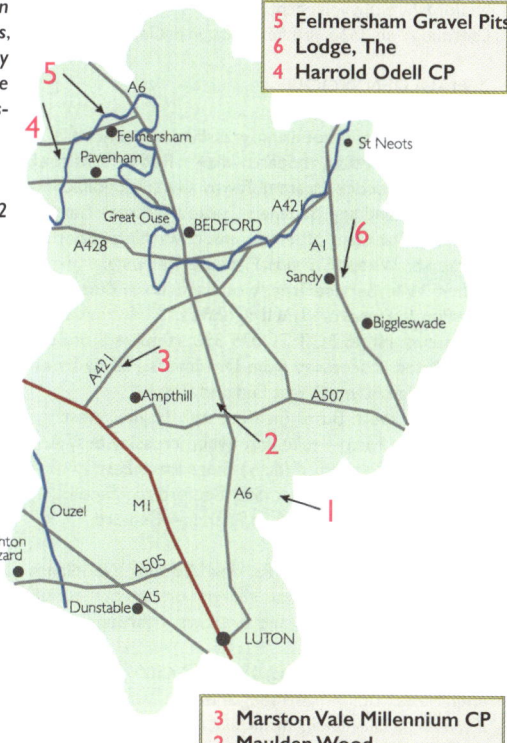

5 **Felmersham Gravel Pits**
6 **Lodge, The**
4 **Harrold Odell CP**

3 **Marston Vale Millennium CP**
2 **Maulden Wood**
1 **Pegsdon Hills and Hoo Bit**

Having journeyed from Kent, as you do, take the M1 N from the M25 and leave at J10, taking the A1081 and then A505 for Hitchin.

1 PEGSDON HILLS AND HOO BIT NATURE RESERVE
Beds, Cambs & Northants Wildlife Trust.
Habitats: Chalk grassland, scrub and woodland.
Birds: Spring: Wheatear, Ring Ouzel, Tree Pipit, Yellowhammer. *Summer:* Turtle Dove, Grey Partridge, Lapwing, Skylark. *Winter:* Brambling, Stonechat, winter thrushes, raptors inc Buzzard.
Other: Dark Green Fritillary, Dingy & Grizzled Skippers, Chalkhill Blue, Brown Argus and Small Heath butterflies. Glow Worm. Plants inc Pasqueflower in spring, Fragrant & Common Spotted Orchids.
Directions: SG5 3JS; TL 118 302 (lay-by). Five miles W of Hitchin. Take B655 from Hitchin towards Barton-le-

Bedfordshire

Clay. Turn R to Pegsdon then immediately L and park in lay-by. Reserve entrance across B655 via footpath.
Public transport: None.
Visiting: Open all hours. Tracks/paths can be steep and uneven. The Icknield Way runs along S edge
Contact: BCN WT: 01234 364 213;
bedfordshire@wildlifebcnp.org
Continue W on B655, join A6 in Barton-le-Clay, head N.

2 MAULDEN WOOD

Forestry England
Habitats: Ancient woodland, grassland, some heathland.
Birds: *All year:* Buzzard, Sparrowhawk, Red Kite, Kestrel, Hobby, Woodcock (scarce), Tawny Owl, Redpoll, common woodland spp. *Summer:* Cuckoo (scarce), Garden Warbler, Blackcap, other common warblers, Spotted Flycatcher. *Winter:* Corvids, Fieldfare, Redwing.
Other: Wild Service Tree, woodland flora. Butterflies (inc Purple Emperor) and dragonflies.
Directions: MK45 3QT; TL 075 390. 10 miles S of Bedford. Wood is accessed from Deadman's Hill lay-by off A6 between Haynes West End and Clophill.
Public transport: Buses (nearest stop: Haynes West End, Oxleys Farm—*take care* when crossing busy A6): MK1 Bedford to Luton (daily). Stagecoach East (0345 241 8000); 44 (Mon-Sat) Bedford to Amptill. Grant Palmer (01525 719 719). Train—Bedford (10 miles).
Visiting: Open all hours. Parking: Working Woodlands Centre & car park (small charge) or car can be left in lay-by. Various paths and bridleways through wood. Picnic area.
Contact: Forestry England: 0300 067 4500;
enquiries.eastfd@forestryengland.uk
If you don't fancy taking minor roads W. Continue N on A6. Just S of Bedford, join A421 and head SW back towards M1.

3 MARSTON VALE
MILLENIUM COUNTRY PARK

Marston Vale Trust
Habitats: Millenium Country Park (575 acres) two lakes, Stewartby Lake and The Pillinge, reedbeds, woodland, hawthorn scrub, ponds and wet grassland.
Birds: *Spring:* Passage waders and terns (Black & Arctic Terns), hirundines, Wheatear, Whinchat, Osprey and Little Gull. *Summer:* Ten species of breeding warblers, Hobby, Turtle Dove, Nightingale, Bearded Tit, Cuckoo, Barn Owl, Marsh Harrier, Bittern, Water Rail, Kingfisher and common wildfowl. *Autumn:* Passage waders and terns. *Winter:* Bittern, Peregrine Falcon, Siskin, Redpoll, Stonechat, Snipe, gulls inc Caspian, Yellow-legged & Mediterranean Gulls, thrushes, wildfowl (Gadwall, Shoveler, Pochard, Teal and Tufted Duck), Little & Great Crested Grebes. Rarer species can inc divers, grebes, Common Scoter, Smew and Scaup. Rarities: Glossy Ibis, Purple Heron and White Stork.

Other: Dingy & Grizzled Skipper butterflies, excellent for dragonflies. Variety of flora inc Bee & Pyramidal Orchids and stoneworts.
Directions: MK43 0PS; TL 004 417. SW of Bedford off A421 at Marston Moretaine. Only five minutes from J13 of M1, along A421 towards Bedford. Look for brown tourist signs for the Forest Centre.
Public transport: Trains—Millbrook and Stewartby, 20 minutes walk to Forest Centre.
Visiting: Car parking, coach parking (book in advance)—charges apply—closes at 5pm. Forest Centre (cafe bar, gift shop, art gallery) open weekdays 9am-5pm, weekends 10am-5pm. Reduced hours in winter (closed 25/26 Dec, 1 Jan). Pedestrian access to park at any time. 8 miles of surfaced trails and 1.25 mile trail round the Wetlands Nature Reserve (entry charge, no dogs), which is a level path with a compacted, loose stone surface inc two hand gates with top latches with wheelchair and pushchair access. Four hides with level or ramped access.
Contact: Forest Centre: 01234 767 037;
info@marstonvale.org; www.marstonvale.org
Return to A6 and continue N.

4 HARROLD-ODELL COUNTRY PARK

Bedford Borough Council
Habitats: Gravel pit, reed swamp, woodland, wet woodland, 0.75 mile of riverbank and meadow along Great Ouse.
Birds: *All year:* Great Crested Grebe, Grey Heron and Little Egret, common wildfowl, Kingfisher, Grey Wagtail, common woodland/scrub spp. *Spring/summer:* Common Sandpiper, Common Tern, Cuckoo, hirundines, warblers. *Autumn passage:* Occasional waders, terns. *Winter:* Wildfowl (inc Goosander, Goldeneye), Snipe, Redwing, Fieldfare, Siskin, Redpoll.
Other: Otter, Fox. Grass Snake. Damsel- & dragonflies.
Directions: MK43 7DS; SP 956 566. 7.5 miles NW of Bedford. Take A6 N from Bedford, turn L for Oakley and then R for Pavenham. Go through Pavenham and turn R for Carlton. Through Carlton, cross over narrow bridge into Harrold. Park is signed on R, just beyond bridge.
Public transport: Bus: 25 Bedford (bus station) to Harrold/Rushden (not Sun/bank hols), Grant Palmer: 01525 719 719. Train—Bedford.
Visiting: Open all year. Car park with disabled spaces—free/donation welcomed (over-spill car park closes 5pm). Disabled access to visitor centre, toilets (9am-5pm), cafe (9am-4pm). Main path suitable for wheelchairs/pushchairs, kissing gates have RADAR key access. Two hides (wheelchair access). Wheelchairs available for loan.
Contact: Bedford Borough Council: 01234 720 016;
hocp@bedford.gov.uk
Head back to Sharnbrook and A6, passing to N of

5 FELMERSHAM GRAVEL PITS

Beds, Cambs & Northants Wildlife Trust.
Habitats: Open water, woodland and grassland.
Birds: Wildfowl inc Great Crested Grebe, Tufted Duck, Teal. Grey Heron, Kingfisher, Reed Bunting. *Summer:* Sedge & Willow Warblers, Blackcap, Chiffchaff.
Other: 18 spp dragonflies have bred, White-letter Hairstreak. Interesting flora inc Whorled Water-milfoil, Bladderwort. Otter, Grass Snake.
Directions: MK44 1JW; SP 987 583. 500 yards N of Felmersham, seven miles N of Bedford. Take A6 N from Bedford, in Milton Ernest turn L to Felmersham (two miles). Through the village, continue N across river, continue along causeway for 450 yards to parking area. Access via kissing gate.
Public transport: Bus: 50 Bedford to Rushden/Kettering stops at Felmersham (continue on foot over causeway). Stagecoach.
Visiting: Open all hours. Less well used paths may be a little overgrown. Dogs under control.
Contact: BCN WT: 01234 364 213;
bedfordshire@wildlifebcnp.org
Head S on A6, then E on A603 for Sandy, then B1042.

6 THE LODGE, SANDY

RSPB
Habitats: 550 acres, mixture of woodland, heathland and acid grassland. Includes formal gardens of RSPB's UK HQ. New areas being restored to heathland.
Birds: *All year:* Woodpeckers, woodland birds. *Spring/summer:* Hobby, Nightjar, Spotted Flycatcher, breeding common woodland species and warblers. *Winter:* Winter thrushes.
Other: Natterjack Toad, rare heathland insects. Particularly good site for fungi (600 spp) and lichens. Garden pools good for dragonflies.
Directions: SG19 2DL; TL 191 485. Reserve lies one mile E of Sandy, signposted from the B1042 road to Potton.
Public transport: Bus: 73 (not Sun) Bedford to Sandy, one mile from Sandy Market Place. Stagecoach. Train—Sandy (0.5 mile). Walk in, part is along trail through heathland restoration.
Visiting: Reserve open daily 7am-7pm. Visitor Hub: shop (with refreshments) generally open 9:30am-5pm (February-end October), 9:30am-4:30pm (November–end January), cafe typically open 10am-4pm. Toilets (inc disabled). Car park charge for non-members (free if only visiting shop). Five miles of nature trails. One bridleway (0.5 mile) and gardens are partly wheelchair/pushchair accessible. Cycle racks. Dogs only allowed on bridleway. Coach parking at weekends by arrangement.
Contact: RSPB: 01767 693 333;
thelodgereserve@rspb.org.uk
*Then continue E on B1042 to junction with A1198. Turn S for Royston and **Hertfordshire**.*

Hertfordshire

The first breeding record of Little Ringed Plover in the UK (1938) and the first breeding record of Black-necked Grebe in England (1919) were in the county. The Wildlife Trust manages over 40 nature reserves offering residents of this urbanized Home County a welcome taste of the countryside. The wetland habitats of the Lee Valley have regular wintering Bittern and other interesting species can turn up here, whilst the Tring Reservoirs are still one of the best sites in the county.

Bird Atlas/Avifauna
Birds of Hertfordshire
Ken W Smith, Chris W Dee, Jack D Fearnside & Mike Ilett (Herts NHS, 2015).

Bird Recorder
Chris Ruis: birdrecorder@hnhs.org

Bird Report
Hertfordshire Bird Report (1980-), from HNHS—David Utting (Sec), 250 Sandridge Road, St Albans, AL1 4AL: 01727 762 855; secretary@hnhs.org

BTO Regional Representative
Martin Ketcher
Wetland Bird Survey (WeBS)
Local Organizer: webs@bto.org
Hertfordshire (excl. Lee Valley)
Martin Ketcher
Lee Valley (Greater London/Essex/Hertfordshire)
Cath Patrick

Club
Hertfordshire Natural History Society (1875; 530) /
Hertfordshire Bird Club (1971)
David Utting (Sec), 250 Sandridge Road, St Albans, AL1 4AL: 01727 762 855; secretary@hnhs.org;
www.hnhs.org/herts-bird-club/home
Meetings: Annual Herts Bird Conference—contact/ see website for details.

Ringing Groups/Bird Observatory
Maple Cross RG.
Runnymede RG:
https://runnymededuringing.blogspot.com
Rye Meads RG: via website; www.rmrg.org.uk
Southern Colour Ringing Group:
chair: ntgg_sightings@hotmail.co.uk
southern-colour-ringing-group.org.uk
Tring RG: https://tringringinggroup.blogspot.co.uk

RSPB Local Groups

Harpenden (1974; 100)
Geoff Horn geoffrhorn@yahoo.co.uk;
https://group.rspb.org.uk/harpenden/
Meetings: 8pm, (usually) 2nd or 3rd Thursday of the month (Sep-Apr). All Saint's Church Hall, Station Road, Harpenden, AL5 4UU.

Hemel Hempstead (1972; 90)
Mary Attwood: maryattwood671@gmail.com;
https://group.rspb.org.uk/hemelhempstead/
Meetings: 7:45pm, 1st Tuesday of the month (Sep-Nov) St Paul's Church, Chipperfield, WD4 9BS and Dec-Jun: 1st Monday of the month Chipperfield Village Hall, Chipperfield, WD4 9BS. Dates may be adjusted to allow for Bank Holidays.

Hitchin & Letchworth (1972; 75)
Martin Johnson: martinrjspc@hotmail.com;
https://group.rspb.org.uk/hitchinandletchworth
facebook: RSPB-Hitchin-and-Letchworth-Local-Group
Meetings: 7:30pm, 1st Friday of the month
(Sep-May). Letchworth Settlement, 229 Nevells Rd, Letchworth, SG6 4UB.

Potters Bar & Barnet (1977; c.100)
Ian Sharp: Pbandb.RSPB@gmail.com;
https://group.rspb.org.uk/pottersbarandbarnet/
Meetings: 2pm, one Wednesday of the month (Sep-Jun). St Johns URC Hall, Mowbray Rd, Barnet, EN5 1RH and 7:30pm, one Friday of the month (Sep-Jun). Our Lady & St Vincent Church, 243 Mutton Lane, Potters Bar, EN6 2AT—contact/ see website for details.

South East Hertfordshire (1971; 200)
Stan Kitchiner: se_herts_RSPB@yahoo.co.uk;
https://group.rspb.org.uk/southeasthertfordshire/
Meetings: 8pm, last Tuesday of the month
(Sep-Jun, 3rd Tues in Dec). United Reformed Church, Mill Lane, Broxbourne, EN10 7BQ.

St Albans (1979; open to all)
Fran Fullerton: st-albans-RSPB@hotmail.co.uk;
https://group.rspb.org.uk/stalbans/
Meetings: Monthly weekend/midweek bird walks—contact/see website for details.

Stevenage (1982; -)
Trevor Storey: trevorstorey54@gmail.com; or bazjas@ntlworld.com
https://group.rspb.org.uk/stevenage/
Meetings: 7:30pm, 3rd Friday of the month
(Sep-Nov/JMar-May). Friends Meeting House, Cutty's Lane, Stevenage, SG1 1UP. Outdoor meetings (Sep-Jun) posted in RSPB Stevebage website.

Stort Valley (2008; 35)
Peter Allen: peter2349@sky.com;
https://group.rspb.org.uk/stortvalley/
Meetings: 7:30pm, 2nd Tuesday of the month (Sep-Jul).
Bishops Park Community Centre,
2 Lancaster Way, Bishop's Stortford, CM23 4DA.

Watford (1974; 150)
Janet Reynolds: watfordrspb@gmail.com;
https://group.rspb.org.uk/watford/
Meetings: 8pm, 2nd Wednesday of the month (Sep-Jun). The Stanborough Centre, 609 St Albans Road, Watford, WD25 9JL.

Wildlife Trust

Hertfordshire and Middlesex Wildlife Trust (1964; 22,000)
Grebe House, St Michael's, Street, St Albans, Herts, AL3 4SN: 01727 858 901; info@hmwt.org;
www.hertswildlifetrust.org.uk

Entering on the A1198 from Bedfordshire, Take A505 just N of Royston.

1 THERFIELD HEATH LNR
Conservators of Therfield Heath
Habitats: Natural chalk/grass downland.
Birds: Noted stop-off site for migrants such as Ring Ouzel and Wheatear. *Spring/summer:* Breeding Grey Partridge, Skylark, Whitethroat, Lesser Whitethroat, Meadow Pipit and Spotted Flycatcher. Good selection of raptors seen regularly, inc Red Kite.
Other: 28 spp butterflies inc increasingly rare Chalkhill Blue. Several orchid spp, Pasqueflower and variety of chalk grassland flowers.
Directions: SG8 5BG; TL 335 400. Common land SSSI lies west and south of Royston and is accessed from A505 (Baldock Road).
Public transport: Train—Royston, 15 mins walk.
Visiting: Open all hours. Open downland walks, golf course and sports fields.
Contact: Conservators of Therfield Heath: clerk@therfieldheath.org.uk;
www.therfieldheath.org.uk
Continue on A505 through Luton and across M1. At junction with A5183 in Dunstable, go straight across and continue on B489 to Tring.

2 TRING RESERVOIRS
Canals and Rivers Trust/Hertfordshire and Middlesex Wildlife Trust. [Water Treatment Works lagoon—Thames Water].
Habitats: Four reservoirs with surrounding woodland, scrub and meadows. Two of reservoirs have extensive reedbeds. WTW lagoon with islands and dragonfly scrape, surrounding hedgerows and scrub.
Birds: Spring/summer: Breeding water birds, Common Tern and heronry. Regular Hobby, Black Terns and Red Kite, warblers inc Cetti's. Occasional Marsh Harrier, Osprey. *Autumn/winter passage:* Waders, occasional White-winged Tern. *Winter:* Gull roost, large wildfowl flocks, bunting roosts, Bittern.
Other: Black Poplar trees, locally rare plants in damp ar-

Hertfordshire

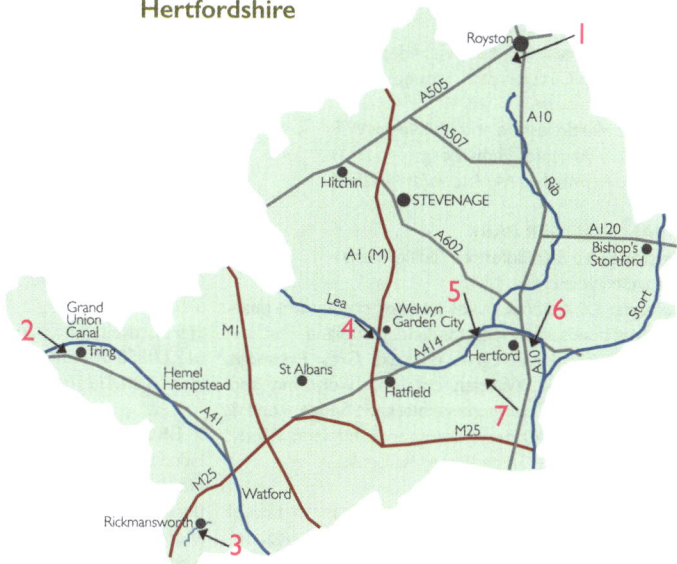

eas. 18 spp dragonflies inc Black-tailed Skimmer, Ruddy Darter and Emerald Damselfly. Holly Blue and Speckled Wood butterflies. Chinese Water Deer, Daubenton's, Natterer's and both spp. Pipistrelle bats.

Directions: HP23 4NW; SP 904 134. Reservoirs two miles NW of Tring, all accessible from B489, which crosses A41 Aston Clinton by-pass. *Exit only from south-bound by-pass.*

Public transport: Bus: 164 (not Sun) Aylesbury to Tring (circular), alight Tringford Road. (0.9 miles to Wilstone, 0.4 miles to Startops). Redline Buses (01296 426 786). Train— Tring (3.8 miles to Wilstone, 2.7 miles to Startops).

Visiting: Reservoirs: Marsworth, Startops End, Tringford, Wilstone, open all hours. Coaches can only drop off and pick up, contact for advice. Car parks: at Wilstone (free, height barrier), at Startop's End (pay & dispaly). Hides on all reservoirs. Disabled access from car park at Startops/Marsworth Reservoirs, as well as WTW Lagoon Hide.

Tring is in Hertforshire but the county boundary with Buckinghamshire runs close to the town. These reservoirs are in Hertfordshire but College Lake, just a few hundred yards to NE, is in Buckinghamshire.

Contact: Hertfordshire and Middlesex WT: 01727 858 901; info@hmwt.org
From S of Tring take A41 to M25 and then A404 at J16.

3 STOCKER'S LAKE

Herts & Middlesex Wildlife Trust
Habitat: Lake (part of Colne Valley system).
Birds: Common waterfowl, Great Crested Grebe, Egyptian Goose, Kingfisher, Little Egret, Cetti's Warbler, Reed Bunting. *Spring/summer:* Common Tern, heronry. *Autumn/Winter:* Wildfowl, inc Pochard, Shoveler, occa-

sional Smew, Redpoll, Siskin.

Directions: WD3 1NB; TQ 057 939 (Aquadrome car park). S edge of Rickmansworth. From A404, turn on to Harefield Road, after one mile turn R on to Frogmore Lane & car park.

Public transport: Bus: R1/R2 Maple Cross to Mount Vernon Hospital (via Rickmansworth)—alight The Grove (nr Tesco). Red Eagle Buses. Train—Rickmansworth, one mile.

Visiting: Open all hours. Large car park at adjacent Rickmansworth aquadrome. Circular path around lake, two miles, three hides. Cafe at nearby Bury Lake. Dogs on lead.

Contact: Hertfordshire and Middlesex WT: 01727 858 901; info@hmwt.org
Return to M25 and junction with A1(M).

4 LEMSFORD SPRINGS

Hertfordshire and Middlesex Wildlife Trust.
Habitats: Shallow spring-fed lagoons/old cress bed, woodland and meadow.
Birds: Spring/summer: Little Egret, Kingfisher, Reed Bunting. *Autumn/Winter:* Green Sandpiper, Snipe, Jack Snipe, Water Rail, Redpoll, Siskin.
Other: 50 spp water snail.
Directions: AL8 7TN; TL 222 123. Leave A1(M) at J4 and take A6129 heading N past Stanborough. Turn L on roundabout (B653 towards Wheathampstead) then L on to B197 at next roundabout (signed Welwyn). Continue to next roundabout, turn L into Lemsford Village (road). Reserve entrance (wooden gates) at junction, 50 yards off roundabout (park in cul-de-sac).
Public transport: Train—Welwyn Garden City, 1.5 miles.
Visiting: Open all hours but gate locked, access by key

(contact the Trust: see below). Hides, inc one with disabled access. Circular path around lagoons (c.1 mile). No dogs.

Contact: Hertfordshire and Middlesex WT: 01727 858 901; info@hmwt.org

Return to A1(M), then A414 towards Hertford.

5 PANSHANGER PARK

Hertfordshire & Middlesex Wildlife Trust/Tarmac/Maydencroft.

Habitats: 1,000 acres, lakes (former sand/gravel quarry), river, ponds, reedbed, grassland, woodland.

Birds: All Year: Little Egret, Buzzard, Grey Partridge, Kingfisher, Cetti's Warbler, common woodland spp. *Summer:* Hobby, Common warblers inc Sedge, Reed & Garden. *Passage:* Osprey, Common Sandpiper. *Winter:* Wildfowl, Lapwing, Snipe, Water Rail, gulls.

Other: 19 spp dragonflies.

Directions: SG14 2WN; TL 306 124. Lies on W side of Hertford, just off N side of A414—turn off roundabout into Thieves Lane, car park entrance immediately on L (by white board).

Public transport: Various buses from Hertford to Welwyn Road, just NE of park (walk down Thieves Lane). Train—Hertford North—0.6 mile walk to W.

Visiting: Open all year. Car park (small charge), height barrier. 15 miles of paths—permissive paths can be subject to closure, Dragonfly Trail, Oak Trail. Dogs under control/on lead near stock.

Contact: Maydencroft (manages site on behalf of Tarmac): 01462 420 851; panshangerpark@maydencroft.co.uk

Hertfordshire and Middlesex WT (volunteering/events): panshanger@hmwt.org

Continue on A414 through Hertford to A10, then S.

6 RYE MEADS

RSPB/Hertfordshire and Middlesex Wildlife Trust.

Habitats: Beside River Lee—marsh, willow scrub, pools, scrapes, lagoons and reedbed.

Birds: Summer: Breeding Water Rail, Tufted Duck, Gadwall, Common Tern, Kestrel, Kingfisher, Little Ringed Plover, nine species of warblers. Hobby. *Autumn:* Birds on passage inc Green Sandpiper, Teal and Snipe. *Winter:* Bittern (rare), Shoveler, Teal, Water Rail, Snipe, Jack Snipe, Redpoll and Siskin.

Other: Fen vegetation, invertebrates and reptiles.

Directions: SG12 8JS; TL 389 103. Take Hoddesdon turn off A10 and follow brown duck signs. Near Rye House railway station.

Public transport: Bus: 410 (not Sun) Harlow to Waltham Cross alight Rye Road/Rye Park, 0.5 mile. Trustybus. Train—Rye House, 0.4 mile.

Visiting: Currently open Sun-Thur (not Dec 25/26) 9am-5pm/dusk if earlier. Gates are locked when the reserve is closed. Car park (charge for non-members),

visitor centre—staffed reception, drinks machine, classrooms, toilets. Nature trails, picnic area, bird feeding area, RSPB has 5 hides and 1 on HMWT reserve that can be accessed, plus 1 viewing screen. Disabled access to visitor centre, toilets, trails. No dogs, except guide dogs. Access to HMWT site.

At the time of publication, the RSPB was still reviewing the management of the reserve, so please check their website before travelling.

Contact: RSPB: 01992 708 383; rye.meads@rspb.org.uk;

Hertfordshire and Middlesex WT: 01727 858 901; info@hmwt.org

Head S on A1170, Broxbourne Woods to W of A10.

7 BROXBOURNE WOODS NNR

Hertfordshire County Council/Woodland Trust

Habitats: Woodland. NNR made up of four woods: Bencroft and Broxbourne (Herts CC), Hoddesdonpark and Wormley (Woodland Trust).

Birds: All year: Woodcock, Sparrowhawk, Buzzard, 3 spp woodpeckers, Tawny Owl, variety of finches inc Hawfinch, thrushes and woodland species inc Marsh & Willow Tits. *Summer:* Cuckoo, warblers inc Garden. *Winter:* Siskin, Redpoll, Crossbill.

Other: Woodland flora, butterflies. Dormouse.

Directions: EN10 7QP; TL 330 064 (Bencroft Wood, East car park/centre of area). E of Broxbourne. From Broxbourne (A1170) turn into Bell Lane (follow brown sign to Paradise Wildlife Park), continues into Baas Hill (goes over A10) then into White Stubbs Lane—car park on L, just past wildlife park.

Public transport: None.

Visiting: Other car parks: Bencroft Wood West (continue along White Stubbs Lane 0.3 miles on L, TL 326 064); Broxbourne Wood East (turn R after Bencroft East, car park at T-junction, TL 327 069); Broxbourne Wood West (turn L at T-junction, 0.3 mile on R, TL 324 071). All have height barriers.

Bridleways, paths and rides throughout the area.

Contact: Hertfordshire County Council: 01992 588 433;

northeast.cms@hertfordshire.gov.uk

Woodland Trust: 0330 333 3300; england@woodlandtrust.org.uk

Essex

This is a large county where the Wildlife Trust manages 87 nature reserves. The RSPB's coastal reserves at Rainham Marshes and Old Hall Marshes attract a wide range of species including wintering raptors and many parts of the coast (including the Naze and Bradwell, with its Bird Observatory) attract migrants on spring and autumn passage, including rarities. Sea-

watching along the Thames, off Southend Pier, can be rewarding. Away from the coast, Abberton Reservoir holds important numbers of wintering wildfowl and wader passage can be good. Explore the ancient woodland of Epping Forest, which lies close to London.

Bird Atlas/Avifauna
The Birds of Essex
Simon Wood
(Christopher Helm, 2007).

Bird Recorder
Michael Tracey, Robins, Hayhouse Rd, Earls Colne, Colchester, CO6 2PD: 07500 866 335; ebwsrecorder@gmail.com

Bird Report
Essex Bird Report (1949/50-), from EBWS: info.ebws@gmail.com

BTO Regional Representatives
North-East
John Fell
North-West
Ade Jevans
South
Tony Porter
Wetland Bird Survey (WeBS)
Local Organizers: webs@bto.org
Crouch/Roach Estuary and South Dengie
Sean Murphy
Essex (Other Sites) &
South Blackwater and North Dengie
Anthony Harbott
Hamford Water
Leon Woodrow
Lee Valley
See **Hertfordshire**
North Blackwater
John Fell
Swale Estuary
See **Kent**
Medway Estuary
See **Kent**
Thames Estuary (Foulness)
Chris Lewis
Thames Estuary (Hoo)
See **Kent**

Club
Essex Birdwatching Society (1949; 750)
Peter Dwyer (Membership Sec):
ebwsmembership@gmail.com; www.ebws.org.uk
Meetings: 8pm, 1st Friday of the month (Sep-Apr). Quaker Meeting House, 82 Rainsford Road, Chelmsford, CM1 2QL—has blue badge parking.

Ringing Groups/Bird Observatory
Abberton Reservoir RG
Bradwell Bird Observatory RG--see entry
North Thames Gull Group: www.ntgg.org.uk
Southern Colour Ringing Group:
www.southern-colour-ringing-group.org.uk
Thames Estuary RG

RSPB Local Groups
Chelmsford and Central Essex (1975; 360)
Sue McClellan: suem@idnet.com;
https://group.rspb.org.uk/chelmsford/
Meetings: Zoom talks to continue for forseeable future—contact/see website for details.
South East Essex (1983; 110)
Caroline Reay: rspbseelg@gmail.com;
https://group.rspb.org.uk/southeastessex/
Meetings: Currently no indoor meetings held—contact/see website for details.

Wildlife Trust
Essex Wildlife Trust (1959; 40,000)
Abbotts Hall, Maldon Road,
Great Wigborough, Colchester, CO5 7RZ:
01621 862 960; enquiries@essexwt.org.uk;
www.essexwt.org.uk

If entering Essex round the M25 from **Hertfordshire,** *leave at J with M11, then exit M11 at J5. L on to A113 and then R on to A1112. Approach from N.*

1 HAINAULT FOREST COUNTRY PARK
The Woodland Trust/London Borough of Redbridge/ Vision Redbridge Culture & Leisure
Habitat: Ancient woodland, grassland, scrub, lake.
Birds: c.160 spp recorded. *All year:* Common woodland spp & waterfowl. Rose-ringed Parakeet, Tawny Owl, Green Woodpecker. *Spring/summer:* Turtle Dove, Cuckoo, Nightingale, warblers inc Wood. *Autumn/winter:* Brambling, winter thrushes.
Other: Bats, butterflies, bluebells.
Directions: IG7 4QN; TQ472 923 (main car park/facilities). Three miles NW of Romford. From A12 take A1112 N towards Chigwell. After 2.35 miles turn R across dual carriageway into main entrance. Alternatively, continue to end of Romford Road, turn R on to Lambourne Road/Manor Road for two Woodlnd Trust car parks (on R).
Public transport: Bus: 247 (Romford station) stops by main entrance. TFL (0343 222 1234; www.tfl.gov.uk).
Visiting: Open daily, parking charges at main car parks (cash-free Ringo payments) or free in Woodland Trust car parks—open 8am closing times vary. Visitor centre, gift shop (10am-4pm), cafe (9am-6pm), toilets, outdoor play area. Network of trails. Activities.

Contact: Hainault Forest/Hainault Forest Country Park:
hainault@woodlandtrust.org.uk
hainaultforest@visionrcl.org.uk
S on A1112 to Rainham

2 RAINHAM MARSHES
RSPB
Habitats: Former MoD shooting range, largest area of lowland wetland remaining along the Thames.
Birds: Spring: Marsh Harrier, Hobby, Wheatear, hirundines and other migrants. *Summer/autumn:* Many waders, inc Black-tailed Godwit, Whimbrel, Greenshank, Snipe, Lapwing, Avocet. Yellow-legged Gull. Hunting Merlin and Peregrine Falcon. *Winter:* Waders, wildfowl, Water Pipit, Short-eared Owl, Little Egret. Penduline Tit not seen recently, Bearded Tit fairly regular.
Other: 21 spp dragonfly, inc Hairy Dragonfly, Scarce Emerald and Small Red-eyed Damselfly. Marsh Frog, Water Vole, Water Shrew, Fox, Stoat, Weasel, 32 spp butterflies and 13 spp Orthoptera. Deadly Nightshade, Flowering Rush.
Directions: RM19 1SZ; TQ 547 787. Off New Tank Hill Road (A1090) in Purfleet, just off A1306 between Rainham and Lakeside. This is accessible from Aveley, Wennington and Purfleet junction of A13 & J30/31 of M25.
Public transport: Bus: 44 Grays to Lakeside. Ensignbus (01708 865 656)/Arriva (on Sun). Train—Purfleet. Reserve is 20 mins walk along riverside path (signposted).
Visiting: Open 9:30am-5pm (Feb-Oct), 9:30am-4:30pm Nov-Jan (not 25/26 Dec). Entry fee for non-RSPB members. Car park (four Blue Badge spaces). Award-winning visitor centre with disabled toilets, picnic area, wildlife garden and children's playground. Future operation of centre under review; no longer has cafe or shop. Four hides. Three signposted trails, suitable for wheelchairs and pushchairs. Guided walks—check RSPB website for details. Dogs allowed only on Thames riverside path.
Contact: RSPB: 01708 899 840;
rainham.marshes@rspb.org.uk
Head E on A13, then take B1007 N. The L on to B148.

3 LANGDON NATURE DISCOVERY PARK
Essex Wildlife Trust
Habitats: Woodland, meadows, lakes, former plotland gardens. Part of wider Langdon Hills area.
Birds: All year: Common passerines (inc 3 spp Woodpeckers). *Summer:* Nightingale, warblers. *Winter:* Woodcock, Thrushes and finches.
Other: 30 spp butterflies. Weasel. Great Crested Newt.
Directions: SS16 6EB; TQ 659 873. Langdon Hills, W of Basildon. From A127 take B148 (to Laindon) then after 200 yards turn R (signed to Hordon on the Hill)—reserve 1.5 miles on L.
Public transport: None to visitor centre.
Visiting: Car park (free), visitor centre and shop open daily 10am-5pm. Toilets. Various trails, routes and other

car parks scattered through wider area,
Contact: 01268 419103; langdon@essexwt.org.uk
Continue E on A13, then A130 and A127. N of Southend take minor road to Rochford.

4 WALLASEA ISLAND
RSPB
Habitat: 1,830 acres of lagoons, mudflats, saltmarsh and grassland, including new intertidal Jubilee Marsh created using spoil excavated during the building of the Elizabeth Line. 250 acres added in 2025 but not yet fully integrated into the reserve
Birds: Spring/summer: Yellow Wagtail, Corn Bunting, Common Tern, Mediterranean Gull, Ringed Plover, Avocet *Winter:* Grey Plover, Knot, Golden Plover, both godwits, Pintail, Shoveler, Hen Harrier Short-eared Owl.
Other: Common Seal, Brown Hare, Marbled White, Wall, Gatekeeper; Shrill Carder Bee, Brown Banded Carder Bee.
Directions: SS4 2HD; TQ955 945. Take Ashingdon Road from Rochford. Turn R along Brays Lane. At the end turn R into Creeksea Ferry Lane, pass through green gates at its end and follow access road to car park.
Public transport: Bus: 60A from Rochford to Wallasea Island. Train—Rochford (6 miles), then 60A bus. In summer train to Burnham-on-Crouch, then boat to Wallasea Marina (1 mile).
Visiting: Car park (charge but free for members), reserve free and open 8am-8pm or dusk, if earlier. 2 Blue Badge spaces. Bicycle racks, no coaches. 3 unsurfaced trails from car park, accessed through wheelchair-friendly kissing gate, then ramp to sea wall. 3 further, part surfaced circular trails. 1 hide, 4 viewpoints, benches throughout reserve. Accessible toilets in car park.
Contact: RSPB: 01702 669346; wallasea@rspb.org.uk
Head back W on minor roads parallel to River Crouch to Hullbridge and Battlesbridge, where cross the Crouch, and then take Hawk Hill to A125 double roundabout. 3rd exit then 2nd exit on to Main Road heading N for Rettendon parallel to new A130.

5 HANNINGFIELD RESERVOIR
NATURE DISCOVERY PARK
Essex Wildlife Trust/Essex and Suffolk Water
Habitats: 110 acres mixed woodland with grassy glades & rides, adjoining 870 acre Hanningfield Reservoir.
Birds: All year: Common wildfowl and woodland spp. *Spring/Summer:* Hobby, Osprey, Common Tern, vast numbers of hirundines feeding over reservoir, common warblers. *Passage:* waders. *Winter:* Wildfowl (inc Pochard, Goldeneye), large gull roost.
Other: Spectacular displays of Bluebells in spring. Dragonflies around ponds. Grass Snake and Common Lizard sometimes bask on rides.
Directions: CM11 1WT; TQ 725 971. Three miles N of

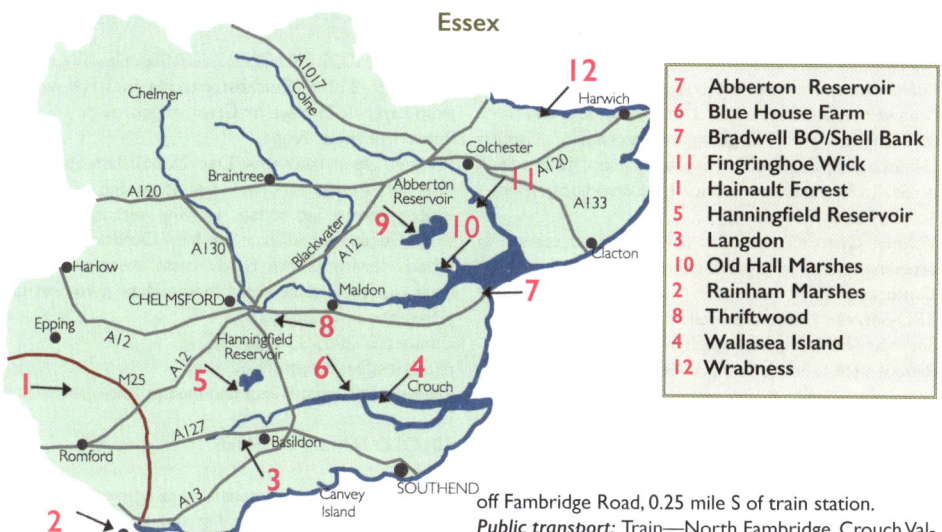

Wickford. Exit off Southend Road (Old A130) at Rettendon on to South Hanningfield Road. Follow this for two miles (passing under A130) until reaching the T-junction with Hawkswood Road. Turn R—entrance to visitor centre & reserve is one mile on R.

Public transport: Bus: 14 (not Sun) Chelmsford to Wickford. First Essex. Alight at Downham village and walk 0.5 mile down Crowsheath Lane.

Visiting: Open daily (not 25/26 Dec) 9am-5pm (4pm Nov-Jan). Voluntary entrance donation. Car park with disabled and coach parking. Visitor centre, toilets, shop, refreshments, education room. Picnic area, four hides (one adapted), nature trails. No dogs. No cycling.

Contact: 01268 711 001; hanningfield@essexwt.org.uk
Return to Rettendon and then minor roads (Buckhatch and Creephedge Lanes) to South Woodham Ferrers.

6 BLUE HOUSE FARM NATURE RESERVE

Essex Wildlife Trust

Habitats: 708 acre farm. Coastal grazing marsh and arable. 100 acres of of wetland creation. Overlooks River Crouch (tidal).

Birds: All year: Pochard, Little Egret, Buzzard, Marsh Harrier, Lapwing, Redshank, Barn Owl, Skylark, Bearded Tit, Reed & Corn Buntings. *Spring/summer:* Cuckoo, Little Ringed Plover, Avocet, Common Tern, Hobby, Reed & Sedge Warblers. Yellow Wagtail, *Spring/autumn passage:* Green, Common & Wood Sandpipers, Spotted Redshank, Ruff. Wheatear. *Winter:* Wildfowl and waders inc Brent Goose, Teal, Wigeon, Golden Plover, Dunlin. Peregrine Falcon, Merlin, Short-eared Owl, winter thrushes.

Other: Butterflies, dragonflies. Water Vole, Brown Hare.
Directions: CM3 6GU; TQ 857 969. 2.5 miles E of South Woodham Ferrers. Take B1012, after three miles turn R to North Fambridge. Access to reserve via track on L

off Fambridge Road, 0.25 mile S of train station.

Public transport: Train—North Fambridge. Crouch Valley line from Wickford, Greater Anglia.

Visiting: Open all hours. Small car park. Permissive grass path passes around farm, access to three hides and links with seawall creating 2.5 mile circular route (steps onto seawall). Dogs permitted on public footpath from car park to seawall (on lead) but not on reserve.

Contact: Essex WT: 01621 740 687;
admin@essexwt.org.uk

Continue E on B1012 and then B1010 to Burnham-on-Crouch. Then N on B1021 to Bradwell-on-Sea.

7 BRADWELL BIRD OBSERVATORY/ SHELL BANK
inc. the Dengie Peninsula Coast

Essex Birdwatching Society

Habitats: Mudflats, saltmarsh, 30 acres of shellbank. Mouth of Blackwater estuary.

Birds: Spring/autumn: good passage of migrants. *Summer:* Small breeding population of terns and other estuarine species, Yellow Wagtail, Reed Bunting and Linnet. *Winter:* Wildfowl inc Brent Goose, Red-throated Diver, Red-breasted Merganser, large numbers of waders (more than 20,000), Snow Bunting now scarce, Twite and Shore Lark now very scarce. Hen Harrier, Merlin, Peregrine Falcon all year as breeds in area. Scarce migrants observed most years: Red-breasted Goose, Black Brant.

Other: Variety of dragonflies (inc Hairy Dragonfly and, possibly, Scarce Emerald Damselfly. Willow Emerald recorded in area).

Directions: CM0 7PW; TM 035 081. BBO is located on edge of Bradwell Shell Bank nature reserve on the Othona Community property, north of St. Peter's Chapel and the public car park (not regularly manned, however anyone can access the seawall and survey the area). Parking at end of East End Road. Bradwell-on-Sea: the public car park is at Eastlands Farm, East End Road,

Essex

Bradwell on Sea, CM0 7PW
Public transport: Nearest bus stop The Kings Head, Bradwell on Sea (just under 1 mile). Bus: 3, Chelmsford to Tillingham; 104, Tillingham to Burnham on Crouch D1 (not Sun) Bradwell on Sea to Maldon; 45 Bradwell on Sea to Burnham on Crouch (not weekends). Train— Southminster 5.6 miles).
Visiting: Open all year. Car park. Keep to seawall in breeding season to prevent disturbance.
Contact:
BBO Secretary: info.bradwellbirdobs@gmail.com; Secretary EBWS: info.ebws@gmail.com
Retrace steps to South Woodham Ferrers, then N on B1418.

8 THRIFT WOOD NATURE RESERVE
Essex Wildlife Trust
Habitats: Ancient woodland, raised bog.
Birds: All year: 3 spp woodpeckers, (Lesser Spotted no longer definite), Mistle Thrush, Bullfinch other common woodland spp. *Summer:* Nightingale, common warblers. *Other:* Great Crested Newt. Ancient woodland plants. Wood-ant, butterflies.
Directions: CM3 4HW; TL 790 017. Six miles SE of Chelmsford. Take A414 from Chelmsford, turn R at Danbury to Bicknacre. Leave Bicknacre on B1418— 0.25 mile after the Drunken Dragon pub, pull off main road by reserve entrance.
Public transport: Bus: 36 (daily) from Chelmsford-South Woodham. Bus stop by reserve entrance ('Bicknacre opp. Thrift Wood' stop). First Essex.
Visiting: Open all hours. No car parking, can pull off main road by entrance (limited space). Circular paths.
Contact: 01621 740 687; enquiries@essexwt.org.uk
Return to A414, then A12 for Colchester. Take B1024 into Kelvedon, then B1023 on R to Tolleshunt D'Arcy, whence take B1026 (Station Road) and stay on it until Visitor Centre and car park.

9 ABBERTON RESERVOIR
Essex Wildlife Trust
Habitats: 62 acres on edge of expanding 1,200 acre reservoir, with wader-friendly muddy margins.
Birds: Spring: Passage waders, terns, birds of prey. *Summer:* Tree-nesting Cormorant colony, raft-nesting Common Tern. Hobby, Yellow Wagtail, warblers, Nightingale, Turtle Dove, Skylark, Corn Bunting. *Autumn:* Red-crested Pochard, waders, rarities. *Winter:* Nationally important for Coot, Mallard, Teal, Wigeon, Shoveler, Gadwall, Pochard, Tufted Duck, Goldeneye. Goosander regular; Smew and Bittern occasional. Golden Plover and Lapwing flocks on surrounding fields.
Other: Dragonflies inc Broad-bodied Chaser, Small Red-eyed damselfly. Butterflies inc Brown Argus, Purple Hairstreak and Purple Emperor. Roesel's Bush-cricket. Brown Hare, Great Crested & Smooth Newts, Wasp Spider.

Directions: CO2 0EU. TL 962 177. Six miles SW of Colchester on B1026 (Colchester to Maldon). Follow signs from Layer-de-la-Haye or Great Wigborough.
Public transport: None.
Visiting: Open daily (not Dec 25/26) 9am-5pm (4pm Nov-Jan). Ample parking, inc disabled and coach bays. Visitor centre inc toilets, viewing veranda, cafe and shop. Electric wheelchair for hire. Outdoor play area. Good viewing where roads cross reservoir. Nature trails with panoramic views, three hides—two overlook water, one in woodland.
Contact: 01206 738 172; enquiries@essexwt.org.uk
Return to Tolleshunt D'Arcy and then as below.

10 OLD HALL MARSHES
RSPB
Habitats: 1,560 acres, coastal grazing marsh, reedbed, open water, saline lagoon, saltmarsh and mudflat.
Birds: Summer: Avocet, Redshank, Lapwing, Pochard, Shoveler, Marsh Harrier, Bearded Tit and Barn Owl. *Passage:* Waders inc Whimbrel, Spotted Redshank, Green Sandpiper. Yellow Wagtail, Whinchat and Wheatear. *Winter:* Wildfowl inc Brent Goose, Wigeon, Teal, Shoveler, Goldeneye, Red-breasted Merganser. Waders, Merlin, Hen Harrier, Short-eared Owl and Twite.
Other: Brown Hare, Water Vole, Hairy Dragonfly, Scarce Emerald Damselfly, Ground Lackey moth, Cream Spot Tiger, 24 spp butterflies (inc White-letter Hairstreak), Yellow Meadow Ant.
Directions: CM9 8TP; TL 959 122. Overlooks River Blackwater, SW of Colchester. From A12 take B1023, via Tiptree to Tolleshunt D'Arcy. Turn L at village maypole then R into Chapel Road (back road to Tollesbury). After c.1 mile, turn L into Old Hall Lane. Continue up Old Hall Lane, through iron gates and follow signs straight ahead to car park.
Public transport: Bus: 95 (not Sun) Maldon to Tollesbury (then two mile walk along seawall). Hedingham (01206 769 778).
Visiting: Car park open 9am-5pm (Mon-Fr)/dusk if earlier, when car park gates locked. No coaches. Do not park in the lane. Alternative parking in Tollesbury when car park closed. Two trails—3 miles and 6.5 miles, open 7 days a week. Viewing screens overlooking saline lagoon area at E end of reserve. No wheelchair access or facilities. Dogs under control allowed on footpaths.
Contact: RSPB: 01621 869 015; oldhallmarshes@rspb.org.uk
Take minor road on R for Great Wigborough from B1026 between Tolleshunt D'Arcy and Abberton Reservoir. Continue to Peldon and then Abberton, where cross B1025 into Fingringhoe Road.

11 FINGRINGHOE WICK NATURE DISCOVERY PARK

Essex Wildlife Trust.

Habitats: Old gravel pit, large lake, many ponds, sallow/birch thickets, young scrub, reedbeds, saltmarsh, gorse heathland.

Birds: 200 spp recorded. *Spring/summer:* Nightingale, Marsh Harrier, Hobby, Turtle Dove, Cuckoo, Green & Great Spotted Woodpeckers and good variety of warblers in scrub. *Autumn/winter:* Brent Goose, waders inc Avocet and Golden Plover, Peregrine Falcon, Merlin, Hen Harrier, Kingfisher, Little Egret. Little Grebe, Water Rail, Mute Swan, Teal, Wigeon, Shoveler, Gadwall.

Other: Swathes of Sea Lavender in summer among 350 plant spp. Numerous dragonflies and butterflies.

Directions: C05 7DN. TM 048 192. Reserve signposted from B1025 to Mersea Island, five miles S of Colchester.

Public transport: Nearest buses (174/175) to Fingringhoe, then 45 mins walk along Gravel Pit Trail to reserve.

Visiting: Open daily (not 25/26 Dec) 9am-5pm (4pm Nov-Jan). Car park. Voluntary entrance donation. Visitor centre—toilets (inc baby changing facilities, easy access toilet), shop, observation room/displays overlooking saltmarsh. One wheelchair available. Seven hides, nature trails. Dogs on leads, limited to dog walk area at edge of reserve.

Contact: 01206 729 678;
fingringhoe@essexwt.org.uk
Return to A12 and then A120 E towards Harwich, exit L on to B1352.

12 WRABNESS NATURE RESERVE

Essex Wildlife Trust

Habitats: 60 acres, grazed grassland and open scrub overlooking wader and wildfowl feeding grounds in Jacques Bay.

Birds: Spring/summer: Nightingale, Whitethroat, Turtle Dove, Bullfinch, Yellowhammer. *Winter:* Brent Goose, Shelduck, Wigeon, Pintail, Black-tailed Godwit, Grey Plover, Dunlin, Turnstone and Curlew. Short-eared & Barn Owls hunt over grassland.

Other: Wildflowers, good range of butterflies and dragonflies.

Directions: CO11 2TD; TM 167 314. Lies on southern bank of Stour estuary. From B1352 between Bradfield and Wrabness turn down Whitesheaf Lane to reserve. Car park is on L just beyond railway bridge.

Public transport: Bus: 103 Colchester to Harwich, (not Sun) alight Wrabness. First Essex. Train—Wrabness—one mile walk from reserve on public footpath.

Visiting: Open all year. Car park, hide. Hard-surfaced path around site suitable for wheelchairs (RADAR NKS key required for gates).

Contact: 01621 740 687; enquiries@essexwt.org.uk
Head back to Colchester on A120 then take A12 N. Exit at J31 on to B1070 for Hadleigh and Suffolk.

Suffolk

The coastal hot-spots tend to get most attention from birdwatchers. The county has always been the stronghold of iconic birds like Bittern, Avocet and Marsh Harrier, which were largely associated with Havergate Island and Minsmere, but are now more widespread. Away from the coast, the Suffolk Brecklands are worth a visit and there are other inland sites good for birds among the Wildlife Trust's 50 reserves.

Bird Atlas/Avifauna
The Birds of Suffolk
Steve Piotrowski
(Christopher Helm, 2003)

Bird Recorders
North East
Richard Walden: bird-ne@sns.org.uk
South East
Steve Fryett: 07593 382 082; bird-se@sns.org.uk
West
Chris Gregory, 3 Mount Road, Bury St Edmunds, IP32 7BH: 01284 722 950; bird-w@sns.org.uk
Rarities
David Walsh: davidfwalsh@hotmail.com

Bird Report
Suffolk Birds (1950-), from Suffolk Naturalists' Society, c/o The Hold, 131 Fore Street, Ipswich, IP4 1 LR.
enquiries@sns.org.uk
https://sns.org.uk/store/Books-&-Publications

BTO Regional Representative
Mick Wright
Wetland Bird Survey (WeBS)
Local Organizers: webs@bto.org
Alde Complex
Ian Castle
Alton Water
John Glazebrook
Blyth Estuary (Suffolk)
Will Russell
Deben Estuary
Nick Mason
Orwell Estuary
Mick Wright
Stour Estuary
Rick Vonk
Suffolk (Other Sites)
Alan Miller

Clubs
Suffolk Bird Group (1973; 440)
Katya Bathgate (Secretary): info@suffolkbirdgroup.org;

www.suffolkbirdgroup.org
Meetings: 7:30pm, usually the 4th Thursday of the month (Sep-Apr, not Dec). Hintlesham Community Hall, George Street, Hintlesham, IP8 3PS. Contact/ see website for details.
Waveney Bird Club. (n/a; 185)
Rebecca Bedwell (Sec), Garden Cottage, Great Common Lane, Ilketshall St Andrew, NR34 8JB: 01986 781 436;
secretary@waveneybirdclub.com;
www.waveneybirdclub.com
Meetings: 7:30pm, usually 2nd Tuesday of the month (Sep-Mar). The Maltings Pavilion, Pirnhow Street, Bungay, NR35 2RU. Contact/see website for details.

Ringing Groups/Bird Observatory
Dingle Bird Club:
Kessingland RG
Lackford RG
Little Ouse RG
Waveney RG
Landguard Bird Observatory
(ringing as *Landguard RG*).
Landguard Bird Observatory, View Point Road, Felixstowe, IP11 3TW: landguardbo@yahoo.co.uk; www.lbo.org.uk

RSPB Local Groups
Ipswich (1975; 150)
Timothy Kenny: ipswichrspblocalgroup@yahoo.com; https://group.rspb.org.uk/ipswich/
Meetings: 7:30pm, 2nd Thursday of the month (Sep-Apr). St Andrews Church Hall, The Street, Rushmere, Ipswich, IP5 1DH.
Woodbridge (1987; 200)
Paul Hetherington: rspbwoodbridge@paulandgill.com; https://group.rspb.org.uk/woodbridge/
Meetings: 7:30pm, 1st Thursday of the month (Oct-May). Woodbridge Community Hall, Station Road, Woodbridge, IP12 4AU.

Wildlife Trust
Suffolk Wildlife Trust (1961; 27,000)
Brooke House, The Green, Ashbocking, Ipswich, IP6 9JY: 01473 890 089; teamwilder@suffolkwildlifetrust.org; www.suffolkwildlifetrust.org

If entering from **Essex** *on A12 and B1070, turn R off High Street in Hadleigh into Angel Street. At junction with A1071, turn R. Car park 1 mile on L.*

1 WOLVES WOOD
RSPB
Habitats: Woodland.
Birds: All year: Common woodland spp, Marsh Tit, Sparrowhawk. *Spring/summer:* Nightingale, warblers inc

Garden. *Autumn/winter:* Woodcock, Redwing, Fieldfare, Siskin, Redpoll.
Other: Butterflies, dragonflies.
Directions: IP7 6BG; TM 054 437. W of Ipswich. Take A1071 from Ipswich towards Hadleigh. Reserve signposted on R, one mile before Hadleigh.
Public transport: Bus: 90/91 Ipswich to Hadleigh. Beestons (01473 823243). Ask driver to stop at reserve entrance but if won't, take public footpath/bridleway NE from centre of Hadleigh (passes Durrant's Farm). Train—Ipswich (eight miles).
Visiting: Open all hours. Car park open 9am-6pm (or dusk if earlier). Cycle rack, nature trail—one mile loop. No dogs permitted (except assistance dogs).
Contact: RSPB: 01206 391 153; stourestuary@rspb.org.uk
E on A1071 to junction with A1214. Turn R and at A12/14 intersection, take A14 for Felixstowe.

2 TRIMLEY MARSHES NATURE RESERVE
Suffolk Wildlife Trust
Habitat: Coastal and floodplain grazing marsh, reedbed.
Birds: 240+ spp recorded. *All year:* Marsh Harrier, Water Rail, Avocet, Lapwing, Redshank, Bearded Tit. *Spring/summer:* Hobby, hirundines, common warbler spp. *Winter:* Wildfowl and waders inc Brent & White-fronted Geese, Pintail, Grey Plover, Knot. Possible divers and scarcer grebes, Bittern, Hen Harrier, Merlin, Short-eared Owl. *Spring/autumn passage:* Osprey, terns inc Black & Little, waders inc Greenshank and Curlew Sandpiper, passerines.
Other: 19 spp dragonflies and 27 spp butterflies.
Directions: IP11 0UD; TM 262 355. W side of Felixstowe, reached from Trimley St Mary. Leave A14 at J59 (Trimley) along Howlett's way. After 300 yards turn L for Trimley St Mary (brown nature reserve sign). After 0.5 mile turn R (Station Road then Cordy's Lane), follow to parking area at end of lane.
Public transport: Bus: 75/77 Ipswich-Felixstowe, alight at Trimley station. From Trimley St Mary and Trimley station c.2 mile walk (approx 45 minutes) to reserve entrance down Cordy's Lane. First Eastern Counties. Train—Trimley (located on Cordy's Lane).
Visiting: Open all year, dawn-dusk. Free car park on Cordy's Lane, 2 mile/c.45 min walk to the reserve entrance. Accessible parking available at reserve office with prior booking. 6 mile circular trail available taking in nearby Levington Lagoon Nature Reserve. Bird hides and viewing platforms. Dogs on short leads allowed in some areas.
Contact: teamwilder@suffolkwildlifetrust.org
The other side of Felixstowe.

3 LANDGUARD BIRD OBSERVATORY
Landguard Conservation Trust
Habitats: Adjoining LNR, composed of close grazed

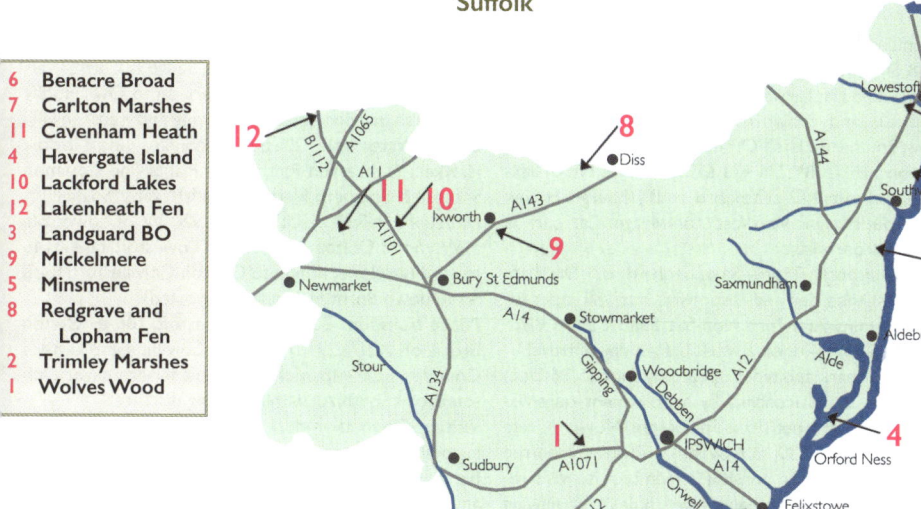

turf, raised banks with holm oak, tamarisk, etc.

Birds: Common, scarce and occasionally rare migrants pass through area, esp spring and autumn. In *summer/autumn* look for seabird/wildfowl movements offshore. **Other:** 26 spp dragonflies and 32 spp butterflies. Several small mammal spp plus sightings of seals and cetaceans off-shore. Nationally rare Stinking Goosefoot.

Directions: IP11 3TW; TM 283 317. On Landguard peninsula, off View Point Road S of Felixstowe town centre. Housed in wartime emplacements alongside Languard Fort.

Public transport: Buses and trains to Felixstowe town centre (1.5 miles away). 77 bus from Ipswich to Landguard Point via Felixstowe.

Visiting: Open all year providing there is a member on site to give access—contact in advance to make arrangements. Migration watch point and ringing station. **Contact:** Landguard Bird Observatory, View Point Road, Felixstowe, IP11 3TW: landguardbo@yahoo.co.uk (enquiries or to arrange a visit); www.lbo.org.uk
Return to A14 and at J58 take A12 towards Lowestoft.

4 HAVERGATE ISLAND
RSPB

Habitats: Small island: shallow brackish water, lagoons with islands, mudflats, saltmarsh. Part of Orfordness-Havergate Island NNR on Alde/Ore estuary.

Birds: The site to which Avocets returned to the UK in the 1940s. *Summer:* Breeding gulls, Common & Sandwich Terns, Avocet, Shelduck and Oystercatcher. Flock of Spoonbills present from mid-Jul onwards. *Winter:* Wildfowl and waders inc Wigeon, Teal, Pintail, Shoveler, Avocet, Lapwing and Black-tailed Godwit. Barn & Short-eared Owls, Marsh Harrier.

Other: Brown Hare.

Directions: IP12 2B; TM 425 495. Orford is 10.5 miles E of Woodbridge, signposted off A12.

Public transport: None.

Visiting: Pre-booked 20-min boat crossings (for max. 12 people) from Orford Quay—leaves at 10am, returns at c.3:20pm on first Sat of month (not May/Jun/Jul) and special event weekends (see RSPB website). Bookings made via RSPB website. Reduction for RSPB members. Park in Orford's pay & display car park next to quay. On the island: Compost toilet with alcohol handwash—no running water, picnic area, five hides, one viewing screen, visitor trail (approx 1.25 miles).

Contact: RSPB: 01728 688 959; havergate.island@rspb.org.uk
Return to A12 and continue N.

5 MINSMERE
RSPB

Habitats: Coastal lagoons, 'the Scrape', freshwater reedbed, grazing marsh, vegetated dunes, heathland, arable reversion and woodland.

Birds: All year: Marsh Harrier, Bearded Tit, Bittern, Cetti's & Dartford Warblers, Little Egret, Great White Egret, Lapwing. *Summer:* Breeding Hobby, Avocet, Lapwing, Redshank, Common, Sandwich & Little Terns (occasional), Mediterranean Gull, Sand Martin, warblers, Nightingale, Nightjar, Woodlark, Stone Curlew (sometimes visible—ask at visitor centre to minimize disturbance). *Autumn/spring:* Passage waders inc Black-tailed Godwit, Spotted Redshank, Ruff, Green, Common, Wood & Curlew Sandpipers, Little Stint, Whimbrel, Spoonbill. Regular Wryneck, Red-backed Shrike, Yellow-browed Warbler. *Winter:* Wildfowl inc Bewick's & Whooper Swans, White-fronted Goose (scarce), Smew (scarce), Hen Harrier (scarce), Water Pipit. Starling murmuration. **Other:** Red & Muntjac Deer, Otter, Water Vole, Badger.

Dragonflies inc Emperor, Norfolk Hawker, Willow Emerald & Small Red-eyed Damselfly. 27 spp butterflies inc Silver-washed Fritillary, White Admiral, Purple & Green Hairstreaks and Brown Argus. Adder. Antlion. Marsh Mallow, Southern Marsh Orchid.
Directions: IP17 3BY; TM 473 672. Six miles NE of Saxmundham. From A12 at Yoxford or Blythburgh. Follow brown tourist signs via Westleton village. Car park is two miles from village.
Public transport: Train—Saxmundham or Darsham (five miles) then demand-responsive bus will meet local buses/trains 7am-7pm, Mon-Sat. Suffolk Links Blyth (01728 635 938)—book a week before day of travel.
Visiting: Car park and hides open daily (not 25/26 Dec) dawn-dusk. Groups/coaches by appointment only. Visitor centre/shop open 9am-5pm (4pm Nov-Jan), cafe open 10am-4pm (3:30pm Nov-Jan). Visitor centre (free entry)—entry fee for non-RSPB members to visit reserve (adults £10). Car park, seven hides and viewing platform, toilets (inc disabled). Volunteer guides, guided walks and family events (see RSPB website). Limited access for dogs.
Contact: RSPB: 01728 648 281; minsmere@rspb.org.uk www.rspb.org.uk/monsmere
Continue N on A12.

6 BENACRE BROAD NNR

Natural England
Habitats: 970 acres, coastal, woodland, saline lagoons, reedbeds and heathland.
Birds: 100 spp of breeding birds, inc Marsh Harrier, Bearded Tit, Water Rail and wildfowl. Bittern breeds irregularly. Woodlark, Hobby and Wheatear breed on heathland areas and Little Terns fish off the coast. *Winter:* Shorelark possible on cliff-top areas, winter thrushes.
Other: Lagoon Shrimp, Starlet Sea-anemone, Yellow-horned Poppy, Grey Hair Grass.
Directions: NR34 7JW; TM 522 820. (Covehithe) On coast S of Kessingland. From A12 at Wrentham take minor road to Covehithe. Park near Covehithe church.
Public transport: None.
Visiting: Open all hours on permissive paths. Cliff top from Covehithe unstable, proceed with care. Elevated bird hide on southern edge of Broad—if sea has breached sandbar it is not possible to reach hide from north. Dogs on lead. Telescope needed for best views.
Contact: Natural England: 01502 676 171
Continue on A12. As approach Lowestoft take A1117 from roundabout to A146. Turn L on A146 then as below.

7 CARLTON MARSHES

Suffolk Wildlife Trust
Habitats: 1,000 acres, meadow, fen, wet grassland, reedbed, marsh and woodland (together with Oulton Marsh).

Birds: 150+ spp with wide range of wetland and broadland birds inc Grasshopper, Reed, Sedge & Cetti's Warblers, Bearded Tit, Barn Owl, Short-eared Owl, Hobby and Marsh Harrier. Breeding Lapwing and Redshank.
Other: Water Vole, 22 spp dragonflies (inc Norfolk Hawker) & rare Fen Raft Spider. Plants (inc Common Spotted & Southern Marsh Orchids), Water Soldier.
Directions: NR33 8HU; TM 508 920. W of Lowestoft, at W end of Oulton Broad. From Lowestoft, take A146 toward Beccles continue to Carlton Colville. Turn R off A146 down Burnt Hill Lane (signposted).
Public transport: Bus: From Lowestoft, 106 to Oulton Broad or X21/X22 to Carlton Colville. First Eastern Counties. Train—Ipswich-Lowestoft service, alight Oulton Broad South. All within walking distance.
Visiting: Open dawn-dusk, free car park with EV charging points and spaces suitable for coaches. Fully accessible visitor centre, cafe serving drinks and lunches, shop and toilets including a Changing Places toilet. Keep to marked trails. Firm path around part of marsh, inc easy access gates. Wheelchair-friendly trail with asphalt path and boards. Mobility Scooter hire available. Dogs on short leads allowed in some areas.
Contact: 01502 359 480; carlton.centre@suffolkwildlifetrust.org
Continue on W A146. Then take A143 to Diss and continue on it to W.

8 REDGRAVE AND LOPHAM FEN NNR

Suffolk Wildlife Trust
Habitats: Calcareous fen with open water areas, wet acid heath, river corridor, scrub and woodland.
Birds: All year: Water Rail, Snipe, Teal, Shelduck, Gadwall, Woodcock, Sparrowhawk, Kestrel, Great Spotted & Green Woodpeckers, Tawny, Little & Barn Owls, Kingfisher, Bearded Tit, Willow & Marsh Tits, Reed Bunting. *Summer:* Hobby, warblers inc. Reed, Sedge and Grasshopper, Spotted Flycatcher, plus large Swallow and Starling roosts. *Winter/occasionally on passage:* Marsh Harrier, Greenshank, Green Sandpiper, Shoveler, Pintail, Garganey, Jack Snipe, Bittern, Little Ringed Plover, Oystercatcher, Wheatear, Stonechat & Whinchat.
Other: Otter, Water Vole, Roe, Muntjac & Chinese Water Deer, Stoat, Pipistrelle & Natterer's Bats. Great Crested Newt, Grass Snake, Adder, Slow Worm, Common Lizard. 300+ spp flowering plants. 27 spp butterflies inc Purple & Green Hairstreaks and Brown Argus. 20+ spp dragonfly inc Emperor & Hairy Dragonfly, Black-tailed Skimmer and Scarce Emerald Damselfly. Fen Raft Spider.
Directions: IP22 2HX; TM 052 803. Five miles W of Diss, signposted and easily accessed from A1066 and A143, car park on minor road off the B1113.
Public transport: None.
Visiting: Open all year, dawn-dusk. Car park with coach space, area for bikes. Toilets. Keep to marked trails. Cir-

cular trail can be muddy after heavy rain, boarded in some areas—not wheelchair accessible. Dogs on short leads.

Contact: teamwilder@suffolkwildlifetrust.org
Continue SW on A143.

9 MICKLE MERE

Suffolk Wildlife Trust
Habitats: 40 acre, wet meadow, open water, reedbed.
Birds: All Year: Barn & Little Owls. *Summer:* Breeding Lapwing, Redshank, Shelduck. *Passage:* Waders inc Bar-tailed Godwit, Little Ringed & Ringed Plovers, Green-shank, Green & Common Sandpiper, Ruff. Garganey, Black Tern. *Winter:* Wildfowl inc Teal, Wigeon, Gadwall, Shoveler.
Other: Otter.
Directions: IP31 3NB; TL 937 696. Immediately S of Ix-worth. From A143 take turn to Pakenham Water Mill. Park here and turn L, walk 100 yards along road to reserve entrance on R (care, narrow road).
Public transport: None.
Visiting: Open all year, dawn-dusk. Viewing only from hide—short path from road to hide, suitable for wheel-chair/pushchair use. No dogs.
Contact: teamwilder@suffolkwildlifetrust.org
Continue on A143 to Bury St Edmunds, then take A1101.

10 LACKFORD LAKES
NATURE RESERVE

Suffolk Wildlife Trust
Habitats: 161 acres, restored gravel pit with lakes, la-goons, islands, willow scrub, reedbed, wet woodland and unique Breckland fen.
Birds: Spring/autumn: Migrants, raptors inc Osprey. *Sum-mer:* Breeding Lapwing, Shelduck, Little Ringed Plover and reedbed warblers. Nightingale, Turtle Dove, Hobby. *Winter:* Bittern, Water Rail, Bearded Tit. Large gull roost. Wide variety of wildfowl inc Goosander, Pochard, Tuft-ed Duck, Shoveler and waders.
Other: Otter. 17 spp dragonflies inc Hairy and Emperor. Early Marsh and Southern Orchid.
Directions: IP28 6HX; TL 801 706. Five miles NW of Bury St Edmunds. Access via track off N side of A1101, between Lackford & Flempton.
Public transport: Bus: 16 Bury St Edmunds-Newmarket, alight at Lackford or Flempton, walking distance. Ste-phensons of Essex (01440 704583).
Visiting: Open all year, dawn-dusk. Visitor Centre and car park open 10am-5pm. Coaches by pre-arrangement. Visitor Centre with cafe serving drinks and light lunch-es, shop, toilets and viewing areas. Keep to marked trails. Bird hides and viewing platforms. Dogs on short leads allowed on Sayer's Beck trail only.
Contact: 01284 728 706;
lackford.centre@suffolkwildlifetrust.org
Continue NW on A1011 to Mildenhall.

11 CAVENHAM HEATH NNR

Natural England
Habitats: Breckland heath, woodland, wet woodland scrub, fen, riverside meadow.
Birds: 280+ species. *Spring/summer:* Hobby, Nightjar, Tree Pipit, Woodlark, Wheatear (passage), warblers. *On river:* Reed & Sedge Warblers, Kingfisher, Grey Wagtail. *Autumn:* pre-migration roost Stone Curlew. *Winter:* Woodcock, winter thrushes, Siskin, Redpoll; Hen Harri-er, Great Grey Shrike both very occasional.
Other: Adder. Butterflies. Fungi.
Directions: IP28 6TB; TL 747 720. 2.5 miles SE of Mild-enhall, straddling unmade public road between Ickling-ham and Tuddenham. Head S from Mildenhall on A11, turn L to Tuddenham. At Tuddenham, turn L off High Street into The Green, continue c.0.6 mile to main car park. Another parking area one mile further along track by Temple Bridge. Access to site (except Woodland Trail) is to S of this track.
Public transport: Bus: 355 Bury St Edmunds-Mildenhall via Icklingham/walk down West Street (Mon-Sat) or 357 (limited service) Bury St Edmunds-Mildenhall stops at Tuddenham (The Green). Mulleys Motorways (01284 702 830).
Visiting: Three trails, marked by trail points: to S of track—'Heathland Trail' 2.5 miles and 'Wetland Trail' 0.8 mile; to N of main car park—'Woodland Trail' 1.5 miles. Dogs on lead/under control.
Minor road off A1011 on L in Icklingham runs to River Lark and there is then a footbridge into reserve from NE.
Contact: Natural England: 01638 721 329;
brecklandnnr@naturalengland.org.uk
Return to Mildenhall than N on A1065.

12 LAKENHEATH FEN

RSPB
Habitats: Reedbed, riverside pools, poplar woods.
Birds: Kingfisher. *Spring/summer:* Cuckoo, Garganey, Bittern, Common Crane (breed, increasingly present in winter), Marsh Harrier, Hobby (up to 40), Raven (reg-ular recently), Grasshopper, Reed & Sedge Warblers. *Autumn:* Harriers, Bearded Tit. *Winter:* Wildfowl inc Whooper Swan (primarily roosting in Hockwold Wash-es, peak '25 count 4,400), Merlin, Barn Owl. 10+ Cattle Egrets in recent years and 30/40+ Great White & Little Egrets. In years when river low, pools and exposed mud a magnet for waders and passage migrants. Caspian Tern and Glossy Ibis in '25. Breeding Lapwing and Red-shank. 60+ wintering Snipe. Regular Avocet, Black-tailed Godwit, Dunlin, Greenshank, Green, Common & Wood Sandpipers. Good gull flocks in wetter years, can include Caspian, Yellow-legged & Little Gulls.
Other: 15+ spp dragonflies and damselflies, inc Hairy Dragonfly and Scarce Chaser. Range of fenland plants inc Water Violet, Common Meadow-rue and Fine-

leaved Water Dropwort. Roe Deer, Otter and Water Vole.

Directions: IP27 9AD; TL 724 865. W of Thetford, straddling the Norfolk/Suffolk border. From A1065, head N on B1112 to Lakenheath and then two miles further. Entrance is on L, after level crossing.

Public transport: Bus: 200/201 Thetford-Brandon stop at Lakenheath, then two mile walk to reserve. Coach Services. Train—weekends-only some trains on Norwich-Ely service stop at Lakenheath (path links station to Visitor Centre).

Visiting: Reserve open daily dawn-dusk. Entrance fee for non-RSPB members (free if just visiting visitor centre), group bookings welcome—coaches must book in advance. Visitor centre and toilets (inc disabled) open 9am-5pm (4pm winter) daily. Check website/call to check opening hours over Christmas. Events programme. Four viewpoints, one hide, picnic area, four nature trails over varied terrain—possible for wheelchairs. Dogs restricted to public footpaths.

Contact: RSPB: 01842 863 400;
lakenheath@rspb.org.uk
Return to Mildenhall, then head NW on A1101 for Welney and Norfolk.

Norfolk

The county has long been regarded as the best birdwatching spot in the UK and with such iconic sites as Cley, Titchwell, The Broads and Breckland it is hard to dispute this. A visit to this east coast county, no matter at what time of the year, will always produce an excellent selection of birds. There are breeding Bittern, Crane and Stone Curlew, passage and wintering waders in their thousands, plus plenty of wintering geese. During spring/autumn migration many common, scarce and rare species pass through, and a 'first for Britain' wouldn't be unexpected.

Bird Atlases/Avifauna
The Norfolk Bird Atlas: Summer and Winter Distributions 1999-2007
Moss Taylor & John H Marchant
(BTO 2011).
The Birds of Norfolk
Moss Taylor, Michael Seago, Peter Allard & Don Dorling
(Christopher Helm, 1999/rep 2007).
The Birds of Blakeney Point
Andy Stoddart, Steve Joyner & James McCallum
(Wren Publishing, 2005).

Bird Recorder
Neil Lawton, Scolt Head Boatshed, Harbour Way, Brancaster Staithe, PE31 8BW: norfolkbirdrecs@gmail.com

Bird Reports
Norfolk Ornithologists' Association Annual Report (1962-), from NOA, Broadwater Rd, Holme-Next-the-Sea, Hunstanton, PE36 6LQ: info@noa.org.uk
Norfolk Bird & Mammal Report (1953-), from NNNS—Tony Leech, 3 Eccles Road, Holt, NR25 6HJ: membership@nnns.org.uk
Nar Valley Ornithological Society Annual Report (1977-), from NARVOS: enquiries@narvos.org.uk
North East Norfolk Bird Club Report (2015-; £5 most recent report, £3 earlier reports + p&p), from NENBC—Carol: nenbc@aol.co.uk.

BTO Regional Representatives

North-East
Chris Hudson:
North-West
Nick Gallichan
South-East
Rachel Warren
South-West
Vincent Matthews
Wetland Bird Survey (WeBS)
Local Organizers: webs@bto.org
Breydon Water
Anthony Bentley
Norfolk (excl Estuaries)
Mark Clay
North Norfolk Coast
Neil Lawton
The Wash (Norfolk/Lincolnshire)
Jim Scott

Clubs
Norfolk Ornithologists' Association (1970; 1,500)
Sophie Barker (Warden/Secretary), Broadwater Rd, Holme-Next-the-Sea, Hunstanton, PE36 6LQ: 01485 525 406;
info@noa.org.uk; www.noa.org.uk
Meetings: AGM held in Sep.
Norfolk & Norwich Naturalists' Society (1869; 630)
NNNS Secretary, 56 The Red House, 41 Palace Road, Ripon, North Yorkshire HG4 1FA: 01508 489 551;
membership@nnns.org.uk;
www.norfolknaturalists.org.uk
Meetings: 7:30pm, 2nd & 4th Tuesdays of the month Oct-Mar (not 4th in Dec), St Andrew's Hall, Church Lane, Eaton, NR4 6NW—contact/see website for details.
Cley Bird Club (1986; 450)
Register via the website.
William Earp (Membership Sec) c/o 11 Weynor Gardens, Kelling, Holt, Norfolk NR25 7EQ:
cleybcmembership@gmail.com;
www.cleybirdclub.org.uk
Meetings: 7:30pm, variable days (Oct-Mar). Cley Village Hall, The Fairstead, Cley, NR25 7RJ.

Contact/see website for details.

Nar Valley Ornithological Society (1976; 145)
Paul Fuller (Chairman): 07999 857 209;
paul.fuller123@btinternet.com; www.narvos.org.uk
Meetings: 7:30pm, last Wednesday of the month (all year, not Dec). Assembly Room, 1 Market Place, Swaffham, PE37 7AB.

North-East Norfolk Bird Club (2015; 440)
Colin Blaxill, (Membership Sec), Caitlins, Bernard Close, High Kelling, Holt, NR25 6QY: 01263 711 718;
colin.blaxill@hotmail.co.uk; www.nenbc.co.uk
Meetings: 7:30pm, last Thursday of the month (Sep-Nov, Jan-Apr, plus a social event in Dec). Gresham Village Hall, Gresham, NR11 8RF.

Wensum Valley Birdwatching Society (2003; 150)
Chair: Alan Hughes: wvbs.memberships@gmail.com; www.wvbs.co.uk
Meetings: 7.15pm, 3rd Thursday (usually) of the month. Great Witchingham Village Hall, Hubbards Loke, Lenwade, NR9 5AZ.

Ringing Groupa/Bird Observatory
BTO Nunnery RG
East Norfolk RG
www.eastnorfolkringinggroup.blogspot.co.uk
North Norfolk RG
North West Norfolk RG: www.nwnrg.co.uk
South West Norfolk RG
Thetford Forest RG
UEA RG: www.uearg.blogspot.co.uk
Wash Wader Research Group:
via website; www.wwrg.org.uk
Holme Bird Observatory (ringing as *NOA RG*):
www.noa.org.uk/blog

RSPB Local Group
No Groups.

Wildlife Trust
Norfolk Wildlife Trust (1926; 38.000)
Bewick House, 22 Thorpe Road, Norwich, NR1 1RY:
01603 625 540; info@norfolkwildlifetrust.org.uk;
www.norfolkwildlifetrust.org.uk

*Entering Norfolk from **Suffolk** on the A110 I takes you to*

1 WELNEY WETLAND CENTRE
WWT
Habitats: 1,000 acres, washland reserve, spring damp meadows, winter wildfowl marsh (SPA, Ramsar site, SSSI, SAC). Additional 200 acres of recently created wetland habitat next to visitor centre.
Birds: All year: Local Cranes regularly seen, esp. post-breeding birds. *Spring/summer:* Common Tern, Avocet, Lapwing, Black-tailed Godwit, House Martin, occasional rarities. *Autumn:* Waders inc Little Stint, Ruff and Curlew Sandpiper. *Winter:* Bewick's and Whooper Swans, wintering wildfowl.

Other: Purple Loosestrife, Meadow Rue, mixed grasses. Dragonflies inc Scarce Chaser, Emperor, Banded Demoiselle, Small Red-eyed damselfly. 400 spp moths inc Goat Moth. Butterflies inc Brown Argus.
Directions: PE14 9TN; TL 546 944. Hundred Foot Bank, 12 miles N of Ely, signposted from A10 and A1101. Check if A1101 is flooded in winter before setting off.
Public transport: None.
Visiting: Open daily (not Dec 25). Free car and coach parking. 9:30am-5pm (last entry 4:30pm) Mar-Oct, 10am-5pm (last entry 4:30pm) Mon-Wed & 10am-8pm (last entry 6:30pm) Thurs-Sun Nov-Feb). Entrance fee—WWT members free. Visitor centre (wheelchair-friendly), Blue Badge parking, wheelchairs for hire (electric scooter/manual chairs), lifts, disabled toilets, ramps. Large, heated observatory and five hides. Cafe open, 9:30am-4:30pm Mar-Oct, 10am-4:30pm Mon-Wed & 10am-6pm Thurs-Sun Nov-Feb. Access roads and paths to remote hides may be flooded, so check before visiting. No dogs allowed.
Contact: WWT Welney: 01353 860 711;
info.welney@wwt.org.uk
Return to Mildenhall, then A1065 for Moldenhall

2 WEETING HEATH
Norfolk Wildlife Trust
Habitats: Breckland grass and lichen heath.
Birds: Spring/summer: Stone Curlew (main attraction), Lapwing, Little Owl, Hobby, Woodlark, Tree Pipit, Spotted Flycatcher, Crossbill.
Directions: IP26 4NQ; TL 757 881. W of Brandon on Norfolk/Suffolk border. Head N from Brandon on A1065 to Mundford. Cross railway line on outskirts of town, then turn L to Weeting and Methwold. In Weeting, turn L to Hockwold cum Wilton—reserve is signposted off this road.
Public transport: Bus: 40 from Brandon to Weeting (Thetford-Brandon-King's Lynn. Limited services Mon-Fri, only one on Sat). Coach Services (01842 821 509). Train—Brandon.
Visiting: Open daily mid-Mar to end Jul (9:30am-4pm). Car park with coach parking (groups welcome but book first). Entrance fee for non-members, members and children free. Visitor centre open daily toilets, shop, refreshments, hides, live webcam. Disabled access to visitor centre and hides. Reserve/visitor centre opening extended into Aug if Stone Curlews are still nesting.
Contact: Weeting Heath Visitor Centre: 01842 827 615; Norfolk WT: 01603 625 540;
info@norfolkwildlifetrust.org.uk
Return to Brandon, Take B1107 for Theford. At A11 roundabout, go straight across (2nd exit) on to A134.

3 NUNNERY, THE
British Trust for Ornithology HQ
Habitats: Flooded gravel workings, flood meadows, wet

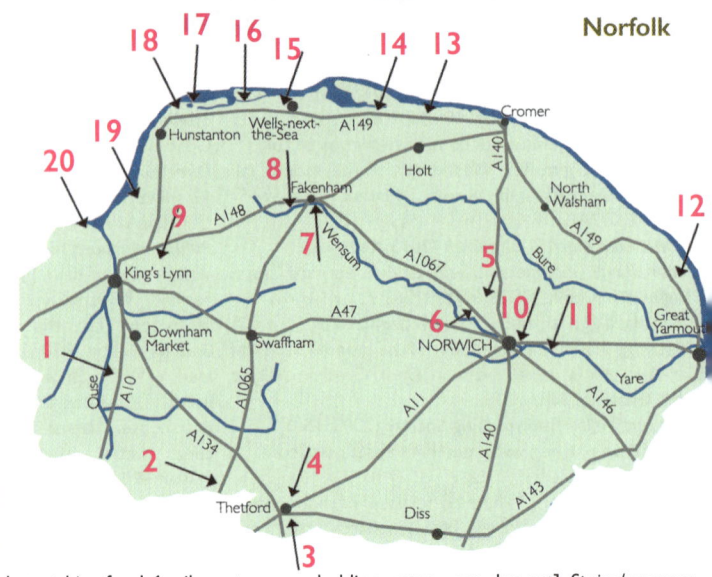

woodland, dry, sandy heathland stretching for 1.6 miles along Rivers Little Ouse & Thet.

Birds: 60 spp breed. Common woodland and wetland spp inc Marsh Tit and Curlew. Cetti's Warbler now common, Willow Warbler rare. Purple Heron, Bittern and, infamously, Black-bellied Dipper have been recorded. Species list still showing Lesser Redpoll (tut tut, get with the message).

Other: Water Vole, Otter, Grass Snake, Common Lizard. Tower Mustard, Mossy Stonecrop.

Directions: IP24 2PU; TL 873 823. A134 from Bury St Edmunds joins A11 (Newmarket-Norwich) to the W of Thetford. From the A134 (Bury Road), take Nun's Bridges Road, which runs NE to the centre of Thetford, 1.5 miles from junction with A11. BTO offices 600 yards to S of road just before bridge over Little Ouse.

Public transport: Bus: 84/86, Thetford to Bury St Edmunds runs along Bury Road, Coach Services (01842 821509; info@coachservicesltd.co.uk). Train—Thetford, then c.1 mile walk.

Visiting: Car park at BTO offices, open dawn to dusk, free. Toilets at Nunnery Place (9am-5:30pm Mon-Thur; 5pm Fri). Trails, only one wheelchair accessible, one hide. Dogs on lead. Immediately adjacent to 171 acre **Barnham Cross Common** (grass and heathland, Thetford Town Council/MoD).

Contact: 01842 750 050; info@bto.org

4 EAST WRETHAM HEATH

Norfolk Wildlife Trust.

Habitats: Breckland grass-heathland, woodland and scrub, meres.

Birds: All year: Common wildfowl, Little Grebe, Curlew, Woodcock, Tawny & Barn Owl, Kingfisher, Skylark, Redpoll, Siskin, Yellowhammer. [Waterfowl numbers subject to meres holding water—can dry out]. *Spring/summer:* Hobby, Cuckoo, Nightjar, Long-eared Owl, Woodlark, Tree Pipit, Redstart, Willow Warbler, Spotted Flycatcher, Crossbill. *Spring/autumn:* Passage wildfowl and waders. *Occasional:* Stone Curlew, Goshawk.

Other: Stoat, Roe Deer and Muntjac. Grass Snake, Adder. Essex Skipper.

Directions: IP24 1RU; TL 913 887. Four miles NE of Thetford. Leave Thetford on A1075 towards Watton, reserve car park on L after c.3 miles (signposted).

Public transport: Bus: 81 Thetford-Watton—very limited service (Mon-Fri) stops East Wretham. Train—Thetford 4.5 miles.

Visiting: Open daily dawn-dusk. Trail from car park. A public footpath crosses the reserve (all spp can be seen from this path if reserve closed, lay-by at TL 911 883). Hide overlooks Langmere, viewing shelters at Fenmere and Ringmere. Dogs on leads/under control at all times (see any restrictions on site).

Contact: Norfolk WT: 01603 625 540; info@norfolkwildlifetrust.org.uk

Continue on A1075 to junction with A47. Head E for Norwich, continuing on A1074 to junction with A140. Head N on A140, the A1270.

5 BUXTON HEATH

Norfolk Wildlife Trust.

Habitats: 165 acres, heathland, ponds, woodland.

Birds: All Year: Common scrub and woodland spp. *Spring/ Summer:* Woodcock, Hobby, Nightjar, Cuckoo, Turtle Dove (possible), Tawny Owl, Woodlark, Stonechat, Grasshopper Warbler, Lesser Whitethroat, Linnet, Yellowhammer, Reed Bunting. *Winter:* Jack Snipe (scarce), Snipe, winter thrushes.

Other: Adder, Common Lizard. Dragonflies and butterflies (inc Silver-studded Blue and White Admiral). Glow-

worm, Bog Bug Cricket, Wolf Spider. Fungi.
Directions: NR10 4DA; TG 172 213. Eight miles N of Norwich. From A1270, N of Norwich, take B1149 (to Holt/Horsford) and continue for 4.5 miles then turn R (sign for Buxton Heath)—car par 100 yards on L.
Public transport: None.
Visiting: Open all hours. Small car park, height barrier. Stay on tracks. Dogs on leads.
Contact: Norfolk WT: 01603 625 540; info@norfolkwildlifetrust.org.uk
Or head NW from A140 on A1067 up the Wensum Valley to:

6 SPARHAM POOLS
Norfolk Wildlife Trust
Habitats: 30 acres, one of a cluster of flooded gravel pits N of the Wensum. Reed-fringed, islands, woodland.
Birds: Kingfisher, *Summer:* Common Tern. *Winter (mainly);* Gadwall, Shoveler, Pochard, Tufted Duck, Goldeneye, Goosander.
Other: Green Hairstreak, Red-eyed Damselfly.
Directions: NR9 5QY; TG 073 179. Leave the A1067 c.13 miles NW of Norwich and take road for Lyng. Car park on L after c.1 miles, before you cross the Wensum and enter Lyng.
Public transport: X29 Fakenham-Norwich, every day, runs along A1067 stopping at turn for Lyng, First Bus (0345 646 0707; firstbus.co.uk/easterncounties).
Visiting: Open all hours, free, no facilities. Circular trail around main pool. Public footpath along N edge of reserve other pools to E (not part of reserve). Assistance dogs only.
Contact: Norfolk WT: 01603 625 540; info@norfolkwildlifetrust.org.uk
Continue along A1067 towards Fakenham.

7 PENSTHORPE NATURAL PARK
Privately owned, linked to
Pensthorpe Conservation Trust
Habitats: 700 acres, including 250 acres farmed for nature. Series of flooded gravel pits along River Wensum, islands, scrapes and wetland. Woodland. Wildlife Garden.
Birds: All year: Gadwall, Mallard, Shoveler, Pochard, Grey & Red-legged Partridges, Great Crested & Little Grebes, Water Rail, Sparrowhawk, Barn, Tawny & Little Owls, Kestrel, Marsh Tit, Cetti's Warbler. *Summer:* Avocet, Little Ringed Plover, Lapwing, Mediterranean Gull, warblers. *Winter:* Wigeon, Teal, Goldeneye, Bittern, Snipe, Woodcock.
Other: Large wildflower meadow on floodplain of Wensum. Bluebells in ancient woodland.
Directions: NR21 0LN; TF 947 292 (car park). To S of A1067 (Norwich-Fakenham) 0.5 mile to the E of the outskirts of Fakenham.
Public transport: X29 Fakenham-Norwich, every day,

runs along A1067 stopping at turn for Penshorpe NP, First Bus (0345 646 0707; firstbus.co.uk/easterncounties).
Visiting: Open every day 10am-5pm (cafe opens 9am), charge, memberships available. Various attractions, inc wader aviary, cafe shop, several trails, some wheelchair accessible, 7 hides. In reserve, assistance dogs only. Elsewhere, dogs allowed.
Contact: 01328 851 465; info@pensthorpe.com
Just to the W of Fakenham, off the A148 for King's Lynn.

8 SCULTHORPE MOOR
Hawk & Owl Trust
Habitats: 200 acres, fen and wetland, meadow, wood, with 52 acres set aside for Beavers. Other meadows around Fakenham being managed to boost small mammal populations and owl boxes installed.
Birds: Although an area of N Norfolk wetland and woodland with all the species you might expect, the focus of Trust's wok is on birds of prey. Those present include: Sparrowhawk, Marsh Harrier, Red Kite, Kestrel, Hobby. Barn, Tawny & Little Owls.
Other: Beaver.
Directions: NR21 9GN; TF 900 305, just to S of A148 in village of Sculthorpe. Turn down Turf Moor Road 0.75 mile W of roundabout where A148 (King's Lynn to Fakenham) and A1065 meet to W of Fakenham. Reserve extends S to River Wensum.
Public transport: Bus: 49/49A, King's Lynn to Fakenham stops on A148 near Turf Moor Road turning, Lynx Bus (talk2us@lynxbus.co.uk).
Visiting: Car park 9:30am-4pm every day. Entry by donation. Visitor Centre, shop, cafe. Visitors on site before 4pm can stay until 8pm. Toilets. Extended visiting hours for members. 6 hides, 3 miles of trail suitable for wheelchairs, boardwalk. Grazing livestock, assistance dogs only.
Contact: 01328 856 788; enquiries@hawkandowltrust.org.uk
www.sculthorpe.hawkandowltrust.org.uk
Continue W on A148 and then A149.

9 ROYDON COMMON
Norfolk Wildlife Trust
Habitats: Heathland, acid grassland, carr and woodland. Adjoins Tony Hallatt Memorial Reserve, part of NWT's Gaywood Valley Living Landscape.
Birds: All year: Grey Partridge, Lapwing, Snipe, Woodcock, Curlew, Barn Owl, common scrub spp. *Spring/summer:* Hobby, hirundines, Nightjar, Woodlark, Tree Pipit, Nightingale, warblers. *Autumn/winter:* Marsh & Hen Harrier, Merlin, Jack Snipe, Redwing, Fieldfare.
Other: 16 spp dragonflies, 30 spp butterflies, 450 spp moths. Heathland flora. Brown Hare, Raft Spider.
Directions: PE31 6DB; TF 680 229 (west car park); PE32 1AP; TF 697 228 (east car park). E of King's Lynn. Take

A149 from Kings Lynn to Fakenham, then A148 off Rising Lodge roundabout, turn R after 300 yards for Roydon (Lynn Road). Both car parks on R after 0.6 and 1.7 miles).

Public transport: Bus: 48 Kings Lynn to Grimston. Stops 1.5 miles from 2nd car park (last 300 yards on road, no footpath). Lynx Bus (01553 611 955).

Visiting: Open all hours. Raptor watch point (and Nightjars) access from first car park; Nightingales from 2nd car park. No facilities. Various sandy tracks across heath. Dogs on lead (Mar-Jul), under close control at other times.

Contact: Norfolk WT: 01603 625 540; info@norfolkwildlifetrust.org.uk

Or, instead of heading NW from Norwich, at 6 you could head E on A47.

10 WHITLINGHAM COUNTRY PARK

Whitlingham Charitable Trust

Habitats: Wetland, lake, woodland, grassland, adjacent to River Yare.

Birds: All year: Common woodland spp, Egyptian Goose, Cormorant, Great Crested Grebe, Water Rail, Kingfisher, Cetti's Warbler. *Spring/summer:* Common Tern, common warblers inc Reed & Sedge. *Passage:* Common Sandpiper, Arctic Tern, occasional Black Tern, Little Gull. *Winter:* Wintering wildfowl & waders inc Goldeneye, Snipe, Bittern, Great White Egret, Little Egret, gulls, Siskin, Redpoll, Occasional scarce divers, grebes, ducks. *Other:* Norfolk Hawker dragonfly.

Directions: NR14 8TR; TG 254 078. Two miles SE of Norwich city centre (near village of Trowse). From A47/A146 interchange take A146 for Norwich. At next T-junction turn R on to A1054, then R at next roundabout towards Trowse then L into Whitlingham Lane & follow road to main car park/facilities.

Public transport: Bus: 40/41A from Norwich city centre, stop at Trowse. First Eastern Counties. Train—Norwich.

Visiting: Open daily. Pay & display car park, bike racks. Cafe open 9am-5pm. Picnic area. Circular walk around Great Broad, inc bird hide, also woodland and meadow walks. Dogs welcome but must be on lead in Conservation Area.

Contact: Whitlingham Country Park: via website; www.whitlinghamcountrypark.com

Continue on A47.

11 STRUMPSHAW FEN

RSPB

Habitats: Reedbed/reedfen, wet grassland, woodland.

Birds: Summer: Water Rail, Bittern, Great White & Little Egrets, Crane, Bearded Tit, Marsh Harrier, Hobby, Kingfisher, Cetti's & Grasshopper Warblers and other reedbed birds. *Winter:* Bittern, wildfowl, Marsh Harrier (roost), Hen Harrier now scarce.

Other: Rich fen flora—4 spp orchid, inc Marsh Helle-

borine and Narrow-leaved Marsh Orchid. Otter, Chinese Water Deer and Water Vole. Swallowtail, White Admiral, Silver-washed Fritillary and White Letter Hairstreal butterflies. Norfolk Hawker, Scarce Chaser, Lesser Emperor and Variable Damselfly among 20 dragonfly spp.

Directions: NR13 4HS; TG 341 065. Six miles E of Norwich. Approach off A47 Great Yarmouth road—take roundabout to Brundell and continue on same road towards Strumpshaw. Just after Strumpshaw sign turn R into Stone Road and R again into Low Road. Car park 0.3 mile on R.

Public transport: Bus: 15 & 15A from Acle/Lingwood-Norwich-Wymondham—stops 0.5 mile from reserve. First Norfolk & Suffolk (08456 020 121). Train—Brundall, c.1.5 miles from reserve or Buckenham (weekends only).

Visiting: Open daily (not 25 Dec), dawn-dusk. Entry fee for non-RSPB members. Reception hide and information centre open 9:30am-5pm Apr-Sep, 10am-4pm Oct-Mar, drinks/snacks available. Toilets, two other hides, trails. Guide dogs only. Limited wheelchair access—phone for advice.

Contact: RSPB: 01603 715 191; strumpshaw@rspb.org.uk

Mid Yare NNR

Strumpshaw Fen, lying to the N of the Yare, is at the NW end of the **Mid Yare NNR,** which also includes **Buckenham Marshes** (TG 351 056) to the SE of but not contiguous with **Strumpshaw Fen** and then, further SE, **Cantley Marshes,** (TG 381 037) these two both being on the N side of the Yare. Then, back to the NW, on the opposite side of the Yare to Strumpshaw Fen and round a bend in the river, the NNR also includes **Surlingham Church Marsh** (TG 304 066). All four marshes that make up the **Mid Yare NNR** are managed by the RSPB and they cover a total area of 1,930 acres. The Surlingham Marshes facing Strumpshaw Fen across the Yare are not managed by the RSPB but one section, **Wheatfen Broad,** is a reserve managed by the Ted Ellis Trust.

A railway line running NW to SE from Norwich and roughly parallel to the Yare forms the NE boundary of the reserves to the N of the Yare. A minor road runs from Strumpshaw to Buckenham station, where there is a car park. A track runs from the station car park to a riverside hide and there are trails along the river bank. Buckenham Marshes have winter roosts of Jackdaws and Rooks, as welll as flocks of wildfowl, including the UK's only flock of Taiga Bean Geese. The next station along the line is Cantley. There is no direct road to Cantley from Buckenham but the village can be reached by the B1140 off the A47 between Norwich and Acle. A path leads from the station to the river and along the embankment. Buckenham and Cantley have less open water and reedbed than Strumpshaw but more ditches and wet meadows are managed for breeding waders in summer and widfowl in winter.

There is no road or ferry crossing in this part of the Yare and so **Surlingham Church Marsh**, which, in any event, does not face Strumpshaw Fen but lies upstream and round a bend in the Yare, needs to be approached from Norwich via a different road from the other three marshes. Take the A146 Loddon Road off the A47 in Trowse Newton, then 1st L on to Kirby Road, follow this, forking L for Surlingham, not R for Bramerton. As you enter Surlingham turn L for church. Footpath leads to reserve from church. Open all hours, free, no facilities. Circular trail around reedbed, fens and pool, with the Yare on one side.

Returning to the A47, continue on it to Acle, whence take A1064, branching L on to B1152 in Billockby. Join A149 just S of Bastwick. Then follow directions below.

12 HICKLING BROAD NNR

Norfolk Wildlife Trust.

Habitats: Largest and wildest of the Norfolk Broads with open water, reedbed, fen, grazing marsh and woodland.

Birds: All year: Bittern, Pochard, Water Rail, Cetti's Warbler, Bearded Tit. *Nov-Feb:* Raptor roost at Stubb Mill, provides excellent views of raptors flying in to roost. Likely spp inc Marsh & Hen Harriers, Merlin, Crane and Pink-footed Goose. *Autumn/winter:* Wildfowl inc Shoveler, Teal and Goldeneye.

Other: Swallowtail butterfly, Norfolk Hawker dragonfly, Marsh Orchid.

Directions: NR12 0BW; TG 428 222. Approx four miles SE of Stalham, just off A149 Yarmouth Road. From Hickling village, follow brown badger tourist signs into Stubb Road at Greyhound Inn. Follow Stubb Road for another mile and turn R at end for nature reserve.

Public transport: Bus: 34 Stalham to North Walsham—stops in Hickling village. Sanders Coaches (01263 712 800). 25 min walk to reserve.

Visiting: Open daily dawn-dusk. Car & coach parking, groups welcome. Visitor centre open daily 10am-5pm Mar-Oct and 11am-4pm Nov-Feb (not 24/25 Dec). Entrance fee charged for reserve, NWT members/ children free. Shop, refreshments, toilets. Picnic area, boardwalk trail through reedbeds to open water, hides—disabled access to broad, boardwalk and toilets. Dogs only allowed on Weaver's Way footpath. Water trail boat trips May to Sep (additional charge—booking advisable).

Contact: Hickling Broad Visitor Centre: 01692 598 276; Norfolk WT: 01603 625 540; info@norfolkwildlifetrust.org.uk

Returning to the A149 and heading N and then W pararllel to the coast, it links a string of reserves along the N Norfolk coast. The Norfolk Coast Path, soon to be incorporated into the King Charles III England Coast Path, also runs along the N Norfolk coast and through or alongside the edge of the following coastal reserves—sometimes along the edge of the dunes and beach, sometimes inside the salt marshes. From E to W along the A149:

13 CLEY MARSHES NNR

Norfolk Wildlife Trust

Habitats: Reedbeds, salt and freshwater marshes, pools/ scrapes and shingle ridge with international reputation as one of finest birdwatching sites in Britain.

Birds: Breeding: Avocet, Marsh Harrier, Spoonbill, Bearded Tit. *Spring/Autumn:* waders—most common species and regularly less common spp inc Ruff, Wood Sandpiper, Spotted Redshank, Temminck's & Little Stint. Common/scarce passage migrants and rarities can turn up any time. *Winter:* large numbers of wintering wildfowl inc Wigeon, Teal, Pintail and Brent Goose. *Offshore*—divers, grebes, sea duck.

Directions: NR25 7SA; TG 054 440. Situated four miles N of Holt on A149 (Coast Road), 0.5 mile E of Cley-next-the-Sea. Visitor centre and car park on inland side of road.

Public transport: Bus: Coasthopper CH1 service Cromer-Sheringham-Wells stops at Cley. Sanders Coaches (01263 712 800). Connections for train and bus services at Sheringham.

Visiting: Open dawn-dusk. Visitor Centre open daily, (not 24/25 Dec) 10am-5pm/4:30pm (Nov-Feb). Environmentally-friendly visitor centre (wheelchair accessible) incorporates observation area, interactive interpretation inc remotely controllable wildlife camera, toilets, cafe (closes 30 min before centre) and sales area. Free admission to visitor centre, entrance fee charged for reserve (NWT members/children free). Five hides (three with wheelchair access), boardwalk and information boards, audio trail. Wildlife detective bumbags for children, free to hire. Reserve leaflet, regular events. No dogs on reserve but can walk Beach Road, along shingle bank and East bank.

Contact: NWT Cley Marshes Visitor Centre: 01263 740 008;

Contact: Norfolk WT: 01603 625 540; info@norfolkwildlifetrust.org.uk

14 BLAKENEY NNR

National Trust

Habitats: Saltmarsh, dunes, sand and mudflats.

Birds: Breeding: Colonies of Common, Arctic, Sandwich & Little Terns, as well as Black-headed and, sometimes, Mediterranean Gulls breed on the beach at Blakeney Point. Ringed Plover, Oystercatcher, Avocet and Redshank breed in the dunes and on the beach

Other: Largest Grey Seal colony in England.

Directions: NR25 7ND; TG 028 442 Blakeney Quay, pay & display NT members free, managed by Blakeney Parish Council, turn into Blakeney High Street off A149, Quay at end of High Street. NR25 7BH; TG 006 442 Morston Quay, NT, charge but members free, Quay Lane, N off A149 in Morston. NR23 1QE; TF 965 439 Stiffkey Salt Marshes, free, turn down Green Way to W of Stiffkey.

Public transport: Coasthopper CH1 service Cromer-Sheringham-Wells stops at Blakeney. Sanders Coaches (01263 712 800). Connections for train and bus services at Sheringham.

Visiting: Morston and Stiffkey Salt Marshes to S of Blakeney Channel. Blakeney Point, sand and shingle spit, to N. The Point is NT but accessed on foot from Cley (NWT), closed to dogs during bird breeding and seal pupping seasons. Toilets at Morston and Blakeney Quay car parks. Reserve open dawn-dusk. Wildlife watching trips (charge) to Blakeney Point depart from Morston Quay. No landings.

Contact: 01263 740 241; norfolkcoast@nationaltrust.org.uk

15 HOLKHAM NNR

Holkham Estate/Natural England

Habitats: 10,000 acres, sandflats, dunes, marshes, pinewoods, reclaimed saltmarsh.

Birds: All year: Marsh Harrier, Grey Heron, Lapwing, Barn Owl, Kestrel. *Summer:* Breeding Little Tern (record year in '25), Spoonbill (largest colony in UK), Great White & Cattle Egrets, Oystercatcher and Ringed Plover (no Snipe for last 4 years). *Passage:* Migrants, inc Yellow Wagtail, Wheatear, Cuckoo and many unusual species. *Winter:* Wildfowl, inc Brent (7,000), Pink-footed (up to 60,000) & White-fronted Geese, up to 13,000 Wigeon. Shore Lark and Snow Bunting. No longer Twite.

Other: Seablite bushes, attractive to incoming migrant birds, Sea Aster and Sea Lavender. Antlion.

Directions: NR23 1RH; TF 890 447. Three miles W of Wells on A149. From Holkham village turn down Lady Ann's Drive (opposite entrance to Holkham Hall) to park. More parking at end of Wells Beach Road in Wells and at Burnham Overy.

Public transport: Bus: Coastliner 36 King's Lynn-Hunstanton-Fakenham stops at Holkham. Lynx Bus (01553 611 955).

Visiting: Unrestricted, keep to paths and off grazing marshes/farmland. Pay & display parking, two hides. Disabled access.

Contact: Holkham Estate, Holkham Nature Reserve: 01328 800 730; info@holkham.co.uk

16 SCOLT HEAD ISLAND NNR

National Trust & Norfolk Wildlife Trust
(managed by Natural England)

Habitats: Sand and shingle barrier island with dunes, saltmarsh, mudflat. Similar to Blakaney Point: sand and shingle on the N seaward facing side with tidal salt-marsh and mudflat on the sheltered S side; but, whereas Blakeney is a spit connected to the mainland, Scolt is a tidal island, although there will most likely be wading even at low tide.

Birds: Summer: Arctic, Common, Sandwich & Little Terns (one third of UK's breeding Sandwich Terns). Black-headed & Mediterranean Gulls, Oystercatcher, Avocet (visiting), Redshank, Ringed Plover, Water Rail. *Passage/Winter:* Grey & Golden Plovers, Lapwing, Turnstone, Greenshank, Ruff (occasional), Bar & Black-tailed Godwits, Curlew, Knot, Dunlin, Curlew Sandpiper.

Other: Sea Lavender, Sea Heath.

Directions: Quayside at Burnham Overy Staithe: PE31 8FF; TF 844 443. A149 runs through Burnham Overy Staithe, Quayside a short distance to N.

Public transport: Bus: Coastliner 36 King's Lynn-Hunstanton-Fakenham stops at Burnham Overy Staithe. Lynx Bus (01553 611 955).

Visiting: Free parking at Burnham Overy Staithe Quayside but may flood at high tide. At low tide, can walk from Burnham Overy Staithe BUT check tides before trying. Apr-Sep, a ferry (charge) runs from Burnham Overy Staithe. Runs 1.5 hours either side of high water, advisable to book in advance. Island uninhabited apart from two huts in W half, one dating from 1920s, one from the early 20C, occupied seasonally by wardens. No facilities. No dogs on island mid Apr-mid-Aug. W end of island closed to visitors during breeding season.

Contact: Contact: 0300 060 3900; enquiries@naturalengland.org.uk

17 TITCHWELL MARSH

RSPB

Habitats: Freshwater reedbed and fresh water lagoons, extensive salt marsh, dunes, sandy beach with associated exposed peat beds.

Birds: Spring/summer: Breeding Avocet, Bearded Tit, Bittern, Marsh Harrier, Reed Sedge & Cetti's Warbler, Redshank, Ringed Plover and Common Tern. *Summer/autumn:* Passage waders inc Knot, Curlew, Wood & Green Sandpiper, Little Stint, Spotted Redshank. *Winter:* Brent Goose, Hen/Marsh Harrier roost, Snow Bunting. *Offshore* Common & Velvet Scoter, Long-tailed Duck, Great Northern & Red-throated Divers.

Other: 25 spp butterflies, inc all the common spp, plus Essex Skipper and annual Clouded Yellow. 21 spp dragonflies, inc Small Red-eyed Damselfly. Good diversity of saltmarsh plants inc Shrubby Sea-blite and three spp Sea Lavender.

Directions: PE31 8BB; TF 750 438. E of Hunstanton, signposted off A149.

Public transport: Bus: Coastliner 36, King's Lynn-Hunstanton-Fakenham stops at Titchwell. Lynx Bus (01553 611 955).

Visiting: Trails always open. Public toilets open 9am-5pm. Free car park, limited coach parking. Entry charge for non-members. Visitor centre open daily (not 25/26 Dec) 9:30am-4:30pm, information desk, cafe, shop—large selection of optics, birdfood and books. Four hides. Three signposted trails, suitable for wheelchairs, but beach not accessible (wheelchairs available, no charge). Groups by appointment. Dogs on leads only on west bank path (public path).
Contact: RSPB: 01485 210 779; titchwell@rspb.org.uk
Two separately owned/managed but immediately adjacent reserves, accessed via the same road and sharing some facilities. The Holme Bird Observatory is also the headquarters of the Norfolk Ornithologists' Association.

18 HOLME BIRD OBSERVATORY/ HOLME DUNES
Norfolk Ornithologists' Association/
Norfolk Wildlife Trust
Habitats: NOA bird observatory reserve 13 acres, NWT reserve 500 acres. Beach, saltmarsh, pools, dunes covered by pine and scrub on headland between sea and brackish lagoon (Broad Water), water level controlled by sluice. NNR, SSSI, Ramsar.
Birds: 320 spp+ recorded by Observatory since opened in 1962. Location on headland between N Norfolk coast and Wash good for a wide range of migrants, including rarities, spring and autumn. *All year:* Marsh Harrier. *Summer:* Avocet visit, Little Tern breed. *Winter:* Large numbers of Pink-footed & Brent Geese and Wigeon, Golden Plover and Lapwing on marshes, wildfowl on pools. Waders inc Bar-tailed Godwit and Knot on beach. Flocks of Snow Bunting and Twite. Peregrine Falcon and Merlin. Seawatching from Observatory hide; systemtic monitoring since 2005.
Other: Moth trapping.
Directions: PE36 6LQ; TF 714 449. Take A149 N from Hunstanton. Signed on L just before Holme next the Sea. Turn R at end of road and follow gravel track to reserve Visitor Centre and adjacent car park. Continue E through gate for Observatory car park
Public transport: Bus: Coastliner 36, King's Lynn-Hunstanton-Fakenham stops at Holme next the Sea, Lynx Bus (01553 611 955).
Visiting: Charges for both sites but free for respective members. If visiting Observatory, do not need to pay to cross NWT reserve. Observatory manned and open daily all year. Toilet facilities limited. Observatory and adjacent viewing platform are wheelchair accessible. Raised seawatching hide, 5 further hides. Active ringing (mist nets, Heligoland, also moth traps) and seawatching programme. The larger NWT reserve open every day except 25 Dec 10am-5pm (or dusk if earlier); Visitor Centre (toilets, cafe) open 10am-5pm Mar-late Oct, 4pm late Oct-Feb. Closed 24/25 Dec. Cafe closes 30 min before Centre. Network of permissive and public footpaths, 6 hides, grazing livestock. Keep dogs on lead (cattle, ground-nesting birds). Assistance dogs only in Visitor Centre.
Contact: NOA: 01485 525 406; info@noa.org.uk
NWT: 01485 525 240

19 SNETTISHAM
RSPB
Habitats: Intertidal mudflats on E side of Wash, saltmarsh, shingle beach, brackish lagoons and unimproved grassland/scrub. Highest tides best for good views of waders.
Birds: *Summer:* Breeding Mediterranean Gull, Ringed Plover, Redshank, Avocet, Common Tern. Marsh Harrier regular. *Autumn/winter/spring:* Waders—particularly Knot, Bar & Black-tailed Godwits, Dunlin, Grey Plover. Wildfowl—particularly Pink-footed (40,000) & Brent Geese, Wigeon, Gadwall, Goldeneye. Peregrine Falcon, Merlin, Hen Harrier, Short-eared Owl. Passage migrants in season.
Other: Yellow Horned Poppies and other shingle flora along the beach.
Directions: PE31 7RA; TF 650 328. Car park two miles along Beach Road, signposted off A149 S of Hunstanton, opposite Snettisham village.
Public transport: Bus: Coastliner 36 service King's Lynn-Hunstanton-Fakenham stops at Snettisham. Lynx Bus (01553 611 955).
Visiting: Open all hours. Car park (charge to non-members), three trails, two hides. Coach groups by prior arrangement (contact Titchwell Reserve). Dogs on lead.
Contact: RSPB: 01485 210 779; snettisham@rspb.org.uk
The A149 continues S past Snettisham to its junction with the A17 to the SE of King's Lynn.

20 WASH, THE NNR
Natural England
Habitats: 21,930 acres saltmarsh (10% of England's total), mudflat and sand, pierced and flanked by the outflows of the Rivers Great Ouse, Nene and Welland.
Birds: Barn Owl, Marsh Harrier. *Breeding:* Redshank, Oystercatcher, Skylark, Reed Bunting. *Autumn/Winter/Spring:* Pink-footed & Brent Geese, Wigeon, Teal. Curlew, Knot, Dunlin. Hen Harrier, Short-eared Owl. Twite, Linnet.
Other: Large population of Common Seals. Halophytes such as Sea Aster and Sea Lavender.
Directions: Occupies SE corner of The Wash between RSPB **Snettisham** (see above) on E coast of The Wash and the mouth of the River Nene. A small separate area of the NNR (Kirton Marsh) lies in the SW corner of The Wash to the N of the River Welland, immediately to the SW of RSPB **Frampton** (see Lincolnshire). Most of the NNR lies in Norfolk, a small part in Lincolnshire. The A17 runs from King's Lynn, on the Great Ouse,

to Sutton Bridge on the Nene and on to the Welland upstream of Kirton Marsh. Minor roads run N from the A17 to the S shore of The Wash and the NNR. Main car parks at Ongar Hill PE34 4JF; TF 583 248 (take Station Road from A17 for Terrington St Clement. As you enter village take a dogleg R then L on to Churchgate Way. At Churchfield turn R on to Newgate Way. After 0.75 mile, turn L on to Rhoon Road. Fork R after 1 mile, continue for 1.8 miles to car park. Footpath (Peter Scott Walk) to coastal embankment. Two car parks at Guys Head and Lutton Leam on either side of the Nene at PE12 9NR; TF 492 257, reached by minor roads running N on either side of the Nene from Sutton Bridge. A car park for Kirton Marsh in the SW corner of The Wash is reached by minor roads running SE from Kirton

Public transport: Buses do run between King's Lynn and Sutton Bridge but it is up to a 5 mile walk to the coastal embankment. Train—King's Lynn.

Visiting: England's largest NNR and the largest area of wetland in the UK. The King Charles III Coastal Path runs along the coastal embankment between farmland and saltmarsh on the E and S edges of the NNR. Not suitable for wheelchairs. To the E of the Great Ouse the path leads from the docks to the mouth of the River Babingley. Boardwalk out into marsh. After crossing the Great Ouse, the path, once known here as the Peter Scott Walk, runs along the S shore of The Wash to the Nene and can be reached from the Ongar Hill and Guys Head car parks. Disabled access to a screen hide at Kirton Marsh. The NNR itself is open all hours and free. No facilities but toilets and refershments in King's Lynn and Sutton Bridge.

Contact: 0300 060 4702; enquiries@naturalengland.org.uk

Lincolnshire

The coast of this large, sparsely populated rural county stretches from the Humber in the north to the Wash in the south-east; and a number of sites along it, including Tetney Marshes, Frieston Shore and Gibraltar Point, hold huge numbers of wintering wildfowl and waders, as well as attracting spring/autumn passage migrants. Agricultural land dominates the interior but there are also a number of reservoirs and gravel pits that can produce a good selection of interesting birds.

Bird Atlases/Avifauna
Birds of Lincolnshire
Colin Casey, John R Clarkson, Phil Espin & Phil A Hyde (Lincolnshire Bird Club, 2021).
The Lincolnshire Bird Atlas 1980-1999:
an historical perspective
Lincolnshire Bird Club
(Lincolnshire Bird Club, 2020)

Bird Recorder
Phil Hyde, The Hawthorns, Legbourne, Louth, LN11 8NH: 01507 607 998; philhyde55@gmail.com
Bird Report
Lincolnshire Bird Report (1979-),from LBC—Bill Sterling, 'Newlyn', 5 Carlton Avenue, Healing, NE Lincs DN41 7PW: sales@lincsbirdclub.co.uk

BTO Regional Representatives
East
Philip Espin
North
Chris Gunn
South
Joanne Whitley
West
Howard Gannaway
Wetland Bird Survey (WeBS):
Local Organizers: webs@bto.org
Humber Estuary (Inner South)
Keith Parker:
Humber Estuary (Mid-South)
Mike Pilsworth:
Humber Estuary (North) See **Yorkshire**.
Humber Estuary (Outer South)
Owen Beaumont:
North Lincolnshire (Inland)
Chris Gunn:
South Lincolnshire (Inland Inc. Peterborough)
Joanne Whitley
The Wash (Norfolk/Lincolnshire) See **Norfolk**.

Clubs
Lincolnshire Bird Club (1979; 500)
Peter Locking (Hon Sec), 2, Sandy Lane, North Somercotes, Louth, Lincs, LN11 7QP: 0790 0081 049; jackieandpete@hotmail.co.uk; www.lincsbirdclub.co.uk
Meetings: Held occasionally—sometimes jointly with other groups such as BTO or Lincolnshire Naturalists' Union. AGM in Mar or Apr with a guest speaker. Contact/see website for details.
Lincolnshire Naturalists' Union (1893; n/a)
c/o Lincolnshire Wildlife Trust, Banovallum House, Manor House Street, Horncastle, LN9 5HF: 01507 526 667; info@lnu.org; www.lnu.org
Meetings; 2pm, Saturdays (winter)—contact/see website for details. Whisby Education Centre, Whisby Nature Park, Moor Lane, Thorpe on the Hill, Lincoln, LN6 9BW.

Ringing Groups/Bird Observatory
Mid Lincs RG
Wash Wader Research Group:
via website; www.wwrg.org.uk

Lincolnshire

Gibraltar Point Bird Observatory
Kevin Wilson (Coastal Officer) Sykes Farm, Gibraltar
Point Nature Reserve, Skegness, PE24 4SU:
01754 802 440; kwilson@lincstrust.co.uk;
Bird Observatory Blog:
www.gibraltarpointbirdobservatory.blogspot.com

RSPB Local Groups
Grimsby (1986; n/a)
Martin Francis: martin.francis2@ntlworld.com;
https://group.rspb.org.uk/grimsby/
Meetings: 7:30pm, 3rd Monday of the month (Sep-Jun).
Holy Trinity Parish Hall, 2 Machray Place, Grimsby Road,
Cleethorpes, DN35 7LH.
Lincoln (1974; 150)
Graham Mumby-Croft: info@lincolnrspb.org.uk;
www.lincolnrspb.org.uk/
facebook:www.facebook.com/groups/
649184110570736   Instagram: rspb_lincoln
Meetings: 7:30pm, 2nd Thursday of the month (Sep-May).
Bishop Grosseteste University, Longdales Road, Lincoln,
LN1 3DY.
Field trips to various locations on the 2nd Sunday of
each month (Sep-May) and a Walk With Nature at
Hartsholme Country Park, Lincoln on the 1st Sunday
of every month.
South Lincolnshire Social Group (1987; n/a)
Neil Oakman (chair): neil.oakman@rspb.org.uk and
RSPBsouthlincs@gmail.com;
https://group.rspb.org.uk/southlincolnshire/
Meetings: This is a Social rather than a Local Group—
contact/see website for details of activities which in-
clude walks and Wash boat trips.

Wildlife Trust
Lincolnshire Wildlife Trust (1948; 26,000), Banovallum
House, Manor House Street, Horncastle, LN9 5HF:
01507 526 667; info@lincstrust.co.uk;
www.lincstrust.org.uk

*The A17 runs across the SE side of The Wash from King's
Lynn to a crossroads with the A16. to the SW of*

1 FRAMPTON MARSH
RSPB
Habitats: Saltmarsh, wet grassland, freshwater scrapes,
developing reedbed.
Birds: Summer: Breeding Redshank, Avocet, Lapwing,
Skylark, Little Ringed Plover, Ringed Plover, Sand Martin
and several spp of duck. *Passage:* Waders (inc Green-
shank, Curlew Sandpiper, Wood Sandpiper, Little & Tem-
minck's Stints, Ruff and Black-tailed Godwit), Marsh
Harrier and Hobby. *Winter:* Wildfowl inc Whooper
Swan, Dark-bellied Brent Goose and Wigeon, Hen
Harrier, Short-eared Owl, Merlin, Lapwing and Golden
Plover, Kingfisher, Lapland Bunting, Twite.

Other: Water Vole, Brown Hare, Stoat. Dragonflies
inc Emperor, hawkers, chasers and darters. Common
butterflies inc Wall Brown, Painted Lady and Speckled
Wood. Scarce Pug, Star Wort and Crescent Striped
moths on saltmarsh. Important brackish water flora
and fauna inc nationally scarce Spiral Tassleweed and
several rare beetles.
Directions: PE20 1AY; TF 356 392. Four miles SE of Boston. From A16 follow signs to Frampton then Frampton
Marsh.
Public transport: None.
Visiting: Reserve open all hours. Visitor centre, inc.
toilets, open daily 9am-4pm (closed 24-26 Dec). Cafe
serving sandwiches and light meals, hot and cold drinks,
cakes and ice creams, Binocular hire. 60-space car park
(free for RSPB members and Blue Badge holders), four
spaces for disabled visitors, bicycle rack, benches, viewpoints. Footpaths and three hides open all hours, all
suitable for wheelchairs. Two mobility scooters available to borrow.
Contact: RSPB: 01205 724 678;
lincolnshirewashreserves@rspb.org.uk
Head NE on A16 past Boston, then A52 for Skegness

2 GIBRALTAR POINT NNR
AND BIRD OBSERVATORY
Lincolnshire Wildlife Trust
Habitats: Sand dune grassland and scrub, saltmarsh and
mudflats, freshwater marsh, lagoons.
Birds: Large scale visible migration during spring and
autumn passage. Internationally important populations
of non-breeding waders between Jul and Mar (peak
Sep/Oct). Winter flocks of Brent Geese, Shelduck and
Wigeon on flats and marshes with Hen Harrier, Mer-
lin and Short-eared Owl often present. Red-throated
Divers offshore (peak Feb). Colonies of Little Tern and
Ringed Plover in summer. 100+ spp can be seen in a day
during May and Sep. Can be a good passage of autumn
seabirds during northerly winds.
Other: Grey & Common Seal colonies, with Harbour
Porpoises offshore most months. Patches of Pyramidal
Orchids. Butterflies inc Brown Argus and Green Hair-
streak. 18 spp of breeding dragonfly.
Directions: PE24 4SU; TF 556 580. Three miles S of
Skegness, signposted from town centre.
Public transport: Train—Skegness (3.5 miles). Cycle
route from Skegness.
Visiting: Open dawn-dusk all year. Charges for parking,
car park closed at dusk. Free admission to reserve.
Some access restrictions to sensitive sites at S end. Visitor centre and cafe open 10am-3pm (Nov-Mar) 10am-
4pm (Apr-Oct), may stay open later during busy periods), toilets, shop. Public hides overlook freshwater and
brackish lagoons. Wash viewpoint overlooks saltmarsh
and mudflats. Most hides suitable for wheelchairs, as
well as surfaced paths. Dogs on leads at all times—not

Lincolnshire

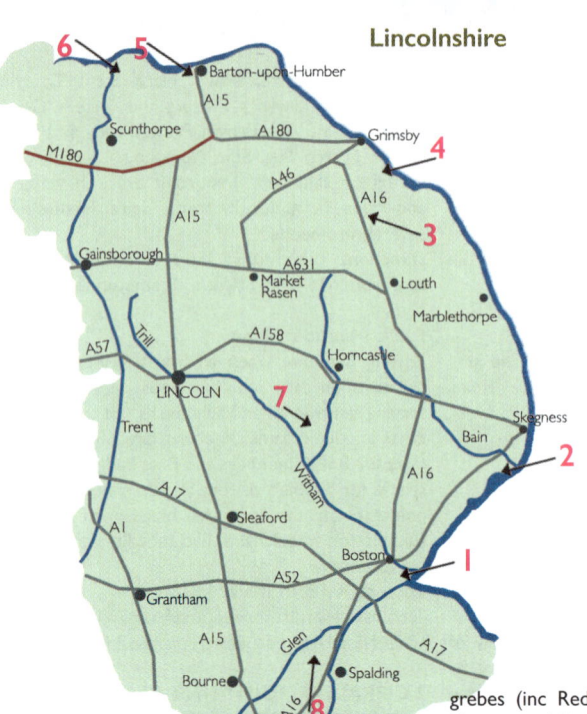

permitted on beach from 1 Apr to 1 Sep. Access for coaches. Day visit groups must be booked in advance. The Wash Study Centre is an ideal field centre for bird-watching/natural history groups in spring, summer & autumn.

Contacts:
Education Team and day visit bookings:
01754 762 763; gibeducation@lincstrust.co.uk
Gibraltar Point Bird Observatory
Kev Wilson: 01754 802 440; kwilson@lincstrust.co.uk;
http://gibraltarpointbirdobservatory.blogspot.com
Vistor Centre: 01754 898 057; gibvc@lincstrust.co.uk
A 1028 NW from Skegness to A16, then head N.

3 COVENHAM RESERVOIR

Anglian Water
Habitats: 200 acre concrete-sided reservoir, raised above surrounding low-lying farmland, small areas of trees.
Birds: All year: Barn Owl. *Spring/Summer:* Yellow Wagtail, Wheatear, Ring Ouzel, Black Redstart possible on passage; Cuckoo, Tree Sparrow breeding but summer birds fairly limited. *Autumn:* Waders, inc Common Sandpiper, Ruff, Curlew Sandpiper and Little Stint, more unusual waders may inc Red-necked & Grey Phalaropes and Purple Sandpiper. Also Black-necked Grebe, Black Tern and Little Gull. *Winter:* Good variety of waterfowl inc Goldeneye, Pochard, Pintail and regular Smew, Common Scoter and Long-tailed Duck plus divers,

grebes (inc Red-necked), gulls and occasional geese. Short-eared Owl, finch flock with occasional Brambling and Tree Sparrow. Has attracted regular rarities inc Red-breasted Goose, American Wigeon, Ring-necked Duck and White-winged Tern.
Directions: LN11 0XX; TF 340 962. Five miles N of Louth. Take minor road (Pear Tree Lane) off A16 just S of Ludborough. Continue for two miles to junction—go over junction (into Bull Bank) for a further 0.5 mile to car park on R.
Public transport: None.
Visiting: Open all hours. Top of reservoir bank reached by steps from car park, path goes around it.
Contact: none.
Continue N on A16. At roundabout N of New Waltham take A1098, 2nd exit.

4 TETNEY MARSHES

RSPB
Habitats: Coastal mudflats, salt marsh, dunes and saline lagoons.
Birds: Summer: Breeding Redshank, Skylark, Reed Bunting. *Winter:* Brent Goose, Golden & Grey Plovers, Knot, Bar-tailed Godwit. Marsh & Hen Harriers, Peregrine Falcon, Merlin, Short-eared Owl, Twite. *Spring/Autumn Passage:* Migrant passerines. Skuas, seaduck, divers offshore (but distant).
Other: Lagoon Sand Shrimp. Blue Sea Lavender.
Directions: DN36 4HE; TA 336 050. S of Grimsby. Take A1098 along Cleethorpes seafront, then follow Kings Road (by leisure centre) until roundabout for Thorpe Park and take exit into Anthony's Bank Road. Continue

past Thorpe Park and into Humberston Fitties holiday village—continue through one way system until car park. Alternative parking at Horseshoe Point DN36 5UU; TA 381 018. Follow brown tourist sign off A1031 (Sheepmarsh Lane, just S of North Cotes).

Public transport: Bus: 9 &10 Grimsby to Cleethorpes North Sea Lane (1.4 miles from car park through holiday village). Stagecoach: 0345 241 8000. Train—Cleethorpes (3.5 miles).

Visiting: Restricted access, site covered daily by tides—only view reserve from car parks at Humberston Fitties and Horseshoe Point or from official footpaths on flood banks. Humberston Fitties owned by NE Lincs Council (free), open 9am-7pm summer, 4pm winter.

Spurn Point in **Yorkshire (East Riding)** is directly opposite on the other side of the Humber.

Contact: RSPB: 01405 704 665;
blacktoft.sands@rspb.org.uk
Take A180 W from Grimsby to A15, the N.

5 FAR INGS NNR

Lincolnshire Wildlife Trust

Habitats: Flooded pits, reedbed, meadow and scrub.

Birds: *All year:* Grey Heron, Bittern, Water Rail, Marsh Harrier, Barn Owl, Kingfisher, Bearded Tit, Cetti''s Warbler. *Spring/summer:* Hobby, Common Tern, Cuckoo, hirundines, warblers inc Whitethroat, Lesser Whitethroat, Reed, Sedge & Garden. *Autumn/winter:* Waders and wildfowl inc Pink-footed Goose, Goldeneye, Teal, Dunlin, Snipe and Redshank. Short-eared Owl, Fieldfare, Redwing, Starling (murmuration).

Other: Butterflies & dragonflies.

Directions: (off Far Ings Road) Ness End Farm DN18 5RG; TA 011 229. Visitor Centre DN18 5RF; TA 018 229. 1 mile NW of Barton-on-Humber. Leave A15 S of Humber Bridge taking A1077 into Barton-on-Humber. Turn L on to B1218 and follow road round to R. Continue 0.5 mile and turn L into Far Ings Road (brown sign) to Visitor Centre/Ness End Farm entrances.

Public transport: Train—Barton-on-Humber. Head N from station, turn L along Far Ings Road to Visitor Centre entrance (1 mile—*care*, no pavement). Alternatively, continue N from station to Humber, turn L along coast path to Visitor Centre (1.25 miles).

Visiting: Reserve open all hours. Car parks (free): Ness End (8am-6pm, or dusk if earlier) and Visitor Centre (9am-5pm). Visitor Centre open Wed-Sun 10am-4pm, not 24-30 Dec). Shop, refreshments, toilets, bike racks (no cycling on reserve). Three waymarked circular trails (0.5-2 hours) and hides—some suitable for wheelchairs. No dogs permitted on reserve.

Contact: Lincolnshire WT, Reserve: 01652 634 507; farings@lincstrust.co.uk
Visitor Centre: 01652 637 055;
faringscentre@lincstrust.co.uk
Take A1077 W.

6 ALKBOROUGH FLATS

North Lincolnshire Council

Habitats: 1,111-acre managed realignment created by breaching river defences to protect homes from flooding. Intertidal mudflats, reedbeds, grasslands, arable land.

Birds: 200 spp. Lying on a key migration route, geese and ducks are attracted in large numbers. Long-billed Dowitcher, Lesser Yellowlegs and Marsh Sandpiper are amongst the site's total of 40 wader spp. *Spring/autumn:* passage waders (Avocets in autumn). *Summer:* Marsh Harriers have attempted to breed, Little Egret, Bearded Tit, Reed Warbler, Water Rail. Spoonbills are regular. *Winter:* Huge flocks of Lapwings (10,000 regularly) and Golden Plover (up to 14,000 but 5,000–10,000 regular), plus Marsh & Hen Harriers, Peregrine Falcon, Merlin, Teal, Wigeon, Black-tailed Godwit. Large flock of Barnacle Geese can be seen at nearby Whitton Sands.

Other: Roe Deer, Badger, Brown Hare, Water Vole, Otter, Fox. Wall Brown among butterflies and Black-tailed Skimmer among dragonflies.

Directions: DN15 9JN; SE 887 224, main car park. Located on S bank of Humber where Rivers Trent and Ouse meet to form the Humber. Follow brown tourist signs to Alkborough Flats from A1077 near Winterton. Reach two car parks by following the duck signs through Alkborough village. Car park at bottom of Prospect Lane is mainly for disabled visitors. Main car park off Whitton Road, just N of Alkborough village. Site also accessible via a permissive footpath from Julian's Bower, Back Street, Alkborough.

Public transport: Bus: 60 (not Sun) Scunthorpe to Alkborough. Stagecoach.

Visiting: Open all hours. Five miles of public footpaths (two miles wheelchair-friendly), three hides, with wheelchair access. On other side of Trent from **Blacktoft Sands** in **Yorkshire (East Riding).**

Contact: Site Manager: 01724 721 269.

Return to A1077, S to M181, then M180, then A15 to Lincoln. SE of Lincoln exit A15 on B1188 to Metheringham (6 miles), then B1189 to B1191. Turn L

7 KIRKBY MOOR

Lincolnshire Wildlife Trust

Habitats: Remnant heathland, mixed woodland (with adjacent coniferous plantation).

Birds: *All Year:* Sparrowhawk, Woodcock, Little & Tawny Owl, 3 spp woodpeckers, Willow Tit, Redpoll, Bullfinch. *Summer:* Cuckoo, Hobby, Turtle Dove, Nightjar, Woodlark, Redstart, warblers inc Garden and Lesser Whitethroat. *Winter:* Crossbill, Brambling, Siskin, winter thrushes, occasional Firecrest.

Other: 250 spp plants, 275 spp moths, 20 spp Butterflies, 11 spp dragonflies. Adder, Common Lizard, Bog Bush-cricket.

Directions: LN10 6YY; TF 225 629. Between Woodhall Spa and Kirkby-on-Bain (B1191), entrance gate opposite turn to Wellsyke Lane (0.9 mile W of Kirkby-on-Bain). Car park at end of track through reserve, near to reservoir (or park carefully by road if gate closed). Site adjacent to Ostler's Plantation, parking here as well (Forestry England).

Public transport: Bus: IC5 Lincoln-Boston passes through Woodall Spa (not Sun). Brylane Travel (01205 364 087).

Visiting: Open all hours, car park, two waymarked routes (close gates behind you), hide overlooking small reservoir. Rough terrain, no wheelchair access. No dogs.

Contact: Lincolnshire WT: 01507 526 667; info@lincstrust.co.uk

Take B1191 to A15 then S through Bourne. Leave A15 at Baston, taking minor road on L for Pode Hole.

8 WILLOW TREE FEN

Lincolnshire Wildlife Trust

Habitats: Formerly extensively farmed arable land, now shallow meres, flooded pastures, hay meadows, reed-beds.

Birds: All year: Crane (first bred in 2020), now virtually resident. 3 spp of Egrets can be regular. Barn Owl, Reed Bunting, *Summer:* Sedge & Reed Warbler. Winter: Common wildfowl. Whooper Swan, occasional Bewick's, Lapwing, Golden Plover, Snipe, Marsh & Hen Harriers, Short-eared Owl.

Other: Great Water Parsnip, Spined Loach, Otter, Dragonflies, inc Hairy.

Directions: PE11 3JH; TF181 213. W of Spalding, Take A151 to Bourne, at Pode Hole turn L on to minor road towards Baston. Continue for two miles to viewing area off Counter Drain Drove, opposite Bank House Farm.

Public transport: None.

Visiting: As this is a small site and cranes are easily disturbed, access to the reserve is now restricted. View from small car park/viewing area open daily 9am-7pm in summer, 9am-dusk in winter. Volunteer presence when Cranes are breeding. No dogs on reserve inc car park & viewing area.

Contact: Lincolnshire WT: 01507 526 667; info@lincstrust.co.uk

Cambridgeshire

The Fens have a number of superb wetlands well known for wintering wildfowl, owls and raptors: the Nene Washes offer the chance of Cranes, breeding Black-tailed Godwits, Spotted Crakes and introduced Corncrakes in summer whilst the Ouse Washes hold the largest inland concentration of wintering wildfowl in the UK. Grafham Water often attracts scarce species, while Paxton Pits is probably the best place in the country to actually see (as well as hear) Nightingales.

Bird Atlas/Avifauna

Cambridgeshire Bird Atlas 2007-2011
Louise Bacon, Alison Cooper & Hugh Venables (Cambridge Bird Club, 2013).
The Birds of Cambridgeshire
PMM Bircham
(Cambridge University Press, 1989/pbk ed 2009)

Bird Recorder

Jon Heath, 50 Lovell Road, Cambridge, CB4 2QR: 07422 664 881; recorder@cambridgebirdclub.org.uk

Bird Report

Cambridgeshire Bird Report (1927-), from CBC—https://www.cambridgebirdclub.org.uk/publications/annual-bird-reports

BTO Regional Representative

Cambridgeshire
Claire Thorpe
Huntingdon and Peterborough
Drew Lyness
Wetland Bird Survey (WeBS)
Local Organizers: webs@bto.org
Cambridgeshire (inc. Huntingdonshire)
Bruce Martin
Nene Washes
Vacant
Ouse Washes
Paul Harrington

Clubs

Cambridgeshire Bird Club (1925; 330)
Andy Merryweather, (Membership Sec),
6 Lewis Crescent, Abington, Cambridge, CB21 6AG: membership@cambridgebirdclub.org.uk; www.cambridgebirdclub.org.uk
Meetings: 7:30pm, 2nd Friday of the month (Sep-May) plus summer field trips. Indoor meetings held at Wilkinson Room, St John's Church, Hills Road, Cambridge, CB2 8RN.
Talks are occasionally held via zoom—see Meetings page on website for details.
Peterborough Bird Club (1998; 76)
Keith Lievesley, Southfields, Marholm Road, Ufford, near Stamford, PE9 3BL: 01780 740 679; membership@peterboroughbirdclub.com; www.peterboroughbirdclub.com
Meetings: 7:30pm, last Wednesday of the month (Oct-Apr, not Dec), St.Mark's Church Hall, 82 Lincoln Road, Peterborough, PE1 2SN, full programme of outdoor meetings, some weekend trips—see website for details.

Ringing Groups/Bird Observatory

Kingfisher Bridge RG
South Cambridgeshire RG

Upper Cam RG
Wicken Fen RG

RSPB Local Groups
Cambridge (1977; 60)
Tony Corps: rspbcambridge@outlook.com;
https://group.rspb.org.uk/cambridge/
Meetings: 7.30pm, 3rd Wednesday of the month (Sep-Nov/Jan-May). Wilkinson Room, St John the Evangelist, Hills Road, Cambridge, CB2 8RN.
Huntingdonshire (1982; 70)
Heather Twinn: rspbhuntslocalgroup@outlook.com;
https://group.rspb.org.uk/huntingdonshire/
Meetings: 7:30pm, last Wednesday of the month (Sep-Apr, Dec may be earlier in month). The Free Church, St Ives, Market Hill, St Ives, PE27 5AL.

Wildlife Trust
See **Bedfordshire.**

If entering from Lincolnshire, continue on A15 S to Peterborough and then A47 W.

1 CASTOR HANGLANDS NNR
Natural England
Habitats: Woodland, limestone grassland, scrub, ponds and wetland.
Birds: All year: Common woodland spp. inc 3 spp. woodpeckers. *Summer:* Woodcock, Cuckoo, Nightingale, warblers inc Garden & Grasshopper, Turtle Dove, Hawfinch.
Other: Rare plants inc Crested Cow-wheat, Lesser Water-plantain, Man Orchid, Narrow-leaved Water Dropwort. Butterflies inc Black Hairstreak, 18 spp dragonflies. Grass Snake, Harvest Mouse.
Directions: PE6 7EN; TF 110 023 (Southey Wood car park). Four miles W of Peterborough. For Southey Wood—take A47 from Peterborough, turn R on to Sutton Heath Road (signed to Southorpe/Ufford) and R again on to Langley Bush Road towards Helpston—car park on L after 2 miles.
Public transport: None.
Visiting: Open all hours. Parking available in Forestry Commission site at Southey Wood, (0.3 mile walk to reserve—take bridleway opp car park, after 125 yards take bridleway to L across field into N end of NNR). Bridleways and paths, can be wet. No facilities.
Contact: Natural England: 0300 060 3900;
enquiries@naturalengland.org.uk
Head W on A47 then S on A1(M).

2 GREAT FEN, THE
BC&N Wildlife Trust/Natural England Environment Agency/Hunts District Council
Habitats: Pools formed from clay pits at Ramsey Heights; extensive birch forest (largest in lowland Britain) and reedbed at Holme Fen; mixed woodland, open waters, fen and grassland at Woodwalton.
Birds: Wide variety of common wildfowl, plus Kingfisher, Grey Heron, Bittern and wintering Goosander on meres. Marsh Harriers breed in reedbed, along with Bearded Tit & Cetti's Warbler. Hen Harriers visit in winter. Common Crane observed in recent years. Wet meadows at Darlow's Farm attractive to breeding Lapwing, Snipe and Redshank and wintering Whooper & Bewick's Swans.
Other: Great Crested Newt and rare beetles at Ramsey Heights. Otter, Brown Hare, deer spp, Water Vole. Scarce Chaser dragonfly, Small Copper and White Admiral butterflies. Wide variety of bog and heath plants.
Directions: PE26 2RS; TL 245 848 (Ramsey Heights), plus Holme Fen NNR and Woodwalton NNR (Chapel Road, Ramsey Heights), S of Peterborough, lying between A1 in west and Ramsey. B660 runs through centre of Great Fen.
Public transport: Bus: 31 (Mon-Sat) Peterborough to Ramsey stops at end of Chapel Road, 0.5 mile from Countryside Centre. Stagecoach.
Visiting: Open all hours, views over farmland linking sites—Ramsey Heights Nature Reserve, Woodwalton Fen NNR, Holme Fen NNR and New Decoy Farm. Great Fen will eventually occupy 9,140 acres. All have waymarked trails—grassy paths mostly level. Countryside Centre at Ramsey Heights (open 9am-4pm), toilets. Hides at Woodwalton and Holme Fen. Dogs on leads.
Contact: Great Fen Team: 01487 710 420;
info@greatfen.org.uk; www.greatfen.org.uk
Head N up A1(M). Take A15 and J16 and then A605.

3 NENE WASHES
RSPB
Habitats: 2,000 acres of wet grassland with ditches—often flooded.
Birds: Spring/early summer: Common Crane breed on Washes. Corncrake release scheme, plus Spotted Crake. UK's top site for breeding Black-tailed Godwit. Other breeding waders (inc Lapwing, Redshank and Snipe). Duck (inc Garganey), Marsh Harrier, Hobby, Yellow Wagtail and Tree Sparrow. *Autumn/winter:* Waterfowl in large numbers inc Bewick's Swan, Pintail, Shoveler. Barn & Short-eared Owls, Marsh & Hen Harriers, Common Crane flocks.
Other: Water Vole, Otter, Water Violet, Flowering Rush and Fringe Water Lily.
Directions: PE7 2DD; TL 318 991. Reserve is eight miles E of Peterborough and NE of Whittlesey. Car park at end of Eldernell Lane, N off A605 E of Coates.
Public transport: Bus: 33 (not Sun) Peterborough to Chatteris runs on A605, alight at Coates, walk down Eldernell Lane (c. one mile). Stagecoach.
Visiting: Open all hours along South Barrier Bank, accessed at Eldernell. Small car park at end of Eldernell Lane—one coach max so group visits along central

Cambridgeshire

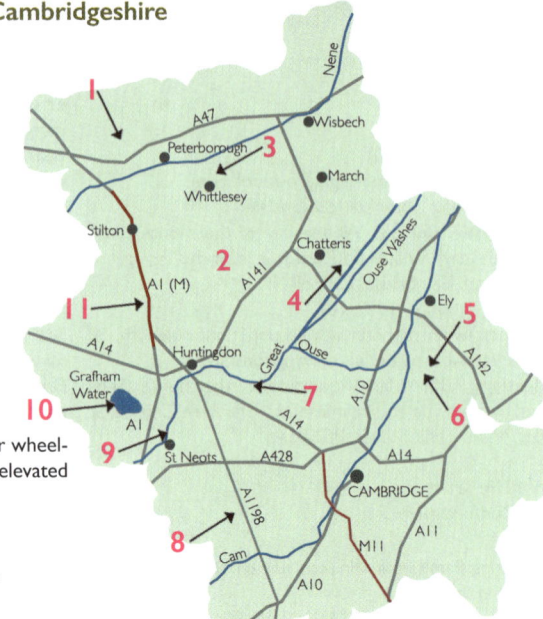

path by arrangement. No access to fields or for wheel-chairs along bank. Nene Valley Way path offers elevated views over reserve.

Contact: RSPB: 01733 205 140;
charlie.kitchin@rspb.org.uk
Continue on A605 E to junction with A141, then S.

4 OUSE WASHES
RSPB

Habitats: Lowland wet grassland, seasonally flooded. Open pool systems in front of some hides.

Birds: Summer: 70 spp breed inc Great White Egret, Black-tailed Godwit, Avocet, Lapwing, Redshank, Snipe, Shoveler, Gadwall, Garganey, Spotted Crake, Hobby, Marsh Harrier, Yellow Wagtail. *Autumn:* Passage waders inc Wood & Green Sandpipers, Spotted Redshank, Greenshank, plus Crane, Egrets and Marsh Harrier. *Winter:* Large number of wildfowl (up to 100,000 birds) inc Bewick's & Whooper Swans, Wigeon, Teal, Shoveler, Pintail, Pochard, Goldeneye.

Other: Good range of dragonflies, butterflies and fen-land flora.

Directions: PE15 0NF; TL 471 860. Between Chatteris and March on A141, take B1093 to Manea. Reserve signposted from Manea. Reserve office and visitor centre located off Welches Dam.

Public transport: None to reserve entrance. Buses and trains stop at Manea, three miles from reserve.

Visiting: Open all hours. Car park (inc two disabled bays, groups welcome—space for two small 36-seat coaches, large coaches can't pass final bend to reserve). Access reserve from visitor centre (open daily 9am–5pm, not 25/26 Dec), toilets, hot drinks. 5 hides (open all hours) overlook reserve—Welches Dam hide (with disabled access) 350 yards from visitor centre, rest up to 1.8 miles away. Welches Dam to public hides approached by marked paths behind boundary bank. Dogs on leads.

Contact: RSPB: 01354 680 212;
ouse.washes@rspb.org.uk
Head S to Charteris on A141, then A142 to Ely. Continue on A142 or S on A10 at Ely.

5 KINGFISHERS BRIDGE NATURE RESERVE
The Kingfisher's Bridge Wetland Creation Trust

Habitats: Wetland creation project—250 acres of former farmland, now a wetland mix of grass, lakes, reed-bed and scrub bordered by the River Cam.

Birds: 210+ spp, 90+ spp breed. *All year:* Bittern, egrets, Lapwing, Snipe, Water Rail, Marsh Harrier, Barn & Little Owls, Kingfisher, Bearded Tit, Cetti's Warbler. *Spring/summer:* Hobby, Grasshopper, Sedge & Reed Warblers. *Passage/winter:* Wildfowl and waders inc Wigeon, Teal, Pochard, Golden Plover, Ruff.

Other: Water Vole, Otter, Badger, Brown Hare. Bats, moths, dragonflies. Fen plants inc Water Germander. Grazing Highland cattle, Konik horses and Water Buffalo.

Directions: CB7 5XL; TL 547 729. 16 miles NE of Cambridge. From A10 at Stretham or A142 S of Soham take A1123. Look for brown sign to **Kingfisher's Bridge Nature Reserve** (opposite turning to Upware).

Public transport: Train—Ely then four miles on foot/bike. Turn R out of station, walk 0.25 miles to E side of river, head S via Fen Rivers Way.

Visiting: Open daily, dawn to dusk. Liable to closure at any time for management work and closed 2nd Tues Nov, 1st Tues Dec/Jan—advisable to check if travelling far. Car park (donation requested). Various paths (inc 2.2 miles circular walk, closed Mar-Jun to avoid disturbance to breeding birds), hides and viewing points. Visitor centre, toilets, cafe and gift shop. Guided walks and tours—booking essential.

Contact: Reserve manager: 07842 782 177;
james.moss@kingfishersbridge.org;

www.kingfishersbridge.org
A short distance further along A1123

6 WICKEN FEN NNR
National Trust
Habitats: Internationally important wetland, inc open fen meadows, sedge fields, grazing marsh, partially flooded wet grassland, reedbed, scrub, woodland.
Birds: Spring: Passage waders and passerines. *Summer:* Marsh Harriers, Hobbies, waders and warblers. *Winter:* Wildfowl, Hen Harriers roost on Sedge Fen, Marsh Harrier, Bittern, Barn & Short-eared Owls, Cetti's Warbler.
Other: 9,000+ spp recorded inc 22 spp dragonflies, 27 spp butterflies, 1,200+ spp moths. Water Vole, Otter.
Directions: CB7 5XP; TL 564 706. Lies 17 miles NE of Cambridge and 10 miles S of Ely. From A10 drive E along A1123 to Wicken, turn R in village (signposted).
Public transport: None.
Visiting: Open daily dawn-dusk daily (not 25 Dec). Disabled parking in main car park (close to visitor centre), coach parking limited (groups need to book). Parking/entry fee for non-NT members. Visitor centre, shop and cafe open daily (10am-5pm/dusk in winter). Toilets (inc disabled), 9 hides (3 equipped for wheelchairs), boardwalk (suitable for wheelchairs), footpaths, cycle route (NCN Route 11 passes through reserve). National Dragonfly Centre open weekends during summer.
Contact: Wicken Fen Visitor Centre: 01353 720 274; wickenfen@nationaltrust.org.uk
Return on A1123 to A10, cross it and continue on A1123 to turning on R (Bluntisham Road) into Needingworth..

7 OUSE FEN
RSPB/Brice Aggregates
Habitats: A working sand and gravel quarry being developed into a vast nature reserve (1,700 acres) but currently final completion of the project may be delayed until 2038. Reedbed and open water with dry grassland surrounds predominate but also a restored gravel pit lake (Barleycroft) and lowland wet grassland (Berry Fen). Potentially, the UK's largest reedbed (1,136 acres).
Birds: Spring/summer: Breeding Cormorant, Bittern, Grey Heron, Little & Cattle Egrets, Common Crane, Lapwing, Redshank, Oystercatcher, Great Crested & Little Grebe, Pochard, Red-crested Pochard, Garganey, Skylark, Linnet, Yellowhammer, Marsh Harrier, Hobby, Buzzard, Red Kite, Common Tern, Black-headed Gull, Reed Bunting, Bearded Tit and incoming migrants inc Reed & Sedge Warblers, hirundines; passage Black-tailed Godwit, Ruff, Garganey, Arctic, Black & Common Terns. *Autumn:* Passage waders inc Green Sandpiper, increasing numbers of common wildfowl and incoming winter thrushes. *Winter:* Good numbers of Mute Swan, Gadwall, Tufted Duck, Wigeon and Pochard and occasional Smew. Starling murmuration and Harrier roost. Large number of Little Egret, plus flocks of tits, finches and buntings. Barn Owl and Bittern regular; Short-eared Owl, Hen Harrier and Peregrine Falcon occasional.
Other: Brown Hare, Chinese Water, Roe & Muntjac Deer. Otter and Water Vole. 25 spp of dragon- and damselfly inc Green-eyed Hawker and Lesser Emperor.
Directions: PE28 3PS; TL 396 743. Located at Needingworth, near St Ives. Exit A14 at J24, take A1307 towards Huntingdon. Take A1096 at next roundabout. Go straight over three roundabouts. At 4th take 3rd exit (A1123). Cross over next roundabout, then next R into Bluntisham Road. After 400 yards, turn L into reserve.
Public transport: Bus 301 St Ives-Earith (Mon-Sat, limited service) Dews Coaches (01487 740 241). Walk E towards Earith Bridge via A1123. At the EA boosting lock follow footpath to site perimeter canal, whence entrance/car park visible to E.
Visiting: Open 7am-8pm spring/summer; dawn-dusk autumn/winter. Automatic gate restricts access to reserve/car park outside opening hours. Car park (currently free), height barrier—no coaches. Two way-marked visitor trails, two viewpoints (one screened).
Contact: RSPB: 01954 233 260; ousefen@rspb.org.uk
Return to A1307, then A1198 towards Royston.

8 HAYLEY WOOD
Beds, Cambs & Northants Wildlife Trust
Habitats: Ancient coppice woodland.
Birds: All Year: Common woodland birds inc woodpeckers and Treecreeper. *Summer:* warblers, Spotted Flycatcher. *Winter:* Redwing & Fieldfare.
Other: Ancient woodland flora inc largest Oxlip woods on chalky boulder clay in Britain. 540 spp fungi. Silver-washed Fritillary. Muntjac, Fallow Deer, Badger.
Directions: CB23 2UR; TL 294 537. 8.5 miles NW of Royston. Take A1198 N from Royston, turn L on to B1046 (School Lane) towards Gransdens. Continue 1.8 miles until reach a water tower (park carefully opposite the tower). Track signposted to reserve (300 yards to entrance).
Public transport: None.
Visiting: Open all hours. Has a recorded history of over 700 years. A working woodland—take notice of any warning signs. Good level paths around the site but can be very muddy in winter.
Contact: BCN WT: 01954 713 500; cambridgeshire@wildlifebcnp.org
Continue on B1046 to St Neots. In centre of St Neots take B1041 N to Little Paxton.

9 PAXTON PITS NATURE RESERVE
Huntingdonshire District Council/
    Friends of Paxton Pits
Habitats: 190 acres, lakes, riverside, reedbed, meadows, scrub, woodland. SSSI

Birds: 235 spp, 70 spp breed. *Spring/summer:* Cuckoo, Great White & Little Egrets, Kingfisher, Common Tern, Sparrowhawk, Hobby, Grasshopper, Sedge & Reed Warblers, Lesser Whitethroat. Large Cormorant colony. *Winter:* Wildfowl inc Smew, Goldeneye, Goosander, Gadwall, Pochard, Tufted Duck, Shoveler.

Other: Wildflowers, 29 spp butterflies and 25 spp dragon- and damselflies (BDS Dragonfly Hotspot). Common Spotted Orchids along meadow trail. Otters use reserve.

Directions: PE19 6ET; TL 196 629. Access from A1 at Little Paxton, two miles N of St Neots. Reserve signposted from edge of Little Paxton.

Public transport: Bus: 66 (not Sun) St Neots and Huntingdon to Little Paxton. Stagecoach. Train—St Neots (two miles—can walk along Ouse Valley Way.)

Visiting: Reserve open all hours. Car park—coaches/groups by arrangement, cycle racks. Wheelchair-accessible visitor centre/toilets, small shop—books, bird seed/feeders etc. and light refreshments, open 10am-4:30pm (not 25 Dec)—subject to volunteer availability. 4 hides (always open), marked nature trails. Many paths suitable for wheelchairs, but muddy when wet. Dogs must be under control at all times and on leads Feb-Aug.

Contact: The Rangers, Paxton Pits Nature Reseve, High Street, Little Paxton, St Neots, Cambs PE19 6ET: 01480 406 795; paxtonpits@huntingdonshire.gov.uk; www.paxton-pits.org.uk

Return to A1 and head N to Buckden

10 GRAFHAM WATER

Beds, Cambs & Northants Wildlife Trust

Habitats: Open water, lagoons, reedbeds, wet mud and willow carr, ancient and plantation woodland, scrub, species-rich grassland.

Birds: All year: Common woodland birds. *Spring/summer:* Breeding Nightingale, Reed, Willow & Sedge Warblers, Common & Black Terns. *Autumn:* Passage waders. *Winter:* Waders inc Common Sandpiper and Dunlin, Great Crested Grebe. Wildfowl inc large flocks of common species, plus Shelduck, Goldeneye, Goosander and Smew, gulls (can be up to 30,000 roosting in mid-winter). *Rarities:* Have inc Wilson's Phalarope, Ring-necked Duck, Great Northern Diver, Glaucous, Iceland & Mediterranean Gulls.

Other: Bee, Common Spotted & Early Purple Orchids, Common Twayblade (in woods), Cowslip. Common Blue and Marbled White butterflies, dragonflies inc Broad-bodied Chaser, voles, Grass Snake.

Directions: PE28 0BX; TL 143 671. Follow signs for Grafham Water from A1 at Buckden or A14 at Ellington. Follow B661 road towards Perry & Staughtons to West Perry. As you leave village, Anglian Water's Mander car park is signposted on R.

Public transport: Bus: 400 (Mon-Fri) Huntingdon Circu-

lar to West Perry. Go-Whippet (01954 230 011).

Visiting: Open all year (not 25 Dec). Car parks (8am-dusk) Use Plummer car park for lagoons, Marlow car park for dam area (good for waders/vagrants)—pay & display, disabled parking. Visitor centres at Mander and Plummer car parks with restaurants, shops and toilets. Six bird hides in nature reserve: three in bird sanctuary area, two in wildlife garden accessible to wheelchairs, further hide overlooks islands/scrapes in settlement lagoons. Cycle track through reserve also accessible to wheelchairs. No dogs in wildlife garden, on leads elsewhere.

Contact: Grafham Water Nature Reserve: 01480 811 075; grafham@wildlifebcn.org

Return to A1 and head N past Huntingdon towards Peterborough.

11 AVERSLEY WOOD

Woodland Trust

Habitats: Woodland.

Birds: All year: Red Kite, Buzzard, Marsh Tit, 3 spp Woodpeckers, Firecrest, common woodland spp. *Spring/summer:* Cuckoo, Grasshopper and common warblers.

Other: Bluebells, other woodland flora. Butterflies (inc. Silver-washed Fritillary). Fungi. Muntjac.

Directions: PE26 5GR; TL 170 828 (Sawtry parking). 10 miles S of Peterborough. A1 from S: leave at J15, take 2nd exit at roundabout (Green End Road), then 3rd L (St Judith's Lane), continue to car park by playing field. A1 from N: leave at J15, on to Old North Road, take 2nd exit at first roundabout and 2nd exit at second roundabout (St Andrew's Way—crosses over motorway). At next roundabout, take 1st exit (Fen Lane), then at next roundabout take 3rd exit (Green End Road) then 3rd L (St Judith's Lane).

Public transport: Bus: 904 Peterborough to Huntingdon (not Sun/bank holidays), alight Beaumaris Road stop in Sawtry and walk route from St Judith's Lane. Stagecoach East (0345 241 8000).

Visiting: Open all hours. Car park in St Judith's Lane, Sawtry (20 min walk along grassy path to entrance). 3.5 miles of paths—can be muddy wet, steep in places.

Contact: Woodland Trust: 0330 333 3300; enquiries@woodlandtrust.org.uk

Return to J15 of A and take B1043 running N parallel to A to junction with B660. Turn L and follow B660 to J16 of A14. Head W for Thrapston and enter **Northamptonshire.**

Northamptonshire

Reservoirs and old mineral workings make up much of the birdwatching interest in the county, including the Nene Wetlands, Stanwick Lakes, Pitsford Water and Hollowell reservoirs—all attract a good selection of wildfowl, especially in winter. Buzzard and introduced Red Kites are spreading.

Bird Recorder
Jon Cook, 16 Church Hill, Hollowell, Northampton, NN6 8RR: joncooknorthantsbirds@gmail.com

Bird Report
Northants Birds (1969-), from NBC—RW Bullock, 81 Cavendish Drive, Northampton, NN3 3HL: robertbullock25@hotmail.com

BTO Regional Representative
Drew Lyness
Wetland Bird Survey (WeBS)
Local Organizers: webs@bto.org
Nene Valley
Steve Brayshaw:
Northamptonshire (excl. Nene Valley)
Vacant

Club
Northamptonshire Bird Club (1973; 50)
Eleanor McMahon (Sec), Oriole House, 5 The Croft, Hanging Houghton, NN6 9HW: 07780 603 290; eleanor1960@btinternet.com;
www.northantsbirdclub.blogspot.com
Meetings: 7:30pm, 1st Wednesday of the month (all year). The Lodge, Pitsford Water, 7 Brixworth Road, Holcot, NN6 9SJ.

Ringing Groups/Bird Observatory
Northants RG
Rockingham Forest RG
Stanford RG: www.stanfordrg.org.uk

RSPB Local Group
Mid Nene (1975; 300)
Ian Wrisdale: wrisdale1@tiscali.co.uk;
https://group.rspb.org.uk/midnene/
Meetings: 7:30pm, 3rd Thursday of the month (Sep-Mar). The Saxon Hall, Thorpe Street, Raunds, Wellingborough, NN9 6LT.

Wildlife Trust
See **Bedfordshire**

Nene Valley Wetlands: a sequence of wetlands formed out of flooded gravel pits running NE to SW along the Nene Valley. Entering Northamptonshire from Cambridgeshire brings you first to

1 TITCHMARSH
Beds, Cambs & Northants Wildlife Trust
Habitats: 178 acre, former gravel pit, two lagoons, islands on larger. Scrub, grassland and woodland. Further lagoons and streams adjacent to but outside reserve.
Birds: Breeding: Great Crested Grebe, Lapwing, Oystercatcher, Common Tern, Grey Heron, Bittern, Hobby, Kingfisher, Cetti's Warbler, Reed Warbler, Nightingale, Yellow Wagtail. *Passage:* Black-tailed Godwit, Ringed Plover, Dunlin, Whimbrel. *Winter:* Goosander, Shoveler, Gadwall, Wigeon, Teal, Tufted Duck.
Other: Otter, Water Shrew, Harvest Mouse. Hairy and Emperor Dragonflies.
Directions: NN14 3EE; TL 006 812. Heading towards Peterborough, leave the A605 at Thorpe Waterville, 2.5 miles N of Thrapston intersection with A14, taking road for Aldwincle. 1st L after church into Lowick Road. Car park after 300 yards on L.
Public transport: Bus: 94, Rushden-Oundle stops in Aldwincle (Mon-Fri), Stagecoach Midlands (0345 241 8000).
Visiting: Open all hours, free. No facilities, most paths not suitable for wheelchairs. Circular trail round perimeter, 5 hides (none wheelchair accessible). Grazing cattle and sheep, keep dogs on lead. Nene Valley Way runs along W edge of reserve.
Contact: BCN WT: 01604 405 285;
northamptonshire@wildlifebcn.org
Head S on A605 to Thrapston and then A45.

2 STANWICK LAKES
Rockingham Forest Trust
Habitats: 740 acres, countryside park includes a Ramsar-designated wetland on site of former quarry, part of Nene Valley Special Protection Area, inc reedbeds, hedgerows, grazed areas. SSSI
Birds: All year: Little Egret, Kingfisher, Green & Great Spotted Woodpeckers, Grey Wagtail, Cetti's Warbler, Barn Owl. *Spring/summer:* Waders (inc Oystercatcher (breeding), Little Ringed Plover, Green Sandpiper, Greenshank). Hobby, Yellow Wagtail, hirundines, migrant warblers. *Autumn/winter:* Wildfowl inc. Pintail, Goldeneye, Goosander. Bittern. Redpoll, Siskin.
Other: Otter, Grass Snake, 150 spp.moths, dragonflies.
Directions: NN9 6GY; SP 967 715. Entrance off the A45, eight miles N of Wellingborough.
Public transport: Village Hopper visits from W of county on Sat and School holidays. Request stop on Chatty Bus Corby-Rushden Lakes route.
Visiting: Open daily (not 25 Dec) 7am-7pm (Mar & Oct), 8pm (Apr-Sep); 5pm (Nov-Feb). Visitor centre

open daily (not 25/26 Dec) 10am-5pm (Mar-Oct), 10am-4pm weekdays/5pm weekends and school holidays (Nov-Feb). Charges for car and coach parking. All paths, visitor centre, gift shop, toilets and bird hide are wheelchair accessible. Disability scooter hire available.

8	Daventry
3	Nene Wetlands
5	Pitsford Water
6	Salcey Forest
2	Stanwick Lakes
7	Storton's Pits
4	Summer Lays
1	Titchmarsh

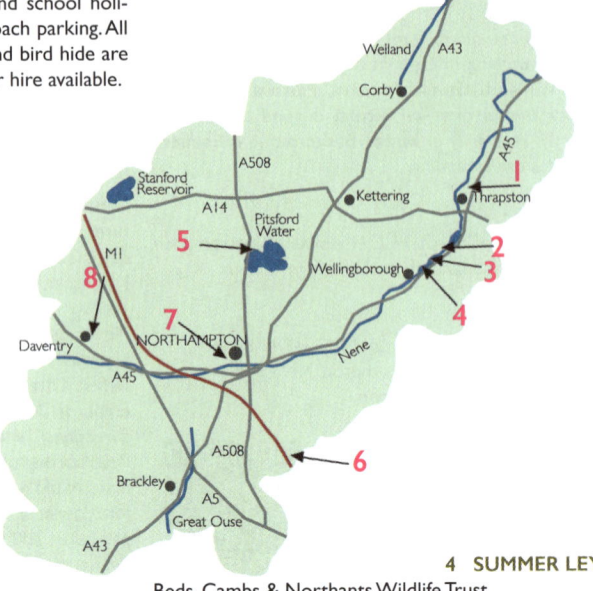

Contact: Rockingham Forest Trust:
01933 625 522;
info@rftrust.org.uk
Continue S on A45, Cross A6 and then

3 NENE WETLANDS
NATURE RESERVE
Beds, Cambs & Northants Wildlife Trust.
Habitats: Part of upper Nene valley floodplain, complex of old gravel pits, rough grassland, lakes, reed, scattered scrub, woodland. Joins up individual sites inc. *Irthlingborough Lakes and Meadows, Ditchford Lakes and Meadows, Higham Ferrers Pits.*
Birds: Great Crested & Little Grebes, Grey Heron, Redshank, Oystercatcher, Snipe. *Summer:* Common Tern, Cuckoo, Nightingale, Reed, Sedge & Cetti's Warblers, Swift, House Martin. *Autumn/Winter:* Wildfowl inc Teal, Wigeon, Gadwall, Tufted Duck, Curlew, Common Sandpiper.
Other: Hairy Dragonfly, Grass Snake, Otter. Plants inc Marsh Woundwort, Dropwort, Great Burnet.
Directions: NN10 6FA; SP 938 679 (Visitor Centre). From Northampton, take A45 towards Rushden and Higham Ferrers. Take exit to Rushden Lakes Retail Park.
Public transport: Bus: 45, 49, 50, X46/47 from various towns inc. Northampton, Wellingborough, Kettering, Bedford to Retail Park. Stagecoach.
Visiting: Car parking at the Rushden Lakes Retail Park (five hrs max.). Visitor centre open daily (not 25 Dec) 10am-5pm, toilets, cafe, shop. Reserve map available showing access points, inc disabled routes. Dogs on leads.
Contact: BCN WT: 01933 779 587;
nenewetlands@wildlifebcn.org
Continue on A45 past A509 to

4 SUMMER LEYS
Beds, Cambs & Northants Wildlife Trust
Habitats: Flooded gravel pit, 116 acres, shallow margins, scrapes, ponds with islands, reedbed, grassland and wet woodland. SSSI & SPA.
Birds: Great White Egret, Glossy Ibis (occasional), Marsh Harrier, Kingfisher, Reed Bunting. *Summer:* Cuckoo, Common Tern, Oystercatcher, Redshank, Lapwing, Little Ringed Plover (breed on islands), Hobby, Yellow Wagtail. *Passage:* Ringed Plover, Greenshank, Green & Common Sandpiper. Smaller numbers of other waders. *Winter:* Gooseander, Gadwall, Wigeon, Teal, Shoveler, Pochard, Tufted Duck, Goldeneye, Smew (occasional). Golden Plover, Lapwing. Peregrine Falcon, Siskin.
Other: Otter (occasional), 16 spp dragon- and dameselflies.
Directions: NN29 7TD; SP 886 634. Take B573 Great Doddington exit from A45, follow brown 'Summer Leys Nature Reserve' signs. Car park at S edge of reserve off Great Doddington-Wollaston minor road.
Public transport: Bus: X47 Wellingborough-Great Doddington, then 1.25 mile walk, Stagecoach (0345 241 8000).
Visiting: Reserve open all hours. Car park (charge for non-members, members must register cars in advance) open 5am-11pm. Visitor centre open 10am-4:30pm, Thur-Sun (+Bank Hol Mon). Toilets (inc accessible) same hours as Visitor Centre. Shop, cafe, picnic area, accessible trails, some grass sections and kissing gates, can be muddy. RADAR keys available. 2 mile circular walk. 4 hides (wheelchair accessible), 2 viewing screen. Grazing livestock, dogs on lead.
Contact: 01604 405 285; summerleys@wildlifebcn.org

Northamptonshire

Continue on A45, then take A43 N.

5 PITSFORD WATER

Anglian Water/Beds, Cambs & Northants Wildlife Trust
Habitats: Open water (300 acres), marginal vegetation and reed grasses, wet woodland, grassland, mixed woodland.
Birds: Typically 165-170 spp annually with a total list of over 250 spp. *Summer:* Breeding terns, grebes, herons, warblers. *Autumn:* Waders if water levels suitable. *Winter:* Up to 10,000 wildfowl, feeding station (Tree Sparrow and occasional Corn Bunting).
Other: 32 spp butterflies, 392 spp macro moths, 21 spp dragonflies, 377 spp flora, 404 spp fungi, 105 spp bryophytes. Harvest Mouse, Brown Hare.
Directions: NN6 9SJ; SP 787 699. Five miles N of Northampton. From A43 take turn to Holcot and Brixworth. From A508 take turn to Brixworth and Holcot.
Public transport: None.
Visiting: Reserve (N of causeway) open all year to permit holders. Wildlife Trust members can apply for free permit from HQ. Non-members can obtain day permits from fishing lodge, open mid-Mar to mid-Nov from 8am-dusk. Winter opening times variable, check in advance. No dogs. Disabled access from Lodge to first hide. Toilets available in Lodge, 15 miles of paths, eight hides and car parking.
Contact: BCN WT: 01604 405 285; northamptonshire@wildlifebcn.org
Pitsford Water Fishing Lodge, Brixworth Road, Holcot, Northampton, NN6 9SJ: 01604 781 350; fishing@anglianwater.co.uk
Return to A45, to S of Northampton at last exit before M1.

6 SALCEY FOREST

Forestry England
Habitats: Woodland inc ancient oak trees.
Birds: All year: Common woodland spp inc 3 spp. woodpeckers, Marsh & Willow Tits. Buzzard, Kestrel, Sparrowhawk, Tawny Owl. *Spring/summer:* Woodcock, Cuckoo, Spotted Flycatcher, common warblers. *Winter:* Siskin, Redpoll.
Other: Butterflies.
Directions: NN7 2HX; SP 794 516. 7 miles SE of Northampton. From J15 M1, take A45 towards Northampton then slip road marked Wootton, 1st exit on roundabout to cross over A45. Go across next roundabout, for Quinton. At next roundabout 3rd exit on to Wootton Road and then through Quinton to edge of Forest. Car park is 0.5 mile on L (after kennels).
Public transport: Bus: 33/33A Northampton to Milton Keynes stops at car park. Arriva Beds & Bucks (0344 800 4411). Train—Northampton.
Visiting: Open all year (not 25 Dec). Car park (charge/membership available) open 8am-9pm Apr-Oct, 7pm Feb-Mar 5pm Nov-Jan. Cafe, toilets, play area, informa-

tion point, cycle hire, network of rides and three way-marked trails (0.75—easy access, 1.5, 6.0 miles).
Contact: Forestry England: 0300 067 4340; salcey@forestryengland.uk
Return to A45 for Northampton and then A4500.

7 STORTON'S PITS

Beds, Cambs & Northants Wildlife Trust
Habitats: Grassland, wetland/old gravel pits.
Birds: All year: Great Crested Grebe, Red Kite, Sparrowhawk, Tawny Owl, Kingfisher, Cetti's Warbler, Bullfinch, Reed Bunting. *Summer:* Common Tern, Cuckoo, Whitethroat, Reed & Sedge Warblers. *Winter:* Common wildfowl, Water Rail, Snipe, Woodcock, Fieldfare, Redwing, Redpoll.
Other: Butterflies and dragonflies. Frog and Toad, Fox.
Directions: NN5 4AB; SP 728 600. W side of Northampton (Sixfields). From A4500 turn S on to A5076. At roundabout take 1st L then take 3rd exit at next roundabout. Follow this road (under height barrier) to Fisherman's car park.
Public transport: Bus: 18 Waterside to Sixfields (stops opposite football ground). Uno (01604 892 986). Train—Northampton (bus stop outside on Station Approach).
Visiting: Open all hours. Park in Fisherman's car park. Section of surfaced path leads to viewing platform, other paths can be soft/uneven in places (not suitable for wheelchairs/pushchairs). Dogs on lead.
Contact: BCN WT: 01604 405 285; northamptonshire@wildlifebcn.org
Return to A4500, then A45 for Daventry. At outskirts of Daventry, take A425 round NE edge

8 DAVENTRY COUNTRY PARK

Daventry District Council
Habitats: Reservoir, woodland, meadows, orchard.
Birds: 200+ spp. *All Year:* Great Crested Grebe, Gadwall, woodland/scrub spp. *Summer:* Common Tern, warblers. *Winter:* Wildfowl inc Pochard, Shoveler, Wigeon, Goldeneye, Goosander plus occasional scarcer spp, inc. Scaup, Long-tailed Duck. Gulls—check for scarce spp Lapwing, Golden Plover, Snipe depending on water levels. Siskin, Redpoll. Site has regularly turned up scarcer/rare spp esp waders.
Other: Grass Snake, amphibians.
Directions: NN11 2JB; SP 577 641. Located off Northern Way (A425), 1 mile NE of Daventry town centre.
Public transport: None to Park.
Visiting: Car park open daily (charge). Cafe 9am-5pm Mon-Sat (summer) and 9am-2pm (winter, Sundays and bank holidays). Toilets (inc disabled) open 9am-5pm (4pm winter). Facilities closed 25 Dec/1 Jan). Three circular trails inc.around reservoir (2.5 miles).
Contact: Daventry District Council: 01327 871100.

Leicestershire and Rutland

Rutland, England's smallest historic county, and its larger neighbour are well served with reservoirs, including Cropston, Eyebrook and Swithland, which all attract wintering wildfowl and a regular spring Black Tern passage. The jewel in the crown though is Rutland Water where Ospreys have been successfully reintroduced. Huge numbers of wildfowl and a good selection of passage waders can be found here. The Wildlife Trust manages 35 nature reserves covering a broad range of habitats spread across the counties.

Bird Atlases/Avifauna
Rutland Breeding Bird Atlas 2008-2011
Terry Mitcham (Spiegl Press, 2013)
The Birds of Leicestershire and Rutland
Rob Fray, Roger Davies, Dave Gamble, Andrew Harrop & Steve Lister (Christopher Helm, 2009).

Bird Recorder
Carl Baggott, 72 New Street, Earl Shilton, LE9 7FR: cdbaggott@gmail.com

Bird Report
Leicestershire & Rutland Bird Report (1946-), from LROS Mrs S Graham: JSGraham83@aol.com

BTO Regional Representative
David Wright
Wetland Bird Survey (WeBS)
Local Organizers: webs@bto.org
Leicestershire & Rutland
(excl. Rutland Water)
Brian Moore
Rutland Water
Tim Appleton:

Club
Leicestershire & Rutland Ornithological Society (1941; 527) Peter Williams (Sec): 07809 337 229; secretary@lros.org.uk; www.lros.org.uk
Meetings: 7.30pm, (usually) 1st Friday of the month (Oct-May). The Hall of St. Anne's, Letchworth Road, Leicester LE3 6FN. Some talks are via zoom.
Rutland Natural History Society (1965; 150)
Tricia Marston (Membership Sec), 42 Church Street, Braunston, Oakham. LE15 8QT: 01572 756 870; rnhsmembers@gmail.com; www.rnhs.org.uk
Meetings: 7:30pm, 1st Tuesday of the month (Oct-Apr). Contact/see website for venue.
South Leicester Birdwatchers (2006; 30)
Roger Keightley: hello@southleicesterbirdwatchers.uk; www.southleicesterbirdwatchers.uk/
Meetings: 6:45pm, 2nd Tuesday of the month (Sep-Jun). Blaby & District Social Centre & Village Hall, Leicester Road, Blaby, Leicester, LE8 4GQ.

Ringing Groups/Bird Observatory
Rutland Water RG
Stanford RG: www.stanfordrg.org.uk

RSPB Local Group
Leicester (1969; 1,000/area)
Graham Heninghem:
graham.heninghem@hotmail.co.uk;
https://group.rspb.org.uk/leicester/
Meetings: 7:30pm, 3rd Friday of the month (Sep-May, not Dec). Leicester Bowling Club, Kenwood Road, Leicester, LE2 3PL.

Wildlife Trust
Leicestershire & Rutland Wildlife Trust (1956; 19,000)
The Old Mill, 9 Soar Lane, Leicester, LE3 5DE: 0116 262 9968; info@lrwt.org.uk; www.lrwt.org.uk

5	Bradgate Park and Cropstone Reservoir
7	Cossington Meadows
2	Fosse Meadows
3	Hicks Lodge
4	Kelham Bridge
1	Rutland Water
6	Swithland Reservoir
8	Watermead CP

*Why save the best till last? In **Northamptonshire** head back from Daventry to Northampton and then take A43 for Kettering and then A6003 to Oakham.*

1 RUTLAND WATER
Anglian Water/Leics & Rutland Wildlife Trust

Habitats: Ramsar-designated reservoir, lagoons, scrapes, reedbeds, woods, meadows, plantations.

Birds: Spring/autumn: Outstanding wader passage, up to 28 spp. Wide range of raptors, owls, passerine flocks, terns (Black, Arctic, breeding Common, occasional Little & Sandwich). *Summer:* Ospreys among 70 breeding spp. *Winter:* Up to 28 spp wildfowl inc internationally important numbers of Gadwall and Shoveler. Goldeneye, Smew, Goosander, rare grebes, Great Northern, Black & Red-throated Divers, Ruff.

Other: Otter, Badger, Fox, Weasel, Stoat. Up to 20 spp dragonflies and 24 spp butterflies.

Directions: Two nature reserves on site.

1—*Egleton Reserve* LE15 8BT; SK 878 075, from Egleton village off A6003 or A606 S of Oakham.

2—*Lyndon Reserve* LE15 8RN; SK 894 058, S shore, E of Manton village off A6003 S of Oakham. Follow 'nature reserve' signs to car park.

Public transport: Train—Oakham c.two miles.

Visiting: Day permits available. Reduced admission for disabled visitors and carers.

1—*Egleton:* The Anglian Water Bird Watching Centre—open daily (not 25/26 Dec), 9am-5pm, (4pm, Nov-Jan). Centre has toilets and disabled access, mobility scooter for hire, good network of paths. 31 hides (disabled access possible to 12 of them). Badger-watching hide, book through centre. No dogs.

2—*Lyndon:* Centre open daily 9am-5pm, mid-Mar to mid-Sep—car park open to 8pm. Interpretation centre, toilets (inc disabled), paths, use of a mobility scooter. 7 hides, 4 accessible to wheelchairs. Dogs on short lead.

Contact: 1—Egleton: 01572 770 651;
2—Lyndon: 01572 737 378; info@lrwt.org.uk

Leave Rutland and cross S Leicestershire by heading S to Corby on the A6003 and then W on A427 and A4304 to J20 on M1, across M1 and then A4303 to A5. Take B4114 for Sharnford on R off A5.

2 FOSSE MEADOWS NATURE AREA
& ARBORETUM
Blaby District Council

Habitats: Grassland, woodland, inc Arboretum, river, lake, pond.

Birds: All year: Common woodland spp, Kingfisher, Barn, Tawny & Little Owls, Green Woodpecker, Marsh Tit. *Spring/summer:* Common warblers, Sand Martin, Spotted Flycatcher. *Winter:* Snipe, occasional Woodcock, winter thrushes, Siskin, Redpoll.

Other: Brown Hare, Water Vole.

Directions: LE10 3AB; SP 489 909. Four miles SE of Hinckley, located off Fosse Way—Roman Road, SE of Sharnford. From J1 of M69, take A5 towards M1. After 1.75 miles, turn L on to B4114 for Sharnford, drive through village, turn R (Frolesworth Road), then first R (narrow road, signed **Fosse Meadow**).

Public transport: None.

Visiting: Open all year—early morning visit best. Car park open 6am-8pm (summer), 7am-4pm (winter). Network of public paths, marked permissive bridleway around site, two wheelchair friendly gates and portable/accessible toilet on site. Two hides, Sand Martin artificial bank, riverside walk. Picnic area, children's play area, coffee van.

Contact: 0116 275 0555; via website; www.blaby.gov.uk

Return to A5 and continue N to M42 and then A42.

3 HICKS LODGE
Forestry England

Habitats: New native woodland, rough grassland, seasonally-grazed open fields, lakes and ponds. Largest lake has two small islands, one managed for Little Ringed Plover, other ground-nesting spp.

Birds: Raptors inc Buzzard, Sparrowhawk, Red Kite, Kestrel, Hobby and Peregrine Falcon. Common wildfowl in winter, plus a good range of finches inc Crossbill, buntings, tits and summer warblers. Wader records inc Bar-tailed Godwit, Greenshank, Ringed & Little Ringed Plovers, Common Sandpiper, Oystercatcher, Temminck's Stint, Lapwing and Golden Plover. *Passage:* migrants inc Black Tern, Cuckoo, Wheatear, Whinchat, Stonechat, Spotted Flycatcher and hirundines.

Directions: LE65 2UP; SK 329 155. Within National Forest, approx 0.5 miles from Moira village. Follow brown tourist signs for National Forest Cycle Centre from Moira, Ashby-de-la-Zouch and from J12 of A42.

Public transport: None.

Visiting: Open all year: 8am-8pm. Height barrier at main entrance is removed when open, so no vehicle restrictions. Pay & display car park with 5 designated disabled bays. On-site forest centre with small cafe (open 9am-5pm), toilets (inc disabled and baby-changing facilities) and cycle hire. All-ability trails and cycle trails. Most birdwatching activity occurs in front of main centre, around Hicks Lodge Loop and on the ponds/lakes and open fields. Hide, Sand Martin wall.

Contact: Forestry England: 0300 067 4340; info_nationalforest@forestry.gsi.gov.uk

Continue N on A42 to J13, then A511 to Coalville and S on A447.

4 KELHAM BRIDGE
Leicestershire & Rutland Wildlife Trust

Habitats: Wetland/open water, reedbed, scrubby grassland, wet woodland.

Birds: All year: Grey Partridge, Little Owl, Kingfisher, Cetti's Warbler, Willow Tit. *Spring/summer:* Little Ringed

Plover, Hobby, Sand Martin, warblers (inc Reed, Sedge, Garden & Grasshopper, Whitethroat). *Autumn/winter:* Green Sandpiper, Snipe, Jack Snipe (occ). Wildfowl inc Teal and Wigeon. Interesting migrants also turn up inc Garganey, Osprey, Merlin, Marsh Harrier, Short-eared Owl and Yellow Wagtail.
Other: 16 spp dragonflies, 19 spp butterflies. Otter, Water Shrew, Harvest Mouse.
Directions: LE67 2AN; SK 405 120. Between Coalville and Ibstock, c.0.6 mile N on A447 from Ibstock. Park on grassy verge to R of entrance. A narrow stile takes you behind sewage treatment works to reserve.
Public transport: None.
Visiting: Open all hours. Two hides, viewing points, noticeboard. Paths can be boggy. Dogs on lead.
Contact: Contact: Leics & Rutland WT: 0116 262 9968; info@lrwt.org.uk
Return to Coalville, then A511 and A50 to A56 NW of Leicester.

5 BRADGATE PARK AND CROPSTON RESERVOIR

Bradgate Park Trust
Habitats: Semi-natural moorland, woodland, river. Deer Park, est in 13C. Reservoir.
Birds: All year: Great Crested Grebe, Mandarin, owls (Barn, Little, Tawny), Kingfisher, Skylark, Stonechat, Grey Wagtail, common woodland spp. *Summer:* Common Tern, Cuckoo, Meadow Pipit, Yellowhammer. *Passage:* Waders (inc Green & Common Sandpiper), Black Tern. *Winter:* Wildfowl inc Goldeneye, gulls (worth checking out), Redwing, Fieldfare.
Other: Red & Fallow Deer, bats.
Directions: Car parks—(1) Newtown Linford LE6 0HB; SK 523 097 (2) Hunts Hill LE6 0AH; SK 523 117 (3) Hallgates—closest to reservoir LE7 7HQ; SK 543 113. Lies NW of Leicester—from A46 go into Anstey and head to Newtown Linford for (1 & 2) or Cropston for (3).
Public transport: Bus: 125 Leicester to Coalville (Mon-Sat) Midland Classic (01283 500 228); 29B (Sun/Bank Hol) Arriva Midland (0344 800 4411), stops Newtown Linford.
Visiting: Three main car parks (pay & display), open 8am-8:30pm summer (sunset at other times), all have toilets. Reservoir can be viewed from park or from Reservoir Road (E side). Deer Barn cafe (10am-5pm Apr-Oct, 4pm Nov-Mar); visitor centre (weekends/school holidays 11am-4pm) and toilets—located in centre of park. Talks and walks available. Dogs under control at all times, must be on leads in some areas. Deer sanctuary area—no public access.
Contact: Bradgate Park Trust: 0116 236 2713; www.bradgatepark.org
Return to A46, head N, then take A6. Or take minor road from Cropston to Swithland and then E to

6 SWITHLAND RESERVOIR

Severn Trent Water
Habitats: Large reservoir divided by Great Central Railway line, small area of woodland (Buddon Wood).
Birds: Common wildfowl are regular and has produced sea duck inc Common Scoter, Scaup and Long-tailed Duck, and occasional divers. Black-necked Grebe seen in late summer/autumn, Mediterranean Gull is annual, Black Tern on Spring passage. High water levels curb wader sightings but Kingfishers are regular and Ravens usually seen daily. 3 spp woodpeckers are in Buddon Wood, along with a range of woodland spp, Buzzard, Sparrowhawk, Peregrine Falcon and Hobby (summer). Good track record of rarities in recent years.
Other: Buddon Wood along Kinchley Lane is good for Purple Hairstreak butterfly and Orange Underwing moth—look for the latter around Silver Birch.
Directions: LE7 7SE; SK 561 131. Lies S of Quorn, W of A6 (Leicester to Loughborough road). Use minor road between Swithland and Rothley for S section. For N section take Kinchley Lane along E shore to the dam.
Public transport: None.
Visiting: View from roads.
On other side of A6 and slightly S

7 COSSINGTON MEADOWS

Leicestershire & Rutland Wildlife Trust
Habitats: Deep lakes, shallow pools, lowland meadow and pasture, wet grassland, reedbed, scrub.
Birds: All year: Great Crested Grebe, Red-legged Partridge, Kingfisher, Reed Bunting. *Spring/autumn:* Waders inc Common & Green Sandpipers, Ringed & Little Ringed Plovers, Redshank, Dunlin and Ruff. *Summer:* Sedge, Reed & Grasshopper Warblers. *Winter:* Wildfowl inc Teal, Wigeon, Goosander, Snipe, Jack Snipe, Green Sandpiper, Short-eared Owl, winter thrushes, Redpoll. Occasional rarities.
Other: Dragonflies, butterflies, Grass Snake.
Directions: LE7 7NQ; SK 597 130. N of Leicester, W of village of Cossington, alongside River Soar. N on A6 from Leicester, take old A6 to Rothley, turn R at crossroads into Cossington Road becoming Syston Road. Park off road outside main entrance or in small public car park adjacent to Cossington Parish Church.
Public transport: Bus: 2 (not Sun) Loughborough to Leicester stops in Cossington (alight at Garden Centre and walk along main road towards Rothley to reserve main entrance (0.3 mile). Kinchbus (01509 815 637). Train—Sileby (on Leicester-Loughborough line) 1.2 mile walk to reserve entrance by church in Cossington.
Visiting: Open all hours.
Contact: Leics & Rutland WT: 0116 262 9968; info@lrwt.org.uk
Head S on A6 then A46 E

8 WATERMEAD COUNTRY PARK

Leicestershire County Council

Habitats: River Soar and Grand Union Canal, 12 lakes and pools, reedbeds (one of largest in Midlands), wildflower meadow, woodland. Park stretches for nearly two miles. Wanlip Meadows can be viewed from Plover Hide.

Birds: 200 spp, inc common wildfowl, Little Egret, Kingfisher, Water Rail, Cetti's Warbler. *Passage:* Garganey and Black Tern. Wanlip Meadows very good for waders, inc Little Ringed Plover and is county's best site for Temminck's Stint. *Winter:* Bittern, Caspian Gull, Yellow-legged Gull, thrushes.

Other: Otters regular, but elusive. Emperor and other dragonfly spp.

Directions: LE7 1AD; SK 608 113. Located off Wanlip Road, Syston (off A46 or A607), 6 miles N of Leicester city centre. Watermead CP (South) is managed by Leicester City Council.

Public transport: Bus: 5/5A/6 from Leicester to Syston/East Goscote/Melton, regular daily. Get off at Alderton Close for S or walk from Syston for N. Arriva. Train—one mile from Syston.

Visiting: Open all year, 7am-dusk. Wanlip Road gives access to four car parks (fees payable), S entrance in Alderton Close, Thurmaston. Wheelchair access on five miles of surfaced tracks. RADAR key needed by mobility scooter riders to negotiate kissing gates on perimeter track. Toilets, inc disabled. 4 bird hides (in nature reserve), Sand Martin nesting wall.

Contact: 0116 305 5000; countryparks@leics.gov.uk; www.leicscountryparks.org.uk

Head N along A46 to Nottinghamshire.

Nottinghamshire

The county has numerous gravel pits, which attract waterfowl and gulls in good numbers and from time to time turn up scarce species: there are various sites in the Trent Valley, the Idle Valley and the RSPB's reserve at Langford Lowfields, near Newark. Nightjar and Woodlark can be found on remnant pockets of heathland and raptor watching around Sherwood Forest, may produce sightings of Honey Buzzard, Goshawk and Osprey. Hawfinch winter in Clumber Park.

Bird Atlas/Avifauna

Birds of Nottinghamshire

Nick Crouch, Jason Reece, Bernie Ellis, Chris du Feu, David Parkin

(Liverpool University Press, 2019).

Bird Recorder

Keith Rainford: Bullfinch194@gmail.com

Bird Report

Birds of Nottinghamshire (1943-), from NB—Jenny Swindells, 21 Chaworth Road, West Bridgford, Nottingham, NG2 7AE: 0115 9812 432; j.swindells@btinternet.com

BTO Regional Representatives

Joanne Whitley

Wetland Bird Survey (WeBS)

Local Organizer: webs@bto.org

Mike Hill

Clubs

Nottinghamshire Birdwatchers (1935; 277)

Jenny Swindells (Sec), 21 Chaworth Rd, West Bridgford, Nottingham, NG2 7AE: 07763 110 758; j.swindells@btinternet.com; www.nottsbirders.net

Meetings: Contact/see website for details.

Lound Bird Club (1990; 100)

Gary Hobson: 07464 964 879; ghlbc@hotmail.co.uk; www.loundbirdclub.co.uk

Meetings: Regular winter meetings and summer walks—contact/see website for details.

Netherfield Wildlife Group (1999; 130)

NWG, c/o 4 Shellburne Close, Heronridge, Nottingham, NG5 9LL. Neil Matthews (Memb Sec): neilmatthews7@yahoo.co.uk; www.gedlingconservationtrust.org/netherfield-lagoons/netherfield-wildlife-group/

Meetings: AGM held in Nov.

Wollaton Natural History Society (1976; 70)

via website;

Nigel Downes (Bird Group): 0115 944 4671; www.spanglefish.com/wollatonnaturalhistory

Meetings: 7:30pm, 3rd Wednesday of the month (Sep-Jun). St Leonards Community Centre, Bramcote Lane, Wollaton, HG8 2ND.

Ringing Groups/Bird Observatory

Birklands RG

North Notts RG: Adrian Blackburn (sec): 01777 706 516 & 07718 766 873; adrian.blackburn@sky.com

South Notts RG: www.southnottsringinggroup.blogspot.co.uk

Treswell Wood Integrated Population Monitoring Group:

www.treswellwoodipmg.org

RSPB Local Groups

Mansfield (1986; 40)

Diane Bartlam: dianeashplorers@hotmail.co.uk; https://group.rspb.org.uk/mansfield/

Meetings: 7:30pm, 1st Wednesday of the month (Sep-Jun). Mansfield Methodist Church, Big Barn Lane, Mansfield, Nottinghamshire, NG18 3LJ.

Nottingham (1974; 120)
John Forester: RSPBnottmlginfo@gmail.com;
https://group.rspb.org.uk/nottingham/
Meetings: 7pm, 1st Monday of the month (Sep-May).
The International Community Centre, 61b Mansfield
Road, Nottingham, NG1 3FN.

Wildlife Trust

Nottinghamshire Wildlife Trust (1963; 11,000)
The Old Ragged School, Brook Street, Nottingham,
NG1 1EA: 0115 958 8242; info@nottswt.co.uk;
www.nottinghamshirewildlife.org

4	**Idle Valley**
6	**King's Mill Reservoir**
2	**Langford Lowfields**
1	**Netherfield Lagoons**
5	**Sherwood/Budby Forest**
3	**Tresswell Wood**

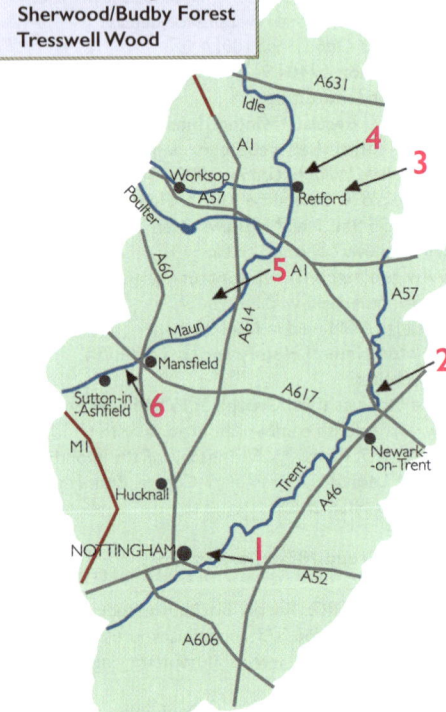

*Entering Nottiinghamshire on the A46 from Leicestershire,
take A6097 W once past Nottingham. Then, at roundabout
with A612, take 1st exit and approach from N.*

1 NETHERFIELD LAGOONS

Gedling Conservation Trust
Habitats: Trent Valley gravel pits.
Birds: Scarce/rare spp can turn up at anytime. *All year:*
Common waterfowl, Willow Tit. *Summer:* Little Ringed
Plover, Common Tern, Cuckoo, nine spp breeding war-

blers, hirundines. *Passage:* Waders (esp autumn) inc.
Ruff, Greenshank, Dunlin, terns, migrants inc Wheatear,
Whinchat, Yellow Wagtail. *Autumn/winter:* Wildfowl inc
Goosander, Goldeneye, Pochard and gulls. Golden Plov-
er and Lapwing in good numbers. Bittern, Water Rail,
Long-eared & Short-eared Owls, Stonechat, winter
thrushes.
Other: Dragonflies, orchids.
Directions: NG4 2PE; SK 688 411. Four miles SE of
Nottingham. Approach from A612 Colwick Loop Road
via Victoria Retail Park. Take Teal Close, L off second
roundabout, park near end opposite the CEM facto-
ry gates. Cross Ouse Dyke and walk to R along its N
bank until reaching foot bridge (c.0.5 mile). Cross back
across foot bridge to enter reserve.
Public transport: Bus: 50 Nottingham (from stop W1
Victoria Centre) 24 (from stop K1 King Street) both
to Victoria Retail Park (Morrisons)—short walk to Teal
Close. Nottingham City Transport (0115 950 6070).
Train—Netherfield (one mile).
Visiting: Open all hours. Membership of Netherfield
Wildlife Group available.
Contact: GCT: GedlingCT@gmail.com;
www.gedlingconservationtrust.org
Return to A46 and head towards Newark.

2 LANGFORD LOWFIELDS

RSPB/Lefarge Tarmac.
Habitats: RSPB/Tarmac working to create East Midlands' largest reedbed. The site currently covers 300
acres of restored land that was formerly a sand and
gravel quarry. Reedbed, ponds, islands, mature woodland, flower-rich meadow scrub.
Birds: Summer: Bittern, mixed edgret flocks, 10 spp
warbler, inc Cetti's, Grasshopper and regionally important numbers of Reed & Sedge. Cuckoo, Bearded Tit
(occasional), Marsh Harrier, Hobby, hirundines. *Winter:*
Large waterfowl numbers, Starling roosts.
Other: Badger, Brown Hare, 27 spp butterflies, 20 spp
Odonata.
Directions: NG23 7QL; SK 821 601. Lies NE of New-
ark-on-Trent. From A1 take A46 (signposted to Lincoln)
and then turn on to A1133 (to Collingham). After 2.5
miles turn L into Cottage Lane—gated car park 50
yards along the lane (height restriction, 7 ft, contact
prior to visit if required).
Public transport: Bus: 367 Newark-Collingham will
stop near to Cottage Lane junction on request. Travel
Wright (01636 703 813).
Visiting: Cottage Lane car park open dawn-dusk. Small
Beach Hut located 0.8 mile from car park where nature
trails start, open daily, if volunteers available. Benches at
key points overlooking reedbed, Floating Bridge, boardwalk, 360° Viewing Area. No toilets.
Contact: RSPB: 01636 893 611;
langford.beckingham@rspb.org.uk

Nottinghamshire

www.rspb.org.uk/langfordlowfields
Return to A1. Head N and the leave on A638 for Retford at Markham Moor.

3 TRESSWELL WOOD NATURE RESERVE
Nottinghamshire Wildlife Trust
Habitats: 120 acres, Ash, Oak, Maple woodland, Hazel, Field Maple, Sallow and Guelder Rose understorey. Ponds
Birds: Bird ringing programme site since 1972, CBC site since 1976. Nest boxes. Common woodland spp inc Woodcock, Great & Lesser Spotted Woodpecker, Garden Warbler, Spotted Flycatcher.
Other: Reintroduced Dormouse, Great Crested & Smooth Newts, Speckled Bush Cricket, 12 spp water beetle. Ancient woodland species such as Wood Anemone, Bluebells and Primrose; Marsh Marigold, Yellow Iris and Water Crowfoot in ponds.
Directions: DN22 0ED; SK 761 798. Take Grove Road on R as enter Retford on A638 from S. Pass through Grove, then take Wood Lane on R. Reserve on R between Grove and Tresswell.
Public transport: Train—Retford, served by 2 lines. 3 miles.
Visiting: Open all hours, free, no facilities. Limited parking at entrance to wood, etxensive network of paths. Dogs under control.
Contact: Nottinghamshire Wildlife Trust: 0115 958 8242; info@nottswt.co.uk
Return to A638, head N through Retford then turn R

4 IDLE VALLEY
Nottinghamshire Wildlife Trust/Tarmac/Private
Habitats: Former sand and gravel quarries, restored gravel workings, conservation grazed areas, woodland, reedbed, river valley, farmland, scrub, willow plantations, open water.
Birds: 250+ spp. *Summer:* Gulls, terns, wildfowl and waders inc breeding Little Ringed Plover and Redshank. *Passage:* Waders, terns, passerines and raptors. *Winter:* Wildfowl, gulls, raptors. Wider valley has been good for rarities, which have inc Broad-billed Sandpiper, Great White Egret, Baird's Sandpiper and Steppe Grey Shrike in recent times.
Directions: DN22 8SG; SK 689 830. S end of reserve is 0.5 mile N of Retford off A638 to Barnby Moor, via entrance to Tarmac. Rural Learning Centre is on R.
Public transport: Bus: 27 Retford to Misson passes reserve entrance. Stagecoach.
Visiting: Open all year, 9am-5pm. Car park (donation welcome). Idle Valley Rural Learning Centre has toilets and cafe open 10am-4pm. 4 walking routes, many wheelchair accessible. 6 viewing screens, 2 overlooking Chainbridge NR Scrape, two at Neatholme Scrape and single screens at Neatholme Fen and Neatholme Pit. 2 hides in Chainbridge Wood.

Contact: Idle Valley Rural Learning Centre, Great North Road, Retford, DN22 8RQ: 01777 858 245; info@nottswt.co.uk
Return to Retford and in the centre of town take A629 E to Ranby and junction with A1. Head S to junction with A614, continue S on A614 to its junction with A6075 and A616. These form two sides of a triangle enclosing

5 SHERWOOD FOREST NNR/ BUDBY SOUTH FOREST
The RSPB manages most of the Sherwood Forest NNR, which includes Budby South Forest. (Forestry England manage a part of the NNR, as well as adjacent land to the West.) Boundary and trail markers should indicate which land you access.
Habitats: Heathland, acid grassland, rough grassland, ancient woodland and tree pasture.
Birds: All Year: Common woodland spp, 3 spp woodpeckers. *Spring/summer:* Woodcock, Nightjar, Hobby, Long-eared Owl, Tree Pipit, Woodlark, Redstart, Spotted Flycatcher, warblers, Linnet, Yellowhammer. *Winter:* Redpoll, Siskin, Crossbill.
Other: Veteran Oak trees inc 'The Major Oak' (1,000 years old), fungi.
Directions: NG21 9QB (main car park); SK 626 675. E of Ollerton, between A6075 and A616 (20 miles N of Nottingham). From village of Edwinstowe, follow signs to Sherwood Forest Visitor Centre, N on B6034.
Public transport: Bus: 'Sherwood Arrow' from Nottingham City Centre-Ollerton, stops at Visitor Centre (daily). From Mansfield: 14 and 15A to Edwinstowe (not Sun/bank hols). Stagecoach.
Visiting: Main car park, across road from Visitor Centre (charge, RSPB members free—except during Robin Hood Festival/major events). Sherwood Forest Visitor Centre—open daily (not 25 Dec) 10:30am-5pm (Mar-Oct) 4:30pm Nov-Feb). Toilets (inc disabled), cafe, shop. Trails, events. Dogs on lead in breeding season/under control at other times. Parking for RSPB Budby South Forest section—0.5 mile past Visitor Centre on L—200 yards before junction—pull-in serves as parking area for 8 vehicles (max).
Contact: Sherwood Forest VC: 01623 677 321; sherwoodforest@rspb.org.uk; www.Visitsherwood.co.uk
Continue on A6075 round N of Mansfield to junction with A617, head S.

6 KING'S MILL RESERVOIR
Ashfield District Council
Habitats: Open water, maintained by River Maun, edged with woodland and scrub, patches of reedbed, grassland.
Birds: 220 spp recorded. *All year:* Common wildfowl, Great Crested & Little Grebes, Grey Heron, Kingfisher, Grey Wagtail, Reed Bunting, common woodland spp.

Spring/summer: Common Sandpiper, Common & Black Terns, Wheatear, (passage). Hirundines, warblers inc Whitethroat, Lesser Whitethroat, Reed, Sedge, Garden & Grasshopper. *Winter:* Wildfowl inc Teal, Wigeon, Shoveler and Goldeneye. Snipe, Water Rail, gull roost—worth checking for scarcer spp. Fieldfare, Redwing. *Other:* Water Vole.

Directions: NG17 4PA. Car park at SK 516 593. Located between Sutton-in-Ashfield and Mansfield. From A38 (King's Mill Road E) take A617 towards Newark (Reservoir signposted). Car park entrance on L.

Public transport: Regular buses between Mansfield and Sutton-in-Ashfield stop on A38 by King's Mill hospital—pedestrian access to Reservoir from here. Trentbarton (01773 712 265). Train—Mansfield.

Visiting: Open all year. Pay & display car park. Visitor centre, cafe (9am-4pm), toilets. Hard surfaced path (1.5 miles) circles the Reservoir with views to water. Can be busy, also has sailing activities.

Contact: Ashfield District Council: 01623 450 000; info@ashfield.gov.uk

Head N on A617 towards Derbyshire.

Derbyshire

The majority of the Peak District National Park—where Red Grouse, a variety of raptors, Redstart, Pied Flycatcher and Wood Warbler can be found—falls within the county's borders. Water bodies in the southern half of the county, including Carsington Water, Ogston and Foremark Reservoirs, hold a good selection of wintering waterfowl as well as large gull roosts that are always worth checking out.

Bird Atlas/Avifauna
The Birds of Derbyshire
RA Frost & Steve Shaw
(Liverpool University Press, 2014)

Bird Recorders
Joint Recorder (rarities): Mark Beevers,
11 Chatsworth Close, Bolsover, S44 6XJ:
07816 912 725;
markbeev@aol.com
Joint Recorder (rare breeding birds). Roy Frost,
66 St Lawrence Road, North Wingfield, Chesterfield,
S42 5LL: 01246 850 037; frostra66@btinternet.com
Joint Recorder (Annual Report, editor):
Anthony Garton: 07879 947 804;
tonygarton13@sky.com

Bird Reports
Derbyshire Bird Report (1955-), from DOS—Paul Buckley: Bridge House, Woodshop Lane, Swarkestone, Derbyshire, DE73 7JA: 01332 700 574; paulbuckley728@btinternet.com:

www.derbyshireos.org.uk
Carsington Bird Club Annual Report (1992-), from CBC—Gary Atkins: 01335 370 773; garyatkins@aol.com
Ogston Bird Club Report (1970-), from OBC—Val Jones (Gen Sec): vallers99@outlook.com

BTO Regional Representatives
North
Jonathan Potts
South
Drew Lyness
Wetland Bird Survey (WeBS)
Local Organizer: webs@bto.org
Kelvin Lawrence & Layla Alexandra

Clubs
Derbyshire Ornithological Society (1954; 614)
Steve Thorpe (Sec), 42 Woodland Avenue, Breaston, Derby, DE72 3AN: 07815 784 642:
derbyshirebirders@gmail.com;
www.derbyshireos.org.uk
Meetings: 7:30pm, usually last Friday of the month (Sep-Mar), various venues—contact/see website for details.
Bakewell Bird Study Group (1987; 75)
Brian Shaw (Chairman): 07768 928 432;
drgbshaw@gmail.com;
www.bakewellbirdstudygroup.org.uk
Meetings: 7:30pm, 2nd Monday of the month (Sep-May). Friends Meeting House, Chapel Lane, Bakewell, DE45 1EL.
Buxton Field Club (1946; 130+)
via website; www.buxtonfieldclub.org.uk
facebook: Buxton Field Club-wildlife and nature enthusiasts; Youtube: @buxtonfieldclub
Meetings: Autumn/winter; site visits (spring/summer) as per programme—contact/see website for details.
Carsington Bird Club (1992; 100)
David Horsley (Membership Sec), 26, Greenway, Hulland ward, Ashbourne Derbyshire, DE6 3FE: 01335 370 740 or 07900 597 230; daveat2602@hotmail.com; www.carsingtonbirdclub.co.uk
Meetings: 7:30pm, 3rd Tuesday of the month (Sep-Mar). The Henmore Room, Carsington Water Visitor Centre, Big Lane, Ashbourne, DE6 1ST.
Ogston Bird Club (1969; 655)
Val Jones (Gen Sec): vallers99@outlook.com;
www.ogstonbirdclub.co.uk
Meetings: Contact/see website for details.

Ringing Group/Bird Observatory
Sorby Breck RG: www.britishringers.co.uk
Souder RG
South Manchester RG

Derbyshire

RSPB Local Groups
Chesterfield (1987; 120)
Wendy Dyson: wendy2002khan@gmail.com;
https://group.rspb.org.uk/chesterfield/
Meetings: 7:15pm, (usually) 1st Monday of month.
St Thomas's Centre, Chatsworth Road, Chesterfield,
S40 3AW.

Derby (1974; 270)
Max Maughan: RSPBlocalgroupderby@gmail.com;
https://group.rspb.org.uk/derby/
Meetings: 7.30pm, 2nd Wednesday of the month (Sep-
Apr). The Grange Banqueting Suite,
457 Burton Rd, Littleover, Derby, DE23 6XX.

Wildlife Trust
Derbyshire Wildlife Trust (1962; 14,000)
Sandy Hill, Main Street, Middleton, Matlock, DE4 4LR:
01773 881 188; enquiries@derbyshirewt.co.uk;
www.derbyshirewildlifetrust.org.uk

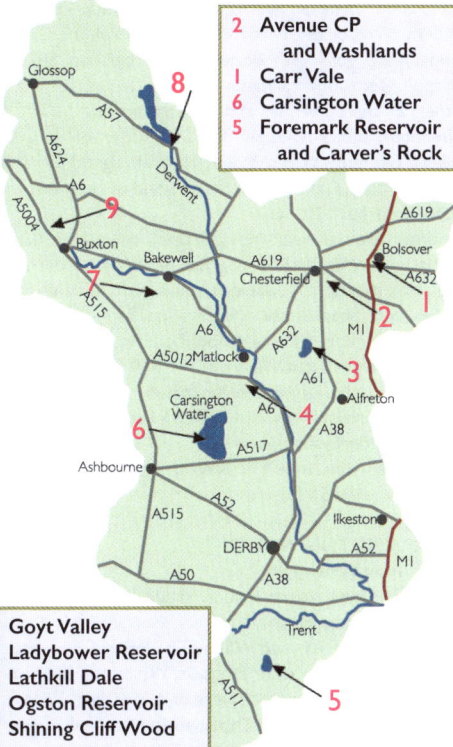

> 2 **Avenue CP**
>   **and Washlands**
> 1 **Carr Vale**
> 6 **Carsington Water**
> 5 **Foremark Reservoir**
>   **and Carver's Rock**

> **Goyt Valley**
> **Ladybower Reservoir**
> **Lathkill Dale**
> **Ogston Reservoir**
> **Shining Cliff Wood**

*Entering Derbyshire from **Nottinghamshire** on the A617,
take B6417 in Pleasley for Bolsover, turning L on to A632.*

1 CARR VALE NATURE RESERVE
Derbyshire Wildlife Trust
Habitats: Lakes, wader flashes, reedbed, sewage farm,
scrub, arable fields.

Birds: Up to 150 spp annually, long list of rarities. *Spring/
autumn:* Migrants inc pipits and thrushes. In *Sep*, Swallows gather in the marsh in a large roost of 1,000-2,000
birds, which often attracts Hobby. *Early summer:* Breed-
ing birds inc Gadwall, Skylark, Reed & Sedge Warblers,
Whitethroat and Yellowhammer. *Winter:* Large numbers
of wildfowl inc flocks of Teal and Wigeon, Water Rail.
Flocks of finches and buntings.
Other: Dragonflies, Brown Hare, Harvest Mouse, Water
Shrew, Grass Snake.
Directions: S44 6GA; SK 459 702. 0.75 mile W of
Bolsover on A632 to Chesterfield. Turn L at rounda-
bout (follow brown tourist signs) into Riverside Way.
Use the County Council's Peter Fidler car park off Riv-
erside Way.
Public transport: Bus: 82, 82A & 83 serve roundabout
on A632 and 83 serves Villas Road—from Chesterfield
(Stephenson Place). Stagecoach.
Visiting: Open all year. Car park, coach parking on ap-
proach road, good disabled access, paths, three viewing
platforms, hides. Follow waymarked footpath around
Peter Fidler reserve. Dogs only on leads.
Contact: Derbyshire WT: 01773 881 188;
enquiries@derbyshirewt.co.uk
Continue W on A632 to Chesterfield, then take A61 S.

2 THE AVENUE COUNTRY PARK
AND WASHLANDS
Derbyshire Wildlife Trust/The Land Trust
Habitats: Restored coking works—Country Park 225
acres, Washlands 42 acres—more under development.
Woodland, grassland, reedbed, ponds.
Birds: All year: Little Grebe, Lapwing, Barn Owl, King-
fisher, Skylark, Yellowhammer. *Summer:* Warblers inc
Grasshopper, Reed & Sedge, Whitethroat. *Winter:* Wild-
fowl, Snipe, mixed bird flocks. Bittern and Goosander
occasional.
Other: Butterflies and dragonflies. Water Vole, Great
Crested Newt, Grass Snake.
Directions: Country Park: S42 6FY; SK 388 680; Wash-
lands: S42 6NG; SK 396 670. Adjoining sites on SE edge
of Chesterfield. Leave Chesterfield for Clay Cross on
A61. At Wingerworth, turn L at roundabout into Hornbeam Drive. Country Park car park on L. For Washlands park in CP car park and walk or continue S on
A61 for 0.5 mile, turn L into Mill Lane—park just after
houses and walk to entrance.
Public transport: Bus: 51 (daily) Chesterfield to Clay
Cross/Danesmore—alight at the Avenue (for CP) or
Nottingham Drive (for Washlands). Stagecoach.
Visiting: Country Park car park (free, may be closed
outside daylight hours). Variety of multi-user paths—access to all main entrances via squeeze stiles (OK for
wheelchairs/smaller mobility scooters). Other recrea-
tional users on site inc sports pitches, cycling, horse
riding. Dogs on lead.

Washlands: Open all hours. Viewing screens. Various footpaths inc boardwalk. 80% of reserve suitable for wheelchairs. Dogs on lead.

Contact: Derbyshire WT: 01773 881 188; enquiries@derbyshirewt.co.uk
Continue S on A61.

3 OGSTON RESERVOIR
Severn Trent Water/Ogston Bird Club
Habitats: Open water, pasture, mixed woodland.
Birds: All year: 3 spp woodpeckers, Little & Tawny Owls, Kingfisher, Grey Wagtail. *Summer:* Warblers. *Passage:* raptors (inc Osprey), terns and waders. *Winter:* Good numbers of wildfowl, tit and finch flocks. Gull roost attracts thousands of birds inc regular Glaucous and Iceland Gulls. Top inland site for Bonaparte's Gull and also attracts birds from Caspian/Herring Gull complex.
Directions: DE55 6FL; SK 374 610. From Matlock, take A615 E to B6014, just after Tansley. From A61 (Alfreton to Chesterfield road), at White Bear pub, Stretton turn on to B6014 towards Tansley, cross railway, take L fork in road and continue over hill. Reservoir is on L after hill.
Public transport: Bus: 63/63A (not Sun) Chesterfield to Matlock, both serve N end of reservoir. Hulleys (01246 582 246).
Visiting: View from roads. Three car parks on N, S & W banks. Public hide (wheelchair access) reached from west bank car park (also suitable for smaller coaches). Heronry in nearby Ogston Carr Wood (private) viewable from Ogston new road, W of reservoir. Ogston BC organizes monthly guided walks (see website for details) and members have access to three hides, (two wheelchair accessible) as well as club's own 3.5 acre Jim Mart Nature Reserve, three miles N of Ogston.
Contact: Val Jones (General Secretary, OBC): vallers99@outlook.com; www.ogstonbirdclub.co.uk
Return to A61, continue on A61 and then A38, taking A610 at Ripley W to A6. Head N on A6 towards Matlock.

4 SHINING CLIFF WOOD
Forestry England
Habitats: Broadleaf and conifer woodland. Programme to remove infected larch and pine running until 2028.
Birds: All year: Common woodland spp, inc 3 spp woodpecker, Woodcock. *Spring/summer:* Warblers inc Wood & Garden, Redstart, Spotted Flycatcher. *Winter:* Check feeding flocks for Firecrest. Winter thrushes, Hawfinch, Brambling, Redpoll, Siskin. [Nearby: canal path—Dipper, Kingfisher, Grey Wagtail; river—Goosander].
Other: Woodland flora inc Bluebell display.
Directions: DE56 2SR; SK 337 524. Located N of Belper on the A6 to Matlock. Access Wood from footpaths along minor road between Ambergate and Alderwasley.
Public transport: Bus:142 Belper to Alfreton stops at Ambergate (not Sun). Littles Travel (0115 932 8581).

Train—Whatsandwell & Ambergate (walk canal footpath between them, a Derbyshire Wildlife Trust reserve). From Ambergate, walk S on A6, turn R into Holly Lane and pick up public footpaths into the reserve.
Visiting: Open all hours. No formal parking facilities. Access to wood by public footpaths. Circular waymarked trail—passes by remains of 'Betty Kenny [Yew]' Tree', said to be 2,000 years old.
Contact: Forestry England: 0300 067 4340; central.district@forestryengland.uk
Continue S to Derby on A6, round it on A38 and A5111, then E on A50. Exit S at J3 on A514

5 FOREMARK RESERVOIR
AND CARVER'S ROCK NR
Severn Trent Water/Derbyshire Wildlife Trust
Habitats: FR—open water, coniferous woodland. CR—marsh, deciduous woodland, heathland.
Birds: All Year: Little & Great Crested Grebes, Woodcock, Barn, Little & Tawny Owls, Kingfisher. *Passage:* waders, terns, birds of prey. *Winter:* Wildfowl (inc Goosander) and gulls with occasional scarcer spp, Siskin, Redpoll. Occasional rarities.
Other: 27 spp butterflies and 300 spp moths.
Directions: DE65 6EG; SK 336 242. Reservoir is five miles S of Derby, W of A514 at Ticknall (signed to reservoir/Milton), **Carver's Rocks** at S end of reservoir.
Public transport: None.
Visiting: Open all year (not 25 Dec), dawn-8pm (last admission 5pm). Pay & display car park (annual permit available), toilets (inc disabled), some paths suitable for wheelchairs. Snack kiosk open Fri-Sun, Bank Hol Mondays and weekdays during school holidays.
Contact: Severn Trent Water: 01332 865 081; staunton.foremark@severntrent.co.uk
Contact: Derbyshire WT: 01773 881 188; enquiries@derbyshirewt.co.uk
Retrace steps and take A52 NW of Derby from A38. At Ashbourne take B5035.

6 CARSINGTON WATER
Severn Trent Water
Habitats: Open water, islands, small reedbed, mixed woodland, scrub, grassland.
Birds: 220+ spp. *All year:* Willow Tit. *Spring:* Good passage inc Yellow & White Wagtails, Whimbrel, Black & Arctic Terns. *Summer:* Warblers and breeding waders (inc Little Ringed Plover). Ospreys often stop-off during migration. *Winter:* Wildfowl and a large gull roost, possibility of divers and scarce grebes.
Other: Species-rich hay meadows, ancient woodlands with Bluebells, three spp orchid, five spp bat, 21 spp butterflies, Water Vole.
Directions: DE6 1ST; SK 241 515 (visitor centre). Off B5035 Ashbourne to Wirksworth road.
Public transport: Bus: 110/111 (not Sun), Matlock to

Ashbourne. Yourbus (01773 714 013).

Visiting: Open all year (not 25 Dec). Three car parks: Visitor Centre (pay & display 7:30am-8pm or 7pm Oct-Mar); Sheepwash and Millfields (reduced rates, open 8am, close same time as Visitor Centre car park). Visitor centre (open 10am-6pm Apr-Sep, 10am-5pm Oct-Mar) has four shops (inc RSPB), exhibition, restaurant, play area and toilets. Good access for wheelchairs (can borrow at visitor centre), mobility scooters for hire. 4 bird hides. Cycle and boat hire.

Contact: Carsington Water Visitor Centre: 0330 6780 701; carsingtonwater@severntrent.co.uk; www.carsingtonbirdclub.co.uk

Continue NE on B5035 to Cromford, then NW on A6 to Bakewell.

7 LATHKILL DALE (DERBYSHIRE DALES NNR)

Natural England (East Midlands Team)

Habitats: One of five Dales in NNR. River, crags, valley woodland, limestone grassland and scrub.

Birds: All year: Kingfisher, Dipper, Grey Wagtail, Raven, common woodland spp. *Spring/summer:* Wheatear, Spotted Flycatcher, Redstart, common warblers.

Other: Jacob's Ladder, limestone flora. Water Vole.

Directions: 2 miles SW of Bakewell between Over Haddon, Monyash and Youlgreave. Car parks: Over Haddon (DE45 1HZ; SK 203 664) and Moor Lane, near Youlgreave (DE45 1LU; SK 194 644). Roadside parking close to Monyash (west end of reserve on B5055, 0.5 mile E of Monyash (SK 157 665).

Public transport: Bus: 178 (not Sun) Bakewell circular stops at Over Haddon and Monyash. Hulleys (01246 582 246).

Visiting: Open all hours—public rights of way and permissive paths. Pay & display car park and toilets in Over Haddon. Some paths are narrow/rocky—easier route from the E side (Over Haddon). Dogs allowed under control (keep out of river!)—access may be restricted to certain areas due to livestock or at nesting times.

Contact: Natural England (Derbyshire Dales NNR), 10 Arden House, Deepdale Business Park, Bakewell, DE45 1GT: 01629 810 509; kevin.bull@naturalengland.org.uk

Take A619 N from Bakewell, then the A623 N at Baslow, leaving on A625 for Sheffield in Calver. Leave A625 on A6187 W for Hathersage and then the A6013 N to the A57, taking you past the dam and the E end of

8 LADYBOWER WOOD
AND RESERVOIR

Derbyshire Wildlife Trust/Severn Trent Water

Habitats: Upland oakwood, moorland. The reservoir adjoins Derwent and Howden Reservoirs to N.

Birds: (General area) *All Year:* Red Grouse, Goshawk, Sparrowhawk, Peregrine, Dipper, Grey Wagtail, Raven, Crossbill, common woodland spp. *Spring/Summer:* Curlew, Golden Plover, Ring Ouzel, Pied Flycatcher, Red-

start, Tree Pipit, Wood Warbler. *Passage:* Occasional Dotterel. *Winter:* Wildfowl inc Pochard, Goosander, Goldeneye, Tufted Duck. Hen Harrier, Merlin. Redwing, Fieldfare, Redpoll.

Other: Fungi, lichen. Mountain Hare.

Directions: S33 0AX; SK 204 865 10 miles W of Sheffield. Head W on A57 to Ladybower Inn just before reservoir. Park here or turn L, just beyond, on A6013 to Heatherdene car park (S33 0BY; SK 201 859).

Public transport: Buses: 256 Sheffield-Castleton (Mon-Sat); 257 Sheffield-Bakewell (Mon-Sat) and 258 (Sun)—all stop at Ladybower Inn and by Heatherdene. Hulleys of Baslow (01246 582 246).

Visiting: Open all hours. Pay & display car parks at Heatherdene (toilets) and Ladybower Inn where public bridleway leads to wood (difficult terrain, best to view from bridleway). Further up the valley: pay & display car park and visitor centre (toilets/refreshments kiosk) at Fairholmes (SK 171 893: 01629 816527)—signposted from A57 'Derwent Valley Dams'. A 5.5 mile circular walk around Ladybower starts here.

Contact: Derbyshire WT: 01773 881 188; enquiries@derbyshirewt.co.uk

Return to Calver (see above) on the A623, then head W to its junction with A5004 and approach from the opposite direction to the instructions below.

9 GOYT VALLEY

Forestry England

Habitats: River Goyt, two reservoirs, mixed conifer/broadleaved woodland, moorland.

Birds: Spring/summer: Breeding Wood Warbler, Pied & Spotted Flycatchers, Tree Pipit, Redstart, Cuckoo, Nightjar on restock areas and common woodland spp; Long-eared Owl and Goshawk also present. Dipper and Grey Wagtail on river, Common Sandpiper on Errwood Reservoir. Red Grouse, Curlew, Short-eared Owl, Whinchat and Ring Ouzel breed on moorland areas.

Directions: SK17 6SX (Errwood Hall car park, SK 011 748) for woodland birds, Derbyshire Bridge (SK 018 716) for moorland birds. From Buxton head N on A5004 (Manchester Road), then bear L on Goyt's Lane to Errwood Hall one-way system, between Errwood car park and Derbyshire Bridge.

Public transport: Train—Whaley Bridge and Buxton, both c.3 miles from Errwood Reservoir.

Visiting: Open all year. Toilets at Derbyshire Bridge and Bonsal Cob. Several picnic sites. Footpath between Errwood Hall and Goyt's Clough Quarry. Use Old Coach Road for walk between Derbyshire Bridge and Burbage.

Contact: Forestry England: 0300 067 4340; central.district@forestryengland.uk

Contact: Derbyshire WT: 01773 881 188; enquiries@derbyshirewt.co.uk

Though still in Derbyshire, you are very close the border with Cheshire, just as at Ladybower you were close to Yorkshire, should wish to begin your exploration of those counties. We, however, are going to return to Buxton and take the A54 and A53 for Leek and cross the border into Staffordshire

Staffordshire

The reservoirs of Belvide, Blithfield and Croxall Lakes are worth a visit for wintering wildfowl and gulls, as well as passage waders. Red Grouse are found on the moors of the southern end the Peak District National Park, in the northern part of the county; and in the dales and valleys, Lesser Spotted Woodpecker, Dipper, Redstart and Pied Flycatcher can be found. The mixture of habitats of Cannock Chase are good for Nightjars, Woodlark and Goshawk, with an occasional Great Grey Shrike in winter.

Bird Atlas/Avifauna
See Warwickshire and West Midlands.

Bird Recorder
Nick Pomiankowski, 22 The Villas, West End, Stoke-on-Trent, ST4 5AQ: 01782 849 682;
staffs-recorder@westmidlandbirdclub.org.uk

Bird Report
See Warwickshire and West Midlands

BTO Regional Representatives
North, South & West
Chloe Pritchard
Wetland Bird Survey (WeBS)
Local Organizer: webs@bto.org
Scott Petrek:

Club
West Midland Bird Club (Stafford Branch)
Chris Evans (Chairman):
stafford@westmidlandbirdclub.org.uk;
www.westmidlandbirdclub.org.uk/stafford
Meetings: 7:30pm, Walton on the Hill Village Hall, Greengore Lane, Stafford. ST17 0LD—contact/see website for details.
Field Trips: For both Stafford and Birmingham book via: https://www.westmidlandbirdclub.org.uk/field-trips

Ringing Group/Bird Observatory
Belvide RG
South Manchester RG
West Midlands RG:
via website: www.westmidlandsringinggroup.co.uk

RSPB Local Group
Burton and South Derbyshire (1973; 25)
Dave Lummis:
burtonandsouthderbyshirerspb@btinternet.com;
https://group.rspb.org.uk/burton/
Meetings: 7:30pm, 2nd Wednesday of some months (Sep-May)—contact/see website for details.
All Saint's Church Hall, Branston Road, Burton-on-Trent, DE14 3BY.
Lichfield and District (1977; 1150)
Andy Clarke: rspblichfieldgroup@gmail.com;
https://group.rspb.org.uk/lichfield/
Meetings: 7:30pm, 2nd Tuesday of the month (Sep-May). Guildhall, Bore Street, Lichfield, WS13 6LU.
North Staffs (1982; 200)
Joan Hudson: joan.hudson1@gmail.com;
https://group.rspb.org.uk/northstaffordshire/
Meetings: 7:30pm, 3rd Wednesday of the month (Sep-May). Wade Conference Centre/Medical Institute, Hartshill Road, Stoke-on-Trent, ST4 7NY.

Wildlife Trust
Staffordshire Wildlife Trust (1969; 18,000)
The Wolseley Centre, Wolseley Bridge, Stafford, ST17 0WT: 01889 880 100; info@staffs-wildlife.org.uk;
www.staffs-wildlife.org.uk

Entering Staffordshire on the A53 from Buxton towards Leek (remember your coming from the opposite direction to the instructions below) you come to

1 ROACHES, THE
Staffordshire Wildlife Trust
Habitats: 976 acres—woodland, upland acid grassland and rush pasture.
Birds: All year: Red Grouse, Peregrine, Meadow Pipit, Raven. *Summer:* Curlew, Cuckoo, Redstart, Wheatear, Whinchat, Stonechat, Skylark. *Winter:* Winter thrushes.
Other: Green Hairstreak.
Directions: ST13 8UA; SK 004 621 (lay-by parking at Rockhall, near Upper Hulme. 4 miles N of Leek. Take A53 N from Leek towards Buxton. Turn L at Upper Hulme, continue for 1.25 miles to lay-by parking at Rockhall.
Public transport: None.
Visiting: Lay-by parking at Rockhall or alternatively use small car park at Gradbach (near Youth Hostel, SK17 0SU; SJ 997 662); reached from A53 (turn L by sign to 'New Inn', through Flash (bearing L after church, Youth Hostel signposted). From car park, walk S into less visited N end of site. Dogs on leads—keep out of pools.
Contact: Staffordshire WT: 01889 880 100;
info@staffs-wildlife.org.uk
Continue S to Leek

2 COOMBES VALLEY
RSPB

Habitats: Steep-sided valley with Sessile Oak woodland, unimproved pasture, meadow.

Birds: Jan-Mar: Displaying birds of prey. *Spring:* Woodcock, Dipper, Grey Wagtail and common woodland spp joined by migrant Wood Warbler (occasional) Pied & Spotted Flycatchers, Redstart. *Autumn/winter:* Redpoll, Siskin, winter thrushes.

Other: Bluebells, various butterflies, Slow Worm.

Directions: ST13 7EU; SK 009 534. 3 miles SE of Leek. From Leek take A523 towards Ashbourne. After Bradnop, turn R on minor road (cross a railway line) to Apesford and follow signs to reserve.

Public transport: Possible demand responsive bus service provided by Moorlands Connect (www.moorlandsconnect.co.uk).

Visiting: Open daily (not 25 Dec). Main car park 9am-5pm, (charge, RSPB members free), some parking away from main car park. Visitor Cenre staffed by vounteers, opening hours depend on volunteer availability. Mostly covered Apr-Oct. Toilets (automatic timer, 8am-6pm). Coaches by prior arrangement. Cold drinks and snacks when Visitor Centre open. No dogs except on public footpaths. Several trails, I suitable for wheel-/pushchairs.

Contact: RSPB: 01538 384 017; CoombesValleyandConsallWoods@rspb.org.uk

Probably simplest to return to Leek and take A520, then A520 to Cheadle.

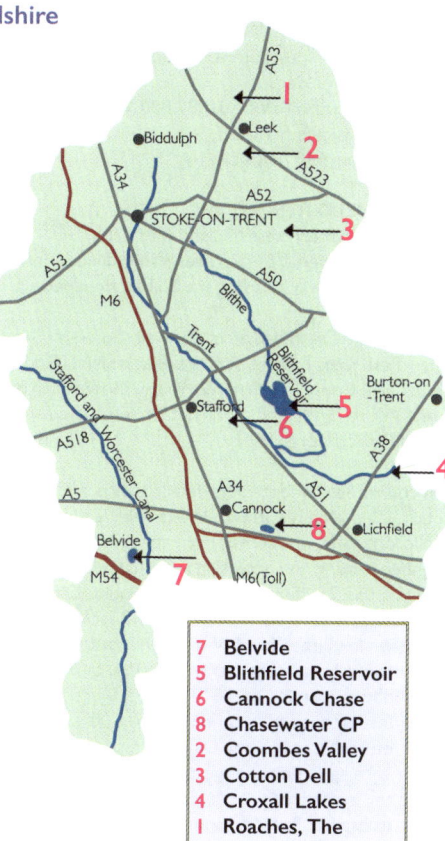

7	**Belvide**
5	**Blithfield Reservoir**
6	**Cannock Chase**
8	**Chasewater CP**
2	**Coombes Valley**
3	**Cotton Dell**
4	**Croxall Lakes**
I	**Roaches, The**

3 COTTON DELL
Staffordshire Wildlife Trust

Habitats: Ancient woodland, grassland.

Birds: All year: Common woodland spp, Tawny Owl, 3 spp Woodpeckers, Dipper, Grey Wagtail. *Spring/summer:* Pied & Spotted Flycatchers, Wood Warbler and common summer warblers, Redstart.

Other: Fungi, woodland flora. Logjammer Hoverfly.

Directions: ST10 3AG; SK 052 445. 3 miles E of Cheadle. From A522 take B5417 towards Oakamoor. On approaching Oakamoor (just past church/on L) turn R into Mill Road (picnic sign/50 yards—park here). From car park, walk over grassy area, crossing River Churnet by footbridge, cross B5417 at old lime kilns and head up narrow track opposite (passing a few houses). Reserve entrance is 380 yards up this track (0.5 mile from car park).

Public transport: Bus: 32/32X Uttoxeter-Hanley (stops in Oakamoor). D&G Bus (01782 332 337).

Visiting: Open all hours. Paths (uneven), circular trail paths (on steep hillsides at times).

Contact: Staffordshire WT: 01889 880 100; info@staffs-wildlife.org.uk

Return to Cheadle and take A522 to Uttoxeter. Then A50 and A511 to Burton-on-Trent and then head S on A38.

4 CROXALL LAKES
Staffordshire Wildlife Trust

Habitats: Two large lakes formed from gravel pits at junction of Rivers Tame, Trent and Mease, and shallow pools, wader scrapes, reedbeds.

Birds: Spring/summer: Breeding spp inc grebes, waders such as Redshank, Oystercatcher, Ringed Plover and Lapwing. *Winter:* Substantial numbers of wildfowl, inc Wigeon, Teal, Goldeneye, Shoveler and occasional Smew. Between Nov and Jan, Short-eared Owls hunt over rough ground.

Other: Otter, Water Vole and Harvest Mouse present but dragonflies will be easier to see.

Directions: WS13 8QX; SK 189 139. From Lichfield head N on A38, following signs for National Memorial Arboretum. At NMA entrance, continue over river bridge and turn L on second track into car park.

Public transport: Bus: 812 (not Sun) Lichfield to Alrewas (1.2 miles from reserve). Midland Classic (01283 500 228).

Visiting: Open all hours, except to restricted areas. Small car park (8am-5pm), 2 bird hides. Kissing gate at entrance wide enough for wheelchairs. Surfaced access track, leading to hide overlooking main lake. Wheelchair ramps to both hides but woodland path uneven. Restricted areas for dogs.

Contact: Staffordshire WT: 01889 880 100; info@staffs-wildlife.org.uk
Take A513 from A38 to Rugeley.

5 BLITHFIELD RESERVOIR

South Staffs Water/West Midland Bird Club

Habitats: Y-shaped, 781 acre reservoir, divided into 2 basins by causeway carrying the B5103. Reedbed, parially wooded margins.

Birds: Great Crested Grebe, Gadwall, Common Sandpiper, Red Kite, Kestrel. *Passage:* Black-tailed Godwit, Black Tern, Osprey. *Autumn & Winter:* Goosander and Great White Egret. For more details see: https://west-midlandbirdclub.org.uk/
Other:

Directions: See website for detailed map and access details. Main North Entrance WS15 3PH leads to main public car park and access road to exclusive WMBC member parking and access. Main East Entrance WS15 3DX; SK 053 250 South Staffs Water Estate Office and Dam End. The reservoir lies between Rugeley and Abbots Bromley. Either head N on B5013 out of Rugeley, cross causeway to T-junction with B5194, or head NW from Abbots Bromley on B514 to said T-juction. From this T-junction head NW on B5013 for 600 yards, then fork L on to Newtonhurst Lane for just under 1 mile before turning L down drive to the Main North Entrance and access road.

Public transport: Bus: 63 Cannock to Uttoxeter runs between Rugeley and Abbots Bronley (Mon-Sat not Bank Holidays) but not over causeway,;walk from Abbots Bromley, Chaserider. Train—Rugeley.

Visiting: Only open to WMBC members, who must carry membership card on visit and display car sticker/park in designated parking areas shown in WMBC map. No individual day permits. Two car parks along drive to The Cottages/P2 (toilets). Car parks at either end of causeway. Sailing in basin to SE of dam, club by dam. 11 hides around shore of the 2 bays of NW basin. Several locked gates requiring key across reserve paths.

Contact: Mark Sumnall: blithfield@westmidlandbirdclub.org.uk
Return to Rugeley.

6 CANNOCK CHASE

Forestry England

Habitats: Woodland, heathland, scrub.

Birds: All Year: Goshawk, Sparrowhawk, Woodcock, Tawny & Long-eared Owls, 3 spp woodpeckers, Woodlark, Willow Tit, Raven, common woodland spp. *Spring/summer:* Hobby, Cuckoo, Nightjar, Tree Pipit, Redstart, Stonechat, warblers, Pied Flycatcher, Crossbill. *Autumn/winter:* Snipe, winter thrushes, Brambling, Siskin, Redpoll, occasional Great Grey Shrike, Hen Harrier.

Other: Fallow & Muntjac Deer. Butterflies inc Green Hairstreak & Small Pearl-bordered Fritillary.

Directions: WS15 2UQ; SK 018 171 (Birches Valley Forest Centre). The Chase is located between Stafford-Rugeley-Cannock (A513-A460-A34). Various car parks are scattered through area. Sherbrook Valley-Brocton Coppice-Seven Springs (SK 004 204) area is particularly worth a visit.

Public transport: For Forest Centre. Train—Rugeley (two miles).

Visiting: Forest Centre—open 7:30am-9pm (or dusk, changes monthly). Car park (ANPR, pay on exit), cafe, toilets inc disabled access, cycle hire, activities, trails. There is a Go Ape activity centre on site as a separate operation.

Contact: Forestry England: 0300 067 4340; info-cannock@forestryengland.uk
Take A460 to Cannock and then A5 W.

7 BELVIDE

Managed by West Midland Bird Club

Habitats: Reservoir with muddy margins, depending on water levels, marsh, reedbed, woodland, unimproved pasture, scrub.

Birds: Breeding and passage: waders (up to 12 spp in a day when conditions are right) and terns. Warblers breed in reedbeds and hedgerows. *Winter:* Holds SSSI status for wintering wildfowl. Gull roost sometimes inc Glaucous or Iceland Gulls. Recent scarcities inc Sabine's Gull, White-winged & Whiskered Terns and Spotted Sandpiper.

Other: Dragonflies.

Directions: ST19 9LX. SJ 870 098. Entrance and car park on Shutt Green Lane, Brewood (S of A5), 7 miles NW of Wolverhampton.

Public transport: Bus: 877/878 (Mon-Fri) Wolverhampton to Brewood (walk down Shutt Green Lane). Select Bus Services (01785 330 764).

Visiting: Parking for 25-30 cars, 6 hides (5 fully accessible), hard surface path runs length of reserve. Access exclusively through WMBC membership (lock combination issued to members). Individual day permits cannot be issued; visits by organized groups can be made by pre-arrangement.

Contact: West Midland BC Permit Sec for group permits: permits@westmidlandbirdclub.org.uk;
Return to Cannock.

8 CHASEWATER COUNTRY PARK

Staffordshire County Council

Habitats: Reservoir, heath, scrub, woodland, reedbed.

Birds: All year: Great Crested Grebe, common waterfowl, Kingfisher, Willow Tit. *Summer:* Common warblers, hirundines. *Spring/autumn passage:* Waders and terns. *Winter:* Wildfowl and gulls, Snipe, occasional Jack Snipe, finches.

Other: Dragonflies.

Directions: WS8 7NL; SK 037 071. Four miles SE of Cannock. Follow the brown tourist sign off A5 at Brownhills into Pool Lane.

Public transport: Bus: Brownhills to Cannock services pass Brownhills junc A5/A452, 0.75 mile walk to reserve.

Visiting: Car park—charge. Visitor centre open weekdays 9am-4pm; shop/cafe open 10am-4pm Apr- Sep, 5pm Oct-Mar. Toilets open 11am-3pm.

Contact: Staffordshire County Council 01543 370 737; chasewater.ic@staffordshire.gov.uk

Continue on A5

Warwickshire and West Midlands

The river valleys and gravel pits are Warwickshire's main focus for birds. Tame Valley sites, including Ladywalk, Draycote Water and Brandon Marsh all attract a selection of wintering wildfowl and passage waders, whilst Cetti's Warbler is well established at Brandon Marsh. In contrast to Warwickshire's largely rural setting, the West Midlands is heavily urbanized but, despite this, Sutton Park (one of the largest urban parks in Europe) and Sandwell Valley attract a good selection of birds.

Bird Atlas/Avifauna

The New Birds of the West Midlands
Graham and Janet Harrison
covers Staffordshire, Warwickshire, Worcestershire and the former West Midlands county
(West Midland Bird Club, 2005).

Bird Recorders

Warwickshire
Chris Hill, 57 Lower Cape, Warwick, CV34 5DP:
07900 473 911;
warks-recorder@westmidlandbirdclub.org.uk
West Midlands
Steve Haynes: The Stables, Windmill Hill Farm,
Leamington Spa, CV33 9LB:
west-mids-recorder@westmidlandbirdclub.org.uk

Bird Report

The Birds of Staffordshire, Warwickshire, Worcestershire and the West Midlands (1934-), from The Birders Store
www.birders-store.co.uk
or further info from:
secretary@westmidlandbirdclub.org.uk

BTO Regional Representatives

Warwickshire
Annette Jarratt-Knock
Birmingham and West Midlands
Steve Davies
Wetland Bird Survey (WeBS)
Local Organizers: webs@bto.org
Warwickshire
Matthew Griffiths
West Midlands
Jamie Hicken

Clubs

West Midland Bird Club (1929; 2,600)
(Staffs, Warks, Worcs & the West Midlands.) c/o Gibson House, Hurricane Court, Hurricane Close, Stafford, ST16 1GZ: secretary@westmidlandbirdclub.org.uk; www.westmidlandbirdclub.org.uk
Meetings: Contact/see website for branch details.
Field Trips: For both Stafford and Birmingham book via: https://www.westmidlandbirdclub.org.uk/field-trips
Nuneaton & District Birdwatchers' Club (Nuneaton Bird Club) (1950; 50)
Mark Maddox, 104 Ridge Lane, Nuneaton, CV10 0RD: 07704 946 226; nuneatonbirdclub1@outlook.com; www.nuneatonbirdclub.wordpress.com
Meetings: 7.30pm, 3rd Thursday of the month (Sep-Apr). Chilvers Coton Heritage Centre, Avenue Road, Nuneaton, CV11 4LU.

Ringing Groups/Bird Observatory

Arden RG
Brandon RG
Birmingham University RG:
www.birmingham.ac.uk/research/activity/ornithology/people/ringing-group/index.aspx
Mercian RG
West Midlands Ringing Group:
www.westmidlandsringinggroup.co.uk

RSPB Local Groups

Coventry & Warwickshire (1969; 80)
Jo Rooney: covandwarksbirding@gmail.com;
https://group.rspb.org.uk/coventryandwarwickshire/
Wildlife Talks: 7:30pm, 4th Friday of the month (Sep-May unless otherwise stated). Baginton Village Hall, Frances Road, Baginton, CV8 3AB. Local nature walks: 2nd Wed of the month Sep-May.
Solihull (1983; 2,600)
Sophie Curtis: sophie.rspbsolihull@gmail.com;
https://group.rspb.org.uk/solihull/
Meetings: 7:30pm, (usually) 1st Thursday of the month (Sep-Apr). Bentley Heath Community Hall, Widney Road, Bentley Heath, Solihull, B93 9BQ.
Sutton Coldfield (1986; 250)
Tony Green: tonygreen777@hotmail.co.uk;

Warwickshire and West Midlands

https://group.rspb.org.uk/suttoncoldfield/
Meetings: 7:30pm, 1st Monday of the month (Sep-May, not Jan). Bishop Veseys Grammar School, Lichfield Road, Sutton Coldfield, B74 2NH.
Walsall (1971; n/a)
Michael Pittaway: chair@rspb-walsall.org.uk;
www.rspb-walsall.org.uk/
Meetings: 7:30pm, 3rd Wednesday of the month (Sep-May, earlier in Dec). Central Hall Methodist Church, Ablewell Street, Walsall, WS1 2EQ.

Wildlife Trust
Warwickshire Wildlife Trust (1970; 26,000)
Brandon Marsh Nature Centre, Brandon Lane, Coventry, CV3 3GW: 02476 302 912:
enquiries@wkwt.org.uk;
www.warwickshire-wildlife-trust.org.uk

7	**Brandon Marsh**
9	**Draycote Water**
4	**Harborne**
5	**Ladywalk**
6	**Middleton Lakes**
8	**Ryton Wood**
2	**Sandwell Valley CP**
3	**Sandwells Valley RSPB**
1	**Sutton Park**
10	**Ufton Fields**

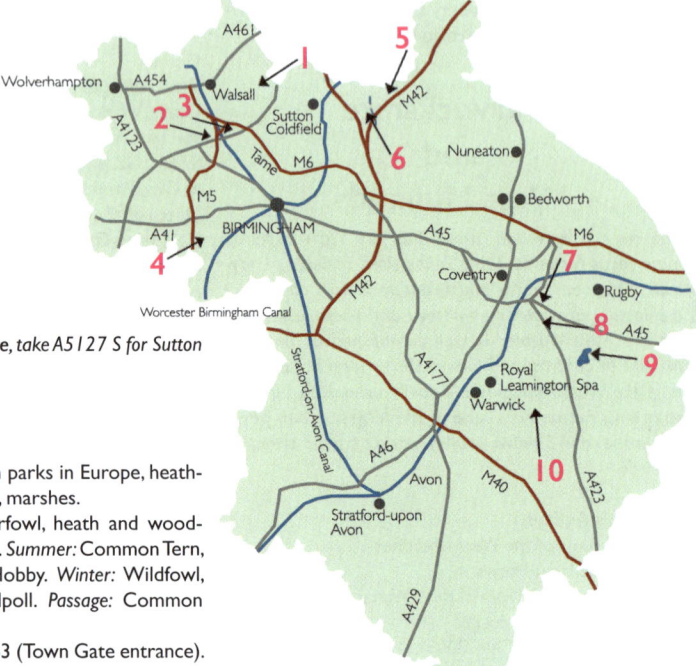

*Entering on A5 from **Staffordshire**, take A5127 S for Sutton Coldfield*

1 SUTTON PARK NNR
Birmingham County Council
Habitats: One of largest urban parks in Europe, heathland, woodland, lakes, wetlands, marshes.
Birds: All year: common waterfowl, heath and woodland spp, Kingfisher, Tawny Owl. *Summer:* Common Tern, Cuckoo, breeding warblers. Hobby. *Winter:* Wildfowl, Snipe, Woodcock, Siskin, Redpoll. *Passage:* Common Sandpiper, migrants.
Directions: B73 6BU; SP 116 963 (Town Gate entrance). 6 miles N of Birmingham city centre, Maney area of Sutton Coldfield. A5127 runs N-S a short distance from E edge of Park.
Public transport: Train—Sutton Coldfield (400 yards from Town Gate entrance).
Visiting: Park gates open by 9am until dusk. Several entrances to park and a number of car parks (charge Easter-Sep, Sun and bank hols/rest of year free). Visitor centre, toilets, shop open daily 10am-6pm (to 4:30 in winter). Various refreshments. Events. Grazing animals, dogs under control.
Contact: Visitor Centre/Rangers Office: 0121 355 6370
Continue on A5127 to J6 of M6. At J7 take A34 S, then A4041 W. Just before this crosses M5, take Forge Lane on L to car parks

2 SANDWELL VALLEY COUNTRY PARK
Sandwell Metropolitan Borough Council
Habitats: 1,800 acres pools, woodlands, grasslands, inc 3 Local Nature Reserves.

Birds: All year: Grey Heron (small heronry), Great Crested Grebe, Lapwing, Reed Bunting, Great Spotted & Green Woodpeckers, Sparrowhawk, Kestrel, Rose Ringed Parakeet. *Spring:* Little Ringed Plover, Oystercatcher, up to eight spp breeding warbler, passage migrants. *Autumn:* Passag migrants. *Winter:* Goosander, Shoveler, Teal, Wigeon, Snipe, Cormorant.
Other: Common Spotted & Southern Marsh Orchid. Ringlet butterfly. Water Vole, Weasel, Muntjac.
Directions: B71 4BG (Sandwell Valley Visitor Centre). Main entrances off Salter's Lane (SP 013 918) or Forge Lane (SP 022 930). Located approx 1 mile NE of West Bromwich town centre.
Public transport: Bus: 45/46 West Bromwich to Walsall/ Great Barr. National Express, West Midlands. West Bromwich Central Metro stop (1 mile).
Visiting: Car parks open 8am-sunset, coaches by ap-

pointment. Visitor centre, toilets, shop, cafe, kitchen garden at Sandwell Valley Visitor Centre open daily (not Christmas period) 10am-4pm winter; 10am-5pm summer. Good footpaths around LNR's and much of the country park. Wheelchair access to Priory Woods LNR, Forge Mill Lake LNR and other parts of the country park. 20 acre RSPB reserve nearby (see below).
Contact: Sandwell Valley CP: 0121 569 3070; visitor_Services@sandwell.gov.uk
Nearby

3 SANDWELL VALLEY RSPB
RSPB
Habitats: Open water, wet grassland, reedbed, dry grassland, scrub.
Birds: Summer: Lapwing, Little Ringed Plover, Whitethroat, Sedge & Reed Warbler, Willow Tit. *Winter:* Wildfowl inc Goosander. Water Rail, Snipe, Jack Snipe, woodpeckers, Bullfinch. *Passage:* Sandpipers, Common Tern, Yellow Wagtail, chats.
Directions: B43 5AG; SP 035 928. Great Barr, Birmingham. Follow signs S from M6 J7 via A34. Take R at 1st junction on to A4041. Take 4th L on to Hamstead Road (B4167), then R at 1st mini roundabout onto Tanhouse Avenue.
Public transport: Bus: 16W Birmingham to West Bromwich and 16 to Hamstead (ask for Tanhouse Avenue). Diamond. Train—Hamstead.
Visiting: Pedestrian access open at all times. Visitor centre/car park (open Tues-Sun, 10am-5pm summer (4pm winter), toilets (inc disabled), light refreshments. Car park charge, members free/contact for coach parking. Way-marked trails, most paths accessible to assisted and powered wheelchairs with some gradients (phone for further info). Viewing screens. Hide open when staff/volunteers available (Tues-Sun, 10:30am-3pm)—hide can be hired outside of opening hours. Dogs on leads.
Contact: RSPB: 0121 357 7395; sandwellvalley@rspb.org.uk
Stay on M6 to junction with M5, head S on M5 leave at J1. Take A4252 and then A4030 S to Harborne. Turn L into Gilhurst Road as enter Harborne.

4 HARBORNE
West Midlands Bird Club
Habitats: Small, 10-acre reserve of regenerating Oak woodland and conifer plantation flanking Chad Brook 3 miles from centre of Birmingham.
Birds: Buzzard, Green & Great Spotted Woodpeckers, Lesser Spotted has been reported. Raven, Long-tailed Tit, Goldcrest, Wren Nuthatch, Song Thrush, Grey Wagtail, Greenfinch. *Summer:* Swift.
Other:
Directions: B17 8PL; SP 033 853. Harborne Walkway runs along NE side. Enter Harbourne Walkway from Gilhurst Road. Walk S for 400 yards, path on R runs

down to Chad Brook. Gated entrance on L at bottom. Access code required.
Public transport:
Visiting: WMBC members or annual permit holders only. Annual Permits for this site (only) are available via https://www.westmidlandbirdclub.org.uk/. For group visits contact the permit secretary at permits@westmidlandbirdclub.org.uk. Open all hours, no facilities.
Contact: Paul Bateman: harborne@westmidlandbirdclub.org
Return to M5/M6 and head E to M42.

5 LADYWALK RESERVE
West Midland Bird Club
Habitats: 123 acres, floodplain, reedbed, woodland within a loop of River Tame.
Birds: 200+ spp. *Spring/summer:* Passage waders inc Greenshank, Curlew, godwits and plovers, hirundines and other migrants. *Winter:* Hundreds of wildfowl, inc Wigeon, Teal, Shoveler, Goldeneye, Goosander. Water Rail and Woodcock regular, lots of small bird activity at feeding stations. Up to 4 Bitterns in recent years, Siskin, Redpoll and winter thrushes.
Other: Five spp orchid, inc county's only known colony of Marsh Hellebore and locally rare Yellow Bird's Nest. Butterflies plentiful and 16 spp dragonflies.
Directions: B46 2BS; SP 211 916. Next to the Hams Hall distribution site, in Tame Valley—10 miles from Birmingham city centre. From J9 of M42, head S on A446 to Hams Hall Distribution Centre. Follow Faraday Avenue to reserve. WMBC members can use the club's car park at the entrance to the reserve.
Public transport: None.
Visiting: Access to the site is via the coded gate. Codes are only provided to members. Reserve open only to WMBC members, but other groups can organize visits with Permit Sec. Non-members can observe site from public footpaths E of River Tame. No easy access on site for disabled visitors. Display permits on dashboard if using secure car park. Dogs not allowed. 6 bird hides, inc elevated River Walk Hide. Other screens for close-up viewing. Circular footpath (1.6 miles).
Contact: W Midland BC Permit Sec: permits@westmidlandbirdclub.org.uk; *no permits issued to individual non-members—groups only.*
Nearby.

6 MIDDLETON LAKES
RSPB
Habitats: Former quarry, lakes, reedbeds, meadows, woodland.
Birds: All year: Great White Egret, Bittern (booming), Barn Owls regularly seen and Cetti's Warbler frequently heard, Kingfisher. *Spring:* Garganey, waders, Lesser Spotted Woodpecker. *Summer:* Heronry (30+ pairs), Avocet, Little Ringed Plover, Redshank, Oystercatcher.

Lesser Spotted Woodpecker, 10 spp warbler inc Grasshopper, Lapwing, hirundines and woodland spp. *Autumn:* Osprey and other passage migrants. *Winter:* Peak numbers of wildfowl and waders. Marsh Harrier becoming more common, Peregrine Falcon.

Other: Bee orchid, Bluebells and spring flowers, Grass Snake. 20+ spp dragonfly, 25 spp butterfly inc White-letter Hairstreak, moths.

Directions: B78 2BB; SP 192 967. Reserve lies in Tame Valley, S of Tamworth, next to Middleton Hall. Leave M42 at J9 on to A446, then A4091 and finally into Bodymoor Heath Road. NB: Access shared with Aston Villa FC, drive past football ground for reserve car park.

Public transport: Train—Wilnecote, 2.5 miles.

Visiting: Open daily dawn/dusk. Car park (open 8am-5pm; Nov-Feb 8:30am-4pm) for 50—parking charge/ members free, cycle racks. 4 trails ranging from 500 yards to 2 miles. Surfaced path from car park to Middleton Hall. Other paths are not surfaced but generally flat. Playmeadow Trail not suitable for wheelchairs. 5 viewing screens. Lookout hide open to view northern scrapes (see RSPB website for lock combination number). Dogs allowed on leads in parts of site. Nearest toilets at Middleton Hall.

Contact: RSPB: 01827 259 454; middletonlakes@rspb.org.uk

Leave M42 at J6 and take A45.

7 BRANDON MARSH

Warwickshire Wildlife Trust

Habitats: 260 acres, pools, marsh, reedbeds, willow carr, scrub and small mixed woodland.

Birds: 230+ spp. *All year:* Cetti's Warbler, Kingfisher, Water Rail, Gadwall, Little Grebe, Buzzard. *Spring/summer:* Little Ringed Plover, Garden & Grasshopper Warblers, Whitethroat, Lesser Whitethroat, Hobby, Whinchat, Wheatear. *Autumn/winter:* Bittern, Dunlin, Ruff, Snipe, Greenshank, Green and Common Sandpipers, Wigeon, Shoveler, Pochard, Goldeneye, Siskin, Redpoll.

Other: 500 plant spp, Badger, Otter, Great Crested Newt. 20+ spp butterflies and 18 spp dragonflies.

Directions: CV3 3GW; SP 386 758. 3 miles SE of Coventry, 200 yards SE of A45/A46 J (Tollbar End). Turn E off A45 (after Texaco garage) into Brandon Lane. Reserve entrance signposted 1.25 miles on R.

Public transport: Bus: 21 Coventry to Willenhall/Tollbar End, then 1.25 miles walk. National Express, Coventry.

Visiting: Open 9.30am-4:30pm weekdays, 10am-4:30pm weekends (closes 4pm, Oct-Mar). Only Trust members can visit site outside these hours. Entrance charge (free to WT members). Visitor centre, tea-room (open 10am-4pm daily), shop, toilets, nature trails, 8 hides. Wheelchair access to nature trails and Wright hide. No dogs. Parking for coaches, by arrangement.

Contact: Warwickshire WT: 024 7630 2912; enquiries@wkwt.org.uk

Take A45.

8 RYTON WOOD

Warwickshire Wildlife Trust

Habitats: 210 acre, semi-natural ancient woodland.

Birds: All year: Buzzard, Sparrowhawk, Tawny Owl, common woodland spp. *Summer:* Common warblers inc. Garden, Spotted Flycatcher. *Winter:* Woodcock, Redpoll, Corvid roost. Check out Ryton Pools for wildfowl.

Other: 570 spp moths. Butterflies (inc White Admiral, Purple Hairstreak and Silver-washed Fritillary).

Directions: CV8 3EP; SP 386 728. 4.5 miles SE of Coventry. From A46 Coventry bypass take A45 to Ryton roundabout. Turn L on to A445, go straight over next roundabout, entrance to Ryton CP one mile on L.

Public transport: Bus: 25/25A (not Sun) Coventry to Rugby (Ryton-on-Dunsmore/Sky Blue Connection stop), 0.6 mile walk along A445 to pedestrian access to Ryton Pools. National Express Coventry (0121 254 7272).

Visiting: Open all hours. Reserve accessed from Ryton Pools Country Park (with visitor centre, cafe, toilets). Extensive network of paths and rides, waymarked walks. Dogs on lead.

Contact: Warwickshire Wildlife Trust: 024 7630 2912; enquiries@wkwt.org.uk

Return to A45 and continue E. At start of M45 take B4429, then R on minor road over M45 to Thurlaston.

9 DRAYCOTE WATER

Severn Trent Water

Habitats: Large storage reservoir, surrounded by grassland, wooded areas.

Birds: All year: Farmland and woodland spp in surrounding countryside. *Spring and autumn passage:* inc waders, Black & Arctic Terns and Ospreys. *Winter:* Wide range of common wildfowl, regular sightings of less common spp such as Smew, Scaup and Black-necked Grebe. Gull roost can number in excess of 50,000 birds, scarcer spp often seen.

Directions: CV23 8AB; SP 462 685. Reservoir and 20-acre country park situated near Dunchurch, 3.5 miles SW of Rugby off the A426.

Public transport: Bus: 63 Rugby to Leamington Spa stops at Kites Hardwick/Draycote Water. Stagecoach.

Visiting: Open daily (not 25 Dec) 7:30am-8pm (Apr-Sep), 7:30am-dusk (Oct-Mar). Cars must stop at pay & display car park—disabled parking allowed at Toft, close to bird hide. Visitor centre, toilets, cafe open 10am-6pm (Apr-Sep), 4pm (Oct-Mar). Access to reservoir on foot or bicycle only. 5 mile road surrounding reservoir. Paths good for wheelchairs. Dogs only in Country Park.

Contact: Draycote Water, Kites Hardwick, Warwickshire CV23 8AB: 01788 811 107; draycotewater@severntrent.co.uk; www.draycotebirding.co.uk

Return to A45 and head for Coventry., leave on B4453. Continue to junction with A425 to SE of Leamington Spa.

10 UFTON FIELDS

Warwickshire Wildlife Trust

Habitats: Grassland, woodland, pools.

Birds: All Year: Little Grebe, Tufted Duck, Buzzard, Kingfisher, Bullfinch, Reed Bunting, *Summer:* Hobby, Cuckoo, warblers inc Sedge & Reed. *Winter:* Wildfowl inc Goosander, Wigeon—both scarce, Snipe, Woodcock, winter thrushes, Siskin, Redpoll

Other: 28 spp. butterflies, 14 spp dragonflies, bats, Muntjac, Great Crested Newt, Grass Snake.

Directions: CV33 9PU; SP 378 615. E of Leamington Spa. Take A425 towards Southam, at Ufton turn R into Ufton Fields Lane to car park (0.5 mile).

Public transport: Bus: 63 Leamington Spa-Rugby (daily) pass Ufton, alight at 'bus shelter' stop and walk 0.5 mile along Ufton Fields Lane. Stagecoach Warwickshire (01604 676 060),

Visiting: Open all hours. Small car park (height restriction). Paths are wheelchair accessible but there are wooden kissing gates at path entrance (not suitable for mobility scooters). 1.25 mile trail, two hides. Dogs under control at all times.

Contact: Warwickshire WT: 024 7630 2912; enquiries@wkwt.org.uk

Worcestershire

A largely rural county, the Wildlife Trust manages a range of habitats on more than 75 reserves. There is only one sizeable reservoir (Bittell) but there are excellent wetlands to explore at Upton Warren and Bredon's Hardwick. The best area to find the widest range of woodland species, including Wood Warbler, Pied Flycatcher and the more elusive Hawfinch, is the Wyre Forest to the west of Kidderminster.

Bird Atlas/Avifauna
See **Warwickshire and West Midlands**

Bird Recorder
Craig Reed, 27 Meadow Rise, Bewdley, DY12 1JP: worcs-recorder@westmidlandbirdclub.org.uk

Bird Report
See **Warwickshire and West Midlands**

BTO Regional Representatives
Steve Davies:
Wetland Bird Survey (WeBS)
Local Organizer: webs@bto.org
Chris North

Club
See **Warwickshire and West Midlands**.

Ringing Groups/Bird Observatory
West Midlands RG:
www.westmidlandsringinggroup.co.uk
Wildgoose RG
Wychavon RG

RSPB Local Group
Worcester and Malvern (1980; 300)
Nick Skilbeck:
localgroup@worcestermalvernrspb.org.uk;
https://group.rspb.org.uk/worcester/
Meetings: 7:30pm, 2nd Wednesday of the month (Sep-May). Powick Village Hall, on A449, Powick, Worcester, WR2 4RT.

Wildlife Trust
Worcestershire Wildlife Trust (1967; 23,500)
Lower Smite Farm, Smite Hill, Hindlip, Worcester, WR3 8SZ: 01905 754 919;
enquiries@worcestershirewildlifetrust.org;
www.worcswildlifetrust.co.uk

Enter from Warwickshire on M42. Take A441 at J2. 4 miles S of Redditch take B4090 W to Feckenham.

1 FECKENHAM WYLDE MOOR NATURE RESERVE

Worcestershire Wildlife Trust

Habitats: Fen meadows, reedbed, woodland, pools.

Birds: All year: Little Grebe, Buzzard, Barn Owl, Reed Bunting. *Spring/Summer:* Kingfisher, Cuckoo, Hobby, Reed & Sedge Warblers. *Winter:* Snipe, Siskin, Redpoll, winter thrushes.

Other: 17 spp dragonflies. 150+ spp flora (inc Marsh Arrowgrass and Fen Bedstraw). Grass Snake.

Directions: B96 6JL; SP 012 606 (reserve). Park in Feckingham village car park (Turton Gardens, off High Street) and walk to reserve (c.15 mins). From car park turn R back to main road, turn L then R into Moor Lane. Reserve entrance is 0.5 mile on R.

Public transport: None.

Visiting: Open dawn-dusk. Circular trail (1 mile, leaves reserve and re-enters—leaflet available), 2 hides. Dogs on lead.

Contact: Worcestershire WT: 01905 754 919; enquiries@worcestershirewildlifetrust.org

Continue W on B4090 and then B4091. At junction with A38, head N.

2 THE CHRISTOPHER CADBURY WETLAND RESERVE AT UPTON WARREN

Worcestershire Wildlife Trust

Habitats: Fresh and saline pools with muddy islands,

Worcestershire

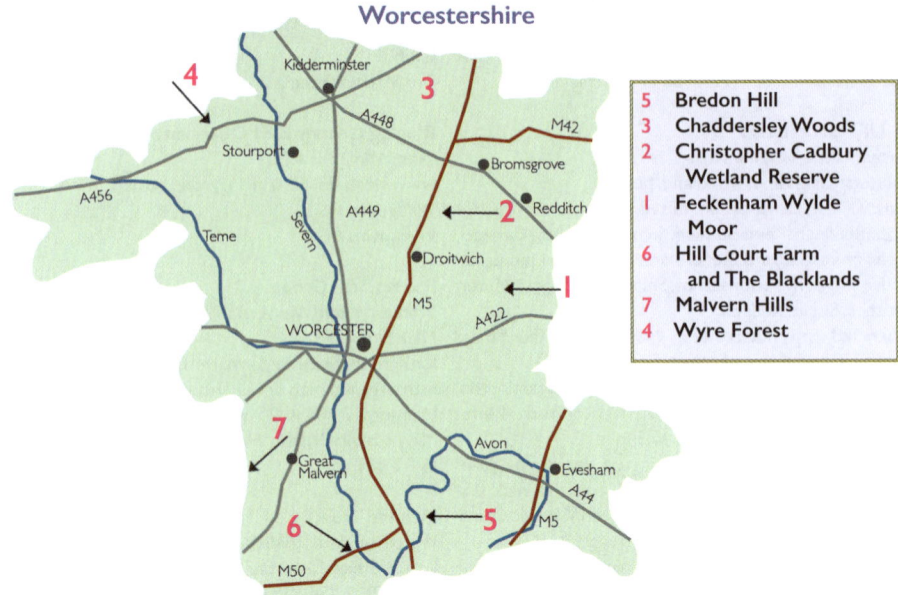

5	Bredon Hill
3	Chaddersley Woods
2	Christopher Cadbury Wetland Reserve
1	Feckenham Wylde Moor
6	Hill Court Farm and The Blacklands
7	Malvern Hills
4	Wyre Forest

some woodland, scrub.

Birds: Spring/autumn: Passage waders, occasional Black Tern, Osprey. *Summer:* Breeding Oystercatcher, Avocet, Redshank, Little Ringed Plover, Common Tern, Cetti's, Sedge & Reed Warblers. Hobby nearby. *Winter:* Wildfowl, Bittern, Water Rail, Snipe.

Other: Saltmarsh plants, dragonflies.

Directions: B61 7ET; SO 936 677. 2 miles S of Bromsgrove on A38. Leave M5 at J5 and head N on A38, take 3rd exit at first roundabout.

Public transport: Bus: 144 Birmingham to Worcester passes reserve entrance. First Bus.

Visiting: Christopher Cadbury Wetland Reserve consists of Moors Pools (freshwater) and Flashes Pools (saline). Open dawn-dusk. The Flashes car park open 9am-4:30pm (Apr-Sep) and 10:30am-3pm (Oct-Mar). May be open outside these hours but please check noticeboard in car park for daily closing times. The Moors car park open dawn-dusk. Non-members must obtain a day permit from the Trust's online shop, volunteers on site or the Boatshack Cafe (at The Flashes car park). Trust members should carry membership card. 7 hides, maps at entrances, paths can be very muddy. Disabled access to 2 hides at The Moors only by prior arrangement (3rd hide available during same hours as car park). Coach parking at Aztec Adventure by arrangement. No dogs.

Contact: Worcestershire WT: 01905 754 919; enquiries@worcestershirewildlifetrust.org

Head N to Bromsgrove on A38, then W on A448.

3 CHADDERSLEY WOODS NNR

Worcestershire Wildlife Trust

Habitats: Woodland (W side: planted broadleaf and co-nifer; E side: ancient woodland).

Birds: All Year: Sparrowhawk, Tawny Owl, Woodcock, common woodland spp. Crossbill (conifer areas). *Summer:* Common warblers. *Winter:* Redwing, Fieldfare.

Other: Butterflies, ancient woodland flora. Land Caddis.

Directions: B61 9EG; SO 914 736. Between Bromsgrove and Kidderminster, 1.5 miles N of Woodcote Green. Take Woodcote Lane from A448 Kidderminster-Bromsgrove road, after 0.6 mile take L fork (Woodcote Green Lane) continue for 0.5 miles to reserve entrance—park in lay-bys.

Public transport: None—local bus runs along A448 but not safe to walk from bus stop.

Visiting: Open all hours. Extensive network of paths and rides (mainly W side of reserve). Main track is stoned, others not suitable for wheelchairs/buggies. Dogs on lead.

Contact: Worcestershire WT: 01905 754 919; enquiries@worcestershirewildlifetrust.org

Continue in to Kidderminster on A448, then A456.

4 WYRE FOREST NNR

Natural England/Forestry England/Worcs Wildlife Trust

Habitats: Ancient coppice Oak woodland, conifer areas, Birch heath, lowland grassland, stream. The country's largest woodland NNR.

Birds: Breeding birds inc Redstart, Pied Flycatcher, Wood Warbler, Buzzard and Raven, with Dipper, Grey Wagtail and Kingfisher on larger streams.

Other: Mammals inc Fallow, Roe & Muntjac Deer, Polecat, Otter, Mink, Yellow-neck Mouse, Dormouse, Water Shrew and voles. Several bat spp inc Pipistrelle and Daubenton's. Important for invertebrates inc England's largest colony of Pearl-bordered Fritillary butterfly.

Worcestershire

Directions: DY14 9XQ; SO 750 740 (Callow Hill/Discovery Centre). On A456 Kidderminster to Tenbury Wells road, three miles west of Bewdley.

Public transport: Bus: 291 (not Sun) Kidderminster to Bewdley/Tenbury Wells stops at Callow Hill/DC. R&B Travel (01584 890 770). Train—Kidderminster.

Visiting: Keep to paths. Toilets and refreshments (with disabled access). Several waymarked trails (some suitable for wheelchair users), regular guided walks, family cycle routes through reserve.

On **Shropshire** border.

Contact: Wyre Forest NNR, Natural England Office, Lodge Hill Farm, Dowles Brook, Bewdley DY12 2L: 01299 400 686

Head S from Kidderminster on A449 and A44 to Evesham.

5 BREDON HILL NNR

Natural England

Habitats: Wood pasture, nearby farmland, woodland

Birds: All year: Red Kite, Skylark, Stonechat, Marsh Tit, Yellowhammer. *Spring/summer:* Redstart, Tree Pipit, Spotted Flycatcher, common warblers. *Spring/autumn passage:* Wheatear, Whinchat, Ring Ouzel—occasional Dotterel (not annual). *Autumn/winter:* Winter thrushes, Brambling, Crossbill—rarities inc Hen Harrier, Short-eared Owl, Great Grey Shrike.

Other: 230 invertebrate spp inc Violet Click Beetle & 6 rare spp of fly. Herb-rich unimproved grassland.

Directions: WR10 3DN; SO 953 402. 6 miles SW of Evesham, take A46, turn R and follow sign to Elmley Castle. At T-junction turn L into Main Street. Park in village or turn L by Queen Elizabeth Inn to small car park 200 yards on L (at picnic place). Walk up Hill Lane (by Inn) and take footpath at end of lane to top of Bredon. Access to parts of the hill restricted due to sensitive flora and fauna.

Public transport: None.

Visiting: Open all hours, on public rights of way. Can be a good migration watch point—early morning best, especially Sept/Oct.

Contact: Natural England: 07919 995 036;

Continue W on A46 and then A438.

6 HILL COURT FARM AND THE BLACKLANDS— THE ANDREW FRASER RESERVE

Worcestershire Wildlife Trust

Habitats: Wet grassland, hay meadow, scrub, scrape.

Birds: All Year: Barn Owl, Skylark, Yellowhammer. *Spring/summer:* Lapwing, Redshank, Curlew, Reed Bunting. *Autumn/winter:* Wigeon, Teal, Pintail, Peregrine, Woodcock, Green Sandpiper, Snipe.

Other: Brown Hare, butterflies.

Directions: GL20 6BD; SO 825 355. From A4104 take B4211 to Longdon, Turn R into Bear Lane then R again into Marsh Lane (0.6 mile to parking area). From A438 take B4211 towards Longdon, after crossing under

M50. Turn L into Marsh Lane (1 mile to parking area).

Public transport: None.

Visiting: Open dawn-dusk (permissive path). Parking space for 2/3 cars on Marsh Road by Longdon Brook. Access restricted to a permissive path (muddy/slippy when wet) to a viewing screen overlooking a scrape. Public bridleway between Marsh Road and Robertsend (runs along a high ridge) gives excellent views of reserve (0.6 mile E from parking area, opposite Bear Lane turn).

Contact: Worcestershire WT: 01905 754 919; enquiries@worcestershirewildlifetrust.org

*Continue N on B4211 then W on A4104 to Little Malvern and the A449. Head N on A449 to Great Malvern along the Malvern Hills, which straddle the **Worcestershire/Herefordshire** border.*

7 MALVERN HILLS

Malvern Hills Trust

Habitats: Grassland on hilltops, mixed woodland, scrub, quarries, small reservoirs and lakes.

Birds: Raptors inc Buzzard, Sparrowhawk, Peregrine Falcon, Hobby. Ravens nest in quarries. Wooded areas hold all expected common spp., breeding flycatchers and warblers, 3 spp woodpeckers and Tree Pipit on woodland edge. A few Nightingales hang on in areas of dense scrub, which also hold chats, pipits and Linnet. *Spring passage:* inc Wheatear, Ring Ouzel (best in Happy Valley between Worcestershire Beacon and North Hill) and more rarely, Dotterel. *Autumn passage:* Good range of migrants heading south. A winter highlight is Snow Bunting on the highest hills.

Other: Lesser Horseshoe & Barbastelle Bats, Polecat, 25 spp butterflies, inc High Brown Fritillary. Broad range of plants inc Blinks, Crosswort and Common Spotted Orchid.

Directions: WR13 6DW (British Camp car park). SO 763 403. An 8 mile long range of hills and commons lying S and W of Great Malvern, covering *c*.3,000 acres.

Public transport: None.

Visiting: Open all year. Many car parks (mainly open 6am-11pm)—charges/annual permit available. Public toilets with disabled access opposite British Camp car park (A449 Worcester Road). Two easy-access trails at Earnslaw (450 yards) and Blackhill (250 yards). Best birdwatching areas inc Castlemorton Common and Midsummer Hill.

Contact: Malvern Hills Trust, Manor House, Grange Road, Malvern WR14 3EY: 01684 892 002; info@malvernhills.org.uk; www.malvernhills.org.uk

Or turn L at Little Malvern and head SW on A449 into Herefordshire.

Herefordshire

Central Herefordshire is a broad basin formed by the Rivers Wye and Lugg, which join just to the S of Hereford, fringed by the Black Hills of the Welsh border to the W, the Malverns on the Worcestershire border to the E and the hills of S Shropshire to the N.

Bird Atlas/Avifauna
The Birds of Herefordshire 2007-2012: An Atlas of Their Breeding and Wintering Distributions
Mervyn Davies, Peter Eldridge, Chris Robinson, Nick Smith & Gerald Wells (Liverpool University Press, 2014)

Bird Recorder
Mike Wheeler, 6, Watling Street, Leintwardine, Craven Arms. SY7 0LW; 07751 524 771; mike.leintwg@gmail.com

Bird Report
The Birds of Herefordshire (1951-), from HOC.
For reports up to 2023: Mervyn Davies, Hunters Moon, Bishopstone, Hereford, HR4 7JE: 07887 485 984; mervyn.davies88@gmail.com
From 2024 onwards: David Allen (editor), Westcombe Cottage, Bircher, Leominster, HR6 0BT: 07794 354 710; davidallen651@outlook.com

BTO Regional Representative
Chris Robinson
Wetland Bird Survey (WeBS)
Local Organizer: webs@bto.org
Chris Robinson

Club
Herefordshire Ornithological Club (1950; 280)
Mike Bound (Membership Sec), 34 The Rugg, Leominster, Herefordshire HR6 8TE: 07974 158 591; hocmembership@gmail.com; www.herefordshirebirds.org
Meetings: On zoom or 7:00pm, last Thursday of the month (Sep-Mar). Saxon Hall, Hoarwithy Road, Putson, Hereford HR2 6HE. Contact/see website for details.

RSPB Local Group
No Groups

Wildlife Trust
Herefordshire Wildlife Trust (1962; 8,000)
Queenswood Country Park & Arboretum, Dinmore Hill, Nr Leominster, HR6 0PY: 01432 356 872; enquiries@herefordshirewt.co.uk; www.herefordshirewt.org

*Entering from **Worcestershire** on the A449, take the B4224 NW towards the Woolhope Dome and then Hereford.*
To the E and SE of Hereford, on the other side of the Lugg and Wye, the Woolhope Dome is the remnant of an eroded anticline comprising a central dome to the NW of Woolhope (7.5 miles SE of Hereford), an incomplete surrounding ring of hills and intervening dip. It is an area of ancient hillside woods and hedgerow enclosed fields. The Herefordshire

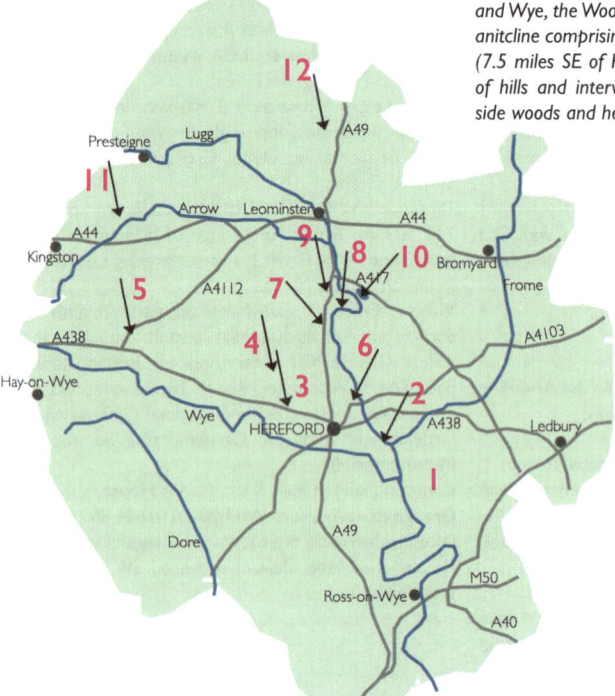

10	Bodenham Lake
3	Brockhall Gravel Pits
4	Credenhill Park Wood
2	Hampton Meadow
1	Lea and Paget's Wood
6	Lugg Meadows
12	Mortimer Forest
8	Oak Tree Farm
9	Queenswood
5	Sturts, The
11	Titley Pool
7	Wellington Gravel Pits

Wildlife Trust has a number of reserves on and around the Dome including:

1 LEA & PAGET'S WOOD

Herefordshire Wildlife Trust

Habitats: 27 acres, semi-natural ancient broadleaved woodland on slopes of hill. Sessile Oak and Ash, with Hazel and Field Maple understorey. SSSI

Birds: Common woodland sp inc 3 spp woodpecker, Wood Warbler, Pied Flycatcher.

Other: White Admiral, Wood White, Silver-washed Fritillary. Woodland flowers in spring.

Directions: HR1 4QA; SO 593 345. Head SE from Hereford through Tupsley on the B4224, After Fownthorpe take Hawker's Lane on L. Park in lay-by at top of ridge.

Public transport: Bus: 453/454, Hereford to Fownhorpe and Woolhope (not Sun), Yeomans Travel (01432 356 201). Walk from Fownthorpe, c.1.25 miles.

Visiting: Dawn-dusk, free, no facilities (but pub in Fownthorpe). Wye Valley Walk runs to NE of Fownthorpe and then over crest of the hill. No surfaced paths and no wheelchair access. Main path low-lying, damp and can be muddy. Disused quarry with steep drops. Dogs on lead.

Contact: reserves@herefordshirewt.co.uk

If approaching Hereford from Woolhope Dome and along B4224, you pass through Hampton Bishop after crossing the Lugg and before reaching the Wye.

2 HAMPTON MEADOW

Herefordshire Wildlife Trust

Habitats: 62 acres, two fields: a large traditional hay meadow (a Lammas Meadow) and a smaller area of permanent pasture. Floods in winter. At confluence of Rivers Lugg and Frome.

Birds: Breeding: Curlew, Kingfisher, Skylark, Sand Martin, Reed Bunting. Winter: Flocks of ducks and gulls. Occasionally may include Bewick's Swan.

Other: Sweet Vernal Grass, Pepper Saxifrage.

Directions: HR1 4DF; SO 560 391. Park in Hampton Bishop to N of B4224 between Hereford and Mordiford.

Public transport: Bus: 453/454, Hereford to Fownhorpe and Woolhope (not Sun), stops in Hampton Bishop, Yeomans Travel (01432 356 201).

Visiting: Follow footpath N from village to bridge over river. Public footpaths across reserve but from 1 Mar to 31 Jul no access to reserve other than these paths. At other times open all hours, free. No facilities, though pub in Hampton Bishop. Seasonal grazing. Dogs on lead during breeding season or with livestock, otherwise under close control. No surfaced paths, not suitable for wheel/pushchairs. Steep riverbanks.

Contact: David Hutton: reserves@herefordshirewt.co.uk

Either continue into Hereford and then take A438 off A49.

3 BROCKHALL GRAVEL PITS

Duchy of Cornwall

Habitats: Flooded gravel pit, margins mix of meadow and woodland. E end deeper (angling). Water levels now lower than in past and several islands at W end.

Birds: All year: Gadwall, Great Crested & Little Grebes, Green Woodpecker. Passage: Little Gull (often recorded) Green & Common Sandpipers, Little Ringed Plover, Dunlin, Ruff, Greenshank plus scarcer waders and grebes (occasional). Winter: Wildfowl inc occasional Pintail and Pochard. First county records for Great White Egret and Spoonbill.

Other:

Directions: HR4 7QS; SO 453 423. Head NW from Hereford on A438. 3.6 miles after leaving the A49 in Hereford, park in lay-by on L (heading W) in Sugwas Pool. Cross road and walk W for 200 yards, branching R on to lane. Almost immediately take footpath on R between two houses. Follow through wood and across meadow to gravel pit

Public transport: Bus: 71/71B (not Sun or Bank Holidays, operated by Sargeants Brothers) Hereford to Credenhill, leaves A438 1.25 miles before footpath into reserve in Sugwas Pool. Credenhill is to N of gravel pit but SAS HQ between village and gravel pit.

Visiting: Free, open all hours, no facilities at gravel pits. Permissive paths around perimeter.

Contact:

Continuing along the lane taken off A438 rather than taking the footpath through the wood and across the meadow leads you past **Kenchester Pools**, a cluster of several small pools.

Leave A438 in Kings Acre before reaching Sugwas Pool (see above), taking A480 on R, just past garden centre.

4 CREDENHILL PARK WOOD

Woodland Trust

Habitats: 235 acre ancient woodland, mix of conifer and broadleaf with understorey. Some clear fell on hill summit (725 ft), steep slopes.

Birds: Common woodland spp inc Sparrowhawk, Tawny Owl, Raven, Marsh & Long-tailed Tits, Nuthatch, Treecreeper. Summer: Garden Warbler, Tree Pipit. Passage: Spotted Flycatcher, Redstart, Stonechat. Winter: Occasional Woodcock.

Other: Fallow Deer, Muntjac, Silver-washed Friillary

Directions: SO 455 440. Leave A480 in centre of Credenhill, taking road running NE from opposite Cross Farm for Tillington. After 200 yards car park on L.

Public transport: Bus: 71/71B (not Sun or Bank Holidays) Hereford to Credenhill, Sargeants Brothers.

Visiting: Open all hours, free, no facilities but shop in Credenhill and pub in Tillington. Surfaced circular path from car park. Unsurfaced tracks run to summit.

Contact: www.woodlandtrust.org.uk
Continue on A438. You can also approach from N on A44 and then A4412 from Leominster.

5 THE STURTS, NORTH, EAST & SOUTH

Herefordshire Wildlife Trust
Habitat: Three separate reserves located close to each other on the flood plain of the Wye. Wet unimproved grassland with drier ridges, ponds and ditches, enclosed by old hedges. Prone to winter flooding. **North:** 52 acres, 7 fields **East:** 6 fields, 15 acres. **South:** 52 acres on W edge of **Letton Lakes.**
Birds: Hedgerow and farmland species inc Long-tailed Tit, Marsh Tit, Whitethroat, Lesser Whitethroat (occasional), Reed Bunting, Yellowhammer. *Winter:* Snipe, Jack Snipe, Lapwing. Wildfowl during flooding.
Other: Ruddy & Common Darters, Large Red Damselfly. Wide variety of fungi, 28 spp Waxcaps. Wet grassland flora.
Directions: **North:** HR3 6NY; SO 338 482. **East:** HR3 6QA; SO 341 478. **South:** HR3 6QA; SO 340 475. Take the A438 NW from Hereford. 11.75 miles after leaving junction with A49, take a minor road on R for Ailey. The reserves lie to the W of this road and to the S of Ailey, which is 1.5 miles N of the turning.
Public transport: None.
Visiting: All three are open dawn to dusk, free, no facilities. For **South** park on verge 0.6 mile from A438, by the Old School House, Waterloo. For **East**. The fields that form the reserve are immediately adjacent to the road N of a track on L after the Old School House and a pond, For **North**, continue to the minor road on L leading to Ailey. Take this road, just past Ailey Farm (don't be distracted by Upper Ailey and Lower Ailey Farms) there is a track on L with limited parking leading to reserve. Ground can be damp and prone to flooding, footpaths but no surfaced paths. Not suitable for wheelchairs. Do not trample vegetation in wetter areas, Keep to field margins when hay growing. Seasonal grazing, keep dogs on lead.
Contact: Luke Osman
reserves@herefordshirewt.co.uk
Letton Lakes, an area of farmland on the Wye floodplain that is prone to flooding in winter, is nearby.

Or, after 2 Hampton Meadow return along B4224 to Mordiford and then take L in centre of village and L again after 1 mile. Turn L for Lugwardine along Larport and then Tidnor Lane. At junction with A438 turn L for Hereford and park opposite Cock of Tupsley (see below).

6 LUGG MEADOWS, UPPER & LOWER

Herefordshire Wildlife Trust
Habitats: 114 acres, a long, narrow strip of meadow on flood plain of the Lugg. A rare surviving example of a Lammas Meadow. SSSI.

Birds: Kingfisher *Summer:* Curlew, Skylark, Sand Martin, Yellow & Grey Wagtails. *Passage:* Lapwing, Black-tailed Godwit, Greenshank, Redshank, Common Sandpiper. Snipe, *Winter:* Mute, Whooper & possible Bewick Swans, grey geese, Wigeon, Shoveler, Teal, Mallard, gull roost when meadows flooded may include Common, Caspian, Yellow-legged & Mediterranean Gulls. Peregrine Falcon, Merlin
Other: Otter. 20 spp grass, Snake's Head Fritillary, Narrow-leaved Dropwort.
Directions: HR1 1UT; SO 527 411. Take A38/Ledbury Road E out of Hereford. Park in lane opposite the Cock of Tupsley pub (corner of Ledbury and Hampton Dene Roads). Walk along lane to entrance.
Public transport: Bus: 476 Hereford to Ledbury stops opposite Cock of Tupsley, DRM Bus (01885 483 939; drm@drmbus.com). Train—Hereford.
Visiting: Open dawn-dusk (may be restrictions during breeding season), free. No facilities on reserve. From entrance at S end reserve stretches N along Lugg to its confluence wuth the Little Lugg. No restrictions on access to Upper Lugg Meadow, but do not walk in growing hay (late-Apr-Jul). Keep to public rights of way in Lower Lugg Meadow Mar-Jul. May flood up to depth of 3 ft for much of winter. No surfaced paths or wheelchair access. Seasonally grazed by sheep and cattle and ground-nesting birds, so keep dogs on lead.
Contact: David Hutton:
reserves@herefordshirewt.co.uk
Heading N from Hereford on the A49 along the Lugg Valley.

7 WELLINGTON GRAVEL PITS

Tarmac
Habitats: Flooded gravel pits, mudflats, wooded margins, islands.
Birds: Little Egret, Great Crested Grebe, Kingfisher, Barn & Little Owls. *Summer:* Little Ringed Plover, Common Sandpiper, Cetti's, Willow, Reed & Sedge Warblers. *Passage:* Cuckoo, Green Sandpiper. *Winter:* Pochard, Teal, Shoveler, and Gadwall. Starling murmuration
Directions: HR4 8BY; SO 507 483. Take A49 N out of Hereford, after 4 miles turn E into Orchard Green. Site is on R after c.0.5 mile.
Public transport: Bus: 492 Hereford to Leominster runs along A49. Several stops in Wellington to W of A49, Gravel pits to E. Yeomans Travel (01432 356 201). Train—Hereford.
Visiting: Still being actively quarried. Book in at porta-cabin (7am-4:30pm Mon-Fri; 8am-1pm Sat) by weighbridge. Free, no facilities but cafe and toilet facilities in garden centre on other side of A49 or in Wellington village. Public rights of way across site and outside opening hours can enter via footpath from A49. Hide beside main lake.
Contact: Tarmac: 01275 512 903;
swswsales@tarmac.com

Planning approval has just been granted to the Wye Valley Group for a new gravel and sand quarry in Wellington. The quarry has a projected operating life of 10 years, after which it will be restored as wetland and grassland for wildlife. Roll on *The Birdwatcher's Yearbook 2036.*

6 Lugg Meadows and the following three reserves along the A49 and the River Lugg to the N of Hereford make up the Trust's **Lugg Living Landscape** project.

8 OAK TREE FARM

Herefordshire Wildlife Trust

Habitats: 30 acres, purchased in 2020. Work in progress. On S side of Dinmore Hill, meadows sloping down to Lugg, pools, scrapes and wet grassland created along river. Reedbed.

Birds: Oystercatcher, Lapwing, Barn Owl, Kingfisher.

Other: Otter. Dark Green Fritillary. Wet grassland planted in 2022 and 2023 with wildflowers for pollinators such as bumblebees.

Directions: HR1 3JP; SO 507 506. Immediately off A49 as road starts to climb Dinmore Hill

Public transport: Bus: 492 Hereford to Leominster runs along A49, stops at start of climb up Dinmore Hill. Yeomans Travel (01432 356 201). Train—Hereford.

Visiting: Open dawn to dusk, free, two permissive paths to hides. Paths unsurfaced and steep. No public access to rest of site. Not currently suitable for wheel- or pushchairs. Grazed seasonally, no dogs.

Contact: Rosie Wilson: 07341 736 188; reserves@herefordshirewt.co.uk

9 QUEENSWOOD COUNTRY PARK & ARBORETUM

Herefordshire Wildlife Trust

Habitats: 123 acres native woodland and 47 acre tree collection. SSSI.

Birds: Common woodland spp inc 3 spp. woodpecker, Sparrowhawk, Tawny Owl, Raven, Marsh Tit, Goldcrest, Siskin. *Summer:* Willow, Wood & Garden Warblers, Spotted Flycatcher. *Spring/autumn:* Cuckoo, Chiffchaff. *Winter:* Woodcock, Redpoll, Common Crossbill. Occasional Waxwing.

Other: Dormouse. Purple Hairstreak, Silver-washed Fritillary. Tree collection

Directions: HR6 0PY; SO 5016 504. Take the A49 N from Hereford, the Arboretum and its car park are immediately to L of road on Dinmore Hill.

Public transport: Bus: 492 Hereford to Leominster runs along A49. Stops outside the Country Park. Yeomans Travel (01432 356 201). Train—Hereford.

Visiting: Entry free dawn-dusk, pay & display car park, visitor centre open 10am-4pm, closed 25 Dec. Gift shop, cafe (9am-4pm, kitchen closes 3:30pm), accessible toilets. Main trails surfaced and wheelchair accessible. Dogs permitted, keep under control, clean up mess.

Contact: Rosie Wilson: 07341 736 188; reserves@herefordshirewt.co.k

Instead of staying on A49 take minor road for Bodenham on R at start of climb up Dinmore Hill.

10 BODENHAM LAKE LNR

Herefordshire Wildlife Trust

Habitats: 50 acre lake (reserve totals 111 acres), former gravel pit. margins reprofiled in 2018 to allow planting of reeds, wooded and treeless islands. Meadows. orchards. Adjacent to River Lugg. SSSI

Birds: 170 spp recorded. Great Crested & Little Grebes, Water Rail, Hobby, Kingfisher, Lesser Spotted Woodpecker, Reed Warbler. *Passage:* Cuckoo, Green & Common Sandpipers, Osprey. *Winter:* Wigeon, Goldeneye, Teal, Shoveler, Pintail, Pochard, Gadwall.

Other: Otter, dragonflies. Common Toad, (migration along historic routes in spring). Pyramidal & Bee Orchids

Directions: HR1 3JT; SO 529 512. Take A49 N from Hereford, turn R for Bodenham village, signposted to Railway Inn. Reserve on R, a short distance after pub, not as far as War Memorial.

Public transport: Bus: 426 Hereford-Leominster stops in Bodenham (not Sun), Yeomans Travel (01432 356 201). Train—Hereford.

Visiting: Open dawn-dusk, car park (charge), easy access paths from car park round part of lake. 2 hides. W end of reserve closed to public but viewable from hides to E. Seasonal sheep grazing, dogs on lead.

Contact: Rosie Wilson: 07341 736 188; reserves@herefordshirewt.co.k

Return to the A49 along the minor road followed to reach Bodenham or continue along it to its junction with the A147. Turn L and follow A147 to its junction with A49 N of Dinmore Hill. If you continue N on the A49 to Leominster you can then take the A44 West for Kington.

11 TITLEY POOL

Herefordshire Wildlife Trust

Habitats: 22 acres, one of Herefordshire's largest natural bodies of water in an area of hollows and hills formed from glacial debris. Fringing pasture and woodland. Other nearby pools.

Birds: Mute Swan, Great Crested Grebe, Barn & Little Owls, Kingfisher, Green Woodpecker, Treecreeper. *Summer:* Water Rail, Little Grebe, Willow Warbler, Pied Flycatcher, Redstart. *Winter:* Teal, Tufted Duck, Pochard, Goosander, Redpoll, Siskin.

Other: Orange Tip, Green-veined White, Speckled Wood and Gatekeeper.

Directions: HR5 3RL; SO 325 595. 10 miles W of Leominster. Take the B4355, 2nd exit from 2nd roundabout after A44 enters Kington. After 2.75 miles (just before Titley (pub), turn L at Balance Farm. Minor road running W takes you N of Pool. After 0.5 mile turn L and follow

track around end of pool to parking place on S side.
Public transport: Bus: 41 Kington to Knucklas stops in Titley (not Sun), Sargeants Brothers.
Visiting: Open dawn to dusk, free, no facilities. Permissive path, unsurfaced, not suitable for wheelchairs, along S side of pool and to hide. No dogs
Contact: reserves@herefordshirewt.co.uk
At Leominster, rather than heading W, you could continue N on the A49.

12 MORTIMER FOREST

Forestry England
Habitats: 2,500 acres, mostly conifer, some broadleaved, and planted since 1920s on steep hillsides rising to a high point of over 1,200 ft, with open areas.
Birds: Common woodland spp inc Woodcock, Goshawk, Raven, Marsh & Willow Tit, Common Crossbill. *Summer:* Cuckoo, Garden Warbler, Spotted Flycatcher, Tree Pipit. *Winter:* Large flocks of Redpoll, Siskin and Goldfinch, mixed tit flocks with Coal Tit, Goldcrest, possible Nuthatch and Treecreeper. Occasional Hawfinch.
Other: Long-haired Fallow Deer
Directions: Head N from Leominster on A49, three car parks. All are free, Black Pool and Vinnalls open dawn-dusk, every day, Whitcliffe 8am-3pm Mon-Fri. Southernmost one is Black Pool SO 496 717, leave A49 c.2 miles S of Ludlow. and take B4361 on L for Overton. There is a sharp L on the road after just under a mile, pass through Overton and car park on R a mile after sharp turn. For two northern car parks return to the sharp turn in the B4361 and continue N towards Ludlow on what is Overton Road. As you enter Ludlow, just before you cross the River Tem, turn L on to Whitcliffe Road, ignore the first car park on your L overlooking a bend in the river and continue to the Whitcliffe car park (SY8 2HD; SO 495 741) on R up forest road off what is now Killhorse Lane. For third car park, Vinnalls (SO 474 731) continue 1.5 miles along from Killhorse Lane, up forest road on R.
Public transport: Bus: 490 Leominster to Ludlow, stops in Overton and Ludlow, Sargeants Brothers. Train— Ludlow.
Visiting: Free, see above for car park opening times, picnic areas, no toilets. Car parks on N and S edges of forest and connected by a network of trails of varying lengths. Most have steep sections and can be muddy but a short loop from Vinnalls is surfaced.
Contact: 0300 067 4800;
westengland@forestryengland.uk
Contact: Forestry England: 0300 067 6977;
Mortimer Forest straddles the Herefordshire/Shropshire border, with the northernmost of its 3 car parks being in Shropshire.

Shropshire

The upland moorland of the South Shropshire Hills, bordering Wales to the west and part of the area known as the 'Welsh Marches', holds Red Grouse, Dipper and Ring Ouzel. Passage Dotterel may occasionally be seen. The fertile lowland valleys, extensive farmland and mixed woodland offer a good range of species, whilst a cluster of water bodies in the north, near Ellesmere, attract wintering wildfowl and gulls. For their part, Venus Pools, Wood Lane and Chelmarsh offer passage waders.

Bird Atlas/Avifauna
The Birds of Shropshire
Leo Smith
(Liverpool University Press, 2019)

Bird Recorder
John Martin, 39 Sandygate Avenue, Shrewsbury, SY2 6TF: 07443 544 962; soscountyrecorder@gmail.com

Bird Report
Shropshire Bird Report (1956-), from SOS— WebManager@shropshirebirds.co.uk

BTO Regional Representatives
Jonathan Groom
Wetland Bird Survey (WeBS)
Local Organizer: webs@bto.org
Martin George

Club
Shropshire Ornithological Society (1955; 1,000)
Mim Elliot-Smith (Sec): secretary@shropshirebirds. co.uk;
www.shropshirebirds.com
Meetings: 7:15pm, 1st Wednesday of the month (Oct-Mar). Bayston Hill Memorial Hall, Lyth Hill Road, Bayston Hill, Shrewsbury, SY3 0DR.

Ringing Groups/Bird Observatory
Chelmarsh RG: www.chelmarshrg.blogspot.co.uk
Shropshire RG: www.shropshirerg.wordpress.com
West Midlands RG: www.westmidlandsringinggroup. co.uk

RSPB Local Groups
Shropshire (2021; 46)
Yvonne Mancey: shrewsburyRSPBgroup@gmail.com; https://group.rspb.org.uk/shropshire/
Meetings: 7:15pm, 4th Tuesday of the month (Sep-Apr, not Dec). Bayston Hill Memorial Hall, Lyth Hill Rd, Shrewsbury, SY3 0DR.
South Shropshire (2004; 140)

Carol Wood: carolwood772@outlook.com; https://group.rspb.org.uk/southshropshire/
Meetings: 7:30pm, 3ʳᵈ Wednesday of the month (Sep-Apr). Wistanstow Village Hall, Near Craven Arms, SY7 8DQ.

Wildlife Trust
Shropshire Wildlife Trust (1962; 9,000).
193 Abbey Foregate, Shrewsbury, SY2 6AH: 01743 284 280;
enquiries@shropshirewildlifetrust.org.uk;
www.shropshirewildlifetrust.org.uk

Fenn's, Whixall and
  Bettisfield Mosses
Priorslee Lake
Stiperstones, The
Venus Pool
Wood Lane

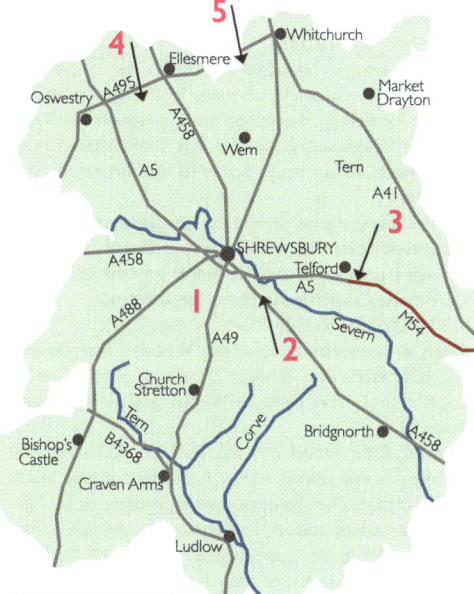

MORTIMER FOREST
Entry formerly placed in Shropshire now moved to **Herefordshire**, since two of the three car parks and most of the actual forest are in Herefordshire, not Shropshire. Head into Ludlow from the Forest and continue N on A49, taking the A489 NW just N of Craven Arms and then the A488

1 STIPERSTONES NNR, THE
Natural England
Habitats: Heathand, upland oak woodland, acid grass-land, hay meadow, mire and swamp.
Birds: All year: Red Grouse, Red Kite, Woodcock, Sky-lark, Raven, Stonechat. *Spring/summer:* Lapwing, Snipe,

Curlew, Hobby, Cuckoo, Tree Pipit, Redstart, Whinchat, Wheatear, Ring Ouzel, Pied Flycatcher, Wood Warbler. *Winter:* Thrushes, Siskin, Redpoll.
Other: Fungi. Brown Hare. Hairy Wood Ant.
Directions: Two miles E of A488 which runs parallel to The Stiperstones Ridge. NNR car park: SY5 0NL; SO 369 976; The Bog car park: SY5 0NG; SO 356 979; Snail-beach car park: SY5 0NZ; SJ 373 022 (Snailbeach).
Public transport: Stiperstone Shuttle from Church Stretton (01743 254 740) currently operating reduced service. Go to www.shropshirehills-nl.org for latest schedule. Train—Church Stretton.
Visiting: Open all hours. Three car parks (The Bog, Snailbeach and main NNR). The Bog Visitor Centre (toilets inc disabled), offers cakes and drinks. Currently operating reduced hours. Visit www.bogvisitorcentre. com for latest information. Toilets at Snailbeach (all year). 'The Stiperstone Stomp' is a five mile trail from the NNR car park, along the ridge to Habberley village. Unfortunately, given the currently reduced shuttle bus service, a five mile stomp risks turning into a ten mile there-and-back trudge.
Contact: Natural England: 01743 792 294; stiperstones.events@naturalengland.org.uk
The N-S ridges of the Stiperstones and Long Mynd that lie between the A488 and the A49 mean there are no major roas running E-W until the A488 enters Shrewsbury. Probably safest and quickest to eschew the minor roads, jead into Shrewsbury on the A488, head E on the A5 and then SE on the A458

2 VENUS POOL
Shropshire Ornithological Society
Habitats: 67 acres, pool, several islands, open shore-line, marshy grassland, hedgerows, woodland, scrub, species-rich meadows, field growing bird-friendly crops.
Birds: Noted for wintering wildfowl, passage waders and occasional county rarities, inc Black-necked Grebe, Purple Heron, Spoonbill, Red Kite and Woodlark. *All year:* Common ducks and waterfowl, passerines, inc Tree Sparrow. *Spring/summer:* Passage waders inc Cur-lew, Ringed Plover, Dunlin, Redshank, Green & Common Sandpipers, both godwits. *Passage:* Black Tern, breeding Oystercatcher, Little Ringed Plover, Lapwing, warblers, hirundines. *Autumn:* Wader passage can inc Little Stint, Greenshank, Green, Wood, Curlew & Common Sand-pipers, and possible rarities. *Winter:* Occasional Bittern. Geese inc occasional White-fronted. Ducks inc Wigeon, Teal, Pintail, Shoveler, Pochard, Goosander (up to 50 in evening roosts) and occasional Goldeneye. Water Rail, vagrant raptors and owls, winter thrushes and large passerine flocks inc Redpoll, Linnet, Tree Sparrow, Reed Bunting and Yellowhammer.
Directions: SY5 6JT; SJ 548 062. Six miles SE of Shrews-bury in angle formed by A458 and minor road leading S to Pitchford. Entrance is 0.5 mile along minor road

which leaves A458, 0.5 mile SE of Cross Houses.

Public transport: Bus: 436 Shrewsbury to Bridgnorth, stops at Cross Houses, one mile walk from Venus Pool (partly along busy main road). Arriva Midlands North.

Visiting: Car park with height barrier, also small parking area for disabled visitors close to Main Hide. 5 hides (2 for SOS members only). Information boards. Public access inc 3 hides (pool-side, feeder and woodland/meadow). Please keep to footpaths shown on notice boards. Wheelchair-friendly paths to main hide and feeder hide. No dogs allowed.

Contact: www.shropshirebirds.com/index/guide-to-birding-sites/venus-pool-reserve/
Continue on A458 to Much Wenlock, whence take A4169 N to Telford and junction with A422. Head N and then R on to A464 to J4 with M54.

3 PRIORSLEE LAKE

Severn Trent Water/Friends of Priorslee Lake

Habitats: A man-made balancing lake, surrounded by woodland, rough grassland and three reedbeds.

Birds: 125+ spp (45 spp breeding). *Summer:* Warblers, inc Cetti's Reed & Garden Common Whitethroat. *Winter:* The nearby landfill site is long gone but gulls still stop off. Yellow-legged, Caspian & Great Black-backed occur most years. Check the wildfowl for less common spp such as Goosander and Goldeneye. Often Water Rail, finches, with Siskin in woodland, tits.

Other: Wide range of butterflies, dragonflies and other insects. Southern Marsh, Bee & Common Spotted Orchids.

Directions: TF2 9NS; SJ 720 095 (Teece Drive). In Telford between M54 and A5. Leave M54 going N (B5060) at J4 and park in lay-by (100 yards from J4) overlooking the lake. Alternatively park on lay-by alongside Teece Drive, Priorslee, Telford (very busy during school run) and walk forward. The Flash, Priorslee is a slightly smaller lake half a mile distant. Follow the stream that comes in at W end of Priorslee Lake or head for Derwent Drive, Priorslee.

Public transport: Teece Drive entrance is about two miles from Telford bus station, 1.25 miles from Telford train station.

Visiting: Open all hours. A permissive path around lake—can be muddy when wet. There is a public footpath around The Flash.

Contact: http://friendsofpriorsleelake.blogspot.co.uk
Return to Shrewsbury, then, from by-pass, take A528 for Ellesmere.

4 WOOD LANE

Shropshire Wildlife Trust

Habitats: 37 acre reservoir. Worked out sand and gravel pit (adjacent working quarry) with lagoons, islands and wetland.

Birds: 180+ spp recorded, 40 *breed* inc Little Ringed

Plover, Lapwing, Tree Sparrow, Yellowhammer. Large Sand Martin colony. *Passage:* Waders inc Greenshank, Redshank, Curlew, Whimbrel, Black-tailed Godwit, Green Sandpiper, Dunlin, Little Stint.

Other:

Directions: SY12 0KY; SJ 425 330. Take road for Colemere at Spunhill crossroads on A528 1.5 mile S of Ellesmere, Reserve car park (Tudor Griffiths) 0.75 mile.

Public transport: Bus: 501 Ellesmere-Shrewsbury (not Sun) runs along A528 but nearest stop in Ellesmere, Lakeside Coaches (01691 622761).

Visiting: Open all hours, free but permit required for entry code for 2 accessible hides. No facilities. Flat, some muddy areas. Working quarry, nearby vehicles may cross paths. No grazing animals, no dogs.

Contact: 01743 284280;
enquiries@shropshirewildlifetrust.org.uk
There are several nearby meres to the SE of Ellesmere that are not designated as nature reserves but that might be visited in conjunction with Wood Lane. They include:

White Mere:

SY12 0HU; SJ 415 332.

65 acres, margins wooded in parts, it lies to the S of the Spunhill crossroads, 1.5 miles S of Ellesmere, in the corner formed by the minor road to Spunhill and the A528 for Shrewsbury. An SSSI, it is immediately to the W of the A528 but is also home to the Shropshire Sailing Club.

Continue along the minor road from the Spunhill crossroads past Wood Lane. Do not take sharp L after Wood Lane but veer L at fork and continue to free car park of

Colemere Countryside Heritage Centre:
SY12 0QW; SJ436 328.

Open all hours, free, picnic site. Wooded margins and two hay meadows.

Snipe, Curlew on passage. *Wintering* Goldeneye and Pochard.

Take A495 for Whitchurch NE from the A528, entering Cheshire in the process, although, by the time you reach Whitchurch you will have returned to Shropshire. The following 3 mosses straddle the Shropshire/Cheshire border but, since Shropshire has just been stripped of Mortimer Forest for this edition, their entry is placed in Shropshire.

5 FENN'S, WHIXALL AND BETTISFIELD MOSSES

Natural England

Habitats: 2,000 acres of raised peatland meres and mosses. Llangollen Canal runs through middle

Birds: *All year:* Kingfisher, Skylark, Linnet. *Spring/summer:* Breeding Teal, Mallard, Nightjar, Hobby, Curlew, Tree Sparrow. *Winter:* Short-eared Owl.

Other: Water Vole, Brown Hare, Polecat, Adder, 670 spp. moths, 27 spp butterflies, nationally important for dragonflies (29 spp), inc White-faced Darter, 18 spp bog moss.

Directions: Fenn's Bank SY13 3NY; SJ 505 366. 4 miles SW of Whitchurch, to S of A495 between Fenn's Bank, Whixall and Bettisfield. Roadside parking at entrances, car parks at Morris's Bridge, Roundthorn Bridge, World's End and a large car park at Manor House. Disabled access by prior arrangement along railway line.
Public transport: None.
Visiting: Permit required except on Mosses Trail routes. Information panels at main entrances and leaflets are available when permits are applied for. 3 interlinking Mosses Trails explore the NNR and canal from Morris's and Roundthorn bridges.
Contact: Natural England, Manor House NNR Base: 0300 060 0269; peter.bowyer@naturalengland.org.uk
Continue into Whitchurch and head for **Cheshire** *on either the A41 (by-pass) or A49.*

Cheshire and Wirral

Spectacular numbers of waders can be seen along the Dee & Mersey estuaries during passage times and the winter (rising tides bring the birds in closer). During north-westerly autumn gales Leach's Petrels are pushed in to the tip of the Wirral peninsula, probably the best place in the UK to see them away from their breeding grounds. The north-eastern border of the county abuts the Peak District National Park.

Bird Atlases/Avifauna
Rare and Scarce Birds in Cheshire and Wirral
Allan Conlin & Eddie Williams
(privately published, 2017).
Birds in Cheshire and Wirral:
A Breeding and Wintering Atlas
David Norman
(Liverpool University Press, 2008).

Bird Recorder
Jane Turner: countyrec@cawos.org

Bird Report
Cheshire & Wirral Bird Report (1964), from CAWOS—David Hiley, 23 Greenfield Road, Waverton, Chester, CH3 7NE: 07484 836 652; davidhiley@cawos.org

BTO Regional Representatives
Mid, The Wirral
Paul Miller
North and East, South
Hugh Pulsford:
Wetland Bird Survey (WeBS)
Local Organizers: webs@bto.org

Cheshire (North)
Vacant
Cheshire (South)
Paul Miller

Clubs
Cheshire & Wirral Ornithological Society (1988; 270)
David Hiley (Sec): info@cawos.org; www.cawos.org
Meetings: Meetings by zoom or in person. Contact/see website for details.
Knutsford Ornithological Society (1974; 38)
Karina Stanley (Sec): 01565 634 417;
secretary@10X50.com; www.10x50.com
Meetings: 8pm, 4th Friday of the month (Sep-Apr). Jubilee Hall, 18-24 Stanley Road, Knutsford, WA16 0GP. Monthly field trips (Sep-Jul),
monthly evening walks (May-Jul)
Lancashire & Cheshire Fauna Society
See Lancashire.
Mid-Cheshire Ornithological Society (1962; 65)
Secretary: via website; www.midcheshireos.co.uk
Meetings: 7:45pm, 2nd Friday of the month (Oct-Apr). Cuddington and Sandiway Village Hall, Norley Road, Cuddington, CW8 2LB.
Nantwich Natural History Society (1979; 80)
Roger Crow: 07393 367 978; roger.crow@hotmail.co.uk
Meetings: No indoor meetings but regular social evenings relating to field work and surveys, usually in The Vine Pub, 42 Hospital Street, Nantwich, CW5 5RP.
South East Cheshire Ornithological Society (1964; 109)
Jean Harrison (Sec): via website; www.secos.org.uk
Meetings: 7:30pm, 2nd Friday of the month (Sep-Apr). Ettiley Heath Church Community Centre, Elton Road, Ettiley Heath, Sandbach, CW11 3NE.
Wilmslow Guild Birdwatching Group (1965; 65)
All members of the WGBG are required to be members of the Wilmslow Guild: 01625 523 903.
info@guildlifelonglearning.org;
www.guildlifelonglearning.org/
Stuart Mollison (Chairman WGBG): 07505 254 306; rsm898@gmail.com; http://wgbwcopy.wikidot.com/wgbg
Meetings: 7:30pm, usually 1st or 2nd Thursday of the month (Sep-Apr). Wilmslow Guild, 1 Bourne Street, Wilmslow, SK9 5HD.
Wirral Bird Club (1977; 100)
Bill Wonderley: 07795 148 140;
wirralbirdclub77@gmail.com;
www.wirralbirdclub.com
Meetings: 7:30pm, 4th Thursday of the month (Sep-Nov and Jan-Jul). St Bridget's Church Centre, Church Road, West Kirby, Wirral, CH48 7HL.

Ringing Groups/Bird Observatory

Cheshire Swan Study Group:
cheshireswansightings@gmail.com
www.cheshireswanstudygroup.wordpress.com
South Manchester RG
Hilbre Bird Observatory
Phil Woollen: secretary@hilbrebirdobs.org.uk;
http://hilbrebirdobs.blogspot.com

RSPB Local Groups

Chester (1988; 140)
Dot Seed: rspbchester@googlegroups.com;
https://group.rspb.org.uk/chester/
Meetings: 7:30pm, 3rd Wednesday of the month (Sep-Apr). Christleton Parish Hall, Village Road, Christleton, CH3 7AS.
Macclesfield (1979; 130)
secretary@macclesfieldRSPB.org.uk;
https://group.rspb.org.uk/macclesfield/
Meetings: No longer held. Focus on fundraising.
Wirral (1982; 100)
Jeremy Bradshaw: wirralrspblocalgroup@gmail.com;
https://group.rspb.org.uk/wirral/
Meetings: 7:30pm, 1st Thursday of the month (Sep-Jun). Hoylake Community Centre, Hoyle Road, Hoylake, Wirral CH47 3AG.

Wildlife Trust

Cheshire Wildlife Trust (1962; 17,500)
Bickley Hall Farm, Bickley, Malpas, SY14 8EF:
01948 820 728; reserves@cheshirewt.org.uk;
www.cheshirewildlifetrust.org.uk

Entering Cheshire from Whitchurch.

1 BICKLEY HALL FARM

Cheshire Wildlife Trust
Habitats: 215-acre working organic farm & CWT HQ with hay meadows, wet grassland, margins, wild bird seed crops, ponds, hedgerows.
Birds: All Year: Stock Dove, Barn & Little Owls, Yellow-hammer, Reed Bunting. *Spring/Summer:* Lapwing (scarce breeder), Quail (rare), Hobby, Cuckoo, Yellow Wagtail. *Winter:* Teal, Wigeon, Lapwing, Snipe, Green Sandpiper, Stonechat, winter thrushes. Finches etc using stubble (inc. Brambling, Tree Sparrow, Linnet).
Other: 21 spp butterflies, 18 spp Dragonflies. Great Crested Newt.
Directions: SY14 8EF; SJ 529 476. Four miles N of Whitchurch. Take A41 or A49 N from Whitchurch, turn in to Bickley Lane from either road. Look for CWT sign on S side of road.
Public transport: None.
Visiting: Sandstone Trail walking route accessible all hours (off Bickley Lane). Parking, toilets and other routes open Mon-Fri 10am-3pm. Circular trail around farm, hide overlooking Bar Mere. Out of hours parking on Bickley Lane where Sandstone Trail crosses road.
Contact: Cheshire Wildlife Trust: 01948 820 728; info@cheshirewt.org.uk
Continue on A41 to Chester and then A450.

2 DEE ESTUARY
(BURTON MERE WETLANDS)

RSPB
Habitats: Former farm and fishery now converted to freshwater wetland, mixed farmland and woodland.
Birds: Little Egret, Great White Egret now breeding and

9	Alderley Woods
1	Bickley Hall Farm
2	Burton Mere Wetlands
7	Delamere Forest

6	Frodsham Marsh
5	Gowy Meadows
3	Hilbre Island
4	North Wirral Coastal Park
8	Trentabank Reservoir
10	Woolston Eyes

winter roosts in double figures, Cattle Egret has bred twice, Bittern regular and bred in '22. *Spring/summer:* Avocet, Grasshopper Warbler, Lesser Whitethroat and other commoner warblers, passage Black-tailed Godwit, Spotted Redshank and regular Mediterranean Gull. Hobby, Marsh Harrier, Spoonbill (bred in '25). *Autumn:* Passage waders inc Little Stint, Ruff, Spotted Redshank, Green, Curlew & Wood Sandpipers. *Winter:* Whooper & Bewick's (now very scarce) Swans, Teal, Water Rail, Hen Harrier, Fieldfare, Redwing, Water Pipit, Linnet, Brambling (not regular).

Other: Extensive butterfly list. Pipistrelle, Noctule, Daubenton's Bats, Water Vole, wide array of orchids. Red-eyed Damselfly.

Directions: CH64 5SF; SJ 319 739. Located on the Wirral. From Chester High Road (A540) follow signs for Burton Mere Wetlands. Turn down Puddington Lane, reserve's entrance is just outside Burton Village.

Public transport: Bus: 22A stops in Burton Village but not Sun; 487 Liverpool (Whitechapel) to bus stop at Ness Botanic Gardens, 1.5 miles from reserve. Arriva in North West.

Visiting: Open daily 9am-9pm/dusk if earlier. Large car park, not suitable for coaches/larger minibuses (groups should ring for advice). Visitor centre open 9:30am-5pm (4:30pm Nov-Jan). Admission charge for non-RSPB members. Refreshments, toilets inc disabled. 3 hides and 3 viewing screens overlooking pools and wetland area, picnic tables. Signposted trails—wheelchair access to footpaths and hides. Guided walks and binocular hire. Guide dogs only.

Contact: RSPB: 0151 353 2720;
deeestuary@rspb.org.uk
Continue along A540 to NW tip of the Wirral.

3 HILBRE ISLAND LNR

Wirral Council

Habitats: Sandflats, rocky shore and open sea.

Birds: *Late summer/autumn:* Seabird passage inc Gannets, terns, skuas, shearwaters and after NW gales good numbers of Leach's Petrel. *Passage:* Migrants. *Winter:* Wader roosts at high tide, Purple Sandpiper, Turnstone, sea ducks, divers, grebes.

Other: Nationally scarce Rock Sea-lavender and Sea Spleenwort. Field Vole, Grey Seal. Whales and dolphins.

Directions: CH48 0QG. SJ 208 866 (Dee Lane, West Kirby). SJ 184 880 (main island). 3 tidal islands in mouth of Dee Estuary. Park in West Kirby on A540 Chester to Hoylake road. Follow brown Marine Lake signs to Dee Lane pay & display car park (or free parking along promenade). Coach parking available in West Kirby.

Public transport: Bus: 437 Liverpool (Union Court) to West Kirby, within 0.5 mile of Dee Lane slipway. Arriva in North West. Train—West Kirby.

Visiting: 2 mile walk across sands from Dee Lane slipway—**DO NOT** cross either way within 3.5 hours of high water—*check* noticeboard at slipway for tide times and suggested safe routes. No disabled access. Permit required for groups of six or more (apply to Wirral Country Park Visitor Centre—see below). Composting toilets on main island (Hilbre) and at Wirral Sailing Centre (end of Dee Lane, West Kirby). Leaflets and tide times available at Visitor Centre. Visits to Hilbre Bird Observatory by prior appointment only.

Contact: Wirral Country Park Visitor Centre, Station Road, Thustaston, Wirral CH61 0HN: 0151 648 4371; wcp@wirral.gov.uk
Hilbre Island Bird Observatory:
secretary@hilbrebirdobs.org.uk;
http://hilbrebirdobs.blogspot.co.uk
Take A540 (Meols Drive) and then A553 (Market Street) to Moreton.

4 NORTH WIRRAL COASTAL PARK

Wirral Council

Habitats: Saltmarsh.

Birds: Important as a feeding and roosting site for passage and wintering flocks of waders, wildfowl, terns and gulls inc wintering Knot (20,000+), Bar-tailed Godwit (2,000+) and Dunlin (10,000). Redshank (1,000+) and Turnstone (500+) feed on the rocky shore at Perch Rock and on rocky sea walls. Oystercatcher (500+), Curlew, Grey Plover and Black-tailed Godwit regularly roost here in relatively high numbers. Small numbers of wildfowl, inc Common Scoter, Scaup and Goldeneye, Red-throated Diver and Great Crested Grebe also frequently winter.

Other: Sea Holly, Marram Grass, Storksbill, Burnet Rose and rarities like the Isle of Man Cabbage. One of two known sites in world for very rare British subspecies of Belted Beauty moth.

Directions: CH46 4TA; SJ 241 909. Located between outer Dee and Mersey Estuaries. From Moreton take A553 E, then A551 N. Turn L on to Tarran Way South then R on to Lingham Lane. Parking available by lighthouse. Foreshore can be viewed from footpath which runs alongside.

Public transport: Bus routes along Leasowe Road, Pasture Road and Harrison Drive. Train—area served by Grove Road (Wallasey), Leasowe, Moreton, and Meols Merseyrail stations.

Visiting: Open all hours. Various car parks, toilet blocks, picnic areas, extensive network of footpaths and public bridleways. Wirral Country Park Visitor Centre open daily (not 25 Dec) 10am-4:45pm, located Heswall and West Kirby, off A540—has toilets, hide, cafe, kiosk (all wheelchair accessible).

Contact: Wirral Country Park Visitor Centre, Station Road, Thustaston, Wirral CH61 0HN: 0151 648 4371; wcp@wirral.gov.uk
Hilbre Island Bird Obs:
secretary@hilbrebirdobs.org.uk;

http://hilbrebirdobs.blogspot.co.uk
Take M53 back SE along Wirral.

5 GOWY MEADOWS

Cheshire Wildlife Trust
Habitats: Lowland grazing marsh.
Birds: 160 spp recorded. *All year:* Cetti's Warbler, Stonechat. *Spring/summer:* Common warblers inc Reed & Sedge. *Winter:* Wildfowl, inc Shoveler, Pintail, Pink-footed Goose, Green Sandpiper, Jack Snipe.
Other: Otter, Water Vole, 360 spp moths, 83 spp hoverfly, Lesser Silver Water Beetle, Pond Mud Snail. Butterflies, dragonflies,
Directions: CH2 4HU; SJ 441 745. E of Ellesmere Port. Take A5117 from Ellesmere Port/J10 of M53 and head E, turn R for Thornton-le-Moors. Park on L by church—entrance other side of road.
Public transport: Bus: 2, Chester to Runcorn picks up at Ellesmere Port Bus Station, then alight at Thornton-le-Moors (not Sun). Stagecoach. Train—Ellesmere Port.
Visiting: Open all year. 2.5 miles of walking trails across reserve (not suitable for wheelchairs). Dogs on lead.
Contact: Cheshire Wildlife Trust:
01948 820 728; info@cheshirewt.org.uk
Take M56 from M53. Exit for Frodsham at J12.

6 FRODSHAM MARSH

Manchester Ship Canal Company
Habitats: Saltmarsh, mudflats, embanked tanks to hold river dredgings, reedbeds, farmland and river.
Birds: 20+ spp wader, inc large flocks of Redshank, Black-tailed Godwit, Dunlin. *Summer:* Breeding Oystercatcher, Ringed & Little Ringed Plovers, Grasshopper, Sedge & Reed Warblers. *Autumn:* Hobbies hunt. *Winter:* Wildfowl, inc Whooper Swan, Pink-footed Goose, Shelduck, Pochard, Pintail, Wigeon and other common species, Raven, Short-eared Owl, Hen Harrier, Peregrine Falcon. Passage migrants inc wagtails, pipits, terns, Garganey, Wheatear and Whinchat.
Directions: WA6 7BN; SJ 511 779 (Marsh Lane), SJ 520 785 (Weaver Bend/Ship Street). Large area of mixed habitat lying alongside Manchester Ship Canal, SW of Runcorn. Close to Frodsham town centre. Take Ship Street, off High Street, turn L into Weaver's Lane and cross over M56 (to access Weaver's Bend). Take Marsh Lane, off Main Street, take R fork at Marsh Green Cottages and cross over M56. (to access main marsh).
Public transport: None.
Visiting: Open all hours. Park just before concrete bridge, walk along grassy track to barrier gates and then towards vantage points overlooking Rivers Mersey and Weaver. Wheelchair access difficult.
Contact: None.
Either continue on M56 and junction with M6 and go straight to 10 Woolston Eyes or take B5152 S from Frodsham town centre to

7 DELAMERE FOREST

Forestry England
Habitats: Woodland (broadleaved and conifer), lake, remnant heathland.
Birds: All year: Common woodland spp, inc Redpoll, Siskin. Crossbill. *Summer:* Black-headed Gull colony on Blakemere (lake), warblers, Pied & Spotted Flycatchers, Redstart. *Winter:* Wildfowl inc Mandarin, Wigeon, Teal, Gadwall and Goosander.
Other: Dragonflies inc White-faced Darter. Common Lizard, bats.
Directions: CW8 2HZ; SJ 548 705. Take A51/A54 from Chester then A556. After 1.2 miles turn L on to B5152, entrance to Forest Centre is one miles on L.
Public transport: Train—Delamere (regular services between Chester and Manchester)—short walk to Forest Centre.
Visiting: Open daily (not 25 Dec), 8am-8pm summer, 6pm winter. 3 pay & display car parks—Forest Centre (next to facilities), Treetops (next to Delamere station), Whitefield (on B5152 N of Delamere). Visitor centre, cafe, toilets inc disabled. Trails, information, events, cycle hire. Also free car park (Barnsbridge)—continue on B5152 to Hatchmere, turn L on to Ashton Road, car park on L (some lay-by parking on Ashton Road).
Contact: Forestry England: 0300 067 4340; delamere@forestryengland.uk
Continue S on A5152 to junction with A556. Head E to junction with A5033. From Knutsford take A537 for Macclesfield.

8 TRENTABANK RESERVOIR

Cheshire Wildlife Trust
Habitats: Reservoir surrounded by conifer plantation. [Other reservoirs in area (viewable from roads) and further access into Macclesfield Forest.]
Birds: Small heronry. *All year:* Raven, Crossbill, common coniferous woodland spp. *Spring/autumn:* (when water levels expose the banks) Green Sandpiper, Little Ringed Plover. *Summer:* Common Sandpiper, Woodcock (roding). *Winter:* Wildfowl inc Goldeneye, Goosander.
Other: Red Deer, variety of butterflies and dragonflies.
Directions: SK11 0NS; SJ 961 711. Three miles SE of Macclesfield. Head out of Macclesfield on A537 Buxton Road, take minor road signposted Tegg's Nose Country park. After 0.7 miles turn R and continue to Langley, turn L at T-junction. After another 0.8 miles turn R (by Ridgegate Reservoir) and then L for 250 yards to reservoir car park/visitor centre.
Public transport: None.
Visiting: Open all year. The woodland trail and heronry viewpoint is opposite car park entrance. Access to reservoir itself is by permit only. Visitor centre may be open on selected weekends. Toilets. Dogs on leads.
Contact: Cheshire Wildlife Trust:
01948 820 728; info@cheshirewt.org.uk

Return to Macclesfield, take B5087 for Alderley Edge.

9 ALDERLEY WOODS
National Trust
Habitats: Woodland on red sandstone escarpment, lowland heath, grassland, ponds, wildflower meadow
Birds: Common woodland birds inc Tawny Owl, 3 spp woodpeckers. *Spring/summer:* Woodcock, Redstart, Tree Pipit, Pied & Spotted Flycatchers, Wood Warbler and other common warblers. *Winter:* Thrushes, finches.
Other: Polecat. 7 spp bat. 20+ spp butterflies. Rare Bryophytes
Directions: SK10 4UB; SJ 859 772. 1.5 miles E of Alderley Edge village (off A34, S of Manchester) on B5087, Macclesfield Road. Car Park on L just past The Wizard Tea Room.
Public transport: Bus: 130 Macclesfield-Alderley Edge. Alight at Nether Alderley Primary School, follow Bradford Lane to Macclesfield Road. D&G Bus (01270 252 970). Train—Alderley Edge, 1.5 miles from car park.
Visiting: Woods open all hours. Pay & display car park with information open 8am-8pm (closes 5pm in winter, when clocks change), no coaches. Toilets. 5 waymarked colour-coded trails (each 1-2 miles).
Contact: National Trust: 01625 584 412; alderleyedge@nationaltrust.org.uk
From Alderley Edge take B5085 to Knutsford and then A5033 and A556 to J19 of M6. Head N.

10 WOOLSTON EYES
Woolston Eyes Conservation Group
Habitats: Wetland, marsh, scrubland, wildflower meadow areas.
Birds: 244 spp. *Breeding:* Black-necked Grebe, variety of duck, good number of warblers inc Grasshopper, raptors (Merlin, Peregrine Falcon, Marsh Harrier). *Passage:* Waders. *Winter:* Wildfowl, winter thrushes.
Other: 25 mammal spp inc 5 spp bat. 278 spp Lepidoptera inc 27 spp butterflies. 23 spp dragonflies. Notable plants inc Pyramidal, Marsh & Bee Orchids, Helleborine, Snakeshead Fritillary and Cowslip.
Directions: WA4 1PD; SJ 654 888. E of Warrington between River Mersey and Manchester Ship Canal. Off J21 of M6, take New Manchester Road (A57), take 2nd L into Weir Lane (footpath only)—do not park at bottom end of Weir Lane. Vehicle access via Thelwell Lane, Latchford—permit and key required: WA4 1PD SJ 638 873.
Public transport: Buses from Warrington Bus Interchange. (Weir Lane) 3 to Martinscroft. (Thelwall Lane), 1 or 2 to Westy (Whitley Ave) and walk to E end of Thelwall Lane. Warrington's Own Buses (01925 634 296).
Visiting: Open all year from 8am-dusk. Permits required—apply online from website. Hides and raised platform. Dogs on lead—pick up waste and take away with you.

Contact: via website; www.woolstoneyes.com
You are now just to the W of Manchester.

Manchester (Greater)

Despite being a largely urban area, there are some excellent sites for birdwatching. The former colliery workings of Pennington and Wigan Flashes are probably the best all-round sites, with a wide range of species including, from time to time, rarities. Dipper and a good selection of woodland birds, including Pied Flycatcher, can be found at Etherow Country Park.

Bird Recorder
Ian McKerchar, 42 Green Ave, Astley, Manchester, M29 7EH: 01942 701 758 & 07958 687 481; ianmckerchar1@gmail.com

Bird Reports
Birds In Greater Manchester (1959-2012), publication ceased and back copies no longer available from Bird Recorder.
The Greater Manchester area is covered by: www.manchesterbirding.com
Leigh Ornithological Society Bird Report (1971-), latest report for members only, then as download from website after a year: www.leighos.org.uk

BTO Regional Representatives
Nick Hilton:
Wetland Bird Survey (WeBS)
Local Organizer: webs@bto.org
Tim Wilcox

Clubs
Altrincham and District Natural History Society (1908; 25) Mike Pettipher (Chairman): info@altnats.org.uk; www.altnats.org.uk
Meetings: 7:30pm, usually 2nd Tuesday of the month (Sep-Apr). The Jubilee Centre, The Firs, Bowdon, Altrincham, WA14 2TQ. Some talks via zoom—contact/see website for details.
Leigh Ornithological Society (1971; 90)
Paul Pennington (Chairman):
 leighos.chairman@gmail.com;
www.leighos.org.uk
LOS Young Birders: www.losybc.blogspot.co.uk
Meetings: 7:30pm, 1st Friday of the month (c.10 talks Sep-May)—contact/see website for details. Derby Room, Leigh Library, Turnpike Centre, Civic Square, Leigh, WN7 1EB.

Rochdale Field Naturalists' Society (1874; 100+)
Ian Short (Secretary): rfns_enquiries@btinternet.com;
www.rochdalefieldnaturalists.org.uk
Meetings: 7:30pm, usually 2nd Thursday of the month
(Sep-Apr). Cutgate Baptist Church, Edenfield Rd, Roch-
dale, OL11 5AQ, also local walks and coach/car trips.
Contact/see website for details.

Ringing Groups/Bird Observatory
Leigh RG
South Manchester RG

RSPB Local Groups
High Peak (1974; 100)
David Knass: highpeakgroup2@gmail.com;
https://group.rspb.org.uk/highpeak/
Meetings: 7:30pm, 3rd Monday of the month (Sep-May,
not Dec). Marple Senior Citizens Hall, Memorial Park,
Marple, Stockport, SK6 6BA.
Stockport.(1979; 100)
Martin Durrell: stockportrspblocal@gmail.com;
https://group.rspb.org.uk/stockport/
Meetings: 7:30pm, 2nd Monday of the month (Sep-May).
Stockport Masonic Guildhall, 169-171 Wellington Road
South, Stockport, SK1 3UA.
Manchester Swift Project
The nascent Salford Local Group has metamorphosed
into a Mancester Swift Project. This has a facebook page
but I won't follow any link to facebook as a matter of
principle. For more info you can e-mail:
Alasdair.Mckee@rspb.org.uk

Wildlife Trust
See **Lancashire and North Merseyside.**

As with **London**, no attempt is made here to guide you from
site to site. They are, very roughly, arranged in an anti-clock-
wise circle leading you from **Cheshire** to **Lancashire**. To
visit any individual site, follow the instructions in the relevant
Directions section.

1 PENNINGTON FLASH COUNTRY PARK

Wigan Council
Habitats: Lowland lake, ponds and scrapes, fringed with
reeds, rough grassland, scrub and woodland.
Birds: 240+ spp inc many county firsts and rarities. All
year: Waterfowl. Feeding station attracts Willow Tit,
Stock Dove and up to 40 Bullfinches. Spring/autumn
passage: Waders (14+ spp) and terns (4+ spp). Summer:
Breeding inc Common Tern, Ringed & Little Ringed
Plover, nine spp warbler. Winter: Peregrine Falcon, Merlin, large gull roost (with occasional white-winged gulls),
Siskin, Brambling.
Other: Several spp orchid inc Bee Orchid. Wide variety
of butterflies and dragonflies.
Directions: WN7 3PA; SJ 640 990. One mile from Leigh
town centre and well signposted from A580 East Lancashire Road. Main entrance on A572 (St Helens Road).
Public transport: Bus—one mile from Leigh bus station,
589 and 590 stop on St Helens Road near entrance
to park. Transport for Greater Manchester (0161 244
1000).
Visiting: Park open all hours. Main car park pay & display (coach parking/group visits available if booked in
advance) Toilets (inc disabled) and information point
open 9am-dusk (not 25 Dec), catering. Main paths flat,
suitable for disabled. Seven hides, nature trails. Site leaflet available.
Contact: Wigan Council: 01942 489 007.

2 GATLEY CARRS

Stockport Metropolitan Borough Council
Habitats: Woodland, grassland, willow carr, scrub,
ponds, stream.
Birds: All year: Common woodland spp, Grey Heron,
Buzzard, Sparrowhawk, Ring-necked Parakeet, Tawny
Owl, Kingfisher, Bullfinch. Summer: Blackcap, Whiteth-
roat, Willow Warbler, Chiffchaff, possible Redstart, Pied
Flycatcher. Winter: Snipe, Grey Wagtail, Redwing, Field-
fare.
Other: Butterflies, dragonflies.
Directions: SK8 4BL; SJ 842 888. S of Manchester in
Gatley. From A34 (S of M60) turn R on to A560 (Gat-
ley Road). Continue until reaching old Tatton Cinema/
Horse & Farrier pub (on R)—brown sign here (**Gatley
Carrs**)—R into Old Hall Road, L into Brookside Road
and continue to car park.
Public transport: Bus—various services to Gatley.
Train—Gatley (0.3 mile walk to reserve entrance
along Cambridge Road/Brookside Road). Transport for
Greater Manchester (0161 244 1000).
Visiting: Open all hours. Car park, locked at dusk. Various paths, dipping pond. Much of management carried
out by volunteer group… new members always welcome
Contact: Gatley Carrs Conservation Group:
enquiries@gatleycarrs.org.uk;
www.gatleycarrs.org.uk/index.shtml

3 ETHEROW COUNTRY PARK

Stockport Metropolitan Borough Council
Habitats: River Etherow, woodlands, marshy area,
ponds and surrounding moorland.
Birds: 100+ spp inc Sparrowhawk, Buzzard, Woodcock,
3 spp woodpeckers, Dipper, warblers inc Wood & Gar-
den, Pied Flycatcher, Winter: Brambling, Siskin, Water
Rail. Merlin and Raven over hills.
Other: 200 spp of plants.
Directions: SK6 5JD; SJ 965 908. Site lies at halfway
point on 12-mile Valley Way Footpath linking Stockport

4	Chorlton Water Park
3	Etherow Country Park
2	Gatley Carrs
I	Pennington Flash CP
5	Wigan Flashes

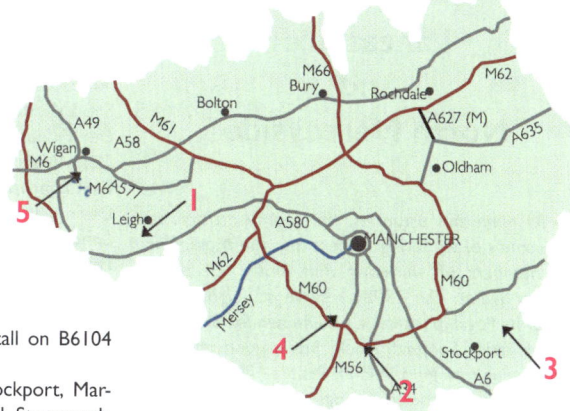

and Woolley Bridge. Situated at Compstall on B6104 near Romiley, Stockport.

Public transport: Bus: 383 and 384 Stockport, Marple/Romiley circular—alight at Compstall. Stagecoach. Train—Romiley and Marple Bridge.

Visiting: Parkland open all hours—permit required for conservation area (contact first for info). Pay & display car park. Visitor centre open (not 25 Dec) 11am-4pm (when possible), cafe (10am-4pm summer, 10am-3pm winter) and toilets. 1 hide, nature trail, Keep to paths. Motorized wheelchairs available (free), book in advance. *Contact:* Etherow Country Park Visitor Centre: 0161 427 6937.

4 CHORLTON WATER PARK LNR

Manchester City Council

Habitats: Lake, woodland, grassland.

Birds: Summer: Common wildfowl, Grey Heron, Great Crested Grebe. *Winter:* Wldfowl inc Tufted Duck, Pochard, Goldeneye, Goosander. Kingfisher, Siskin plus occasional rarities. Barlow Tip (W side of lake)—warblers in summer, Woodcock, Jack Snipe, Short-eared Owl possible in winter .

Directions: M21 7WH; SJ 824 916. S of city centre. Head S on A5103. Turn R on to A5145 (Barlow Moor Road) then after 350 yards turn L into Maitland Avenue—free parking at the end of this road.

Public transport: Metrolink Tram stop—Barlow Moor Road, Chorlton (0.6 miles). Buses: 23 (Trafford Centre-Stockport), 86 (Chorlton-Piccadilly Gardens) & 766 (Davyhulme-Hale Barns) all travel along A5145 (alight at Aldermary Road stop and walk 50-100 yards W to Maitland Ave).

Visiting: Open dawn-dusk. Car park, toilets, network of accessible paths, picnic benches.

Contact: Manchester City Council, parks@manchester.gov.uk
Friends of Chorlton Water Park:

5 WIGAN FLASHES

Wildlife Trust for Lancs, Manchester & N. Merseyside/ Wigan Council

Habitats: Open water, reedbed, fen, rough grassland, wet woodland and scrub. 650 acres.

Birds: 200+ spp *Summer:* Nationally important for Willow Tit. Common Tern, Water Rail, Reed, Sedge, Cetti's & Grasshopper Warblers, Kingfisher. *Passage:* Black Tern. *Winter:* Bittern, wildfowl, especially diving duck and Gadwall.

Other: Interesting orchids, 6 spp inc Marsh and Dune Helleborine. One of UK's largest feeding assemblage of Noctule Bats. Water Vole. 18 spp dragonflies, has inc Red-veined Darter.

Directions: WN3 5NY; SD 585 030. Leave M6 at J25 head N on A49, turn R on to Poolstock Lane (B5238)—car park 0.75 mile on R. Also parking on Welham Road—after turning into Poolstock Lane turn R (0.3 mile) into Carr Lane then L into Welham Road, just before school. Can access reserve from banks of Leeds and Liverpool Canal.

Public transport: Bus: 607 Wigan to Ashton Heath passes along Poolstock Lane. Diamond Bus North West (01942 888 893).

Visiting: Open all hours. Poolstock Lane car park has 300 spaces—access for coaches, contact reserve manager. Network of footpaths, areas suitable for wheelchairs. Six hide screens.

Contact: WT for Lancashire, Manchester & N. Merseyside; 01942 233 976; mchampion@lancswt.org.uk

Lancashire and North Merseyside

With its numerous estuaries, the county attracts tens of thousands of wintering waders and the Mosses hold large numbers of wintering Pink-footed Geese and Whooper Swans. The RSPB's reserve at Leighton Moss is one of its flagship reserves, well known for Bittern and Marsh Harrier. Seaforth Docks has a good reputation for attracting rare gulls. Inland, Pendle Hill regularly attracts Dotterel on spring passage.

Bird Atlases/Avifauna
The Birds of Lancashire and North Merseyside
Steve White, Barry McCarthy & Maurice Jones (Hobby Publications, 2008).
Atlas of Breeding Birds of Lancashire and North Merseyside 1997-2000
Robert Pyefinch & Peter Golborn (Hobby Publications, 2001).

Bird Recorder
Steve White, 102 Minster Court, Crown Street, Liverpool, L7 3QD: 0151 707 2744;
stevewhite102@btinternet.com

Bird Reports
Lancashire Bird Report (1914-), from LACFS—Dave Bickerton (Hon Sec), 64 Petre Crescent, Rishton, Blackburn, BB1 4RB: sec@lacfs.org.uk
Birds of Lancaster and District (1959-), from LDBWS—Dan Haywood (Sec): ldbws.info@gmail.com
01254 679 094; blackburnbirdclub@gmail.com
Chorley and District Natural History Society Annual Report (1975-), published online:
www.chorleynats.org.uk
East Lancashire Ornithologists' Club Bird Report (1982-), from ELOC—David Chew (Sec), Lower Wheathead Barn, Wheathead Lane, Blacko, Nelson, BB9 6PD: 01282 695 649; djchew@btinternet.com
Fylde Bird Report (1983-), from FBC—online:
www.fyldebirdclub.org

BTO Regional Representatives
East Lancashire
Helen Whitehead
Merseyside
Drew Lyness
North-West Lancashire
Drew Lyness
South Lancashire
Mark & Heather Walsh

Wetland Bird Survey (WeBS)
Local Organizers: webs@bto.org
Alt Estuary
Steve White
Dee Estuary (Clwyd/Merseyside)
Colin Wells:
East Lancashire and Fylde
David Jefferies
Lancashire—North (Inland)
Peter Marsh
Lancashire—West (Inland)
Mark Walsh
Mersey Estuary
Dermot Smith
Merseyside (Inland)
David Broome
Morecambe Bay (North)
See **Cumbria**
Morecambe Bay (South) & River Lune
Jean Roberts
Ribble Estuary
Ken Abram

Clubs
Lancashire and Cheshire Fauna Society (1914; 220)
Dave Bickerton (Hon Sec), 64 Petre Crescent, Rishton, BB1 4RB: 07779 822 091; sec@lacfs.org.uk; www.lacfs.org.uk
Meetings: No indoor meetings held except the AGM on the 1st Saturday of Mar.
Blackburn Bird Club (1991; 100)
John Collins (Sec): 01254 208 479; blackburnbirdclub@gmail.com; www.blackburnbirdclub.com
Meetings: 7:30pm, normally 1st Monday of the month (Oct-Apr). Feniscowles Methodist Church, Preston Old Road, Blackburn, BB2 5ER.
Chorley and District Natural History Society (1979; 150)
Paul West (Sec): secretary@chorleynats.org.uk; www.chorleynats.org.uk
Meetings: 7:30pm, 3rd Thursday of the month (Sep-Apr). St Mary's Parish Centre, West Street, off Devonshire Road, Chorley, PR7 2SR.
East Lancashire Ornithologists' Club (1955; 70)
Adrienne Lancaster (Sec): elocsecretary@gmail.com; www.eastlancsornithologists.org.uk
Meetings: 7:30pm, 1st Tuesday of the month (Sep-May). Higham Village Hall, Higham Hall Road. BB12 9EU.
Fylde Bird Club (1982; 240)
Paul Ellis (Sec), 22 Beach Rd, Preesall, Poulton le Fylde, FY6 0HQ: 07788 264 116; fyldebirdclub@gmail.com; www.fyldebirdclub.org
contact/see website for details.
Fylde Naturalists' Society (1946; 90)
Julie McGough (Sec): 01253 883 785;

secretary@fyldenaturalists.co.uk;
www.fyldenaturalists.co.uk
Meetings: 7:15pm, 2nd Wednesday of the month (Sep-Mar). Forest Gate Baptist Church Hall, off Whitegate Drive, Blackpool, FY3 9AW.

Lancaster and District Birdwatching Society (1959; 200)
Dan Haywood (Sec): ldbws.info@gmail.com;
www.lancasterbirdwatching.org.uk
Meetings: 7:30pm, last Monday of the month (Sep-Nov/Jan-Mar)—contact/see website for details.

Merseyside Naturalists' Association (1938; 100)
Sabena Blackbird (Chairman), 18 Ludlow Grove, Bromborough, Wirral CH62 7JH: chairman@mnapage.info;
www.mnapage.info
Meetings: Contact/see website for details.

Preston Society Bird Watching & Natural History
(1876/Preston Scientific Society; 100). Secretary:
07565 497 065; via website; www.prestonsociety.co.uk
Meetings: 7:30pm, Monday evenings (Oct-Mar). St. Mary's Church, Church Avenue, Penwortham, PR1 0AH, plus monthly walks and reserve visits.
Monday evening walks in spring and summer.

Rossendale Ornithologists' Club (1976; 175 online)
http://rocforum.activeboard.com
Meetings: 7:15pm, 3rd Monday of the month (check the forum for details). Weavers Cottage, Bacup Road, Rawtenstall, BB4 7NW.

Ringing Groups/Bird Observatory
Fylde RG
Merseyside RG: www.merseysiderg.org.uk
North Lancashire RG (inc *North Heysham Bird Obs*):
www.heyshamobservatory.blogspot.com
South West Lancs RG

RSPB Local Groups
Bolton (1978; 60)
Terry Delaney: terry.delaney@sky.com;
https://group.rspb.org.uk/bolton/
Meetings: 7:30pm, 2nd Thursday of the month (Sep-Apr). Harwood Methodist Church, Longsight, Harwood, Bolton, BL2 3HX.
Liverpool (1972; 155)
Kevin Parr: kevinparr@aol.com;
https://group.rspb.org.uk/liverpool/
Meetings: 7:30pm, 3rd Monday of the month (Sep-Apr, usually 1st Monday in Dec). Mossley Hill Parish Church Hall, Rose Lane, Liverpool, L18 8DB.
Southport (1974; 79)
Ian Wright: iwrightstretton@aol.com;
https://group.rspb.org.uk/southport/
Meetings: 7:45pm, 3rd Friday of the month (Sep-May). Birkdale United Reformed Church hall, Grosvenor Road, Southport, PR8 2ET.
Wigan (1972; 140)

Neil Martin: neimaz07@yahoo.co.uk;
https://group.rspb.org.uk/wigan/
Meetings: 7:45pm, 2nd Tuesday of the month (Sep-Apr). St Anne's Parish Hall, Church Lane, Shevington, Wigan, WN6 8BD.

Wildlife Trust
The Wildlife Trust for Lancashire, Manchester and North Merseyside
(1962; 28,000)
The Barn, Berkeley Drive,
Bamber Bridge, Preston,
Lancs PR5 6BY:
01772 324 129;
info@lancswt.org.uk;
www.lancswt.org.uk

W of Manchester, N of Liverpool at A59/M57/M58 intersection.

1 LUNT MEADOWS
Wildlife Trust for Lancashire, Manchester & N Merseyside.
Habitats: Open water/pools, reedbeds, grassland, small orchard—along the River Alt.
Birds: *All year:* Marsh Harrier, Peregrine Falcon, Barn Owl, Kingfisher, Bearded Tit, Reed Bunting. *Spring/summer:* Shelduck, Oystercatcher, Avocet, Little Ringed & Ringed Plovers. Hobby, Grasshopper, Reed & Sedge Warblers. *Passage:* Common & Green Sandpipers, Ruff, Greenshank, Black-tailed Godwit, Black Tern. *Winter:* Wildfowl and waders, Short-eared Owl.
Other: Water Vole.
Directions: L29 8YA; SD 355 021. Lies just to W of Maghull. From A59/M57/M58 interchange take A5758. At roundabout, turn L (A565) then L at traffic lights towards Netherton (Green Lane). Continue to T-junction, turn L (B5422 to Maghull). In Sefton turn L into Bridge Lane (brown sign to The Punchbowl) continue on this road (1 mile) to reserve entrance on R.
Public transport: Bus: 133 (not Sun) from Waterloo Interchange-Kirkby, stops at Lunt village. Cumfybus (0151 236 7676—Merseytravel network).
Visiting: Open all hours. Car park (free) open 9:30am-5:30pm (summer), 9:30am-4:30pm (winter)—if locked, park by entrance gate—do not park in surrounding lanes to access reserve Disabled parking available. Accessible Learning Centre. Opening hours for Sunshine Tea Rooms posted on Trust website. Toilets. Outside opening hours padlocked (code available on request) composting toilet available. Paths (unsurfaced, can be rough), viewing screens, hide. Dogs on lead.
Contact: WT for Lancashire, Manchester & N. Merseyside; luntinfo@lancswt.org.uk
Head N on A59, in Burscough take Red Cat Lane (becomes Fish Lane) on L, just after station.

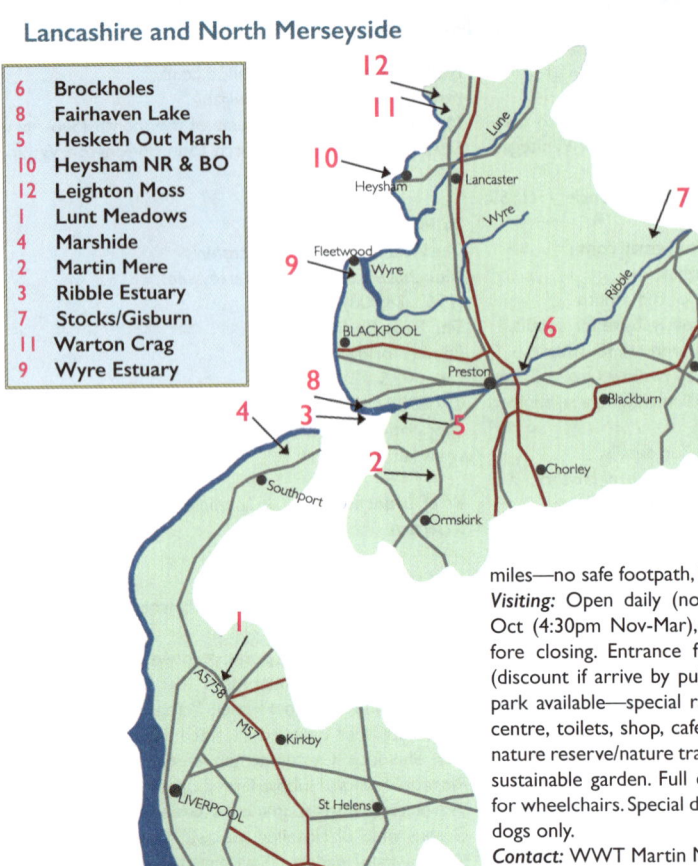

miles—no safe footpath, have to walk along a road).

Visiting: Open daily (not 25 Dec) 9:30am-6pm Apr-Oct (4:30pm Nov-Mar), last admission one hour before closing. Entrance fee for non-WWT members (discount if arrive by public transport or bike), coach park available—special rates for coach parties. Visitor centre, toilets, shop, cafe, education centre, play area, nature reserve/nature trails, hides, waterfowl collection, sustainable garden. Full disabled access, hides suitable for wheelchairs. Special dawn and evening events. Guide dogs only.

Contact: WWT Martin Mere Wetland Centre: 01704 895 181; info.martinmere@wwt.org.uk

*Continue on Fish Lane to junction with B5246. head N and when join A565 head W for Southport, approaching from N (i.e. Marside end), with the **Ribble Estuary NNR** across the marshes to your R.*

2 MARTIN MERE
WWT

Habitats: Open water, wet grassland, moss, copses, reedbed, parkland.

Birds: Spring: Ruff, Shelduck, Little Ringed & Ringed Plovers, Lapwing, Redshank. *Summer:* Marsh Harrier, Garganey, hirundines, Tree Sparrow. Breeding Avocet, Lapwing, Redshank, Shelduck. *Autumn:* Pink-footed Goose, waders on passage. *Winter:* Whooper & Bewick's Swans, Pink-footed Goose, various ducks, Ruff, Black-tailed Godwit, Peregrine Falcon, Hen Harrier, Tree Sparrow.

Other: Whorled Caraway, Golden Dock, Tubular Dropwort, 300 spp moth.

Directions: L40 0TA; SD 428 145. Off Fish Lane, Burscough, six miles N of Ormskirk via Burscough Bridge (A59). 20 miles from Liverpool and Preston. Signposted from: J8 M61, J3 M58, J27 M6.

Public transport: Train—Burscough Bridge (2.5 miles) or Burscough Junction (three miles—walk to Burscough Bridge station first). New Lane Station (1.2

3 RIBBLE ESTUARY NNR
Natural England

Habitats: One of England's largest areas of saltmarsh and mudflats.

Birds: Winter: High water wader roosts of Knot, Dunlin, Black-tailed Godwit, Oystercatcher and Grey Plover are best viewed from Southport, Marshside, Lytham St Annes. Pink-footed Geese and wintering swans are present in large numbers from Oct-Feb on Banks Marsh and along River Douglas respectively. Banks Marsh can be viewed from public footpath which runs along sea defence embankment from Crossens Pumping Station to Hundred End. Large flocks of Wigeon, for which site is renowned, can be seen on high tides from Marshside but feed on saltmarsh areas at night. Good numbers of raptors.

Directions: PR4 6XH; SD 380 240 (S side). Lies c.4.5 miles W of Preston, stretching on both sides of River

Ribble as far as Lytham St Anns (N side) and Crossens (S side). Take A584 and minor roads for north bank, A59/A565 and minor roads for south bank.

Public transport: Bus: 2 Preston to Southport and 68 Preston to Lytham St Anns. Stagecoach.

Visiting: Public footpaths open all hours, no access to saltmarsh itself. See the following sites adjacent to and offering views over the NNR: **Marshside, Hesketh Out Marsh. Fairhaven Lake Discovery Centre**

Contact: Natural England: 01704 578 774; dave.mercer@naturalengland.org.uk

The A565 takes you first to

4 MARSHSIDE
RSPB

Habitats: Coastal grazing marsh, saltmarsh and lagoons.

Birds: All year: Lapwing, Redshank, Black-tailed Godwit, Skylark. *Spring:* Breeding waders, inc Avocet and wildfowl, Garganey, Black-headed Gukk, migrants. *Autumn:* Migrants. *Winter:* Wildfowl inc Pink-footed Geese, waders inc Golden Plover, raptors inc Marsh & Hen Harriers, Sparrowhawk. Short-eared Owl. Merlin, Peregrine, Kestrel.

Other: Brown Hare, various plants inc Marsh Orchid, Migrant Hawker dragonfly.

Directions: PR9 9PJ; SD 353 205. From Southport, follow minor coast road Marine Drive N (1.5 miles from Southport Pier) to small car park by sand works.

Public transport: Bus: 44 Southport to Crossens, alight at Marshside, Elswick Road stop. Walk 0.5 mile (towards the coast) to reserve entrance. Arriva in North West.

Visiting: Open all year 8:30am-5pm (dusk if earlier), car park charge for non-members—coach parties should book in advance. Visitor centre, toilets (inc disabled), two hides (both glazed, one doubling as visitor centre), trails accessible to wheelchairs, two viewing screens, one raised viewing platform. Dogs not permitted on path to Nel's hide or in the hides, keep on leads elsewhere.

Contact: RSPB: 01704 211 690; ribble.reserves@rspb.org.uk

Marshide lies at mouth of Ribble, on S side. Hesketh Out Marsh is a continuation NE of the saltmarsh and mudflats upstream on S side of Ribble.

5 HESKETH OUT MARSH
RSPB

Habitats: Farmland returned to saltmarsh between 2007 and 2017. Overlooking Rivers Ribble and Douglas, both tidal.

Birds: Redshank, Skylark. *Spring:* Avocet, Arctic & Common Terns. *Winter:* Wildfowl inc Pink-footed Goose, Whooper Swan. Hen & Marsh Harriers, Buzzard, Short-eared Owl, Peregrine Falcon.

Other: Brown Hare

Directions: PR4 6XQ; SD 421 251. From roundabout

on A565 at N end of Southport take Banks Road. It and continuations run parallel to edge of marsh, becoming Marsh Road and Shore Road. Take Dib Road running to edge of marsh, where there is a small car park at the above grid reference.

Public transport: Bus: 2 Preston to Southport stops on Shore Road (1 mile walk along footpath), Arriva. Train—Southport, Rufford, Preston.

Visiting: Reserve open all hours, free. Car park 8am-6pm. No facilities. A short nature trail, suitable for wheel and pushchairs, benches, picnic area. Footpaths, including King Charles III England Coast Path, which runs between farmland and marsh. Stay on paths. Dogs allowed on footpaths, keep under control.

Contact: RSPB: 01704 211 690; ribble.reserves@rspb.org.uk

E on A565 to Preston but before heading for N side of Estuary (see Fairhaven) continue through Preston to M6 J31.

6 BROCKHOLES
Wildlife Trust for Lancashire, Manchester & N Merseyside

Habitats: Created from disused gravel pits, alongside River Ribble. Now features open water, reedbeds, wet grassland and woodland.

Birds: Spring/summer: Breeding Great Crested Grebe, Lapwing, Redshank, Skylark, Reed & Sedge Warblers, Reed Bunting. *Passage:* waders inc Turnstone, Grey Plover, Greenshank, Whimbrel, Curlew, Wood, Green & Curlew Sandpipers and Black-tailed Godwit. *Winter:* Good for wildfowl, inc Pochard, Pintail, Goldeneye and Teal.

Other: Brown Hawker and Emperor dragonflies.

Directions: PR5 0AG; SD 588 306. Site in Preston New Road, Samlesbury, adjacent to J31 of M6. From S take A59 towards Blackburn and then first exit, signposted to reserve, and follow under southbound slip road north of River Ribble.

Public transport: Buses run close to entrance. Video with instructions for walking from nearest bus stop: https://www.youtube.com/watch?v=aJXY_iiJm48

Visiting: Gates to reserve open 6am-9pm—car park charges, inc members. Car park closes 7pm in winter. Safe pedestrian route to reserve from centre of Preston follows Guild Wheel. Visitor Village open 10am-4pm all year. The village is a cluster of buildings made from sustainable materials with a village store and shop, cafe, adapted toilets. Cafe open 10am-4pm Thur-Sun, daily during school holidays. Most paths are level and surfaced—wheelchair-friendly (for larger wheelchairs, refundable deposit required for keys to access gates bypassing kissing gates), hides, Sand Martin wall, children's play area. Guided tours available, booking required. No dogs.

Contact: WT for Lancashire, Manchester & N. Merseyside: 01772 872 000; info@brockholes.org

Whilst at J31, cross over for A59 and A671 to Clitheroe.

7 STOCKS RESERVOIR/GISBURN FOREST

United Utilities

Habitats: Reservoir, coniferous and deciduous woodland. *Birds: Spring passage:* Waders (28 spp recorded inc I breeding), terns (inc Black). *Spring/summer:* Osprey, Redstart, Pied Flycatcher, Grasshopper and occasional Wood Warblers, Whinchat, Stonechat, Crossbill. *Winter:* Gull roost, mainly Black-headed & Common, Brambling. Regular raptors inc Buzzard, Hen & Marsh Harriers, Hobby, Red Kite, Goshawk.

Other: Rare mosses and liverworts.

Directions: BB7 4TS; SD 732 565. Nine miles N of Clitheroe. Take B6478 from Clitheroe through Waddington/Newton-in-Bowland/Slaidburn. At Slaidburn, continue for 3.25 miles, turn L and follow road another 2 miles to reservoir/forest and School Lane (reservoir) car park. Forest car parks at Cocklet Hill and Gisburn Forest Main Car Park (both en-route to reservoir).

Public transport: None.

Visiting: Open dawn-dusk. Hide near car park. Eight mile circular walk possible around reservoir. Various trails around forest. Cafe (Thur-Sun, 10am-4pm) and toilets at Gisburn Forest Main Car Park. Parking charges.

Contact: Forest of Bowland AONB: 01200 448 000; www.forestofbowland.com/
Forestry England: 01200 446 387;
enquiries.northengland@forestryengland.uk
Return to Preston and the head W on A583 and A584 to Lytham St Annes at mouth of Ribble on N side.

8 FAIRHAVEN LAKE DISCOVERY CENTRE

Fylde Borough Council

Habitats: Lake with islands behind sea wall, mudflats.

Birds: Primarily a view point for looking out over the Ribble estuary from the N side. Mix of species as for other Ribble reserves.

Directions: FY8 1BD; SD. 341 274. Lake and Visitor Centre behind sea wall on N side of Ribble in Lytham St Anne's at mouth of estuary. Take A583 from Preston, exit it on A584 and continue to Lytham.

Public transport: In centre of Lytham St Anne's

Visiting: The Visitor Centre has closed following the withdrawal of the RSPB but Fylde Borough Concil has taken it over and plans to re-open in early 2026. Details of opening hours not available at time of going to press. Three 24-hr car parks: Inner Promenade, Stanner Bank & St Paul's. Run by Council, charges. Smooth, level trail around lake suitable for wheelchairs/pushchairs; benches, no hides. Toilets (inc. disabled) not on reserve but nearby. Dogs on lead.

Contact: 01253 229225; nick.skiba@fylde.gov.uk
Continue on A584, then, N of Blackpool turn R on to B5412 (Victoria Road West), then as below.

9 WYRE ESTUARY COUNTRY PARK

Wyre Council

Habitats: Tidal estuary, saltmarsh, adjacent grassland, woodland, scrub.

Birds: (wider area). *Spring/autumn passage:* Waders (inc Sanderling, Ringed Plover, Whimbrel, Greenshank, Knot), migrants inc Ring Ouzel, Wheatear, Whinchat, hirundines. *Summer:* Warblers (inc Reed & Sedge). *Autumn passage (offshore):* shearwaters, skuas, terns, Storm & Leach's Petrels possible in SW gales. *Winter:* Nationally important for Pink-footed Goose, Teal, Black-tailed Godwit, Redshank. Red-throated Diver, Great Crested Grebe, Eider, Red-breasted Merganser, other waders (inc Lapwing, Jack Snipe, Snipe. Merlin, Peregrine Falcon, Redwing, Fieldfare, finches, Snow Bunting.

Other: Saltmarsh flora, dragonflies.

Directions: FY5 5LR; SD 356 431. Estuary lies to E of Fleetwood/Blackpool. From A585 take B5412 from the Skippool junction by River Wyre Hotel, turn R on to Stanah Road and continue into River Road to park (signed for **Wyre Estuary CP**).

Public transport: Bus: 74 Fleetwood to Preston, alight at Lambs Road (Thornton-Cleveleys), then a 20 min walk along Stanah Road to River Road. Coastliner Buses (01253 761 739). Train—Poulton-le-Fylde.

Visiting: Car park (free), toilets, cafe, walking and cycle trails. Events and activities. Area is southern boundary of Morecambe Bay, other nearby sites worth visiting around estuary: Rossall Point and Knott End (seawatching), Skippool, Arm Hill-Barnaby Sands, Wardleys.

Contact: Wyre Estuary CP, Duty Ranger: 07976 650 803;
countrysideservice@wyre.gov.uk
Follow directions to M6, leave at J34 on A683.

10 HEYSHAM NR AND BIRD OBSERVATORY

Wildlife Trust for Lancashire, Manchester & N Merseyside/EDF Energy Estates

Habitats: Wetland, acid grassland, alkaline grassland, foreshore.

Birds: 170+ spp annually. *Summer:* Good variety of breeding birds (inc 8 spp warbler on reserve). *Passage:* Passerines when conditions right—two or three scarce land-birds annually, esp Yellow-browed Warbler. Good seabird passage in spring, esp Arctic Tern. Storm Petrel and Leach's Petrel during strong onshore (SW-WNW) winds in mid-summer and autumn respectively.

Other: Notable area for dragonflies—Red-veined Darter has bred for several years at nearby Middleton Community Woodland main pond SD 418 592 (mid-Jun to mid-Jul). Bee Orchid.

Directions: LA3 2UW; SD 407 601. W of Lancaster. Take A683 to Heysham port. Turn L at traffic lights by Duke of Rothesay pub, then first R after 300 yards.

Public transport: Buses from Lancaster to various Heysham sites within walking distance (ask for nearest stop to the harbour). Train services connect with nearby **Isle of Man** ferry terminal.

Visiting: Pedestrian access at all times, car park open 9am-5pm or dusk if earlier—map in car park. Limited disabled access. No dogs on main reserve but extensive off-lead area nearby. No manned visitor centre or toilet access, but someone usually in reserve office in morning (next to main car park).

Contact: WT for Lancashire, Manchester & N. Merseyside; Reserve Warden, Heysham Nature Reserve: 01524 855 030; rneville@lancswt.org.uk Check out observatory's blogpot for virtually daily updates and detailed map at bottom of page.
http://heyshamobservatory.blogspot.co.uk/
Return on A683 to A6, then N on A6.

11 WARTON CRAG
Wildlife Trust for Lancashire, Manchester & N Merseyside

Habitats: Woodland and grassland, limestone cliffs.

Birds: Buzzard, Peregrine Falcon, Kestrel, Raven, Marsh Tit, common woodland spp, common summer warblers, winter thrushes.

Other: Limestone and woodland flora, lichens. Butterflies (inc Pearl-bordered & Small Pearl-bordered Fritillaries).

Directions: LA5 9RB; SD 494 730. 1.25 miles NW of Carnforth. From A6 in Carnforth turn into Market Street, continue past train station, through Millhead to Warton. Turn L on to Crag Road by George Washington pub—car park on R.

Public transport: Bus: 49 runs between Carnforth and Warton (not Sun/bank holidays). Stagecoach (0345 241 8000). Train—Carnforth.

Visiting: Open all hours. Free parking on Crag Road (height barrier). Reserve rises steeply from car park—rocky paths and steep walks. Dogs under close control.

Contact: WT for Lancashire, Manchester & N. Merseyside; Reserve Warden: 01524 885 030; rneville@lancswt.org.uk
Continue along Crag Road to

12 LEIGHTON MOSS
RSPB

Habitats: Reedbed, shallow meres, woodland and scrub. Saltmarsh pools separated by *c.*1 mile.

Birds: All year: Bittern, Bearded Tit, Cetti's Warbler. Water Rail, Shoveler, Gadwall, Marsh Tit, Little Egret. *Summer:* Breeding Marsh Harrier, Reed & Sedge Warbler. Avocet at saltmarsh pools. *Passage:* Black-tailed Godwits in spring (good numbers), Greenshank, Ruff and godwits in autumn. *Winter:* Large flocks of Starlings roosting, Peregrine Falcon and Merlin hunt overwintering wildfowl.

Other: Otter, Red Deer.

Directions: LA5 0SW; SD 478 750. Four miles NW of

Carnforth. Leave M6 at J35. Take A6 N towards Kendal and follow brown signs for **Leighton Moss** off A6.

Public transport: Train—Silverdale station is 250 yards from reserve (on Manchester Airport to Barrow line).

Visiting: Open daily, dawn-dusk. Entry fee for non-members (half-price if arriving by cycle or public transport). Visitor centre/cafe (free entry) open 9:30am-5pm/4:30pm Dec-Jan (not 25 Dec)—shop, cafe (stair lift available), toilets (inc disabled), binoculars for hire. 3 signposted nature trails, 7 hides (some wheelchair access). Dogs restricted to Causeway public footpath.

Contact: RSPB: 01524 701 601;
leighton.moss@rspb.org.uk

Isle of Man

Although listed here as part of Northern England, the Isle of Man, like the Channel Islands, is a self-governing Crown Dependency. Situated in the Irish Sea, it is 33 miles long, 13 wide and has a land area of 222 square miles. A number of small islands, most notably the Calf of Man, lie in close proximity. There are hills in the S and N divided by a central valley running roughly E-W, with low ground at the N tip. The highest point, Snaefell, rises to just over 2,000 ft.

Bird Atlas/Avifauna
Manx Bird Atlas: An Atlas of Breeding and Wintering Birds on the Isle of Man
Chris Sharpe
(Liverpool University Press, 2007).

Bird Recorder
David Kelly: 07624 291 661; davidkelly737@hotmail.com

Bird Reports
Calf of Man Bird Observatory, from MNH—Manx National Heritage Shop, Manx Museum, Kingswood Grove, Douglas, IM1 3LY: 01624 648 000; enquiries@mnh.im
Manx Bird Report (1972-), published in *The Peregrine* (journal): 01624 861 130; enquiries@manxbirdlife.im

BTO Regional Representatives
David Kennett
Wetland Bird Survey (WeBS)
Local Organizer: webs@bto.org
David Kennett

Clubs
Manx Birdlife
Laxey & Lanan Commissioners Offices, 35 New Road, Laxey, Isle of Man IM4 7BG: 01624 861 130;
enquiries@manxbirdlife.im; www.manxbirdlife.im

Manx Bird Club (1997; 150)
Janet Thompson (Sec), Cott ny Greiney, Beach Road, Port St Mary, IM9 5NF: 07624 428 953; thompsonjanet57@gmail.com;
www.manxbirdlife.im/manx-ornithological-society
Meetings: 7:30pm, 1st Tuesday of the month (Oct-Mar). Union Mills Methodist Chapel, Strang Road, Union Mills IM4 4NL. Field trips throughout year. Contact Janet Thompson for details.

Ringing Groups/Bird Observatory
Manx RG
Calf Of Man Bird Observatory
Eleanor Grover (Ornithological Warden): calfbirdwarden@mwt.im;
www.manxnationalheritage.im/visit-2/stay-with-us/calf-of-man-bird-observatory
Accommodation bookings handled by Island Escapes: 01624 830 200; visit@islandescapes.im;
www.islandescapes.im/property/563693

RSPB Local Group
No Group

Wildlife Trust
Manx Wildlife Trust (1973; 1,347)
7-8 Market Place, Peel, Isle of Man IM5 1AB:
01624 844 432; enquiries@mwt.im;
www.mwt.im

For the fit amongst you, a 90 mile footpath, the Raad ny Foillan, runs along the coast around the entire island. There are a few forced detours, the occasional river to ford and a total of over 12,000 ft to climb...

All bus services on the Isle of Man operated by Bus Vannin for Isle of Man Transport (https://www.iombusandrail.im)

A number of the following reserves have been acquired in the last few years and are still developing following the change in management regime and will continue to do so for years to come, offering visitors the opportunity to witness the impact of conservation in action.

9	**Ayres**
1	**Calf of Man BO**
7	**Close Sartfield and Ballaugh**
5	**Creg y Cowen**
8	**Cronk y Bing**
3	**Dalby Mountain**
6	**Glen Audlyn**
11	**Glen Dhoo**
4	**Glion Darragh**
2	**Langness**
10	**Point of Ayre**

1 CALF OF MAN BIRD OBSERVATORY
Manx Natural Heritage/Manx Wildlife Trust
Habitats: Uninhabited 630 acre island but Observatory manned from March to November Unimproved grass and heather, rocky shores, cliffs.
Birds: 36 spp. breed inc Common Eider, Shag, Great Black-backed Gull, Manx Shearwater (increasing following rat eradication programme), Chough, Wheatear.
Other:
Directions: SC 156 658. Half a mile off S tip of Isle of Man reached by boat from Port St Mary or Port Erin.
Public transport: None.

Visiting: Day trips: Calf of Man boat from Port St Mary (07624 490 615), operates all year, weather permitting; Shona Boat Trips from Port Erin (07624 322 765), operates May-Sept. Hostel accommodation available Jun-Aug. Book accommodation through Island Escapes (01624 830 200; www.islandescapes.im) *but book outward and return boat trips separately!*
Contact: Manx Natural Heritage, Douglas, Isle of Man, IM1 3LY: 01624 648 000; enquiries@mnh.im;
www.manxnaturalheritage.im
Calf of Man Bird Observatory Warden:
calfbirdwarden@mwt.im
Head E from Port St Mary on the A5, passing through Castletown, for Derbyhaven. on A12.

2 LANGNESS
Manx Birdlife
Habitats: 2 mile long rocky peninsula joined to mainland by narrow neck at Derbyhaven. N part occupied

by golf course. Rocky shore, sand, mudflat, saltmarsh and coastal grass. 60 acres acquired as reserve 2025. ASSI.

Birds: 202 spp recorded inc Pale-bellied Brent Goose, Teal, Curlew, Ringed, Grey & Golden Plovers, Knot, Ruff, Whimbrel, Bar & Black-tailed Godwits, Little Egret, Short-eared Owl. Temminck's Stint, Buff-breasted Sandpiper, Chough.

Other: Lesser Mottled Grasshopper (only British site), 15 spp butterfly.

Directions: IM9 1AU (golf club), SC 284 660 (car park). Minor road from Derbyhaven, fork R at ruined building, continue to car park.

Public transport:

Visiting: Open all hours, network of paths, free. No facilities but cafe at Castletown Golf Club, public toilets in Castletown. Dogs under control, clean up mess.

Contact: enquiries@manxbirdlife.im

Instead of heading E from Port St Mary take the A36. At the Round Table crossroads turn L on to the A27

3 DALBY MOUNTAIN
Manx Wildlife Trust

Habitats: 122 acres of heather moorland and blanket bog in the island's southern hills.

Birds: Curlew, Snipe, Hen Harrier, Grasshopper Warbler.

Other: Orchids, Cotton Grass.

Directions: SC 232 765. Small car park on L just over 1 mile NW of Round Table crossroads or 1.6 miles SE of Dalby, when car park on R.

Public transport: None.

Visiting: Open all hours, free, no facilities. Keep to public footpaths. Dogs on lead,

Contact: 01624 844 432; enquiries@mwt.im

Continue along the A27, pass through Dalby itself, and then at Peel turn R on to the A1 for Douglas. As you enter Union Mile turn L on to the A22. After 0.5 miles turn L on to A23 and then, after another 0.75 mile, turn R at Mount Rule on to B22 and follow directions in following entry.

4 GLION DARRAGH
Manx Wildlife Trust

Habitats: 170-acre conifer plantation on the sides of the valley of the River Glass with remnants of the original Oak-Hazel wood. Acquired in 2024. Extensive areas of windbown conifer following the storms of winter 24/25. will be restored as temperate rainforest.

Birds: Woodcock, Sparrowhawk, Long-eared Owl, Coal Tit, Goldcrest, Treecreeper, Crossbill.

Other: Hairy Woodrush.

Directions: IM4 5HA; SC 350 813. If coming from Douglas, leave on A23, cross junction with A22 and then, after another 0.75 mile turn R at Mount Rule on to B22 for Baldwin. Park in Baldwin village after 1.25 miles.

Public transport: None.

Visiting: Open all hours, free, no facilities. Keep to paths.

Steep in places. Dogs on lead.

Contact: 01624 844 432; enquiries@mwt.im

Return to junction with A22, turn L and then, after 0.67 mile turn L on to B21 and follow directions in following entry.

5 CREG Y COWIN
Manx Wildlife Trust

Habitats: 107-acre sheep farm on S slopes of central range now being planted to form new temperate rainforest. Planting due to finish in 2026/7. Once trees established, cattle and sheep will be introduced to create woodland pasture.

Birds: Long-eared Owl, Willow Warbler, Meadow Pipit.

Other: Round-leaved Sundew.

Directions: IM4 5ER; SC 380 840. Park at Windy Corner (SC 390 844) on A18 running from Douglas to Ramsey, above the new reserve. Or, leave Douglas on the A22 and then, after crossing the River Glass, turn R on to the B21 and head N beside the River Baldwin. Park in East Baldwin.

Public transport: None.

Visiting: Open all hours, free, no facilities. No access by car to reserve (park on A6 above reserve) or walk in along footpath from East Baldwin (SC 375 836) through reserve and up slope to Windy Corner. Dogs on lead.

Contact: 01624 844 432; enquiries@mwt.im

Carry on along the A18 over the watershed and into Ramsey. Taking the A3 W out of Ramsey will take past a series of reserves, starting with...

6 GLEN AULDYN
Manx Wildlife Trust

Habitats: 1,120 acre upland valley running SW to NE on NE slopes of Snaefell massif, acquired in 2025. 7.25 miles of mountain stream, bracken-covered valley sides, moorland.

Birds: Curlew, Jack Snipe, Woodcock, Buzzard, Hen Harrier, Peregrine Falcon, Kestrel. Skylark, Mistle Thrush, Meadow Pipit, Reed Bunting.

Other: Butterwort, Round-leaved Sundew.

Directions: IM7 2AH; SC 424 923. Head W out of Ramsey on A3. 0.75 miles from town centre take B19, signposted Glen Audlyn (hamlet), park a short distance along this road in Milntown Estate car park (SC 438 942). There is no parking in the valley

Public transport: None.

Visiting: No parking on reserve. Open all hours, free, no facilities. Source of river is 3.4 miles SW of and 1,400 ft higher than car park. A number of greenlanes (not suitable for on-road or heavy off-road vehicles) and public rights of way traverse reserve. Dogs, on a short lead, only allowed on footpaths and greenlanes.

Subject to surveys and permissions, tree planting will start in 2027 to recreate a native temperate rainforest. Once trees are established, grazing animals will be introduced to create wood pasture.

Contact: 01624 844 432; enquiries@mwt.im
Return to the A3, which runs E-W across the N end of the island from Ramsey. The Curragh wetland, surrounded by several reserves, lies Immediately to the N of it, between Sulby and Ballaugh.

7 CLOSE SARTFIELD & BALLAUGH MEADOWS

Manx Wildlife Trust
Habitats: Six internationally important orchid fields (30 acres) of damp, traditionally managed (late cut, then grazed by sheep) hay meadow. ASSI & Ramsar site.
Birds: Breeding: Water Rail (probable), Curlew, Sedge, & Grasshopper Warblers, Whitethroat, Redpoll, Reed Bunting. *Winter:* Hen Harrier, Woodcock.
Other: May to early July huge numbers of orchids in bloom in hay meadows: Heath Spotted, Early Marsh, Common Spotted, Northern Marsh, Greater Butterfly and Common Twayblade. Royal Fern
Directions: SC 358 956; Take the B9 off the A3 to the E of Ballaugh. After just over 1 mile take 3rd minor road on R. Reserve entrance 25 yards down track on R after just over another mile.
Public transport: None.
Visiting: Car park, hide tower and boardwalks thereto open all hours, no facilities. Walks wheelchair accessible. Rest of reserve open June-Aug. Assistance dogs only.
Contact: 01624 844 432; enquiries@mwt.im
Close Sartfield lies on the NW edge of the Curragh wetland—the island's largest wetland and a Ramsar site. Much of the Curragh is owned by Manx Natural Heritage. The Curragh is a mosaic of willow and bog myrtle scrub, sphagnum bog, open water and hay meadows.

The Manx Wildlife Trust has three other, largely hay-meadow reserves on the margins of the Curragh that can be visited by appointment: Close Umpson (2.5 acres), Goshen (47 acres) and Moaney and Crawyn's Meadows (2.5 acres).

Once you've had your fill of hay meadows, rejoin the B9 and continue N to its junction with A10 at The Cronk. Then head NE along A10 for 4.3 miles. Just before The Lhen, where the A10 turns sharp R, take a L turn down track towards coast.

8 CRONK Y BING

Manx Wildlife Trust
Habitats: 17 acres at W end of The Ayres dune system. ASSI
Birds: 116 spp. recorded. *Breeding:* Ringed Plover, Oystercatcher. Isle of Man's largest Common Gull roost. *Autumn:* Curlew, Sanderling, Dunlin onshore. Divers, grebes, seaducks, skuas, all offshore.
Other: Pyramidal Orchid.
Directions; NX 378 016. Alternatively, if not following the itinerary from the Curragh wetlands, take the A9 NW out of Ramsey for Andreas, and then the A19 from

Andreas. The A19 joins the A10 just before a sharp L bend where you exit for the car park, which is 300 yards down a track into the dunes.
Public transport: None.
Visiting: Open all hours, free, no facilities. Car park adjacent to reserve not owned by MWT. Terrain rough, not suitable for wheelchairs. No dogs.
Contact: 01624 844 432; enquiries@mwt.im
Return to the A10 and turn L to follow it NW along the coast. If you are following this itinerary and are approaching from the W you will come first to the turning on the L at Ballakinnag for Roe Point (1.25 miles from Cronk y Bing) and then, after a further 1.75 miles to the turning on L for Ballaghennie and the Nature Discovery Centre.

9 AYRES, THE NNR

Manx Natural Heritage/
Department for Environment, Food and Agriculture
Habitats: 673 acres of shingle beach, dunes, dune grassland, lichen heath. gorse scrub and conifer plantation. 5 miles of coastline between Cronk-y-Bing to W and Point of Ayres to E. ASSI
Birds: Breeding: Shoveler, Curlew, Ringed Plover, Arctic & Little Terns, Sparrowhawk, Long-eared Owl, Kestrel, Skylark, Willow Warbler, Whitethroat, Stonechat, Linnet. *Summer, non-breeding:* Gannet, Kittiwake, Artcic Skua, Marsh Harrier, Short-eared Owl, Kestrel, Chough. *Passage:* Sanderling, Dunlin, Knot, Redshank, Black & Bar-tailed Godwits, Osprey. *Winter, offshore:* Great Northern Red & Black-throated Divers.
Other: Scarce Crimson and Gold Moth, Heath Beefly.
Directions: If starting from Ramsey, head N on the A10. Stay on A10 through Bride and then for:
Nature Discovery Centre: IM7 4BF; NX 435 038. Turn R after 0.75 mile on to minor road for Ballaghennie. Nature Discovery Centre car park is in the dunes at end of this (rough) road after 1.25 miles. There is another car park mid-way along the road, as it enters the dunes, at NX 436 034.
Rue Point: NX 407 032. Continue W on A10 for a further 1.75 miles, then turn R on to minor road for Ballakinnag. Car park at coast at the end of this road after 1.3 miles. another car park, mid way along this road at NX 414 030.
Public transport: Bus: 20/circular bus service from Ramsey passes along A10 (occasional, 1 mile walk from road).
Visiting: The NNR and car parks open all hours, free. The **Nature Discovery Centre** is operated by the Manx Wildlife Trust. Open early May to mid September, it has a shop (not selling refreshments) and toilets (not wheechair accessible). Three trails (mixture of surfaces, some steps) through the dunes start from the **Centre** and there is a raised viewing platform. Dogs on lead. An area of the dunes is owned by the Manx National Trust.
Contact: NNR warden: 07624 365 131;

Nature Discovery Centre: 01624 844432; enquiries@mwt.im

If you have been following the itinerary and approached from the W, rejoin the A10 and turn L for Bride. After 0.75 mile, in the centre of Bride, turn L on to A16 and head NE for the Point of Ayre, following the directions in the following entry.

10 POINT OF AYRE

Manx Birdlife

Habitats: 105 acres of reclaimed sand and gravel workings. Two lakes with islands and smaller pools. Scrub.

Birds: 200 spp recorded (Avocet was 200). Eider, Pochard, Little Tern, Sand Martin (artificial nest wall). Common Tern (not currently breeding on island) attempted to breed on tern rafts in 2024. Warblers in scrub. Seawatching offshore.

Other: Bat house on stilts, dragonflies, orchids.

Directions: IM7 4BS; NX 461 044. If starting from Ramsey, head N on A10 and then turn R on to A16 (signposted for Point of Ayre) in Bride. Pass through Cranstal. Point of Ayre itself, where there is a lighthouse and a car park, is the low NE tip of the island lying to the E of **The Ayres NNR**. After 2.75 miles, on the L, just before the point, there is an aggregates quarry, part of which has been undergoing redevelopment as a reserve since 2019.

Public transport: Bus: 20/circular bus service from Ramsey passes through Bride (occasional).

Visiting: Open to individuals Wed & Sat 9am to dusk. groups by arrangement at other times. No facilities 4 view points and hide linked by trail. Paths level but uneven. No dogs.

Contact: 01624 861130; pointofayre@manxbirdlife.im

Alternatively, if you prefer upands to wetlands and dunes, wind back to **6** *and stay on the A3 rather than taking the B9 for* **Close Sartfield**. *At Ballaugh turn L*

11 GLEN DHOO

Manx Wildlife Trust

Habitats: 25 acres of meadow and upland pasture surrounded by conifer plantation in steep-sided upland valley

Birds: Hen Harrier, Peregrine Falcon, Stonechat, Meadow Pipit.

Other: Upland acid grassland, rush pasture. Orchids.

Directions: Follow minor road S through Ballaugh for c.1 mile to conifer plantation car park. Then a walk of another mile along green lane beside stream to reserve.

Public transport: None.

Visiting: Open all hours, free, no facilities. Grazing animals, dogs on lead.

Contact: 01624 844 432; enquiries@mwt.im

On returning to the A3, if you decide you do fancy some wetlands after all, you can turn R and then take the B9 on the L for 7 **Close Sartfield**, *or you can cross the A3 and take the A10 heading N to The Cronk (1.75 miles). This is where the B from 7 Close Sartfield joins the A10. From then on follow the route to* **8 Cronk Y Bing**.

The A3 continues on from Ballaugh to Kirk St Michael, where the A4 from Peel joins it. It would therefore be possible to remain on the W side of the island and take the A4 N from Peel after **3 Dalby Mountain** *and make straight for the reserves at the N tip of the island.*

Yorkshire

Bird Atlases/Avifauna

The Birds of Spurn
Andy Roadhouse
(Spurn Observatory Trust, 2016)
Breeding Birds of the Sheffield Area including the North-east Peak District
David Wood & Richard Hill
(Sheffield Bird Study Group, 2013)
Birds of the Huddersfield Area
Paul & Betty Bray
(Huddersfield Birdwatchers Club, 2008)
The Birds of Yorkshire
J Mather
(Croom Helm, 1986)

Bird Recorders

Yorkshire
(Rarities Committee Sec). Thomas Willoughby:
YNURCDescriptions@outlook.com
East Yorkshire
Jacob Spinks: 07724 648 487; spinksy72@gmail.com
North Yorkshire
Keith Wimbush: kwim473@gmail.com
South Yorkshire
Martin Wells, 715 Manchester Road, Stocksbridge, Sheffield, S36 1DQ: 0114 288 4211;
martinwells@barnsleybsg.plus.com
West Yorkshire
Jacob Spinks: 07724 648 487; spinksy72@gmail.com

Bird Reports

Yorkshire Bird Report (1940-), from Yorkshire Naturalists' Union: www.ynu.org.uk/join-the-ynu/shop
Birds in Huddersfield (1966-), from HBWC—Hazel Sill, Wards End Farm, Marsden, Huddersfield HD7 6NJ: 07854 739 646; hazelsill@hotmail.com
Birds in the Sheffield Area (1973-), from SBSG - Martin Hodgson, membership@sbsg.org
Bradford Ornithological Group Report (1987-), online—download from: www.bradfordbirding.org/reports
Filey Bird & Wildlife Report (1976-), from FBOG—Margaret Denny (Treasurer): treasurer@fbog.org.uk

Flamborough Bird Observatory Annual Report, online only, available to Friends of FBO.
Scarborough District—download online from: www.scarboroughbirding.co.uk
Spurn Wildlife (1991-), from Spurn Bird Observatory Trust, Kew Villa, Kilnsea, HU12 0UB: 01964 650 479; info@spurnbirdobservatory.co.uk
Swillington Ings Bird Group Annual Report: Free to members. www.sibg1.wordpress.com
York Ornithological Club Report (1966-), from YOC: Jane Chapman: editor@yorkbirding.org.uk

BTO Regional Representatives
Bradford
Mike Denton:
East & Hull
Brian Walker
North-East
Nicholas Gibbons
South-East & South-West
Grant Bigg
York
Rob Chapman
Central, Leeds & Wakefield,
North-West & Richmond
Drew Lyness
Wetland Bird Survey (WeBS)
Local Organizers: webs@bto.org
East Yorkshire & Scarborough (excl. The Humber)
Alan Burnham
Harrogate & Yorkshire Dales
Vacant
Huddersfield & Halifax Area
Vacant
Humber Estuary (North)
Nick Cutts
Leeds Area
Paul Morris
South Yorkshire
Grant Bigg
Wakefield Area
Peter Smith

Clubs
Yorkshire Naturalists' Union (1861; 500)
Hannah Whitaker/Clare Langrick:
membership@ynu.org.uk; www.ynu.org.uk
Meetings: No indoor meetings held.
Bradford Ornithological Group (1987; 55)
Shaun Radcliffe (Chairman), 8 Longwood Avenue, Bingley, Bradford, BD16 2RX: 01274 770 960;
shaun.radcliffe@btinternet.com;
www.bradfordbirding.org
Meetings: No indoor meetings.
Doncaster & District Ornithological Society (n/a; 20)
Chris Robinson: 07534 271 254; Sabsgull@hotmail.co.uk;

www.doncasterbirding.co.uk/wordpress/
Meetings: 7:15pm, last Thursday of the month (Sep-Nov, Jan-May). Potteric Carr Visitor Centre, Mallard Way, Doncaster DN4 8DB.
Harrogate & District Naturalists' Society (1947; 210)
Sue Coldwell (Gen Sec), 4 Abbots Way, Knaresborough, HG5 8EU: gensec@hdns.org.uk; www.hdns.org.uk
Meetings: 7:30pm fortnightly (Oct-Mar). Friends Meeting House, 12A Queen Parade, Harrogate HG1 5PP. Contact/see website for details.
Huddersfield Birdwatchers' Club (1966; 80).
Hazel Sill (Membership Sec), Wards End Farm, Marsden, Huddersfield HD7 6NJ: 07854 739 646; hazelsill@hotmail.com;
www.huddersfieldbirdwatchersclub.co.uk
Meetings: 7:30pm, usually 1st or 2nd Tuesday of the month (Sep-May). Reception Room, Town Hall, Ramsden Street, Huddersfield, HD1 2TA.
Rotherham & District Ornithological Society (1974; 80)
RDOS, c/o Galaxy Four, 493 Glossop Road, Sheffield, S10 2QE: via website; www.rotherhambirds.co.uk
Meetings: 7pm, 2nd Friday of the month (Sep-Apr). Herringthorpe United Reform Church Hall, Wickersley Road, Rotherham, S60 4JN.
Scarborough Birders (1993; 130)
Nick Addey (Chairperson): nickaddey@dsl.pipex.com;
www.scarboroughbirding.co.uk
Free membership for under 25s.
Meetings: Occasional field meetings for members—contact/see website for details.
Sheffield Bird Study Group (1972; 400)
Jill Greenwood (Sec): Secretary@sbsg.org; www.sbsg.org
Meetings: 7:15pm, 2nd Wednesday of the month (Sep-May).
Diamond Building—Lecture Theatre 2, Sheffield University, 32 Leavygreave Road, Sheffield, S3 7RD. Offers free membership to under-25's.
SK58 Birders (1992; 50)
Paul Tennyson (Chairman), 16/18 Sheffield Road, South Anston, Sheffield, S25 5DT: 01909 569 409;
chair@sk58birders.com; www.sk58birders.com
Meetings: 7:30pm, last Tuesday of the month (Sep-Nov and Jan-May). The Loyal Trooper Inn, Sheffield Road, South Anston, Sheffield, S25 5DT.
Sorby Natural History Society (1918; 400)
General enquiries: secretary@sorby.org.uk;
www.sorby.org.uk
(Ornithology Group): Secretary—Andrew Darby ornithology@sorby.org.uk
www.sorby.org.uk/groups/sorby-ornithological-recording-group/
Meetings: Contact/see website for details.
Swillington Ings Bird Group (1989; 300)
Alex Aylward (Sec): via website;
www.sibg1.wordpress.com

No longer hold indoor meetings but Sightings and Chat WhatsApp groups. Bimonthly digital newsletter, printed annual report.

Wakefield Naturalists' Society (1851; 30):
via website; http://wakefieldnaturalists.org
Meetings: 7:30pm, 2nd Tuesday of the month (Sep-Apr). Quaker Meeting House, Thornhill Street, Wakefield, WF1 1NQ.

York Ornithological Club (1965; 180)
Tim Godson (Sec): secretary@yorkbirding.org.uk;
www.yorkbirding.org.uk
Meetings: 7:30pm, 1st Tuesday of the month (Sep-May, by zoom in Jan/Feb). St Olaves Church Hall, Marygate Lane, Marygate, York, YO30 7DS.

Ringing Groups/Bird Observatories
Barnsley RG: www.barnsleybirds.blogspot.com
Doncaster RG
East Dales RG:
www.eastdalesringinggroup.wordpress.com
Humber Wader RG
Pickering Forests RG
Sorby Breck RG: www.britishringers.co.uk
Swaledale RG
Wintersett RG
Filey Bird Observatory & Group (1977; 165)
Mark Moore (Secretary): 07923 349 880;
secretary.fbog@gmail.com; www.fbog.org.uk
Flamborough Bird Observatory
Tony Hood, FBO Sec., 9 Hartendale Close, Flamborough, East Yorkshire, YO15 1PL
info@flamboroughbirdobs.org.uk;
www.flamboroughbirdobs.org.uk
Spurn Bird Observatory
Paul Collins (Warden), Spurn Bird Observatory, Easington Road, Kilnsea, Hull, HU12 0UB: 01964 650 479;
pcnfa@hotmail.com www.spurnbirdobservatory.co.uk
Acommodation enquiries: as above;
accommodation.spurnbirdobs@hotmail.com

RSPB Local Groups
Airedale & Bradford (1972; n/a)
Paul Barrett: abrspb@blueyonder.co.uk;
https://group.rspb.org.uk/airedaleandbradford/
Meetings: 7pm, 2nd Friday of the month (Sep-Apr). Kirkgate Centre—contact/see website for details.
Doncaster (1984; 70)
Steve Pynegar: rspbdongroupleader@gmail.com;
https://group.rspb.org.uk/doncaster/
Meetings: 7pm, 2nd Wednesday of the month (Sep-May). Armthorpe Community Centre, Armthorpe, Doncaster, DN3 3AG.
East Yorkshire (1986; 120)
David Woodmansey: eastyorksRSPB@yahoo.co.uk;
https://group.rspb.org.uk/eastyorkshire/
Meetings: 7:30pm, 4th Tuesday of the month (Sep-Apr,

not Dec). North Bridlington Library, Martongate, Bridlington, YO16 6YD.
Harrogate District (2005; 100)
Bill Sturman: billsturman@outlook.com;
https://group.rspb.org.uk/harrogate/
Meetings: 7:30pm, 2nd Monday of the month (Sep-Apr). Christ Church Parish Centre, The Stray, Harrogate, HG1 4SW.
Huddersfield & Halifax (1981; 40)
David Hemingway: d.hemingway@ntlworld.com;
https://group.rspb.org.uk/huddersfieldandhalifax/
Meetings: 7:30pm, 3rd Wednesday of the month (Sep-May). New North Road Baptist Church, New North Parade, Huddersfield, HD1 5JU.
Hull & District (1983; 50)
John Hallam: jobar.hull@hotmail.co.uk;
https://group.rspb.org.uk/hull/
Meetings: 7:30pm, 2nd Tuesday the month (Sep-Apr). Men in Sheds, Haltemprice, Community Centre, First Lane, Anlaby HU10 6UE.
Leeds (1974; 430)
Simon Reeve: rspbleeds@googlemail.com;
https://group.rspb.org.uk/leeds/
Meetings: 7:15pm, usually 3rd Wednesday of the month (Sep-Apr). St Chad's Parish Centre, Otley Road, Leeds LS16 5JT. Local walks and weekend coach trips (autumn-early summer).
Richmondshire & Hambleton (2005; 85)
Teresa Quinn: tquinn53@btinternet.com
https://group.rspb.org.uk/richmondshireandhambleton/
Meetings: 2pm & 7:30pm on various weekdays Sept/Oct-Mar. Village/church halls in various locations throughout the area, such as Leyburn, Northallerton, Bedale, Tunstall—contact/see website for details.
Sheffield (1982; 250)
RSPBsheffield@googlegroups.com;
https://group.rspb.org.uk/sheffield/
Meetings: 7:15pm, 1st Thursday of the month (Sep-May). Central United Reformed Church, 60 Norfolk Street, Sheffield, S1 2JB.
Skipton (1986; 100)
David Adam: david@davidwadam.co.uk;
https://group.rspb.org.uk/skipton/
Meetings: 7:30pm, 2nd Wednesday of the month (Sep-Apr). Skipton Baptist Church Hall, The Church Hall (at Rectory Lane exit of car park), Rectory Lane, Skipton, North Yorkshire, BD23 1ER.
Wakefield District (1987; 40)
Duncan Stokoe: duncanstokoe@gmail.com;
https://group.rspb.org.uk/wakefield/
Meetings: 7:30pm, 4th Thursday of the month (Sep-Apr). St Austin's Church, Wentworth Terrace, Wakefield, West Yorkshire, WF1 3QN.
York (1972; 200 households)
Barbara Cromack: rspbyorklocalgroup@gmail.com;
https://group.rspb.org.uk/york/

Meetings: In hall talks: 2:15pm/7:30pm, Clements Hall, Nunthorpe Road, York, YO23 1BW, and via zoom—contact/see web site for details.

Wildlife Trusts

Sheffield and Rotherham Wildlife Trust (1985; 6,000) 37 Stafford Road, Sheffield, S2 2SF: 0114 263 4335; mail@wildsheffield.com; www.wildsheffield.com

Yorkshire Wildlife Trust (1946; 45,000) 1 St George's Place, Tadcaster Road, York, YO24 1GN: 01904 659 570; info@ywt.org.uk; www.ywt.org.uk

Yorkshire Reserves: South & West

Despite being located in the heart of the industrial north and its numerous towns, the area still offers birdwatchers a surprising number of interesting sites. As the result of the area's industrial past, there are many water meadows and marshes (known as 'Ings'). Sites such as RSPB Fairburn Ings (next to the A1), Potteric Carr, RSPB Old Moor and Bolton Ings have something to offer throughout the year.

Entering from Lancashire, take the A65 from J36 of the M6 for Skipton., veering S on A629 and then the A6033 at Haworth for Hebden Bridge.

1 HARDCASTLE CRAGS

National Trust
Habitats: 395 acres, unspoilt wooded valleys, ravines, streams, hay meadows and moorland edge.
Birds: All year: Sparrowhawk, Kestrel, Tawny, Barn & Little Owls, Green & Great Spotted Woodpeckers, Dipper, Grey Wagtail, Jay and other common woodland species. *Spring/summer:* Cuckoo, Redstart, Lesser Whitethroat, Garden Warbler, Blackcap, Wood Warbler, Chiffchaff, Spotted & Pied Flycatchers.
Other: Northern Hairy Wood Ant, Moss Carder Bee, Tree Bumblebee, Killarney Fern, Brittle Bladder Fern, Roe Deer, 8 spp bat.
Directions: HX7 7AL; SD 988 291 (Midgehole car park). From Hebden Bridge follow National Trust signs to A6033 Keighley Road. Follow for 0.75 mile. Turn L at National Trust sign to car parks. Alternative pay & display car park at Clough Hole (HX7 7AZ; SD 969 298)) on Widdop Road, Heptonstall.
Public transport: Bus/train to Hebden Bridge, then one mile walk to Midgehole. Sat/Sun and bank holidays bus (approx. May-Oct) 906 Widdop Reservoir-Hardcastle Crags-Hebden Bridge. TLC Travel (0113 245 7676).
Visiting: Open all year. Two small car parks, NT car park

charges—free for members and disabled badge holders. Cycle racks, several waymarked trails. Gibson Mill visitor centre has toilets, cafe, exhibitions and limited disabled parking (pre-book). Dogs under control.
Contact: National Trust, Hardcastle Crags: 01422 846 236; hardcastlecrags@nationaltrust.org.uk
E on A646 from Hebden Bridge to Halifax then S on A629.

2 INGBIRCHWORTH RESERVOIR

Yorkshire Water
Habitats: Reservoir, small strip deciduous woodland.
Birds: *Spring/summer:* Whinchat, warblers, woodland birds, House Martin. *Spring/autumn passage:* Little Ringed & Ringed Plovers, Dotterel, other waders, Common, Arctic & Black Terns, Yellow Wagtail, Wheatear. *Winter:* Wildfowl, Golden Plover, waders, occasional rare gulls such as Iceland or Glaucous, Grey Wagtail, Fieldfare, Redwing, Brambling, Redpoll.
Other: Woodland wildflowers, inc. Bluebells.
Directions: S36 7GS; SE 217 062. Leave M1 at J37 and take A628 towards Manchester. After five miles turn R at roundabout on to A629 Huddersfield road. Drive 2.5 miles to Ingbirchworth. Turn L into Wellthorne Lane (signed to 'Inn'). Park on roadside just past The Fountain Inn, continue on foot to where road bears L (to cross the dam), go straight forward here on to track, which follows N edge of reservoir. Can also walk across dam and on to a footpath through narrow strip of woodland at end of dam.
Public transport: Bus: 24 Barnsley to Ingbirchworth (Mon-Sat). Stagecoach.
Visiting: Open all year. Car park, picnic tables. One of few reservoirs in area with footpath access.
Contact: Recreation Officer, Yorkshire Water: Geoff.D.Lomas@yorkshirewater.co.uk
S on A629, then A61—then as below but from N.

3 GRENO WOODS

Sheffield & Rotherham Wildlife Trust
Habitats: 420 acres, ancient woodland, some heathland.
Birds: Inc wider area *All year:* Common woodland spp. Tawny Owl, Willow Tit, Crossbill. *Summer:* Woodcock, Nightjar, Cuckoo, warblers inc Whitethroat and Willow Warbler, Tree Pipit. *Winter:* Winter thrushes, Stonechat, Redpoll. *Caution: the S&RWT has not responded to requests for updates.*
Other: Woodland plants inc Bluebells and Cow Wheat.
Directions: S35 7DS; SK 325 949. Lies on N outskirts of Sheffield (adjacent to Wharncliffe and Wheata Woods—covering total area of 1,739 acres). Head N from Sheffield on A61 (Penistone Road) until it becomes Halifax Road, then turn L into Foxhill Road—continue on to Main Street and then on to Woodhead Road. After one mile, Forestry England car park is on L. Most of wood lies between Woodhead Road and A61.
Public transport: Bus: 85 runs from Sheffield city centre

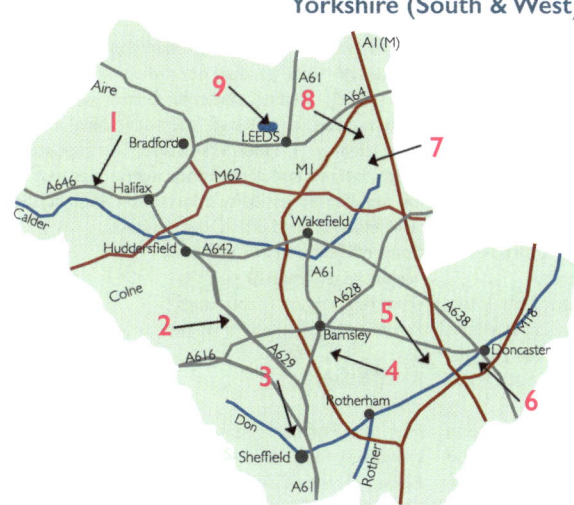

Yorkshire (South & West)

5	**Denaby Ings**
9	**Eccup Reservoir**
7	**Fairburn Ings**
3	**Greno Woods**
1	**Hardcastle Crags**
2	**Ingbirchworth Reservoir**
4	**Old Moor (Dearne Valley)**
6	**Potteric Carr**
8	**St Aidan's**

to Grenoside village. 86 runs along the A61 with stops adjacent to reserve. Stagecoach.

Visiting: Open all hours. Network of footpaths and bridleways—also three downhill mountain bike trails.

Contact: Sheffield & Rotherham Wildlife Trust: 0114 263 4335; mail@wildsheffield.com

A61 N, cross M1 at J36 then A6195 to

4 OLD MOOR (DEARNE VALLEY)
RSPB

Habitats: Lakes and lowland wet grassland, wader scrape and reedbeds.

Birds: All year: Kingfisher, Barn Owl, Bearded Tit. *Summer:* Breeding Bittern, Marsh Harrier, Hobby, waders, inc. Little Ringed Plover, migrant warblers and wildfowl. *Autumn:* Passage waders. *Winter:* Large numbers of wildfowl inc Gadwall, Teal, Pochard. Peregrine Falcon and Sparrowhawk.

Other: Stoat, Weasel, Pygmy Shrew, wildflowers inc orchids and Adders Tongue Fern.

Directions: S73 0YF; SE 422 022. Old Moor is just off Manvers Way (A633). Leave M1 at J36 and take A61. At next roundabout follow **Old Moor** signs for c.4 miles. From A1(M), take J37 and follow A635 towards Barnsley, then follow **RSPB Old Moor** signs.

Public transport: Bus: X20 to Old Moor reserve from Barnsley-Doncaster (not Sun). Stagecoach (01709 515 151). Train—Wombwell and Swinton stations c.3 miles from reserve.

Visiting: Entrance charge for non-members. Visitor centre open daily (not 25/26 Dec) 9:30am-5pm summer and 9:30am-4pm winter. Cafe open 9:30am-4pm. Shop open 10:30am-4:30pm, toilets, mobility scooter for hire. Two trails with nine hides/viewing screens—suitable for wheelchair users. Guide dogs only.

Contact: RSPB: 01226 751 593; old.moor@rspb.org.uk

A633 to SE, then A6023, leaving on Pastures Road.

5 DENABY INGS
Yorkshire Wildlife Trust

Habitats: Riverside meadows, hay meadows, open water, deciduous woodland, marsh, willows.

Birds: All year: Common woodland birds, inc 3 spp woodpeckers, possible Willow Tit, Corn Bunting, Yellowhammer. *Spring/summer:* Waterfowl, Kingfisher, Barn & Tawny Owls, Sand Martin, Swallow, Whinchat, Grasshopper Warbler, Lesser Whitethroat, Whitethroat, other warblers. *Passage:* Waders, Common, Arctic & Black Terns, Redstart, Wheatear. *Winter:* Wildfowl inc Whooper Swan and Goosander, Jack Snipe and other waders, Grey Wagtail, Fieldfare, Redwing, Brambling, Siskin.

Other: Grass Snake, Bee, Pyramidal & Common Spotted Orchids.

Directions: S64 0JJ; SE 496 008. NE of Mexborough. Take A6023 from Mexborough, turn L down Pastures Road on outskirts of town. After one 1 mile turn R into car park (shortly after crossing River Dearne). Climb flight of concrete steps to enter reserve.

Public transport: Train—Conisbrough or Mexborough, 30 mins to reserve.

Visiting: Open all year. Car park, interpretation panels, 2 hides/1 viewing screen, circular trail. Dogs on leads.

Contact: Yorkshire WT: 01904 659 570; info@ywt.org.uk

At end of Pastures Road, R into Pasture Lane, through Cadeby to Sprotbrough Bridge over Don—Sprotbrough Flash NR immediately upstream. L on to A630 (Sheffield Road). Tale A1(M) S at J36, exit to M18 at J35.

6 POTTERIC CARR
Yorkshire Wildlife Trust

Habitats: Flood plain of River Tome, with reed fen, subsidence ponds, artificial pools, grassland, woodland.

Birds: 230 spp, 102 spp have bred—waterfowl (inc

Shoveler, Gadwall, Pochard), Water Rail, Kingfisher, 3 spp woodpecker, Lesser Whitethroat, Reed & Sedge Warblers, Willow Tit. *Passage/winter:* Bittern, Marsh Harrier, Black Tern, wildfowl and waders.

Other: 21 spp dragonflies, 28 spp butterflies inc Purple Hairstreak and Dingy Skipper. Palmate & Great Crested Newt. Common Spotted & Bee Orchids.

Directions: DN4 8DB; SE 588 005. From M18, J3 take A6182 (Doncaster) and at first roundabout turn R. Entrance and car park are on R after 50 yards.

Public transport: Bus: 72 & 73 from Doncaster Interchange, alight at B&Q on Woodfield Way. Cross White Rose Way, walk down Mallard Way. Cross car park to reserve entrance in Sedum House. First South Yorkshire. Train—Doncaster.

Visiting: Closed Mon, except Bank Hols; Open Tues-Sun and Bank Hols (not 24-27 Dec) 9:30am-5pm. Hot food served until 2:30pm, cafe closes 3:30pm. Snacks, cold drinks, ice creams until 5pm. Car park locked at 5pm but ask (before 5pm) if you would like to stay later. Visitor centre/cafe/shop free, non-members entrance fee to reserve. Groups of 10 or more should book in advance. Toilets in Visitor Centre. *c*.5 miles of paths (3.2 miles accessible to wheelchairs, unassisted), 14 viewing hides (10 suitable for disabled). Guide dogs only.

Contact: Potteric Carr Nature Reserve: 01302 325 736; potteric.carr@ywt.org.uk

Return to M3 then A1(M) N. Leave at J42.

7 FAIRBURN INGS
RSPB

Habitats: Open water, wet grassland, marshland fen scrub, reedbed, reclaimed colliery spoil heaps, woodland.

Birds: All year: Kingfisher, Green Woodpecker, Bullfinch, Willow Tit. Bittern. *Spring:* Garganey, Osprey, Little Ringed Plover, Little Gull, terns five spp (inc Black). Wheatear. *Summer:* Spoonbill, Cattle Egret, nine spp breeding warbler, Grey Heron, Gadwall, Little Ringed Plover. *Autumn:* Thousands of waders on passage (inc Green Sandpiper, Little Ringed Plover, Black-tailed Godwit). *Winter:* Smew, Goldeneye, Goosander, Wigeon. Peregrine.

Other: 28 spp butterflies, 20 spp dragonflies. Leisler's & Daubenton's Bats. Brown Hare, Harvest Mouse.

Directions: WF10 2BH; SE 451 277. 12 miles from Leeds, 6 miles from Pontefract, 3 miles from Castleford. Next to A1246 from J42 of A1(M).

Public transport: Bus: 493 from Pontefract to Fairburn (Mon-Sat). Arriva in Yorkshire. Train—Castleford, 3 miles.

Visiting: Open daily (not 25/26 Dec). Car parking (inc coaches) 9:30am-8pm Feb-Oct, 9:30am-4pm Nov-Jan—charge for non-members (after 30 mins), free for disabled badge holders. Visitor centre/shop open 9am-5pm Mar-Oct, 9am-4pm Nov-Feb. Hot/cold drinks and

snacks available. Toilets inc disabled and baby-changing facilities. Wildlife garden, pond-dipping and mini beast areas, duck feeding platform. Boardwalks leading to Pickup Hide and Kingfisher viewpoint are wheelchair-friendly. 4 hides/4 shelters, 5 signposted trails (both flat and undulating) totalling 6 miles, see website for detailed accessibility information. Mobility Scooter available—call to book. Dogs on leads.

Contact: RSPB: 01977 628 191; fairburnings@rspb.org.uk
www.rspb.org.uk/fairburnings

Return to A1(M), take M1 at intersection.

8 ST AIDAN'S
RSPB

Habitats: Former open cast coal mine—now wetland, woodland, reedbed, meadows.

Birds: All year: Common wildfowl. Peregrine, Barn & Little Owls, Kingfisher, Cetti's Warbler, Bearded Tit. *Spring/summer:* 4,000 prs Black-headed Gull nest. Black-necked Grebe, Bittern, Garganey, Little-Ringed Plover, Avocet, Common Tern, Hobby, Cuckoo, hirundines, warblers inc Garden, Reed & Sedge. *Passage:* Waders inc Greenshank, Little Stint, Green Sandpiper, Black Tern, Wheatear. *Winter:* Wildfowl and waders, Short-eared Owl, Brambling.

Other: Roe Deer, Brown Hare, dragonflies, butterflies.

Directions: LS26 8AL; SE 398 287. 6 miles SE of Leeds. Leave M1 at J46 for Garforth, follow Selby Road/A63. Turn R at roundabout on to A642, Turn L after 1.4 miles into Astley Lane—reserve on R after 1.5 miles.

Public transport: Bus: 168 Leeds to Castleford (daily) alight at Bowers Row stop (Great Preston), 0.2 miles from visitor centre. Arriva.

Visiting: Reserve open dawn-dusk. Car park, inc Blue Badge spaces, 6am-8pm, charge for non-members, bike racks. Visitor centre, toilets (inc accessible toilet) & cafe (10am-5pm, 4pm Nov-Feb). Four trails (one to three miles). Events. Dogs welcome on public footpaths/bridleways on lead.

Contact: RSPB: 01132 320 529; staidans@rspb.org.uk 8

Return to J46 of M1, cross it, 2ⁿᵈ exit from roundabout to A6102. Continue on it round Leeds to A61, head N. Alwoodley Lane after 1 mile on L.

9 ECCUP RESERVOIR
Yorkshire Water

Habitats: Reservoir, woodland.

Birds: All year: Common wildfowl, Red-legged & Grey Partridges, Red Kite, Barn, Little & Tawny Owls, common scrub spp and finches. *Spring/summer:* Cuckoo, hirundines, warblers. *Spring/Autumn:* Passage waders and terns, Hobby. *Winter:* Wildfowl (inc Shoveler, Pochard and Goldeneye), gull roost (check for scarcer spp). Occasional divers and rarer grebes. Siskin, Redpoll.

Directions: LS17 7PL; SE 296 408. On N outskirts of

Leeds, just N of Alwoodley. On-street parking available on Lakeland Drive, off Alwoodley Lane (access from A61, signed to Alwoodley/Adel). Walk back to main road, turn L, walk 50 yards and turn L—Goodrick Lane. Walk down lane (past golf course) to reservoir.

Public transport: Bus: X7 and 7 from Leeds city centre (Infirmary Street) to Alwoodley Ave. Bottom stop on Alwoodley Lane. First Leeds.

Visiting: Open all year round. 4.5 mile circular walk around reservoir—route crosses farmland but mostly on roads/surfaced paths. Red Kite viewpoint.

Contact: None.

Return to A6120, then take A64 for York and, from E of York, the B1228 to Storwood in an angle formed by the Pocklington Canal and the Derwent.

East Riding

Birdwatching here is dominated by the coast. The headlands at Flamborough Head and Spurn Point are magnets for migrants and they regularly turn up rarities, especially in the autumn. Bempton Cliffs are probably the best mainland seabird colony in England, where you can get close to Puffins and Gannets, and an autumn boat trip from Bridlington will find passing shearwaters and skuas. Inland wetland sites offer a different selection of species.

1 LOWER DERWENT VALLEY NNR

Natural England/Yorkshire Wildlife Trust/Carstairs Countryside Trust/Friends of the Lower Derwent Valley

Habitats: Flood meadows (Derwent), pastures, swamp, open water and alder/willow woodland.

Birds: 80+ spp. *Spring/summer:* Breeding wildfowl and waders, inc Garganey and Snipe. Grey Partridge, Spotted Crake, Barn Owl and warblers. *Passage:* waders, inc. Whimbrel, Green Sandpiper. *Winter/spring:* Bittern, 20,000+ waterfowl inc Whooper Swan, wild geese, Teal and Wigeon. Large gull roost. Merlin, Hen Harrier, Peregrine Falcon, finches, buntings.

Other: Pocklington Canal is particularly good for wide range of aquatic plants and animals. Noctule, Daubenton's & Pipistrelle Bats regularly recorded. Water Vole, Pygmy Shrew and Brown Hare.

Directions: YO19 6FE (Bank Island). Six miles SE of York, stretching 12 miles S along River Derwent from Newton-on-Derwent (N) to Wressle (S) and along Pocklington Canal (E). Three main access points: **Bank Island** (Natural England; SE 691 448), **North Duffield Carrs** (SE 697 367) and **Wheldrake Ings** (YWT; YO19 6AX; SE 691 444).

Public transport: Buses (not Sun) 18 York to Wheldrake/North Duffield. East Yorkshire Motor Services, (Busline: 01482 592 929), 36 York to Wheldrake. Pullman (01904 622 992).

Visiting: Open all year, free. Car parks at all sites (can flood), cycle racks Bank Island and North Duffield Carrs. Bank Island—RADAR key toilets, two hides, viewing tower, sightings board. North Duffield Carrs—two hides, wheelchair access. Thorganby—viewing platform. Wheldrake Ings, 390 acres, two hides, Grazing livestock, path level but can be muddy and prone to flooding. No dogs.

Contact: Natural England: 07917 088 021; craig.ralston@naturalengland.org.uk

Continue S on B1228 to A614. Cross Ouse and then M62 on A161 at Goole

2 BLACKTOFT SANDS

RSPB

Habitats: Second largest tidal reedbed in UK, saline lagoons, lowland wet grassland, willow scrub.

Birds: 270 spp. *Summer:* Breeding Bittern, Avocet, Marsh Harrier, Bearded Tit, Reed & Sedge Warblers, Tree Sparrow. *Passage:* Waders (exceptional list inc rarities). *Winter:* Wildfowl, Hen Harrier, Merlin, Peregrine Falcon.

Other: Water Vole. Dragonflies and damselflies inc Black-tailed Skimmer, Four-spotted Chaser, Large Red Damselfly. Marsh Sow Thistle easily seen from footpaths in summer. Rare Brown-veined Wainscot moth.

Directions: DN14 8HR; SE 843 232. Eight miles E of Goole. Follow brown tourist signs on minor road between Ousefleet and Adlingfleet.

Public transport: Bus: 360/361 from Goole stops at reserve entrance. Stagecoach.

Visiting: Open daily (not 25 Dec) 9am-6pm/dusk if earlier. Charge for non-members. Car park, toilets. Reception hide open daily 9am-4pm Apr-Sep, weekends 9am-4pm Oct-Mar. Light refreshments, binocular hire. 6 hides with wheelchair spaces, 1 viewing screen, footpaths suitable for wheelchairs. Assistance dogs only. Faces **Alkborough Flats** (**Lincolnshire**) across Trent.

Contact: RSPB: 01405 704 665; blacktoft.sands@rspb.org.uk

Cross back to N of Ouse at Goole, E on M62 from J36.

3 NORTH CAVE WETLANDS

Yorkshire Wildlife Trust

Habitats: Former gravel pits converted into various lagoons, inc reedbed, scrub and hedgerows, wet grassland. An expanding site.

Birds: 200+ spp. Bittern now present year round, most noticeable in spring. *Summer:* breeding spp inc Great Crested Grebe, Gadwall, Pochard, Common Tern, Sparrowhawk, Avocet, Little Ringed & Ringed Plover, Oystercatcher, Sedge Warbler and Reed Bunting. Bittern (which have overwintered) bred for first time in '25. Large numbers of Sand Martins feed over reserve in summer. *Winter:* Wildfowl and waders inc Golden Plover, Dunlin, Ruff and Redshank. Tree Sparrow.

Other: Water Vole, dragonflies, several butterfly spp inc

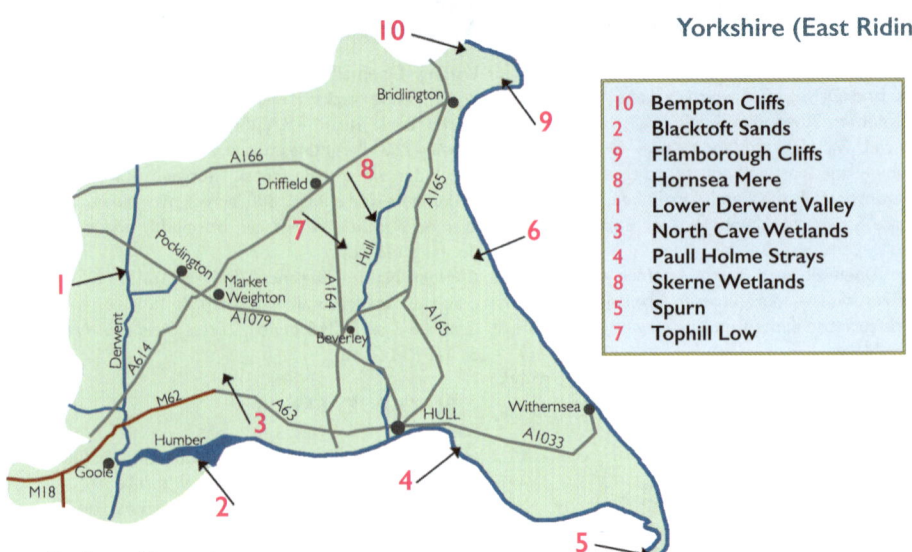

10	**Bempton Cliffs**
2	**Blacktoft Sands**
9	**Flamborough Cliffs**
8	**Hornsea Mere**
1	**Lower Derwent Valley**
3	**North Cave Wetlands**
4	**Paull Holme Strays**
8	**Skerne Wetlands**
5	**Spurn**
7	**Tophill Low**

small colony of Brown Argus.

Directions: HU15 2LY; SE 886 328. NW of North Cave village, c.10 miles W of Hull. From J38 of M62, follow signs to North Cave on B1230. In village, turn L and follow road to next crossroads, then go L and park in Dryham Lane.

Public transport: Bus: X55 (not Sun), 155 to North Cave from Hull/Goole. East Yorkshire Motor Services, (Busline: 01482 592 929).

Visiting: Open all year, car park 7:30am to dusk, composting toilet on site. Little Butty Bus (mobile trailer, Tues-Sun, 8am-2:30pm) on Dryham Lane in the reserve car park. Part of circular footpath is suitable for all abilities, 9 hides, 7 wheelchair accessible. Guide dogs only.

Contact: Yorkshire WT: 01904 659 570; info@ywt.org.uk

Return to J36, then E on A63 through Hull, then A1033.

4 PAULL HOLME STRAYS NATURE RESERVE

Yorkshire Wildlife Trust

Habitats: 260 acres, intertidal saltmarsh and mudflats, lies on N shore of the Humber. Realignment scheme.

Birds: Waders present all year but autumn/winter provide highest numbers and widest range of spp—for best views time visits on rising tide. *All year:* Shelduck, Little Egret, gulls, Barn & Little Owl, Skylark, common scrub spp. *Spring/summer:* Hirundines, Reed & Sedge Warblers, Whitethroat. *Spring/autumn passage:* Avocet, Little Stint, Greenshank, Whimbrel, Green, Common & Curlew Sandpipers. Migrants. Sometimes Gannet, Common Scoter, skuas, terns can be seen in the Humber. *Autumn/ Winter:* Wildfowl (inc Wigeon, Teal). Waders (inc Black-tailed Godwit, Knot, Golden & Grey Plovers, Turnstone, Dunlin, Curlew, Redshank. Stonechat, winter thrushes, Rock Pipit. Occasional Marsh Harrier, Peregrine, Hobby (summer/autumn), Merlin (winter).

Directions: HU12 8AX; TA 181 251. 6 miles SE of Hull. From A1033 follow signs for Fort Paull then continue S on Thorngumbald Road. Car park entrance on R (one mile after entrance to Fort Paull).

Public transport: Bus: 79 Hull to Hedon (not Sun) stops in Paull (can walk to reserve along sea wall). East Yorkshire Buses (01482 325 679). Train—Hull.

Visiting: Open all hours, free. Car park. Permissive footpaths in both directions along seawall (unsuitable for wheelchairs)—hide (to SE) and viewing screen (to NW) from car park. When walking along seawall take care not to flush waders. Dogs on lead.

Contact: Yorkshire WT: 01904 659 570; info@ywt.org.uk

Return to A1033.

5 SPURN NNR

Yorkshire Wildlife Trust

Habitats: Sand dunes with marram and sea buckthorn scrub. Mudflats around Humber Estuary.

Birds: Spring: Many migrants on passage, inc scarce spp such as Red-backed Shrike, Bluethroat. *Summer:* Little Terns feed offshore. *Autumn:* Passage migrants and rarities inc Wryneck, Pallas's Warbler. *Winter:* Large numbers of waders, Shelduck, Brent Goose, Merlin, Peregrine Falcon, Snow Bunting.

Other: Unique habitats and geographical position makes Spurn interesting site for butterflies (25 spp) and moths.

Directions: HU12 0UH; TA 419 149. 26 miles E of Hull. Take A1033 from Hull to Patrington then R on B1445 to Easington—continue on minor road to Kilnsea. Turn R at crossroads towards Spurn Discovery Centre.

Public transport: 'Spurn Explorer' (72) between Hull Interchange and Spurn, weekends and Bank Hols, early Apr-early Nov.

Visiting: Open all year—weather permitting. Pay & display car park (open dawn-dusk) on approach road to reserve, opposite Spurn Discovery Centre (members and Easington parish residents/with permit free). Coaches—book in advance. Centre open 10am-4pm (cafe 10am-3:30pm), toilets (9am-5pm), shop. Hides. Dogs not permitted pst gate on to Point

Contact: Yorkshire Wildlife Trust, Spurn Discovery Centre, Spurn Road, Kilnsea, Hull, HU12 0UH: 01964 650 144; spurn@ywt.org.uk

Return to A1033 and continue to Witherness, then B1242 tracking the coast N to

6 HORNSEA MERE
Wassand Hall

Habitats: Yorkshire's largest body of freshwater, 0.6 mile inland from coast, edged by reedbeds and woodland.

Birds: All year: Common wildfowl. *Spring/autumn passage:* Marsh Harrier, Osprey, Little Gull, terns, White & Yellow Wagtails, Wheatear, maybe rarer spp. *Winter:* Common Wildfowl with a chance of divers, grebes, Long-tailed Duck, Goosander & Pintail.

Directions: HU11 5RJ; TA 174 460 (Hall). 12 miles E of Beverley. Wassand is between Seaton and Hornsea on A1035. Mere can also be viewed from Hornsea—enter town, on to Southgate then take signposted road to car park at Kirkholme Point. B1242 enters Hornsea from S and joins A1035.

Public transport: Bus: 246 Hull-Beverley-Hornsea—ask to stop by Wassand Hall. East Yorkshire Motor Services, (Busline: 01482 592 929).

Visiting: Mere is owned by nearby Wassand Hall (which is open to public on selected days). Cafe on site (limited winter opening), toilets. Hide and woodland trail open daily (not 25 Dec)—see notices for closing times. Hide—charge for electronic code, available from 10:30am at East Lodge, first house after Wassand Estate entrance on R (parking at Hall). Dogs on leads.

Contact: 01964 537 474 or 07767 039 793; info@wassand.co.uk; www.wassand.co.uk; https://hornseamere.wordpress.com/

A1035 W from Hornsea

Take A1035 W to Beverley. then as below (reservoirs are on other side of unbridged River Hull from Hornsea.

7 TOPHILL LOW NATURE RESERVE
Yorkshire Water

Habitats: Adjacent to River Hull, active water treatment works. 300 acres. Two main reservoirs (SSSI), surrounding ponds, marsh, grass and woodland

Birds: 260+ spp recorded (once 269 but Redpolls have been lumped). *Breeding:* Shelduck, Gadwall, Pochard, Shoveler, Great Crested & Little Grebes, Water Rail, Snipe, Little Ringed Plover, Common Tern, Marsh Harrier, Kingfisher, Marsh & Willow Tits, Cetti's & Reed War-blers, Lesser Whitethroat *Passage:* Slavonian & Black-necked Grebes, Temminck's Stint, Common, Green & Wood Sandpipers, Spotted Redshank, Greenshank, Ruff, Osprey. *Winter:* Whooper Swan, geese, ducks inc Red-crested Pochard, Scaup, Goldeneye, Smew; Iceland & Glaucous. Hen Harrier.

Other: Otter, Grass Snake. 20 spp butterflies.

Directions: YO25 9GA; TA 072 485. Off A164 between Beverley and Driffield. In Watton, take Church Lane and head E, following signs for **Toplow Hill Nature Reserve**.

Public transport: Bus: 41, Hull to Bridlington stops in Watton, East Yorkshire (01482 327 142). Then 3.75 mile walk.

Visiting: Car park (charge). Open every day, 9am-6pm (reception hide only open when wardens on site: weekends and most weekdays). Toilets (inc disability access) and 12 hides (6 wheelchair accessible) always open when car park open. Stay on paths, mostly easy access but some sections can be muddy, Mobility scooter available by prior arrangement. No dogs.

Contact: 01377 270690; richard.hampshire@yorkshirewater.co.uk

Return to A164 and N to Driffield, then SE B1249 or, after 6 Hornsea Mere take A1035 N to A165 and junction with B1249, approaching from SE and missing out 7 Tophill Low.

8 SKERNE WETLANDS NATURE RESERVE
Yorkshire Wildlife Trust

Habitats: Wet grassland, chalk streams, old fish ponds, reworked into wet woodland, fen, reedbed, open water.

Birds: All year: Marsh Harrier, Kestrel, Water Rail, Kingfisher, Cetti's Warbler, Reed Bunting. *Autumn:* Green Sandpiper. *Winter:* Bittern, Barn Owl, winter thrushes.

Other: Otter, Water Vole, Grass Snake. Dragonflies, freshwater invertebrates.

Directions: Two areas: YO25 8NX; TA 063 560 (Snake-holme pastures just S of Wansford Bridge off B1249, four miles SE of Driffield); YO25 9HU; TA 057 542 (Skerne Wetlands accessed along farm track just E of Skerne village. Turn S off road, L at fork, R towards Cleaves Farm, then follow track past farm to parking areas.

Public transport: Bus: 136 Driffield to Bridlington stops at Wansford (daily). East Yorkshire Motor Services. No services to Skerne.

Visiting: Open all hours. Parking—roadside lay-by (Wansford) for N section and small car park at end of long farm track (Skerne) for S section. Various tracks, viewing screens, benches (reserve is surrounded by drains and flowing water). Guide dogs only.

Contact: Yorkshire WT: 01904 659 570; info@ywt.org.uk

Return to Driffield, take A614 to Bridlington.

9 FLAMBOROUGH CLIFFS

Yorkshire Wildlife Trust

Habitats: Coastal cliffs, species-rich rough grassland and scrub, farmland.

Birds: Summer: Breeding Puffin, Guillemot, Razorbill, Kittiwake, Shag, Fulmar, Skylark, Meadow Pipit, Linnet, Whitethroat, Yellowhammer, Tree Sparrow, occasional Corn Bunting. Thornwick reedbeds hold Reed & Sedge Warblers and Reed Bunting. *Passage migrants:* Thrushes, warblers, finches, buntings and occasional rarities such as Wryneck and Red-backed Shrike. *Autumn:* Passage divers, grebes and sea duck.

Other: Pyramidal & Northern Marsh Orchids, Harebell, Thrift on cliff tops. Migrant butterflies such as Small Skipper and Painted Lady.

Directions: YO15 1BJ. Car parks: North Landing—TA 238 719 and Thornwick Bay—TA 234 719. Reserve is part of Flamborough headland, approx four miles NE of Bridlington. From Bridlington take B1255 to Flamborough and follow signs for North Landing.

Public transport: Bus: 14 Bridlington to North Landing (not Sun). East Yorkshire Motor Services, (Busline: 01482 592 929).

Visiting: Open all year. Pay & display car parks at North Landing/Thornwick Bay gives access to trails on reserve. Paths not suitable for wheelchairs. Cafe at North Landing (open Apr-Oct, 10am-5pm), toilets.

Contact: Yorkshire WT: 01904 659 570; info@ywt.org.uk

Take B1229 NW from Flamborough.

10 BEMPTON CLIFFS

RSPB

Habitats: Largest mainland seabird colony in UK and only Gannet colony in England. Sea cliffs, farmland, grassland, coastal scrub.

Birds: Breeding numbers in excess of 200,000 between Apr-Jun inc Kittiwake, Gannet, Puffin, Guillemot, Razorbill and Fulmar, some spp start returning to cliffs in Jan. Breeding Tree Sparrow and Corn Bunting. Passage: skuas, shearwaters, terns and passerine migrants.

Other: Harbour Porpoise & Grey Seal regularly offshore. Bee & Northern Marsh Orchids.

Directions: YO15 1JF; TA 197 738. Near Bridlington. Take Cliff Lane N from Bempton village off B1229 to car park and visitor centre.

Public transport: Train—Bempton station 1.25 miles from reserve.

Visiting: Entrance charge for non-members (but cafe and shop free), coaches/minibuses (in advance, or drop off only). Seabird Centre open daily (9.30am-5pm Mar-Oct, 9.30am-4pm Nov-Feb. Toilets (inc disabled), light refreshments, shop, picnic area, binoculars for hire. Cliff-top public footpath with 5 observation points (2 wheelchair accessible). 4 miles of stunning chalk cliffs, highest in county. Short farmland footpath. Dogs on

leads.

Contact: RSPB: 01262 422 212; bempton.cliffs@rspb.org.uk

Continue NW on B1229 to Reighton, the S edge of the Filey Bird Observatory (Yorkshire North) recording area and then A165 to Filey)

Yorkshire Reserves: (North)

The North York Moors hold breeding Red Grouse, waders, raptors and chats, whilst the Lower Derwent Valley is good for birdwatching throughout the year. Seawatching from Filey Brigg in the autumn produces skuas and shearwaters, with divers and grebes becoming more noticeable as the season progresses.

1 FILEY BIRD OBSERVATORY AND GROUP

FBOG/Yorkshire Wildlife Trust (The Dams)

Habitats: 5 reserves owned/managed in area inc wetland, woodland, scrub—attractive to migrants.

Birds: The Dams: Breeding and wintering water birds, breeding Sedge & Reed Warbler and Tree Sparrow. *The Tip:* Important for breeding Skylark, Meadow Pipit, common warblers and Grey Partridge. *Winter:* Buntings, inc Lapland. *Seawatching Hide:* (Jul-Oct) All four skuas, shearwaters, terns. *Winter:* divers and grebes. *Parish Wood:* Common woodland residents and summer migrants inc Grasshopper Warbler, Lesser Whitethroat. Scarce/rare migrants possible at all sites.

Directions: The Observatory recording area lies between coast and A165, centred around Filey town in N and as far as Reighton in S. *Filey Dams* and *East Lea:* YO14 0DG; TA 106 807. *The Old Tip:* YO14 9NU; TA 112 818. *Parish Wood:* YO14 9NU; TA 112 815. *Rocket Pole Field:* YO14 9ES; TA 121 818.

Public transport: Filey bus and train stations within walking distance (1 mile) from each site.

Visiting: Open all hours. Park at end of Wharfedale Road (*Dams/East Lea*), Sycamore Avenue (*Parish Wood/The Old Tip*) or North Cliff Country Park (*Rocket Pole Field* and *Filey Brigg*). Toilets in Country Park (Apr-Oct) and town centre. Two open-access hides at *The Dams* (wheelchair access to Main Hide), one hide on *The Brigg* (for FBOG members only). Nature trails at *The Dams, Parish Wood/Old Tip.* Cliff top walk for seabirds along Cleveland Way. Dogs only in *Parish Wood* and *The Old Tip* (on lead). Events.

Contact: Bird Observatory: membership.fbog@gmail.com; www.fbog.co.uk; Yorkshire WT: 01904 659 570; info@ywt.org.uk

Continue N on A165 and then A171

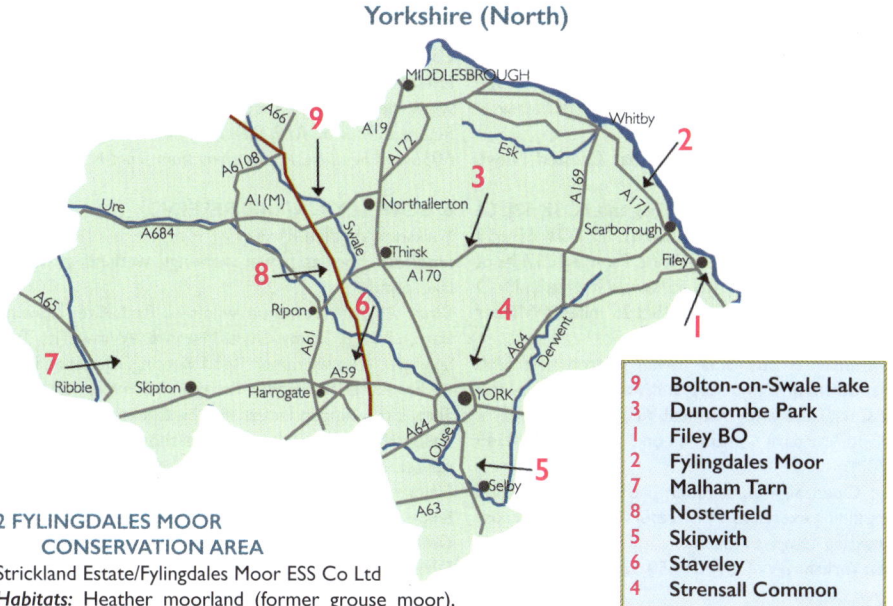

Yorkshire (North)

9	**Bolton-on-Swale Lake**
3	**Duncombe Park**
1	**Filey BO**
2	**Fylingdales Moor**
7	**Malham Tarn**
8	**Nosterfield**
5	**Skipwith**
6	**Staveley**
4	**Strensall Common**

2 FYLINGDALES MOOR CONSERVATION AREA

Strickland Estate/Fylingdales Moor ESS Co Ltd
Habitats: Heather moorland (former grouse moor), with scattered trees, wooded valleys and gulleys. Now managed for wildlife and archaeological remains.
Birds: 80+ common spp inc Kestrel, Lapwing, Snipe, Cuckoo, Meadow Pipit, Grey Wagtail and Wood Warbler. Peregrine Falcon regular. Scarce breeding spp inc Hen Harrier, Merlin, Golden Plover, Red Grouse, Curlew, Wheatear, Stonechat, Whinchat, Skylark, Marsh & Willow Tit, Linnet, Bullfinch, Reed Bunting and Yellowhammer.
Other: Otter, Roe Deer, Brown Hare, Stoat, Weasel and Badger, important for Water Vole. Three spp heather, plus Cranberry, Cowberry, Moonwort and, in wetter parts, Bog Myrtle, Lesser Twayblade, Bog Asphodel, Butterwort, Marsh Helleborine and sundews. Rare orchids and sedges. Insect spp inc Large Heath and Small Pearl-bordered Fritillary butterflies and Emperor Moth.
Directions: YO22 4US; NZ 945 002 (Jugger Howe lay-by). Conservation area covers 6,800 acres within National Park off A171 S of Whitby, stretching between Sneaton High Moor (Newton House Plantation) and coast at Ravenscar.
Public transport: Bus: X93 between Scarborough and Whitby, nearest stop at Flask Inn (approx 1 mile N of Jugger Howe lay-by). Arriva North East (0344 800 4411).
Visiting: Open access. Parking (inc coaches) available at Jugger Howe lay-by on A171. Numerous footpaths inc Jugger Howe Nature Trail, Lyke Wake Walk and Robin Hood's Bay Road.
Contact: None.
Head back S on A169 off A171 just to W of Whitby. and then A170 W at Pickering.
[Alternatively you could decide to carry on NW on A171 to Durham/Tyne & Wear.]

3 DUNCOMBE PARK

Private Estate
Habitats: Wood pasture, woodland, river valley. NNR in grounds of Park managed by Natural England.
Birds: All year: common woodland spp. inc 3 spp woodpeckers, Tawny Owl, Hawfinch. Red Kite, Buzzard, Goosander, Kingfisher, Dipper, Grey Wagtail, Tree Sparrow. *Summer:* Common Sandpiper, Cuckoo, Redstart, warblers inc Wood, Pied & Spotted Flycatchers. *Winter:* Winter thrushes, Siskin, Redpoll, Brambling.
Other: Ancient Trees. Fungi. Spring flora. Otter.
Directions: YO62 5EB. SE 603 831. 0.5 mile W of Hemsley. Signposted off main A170 in Hemsley (down Buckingham Square).
Public transport: Bus: 128 Scarborough to Hemlsey (Mon-Sat, Sun in summer). Scarborough & District (01723 500 064).
Visiting: Open daily Feb to 24 Dec, 10:30am-5pm (start/end dates can vary). Two waymarked trails—country and river. Entry fee payable. National Centre for Birds of Prey is located here—parking.
Contact: Estate Office: 01439 770 213; via website; www.duncombepark.com
Leave A170 just S of Helmsley and take B1363 to the A1237 (York's N by-pass), E for 1.5 miles, then as below.

4 STRENSALL COMMON NATURE RESERVE

Yorkshire Wildlife Trust/(MOD)
Habitats: Heathland.
Birds: All year: Woodcock, Barn, Tawny & Long-eared (scarce) Owls, Marsh & Willow Tits, Common wood/scrub spp. *Spring/summer:* Tree Pipit, Woodlark, Cuck-

oo, warblers inc Grasshopper, Garden, Sedge, Lesser Whitethroat, Whitethroat. Hobby (autumn). *Passage:* Wheatear, Whinchat. Winter: Redpoll, Stonechat, winter thrushes.

Other: Common Lizard, Adder, Great Crested Newt, butterflies, Roe Deer.

Directions: YO32 5UL; SE 635 598 and YO32 5BJ; SE 648 611 (car park 1 and 2 MOD). YO60 7QY; SE 653 618 (car park 3 YWT). NE of York. From A1237 N of York take minor road N (to Earswick/Strensall). MoD car parks 1 and 2 on R after 2.25/3.25 miles. YWT car park 3 on L after 3.75 miles.

Public transport: Bus: 5/5a York to Strensall (daily). Alight at Strensall Camp stop and walk 0.5 mile N (on to Ox Carr Lane after roundabout) to SE corner of MOD land (car park 1 entrance on R). First York (0345 646 0707).

Visiting: Open all hours. MoD: paths may be closed during training exercises. YWT reserve accessed across level crossing. Dogs on lead.

Contact: Yorkshire WT: 01904 659 570; info@ywt.org.uk
Return to A1237, head E, then S on A64. Take A19 for Selby

5 SKIPWITH NNR

Escrick Estate, in conjunction with Natural England
Habitats: Lowland heath, scrub, woodland.
Birds: All year: Woodcock, Long-eared (scarce), Barn & Tawny Owls, common scrub spp. *Spring/Summer:* Nightjar, Cuckoo, Turtle Dove, Tree Pipit, Woodlark, warblers inc Grasshopper & Garden. Whinchat (passage). *Autumn:* Hobby. *Winter:* Snipe, Water Rail, winter thrushes, Stonechat, Siskin, Redpoll.
Other: Dragonflies. Roe & Fallow Deer, Grass Snake, Adder. Fungi.

Directions: 5 miles NE Selby. Three main access points. King Rudding Lane Car Park: YO19 6QL; SE 644 373. From A19 at Riccall turn E down King Rudding Lane to Riccall Grange, follow narrow lane for 1.2 miles (park on L on part of old concrete airfield. Sands Lane Car Park: Y08 5SE; SE 669 377. From A163, west of North Duffield turn N on to Cornelius Causeway, car park 0.9 mile on L. Now also Common Road Car Park: SE 691 420. Turn S from village green.

Public transport: Bus: 18 York to Holme on Spalding Moor stops in Skipwith Village (not Sun). East Yorkshire (https://www.eastyorkshirebuses.co.uk/). From village green bus stop walk S along Common Road and follow narrow road into site.

Visiting: Open all hours. Three waymarked trails. One wheelchair accessible, work being undertaken on others to improve access for motorized wheelchairs. Level terrain but paths can be wet and muddy. One viewing tower (by Sands Lane Car Park). Livestock on reserve. Dogs on leads. Just a few miles W of **Lower Derwent Valley NNR, East Riding.**

Contact: Escrick Park Estate: www.escrick.com; Friends of Skipwith Common: www.friendsofskipwithcommon.org.uk
Return to York on A19, then A59 for Knaresborough. Take 6055 and head NE. Approaching from S not N..

6 STAVELEY NATURE RESERVE

Yorkshire Wildlife Trust
Habitats: Former gravel workings, wetland, grassland, lake, ponds.
Birds: All year: common wildfowl, Red Kite, Lapwing, Barn, Little & Tawny Owls, Marsh & Willow Tits, Tree Sparrow, Yellowhammer, Reed Bunting. Occasional Little Egret, Marsh Harrier, Peregrine. *Summer:* Common Tern, Little Ringed Plover, Hobby, Cuckoo, Sand Martin, Yellow Wagtail, warblers inc Grasshopper. *Winter:* Goosander, Snipe, Water Rail, Long-eared Owl, Redwing, Fieldfare. Occasional Bittern, Short-eared Owl, Jack Snipe.
Other: Otter. Orchids.

Directions: HG5 9LQ; SE 369 630. NE of Harrogate. Take A6055 from J48 of A1 for Boroughbridge, continue on A6055 towards Knaresborough. Enter Minskip turn R after 0.4 miles (opp Village hall) to Staveley. Car park on R just after village sign (continue into village for disabled access by church).

Public transport: Bus: 21 Knaresborough to Roecliffe (not Sun/Bank hol). Alight at Stavelely (Spellow Cres.)— 350 yards walk to car park (*care no pavement for part of way*). Harrogate Bus Co. (01423 566 061).

Visiting: Open all hours. YWT car park (for 12 cars) just outside Staveley village on Minskip Road. Also disabled parking off Main Street, up track by village church (accessed by radar key). Network of surfaced/unsurfaced tracks. 2 hides, 1 has wheelchair access). Dogs on lead.
Contact: Yorkshire WT: 01904 659 570; info@ywt.org.uk
Continue W on A59 to Skipton, then A65.

7 MALHAM TARN

National Trust
Habitats: Upland pasture, woodland, lake (highest in England), limestone outcrops.
Birds: All year: Waterfowl inc Great Crested Grebe, regular gull spp, Peregrine Falcon, Barn Owl. *Spring/Summer:* Oystercatcher, Lapwing, Redshank, Curlew, Redstart, warblers, Twite. *Winter:* wildfowl inc Goldeneye, Pochard, Goosander, Woodcock, Water Rail, winter thrushes, Redpoll, Siskin. *Occasional:* Harriers, Osprey on passage, Whooper Swan and Short-eared Owl (winter).
Other: Water Vole.

Directions: BD24 9PU; SD 894 658 (parking S side of tarn). BD24 9PT; SD 882 671 (parking N side of tarn/ woods. 5 miles NE of Settle, 2 miles NW of Malham. For Malham, take minor road N off A65 at Coniston Cold, 6 miles.

Public transport: Bus—irregular and seasonal Skipton to Malham.

Visiting: Open all hours. Various walks in the area, graded easy to difficult, inc tramper route and circular walk (4.5 miles). No dogs in nature reserve. Nearest facilities in Malham, inc National Park Centre. Malham Cove 1 mile N of village: limestone outcrop/Peregrine Falcon.

Contact: National Trust: 01729 830 416; malhamtarn@nationaltrust.org.uk

Back to Harrogate on A65 and A59, then N to Ripon on A61.

8 NOSTERFIELD LNR

Lower Ure Conservation Trust

Habitats: Wetland grassland and open water, magnesium limestone grassland, gravel banks, hedgerows and scrub.

Birds: 150 spp annually, 225+ spp overall. *Spring/autumn:* up to 30 wader spp annually, terns. *Summer:* breeding spp inc Redshank, Lapwing, Avocet, Curlew, Oystercatcher, Ringed Plover, Mediterranean Gull, Shoveler, Gadwall, Barn Owl, Skylark, Lesser Whitethroat, Tree Sparrow, Linnet, Reed Bunting. *Autumn:* Passage waders inc regular Pectoral Sandpiper. *Winter:* Wildfowl (inc Wigeon, Teal, Greylag and rarer geese), waders inc Golden Plover, Lapwing, Curlew. Peregrine Falcon.

Other: Specialist grassland and wetland flora, inc seven spp orchid, Mudwort, Yellow Rattle, Golden Dock. Butterflies inc White-letter Hairstreak, Brown Argus, Wall and large colony of Common Blue. Dragonflies inc Emperor, Black-tailed Skimmer, Red-veined Darter (has bred). 480+ spp moths. Brown Hare and Water Shrew.

Directions: DL8 2QZ; SE 278 795. 6 miles N of Ripon, between West Tanfield and Nosterfield E of A6108 (Ripon to Masham road) and c.4 miles W of A1. Traversed by B6267.

Public transport: Bus: 159 (Mon-Sat) from Ripon to Masham, alight at West Tanfield (0.5 mile walk to reserve). Hodgsons Coaches (01833 630 730).

Visiting: Open all year. Lower viewing area beyond car park allows viewing from cars only. Coaches, book in advance. Footpath (approx 1 mile) is wheelchair-friendly. 2 disabled-friendly hides, interpretation panels (main hide).

Contact: amy.horton@luct.org.uk (Community Engagement Officer); www.luct.org.uk

E on B6267 to A6055, which runs beside A1(M), then N to Catterick.

9 BOLTON-ON-SWALE LAKE

Yorkshire Wildlife Trust

Habitats: Former sand and gravel quarry. Open water, scrub, surrounding farmland.

Birds: All year: Common wildfowl, Great Crested Grebe. *Passage:* Waders, inc Common Sandpiper, Ruff, Little Stint, Whimbrel. Occasional Osprey. *Winter:* Wildfowl, inc nationally significant numbers of Wigeon, plus Goldeneye, Pochard, Teal, Lapwing, Curlew, Golden Plover.

Directions: DL10 6AH; SE248 987. 0.5 mile N of Catterick. Take A6055 from J52 of A1, then turn R for Brompton-on-Swale. After one mile, turn R at traffic lights on to B6271. Continue for 1.3 miles then turn R along narrow track (Back Lane)—car park 0.7 mile on L. Entrance track to hides on opposite side of lane,

Public transport: None.

Visiting: Open all hours. Access limited to 2 hides reached from car park.

Contact: Yorkshire WT: 01904 659 570; info@ywt.org.uk

From Catterick take A6136 to Richmond and then A6108 to Scotch Corner. Thence A66 to junction with B6277 S of Barnard Castle. Follow to Langdon Beck in **Durham**

Durham/Tyne & Wear

The coastal area around Teesmouth attracts regular migrants during spring and autumn passage, with the occasional rarity thrown in, along with large numbers of wildfowl and waders during the winter. Inland, Upper Teesdale still holds Black Grouse, Ring Ouzel and breeding waders while the Derwent Valley has a good mixture of habitats and birds.

Bird Atlases/Avifauna

The Birds of Durham
Keith Bowey & Mark Newsome
(Durham Bird Club, 2012)
Birds of Cleveland
Martin Blick
(Tees Valley Wildlife Trust, 2009)
*The Breeding Birds of Cleveland:
A Tetrad Atlas 1999-2006*
Graeme Joynt, James Fairbrother & Ted Parker
(Teesmouth Bird Club, 2008)

Bird Recorders

Cleveland
Alan Crossley, 32 Sledwick Road, Billingham, Cleveland TS23 3HU: 07801 751 952;
alancrossley11@outlook.com
Durham
Recorder: Tom Middleton: dbc.records@hotmail.co.uk
Assistant Recorder (Rarities): Vacant
dbc.records@hotmail.co.uk

Bird Reports

Cleveland Bird Report (1974-), from TBC—John Fletcher, 43 Glaisdale Avenue, Tollesby, Middlesbrough, TS5 7PF:

01642 818 825
Birds In Durham (1970-), from DBC—D Sowerbutts, 9 Prebends Fields, Gilesgate Moor, Durham, DH1 1HH: dsowerbutts608@gmail.com

BTO Regional Representatives
Cleveland
Michael Leakey
Durham
David Sowerbutts
Wetland Bird Survey (WeBS)
Local Organizers: webs@bto.org
Cleveland (excl. Tees Estuary)
Chris Sharp
Durham
Anne Donnelly
Tees Estuary
Adam Jones

Clubs
Durham Bird Club (1974; 350)
Richard Cowen (Sec), Rose Cottage, Old Quarrington, DH6 5NN: 07397 862 833; durhambirdclub@gmail.com;
www.durhambirdclub.org.uk
Meetings: Contact/see website for details.
Northumberland & Tyneside Bird Club.
Natural History Society of Northumbria
See Northumberland
Teesmouth Bird Club (1960; 475)
Chris Sharp (Sec), 6 Maritime Avenue, Hartlepool, TS24 0XF: 07765 497 100; chrisandlucia@ntlworld.com;
www.teesmouthbc.com
Meetings: 7:30pm, 1st Monday of the month (Sep-Apr). Stockton Library, Church Road, Stockton, TS18 1TU.

Ringing Groups/Bird Observatory
Durham RG
Durham Dales RG
South Cleveland RG
Tees RG
Whitburn RG

RSPB Local Group
Cleveland (1974; 100)
Jenny Wright: jennyseasonals@gmail.com;
https://group.rspb.org.uk/cleveland/
Meetings: 7:30pm, 2nd Monday of the month (Sep-Apr). Contact/see website for details.

1 WIDDYBANK FELL (NNR)
Natural England
Habitats: Upland, crags, reservoir, river. Part of Moor House—Upper Teesdale NNR.
Birds: All year: Black & Red Grouse, Grey Partridge,

Goosander, Peregrine, Merlin, Raven. *Spring/summer:* breeding waders inc Oystercatcher, Lapwing, Golden Plover, Redshank, Snipe, Curlew, Common Sandpiper. Cuckoo, Dipper, Skylark, Meadow Pipit, Ring Ouzel, Wheatear, Grey Wagtail. *Winter:* Redwing, Fieldfare.
Other: Alpine flora inc Spring Gentian.
Directions: (1) DL12 0HF; NY 847 309 (parking, Langdon Beck). (2) DL12 0HX; NY 810 309 (parking, Cow Green Reservoir). 18 miles NW Barnard Castle. From A67 at Barnard Castle take B6277 (towards Middleton-in-Teesdale). Continue to Langdon Beck. Turn L just before Langdon Beck Hotel. (1) parking 0.6 mile on L. (2) Cow Green Reservoir parking three miles.
Public transport: None.
Visiting: Open all hours. Full eight mile circuit from either parking area is possible—includes steep inclines around Cauldron Snout (falls) section. Alternatively take shorter return walks to falls from either parking area. Leaflet available. *Take care, weather conditions can change rapidly at any season.* Weardale road: turn R 0.5 mile after hotel (brown sign). Reliable area for Black Grouse—stop and scan where safe to do so—do not enter fields. Late Mar-May, early start recommended.
Contact: Natural England, Widdybank Farm: 01833 622 374
Return to Middleton-in-Teesdale, then B6282 and N on B6278 for Stanhope. Head E to Wolsingham on A689.

2 BACKSTONE BANK WOOD/
TUNSTALL RESERVOIR
Northumbrian Water
Habitats: Woodland, reservoir.
Birds: All year: Buzzard, Marsh Tit, common woodland spp. *Spring/summer:* Goosander, Common Sandpiper, Woodcock, Oystercatcher, Tree Pipit, Redstart, Wood Warbler, Pied & Spotted Flycatchers, Grey Wagtail, Siskin.
Other: Woodland flora.
Directions: DL13 3LZ; NZ 064 413 (reservoir car park). 2.5 miles N of Wolsingham, off A689. Head towards Stanhope, just before leaving village, turn R into Leazes Lane and continue to reservoir. Limited roadside parking by dam wall, S end of reservoir—car park another 300 yards on R. Walk over dam to access S end of wood.
Public transport: Bus: 101 Bishop Auckland-Stanhope (Mon-Sat) stops in Wolsingham. Footpaths go up to reservoir from here making an extended walk. Weardale Travel (01388 528 235).
Visiting: Open all hours. Can walk around reservoir and through woodland (2 mile circuit). Longer walks throughout area.
Contact: None.
Take A689 from Wolsingham then A68 to Bishop Aukland.

2	**Backstone Bank Wood/ Tunstall Reservoir**
11	**Derwent Walk and Derwenthaugh**
8	**Hawthorne Dene**
3	**Low Barns**
4	**Margrove Ponds**
5	**Portrack Marsh**
6	**Saltholme**
7	**Teesmouth**
9	**Washington Wetland Centre**
10	**Whitburn Coastal Park**
1	**Widdybank Fell**

3 LOW BARNS

Durham Wildlife Trust

Habitats: Flooded gravel pits, wet grassland, reedbeds, riverbank, woodland.

Birds: All year: Goosander, Kingfisher, Marsh & Willow Tits, Dipper, common woodland spp inc Tawny Owl, Nuthatch. *Spring/summer:* Oystercatcher, Common Sandpiper, Woodcock, hirundines, Redstart, Pied & Spotted Flycatchers, warblers, Grey Wagtail. *Autumn/Winter:* Bittern, Water Rail, Snipe, Lapwing, Green Sandpiper, Barn Owl, Redwing, Fieldfare, Siskin, Redpoll, Crossbill.

Other: Dragonflies.

Directions: DL14 0AG; NZ 161 314. NW of Bishops Auckland. Follow brown tourist signs: off A68 at Witton-le-Wear or off A689 from Bishop Auckland, at High Grange. Reserve one mile either way.

Public transport: None.

Visiting: Open daily 9:30am-4:30pm. Car park (free/donation for non-members), visitor centre open 10am-4pm. Toilets inc disabled, shop, cafe. Pathways and hides suitable for wheelchairs.

Contact: Durham WT: 0191 584 3112; mail@durhamwt.co.uk

A68 to Darlington then E on A67, A1044 and, ultimately, the A171 at Guisborough.

4 MARGROVE PONDS NATURE RESERVE

Tees Valley Wildlife Trust

Habitats: Shallow open water, reedbed, fenland, wet grassland flanked by low, gorse and scrub-covered spoil heaps (once mined for iron ore), disused railway line.

Surrounded by wooded hills.

Birds: 150 spp recorded. Water Rail, Shoveler, Snipe, Sparrowhawk, Goshawk (possible), Peregrine Falcon, Kestrel, Merlin (possible) Willow Tit, Cetti's & Reed Warblers, Lesser Whitethroat, Reed Bunting. *Passage:* Garganey, Ruff, Wood, Green, Common & Pectoral Sandpipers, Osprey, Marsh Harrier, Hobby. *Winter:* Wildfowl, winter thrushes.

Other: Smaller ponds good for amphibians.

Directions: TS12 3BZ (Heritage Centre); NZ 654 162 (main pond). Leave the A171 (Middlesbrough-Whitby) in Charltons, taking the road signed for Margrove Park and Boosbeck. Car park at Margrove Heritage Centre (HQ of TVWT) Walk through village, then track to reserve on L in dip in road. Reserve 300 yards down track.

Public transport: Bus: X93/94 Middlesbrough to Scarborogh stops in Charltons, Arriva North East (0344 800 44 11).

Visiting: Free car parks at Hertage Centre (toilets Mon-Fri, 9am-5pm) and another (small) at start of track to reserve. No facilities at reserve, flat, compacted surface track along SW side of main pond, seat. Another track from Boosbeck at NW end of pond. May flood. Dogs on leads, clean up mess,

Contact: 01287 636382; info@teeswildlife.org

Take 171 W from Guisborough to junction with A66, then W and as below.

5 PORTRACK MARSH SSSI

Tees Valley Wildlife Trust

Habitats: 50 acres of partly reclaimed ponds, reedbed,

341

grassland and scrub on N side of Tees between Tees Viaduct and Barrage.

Birds: *Spring:* Wheatear, Whinchat. *Summer:* Little Grebe, Lapwing, Common Tern, Kingfisher, Sand Martin (nest bank), Willow, Sedge & Grasshopper Warblers, Blackcap, Whitethroat. *Autumn:* Dunlin, Greenshank, Ruff, Black-tailed Godwit, Gadwall, Wigeon. *Winter:* Starling murmuration and roost in reeds. Jack Snipe.

Other: Otter, Grey & Common Seals

Directions: TS17 6QB; NZ 465 193. From A66 follow signs for Tees Barrage, go straight over roundabout, and barrage, turn R into Whitewater Way.

Public transport: Adjacent to Tees Barrage International White Water Course, which is served by several Teeside bus routes: 36, 36A, 58, X10, X12.

Visiting: Free parking off Whitewater Way. Do not use Talpore car park. No facilities but toilets in Talpore. Most paths compacted aggregate and fairly flat, though slope down from entrance. Cycle path along N bank of Tees.

Contact: 01287 636 382; info@teeswildlife.org
Return to A66, head E, then cross Tees again on A19, leave on A1046. Then A178. Visitor Centre 1st L.

6 SALTHOLME

RSPB

Habitats: Wet grasslands, reedbeds, pools with tern islands, wader scrapes.

Birds: *All year:* Lapwing, Peregrine Falcon, Water Rail. *Spring/summer:* Breeding Avocet, Lapwing, Bittern, Great Crested Grebe, common wildfowl, hirundines, Snipe, Skylark, colony of Common Terns. *Autumn:* Various waders inc Black-tailed Godwits and Green Sandpipers, occasional rarer species. *Winter:* Large numbers of wildfowl and waders, inc impressive flocks of Golden Plover and Lapwing. Starling murmuration.

Directions: TS2 1TP; NZ 506 231. N of River Tees between Middlesbrough and Billingham. From A19, take A689 north of Stockton and then A1185. After 4 miles join A178 at mini roundabout. Take 3rd exit and reserve is 250 yards on R.

Public transport: Bus: 1 Middlesbrough-Hartlepool stops outside reserve. Stagecoach.

Visiting: Open daily (not 24-26 Dec) 9:30am-5pm Apr-Oct (4pm Nov-Mar). Large car park, inc Blue Badge spaces and coach parking—charge for non-members. Visitor centre, cafe and shop open 10am-4pm (3:30pm winter). Toilets (inc adapted), picnic areas, bound gravel surfaces to 4 trails, 4 hides. Mobility scooters available to hire. Dogs not allowed.

Contact: RSPB: 01642 546 625; saltholme@rspb.org.uk
Continue on A178.

7 TEESMOUTH NNR

Natural England (Northumbria Team)

Habitats: Grazing marsh, dunes, intertidal sand and mudflats.

Birds: *Spring/summer:* Breeding Ringed Plover, Lapwing, Oystercatcher, Redshank and Snipe. *Passage:* Terns and skuas in late summer, scarce passerine migrants and rarities. *Winter:* Internationally important numbers of waterbirds, inc divers, grebes, waders and Shelduck. Merlin, Peregrine, Short-eared Owl, Twite, Snow Bunting.

Other: Northern area has large Marsh Orchid populations in damp dune grassland. Colony of Common Seals at Seal Sands (pups born in late-Jun).

Directions: Two areas—North Gare, centred on TS25 2DT; NZ 535 276 and Seal Sands—centred on TS25 2BY; NZ 530 260. 3 and 5 miles S of Hartlepool, E of A178. Access to N area from car park at NZ 533 282, 0.5 mile E of A178. Access to S area from A178 bridge over Greatham Creek at NZ 509 254. Car park adjacent to A178 at NZ 508 251. Both car parks can accommodate coaches.

Public transport: Bus: 1 Middlesborough-Hartlepool. Stagecoach. Train—Seaton Carew is 1.25 miles from North Gare car park.

Visiting: Open all hours. N area—no restrictions over most of dunes and North Gare Sands (avoid golf course, dogs must be kept under close control). S area—easy-access path to public hides at NZ 516 255 & NZ 516 252 (no other access). Nearest toilets at Seaton Carew, 1 mile to N and **6 Saltholme** (1 mile to S). Interpretation panels and leaflet.
Teesmouth Field Centre: 01429 853 847;
www.teesmouthfieldcentre.org.uk

Contact: Natural England:
  0191 586 0004;
northumbria.hub@naturalengland.org.uk
Stay on A178 to Hartlepool, then A1086 to Easington.

8 HAWTHORN DENE
   NATURE RESERVE

Durham Wildlife Trust

Habitats: Extensive area of semi-natural habitat situated on magnesium limestone escarpment. Steep-sided ravine woodland and limestone grassland.

Birds: *Summer:* Green Woodpecker, Sparrowhawk, Kestrel, Skylark (important conservation site), Twite, Linnet, Yellowhammer, Whitethroat, Blackcap, Grasshopper Warbler, Tree Sparrow, Reed Bunting. *Passage:* Wheatear, Fieldfare, Redwing, Waxwing, Buzzard, Ringed Plover, Dunlin, Knot, Lapwing. *Winter (coast/offshore):* Wide variety of waders (inc Turnstone, Purple Sandpiper, Redshank, Curlew, Oystercatcher). Common Scoter, Red-throated Diver, Guillemot, Cormorant and Great Crested Grebe.

Other: Good variety of butterflies. Snowdrops, Bluebells and numerous spp orchid, inc Early Purple, Bird's Nest, Lesser Butterfly & Bee. Roe Deer, Badger and Brown Hare.

Directions: SR7 8SH; NZ 424 459. Hawthorn Dene

Meadow located between Easington and Seaham on Durham coast. Leave A19 at Easington or Seaham and join B1432 to Hawthorn village. From N end of village, follow minor road E, signposted 'Quarry Traffic'. After 0.25 mile, road ends at two metal gates. Park on grass verge on opposite side to cottage. Follow track through gate for 350 yards, turn R on to trail into wood.
Public transport: Bus: 22/23 Sunderland to Durham/Hartlepool, pass through Hawthorn. Arriva Durham County. Short walk to reserve entrance.
Visiting: Open all year, footpaths. Dogs on leads.
Contact: Durham WT: 0191 584 3112; mail@durhamwt.co.uk
Back to Easington, take A182 N. In Washington, A195 E.

9   WWT WASHINGTON WETLAND CENTRE
WWT
Habitats: Saline lagoon, tidal river, pools, reedbed, woodland
Birds: Little Egret, Kingfisher, Herring Gull, Water Rail
Breeding: Lapwing, Avocet, Redshank, Common Tern, Grey Heron. *Autumn passage:* Whimbrel, Black-tailed Godwit, Greenshank, Ruff, Dunlin, Common, Green & Wood Sandpipers, Jack Snipe, Snipe. *Winter:* Teal, Goldeneye, Curlew (one of the UK's largest inland freshwater Curlew roosts), Redshank, Woodcock, Redpoll. Willow Tit, Greenfinch, Bullfinch, Mistle Thrush in woodland.
Other: Otters, 7 spp of bat: Noctule, Daubenton's, Brown Long-eared, Whiskered, Common, Nathusius & Soprano Pipistrelle. Common Frog and Toad, Smooth & Great-crested Newts.
Directions: NE38 8LE; NZ 330 562. Stands on N bank of River Wear, 4 miles from A1/A194(M). **N-bound**, leave A1(M) at J64, take A195 (Western Highway, then Northumberland Way) to intersection with A1231, then head E for Sunderland. **S-bound** leave A194(M) at J1, take A182 (Washington Highway) to junction with A1231, head E for Sunderland. In both cases, following brown duck signs, leave A1231 at roundabout to SW of Nissan plant. Take Pattinson Way S. At 1st roundabout, take 1st exit (Barmston Lane), after 200 yards follow Barmston Lane sharp R and then into car park.
Public transport: Bus: Waterview Park government offices immediately behind centre served by 8, 81, 8A, 82, 939. Train—Sunderland.
Visiting: Car park free (accessible spaces), charge for centre. Open Apr-Oct 10am-5:30pm; Nov-Mar; 10am-4:30pm, last admission 1 hour before closing, 7 days a week (closed 25/26 Dec). Cafe (closes 5pm, 4pm winter, hot food served until 3pm), shop, toilets (inc accessible). 6 hides, most step-free access, inner paths tarmacked. Assistance dogs welcome except in Close Encounters and Ganderland.
Contact: 0191 416 5454; info.washington@wwt.org.uk
Take A1321 E, the A183 N from Monkwearmouth.

10   WHITBURN COASTAL PARK
National Trust/South Tyneside Council
Habitats: Clifftop, parkland, scrub.
A premier migration-seawatching site.
Birds: Nearly 300 spp recorded from wider area. *Spring/autumn* are good for seabirds, wildfowl and waders passing offshore, inc divers, ducks, geese and swans, shearwaters, skuas, gulls and terns. On land, common, scarce and occasional rare migrants are regular. *Winter:* Divers, scoter, auks, waders.
Other: Cetaceans.
Directions: Coastal stretch SE of South Shields to Whitburn on A183 coastal road between Souter Lighthouse and Whitburn Point LNR (both parking areas accessed from A183 at: SR6 7NF; NZ 407 638).
Public transport: Bus: E1/E2/E6 South Shields to Sunderland stop in Lizard Lane, Whitburn—short walk through to coast. Stagecoach.
Visiting: Open all hours. Car parks by lighthouse (pay & display/NT members free, 9am-8pm, 6pm Nov-Mar) and LNR. Cafe/shop/toilet at lighthouse (10am-5pm). Nearby Whitburn Conservation Centre has toilets. Plenty of seawatching viewpoints, check out whole area for migrants.
Contact: National Trust: 0191 529 3161; souter@nationaltrust.org.uk
Return to Washington and then A1(M). Head N. Stay on A1 to junction with A694.

11   DERWENT WALK COUNTRY PARK
AND DERWENTHAUGH PARK
Gateshead Council
Habitats: Mixed woodland, river, ponds, meadows.
Birds: All year: Red Kite, Kingfisher. Great Spotted & Green Woodpeckers, Dipper, Nuthatch. *Summer:* Grasshopper Warbler, Lesser Whitethroat, Blackcap, Garden Warbler, *Winter:* Teal, Tufted Duck, Goosander, Marsh Tit, Brambling, Bullfinch, Siskin.
Other: Otter, Roe Deer, Badger, woodland flowers.
Directions: NE39 1AU; NZ 178 604 (Thornley Woodlands Visitor Centre, near Rowlands Gill). NE16 3BN; NZ 199 621 (Swalwell Visitor Centre, on B6317 beside Blaydon Rugby Club). Along River Derwent, 4 miles SW of Newcastle/Gateshead. Several car parks along A694. Derwent Walk follows old rail track for 11 miles from Swalwell to Consett.
Public transport: Buses—various services from Newcastle/Gateshead to Swalwell/Rowlands Gill. Bus stop—Thornley Woodlands Centre. Go North East (0191 420 5050).
Visiting: Open all hours. 2 visitor centres, various car parks. Thornley Woodlands, open daily 10am-3pm (3:30pm Sat/Sun). Parking, toilets, cafe, ranger service. Swalwell, open 10am-3pm Mon-Fri only (not Christmas-New Year or bank holidays). Parking, toilets, information—open subject to staff availability. Hides at Far

Pasture Ponds and Thornley feeding station—keys from Thornley, both accessible to wheelchairs.
Contact: Thornley Woodlands Centre: 01207 545 212; Swalwell Visitor Centre: 0191 414 2106; countryside@gateshead.gov.uk; www.gateshead.gov.uk/article/4393/Derwent-Walk-Country-Park-and-Derwenthaugh-Park
Return to A1, cross Tyne, head W on A69 and enter Northumberland.

Northumberland

This is a county of two halves which offers a fantastic range of birdwatching along the coast and inland. The seabird colonies on the Farne Islands and Coquet Island are teeming with birds that can be seen at close quarters. Coastal sites, such as Holy Island (Lindisfarne), Budle Bay and East Chevington, attract spring and autumn migrants (including rarities) and large numbers of wintering birds. Inland, Kielder Forest is excellent for Crossbills and raptors, including Osprey and Goshawk, while the nearby moors hold a good selection of upland species.

Bird Atlas/Avifauna
Northumbria Bird Atlas
Tim Dean, Dick Myatt, Muriel Cadwallender & Tom Cadwallender
(Northumberland & Tyneside Bird Club, 2015).

Bird Recorder
Tim Dean, 2 Knocklaw Park, Rothbury, NE65 7PW: 01669 621 460; t.r.dean@btinternet.com

Bird Reports
Birds In Northumbria (1970-), from NTBC -
Trevor Blake, 6 Glenside, Ellington, Morpeth, NE61 5LS: 07368 236 268; trevor.1958@live.co.uk
North East Naturalist (1971-), from NHSN, Great North Museum, Hancock, Barras Bridge, Newcastle upon Tyne, NE2 4PT: 0191 208 2790; nhsn@ncl.ac.uk

BTO Regional Representatives
Tom Cadwallender
Wetland Bird Survey (WeBS)
Local Organizers: webs@bto.org
Lindisfarne
Andrew Craggs
Northumberland (Coastal)
Kathy Evans
Northumberland (Inland)
Tim Daley
Clubs
Natural History Society of Northumbria (1829; 2,900+), Great North Museum: Hancock, Barras Bridge, New-

castle upon Tyne, NE2 4PT: 0191 208 2790; nhsn@ncl. ac.uk; www.nhsn.org.uk
Meetings: 6pm, Mondays (Oct-Mar). Curtis Auditorium, Herschel Building, Newcastle University, Newcastle upon Tyne, NE1 7RU.
North Northumberland Bird Club (1984; 160)
Neil Hincliff (Chair): neilskye8@gmail.com;
Paul Ashdown (Sec): ashbauve.pm@gmail.com;
Membership Secretary: m__e_cobb@msn.com
www.northnorthumberlandbirdclub.co.uk
facebook: North Northumberland Bird Club Group
Meetings: 7:30pm, 2nd Friday of the month (Sep-Jun). Bamburgh Pavilion (corner of green below Bamburgh Castle).
Northumberland & Tyneside Bird Club (1958; 270).
Andrew Brunt (Sec), South Cottage, West Road, Longhorsley, Morpeth, NE65 8UY: 01670 788 352;
ntbcorg@gmail.com; www.ntbc.org.uk
Meetings: 7pm, 2nd Thursday of the month (Sep-Apr). Northern Rugby Club, McCracken Park, Great North Road, Newcastle upon Tyne, NE3 2DT, unless indicated otherwise on the website.

Ringing Groups/Bird Observatory
NHS of Northumbria
Northumbria RG: www.northumbriaringinggroup.com

RSPB Local Group
Newcastle upon Tyne (1969; 110)
Peter Weighill: NewcastleRSPBgroup@gmail.com;
https://group.rspb.org.uk/newcastle/
Meetings: Zoom meeting 1st Tuesday of the month (Nov/Dec and Feb/Mar). Also a 'Walk & Talk' meeting in Oct and Apr. Contact/see website for details.

Wildlife Trust
Northumberland Wildlife Trust (1971; 10,000)
Garden House, St Nicholas Park, Jubilee Road, Gosforth,
Newcastle upon Tyne, NE3 3XT: 0191 284 6884; mail@northwt.org.uk; www.nwt.org.uk

Entering from Tyne & Wear

1 ALLEN BANKS
National Trust
Habitats: 620 acres, ancient semi-natural woodland, river.
Birds: 70+ spp. *All year:* Goosander, Buzzard, Dipper, common woodland and farmland birds. *Spring/Summer:* Redstart, Tree Pipit, Warblers, inc Wood & Garden, Pied & Spotted Flycatchers. *Winter:* Winter thrushes, Siskin, Redpoll, Brambling, Hawfinch (scarce).
Other: Red Squirrel, 8 spp bats inc Daubenton's. Woodland flora inc Bluebells and Wild Garlic.

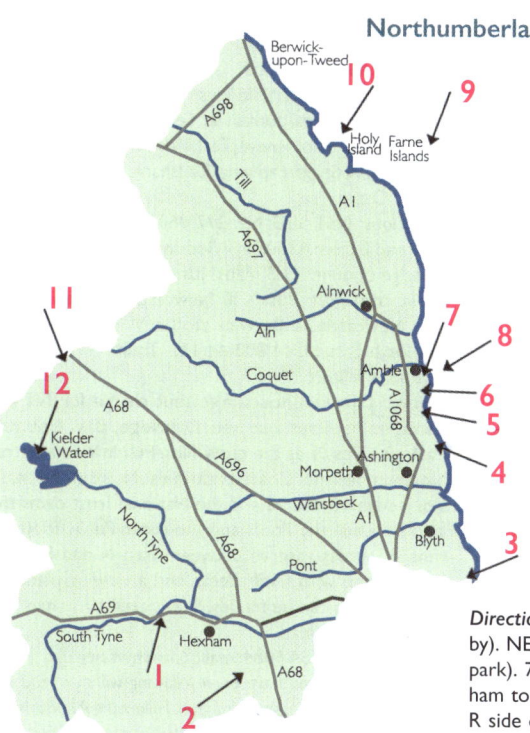

1	**Allen Banks**
8	**Coquet Island**
4	**Cresswell Pond and Foreshore**
5	**Druridge Pools**
6	**East Chevington**
8	**Farne Islands**
7	**Hauxley**
9	**Holburn Moss**
12	**Kielder Water and Forest**
10	**Lindisfarne**
3	**St Mary's Island and Wetland**
2	**Slaley Forest**
11	**Whitelee Moor**

Directions: NE47 7BP; NY 798 640 (but avoid using Sat Nav). 5.5 miles E of Haltwhistle, 3 miles W of Haydon Bridge, signposted off A69 (0.5 mile to S).
Public transport: Bus: 685 Newcastle/Hexham to Brampton/Carlisle stops 0.5 mile away on A69 (alight at Allen Banks, Ridley Hall road end). Stagecoach. Train— Bardon Mill, 1.5 miles.
Visiting: Open dawn-dusk. Pay & display parking (NT members free). Toilets inc. Disabled. Dogs on leads. Three colour-coded walks of varying lengths, totalling over 6 miles.
Contact: National Trust: 01434 321 888; allenbanks@nationaltrust.org.uk
Returning to the A69, head E to Hexham.

2 SLALEY FOREST
Forestry England
Habitats: Woodland—a working forest with rides and clear fell areas. Moorland/farmland around its edge.
Birds: All year: Woodcock, common woodland spp, Siskin, Redpoll, Crossbill. Goshawk, Long-eared & Tawny Owls breed... but hard to see. *Summer:* Nightjar, Cuckoo, Tree Pipit, Redstart, Wood Warbler, common warblers. *Winter:* Redwing, Fieldfare. On adjacent moorland to S: Red Grouse and possible Black Grouse (all year), Whinchat, Wheatear, Merlin, Curlew, Lapwing, Golden Plover (summer), Hen Harrier (winter).
Other: Red Squirrel.

Directions: NE47 0BY; NY 978 551 (B6306 parking lay-by). NE47 0AW; NY 954 551 (Ladycross Quarry car park). 7 miles SE of Hexham. Take B6306 from Hexham to the forest. This road passes parking lay-by (on R side of road). For quarry, turn off B6306 signposted to Ladycross (stay on this narrow road for two miles to parking area).
Public transport: None.
Visiting: Open all hours. Keep to forestry roads/tracks.
Contact: Forestry England: 01388 488 312; enquiries.hamsterley@forestryengland.uk
*Continue E on A69 to A1, head N, then A19 and then as below [on border between **Tyne & Wear** and **Northumberland**].*

3 St MARY'S ISLAND AND WETLAND LNR
North Tyneside Council
Habitats: Small island linked by tidal causeway with grassland, scrub and small wetland on adjacent shore.
Birds: Spring/autumn: Seawatching from island or shore—Gannet, divers, sea duck, geese, Fulmar, shearwaters, skuas, terns, gulls, auks. *Shoreline and adjacent wetland/fields:* Grey Partridge, Snipe, wildfowl, Reed Bunting, waders inc Dunlin, Curlew, Sanderling, Turnstone. *Migrants*—Pied & Spotted Flycatchers, Wheatear, Redstart, Whinchat, warblers, hirundines... anything could turn up inc rarities. *Winter:* Red-throated Diver, Golden & Ringed Plovers, Knot, Purple Sandpiper, Rock Pipit.
Other: Grey Seal, White-beaked & Bottlenose Dolphins, butterflies.
Directions: NE26 4RS; NZ 350 750 (car park). Between Blyth and Whitley Bay. Follow brown tourist signs from A19 Whitley Bay turn-off.
Public transport: Bus: 308 Arriva/309 Cobalt & Coast

Newcastle to Blyth—stop at The Links—Cemetery (short walk to island). GoNorthEast (0191 420 5050). Train—Metro Newcastle to Whitley Bay (two miles). *Visiting:* Pay & display car park, toilets on shore. **NOTE:** Island access depends on safe crossing times. Lighthouse/visitor centre open when tidal access possible—daily May-Oct; weekends/school holidays Nov-Apr. *Contact:* North Tyneside Council, Lighthouse: 0191 643 4777; stmaryslighthouse@northtyneside.gov.uk

DRURIDGE BAY

A 7 mile bay running in a shallow curve from Cresswell in the S to Amble in the N. Sandy beach backed by dunes and areas of marsh and pools further inland. Low rocky headlands at N and S ends.

The A1068 tracks the coast about 1.5 miles inland, with several minor roads running E towards the coast.

The Northumberland Coast Path runs the entire length of the Bay along the inland side of the dunes.

4 CRESSWELL POND AND CRESSWELL FORESHORE

Northumberland Wildlife Trust

Habitats: Two almost adjacent reserves. **Pond:** 50 acres, brackish lagoon, two smaller freshwater ponds and reedbed lying just inside the coastal dunes, SSSI. **Foreshore:** 80 acres of beach up to sand dunes.

Birds: Summer: Coot, Moorhen, Avocet, (bred since 2011), Tree Sparrow, Yellowhammer. *Passage:* Waders. *Winter:* Greylag & Pink-footed Geese, Gadwall, Wigeon, Pochard. Turnstone, Ringed Plover, Sanderling

Other: Otter. Designated an SSSI because brackish conditions result in mix of salt and freshwater invertebrates.

Directions: NE61 5EH; NZ 283 944 (**Pond**). Leave A1068 at roundabout to NW of Ellington and take minor road into village. After 600 yards turn L for Cresswell. 1.5 miles further on, just after holiday park, take L exit at roundabout, follow road along coast. For **Foreshore** use public car park on R at NZ 289 939. For **Pond** continue N to second, small car park (free) on R.

Public transport: Bus: 1 Blyth to Widdrington Station stops in Cresswell, 1 mile S of reserve, Arriva North East (0344 800 44 11).

Visiting: For **Foreshore**, broad track from car park leads to beach. Gap allows locked gate to be bypassed. Above high tide mark, sand is soft. For **Pond**, walk S from second car park to turning for Blackmoor Farm. Turn up track. At farm, enter reserve through gate on R before first building. Follow path and boardwalk to hide. Mostly flat but some steps. Dogs on lead. No facilities at either reserve but toilets and shop in Cresswell.

Contact: 0191 284 6884; mail@northwt.org.uk

Continue N past Cresswell Pond for 1 mile on minor road alongside coast to NT car park for

5 DRURIDGE POOLS

Northumberland Wildlife Trust

Habitats: 60 acres, pools, wet fields.

Birds: Winter: Goldeneye, Teal, Wigeon, Gadwall, Shoveler, Curlew, Snipe, Lapwing, Redshank, Ruff. Stonechat.

Other: Otter

Directions: N61 5EG; NZ 277 960 (car park). Take minor road E from A1608 in Widdrington for NT car park on edge of dunes (1.5 miles) just beyond Druridge.

Public transport: Bus: X20 Newcastle to Alnwick and X18 Newcastle to Berwick stop in Widdrington, Arriva North East (0344 800 44 11). Train—Widdrington Station, 3 miles.

Visiting: Open all hours, free (but charge for NT car park), no facilities but see **Druridge Bay Country Park**, 2 miles N as the crow flies. Pub in Widdrington. Northumberland Coast path runs N from car park along edge of reserve and the National Trust owns the land between the Pools and the coast. Public footpath runs W across reserve between main N and S pools. 2 hides, one with level access, and a viewing platform. Paths flat but can be muddy. Site grazed by ponies and cattle. Dogs on lead.

Contact: 0191 284 6884; mail@northwt.org.uk

The minor road you have been following will now lead you back to the A1068 at Widdrington. Follow the A1068 N to

6 EAST CHEVINGTON

Northumberland Wildlife Trust

Habitats: Ponds and reedbeds created from former open cast coal mine. Areas of scrub and grassland.

Birds: Summer: Skylark, Stonechat, Reed Bunting, Reed, Sedge & Grasshopper Warblers. Marsh Harrier. *Winter:* large numbers of wildfowl, inc Greylag & Pink-footed Geese. Short-eared Owl, Tree Sparrow, Twite. Capable of attracting rarities at any time.

Other: Coastal wildflowers and Dyer's Greenweed in grassland.

Directions: NE61 5BX; NZ 270 990. Near Red Row, overlooking Druridge Bay, off A1068 between Amble and Widdrington—park at **Druridge Bay Country Park** (signposted).

Public transport: Bus: X18 to Red Row (one mile). Arriva in North East.

Visiting: Main access from overflow car park (charge) at **Druridge Bay Country Park** (walk S). 4 hides, plant ID boards. Cafe, toilets and information at Country Park (County Council).

Contact: Northumberland WT: 0191 284 6884; mail@northwt.org.uk

and

DRURIDGE BAY COUNTRY PARK

Northumberland County Council

Habitats: Lake, woodland, 3 miles of the bay but included not so much as a reserve in its own right as for the facilities it offers to those visiting other nearby reserves.

Directions: NE61 5BX; NZ 272 998. Leave A1068 in Hadston, taking minor road E for Country Park (1mile).

Public transport: Bus: X20 Newcastle to Alnwick; X18 from Newcastle to Berwick both stop in Hadston, Arriva North East (0344 800 44 11).

Visiting: 3 car parks (charge) open dawn-dusk. Visitor Centre open 9am-5pm with information centre, shop, toilets and viewing area. Also a cafe open Nov-Mar 10am-3:30pm; 9am-4pm (Sat); 10am-4pm (Sun); Apr-Oct: 10am-4:30pm; 9am-4:30pm (Sat). Separate building has toilet open 24/7.

Contact: 01670 760968; druridgebay@northumberland.gov.uk

Along coast to NE of Country Park another NWT reserve. Linked by King Charles III Coast Path.

7 HAUXLEY

Northumberland Wildlife Trust

Habitats: 65 acres reclaimed from open cast mine. Lake, meadow pasture, woodland. Immediately inland from rocky shore and beach.

Birds: 140 spp annually. Terns inc occasional Roseate, warblers inc Reed, Willow Tit (intermittent), Tree Sparrow, Bullfinch, Reed Bunting. *Passage and winter:* Divers (White-billed recorded), sea duck, Water Rail, Waders inc Bar and Black-tailed Godwits, Grey Plover, Ruff.

Other: Red Squirrel, Otter.

Directions: NE65 0JR (centre of Low Hauxley village, then follow signs); NU 285 023. Leave A1068 just S of Amble, taking minor road to High, then Low Hauxkey.

Public transport: Bus: X20 Newcastle to Alnwick; X18 from Newcastle to Berwick both stop on A1068 near turn to High Hauxley. Arriva North East (0344 800 44 11).

Visiting: Free (charge for parking, car park locked at 5:30pm). Open all year Wildlife Discovery Centre built from straw bales (open 9:30-5:30pm; cafe 10am-4:30; hot food ends 3:30pm), cafe, shop, toilets Circular trail, 6 hides (1 members only). 1 trail and 2 hides wheelchair accessible. Asistance dogs only.

Contact: 0191 284 6884; mail@northwt.org.uk

Return to the A1068 and Amble.

8 COQUET ISLAND

RSPB

Habitats: Small, rocky island off the coast at Amble.

Birds: Breeding: Eider, Puffin, Sandwich, Common Artic & Roseate Terns, Kittiwake. **Sole UK breeding colony of Roseate Terns.**

Other: Grey Seal

Directions: NE65 0FD: NY 267 048 (Amble quayside) Amble is on the A1068 running N from Newcastle to Alnwick. Follow signs for harbour from A1608, park in harbour car parks (charge).

Public transport: Bus: X18 Newcastle-Berwick and X20 Newcastle-Alnwick stop in Amble. Arriva in North East.

Visiting: Landing on the island is not permitted but boat trips from Amble quayside allow viewing from offshore. Puffin Cruises (01665 711 975/07752 861 914; www.puffincruisesamble.com). Trips run all year, weather permitting. Special 90 min birdwatching cruise May-late Jul. There is also CCTV feed from the island in the Northumberland Seabird Centre on the quayside.

Contact: RSPB: 0300 7772 676; www.rspb.org.uk/coquetisland

Return to the A1068 and follow signs in Alnwick to the A1. Join the A1 northbound just outside Alnwick, and then leave the A1 on one of several minor roads running E to Seahouses, the largest of which is the B1341 to Bamburgh and then the B1340 to Seahouses.

8 FARNE ISLANDS

National Trust

Habitats: 15-28 offshore islands, depending on tide.

Birds: Spring/summer: c.23 breeding spp/100,000 pairs of seabirds—Common, Arctic & Sandwich Terns, Puffin, Razorbill, Guillemot, Kittiwake, Eider, Shag. Shearwaters, skuas offshore. Rarities often turn up but usually difficult to see as a visitor.

Other: Large Grey Seal colony, breed late-Oct/early Dec.

Directions: NE68 7TA; NU 219 322 (Seahouses). Access by boat from Seahouses Harbour.

Public transport: Bus: X18 Berwick to Alnwick (few services on Sun). Arriva in North East; 418 (not Sun) Alnwick to Belford. Travelsure (01665 720 955). Trains— Alnmouth and Berwick (then use bus).

Visiting: Four boat companies run trips out of Seahouses. Islands open: Apr, Aug-Sep: Inner Farne 10:30am-5pm. May-Jul: Inner Farne: 1:30pm-5pm. Disabled access possible on Inner Farne, contact Property Manager for details. NT charge to land on islands (free to members)—these charges **DO NOT** include boatman's fees. Toilets on Inner Farne. Dogs may be allowed on boats (check with boatman) but **NOT** allowed on islands.

Contact: National Trust, The Farne Islands, Seahouses, NE68 7SR: 01289 389 244; farneislands@nationaltrust.org.uk

Return to the A1 continue N

9 HOLBURN MOSS

Northumberland Wildlife Trust

Habitats: Raised mire, peat excavations

Birds: Winter: Pink-footed Goose, Wigeon, Grey Plover. Extensive movements between Holburn and **Lindisfarne NNR** to the E.

Directions: TD15 2UJ; NU 050 365. Leave the A1 and head W on the B6353 at Fenwick. After 2.4 miles turn L at a crossroads and take a minor road to Holburn (2.8 miles). Either park in Holburn or continue a further

0.63 mile, then turn L to Holbun Grange and NT car park (charge) for St Cuthbert's Cave.

Public transport: None

Visiting: Open all hours, free (charge at NT car park), no facilities. Follow track from car park for 0.25 to SE entrance (gate and stile), or bridleway from Holburn leading to entrance in NW, again gated. Paths along S edge level but can be muddy. Path over Greenshaw Hill (overlooking mire) narrow and rocky in parts, boggy in others. Dogs on lead.

Contact: 0191 284 6884; mail@northwt.org.uk

Rejoin A1, continue N, then E for the coast at Beal.

10 LINDISFARNE NNR

Natural England

Habitats: Tidal island, dunes, sand, mudflats and salt-marsh, rocky shore and open water. Budle Bay is the area of tidal sand and mudlats between Holy Island and the mainland

Birds: Passage and winter: wildfowl and waders, inc. Pale-bellied Brent Goose, Red-breasted Merganser, Long-tailed Duck and Whooper Swan. Divers, grebes, Merlin. Common, scarce and rare migrants.

Other: Butterflies inc Dark Green Fritillary and Grayling, nine spp orchid inc Coralroot and Lindisfarne Helleborine. Grey Seal.

Directions: TD15 2SS; NU 094 430. Island access lies 2 miles E of A1 at Beal, signposted to Holy Island, 10 miles S of Berwick-on-Tweed.

Public transport: Bus: 477 limited service to Holy Island from Berwick. Border Buses (01289 308 719). WT2 'Lindisfarne Hoppa' service Haggerston/Beal to Holy Island. Woody's Taxis (01289 547 009). Both mainly summer, services fit in with safe crossing times.

Visiting: NOTE—causeway to Holy Island floods at high tide, check safe crossing times BEFORE crossing. Some restricted access (bird refuges). On island—car and coach parking (charge), toilets and visitor centre in village, hide and self-guided trail. New hide with disabled access at Fenham-le-Moor (on mainland).

Contact: Natural England: 01289 381 470

Rejoin A1. At roundabout on outskirts of Berwick-upon-Tweed take 1st L, A698, Stay on A698 for 30 miles (you cross into Scotland at Coldstream), then, at Bonjedward, turn L on to A68 for Jedburgh and Newcastle. Stay on A68, passing through Jedburgh, for 11.75 miles until you reach the English border at Carter Bar.

11 WHITELEE MOOR

Northumberland Wildlife Trust

Habitats: 3,730 acres. Heath and moorland, blanket bog, grassland. 80 scres of deciduous woodland planted since acquired in 1999. Headwaters of River Rede.

Birds: Breeding: Red Grouse, Dunlin, Golden Plover, Hen Harrier, Merlin, Peregrine Falcon, Stonechat. Meadow Pipit, Skylark. Osprey breed on adjoining Catscleugh

Reservoir (Forestry England).

Other: Feral goat. Otter, Common Lizard, Adder

Directions: NT 700 040. Park in car park off A68 at Carter Bar (the ridge that forms the border between England and Scotland with the reserve occupying the slope up to the ridge on the S, English side and to the W of the A68). Path from car park leads along ridge. Two other entry points lower down on English side off A68; the bottom one being a forest track leading into the commercial plantations that are the NE edge of **Kielder Forest**, flanking the Catscleugh Reservoir. This track is drivable, wirh care, but permission required from Forestry England past second gate.

Public transport: Bus: X74 Jedburgh to Newcastle crosses Carter Bar, Peter Hogg of Jedburgh (01835 863755).

Visiting: Open all hours, free, park at Carter Bar (border with Scotland). No facilities. Lightly grazed. Dogs on lead.

Contact: 0191 284 6884; mail@northwt.org.uk

From Carter Bar head S along A68. After you have passed the Catscleugh Reservoir on your R there is a R turn at Cottonshopeburnfoot, whence the Forest Drive (toll, rough surface, 12 miles) leads to

12 KIELDER WATER AND FOREST PARK

Forestry England

Habitats: Largest forest in England (251 sq miles), mainly commercial coniferous/broadleaved woodland. Kielder Water is a 4.25 sq mile reservoir formed by damming the North Tyne.

Birds: Successful Osprey breeding programme since 2009, with some 7 nests today. *All year:* Dipper, Great Spotted & Green Woodpeckers, Tawny Owl, Song Thrush, Jay, Nuthatch, Goldcrest, Siskin. *Spring/summer:* Goshawk, Raven, Chiffchaff, Willow Warbler, Redstart. *Winter:* Crossbill & winter thrushes.

Other: Impressive display of Northern Marsh Orchids at entrance to Kielder Castle. Red Squirrel, Badger, Otter, Roe Deer, seven bat spp.

Directions: NE48 1ER; NY 632 934 (Kielder Castle). The Castle is situated at N end of Kielder Water, NW of Bellingham, 30 miles from Hexham.

Public transport: Bus: 880 (Mon-Sat) Hexham to Kielder Castle. Snaith's Travel (01830 520 609) and Tyne Valley Coaches (01434 602 217); 714 (Sun/bank hol—limited), Newcastle to Kielder Castle). Arriva.

Visiting: Forest open all year, car parks open dawn-dusk. Car parking facilities at Kielder Castle and overflow behind Angler's Arms pub (24-hr parking ticket required)—transferable for all car parks on south shore. Toll charge for 12-mile forest drive (rough surface), closed 1 Dec to end-Apr due to weather conditions. Kielder Castle Information Centre, free exhibition, licensed Kielder Castle Cafe with live wildlife viewing screens, access for disabled and toilets inc baby changing facilities. Many walking/mountain biking trails start from here, ask staff for more info. Kielder Cycle Centre and cycle wash, post office/local shop, Angler's Arms pub, camp site, Kielder Observatory and 24 hour (pay by card) garage. 1 mile multi-access Duke's Trail inc. arboretum and hide where red squirrels can usually be seen. Bakethin Nature Reserve (NW end of reservoir) has dipping pond.

Contact: Forestry England: 01434 250 209; kieldercastle@forestryengland.uk
Ospreys: www.kielderospreys.wordpress.com
www.visitkielder.com
From Kielder itself you can...
*Turn left on to the minor road that runs along the SW side of the reservoir and then the North Tyne before eventually reaching the A69 that runs between Newcastle and Carlisle at a point between 1 Allen Banks and 2 Slaley Forest. You can then do the **Northumberland** circuit all over again or turn W for **Cumbria**.*
*Turn right, head up to the watershed, the border with Scotland, and then follow Liddel Water to the point where it is joined by the Dawston Burn at Saughtree. Here the road joins the B6357. Turn right to head further into the **Scottish Borders**. Turn left for Newcastleton and then **Dumfries and Galloway**.*

And, in future editions of **The Yearbook***...*

ROTHBURY ESTATE
Northumberland Wildlife Trust
The Rothbury Estate lies to the SW of Rothbury, a town to the W of the A697 between Morpeth and Wooler.
In the autumn of 2024 the Northumberland Wildlife Trust, in partnership with the Wildlife Trusts, purchased the first parcel of the 9,400 acre Rothbury Estate and reached agreement to purchase it in its entirety. It is proposed to embark on a programme of landscape-scale habitat restoration.

Cumbria

The Solway attracts wintering wildfowl, including Barnacle and Pink-footed Geese, in their thousands. The Lake District offers a typical range of upland birds and there is an Osprey watch point at Bassenthwaite Lake. The seabird colony at St Bees Head holds a few Black Guillemots and Puffins, whilst Walney Island, with its bird observatory, is a likely place to pick up passage migrants in spring and autumn, which may include the occasional rarity.

Bird Atlas/Avifauna
The Breeding Birds of Cumbria:
A Tetrad Atlas 1997-2001
M Stott, J Callion, I Kinley, C Raven & J Roberts (Cumbria Bird Club, 2002).

Bird Recorder
Chris Hind, 2 Old School House, Hallbankgate, Brampton, CA8 2NW: 07710 272 691;
countyrecorder@cumbriabirdclub.org.uk
Regional Recorders
Allerdale and Copeland
Nick Franklin: 01228 810 413; nickbirder66@gmail.com
Barrow and South Lakeland
Mike Douglas: 07967 935 144;
thedouglasfamily21@yahoo.com
Carlisle and Eden
Peter Howard: 01697 742 206;
carlisleandedenbirdrecorder@cumbriabirdclub.org.uk

Bird Report
Birds and Wildlife in Cumbria (1970-), from CBC—Sue King, The Coach House, Hampsfell Road, Grange over Sands, LA11 6BG: 07879 815 276;
info@cumbriabirdclub.org.uk
Walney Bird Observatory Report (1964-), from WBO—Keith Parkes (Membership Sec), 77 Dalton Lane, Barrow-in-Furness, LA14 4LB: 01229 824 219;
keith.parkes5@gmail.com

BTO Regional Representatives
Colin Gay
Wetland Bird Survey (WeBS)
Local Organizers: webs@bto.org
Cumbria (Excl. Estuaries),
Irt/Mite/Esk Estuaries,
Solway Estuary (Outer South)
Dave Shackleton
Duddon Estuary
Colin Gay
Morecambe Bay (North)
Mike Douglas
Solway Estuary (Inner South)
David Blackledge
Solway Estuary (North)
See *Dumfries and Galloway.*

Clubs
Cumbria Bird Club (1989; 350)
Sue King (Sec), The Coach House, Hampsfell Road, Grange over Sands, Cumbria, LA11 6BG:
07879 815 276; info@cumbriabirdclub.org.uk;
www.cumbriabirdclub.org.uk
Meetings: 7:30pm, 3 indoor meetings Sep-Mar at various venues. AGM at the George Hotel, Devonshire Street, Penrith, CA11 7SU. Contact/see website for details.

Arnside & District Natural History Society (1960's; 300)
Clare Shaw (Sec):
arnsidenaturalhistorysociety@gmail.com;
www.arnsideanddistrictnhs.co.uk
Meetings: 7:30pm, 2nd Thursday of the month (Sep-Apr).
WI Hall, Orchard Rd, Arnside, LA5 0DP.

Ringing Groups/Bird Observatory
Eden RG
Morecambe Bay Wader RG
Watchtree RG: www.watchtree.co.uk
Walney Bird Observatory
Steve Palmer (membership enquiries):
stevejpalmer64@icloud.com;
Recorder: walneyobs@gmail.com;
http://walneybo.blogspot.co.uk
http://walneybo-ringing.blogspot.com/

RSPB Local Groups
North Cumbria (1976; 160)
Richard Dixon: richard.dixon007@btinternet.com;
https://group.rspb.org.uk/carlisle/
Meetings: 7:15pm, (usually) 2nd Wednesday (Sept-Mar).
Wetheral Community Hall, Cumwhinton Road, Wetheral, nr Carlisle, CA4 8HE.
West Cumbria (1986; 72)
Dave Smith: smida@talktalk.net;
https://group.rspb.org.uk/westcumbria/
Meetings: 7:30pm, 1st Tuesday of the month (Sep-Apr).
United Reformed Church, Main St, Cockermouth, CA13 9LU.

Wildlife Trust
Cumbria Wildlife Trust (1962; 15,000).
Plumgarths, Crook Road, Kendal, LA8 8LX:
01539 816 300; mail@cumbriawildlifetrust.org.uk;
www.cumbriawildlifetrust.org.uk

Although ownwed by the Forestry Commission and managed by the Northumberland Wildlife Trust, Butterburn Flow is actually in Cumbria.

1 BUTTERBURN FLOW
Northumberland/Cumbria Wildlife Trusts
Habitats: 1,100 acres, largest of the Border mires, transitional between hummock-hollow and patterned mire. SSSI & SAC. River Irthing flows around its N and E sides, the Butter Burn along the S flank, with the two joining at Butterbrun Farm. Extensive conifer plantations on road to and around Flow but much felling and replanting.
Birds: *Breeding:* Dunlin, Curlew, Peregrine Falcon, Skylark, Medow Pipit.
Other: Cloudberry. Cranberry, Cross-leaved Heath, Sphagnum. Great Sundew, Tall Bog and Few-flowered sedge.

I	**Butterburn Flow**
II	**Campfield Marsh**
5	**Eycott Hill**
7	**Foulshaw Moss**
2	**Geltsdale**
6	**Haweswater**
9	**Hodbarrow**
10	**St Bees Head**
3	**Talkin Tarn**
8	**Walney Island**
4	**Watchtree**

Directions: CA8 7BB (Butterburn Farm); NY 673 763 (slap bang in the middle of the bog) on the border with Northumberland (formed by the Irthing). Leave Hexham-Carlisle A69 at Greenhead and follow the B6318 to Gilsland. To W of Gilsland take minor road heading N. Follow this road past entrance to Gilsland Spa Hotel (currently closed) for 8.75 miles (passing Butterburn Farm) to the high point (990 ft) at NY 660 758 that is the best point to access the bog.
Public transport: None.
Visiting: Open all hours, free, *absolutely* no facilities. No car park but roadside parking by the River Irthing bridge close to Butterburn Farm, c.2 miles before the suggested access point. No paths, terrain difficult and can be very wet. Dogs on lead.
Contact: 01539 816300;
mail@cumbriawildlifetrust.org.uk
Return to B6318. and A69, head W

2 GELTSDALE

RSPB

Habitats: Blanket bog, heath, grassland, native woodland. Two upland farms extending over 13,600 acres and rising to 2,037 ft being managed for wildlife. Active habitat restoration underway

Birds: Breeding: Black Grouse, Golden Plover, Lapwing, Redshank, Curlew, Snipe. Hen Harrier, Merlin, Short-eared Owl. Ring Ouzel.

Other: Red Squirrel.

Directions: CA8 2PN; NY 589 585. At the junction SE of Brampton between the A689 running from the M6 at Carlisle and the A69 from Hexham, take the A689 for Halbankgate. Leave the A689 at Halbankgate and the take the minor road heading SE. The car park is just under 1 mile along this road.

Public transport: Train—Brampton

Visiting: Small car park, no coaches. Visitor centre and toilets 40 min walk from car park (additional blue badge parking by visitor centre). Open all hours (visitor centre & toilets 9am-5pm), free. 5 trails, some through grazed areas, in part uneven or muddy, not wheel/pushcair accessible. Viewing screen overlooking tarn. Dogs on lead

Contact: 01697 746 717; geltsdale@rspb.org.uk

Return to Halbankgate and then Brampton on A69.

3 TALKIN TARN COUNTRY PARK

Carlisle City Council

Habitats: Natural glacial tarn, mature Oak/Beech woodland, orchid meadow (traditionally managed), wet mire and farmland.

Birds: Spring/summer: Spotted Flycatcher, Redstart, Chiffchaff, Wood Warbler. *Winter:* Grebes, swans, Goosander, Gadwall, Wigeon, occasional Smew and Long-tailed Duck. Brambling.

Other: Common Blue Damselfly, Common Darter, Small Copper butterfly, Otter, Red Squirrel.

Directions: CA8 1HN; NY 543 590. Nine miles E of Carlisle. From A69 E at Brampton, go S on B6413 for 2 miles (signposted). Talkin Tarn is on L just after level crossing.

Public transport: Train—Brampton Junction, one mile along footpath.

Visiting: Open all hours. Car park charges, coaches welcome. Tearoom, shop open 10:30am-4pm daily from Easter to Oct half term then Sat/Sun and school holidays until Easter. Toilet. Wheelchair access around tarn. Watersport activities can cause some disturbance to water birds.

Contact: Talkin Tarn Country Park, Tarn Road, Brampton, Cumbria, CA8 1HN: 01228 817 200; talkintarn@carlisle.gov.uk; www.carlisle.gov.uk/talkintarn/

Return to Brampton and then A69 to xentre of Carlisle, then out SW on A595

4 WATCHTREE NATURE RESERVE

Watchtree Nature Reserve Ltd

Habitats: Former WW2 airfield. Woodland, wetland, hay meadow.

Birds: All year: Little Grebe, Tufted Duck, Buzzard, Barn Owl, Skylark, Tree Sparrow, Redpoll, Linnet, Bullfinch, Reed Bunting, Yellowhammer, common woodland spp. *Summer:* Curlew, Sand Martin, Whitethroat, Reed, Sedge & Garden Warblers. *Winter:* Teal, Goldeneye, winter thrushes, finches.

Other: Crested & Palmate Newts, Common Frog, Toad. Brown Hare, Roe Deer, Stoat & Weasel. Occasional Otter. Dragonflies, butterflies, 50 spp water beetles.

Directions: CA5 6NL; NY 304 539. Six miles SW of Carlisle. Take A595/A596 from Carlisle/Wigton. Leave A596 at Whinnow, follow signs for Wiggonby. Turn R just before Wiggonby—reserve 0.5 mile to N of hamlet. Take B5307 from Carlisle—at Kirkbampton turn L towards Wiggonby—reserve c.2 miles on L.

Public transport: None.

Visiting: Open daily 9am-5pm (not 25-27 Dec). Free—donations welcomed. Parking, visitor centre, cafe (10am-4pm), toilets, accessible trails, cycle routes/hire, two hides. Events, education centre. Membership available—access code provided for out of hours visits. Dogs on lead at all times.

Contact: Watchtree NR: 01228 712 539; wnr@watchtree.co.uk

Return to A596/A595 junction and head SW. Continue to Cockermouth and cut back through Lake District on A66 to Keswick. Then approach from W rather than E on A66.

5 EYCOTT HILL

Cumbria Wildlife Trust

Habitats: Upland pasture, flower-rich meadows, moorland, swamps and mires, woodland and scrub.

Birds: Summer: Curlew, Snipe, Peregrine Falcon, Short-eared Owl, Raven, Skylark, Wheatear.

Other: Upland flora inc 20 spp sedge and 18 spp sphagnum moss. Butterflies inc Small Pearl-bordered & Marsh Fritillaries, dragonflies. Dark Deerfly.

Directions: CA11 0XD; NY 393 301. W of Penrith. Take A66 for Keswick from J40 of M6. After 7 miles turn R (signposted Hutton Roof) then L by Sportsman's Inn. Continue for 1.6 miles (through Berrier, car park is on L.

Public transport: None.

Visiting: Open all year. Car park. Cycle racks. Information boards. Waymarked route to summit from car park (0.8 mile)—no surfaced paths/ground uneven and often wet. Dogs on lead.

Contact: Cumbria WT, 01228 829 570; mail@cumbriawildlifetrust.org.uk

Return to Penrith on A66, cross M6, then S on A6. Cross River Eamont, then take B5320 on R. Cross railway in Yanwith then minor road immediately on L to Askham to Bampton.

6 HAWESWATER

RSPB/United Utilities

From 1969 to 2015, Haweswater was home to England's only pair of Golden Eagles. Sadly they are now absent from the country, but the landscape restoration work here is hoping to encourage them back in future.

Habitats: Fells with rocky streams, steep Oak and Birch woodlands.

Birds: *Upland breeders:* Peregrine Falcon, Raven, Ring Ouzel, Curlew, Snipe. *Woodland breeders:* Sparrowhawk, Buzzard, Pied Flycatcher, Wood Warbler, Tree Pipit, Redstart. Breeding Goosander and Dipper around the reservoir and along the rivers. *Winter:* Large gull roost.

Other: Red Deer, Red Squirrel hide, Water Vole, Badger hide.

Directions: No post code; NY 469 108. Mardale Head car park is located at the S end of the reservoir. Go to Bampton village, 10 miles S of Penrith and 5 miles NW of Shap, then head S to Haweswater reservoir and drive along unclassified road beside the reservoir. Road ends at a car park—walk from here.

Public transport: None.

Visiting: Majority of site is open access. The only public car park for the site is at Mardale Head but the other valleys can be accessed from there via a network of public rights of way. Visit: www.wildhaweswater.co.uk for full information.

Contact: RSPB: 01931 713 376;
haweswater@rspb.org.uk

Haweswater is a dead end. There is no vehicular egress to the S. From Bampton take minor road E to Shap and A6. Then S through Kendal and join A590.

7 FOULSHAW MOSS NATURE RESERVE

Cumbria Wildlife Trust

Habitats: Lowland raised mire.

Birds: Breeding Osprey. *All year:* Peregrine, Snipe, Tree Sparrow, Stonechat, Redpoll, Siskin, Reed Bunting. *Spring/summer:* Hobby, Cuckoo, Tree Pipit, warblers. *Winter:* Wildfowl, Marsh & Hen Harrier.

Other: Adder. Dragonflies inc. White-faced Darter. Butterflies inc. large Heath.

Directions: LA11 6SN; SD 458 837. 6 miles SW of Kendal, on A590 between Grange-over-Sands and Kendal. Look for gate entrance on S side of single carriageway section of road. Car park down track.

Public transport: Bus: X6 Kendal to Ulverston (daily), alight at Mill Side (close to reserve entrance). Stagecoach.

Visiting: Open all hours. Small parking area with various boardwalks leading from it inc circular walk. Ground soft/areas of deep water—*stay on boardwalks at all times*. Viewing platform—Ospreys visible from here. Dogs on lead.

Contact: Cumbria WT 01539 816 300;
mail@cumbriawildlifetrust.org.uk

Continue on A590 to Barrow-in-Furness.

8 WALNEY ISLAND

Cumbria Wildlife Trust/Walney Bird Observatory

The Herring Gull colony at Walney Island was where Niko Tingbergen carried out much of his work on Herring Gull behaviour after his move to the UK.

Habitats: Estuarine, saltmarsh, sand dunes, shingle, freshwater and brackish lagoons, scrub and farmland.

Birds: 300 spp. *Spring/autumn:* migrants—island has a proven pedigree for attracting rare and unusual species as well as common spp inc Wheatear, Redstart and Willow Warbler and Tree Sparrow. *Summer:* 1,000 breeding pairs of Herring, Great & Lesser Black-backed Gulls, 30 breeding pairs of Great Black-backed Gull, Shelduck, Eider. Little Tern. Arctic & Sandwich Terns breed nearby and present offshore. *Winter:* Teal, Wigeon, Goldeneye, Redshank, Greenshank, Curlew, Oystercatcher, Knot, Dunlin, Merlin, Short-eared Owl, Twite.

Other: 450 spp of flowering plants—famed for Walney Geranium, but also important for coastal shingle species such as Sea Holly, Sea Rocket and Sea Kale. 550+ spp moths inc sand dune specialities such as Coast Dart & Sand Dart. Grey Seal colony (reserve). Natterjack Toad at North Walney.

Directions: LA14 3YQ; SD 225 620. 6 miles S of Barrow-in-Furness. From Barrow, cross Jubilee Bridge on to Walney Island, turn L at lights. Continue through Biggar village to South End Caravan Park. Follow road for one mile to reserve and Observatory.

Public transport: Bus: 1 Barrow-in-Furness to Biggar Bank, 3.5 mile walk to South End/reserve car park and Obs (along coastal path). Stagecoach.

Visiting: *South Walney CWT Reserve*—open daily (10am-5pm, 4pm in winter)—entrance fee, members free. Coach parking available. Toilets, nature trails, 200 yard boardwalk, hides (two wheelchair accessible). Mobility tramper for hire. No dogs, except assistance dogs. *Observatory*—is located in south but covers whole island. Access to several areas, notably golf course/airfield, is restricted but island's narrow width means most sites are viewable from road or footpaths. Monitoring and ringing of breeding birds/migrants, with ringing opportunities for qualified visitors. For availability contact Observatory.

Contact: Cumbria WT, South Walney: 01229 471 066; mail@cumbriawildlifetrust.org.uk;
Walney Bird Observatory, Coastguard Cottages, Walney Island, Barrow-in-Furness, Cumbria LA14 3YQ: walneyobs@gmail.com;
http://walneybo.blogspot.co.uk

Take A595 N from Barrow-i-F, then A5093 S to Millom.

9 HODBARROW

RSPB

Habitats: Coastal lagoon, limestone grassland (former iron mine), estuary.

Birds: Great Crested Grebe, Red-breasted Merganser. *Summer:* Eider, Black-headed Gull colony, Common, Little & Sandwich Terns, Lesser Whitethroat, Sedge Warbler. *Passage:* Waders, skuas. *Winter:* Wildfowl may inc. Long-tailed Duck, Scaup, winter thrushes.

Other: Dragonflies. Orchids.

Directions: LA18 4JY; SD 174 790. S of Millom. From town square, continue E taking 2nd R (Mainsgate Road signposted for **Hodbarrow RSPB**). Continue for c.0.5 miles, turn L by lagoon for reserve car park.

Public transport: Train—Millom (1.5 miles).

Visiting: Open all hours. Hide (1.5 miles from car park), 3 mile circular walk, picnic area and seating. Nearest facilities in Haverigg/Millom.

Contact: RSPB: 01931 713 376; campfield.marsh@rspb.org.uk

Continue through Millom on A5093 to rejoin A595. Head N along coast. In Egremont take minor road on L to

10 ST BEES HEAD

RSPB

Habitats: Three miles of sandstone cliffs, up to 300 feet high.

Birds: Spring/summer: Largest seabird colony on W coast of England: Fulmar, Cormorant, Guillemot, Razorbill, Puffin, Kittiwake and England's only breeding pairs of Black Guillemot (around Fleswick Bay). Linnet, Stonechat, Whitethroat and Rock Pipit along cliff-top heath areas.

Directions: CA27 0ET; NX 959 118. S of Whitehaven via B3545 to St Bees village. Car park at end of Beach Road.

Public transport: Train—St Bees (0.75 mile).

Visiting: Open all hours. Pay & display car park, toilets next to reserve entrance. Three viewpoints overlook seabird colony—access via three mile cliff-top coast-to-coast footpath (steep in parts). Dogs only on public footpaths.

Contact: RSPB: 01697 351 330; stbees.head@rspb.org.uk

Continue N on A595. To SE of Workington take A596 and then, N of Maryport, the B5300, taking you to the charming Silloth. From Silloth take the B5302 and then B5307 to Angerton. You are working around the mudflats at the mouth of the Rivers Waver and Wampool and crossing a series of mosses and marshes that make up the **South Solway NNR.** *From Angerton, head N on minor road to Anthorn and then follow around Solway coast to*

11 CAMPFIELD MARSH

RSPB

Habitats: Saltmarsh/intertidal areas, open water, raised peat bog, farmland, wet grassland.

Birds: Spring/summer: Breeding Lapwing, Curlew, Redshank, Snipe, Tree Sparrow and warblers. *Spring and autumn:* Passage waders inc Black-tailed Godwit, Whimbrel. Look for Pomarine, Arctic, Great & Long-tailed Skuas over the Solway. *Winter:* Waders (up to 10,000 Oystercatcher among large roosting wader flocks). Wildfowl inc Barnacle & Pink-footed Geese, Shoveler, Scaup, Grey Plover. Hen Harrier.

Other: Roe Deer, Brown Hare. Bog Rosemary, Bog Asphodel, sundews & cotton grass. Large numbers of dragonflies (inc Azure & Emerald Damselflies and Four-spotted Chaser).

Directions: CA7 5AG; NY 197 615. At North Plain Farm, on S shore of Solway estuary, W of Bowness-on-Solway. Signposted on unclassified coast road from B5307 from Carlisle.

Public transport: Bus: 93 from Carlisle terminates at reserve's E end, 1.5 mile walk to North Plain Farm. Stagecoach.

Visiting: Open all hours. Car park at North Plain Farm. Disabled visitors can drive to wheelchair-friendly hide to view high-tide roosts. Small visitor centre—'Solway Wetlands Centre'—open 10am-4pm, manned most weekends. 1 hide, several viewing screens overlooking wetland areas, 3 trails (grass paths, can be muddy). Roadside lay-bys overlook wader roosts.

Contact: RSPB: 01697 351 330; campfield.marsh@rspb.org.uk

SCOTLAND/ALBA
ORGANIZATIONS

BIRD ATLAS/AVIFAUNA
The Birds of Scotland
Ron Forrester & Ian Andrews
(Scottish Ornithologists' Club, 2007)

BIRD REPORT
Scottish Bird Report
(1968-, data online), from:www.the-soc.org.uk/about-us/online-scottish-bird-report

The Scottish headquarters of a number of organizations focusing on birds or where they live are listed here, in advance of the County Directory. Where the organization's UK headquarters is in England, its purpose and activities are presented in the UK/England section and all that is listed here are its Scottish contact details.

BRITISH TRUST FOR ORNITHOLOGY SCOTTISH OFFICE
BTO Scotland's main functions are to promote the work of the Trust and develop wider coverage for surveys in Scotland, by encouraging greater participation in survey work. With a landscape and wildlife so different from the rest of the UK, BTO Scotland ensure that the Trust's work is not just related to the priorities of the UK as a whole but is also focused on the priorities of Scotland. *Contact:* BTO Scotland, Unit 15, Beta Centre, Stirling University Innovation Park, Stirling FK9 4NF: 01796 458 021; scot.info@nto.org
www.bto.org/about-bto/national-offices/bto-scotland

ROYAL SOCIETY FOR THE PROTECTION OF BIRDS (RSPB) SCOTTISH HEADQUARTERS
2 Lochside View, Edinburgh Park, Edinburgh EH12 9DH: 0131 317 4100; RSPB.Scotland@rspb.org.uk

SCOTTISH BIRDS RECORDS COMMITTEE (1984)
Set up by the Scottish Ornithologists' Club to ensure that records of species not deemed rare enough to be considered by the British Birds Rarities Committee, but which are rare in Scotland, are fully assessed; also maintains the official list of Scottish birds.
Contact: SBRC, Mark Wilkinson (Sec)
secy.sbrc@gmail.com
www.the-soc.org.uk/bird-recording/about-sbrc

SCOTTISH ORNITHOLOGISTS' CLUB (1936)
The SOC promotes the study, enjoyment and conservation of wild birds and their habitats across Scotland. The Club has 15 local branches (see County entries), each running a programme of indoor meetings and field trips. Although these events are primarily intended for local branch members, they are also open to members from other branches or to visitors from outside Scotland. The SOC organizes an annual weekend conference in the autumn and a joint SOC/BTO one-day-birdwatchers' conference in the spring. Its quarterly journal, *Scottish Birds,* is free for members. Waterston House, its headquarters, has panoramic views of Aberlady Bay, a prime coastal birdwatching site on the Firth of Forth, just to the E of Edinburgh, and houses a shop, gallery and the George Waterston Library. Drop in if you're passing.
From September to April, the Club runs a programme of monthly talks via Zoom, with the passcode for these talks being sent to all members who have signed up for its e-newsletter. These talks are for members only but membership is not limited to those living in Scotland. To sign up for the newsletter go to:
www.the-soc.org.uk/subscribe or scan this QR code.
Contact:
The SOC, Waterston House,
Aberlady, East Lothian
EH32 0PY:
01875 871 330;
via website;
www.the-soc.org.uk

ASSOCIATION FOR THE PROTECTION OF RURAL SCOTLAND (1926)
Works to protect and enhance Scotland's world renowned landscape and the amenity of the countryside from unnecessary or inappropriate development. The APRS recognizes the needs of those who live and work in rural Scotland and the necessity of reconciling these needs with the sometimes competing requirements of industry and recreation. Members have access to specialist advice, newsletters and regular e-bulletins.
Contact: Association for the Protection Rural Scotland, Dolphin House, 4 Hunter Square, Edinburgh EH1 1QW: 0131 225 7012; info@aprs.scot; http://aprs.scot/

FORESTRY AND LAND SCOTLAND (2019)

F&LS looks after national forests and land to enhance biodiversity, support tourism and increase access to the green spaces that will help improve Scotland's physical and mental health and well-being.

Contact: Forestry and Land Scotland Head Office, Great Glen House, Leachkin Road, Inverness IV3 8NW: 0300 067 6000; enquiries@forestryandland.gov.scot; www.forestryandland.gov.scot

GAME & WILDIFE CONSERVATION TRUST (1931): SCOTTISH OFFICE

Contact: Hopetoun Estates Office, Home Farm, Hopetoun, South Queensferry EH30 9SL; 01312 027 670; scottishhq@gwct.org.uk; www.gwct.org.uk

SCOTTISH FORESTRY (2019)

SF supports the delivery of sustainable Scottish forestry operations including grants for forestry activities and felling permissions.

Contact: Scottish Forestry, Silvan House, 231 Corstorphine Road, Edinburgh EH12 7AT: 0131 370 5250; scottish.forestry@forestry.gov.scot; www.forestry.gov.scot

NATIONAL MUSEUMS SCOTLAND

Entry to the public galleries of Scotland's national museum is free and these are located at Chambers Street, Edinburgh EH1 1JF: 0300 123 6789; www.nms.ac.uk
In addition to what is on display in the public galleries, the museum holds extensive collections of, inter alia, bird specimens. These are held at its Granton site and may be visited by prior arrangement.
The museum very kindly allowed Sylvie Soudan access to its collections of Redpolls as she worked on the images illustrating this edition of **The Yearbook**.

NATIONAL TRUST FOR SCOTLAND (1931)

With a membership of over 300,000 and nearly 4,000 volunteers, the Trust protects and promotes Scotland's natural and cultural heritage for present and future generations to enjoy. Amongst its responsibilities, the Trust looks after listed buildings, gardens/designed landscapes and 76,000ha of countryside - inc. eight National Nature Reserves and 46 Munros (>3,000 ft).

Contact: National Trust for Scotland, Hermiston Quay, 5 Cultins Rd, Edinburgh EH11 4DF: 0131 458 7490; via website; www.nts.org.uk

NATURESCOT (2020)

Formerly Scottish Natural Heritage (1991). Funded by the Scottish Government, to promote and care for Scotland's natural heritage; to enable people to enjoy the outdoors; and to support those who manage it.

Contact: NatureScot HQ, Great Glen House, Leachkin Road, Inverness, IV3 8NW: 01463 725 000; enquiries@nature.scot; www.nature.scot

SCOTTISH OUTDOOR ACCESS CODE

The code, which outlines your rights, responsibilities and how you should behave, can be viewed and downloaded at:
www.outdooraccess-scotland.scot

SCOTTISH WILDLIFE TRUST (1964)

A member of The Wildlife Trusts partnership. The Trust's vision is for 'healthy, resilient ecosystems across Scotland's land and seas.' Its main activities focus on managing over 100 wildlife reserves and four visitor centres; undertaking practical conservation tasks; influencing and campaigning for better wildlife-related policy and action; inspiring people to enjoy and find out more about wildlife. It has a network of 18 local groups and a total of 42,000 members. Contact details for these local groups are listed in the relevant County entries.

Contact: Scottish Wildlife Trust, Harbourside House, 110 Commercial Street, Edinburgh, EH6 6NF. 0131 312 7765; via website; www.scottishwildlifetrust.org.uk

WILDFOWL AND WETLANDS TRUST (WWT)

The WWT has one Wetland Centre in Scotland *Caerlaverock*, Eastpark Farm, Caerlaverock, Dumfriesshire DG1 4RS: 01387 770 200; info.caerlaverock@wwt.org.uk

WOODLAND TRUST

Scottish Office: South Inch Business Centre, Perth, PH2 8BW: 01738 635 544; scotland@woodlandtrust.org.uk

Acknowledgement
The Birdwatcher's Yearbook
would like to thank the National
Museums Scotland and the Senior
Curator of its collection of bird speci-
mens, Martin Stervander, for access
to this collection and for advice in
preparing the paintings of Redpolls.

Dumfries and Galloway

The Solway is nationally important for wintering Barnacle Geese—WWT Caerlaverock and RSPB Mersehead are the best sites to see them along with other wildfowl. Ospreys and Red Kites have colonized and there is a chance of Golden Eagle over upland areas or Hen Harrier on moorland. The Mull of Galloway has fine seabird cliffs.

Bird Recorder
Joint Recorders: Gavin & Alyn Chambers, Tibbie Strand, Carsethorn, Dumfries, DG2 8DS: 07824 636 863; dgrecorder@gmail.com

Bird Report
Birds in Dumfries and Galloway (1987-), published by SOC D&G branches from
Peter Swan, 13 Robb Place, Castle Douglas, DG7 1LW: 01556 502 144; pandmswan@btinternet.com

BTO Regional Representatives

Dumfries
Andy Riches:
Huw Connick (Assistant)
Kirkcudbright
Andrew Bielinski
Huw Connick (Assistant)
Wigtown
Steve Willis
Wetland Bird Survey (WeBS)
Local Organizers: webs@bto.org
Auchencairn & Orchardton Bays
Euan MacAlpine:
Dumfries and Galloway (Other Sites),
Rough Firth, Solway Estuary North
Andy Riches:
Fleet Bay
Ian Bainbridge:
Loch Ryan, Wigtown Bay
Paul Collin

Club
SOC Dumfries Branch (1964; 75)
Heather Stevenson: 01387 248 535;
dumfriessecretary@the-soc.org.uk;
www.the-soc.org.uk/local-branches/dumfries
Meetings: 7:30pm, 2nd Wednesday of the month (Sep-Apr). Dumfries Baptist Church Centre, Gillbrae Rd, Dumfries, DG1 4EJ.
Online talks also held. Contact/see website for details.

SOC Stewartry Branch (1976; 80)
Joan Howie: 01644 420 280;
joanospreys1@btinternet.com;
www.the-soc.org.uk/local-branches/stewartry
Meetings: 7:30pm, 2nd Thursday of the month (Sep/Oct/Apr); 10:30am (Nov-Mar). Village Hall, Balmaclellan (2 miles east of New Galloway), Castle Douglas, DG7 3QE. Online talks also held. Contact/see website for details.
SOC West Galloway Branch (1975; 35)
Geoff Sheppard: 01776 870 685;
geoff.roddens@btinternet.com;
the-soc.org.uk/local-branches/west-galloway
Meetings: Online talks. Contact/see website for details.

Ringing Group/Bird Observatory
North Solway RG

RSPB Local Group
No groups.

Scottish Wildlife Trust Regional Networks
None

Forestry and Land Scotland Regional Office
0300 067 6900;
enquiries.south@forestryandland.gov.scot

Borders Forest Trust
See **Scottish Borders**

KEN-DEE MARSHES
RSPB
The former RSPB reserve at Ken-Dee Marshes has now closed. Do not visit.

Take A75 from M6/A74(M) at Gretna, follow signs after Annan.

1 CAERLAVEROCK
WETLAND CENTRE
The Wildfowl & Wetlands Trust
Habitats: Saltmarsh, grassland, wetland.
Birds: Summer: Osprey, Barn Owl, Skylark, Tree Sparrow, migrant warblers. *Winter:* Wildfowl esp Barnacle (up to 40,000) & Pink-footed Geese, Whooper Swan, Hen Harrier, Merlin.
Other: Natterjack Toad, Badger. Northern Marsh Orchid.
Directions: DG1 4UF; NY 051 656. Overlooks the Solway. From St Michael's church in Dumfries take B725 towards Bankend, following tourist signs. Also signposted from A75 W of Annan.
Public transport: Bus: 6A (not Sun) from Dumfries stops one mile from reserve. Stagecoach West Scotland.
Visiting: Open (not 24-26 Dec), Tues-Sat 10am-4pm winter; times for summer to be announced. Parking

1	**Caerlavrock**
5	**Cairnsmore of Fleet**
12	**Carrifran Wildwood**
7	**Crook of Baldoon**
10	**Glentrool**
13	**Grey Mare's Tail**
3	**Mersehead**
8	**Mull of Galloway**

2	**Stenhouse Wood**
11	**Tarras Valley**
4	**Threave House**
6	**Wigtown Bay**
9	**Wood of Cree**

enquiries@scottishwildlifetrust.org.uk
Then return to A76 and either head NW into **Ayrshire** *or back to Dumfries, cross the Nith and head S on A710.*

for coaches. Charge for non-WWT members. Visitor centre but shop and cafe closed Nov '25. 16 Hides, four towers, heated observatory and sheltered picnic area. Self-catering farmhouse accommodation. Summer meadow walk May-Aug, wild swan feeds Oct-Apr. Assistance dogs only.
Contact: WWT Caerlaverock: 01387 770 200; info.caerlaverock@wwt.org.uk
Take B725 to Dumfries, then take the A76 N to Thornhill.

2 STENHOUSE WOOD
Scottish Wildlife Trust
Habitats: Deciduous woodland
Birds: All year: common woodland birds, Buzzard, Dipper, Grey Wagtail, Willow Tit, Siskin. *Summer:* Redstart, Pied Flycatcher, Wood Warbler. *Winter:* Woodcock, winter thrushes.
Other: Red Squirrel, woodland flora inc Toothwort and Bird's Nest Orchid.
Directions: DG3 4LD; NX 797 931. Six miles W of Thornhill. Take A702 to Tynron. Cross river, turn R at war memorial. After 0.3 mile turn R into no through road—reserve on L after 0.5 mile. Park on grass by reserve sign or in long lay-by beside narrow road.
Public transport: Bus: 212 Moniaive to Thornhill (not Sun)—limited service stops in Tynron. W. Brownrigg (01848 330 203).
Visiting: Open all hours. Unsurfaced path is maintained but steep and uneven in places. Dogs under close control.
Contact: Scottish WT: 0131 312 7765;

3 MERSEHEAD
RSPB
Habitats: Wet grassland, arable farmland, saltmarsh, intertidal mudflats.
Birds: Summer: Breeding birds inc Lapwing, Redshank, Skylark. *Winter:* Whooper Swan, 7-10,000 Barnacle Geese, 2,000 Teal, 1,000 Wigeon, 1,000 Pintail, waders (inc Dunlin, Knot, Oystercatcher), Hen Harrier.
Other: Natterjack Toad, Otter.
Directions: DG2 8AH; NX 928 566. Take A710 S from Dumfries for about 18 miles. Reserve signposted from New Abbey and then on L just before Caulkerbush village. Single track road with passing places runs for one mile to car park, adjacent to visitor centre. From Castle Douglas, take A745, then A711 to Dalbeattie. Follow signs from Dalbeattie before joining A710.
Public transport: Bus: 372 Dalbeattie to Dumfries. Bus stop at Caulkerbush (Southwick) or ask driver to stop at end of access road to reserve c.1 mile from visitor centre, Houstons Coaches (01576 203 874).
Visiting: Dawn-dusk daily (not 25 Dec). Car park (members free, charge for non-members). Visitor centre open 10am-4pm, occasionally unmanned—viewing room, toilets, refreshments (when manned). Wheelchair-friendly hides/trails, open all hours, disabled parking spaces within 450 yards of hides and next to visitor centre.
Contact: RSPB: 01387 780 579;
mersehead@rspb.org.uk
Take A745 to Castle Douglas.

4 THREAVE HOUSE, GARDENS & NATURE RESERVE

National Trust for Scotland

Habitats: Former dairy farm, beside River Dee. Wetland being restored by breaching flood banks, low intensity grazing, removing non-native conifers and broadleaf planting. 200 acre SPA.

Birds: Peregrine, Osprey (nest platform), Red Kite, Willow Tit. *Winter:* Greenland White-front, Pink-footed Geeese, Whooper Swan, Wigeon, Teal, Mallard, Pintail.

Other: 8 spp bat, Red Squirrel, Otter.

Directions: DG7 1RX; NX 746 617 (Threave Nature Reserve car park). For the nature reserve, leave A75 at the roundabout just W of Castle Douglas, taking the minor road NW signposted for Kelton Mains or Threave Castle, not the B736, directly opposite, for Threave House & Gardens. Car park is at Kelton Mains after 600 yards.

Public transport: Bus: 500 Dumfries-Stranraer (Stagecoach West Scotland, 01292 613 500); 501 Dumfries-Kirkcudbright & 502A Castle Douglas-Kirkcudbright (McCalls Coaches, 01576 204 309; enquiries@ mccallscoaches.com) stop at Hightae Farm, 12 min walk to Threave House.

Visiting; Charge for house and garden, NTS members free; nature reserve free. House 10am-3pm; visitor centre, shop, cafe & garden 10am-5pm; reserve dawn-dusk, all year. Facilities at House & Garden. Trails and hides at reserve. Dogs on lead.

Contact: 01556 502 575

Continue W on A75.

5 CAIRNSMORE OF FLEET NNR

NatureScot

Habitats: Moorland rising to 2,333 ft, blanket bog.

Birds: All year: Red & Black Grouse, Peregrine, Merlin, Golden Eagle (occasionally). *Summer:* Curlew, Cuckoo, Swift (nest under viaduct), Stonechat, Wheatear.

Winter: Hen Harrier.

Other: Brown & Mountain Hares, Red & Roe Deer, wild Goat. Dragonflies.

Directions: DG7 2BP; NX 553 637 (Small Info Centre). Eight miles NW Gatehouse of Fleet, whence take B796 N for six miles (signposted) to T-junc, turn R, continue to car park—more parking beyond by Viaduct. Alternatively, continue on A75 along E shore of **Wigtown Bay**. After Creetown, minor road on R for Cairnsmore leads to small car park for summit path 250 yards beyond Graddoch Bridge (NX 463 632).

Public transport: None.

Visiting: Open all hours. Car park, info centre, toilets (wheelchair access)—all open 24-hrs, picnic tables. Trails on to reserve from here. Summit Path (above).

Contact: Reserve Manager: 01557 814 435; nnr@nature.scot

Continue N on A75 to Newtown Stewart, where cross the Cree. Then take A714 S along W side of Wigtown Bay to Wigtown.

6 WIGTOWN BAY LNR

Dumfries and Galloway Council

Habitats: 7,000 acres, largest LNR in Britain—estuary with extensive saltmarsh/merse, mudflats and a freshwater wetland at Wigtown Harbour.

Birds: Summer: breeding Osprey, Peregrine, waders and duck. *Winter:* Internationally important for Pink-footed Goose, nationally important for Curlew, Whooper Swan and Pintail, with major gull roost and other migratory coastal birds. Small Twite flock.

Other: Fish inc Smelt and Shad. Lax-flowered Sea-lavender, Sea Aster.

Directions: DG8 9ED. NX 438 548. Between Wigtown and Creetown, S of Newton Stewart. The A75 runs along E side, with A714 S to Wigtown and B7004 providing views of LNR.

Public transport: Bus: 415 from Newton Stewart to Wigtown. DGC Buses.

Visiting: Open all hours. Main access points: roadside lay-bys on A75 near Creetown, parking at Martyr's Stake (on B7004 just out of Wigtown) and Wigtown Harbour—suitable for coaches. Visitor Centre—open Mon-Sat 10am-5pm (later some days), Sun 2pm-5pm—located in Wigtown County Building has coach parking plus full disabled access, inc lift and toilets. CCTV of Ospreys breeding in Galloway during summer and wetland birds in winter. Hide at Wigtown Harbour overlooking River Bladnoch, saltmarsh and freshwater wetland has disabled access from harbour car park. Another hide at Martyr's Stake car park.

Contact: D&G Council: 0303 333 3000; contact@dumgal.gov.uk

Continue on A714

7 CROOK OF BALDOON

RSPB

Habitats: Lagoon, saltmarsh, mudlflats, restored wet grassland.

Birds: Winter: Mute & Whooper Swans, Barnacle & Pink-footed Geese, Shelduck, Golden Plover. Redwing and Fieldfare. *Summer:* Waders inc Redshank and Lapwing. Wildfowl inc Shoveler. Skylark, Wheatear.

Other:

Directions: DG8 9AQ; NX 445 531. From the centre of Wigtown take the A714 for Port William. At Bladnoch take the 1st exit and cross the river. Stay on A714 for one mile then turn L for Penkiln Saw Mill. Continue on this road past West Mains and East Mains of Baldoon farms, then continue down single lane track to Crook of Baldoon car park.

Public transport: Bus: 415/416 (daily, infrequent Sun) from Wigtown town centre passes minor road off A714. Nearest bus stops are at Bladnoch (c.2.6 miles walk to reserve) and Kirkinner (*c*.2.8 miles walk to reserve) Stagecoach.

Visiting: Open all hours, free. Surfaced path from car park along edge of saltmarsh to S bank of River Bladnoch and to viewing platform by lagoon. No toilets. Conservation grazing. Dogs permitted under close control. RSPB reserve is to S of Wigtown on W shore of Wigtown Bay, whilst **Wigtown Bay LNR** occupies N end of bay from Wigtown to N.

Contact: RSPB: 01776 840 539;

crookofbaldoon@rspb.org.uk

Return to Bladnoch and take B7006 W. At junction with A747 on E shore of Luce Bay head N to A75. Then turn W for Stranraer. In Stranraer take A77 and then A716 for Drummore.

8 MULL OF GALLOWAY
RSPB

Habitats: Sea cliffs, coastal heath.

Birds: *Spring/summer:* Fulmar, Shag, Guillemot, Razorbill, Black Guillemot, Puffin, Kittiwake, Herring Gull, Raven, Hooded Crow, Wheatear, Rock Pipit, Linnet, Twite, Gannet (feeding offshore and nesting on the Scare Rocks) and Peregrine Falcon. *Autumn:* Manx Shearwater and Arctic Skua passing offshore, passerines heading S inc. Linnet, Goldfinch, Meadow Pipit, Skylark, Pied Wagtail and Swallow with scarcer species occasionally turning up. *Winter:* Occasionally winter migrant such as Lapland Bunting.

Other: Harbour Porpoise, Bottle-nosed Dolphins, Grey Seal; butterflies inc Grayling, Wall Brown and Dark Green Fritillary; occasional migrant Dragonflies inc Red-veined Darter and Vagrant Emperor. Flora inc Purple Milk-vetch, Golden Samphire, Spring Squill, Rock Sea-lavender and Adder's Tongue.

Directions: DG9 9HP; NX 156 305. Most southerly tip of Scotland—follow brown signs for five miles from village of Drummore, S of Stranraer.

Public transport: None.

Visiting: Open all hours. Blue Badge parking by Visitor Centre, which is open Easter-Oct, toilets, nature trail, CCTV on cliffs. Small shop in Gallie Craig cafe (not RSPB). Steep stairway to foghorn viewing platform overlooking seabird colonies. Trail uneven. Start/End Rhins of Galloway Coast Path.

Contact: RSPB: 01776 840 539;

mullofgalloway@rspb.org.uk

Head back E on A75 to Newton Stewart.

9 WOOD OF CREE
RSPB

Habitats: Deciduous oak woodland, wood pasture, wet woodland, riverside meadow, streams, moorland.

Birds: *All year:* Sparrowhawk, Buzzard, Barn & Tawny Owls, Great Spotted Woodpecker, Bullfinch, Teal, Dipper, Willow Tit, Black Grouse on moorland. *Spring/Sum-*

mer:, Redstart, Tree Pipit, Pied Flycatcher, Grasshopper, Garden, Wood & Willow Warblers, Chiffchaff, Blackcap, Cuckoo, Whinchat, Stonechat, Linnet, Grey Wagtail, Common Sandpiper. *Autumn/winter:* Whooper Swan, Goldeneye, Goosander, Redwing, Fieldfare, Woodcock.

Other: Otter, Roe Deer, Red Squirrel, Pine Marten, eight spp bats inc. Leisler's. Carpets of Bluebells and Cowwheat within woodland. Large Heath, Purple Hairstreak and Scotch Argus.

Directions: DG8 6SW; NX 381 708. Travel N along minor road from Newton Stewart through Old Minnigaff. Turn L past Monigaff church, continue 3 miles along minor road until reaching Wood of Cree car park or stop at Barclye car park (NX 386 694).

Public transport: None. Closest buses at Minnigaff and Newton Stewart, *c*.4 miles to S.

Visiting: Open all hours. Main car park at Wood of Cree. Keep to trails—1.25 mile waymarked woodland trail can be extended to 3.5 mile walk inc scrubland trail—steep, rough and uneven in parts. Another car park at Barclye has 3 trails, 2 circular ones weaving through open habitats and newly planted woodland, and one longer one linking to Knockman Wood. Dogs under control, esp. during breeding season.

Contact: RSPB: 01776 840 539;

wood.cree@rspb.org.uk

Return to Newton Stewart.

10 GLENTROOL
Forestry and Land Scotland

Habitats: Part of Galloway Forest Park. Loch, waterfalls, conifer and oak woodlands, moorland.

Birds: All year: Common woodland spp, Peregrine Falcon, Hen Harrier, Siskin, Crossbill. *Summer:* Redstart, Pied Flycatcher, Wood Warbler.

Other: Red Squirrel, Roe Deer.

Directions: DG8 6SX; NX 371 786. Eight miles NW of Newton Stewart. Leave A714 at Bargrennan to Glentrool—visitor centre signposted from unclassified road that passes N from village.

Public transport: None.

Visiting: Trails and car park (charge). Toilets, cafe open 10:30am-5pm Easter to end Aug. Various trails, between 1.75 and 5.75 miles. Single track road (with passing places) continues past visitor centre along N side of Loch Trool to two other parking areas.

Contact: Forestry and Land Scotland: 0300 067 6900;

enquiries.south@forestryandland.gov.scot

Continue NW on A714, which reaches the coast at Girvan in Ayrshire. Either start your exploration of Ayrshire or Return to Newton Stewart and take A75 E to Gretna. At Gretna head S on M6 and then take A7 at J44, heading NE for Langholm.

11 TARRAS VALLEY NATURE RESERVE

The Langholm Initiative.

Habitats: Moorland and blanket bog, woodland, river, wood pasture, wetland.

Birds: All year: Red & Black Grouse, Goosander, Goshawk, Hen Harrier, Peregrine Falcon, Barn & Short-eared Owls, Dipper, Crossbill. Golden Eagle (occasional). *Summer:* Oystercatcher, Lapwing, Golden Plover, Curlew, Cuckoo, Redstart, Wheatear, Whinchat, Pied & Spotted Flycatchers, Ring Ouzel, warblers (inc Grasshopper & Wood). *Winter:* Winter thrushes, Brambling.

Other: Feral Goat, Otter, Water Vole.

Directions: DG13 0EO; NY 363 849 (Kiln Green Car Park, Langholm). 18 miles N of Carlisle. Take A7 N from Carlise to Langholm.

Public transport: Bus: X95 Carlisle to Galashiels/Edinburgh runs through Langholm. Borders Buses (01896 754 350).

Visiting: Once part of a grouse moor, the 10,500 acre landholding has been purchased through two large buy-outs by local community development trust, the Langholm Initiative. Facilities are being developed. Main parking and toilets at N of town on A7 (Kiln Green)—walk back into town to access S end of reserve. Also several small informal parking areas on reserve boundaries (no roads through the original purchase) and a small informal visitor car park has recently been developed at Broomholmshiels (NY 381 823). Number of circular walks available.

Beyond the Kiln Green car park, N of the town, a single-track road runs c.8 miles E across the moor from the A7 to Newcastleton and crosses the Tarras Valley. Parking at Tarras Lodge NY 402 873, whence a road serving isolated houses runs N.

Contact: Tarras Valley NR: hello@tarrasvalleynaturereserve.org www.tarrasvalleynaturereserve.org

From Langholm you can take the B709 through Eskdalemuir to Ettrick (25 miles). You are now in the Scottish Borders. Continue E on B709 to Tushielaw)3.25 miles), passing the Ettrick Marshes in the Scottish Borders, At Tushielaw the B709 turns sharp L for the Yarrow valley. Follow it, do not carry straight on on the A7009 or you will end up in Selkirk. At the Gordon Arms crossroads turn L on to the A708 for St Mary's Loch (after which you will re-enter Dumfries and Galloway) and Moffat. On the R of the A708 you will come first to

12 GREY MARE'S TAIL NATURE RESERVE

National Trust for Scotland

Habitats: Moorland, woodland, 197 ft waterfall.

Birds: All year: Red Grouse, Golden Eagle, Goshawk, Sparrowhawk, Buzzard, Red Kite, Peregrine Falcon, Kestrel, Red Grouse, Raven, Dipper, Grey Wagtail, Stonechat, common woodland spp.. *Spring/summer:* Osprey,

Common Sandpiper, Common Gull, Ring Ouzel, Whinchat (now rare). *Autumn/Winter:* Pink-footed Goose (passage), Redwing, Fieldfare, Brambling.

Other: Upland flora. Feral Goat.

Directions: DG10 9LH; NT 187 147. 10 miles NE of Moffat. Take A708 from Moffat towards Selkirk. Can park at woodland sites before reaching reserve car park.

Public transport: None.

Visiting: Open all year. Car park (charge, free for NT members) at entrance to waterfall valley—viewpoint for waterfall (5 mins walk). Trail up to Loch Skeen and beyond. Information available (summer), guided walks. Nearest cafe/toilets 4 miles NE along A708 at James Hogg Memorial/Isthmus of Loch of the Lowes and St Mary's Loch (Common Sandpiper, Oystercatcher, Common Gull, Osprey (possible), Redstart, Dipper, wagtails, Reed Bunting).

Contact: NTS: 01890 771 443; greymarestailnaturereserve@nts.org.uk *and then*

13 CARRIFRAN WILDWOOD

Borders Forest Trust

Habitats: 1,670 acre valley and corrie of the Carrifran Burn, replanted over last 25 years with 750,000+ native trees. Valley sides rise to over 2,300 ft.

Birds: Common woodland spp. The mix of species is changing as the woodland develops but there are also moorland species inc Golden Plover and Dunlin, as well Golden Eagle on the heights above the valley

Other: Native tree species.

Directions: DG10 9LH; NT 160 115. 8 miles NE of Moffat. Take A708 from Moffat towards Selkirk.

Public transport: None

Visiting: Open all hours, free, car park to N of road. Do not park at Carrifran Cottage to S of road. Margins of the Wildwood on the heights abut **Grey Mare's Tail** (q.v.) and **Gameshope** (q.v. **Scottish Borders**). No facilities on site but cafe/toilets 6 miles NE along A708 at James Hogg Memorial/Isthmus of Loch of the Lowes and St Mary's Loch (as above).

Contact: Borders Forest Trust: 01835 830 750; enquiries@bordersforesttrust.org; www.bordersforesttrust.org

Alternatively, when you took the A75 back to Gretna, you could have turned N on to the A74(M), leaving it at J15 for Moffat. Then taken the A708 NE from Moffat, which would have brought you first to **Carrifran***, on the L and then, again on the L,* **Grey Mare's Tail***.*

Ayrshire

The island of Ailsa Craig, which boasts a huge gannetry and plenty of other breeding seabirds, is well worth a boat trip. The shore at Barassie and Troon sees a large build-up of passage waders in spring and autumn—seawatching here in the autumn can be rewarding and white-winged gulls often turn up in winter. Martnaham Loch is good for wildfowl and a range of common species, whilst Turnberry Point offers seawatching, plus Twite. The river valleys and inland woodlands offer other birdwatching opportunities.

Bird Atlas/Avifauna
Arran Bird Atlas 2007-2012:
Mapping the breeding and wintering birds of Arran
Jim Cassels
(Arran NHS, 2014)
Available as a free pdf download from:
www.arranbirding.co.uk/files/Arran-Bird-Atlas-e-book-Dr-Jim-Cassels-compressed.pdf

Bird Recorders
Fraser Simpson, 4 Inchmurrin Drive, Kilmarnock, KA3 2JD: recorder@ayrshire-birding.org.uk
Assistant Recorder: Angus Hogg, 11 Kirkmichael Road, Crosshill, Maybole, KA19 7RJ: 01655 740 317; dcgos@yahoo.com

Bird Report
Ayrshire Bird Report (1976-), from Ayrshire Birding—Anne Dick, Rowanmyle House, Tarbolton, Mauchline, KA5 5LU: a_m_dick@btinternet.com
Available as a pdf download (from 2017 report):
www.ayrshire-birding.org.uk/bird_report
Arran Bird Report (1980-), from ANHS:
arrannaturalhistorysociety@gmail.com

BTO Regional Representatives
Ayrshire and Cumbrae
Dave McGarvie:
Arran
James Cassels
Wetland Bird Survey (WeBS)
Local Organizers: webs@bto.org
Arran
Jim Cassels:
Ayrshire (excl. Isle of Cumbrae)
Dave Grant:
Isle of Cumbrae
Vacant

Club
SOC Ayrshire Branch (1962; 120)
Anne Dick: 07780 927 244; a_m_dick@btinternet.com; www.the-soc.org.uk/local-branches/ayrshire

Meetings: 7:30pm, 2nd Tuesday of the month (Sep-Apr). Monkton Community Church, Main Street, Monkton by Prestwick, KA9 2RN. Monthly online talks also held. Contact/see website for details.
The club branch also sponsors:
www.ayrshire-birding.org.uk

RSPB Local Groups
Central Ayrshire (1978; 85)
Anne Dick: a_m_dick@btinternet.com;
https://group.rspb.org.uk/centralayrshire/
Meetings: No indor meetings in 25/26 but there will field trips.
North Ayrshire (1976; 60)
Laura Montgomerie: hello.narspb@gmail.com;
https://group.rspb.org.uk/northayrshire/
Meetings: 7:30pm, 2nd Friday of the month (Sep-Apr). Ardrossan Civic Centre, 150 Glasgow Street, Ardrossan, KA22 8EU, with effect from Sep '25.

Scottish Wildlife Trust Regional Networks
Ayrshire
Chair: Robbie Mann: swtayrshire@gmail.com;
https://sites.google.com/view/swt-ayrshire-group/home
Meetings: The Horizon Hotel, Esplanade, Ayr KA7 1DT

Forestry and Land Scotland Regional Office
0300 067 6900;
enquiries.south@forestryandland.gov.scot
or, for North Ayrshire
0300 067 6600;
enquiries.central@forestryandland.gov.scot

The A76 from Thornhill in Dumfries & Galloway continues to New Cumnock

1 KNOCKSHINNOCH LAGOONS
Scottish Wildlife Trust
Habitats: Open water, marshland, reedbeds, willow carr, bare mining spoil and birch woodland.
Birds: All year: Common wildfowl, Gadwall, Snipe, Water Rail, Reed Bunting. *Summer:* Warblers inc. Grasshopper, Sedge & Garden Warblers. *Autumn/winter:* Finches and thrushes.
Other: Butterflies and moths, fungi, wild flowers, mining bees.
Directions: KA18 4NF; NS 613 130. W of New Cumnock—car park on B741, 0.3 mile outside of town.
Public transport: Buses—regular from Glasgow, Kilmarnock and Ayr. Train—New Cumnock. On foot signposted from wildlife garden in New Cumnock centre: cross over at community centre then L (off A76) into Castlehill—entrance at end of road.
Visiting: Open all year. Car park. Hides, surfaced paths.
Contact: Scottish WT: 01294 279 376;
enquiries@scottishwildlifetrust.org.uk
Continue W from New Cumnock on A70.

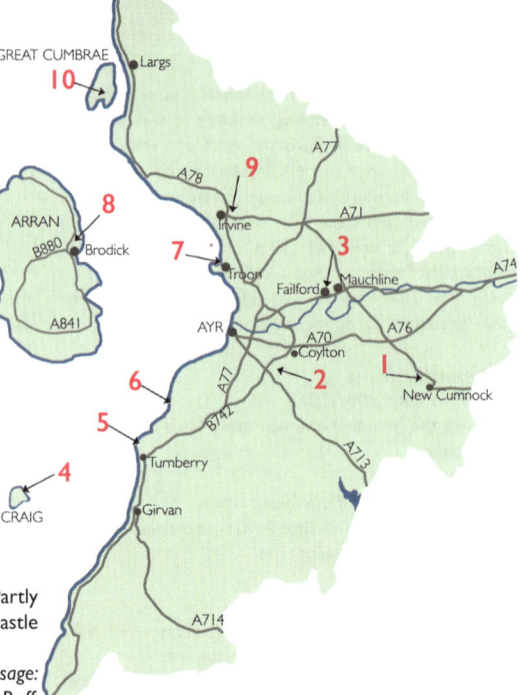

2 MARTNAHAM LOCH

Private

Habitats: Loch, narrow but over a mile long. Partly wooded lakeside. Areas of marshy shore. Ruined castle on S shore (NS 396 173).

Birds: Breeding: Great-crested & Little Grebe. *Passage:* Waders inc. Whimbrel, Black-tailed Godwit, Ruff, Green Sandpiper. *Winter:* Wildowl inc Goldeneye, Long-tailed Duck, Scaup. Gulls inc Glaucous, Icelandic, Mediterranean. Known for rarities.

Other:

Directions: KA6 6EU: NS 396 167 (Martnaham Mains to S of loch). At Coylton on the A70 head SW on B742. After 1.5 miles L turn into minor road around E end of loch (NS 404 177).

Public transport: Bus: 2/X42 (daily) Ayr-Coylton-Cumnock runs along B742. Stagecoach (0345 241 8000).

Visiting: Private, no facilities or wheel chair access. Park in lay-bys or verge, with due concern for passing traffic. Disused railway line runs close to S shore of loch at E end. Other smaller bodies of water on either side of B742.

Contact: None

Head back to Coylton on A70, then N on B730. At the crossroads with the B743 (Ayr-Mauchline road) turn R for Failford.

3 AYR GORGE WOODLANDS

Scottish Wildlife Trust

Habitats: Sandstone river gorge. Broadleaved and mixed woodland.

Birds: Breeding: Great Spotted Woodpecker, Kingfisher, warblers inc Garden & Wood, Redstart, Spotted Flycatcher, Nuthatch, Treecreeper, Jay.

Other: Beetles, moths, spiders, fungi, ancient woodland flora, bats.

Directions: KA5 5TF; NS 460 262 (Failford Inn). Gorge downstream from Failford. B743 Ayr-Mauchline road runs through Failford.

Public transport: Bus: 343 Ayr-New Cumnock stops at Failford Inn daily. Stagecoach (0345 241 8000).

Visiting: Park in lay-bys at Failford and enter at W end of village. Way-marked, surfaced paths, sometimes steep with steps, along the river bank and up through the woods.

Contact: Scottish Wildlife Trust: 01294 279 376; enquiries@scottishwildlifetrust.org.uk

*If you entered Ayrshire on the A714 from Newton Stewart in **Dumfries & Galloway**, it reaches the coast at Girvan.*

4 AILSA CRAIG

Private

Habitats: Volcanic plug (350 ft high) provides nest sites for seabirds.

Birds: Summer: third largest gannetry in UK (up to 36,000 pairs of Gannets). Other breeding seabirds inc Guillemot, Razorbill, Puffin, Black Guillemot, Kittiwake, and also Twite.

Other: Slow Worm.

Directions: KA26 9AJ. NX 181 981 (Girvan Harbour). Island is nine miles offshore. Girvan, nearest town on mainland.

Public transport: None.

Visiting: No formal arrangements—accessible only by boat during summer:

Ailsa Craig Trips/MFV Glorious: 01465 713 219 or

07773 794 358; mccrindlem@aol.com
JAG Charters Ltd: 01465 713 174;
info@seafishingcharterssscotland.com
A77 N from Girvan to Turnberry, then A719.

5 TURNBERRY POINT

Turnberry Golf Club
Habitats: Seawatching, rocky shore, golf links.
Birds: Sea: Passage shearwaters, petrels, scoters, divers, grebes, skuas. *Shore:* Passage wader, White-rumped & Pectoral Sandpipers and Grey Phalarope have been recorded. *Scrub:* Wheatear, Whinchat, Stonechat, Twite.
Directions: KA26 9LT; NS 204 060 (club house). Turnberry Golf Courses lies immediately to the W of the A719 between the villages of Maidens and Turnberry. Members of bird clubs are permitted to park in car park at NS 206 068 (c.5 mile N of club house) off the A719.
Public transport: Bus: 60/360 Ayr-Stranraer. Stagecoach West Scotland.
Visiting: Ayrshire Coastal Path runs from car park across golf course to lighthouse (NS 196 073) and point, as well as S between course and beach.
Contact:
Continue N on A719.

6 CULZEAN CASTLE COUNTRY PARK

National Trust for Scotland.
Habitats: 650 acre estate—shoreline, parkland, woodland, gardens, streams, ponds.
Birds: All year: Good numbers of common woodland species inc Jay, Great Spotted Woodpecker and thrushes. *Spring/summer:* Arriving migrants, esp Blackcap, Chiffchaff and Willow Warbler. Nesting Raven and Gannet on cliffs, Gannet and terns offshore. *Autumn/winter:* Wildfowl on pond inc Little Grebe, Tufted Duck, Goldeneye. Crossbill, regular flocks of winter thrushes. Offshore divers and Eider.
Other: Roe Deer, Otter, Water Vole, several spp of bat. Shoreline SSSI rich in rock pool life.
Directions: KA19 8LE. NS 234 103. 12 miles SW of Ayr off A719.
Public transport: Bus: 60 (Ayr to Girvan) stops at site entrance. One mile walk downhill to castle. Stagecoach West Scotland.
Visiting: Open 9am-5pm. Entrance fee to country park (members free). Three car parks, cafe/shops open daily (not Dec 25/26, Jan 1), children's playground, picnic areas, many footpaths and estate tracks, ranging from unsurfaced woodland paths to metalled roads. Access leaflet available.
Contact: NTS Culzean: 01655 884 455; culzean@nts.org.uk
From Culzean, head N on A719 and then A79 through Ayr. The join A78 and head N. If arriving from Failford, take B743 to junction with A77, then head N to its junction with A78.

7 BARASSIE & TROON

Ayrshire Coastal Path runs around harbour and along sea front.
Habitats: Sea, harbour walls, sandy beach, primarily winter.
Birds: Sea and sands: Divers, Manx Shearwaters, Storm & Leach's Petrels, waders inc. Sanderling, Purple Sandpiper, Bar-tailed Godwit, Twite. *Harbour:* Eider, Red-breasted Merganser, Shag, Cormorant, Black Guillemot, roosting gulls inc Glaucous, Iceland, Mediterranean, Kittiwake,
Directions: KA10 6DH; NS 312 312 (Troon Harbour). To the N of the harbour North Sands extends to Stinking Rocks (NS323 336) and to the S South Sands extends to Meikle Craigs (NS 328 290). The A78 S from Irvine runs c.1.5 mles E of Troon Exit the A78 to the N of Troon and follow the B746 to the sea front at Barassie. At the sea front follow the road S to the harbour.
Public transport: Train—Barassie or Troon. On Glasgow-Ayr line. Stations 500 yards from sea front.
Visiting: Car parks overlooking North Sands, Barassie at NS 325 325; NS 322 314; Troon Harbour NS 307 314; South Sands at NS 315 346, NS 326 300. Sea Watching from the sea front. Toilets at NS 322 308. Cafes in town.
Also, while at Troon
Lady Isle: private island 2.5 miles offshore, no landing without permission but can be circumnavigated. Crackin Sea Tours, Troon: www.crackinseatours.co.uk. Large Herring, Lesser & Great Black-backed Gull colony, Eider. *Winter:* Purple Sandpiper, Dunlin, Turnstone, divers.
Ferries for Arran currently depart from and arrive at Troon Harbour.

8 BRODICK CASTLE COUNTRY PARK AND FOREST

National Trust for Scotland/Forestry and Land Scotland
Habitats: 200 acre park. Broadleaved woodland, meadow, pasture, surrounded by extensive coniferous forest.
Birds: Offshore: Eider, Red-breasted Merganser, divers, Gannet, Common & Black Guillemots. *Shore:* Breeding Shelduck, Common Sandpiper, Redshank, Curlew. *Woodland:* Barn Owl, Warblers inc Wood & Willow, Spotted Flycatscher., finches.
Other: Systematic management of the grounds of Brodick Castle began in 1710 and the gardens now hold many rare plants.
Directions: Take ferry (55 min) from Troon, Ayshire (KA10 6HH; NS 311 316) to Brodick (KA27 8HY; NS 015 378). CalMac (0800 066 5000; enquiries@calmac.co.uk). Turn L out of ferry terminal. Brodick Castle is 2 miles N on A841. At Rosa Bridge roundabout continue on A841 across the river, then over Cnocan Bridge, past the Brewery in Cladach and the gates to the Castle are on the L
Public transport: Bus: 324 runs from Brodick to Lochranza. Stops at Castle entrance. Stagecoach.
Visiting: The Castle Country Park is a National Trust

for Scotland property. Large car park within 200 yards of Castle, diabled parking at Castle. Coach parking available. Charge for non-members. Park open 10am-5pm every day. Castle, shop, cafe open daily Easter/Apr-Oct 10am-5pm; closed Nov-Mar. Leaflets, guided walks. Surrounding coniferous forests on the S & E slopes of Goatfell, Arran's highest hill (2,867 ft), are Forestry and Land Scotland. Paths from Country Park extend into the forests. There is also a car park in Cladach on the A481, S of Castle, with path leading directly into F&LS forests and up Goatfell,

Contact: Brodick Castle: 01770 302 202; BrodickCastle@nts.org.uk

Now you are on Arran.

The A841 runs the length of the E side of the island, minor roads along the W. As with Loch Lomond, the Highland fault Line runs through Arran, with 'highlands' to the N and 'lowlands' to the S.

At the N end, at Lochranza, on the A84, after sampling the whisky—or, more prudently, before—there is a 10 mile circular walk and path S from the distillery up Glean Easan Biorach round the S slopes of Beinn Bhereac and then N along Gleann Diomhan and Glen Catacol, returning to the coast at Fairhaven. Walk along the minor coast road back to Lochranza.

Birds: Red Grouse, Curlew, Golden Eagle, Hen Harrier, Peregrine, Merlin, Wheatear.

Rather than heading back on the ferry from Brodick to Ardrossan it is possible to take a ferry on from Lochranza to Tarbert on the Kintyre peninsula or, in summer, Claonaig, further S on the same peninsula.

Rejoin A78 and head N.

9 EGLINTON COUNTRY PARK

North Ayrshire Council

Habitats: 1,000 acres, river, loch, seasonal damp areas, broadleaved, mixed and coniferous woodland, meadows. Sourlie Wood, a reserve managed by SWT is adjacent.

Birds: Great Crested & Little Grebes, Kingfisher, Dipper, Reed Bunting, Common woodland spp inc Sparrowhawk, Long-tailed Tit, Goldcrest, Treecreeper, Nuthatch, Siskin, Bullfinch. *Summer:* Usual warblers inc Grasshopper, *Passage:* Waders. *Winter:* Whooper Swan, Pink-footed Goose, Goldeneye, Wigeon, Teal, gulls, thrushes.

Other:

Directions: KA12 8TA; NS 320 419. Immediately off Eglinton interchange on A78, 3rd exit N bound, 1st exit S bound. N section of national cycle route 73 traverses park.

Public transport: Bus: 11, Kilmarnock to Ardrossan, stops outside park on Irvine Road (A737). 0.6 mile walk to main visitor facilities, Stagecoach. Train—Irvine (3 miles), Kilwinning (2.5 miles).

Visiting: Park and car parks (inc disabled) open all year,

free. Courtyard, cafe and toilets (inc accessible) open every day: 9:30-4:30pm; Nov-Mar: 10:30am (9:30am Sat)-3:30pm. Extensive network of bridleways and paths, some can be muddy and some slopes. Motorized scooters and wheelers available, free but need to book in advance.

Contact: 01294 551776 (cafe) 01294 554320; eglintoncountrypark@north-ayrshire.gov.uk

Return to A78 and continue to Largs. Harbour immediately off A78.

10 GREAT CUMBRAE

Island

Habitats: Gravel shore, fields, woodland. Highest point on island 417 ft.

Birds: Sea: Eider, Red-breasted Merganser, Shelduck, Cormorant, Shag, Gannet, Fulmar. *Shore:* Redshank, Oystercatcher, Turnstone, Dunlin, Ringed Plover, Common Sandpiper. *Land:* Lapwing, Curlew, Raven, Stonechat, Whinchat. Buzzard, Sparrowhawk, Kestrel.

Other:

Directions: Take ferry (10 min) from Largs, Ayrshire (KA30 8BG; NS 201 595) to ferry terminal on Great Cumbrae KA28 0HQ; NS 184 586. CalMac (0800 066 5000; customerrelations@calmac.co.uk).

Public transport: Frequent island buses, fitted with wheelchair lifts.

Visiting: Can take car on ferry or park in Largs and proceed on foot. Great Cumbrae is 4 by 2 miles and the B896 runs around the island, close to the coast. Eider cluster off N end in May. Bikes can be hired in Millport, 2.5 miles S from ferry terminal (take B899, which branches from B896 opposite jetty for more direct route). Toilets at the ferry terminal and Millport.

Contact:

Clyde

(Dunbartonshire, Glasgow, Lanarkshire, Renfrewshire)

The two RSPB reserves of Lochwinnoch and Baron's Haugh offer a good selection of commoner species throughout the year, with breeding Whinchat at the latter. The Scottish Wildlife Trust's Falls of Clyde reserve has a good selection of woodland birds, with Dippers and Kingfishers along the river. Cloch Point can be good for passing seabirds in late summer/early autumn.

Bird Recorders

John Simpson (Recorder); Val Wilson and John Sweeney (Assistants) all at: clyderecorder@the-soc.org.uk

Clyde Islands (Arran, Bute & Cumbrae)

Bernard Zonfrillo, 28 Brodie Road, Glasgow, G21 3SB: b.zonfrillo@bio.gla.ac.uk

Bird Report
Clyde Birds (Clyde & Clyde Islands) (1973-)
NB: Arran and Cumbrae lie in Ayrshire, Bute in Argyll, also refer to these counties.
Available (none later than 2011) as a download from:
www.birdsinclyde.scot/publications.html

BTO Regional Representatives
Lanarkshire, Renfrewshire and Dunbartonshire
Gordon Brady
Wetland Bird Survey (WeBS)
Local Organizer: webs@bto.org
Clyde Estuary (Glasgow, Renfrewshire, Lanarkshire), Glasgow, Renfrewshire, Lanarkshire
John Clark

Club
SOC Clyde Branch (n/a; 300)
Rebecca Dickson: 07907 833 114;
clydesecretary@the-soc.org.uk;
www.the-soc.org.uk/local-branches/clyde
www.birdsinclyde.scot
Meetings: 7:00pm, 1st Monday of the month (Sep-Apr, but 2nd Mon Sep & Jan). Patrick Burgh Hall, 9 Burgh Hall Street, Partick, Glasgow G11 5LW
Monthly online talks also held—contact/see website for details.
Paisley Natural History Society (1968)
Tom Byars, Chair
PaisleyNaturalHistorySociety@gmail.com
Meetings: 7:30pm, 1st Thursday of the month (Sep-Apr). The Wynd centre, 6 School Wynd, Paisley PA1 2DB.

Ringing Group/Bird Observatory
Clyde RG: www.clyderinginggroup.com

RSPB Local Groups
Glasgow (1972; 140)
Neil Rankine: rspbglasgowgroupleader@gmail.com;
https://group.rspb.org.uk/glasgow/
Meetings: 7:30pm, 2nd Wednesday of the month (Sep-Apr). Renfield St Stephens Church Centre, 260 Bath Street, Glasgow, G2 4JP.
Lanarkshire (1976; 50)
Alex Smillie: contactlanarkshireRSPBgroup@gmail.com;
https://group.rspb.org.uk/lanarkshire/
Meetings: 7:30pm, 3rd Thursday of the month (Sep-May), Motherwell South Parish Church, 11 Gavin Street, Motherwell, ML1 2RL
Renfrewshire (1986; 50)
Rick Bolton: renfrewrspb@hotmail.co.uk;
https://group.rspb.org.uk/renfrewshire/
Meetings: 7:30pm, 3rd Friday of the month (Sep-May) except 2nd Friday Dec. All in-person. The Wynd Centre, 6 School Wynd, Paisley, PA1 2DB

Scottish Wildlife Trust Regional Networks
Glasgow
Chair: Clare Winsch: cwinsch5c@gmail.com;
https://scottishwildlifetrust.org.uk/local-group/glasgow/
Meetings: Hyndland Secondary School, Airlie Theatre, Clarence Drive, Glasgow G12 1RQ. Contact Mike Turner: mgturner@gmail.com for information.
Clarkston and East Kilbride
Info: cek.swt@gmail.com;

Forestry and Land Scotland Regional Office
0300 067 6600;
enquiries.central@forestryandland.gov.scot

*Continue N on the A78 from Largs in **Ayrshire**, turning L on to the A770 shortly after Inverkip.*

1 CLOCH POINT
Lighthouse now privately owned. A770 public road.
Habitats: Firth of Clyde, rocky and stony shore. Tidal.
Birds: Seawatching late summer/early autumn. Skuas, auks, shearwaters
Directions: PA19 1BA; NS 202 758 (lighthouse). The lighthouse stands on the A770 and the Inverclyde Coastal Path, N of Inverkip, 3 miles SW of Gourock.
Public transport:
Visiting: Busy road, no parking at lighthouse. There is a hard shoulder and just to the N of the lighthouse a grassy area overlooking the Clyde. Holiday camp on inland side of A770. There is a garden centre, car park on other side of road and toilets about 0.75 miles S on A770 at NS 204 747.
Return to A78, turn L for Greenock, then as below.

2 CLYDE MURSHIEL REGIONAL PARK
Clyde Muirshiel Regional Park
Directions: PA16 9LS; NS 247 722 (Visitor Centre). Leave the A78 between Greenock and Inverkip at Auchness bridge and take minor road over stream, railway line and then along the side of the Shielhill Glen to the Visitor Centre. Beyond the Centre, at S end of Loch Thom, this road joins the Old Largs Road from Greenock, which runs down the E side of Loch Thom and on to Largs. As this road passes through Overton on the S outskirts of Greenock a side road running W leads to the Overton car park at the N end of the circular trail that follows the Cut around the high ground between the lochs and Greenock.
Public transport: Train—stations at Drumfrochar and Branchton, both within 0.5 mile of the circular route.
Visiting: Car parks (at Visitor Centre NS 247 722; Overton NS 263 749) and trails open all hours. Toilets 9:15am-4pm at Visitor Centre. Ranger-led events. Visitor Centre located at point where Kip Water and the Greenock Cut aqueduct flow out of the Compensation

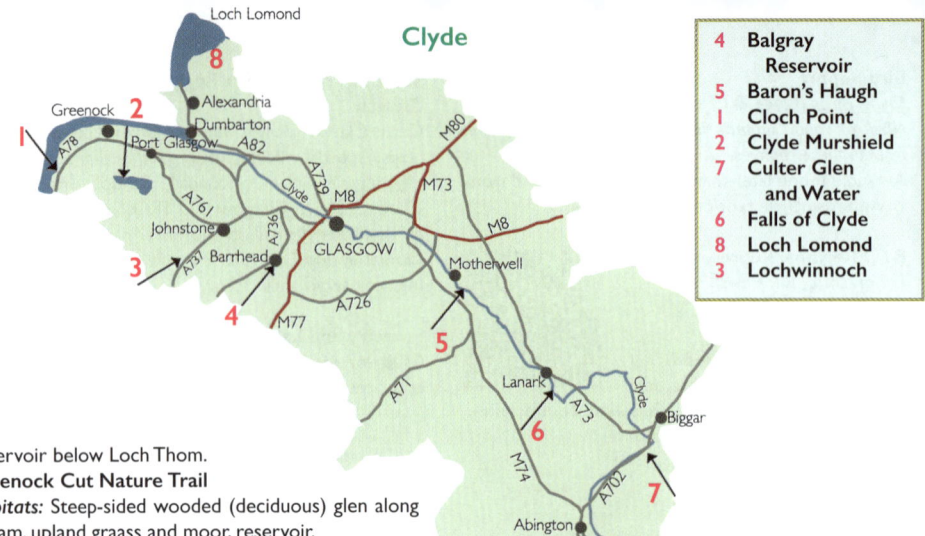

Clyde

4	Balgray Reservoir
5	Baron's Haugh
1	Cloch Point
2	Clyde Murshield
7	Culter Glen and Water
6	Falls of Clyde
8	Loch Lomond
3	Lochwinnoch

Reservoir below Loch Thom.

Greenock Cut Nature Trail

Habitats: Steep-sided wooded (deciduous) glen along stream, upland graass and moor, reservoir.

Birds: Common woodland and scrub spp inc Grasshopper & Sedge Warblers. Tree Pipit, Redstart occasional. Dipper, Grey Wagtail along burn. Curlew and Snipe, Wheatear, Stonechat & Whinchat on hill. *Autumn/winter:* Tit & Goldcrest flocks. Thrushes, possible passage Ring Ouzel. Occasional Osprey fishing on reservoir.

Visiting: 8 mile circular walk follows the Cut but for birds follow the Kip down into wooded Shielhill Glen, then out on to open hill and back to the Visitor Centre along another aqueduct, the Kelly Cut.

Loch Thom

Habitats: Pasture, moor, reservoirs, marsh at S end. Island

Birds: Gull colony (Great Black-backed, Lesser Black-backed, Herring & Common) on island. Common Sandpiper, Oystercatcher, Ringed Plover breed, Passage waders if water levels low. Snipe, Grasshopper Warbler, Reed Bunting in marsh.

Visiting: Path from Visitor Centre runs NE past the Compensation Reservoir and the W & N sides of Loch Thom before joining the Old Largs Road. Follow this road down the E side of the loch to the road at the S end from the Visitor Centre. The Old Largs Road crosses the dam between Loch Thom and the two Gryfe Reservoirs.

Contact: Greenock Cut Visitor Centre: 01475 521 458/529 543

From Greenock take B788 SE. After 6.8 miles, just outside Kilmacolm turn R on to B786 for 7.3 miles to A760.

3 LOCHWINNOCH

RSPB

Habitats: Shallow lochs, marsh, wet grassland, mixed woodland.

Birds: Summer: Breeding Great Crested Grebe, Water Rail, Lapwing, Redshank, Little Ringed Plover, Black-headed Gull, Sedge & Grasshopper Warblers, Spotted Flycatcher, Reed Bunting. *Passage:* Regular migrants inc Black-tailed Godwit, Curlew, Greenshank, Whimbrel, Ringed Plover, Little Ringed Plover, Osprey. *Winter:* Wildfowl inc Whooper Swan, Wigeon, Goosander, Goldeneye, Icelandic Greylag Geese, Hen Harrier, Kingfisher. Recent habitat restoration work has led to increase in scarcer species inc Ruff and Wood Sandpiper. Avocet and Curlew Sandpiper in 2025.

Other: Roe Deer, small mammals, possible Otter, butterflies, moths and dragonflies. Fungi, wild flowers and wetland plants

Directions: PA12 4JF. NS 358 580. 18 miles SW of Glasgow, adjacent to A760 Largs Road, off A737 (Irvine Road). Leave M8 at J28A.

Public transport: Bus: X34/X36 Glasgow to Irvine/Ardrossan, alight Roadhead roundabout, 0.5 mile from reserve. 307 (all week) McGills. Train—Lochwinnoch.

Visiting: Open all hours, free entry (parking charge for non-RSPB members). Visitor centre open daily (not 25/26 Dec, 1/2 Jan) 9:30am-5pm, refreshments, shop, toilets. Three trails, three hides and toilets—all hides and toilets have disabled access.

Contact: RSPB: 01505 842 663; lochwinnoch@rspb.org.uk

Castle Semple Loch & Parkhill Wood immediately to NE Head SW on A737 to Beith, then the B777 to its junction with A736. Approach Balgray from the opposite direction to that given below.

4 BALGRAY RESERVOIR

Scottish Water

Habitats: Open water. Extent of margins and presence

of islands depends on water level. Fringe vegetation. Fed by several streams.

Birds: Passage: Waders inc Whimbrel, Curlew, Black-tailed Godwit, Green Sandpiper (especially if water levels low), Whinchat, Redstart, White Wagtail. *Summer:* Great Crested Grebe, Sedge Warbler, Reed Bunting. Unusual gulls (Iceland, Glaucous) and terns (Black) have been recorded, as well as Slavonian & Black-necked Grebes.

Other:

Directions: G78 2NE; NS 508 573 (car park). At the Dovecothall roundabout on A736 in Barrhead, take Aurs and then Springfield Roads and then, after about a mile, take the 2nd L into Balgraystone Road, pass under the railway line, and then park in the car park.

Public transport: Bus: 3 Neilston to Glasgow, stops in Barrhead on Aurs Road, McGills. Train—New station and car park, Balgray, being built close to reservoir. Due to open in autumn 2026.

Visiting: Free car park. Open all hours. There is a surfaced path suitable for wheelchairs around the S side of the reservoir. This leads to Aurs Road, which runs along the NE side. It is possible to cross Aurs Road (can be busy) and continue along the path past three smaller reservoirs to the NE. Part of Dams to Darnley Country Park

Contact:

Join M77 at J4, head N, then A74(M) E & S.

5 BARON'S HAUGH

RSPB

Habitats: Marshland, flooded areas, woodland, parkland, meadows, scrub, river.

Birds: Summer: Breeding Gadwall, Common Sandpiper, Kingfisher, Sand Martin, Whinchat, warblers inc Garden & Grasshopper. *Autumn:* Excellent for waders (22 spp). *Winter:* Whooper Swan, Pochard, Wigeon, Sparrowhawk.

Other: Otter, Beaver (nearby).

Directions: ML1 2QW; NS 755 552. On SW edge of Motherwell. Take exit for Motherwell from J6 of M74. Bear R at next traffic lights, signposted to Wishaw. Turn R at 3rd mini-roundabout and follow road to junction, turn L, then immediately R to enter reserve.

Public transport: Buses: various from Motherwell stop in Airble estate (0.5 mile from reserve). Train—Airbles c.15 min walk.

Visiting: Open all year. Car park, information boards, two hides (two with steps), four trails. Considerable expansion in the area of wetland visible from hides. Apart from longer circuit (steeper slopes, soft surfaces and gates) most paths are wide and surfaced

Contact: RSPB: 0141 331 0993;
baronshaugh@rspb.org.uk
Leave A74(M) at J7.

6 FALLS OF CLYDE

Scottish Wildlife Trust

Habitats: Reserve stretches along both sides of an ancient gorge, with waterfalls, meadow, wet woodland.

Birds: 100+ spp. *Summer:* Goosander, Kingfisher, Dipper, Jay, Spotted Flycatcher, Grey Wagtail.

Other: Badger, Otter, bats and wild flowers.

Directions: ML11 9DB; NS 881 423 (visitor centre). Reserve covers both sides of the Clyde Gorge from New Lanark to Bonnington Weir c.1 mile S of Lanark. From Glasgow travel S on A74(M) to J7, exit on A72 and follow signs to New Lanark.

Public transport: Bus: 132 Lanark to New Lanark. Stuarts Coaches (not operating at time of going to press, check if service restored: 01555 773 533). Train—Lanark.

Visiting: Reserve open daily, dawn to dusk. From New Lanark car park walk into village, through iron gates and down steps to R of New Lanark Visitor Centre (unstaffed, open Fri-Sun 10am-4pm), admission charge for non-SWT members. Centre wheelchair friendly inc toilet facilities. Woodland trails and range of guided and self-guided walks. Badger watching. Reserve terrain unsuitable for wheelchairs.

Contact: Falls of Clyde Visitor Centre: 01555 665 262;
fallsofclyde@scottishwildlifetrust.co.uk
Continue S on A74(M), take A702 at J13 for Coulter (8.4 miles).

7 CULTER GLEN AND WATER

Habitats: Stream, reservoir, upland grass, heather (especially to E), small deciduous and coniferous plantations at N end.

Birds: All year: Red Grouse, Red Kite, Crossbill. Dipper and Grey Wagtail may move away in winter. *Summer:* Cuckoo, Common Sandpiper, Ring Ouzel, Whinchat, Stonechat, Redstart. Check reservoir for Osprey

Directions: ML12 6QB NT 031 312 (Culter Aller Farm). Minor road (Birthwood Road) heading S leaves A702 in Coulter immediately next to bridge over Culter Water. Follow this road for 2 miles with the river to your R. Park by roadside next to small wood between Culter Aller Farm and Birthwood.

Public transport: Bus: 101 101A 102 Dumfries-Edinburgh (Mon-Sat) stops in Coulter. Houstons Coaches (01576 203 874).

Visiting: Walk S c.2.5 miles on metalled road along glen beside Culter Water to Coulter Reservoir dam at NT 036 275. The track to the reservoir is a very gentle climb but the hills on either side rise some 600 to 750 ft from the path. If you wish to explore further, track runs along N shore of reservoir and then a mile further to source of Culter. Another track runs along S shore. Both involve ascents. When you have finished, retrace steps from reservoir

Contact:

On other side of Glasgow from all the other reseverves in Clyde, perhaps better combined with visits to reserves in Central or on way to Argyll.

8 LOCH LOMOND
RSPB

Habitats: Marshy shores of loch, floodplain, grass- and woodland.
Birds: *Wintering* geese: Greenland White-fronted, Pink-footed & Greylag. *Summer:* Osprey, Grasshopper Warbler, Redstart, Tree Pipit,
Other: Bluebells, ancient woodland.
Directions: GB83 8SB (do not use with sat nav); NS 437 871. Take A811 from Drymen for Balloch and Gartocharn. 200 yards after High Wards Weddings and Dreamwood Cottage on R, the reserve entrance is the next turning on the R. If driving from Balloch on A811 pass through Gartocharn. The reserve is a further 0.7 miles, 160 yards after Drummakill, on L.
Public transport: Bus: 309, Balloch to Balmaha, McColls (01389 754 321). Nearest stop in Gartocharn. 1 mile walk, no pavement, busy road. Train—Balloch, not within walking distance.
Visiting: Trails open all hours. Height restriction at car park, on L as you enter, 9am-5pm, 30 spaces. Reserve free, car park charge for non-members via Pay to Park app. Nature Hub 10am-4pm. Toilets 3, inc accessible and Changing Places. Four trails. All have hardcore surfaces, although there are some sections of boardwalk and steep slopes. Keep dogs on short lead, clean up mess.
Contact: RSPB: 01389 830 670; loch.lomond@rspb.org.uk

Scottish Borders

St Abb's Head has a large summer seabird colony, with a gannetry beginning to establish itself, and migrants moving past in spring and autumn. High ground in the W with extensive conifer plantations, dissected by several river valleys running very roughly W-E; low farmland to E between Cheviots to the S and Lammermuirs to the N. Goosander are present all year, joined in the winter by Whooper Swan, Pink-footed Goose, Goldeneye and other wildfowl. Osprey territories are now into double figures, Goshawk are widespread, especially in the extensive commercial forestry plantations, and reintroduced Golden Eagle are now breeding.

Bird Atlas/Avifauna
Birds in South-east Scotland 2007-2013:
A Tetrad Atlas of the Birds of Lothian and Borders
Ray D Murray, Ian J Andrews & Mark Holling
(Scottish Ornithologists' Club, 2019)

Bird Recorders
David Parkinson: 07979 365 134;
bordersrecorder@gmail.com

Bird Report
Borders Bird Report (1980-), hardcopy/back copies from SOC Borders branch—Malcolm Ross, 24 Netherbank, Galashiels, TD1 3DH:
eliseandmalcolm@btinternet.com
Also downloadable from www.bordersbirds.weebly.com

BTO Regional Representatives
Neil Stratton
Colonial Birds
Malcolm Ross:
Wetland Bird Survey (WeBS)
Local Organizer: webs@bto.org
Neil Stratton

Club
SOC Borders Branch (1980; 166)
Secretary: John Turner: 07702457007;
johnturner652023@btinternet.com;
www.the-soc.org.uk/local-branches/borders
or
www.bordersbirds.weeby.com
Meetings: 7:30pm, 2nd Monday of the month (Sep-Apr). Eildon Suite, Melrose Rugby Club, Greenyards, Melrose TD6 9SA.
Online talks also held. Contact/see website for details.

RSPB Local Group
No Groups.

Ringing Group/Bird Observatory
Borders RG

Scottish Wildlife Trust Regional Networks
Central Borders
swtborderssecretary@gmail.com;
Meetings: 2nd Thursday (Sep-Apr), Langlee Community Centre, Marigold Drive, Galashiels TD1 2LP:
Berwickshire
swtduns@gmail.com
Meetings: Duns Parish Church

Forestry and Land Scotland Regional Office
0300 067 6900;
enquiries.south@forestryandland.gov.scot

Borders Forest Trust
Monteviot Nurseries, Ancrum, Jedburgh TD8 6TU:
01835 830 750; enquiries@bordersforesttrust.org;
www.bordersforesttrust.org

South of Scotland Golden Eagle Project
Restoring Upland Nature (RUN) Over Kirkhope, Selkirk, Scottish Borders, TD7 5JD:
Cat@restoringuplandnature.co.uk
www.goldeneaglessouthofscotland.co.uk

Rather than leaving the A74(M) at J15 and taking the A708 NE from Moffat for Carrifran, head N on A701. Take minor road on R at Tweedsmuir for the Talla Reservoir, at the head of which you will come to

1 GAMESHOPE & TALLA

Borders Forest Trust
Habitats: 4,075 acres of unimproved grassland, peatland and young woodland rising to 2,600 ft. Recently planted with native tree species along Molls Cleuch, the lower reaches of the Gameshope Burn and Talla Water and the S side of the Talla Reservoir. Burns and lochs. Montane scrub habitats are also being restored at higher altitudes.
Birds: Black Grouse, woodland spp. *Summer:* Goosander, Dunlin, Golden Plover, Oystercatcher, Buzzard, Golden Eagle, Osprey, Kestrel, Peregrine Falcon, Skylark, Ring Ouzel, Dipper, Grey Wagtail, Wheatear.
Other: Native tree species.
Directions: ML12 6QP; NT 135 203. Leave the A708 between Selkirk and Moffat at Capercleuch (St Mary's Loch) and take the single track road for Tweedsmuir, skirt the N side of the Megget Reservoir and then descend (steep!) to the head of the Talla Reservoir. At the end of this descent the road turns sharp R and there is lay-by parking alongside the Gameshope Burn.
Public transport: None.
Visiting: Open all hours. No charge. A farm track runs from the lay-by up the valley alongside the Gameshope Burn to the abandoned steading. No permanent paths beyond the steading, no facilities and the terrain is not suitable for wheelchairs. Beyond the steading it is possible to veer SE along a tributary burn into Donald's Cleuch or continue S along the Gameshope Burn to the eponymous loch. To the E and S, Gameshope abuts with **Grey Mare's Tail** (NTS) and **Carrifran Wildwood** (BFT), both in Dumfries & Galloway, to form a 'reserve' of almost 7,500 acres.
Contact: 01835 830 750;
enquiries@bordersforesttrust.org;
Return to Capercleuch and head E on A708 along the Yarrow Valley. At the Gordon Arms, you can either continue straight on for Bowhill and The Haining or turn R on to B709. Follow it to Ettrick and the

2 ETTRICK MARSHES

Ettrick & Yarrow Community Development Company
Habitats: 140 acres mixed woods and conifer plantation on slopes to S of Ettrick, commercial conifers being felled, replanted with native broadleaf. Restored marsh and willow carr along river.
Birds: Goosander, Water Rail, Kingfisher, Sparrowhawk, Tawny Owl, Raven, tits (probably not Willow, claims notwithstanding), thrushes, Redpoll, Siskin, Reed Bunting. *Spring/summer:* Cuckoo, Oystercatcher, Osprey, warblers, inc Wood (occasional), Spotted Flycatcher, Redstart.
Other: Otter, Red Squirrel, Water Vole. Scotch Argus butterfly. Only known UK location of the moth *Apotomis infida*.
Directions: TD7 5HU; NT 295 165 (Hopehouse). From the Scott Monument in the centre of Selkirk take the A707 N and after 0.5 mile turn L on to the B7009 (signposted Ettrickbridge). Follow for 16 miles to the Hopehouse caravan park on the L. Park here or continue 1.5 miles and branch R along minor road to Ettrick 'village'. B7009 turns S here for Lamgholm along R. Tima, which joins Ettrick Water at Ettrick.
Public transport: Very occasional Hunters, Selkirk
Visiting: Open all hours. No charge. Park at Hopehouse caravan park (shop, cafe, toilets), Ettrick village (EYCDC now based in old school, toilets) or about one mile S along Tima. A network of paths runs between the parking places along the edge of the wood to S of river, with boardwalks into the marsh and one hide. There are several footbridges across the Ettrick and Tima including one reached by a path from the Hopehouse car park. Alternatively walk along B7009 on W & N banks of the rivers. The paths are not suitable for wheelchairs and some of the bridges are accessed by steps.
Contact: info@ettrickandyarrow.org.uk;
www.ettrikandyarrow.org.uk
Head back E on B709. Carry straight on for Bowhill or turn R on to B711 for Roberton, via the causeway over the Alemoor Reservoir, and

3 CRAIK FOREST

Forestry and Land Scotland
Habitats: 10,500 acres, mature (some trees over 100 years old) conifer forest. Blocks of different ages interspersed with clear fell and birch/willow scrub. Drained by Borthwick Water. Alemoor Reservoir borders N edge.
Birds: Goosander, Gadwall, Little Grebe, Goshawk, Goldcrest, Stonechat, Dipper, Grey Wagtail, Bullfinch, Crossbill, Redpoll, Siskin. *Spring/summer:* Common Sandpiper, Osprey, Willow Warbler in abundance, Spotted Flycatcher, Redstart, Tree Pipit. *Winter:* Whooper Swan, Wigeon, Teal, Great Crested Grebe.
Other: Red Squirrel.
Directions: TD9 7PS. NT 347 079. Leave A7 at Martins Bridge, SW of Hawick, follow B711 to Roberton (3.25 miles). Just after school, turn left along single track road for 6.5 miles, signposted to Craik Forest.
Public transport: None.
Visiting: Open all hours. Free car park signposted to

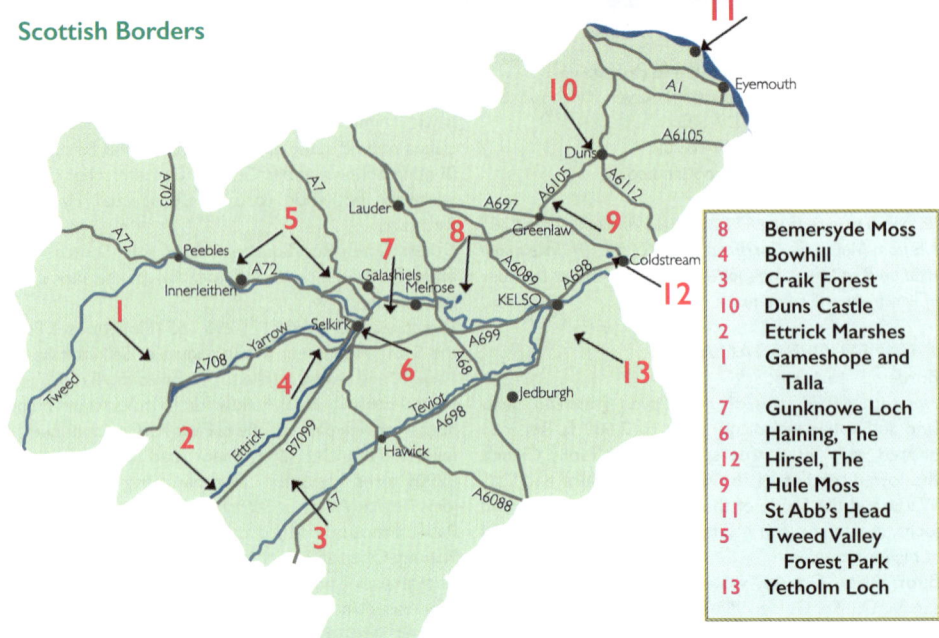

8	**Bemersyde Moss**
4	**Bowhill**
3	**Craik Forest**
10	**Duns Castle**
2	**Ettrick Marshes**
1	**Gameshope and Talla**
7	**Gunknowe Loch**
6	**Haining, The**
12	**Hirsel, The**
9	**Hule Moss**
11	**St Abb's Head**
5	**Tweed Valley Forest Park**
13	**Yetholm Loch**

L of Craik. No facilities beyond picnic tables. Three shortish circular walking trails start from car park—1 wheelchair friendly; but these only cover a small portion of the forest in the vicinity of Craik. Well-made forest roads extend much further. No access for cars but can be walked.

Alternatively, park in lay-bys on the B711 to the W of the causeway over the Alemoor Reservoir, which lies to N of forest. Further plantations to N of B711, walk in along forest roads.

Contact: FLS: 0300 067 6900;
enquiries.south@forestryandland.gov.scot

*If, rather than heading S to **Craik**, you carried on E along the Yarrow (A708) or Ettrick valleys (B7009), the triangle of land at their confluence is occupied by*

4 BOWHILL

Buccleuch Estates

Habitats: Mature woodlands, conifer and broadleaf, meadows, 2 lochs. Open hillside rising to 1,640 ft. Lying between the Yarrow and the Ettrick. Walks along Ettrick.

Birds: Red Grouse, Curlew, Little Grebe, Sparrowhawk, Goshawk, Golden Eagle, Peregrine Falcon, Kingfisher, Raven, Dipper, Redstart, Grey Wagtail, Crossbill.

Other: Red (farmed) and Roe Deer. Red Squirrel, Mountain Hare.

Directions: TD7 5ET; NT 426 279 (car park). Leave Selkirk on the A708 for St Mary's Loch. Half a mile after Philiphaugh, turn L, cross the Yarrow using the General's Bridge, and enter the park. New car park (charge) here

for general estate. Follow the estate road to the main car park (charge to enter grounds) to the N of Bowhill House. It is also possible to enter the park from the S by leaving Selkirk on the B7009 for Ettrick, crossing Ettrick Water at Carterhaugh Bridge and following the B7039 round the margin of the park to the estate road leading to the car park.

Public transport: Infrequent bus service from Selkirk town centre (Scott Monument) to Carterhaugh Bridge on the Ettrick. Cross the bridge and then walk 1.2 miles to the house.

Visiting: Open all year 7am-7pm for general estate but some areas much more restricted opening dates and hours. Several circular trails run from the car park. Facilities in service courtyard of House, when open.

Contact: Ranger:
info@bowhill.co.uk

Both the 708 and the B7009 will take you into Selkirk. Turn L on to the A707 and then A72, and follow along the Tweed Valley to Peebles, passing the

5 TWEED VALLEY FOREST PARK

Forestry and Land Scotland

Habitats: Seven commercially managed coniferous forests, covering a total of 15,720 acres on either side of the Tweed, the longest river in the Borders. Interspersed with farmland and upland.

Birds: Common Sandpiper, displaying Goshawk, Osprey, Sparrowhawk, Dipper, Crosbill, common woodland spp.

Other: Red Squirrel

Directions: The A72 runs W for 16 miles along the Tweed valley from Clovenfords (TD1 3LU; NT 448 364) to Peebles (EH45 8AJ; NT 253 404). The A707 joins from the SE at a roundabout 1 miles SW of Clovenfords. Individual forests (see below), accessed from A72 or A707.

Public transport: Bus X62 Galashiels-Edinburgh runs the length of A72 between Clovenfords and Peebles.

Visiting: Forest car parks open all hours, no charge from E to W: **Yair Hill** off A707 (NT 459 324 & NT 439 349). All rest off A72: **Thornielee** (NT 404 365; view displaying Goshawks in spring above forest to S of Tweed), **Innerleithen** (NT 355 367; NT 336 357), **Caberston** (park Innerleithen), **Cardrona** (toilets, NT 295 385), **Glentress** (toilets, cafe 9am-6pm, EH45 8NB; NT 283 398; NT 287 402; NT 278 412), **Cademuir** (NT 248 384). Extensive network of forest roads and paths. Mountain bike trails in several of the forests.

Contact: FLS: 0300 067 6900;
enquiries.south@forestryandland.gov.scot
Instead of turning L on to A707 in Selkirk, turn R.

6 HAINING, THE
The Haining Charitable Trust
Habitats: 160 acres, artificial loch, reed fringed in places, small marshy area. Surrounded by mature woodland.
Birds: Breeding Great Crested & Little Grebes, Sedge Warbler, Reed Bunting. Common woodland spp. Great Crested Grebe do not winter.
Other: Otter.
Directions: TD7 5LR; NT 469 180. About 0.25 mile from centre of Selkirk on A707. Enter through gates and drive up towards house.
Public transport: Bus Tweedbank to Selkirk. Train— Tweedbank.
Visiting: Grounds open all hours. Park (free) in front of house. Restoration of the house is now nearing completion. Circular walk around lake, suitable for wheel- and pushchairs. Popular with the young mums and dog walkers of Selkirk but only site in Borders where Great Crested Grebe breed. Fishing around but not on loch.
Contact:
Join A7 in centre of Selkirk. Head for Galashiels. At roundabout just outside Galashiels (home of the Great Tapestry of Scotland), take 2nd exit on to A6091. At next roundabout, 1st exit for Tweedbank. Gunknowe signposted.

7 GUNKNOWE LOCH AND PARK
Scottish Borders Council
Habitats: River, loch, parkland, scrub, woodland.
Birds: All year: Goosander, Great Spotted, Woodpecker, Redpoll. *Spring/ summer:* Grey Wagtail, Kingfisher, Sand Martin, Blackcap, Sedge & Grasshopper Warblers. *Passage:* Yellow Wagtail, Whinchat, Wheatear. *Winter:* Wigeon, Tufted Duck, Pochard, Goldeneye, thrushes, Brambling.
Directions: TD1 3SZ. NT 517 345. In Tweedbank, two miles from Galashiels on A6091. Park at Gunknowe Loch (Tweedbank Road, off roundabout on A6091).

Public transport: Bus: X62 Melrose to Galashiels stops in Tweedbank. Borders Buses (01896 754 350).
Visiting: Open all year. Car park, various surfaced paths suitable for wheelchairs.
Contact: Ranger Service: 01835 825 070
Continue E on A6091. Pass Melrose then 2nd exit at A68 roundabout for St Boswell. Then follow directions below.

8 BEMERSYDE MOSS
Bemersyde Estate
Habitats: Long narrow strip of marsh, willow scrub, open water. Once the location of a very large Black-headed Gull colony, the gulls and the Black-necked Grebe are now gone and the moss is drying out and filling in.
Birds: Summer: Breeding spp inc Lapwing, Water Rail, Snipe, Spotted Flycatcher, Stonechat, Tree Sparrow, Yellowhammer, Reed Bunting, Grasshopper & Sedge Warblers. *Winter:* Wildfowl inc large numbers of Wigeon, Teal, Greylag & Pink-footed Geese, Jack Snipe on Moss and adjacent Whitrig Bog to E. *Occasional:* Marsh Harrier (increasingly frequent), Goshawk, Peregrine Falcon, Barn Owl. First Cetti's Warbler in the Scottish Borders recorded here. Cattle Egret and Hawfinch in autumn of '25.
Other: Otter, Water Vole.
Directions: TD6 9DS. NT 614 340. Located 4 miles due E of Melrose, on other side of Tweed. Head S on A68 to St Boswells, turn L on to B6404. Shortly after crossing the Tweed, turn L up hill to Clintmains (entrance to Mertoun House on R) and take minor road to R where main road veers L. Reserve is a mile along this minor road to Maidenhall.
Public transport: Bus: 67 Galashiels to Berwick-up-on-Tweed, stops on B6404 at turn for Clintmains, Borders Buses (01896 754 350)
Visiting: Open all hours, free. Parking for three cars in lay-by on S edge of moss immediately after a sharp bend. Boardwalk leads to wheelchair-friendly bird hide with bird feeders but now with limited views of open water. Continue along minor road and after a sharp L at Whitrighill park on verge opposite a field entrance. Walk round margins of 3 fields (not suitable for wheelchairs) along N edge of moss to a small second hide, with better view of open water. Also view pools and wet pasture of Whitrig Bog to E, especially in winter.
Contact: Management agreement with SWT now expired, future management regime currently undecided.
Continue on B6404 for Kelso, turning R on to B6397 and R again on to A6089. Just to N of Kelso, with park wall of Floors Castle to R, take B6364 on L. Follow to Greenlaw. Then, see below.

9 HULE MOSS
Private estate, hide Scottish Wildlife Trust
Habitats: Heather moorland, scattered pine trees, shal-

low reed-fringed pools.

Birds: Red Grouse, Shelduck, Teal, Wigeon, Goldeneye, Tufted Duck, Snipe. Various raptors may drop in. Raven. *Winter:* Large roosts of Pink-footed Goose, Lesser Black-backed Gull (on passage).

Other:

Directions: TD10 6YT (nearest house); NT 715 489 (hide). From Greenlaw, which stands on the A697, take the A6105 for Duns. After 1.8 miles park in forest road turn off at NT 721 484.

Public transport: Bus: 60 Galashiels-Berwick-up-on-Tweed, daily but infrequent, nearest stops at Polwarth (2 miles on A6105), Borders Buses (01896 754 350).

Visiting: Open all hours. No charge. From turn-off cross low fence beside road and follow fence running to NW across moor for 0.5 mile, then walk beside drainage ditch to hide. Two pools. E one, extensive area of reeds on margin, duck shooting screens. W one less reed, hide at S end, small young birch plantation next to hide. Grouse butts on moor. Active sporting estate. Dogs on lead.

Contact:

Continue on A6105 to centre of Duns.

10 DUNS CASTLE

Duns Estate

Habitats: Two man-made lakes: Heron Pool/Hen Poo and Mill Dam. Woods and parkland.

Birds: All year: Woodland spp inc Great Spotted Woodpecker, Goldcrest. *Summer:* Redstart, Pied Flycatcher and warblers. *Winter:* Wildfowl.

Other: Red Squirrel, Roe Deer, occasional Otter. Woodland rich in wild flowers

Directions: TD11 3NW; NT 778 550. Duns lies W of Berwick-upon-Tweed. From town centre head N on Castle Street & North Castle Street. Alternatively, drive N on A6112 for one mile and turn L on to B6365 to car park on N edge of reserve.

Public transport: Bus: 60 Galashiels-Tweedmouth stops at Duns. Borders Buses (01896 754 350)

Visiting: Grounds open all year. Network of well-marked paths, some suitable for wheelchairs.

Contact: Duns Castle: 01361 883 211; info@dunscastle.co.uk; www.dunscastle.co.uk

From Duns take A6112 to A1 at Granthouses, turn R, then, after 5.5 miles turn L on to B6438.

11 ST ABB'S HEAD

National Trust for Scotland

Habitats: Cliffs, coastal grasslands, freshwater loch.

Birds: Apr-Aug: Seabird colonies with large number of Guillemot & Kittiwake; developing gannetry, with young birds on cliffs until Oct, also Shag, Razorbill, Fulmar, Rock Pipit. *Apr-May* and *Sep-Oct:* Good seawatching: shearwaters *Winter:* Divers, sea duck. *Passage:* Migrant

passerines, inc rarities, especially around Mire Loch, inland from the actual headland. Purple Sandpiper usually present in St Abb's Harbour in winter

Other: Common Rock-rose, Purple Milk-vetch, Spring Sandwort. Northern Brown Argus butterfly. Large Grey Seal colony, up to 2,000 pups late Nov-Dec.

Directions: TD14 5QF; NT 913 674 for car park/bus stop. Take B6438 from A1 for St Abbs, passing through Coldingham.

Public transport: Bus: 235 from Berwick-upon-Tweed. Borders Buses (01896 754 350). Train—Berwick-up-on-Tweed (whence bus) or Reston, closer (4 miles) but no bus.

Visiting: Open all year. Car park (free for members, coach parking arrangements—contact Carol Hamilton Borders Pottery: 07773 347 209. Nature Centre open daily, 9am-5pm Apr-Nov public toilets (inc disabled). All-ability path to viewpoint at Starney Bay. Keep dogs under control, take waste to bins in car park.

Contact: NTS: 01890 771 443; st.abbs@nts.org.uk

Instead of heading to Hule Moss from Kelso, continue of A6089 round Kelso to cemetery roundabout. Take 1st exit, A698 for Coldstream.

12 HIRSEL, THE

Hirsel Estate

Habitats: 500 acre park. Mature trees in parkland, woods, reed-fringed lake.

Birds: Largest concentration and first recorded breeding of Gadwall in Scottish Borders. Other ducks inc occasional Mandarin *Winter:* One of likeliest places in Borders for Hawfinch. Smew, fairly regular of late, Red-necked Grebe has been recorded.

Other:

Directions: TD12 4LP; NT 828 783 (car park). Drive, signposted for The Hirsel, leading to car park runs N from A698 on W edge of Coldstream.

Public transport: A698 main road to Berwick-up-on-Tweed. Several bus lines inc 67. Train—Berwick.

Visiting: Grounds open all hours, charge for parking. Network of roads and paths, some surfaced, One hide, not suitable for wheelchair access, at W end of lake. Good views of lake from grass strip at E end immediately adjacent to car park. Shops, cafe & toilets in steading by car park. Dogs on lead.

Contact: 01555 851536 (not local); office@daestates.co.uk

Take 2nd exit at Cemetery roundabout in Kelso, A698 for Jedburgh, then as below.

13 YETHOLM LOCH

Ownership unclear

Habitats: Wet woodland, shallow, reed-fringed 50 acre loch, streams and ponds.

Birds: Wildfowl inc Wigeon, Gadwall, Goldeneye. Both Smew (winter) and Great White Egret regular recently, with up to 2 or 3 Great White Egret present all year. Water Rail, Little Grebe, Common Gull. Occasional Osprey, Marsh Harrier, Cetti's Warbler recorded recently. *Other:* Otter, Mink.

Directions: TD5 8PD (Lochside House); NT 802 285 (lay-by). On the outskirts of Kelso, at the Sainsbury's roundabout on the A698 Coldstream to Hawick road, take the B6352 for Yetholm. After about six miles turn R down a minor road signposted 'Lochside'. The road bends R after about 200 yards. Park in the lay-by on the L.

Public transport: Bus: 81 (Scottish Borders Council) runs from Kelso Woodmarket to Town Yetholm Mon-Sat, passing minor road to loch. Nearest stop is Town Yetholm, then a one mile walk back along B6352 (road winding and no pavement).

Visiting: Open all hours, free. Path from lay-by—can be muddy—with sections of boardwalk (poor condition, not suitable for wheelchairs) leads to hide halfway along W shore. No dogs. Continue along minor road, up hill past Lochside to look down on willow carr at S end.

Contact: None.

The Lothians
(East, Mid & West)

More than 250 species have been recorded at Aberlady Bay, where thousands of geese gather in winter. The Seabird Centre at North Berwick is worth a visit and a boat can be taken out from here to the gannetry at Bass Rock. The Lammermuir Hills hold a range of upland species including Red Grouse, Whinchat and Ring Ouzel.

Bird Atlas/Avifauna
See **Scottish Borders**

Bird Recorder
Stephen Welch, 25 Douglas Road, Longniddry, EH32 0LQ: 01875 852 802 or 07931 524 963;
lothianrecorder@the-soc.org.uk

Bird Report
Lothian Bird Report (1979-), from SOC Lothian branch—Stephen Hunter:
stephen.lsoc@btinternet.com
BTO Regional Representative
Stephen Metcalfe
Wetland Bird Survey (WeBS)
Local Organizers: webs@bto.org
Forth Estuary (Outer South),
Tyninghame Estuary
Duncan Priddle:
Lothian (excl. Estuaries)
Shawn Waddoups:

Clubs
SOC Lothian Branch (1936, 1,000)
David Parmee: 07769 704 821;
lothiansecretary@the-soc.org.uk;
www.the-soc.org.uk/local-branches/lothian
Meetings: 7:30pm, 2nd Tuesday of the month (Sep-Apr). The Cornerstone Centre, St Johns Church, Princes Street, Edinburgh, EH2 4BJ. [10 March meeting held at Waterston House, Aberlady.]
Monthly online talks also held. Contact/see website for details.
Lothians and Fife Swan and Goose Study Group
See **Fife**

Ringing Group/Bird Observatory
Lothian RG

RSPB Local Group
Edinburgh Area (1974; 270)
Grant Donaldson: edinburghRSPBleader@gmail.com;
https://group.rspb.org.uk/edinburgh/
Meetings: 7:30pm, alternating between a Tuesday and a Wednesday each month (Sep-Apr with Jan/Feb held via zoom). The Nucleus Building, Edinburgh University, The King's Building Campus, Thomas Bayes Road, Edinburgh ED9 3 FG.

Scottish Wildlife Trust Regional Networks
Lothians
Chair: Tim Duffy: chair@swtlothians.org.uk;
https://swtlothians.org.uk
Meetings: Currently online, 7:30pm Thursdays, winter months

Forestry and Land Scotland Regional Office
0300 067 6600;
enquiries.central@forestryandland.gov.scot

Head up A1 from St Abb's Head (Scottish Borders).

1 SKATERAW
East Lothian Council
Habitats: Low, rocky coast, small beach in Skateraw Harbour. Grassland and scrub inland.
Birds: Passage migrants, inc Black Redstart, Wheatear. Pipits and wagtails on beach. Waders inc Purple Sandpiper. Out to sea Kittiwake, terns, auks, possible skuas. Red-throated Diver in winter.
Other: Plants tolerant of lime and salt: Autumn Gentian, White Horehound, Yellow-horned Poppy.
Directions: EH42 1QR; NT 737 754 (Skateraw Harbour car park). Leave A1 on minor road on N side between railway line and Torness power station. Turn R at Skateraw and follow down to sea and car park.
Public transport: None that doesn't involve crossing the A1.

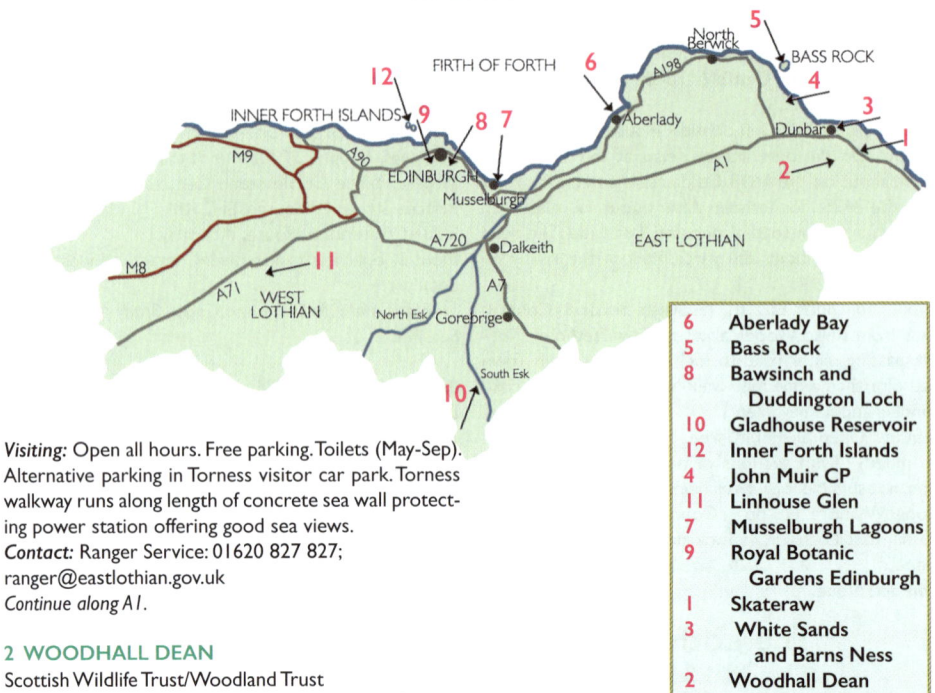

6	**Aberlady Bay**
5	**Bass Rock**
8	**Bawsinch and**
	Duddington Loch
10	**Gladhouse Reservoir**
12	**Inner Forth Islands**
4	**John Muir CP**
11	**Linhouse Glen**
7	**Musselburgh Lagoons**
9	**Royal Botanic**
	Gardens Edinburgh
1	**Skateraw**
3	**White Sands**
	and Barns Ness
2	**Woodhall Dean**

Visiting: Open all hours. Free parking. Toilets (May-Sep). Alternative parking in Torness visitor car park. Torness walkway runs along length of concrete sea wall protecting power station offering good sea views.
Contact: Ranger Service: 01620 827 827;
ranger@eastlothian.gov.uk
Continue along A1.

2 WOODHALL DEAN

Scottish Wildlife Trust/Woodland Trust
Habitats: 155 acres Sessile Oak and Birch wood covering the steep-sided ravines of the Woodhall and Weatherly Burns. Farmland and moorland abut the ravines.
Birds: Common woodland spp, inc Green Woodpecker, Lesser Whitethroat, Spotted Flycatcher, Redstart. Quail, Cuckoo, Merlin, Barn Owl in more open areas.
Other: Adder. Bluebells. Ransoms.
Directions: EH42 1SJ; NT 681 728. Take the minor road for Spott from the Asda roundabout on the A1 S of Dunbar. Turn L in Spott for Woodhall and stay on this road for 2 miles. At this point, just before a steep hill and ford, turn R up a track and park. Do not block access for farm vehicles.
Public transport: None.
Visiting: Open all hours, free. No facilities. Circular trail from entrance, footbridges over burns. Ravine sides steep in places, paths can be muddy. Not suitable for wheelchairs. Dogs under close control (ground nesting birds, adders!)
Contact: Scottish WT: 0131 312 7765;
enquiries@scottishwildlifetrust.org.uk
Return to A1 and continue W.

3 WHITE SANDS AND BARNS NESS

East Lothian Council
Habitats: Rocky, limestone promontory, with lighthouse. Scrub and woodland, sandy beaches and flooded quarry.
Birds: Passage migrants inc rarities, seawatching—Gannet, terns and auks in summer, Great & Arctic Skus, Manx Shearwaters in autumn—winter duck inc Goldeneye, Pochard and Tufted, and geese; waders on beaches and foreshore, along with pipits and wagtails to S of lighthouse. Gulls inc Kittiwake and, occasionally Glaucous and Iceland.
Other: Plants tolerant of lime and salt: Autumn Gentian, White Horehound.
Directions: EH42 1QP; NT 722 771(Barns Ness lighthouse car park). Take the single track road running N from the A1087 about 0.5 mile N of the A1 (other side of main railway line). Follow this road around the fenced off, flooded White Sands quarry and continue a further 0.75 mile to Barns Ness.
Public transport: None that doesn't involve crossing the A1.
Visiting: Open all hours. The minor road off the A1087 takes you first to White Sands—winter ducks and geese on flooded quarry, viewing shelter in NW corner, car park (charge) and toilets between quarry and sea—and then on to Barns Ness car park (charge) inland from the lighthouse—scrub spp, migrants and seawatching but exposed. Area of grassland to S of Barns Ness fenced off to allow conservation grazing over winter. It is no longer possible to drive along minor roads between Barns Ness and **Skateraw** (q.v.).
Contact: Countryside Rangers: 01620 827 827;
ranger@eastlothian.gov.uk
Return to A1 and continue W

4 JOHN MUIR COUNTRY PARK
East Lothian Council
Habitats: 1,730 acres of sand spit, saltmatsh, mudlfats, the estuary of the [East Lothian] Tyne, pine woods.
Birds: All year: Common woodland and scrub spp poss inc Crossbill. *Summer:* Fishing terns. *Autumn to spring:* Variety of waders and ducks on estuary/mudflats. Brent Geese. *Winter:* Twite and, possibly, Shore Lark on salt-marsh. Sea duck and Red-throated Diver off the beach.
Other: 400 spp plants. Butterflies and moths.
Directions: EH42 1XF; NT 652 787 (car park). Take the turning for Dunbar at the Thistly Cross roundabout on the A1. After passing under the railway and over Biel Water take the 3rd exit, the A1087 for Dunbar. Turn L after 0.5 mile and follow signs for Linkfield car park, which is adjacent to the East Links Family Park. Alter-natively, stay on the A1087 for just under another mile and turn L before the Brewery into Shore Road. Then park in the sea front car park (charge) by the mouth of Biel Water.
Public transport: Bus: X7 Edinburgh-Dunbar. East Coast Buses (0131 653 1335). Ask driver to stop near JMCP. Train—Dunbar, 15 min walk to Dunbar Harbour at E end of JMCP.
Visiting: Open all hours. Charge at Linkfield car park, toilets. Walk W through pine woods along the bound-ary of the family Park to the S side of the Tyne estu-ary at the point where the Hedderwick Burn flowed in. Path along estuary offers views over mudflats, Path runs along S side of estuary. Can walk round N end of pine wood and back to car park or out to sand spit (cordoned off in summer, dog walkers at other times).
Located at E end of John Muir Way, a walking trail that traverses Scotland from E to W.
Contact: Ranger Service: 01620 827 827; ranger@eastlothian.gov.uk
Return to A1, head W then A198 on R for North Berwick.

5 BASS ROCK/SCOTTISH SEABIRD CENTRE
Private
Habitats: Sea cliffs.
Birds: Spectacular cliffs hold a massive Gannet colony (up to 150,000 birds, largest in world). Fulmar, Shag, Puf-fin, Guillemot, Razorbill, Kittiwake, Common Tern.
Directions: NT 602 873. Island NE of North Berwick. Scottish Seabird Centre is located in North Berwick Harbour (EH39 4SS; NT554 856).
Public transport: None.
Visiting: Bass Rock is private—contact Seabird Centre/ check website for details of exclusive Bass Rock land-ing trips (inc three hours on island). Terms and con-ditions apply to bookings. Sailings/landings are subject to weather conditions. No facilities on island. Range of other boat trips in Firth of Forth from North Berwick. Seabird Centre—entrance fee: open Jan 10am-4pm; Feb/Mar and Sep/Oct 10am-5pm; Apr-Aug 10am-6pm;

Nov-Dec (not 25 Dec) 10am-4pm. Aquaria, telescope deck and toilets. Free to visit cafe and shop.
Contact: The Scottish Seabird Centre: 01620 890 202; info@seabird.org; boat trips: boats@seabird.org; www.seabird.org
Continue on W on A198 for

6 ABERLADY BAY LNR
East Lothian Council
Habitats: Tidal mudflats, saltmarsh, freshwater marsh, dune grassland, scrub, open sea.
Birds: Summer: Breeding spp inc Shelduck, Eider, Reed Bunting and up to eight spp of warbler. *Passage:* Wad-ers inc Green, Wood & Curlew Sandpipers, Little Stint, Greenshank, Whimbrel, Black-tailed Godwit. *Winter:* Divers (esp. Red-throated), Red-necked & Slavonian Grebes and geese (in autumn 30,000+ Pink-feet roost and feed before moving on), sea duck, waders.
Directions: EH32 0QB; NT 471 804. From Edinburgh take A198 E to Aberlady. Reserve car park is on A198 just to E of Aberlady village.
Public transport: Bus:124/X24 Edinburgh to North Berwick passes reserve (ask to be dropped nearby). East Coast Buses.
Visiting: Open all hours. Small (free) car park and toi-lets. Notice board with recent sightings at end of foot-bridge. Stay on footpaths to avoid disturbance. Disabled access from reserve car park. No dogs.
The Scottish Ornithologists' Club (SOC) HQ, Water-ston House, is located W of Aberlady village, open dai-ly? (not 25/26 Dec, 1 Jan) 10am-4pm inc shop, library, gallery: 01875 871 330.
Contact: Countryside Rangers: 01620 827 827; ranger@eastlothian.gov.uk
Continue W on A198 and then, S of Cockenzie, the B1361 to roundabout with A199. Then as below.

7 MUSSELBURGH LAGOONS
East Lothian Council
Habitats: Reclaimed mudflats—lagoons, grassland, woodland, boating pond, wader scrapes. Views of tidal mudflats and Firth of Forth from sea wall.
Birds: 270 spp recorded in wider area, regular rarities turn up. Good for terns, gulls, waders, sea-ducks and grebes. Offshore: five spp Scoter recorded, Eider, Long-tailed Duck, Red-necked & Slavonian Grebes. Wildfowl and waders inc Goosander, Goldeneye, Ruff, Curlew, Green & Wood Sandpipers, terns inc Black & Roseate. Barn & Short-eared Owls, passage migrants, summer warblers, various passerines.
Other: Wildflowers.
Directions: EH21 7QU; NT 357 734. E of Edinburgh/NE of Musselburgh. From A1 take A199 to Musselburgh. Continue over 1st roundabout then turn R onto B1348 (Prestonpans)—entrance to Musselburgh Lagoons car park 250 yards on L.

Public transport: Bus: 124 Edinburgh to North Berwick (alight Levenhall Links). East Coast Buses. Train—Musselburgh.

Visiting: Open all hours. Various trails, most wheelchair accessible. Hides—three on E side and five on W side overlooking new lagoon. For waders check for rising tides when birds come off mudflats.

Contact: Ranger Service: 01620 827 827; ranger@eastlothian.gov.uk

Continue on A199 to junction with A1, then A1. Turn L off A1 (Milton Road West) on to Duddingstin Road West

8 BAWSINCH RESERVE & DUDDINGSTON LOCH
Scottish Wildlife Trust

Habitats: Edinburgh's only natural freshwater loch (20 acres). Reedbed, marsh, ponds, mixed woodland, flower meadow and scrub. Bawsinch reserve (64 acres) on S edge of loch developed from former industrial wasteland.

Birds: Summer: Largest heronry in the Lothians, breeding swans, geese, ducks, grebes and Water Rail. Kingfisher. Migrants inc Spotted Flycatcher, hirundines, warblers inc occasional Grasshopper Warbler. *Winter:* Bittern (recorded), wildfowl, gulls.

Other: Fox, Water Vole, & Otter. Dragonflies, four spp of amphibians.

Directions: EH15 3 PY; NT 282 726. Two miles from the centre of Edinburgh, below Arthur's Seat. Use car park just W of Duddingston village on Duddingston Low Road (NB: Edinburgh now has a low emission zone, check your vehicle's eligibility: https://www.edinburgh.gov.uk/low-emission-zone)

Public transport: Bus: 42 Edinburgh-Portabello, alight Duddington Villlage (by Holyrood School). Lothian Buses (0131 555 6363).

Visiting: Open access to N shore of loch. S shore and hide by prior arrangement with SWT.

Contact: Scottish WT: 0131 312 7765; enquiries@scottishwildlifetrust.org.uk

Cross the centre of Edinburgh, from Duddingston Loch to the S of Arthur's Seat, round its W side, N to Princes Street and then

9 ROYAL BOTANIC GARDENS EDINBURGH

Habitats: 70 acres of specimen plants at a site in central Edinburgh, pond.

Birds: Kingfisher, Water Rail, Sparrowhawk, Tawny Owl, Nuthatch. Warblers inc Chiffchaff and Blackcap. Blackcap may winter.

Other: 13,000 spp of plants in Edinburgh and the four regional gardens.

Directions: EH3 5NZ NT 244 753 (Arboretum Place parking and main entrance) EH3 5LP (East Gate). The Botanic Garden lies outside the Edinburgh Low Emission Zone. Arboretum Place is a little over 1 mile N of Princes Street.

Public transport: Bus: 8, 9, 23 & 27 from city centre to East Gate; Lothian Buses 29 & 24 to main entrance. Train—Waverley Station, bus or 1.25 mile walk.

Visiting: On street parking (charge), gardens free but charge for plant houses (closed at present for restoration). Open 10am-5pm (4pm Nov-Jan) Last entry 45 min before closing. Cafe open 10am-4pm Feb-Nov. Shop. Toilets (ins accessible). Wheelchair and mobility scooters for hire. Assistance dogs permitted.

Contact: 0131 248 2909; via website; www.rbge.org.uk

To visit the following three sites from central Edinburgh see their Directions sections.

10 GLADHOUSE RESERVOIR
Scottish Water

Habitats: Largest body of freshwater in Lothians, two islands, wooded margins and two plantations. SSSI.

Birds: Breeding: Mallard, Teal, Tufted Duck, Coot, Moorhen, Great Crested & Little Grebes. Osprey. *Winter:* Major roost for Pink-footed & Greylag Goose. Mallard, Wigeon, Teal and Tufted Duck

Other:

Directions: EH23 4TA; NT 300 551 (Gladhouse Mains). Take the A701 S from Edinburgh city centre of the Straiton Junction on the by-pass. Take the L exit (B7026) just after the Gowkley Moss roundabout for Auchendinny. After 3 miles, turn L on to B6372 and follow signs for reservoir. After 3.5 miles turn R on to a minor road at Upper Side. After just over 1 mile turn L on to a minor road running around N side of reservoir and across dam. Parking restrictions here in summer.

Public transport: None.

Visiting: Open all hours, free. No facilities. Limited parking on roads to N of reservoir. Seasonal restrictions. Paths around reservoir, many unpaved, can be muddy.

Contact: 0800 0778 778; Rangers permanently on site.

11 LINHOUSE GLEN
Scottish Wildlife Trust

Habitats: Heath, native woodland, species-rich grassland.

Birds: Grey Partridge, Snipe, Kestrel, Skylark, Dipper. Linnet, Bullfinch, Yellowhammer, Reed Bunting. *Summer:* Curlew, Oystercatcher, Willow Warbler, Spotted Flycatcher.

Other: Brown Hare, Otter, Greater Butterfly and Fragrant Orchids.

Directions: NT 072 643. Take A899 S from J3 of M8. At roundabout, take A71 for West Calder, then 1st L and L again at T junction on to Murieston East Road. Take 4th L (Murieston Road). Then, just before sharp R bend, turn L on to short section of road and park. Walk through gap next to large metal gate. Follow cinder track for 1.25 miles (passing under wooden bridge). At NT 074 647 path on R runs towards Linhouse Water, passing beneath viaduct. Enter NE corner of reserve.

Public transport: Train—Livingston South.

Visiting: Open all hours, free. No facilities. Long, thin reserve linked by level crossing (use with care) on either side of active railway, extending down steep slopes of glen to Linhouse Water.

Contact: SWT Lothians Group:
www. swtlothians.org.uk

12 INNER FORTH ISLANDS
Edinburgh City Council/RSPB

Habitats: Small rocky islands in the inner Forth: Cramond Inchgarvie, Inchholm, Inchkeith, Inchmickery.

Birds: Summer: Guillemot, Razorbill, Puffin, Sandwich Tern.

Other: Grey Seals, dolphins.

Directions: NT 133 784; EH30 9TB (ticket office); Queensferry. Take the A90 W from Edinburgh and then the B924 to Queensferry Pier.

Public transport: Bus: 43/x43 daily St Andrews Square (central Edinburgh)-South Queensferry, then 15 min walk. Lothian Country (0131 555 6363). Train—Dalmeny, then 10 min walk.

Visiting: Free car parking on seafront at South Queensferry. **Maid of the Forth** runs a regular summer ferry service to Inchholm (landing allowed) and a variety of trips around the other islands (no landing). Inchmickery is managed by the RSPB. Toilets at pier, on boat and at Inchholm. Boat gangway not suitable for wheelchairs. Dogs allowed under control.

Contact: Maid of Forth; 0131 331 500;
info@maidoftheforth.co.uk;
www.maidoftheforth.co.uk

Central

(Clackmannanshire, Falkirk, Stirling)

The RSPB reserve at Inversnaid is good for Black Grouse, Redstart, Wood Warbler, Pied Flycatcher and Twite. The feeding station at Argaty provides visitors with close-up views of Red Kite. Cambus Pools attract passage waders and winter wildfowl, while high tide at Kinneil produces good numbers of waders in spring and autumn.

Bird Atlas/Avifauna
The Birds of Clackmannanshire
Neil Bielby, Keith Broomfield & John Grainger
(Scottish Ornithologist's Club, 2014)

Bird Recorders
Upper Forth
Chris Pendlebury, 23 Ochlochy Park, Dunblane, FK15 0DU: 07798 711 134; chrispendlebury@gmail.com
Assistant: Neil Bielby, 56 Ochiltree, Dunblane, FK15

0DF: 01786 823 830; centscotbranch@gmail.com

Bird Report
Upper Forth Area Bird Report (1975-), published Nov in *The Forth Naturalist & Historian*. To purchase journal or a pdf contact Dan Jackman, Newfield, Beancross Road, Grangemouth, FK3 8YL: danieljoan1@virginmedia.com

BTO Regional Representative
Central Scotland
Neil Bielby
Wetland Bird Survey (WeBS)
Local Organizers: webs@bto.org
Central Scotland
(excl. Forth Estuary)
Neil Bielby
Forth Estuary (Inner)
Michael Bell

Club
SOC Central Scotland Branch (1968; 100)
Neil Bielby: 01786 823 830;
centscotbranch@gmail.com
www.the-soc.org.uk/local-branches/central-scotland
Meetings: 7:30pm, 1st Thursday of the month (Oct, Nov, Feb, Mar). The Allan Centre, Fountain Road, Bridge of Allan, FK9 4AT. Online talks also held. Contact/see website for details.

RSPB Local Group
Forth Valley (1995; 50)
forthvalleybirders@gmail.com;
https://group.rspb.org.uk/forthvalley/
Meetings: 7:30pm, 3rd Thursday of the month (Sep-Apr). Hillpark Community Centre, Morrison Drive, Bannockburn, Stirling, FK7 0HZ.

Scottish Wildlife Trust Regional Networks
Callander (n/a; 80)
Callanderswt@gmail.com; https://scottishwildlifetrust.org.uk/local-group/callander/
Meetings: 7:30pm 2nd Thursday of the month; St Andrew's Church Hall, Leny Road, Callander FK17 8AL
Falkirk
01324 229 187; jimhopwood15@outlook.com
Meetings: 7:30pm 3rd Thursday of the month (Sep-Apr); Trinity Church, Falkirk.
Stirling and Clackmannanshire
Chair: Stuart Bence: swt.stirling.clacks@outlook.com
Meetings: 7:30pm 1st Tuesday of the month. Venue varies. Contact/see website:
https://scottishwildlifetrust.org.uk/local-group/stirling/

Forestry and Land Scotland Regional Office
0300 067 6600;
enquiries.central@forestryandland.gov.scot

STIRLINGSHIRE

Tyndrum

Crianlarich

A85

A84

9

Loch Katrine 7 6 Callander

8 A821

5 Loch Venachar 4 Doune A9

Loch Ard Lake of Menteith Teith

Aberfoyle Forth

A81 A811 STIRLING

Loch Lomond

10

CLACKMANNANSHIRE

11 A91

Alloa

12

M9

3 M80 Denny

2 Falkirk

1

FALKIRK

10	Argaty
12	Black Devon Wetlands
11	Cambus Pools
2	Carron Dams
3	Carron Glen
4	Flanders Moss

Leave the M9 heading W from Edinburgh at J5 and take A905 heading N. At 2ⁿᵈ roundabout take 1ˢᵗ exit, the A904.

7	Glen Finglas
1	Kinneil
9	Inversnaid
6	Little Druim Wood
8	Loch Katrine
5	Queen Elizabeth Forest Park

1 KINNEIL LAGOON AND FORESHORE LNR

Falkirk Council (Lagoon)/
The Friends of Kinneil (LNR)

Habitats: Mudflats, tidal lagoon, reedbed, saltmarsh, scrub, mixed woodland at point where River Avon flows into the Forth. Foreshore LNR, a regenerated former industrial site (extensive tree planting), occupies promontory to E and extends as far as Bo'ness Harbour.

Birds: Summer/Breeding: Water Rail, Grasshopper Warbler. Common, Arctic & a few Sandwich Terns over Firth. Recent records of Marsh Harrier and Bearded Tit. *Passage:* Lesser Whitethroat, Wheatear and Whinchat. Large numbers of waders roost in lagoon and around inlet inc: Lapwing, Golden, Grey & Ringed Plovers, Knot, Dunlin, Snipe, Black & Bar-tailed Godwits, Redhank, Spotted Redshank, Greenshank, Little Stint, Curlew Sandpiper, Whimbrel. *Winter:* Gull roost on mudflats. Wildfowl in Lagoon and Firth inc: Sheduck, Pintail, a few Scaup. Great Crested Grebe. Short-eared & Long-eared Owls occasional over grassland.

Directions: EH51 0PY; NS 962 812 (Sewage Works). Access Lagoon via the Sewage Works road running N from A904 between the Grangemouth Chemical Works and Kinneil House on the W edge of Bo'ness. Park by Sewage Works for Lagoon or Snab Lane

(EH51 0PS; NS 988 808) for Foreshore.

Public transport: Bus: F45 Bo'ness-Linlithgow station, McGill's (03330 166 162) Train—Linlithgow.

Visiting: Open all hours, free parking. No facilities at lagoon or LNR but immediately adjacent to town of Bo'ness.

Contact: LNR: friendsofkinneil@googlemail.com; *Continue on A904 towards Falkirk. At roundabout next to Falkirk Grahamston station, take B902.*

2 CARRON DAMS

Scottish Wildlife Trust

Habitats: Partially drained reservoir. immediately to N of River Carron. Fen. Deciduous woodland.

Birds: Water Rail, Kestrel, common woodland spp.

Other: Water Vole, amphibians, Gypsywort, Remote Sedge, Water Plantain.

Directions: FK5 3BL; NS875 826. Take B902 N from

Falkirk to Stenhousemuir. After crossing River Carron, take 3rd exit at New Carron Road roundabout on to Stenhouse Road. Park on this road or side streets.

Public transport: Bus: 2 & 8 run between Falkirk and Stenhousemuir McGill's (03330 166 162). Train— Falkirk Grahamston, Larbert.

Visiting: Open all hours, free. Enter through pedestrian gate on Stenhouse Road. Reserve very wet and boggy, stay on boardwalks.

Contact: SWT Stirling & Clackmannanshire: swt.stirling.clacks@outlook.com

Continue along Stenhouse Road to B905, turn L. Follow b(05 as it takes a sharp L over River Carron. The 3rd exit at roundabout on to A883. After passing denny, take B883.

3 CARRON GLEN

Scottish Wildlife Trust

Habitats: Oak and Ash woodland, along gorge of River Carron.

Birds: Common woodland spp. inc Green Woodpecker & Wood Warbler. Kingfisher, Dipper, Grey Wagtail.

Other: Globeflower, Toothwort, Bluebells.

Directions: FK6 5HJ; NS 785 835. Take B818 for Fintry from Denny ring road. After about 1 mile park in car park at W end of Fankerton.

Public transport: Bus: 8, Denny-Fankerton (daily). McGill's (03330 166 162).

Visiting: Open all hours, free. Park in car park at W end of Fankerton, take footbridge over river to reserve on N side of river. At time of going to press, path to W of bridge closed due to landslip. Path to E open. Gorge sides steep. Take care. Not suitable for wheelchairs. Dogs under close control.

Contact: SWT Callander: Callanderswt@gmail.com

Continue along Carron Valley and B818 for

Carron Valley Reservoir

Reservoir is Scottish Water. Car parks and toilets operated by Forestry and Land Scotland

5 miles further along the B818 towards Fintry. Car park, open all hours, and toilets at NS 723 838, just to E of dam. B818 runs along N side of 3.5 mile long reservoir. Main blocks of coniferous forest on S side of reservoir. Walking trails, inc boardwalk, and lochside hide. Also mountain bike trails.

Birds: Osprey, Crossbill

Contact: 0300 067 6600;

enquiries.central@forestryandlandscotland.gov.scot

Continue on B818 and, at Fintry, turn R on to B822.

4 FLANDERS MOSS NNR

NatureScot

Habitats: Extensive area of raised lowland bog. Fringe of birch woodland.

Birds: Winter: Whooper Swan, Pink-footed, Greylag & Canada Geese. Siskin, Redpoll. *Spring/summer:* Curlew, Lapwing, Golden Plover, Snipe, Redshank, Cuckoo,

Grasshopper & Sedge Warblers, Whinchat, Redstart, Spotted Flycatcher. Raptors may include Hen Harrier and Red Kite.

Other: Adder, lizards. Bog flora.

Directions: FK8 3QJ; NS 648 978. Leave B822 between Thornhill and Kippen 1.5 miles S of Thornhill and take minor road W for further 0.75 mile to car park

Public transport: Bus: C11 Aberfoyle-Stirling (Mon-Fri). First Bus. X10A Glasgow-Stirling. McGill's (03330 166 162). Both stop at Thornhill. Walk from Thornhill, over 2 miles.

Visiting: Car park for cars and coaches at entrance. Water table being kept high. Moss very wet, keep to circular path. Viewing tower.

Contact: Amee Hood: 01786 450 362; nnr@nature. scot

Continue on B822 to Thornhill. Turn L on to A873 for Aberfoyle, passing the only lake in Scotland. Continuing on B822 at Thornhill will take you to Callander.

5 QUEEN ELIZABETH FOREST PARK
THE LODGE FOREST VISITOR CENTRE

The Queen Elizabeth Forest Park is a cluster of individual forests between Loch Lomond and Strathyre. Loch Katrine (q.v.) is one of these forests and the forest around the Lodge is another. The Lodge also serves as the Forest Park's information centre.

Habitats: Broadleaved forest around the Lodge, lake and streams. Further N, the A821 passes across more open upland and conifer plantations.

Birds: Goshawk, Sparrowhawk, Peregrine Falcon. Common woodland spp inc Great Spotted Woodpecker, Long-tailed Tit, Willow Warbler, Goldcrest, Nuthatch, Siskin and Scottish Crossbill.

Other: Red Squirrel, Pine Marten, Pipstrelle, Long-eared and Daubenton's Bats.

Directions: FK8 3SX; NN 520 014. From the centre of Aberfoyle, take the A821 for Callander and climb in a series of switchbacks for about 0.75 mile before turning R into the Lodge.

Public transport: Trossachs Explorer (daily Jul-Sep, trial service in 2025, plans for 2026 currently uncertain) Aberfoyle-Callander, stops at The Lodge.

Visiting: Car park at Lodge (charge). Lodge Visitor Centre, cafe, toilets. Open daily 10am-4:30pm Apr-Oct, 10am-4pm Nov-22 Dec & Mar; 10am-3pm 3 Jan-Feb. Information about Forest Park. CCTV showing bird feeders. Forest trails, some all ability, and Go Ape zip lines. Mobility scooter hire. Dogs allowed in Lodge

Contact: 0300 067 6615;

thelodge@forestryandland.gov.scot

Continue N along A821 over the Duke's Pass.

GREAT TROSSACHS FOREST NNR

Made up of Little Druim Wood, and Glen Finglas, Loch Katrine and Inversnaid.

The owners of these contiguous reserves are coordinating their management plans to create an unbroken area of pasture, woodland and moor covering 56 square miles. The NNR in turn forms part of the Loch Lomond and Trossachs National Park.

At the T junction at the NW corner of Loch Achray, turn R for

6 LITTLE DRUIM WOOD

Woodland Trust Scotland

Little Druim Wood at the foot of Stuc Odhar/Lendrick Hill and N of Loch Venacher forms one part of the Woodland Trust's Glen Finglas holdings.

Habitats: Birch and Oak woodland on side of hill with rocky outcrops. Loch, marsh.

Birds: All year: Great Spotted Woodpecker, Nuthatch. Summer: Common woodland spp., Wood Warbler, Pied Flycatcher, Redstart, Tree Pipit.

Directions: FK17 8HR; NN 549 062 (car park). Turn off A84 W of Callander at Kilmahog on to A821, which runs to N of Loch Venacher. Car park to S of A821 at head of Loch Venacher about 5 miles from Kilmahog. The A821 continues W beyond the car park and after passing Loch Achray turns S and runs to Aberfoyle, about 10 miles on from the car park. If starting from Aberfoyle take this road.

Public transport: Trossachs Explorer (daily Jul-Sep, trial service in 2025 not yet certain for 2026) Aberfoyle-Callander, stops at Brig o'Turk on A821, 0.75 mile from car park.

Visiting: Open all hours, free. Lendrick Hill Visitor Gateway open 10am-4pm Apr-Oct. Toilets, wi-fi. Paths from car park into wood. Wood lies between A821 and head of Loch Venacher, with marshy area on either side of Black Water S of wood and to W of loch. Pub in Brig o'Turk. Pub currently closed but tea room open.

Contact: enquiries@woodlandtrust.org.uk

and

7 GLEN FINGLAS

Woodland Trust Scotland

Habitats: 12,500 acres of glens, moorland, broadleaved woods and upland wood pasture. Long-term broadleaved woodland planting programme.

Birds: Black Grouse, Cuckoo, Osprey, Red Kite, Golden Eagle, Green Woodpecker, Wood Warbler, Nuthatch, Treecreeper, Siskin.

Other: Luing cattle grazing the wood pastures. Red Squirrel, Otter, Pine Marten. Sessile Oak, Scots Pine.

Directions: As for **Little Druim Wood**

Public transport: As for **Little Druim Wood**

Visiting: Visitor Centre at Lendrick Hill—see **Little Druim Wood**. The A821 continues W from Little Druim Wood through Brig o'Turk and the main part of the Glen Finglas estate lies NW of this village, encompassing the glens (Finglas, Meann & Cassaig) and hillside

to the N and E of the Glen Finglas Reservoir. There is further parking in Brig o'Turk. Paths lead from the Visitor Gateway along the lower slopes of Stuc Odhar and from Brig o'Turk to the Finglas Reservoir dam, along the N and E sides of the reservoir and into the 3 glens. Some of the low-level paths are surfaced

The Trust's holdings also include Milton and Bohcastle to the E of the Lendrick Hill Visitor Gateway on the N shore of Loch Venacher.

Contact: enquiries@woodlandtrust.org.uk

Download a walking map from:
https://www.woodlandtrust.org.uk/media/50669/10513-glen-finglas-leaflet-map-a2-v3.pdf

Turn L at the T junction for

8 LOCH KATRINE

Scottish Water/Forestry and Land Scotland

Habitats: 23,700 acres of moorland, broadleaved forest conifer plantations around Lochs Katrine and Arklet. Long-term broadleaved woodland planting programme.

Birds: Similar assemblage to the other sites in the Great Trossachs Forest.

Directions: FK17 8HZ; NN 497 072 (Trossachs Pier car park at Loch Katrine). Turn off A84 W of Callander at Kilmahog on to A821, which runs to N of Loch Venacher. Carry on to the head of Loch Achray. Here, there are car parks at NN 057 068 and NN 509 070 (in the Achray Forest, charges, also Forest and Land Scotland, charges). For the Trossach Pier at the foot of Loch Katrine take the Pass of the Trossachs spur road running NW from Achray View for about 1 mile to the car park (charge).

Public transport: Trossachs Explorer (daily Jul-Sep, trial service in 2025, not yet certain for 2026) Aberfoyle-Callander, stops Loch Katrine.

Visiting: Cafe, toilets, bicycle hire at the Trossachs Pier. Cruise ships (foot passengers and bicylces), including the Sir Walter Scott, offer circular tours or one-way trips to Stronachlachar (NN 404 102), about two thirds of the way along the S shore of Loch Katrine. A minor road runs W from Stronachlachar. Numerous paths, some surfaced. The Great Trossachs path runs from **Inversnaid** (q.v.), in the W, around the N end and shore of Loch Katrine and on to Callander.

Contact: 0300 067 6600;
enquiries.central@forestryandland.gov.scot

From Aberfoyle take the B829, passing Lochs Ard and Chon, for 12 miles to the junction with the minor road running W from Stronachlachar. Turn L on to this minor road for

9 INVERSNAID

RSPB

Habitats: Loch Lomond, woodland, moorland. 2,000 acres rising to 2,530 ft at the summit of Beinn a Choin from near sea level.

Birds: All year: Goosander, Golden Eagle, Peregrine,

Black Grouse, Woodcock, Dipper, Grey Wagtail, common woodland spp. *Summer:* Common Sandpiper, Osprey, Tree Pipit, Redstart, Whinchat, Pied & Spotted Flycatchers, Wood Warbler, Twite. *Winter:* Goldeneye, Redwing, Fieldfare.
Other: Fungi. Pine Marten, Red Deer.
Directions: FK8 3TU; NN 348 096. Remote. See above for directions from Aberfoyle.
Public transport: None.
Visiting: Open all hours. RSPB car park at Garrison Farm (seven spaces) or continue to Inversnaid Hotel (council run car park/40 spaces). Four trails at reserve: upland—1.0 mile (from Garrison Farm); woodland:—0.75 mile (from hotel); West Highland Way—2.5 miles through length of reserve; Great Trossachs Path passes through.
Contact: RSPB: 01389 830 670;
inversnaid@rspb.org.uk
Return to Aberfoyle, and then the A821 and A81 to Callander and then the A820 into Doune. Doune and Argaty are in the historic county of Perthshire but the Stirling Council area, hence their inclusion in Central.

10 ARGATY
Lerrocks Farm
Habitats: Upland livestock farm with areas of deciduous woodland and ponds.
Birds: Red Kite feeding centre, peak numbers in winter. Occasional Osprey. Common wood- and farmland spp.
Other: Red Squirrel, Beaver
Directions: FK16 6EJ; NN 738 039. From Main Street (A820) Doune take King Street (between church and takeaway, brown tourist sign) and follow for about 1 mile. Turn L at bungalow and bus shelter into 'No Through Road'. Follow for 1 mile (narrow and winding). Turn L at Lerrocks Farm. Park in Red Kite Centre car park (do not take the private drive to the farm).
Public transport: Bus: 59 (daily) Stirling-Callander, stops in Doune. McGill's (03330 166 162). Then 2 mile walk. Train—Dunblane, then 3 miles walk.
Visiting: Open 9am-5pm daily. Park at farm. Charges made for viewing feeding and hide. Honesty box for outwith feeding time visit. Booking highly recommended and essential for woodland hides.
Contact: 01786 841 373;
argatyredkites1@btinternet.com
Website and booking: https://argatyredkites.co.uk
Whilst you are at Doune
Doune Ponds Nature Reserve
Doune Community Woodland Group/Moray Estates
Habitats: Former gravel pits in process of being restored as community woodland and ponds.
Birds: Common woodland spp. Waterfowl. Osprey and Mandarin have been reported.
Other: Red Squirrel, fungi
Directions: FK16 6DF (office); NN? 726 018 (car park).

200 yards N of Main Street (A820) Doune, along Station Wynd.
Public transport: Bus: 59 (daily) Stirling-Callender, stops in Doune. McGill's (03330 166 162).
Visiting: Car park off Station Wynd, all ability access to woodland. Paths, hides, viewing platform.
Contact: 01786 841 250;
douneponds@gmail.com
Return to Doune and take A820 to the A9 and then A907.

11 CAMBUS POOLS
Scottish Wildlife Trust
Habitats: Wet grassland, reedbeds and two saline pools.
Birds: *Spring/autumn:* Used extensively by migrants. Wildfowl inc Mute & Whooper Swans, Goldeneye, Teal, Shelduck. Waders inc Black-tailed Godwit, Oystercatcher, Greenshank. Gadwall (have bred), Kingfisher, Yellowhammer & Reed Bunting.
Other: Brown Hare, Stoat, Short-tailed vole, 115 spp of vascular plants. Harbour Porpoise seen in Forth.
Directions: FK10 2PG; NS 846 937. From Stirling, take A907 E towards Alloa. From roundabout drive 0.6 mile to where B9096 leads off to Tullibody. Take minor road (Station Road) R to small village of Cambus.
Public transport: None.
Visiting: Open all year. Cross River Devon by bridge at NS 853 940 and walk down stream on R bank past bonded warehouses. Best viewing around high tide. Bench on S side of W pool. Dogs under control.
Contact: Scottish WT: 0131 312 7765;
enquiries@scottishwildlifetrust.org.uk
Return to A907.

12 BLACK DEVON WETLANDS
RSPB
Habitats: Wet grassland, marshland, open water and shallow pools. Adjacent to the tidal River Forth.
Birds: *All year:* Water Rail, Marsh Harrier, Stonechat, Reed Bunting. *Spring/summer:* Little Ringed Plover, Common Tern, Sand Martin, warblers inc Sedge & Grasshopper. *Winter:* Wildfowl and waders inc Pink-footed Goose, Teal, Shoveler, Shelduck, Goosander, Oystercatcher, Curlew, Lapwing, Snipe, Redshank.
Directions: FK10 1BU; NS 889 919. S edge of Alloa. From A907 take Auld Brig Road, at roundabout take 2nd exit on to Greenside Street. Turn L into Broad Street, then L into Bowhouse Road and L again into Riverside View—reserve reached by public footpath at end of Riverside View.
Public transport: Train—Alloa, one mile.
Visiting: Open all year. No parking facility—park carefully in residential area (Riverside View)—take path to reserve (700 yards). Nature trail, viewing screen, benches. Dogs under close control.
Contact: RSPB: 01324 832 853;
innerforthreserves@rspb.org.uk

Fife

Many of the county's best birdwatching sites are found on the coast. Fife Ness is good for seawatching and autumn migrants; the Eden Estuary holds good numbers of wildfowl and waders throughout the year but especially in winter, whilst wintering flocks of seaduck off Ruddons Point (Largo Bay) often include a Surf Scoter or two amongst the more numerous Common & Velvet Scoters. Tentsmuir offers an unusual mix of woodland (scarce in the county) and coastal habitats. Corn Bunting are recovering strongly in the Neuk of Fife.

Bird Atlas/Avifauna
The Breeding and Wintering Birds of Fife:
An Atlas for 2007-2013
Norman Elkins, Allan Brown, Jim Reid
(SOC, 2016).

Bird Recorders
Fife inc. offshore Islands (North Forth),
except Isle of May
Graham Sparshott, 19 Inverewe Place, Dunfermline, KY11 8FH: 07770 225 440; gsparshott@myyahoo.com
Isle of May
Iain English, 19 Nethan Gate, Chantinghall Road, Hamilton, South Lanarkshire ML3 8NH: 01698 891 788;
i.english.t21@btinternet.com

Bird Reports
Fife Bird Report (1988-), from FBC—online (from 2014) —contact: via website
www.fifebirdclub.org.uk
Isle of May Bird Observatory Report (stand alone reports from 1985; but reports appearing in other publications date back to 1934, the year the observatory was founded), from IMBO—Stuart Rivers, 91 Rowanhill Drive, Port Seton, Prestonpans, East Lothian, EH32 0SX: slr.bee-eater@blueyonder.co.uk

BTO Regional Representatives
Fife
Paul Blackburn
Isle of May
Dawn Balmer
Wetland Bird Survey (WeBS)
Local Organizers: webs@bto.org
Fife (Inland)
Allan Brown: webs@bto.org
Forth Estuary (North)
Vacant—contact WeBS Office.
Tay and Eden Estuary
Paul Blackburn

Clubs
Fife Bird Club (1985; 200)
Malcolm Ware (Membership Sec.), 78 Thistle Street, Dunfermline, Fife KY12 0JA: memsec@fifebirdclub.org.uk
www.fifebirdclub.org.uk
Meetings: Held regularly through the year (usually 7:30 p.m. on a Thursday)—contact/see website for details. Dean Park Hotel, Kirkcaldy, KY2 6HF.
The Fife Bird Club has three locked, member-only hides (Edenside, Fife Ness, Kilconquhar).
SOC Fife Branch (1950; 170)
Caroline Gordon: fifesecretary@the-soc.org.uk; www.the-soc.org.uk/local-branches/fife
Meetings: Online talks held. Fife members may attend the in-person meetings of the neighbouring Tayside branch or any other branch meetings. Contact/see website for details.
Lothians & Fife Swan & Goose Study Group (1978; 12)
Allan and Lyndesay Brown, 61 Watts Gardens, Cupar, Fife KY15 4UG: 01334 656 804; swansallan@gmail.com

RSPB Local Group
No Groups.

Ringing Group/Bird Observatory
Tay RG: www.tayringinggroup.org
Isle Of May Bird Observatory
Mark Newell (Booking Sec): 07909 707971;
bookings@isleofmaybirdobs.org;
www.isleofmaybirdobs.org

Scottish Wildlife Trust Regional Networks
Fife and Kinross
Chair: Andy Cage
secfifekinswt@gmail.com;
https://www.facebook.com/swtfifeandkinrossmc

Forestry and Land Scotland Regional Offices
0300 067 6600;
enquiries.central@forestryandland.gov.scot
or
0300 067 6380;
enquiries.east@forestryandland.gov.scot

Fife Coast & Countryside Trust
The Harbourmaster's House, Hot Pot Wynd, Dysart, Fife, KT1 2TQ: 01592 656 080; ask.us@fifecountryside.co.uk;
www.fifecountrysidetrust.co.uk

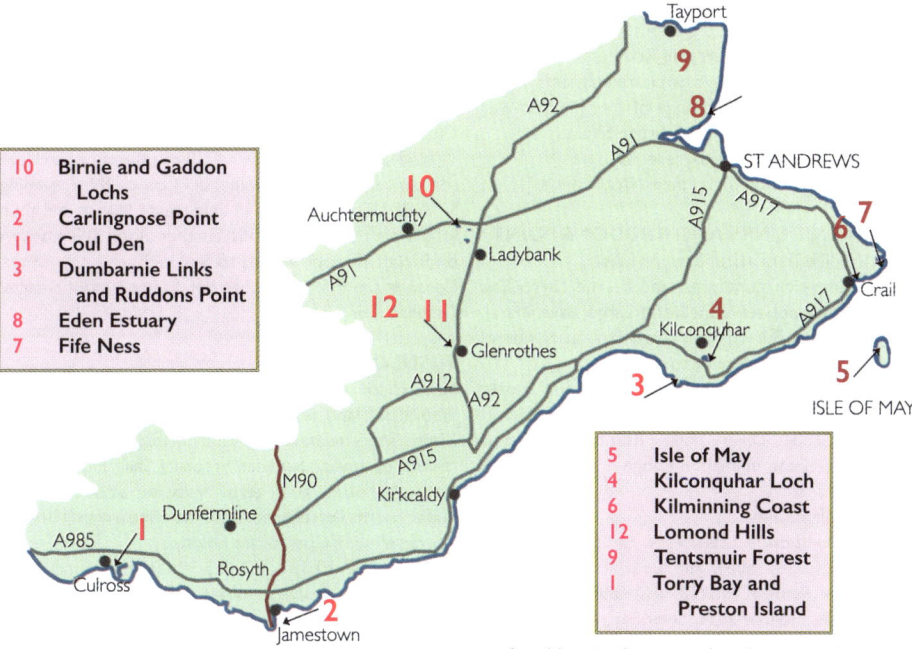

10 **Birnie and Gaddon Lochs**
2 **Carlingnose Point**
11 **Coul Den**
3 **Dumbarnie Links and Ruddons Point**
8 **Eden Estuary**
7 **Fife Ness**

5 **Isle of May**
4 **Kilconquhar Loch**
6 **Kilminning Coast**
12 **Lomond Hills**
9 **Tentsmuir Forest**
1 **Torry Bay and Preston Island**

Entering Fife from W, continue E from Alloa on the A907. At roundabout to E of Clackmannan, take A977 S to junction with A985. Minor road on R from A985 to Culross. From S, use Kincardine Bridge to cross Forth, join A985.

1 TORRY BAY LNR AND PRESTON ISLAND

Formerly Fife Coast & Countryside Trust

Habitats: Island once used for salt extraction, artificial lagoons subsequently built using ash from Longannet power station (now disused). Intertidal mudflats in bay. Tide recedes a long way.

Birds: Common farmland spp along paths. Breeding Lapwing and Shelduck, Water Rail *Autumn:* Large flocks of Greylag & Pink-footed Geese. *Winter:* Island a high tide roost for variety of waders. Usual waders, gulls and wildfowl out on mudflats and Forth. Shelduck, Wigeon, Teal, sometimes Shoveler. Greenshank, Snipe & Jack Snipe. Avocet, Whimbrel, Short-eared Owl and Merlin are amongst the less common species recorded.

Other: Grey & Common Seals.

Directions: KY12 8HL; NS 991 859 (nearest car park, in Culross). Car park immediately to S of Fife Pilgrim's Way at E end of Culross, between Pilgrim's Way and railway line. Adjacent to primary school.

Public transport: Bus: 8A Dunfermline-Culross. Stagecoach. Train—Dunfermline.

Visiting: From car park, cross over railway at NS 994 860 and follow the circular path around the shore of 'island' (actually a peninsula). View the lagoons (fenced off and obscured in parts) and mudflats from this path. Path surfaced but in places rough, railway crossing awkward for wheelchairs. Fife Coastal Path runs E-W on N side.

Contact: FC&CT: 01592 656080

Continue E on A985. Go straight across at interchange with M90 (2nd exit, A921). At next roundabout, take 2nd exit and head S on Chapel Place towards North Queensferry.

2 CARLINGNOSE POINT NATURE RESERVE

Scottish Wildlife Trust

Habitats: Cliff, disused quarry, grassland, gorse. Vantage point for Firth of Forth.

Birds: Spring & autumn: Passage migrants. *Summer:* Fulmar, Common & Arctic Terns, breeding warblers, inc. Lesser Whitethroat.

Other: Field Gentian, Dropwort.

Directions: EH30 9JU (North Queensferry station); NT 135 809. Located in North Queensferry overlooking Firth. Turn off Ferryhill Road into Carlingnose Point and very shortly L into Carlingnose Way. Park at end of Carlingnose Way. If no space for parking, park in Ferrytoll park & pide and walk back along Ferryhill Road.

Public transport: Bus: Numerous buses between Edinburgh to towns N & E of the Forth cross the bridge immediately to the W of North Queensferry. Most do not stop in North Queensferry itself. Best to alight ay the Ferrytoll Park & Ride and walk back along Ferryhill Road. Train—North Queensferry, the other side of the railway from the housing estate and nature reserve.

Visiting: Open all hours. Free. Fife Coastal Path runs through reserve As well as the nature reserve itself, which is immediately behind the shore line, there is

a further area of gorse scrub, the **Ferry Hills**, to the N and rising above North Queensferry. This can be reached by returning to Ferryhill Road and walking up the hill. This is a good vantage point for migrants and in particular a large autumn passage of Tree Pipit, as well as Red-throated Diver, Great & Arctic Skuas.
Contact: www.swt-fife.org.uk/reserve8
Continue E on A921, A955 and then, after, Leven, A915.

3 DUMBARNIE LINKS AND RUDDONS POINT

Scottish Wildlife Trust (Dumbarnie Links)
Habitats: Lime-rich dune grassland behind Largo Bay. Rocky headland between Shell and Largo Bays. Marsh where Cocklemill Burn enters Largo Bay on N side of Ruddons Point. N shore of Firth of Forth.
Birds: Eider, Common, Velvet & (occasional) Surf Scoter, Red-breasted Merganser, Long-tailed Duck. Slavonian & Red-necked Grebes. Divers, mainly Red-throated. Snipe & Jack Snipe winter in marsh. Range of waders, gulls, terns, auks in season.
Other: Rare plants, insects.
Directions: Dumbarnie Links: Free car park in Lower Largo NO 423 026) follow Fife Coastal Park E for c.1 mile. *Ruddons Point:* KY9 1HB; NO 469 004 (car park by road to Elie Holiday Park, Shell Bay. Take A917 between Lower Largo and Elie. SW of Kilconquhar turn SW at a cross roads and follow signs for holiday park.
Public transport: Bus: 95 St Andrews-Leven stops in Kilconquhar and Dumbarnie Golf Course. Stagecoach.
Visiting: Walk along Fife Coastal Path from Lower Largo car park (toilets) to Dumbarnie Links; or walk down track from holiday park car park towards bay, skirt holiday park. Join Fife Coastal Path running round edge of bay and then out on to headland. Extensive facilities in holiday park. Fife Coastal Path connects Dumbarnie Links and Ruddons Point. Dogs under control.
Contact: SWT: secfifekinswt@gmail.com;
https://www.facebook.com/swtfifeandkinrossmc
On the other side of the A917.

4 KILCONQUHAR LOCH

Kilconquhar/Elie Estates & NatureScot
Habitats: 94 acre, shallow freshwater loch on edge of village and close to coast. Water level regulated. Reed-fringed with woods to W, S & E. SSSI.
Birds: Breeding: Great Crested & Little Grebe, Water Rail, Kingfisher, Sedge Warbler and Reed Bunting. *Winter:* Goldeneye, Tufted Duck, Teal. Smew and Scaup possible. Sea close by so Long-tailed Duck, Slavonian Grebe et al may stray.
Directions: KY9 1LF (church); NO 485 020. A917 runs between Upper Largo and Elie. At crossroads 3.75 miles from Upper Largo take minor road L for Kilconquhar. After 0.5 miles, just before church, turn R down lane beside cemetery and park at end in cemetery car park.
Public transport: Bus: 95, St Andrew to Leven Bus Sta-

tion stops in Kilconquhar and Elie. Stagecoach (0345 241 8000).
Visiting: Open all hours, free. No facilities but pub in Elie (1.25 miles). Walk through gate by car park to bank overlooking N shore of loch. Alternatively, The Fife Bird Club has a hide (locked, access for members only) on W side of loch at NO 484 147. Turn off road into village (or park in village and walk back) on to B941 running S. Walk along S edge of 1st field towards loch and then follow path through woods. Further along B941 a path on R runs through woods to S of loch.
Contact: see **Fife Bird Club** details in county contacts.
Continue E on A917.

5 ISLE OF MAY NNR

NatureScot
Habitats: Island, sea cliffs, rocky shoreline.
Birds: Spring/autumn: Weather-related migrations inc. rarities each year. *Summer:* breeding Shag, Eider, Fulmar, Kittiwake, other gulls, terns, auks inc 52,000 pairs of Puffin. Storm Petrel breeding, Manx Shearwater bred in '25, developing Cormorant colony.
Directions: KY10 3RR. NT 655 995 (island). Small island lying five miles E of Anstruther in Firth of Forth.
Public transport: Bus—regular services to Anstruther and North Berwick harbours.
Visiting: Ferries (Apr-Sep). Trips take 4-5 hours, inc time to explore island. From Anstruther (5 miles): Anstruther Pleasure Cruises (07957 585200, info@isleofmayferry.com) and Osprey of Anstruther (07429 454055; info@isleofmayboattrips.co.uk). From North Berwick (13 miles, in East Lothian to S of Forth)—check with Scottish Seabird Centre (01620 890 202).
If staying at Observatory delays getting on/off island are possible due to weather. Keep to paths, no dogs, no camping/fires. Permission required to carry out scientific work or filming.
Contact: Observatory accommodation bookings Sec: Mark Newell: 07909 707 971;
bookings@isleofmaybirdobs.org;
www.isleofmaybirdobs.org
Other enquiries: Reserve Manager: 01738 458 800; nnr@nature.scot
Continue E on the A917.

6 KILMINNING COAST NATURE RESERVE

Crail Community Partnership
Habitats: Arable, small wetland, grazed grassland, meadow, trees and scrub, rocky shore.
Birds: Passage migrant passerines in trees and scrub inc Lesser Whitethroat, Yellow-browed Warbler, Barred Warbler, Red-backed Shrike, Pied Flycatcher, Wheatear, Whinchat, Yellow Wagtail. *Breeding:* Grey Partridge, Corn Bunting. *Autumn:* Golden Plover, Merlin, Skylark, Lapland Bunting.
Other: Grazed to increase range of plants.

Directions: KY10 3XL; NO 632 088 (coastal car park). Take minor road in Crail for Fife Ness and Fife Ness Muir. Immediately after disused airfield turn R down track, pass go kart track, car park at coast.

Public transport: Bus: 95 Leven-St Andrews runs through Crail daily.

Visiting: Open all hours, free. Fife Coastal Path runs through reserve, following coastline. Car park at end of track, other places to pull off track and view grassland and scrub to either side but no facilities. Possible to walk between **Kilminning** and the **Ness**.

Contact: wrlc@st-andrews.ac.uk; https://aboutcrail.wordpress.com
At end of same minor road NE of Crail.

7 FIFE NESS AND FIFE NESS MUIR

Fife Bird Club (Ness/Hide)/Scottish Wildlife Trust (Muir)

Habitats: Rocky headland with lighthouse at easternmost tip of Fife sandwiched between Firths of Tay (to N) and Forth (to S). Fife Ness Muir inland and to NW of Ness is an active ringing site that you pass on your way to the headland. Gorse, Oak and Hazel planted to provide shelter, not yet mature.

Birds: Ness: Primarily autumn sea bird passage—Manx & Sooty Shearwaters, small numbers of Cory's & Balearic Shearwaters possible. Great, Arctic & a few Pomarine Skuas. Storm Petrel, Little Gull. White-billed Diver, Grey Phalarope occasional. *Muir:* Primarily weather-driven (E, SE winds, rain, high pressure over Scandinavia) in the autumn. Yellow-browed Warbler annual, Red-breated Flycatcher and Barred Warbler nearly so. Less pronounced in spring,

Other: Over 30 spp of plants planted to provide shelter and food for migrants.

Directions: KY10 3XN; NO 638 097. In Crail, leave the A917 where it makes a sharp turn and take the minor road running NE past the disused airfield and then the golf club for just under 2 miles.

Public transport: Bus: 95 Leven-St Andrews runs through Crail daily.

Visiting: Free parking in golf club visitors car park by mini roundabout at end of minor road. It is possible to drive past the golf club but parking may be difficult. Be sure not to block access/passing. Walk along path to lighthouse. Fife Bird Club hide (locked, access for members only) at Ness. Fife coastal path runs through reserve, following coastline. Possible to walk between the Ness and **Kilminning** (q.v.).

Contact:
Fife Bird Club memsec@fifebirdclub.org.uk
SWT: secfifekinswt@gmail.com;
https://www.facebook.com/swtfifeandkinrossmc
Return to A917 and continue to St Andrews.

8 EDEN ESTUARY LNR

Fife Coast and Countryside Trust

Habitats: 2,200 acres, mainly intertidal mud and sandflats with saltmarsh, river, reed, sand dunes, wetland.

Birds: Winter/passage: Significant numbers of waders and wildfowl. *Outer estuary*—seaduck inc scoters, Eider, Long-tailed Duck, Red-breasted Merganser & Gannet, terns, skuas. *Mudflats*—Godwits, plovers, sandpipers, Redshank, Shelduck. *River*—Common Sandpiper, Kingfisher, Goosander. Surrounding area attracts Short & Long-eared Owls, Peregrine, Merlin, Marsh Harrier and White-tailed Eagle. Osprey regular visitor.

Other: Northern Marsh Orchid, dune grasses and herbs. Common & Grey Seals, Bottlenose Dolphin, Harbour Porpoise, Brown Hare, Stoat and Otter. Butterflies inc Grayling, Small Pearl-bordered & Dark Green Fritillaries.

Directions: KY16 0UG; NO 450 192 (Eden Estuary Centre). Centre is off main street in Guardbridge, two miles from St Andrews on A91, and from Leuchars via Tentsmuir Forest off A919 (four miles). Use Outhead at St Andrews, off West Sands beach, to access Balgove Bay.

Public transport: Bus—regular services from Cupar, Dundee and St Andrews. Train—Leuchars (1.5 miles),

Visiting: Eden Estuary Centre, Guardbridge open daily (not 25/26 & 31 Dec, 1 Jan) 9am-5pm (4pm Nov-Mar)—access code for centre from local ranger. Locked (code from ranger) George Evans Hide at Balgove Bay: NO 482 181, parking at Pilmuir Links golf course car park. Viewing platform and picnic area at Outhead. There is also a locked Fife Bird Club hide for its members only in the S side of the estuary.

Contact: Dominic Rye, Conservation Officer: 07985 707 593; ask.us@fifecountryside.co.uk
Between Eden Estuary and Firth of Tay. Take A919 N for A91 in Guardbridge. In Leuchars follow Kinshaldy Beach signs for Kinshaldy; or continue on A919 and then take B945 for Morton Lochs.

9 TENTSMUIR FOREST & NNR

Forestry and Land Scotland (Forest) NatureScot (NNR)

Habitats: 3,200 acres of coastal dunes, conifer plantations, loch, mudflat. NNR around lochs to W of FLS plantations and along coastline extending E to Tentsmuir Point.

Birds: Common woodland spp inc possible Crossbill. Osprey, Marsh Harrier occasional, Water Rail. Ducks, inc occasional Garganey. *Autumn:* Possible Shoveler, Pochard, Pintail, occasional Smew. *Tentsmuir Point and offshore:* Large numbers of Eider in winter and roosting Pink-footed Geese.

Other: Red Squirrel.

Directions: Morton Lochs (NS): NO 464 263. Take B945 S from Tayport for 1.5 miles. Turn L on to minor road

(signposted) for another 0.75 mile. *Kinshaldy* (FLS): NO 498 242. Follow Kinshaldy Beach signs from Leuchars.
Public transport: Bus: 42 Dundee-St Andrews stops at Tayport entrance to Tentsmuir and or request at Morton Farm (1 mile walk to Lochs). 54 Glenrothes-Dundee. Both Stagecoach. Train—Leuchars, 3 miles.
Visiting: Morton Lochs (NS) car park invitation to pay, Four wheelchair-accessible hides on N loch, further hide on S loch. Charge (coin and card) at *Kinshaldy* (FLS) car park. Toilets at Kinshaldy. For Tentsmuir Point (NS) park in Tayport and walk E along Fife Coastal Path. Can also walk N along Fife Coastal path through forest from Kinshaldy car park.
Contact: F&LS: 0300 067 6380;
enquiries.east@forestryandland.gov.scot
NatureScot: 01463 725 000; nnr@nature.scot
Take B940 from Tayport and join A92 at S end of Tay Road Bridge. You could either use the bridge to cross the Tay and enter Angus and Dundee or head SW to junction with A91. Then head W on A91.

10 BIRNIE AND GADDON LOCHS
Fife Coast & Countryside Trust
Habitats: Flooded former sand and gravel quarries, strips of woodland around edges.
Birds: Common woodland spp. *Autumn/winter:* Ducks inc Goosander, Goldeneye, Teal, Gadwall, Wigeon and Tufted Duck. Occasional Pochard and Shoveler. Coot, Little & Great Crested Grebes. Lapwing, Snipe and Water Rail. Great White & Little Egret.
Other: Red Squirrel, Otter, Beaver, Fox, Roe Deer, Field Vole. Bats inc Daubenton's and pipistrelles. Frog, Toad, Palmate Newt. Species-rich grasslands with a wide range of butterfly and moth sp.
Directions: KY15 7UT; NO 283 125. Immediately adjacent to the A91 between Cupar and Auchtermuchty. Exit at Collessie, turning S on to the B937. Entrance to reserve c.500 yards on L.
Public transport: Bus: 64 runs between Cupar and Auchtermuchty Mon-Sat. Moffat & Williamson (01382 541 159; enquiries@moffat-williamson.co.uk). Train—Ladybank. 2 miles but 64 bus passes through Ladybank.
Visiting: Open all hours, free. No toilets. Paths around lochs, 2 hides (phone 07485 395 405 for access).
Contact: 01592 656 080;
ask.us@fifecountryside.co.uk
Return to A92 and head S to Glenrothes. The A91 runs to the NW of the Lomond Hills (q.v.).

11 COUL DEN NATURE RESERVE
Fife Coast & Countryside Trust
Habitats: Regenerated industrial site. Woodland. Loch
Birds: Short-eared Owl (on Lomond Hills). Jay, common woodland spp. *Autumn/winter:* Ducks inc Goosander, Goldeneye, Teal, Gadwall, Wigeon and Tufted Duck. Oc-

casional Pochard. Coot. Little & Great Crested Grebes, Water Rail.
Other: Red Squirrel. Dark Green Fritillary. Species-rich grasslands with a wide range of butterfly and moth sp.
Directions: KY7 6FW; NO 270 037 (Calder Court car park). N outskirts of Glenrothes. In Glenrothes, the B969 runs between the motel roundabout on the A911 and the A92. Take the B969.
Public transport: Bus: 5 Markinch station-Glenrothes Bus Station, then 1.5 mile walk. Mon-Sat. Moffat & Williamson. Train—Markinch, then bus 5.
Visiting: Open all hours. Entry free. Circular trail with compacted surface around the reservoir, also from car park along Conland Burn and then S to Pitcairn (toilets, Mon-Fri), recent planting of 80,000 native trees at Formont Hills, with a stile and short steep section; or access from the S to the **Lomond Hills** (q.v.) to NW.
Contact: FC&CT: 01592 656080;
ask.us@fifecountryside.co.uk
The SE edge of the Lomond Hills Regional Park is immediately to the NW of Glenrothes

12 LOMOND HILLS REGIONAL PARK
Regional park; multiple owners
Habitats: 25 square mile regional park, rising to 1,713 ft (West Lomond) and 1,424 ft (East Lomond); moorland, grassland, forests, reservoirs overlooking **Loch Leven** (q.v. **Perth & Kinross**) to SW, Glenrothes to SE and Falkland to N.
Birds & Other: Given area and range of habitats, wide range of species but include: Short-eared Owl, Raven. *Winter:* Whooper Swan
Directions: Car parks on permiter of park in Glenrothes (including **Coul Den** (q.v.), Falkland, Dryside Road (NO 172 069) and Pillars of Hercules (NO 242 082) on A912. Within the boundary of the park, car parks at: Craigmead (NO 227 062) on Hill Road running between Glenrothes and Falkland; Purin Hill (NO 252 058, toilets) minor road running W for 1.5 miles from A912 1 miles SE of Falkland; West Balgothrie/Holl Reservoir (NO 224 034), take The Hazels running N from the A911 to the W of Glenrothes;
Public transport: None within boundary of park. Bus: 36 & 64 run around edge of park between Glenrothes and Falkland (Mon-Sat).
Visiting: Network of paths, some surfaced but others rough and with steep sections or with steps. Keep dogs under control.
Contact: FC&CT: 01592 656080
For more detailed information:
www.fifecountrysidetrust.co.ukplan-your-trip/resources/Inland-leaflets

Perth and Kinross

Loch Leven NNR (including the RSPB's Vane Farm) is the region's best known reserve and has breeding duck and large numbers of wintering geese, ducks and swans. Ospreys fish there too but the well-known watch point of Loch of the Lowes offers views of birds on the nest. Woodland and moorland species are well represented including Woodcock, Redstart, Wood Warbler, Red and Black Grouse (although the latter can be elusive).

Bird Recorder
George Dunbar: 07765 183 697;
pkrecorder@the-soc.org.uk

Bird Report
Perth and Kinross Bird Report (1974-), last published in 2006—digital reports from Scott Paterson: guidedwalks@the-soc.org.uk

BTO Regional Representative
Perthshire
Michael Bell
Kinross
Paul Blackburn
Wetland Bird Survey (WeBS)
Local Organizers webs@bto.org
Loch Leven
Jeremy Squire:
Perth and Kinross (Inland)
Michael Bell:
Tay and Eden Estuary
See **Fife**

Club
Perthshire Society of Natural Science
(1867; Nature Section: 2022: 25).
Nature Section: nature@psns.org.uk
birdsatpsns@btinternet.com; www.psns.org.uk/nature
<u>Meetings</u>: 7:30pm, Wednesday—dates vary (Oct-Mar), AK Bell Library, 17 York Place, Perth, PH2 8EP—contact/see website for details.
SOC Tayside Branch—see **Angus and Dundee**

RSPB Local Group
No Groups.

Scottish Wildlife Trust Regional Networks
Pitlochry and Highland Perthshire
Chair: Mark Aquilina
07796 661 844; markandrosie@btinternet.com;
<u>Meetings</u>: The Tryst, Church Street, Pitlochry PH16 5EB

Forest and Land Scotland Regional Office
0300 067 6380; enquiries.east@forestryandland.gov.scot

Loch Leven and *Vane Farm* lie immediately to the NW of the *Lomond Hills Regional Park* in Fife. Heading W from Glenrothes to SE of Lomond Hills, take B920 on L and then B9097 on for S side of Loch Leven.

1 VANE FARM
RSPB
Habitats: Wet grassland and flooded areas by Loch Leven. Arable farmland, native woodland, moorland. Part of the larger **Loch Leven NNR** (q.v.).
Birds: Spring/summer: Breeding and passage waders (inc Lapwing, Redshank, Snipe, Curlew), hirundines, Great Crested Grebe, Osprey. Farmland birds (inc Skylark and Yellowhammer), Tree Pipit. *Autumn:* Migrating waders on exposed mud. *Winter:* Major fuelling stop for Pink-footed Geese (around 20,000 in late autumn). Whooper Swan (6% of Scotland's wintering population), Bewick's Swan, White-tailed Eagle, finch and tit flocks.
Other: 237 spp butterflies and moths, 25 spp mammal inc. Pipistrelle Bat and Roe Deer.
Directions: KY13 9LX; NT 160 990. Halfway between Perth and Edinburgh, seven miles from Cowdenbeath, signposted two miles E J5 of M90 follow signs for B9097 towards Glenrothes. Drive for approx two miles, car park on R (signposted).
Public transport: Bus—from Edinburgh, Perth and nearby towns to Kinross. Can walk Loch Leven Heritage Trail from here (c.4 miles).
Visiting: Trails and hides open all hours. Free car parking, coach parking available. Visitor centre open daily (not 25/26 Dec, 1/2 Jan) 10am-5pm. Entry fee to reserve, RSPB members free. Disabled access to shop, toilets, cafe (open 10am-4pm) and observation room with telescopes overlooking Loch Leven and reserve. Binocular hire. 1.25 mile Hill Trail through woodland/moorland. Wetland Trail has three hides. Eight-mile cycle path around loch. Other than assistance dogs, dogs not permitted in visitor centre (but can use courtyard) or on Wetland Trail. Permitted on Loch Leven Heritage Trail and Sleeping Giant Path (both accessed from centre).
Contact: RSPB: 01577 862 355; lochleven@rspb.org.uk
*The RSPB reserve forms part of the larger **Loch Leven NNR**, which follows. For rest of NNR, return to M90 and leave at next junction N.*

2 LOCH LEVEN NNR
NatureScot
Habitats: Relatively shallow loch, 3,950 acres wooded margins and fields, islands. Partially drained in 19C.
Birds and Other: Similar assemblage to that already summarized for **Vane Farm**..

4	Ben Lawers
2	Loch Leven
3	Loch of the Lowes
5	Tay Forest Park
7	Tay Reedbeds
6	Tummel Shingle Islands
1	Vane Farm

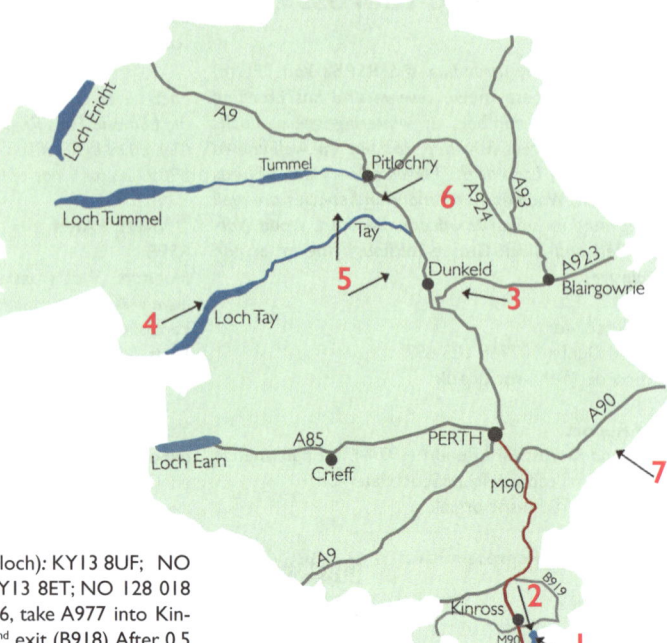

Directions: Kinross (W shore of loch)*:* KY13 8UF; NO 122 017 (Boathouse Pier) or KY13 8ET; NO 128 018 (Kirkgate Park). Leave M90 at J6, take A977 into Kinross. At next roundabout take 2nd exit (B918). After 0.5 mile turn R on to B996. The take 4th L, at mini roundabout, after 100 yards, continue straight on for Kirkgate, veer R for Boathouse Pier. *Findatie* (SE of loch, by canalized outflow of River Leven) KY13 9JLNT 171 993. Leave M80 at J5. Turn R on to B9097 then immediately L on to B996, after 300 yards turn R (back on B9097). Continue on B9097 for 2.5 miles to Findatie, passing RSPB **Vane Farm**.
Public transport: Bus—from Edinburgh, Perth and nearby towns to Kinross.
Visiting: Open all hours. Car parks at Boathouse Pier, Kirkgate (both free and in Kinross) and Findatie. There is also parking at RSPB **Vane Farm** (q.v) on the S shore of the Loch 0.75 mile W of Findatie on the B9097. A car-free 13 mile Heritage Trail runs all around the Loch. Suitable for wheelchairs and mobility scooters, open for cyclists. 3 (Burleigh Sands, Levenmouth, S of Boathouse car park) hides, all wheelchair accessible. Toilets at Kirkgate and Boathouse Pier (9am-7pm, 24 hr with RADAR key, charge).
Contact: Reserve Manager: Jeremy Squire, NatureScot, The Pier, Kinross, KY13 8UF; nnr@nature.scot
Take M90 N to Perth, then continue on A90.

3 LOCH OF THE LOWES

Scottish Wildlife Trust
Habitats: 320 acres, loch, woodland, basin fen.
Birds: Path to SE: Common woodland spp inc Green (recent) & Great Spotted Woodpeckers, Nuthatch, Redstart and Spotted Flycatcher. Also Grasshopper &

Reed Warblers. *Loch:* Breeding Great Crested Grebe, Osprey, Tawny & Barn Owls. *Winter:* Goldeneye, Tufted Duck, Wigeon, occasional Smew and Long-tailed Duck; passing Peregrine Falcon and Marsh Harrier. Snipe, Jack Snipe. Spring influx of Black-headed Gulls
Other: Red Squirrel. Beaver, Roe & Fallow Deer. Pine Marten, Beaver. Rare aquatic plants.
Directions: PH8 0HH (doesn't work with all sat navs, alternatively PH8 0ES); NO 041 435 (visitor centre). Leave A9 on A923, continue on it through the centre of Dunkeld, heading for Blairgowrie. After 2 miles take minor road on R. Car park on L by road after 300 yards. This minor road continues past S shore of Loch. Can walk from through woodland from Dunkeld (2miles) along Fungarth Path.
Public transport: Bus & train—Dunkeld.
Visiting: Visitor centre 120 yards from free car park, bike rack. Car park gate locked at night. Path wheelchair friendly. Vistor Centre (charge, free for SWT members): Nov-Feb: 10:30am-4pm Fri-Sun; Mar-Oct: 10:30am-5pm every day. Toilets. Viewing window in Visitor Centre and 3 loch-side hides (2 open all hours) nearby. CCTV feed of breeding Osprey. *Note: established male died in 2024 and a series pairs attempted but failed to form and breed in 2025. What will happen on 2026?* No circular walk around Loch. Assistance dogs only.
Contact: 01350 727 337;
lochofthelowes@scottishwildlifetrust.org.uk
Webcam: https://scottishwildlifetrust.org.uk/things-to-

do/watch-wildlife-online/loch-of-the-lowes-webcam/
Return to A90 and continue N.

4 BEN LAWERS NNR

National Trust for Scotland

Habitats: Mountain and moorland, river, grassland, woodland and scrub including restored mountain woodlands and willow scrub. 11,100 acres on S & E slopes of massif rising to a summit of 3,984 ft. 7 Munros in the NNR.

Birds: All Year: Ptarmigan, Red & Black Grouse, Red Kite, White-tailed & Golden Eagles, Peregrine Falcon, Merlin, Raven, Hooded Crow, Dipper, Grey Wagtail, common woodland spp. *Spring/summer:* Golden Plover, Cuckoo, Willow Warbler, Skylark, Ring Ouzel, Wheatear, Whinchat, Meadow Pipit. *Winter:* Winter thrushes, Snow Bunting.

Other: Red Deer, Mountain Hare, Red Squirrel, Otter, Beaver. Alpine flora, 600+ spp. lichen. Mountain Ringlet.

Directions: FK21 8TY; NN 614 362 (minor road off A827 to car park). 30 miles NW Perth. Leave A9 at Ballinluig (towards Aberfeldy). After 27.5 miles, turn R on minor road to car park (signed). The road will pass several of the individual forests in the **Tay Forest Park** (q.v.). If approaching from W, leave A85 and take A827 for Killin. After Killin, Loch Tay will be on your R. Seven miles after leaving A85, turn L towards car park.

Public transport: None.

Visiting: Open all year—can get busy with walkers. Car park (charge, members free, road to car park unsuitable for coaches/large vehicles), bike racks. Network of paths on popular routes, some lower paths wheelchair accessible with assistance. Waymarked trails on lower slopes, seven hour round walk to summit. Dogs under close control.

Contact: NTS: 01567 820 988; benlawers@nts.org.uk
https://www.nts.org.uk/visit/places/ben-lawers
Or, rather than going as far W as Ben Lawers on the Tay, explore the

5 TAY FOREST PARK

Forestry & Land Scotland

Habitats: A cluster of separate forests managed by Forestry & Land Scotland flanking the rivers and lochs of the Tay and Tummel valleys, along and to the W of the A9. Some more recent commercial plantations, some with a history of planting going back to the 17C, and incorporating old growth broadleaved and pine forests. In the E, the forests extend from Dunkeld, in the S, to Pitlochry in the N and then W to Rannoch Station.

Birds: See **Faskally** for more detail but essentially the typical assemblage of Scottish coniferous forests inc Capercaillie Goshawk, Crossbill. Osprey on lochs.

Other: Red Squirrel, Pine Marten.

Forests

A brief summary of the location and visiting arrangements is given for each of the individual forests, with a more detailed entry for one of them, **Faskally**, as an exemplar for all the others.

Very roughly, they are arranged in sequence from S to N along the A9 and then from E to W along the Tay and Tummel valleys.

Along the A9.

Craigvinean: PH8 0JR; NO 013 423. Leave A9 W of Dunkeld at sign for Hermitage. Road swings R, car park in 250 yards. Car park free but no toilets, can also park in NTS Hermitage car park but charges for non-members. Originally planted by the Dukes of Atholl. A second free car park further N in same forest at PH8 0JS; NO 003 437, take B898 from A9 at Dalguise junction. Car park 100 yards on L.

Faskally

Habitats: Loch, Oak/Birch woodland.

Birds: All year: Buzzard, Kingfisher, Siskin, Redpoll, common woodland spp. *Summer:* Goldeneye (breeds) Red-breasted Merganser, Common Sandpiper, Dipper, Grey Wagtail, Tree Pipit, Wood & Garden Warblers. *Winter:* Wildfowl (inc Greylag Goose, Pochard, Goldeneye).

Other: Otter, Red Squirrel.

Directions: PH16 5NF; NN 920 592. One mile NW of Pitlochry on B8019. If heading N on A9, signed to Faskally, if heading S follow turn-off for Pitlochry then signs for Faskally.

Public transport: Bus—irregular days/times Pitlochry to Faskally Caravan Park—walk back along B8019 to car park entrance (0.7 mile). Elizabeth Yule Transport. (01796 482 290). Train—Pitlochry (1.2 miles—head W on A924 out of Pitlochry and join B8019 to car park entrance.

Visiting: Open all hours. Car park (free). Two trails (waymarked—0.75 miles wheelchair accessible and 1.5 miles).

Along the Tay and the A827.

Grandtully: PH9 0PY; NN 934 523, at the point where the A827 crosses the Tay at Pitnacree Bridge turn on to the B898, which runs SE on S side of Tay. Grandtully Forest is to your R and the free car park is about 1 mile from the bridge.

Weem: PH15 2JD; NN 839 497. Free car park 0.25 mile W of Weem village (other side of Tay from Aberfeldy) on B846. Shared turn-off with Castle Menzies. No facilities, open all hours.

Drummond Hill: PH15 2HN; free car parks at NN 772 461, toilets and cafe across road in Mains of Taymouth courtyard, and NN 788 478. Above the foot of Loch Tay. Planted with Oak, Birch and Scots Pine in 17C. Capercaillie to be heard and, just possibly, seen; but do not disturb. Continue W along Loch Tay for **Ben Lawers**.

Along the Tummel and to W

Allean: PH16 5RH; NN 857 601 charge for car park, toilets. Leave the A9 at J7 and take the B8019 for

Killiecrankie. Turn L at Garry Bridge and continue on B8019 for Kinloch Rannoch. Allean car park is 7.5 miles along this road on R, with Loch Tummel on L. 0.5 mile beyond the *Queen's View Visitor Centre:* PH16 5NR; NN 865 597. Centre and car parks managed independently of F&LS. Another (free) car park *Tummel Bridge* PH16 5SA; NN 762 596 at the W end of Loch Tummel at the junction of the B8019 and the B846 after it crosses the bridge and runs W to Kinloch Rannoch. *Frenich Wood:* NN 804 565, stretching along the S side of Loch Tummel. There are no car parks or visitor facilities but a minor road leaves the B846 between Aberfeldy and Tummel Bridge just under 2 miles S of Tummel Bridge, cuts back NE to the Loch and then runs E along its S shore, eventually joining the A9 on the W side of Loch Faskally.
Braes of Foss: PH16 5NN; NN 753 557, car park (charge), toilets. Take minor road heading SE from Kinloch Rannoch signposted for Schiehallion. Car park after 6.5 miles. From B846 between Aberfeldy and Tummel Bridge head W for 2.5 miles along minor road signposted for Schiehallion.
Carie/Rannoch: PH17 2QJ; NN 617 571. Free car park, no toilets. 3.5 miles W of Kinloch Rannoch on unclassified South Loch Rannoch road. Immediately adjacent to *Kilvrecht Campsite:* charges for camping. In 2025 was open Apr-Oct. Dates for 26 not yet announced. Encompasses the Black Wood of Rannoch, an area of ancient pine forest exploited for timber for over 200 years. This minor road continues W, crossing the River Gaur at the W end of Loch Rannoch and rejoining the B846. There are further blocks of forest to the SW of it but no classified roads.
On the N side of Loch Rannoch, the B846 continues W from Kinloch, with loch to your left and forest to the right. There are no car parks in this block of forest but there is one at Rannoch Power Station; NN 533 582, at the W edge of the block. The B846 continues W, with further blocks of forest to N, and ends at Rannoch Station on the Fort William line.
Public transport: Bus: 23 Dunkeld-Aberfeldy via Grandtully or Pitlochry, Stagecoach. Bus services from Pitlochry to Aberfeldy or Kinloch Rannoch, Yules Buses (01796 472 290). Rannoch Station-Kinloch Rannoch, Broons Taxis & Dial A Bus (01882 632 331). Coach services to Pitlochry from Inverness, Perth, Glasgow and Edinburgh. Train—stations at Dunkeld (Birnam), Pitlochry and Rannoch.
Contacts:
Forestry and Land Scotland: 0300 067 6380;
enquiries.east@forestryandland.gov.scot
Queens View Visitor Centre: info@queens-view.co.uk
Kilvrecht Campsite: 0300 067 6380;
kilvrechtcampsite@forestryandland.gov.scot
When not visiting the Tay Forests, try the Tummel islands.

6 TUMMEL SHINGLE ISLANDS
Scottish Wildlife Trust
Habitats: Two shingle islands totalling 110 acres, Ballinluig (S) and Tomdachoille (N), lying over a mile apart along the River Tummel. Depending on height of river, 'islands' may be islands or river bank.
Birds: Kingfisher, Common woodland spp. *Summer:* Ringed Plover, Common Tern, Oystercatcher, Redshank, Spotted Flycatcher
Other: 400 spp. of plant recorded inc Lesser Marshwort, Bird's-nest Orchid. Scotch Argus, Common Blue.
Directions: PH16 5NF; NN 963 552 (Tomdachoille). 4.5 miles S of Pitlochry, take the Ballinluig exit from the A9, cross the Tummel on the A827. 0.5 miles after the junction take the minor road running N at Logierat. 0.5 miles along this road there is a parking area at NN 971 526 (do not obstruct access).
Public transport: Bus: 24 Pitlochry-Ballinluig (not Sun). Stagecoach. Train—Pitlochry.
Visiting: Walk another 200 yards N along road and then take path to R down wooded slope to Ballinluig Island. *Note: as of 2025, the footpath to Ballinluig Island has been indefinitely closed by a landslide.* Two miles further N along the road there is a path leading back down to the Tummel alongside Tomdachoille Island. There are no paths on the island itself. *Take care, the shingle can be slippery and the Tummel can run very high.* Open all hours, free, no facilities.
Contact: enquiries@scottishwildlifetrust.org.uk
Head S on A9 to Perth, then take A90 to Dundee.

7 TAY REEDBEDS
RSPB
Habitats: N bank of Tay, longest continuous reedbed in UK. RSPB manages 667 acres and cooperates with local landowners over cutting programme. Arable fields and strips of woodland behind reedbeds but these are not part of reserve.
Birds: All year: Marsh Harrier, Bearded Tit, Water Rail. *Summer:* Reed & Sedge Warblers. Bittern has been recorded. *Autumn:* Hirundine roosts, Hobby possible.
Other: Red squirrel, seals.
Directions: PH2 7SL; NO 266 226. Errol lies S of the A90, close to the Tay, roughly halfway between Perth and Dundee. Follow minor roads signposted for Errol from A90 and park in village.
Public transport: Bus: 16/16A Perth-Dundee stops in Errol. Stagecoach East Scotland. Train—Perth, Dundee.
Visiting: Open all hours, free. Mostly well surfaced 4.5 mile Taybank circular path from Errol (signposted, Station Road) offers views of reedbeds but no access to them. Can be muddy after rain. No parking or facilities on site. Keep dogs under control. Reedbeds abut 'Sure as Death Bank', you have been warned.
Contact: 01577 862 355; lochleven@rspb.org.uk

Angus and Dundee

The Angus glens hold a typical range of upland species, including Golden Eagle, grouse, Ring Ouzel and chats. Marsh Harrier breeds at RSPB Loch of Kinnordy and Ospreys regularly fish there. Montrose Basin is a flagship Scottish Wildlife Trust reserve, with a good selection of wildfowl ever present and waders on passage.

Bird Recorder
Jon Cook, 76 Torridon Road, Broughty Ferry, Dundee, DD5 3JH: 01382 738 495; 1301midget@tiscali.co.uk

Bird Report
Angus and Dundee Bird Report (1985-), from ADBC—via the Bird Recorder—see above.

BTO Regional Representative
Angus
Steve Willis
Wetland Bird Survey (WeBS)
Local Organizers: webs@bto.org
Angus (excl. Montrose Basin)
Jonathan Pattullo
Montrose Basin
Anna Cowie:

Clubs
Angus & Dundee Bird Club (1997; 170)
Jonathan Pattullo (Chair): 07989 971 933;
jonathanpattullo@gmail.com;
www.angusbirding.com/html/adbc.html
Meetings: 7:30pm, 3rd Tuesday of the month (Sep-Apr). Panbride Church Hall, 8 Arbroath Road, Carnoustie, Angus DD7 6BL. Joint meetings sometimes held with other clubs, so contact/see website for details. Monthly guided outings.
SOC Tayside Branch (1960's; 100)
Jan Christin 07506 567 893;
soc_tayside_treasurer@fastmail.co.uk;
www.the-soc.org.uk/local-branches/tayside
Meetings: 7:30pm, 1st Thursday of the month (Sep-Apr). Glasite Hall, St Andrews Parish Church, King Street, Dundee DD1 2JB. Online talks also held. Contact/see website for details.

Ringing Group/Bird Observatory
Tay RG: www.tayringinggroup.org

Local RSPB Group
Dundee (1972; 100)
Darell Berthon: darell.berthon@icloud.com;
https://group.rspb.org.uk/dundee/
Meetings: 7:30 pm, one Wednesday each month (Sep-Nov/Jan-Mar plus AGM Apr and Christmas social

Dec). Glasite Hall, St.Andrew's Parish Church, King Street, Dundee, DD1 2JB.

Scottish Wildlife Trust Regional Networks
Angus and Dundee
Chair: Mark Warnes
info@swtdundeeangus.org.uk;
https://www.swtdundeeangus.org.uk
Meetings: Meffan Museum and Art Gallery, 20, West High Street, Forfar DD8 1BB
North Angus
Chair: Andy Wakelin: 01674 676783;
webmaster@montrosebasin.org.uk;
http://www.montrosebasin.org.uk

Forest and Land Scotland Regional Office
0300 067 6380;
enquiries.east@forestryandland.gov.scot

Just to show you that not every Scottish reserve is 20,000 acres of forest or hillside, head to Dundee on A90.

1 THE MILEY
Scottish Wildlife Trust/Dundee Council
Habitats: A mile of disused railway line, now a single-track footpath with broadleaf woodland, scrub and tall herbs on either side. 4.3 acres.
Birds: Common woodland spp inc Willow Warbler, Great, Blue & Long-tailed Tits, Blackbird, Robin, Dunnock, finches.
Other: Hoverflies, bumblebees, butterflies, moths. Wide variety of wild flowers, inc Marsh Orchid
Directions: DD3 8RX; NO 385 318. Accessible on foot at S end from Loons Road (on street parking) and Clepington Road at N end (disabled access). Middle of reserve can be accessed from Harefield Road (steps).
Public transport: Bus: 202 from Dundee city centre stops at either end of reserve, Moffat & Williamson (01382 541 159; enquiries@moffat-williamson.co.uk).
Visiting: Open all hours, free. No facilities. Interpretation panels at each end. The old Dundee to Newtyle line closed in 1967 ran N through central Dundee to the W of Dundee Law (fort). Work to regenerate it as a city centre nature reserve began in 1992.
Contact: info@swtdundeeangus.org.uk
Take A90 N from Dundee and then A928 to Kirriemuir.

2 LOCH OF KINNORDY
RSPB
Habitats: Loch, marshland, woodland.
Birds: All year: Water Rail, common wildfowl spp common woodland spp. *Spring/summer:* Osprey, Marsh Harrier, Red Kite, Lapwing, Redshank, Curlew, Snipe. Shoveler, Gadwall, Black-headed Gull (colony) Reed & Sedge Warblers. *Winter:* Whooper Swan, Pink-footed &

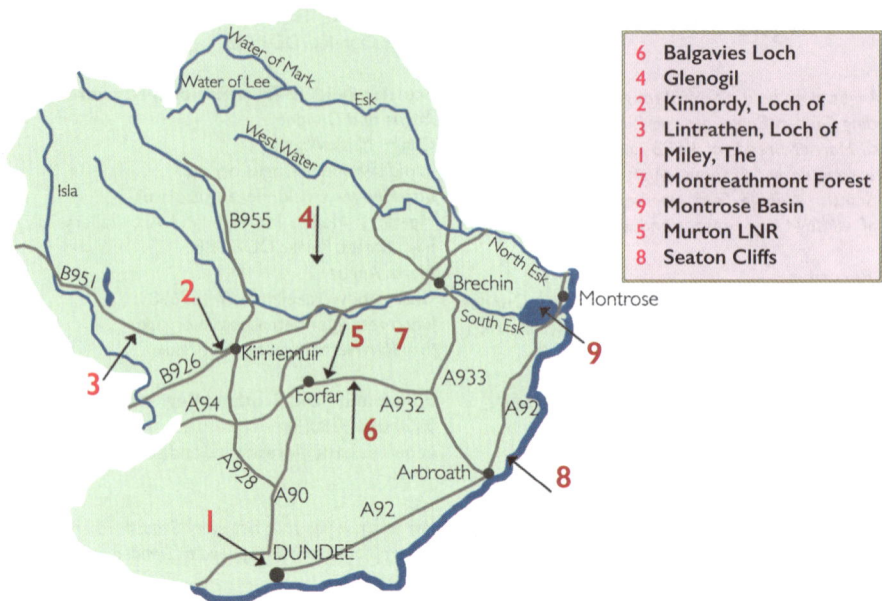

6	Balgavies Loch
4	Glenogil
2	Kinnordy, Loch of
3	Lintrathen, Loch of
1	Miley, The
7	Montreathmont Forest
9	Montrose Basin
5	Murton LNR
8	Seaton Cliffs

Greylag Geese, Goldeneye, Goosander, other wildfowl. Hen Harrier, Kingfisher.

Other: Red Squirrel, Brown Hare, Beavers, bats, Otter.
Directions: DD8 5HT; NO 361 539. One mile W of Kirriemuir on B951 to Glen Isla. Reserve on R.
Public transport: None.
Visiting: Open at all hours. Car park. 12 spaces/one blue badge space. Cycle racks. Three hides, bird feeding station, One linear path (*c.*370 yards) from car park to hides (feasible for pushchairs).
Contact: RSPB: 01577 862 355; lochleven@rspb.org.uk
Continue on B951.

by at NO 286 552, cross road and go through gate to reach 'new' hide.
Public transport: None.
Visiting: Open all hours, free. Minor roads run close to the shore for much of the Loch's perimeter. 2 hides, new, W hide wheelchair accessible. Fishing permitted April-October
Contact:
SWT Angus & Dundee: info@swtdundeeangus.org.uk
Fishing: Lintrathen Angling Club
Return on B951 to Kirriemuir. Then E on B957. At Tannadice turn L on to minor road and follow directions below.

3 LOCH OF LINTRATHEN

Scottish Water/Scottish Wildlife Trust
Habitats: Loch, island, wooded shores. Marshy bay in NW and spit separating off bay to NE, depending on water levels.
Birds: Spring/Summer: Osprey, Great Crested & Little Grebes. *Winter:* Ducks inc Goldeneye, Wigeon, gull roost, Brambling. *Woods around E hide:* Crossbill, Woodcock.
Other: Otter, Beaver
Directions: DD8 5JP; NO 276 555 parking. 8 miles W of Kirriemuir on B951. From Kirriemuir, at Balintore crossroads shortly after passing N end of Loch, at Balintore crossroads, take minor road S along W side of Loch Park by roadside after 500 yards and take forest track to E for 400 yards to raised, 'old' hide. Alternatively, again from Kirriemuir, turn sharp L off B951 after passing saw mill to N of Loch at Foldend. Follow minor road around bay on E side of Loch. Park in small lay-

4 GLENOGIL

Glenogil Estate
Habitats: Moorland rising to 2,300 ft, managed for grouse, steep-sided glen, small reservoir, deep by dam, shallow by inflow of burn, thinned conifer plantations and broadleaved woodland.
Birds: Red & Black Grouse, Golden Plover, Lapwing, Redshank, Snipe, Cuckoo, Wheatear, Whinchat. *On reservoir:* Osprey, Goldeneye, Red-breasted Merganser, Common Sandpiper.
Other: Red Squirrel, Red Deer, Mountain Hare.
Directions: DD8 3SX; NO 667 416. Leave the A90 at Finavon, halfway between Forfar and Brechin. Head N on the B957, just to E of River South Esk. Take 1st R and follow this minor road for just over 1.5 miles to a T junction. Turn L, do not cross Noran Water. Then take either the 1st or 2nd R and continue on this minor road for 3.25 miles to Gelnorgil.
Public transport: None.

Visiting: This is a commercial shooting estate. Avoid the Glorious 12th. Free but limited roadside parking. Numerous estate roads through plantations and up hills, with footbridges over burns.

Contact: Estate office, Auchnacree, By Forfar, Angus, DD8 3SX; 01356 627 327; office@glenogilestate.com

Return to B957 and then A90. Drive into Forfar and then head E on A932

5 MURTON LNR

Murton Trust

Habitats: Several small lochs formed by flooding former sand and gravel pits.

Birds: Common woodland spp inc Long-tailed Tit, Goldcrest. *Passage:* Little Ringed Plover, Black-tailed Godwit, Green & Wood Sandpipers. *Winter:* Snipe. Wildfowl inc Pintail, Shoveler, Wigeon, Teal, Goldeneye.

Other: Otter. Red Squirrel.

Directions: DD8 2RZ; NO 493 512. Immediately to N of A932 2 miles E of Forfar.

Public transport: Bus: 116 Forfar-Montrose, along A932, Stagecoach.

Visiting: Car park 9am-4:30pm, free. Winter 10am-4pm. Tearoom, shop. Educational propgramme. 3 hides. Many of the paths passable for wheelchairs. 0.5 mile W of Loch Rescobie, with **Balgavies Loch** beyond. Further flooded gravel pits between Murtion and Forfar. No dogs.

Contact: 01307 819 491; murtontrust@murtontrust.org.uk; www.murtontrust.org.uk

Continue E of A 932.

6 BALGAVIES LOCH

Scottish Wildlife Trust

Habitats: Shallow loch, reedbeds and willow *carr*.

Birds: Common woodland spp. Water Rail, Great Crested Grebe. Breeding Osprey. Wintering wildfowl.

Other: Red Squirrel, Otter

Directions: DD8 2SE; NO 523 516 car park at W end of loch down track from A932 Forfar-Friockheim, 4.5 miles from Forfar. Signposted viewpoint on N side of A932 a few hundred yards further E.

Public transport: Bus: 27 Forfar-Arbroath, rejoins A932 0.5 mile E of Balgavies Loch; 116 Forfar-Montrose, stops at Balgavies, both Stagecoach.

Visiting: Open all hours, free. Hide 50 yards from car park, wheelchair accessible. Circular path with viewpoints, not suitable for wheelchairs. A minor road runs N off the A932 past E end of loch and then crosses a disused railway line that runs close to N side of Loch as far as the nearby and larger Rescobie Loch to the W. Rescobie Loch has an anglers' boathouse. Busy with anglers in summer and no perimter path. Attracts wildfowl in winter, view with telescope from anglers' car park.

Contact: info@swtdundeeangus.org.uk

To the NE of Balgavies Loch. Take the minor road at E end of loch off the A932 and continue to B9113. Turn R

7 MONTREATHMONT FOREST

Forestry & Land Scotland

Habitats: 1,750 acre, largely coniferous (Pine and Spruce) plantation. Some areas of Birch regeneration. Harvesting by thinning rather than clearfell. Originally planted 1920s on farmland. Largely flat, lowland site with regular grid of forest rides and blocks of different ages. Several small ponds and burns.

Birds: Common woodland spp. Goshawk, Once held Capercaillie but no recent sightings. Nighjar known to be present in East Angus

Other: Red Squirrel

Directions: DD8 2TU; NO 576 529. This point, on the B9113, 7.5 miles E of Forfar, is by Mosstonmuir, roughly halfway across the forest at a junction with a broad ride running NE.

Public transport: Bus: 29 Forfar-Montrose runs along A933. Ask driver to stop. Short's Travel: www.shortstravel.co.uk

Visiting: Open all hours, free. No designated car parks but B9113 from Forfar runs through S section. Fork L on to minor road at SW corner to cut across forest to NE corner. A933 runs N from Friockheim to Brechin along its E edge and A934 runs W from Montrose to a junction with the B9113 and the A933 on the E edge of the forest

Contact: 0300 067 6380; enquiries.east@forestryandland.gov.scot

Take A933 S to Arbroath.

8 SEATON CLIFFS NR

Scottish Wildlife Trust

Habitats: Coastal red sandstone cliffs, caves, stacks,

Birds: Eider, Fulmar Puffin (nearby), Arctic Skua, Arctic & Common Terns, Kittiwake (breeding), Snipe, Curlew. *Passage:* Sabirds offshore.

Other: Cetaceans. Garden Tiger Moth, Small Heath, Small Blue butterflies.

Directions: DD11 5LL; NO 658 412. Take the harbour road from Arbroath, continue through Victoria Park to the St Ninian's Well car park and public toilets at the far end of the promenade.

Public transport: 1.6 miles on foot from Arbroath harbour to the W end of the reserve along the Angus Coastal Path. Arbroath harbour is about 0.25 mile from Arbroath train anf bus stations. Train—Arbroath.

Visiting: Open all hours. Free. Follow the Angus Coastal Route E from car park. The SWT reserve starts at NO 666 416 (Seaman's Grave) and continues E around The Deil's Heid and then N to Carlingheugh Bay as far as the burn at NO 668 424. *Caution, the cliffs are unstable. Do not leave the marked path or proceed beyond 'no*

entry' signs. *Northern section currently closed.*
Contact: info@swtdundeeangus.org.uk
Take A92 from Arbroath to Montrose.

9 MONTROSE BASIN
Scottish Wildlife Trust/Angus Council
Habitats: Estuary, saltmarsh, reedbeds, farmland.
Birds: Summer: breeding Common & Arctic Terns, gulls, Shelduck, Goldeneye, Eider (up to 2,000), Grey Partridge in surrounding fields. Nationally important moulting site for Mute Swan (approx 300 birds). *Winter:* wildfowl and waders (Curlew peak numbers in Aug, Dunlin in Feb). Internationally important for Pink-footed Goose, Knot and Redshank.
Directions: DD10 9TA; NO 700 564. SWT Wildlife Centre on A92, 1 mile S of Montrose. Main car park for western end at Old Mill, Mains of Dun (DD10 9LQ; NO 668 591).
Public transport: Bus: 30 Arbroath-Montrose, request stop outside Visitor Centre. Stagecoach East Scotland. Train—Montrose (1.5 miles).
Visiting: Admission fee (non-members) to visitor centre. Open, daily 10:30am-5pm mid-Feb to Oct and 10:30am-4pm, Fri-Mon, Nov to mid-Feb (not 25/26 Dec and 1/2 Jan). Shop, fair-trade drinks/snacks, toilets, disabled access to centre. Rest of reserve open all the time inc 2 hides on western half of reserve.
Contact: Montrose Basin Wildlife Centre:
01674 676 336;
montrosebasin@scottishwildlifetrust.org.uk

North East Scotland

Troup Head holds Scotland's largest mainland gannetry and, together with Fowlsheugh, has a good variety of other seabirds. The RSPB's Loch of Strathbeg sees the arrival in autumn of huge numbers of Pink-footed Geese. The Ythan Estuary is good for breeding terns, Eider, passage and wintering waders. Inland, Deeside holds most of the typical highland species.

Bird Atlas/Avifauna
The Birds of North-East Scotland Then and Now
Adam Watson & Ian Francis
(Paragon Publishing, 2012)
The Breeding Birds of North-East Scotland
Ian Francis & Martin Cook
(Scottish Ornithologist's Club, 2011)
The Birds of North-East Scotland
ST Buckland, MV Bell & N Picozzi
(North-East Scotland Bird Club, 1990)

Bird Recorder
Ian Broadbent: nescotlandrecorder@the-soc.org.uk

Bird Report
North-East Scotland Bird Report (1974-), from NES-BR—Mark Sullivan: 07966 412 172; geolbird@gmail.com

BTO Regional Representative
Aberdeen
David Gregory
Kincardine and Deeside
Claire Marsden
Wetland Bird Survey (WeBS)
Local Organizer: webs@bto.org
Patrick Cook/Lynne McKenzie:

Club
SOC North-East Scotland Branch (1956; 140).
John Wills: 01467 651 296;
grampian.secretary@the-soc.org.uk;
www.the-soc.org.uk/local-branches/north-east-scotland
Meetings: 7:30pm, 1st Monday of the month (Oct-Apr). Room 1, The Sir Duncan Rice Library, University of Aberdeen, Bedford Road, AB24 3AA. Online talks also held—contact/see website for details.

Ringing Group/Bird Observatory
Grampian RG: www.grampianringing.blogspot.co.uk

RSPB Local Group
Aberdeen and District (1975; 260)
David Leslie: davidleslie77@gmail.com;
https://group.rspb.org.uk/aberdeen/
Meetings: 7:30pm, 2nd Tuesday of the month (Oct-Mar). Large Lecture Theatre, School of Biological and Environmental Sciences, Tillydrone Ave, Aberdeen, AB24 2TZ.

Scottish Wildlife Trust Regional Networks
Aberdeen and Aberdeenshire
Chair: Roger Owen; committee@swtaberdeen.org.uk; https://scottishwildlifetrust.org.uk/local-group/aberdeen/

Forest and Land Scotland Regional Office
0300 067 6380;
enquiries.east@forestryandland.gov.scot

Continue on A92 from Montrose in Angus and Dundee.

1 St CYRUS NNR
NatureScot
Habitats: Inland cliffs, sand dunes provide shelter for grassland plants, beach.
Birds: Breeding: Fulmar, Raven, Grasshopper Warbler. *Autumn:* Waders inc Knot, Ringed Plover, Whimbrel.

North East Scotland

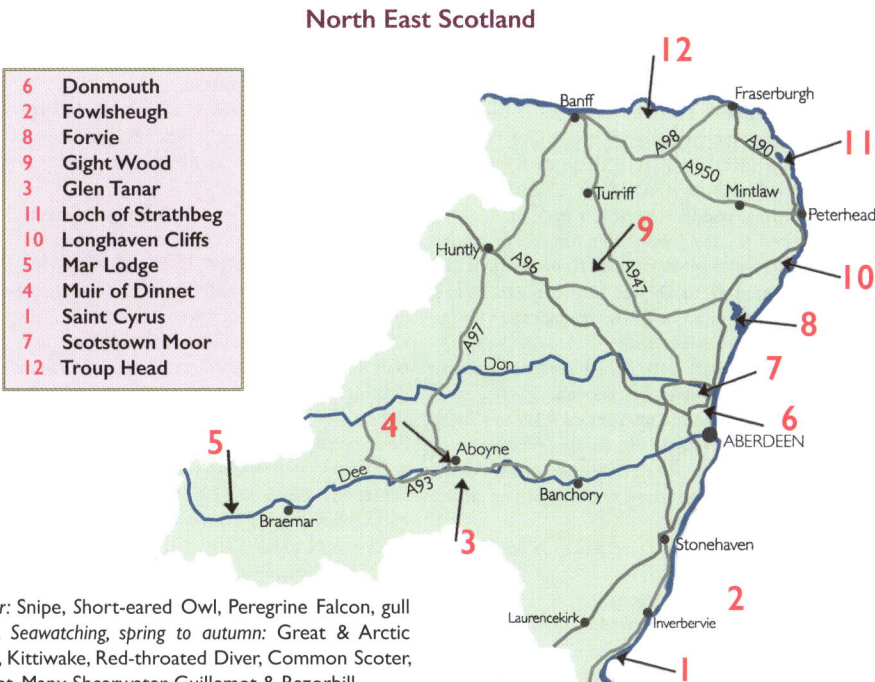

6	Donmouth
2	Fowlsheugh
8	Forvie
9	Gight Wood
3	Glen Tanar
11	Loch of Strathbeg
10	Longhaven Cliffs
5	Mar Lodge
4	Muir of Dinnet
1	Saint Cyrus
7	Scotstown Moor
12	Troup Head

Winter: Snipe, Short-eared Owl, Peregrine Falcon, gull roost. *Seawatching, spring to autumn:* Great & Arctic Skuas, Kittiwake, Red-throated Diver, Common Scoter, Gannet, Manx Shearwater, Guillemot & Razorbill.
Other: 400 spp plants, 500 spp butterflies & moths. All four of Scotland's Grasshopper spp Common Lizard. Cetaceans offshore.
Directions: DD10 0AQ; NO 743 634. Five miles N of Montrose on A92. **St Cyrus NNR** signposted on R immediately after Northwater Bridge over River North Esk. Follow single track road for 1.5 miles for car park and Visitor Centre.
Public transport: Bus: X7 Coastrider Aberdeen-Montrose, nearest stop St Cyrus Village, 1.5 miles, Stagecoach. Train—Montrose, 5 miles.
Visiting: Free. Visitor Centre in Old Lifeboat Station, toilets, open daily Apr-Oct 9:30am-4:30pm, Mon-Fri Nov-Mar 10am-4pm (may be closed during bad weather) Accessible toilet, RADAR key required. 4 trails: Beach, Tyrie, Floo'ery Meads, Estuary, all less than 2 miles long. Mostly firm paths but some rough or steep sections. Stay on paths to avoid damaging plants. Alas, hide overlooking estuary was destroyed during winter storms 23/24. Some areas closed Apr-Aug for ground-nesting birds. Native cattle graze reserve Apr-Oct. Keep dogs under close control, remove mess.
Contact: Theresa Alampo (reserve manager), Old Lifeboat Station, Nether Warburton, St Cyrus, Montrose, DD10 0AQ; 01674 830736; nnr@nature.scot
Continue along A92.

2 FOWLSHEUGH
RSPB
Habitats: Sea cliffs.
Birds: Peregrine regular throughout year. *Summer:* Spec-

tacular 130,000 strong seabird colony, mainly Kittiwake and Guillemot with Razorbill, Fulmar, Puffin. Gannet, Eider and skuas offshore. *Autumn:* Red-throated Diver on sea, terns on passage.
Other: Grey & Common Seals, Bottlenose Dolphin. White-beaked Dolphin and Minke Whale occasional (summer).
Directions: AB39 2TP; NO 879 808. Reserve is three miles S of Stonehaven. From A92 take minor road signposted Crawton. Car park just before end of road.
Public transport: Bus: 747 request stop on A92 Crawton turn-off (Stonehaven to Johnshaven). Stagecoach North East. One mile to reserve entrance.
Visiting: Open all hours, not suitable for wheelchairs. Car park, not suitable for coaches, 200 yards from reserve. Viewing shelter at end of footpath (one mile). Toilets in Stonehaven. Dogs under close control.
Contact: RSPB 01346 532 017;
strathbeg@rspb.org.uk
Take A957 from Stonehaven to A93, turn L on to A93 and head towards Ballater.

3 GLEN TANAR
Glen Tanar Estate
Habitats: Caledonian forest, moorland.
Birds: Best Apr-Sept: Capercaillie, Black & Red Grouse, Ptarmigan, Golden Eagle, Hen Harrier, Merlin, Woodcock, Common Sandpiper, Dipper, Ring Ouzel, Wheatear, Grey Wagtail, Scottish Crossbill, Siskin.

Other: Red Squirrel, Pine Marten, Mountain Hare, Badger. Atlantic Salmon.

Directions: AB34 5EU; NO 481 965. Visitor centre at Braeloine. From Aboyne on A93 cross River Dee at Aboyne Bridge (heading S), turn R on to B976. After one mile, turn L at Bridge and Tower o' Ess into Glen Tanar. Follow this road to reserve car park. *At present, and for the foreseeable future, the bridge at Aboyne is closed to vehicles* (open to pedestrians and cyclists). Continue W to Dinnet, turn L on to B9158, cross Dee, the turn L on to B976 and approach Bridge o' Ess from opposite direction.

Public transport: Bus: 201/202 Aberdeen-Braemar stops in Aboyne and Dinnet. Stagecoach.

Visiting: Visitor Centre (10am-5pm daily, closed Tues), car park, toilets inc wheelchair access, exhibition, information. Events. Network of paths and hides. Follow guidance available from Visitor Centre regarding closed paths, dogs on leads etc.

Contact: Glen Tanar Ranger Service: 01339 886 072; ranger@glentanartrust.org; www.glentanarcharitabletrust.org; Glen Tanar Estate: 01339 886 451; info@glentanar. co.uk; www.glentanar.co.uk

Return to A93 and continue W towards Ballater.

4 MUIR OF DINNET

NatureScot

Habitats: Two freshwater lochs, Pine and Birch woodland, raised bog, moor. The Vat is a giant pothole carved by glacial meltwater. 2,873 acres, SSSI, SAC & SPA.

Birds: Summer: Cuckoo, Osprey, common woodland spp. inc Spotted Flycatcher, Redstart, Tree Pipit, Redpoll & Scottish Crossbill. Water Rail, Goldeneye breed, Great-crested Grebe attempt. *Winter:* The usual suspects.

Other: Dragonflies: Common Hawker, Black Darter, Golden-ringed Dragonfly. Scotch Argus and Pearl-bordered Fritillary.

Directions: AB34 5NB; NO 429 997 Visitor Centre. 2.25 miles W of Dinnet on the A93 Aberdeen-Ballater road take the B9119 N for 1.5 miles to the Burn o'Vat Visitor Centre.

Public transport: Bus: 201/202 Aberdeen-Braemar stops in Dinnet. Stagecoach.

Visiting: Car park, 'invitation to pay', toilets open 24 hrs, picnic and rest areas. Bike rack. Visitor Centre open Mon-Fri 9:30am-4:30pm Apr-Oct; 9:30am-4pm Nov-Mar, may close if weather bad. Four waymarked trails, all are strenuous but lower path to Burn O'Vat is all-accessible. No craft of any description allowed on Loch Kinord March-August or all year on Loch Davan. Keep dogs under close control.

Contact: Simon Ritchie (reserve manager): 01339 881 667; nnr@nature.scot

Continue W along A93 for

5 MAR LODGE NNR

National Trust for Scotland

Habitats: 72,500 acres. Montane (15 Munros, including Ben Macdui), Quoich wetlands, heathland and 7,500 acres of woodland (mix of Pine, plantation and regenerating woodland).

Birds: Black & Red Grouse, Ptarmigan, Cuckoo, Woodcock, Curlew, Snipe, Common Sandpiper, Lapwing, Golden Plover, Dotterel, Dunlin, Osprey, Hen Harrier, Golden & White-tailed Eagles, Long-eared Owl, Peregrine Falcon, Merlin, Raven, Crested Tit, Ring Ouzel, Dipper, Wheatear, Redstart, Spotted Flycatcher, Stonechat, Tree Pipit, Grey Wagtail, 3 spp of Crossbill, Snow Bunting

Other: Red Deer, Otter, Pine Marten, Mountain Hare, Red Squirrel; Adder, Narrow-headed Ant; *Sarcodon* fungi, Stump Lichen; Twinflower.

Directions: AB35 5YJ; NO 097 899 (Mar Lodge itself). Minor road runs W from Braemar (on A93) to S of Dee (Lodge is N of the Dee). Car parks at Linn of Dee, W of the Lodge—continue on minor road, eventually crossing Dee, then turn E on minor road, car park shortly afterwards on L at NO 063 897, 6.75 miles from Braemar to car park—and at Linn of Quoich—continue E on minor road to N of Lodge to car park at NO 118 911, *c*.4 miles from Linn of Dee.

Public transport: Bus: 201 Aberdeen-Braemar, Stagecoach North Scotland

Visiting: Open all hours, free entry but charge for parking (NTS members free). Toilets (Easter-Oct) at Linn of Dee car park. Trails of various lengths and degrees of difficulty lead from car parks. Long distance trails include the 19-mile Lairig Ghru to Speyside (to the NW the NNR abuts **Loch Garten and Abernethy Forest** in **Highlands**), the 22-mile trail along Glen Tilt to Blair Atholl, or the 30-mile one W through Glen Feshie to Kingussie. *Contact:* NTS: 01339 720 163; marlodgeestate@nts.org.uk

Head back E along A93 to Aberdeen.

You could also approach Mar Lodge or depart from it by taking the A93 from/to Blairgowrie in **Perthshire**.

6 DONMOUTH LNR

Aberdeen City Council

Habitats: Mouth of River Don, dunes, scrub, areas of woodland.

Birds: Falls of passage migrants in scrub. Short-eared Owl (likely) Linnet and Stonchat on the links. Mallard, other duck and waders on river, Kingfisher, Dipper and Grey Wagtail. Out to sea: Eider, Long-tailed Duck, scoters, Red-throated Diver. *Summer:* Sandwich, Arctic & Common Terns. Gulls. To N of river scarce passage Wheatear possible in autumn and Curlew and Snow Bunting in winter.

Other: Common & Grey Seals. Common Lizard. Fox & Ruby Toger Moth.

Directions: AB24 ICP; NJ 948 093 In Seaton, sandwiched between beach road running from city centre to A956 at bridge of the Don, with King's Link golf course to S and estuary of River Don to N.

Public transport: Firstbus Aberdeen (0345 646 0707/ route maps| First Bus).

Visiting: Open all hours, free. Park by side of beach road. Hide to N of road overlooking river at NJ 949 093. Possible to walk E along beach to its mouth and then S with golf course to W and open sea to E. Also possible to walk W, across A92 follow the wooded banks of the Don upstream to Brig o' Balgownie, cross river and walk back along N side and then N along beach on other side of river. There is a another small car park at NJ 950 095. Seaton Park, to the S of the Don and W of the A92 is a further area of woods, with a car park, pond and toilets at NJ 941 090.

Contact: ACC Countryside Ranger Service: 01224 067 484; countrysideranger@aberdeencity.gov.uk

Head N on A956. At the 2nd roundabout N of the Don, take 1st exit, The Parlway, then 3rd exit at next roundabout, the B997/Scotstown Road.

7 SCOTSTOWN MOOR LNR

Aberdeen City Council

Habitats: 84 acre SSSI. Ponds, marsh, scrub, grass, heath, plantation

Birds: Pink-footed Goose (winter), Swift, Buzzard, Sparrowhawk, Short-eared & Tawny Owls. Kestrel. Long-tailed Tit, warblers, Stonechat, finches and buntings.

Other: Black Bog Rush, Pipistrelle bats. Northernmost Dragonfly Society hot spot: Common Hawker, Black darter, Emerald Damselfy. Small Pearl-bordered Fritillary, Garden Tiger Moth.

Directions: AB22 8NP; NJ 932 117. Located 4 miles N of Aberdeen city centre. Car park off B997 Scotstown Road. Pedestrian access from Scotstown Road, Dubford Road, Dubford Estate.

Public transport: Bus: 1B, 2 Auchinyell-Scotstown. Firstbus Aberdeen (0345 646 0707 route maps| First Bus).

Visiting: Open all hours. Free. Wide, surfaced paths, some gentle slopes, throughout site.

Contact: ACC Countryside Ranger Service: 01224 067 484; countrysideranger@aberdeencity.gov.uk

Return to A956, take next exit at roundabout, A92/Ellon Road and then A90. Take A975 for Newburgh from A 90 S of Ellon.

8 FORVIE NNR

NatureScot

Habitats: 2,470 acres, estuary, dunes, coastal heath.

Birds: Spring/summer: breeding Eider and terns, migrant waders; seabirds offshore. *Autumn:* Pink-footed Goose, migrant seabirds, waders and passerines, occasional rare spp. *Winter:* waders, wildfowl, inc Whooper Swan, Long-tailed Duck (now occasional), Golden Plover.

Other: Occasional cetaceans offshore, esp. summer.

Directions: 12 miles N of Aberdeen, inc Ythan Estuary. Access: AB41 8RU; NK 034 289 (Forvie Visitor Centre)—three miles NE of Newburgh at Collieston. Waterside car park (AB41 6AB; NK 003 270) one mile N of Newburgh. Waulkmill hide (AB41 8RL; NK 004 287)—turn L off A975 opp. Collieston junction.

Public transport: Bus: 63 Aberdeen to Peterhead (via Cruden Bay) stops in Newburgh and at Collieston crossroads (not Sun). Stagecoach North Scotland.

Visiting: Open all hours, ternery closed Apr to end-Aug. Coach parking at Forvie Visitor Centre: open daily Apr-Oct, toilets, interpretive display. Hide, waymarked trails—short trail and hide wheelchair-accessible.

Contact: NS Reserve Manager: 01358 751 330; forvie@nature.scot

Return to A90. Leave it on B9005 for Ellon. Staying on it, pass through Ellon, crossing the Ythan and continue upstream alongside the Ythan to Methlick.

9 GIGHT WOOD

Scottish Wildlife Trust

Habitats: Ancient Hazel, Oak Cherry and Rowan woodland on steep slopes along N side of River Ythan. SSSI.

Birds: Common woodland spp inc Stock Dove & Buzzard.

Other: Red Squirrel, Otter, Common Pipistrelle and Daubenton's Bat. Bluebells, one of the few areas of ancient woodland left in Aberdeenshire

Directions: AB41 7JA; NJ 823 393. N side of River Ythan 2 miles upstream from Methlick, 3 miles E of Fyvie. Take the B9005 from Methlick for Fyvie and park in the F&LS car park at NJ 833 398 in Badiebath Wood as you pass it on the L. Follow the path through this wood until it emerges opposite Gight Castle. Cross the field (there may be livestock in it) and the entrance to the SWT reserve is next to the Castle. It is a walk of about 0.75 mile from car park to reserve entrance.

Public transport: None.

Visiting: Free, open all hours. No facilities. There is a waymarked path around the central and E end of the reserve. Some sections are steep. No paths in the W part of reserve. There are footbridges across the Ythan but the SWT does not own the woods on the opposite S bank.

Contact: committee@swtaberdeen.org.uk

Return to the A90 (at the roundabout in Ellon take 1st exit, the A920, which leads to A948 and then A90) and head N.

10 LONGHAVEN CLIFFS

Scottish Wildlife Trust

Habitats: 2 miles of red granite coastal cliffs, topped by grass and heath rising to 200 ft. Several flooded disused quarries behind cliff face.

Birds: Breeding seabirds inc Kittiwake, Puffin, Guillemot,

Razorbill, Shag. Clifftop scrub may hold migrant passerines on passage. Pool in disused quarry attracts ducks and geese.

Other: Grey Seals, Cetaceans. Devil's-bit Scabious, Roseroot, Grass-of-Parnassus.

Directions: AB42 0NY; NK 116 394. 4.5 miles S of Peterhead. 2 miles N of Cruden Bay. Take the A90 from the Sandford roundabout S of Peterhead. After c.3.25 miles park in SWT car park on L immediately off A90. If the gate across the path from the car park is open, **DO NOT** drive down path. Gate may be locked at any time.

Public transport: Bus: X63 Peterhead-Aberdeen stops in Longhaven, near the reserve car park. Stagecoach.

Visiting: Free, open all hours, no facilities. Walk c.0.5 mile down path from car park to reserve entrance by disused quarry and then clifftop path, which run to N & S from the entrance. *Caution: clifftop footpath is dangerous and sections are under repair.*

Contact: committee@swtaberdeen.org.uk
Continue N on A90.

11 LOCH OF STRATHBEG
RSPB

Habitats: 2,200 acres, inc. Britain's largest dune loch, with surrounding marshes, reedbeds, grasslands.

Birds: All year: Tree Sparrow. *Spring/autumn:* Avocet, Spoonbill, Marsh Harrier, Garganey, Little Gull, regular Pectoral Sandpiper. Osprey, Common Crane (annual). *Summer:* Common Tern, Water Rail, Corn Bunting. *Winter:* Pink-footed & Barnacle Geese, Whooper Swan, large numbers of duck. Snow Goose and Smew annual. Raptors (inc Hen and Marsh Harriers). Great Northern Diver offshore.

Other: Otter, Badger, Stoat, Roe Deer. Orchids.

Directions: AB43 8QN; NK 055 577. Near Crimond on A90, nine miles S of Fraserburgh. Reserve signposted from village—at T-junction at end of road turn L, after c.0.3 mile turn R at reserve entrance.

Public transport: Bus: 69 Fraserburgh to Peterhead stops in Crimond, one mile from centre. Stagecoach North Scotland.

Visiting: Open all hours (not 25/26 Dec). Visitor Centre open daily (not 25/26 Dec) 9am-5pm, inc observation room, toilets. Wildlife garden, indoor children's area. Tower Pool hide offers panoramic views, open dawn-dusk (0.5 mile from centre). Fen hide (500 yards from airfield car park—footpath from centre to airfield hides open Easter-end Jul). Beach and dune walks accessible from Rattray or St Combs.

Contact: RSPB 01346 532 017; strathbeg@rspb.org.uk
Continue on A90 N. Just S of Fraserburgh take B9032 on L This becomes B9031. Troup Head car park: c.12 miles from A90.

12 TROUP HEAD
RSPB

Habitats: Sea cliffs, farmland.

Birds: Spectacular seabird colony, inc Scotland's largest mainland Gannet colony (2,000+ pairs). Fulmar, Kittiwake, Guillemot, Razorbill, Puffin. Great Skuas may linger in summer. Migrants pass through in spring/autumn.

Other: Impressive common flower assemblage in spring. Cetaceans possible offshore in summer inc. Minke Whale. Brown Hare.

Directions: AB45 3JJ; NJ 822 665. Troup Head is between Pennan and Gardenstown on B9031, E along coast from Macduff. It is signposted off B9031—look for small RSPB signs (and sign for Northfield Farm). At farm go through farmyard and on to a rough track to car park.

Public transport: None.

Visiting: Open all hours, not suitable for wheelchairs. Parking for small number of cars, but not coaches.

Contact: RSPB 01346 532 017; strathbeg@rspb.org.uk

Moray

More than half of the area is over 820 ft above sea level. Lochindorb is the best area of moorland to explore, with breeding grouse, raptors, divers and waders. Extensive woodlands hold Crested Tit (conifer), Tree Pipit and Redstart (birch). Two rivers, the Spey and the Findhorn, flow into the Moray Firth— and the bays at their mouths attract passage waders, terns, Ospreys, seabirds and wildfowl.

Bird Atlas/Avifauna
The Birds of Moray and Nairn
Martin Cook
(Privately published, 2024)

Bird Recorder
Martin Cook, Rowanbrae, Clochan, Buckie, Banffshire AB56 5EQ: 01542 850 296; martin.cook99@btinternet.com

Bird Report
Birds in Moray and Nairn (1999-), online (since 2010), download from www.birdsinmorayandnairn.org

BTO Regional Representative
Melvin Morrison
Wetland Bird Survey (WeBS)
Local OrganizersL webs@bto.org
Lossie Estuary
Bob Proctor
Moray and Nairn (Inland)
David Law:
Moray Basin Coast
Bob Swann

Moray

NB: The BTO region includes Nairnshire but for local government purposes Nairnshire is now part of Highlands.

4 Culbin Forest
5 Culbin Sands
3 Findhorn Bay
2 Loch Spynie
1 Spey Bay

Club

SOC Moray Branch (Moray Bird Club) (2013; 60)
Chris Thomas: moraysecretary@the-soc.org.uk;
www.the-soc.org.uk/local-branches/moray
www.birdsinmorayandnairn.org
Meetings: 7:30pm, 2nd Thursday of the month (Oct-Mar). The Gallery, Elgin Library, Cooper Park, Elgin IV30 1HS. Online talks also held. Contact/see website for details.

RSPB Local Group

No Groups.

Scottish Wildlife Trust Regional Networks

None

Forest and Land Scotland Regional Office

0300 067 6380;
enquiries.east@forestryandland.gov.scot

From **Troup Head**, *return to A9031 and head W, continue on A98. In Fochabers join A96.*

1 SPEY BAY

Scottish Wildlife Trust
Habitats: Tidal, almost enclosed estuary, largest shingle beach in Scotland, coastal grassland, saltmarsh, wet woodland.
Birds: Gulls may include Mediterranean and, in winter, Iceland & Glaucous. Flock largely Herring, Great Black-backed & Common. *Spring:* Red-breasted Mergansers increase before moving inland. *Summer:* Osprey, breeding Arctic & Common Terns. Flock of moulting male Goosander at estuary mouth in late summer. *Passage:* Waders. *Winter:* Wigeon, Teal Goldeneye. Offshore: Eider, Long-tailed Duck, scoters and divers.
Other: Otter, Bottlenose Dolphin.
Directions: IV32 7PJ; NJ 348 655 (Tugnet car park & Scottish Dolphin Centre), E side of Spey. Take B9104 between Mosstodloch and Fochabers. Follow signs for Moray Firth Wildlife Centre. At end of road, fork right for Tugnet car park.
Public transport: Bus: 334 Elgin-Kingston, Moray Council. Train—Elgin.

Visiting: Free, open all hours. Parking (donation, no overnight parking) at Scottish Dophin Centre, which is open Thurs-Mon 10:30am-4pm mid-Feb-June & Sep-Oct; 7 days a week, 10:30am-4pm: Jul&Aug; Nov Thurs-Mon 10:30 am-3:30pm; closed Dec-mid-Feb. For W side of Spey (road bridge S at Fochabers, then take B9015 N) car parks at Kingston: NJ 335 567 & NJ 340 656. Paths unsurfaced but flat. Reserve extends S along Spey on E side to disused railway viaduct over the river at Garmouth.
Contact: 01343 820 339; dolphincentre@whales.org
Continue W on A96 towards Elgin.

2 LOCH SPYNIE

RSPB, Pitgaveny Farms, Spynie Farms
Habitats: Freshwater loch, largest freshwater reedbed in Scotland, marsh, canal, birch and pine woods
Birds: All year: Water Rail. *Spring/summer:* Osprey and Marsh Harrier visit but do not currently breed, breeding Common Tern & Black-headed Gull, Bearded Tit (occasional), Reed Bunting, warblers inc Sedge & Grasshopper. *Winter:* Whooper Swan, Goldeneye, Goosander, occasional Shoveler, Pintail. Greylag & Pink-footed Geese. Woodcock.
Other: Red Squirrel.
Directions: IV30 5BQ; NJ 238 662. Leave the A96 2.6 miles E of the centre of Elgin and head N on the B9103. Alternatively, leave the A941 at the S edge of Lossie-

mouth and head S on the B9103. Just W of Arthur's Bridge over the River Lossie, leave the B9103 and take the minor road for Pitgaveny. After 0.9 mile turn R for Loch Spynie/Scarffbanks Farm. Car park at end of track on R after 0.5 mile.

Public transport: Train—Elgin, then 4 miles along minor roads.

Visiting: Open all hours, free. No toilets. Car park small. 1 separate Blue Badge space further along track with gravel path and ramp to hide halfway along E side of loch. Can walk around S end of loch and reedbeds to old railway line and canal on W side.

Contact: 01346 532 017; strathbeg@rspb.org.uk

Continue W on A96. At roundabout on N edge of Forres take 3rd exit, B9011, which runs N along E side of Findhorn Bay.

3 FINDHORN BAY LNR

Moray Council, NatureScot, local community

Habitats: Almost enclosed, 15,000 acre tidal estuary into which the Findhorn and several burns flow. Almost entirely mudflat at low tide. Narrow opening to sea. Mudflats, sand, saltmarsh. SSSI, SPA

Birds: Summer: Osprey, Arctic, Common & Sandwich Terns, visit bay but don't breed. *Passage:* Pink-footed Geese, Ringed Plover. *Winter:* Redshank, Dunlin, Knot, Sanderling, small numbers of other waders. Wigeon, Teal, Goldeneye, Pintail. *Offshore:* Eider, Long-tailed Duck, Common & Velvet Scoters, divers.

Other: Grey and Common Seals.

Directions: IV36 3YQ; NJ 037 647 (Findhorn Heritage Centre). The B9011 runs along the E side of the Bay from the village of Findhorn, in the N at its mouth, to Kinloss at its SE corner. It then runs SW to join the A96 at Forres c.1 miles S of the Bay. The S side of the Bay can be approached via various minor roads off the B9011 and A96. The Culbin Forest extends along the W side of the Bay

Public transport: Bus: 31 & 31D Forres-Findhorn. Train—Forres, 2 miles to S of Bay.

Visiting: Free, open all hours, dogs under close control. Free car parks in Findhorn (NJ 037 649; NJ 042 649), the Findhorn Foundation and accessible hide (NJ 053 633), Kinlosss (NJ 060 622) and (NJ 027 608). Public toilets in Findhorn and Kinloss.

Contact: www.fblnr.org (website not functioning well).

Continue W on A96.

4 CULBIN FOREST

Forestry & Land Scotland

Habitats: Extensive commercial conifer forest. Birch woodland, a number of ponds and lochs.

Birds: Crested Tit, Common, Scottish &, possibly, Parrot Crossbills. Common woodland spp. Stonechat in felled areas. Tree Pipit and Spotted Flycatcher possible in summer.

Directions: IV36 2TG; NH 997 614, Welhill car park.

Culbin Forest is reached via minor roads running N from the A96 between Nairn and Elgin. If approaching from W, turn L off A96 just after the Brodie Countryfare shop. If from the E turn R for Broom of Moy and Kintessack 1 mile W of Forres. Route to car park signposted from these turnings. If approaching from W the minor road runs along the margin of the forest. Turn L up a forest road before reaching Kintessack for the Cloddymoss car park at NH 981 599

Public transport: Limited, some buses on school days.

Visiting: Open all hours, charge for parking. Wellhill car park has accessible toilets and baby changing facilities. The Forest stretches for nearly 9 miles from W side of **Findhorn Bay LNR** (q.v.) to Nairn and lies behind **Culbin Sands** (q.v.). The Forest can be accesed on foot from the Sands and vice versa. The Forest has an extensive network of gravel tracks, with some steep slopes, and an observation tower, which has steps, at NH 987 624

Contact: 0300 067 6380; enquiries.east@forestryandland.gov.scot

Continue W on A96

5 CULBIN SANDS

RSPB

Habitats: Saltmarsh, sandflats, dunes. SSSI

Birds: Spring: Terns, esp Sandwich, passage waders. *Summer:* Breeding Eider, Ringed Plover, Oystercatcher. Osprey on passage. *Winter:* Common Scoter, Long-tailed Duck, Red-breasted Merganser, Knot, Bar-tailed Godwit. Raptors inc Peregrine, Merlin and Hen Harrier attracted by wader flocks. Roosting geese, Snow Bunting.

Other: Dolphins, Grey & Common Seals in Firth. Otters sometimes seen.

Directions: IV12 5BX; NH 900 576. c.1.5 miles NE of Nairn, overlooking Moray Firth. Use East Beach car park, signed off A96. Follow road through Maggot Road caravan park (car park at end of road). Track along dunes and saltmarsh—from far end of car park take 0.5 mile 'all abilities footpath' to reach reserve.

Public transport: Bus—from Inverness to Nairn, stops in Nairn, one mile W of site. 10, Stagecoach North Scotland. 11, Stagecoach Highlands. Train—Nairn, 1.5 miles W of reserve.

Visiting: Open all hours. Car park with cycle racks, seasonal toilets (inc. disabled, RADAR key).

Contact: RSPB: 01463 715 000; nsro@rspb.org.uk

The A96 continues W to Inverness, whence you can start to explore The Highlands, or head down the Great Glen on the A82 to Fort William and then Argyll. Alternatively, you could head S on the A941 at Elgin, the A940 at Forres or the A939 at Nairn and all of these will connect with the A95, which runs alongside the Spey in The Highlands.

Argyll and Bute

Islands provide the birdwatching highlights for this area—Coll, Tiree, Islay and Mull. Islay is renowned for its wintering wildfowl, which include huge numbers of Barnacle & White-fronted Geese. Choughs, raptors and Corncrakes are other island specialities, although the last of these is more likely to be at the RSPB reserve on Coll. Mull is home to the highest densities of breeding Golden & White-tailed Eagles in Britain. Argyll is also deeply penetrated by sea lochs and has extensive forests, many commercial, but some native ancient woodland. Two clusters of these forests are featured here as examples, but there are many more. It is also, very definitely, t'other side of the Highland fault line.

Bird Atlases/Avifauna
Birds of Argyll
Tristan ap Rheinallt, Clive Craik, P Daw, B Furness, S Petty & D Wood
(Argyll Bird Club, 2007)
The Birds of Colonsay and Oronsay:
An Island Avifauna and Bird Atlas.
David Jardine, Mike Peacock & Ian Fisher
(privately published, 2017)
The Birds of Bute: A Bird Atlas and Local Avifauna
Ronald Forrester, Ian Hopkins & Doug Menzies
(Buteshire NHS, 2012).

Bird Recorders
Jim Dickson, 11 Pipers Road, Cairnbaan, Lochgilphead, Argyll PA31 8UF: 07985 726 209;
Argyllbirder@outlook.com
Assistant: Malcolm Chattwood, 1 The Stances, Kilmichael Glassary, Lochgilphead, Argyll PA31 8QA: 07422 718 533
abcrecorder@outlook.com
Bute (also see Clyde Islands, Clyde)
Bernard Zonfrillo, 28 Brodie Road, Glasgow, G21 3SB:
b.zonfrillo@bio.gla.ac.uk

Bird Report
Argyll Bird Report (1980/83-), from ABC—back copies David Harris, Beech Hill, Inverneill, Lochgilphead, Argyll, PA30 8ES: 07974 430 001;
treasurer@argyllbirdclub.org
Now produced as a pdf download—see website:
www.argyllbirdclub.org/publications/the-argyll-bird-report

BTO Regional Representatives
Argyll Mainland, Bute and Gigha
Nigel Scriven
Argyll (Mull, Coll, Tiree & Morvern)
Ewan Miles
Assistant: Rachel French

Islay, Jura and Colonsay
David Wood:
Wetland Bird Survey (WeBS)
Local Organizers: webs@bto.org
Argyll Mainland, Mull
Nigel Scriven:
Bute
Ian Hopkins:
Islay, Jura & Colonsay
David Wood:
Tiree and Coll
John Bowler

Clubs
Argyll Bird Club (1985; 270)
Nigel Scriven, 14 Taylor Avenue, Kilbarchan, Johnstone PA10 2LS: 01505 706 652; chairman@argyllbirdclub.org;
www.argyllbirdclub.org
Meetings: All-day indoor meetings are held on a Saturday in early Mar and early Nov each year—contact/see website for details. Monthly field trips throughout the year.
Mull Wildlife Group
(formerly *Mull Bird Club*, 2023; 150+)
Jenny Jackson (Sec): 07840 968 987;
mullwildlifegroup@gmail.com;
www.mullwildlifegroup.co.uk
Meetings: 7:30pm, 3rd Friday of the month (Sep-Apr). Salen Church Hall, PA72 6JF. Contact/see website for details.

Ringing Group/Bird Observatory
Treshnish Isles Auk RG
Machrihanish Observatory
David Milward, Warden: 07737 985874;
machobservatory@yahoo.com

RSPB Local Group
None

Scottish Wildlife Trust Regional Networks
Argyll and Lochaber
Chair: Tony Mitchell-Jones: 01631 710559
https://www.swtalg.org.uk

Forest and Land Scotland Regional Offices
for Argyll S & E of Loch Fyne
0330 067 6600;
enquiries.central@forestryand land.gov.scot
for Argyll N & W of Loch Fyne and the islands
0330 067 6650;
enquiries.west@forestryand land.gov.scot

3	**Argyll Forest Park**
1	**Ben Lui**
15	**Coll**
12	**Fishnish**
2	**Glasdrum**
10	**Largiebann**
13	**Loch an Tòrr and Quinish Forest**
7	**Loch Gruinart**
11	**Machrihanish**
4	**Mid Argyll and Kintyre Forests**
5	**Moine Mhor**
9	**Oronsay**
6	**Taynish**
8	**The Oa**
14	**Treshnish Isles**

Drive N on A82 from **Clyde** *along the side of Loch Lomond to Crianlarich. Bear L on A85 to Tyndrum.*

1 BEN LUI, former NNR

DeNNRed by NatureScot

Habitats: Mountain massif with 4 Munros rising to 3,707 ft, cliff, rocky outcrop, upland grass. SSSI & SAC. Woodland flanking the lower reaches of the River Cononish.

Birds: Not a particular avian hotspot but included here as a high, well defined massif with a range of habitats and altitudes on the borders of Argyll and Stirlingshire. Expect the usual Scottish upland and woodland suspects but not to excess.

Other: Red Deer, Red Squirrel, Mountain Hare, Pine Marten, Wildcat. Specialist, low acid soil alpine flora....

Directions: FK20 8RZ; NN 344 292, Tyndrum Community Wood car park off A82 at Dalrigh, S of Tyndrum.

Public transport: Bus: S60, Stirling-Tyndrum, stops in Tyndrum but no stops between Crianlarich and Tyndrum, Midland Bluebird; 978, Edinburgh-Oban stops in Tyndrum; 975 Glasgow-Oban stops in Tyndrum, two latter operated by Scottish Citylink. Train—Tyndrum Lower Station (Oban branch of West Highland line), then walk S through forest from Tyndrum for just over 1 mile along the West Highland Way to join the Cononish farm track, which runs W from Community Wood car park, shortly after it leaves the car park. Alternatively, head SW from the station along a track through the forest that joins the Cononish track further W.

Visiting: Open all hours, free, no facilities in reserve but toilets, hotels and information office in Tyndrum. After parking at the Dalrigh car park walk W along Cononish farm track. The farm is 2.8 miles along the track, which continues on W beside the River Cononish to the mouths of the corries on the E side of Ben Lui. This is not a walking guide, but the ascent from the end of the track to the summit of Ben Lui involves a climb of around 2,600 ft.

Contact:

Continue W on A85 from Tyndrum. After 30 miles, cross the mouth of Loch Ettive on the Connel bridge and follow A828, as below.

2 GLASDRUM NNR

NatureScot

Habitats: Ancient Oak, Hazel & Birch rain forest on steep, S facing slope, with open glades.

Birds: Common woodland spp inc Wood Warbler, Redstart, Pied Flycatcher.

Other: Lichens inc Norwegian Specklebelly, mosses, ferns. Over 20 spp butterflies inc. Chequered Skipper, Pearl-bordered Fritillary, Mountain Ringlet.

Directions: PA38 4BQ; NN 002 454. At roundabout on A828 just N of Creagan Bridge turn E and follow minor road along N shore of Loch Creran. Car park is 1.7 miles from roundabout on N side of road

Public transport: Bus: 918 Oban-Fort William stops at Creagan Bridge. West Coast Motors (01586 552 319)

Visiting: Open all hours, free, no facilities. Circular trail up hillside. Path narrow, steep, some steps and bridges. Keep dogs under close control.

Contact: 0131 316 290; nnr@nature.scot

Forests cover much of Argyll and the following two entries are for two forest parks, each of which is composed of a

number of separate individual forests. The entries focus on locations and visiting arrangements rather than the birds and wildlife of the various forests so that you can make a start on exploring them for yourself. Expect the usual Scottish woodland assemblage depending upon the features of the particular forest and the presence or absence of other habitats besides woodland.

3 ARGYLL FOREST PARK
Forestry and Land Scotland
Habitats: Conifer forests, lochs, hillside.
Scotland's first forest park. Many of these forests date from Victorian landscaping and have stands of N American conifers that are now mature.
Forests:
Cluster of forests between Lochs Lomond and Fyne on the peninsulas between the sea lochs running N from the Firth of Clyde.
Tarbet Isle: G83 7DG; free car park at NN 327 054, to W of A82 N of Tarbet. Scots Pine forest on W shore of Loch Lomond opposite islet in Loch and Ben Lomond on E shore. Rather than continuing N on A82 at Tarbet, turn W on to the A83. The road is flanked by birch woods on the lower slopes *Cruach Tairbeirt* as it runs along the pass between between Tarbet on Loch Lomond and Arrochar on Loch Long. Car parks in either Arrochar or Tarbet. Trails between Arrochar and Arrochar & Tarbet station and along flanks of hill. Access to trails via underpass at station.
Arrochar: PA27 7AP; NN 295 048 & NN 298 048, car parks (not F&LS, charge) to the S of the A83 at the head of Loch Long, between Arrochar and Succoth. Arrochar forest on W side of Loch Long to N of Glen Croe and A83. Trail linking it to Ardgarten, walks up through forest on flanks of The Cobbler/Ben Arthur to summits and trails along Glen Loin. Toilets, shops, cafes in Arrochar village.
Ardgarten: G83 7AS (1 mile W of car park); NN 269 037, free car park immediately to S of A83 3 miles W of Arrochar towards the Rest and Be Thankful. Toilets and picnic site. Trails through commercial forest on W shore of Loch Long, N of junction with Loch Goil. A little further along the A83 you reach the car park for...
Honeymoon Bridge: G83 7AS; NN 248 043. Free car park on N side of A83, tight turn if coming from W. Nearest toilets at Ardgarten, shop and cafe in Arrochar. Trail up The Cobbler/Ben Arthur from the S more challenging than the one from *Arrochar* (q.v.).
Note: After Ardgarten the A83 climbs to The Rest and Be Thankful pass. The road is subject to frequent closures due to rockfalls and engineering work designed to but never actually succeeding in solving the problem.
Lochgoilhead: PA24 8AQ. Continue along the A83 past Ardgarten and then take the B828 The Rest and Be Thankful. There are car parks at NN 299 074 at the TR&BT and at NN 228 069 at the start of the B828. At

the junction with the B839 do not turn R and descend the Hell's Glen (the clue's in the name, why would you?) but continue straight on and follow the Goil until you reach Lochgoilhead. Free car park at Lochgoilhead Arboretum at NN 233 016. Toilets and cafe in village. Duke's Path to E of village leads to Donich Falls amidst mature conifers. 57 mile Loch Lomond & Cowal Way passes through forest. A minor road runs S along the W side of Loch Goil to Carrick Castle and it is possible to walk (but not drive) N from *Ardentinny* (q.v.) to Carrick Castle.
Glenbranter: PA27 8DJ; two free car parks at NS 112 976 (visitor centre, leaflets, toilets, picnic area, hide); NS 106 968. If approaching from N continue along the A83 from TR&BT and take the A815 at Strachur on the E side of Loch Fyne continue on the A815, do not take the A816. The Glebranter Visitor Centre is c.3.5 miles from Strachur. Turn R off A815 into Glenbranter and follow village roads to car park. Owned, a century ago, by Sir Harry Lauder. Mature trees, several walking and cycle trails along glens, up hills, including one around *Loch Eck* (q.v.).
Loch Eck: Continue on along the A815. PA32 8SG; two free car parks and picnic areas on the forested E side of Loch Eck at NS 142 947 & NS 142 931 (Whistlefield, inn, minor road for *Ardentinny* q.v.). Along with Loch Lomond, Lock Eck is the only place where Scotland's rarest freshwater fish, the Powan, is found.
Benmore: Continue along A815 to past the S end of Loch Eck, which is drained by the Eachaig. The Benmore Estate was planted in the 19C with N American conifers and now features mature Californian Redwoods, Douglas Firs and Western Hemlocks. PA23 8QU; NS 144 855 (*Benmore Botanic Garden*, one of the regional gardens of the Royal Botanic Gardens Edinburgh. Toilets, cafe). Immediately to W of A815. Walking and cycling trails to E, these include access to the cycling trail around Loch Eck (*Glenbranter, Loch Eck* q.v.). Dunoon-Inverary bus stops at entrance. 1 mile further along A815...
Puck's Glen: Part of Benmore Estate. PA23 8QT; free car park at NS148 839. Nearest toilets at Benmore Botanic Garden. Walkway up forested gorge with waterfalls. Dunoon-Inverary bus stops on request at entrance. Continue along A815 towards Dunoon and Ardbeg take A880 for...
Kilmun Arboretum: PA23 8SJ (*does not* give access to *Puck's Glen* q.v); NS 164 823 free car park. Toilets in village of Kilmun. 150 tree spp in arboretum, used to trial species for timber production. Network of firm paths. Continue along A880 and then minor road to...
Ardentinny: PA23 8TS; NS 192 886, charge for car park. Toilets at picnic site. Car park and picnic site to N of Ardentinny village. If approaching from *Loch Eck* (q.v.) take minor road for Ardentinny at Whistlefield. If approaching from Dunoon, head N from Dunoon on A815. Then take A880 at Ardbeg and continue along

coast round Strone Point, staying on the same road all the way to Ardentinny village. Car park to N of village. Commercial forest along W shore of Loch Long. 3 marked trails, longest 2 miles, some rough/steep sections. Buses from Dunoon to Ardentinny.

Corlarach: PA23 7LN; NS 163 765 free car park to W of Kilbride Rd in Dunnon. Turning just S of Holy Trinity Episcopal Church. Dunoon can be reached from the N by continuing S on the A815 from *Benmore* (q.v.) or by foot or vehicle ferry from Gourock. Several walking and cyling trails from car park. Ruined farms on the hills to the S & W above Dunoon, now turned over to conifer plantations.

Ardyne: PA23 7UH; NS 113 689. Free car park at the SW corner of the *Corlarach* (q.v.) forests W and S of Dunoon and trail runs between the two. Take A815 S from Dunoon to Toward Point at the S end of the peninsula. Do not go all the way to the Point but veer R on the A815, which becomes a minor road shortly thereafter and head for Toward Quay 1.25 miles W. At this point road turns sharp N (do not continue W to Ardyne Point) and car park 0.7 mile N.. Minor road continues N along E side of Loch Striven but it is not possible to drive its full length

Public transport: Vehicle ferry across Clyde from Gourrock to Hunter's Quay (N of Dunoon) and passenger ferries from Kempock Point (E of Gourrock) to Dunoon and Kilcreggan. Bus services between Glasgow and Helesnburgh; 926 runs from Glasgow to Tarbert on Loch Lomond, across the N end of Lochs Long and Fyne and S along W side of Loch Fyne. Train—Helensburgh.

Contact: for forests S & E of Loch Fyne
0330 067 6600;
enquiries.central@forestryand land.gov.scot
for forests N & W of Loch Fyne
0330 067 6650;
enquiries.west@forestryand land.gov.scot

4 MID ARGYLL AND KINTYRE FORESTS
Forestry and Land Scotland
Habitats: Forests, largely conifer and small lochs.
Forests:
These forests are clustered around Lochgilphead and south through Knapdale and into Kintyre.
To the NE of Lochgilphead.
Ardcastle: PA31 8SB NR 943 919 car park charges, open all hours. Take forest road S off A83 between Minard and Loch Gair, 1.6 miles NE of the hotel in Lochgair. Car park is 300 yards along forest road on R. Trails lead from it through commercial forest down to Loch Fyne, with the inlet of Loch Gair to the W of the forest (the village of Lochgair is to the E of the Loch). Eider on Loch. Common Seals, Otter, Pine Marten. Sika Deer.
Public transport: Bus: 926, Glasgow to Campbelltown.

Knapdale Forests
A group of forests stretching across the peninsula between Crinan and Lochgilphead, fringing Moine Mhor NNR *and S to Taynish NNR.*
'Knapdale' refers to the terrain of outcrops (knaps) and hollows (dales) often filled with small lochs. Similar, though more heavily forested, to the 'cnoc and lochan' country of Sutherland.
Achnabreac: PA31 8RE; NR 852 908, car park, charge. Head N on the A816 from Lochgilphead towards Oban. Take forest road to E shortly after passing junction with B841 at Cairnbaan. After 0.5 mile turn R into car park. Nearest facilities in Lochgilphead (2.5 mile to S). Mix of commercial conifer plantation and remanants of ancient Oak woodland. Other side of A816 from Moine Mhor NNR (q.v.). Alternatively, leave the A816 at Cairnbaan and take the B841 for Crinan and Tayvallich.
Dunardry: PA31 8UE NR 824 808 Dunardry free car park, immediately S of B841 at E end of Dunardry locks. PA31 8UH; NR 819 903 Green Gate Loop free car park, turn L off B841 after F&LS Cairnbaan Workshops and follow road uphill for c.1 mile. Crinan Canal runs along N edge of forest, with Moine Mhor (q.v.) on other side of road for much of length. Network of trails through forests and lochs to S of canal, including one up the gorge of the Dunardy Burn, rising to Cruach More (214m).
Crinan: PA31 8SS; NR 783 942 & NR 788 943 free car parks, toilets, refreshments. Continue along B841 from Dunardry past Bellanoch to Crinan. Mix of ancient Oak, Hazel, Birch and conifer plantation. Trails lead from Crinan up to Castle Dounie (170m).
Barnluasgan: PA31 8PS; NR 791 911 car park, charges, open all hours, no facilities. Continue along B841 from Dunardry. At Bellanoch bear left on B8025 to Tayvallich, not Crinan. after c.1 mile turn L to Achnamara. Barnluasgan car park is just after junction on L. Hazel woods, non-native conifers being cleared. small lochs. Reintroduced Beavers. Red Squirrel, Lichens, Osprey
Gleann a Gealbhan: PA31 8PG; NR 783 906 free car park, nearest facilities are in Crinan or Tayvllich. The car park is c.0.5 mile further along the B8025 from the Barnluasgan junction. Larch woods, a ruined clearance village and lochs.
Public transport: Bus: 429, 425/426 Lochgilphead to Oban and Lochgilphead to Tayvallich
Barnaline: PA35 4AB; NM 969 139 free car park. From Lochgilphead Continue N on the A816 past Achnabreac (q.v.)1 mile to N of Kilmartin take B840 E for Dalavich. After just under 3 miles, between Lochs Ederline and Awe, turn L on to a minor road at Ford and follow this along N shore of Loch Awe and through the Inverliever Forest for c.9.5 miles to Dalavich. Continue for another 0.75 miles to Barnaline Lodge and the car park is down a forest road to L just before bridge over River Avich. Although there are extensive commercial forests along

the N side fo Loch Awe, the area around Barnaline is a large area of ancient Oak and Scots Pine flanking the River Avich, which connects Lochs Avich and Awe.

Kintyre Forests
Instead of heading N from Lochgilphead, take the A83 heading S for just under 13 miles to
Tarbert: Parking in the village of Tarbert, toilets, shops, restaurants, ferry to Arran (East Tarbert Loch). Visitor Information Centre on Harbour Street (A8015) just to E of T-junction with A83 PA29 6UD; NR 865 686. 100 yards beyond Information Centre turn R for castle ruins. 2 trails through heather and bracken climb hills above Tarbert. Also start of 100 mile Kintyre Way, a trail that criss-crosses the Kintyre peninsula to Dunaverty (NR 687 075) at the S tip before running back N to **Machrihanish** (q.v.).
Continue S on A83 for around 5 miles Kennacraig (ferries to Islay and on to Colonsay), then take B8001 for 5 miles to Claonaig (summer ferry to Arran) and then the B842 for 13 miles to Bridgend. Turn L on to B879 for 1.5 miles to.
Carradale: PA28 6SB NR Port na Storm car park (charge). On L as enter village. Start of Deer Hill Trail through forest and open hill up Cnoc nan Gabhar (755 ft) above village. Golden Eagle, Red & Black Grouse. Possible Basking Shark out to sea. Toilets, shops and cafes in Carradale, which is on the Kintyre Way.
Alternatively, 2.25 miles before Bridgend, Grianan car park (charges) PA28 6QJ; NR 798 413 is 300 yards E of B842 along a forest road. Start of trails through N part of Carradale Forest.
Public transport: Bus: Campbelltown-Carradale.
Visiting:
Contact: 0330 067 6650;
enquiries.west@forestryand land.gov.scot
Take the A816 from Lochgilphead to Oban and entries structured as normal.

5 MOINE MHOR NNR
NatureScot
Habitats: Raised bog, tidal flats, saltmarsh, fen, alder carr, ancient oak woodland
Birds: Red-breasted Merganser, Goosander. Snipe, Redshank, Short-eared Owl, Peregrine Falcon, Kestrel, Raven, Reed Bunting. *Summer:* Cuckoo, Common Sandpiper, Osprey, Wood, Willow, Garden & Grasshopper Warblers, Stonechat, Whinchat, Tree Pipit, Redstart. *Winter:* Black Grouse, Greenland White-fronted Goose. Hen Harrier roost.
Other: Large Heath, Scotch Argus, Marsh Fritillary, 10 spp dragonfly. Sundews.
Directions: Two separate areas of raised bog, North and South, served by two car parks, both reached from the A816, Lochgilphead-Oban road.
North area and car park: PA31 8QF (East Lodge, Poltalloch); NR 826 959. Leave the A816 at Slockavullin (7

miles N of Lochgilphead and follow the B8045 for 1.25 miles. The car park is just S of the East Lodge crossroads on the L. Alternatively, take the minor road off the A816 at Ballymeanoch (6 miles N of Lochgilphead) and, after 0.7 mile, turn L at the East Lodge crossroads.
South area and car park: PA31 8SU (Dunadd fort); NR 837 936. 4.5 miles N of Lochgilphead, take the minor road from the A816 signposted for Dunadd. The car park is 600 yards along this road, just after crossing the River Add.
Public transport: Bus: 429, Lochgilphead-Kilmartin, stops along A816; 425/426 Lochgilphead-Tayvallich takes the B841 along the Crinan Canal and S boundary of the NNR, cross canal at Islandadd Bridge, Bellanoch or at the Dunardy Locks. Both services West Coast Motors (01586 552 319).
Visiting: Open all hours, free, no facilities. N car park in native woodland, with Tileworks Trail boardwalk into moss. Keep to paths, raised bogs are 90% water, 10% sphagnum! Kilmartin Burn and River Add form W boundary for much of both areas, with moss traversed by drainage ditches, many now dammed, and Add estuary in SW corner. The Crinnan canal and towpath run along S margin of S area. Dunadd hill, by S car park, offers views over the moss.
Contact: Heather Goodwin (reserve manager): nnr@nature.scot
B841 (see below) runs along S edge of Moine Mhor.

6 TAYNISH NNR
NatureScot
Habitats: Ancient Oak woodland, open glades grazed by cattle, heath, saltmarsh, shoreline
Birds: Woodcock. Little Grebe, Sparrowhawk, Kestrel, Common woodland, inc Goldcrest, Treecreeper, Crossbill. *Summer:* Cuckoo, Sedge, Garden, Grasshopper, Willow & Wood Warblers, Blackcap, Whitethroat, Redstart, Spotted Flycatcher, Tree Pipit. *Winter:* Whooper Swan, Goldeneye on Lochan Taynish.
Other: Otter, Red Squirrel. Dragonflies, 20 spp butterfly inc Marsh Fritillary. White Wood Anemones, Bluebells.
Directions: Centre of nearest village, Tayvallich, PA31 8PW; reserve car park NR 737 852. If travelling from Lochgilphead, take the B841 from the A816 Lochgilphead-Oban road at Cairnbaan c.2 miles N of Lochgilphead. Follow the B841 for 3 miles. Just past Bellanoch turn L on to the B8025 and follow to Tayvallich. In Tayvallich turn R on to a minor road past school and follow for just over a mile to reserve car park. If travelling from Oban, leave the A816 c.1 mile S of Kilmartin and take the B8025 across the **Moine Mhor NNR** (q.v.) and join the B841 at Bellanoch. Then proceed as from Lochgilphead.
Public transport: Bus: 425/426 Lochgilphead-Tayvallich West Coast Motors (01586 552 319).
Visiting: Free, open all hours, nearest facilities in Tayval-

lich (pub, cafe, toilets). Network of paths.
The road to Tayvallich and Taynish passes by and through several of the **Mid Argyll and Kintyre Forests** (q.v.).
Contact: Heather Goodwin (reserve manager): nnr@nature.scot
From Lochgilphead, head S on A83. At Kennacraig take ferry to Islay.

7 LOCH GRUINART, ISLAY
RSPB
Habitats: Lowland wet grassland, sea loch, farmland, moorland.
Birds: All year: Birds of prey, esp Hen Harrier and Peregrine Falcon, Chough feed in nearby fields. *Spring/summer:* Displaying Snipe, Lapwing, Curlew and Redshank. Corncrake. *Sep-Nov:* Passage migrants and arriving wildfowl. *Oct-Apr:* Large numbers of Barnacle & White-fronted Geese, other wildfowl and waders.
Other: Otter, Red & Roe Deer. Marsh Fritillary butterfly.
Directions: PA44 7PP; NR 275 672. On N coast of Islay, NW of Bridgend. Bridgend is 7.5 miles from Port Askaig on the A846 and 13.25 miles from Port Ellen at the other end of the A846. At Bridgend take the A847 to Bruichladdich. After 2.75 miles take B8017 on R, signposted to reserve. Visitor Centre is 3.75 miles from turn-off.
Public transport: Ferry from Kennacraig to Port Askaig (N end of Islay) or Port Ellen (S end of Islay)—Caledonian MacBrayne (08705 650 000; www.calmac.co.uk)
Visiting: Open all hours. Car parking at centre and start of trails, coaches at visitor centre only. Visitor centre open daily 10am-5pm (not Christmas/New Year). Toilets (inc disabled), two hides, two trails, viewpoints. Disabled access to south hide, viewing area. No dogs in hides and under close control on trails.
Contact: RSPB: 01496 850 505: loch.gruinart@rspb.org.uk
Having made it to Islay

8 THE OA, ISLAY
RSPB
Habitats: 330 ft high sea cliffs, rocky shore, grass and moorland rising to 663 ft, freshwater lochs, fields planted for Twite. 4,770 acre SPA.
Birds: Corncrake, Golden Eagle, Hen Harrier, Peregrine Falcon, Chough, Raven. *Summer:* Guillemot, Black Guillemot, Razorbill, Red-throated Diver, Curlew, Kittiwake. Grasshopper Warbler, Stonchat, Whinchat. *Winter:* Greenland White-front Goose, Twite flocks, very occasional Snow & Lapland Buntings.
Other:
Directions: PA42 7AU; NR 281 422. The Oa is the peninsula at the S end of Islay, close to Port Ellen. If landing at Port Ellen, take A846 for Bridgend, after 0.4 mile turn L on to minor road for Risabus and, finally, Upper Killeyan, and follow for 6.25 miles. If landing at Port Askaig,

take A846 for *c*.21 miles to Port Ellen, turning R just before Port Ellen on to minor road referred to above.
Public transport: Ferry from Kennacraig to Port Askraig (N end of Islay) or Port Ellen (S end of Islay)—Caledonian MacBrayne (08705 650 000; www.calmac.co.uk). Nearest bus stop Port Ellen.
Visiting: Open all hours, free, no facilities. Car park has 18 places. Dogs on lead during breeding season. Clean up mess. Respect Scottish Outdoor Access Code.
Contact: 01496 300 118; the.oa@rspb.org.uk
Onward ferry from Port Askaig to Colonsay.

9 ORONSAY
Oronsay Estate (owner)/RSPB (management)
Habitats: Machair, grazing pasture, rocky shores, sand. Reserve covers entire island.
Birds: Corncrake, Rock Dove, waders, especially on passage, seaduck, Hen Harrier, Golden Eagle, Merlin, Peregrine Falcon, Chough, Raven. *Winter:* Geese inc Barnacle, Brent & White-fronted. Twite, Snow & Lapland Buntings.
Other: Machair vegetation, grazing by hill sheep and Luing cattle.
Directions: PA61 7YS; NR 349 889. Take B8086 from pier at Scalasaig, after just under 1 mile turn L and drive 2 miles along B8085 to car park (5 places) at end of road.
Public transport: None on island. Car ferry to Colonsay from Oban (daily, Apr-mid-Oct; 4/week mid-Oct-Mar) or Kennacraig on mainland and Port Askaig on Islay (2/week). Both Caledonian MacBrayne (08705 650 000; www.calmac.co.uk). Also flights to and from Oban.
Visiting: Free, open all hours, no facilities. Working farm, obey all signs, keep to paths. 1.5 miles from Colonsay, only accessible via strand for 2 hours either side of low tide. Do not attempt to drive across. Park at car park on Colonsay, then walk. Check conditions before crossing. Dogs under close control. Respect Scottish Outdoor Access Code.
Contact: 01951 200 367; oronsay@rspb.org.uk and Info@visitcolonsay.co.uk
Of you didn't take the ferry at Kenncraig or have returned to it from the islands, continue S on A83.

10 LARGIEBANN NR
Scottish Wildlife Trust
Habitat: Bog, heath, acid grassland, native woodland . steep cliffs along 4 miles of coastline. 3,950 acres rising to 1,463 ft at Cnoc Moy
Birds: Black Grouse, breeding seabirds, Eider, Curlew, Lapwing, Snipe, Golden Eagle, Kestrel, Willow Warble, Skylark, Spotted Flycatcher, Bullfinch, Crossbill.
Other: Otter, Grey Seal. Common Lizard. Grayling, Small Heath, Garden Tiger Moth.
Directions: PA28 6RL; NR 614 143. Open all hours, free. Take B842 from Campbeltown. **Do not** take B843

for **Machrihanish** (q.v.) at Stewarton but continue on B842. 2.25 miles after Stewarton turn R on to a minor road to Homeston. Follow this road for 3.4 miles (much of it through plantation with blocks of differing ages). Then turn R along a forest road and Largiebann farm is 2.3 miles along this road. *There is no vehicular access to the farm and active forest operations are ongoing in the plantations. Do not park on a public road in such a way as to obstruct timber wagons!*

Public transport: None

Visiting: Open all hours, free. No facilities. Working sheep farm. Keep dogs on lead. Largienbann is only 4 miles S of **Machrihanish** (q.v.) but there is no direct track between them that is passable for vehicles. However the farm is traversed by the Kintyre Way walking trail, which ends there. *Given the limitations on vehicular access, walking in along the Kintyre Way may be the best option but note that although the Way exists the council has ceased to maintain it.*

Contact: enquiries@scottishwildlifetrust.org.uk
Return to Stewarton, then as below.

11 MACHRIHANISH SEABIRD/ WILDLIFE OBSERVATORY

Machrihanish Seabird and Wildlife Observatory

Habitats: Marine, rocky shore, upland habitats.

Birds: Summer: Golden Eagle, Peregrine, Storm Petrel, Twite. *Autumn:* Passage seabirds and waders. On-shore gales/squalls often produce inshore movements of Leach's Petrel and other scarce seabirds, inc Balearic Shearwater, Sabine's Gull, Grey Phalarope. *Winter:* Great Northern Diver, Purple Sandpiper, Turnstone, occasional Glaucous and Iceland Gulls.

Other: Grey and Common Seals, Bottlenose Dolphin, Otter, Wild Goat.

Directions: PA28 6PZ; NR 608 209. SW Kintyre, Argyll. Six miles W of Campbeltown on B842, then B843 to Machrihanish. Signposted from village.

Public transport: Bus from Campbeltown, West Coast Motors (01586 552 319).

Visiting: Seawatching hide open most mornings all year round. E-mail or message to be sure if travelling long distance. Outside platforms open 24/7. Parking for three cars. Coach parking. Toilets in nearby village. Wheelchair access. Dogs welcome.

Contact: David Milward, Warden: 07737 985874; machobservatory@yahoo.com
www.machrihanishbirdobservatory.org.uk
facebook: Machrihanish seabird observatory
Return to Lochgilphead and then A816 for Oban and ferry to Mull.

12 FISHNISH

Forestry and Land Scotland

Habitats: Commercial conifer plantation, rocky shore overlooking Sound of Mull.

Birds: Gannet, Oystercatcher, terns, White-tailed Eagle, Crossbill.

Other: Otter, Dolphin, Porpoise.

Directions: PA65 6BA (on A849); NM 661 424 (hide). Vehicle ferries from Oban to Craignure or across the Sound of Mull from Lochaline (in **The Highlands**). If arriving by ferry from Lochaline, park in hide car park (not at pier) 0.25 mile from pier on L. If on A849 from Craignure, take A884 5 miles NW of Craignure for the car ferry to Lochaline. After 0.5 mile take forest road on R for hide.

Public transport: Bus: 95, 495 Craignure to Tobermory stops on A849 at Lochaline ferry turn-off, West Coast Motors (01586 552319; enquiries@westcoastmotors. co.uk). 0.5 mile walk

Visiting: Free car park, open all hours. Toilets at ferry pier. Hide on shore, 20 yards from car park. Two trails with slopes and muddy sections

Contact: 0300 067 6650;
enquiries.west@forestryandland.gov.scot
Continue on A849 to Tobermory

13 LOCH AN TÒRR & QUINISH FOREST

Forestry and Land Scotland

Habitats: Commercial plantation, moorland, streams, freshwater and sea lochs.

Birds: Snipe, Woodcock, Comon Sandpiper, Black Guillemot, White-tailed & Golden Eagles, Hen Harrier, Short & Long-eared Owls. Wood & Willow Warblers, Goldcrest, Stonechat, Tree, Meadow & Rock Pipits, Crossbill, Redpoll, Siskin. Goldeneye in winter.

Other: Red Deer. Fossilized Palms.

Directions: PA75 6GN; NM 434 523 (car park above Dervaig, NM 450 526 (hide overlooking S end of Loch an Tòrr. Take the B8073 from the outskirts of Tobermory for Calgary. After 4.75 miles, just after passing the S end of Loch an Tòrr, there is a forest road on R. The hide is 350 yards up this road, to the W of the S end of the loch. There is a limited amount of space to park at the entrance to the forest road. Continue another 2.25 miles and, as you enter Dervaig turn R (Kilmore Terrace) past Bunkhouse and climb hill to car park for Quinish Forest.

Public transport: Bus: 494 Tobermory to Calgary, stops at Dervaig. West Coast Motors (01586 552319; enquiries@westcoastmotors.co.uk).

Visiting: Open all hours, car park free. No facilities but toilets and refreshments in Dervaig and Tobermory. No waymarked trails but network of forest roads crossing plantation-clad ridge and moorland between Quinish car park above Dervaig to W and loch-side hide to E. The Mingary Burn runs N from Loch an Tòrr down Glen Gorm to the E of the ridge to Loch Mingary.

Contact: 0300 067 6650;
enquiries.west@forestryandland.gov.scot
Since you are in Dervaig, the closest departure point for the

Treshnish Isles would be Tobermory; but this would entail the longest sea trip.

14 TRESHNISH ISLES
National Trust for Scotland
Habitats: Eight uninhabited islands four miles W of Mull. Grassland, sea cliffs. Entire archipelago an SSSI. Sea of Hebrides MPA
Birds: Breeding: Fulmar, Guillemot, Razorbill, Puffin, Shag, Kittiwake, skuas
Other: Basking Shark, Minke Whale; Bottlenose & Common Dolphin.
Directions: No post code, as uninhabited; NM 279 417 (Lunga, largest island). Various tour operators offer trips departing from, inter alia, Fionnphort, Tobermory and Ulva Ferry on Mull, Iona, and Kilchoan and Oban on the mainland.
Public transport: Tour operators include:
Staffa Tours: 07732 912 370 & 07831 885 985; www.staffatours.com.
Turus Mara: 01688 400 242 or 297; info@turusmara.com; www.turusmara.com
Visiting: Islands open all hours but check with tour operators whence and when boat trips are running. NTS does not charge for landing but tour operators charge for trips. No facilities on islands. Largest island Lunga easiest to land on.
Contact: 07523 268 780; 07717 581 405; Treshnishisles@nts.org.uk
Return to Oban to catch the ferry for

15 COLL RESERVE
RSPB
Habitats: Sand dunes, beaches, machair grassland, moorland, farmland.
Birds: Spring: Great Northern Diver offshore. Corncrake arrive in late Apr. Displaying waders, inc Redshank, Lapwing, Snipe. *Summer:* Auks offshore, plus Gannet, shearwaters and terns. *Autumn:* Barnacle & Greenland White-fronted Geese arrive, thrushes on passage. Waders. *Winter:* Long-tailed Duck, divers offshore. Hunting Hen Harrier and Merlin. Twite.
Other: Good for cetaceans and Basking Shark. Otter, 300+ spp machair wildflowers inc rare orchids, Great Yellow Bumblebee, Belted beauty Moth, Short-necked Oil Beetle.
Directions: PA78 6TB; NM 167 563. By ferry from Oban to Coll. Take B8070 W from Arinagour for five miles. Turn R at Arileod. Continue for about 1 mile. Park at end of road. Reception point at Totronald.
Public transport: Ferry from Oban—Caledonian MacBrayne (08705 650 000; www.calmac.co.uk)
Visiting: Open all year. Free. Two car parks, info bothy at Totronald. Corncrake viewing bench. Natural site with unimproved paths not suitable for wheelchairs. Avoid walking through fields and crops. Grazed by livestock,

keep dogs on lead.
Contact: RSPB: 01879 230 301; glasgow@rspb.org.uk

Highlands

(council area, not geomorphological unit)

A range of habitats that are unique in Britain hold such scarce species as Dotterel, Ptarmigan and Snow Buntings, on the high tops, Capercaillie, Crested Tit, and the endemic Scottish Crossbill in the Caledonian pine forests. The boggy Flow Country of Caithness and Sutherland attracts breeding Red and Black-throated Divers, Common Scoter and Greenshank. Handa Island holds important numbers of seabirds.

Bird Atlases/Avifauna
Birds of Caithness,
including The Breeding & Wintering Atlas 2007-2012
P Davey, S Manson, E Maughan, D Omand & J Smith (Caithness SOC, revised ed 2017—was published as a dvd in 2015)
Sutherland Birdlife
Fraser Symonds & Alan Vittery (Independent Publishing Network, 2016)
Birds of Eigg
John Chester (Isle of Eigg Heritage Trust, 2013)
Skye Birds
RL McMillan (Skye-Birds.com, 2nd ed 2009]
The Birds of Badenoch and Strathspey
Roy Dennis (Colin Baxter Photography Ltd, 1995)

Bird Recorders
Caithness
Rob Hughes, St Clair, Auckengill, KW1 4XP: 07714 196 433; xema_sabini@hotmail.co.uk
Highland [covers Ross-Shire, Inverness-shire, Sutherland, Badenoch and Strathspey, Lochaber, Lochalsh and Skye but not Caithness]
John Poyner, 6 Mackenzie Crescent, Nethybridge, Highland PH25 3DU: 01479 821 357; highlandrecorder@yahoo.com

Bird Reports
Caithness Bird Report (1983-97), no longer published but latest report can be downloaded from: www.the-soc.org.uk/bird-recording/local-recorders-network/areas/caithness
Highland Bird Report (1995-), available online: www.highlandbirds.scot/highland-bird-report.html Hard copies of various editions between 2003 and 2023 can be purchased from Carol Miller: carol.miller1230@outlook.com

BTO Regional Representatives
Caithness
Donald Omand:
Inverness (East and Speyside),
Inverness (West)
Hugh Insley
Ross-shire
Simon Cohen
Rum, Eigg, Canna and Muck
Bob Swann
Skye
Jonathan Jones
Sutherland
Iain Plumtree
Wetland Bird Survey (WeBS)
Local Organizers: webs@bto.org
Badenoch and Strathspey
Vacant
Caithness
Sinclair Manson
Lochaber
Calum and Kirstie Ross
Skye
Jonathan Jones
Sutherland (excl. Moray Basin)
Vacant
West Inverness and Wester Ross
Andy Douse

Clubs
East Sutherland Bird Group (1976; 120)
Fraser Symonds, Old Schoolhouse, Balvraid, Dornoch, Sutherland IV25 3JB: 01408 633 922;
esbirdgroup@gmail.com
Meetings: 7:30pm, last Monday of the month (Oct/Nov, Jan-Mar). Golspie Community Centre, Back Rd, Golspie, Highland KW10 6TL
SOC Caithness Branch (n/a; 40)
Nina O'Hanlon: 07810 300 392;
caithnesssecretary@the-soc.org.uk;
www.the-soc.org.uk/local-branches/caithness
Meetings: 7:30pm, 1st Wednesday of the month (Sep-Apr). Castletown Heritage Centre, Harbour Road, Castletown, Caithness KW14 8TG. Monthly online talks also held. Contact/see website for details.
SOC Highland Branch (1955; 280)
Mary Galloway: 07598 320 978;
highlandsecretary@the-soc.org.uk;
www.the-soc.org.uk/local-branches/highland
www.highlandbirds.scot
Meetings: 7:30pm, 1st or 2nd Tuesday of the month (Sep-Apr). Culloden Library, Keppoch Road, Culloden, IV2 7LL. Monthly online talks also held. Contact/see website for details.

Ringing Groups/Bird Observatory
Canna RG
Highland RG

RSPB Local Group
None.

Scottish Wildlife Trust Regional Networks
North of Scotland
Chair: Dan Puplett: swtnosgroup@gmail.com

Forest and Land Scotland Regional Office
for Highlands S of Knoydart
0330 067 6650;
enquiries.west@forestryand land.gov.scot
for all other parts of Highlands
0330 067 6100;
enqiuries.north@forestryandland.gov.scot

If you decided to head for The Highlands rather than dallying in Argyll, take the A82 at Tyndrum

1 GLEN COE NNR
National Trust for Scotland
Habitats: 13,900 acres of mountain (8 Munros), moorland, woodland, river and loch.
Birds: Ptarmigan, Snow Bunting. Woodcock, Snipe Common Sandpiper, Golden Eagle, Sparrowhawk, Tawny Owls, Peregrine Falcon, Wood Warbler, Dipper, Grey Wagtail, Redpoll, Siskin. *Winter:* Whooper Swan
Other: Mountain Hare, Red Deer.
Directions: PH49 4HX NN 112 575 Visitor Centre immediately off A82, which runs length of Glen Coe. Traffic-free cycle paths between Oban, Glencoe village, NNR Visitor Centre
Public transport: Buses run between Kinlochleven and Fort William via Glencoe, 1.25 miles to the W of the NNR; Bus twice/day Oban to Ballachulish; 405 bus from Oban connects with 144 buss to Glencoe at Duror on schoolday mornings. Long distance buses runs along the A82 through the NNR between Glasgow and Fort William. Train stations at Oban, Fort William, Crianlarich/ Bridge of Orchy and bus service via Glencoe between them.
Visiting: NNR open all hours, free, charge for car park. NTS members free. Visitor Centre & Cafe open 10am-4pm, closed 24-26 Dec & 1 Jan. In summer Visitor Centrer 9:30am-5pm. Step-free access to all areas. Dogs welcome. The Visitor Centre is at the lower, W end of the Glen, in a wooded area just before the village of Glencoe. Toilets inc accessible. Short walks with compacted surfaces aroiund Centre. Further car parks along the A82 in or on the edge of the NNR: NN 128 564; NN 168 569; NN 188 562; NN 213 560; NN 221 563 and at Dalness, on the minor road that

Highlands

6	Beinn Eighe and Loch Maree Isles
8	Ben Mor Coigach
13	Broubster Leans
4	Canna and Sanday
10	Cape Wrath
19	Craigellachie
16	Corrimony
12	Dunnet Head
11	Forsinard Flows
17	Glen Affric
2	Glenborrodale
1	Glen Coe
9	Handa
20	Insh Marshes
7	Inverbroom
3	Isle of Rum
21	Loch Garten and Abernethy Forest
18	Loch Ruthven
14	Nigg Bay
5	Sconser, Strathaird and Torrin
15	Udale Bay

branches SW off the A82 to run alongside River Etive on the S edge of the NNR: NN 166 511. Most of the NNR lies to the S of the A82, although it does includes the N slopes of the Glen up to the ridge line between Sron Garbh and Sgor nam Fiannaidh. 37 miles of paths around reserve.
Contact: NTS: 01855 811307; glencoe@nts.org.uk
Contnue on A82 to Fort William.

2 GLENBORRODALE
RSPB
Habitats: Scottish rainforest upland, coastal (Loch Sunart).
Birds: All year: common woodland spp, Eider, Raven. Occasional Golden & White-tailed Eagles, Buzzard and Merlin. *Spring/summer:* Cuckoo, Tree Pipit, Skylark, Whinchat, Redstart, Spotted Flycatcher, Wood, Willow, Garden & Grasshopper Warblers, Blackcap. *Winter:* Winter thrushes, Woodcock, Snipe.
Other: Butterflies inc Chequered Skipper, Pearl-bordered and other Fritillaries, Scotch Argus. Dragonflies

inc Highland Darter and Northern Emerald. Red & Roe Deer, Grey and Common Seals, Otter, Pine Marten. Lichen and Bryophyte assemblages.
Directions: PH36 4JP. NM 595 615. From Fort William take A830 toward Mallaig, turn L on to A861 (after 10 miles or 22.5 miles). From either route (some narrow roads) take B8007 at Salen to Glenborrodale—car park just W of village.
Public transport: None.
Visiting: Open all hours. Small car park, nature trails, guided walks.
Contact: RSPB: glenborrodale@rspb.org.uk
Or continue on A830 to Mallaig (Ferry Terminal: PH41 4QD).

3 ISLE OF RUM NNR
NatureScot
Habitats: Island—wild/rugged dominated by mountains. Blanket bog, grassland, woodland, wet and dry heath, scree and rocky slopes.
Birds: Breeding: Golden & White-tailed Eagles, Merlin, Hen Harrier, Peregrine Falcon, Golden Plover, Twite. Red-throated Diver, 70,000 pairs Manx Shearwater and small number of other seabirds inc Guillemot, Razorbill,

Fulmar, Kittiwake.

Other: Red Deer, Wild Goat. 2,000+ spp invertebrates inc 11spp dragonfly, 19 spp butterfly.

Directions: PH43 4RR; NM 360 976.

Public transport: Ferry from Mallaig to Rum—Caledonian MacBrayne (0800 066 5000; www.calmac.co.uk). No cars permitted on island—parking for ferry passengers in Mallaig.

Visiting: NS owns and manages most of island. Isle of Rum Community Trust owns some property and land in and around village at Kinloch. Access all hours. Visitor centre on lower shore road near old pier, open daily in summer. Toilets at village campsite (10 mins from ferry terminal). Otter hide one mile through woods to S of main pier.

Contact: NS: 0131 314 4181; nnr@nature.scot

4 CANNA & SANDAY

National Trust for Scotland

Habitats: Canna (2,800 acres) and Sanday (450 acres), whhich are linked by causeway, form the Small Isles archipelago in the Inner Hebrides. Working farms, sea cliffs. SSSI, SPA.

Birds: Breeding: Kittiwake, Fulmar, Kittiwake Razorbill, Puffin, Possible Black Guillemot. Slight recovery in Manx Shearwater colony since rat eradication. Great Skua. Small flocks of various waders and sea duck. White-tailed & Golden Eagles.

Other: Cetaceans.

Directions: PH44 4RS; NG 278 050

Public transport: Ferry from Mallaig to Canna (19 miles) —Caledonian MacBrayne (0800 066 5000; www. calmac.co.uk). No cars permitted on island—parking for ferry passengers in Mallaig.

Visiting: Open all hours, free. Accommodation available on island, pre-booking advisable. Community shop (limited range), cafe. Grazing livestock, dogs under close control.

Contact: 01463 732 621

Return to A82, head N and then take A87 to Kyle of Lochalsh for bridge to Skye.

Alternatively, there is a ferry service between Mallaig and Armadale on the Sleat peninsula of southern Skye.

5 SCONSER, STRATHAIRD AND TORRIN

John Muir Trust

Habitats: Three adjacent estates stretching from the N to the S coasts of Skye, totalling 29,640 acres and encompassing coast, crofting land, blanket bog, woodland and mountains, including most of the Red Cuillins, rising to Blà Bheinn (3,077 ft)

Birds: Breeding: Golden & White-tailed Eagles, Scottish Crossbill, Ptarmigan, Red Grouse, Siskin. *Summer:* Black & Red-throated Divers, Golden Plover, Dipper, Red-wing, Snow Bunting.

Other: Programme of felling commercial Sitka plan-

tations and replacing with native broadleaf woodland (Aspen, Hazel, Ash). Red Deer.

Directions & Visiting: The A87 runs from the Skye Bridge at Kyle of Lochalsh to Portree along the N coasts of the **Sconser** and **Torrin** estates. On the A87, from E to W, there are car parks at: NG 534 267 by the waterfalls at the head of Loch Ainort. NG 532 280 by the waterfalls on the Allt Mhic Mhoirein. IV48 8TD; NG 523 321 Sconser Pier (Caledonian MacBrayne vehicle ferry to Raasay). IV47 8SW; NG 485 298, Sligachan Hotel. For **Strathaird**, to the S, take the B8083 at Broadford. After 5 miles pass through Torrin, round the head of Loch Slapin, and then S to the car park at NG 562 216 at the start of the footpath up Blà Bheinn. Continue S on the B8083 to the car park past Strathaird House at NG 545 173. Paths from this car park lead up to the S ridge of Blà Bheinn, N to Sligachan or W past Loch Coruisk to the Black Cuillins. Continuing S, the road ends at the car park at Elgol at NG 518 136. A path runs from Elgol up the W side of the Strathaird peninsula alongside Loch Scavaig. There is a total of over 40 miles of paths across the three estates.

Public transport: Bus: 52 Portree-Broadford stops at Sligochan and Sconser Stagecoach; 55 Broadford-Elgol (Mon-Fr) stops in Torrin and near Strataird House, Stagecoach.

Contact: 01796 470 080.

Return to Kyle of Lochalsh and take A87 E. After 5 miles head N on A890 (single-track sections). Stay on it to Achnasheen. Turn L on to A832 for Kinlochewe

6 BEINN EIGHE AND
LOCH MAREE ISLANDS NNR

NatureScot

Habitats: Caledonian forest, moorland, mountain tops, freshwater loch shore.

Birds: All year: Golden & White-tailed Eagles, Scottish Crossbill, Ptarmigan, Red Grouse, Siskin. *Summer:* Black & Red-throated Divers, Golden Plover, Dipper, Red-wing, Snow Bunting.

Other: Wide range of dragonflies inc Northern Emerald, Golden-ringed and Common Hawker. Red Deer, Pine Marten, Mountain Hare.

Directions: NH 019 630; IV22 2PD. Complex mountain massif. Visitor centre two miles NW of village of Kinlochewe, Wester Ross, 50 miles from Inverness and 20 miles from Gairloch on A832.

Public transport: Bus—very limited, Inverness to Kinlochewe.

Visiting: Open all hours. Visitor centre open 10am-5pm Mar-Oct (01445 760 258). Toilets. Two woodland trails from visitor centre. From shore of Loch Maree (continue N on A832 to Coille na Glas-Leitir)—self-guided woodland walk and mountain trail—leaflets from visitor centre.

Contact: NS: 01463 701 660; nnr@nature.scot

Head W on the A832. It's a longer route than heading E but it will take you through...

7 INVERBROOM

Scottish Wildlife Trust

Habitats: 18,816 acres of peatland, semi-natural ancient woodland, lochs, lochans, farmland. Former sporting estate purchased by the Trust in 2025.

Birds and Other: Estate only just taken in to Trust ownership, awaiting news of plans for habitat restoration and changes in management regime. Look out for these in **2027 Yearbook**.

Directions: From the A835 take the A832 for Corrieshalloch Gorge. Road runs SW for 3 miles along edge of reserve before turning NW through centre of reserve.

Public transport: Bus: 961 (infrequent, weekdays only, must be booked in advance) Inverness to Ullapool stops near A832/A835 junction, Scottish Citylink (www.citylink.co.uk).

Visiting: The Lochivraon bothy (NH 117 734) at the W end of Loch a' Braoin is currently closed for safety reasons.

Contact: swtnosgroup@gmail.com

When A832 joins A835, turn L for Ullapool. Road is now running along E edge of the Inverbroom estate.

*At Ullapool, rather than continuing on the A835, you can take the ferry for Stornoway (**Outer Hebrides**).*

8 BEN MOR COIGACH

Scottish Wildlife Trust

Habitats: 15,000 acres, high peaks (Ben Mor 2,438 ft), moor, marsh, freshwater lochs, areas of open woodland, croftland, coast.

Birds: Eider, Shag, Redpoll. *Spring/summer:* Red & Black-throated Divers, Cuckoo, Teal, Lapwing, Ringed Plover, Black Guillemot, Whinchat, Stonechat, Wheatear. *Winter:* Barnacle Geese,

Other: Pine Marten, Otter, Water Vole, Red Deer. Common Juniper, Cross-leaved Heath, Round-leaved Sundew.

Directions: IV26 2YG; NC 027 082 (Summer Isles Hotel, Achiltibuie). Take the A835 N from Ullapool. Turn on to minor road for Achiltibuie at Drumrunie 9.5 miles N of Ullapool. The reserves starts at the E end of Loch Lurgainn. However, the road itself runs outside the reserve along the N shores of Lochs Lurgainn and Osgaig (the reserve boundary runs along the middle of Lurgainn and the E shore of Osgaig) before curving round, entering the reserve, which lies between Loch Lurgainn and the mouth of Loch Broom, and then running SE to Achiltibuie.

Public transport: Bus: 811 Ullapool-Achiltibuie, infrequent, not weekends. D&E Coaches (www.decoaches.co.uk). 809 Ullapool-Strathcanaird & Drumrunie, infrequent, 7 days a week. Rapsons Highland (www.georger-

apsontravel.com).

Visiting: Open all hours, free. Hotel at Achiltibue. 7 mile Postman's Path along coast and S slopes of Coigach massif between Strathcanaird on A835 and Coulnacraig or Achduart (which is where the minor road to Achiltibuie terminates). Challenging in good weather; dangerous in bad weather.

Contact: swtnosgroup@gmail.com

Since you've made it to Achiltibuie...

Just before you reach Achiltibuie a minor road runs NW to Polbain and Altandhu (pub). Between Polbain and Altandhu a road on L runs down to Dorney Bay, whence, at low tide it is possible to walk across to the machair-covered (might there be Corncrake?) **Isle Ristol**, the innermost of the Summer Isles. Further out, at the mouth of Loch Broom and passed by ferries to the **Outer Hebrides**, lies **Priest Island** (RSPB), with a large Storm Petrel colony

Continue on A835, A837 and then A894.

9 HANDA

Scourie Estate/Scottish Wildlife Trust

Habitats: Island—sea cliffs, blanket bog and heath, small sandy beaches, coastal grassland.

Birds: Spring/summer: 100,000 seabirds: largest Razorbill and second largest Guillemot colony in Britain. Nationally important for Kittiwake, Arctic & Great Skuas. Puffin, Shag, Fulmar, Arctic Terns; Common & Sandwich Terns visit.

Directions: IV27 4SS; NC 164 488 (Tarbet). Island accessible by boat from Tarbet, near Scourie—follow A835/A894 N from Ullapool for 40 miles. Turn L down single track road, another three miles to Tarbet.

Public transport: Post bus (hail & ride) 806 (Mon-Fri) Lairg to Durness via Scourie. No transport between Scourie and Tarbet (three miles). The Far North Bus (07782 110 007). Train—Inverness to Lairg connects with service.

Visiting: Open Apr-Aug, no Sun sailings (and subject to weather). Ferry runs 9:30am-4:45pm (last boat to island at 2pm)—part of ferry ticket price goes to SWT. Visitors given introductory talk and leaflet with map on arrival. Three mile circular path, visitor shelter, compost toilet. Not suitable for disabled due to uneven terrain. No dogs.

Contact: Handa Ranger (Apr-Aug): 07920 468 572; handaranger@scottishwildlifetrust.org.uk; Ferry operator: Roger Tebay: 07780 967 800; info@handa-ferry.com

Continue on A894 and then A838 (mainly single track).

10 CAPE WRATH

Ministry of Defence/Ozone Cafe/Cape Wrath Mini Bus

The name Wrath is not a reference to exploding bombs or Atlantic storms. It derives from an Old Norse word meaning 'turning point'.

Habitats: Sea Cliffs, wet moorland. freshwater lochs. SSSI & SPA

Birds: Summering Great Northern, breeding Red & Black-throated Divers. Puffin, Guillemot, Black Guillemot, Razorbill, Cormorant, Shag, Great & Arctic Skuas, Greenshank, Dunlin, Golden Plover, Ringed Plover, Golden & White-tailed Eagles, Osprey. And don't forget Spotted Flycatcher, Redpoll.

Other: Otter, cetaceans.

Directions: IV27 4QF; NC 378 662, East Keoldale Pier. 1.75 miles SE of Durness, take the minor road to the W for Keoldale from the A838 Laxford Bridge-Durness road.

Public transport: Bus: 805 Inverness-Durness (The Durness Bus), infrequent.

Visiting: Free car park at East Keoldale Pier, passenger ferry across Kyle of Durness (charge), then 11 mile walk to Cape Wrath or mini bus (charge). The ferry service (May-Sep) across the Kyle is subject to weather and tidal conditions. Most of the land W of the Kyle of Durness and N of Sandwood Bay on the W coast is owned by the Ministry of Defence and exercises are conducted with live ammunition. When exercises are in progress, the mini van service to Cape Wrath is suspended and walking through the marked Danger Area is prohibited. The Ozone Cafe in the lighthouse at Cape Wrath is open 24/7, 365 days a year.

Alternatively, you can walk in across the firing range from the S, although there is no established path N of Sandwood Bay. Leave the A838 at Riconich and take the B801 for Kinlochbervie. Just before Kinlochbervie take a minor road on the R for Oldshoremore (I have swum amidst a raft of Red-hroated Divers fishing off the beach at Oldshoremore) and then on to Blairmore. Park in the John Muir Trust car park (IV27 4RU, NC194 601, toilets, charge) and take the path (surfaced for much of the way) to Sandwood Bay (4 miles). It is then a further 6 miles, as the Hoodie flies, to Cape Wrath; BUT there are several rivers to cross, hills to climb or go round, much of the terrain is boggy and about half the route lies within the firing area. You have been warned.

Contact: Cape Wrath Mini Bus: 07534 591 124; info@visitcapewrath.com; www.visitcapewrath.com Cafe: 01971 511 314

Continue E on A838, then A836 after Tongue. At Melvich take A837 S.

11 FORSINARD FLOWS
RSPB

Habitats: Blanket bog, upland hill farm. The RSPB's largest reserve at 52,000 acres.

Birds: All year: Red Grouse, Golden Eagle, Raven and Buzzard. *May-Jul:* Join a guided walk for best chance of Red-throated Diver, Golden Plover, Greenshank, Dunlin, Hen Harrier, Merlin, Short-eared Owl, Dipper.

Other: Red Deer, Otter, Water Vole, Azure Hawker dragonfly, Emperor Moth, bog plants inc sundews.

Directions: KW13 6YT; NC 891 425. 30 miles SW of Thurso on A897. From S turn off A9 at Helmsdale (24 miles) or from N coast road turn off A836, two miles E of Melvich (14 miles).

Public transport: Train—Forsinard station, between Inverness and Thurso.

Visiting: Open all hours. Contact reserve office during breeding season (mid-Apr/end-Jul) and during the deer stalking season (Jul-Feb 15) for advice; and to enquire about guided walks for best chance of seeing the reserve's specialities. Visitor centre situated in Forsinard station open daily 9am-5pm, Apr-Oct. Wheelchair access to centre and toilet. Two self-guided trails open all year. Boardwalk access to viewpoint on Dubh Lochan Trail (one mile walk). Forsinain Trail starts at roadside car park four mile N of Forsinard (four mile walk). Stay on trails. Dogs under control at all times.

Contact: RSPB: 01641 571 225; forsinard@rspb.org.uk *Return to A836 and continue E to Thurso. At Thurso (Scrabster), take the ferry for Stromness, Orkney, or continue on A836 for*

12 DUNNET HEAD
RSPB

Habitats: Northernmost headland on mainland Britain. Cliffs, coastal grassland, heath. Views over Pentland Firth to the Orkneys. SSSI, SPA.

Birds: Spring/summer: Puffin, Razorbill, Guillemot, Fulmar, Kittiwake, Great & Arctic Skuas. Wheatear, Twite. Passage passerines.

Other: Spring Squill, Thrift, Roseroot. Cetaceans in Pentland Firth.

Directions: KW14 8XS; ND 202 766. At Dunnet, take B855 N from A836 for 4.5 miles to Brough and on to Dunnet Head car park.

Public transport: Bus: 80 Thurso-John o Groats stops in Brough (3 mile walk, not Sun), Stagecoach North Scotland. Train—Thurso.

Visiting: Open all hours, free. Trail to clifftop viewpoint is wheelchair accessible. No toilets. Keep dogs under close control, especially during breeding season for ground-nesting birds. Clean up mess.

Contact: RSPB: 01463 715 000; nsro@rspb.org.uk *Or take B874 and head SW for*

13 BROUBSTER LEANS
RSPB

Habitats: 740 acre floodplain of Forss Water: wet grassland, pools, channels, grazed rush pasture.

Birds: Red & Black-throated Divers, Common Scoter, Greenshank, Curlew, Dunlin Common Sandpiper, Golden Plover, Lapwing, Hen Harrier, Short-eared Owl, Twite. *Winter:* Whooper Swan, Greenland White-fronted Goose.

Highlands

Other: Great Yellow Bumblebee.
Directions: KW14 7RB; ND 032 605. head SW on B874 from Thurso for c.7 miles. At Shebster take minor road due S for c.2.5 miles.
Public transport: Bus: 73 Thurso-Shebster (Mon-Sat). Stagecoach North Scotland.
Visiting: Open all hours, free. Roadside car park has 3 spaces. No facilities
Contact: RSPB: 01463 715 000; nsro@rspb.org.uk
Return to Thurso and head S on A9 and two reserves on either side of the Cromarty Firth.

14 NIGG BAY
RSPB
Habitats: Extensive tidal mudflats and saltmarsh.
Birds: Winter: Waders inc Oystercatcher, Redshank, Dunlin, Knot, Bar-tailed Godwit, sometimes Lapwing, Golden Plover. Ducks inc. Wigeon, Shelduck, 100+ Pintail.
Other:
Directions: IV191PG; NH 806 731 reserve car park. At Nigg roundabout on A9 exit on to B9175. Reserve car park is on R after 3.75 miles.
Public transport: Bus: 25X Inverness-Tain passes reserve car park. Stagecoach. Train—Fearn, 4.5 miles away.
Visiting: Open all hours, free. Car park has 4 spaces, 1 Blue Badge, 2.1 m height barrier. Flat 150m path to single wheelchair-accessible (ramp, 2 wheelchair bays) hide overlooking bay. No toilets. Keep dogs under control, on a lead during breeding season, clear up mess.
Contact: RSPB: 01463 715 000; nsro@rspb.org.uk
In summer, continue S along B9175 to Nigg Ferry, where there is a half-hourly vehicle ferry across the Firth to Cromarty. After crossing, taking the B9163 W along the S shore of the Cromarty Firth to Jemimaville and **Udale Bay** *(q.v.). When ferry not running, continue on A9, cross over firth on bridge. Take minor road on L immediately after crossing bridge and head NE along shore.*

15 UDALE BAY
RSPB
Habitats: Wet, cattle-grazed grassland, saltmarsh, tidal mudflat.
Birds: All year: Curlew, Redshank, Lapwing, Oystercatcher. *Summer:* Common Tern, Shelduck. *Autumn/winter:* Pink-footed & Greylag Geese, Wigeon, Teal, Red-breasted Merganser, Slavonian Grebe, Eider. A large flock of Scaup regularly present. Dunlin, Knot, Bar-tailed Godwit.
Other: Eelgrass.
Directions: IV7 8LU; NH 708 661 (bird screen/RSPB car park). Take B9169 for Culbokie off the A9 2 miles S of Cromarty Bridge. After Culbokie the B9169 joins the B9163. Follow this road to Balblair. At Balblair you can take a minor road on L for the Highland Council car park at Newhall Point (NH 703 671) or turn S. After

0.5 mile there is a L turn at Kirkmichael along a minor road that leads to an RSPB parking area and bird screen at NH 708 661). A further 0.5 mile the B9163 turns sharp L (do not carry straight on on the B9160) and then after another 0.5 mile you reach the Highland Council lay-by and bird hide at (NH 712 651). Continue E through Jemimaville and after 0.5 mile there is a further Highland Council car park at Ivy Cottage at NH 728 653.
Continue along the B9163 to Cromarty and the Nigg Ferry for **Nigg Bay** (q.v.).
Public transport: Bus: 21C, 26, 121,126, 425 variously from Inverness and Cromarty all stop in Jemimaville
Visiting: Open all hours, free, no facilities. See the *Directions* section for the locations of the car parks. The car parks at Newhall Point and Ivy Cottage offer views of the Cromarty Firth (terns, ducks), those at the bird screen and hide offer views over the tidal mudflats (waders around high tide). Keep dogs under control, on a lead during breeding season, clear up mess.
Contact: RSPB: 01463 715 000; nsro@rspb.org.uk
Continue on A9 to Inverness, then A82 to Drumnadrochit, whence the A831.

16 CORRIMONY
RSPB
Habitats: 3,782 acres, Caledonian forest, moorland, blanket bog.
Birds: Spring/summer: Red-throated Diver, Goosander. Greenshank, Black & Red Grouse, Tree Pipit, Whinchat, Crested Tit, Scottish Crossbill, occasional Golden Eagle and Osprey. *Autumn/Winter:* Whooper Swan, Pink-footed Goose, Woodcock.
Other: Red Deer, Pine Marten, many orchids in Jul.
Directions: IV63 6TW (Corrimony village); NH 384 303 (car park). Lies 22 miles SW of Inverness between Cannich and Glen Urquhart, off A 831. Park in Corrimony Cairns car park.
Public transport: Bus: 17 (not Sun) from Inverness to Cannich stops 1.5 miles from reserve (request stop). Stagecoach Highlands.
Visiting: Open all hours. Waymarked trail (8.5 miles) passes through farm, suitable for wheelchairs but unimproved paths may not be suitable. Leave gates as you find them.
Contact: RSPB: 01463 715 000; nsro@rspb.org.uk
Continue along the A831 for.

17 GLEN AFFRIC NNR
Forestry & Land Scotland
Habitats: Ancient Caledonian, Pine Oak & Hazel forest (third largest remnant of Caledonian forest), commercial plantations, lochs, moor. Totalling 43,225 acres.
Birds: Red & Black-throated Divers, Red & Black Grouse, Capercaillie, Ptarmigan, Golden Plover, Dotterel, Greenshank, Osprey, Hen Harrier, Golden Eagle.

Merlin, Crested Tit, Wood Warbler, Common & Scottish Crossbills.

Other: Wildcat, Red Deer.

Directions: IV4 7LN; NH 338 318, Cannich, where there is parking, a camp site, pub and toilets; downstream from Loch Beinn a' Mheadhoin on the River Glass and 10 miles as the Hoodie flies from the River Affric car park at the head of the Loch. Cannich is on the A831, 12 miles W of Drumnadrochit (on A82 on W side of Loch Ness) and *c.*17 miles SW of Beauly, which is W of Inverness.

Forests:

Dog Falls: NH 283 283 car park (charge), toilets (all year). Take minor road (much of it single track) SW from Cannich along the Rivers Glass and Affric (not the more northerly minor road along the River Cannich) to Fasnakyle and beyond for 4.5 miles. Scots Pine, Birch and Oak wood. Waterfalls. 3 marked trails, all strenuous. Carry on along the minor road to the dam (Loch Beinn a' Mheadhoin is a natural loch that has been dammed to enlarge it) and then through forest along the N shore to.

Loch Beinn a' Mheadhoin: Short forest road on L leads to free car park and picnic area at NH 247 262 beside the Loch amidst Scots Pine and Birch. No toilets. Artificial floating reed-fringed floating islands for breeding Black-throated Divers.

There is a second car park (charge) at NH 217 243 just E of the Chisholm Bridge in the N side of the Loch. This is the starting point for trails up the mountains to the N.

River Affric: Car park (charge) and toilets (Apr-Oct) at NH 201 233 on the isthmus between Loch Beinn a' Mheodhoin and Loch Affric, which are linked by the River Affric. The minor road ends here and only estate roads go further W. Two short marked trails with rough sections from this car park and also an 11 mile trail around Loch Affric to the W of the car park

Plodda Falls: IV4 7LY (on route, not at); NH 279 238 free car park. Leave A831 at sharp R bend just before bridge over River Affric on E edge of Cannich and take minor road on L for Tomich. Car park is *c.*6.5 miles along this road, which becomes a forest road after Tomich. Waterfall and mature Douglas Fir and other N American species planted in 19C.

Public transport: Bus: 17 Inverness-Drumnadrochit-Cannich-Tomich Hotel (not Sun), Stagecoach.

Contact: 0300 067 6100; enquiries.north@forestryandland.gov.scot

To the W of the Foresty & Land Scotland forests in Glen Affric, at the upper end of the Glen, the National Trust for Scotland owns the 9,140 acre West Affric estate and, further W again, the Kintail and Glomach estates. The old drove road from Skye to Dingwall crosses the West Affric estate, where Birch and Rowan are re-establishing themselves.

Several private estate also hold blocks of land in Glen Affric. Return to Drumnadrochit via the A831 and then Inverness on the A82. Thence head S on the A9.

18 LOCH RUTHVEN

RSPB

Habitats: Freshwater, sedge-fringed loch, Birch wood.

Birds: Common woodland spp, breeding Red-throated Diver, Slavonian Grebe. Management of reserves focuses on Slavonian Grebe (Schedule 1), observe directions on site.

Other:

Directions: IV2 6UA; NH 638 281. Take the B851 from the A9 S of Inverness. At East Croachy, after 8 miles, turn R on to minor road. Reserve car park is 1 mile on L.

Public transport: Bus: 14 to East Croachy (infrequent). 1 mile to reserve. D&E Coaches (01463 222 444).

Visiting: Car park (8 places) open 8am-8pm, free. No cycle racks or toilets. 500 yards trail from car park to hide and viewing screen, narrow in places, sections of boardwalk, Keeps dogs under close control. Clean up mess.

Contact: RSPB: 01463 715 000; nsro@rspb.org.uk
Return to the A9.

19 CRAIGELLACHIE

NatureScot

Habitats: Upland Birch woodland with Hazel, Rowan and other deciduous trees, some Pine; open glades, lochans, ascending to rocky crags. Some heath on higher ground.

Birds: Very occasional Red & Black Grouse, Peregrine Falcon (present but no longer nesting). Common woodland spp, Chiffchaff, Willow & Wood Warbler Spotted & Pied Flycatchers, Redstart, Tree Pipit. Little Grebe on lochans, occasional Goldeneye in winter.

Other: Red & Roe Deer. Mountain Hare on higher ground. Highland Darter, Golden-ringed Dragonfly, Rannoch Sprawler and Kentish Glory (moths).

Directions: PH22 1PR; NH 893 119 (Youth Hostel). Immediately to W of A9 at S end of Aviemore on the other side of the road from the town. Park in Youth Hostel car park (signed).

Public transport: Bus: Heather Hopper service throughout Cairngorms. Nearest stop Aviemore station. Train—Aviemore, 0.6 mile walk.

Visiting: Open all hours, free. Facilities in Aviemore. From car park take underpass beneath A9 to reserve and start point of four trails. These become steeper, and can be muddy, as you ascend to viewpoint on first ridge. Highest point, 1,752 ft, further W. Keep dogs under close control.

Contact: Ian Sargent: 01463 725 203; nnr@nature.scot
Continue S on A9.

20 INSH MARSHES

RSPB

Habitats: 2,500 acre, marsh, woodland, river, open water.

Birds: Spring/summer: Osprey, Waders (inc Lapwing, Snipe, Curlew, Redshank), wildfowl (inc Goldeneye and Wigeon), Wood Warbler, Redstart, Tree Pipit. *Winter:* Hen Harrier, Whooper Swan, Greylag Goose, Teal, Wigeon, other wildfowl.

Other: Roe Deer. Black Darter dragonfly and Northern Brown Argus butterfly along Invertromie trail. Five spp orchid in Tromie Meadow.

Directions: PH21 1NTS; NN 775 998. In Spey Valley. From A9 take exit to Kingussie. Follow B970 S from village and then beyond Ruthven Barracks. Entrance to reserve is 0.6 mile further on.

Public transport: Bus: 32 Newtownmore to Carrbridge stops at Kingussie. Stagecoach Highlands. Train—Kingussie. Both 1 mile.

Visiting: Open all hours. Car park, coach parking. Disabled access to unmanned information viewpoint. Two hides, three trails.

Contact: RSPB: 01540 661 518; insh@rspb.org.uk

Head back N up the A9 and then, after Aviemore, turn R on to A95. After 3.5 miles turn R on to minor road for Boat of Garten.

21 LOCH GARTEN AND ABERNETHY FOREST

RSPB

Habitats: Loch Garten is the site of the Osprey's return to the UK as a breeding bird in 1954. Caledonian pine forest, moorland, extending S to top of the Cairngorm massif.

Birds: Spring/summer: Ospreys nesting from Apr-Aug, Crested Tit, Redstart, Spotted Flycatcher, Tree Pipit, 3 Crossbill spp, Great Spotted Woodpecker, Siskin from Nature Centre. On lochs—Wigeon, Goldeneye and Common Sandpiper. *Autumn/winter:* Greylag and Pink-footed Geese roost on lochs, Whooper Swan, various duck spp, Fieldfare and Redwing. Wider Abernethy reserve: Golden & White-tailed Eagles, Goshawk, Capercaillie Black & Red Grouse, Ptarmigan, Dotterel, Snow Bunting.

Other: Red Squirrel, Red & Roe Deer, Otter, Pine Marten. Species typical of Caledonian pine woods inc Tooth fungi on track to Nature Centre; Creeping Lady's Tresses, Twinflower, Crowberry, Common Cow-wheat; Narrow-headed Wood Ant, Shining Guest Ant; bryophytes and lichens.

Directions: PH25 3HA; NH 978 183. 2.5 miles from Boat of Garten, eight miles from Aviemore. Off B970, follow 'RSPB Loch Garten Centre' road signs (Centre only open Apr-Oct).

Public transport: Bus: 34, Aviemore to Grantown on Spey, nearest stop is on B970 (ask for Raebreck junc-

tion)—from here dedicated footpath leads to Nature Centre (1.6 miles). Stagecoach Highland.

Visiting: Nature Centre (overlooking Osprey nest) open daily 10am-5pm, last entry 4:30pm, Apr-Aug; 10:30am-3:30pm, last entry 3pm Sep-Oct; closed Nov-Mar. Entrance fee, RSPB members free. Optics, CCTV live feeds from various cameras, displays, talks and activities, light refreshments. Accessible toilets at Nature Centre and toilets at Loch Garten (all open when Nature Centre open). Changing Places accessible toilet at Loch Garten car park accessed with RADAR key. Disabled access. Assistance dogs only. On reserve: multiple trails open all year, some with benches. Dogs on leads in forest (Apr-Aug) and on mountain tops (May-15 Aug).

Contact: RSPB: 01479 821 409 (Reserve);01479 831 476 (Nature Centre); abernethy@rspb.org.uk

The S margin of the Abernethy Forest NNR abuts Mar Lodge NNR in North East Scotland.

Outer Hebrides

[na h-Eileanan Siar]

The stronghold of the Corncrake in Britain... they can usually be heard easily enough but are much harder to see! May sees a strong passage of Long-tailed and Pomarine Skuas past RSPB Balranald. Black Guillemot, Hen Harrier, Short-eared Owl, Twite and passage waders provide added interest.

Bird Recorder

Vacant

recorder@outerhebridesbirds.org.uk;
www.outerhebridesbirds.org.uk

Bird Report

Outer Hebrides Bird Report (1997-), from Outer Hebrides Birds—contact Bird Recorder—see above.

BTO Regional Representatives

Benbecula and The Uists
Stephen Willis
Lewis and Harris
Emma Niederberger
Wetland Bird Survey (WeBS)
Local Organizer: webs@bto.org
Lewis and Harris, Benbecula and The Uists
Both vacant

Ringing Group/Bird Observatory

Shiants Auk RG

Outer Hebrides

RSPB Local Group
No Groups

Scottish Wildlife Trust Regional Networks
None

Forest and Land Scotland Regional Office
0330 067 6100;
enqiuries.north@forestryandland.gov.scot

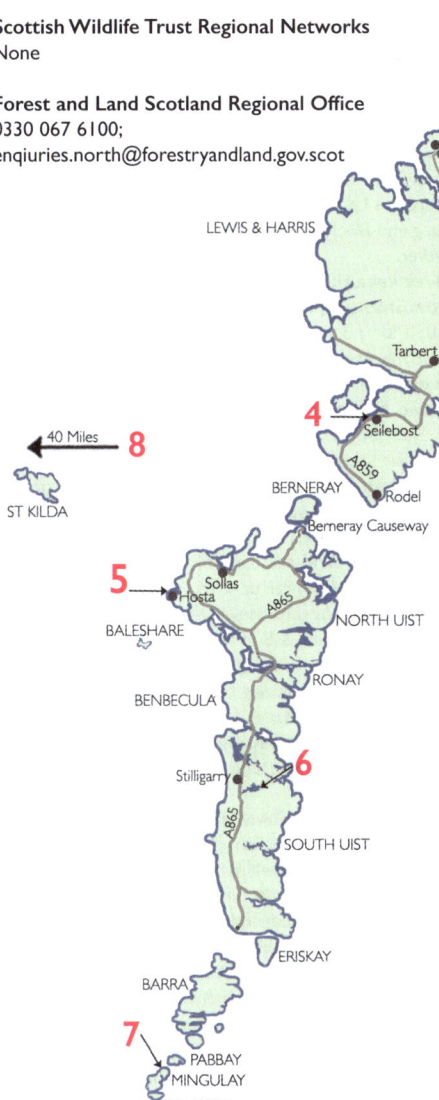

5	**Balranald**
6	**Loch Druidibeg**
3	**Loch na Muilne**
2	**Loch Stiapabhat**
7	**Mingulay, Pabbay and Berneray**
8	**Saint Kilda**
I	**Shiant Islands**
4	**Sound of Taransay**

At low tide North Uist is separated from the island to the S, Benebecula, by a narrow channel, which is crossed by a causeway, and another one crosses the channel separating Benbecula from the island further S, South Uist. At the S end of South Uist a ferry service runs from Coilleag on Eriskay (a small island connected by causewayy to South Uist) to Aird Mhòr on Barra, the southernmost of the main islands. In addition to these main islands, there are numerous smaller ones. The system of causeways and ferries means that it is possible to drive the length of the archipelago from its northern tip at Butt of Lewis to Barra, the southernmost of the main islands, a distance of c.118 miles.

There are a number of ferry services connecting the mainland with various destinations along the length of this archipelago and, given the distances involved, you might want to choose a service that lands you close to your final destination. The **Public transport** sections of the following entries identify the closest ferry port to each of the featured reserves but you could of course choose to land at a different port and use the road network connecting the islands to drive to it.

All the ferry services to and from the mainland or Inner Hebrides or between the main islands of the Outer Hebrides are operated by:

> **Caledonian MacBrayne**
> **0800 066 5000**;
> enquiries@calmac.co.uk;
> www.calmac.co.uk

If you caught the ferry to Stornoway, get straight back on a boat and visit

The arc described by the Outer Henrides stretches for c.130 miles from the Butt of Lewis in the N to Berneray, the southernmost island of the archipelago. The largest and northernmost island in the archipelago is known as Lewis in its northern part and Harris in its southern. It is separated from the next large island south, North Uist, by the Sound of Harris, which is crossed by a vehicle ferry running between Leverburgh and a slipway at the N end of the Berneray causeway (a different Beneray from the island at the S tip of the chain), which connects the slipway with North Uist.

1 SHIANT ISLANDS

Tom Nicolson

Habitats: Group of small islands with sea cliffs 4 miles E of Harris.

Birds: 10% of UK Puffins and 7% of UK Razorbills breed on the Shiants. Also Guillemot, Fulmar, Kittiwake, Great Skua. Storm Petrel breeding following eradication of rats, but Manx Shearwater yet to.

Other: The Seabird Recovery Project (2014-18) successfully eradicated Black Rats from the islands. Do nothing to allow Brown Rats or other predators to take their place. Cetaceans, Basking Shark.

Directions: NG 416 978. Charter boats (think about sharing, it won't be cheap) from Leverburgh, Stornoway, Portree and Ullapool. Sea Harris, Stornoway Safari, Isle of Harris Sea Tours run from Leverburgh and Stornoway. 45 mile round trip.

Public transport: Ferry from Uig to Tarbert or Ullapool to Stornoway, with direct mainland bus service from Glasgow or Inverness. .

Visiting: Free, but tricky, to land (recommended to view birds from sea). The cliffs are dangerous. No facilities (not even electricity) on islands. There is a house that can be stayed in with a small donation to help with upkeep. You need to bring all supplies—and no rats—with you.

Contact: www.shiantisles.net/visit

On returning to Stornoway

2 LOCH STIAPABHAT LNR

Galson Estate Trust/RSPB

Habitat: Shallow, nutrient-rich freshwater loch, fringing vegetation, marsh, machair. SSSI, SPA.

Birds: Breeding: Little Grebe, Lapwing, Snipe, Redshank, Oystercatcher, Moorhen, Mallard, Corncrake, Black-headed Gull, Sedge Warbler, Reed Bunting. *Spring and Autumn passage:* Golden Plover, Whimbrel, Curlew, Ruff, Black-tailed Godwit, Dunlin, Greenshank, Wheatear. *Winter:* Barnacle & Pink-footed Geese, Wigeon, Pintail, Teal, Shoveler, Goldeneye, Tufted Duck. *All year:* White-tailed Eagle, Hen Harrier, Short-eared Owl, Whooper Swan, Grey Heron.

Other: Otter, Wetland flora. Mink and problems associated therewith.

Directions: HS2 0SH (office); NB 523 642 (sports centre car park). Take the A857 N from Stornoway for Port of Ness. Remain on it for 27 miles, turning sharp R at Barvas. 0.75 mile from Port of Ness, turn L on to the B8013. Sports Centre car park is 0.5 mile on L

Public transport: Bus: W1 Stornoway-Ness passes the B8301 turning (not Sun), Lochs Motor Transport. Ferry from Ullapool to Stornoway.

Visiting: Free, open all hours. Cross B8013 from car park, enter reserve through gate and follow path and boardwalk for 350 yards to hide. No toilets, nearest in Port of Ness, 1.25 miles by road. The Butt of Lewis, the island's northernmost point is 1.75 miles further along the B8013.

Contact: 01851 850 411; office@uogltd.com

Instead of turning R at Barvas, turn L for

3 LOCH NA MUILNE

RSPB

Habitat: Coastal lochs, wetland, heath

Birds: 9 spp of breeding waders inc Red-necked Phalarope. *Winter:* Whooper Swan, Golden Plover possible scarcities i.e. Ring-necked Duck. *Coast:* Breeding Fulmar, Shag and Black Guillemot. Gannet offshore.

Other:

Directions: HS2 9DB; NB 310 494. Take the A857 N from Stornaway for 12 miles. At Barvas turn L on to the A858 for c.3 miles and then turn R into Arnol. Drive past the Arnol Blackhouse Museum to RSPB car park at end of road.

Public transport: Bus: W1 Stornoway-Ness stops at Barvas (not Sun), Lochs Motor Transport. W2 West Circular from Stornoway stops in Arnol (not Sun), Hebridean Transport (01851 705 050). Ferry from Ullapool to Stornoway.

Visiting: Free, open all hours. Use RSPB (3 places) not Historic Scotland car park. No toilets. 400 yard waymarked path from car park to viewing point overlooking loch. Path beyond viewing point to coast and then coastal paths to N & S of reserve for views of breeding sea birds. Ground nesting birds, keep dogs under close control. especially diuring the breeding season and keep to waymarked trails.

Contact: 01876 714 040; outerhebrides@rspb.org.uk

Continue on A858 to junction with A859, then head S.

4 SOUND OF TARANSAY

Open access

Habitats: Machair, shell sand, dunes, sheltered waters between W of Harris and island of Taransay. SSSI.

Birds: Summer: Corncrake, Lapwing, Oystercatcher, Common, Arctic & Little Tern, Stonechat, Wheatear, Twite. *Autumn/Winter/Spring:* Great Northern Diver, Slavonian Grebe, Common & Surf Scoter, Eider, Long-tailed Duck, Golden Plover, Snow Bunting, Twite.

Other:

Directions: HS3 3HP; NG 064 974 parking area by Old School, Seilebost, take minor road off A859, roughly 10 miles from Tarbert or 11 miles from Leverburgh.

Public transport: Bus: W10, Stornoway-Leverburgh (not Sun), stops at by School Road, Seilebost, Lochs Motor Transport (01851 860 288; info@lochsmotortransport.co.uk).

Visiting: Free and open all hours, no facilities.

Contact: None.

Take ferry from Leverburgh to Berneray and then North Uist. Head W on A865.

5 BALRANALD

RSPB (North Scotland)

Habitats: Freshwater loch, machair, coast, crofts.

Birds: Spring: Skuas and divers at sea, waders inc Purple Sandpiper, Turnstone, Dunlin. *Summer:* Corncrake, Lapwing, Oystercatcher, Dunlin, Ringed Plover, Redshank, Snipe, terns, Corn Bunting. *Autumn:* Hen Harrier, Peregrine, Greylag Goose. *Passage:* Pomarine & Long-tailed Skuas. *Winter:* Whooper Swan, Barnacle & Greylag Geese, Wigeon, Teal, Shoveler, Merlin, Twite, Snow Bunting. Golden & White-tailed Eagles more regular.

Other: Blanket bog and machair plants reach their peak in Jul. Look for rare Great Yellow Bumblebee on wildflowers. Otters on freshwater lochs.

Directions: HS6 5DL. NF 706 707. On W coast of North Uist, three miles N of Bayhead. Follow A865 N from Clachan towards Sollas. Take L turn for Hogha Gearraigh township and another L for signposted visitor centre prior to reaching Hogha Gearraigh.

Public transport: Bus—runs across Outer Hebrides—DA Travel (01878 700 599)—contact on morning of travel to ensure bus will stop at Balranald. Ferry from Mallaig or Oban to Lochboisdale (S Uist) or Uig (Skye) to Lochmaddy (N Uist).

Visiting: Open all hours. Visitor centre open all year. Toilets (inc disabled), group bookings welcome. Marked circular nature trail (three miles), not suitable for wheelchairs. Dogs on leads.

Contact: RSPB: 01876 714 040;
outerhebrides@rspb.org.uk
Continue S on A865.

6 LOCH DRUIDIBEG NNR

Stòras Uibhist (community ownership)/RSPB (Scotland) *Habitats:* 4,142 acres, coast, freshwater lochs, marshes, machair, moorland.

Birds: Spring/autumn: Migrant waders and wildfowl. *Summer:* Breeding waders, breeding White-tailed Eagle and Hen Harrier, Red- & Black-throated Divers, Red-breasted Merganser, Cuckoo, Greylag Goose, Short-eared Owl wildfowl and terns. *Winter:* Whooper Swan, waders, wildfowl, raptors inc Golden Eagle and Hen Harrier.

Directions: HS8 5RS. NF 789 382. Lies just N of Kildonan on South Uist. Whether approaching from N or S, turn off A865 at Stillgarry on to B890 road for Loch Sgioport. Track is 1.5 miles further on—park at side of road.

Public transport: Bus: W17 (not Sun) Benbecula to Lochboisdale stops at Stillgarry. DA Travel (01878 700 357 or 01878 700 599). Ferry from Mallaig to Lochboisdale.

Visiting: Open all year. View part of reserve from public roads but parking and turning areas for coaches beyond the car park are limited. Several tracks and one walk covering a range of habitats—most not suitable for wheelchairs. Stout footwear essential.

Contact: RSPB: 01876 714 040;
outerhebrides@rspb.org.uk

7 MINGULAY, PABBAY AND BERNERAY

National Trust for Scotland

Habitats: Three islands to S of Barra (do not confuse with Pabbay and Berneray to the N of North Uist). High cliffs, grassland.

Birds: Breeding: Puffin, Razorbill, Guillemot, Fulmar, Corncrake, Snipe, Ringed & Golden Plover, Arctic Tern, Kittiwake, Great & Arctic Skua. Golden Eagle, White-tailed Eagle, Short-eared Owl.

Other: Otter, Dolphin, Porpoise, Basking Shark. Great Yellow Bumblebee and Moss Carder Bee. Common Blue and Grayling butterflies.

Directions: NL 560 830 (Mingulay). Mingulay. the central and largest island, is 11.5 miles SW of Castle Bay, Barra as the Gannet flies.

Boat trips from Barra to or around islands.

Hebridean Sea Tours: 01871 817 803;
info@hebrideanseatours.co.uk

Mingulay Boat Trip: www.mingulayboattrips.com.

Public transport: Ferry from Oban to Castle Bay, Barra.

Visiting: Now uninhabited. Open all hours, landing permitted and free but ensure you do not bring any uninvited guests. Landing is on rocky foreshore, no pier. Camping permitted. No facilities or mobile phone signal. No trails. In places, the cliffs are high and dangerous. Maintain distance from ground-nesting birds. Ideally, do not bring dogs but, if do, keep under close control.

Contact: National Trust for Scotland: 0131 385 7490;
via website: www.nts.org.uk

8 ST KILDA NNR

National Trust for Scotland

Habitats: Archipelago of four islands—Hirta, Soay, Dùn & Boreray—plus a number of islets and stacks. Very high cliffs, stacks, grassy slopes. No resident human population. SSSI, SAC, SPA

Birds: Endemic St Kilda Wren, *Breeding:* Eider, Gannet, Leach's Storm Petrel, Storm Petrel, Manx Shearwater, Fulmar, Puffin, Guillemot, Black Guillemot, Razorbill, Shag, Snipe, Kittiwake, Great & Arctic Skuas. Meadow & Rock Pipits, Wheatear, Starling. *Migrants and vagrants:* Assorted Holarctic species, particularly Redwing, Pink-footed Goose, Snow Bunting, Woodcock amongst many others. 280 spp. recorded to date. The colonies of several of the breeding seabirds are amongst the largest in the world but there have been recent declines in some species, further exacerbated by HPAIV. One of the stacks in the archipelago was the site of the last UK record for the Great Auk.

Other: Endemic and now feral Soay sheep, no terrestrial predators. Endemic subspecies of Fieldmouse.

Directions: NF 089 995, 40 miles W of Outer Hebrides

in Atlantic. A number of companies run trips to St Kilda from the Outer Hebrides or, although the trips take longer, Skye or the mainland. These include:
Hebridean Sea Tours, from Castle Bay, Barra: www.hebrideanseatours.co.uk
Kilda Cruises, from Leverburgh, Harris: www.kildacruises.co.uk
Sea Harris, from Leverburgh, Harris: www.seaharris.com
Uist Sea Tours, most trips from Pol na Cran, Benbecula www.uistseatours.co.uk
Public transport: If setting off from the outer Hebrides you need to first reach your departure point by ferry from the mainland.
Visiting: Open all hours. Toilets and drinking water on Hirta but no shops or cafes. Drones not permitted, no mobile phone signal. No dogs or other pets. Only open boats that can be checked for rats allowed alongside pier and only during daylight. Small campsite (charge) on Hirta In 2025 open 23 Apr-9 Aug & 19 Aug-13 Sep, check website for 2026: https://www.nts.org.uk/visit/places/st-kilda
Contact: 01463 232034; stkildainfo@nts.org.uk

Orkney

Breeding seabirds, moorland specialities and passage migrants make the islands an attractive destination. Hen Harriers breed in good numbers and other scarce breeders include Whimbrel, Great & Arctic Skuas and Red-throated Diver. For seabirds, Marwick Head (mainland) and North Hill (Papa Westray) are worth a visit. A stay at the North Ronaldsay Bird Observatory offers the chance to look for rare migrants in spring and autumn.

Bird Atlas/Avifauna
The Birds of Orkney
C Booth, M Cuthbert & P Reynolds
(The Orkney Press, 1984).

Bird Recorder
Steve Dudley, Westray, Orkney, KW17 2DW: orkneybirdrecorder@gmail.com

Bird Report
Orkney Bird Report (1974-), from Orkney Bird Report Group, via the Bird Recorder—see above.
North Ronaldsay Bird Observatory Bird Report (2011-), from NRBO, Twingness, North Ronaldsay, Orkney KW17 2BE: 01857 633 200; enquiries@nrbo.org.uk

BTO Regional Representative
Stephen Willis
Wetland Bird Survey (WeBS)
Local Organizer: webs@bto.org
Vacant

Club
SOC Orkney Branch (1993; n/a).
Helen Aiton: 07872 904180; helendavidaiton@hotmail.co.uk; www.the-soc.org.uk/local-branches/orkney
Meetings: 7:30pm, 1st Thursday of the month (Oct-Mar; Dec-Feb online). The Corner Room, Ground Floor, King Street Halls, 6 King Street, Kirkwall KW15 1JF. Additional, club-wide monthly online talks also held. Contact/see website for details.

Ringing Group/Bird Observatory
Orkney RG
Sule Skerry RG
North Ronaldsay Bird Observatory
Alison Duncan (Warden), Twingness, North Ronaldsay, KW17 2BE: 01857 633 200; enquiries@nrbo.org.uk; www.nrbo.org.uk

RSPB Local Group
No Groups.

Scottish Wildlife Trust Regional Networks
None

Forest and Land Scotland Regional Office
Apart from gardens, there are almost no trees on Orkney.

Getting to Orkney
Northlink Ferries (0800 111 4422; www.northlinkferries.co.uk) operates vehicle ferries between Scrabster (Thurso) and Stromness (Mainland). Some Aberdeen-Lerwick (Shetland) services call at Hatston/Kirkwall (Mainland).

Pentland Ferries (01856 831 226; www.pentlandferries.co.uk) operates vehicle ferries to and from Gills Bay (Caithness) and St Margaret's Hope (South Ronaldsay, linked to Mainland by causeway).

Flights: a number of airlines connect Kirkwall (Mainland) to various destinations. Flights from Kirkwall to the smaller islands are via Longanair (see below).

Map labels: **PAPA WESTRAY**, **ROUSAY**, **EGILSAY**, **SHAPINSAY**, **Balfour**, **KIRKWALL**, **Brough Head**, **MAINLAND**, **Moaness**, **HOY**, with road labels B9064, A967, A966, A964, A9041 and numbered reserve markers 11, 13, 3, 1, 2, 4, 5, 6, 7, 8, 9, 10.

3	Birsay Moors
1	Brodgar
2	Cottascarth and Rendall Moss
6	Hobbister
7	Hoy
5	Marwick Head
10	Mill Dam
12	North Hill
13	North Ronaldsay BO
11	Noup Cliffs
9	Onziebust
4	The Loons and Loch of Banks
8	Trumland

Getting around Orkney

Buses

All buses on **Mainland** are operated by **Stagecoach** (01856 870 555; www.stagecoachbus.com) on behalf of Orkney Islands Council. Apart from the centre of Kirkwall and Stromness, buses will pick up and drop off on request at any safe spot.

Ferries

Ferry services between Mainland and 13 islands are operated by **Orkney Ferries Ltd** (01856 872 044; www.orkneyferries.co.uk).

Flights

Air services from Kirkwall airport to 6 northern islands operated by **Loganair Ltd** (01856 872 494; www.loganair.co.uk).

1 BRODGAR, MAINLAND

RSPB

Habitats: Two large lochs, grazed grassland.
Birds: Breeding: Lapwing, Redshank, Curlew, Snipe, Shoveler, Pintail. *Winter:* Wildfowl inc Scaup, Red-breasted Merganser, Long-tailed Duck. Possible Slavonnian Grebe.
Other: Great Yellow Bumblebee.
Directions: KW16 3JZ; HY 293 137. On Mainland. Take the B9055 off the A966 Stromness-Kirkwall road, 4.7 miles from Stromness or 10 miles from Kirkwall. The B9055 runs NW along a narrow isthmus between Lochs Stenness and Harray. Car park is 1.5 miles along B9055 on R (shared with Ring of Brodgar archaeological site, Historic Scotland), no height restrictions. Reserve itself is to SW of car park along a rough path.
Public transport: Bus: X1.
Visiting: Open all hours, free, no facilities. Dogs under close control, clean up mess.
Contact: 01856 850 176; orkney@rspb.org.uk www.rspb.org.uk/brodgar
Continue along the B9055 for **The Loons and Loch of Banks** *(q.v.) and for* **Marwick Head** *(q.v.).*

2 COTTASCARTH AND RENDALL MOSS, MAINLAND

RSPB

Habitats: Moorland, mire, wet heath, blanket bog, willow scrub, grassland.
Birds: Summer: Curlew, Snipe, Merlin, Hen Harrier, Short-eared Owl, Great & Arctic Skua, Cuckoo, Raven, Stonechat, common moorland spp.
Other: Moorland flora.
Directions: KW17 2PA; HY 369 195. On Mainland. 4.5

miles N of Finstown off A966. Take minor road W at Norseman village, signposted RSPB **Cottascarth,** then turn R at Settisgarth, following signs for reserve. Road passes through farmyard at Lower Cottascarth Farm (follow the signs for hide) to car park just above it.
Public transport: Bus: 6 Kirkwall to Tingwell stops at Norseman (2 miles).
Visiting: Open all hours. Small car park (3+1 Blue Badge spaces). Eddie Balfour hen harrier hide at Cottascarth, 700 yards from car park. Working farm—request not to bring dogs but if do keep under close control.
Contact: RSPB: 01856 850 176; orkney@rspb.org.uk; www.rspb.org.uk/cottascarth
Continue along A966 for

3 BIRSAY MOORS, MAINLAND
RSPB
Habitats: Moorland, blanket bog, grazed grassland, lochans.
Birds: Breeding: Red-throated Diver, Dunlin, Golden Plover, Curlew, Hen Harrier, Short-eared Owl. *Winter:* Large communal Hen Harrier roost.
Other: Orkney Vole (subspecies of Common Vole).
Directions: KW17 2PL; HY 349 244 (lay-by). Head N from the A965 between Stromness and Kirkwall, taking either the A966 at Finstown or the A986 between Finstown and Stromness. If taking the A966, turn L at Stenso after c.8.75 miles and take the B9057. Park in lay-by after 1.25 miles. From A986, turn R at Dounby after 5.5 miles on to B9057. Park in lay-by after 4.5 miles
Public transport: Bus: 6, passes through Evie (near turning for hide); 7 & 8S pass through Dounby (4.5 miles W of lay-by)
Visiting: Open all hours, free, no facilities, no trails across moor. View from lay-by on B9057; hide at HY 345 249 (parking 70 yards away, path to hide or drop off for disabled), turning in Evie at HY 357 266, then follow signs; lay-by in Durkadale at HY 308 244 on minor road running NW from B9057. Ground-nesting birds, keep dogs under close control and clean up mess. Wind turbines on NE margin of reserve.
Contact: 01856 850 176; orkney@rspb.org.uk www.rspb.org.uk/birsaymoors
Instead of turning R off the A986 at Dounby continue N and you will pass **Loch of Banks** *on your L just before the junction with the A967. The A967 and the disused airfield at Isbister separate the* **Loch of Banks** *from Isbister Loch and the rest of* **The Loons** *reserve.*

4 THE LOONS AND LOCH OF BANKS, MAINLAND
RSPB
Habitats: Open water, marshy grassland, swamp fen, mire, reedbed. Orkney's largest remaining wetland.
Birds: White-fronted Goose, Pintail, Water Rail. Redshank, Curlew, Black-tailed Godwit, Lapwing.

Other: Great Yellow Bumblebee.
Directions: KW17 2NB; HY 246 242. A short distance to the N of the junction of the A986 and A967 a minor road runs W to the B9056 and joins it in Marwick. Small car parks off this road at HY 254 246 for the listening wall and HY 247 242 for the hide, ramp from car park to hide.
Public transport: Bus: 8 passes Loch of Banks; 7 passes the Marwick end of minor road on which hide and listening wall are located. 0.3 mile walk to hide, 0.7 mile to listening wall.
Visiting: Open all hours, free, no facilities. One hide and one concave listening wall that focuses bird calls. Keep dogs under close control and clean up mess.
Contact: 01856 850 176; orkney@rspb.org.uk www.rspb.org.uk/theloons
To W of B9056.

5 MARWICK HEAD, MAINLAND
RSPB
Habitats: Rocky bay, sandstone sea cliffs. The Choin low-tide lagoon good for waders and ducks.
Birds: May-Jul: up to 25,000 seabirds. Large numbers of Kittiwake and auks, inc Puffin, also Fulmar and a Gannet colony, skuas, Rock Dove, Raven, Rock Pipit, Short-eared Owl. *Winter:* Purple Sandpiper, Turnstone, Ringed Plover.
Other: Cetaceans possibility from Marwick with Harbour Porpoise and Minke Whale occasionally seen. Beach path for Great Yellow Bumblebee in Aug.
Directions: KW17 2NB; HY 229 240 (Marwick car park). Lies four miles N of Skara Brae (neolithic village) on W coast of mainland Orkney, NW of Dounby. Path N from Marwick Bay, or from council car park at Cumlaquoy at HY 232 251 (best for Kitchener Memorial).
Public transport: Bus: 8S (Mon, Thurs, Sat—limited) serves Marwick.
Visiting: Open all year. Info board in Marwick car park. Cliff top path. Rough terrain not suitable for wheelchairs.
Contact: 01856 850 176; orkney@rspb.org.uk www.rspb.org.uk/marwickhead
Return to Kirkwall.

6 HOBBISTER, MAINLAND
RSPB
Habitats: Moorland, cliffs, saltmarsh, sandflats.
Birds: Red-throated Diver, Red-breasted Merganser, Curlew, Black Guillemot. Short-eared Owl, Hen Harrier. Twite, Stonechat. *Winter:* Possible views of Great Northern Diver in Scapa Flow.
Directions: KW17 2RA; HY 395 069. Off A964, 3.1 miles SW of Kirkwall between the road and the coast of Scapa Flow.
Public transport: Bus: 2 runs along A964 past reserve.
Visiting: Free, open all hours. No facilities apart from

toilets at Waukmill Bay. Two car parks reached by minor roads running S from A964: HY 395 069 (close to A964) and further W at HY 382 068 overlooking Waukmill Bay, further from A964. Circular, rough, often muddy 2 mile trail. Keep dogs on lead, clean up mess.
Contact: 01856 850 176; orkney@rspb.org.uk www.rspb.org.uk/hobbister

7 HOY
RSPB
Habitats: 9,680 acres covering entire NW of Hoy: sea cliffs, moorland.
Birds: All year: Hen Harrier. *Summer:* Red-throated Diver, White-tailed Eagle, Fulmar, Puffin, Guillemot, Razorbill, Kittiwake, Black Guillemot, Arctic & Great Skuas, Stonechat. *Autumn/winter:* Finches and thrushes, Great Northern Diver, Long-tailed Duck, Merlin.
Other: Primroses and Arctic alpine flowers. Old Man of Hoy landmark.
Directions: KW16 3NJ; HY 222 034. Hoy reached from Mainland by car ferry from Houton to Lyness (S of Hoy); or Stromness passenger ferry to Moaness (N of Hoy), 1.5 miles to N part of reserve). From Lyness ferry turn R (signposted **Hoy**) on to B9047 and take first L after 8.5 miles (signposted Dwarfie Stone) toward Rackwick. Car parks at Dwarfie Stone and Rackwick beach.
Public transport: Bus (limited)—Hoy Community Bus service: 01856 701 356 (office), 07833 777 760 (driver); www.hoyorkney.com.
Visiting: Access all hours. Local car parks (not RSPB). Three trails—five miles to Old Man of Hoy and back to Rackwick; 2.5 miles Old Post Road (crosses moorland); and 0.6 mile return path to Dwarfie Stone. Rough terrain not suitable for wheelchairs. Dogs under control at all times.
Contact: 01856 850 176; orkney@rspb.org.uk www.rspb.org.uk/hoy

8 TRUMLAND, ROUSAY
RSPB
Habitats: 1,070 acres of rocky outcrops (hamars), upland heath, moorland, willow scrub.
Birds: Red-throated Diver, Hen Harrier, Merlin, Short-eared Owl
Other: Alpine Bearberry, Round-leaved Wintergreen. Orkney Vole, Otter.
Directions: KW17 2PU; HY 438 279. No car park at reserve. Walk up hill from pier, bearing L. At T junction at Trumland House, turn R. Look for wooden bridge and RSPB sign on L after 660 yards.
Public transport: Vehicle ferry from Tingwall, Mainland to Brinian Pier.
Visiting: Free, open all hours, no facilities but toilets and pub by pier. One rough 3 mile trail to Knitchen Hill and Blotchnie Fiold (climb of 800+ ft from Pier). Dogs on lead during breeding season and grazed areas, clean up mess.
Contact: 01856 850 176; orkney@rspb.org.uk www.rspb.org.uk/trumland

9 ONZIEBUST, EGILSAY
RSPB
Habitats: Mixed grassland farm, wetland, lochans, rocky and sandy shores.
Birds: Corncrake, Lapwing, Redshank, Curlew Black-tailed Godwit. *Winter:* Wigeon, Teal, Turnstone.
Other: Great Yellow Bumblebee, Buff-tailed Bumblebee.
Directions: KW17 2QD; HY 468 301. Park at pier and then walk; or drive (roads narrow) 0.5 mile to crossroads and park at community centre near reserve entrance.
Public transport: Ferry from Tingwall, Mainland to Skaill Taing. No buses on island.
Visiting: Open all hours, free, no facilities, toilets at pier. Trail, rough in places, due E from pier past community centre to opposite coast or turn R at community centre and walk down centre of island for 1.3 miles to Onziebust Farm along single track road.
Contact: 01856 850 176; orkney@rspb.org.uk www.rspb.org.uk/onziebust

10 MILL DAM, SHAPINSAY
RSPB
Habitats: Open water, marshy fen, mire, flower-rich grassland, small area of heath.
Birds: Spring/Summer: Shoveler, Tufted Duck, Wigeon, Teal, Redshank, Curlew, Snipe, Lapwing. *Winter:* Whooper Swan, Wigeon, Teal, Shoveler, Pintail, Gadwall. Sparrowhawk, Hen Harrier, Merlin, Peregrine,.
Other: Red Marsh Cinquefoil, Pink Bogbean, Yellow Flag Iris
Directions: KW17 2RA; HY 483 177. Take B9059 from Balfour Pier, turn L on to minor road after 0.4 mile. Hide and car park 0.6 mile along road on R.
Public transport: Vehicle ferry from Kirkwall to Balfour on Shapinsay.
Visiting: Free, hide open all hours, no access to reserve. Hide wheelchair accessible. Dogs allowed in hide, clean up mess.
Contact: 01856 850 176; orkney@rspb.org.uk www.rspb.org.uk/milldam

11 NOUP CLIFFS, WESTRAY
RSPB (East Scotland)
Habitats: Cliffs rising to 250 ft.
Birds: The largest seabird colony in Orkney. Gannet, Guillemot, Razorbill, Puffin, Fulmar, Kittiwake. Arctic Tern, Great & Artic Skuas. Rock Dove, Raven, Rock Pipit.
Other: Dolphin.
Directions: KW17 2DW; HY 393 498. Take B9066 from Sulland Pier for 7 miles to Pierowall. Turn W on

to minor road signposted for **Noup Cliffs** at school. Turn L at junction after Noltland Castle. Follow road uphill to Noup Farm. Unless driving 4x4, stop here or at previous farm, Backarass. If in 4x4, a gravel path leads another 1.5 miles to Noup Lighthouse, car park at the reserve entrance.

Public transport: Vehicle ferry from Kirkwall to Sulland Pier, Westray. Westray Public Bus, M& J Harcus (07789 034 289; www.westraybusservice.co.uk). Flights—Loganair flies to Westray from Kirkwall.

Visiting: Free, open all hours, no facilities. Noup Coastal Trail over rough ground part of longer 5 mile West Westray cliff walk from Noup Head to Kirbest. If parked at Backarass Farm can walk to Noup Head and then back along Coastal Trail (4.25 miles). Keep dogs on lead, clean up mess.

Contact: 01856 850 176; orkney@rspb.org.uk
www.rspb.org.uk/noupcliffs

Passenger ferry links Westray and Papa Westray and you can even take the world's shortest flight, from Westray to Papa Westray, courtesy of Loganair.

12 NORTH HILL, PAPA WESTRAY
RSPB
Habitats: Sea cliffs, maritime heath.
Birds: Summer: Close views of Puffin, Guillemot, Razorbill and Kittiwake. Black Guillemot nest under flagstones around reserve's coastline. Small colonies of Arctic Tern. Arctic & Great Skuas. Breeding Lapwing, Redshank and Snipe in grazed areas. *Winter:* Gannet, Fulmar, Eider and winter thrushes.
Other: One of best areas (Fowl Craig) to see Scottish Primrose (primula scotica)—two flowering periods that just overlap (May to Aug). Whales on migration in autumn, inc Orca, Grey & Common seals.
Directions: KW17 2BU; HY 495 538. From pier or airfield travel N along main road. From shop/hostel, take road N to junction at Holland Farm and turn R on to main road. Continue past Rose Cottage to reserve entrance.
Public transport: Ferry—Kirkwall to Papa Westray (car ferry, Tues and Fri). Pierowall (Westray) to Papa Westray passenger ferry (daily). Flights—daily (end-Feb-Oct) from Kirkwall to Papa Westray.
Visiting: Access all hours. Limited parking. Two trails (Coastal—3.5 miles, around N peninsula of Papa Westray) and Fowl Craig (1.5 mile loop for nesting seabirds). Also, additional short walk (200 yards each way) to North Hill hide. Not suitable for wheelchairs. Trail guide and info available in hide.
Contact: 01856 850 176; orkney@rspb.org.uk
www.rspb.org.uk/northhill

13 NORTH RONALDSAY BIRD OBSERVATORY
North Ronaldsay Bird Observatory
Habitats: Crofting island at NE extremity of archipela-

go with a several eutrophic and oligotrophic wetlands and lochs. Sandy bays and rocky shores. A number of gardens with bushes and trees that attract migrants.
Birds: Spring/autumn: Prime migration site inc many rarities and sub-rarities. Walled gardens concentrate passerines. *Summer:* Breeding seabirds, wildfowl and waders. *Winter:* Waders and wildfowl inc Whooper Swan. Divers, seaduck. Late summer passage of auks, shearwaters, Storm Petrels, skuas, terns, Kittiwake.
Directions: KW17 2BE; HY 748 524. Observatory in SW of island, at Twinness.
Public transport: Ferry—Kirkwall to North Ronaldsay (car ferry, Tues & Sat May-Sep, Sat only Oct-Apr). Flights—daily all year from Kirkwall to North Ronaldsay.
Visiting: Open all year (not Christmas). Guest house and hostel accommodation, also camping, fully licenced restaurant, cafe and shop. Five Heligoland traps. Seawatching hide at N end of island for movement between North Sea and Atlantic.
Contact: North Ronaldsay BO: 01857 633 200; enquiries@nrbo.org.uk; www.nrbo.co.uk

Shetland

With its large seabird colonies, a summer visit to Britain's most northerly islands will always be a fantastic experience. Apart from the huge numbers of the common species, Arctic and Great Skuas breed here—particularly around Hermaness (Unst)—an evening visit to the small island of Mousa is a great way to catch up with the largely nocturnal Storm Petrel. The islands, in particular Fair Isle, always attract a large number of spring and autumn migrants, some common, some not, and many of Britain's 'firsts' have been recorded here.

Bird Atlas/Avifauna
The Birds of Shetland
P Harvey, M Pennington,
K Osborn, R Riddington, P Ellis, M Huebeck & D Okill (Christopher Helm, 2004)

Bird Recorder
Mike Pennington, 9 Daisy Park, Baltasound, Shetland ZE2 9EA 07901617119; penningtonunst@btinternet.com; recorder@shetland birdclub.co.uk

Bird Report
Shetland Bird Report (1969-), from SBC:
reports@shetlandbirdclub.co.uk
Fair Isle Bird Observatory Report (1949-),
available to download online (donation welcomed) at:
www.fairislebirdobs.co.uk/shop_books.html

Shetland

BTO Regional Representative
Stephen Willis
Wetland Bird Survey (WeBS)
Local Organizer
Rory Tallack
webs@bto.org

Club
Shetland Bird Club (1973; 260+)
Helen Moncrieff (Secretary):
secretary@shetlandbirdclub.co.uk;
www.nature-shetland.co.uk
<u>Meetings</u>: Regular evening talks or socials - contact/see website for details.

Ringing Group/Bird Observatory
Shetland RG
Fair Isle Bird Observatory
Fair Isle Bird Observatory, Fair Isle, Shetland ZE2 9JU: info@fairislebirdobs.co.uk; www.fair-islebirdobs.co.uk

RSPB Local Group
No Groups

Scottish Wildlife Trust Regional Networks
None

Forest and Land Scotland Regional Office
There are no trees on Shetland.

Getting to Shetland
Northlink Ferries (0800 111 4422; www. northlinkferries.co.uk) operates vehicle ferries between Aberdeen and Lerwick (Shetland). Some of these services also call at Hatston/Kirkwall (Mainland, Orkney).
Flights: A number of airlines, serving various destinations, fly to and from the Shetlands. The main airport for flights to and from the Shetlands is Sumburgh, linked by the A970 to Lerwick, the capital, and Tingwall, the main airport for inter-island flights, including to and from Fair Isle.

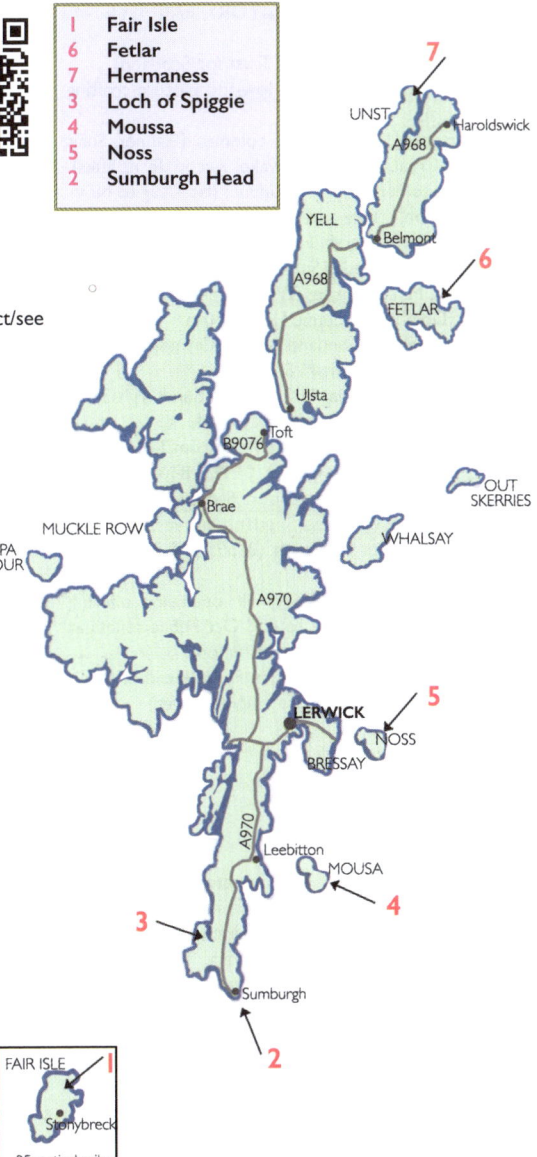

1	Fair Isle
6	Fetlar
7	Hermaness
3	Loch of Spiggie
4	Moussa
5	Noss
2	Sumburgh Head

Getting around Shetland
Ferries
Ferry services between the main inhabited islands, apart from Mainland to Foula, are operated by
Shetland Islands Council (01806 244 200; ferries@shetland.gov.uk; www.shetland.gov.uk/ferries)

Flights
*Inter-island flights are operated under contract to **Shetland Islands Council** by Airtask Group Ltd (01595 840 246; lwk.ops@airtask.com; www.airtask.com. Tingwall airport near Lerwick serves as the Mainland hub for inter-island flights.*
Shetland Council website: www.zettrans.org.uk/travel for public transport information

1 FAIR ISLE BIRD OBSERVATORY, FAIR ISLE

Fair Isle Bird Observatory
(island owned by the National Trust for Scotland)
Habitats: Heather moor and lowland pasture/crofting land, sea cliffs.
Birds: Summer: Large seabird colonies (Gannet, Shag, Arctic & Great Skuas, Kittiwake, Arctic Tern, auks). *Spring* (Apr to early-Jun) and *Autumn* (late-Aug to Nov): many common, scarce and rare migrants
Other: Northern Marsh, Heath Spotted and Frog Orchid, Lesser Twayblade, Small Adders Tongue, Oyster Plant. Orca, Minke Whales, White-backed, White-sided & Risso's Dolphins. Endemic Field Mouse.
Directions: SW of Shetland/NE of Orkney—midway between them, access from Shetland.
Public transport: Regular UK flights to Sumburgh, Shetland or ferry from Aberdeen to Lerwick.
To Fair Isle: By air—Airtask services from Tingwall (nr Lerwick)—contact for details: 01595 840 246; lwk.ops@airtask.com *By sea*—Good Shepherd ferry (12 passengers) from Grutness, Shetland on Tues, Thurs, Sat (May-Sep)—contact for details (01595 760 363; neilthomson1951@gmail.com).
Visiting: Observatory now rebuilt, open and offering accommodation from Apr to end Oct Public toilets at the airstrip and Stackhoull Stores (shop).
Contact: Fair Isle Bird Obs: Alex Penn (Head of Ornithology); Steve Holgate (Hospitality Manager) info@fairislebirdobs.co.uk; www.fairislebirdobs.co.uk

2 SUMBURGH, MAINLAND

RSPB
Habitats: Sea cliffs, grassland.
Birds: Spring/summer: Eider, Oystercatcher, Fulmar, Shag, Guillemot, Puffin, Kittiwake. Wheatear, Twite, Rock Pipit. Migrants. *Autumn passage:* Many migrants move through area—regulars inc Whinchat, Redstart, Pied & Spotted Flycatchers, common warblers. Always chance of rarities turning up.
Other: Grey Seal. Cetaceans offshore.
Directions: ZE3 9JN; HU 407 079. Southern tip of mainland Shetland.
Public transport: Bus: 6/6E Lerwick to Sumburgh Airport (two miles from reserve). J and D S Halcrow (Mon-Sat) and R Robertson & Son (late service Mon-Sat and Sun service).
Visiting: Reserve open all hours. Viewing points inc accessible sheltered viewing area/seating. Lighthouse complex operated by Shetland Amenity Trust. Open Thurs-Mon, 10am-5pm (Apr-Sep) with visitor centre, cafe, shop, toilets: 01595 694 688; www.sumburghhead.com
Contact: RSPB: 01950 460 800; shetland@rspb.org.uk
Head N on A970.

3 LOCH OF SPIGGIE, MAINLAND

RSPB
Habitats: Two, shallow, nutrient-rich lochs, once a sea inlet. Adjoining marshland between lochs and farmland. SSSI, SPA.
Birds: Summer: Red-throated Diver, Eider, Moorhen, Lapwing, Curlew, Snipe, Redshank, Oystercatcher, Arctic Tern, Great Skua. *Autumn:* Black-tailed Godwit, Ruff, Wigeon *Winter:* Great Northern Diver, Whooper Swan, Teal, Wigeon. Long-tailed Duck, Slavonian Grebe
Other: Slender-leaved Pond Weed.
Directions: ZE2 9JE; HU 371 177. Take B9122 W from A970 Lerwick-Sumburgh road. After 1.25 miles take single-track minor road heading NW in South Scousburgh. This takes you across isthmus separating Loch Spiggie from Muckle Sound before turning S and running to the W of the Loch.
Public transport: Bus: 6, Lerwick-Sumburgh Airport, J & DS Harlow, alight at Robin's Brae. 2.5 mile walk to reserve.
Visiting: Free, open all hours, no facilities. Hide (wheelchair accessible) and small parking area at N end. No access to lochside but can view from road, which runs close to loch. View from passing places but take care not to block traffic. Keep dogs under close control/on a lead in breeding season or near livestock.
Contact: RSPB: 01950 460 800; shetland@rspb.org.uk
Return to A970 and continue N.

4 MOUSA, MOUSA

RSPB
Habitats: Island, uninhabited since 19C. Grassland, rocky shores. lochans. SSSI, SAC.
Birds: Breeding: One of UK's largest Storm Petrel breeding colonies. Red-throated Diver, Eider, Puffin, Black Guillemot, Shag, Snipe, Ringed Plover, Redshank, Oystercatcher, Dunlin. Arctic Tern, Arctic & Great Skua. Endemic Shetland Wren, Shetland Starling.
Other: Harbour & Grey Seals.
Directions: ZE2 9HP; HU 435 249 (Sandsayre Pier). Leave A970, Lerwick-Sumburgh road in Sandwick and take minor road for Leebitten and Sandsayre Pier. Car park at pier.
Public transport: Bus: 6A, Lerwick-Sandwick; 6 Lerwick-Sumburgh, nearest stop 10 minute walk to pier, J & DS Harlow
Visiting: Reserve is free, open all hours. Toilets at pier, not on island. Access from Sandsayre Pier, Mainland is via Mousa Boat (charge inc RSPB members, cash only) early Apr-early Sep (not Sat). Dusk trips are also offered (premium rate, May-Jul) for Storm Petrel viewing. Stay on marked trail. RSPB allows dogs on reserve under control/on lead but check with boat operator if allowed on boat.

Contact: RSPB: 01950 460 800; shetland@rspb.org.uk
Mousa Boat: 07901 872 339; info@mousa.co.uk;
www.mousa.co.uk
Continue on A970 to Lerwick.

5 NOSS NNR, NOSS
NatureScot

Habitats: Dune and coastal grassland, moorland, heath, blanket bog, sea cliffs.

Birds: Spring/summer: Breeding Fulmar, Shag, Gannet, Arctic Tern, Kittiwake, Herring & Great Black-backed Gulls, Great & Arctic Skuas, Guillemot, Razorbill, Puffin, Black Guillemot, Eider, Lapwing, Dunlin, Snipe, Wheatear, Twite plus migrants.

Other: Grey & Common Seals, Otter, Harbour Porpoise, Killer Whales (annual).

Directions: ZE2 9ES; HU 525 408 (Bressay parking for Noss). Take car ferry to Bressay from Lerwick and follow signs for Noss (3.2 miles). At end of road, walk to shore (600 yards), where inflatable, passenger-only ferry to island will collect you. If red flag is flying, island is closed due to sea conditions.

Public transport: None.

Visiting: Car park on Bressay side. Access to island, subject to weather, by small inflatable 10am to 5pm, May to end-Aug (not Mon or Thurs). Daily update on crossings by 9am—Noss Ferry Line: 0800 107 7818. Visitor centre, toilets (open during sailing times). Steep, rough track down to ferry. Walk around island c.3 hours. No dogs on ferry.

Contact: NS Reserve Manager: 01595 693 345; nnr@nature.scot

6 FETLAR, FETLAR
RSPB

Habitats: Mires, lochs

Birds: Red-throated Diver, Golden Plover, Red-necked Phalarope, Whimbrel

Other: Serpentine heath. Otters (best viewed at Hamars Ness ferry terminal).

Directions: ZE2 9DJ; HU 658 898. Ferry service to Hamars Ness, NW tip of island. Take the only road out of 'town' and drive S for 1 mile. Turn L on to B9088 and stay on it for 5 miles. Park in small car park W of Loch Funzie.

Public transport: Vehicle ferry from Wick of Gutcher, Yell or Wick of Belmont, Unst to Hamars Ness. No buses on Fetlar.

Visiting: Open all hours (reserve), hide open all year, free. Hide 500 yards from car park, also seasonal viewpoint from roadside at Mires of Houbie, May-Aug.

Contact: RSPB: 01950 460 800; shetland@rspb.org.uk

7 HERMANESS NNR, UNST
NatureScot.

Habitats: Sea cliffs, moorland/grassland, blanket bog.

Birds: Summer: 100,000 seabirds. Fulmar, Gannet, Shag, Guillemot, Razorbill, Puffin, Kittiwake. Arctic & Great Skuas, Dunlin, Golden Plover, Snipe.

Other: Spring Squill. Grey Seal.

Directions: ZE2 9EQ; HP 612 149. On northern island of Unst (from Lerwick via Yell and Unst ferries). On Unst, head N on A968 through Baltasound, turn on to B9086 just before Haroldswick signposted Burrafirth and Hermaness. Continue to fork in road, go straight to reserve car park.

Public transport: None to reserve (bus—Lerwick to Baltasound but overnight stay needed).

Visiting: Access all hours. Walk to cliffs starts in car park (notice board/leaflets). Gravel path N to Winnaswarta Dale then boardwalk takes you across reserve to western cliffs—keep to boardwalk to avoid damaging vegetation (moderate walk). Can explore coast from cliffs (strenuous walk), N tip overlooks Muckle Flugga (UK's most northerly lighthouse).

Contact: NS Reserve Manager: 01595 693 345;

Female [Common] Redpoll
Sylvie Soudan
Instagram: Sylvie.Soudan

WALES/CYMRU
ORGANIZATIONS

BIRD ATLAS/AVIFAUNA

The Birds of Wales/Adar Cymru
Rhion Pritchard, Julian Hughes, Ian M Spence,
Bob Haycock & Anne Brenchley
(Liverpool University Press, 2021)

BIRD REPORT
The Welsh Bird Report is published in *Birds in Wales/ Milvus,* from the Welsh Ornithological Society:
wbr@birdsin.wales
Recent years are available to download from:
www.birdsin.wales/welsh-bird-report

The UK/Welsh headquarters of a number of organizations focusing on birds or where they live are listed here, in advance of the County Directory. Where the organization's UK headquarters is in England, its purpose and activities are presented in the UK/England section and all that is listed here are its Welsh contact details.

BIRD OBSERVATORIES COUNCIL (1946)
The BOC co-ordinates and promotes the work of bird observatories at a national level. All accredited bird observatories (20 at present) affiliated to the Council undertake a ringing programme and provide a ringing experience to those interested. Most are also able to provide accommodation for visiting birdwatchers.
Contact: All enquiries: Steven Stansfield, Cristin, Bardsey Island, Pwllheli, LL53 8DE: 07855 264 151;
info@birdobscouncil.org.uk;
www.birdobscouncil.org.uk

BRITISH ORNITHOLOGISTS' UNION (1858)
The BOU is one of the world's oldest and most respected ornithological societies. It aims to promote ornithology within the scientific and birdwatching communities, in Britain and around the world and this is largely achieved by the publication of its quarterly international journal of avian science, *Ibis.* It runs an active programme of conferences, meetings and seminars covering ornithological topics and issues of the day—the proceedings are published free on the BOU website. Via social media (see website for links), the BOU acts as a global ornithological hub providing details of newly published research articles, conferences, PhD opportunities, jobs and more. Work being undertaken around the world may include research projects that have received financial assistance from the BOU's on-going programme of Small Research Grants and Career Development Bursaries (for ornithology students). The BOU's Records Committee (see below) maintains

the official British List. The BOU previously published a series of country/island group 'BOU checklists'.
Contact: British Ornithologists' Union, P.O. Box 79, Pembroke, SA72 9AX: via website; www.bou.org.uk

BRITISH ORNITHOLOGISTS' UNION RECORDS COMMITTEE
A standing committee of the BOU, BOURC's function is to maintain the 'British List', the official list of birds recorded in Great Britain (the up-to-date list, which currently follows the IOC World Bird List, can be viewed on the BOU website and, as of the date this edition went to press, it is this list, in terms of the species that are included, that forms the basis for the checklist published in this **Yearbook,** although the sequence followed here, as explained in the *Checklist* section, is now that of AviList v25). Where vagrants are involved, it is concerned only with those which relate to potential additions to the British List (i.e. first records). It also examines, where necessary, important pre-1950 records, monitors introduced species for possible admission to/ deletion from the List. BOURC reports are published in *Ibis* and on the BOU website.
Contact: BOU—as above.

BRITISH TRUST FOR ORNITHOLOGY WALES/CYMRU
BTO Wales/Cymru provides a Welsh voice for the BTO and a focus on Welsh priorities.
BTO Wales/Cymru, Thoday Building, Deiniol Road, Bangor, Gwynned LL57 2UW: 01248 383 285;
wales.info@bto.org;
www.bto.org/about-bto/national-offices/bto-wales

ROYAL SOCIETY FOR THE PROTECTION OF BIRDS (RSPB) WELSH HEADQUARTERS
Wales Headquarters: Castlebridge 3, 5-19 Cowbridge Road East, Cardiff CF11 9AB: 029 2035 3000;
cymru@rspb.org.uk

WELSH ORNITHOLOGICAL SOCIETY (1988)
Promotes the study, conservation and enjoyment of birds throughout Wales. Runs the Welsh Records Panel which maintains the Welsh bird list. Publishes the journal *Milvus* (formerly *Birds in Wales*), the annual Welsh Bird Report and the annual *Scarce and Rare Birds in Wales Report*. Organizes an annual conference.
Contact: WOS: web@birdsin.wales; www.birdsin.wales

WILDLIFE AND WETLANDS TRUST (WWT)
The WWT has one Wetland Centre in Wales.
Llanelli Wetland Centre, Llwynhendy, Llanelli, Car-

marthenshire SA14 9SH: 01554 741 087; info.llanelli@wwt.org.uk

CAMPAIGN FOR THE PROTECTION OF RURAL WALES (1928)

CPRW aims are to help the conservation and enhancement of the landscape, environment and amenities of the countryside, towns and villages of rural Wales and to form and educate opinion to ensure the promotion of its objectives. It gives advice and information on matters affecting protection, conservation and improvement of the visual environment. Publishes *Rural Wales*. *Contact:* CPRW, Ty Gwyn, 31 High Street, Welshpool, Powys SY21 7YD: 01938 552 525; info@cprwmail.org.uk; www.cprw.org.uk

NATURAL RESOURCES WALES (2013)/ CYFOETH NATURIOL CYMRU

Natural Resources Wales brought together the work of the Countryside Council for Wales, the Environment Agency Wales and the Forestry Commission Wales, as well as some functions of the Welsh Government. Its purpose is to ensure that the natural resources of Wales are sustainably maintained, enhanced and used, now and in the future. *Contact:* Natural Resources Wales: 0300 065 3000 (Mon-Fri, 9am-5pm); to report an environmental incident: 0300 065 3000 (24 hrs); to check flood warnings—Floodline: 0345 988 1188 (24 hrs):
enquiries@naturalresourceswales.gov.uk; www.naturalresources.wales.gov.uk

WOODLAND TRUST/COED CADW

Wales: Castle Court, 6 Cathedral Road, Cardiff, CF11 9LJ. 029 2002 7732; wales@woodlandtrust.org.uk

Female [Lesser] Redpoll
Sylvie Soudan
Instagram: Sylvie.Soudan

Pembrokeshire

In spring and summer, the steep wooded valleys through the area are good for Red Kite, Redstart, Pied Flycatcher and Wood Warbler. Summer boat trips run to the seabird islands of Ramsey, Skomer (daily) and Skokholm (no day trips/residential only), getting you close to the huge Welsh seabird colonies.

Bird Atlases/Avifauna
Atlas of Breeding Birds in Pembrokeshire 2003-07
Annie Haycock et al.
(Pembrokeshire Bird Group, 2009)
Birds of Pembrokeshire
Jack Donovan & Graham Rees
(Dyfed Wildlife Trust, 1994)

Bird Recorders
Recorder: Jon Green, Crud Yr Awel, Bowls Road, Blaen-porth, Ceredigion SA43 2AR: 07896 315 711;
jonrgreen1990@gmail.com

Bird Report
Pembrokeshire Bird Report (1981-), download from website: www.pembsbirds.blogspot.com or
https://pembsavifauna.co.uk/bird-reports/
Skokholm Bird Report (1981-), download from website: www.welshwildlife.org/about-us/skokholm-reports/

BTO Regional Representatives
Bob Haycock
Wetland Bird Survey (WeBS)
Local Organizer: webs@bto.org
Annie Haycock:

Club
Pembrokeshire Bird Group (2006; 40)
Chris Taylor: 07773 797 559;
chris@pembrokeshirecoast.org.uk
Dean Maiden: 07779 905 995; ocdean54@gmail.com
www.pembsbirds.blogspot.com/ or
https://pembsavifauna.co.uk
Meetings: Occasional activities—contact/see website for details.

Ringing Group/Bird Observatory
Skokholm RG
Pembrokeshire RG
www.birdringingpembrokeshire.blogspot.com
Skokholm Bird Observatory
Richard Brown/Giselle Eagle (Wardens),
The Welsh Wildlife Centre, Cilgerran, Cardigan SA43 2TB: 01239 621 212 (wardens: 07971 114 303);

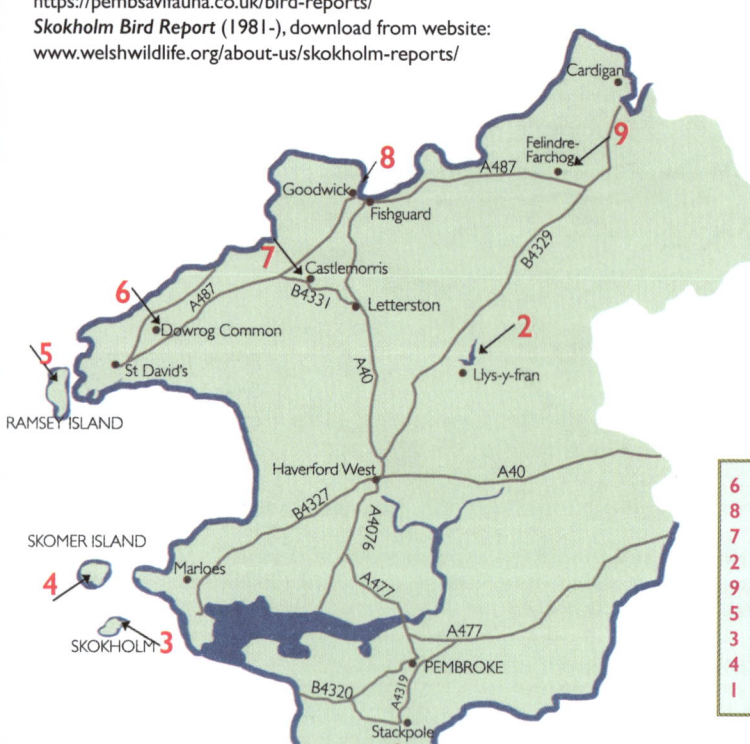

6	Dowrog Common
8	Goodwick Moor
7	Llangloffan Fen
2	Llys-y-Fran Lake
9	Pengelli Forest
5	Ramsey Island
3	Skokholm
4	Skomer
1	Stackpole

skokholmwarden@gmail.com;
www.skokholm.blogspot.co.uk
Accommodation: 01656 724 100;
islands@welshwildlife.org
www.welshwildlife.org/visit/skokholm-island

RSPB Local Group
No Groups.

Wildlife Trust
Wildlife Trust of South and West Wales (2002; 9,000)
The Nature Centre, Fountain Road, Tondu, Bridgend,
Mid-Glamorgan CF32 0EH: 01656 724 100;
info@welshwildlife.org; www.welshwildlife.org

1 STACKPOLE NNR
National Trust in partnership with Natural Resources
Wales
Habitats: Limestone cliffs, dunes, woodland, scrub, shallow freshwater lakes.
Birds: All Year: Shag, Cormorant, Peregrine, Kingfisher, Chough, Raven, Stonechat, common woodland spp.
Spring/Summer: Manx Shearwater and Gannet (offshore), breeding Fulmar, Kittiwake, auks inc Puffin. Migrants inc Wheatear, Ring Ouzel. *Winter:* Red-throated & Great Northern Divers, Wildfowl inc Goldeneye, Goosander. Bittern, Water Rail, Lapwing, Curlew, Golden Plover, Hen Harrier.
Other: Dragonflies, 30+ spp. Butterflies, coastal flora, fungi, 12 spp. Bats inc. Greater Horseshoe. Otter.
Directions: SA71 5LS; SR 991 958 (Stackpole Quay car park). Others at Broad Haven South/Bosherston Lakes (SA71 5DR), Stackpole Court (SA71 5DE). Five miles S of Pembroke. Take B4319 from Pembroke to Stackpole and Bosherston—various entry points on to estate.
Public transport: Bus: 387/388, limited summer/winter services from Pembroke. Pembrokeshire CC (01437 764 551). Train—Pembroke (six miles)
Visiting: Some restrictions, military training areas—observe notices. Pay & display car parks open dawn-dusk (NT members free). Refreshments at Stackpole, various toilets. Walking trails. Check for disabled access—various facilities. Dogs on leads where stock grazing.
Contact: National Trust: 01646 623 110;
stackpole@nationaltrust.org.uk
NRW: 0300 065 3000;
enquiries@naturalresourceswales.gov.uk
Return to Pembroke. Then A477 & A4076 to Haverfordwest.

2 LLYS-Y-FRAN LAKE
Welsh Water
Habitats: Reservoir, farmland, woodland, scrub.
Birds: All year: Common woodland spp, Red Kite, Peregrine Falcon, Kingfisher, Raven, Dipper. *Spring/summer:* Regular sightings of Osprey, hirundines, Willow War-

bler, Redstart, Spotted Flycatcher. *Autumn:* Common & Green Sandpipers. *Winter:* Wildfowl inc Goldeneye, Wigeon, Teal. Gulls, occasional divers, scarcer grebes. Winter thrushes.
Other: Otter, Polecat. Butterflies.
Directions: SA63 4RR; SN 040 244. 11 miles NE of Haverfordwest. Take B4329 from Haverfordwest, fork R in Crundale. After just over 7 miles turn sharp L for hamlet of Llys-y-Fran by dam at S end of reservoir.
Public transport: None.
Visiting: Open daily—gates open at 6am. Car park free for 1 hour, then charges. Visitor centre, cafe, gift shop (9am-5pm Apr-Sep; 10am-4pm Oct-Mar, closed 24-26 Dec). Toilets, bike hire, adventure activities, camping. Circular trail around reservoir (6.25 miles).
Contact: Welsh Water: 01437 532 273;
llysyfran@dwrcymru.com; https://.llys-y-fran.co.uk
Return to Haverfordwest.

3 SKOKHOLM NNR
The Wildlife Trust of South & West Wales
Habitats: Cliffs, bays and inlets. Scrub for migrants.
Birds: Spring: Manx Shearwaters arrive at end of Mar (89,000 pairs). *Summer:* Internationally important colonies of Razorbill, Puffin, Guillemot, Storm Petrel, Lesser Black-backed Gull. *Passage:* Migrants inc rare species.
Other: Grey Seal, Harbour Porpoise, Common and Risso's, occasional Bottlenose Dolphins, nationally rare moths.
Directions: SA62 3BJ; SM 760 089 (Marloes/ Martin's Haven parking). 15 miles SW of Haverfordwest. Take B4327, turn-off for Marloes, continue two miles past village to embarkation point at Martin's Haven (National Trust car park, fee payable).
Public transport: Train—Milford Haven.
Visiting: No day visitors, residential stays available Apr-Sep (bookings open in autumn for following season). Bird Observatory welcomes visiting ringers. Self-catering accommodation for up to 20 people, small shop selling basic foodstuffs. Boat fare paid online or over phone to boatman.
Contact: Main Office and Island Bookings (Mon-Fri 9am-5pm): 01656 724 100; islands@welshwildlife.org

4 SKOMER
The Wildlife Trust of South & West Wales
Habitats: Sea cliff, freshwater ponds.
Birds: Summer: World's largest Manx Shearwater colony (350,000+ pairs). Puffin (until end Jul), Guillemot, Razorbill, (until mid Jul), Kittiwake (until end-Aug), Lesser Black-backed Gull, Fulmar, Short-eared Owl, Chough, Peregrine Falcon, Buzzard, migrants (inc. rarities).
Other: Grey Seal, Harbour Porpoise, Common Dolphin.
Directions: See **Skokholm NNR**
Public transport: Puffin Shuttle arrives from St Davids at 10:15am for 11am departures. Fflecsi bookable bus

service runs in area.

Visiting: Island open Apr-Sep (Easter if earlier). Information centre, toilets, two hides, booklets, guides, nature trails. Take water/food. Not suitable for infirm (87 steep landing steps/rough ground).

Day visitors: (not Mon, max 250 tickets per day, on-line booking: https://www.pembrokeshire-islands.co.uk/boat-trips/land-on-skomer/) Island landing fee, payable online. Boats leave between 10am & noon—returning 3pm onwards. No dogs.

Overnight visitors: Boat sails at 9am—booking essential (bookings open in autumn for following season)/length of stay conditions apply.

Contact: See **Skokholm NNR**

Return to Haverfordwest, then A487 for St Davids.

5 RAMSEY ISLAND
RSPB

Habitats: Acid grassland, maritime heath, sea cliffs.

Birds: All year: Peregrine, Raven, Chough. *Spring/summer:* cliff-nesting auks (Guillemot, Razorbill), Kittiwake, Fulmar, Shag, Stonechat, Wheatear, Skylark, Linnet, Little Owl. *Passage:* Regular migrants, occasionally scarce or rare spp.

Other: Largest Grey Seal colony in south-west Britain, Red Deer, Harbour Porpoise.

Directions: SA62 6PY; SM 721 249 (mainland). One mile offshore from lifeboat station at St Justinians, two miles west of St Davids, Pembrokeshire.

Public transport: Bus: T11 (not Sun) from Haverfordwest to St Davids (Richards Bros: 01239 613 756) and then 403 Celtic Coaster St David's to St Justinians, May-Sep (Sarah Bell: 07828 940 955). Train—Haverfordwest.

Visiting: Coach and car parking at St Justinians (ask boat company for advice/options). Island open daily 10am-4pm, weather permitting, Apr 1st/Easter if earlier) to Oct. Boat fare, plus RSPB landing fee for non-members.. Small RSPB visitor centre/shop selling snacks and hot/cold drinks. Compost toilets—five minute walk uphill from harbour. 3.5 mile circular trail (or two shorter walks)—rugged in parts. Introduction from resident wardens. Guided walks available. No wheelchair access. Boat—sails from lifeboat station at 10am & 12pm, returns at 4pm. *At time of going to press (October 2025), restrictions on visiting due to closure of lifeboat station. Check current situation before making plans.*
To book: Thousand Island Expeditions: 01437 721 721; info@thousandislands.co.uk
Contact: RSPB: 07836 535 733;
ramsey.island@rspb.org.uk
Return to St Davids and head NE

6 DOWROG COMMON
Wildlife Trust of South & West Wales/National Trust

Habitats: Pools, wet & dry heath, fen, 250 acres. SSSI, SAC.

Birds: Breeding: Grasshopper & Sedge Warblers, Reed Bunting: *Winter:* Bewick's & Whooper Swan, Teal, Wigeon, Shoveler, Snipe, Water Rail. Hen Harrier (roost), Merlin, Short-eared Owl.

Other: Water Shrew. Marsh Fritillary, Scarlet Tiger Moth, Small Red Damselfly, Hairy Dragonfly, Scarce Blue-tailed Damselfly. Yellow Centaury, Pale Dog-violet, Wavy St John's Wort, Three-lobed Crowfoot, Pilwort, Lesser Butterfly Orchid

Directions: SA62 6PN; SM 772 275. Take A487 heading NE from centre of St David's. After just over 2 miles, take reflex L turn on to minor road running NW. This crosses the reserve. Small parking area is 0.8 miles along this road on L by cattle grid

Public transport: None. Close to St David's but walk along road not pleasant.

Visiting: Free, open all hours. Car park in middle of N edge. Very wet in places and at times. Not suitable for wheelchairs. Keep dogs on lead, clean up mess.

Contact: WT of S&W Wales: 01656 724 100; info@welshwildlife.org; www.welshwildlife.org
Return to the A487, head NE and take B4331 on R just past Mathry.

7 LLANGLOFFAN FEN NNR
The Wildlife Trust of South & West Wales/ Natural Resources Wales

Habitats: Open water, fen, wet heath, carr, semi-improved pasture SSSI, SAC. One of Wales's largest remaining valley mires, W end WTS&WW, E end NRW.

Birds: Corncrake, Quail, Spotted Crake, Water Rail. Barn Owl, Hen Harrier, Grasshopper Warbler.

Other: Otter, Polecat, Water Vole. River & Brook Lamprey. Marsh Cinquefoil.

Directions: SA62 5ER; SM 895 316. Leave the A40 Haverfordwest-Fishguard road at Letterston and take the B4331. In Castlemorris either turn R on to minor road for 0.25 mile and park in lay-by, NRW entrance on R just before stone bridge, or go straight on and small WTS&WW car park on R after c.0.5 mile. Llangloffan itself is to NE of reserve.

Public transport: Bus: 411, Haverford West-Fishguard Square, Richard Bros (01239 613 756).

Visiting: Free, open all hours, no facilities. Circular trail and boardwalk to 1 hide in WTS&WW section, circular boardwalk in NNR, dogs on lead, not suitable for wheelchairs.

Contact: WT of S&W Wales: 01656 724 100; info@welshwildlife.org; www.welshwildlife.org
NRW: 0300 065 3000;
enquiries@naturalresourceswales.gov.uk
Return to either A487 or A40 to FishgUARD.

8 GOODWICK MOOR
The Wildlife Trust of South & West Wales

Habitats: Reedbed, flood plain mire, carr, ditches and

streams. Liable to flooding at high tide. 44 acres.
Birds: Sparrowhawk, Kestrel, Stonechat. *Summer:* Willow, Sedge & Reed WarblerS, *Winter:* Snipe, Siskin. Bittern & Cetti's Warbler have been recorded.
Other: Otter, Water Vole. Sea Rush, Sea Aster, Common Cotton Sedge, Royal Fern.
Directions: SA65 9PL; SM 947 374. Adjacent to A40 between centre of Fishguard and Goodwick, immediately behind beach. Entrance along track and over footbridge from A40 (SM 949 375) beside Seaview Hotel. Car parks at SM 949 376 & SM 947 379.
Public transport: Bus: 410, 404; Strumble Shuttle from (Pembrokeshire Coast National Park: 01437 720 392), all from Fishguard Square.
Visiting: Now open all hours after being closed for 6 years, free, no facilities (toilets outside reserve on sea front). 500 yard boardwalk through reserve. Wildlife pond. Not suitable for wheelchairs. Dogs on lead.
Contact: WT of S&W Wales: 01656 724 100; info@welshwildlife.org; www.welshwildlife.org
Rejoin A487, head NE.

9 PENGELLI FOREST
The Wildlife Trust of South & West Wales
Habitats: Ancient Oak woodland. SSSI SAC
Birds: *All year:* Sparrowhawk, Buzzard, Tawny Owl, common woodland spp. *Summer:* Cuckoo, Redstart, Wood Warbler, Spotted & Pied Flycatchers. *Winter:* Woodcock, winter thrushes, Brambling.
Other: Polecat, Dormouse, 8 spp bats, butterflies inc Silver-washed Fritillary, White-lettered and Purple Hairstreaks, ancient woodland flora.
Directions: SA41 3PU; SN 122 395. Leave A487 Cardigan to Fishguard road just E of Felindre Farchog along unclassified road (*CARE*—tight turn if approaching from E)—reserve entrance *c.*1.5 miles along narrow lane following foot of hill (around Iron Age mound of Castel Henllys), once across a ford, access gate is 0.3 mile, park on road by gate.
Public transport: Bus: T5 (not Sun) Cardigan to Fishguard stops at Felindre Farchog (then walk road route to forest). Richard Bros (01239 613 756).
Visiting: Open all hours. Easy walks near entrance but no wheelchair access, paths steeper elsewhere.
Contact: WT of S&W Wales: 01656 724 100; info@welshwildlife.org

Ceredigion

Ceredigion occupies the coast of Cardigan Bay between the Teifi and Dovey estuaries, with the Welsh Wildlife Centre (Cardigan) at its south western tip being good for wintering wildfowl and waders. Further inland, along the flanks of the Cambrian Mountains, there are fens and mires, as well as steep wooded valleys that are good for Red Kite, Redstart, Pied Flycatcher and Wood Warbler.

Bird Atlas/Avifauna
Birds of Ceredigion
Hywel Roderick & Peter Davis
(Wildlife Trust of South & West Wales, 2010)

Bird Recorder
Russell Jones, Bron y Gan, Talybont, Ceredigion SY24 5ER: 07735 497 393; russellbronygan@outlook.com

Bird Report
Ceredigion Bird Report (1982/85), from 2017 available as a download from website:
www.birdsin.wales/county-map/ceredigion

BTO Regional Representative
Naomi Davis
Wetland Bird Survey (WeBS)
Local Organizer: webs@bto.org
Ceredigion (inc Dyfi Estuary)
Russell Jones:

Club
None

RSPB
No Groups

Ringing Group/Bird Observatory
Mid-Wales RG: https://midwalesringers.blogspot.com
Teifi RG: www.teifimarshbirds.blogspot.co.uk

Wildlife Trust
Wildlife Trust of South and West Wales (2002, 9,000)
The Nature Centre, Fountain Road, Tondu, Bridgend, Mid-Glamorgan CF32 0EH: 01656 724 100; info@welshwildlife.org; www.welshwildlife.org

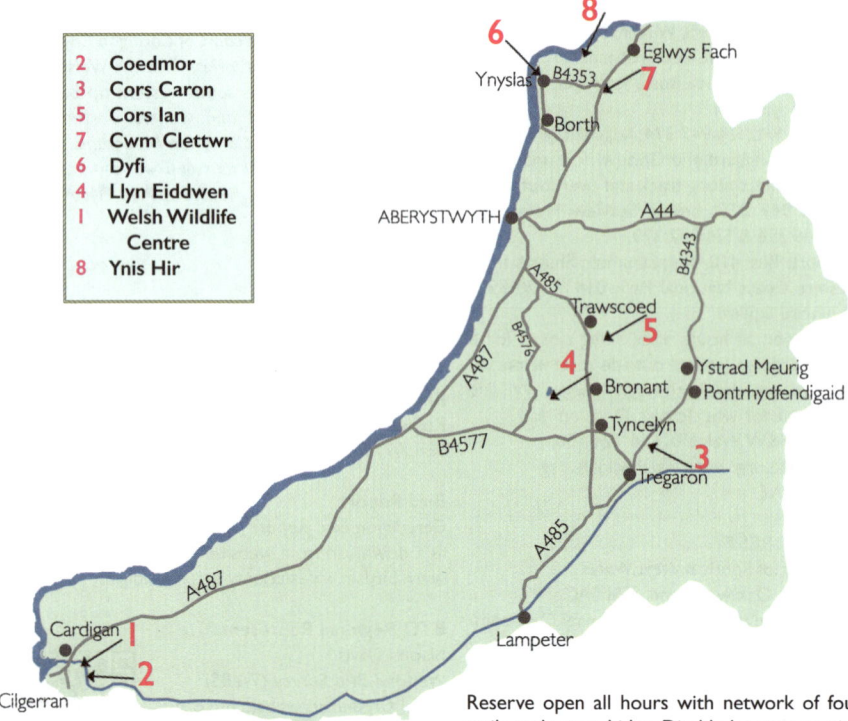

2	Coedmor
3	Cors Caron
5	Cors Ian
7	Cwm Clettwr
6	Dyfi
4	Llyn Eiddwen
1	Welsh Wildlife Centre
8	Ynis Hir

1 WELSH WILDLIFE CENTRE/TEIFI MARSH NR

The Wildlife Trust of South & West Wales

County boundary cuts through marshes. Marshes partly in Ceredigion, partly Pembrokeshire. Wildlife Centre itself is right on boundary but actually in Pembrokeshire.

Habitats: Wetlands, marsh, swamp, reedbed, open water, creek (tidal), river, saltmarsh, woodland.

Birds: *Summer:* Breeding Kingfisher, gulls, Sand Martin, Great Spotted Woodpecker, Redstart, Cetti's Warbler. *Winter:* Wildfowl inc Teal, Wigeon and Mallard. Water Rail, Curlew, Snipe, Lapwing and Peregrine Falcon. Occasional Bittern and Red Kite.

Other: Otter, Water Shrew, Sika & Red Deer, good variety dragonflies.

Directions: SA43 2TB; SN 188 451. Visitor centre 1.25 miles from Cilgerran, two miles SE of Cardigan. River Teifi is N boundary. Signposted from A478 Cardigan to Tenby road. Close to junction of A487 and A478.

Public transport: Bus: 430 (not Sun) Cardigan to Narberth, alight at Cilgerran, then walk to centre. Richards Bros (01239 613 756).

Visiting: Free parking for WTSWW members, charge for non-members payable in car park. Visitor centre/cafe/shop open 10am-4pm Wed-Sun plus some Bank Holiday Mon (closed Christmas and New Year week).

Reserve open all hours with network of four nature trails and seven hides. Disabled access to visitor centre, paths and four hides. Dogs on leads. Events during school holidays for children.

Contact: Welsh Wildlife Centre: 01239 621 600; wwc@welshwildlife.org;
facebook page: Welsh Wildlife Centre
On the other side of the Teifi and just upstream.

2 COEDMOR NNR

Natural Resources Wales

Habitats: Steep-sided gorge with remnant of ancient, mainly but not exclusively, Sessile Oak woodland.

Birds: The West Wales specialities of Wood Warbler, Redstart, Pied Flycatcher.

Other: Otter, 31 spp. butterfly, 200 spp. lichen.

Directions: SA43 2LG; SN196 445 (lay-by at start of gorge walk). Take A484 from Cardigan for Carmarthen. After just over 1 mile turn R at crossroads in Llangoedmor. Road becomes single track. After 0.5 mile lay-by on R at start of gorge walk. look out for map and information board. For Coedmor Mansion (gardens also part of NNR) continue along road for 0.25 mile and then along track when road turns L. Small parking area for gardens after another 0.25 mile.

Public transport: Bus: 460, Cardigan-Carmarthen (not Sun or Bank Holidays), Richard Bros (01239 613 756)/ Morris Travel (01267 235 090).

Visiting: Free, open all hours, no facilities. Short path down steep-sided gorge of tributary of Teifi. The reserve extends beyond this gorge along the steep sides of the Teifi itself and includes the gardens of Coedmor Mansion on more level ground above the gorge. Trails through the gardens but Mansion privately owned. Steep slopes not suitable for wheelchairs. Dogs on lead.
Contact: NRW: 0300 065 3000;
enquiries@naturalresourceswales.gov.uk
From Cardigan take the A484, then the A475 and then the A485 to the edge of the Cambrian Mountains, where at the other end of the Teifi, after it flows down from Llyn Teifi, lies

3 CORS CARON NNR
Natural Resources Wales
Habitats: Three raised bogs, reedbed, fen, wet grassland and woodland, areas of open water on floodplain of Teifi. 2,000 acre SAC
Birds: Curlew, Red Kite, Hen Harrier, Skylark.
Other: Adder.
Directions: SY25 6JF; SN 692 625 (main car park). Leave the A485 in Tregaron and take the B4343 running NE for Pontrhydfendigaid. Main car park after 2 miles on L on E edge of bog. Small car parks also at Maesllyn farm (SN 695 631)—600 yards further along B4343, then turn L up farm track—and Ystrad Meurig Station Yard (SN 711 673)—take B4340 at Pontrhydfendigaid, after just over 1.25 miles land on left in Ystrad Meurig leads to Yard.
Public transport: Bus: 585 Lampeter-Aberystwyth stops in Tregaron (not Sun or Bank Holidays), Lloyds Coaches (01654 702 100); T21 Tregaron-Aberystwyth travels along W & N of NNR and stops at Ystrad Meurig (not Sat or Sun), Evans Coaches (01974 298 546).
Visiting: Free, open all hours, no facilities. Circular boardwalk across SE bog to hide (both wheelchair accessible) running from walk along disused railway (suitable for wheelchairs) on E edge. Main car park adjacent to disused railway, which runs to Ystrad Meurig Station Yard at N end of bog. Keep dogs under control.
Contact: NRW: 0300 065 3000;
enquiries@naturalresourceswales.gov.uk
Rather than leaving the A485 in Tregaron, continue N towards Bronant and, ultimately, Aberystwyth.

4 LLYN EIDDWEN
The Wildlife Trust of South & West Wales
Habitats: Upland, shallow, mesotrophic lake with bog to N and S, acidic grassland and heath.
Birds: Winter: Whooper Swan, Coot, Pochard, Wigeon, Teal. Black-throated Diver and the now lumped Green-winged Teal have been recorded.
Other: Water Vole. Awlwort.
Directions: SY23 4JH; SN 608 672. Between Tyncelyn and Bronant take any one of several minor roads running W from the A485 towards Bontnewydd, passing

through it. After a further 0.8 mile take minor road on R running N to Trefenter. This road runs along the E side of the lake. Roadside parking area just N of cattle grid at N end of lake
Public transport: Bus: 588 Aberystwyth-Lampeter stops in Trefenter (not Sat or Sun) Evans Coaches (01974 298 546).
Visiting: Open all hours, free, no facilities. Public footpath along ridge to W of lake. Ground very soft in places in boggy areas, not suitable for wheelchairs. Dogs on lead.
Contact: WT of S&W Wales: 01656 724 100;
info@welshwildlife.org; www.welshwildlife.org
Instead of heading W off the A485, continue to Lledrod.

5 CORS IAN
The Wildlife Trust of South & West Wales.
Habitats: Upland valley mire and gorse hillside.
Birds: Buzzard, Red Kite, Barn Owl, Raven, Stonechat, Reed Bunting. Summer: Pied & Spotted Flycatchers, Redstart, Whinchat, Grasshopper, Garden & Willow Warblers.
Other: Dragonflies (inc Emperor, Keeled Skimmer, Common Hawker). Butterlies (inc Small Pearl-bordered Fritillary). Marsh flora. Water Vole, Polecat, Otter.
Directions: SY23 4HX; SN 669 695. 1.5 miles E of Lledrod. Leave A485 SE along minor road in Lledrod. After 1.8 miles turn L (towards Trawscoed/Crosswood)—off-road pull in on R after 470 yards (entrance to reserve).
Public transport: None.
Visiting: Open all hours. Public footpath runs along S boundary from parking area and various permissive paths lead up to hill top. Ground is wet—keep out of mire, view from path. Not suitable for wheelchairs. Dogs on lead.
Contact: WT of S&W Wales: 01656 724 100;
info@welshwildlife.org
The A485 eventually joins the A487 for Machynlleth just S of Aberystwyth and this will take you to.

6 DYFI NNR
Natural Resources Wales
Habitats: Tidal estuary, dunes, saltmarsh, mudflats. 5,000 acres of wetland on the S side of the Dyfi/Dovey estuary.
Birds: Spring: Nightjar. Autumn: Passage waders. Winter: Wildfowl inc Greenland White-fronted Goose, Sanderling, Golden Plover, Red Kite, Hen Harrier, Merlin, Peregrine Falcon.
Other: Common & Sand Lizards, Grass Snake, Adder. Vernal Mining Bee. Bee & Marsh Orchids. *Cors Fochno:* Rosy Marsh Moth, Large Heath Butterfly, Bog Bush-cricket, Small Red Damselfly, Bog Raft Spider. Bog Cotton, Bog Asphodel, Bog Myrtle, Sundews.
Directions: SY24 5JZ; SN610 941 *Ynyslas* car park. Take the A487 from Aberystwyth for Machynlleth. In Bow

Ceredigion

Street turn L on to B4353 (signposted Borth). After 2.5 miles R at roundabout, take road parallel to sea for 2 miles then L in Ynyslas and continue on minor road parallel to sea (do not bear right in Ynyslas). Car park is 1 mile along this road. *Alternatively,* you can bear R at Ynyslas and continue for *c.*2 miles, then turn R through a gated entrance (close gate after you) and drive 700 yards for the *Cors Fochno* parking area (free) at SY24 5LB; SN 633 922. This car park can also be reached by continuing on the A487 to Tre'r-ddôl amd then turning L on to B4353. Gated entrance is 1.5 miles on L.
Public transport: Bus: 512 Aberystwyrh-Ynyslas (not Sun or Bank Holidays), Mid Wales Travel. (01970 828 288, enquiries@midwalestravel.co.uk; www.midwalestravel.co.uk) Train—Borth.
Visiting: Ynyslas visitor centre (SN 610 941) car park (charge) floods at high tide, see notices, remove cars before high tide. Shop and cafe closed March '25, consulting over possible future operators. Reserve free, open all hours. Red-flagged beach, do not swim or use inflatables. Toilets. Several waymarked trails and Ynyslas is one end of the Ceredigion Coast Path. The *Cors Fochno* part of the Dyfi NNR is a raised bog also known as 'Borth Bog'. There is a circular boardwalk around the bog but no facilities. Dogs under control at Ynyslas, especially when and where sheep grazing or birds nesting; no dogs at Cors Fochno,
Contact: 01970 872 901;
ynyslas@cyfoethnaturiolcymru.gov.uk
Further along the A487.

7 CWM CLETTWR
The Wildlife Trust of South & West Wales
Habitats: Regenerating broadleaf, with heather and gorse, and mature broadleaf (Sessile Oak and Ash) SSSI mainly to N of the steep-sided ravine of the Afon Clettwr.
Birds: Sparrowhawk, Dipper, Nuthatch, Grey Wagtail. *Summer:* Redstart, Pied Flycatcher, Wood Warbler.
Other: Polypody, Oak and Beech Ferns.
Directions: SY20 8PT (Soar Chapel); SN 666 922. rather than turning L off the A487 in Tre'r-ddôl, for **Cors Fochno**, take the minor road into the centre of the village and then turn R by Soar Chapel up the steep hill. Park off road on R near top of hill.
Public transport: Bus: X28/T2 Aberystwyth-Machynlleth, Lloyds Coaches (01654 702 100) stops in Tre'r-ddôl.
Visiting: Free, open all hours. Minor road and car park along N edge of reserve. Public and permissinve paths, steep sections not suitable for wheelchairs. Clettwr forms S boundary for most of reserve with one block to S of river. Dogs no lead.
Contact: WT of S&W Wales: 01656 724 100;
info@welshwildlife.org; www.welshwildlife.org
Continue along A487 towards Machynlleth. Ynys Hir lies im- *mediately to the NE of the Dyfi NNR, on the S side of the Dyfi estuary.*

8 YNYS HIR
RSPB
Habitats: Estuary, freshwater pools, woodland and wet grassland.
Birds: All year: Red Kite, Buzzard, Little Egret, Teal, Lapwing. *Spring/summer:* Redstart, Pied Flycatcher, nine spp warbler inc Grasshopper & Wood. *Winter:* Greenland White-fronted & Barnacle Geese, Wigeon, Hen Harrier.
Other: 16 spp dragonflies inc Small Red Damselfly and-Golden-ringed Dragonfly. Butterflies inc Dark Green Fritillary, Brimstone and Speckled Wood. Otter, Brown Hare.
Directions: SY20 8TA; SN 681 960. Car park is one mile from Eglwys-fach village, off A487, six miles SW of Machynlleth.
Public transport: Bus T2 & T28 Machynlleth to Aberystwyth, alight Eglwys-fach. Lloyds Coaches (01654 702 100). Train—Machynlleth.
Visiting: Open Wed-Sun **only** (dawn-dusk). Visitor Centre 10am-4pm (not Christmas period). Prior-booked coaches welcome, call for parking info. Drinks/light refreshments, toilets. Entrance fee for reserve, members free. Three trails, five hides, two viewpoints. Not suitable for wheelchair/mobility scooters. Check website (www.rspb.org.uk/ynys-hir) for accessibility statement. No dogs.
Contact: RSPB: 01654 700 222; ynyshir@rspb.org.uk
Continue along A487 for Machynlleth and **Gwynedd**.
Or return to Aberystwyth, then take the A485 and then A484 S to **Carmarthenshire**.

Carmarthenshire

Dunes, mires and wetlands on the north shore of the Bristol Channel between the estuary of the Tywi and the Burry inlet at the mouth of the Loughor. The valley of the Tywi runs NE between the SE slopes of the Cambrian Mountains to the W and The Black Mountain to the E. Extensive forests that are a mix of ancient woodland and recent plantation on the sites of old forests cover the flanks of these mountains.

Bird Atlas/Avifauna
None.

Bird Recorder
Gary Harper, Maesteg, Capel Seion, Drefach, Llanelli, SA14 7BS: 07748 970 124;
gary.harper3@gmail.com

Bird Report
Carmarthenshire Birds (1982-), from CBC

BTO Regional Representative
Gethin Jenkins-Jones
Wetland Bird Survey (WeBS)
Local Organizer: webs@bto.org
Alan Seago:
Burry Inlet (North)
Alan Seago:

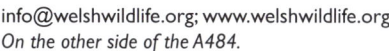

Club
Carmarthenshire Bird Club (2003; 140+)
Sian Rees-Harper (Sec), Maesteg, Capel Seion, Drefach, Llanelli, SA14 7BS: 07748 970 124
gary.harper3@gmail.com;
www.carmarthenshirebird.club
Meetings: 7:30pm, on a Wednesday (Oct-Mar). WWT Penclacwydd, Llanelli, SA14 9SH. Contact/see website for details.

Ringing Group/Bird Observatory
None

RSPB Local Group
No Groups.

Wildlife Trust
Wildlife Trust of South and West Wales (2002; 9,000)
The Nature Centre, Fountain Road, Tondu, Bridgend, Mid-Glamorgan CF32 0EH: 01656 724 100;
info@welshwildlife.org; www.welshwildlife.org

1 FFRWD FARM MIRE
Wildlife Trust for South & West Wales
Habitats: Relict sand dune, fenland, reedbed, open water.
Birds: Summer: Mallard, Moorhen, Water Rail, Reed, Sedge, Cetti's & Willow Warblers, Reed Bunting. *Winter:* Teal, Snipe; occasional Bittern, Marsh Harrier, Peregrine Falcon.
Other: Water Vole (recorded). Scarcer water plants: Bird's-foot, Floating Club-rush, Tubular Water Dropwort, Water Dock.
Directions: SA16 0EZ; SN 418 029 (intersection of minor road, disused railway line and towpath near Ty Mawr. Lies in triangle formed by A484 (Burry Port-Kidwelly) and B4317.
Public transport: Bus: X11 Swansea-Carmarthen stops at end of B4317 (not Sun), First Bus (www.firstbus. co.uk). Train—Pembrey & Burry Port (4 miles).
Visiting: Limited parking on roads running along edges of reserve. No public access to reserve but a disused railway runs N-S along one edge and St Illtyd's Way E-W along towpath of disused canal forms another boundary. Possible to view the reserve from these paths. No facilities.
Contact: WT of S&W Wales: 01656 724 100;

info@welshwildlife.org; www.welshwildlife.org
On the other side of the A484.

2 PEMBREY COUNTRY PARK
Carmarthenshire County Council
Pembrey Country Park offers a number of leisure activities and also visitor facilities that are shared with several reserves that form part of or are adjacent to it.
Habitats: 500 acres of park and woodland.
Birds: Common woodland spp inc Goshawk, Sparrowhawk, Buzzard and Red Kite. Siskin and small numbers of Redpoll best looked for on paths by miniature railway.
Other: Areas of woodland managed for butterflies inc Silver Washed Fritillary and Grizzled Skipper.
Directions: SA16 0EJ; SN 400 001 (PCP car park 1). Take A484 from Llanelli for Bury Port. Turn L after 5 miles, follow brown signs for 1 mile to PCP.
Public transport: Bus: X11 Swansea-Carmarthen stops in Pembrey (not Sun), First Bus (www.firstbus.co.uk). Train—Pembrey & Burry Port (4 miles).
Visiting: Park: 6am-10pm; Visitor Centre: 10am-4pm. Charge for car park. Campsite, cafe, toilets (by the car park, wheelchair accessible. The car parks extend along the far edge of the Park from the entrance, behind the beach, from the edge of the Forest NNR in the NW to the Burrows in the SE. Three nature trails. Dogs allowed but keep under control.
Contact: 01554 742 423 (8am-4pm);
infopembrey@carmarthenshire.gov.uk

2a PEMBREY FOREST NNR
Natural Resources Wales
Habitats: 2,423 acres of forest, largely Corsican Pine, planted 1929-54 on sand dunes.
Birds: Crossbill, Long-eared Owl.
Other: Grizzled Skipper, Marsh Fritillary butterflies.
Directions: SA16 0EJ; SN 400 001 (PCP car park 1). See Pembrey Country Park.
Public transport: See **Pembrey Country Park**.
Visiting: Open all hours, free but car parks subject to PCP conditions, see above. Nearest car park to Shells & Pines trail is PCP car park 1. On the site of a WWI ammunition factory. The waymarked Shells & Pines trail starts beyond PCP car park 1 and follows the factory's old train tracks. The Wales Coast Path goes through the Forest and along the beach.
Contact: NRW: 0300 065 3000;
enquiries@naturalresourceswales.gov.uk

2b PEMBREY BURROWS & SALTINGS LNR
Carmarthenshire County Council
Habitats: 670 acres of active sand dunes and saltmarsh Beach and sea to S, creek to N, estending as far as Pembrey Harbour. SSSI & SAC.
Birds: Over 101 spp recorded. Best for spring migrants

3	**Ash Pits and**
	Pwell Lagoon
6	**Brechfa Forest**
8	**Crychan Forest**
5	**Dinefwr**
1	**Ffrwd Farm Mire**
9	**Gwenffrwd Dinas**
4	**Llanelli Wetland**
	Centre
2	**Pembrey**
7	**Talley Lakes**

on dunes and beach. Scrubby areas for warblers. Large Mediterranean Gull roost Aug/Sep, best viewed from Old Pembrey Harbour, where Osprey possible early autumn. Marsh & Hen Harriers in winter.

Other: Rare dune plants and insects. Orchids late Apr to end June. Butterflies and Dragonflies June to Sep.

Directions: SA16 0EJ; SS 407 998 (at SE end of row of PCP car parks). See **Pembrey Country Park.**

Public transport: See **Pembrey Country Park.**

Visiting: Open all hours, free but see **Pembrey Country Park** for conditions if use one of its car parks. Facilities in Country Park. The Burrows run E from the edge of the Country Park, just beyond the car park. They are grazed by cattle, keep dogs under control. Please follow signage and keep off saltmarsh at all times.

Contact: 01554 742 423 (8am-4pm); infopembrey@carmarthenshire.gov.uk

Continue along the A484.

3 ASH PITS & PWLL LAGOON LNR

Carmarthenshire County Council

Habitats: Former settling lagoons for pulverized fuel ash from Carmarthen Bay Power Station (demolished), reed, wet woodland, fen.

Birds: Summer: Mallard, Tufted Duck, Little & Great Crested Grebes, Reed, Sedge & Cetti's Warblers, Reed Bunting. *Winter:* Pochard, Water Rail.

Other: History of lagoons means unusual mix of lime-loving and lime-hating plants.

Directions: SA15 4BD; SN 474 010 (King George's Playing Field car park to E of LNR). Heading E along the A484 from Burry Port to Llanelli, turn R in Pwll down the lane leading to the King George's Playing Field car park, which is immediately before the sewage works.

Public transport: Bus: X11 Swansea-Carmarthen stops

in Burry Port (not Sun), First Bus (www.firstbus.co.uk). Train—Pembrey & Burry Port (1 mile).

Visiting: Open all hours, free, no facilities. LNR lies between A484 and disused railway line to N, and railway line to S between it and shore. Welsh Coast Path crosses railway line and runs along S edge of LNR. Trails around lagoons. Many surfaced and wheelchair accessible.

Contact: 01554 742 423 (8am-4pm); infopembrey@carmarthenshire.gov.uk

Continue on the A484 and take the B4303 (2nd exit) at the Sandy roundabout and continue on this road until you reach the Wetland Centre from the W as opposed to the E as in the directions in the following entry.

4 LLANELLI WETLAND CENTRE

The Wildfowl & Wetlands Trust.

Habitats: Inter-tidal mudflats, saline lagoons, reedbeds, freshwater pools, scrapes, saltmarsh, international waterfowl collection.

Birds: All year: Kingfisher, Black-tailed Godwit and Little Egret. Short-eared, Tawny & Barn Owls, Marsh Harrier, Peregrine Falcon. *Winter:* Up to 50,000 waterbirds, inc Pintail, Wigeon, Teal, Spoonbill, Curlew, Oystercatcher, Redshank.

Other: Bee & Southern Marsh Orchids, Yellow Bartisa. 22 spp Dragonflies and Damselflies. Water Vole, Otter.

Directions: SA14 9SH; SS 532 985. Overlooks estuary near Llanelli on B4304. Leave M4 at Junc 48. Signposted from A484, E of Llanelli.

Public transport: Train—Llanelli station two miles.

Visiting: Free car/coach parking. Open daily (not 24/25 Dec) 9:30am-5pm (car park locked at 5 pm). Entrance fee, WWT members free. Visitor centre fully accessible with toilets, hides, cafe, shop, education facilities. Mobility scooters/wheelchairs available to hire. Centre has level access and hard-surfaced paths.

Contact: WWT Llanelli Wetland Centre: 01554 741 087;

info.llanelli@wwt.org.uk

From the centre of Llanelli take the A476 for Llandeilo;

5 DINEFWR/DYNEFOR CASTLE WOODS

Wildlife Trust for South & West Wales

Habitats: Two areas of ancient, semi-natural deciduous woodland on steep slopes overlooking Tywi and floodplain. 62 acres, SSSI.

Birds: Summer: Sparrowhawk, Tawny Owl, common woodland spp inc all 3 woodpeckers (few recent reports of Lesser Spotted), Pied & Spotted Flycatchers, Redstart. On floodplain, Goosander, Pochard, Shoveler, Mallard, Teal, Tufted Duck, with Whooper Swan, Wigeon & Pintail in winter. Great White Egret now regular in winter.

Other: Comma, Silver-washed Fritillary, Speckled Wood amongst the butterflies. Bluebells Dog's Mercury, Primrose, Wood Anemone & Toothwort.

Directions: SA19 6RP; SN 627 225 (Fire Station car park). If approaching on A476, this joins A483 at Ffairfach, just S of Llandeilo. As you enter Llandeilo turn L into Carmarthen Street, which become Carmarthen Road. Can park next to Fire Station (but see note below) on right. If approaching on A40, turn S into Carmarthen Road *c.*0.75 mile W of town centre.

Public transport: Bus: X13 from Swansea; 280 Carmarthen-Llandovery. Train—Llandeilo.

Visiting: Open all hours, reserve itself free. Park in Newtown House car park (National Trust, charge but free for NT & WTS&WW members; toilets). If you park elsewhere and then walk down Dinefwr Park Drive, you are crossing NT land and may be charged, so might as well park in NT car park. Alternatively, park in Bridge Street, which has direct access to Trust woods. Trails through reserve. Some paths steep. Wheelchair access only at bottom but even there ground uneven.

Floodplain hide wheelchair accessible but path rough.
Contact: WT of S&W Wales: 01656 724 100; info@welshwildlife.org; www.welshwildlife.org
Join A40 N of Llandeilo and head W.

6 BRECHFA FOREST NNR

Natural Resources Wales

Habitats: 16,055 acres forest. Once (post-1283) the Royal Forest of Glyn Cothi, planted with conifers in 20C.

Birds: Common woodland and woodland edge spp, inc Nightjar, Red Kite, Goshawk, Barn Owl, Peregrine Falcon, Wood, Garden & Grasshopper Warblers, Lesser Whitethroat, Spotted & Pied Flycatchers, Redstart, Hawfinch.

Other: Red Squirrel, bats.

Directions: SA32 7RA; SN 525 303 (Ty Mawr hotel in centre of Brechfa). Leave the A40 at Nantgaredig (5.8 miles E of Carmarthen, 9.4 miles W of Llandeilo) and take the B4310 N for c.6.75 miles to the centre of the village of Brechfa—hotel, parking, toilets. Brechfa itself is not in the forest, which takes the form of a broken belt to the N of the village, running from SW to NE.

Public transport: Bus: 282 Carmarthen-Brechfa (not Sun), Morris Travel (01267 235 090).

Car parks:

Byrgwm: SA32 7RD; SN 545 315. Continue along B4310 past the centre of Brechfa for 1.75 mils. Car park on L up forest road. Open all hours, free, no facilities. I walking and 4 mountain bike trails from car park. Walking trail closed in 2025.

Abergorlech: SA32 7SJ; SN 586 337. Continue along B4310 past Byrgwm for 3 miles. Car park, open all hours, free, on L of road, pub, toilets. 3 walking and I mountain bike trail. The easiest of the walking trails

Looking SW over the Burry Inlet from above the Wetland Centre towards Llanrhidian Marsh in West Glamorgan.

might be wheelchair accessible.

Tower: SA39 9EJ; SN 495 354, fire tower at N edge of forest. Take A484 for Llandeilo out of Carmarthen. At roundabout after hospital take A485 for Lampeter. After c.10 miles turn R on to minor road in New Inn, signposted for Brechfa. Parking area on R after 1.75 miles. If you stay on this road you will reach Brechfa after another c.4.6 miles, passing through the following two car parks on the way. Parking here is open all hours, free but with facilities. You can follow forest roads from here that will connect up with trails from the car parks further S.

Keepers: SA32 7BW; SN 522 319. In Brechfa turn L on to minor road by village shop, signposted for New Inn (see above). Car park 1.5 miles on L. Open all hours, free, no facilities. I short and I long trail from here, with long trail completing a circuit of the N part of the forest

Gwarallt: SA32 7BW; SN 520 322. Car park is 500 yards on from **Keepers.** On R up forest road. Open all hours, free, no facilities. I easy trail suitable for wheelchairs.

NE margin of forest, flanking the River Melinddwr: SN 586 378. Continue along B4310 past Abergorlech for 2.7 miles to Llansawel. By pub, turn sharp L on to B4337. After 2.3 miles bridge on L crosses Melinddwr and leads to forest road. Turn R on to forest road, car park on R. Open all hours, free no facilities. Toilets in Llansawel.

Contact: NRW: 0300 065 3000; enquiries@naturalresourceswales.gov.uk

Instead of turning sharp L in Llansawel, turn R and follow B4337 though village. After crossing the Cothi it joins the B4302. Turn R and approach Talley Lakes from N.

7 TALLEY LAKES

Wildlife Trust for South & West Wales (leased from RSPB)

Habitats: Two small, connected lakes separated by an isthmus, reedbed, Alder & Willow Carr. 62 acres

Birds: *Summer:* Mute Swan, Great Crested Grebe, Tufted Duck, Pochard. Spotted & Pied Flycatchers. *Winter:* Whooper & Bewick Swans, Red-necked Grebe, Scaup, Smew (have been recorded)

Other: Emperor Dragonfly. Shoreweed & Bladder Sedge recorded in 1773 and still present. Southernmost location of Water Sedge.

Directions: SA19 7AX; SN632 328 (Talley Abbey car park). 7 miles N of Llandeilo on B4302. In Talley take minor road for abbey, where B road turns sharp R. Off-road parking at abbey

Public transport: None.

Visiting: Open all hours, no facilities. Footpath across private land from gate on road, past abbey to a stile between lakes. Hide on isthmus. Not suitable for wheelchairs. Dogs on lead.

Contact: WT of S&W Wales: 01656 724 100; info@welshwildlife.org; www.welshwildlife.org

Continue S on B4302 to junction with A40 just N of Llandeilo, then head NE along A40 to Llandovery.

8 CRYCHAN FOREST NNR

Natural Resources Wales

Habitats: Between Cambrian Mountains and Brecon Beacons, bought by Forestry Commission in 1930s. Conifer plantations together with Oak, Ash, Beech & Hazel. Old drove roads.

Birds: Nightjar, Honey Buzzard, Goshawk, Red Kite. Common woodland spp.

Other:

Directions: The Crychan Forest lies NE of Llandovery, with the A483 to Llanwrtyd Wales running along its NW edge. The A40 runs E-W between Llandovery and Brecon to the S of it. Toilets, shops, cafes and information centre in Llandovery.

Public transport: Bus: X14 runs between Llandovery and Llanwrtyd Wells, various stops between them but then walk to forest. Fridays only. Celtic Travel (01686 412 231). Train—Llandovery.

Car parks:

The first three car parks are off the A483 and lie in the NW block of the forest. Follow old tracks that used to link farms before forest planted. All four car parks are open all hours and free. There are no facilities at any of them.

Cefn Farm: SA20 0YS; SN 813 387. Take the A483 NE from Llandovery for Llanwrtyd Wells. After 4.5 miles (just before Cynghordy and 6.8 miles before Llanwrtyd Wells), take minor (Roman) road veering E for Tirabad. After 50 yards take single track road on R. Follow for 1.25 miles. Car park is up track on L.

Esgair Fwyog: SA20 0YS; SN 837 412. Instead of turning off minor road, continue for 2 miles, car park is on R. The Heart of Wales Line trail runs past the car park.

Brynffo: SA20 0YT; SN 848 410. 1 mile further beyond Esgair Fwyog, take a forest road on R. Car park is 150 yards along road on R. If you go past the turning for Brynffo Farm, you have gone too far.

The fourth car park is at the S edge of the SE block of forest, the Halfway Forest.

Halfway: SA20 0SE; SN 835 330 car park. 300 yards up a forest road to N of A40 (brown sign for Crychan Forest Trails), 5.25 miles SE of Llandovery, right on the county boundary. 2 waymarked walking trails.

Contact: NRW: 0300 065 3000; enquiries@naturalresourceswales.gov.uk

The Crychan Forest lies to the SE of the A483. To the N there is.

9 GWENFFRWD-DINAS

RSPB

Habitats: Hillside oak woods, streams and bracken

slopes. Spectacular upland scenery.

Birds: All year: Red Kite, Buzzard, Peregrine, Raven, Goosander, Dipper, Grey Wagtail, Marsh Tit and 3 spp woodpeckers (Lesser not reported for some years! Your chance to earn the warden's gratitude). *Summer:* Common Sandpiper, Cuckoo, Pied Flycatcher, Wood Warbler, Redstart, Tree Pipit.

Other: Golden-ringed Dragonfly, Purple Hairstreak, Silver-washed Fritillary, Wilson's Filmy Fern.

Directions: SA20 0PG; SN 788 471. N of Llandovery. From A483 take B road signposted to Llyn Brianne Reservoir and then follow signs to reserve, which lies between Cynghordy and Llanwrda.

Public transport: None.

Visiting: Public nature trail at Dinas open dawn-dusk. Car park and information board at start of trail, coach parking can be arranged. Nature trail inc a boardwalk. Other parts of trail are rugged. No sections suitable for wheelchairs. Toilets at Llyn Brianne reservoir car park (one mile N).

Contact: RSPB: 02920 353 000; gwenffrwd.dinas@rspb.org.uk

The reserve is right on the county boundary with Breconshire. Return to A483 and head NW for Llanwrtyd Wells in Breconshire.

Alternatively, on leaving the Wetland Centre, do not head for Llandeilo. Instead head E on the A484, cross the River Loughor into West Glamorgan, then take a R at Stafford Common and double back on the B4295 along the S side of the Loughor estuary to Whiteford Burrows and Llanrhidian Marsh (see West Glamorgan).

West Glamorgan

Gower's coastline has breeding seabirds, Peregrines and Chough, with Dartford Warbler also present. Offshore, there are thousands of Manx Shearwaters. Llanrhidian Marsh runs along north side of the peninsula and faces the coast of Carmarthenshire across the Burry inlet, whilst the south side overlooks the Bristol Channel.

Bird Atlas/Avifauna
An Atlas of Breeding Birds in West Glamorgan
DK Thomas
(Gower Ornithological Society, 1992)

Bird Recorder
Gower/Swansea and Neath Port Talbot
Ed Hunter. goweros23@gmail.com

Bird Report
Gower Birds (1968-), from GOS—Jeremy Douglas-Jones, 14 Alder Way, West Cross, Swansea, SA3 5PD: 01792 551 331; jeremy@douglas-jones.biz

BTO Regional Represenatives
Dr Alan Seago
Wetland Bird Survey (WeBS)
Local OrganizerL webs@bto.org
West Glamorgan
Vacant

Club
Gower Ornithological Society (1956; 200)
Jeremy Douglas-Jones (Sec), 14 Alder Way, West Cross, Swansea, SA3 5PD: 01792 551 331;
jeremy@douglas-jones.biz; www.gowerbirds.org.uk
Meetings: Contact/see website for details.

Ringing Group/Bird Observatory
Gower RG:
www.gowerbirds.org.uk/category/gower-ringing-group

RSPB Local Group
Swansea & District (1985; 60)
Maggie Cornelius: rspbswandistgrp@gmail.com;
https://group.rspb.org.uk/swanseaanddistrict/
Meetings: Contact/see website for details.

Wildlife Trust
Wildlife Trust of South & West Wales (2002; 9,000). The Nature Centre, Fountain Road, Tondu, Bridgend, Mid-Glamorgan CF32 0EH: 01656 724 100; info@welshwildlife.org; www.welshwildlife.org

I WHITEFORD BURROWS & LLANRHIDIAN MARSH NNR
National Trust
Habitats: Sand dunes, salt marsh, tidal mudflats. SSSI, SAC, SPA
Birds: Summer: Reed & Sedge Warblers. Wintering waders and wildfowl: Curlew, Redshank, Snipe, Oystercatcher, Golden Plover, Lapwing, Knot, Pintail.
Other: Scarlet Tiger Moth, Narrow-mouthed Whorl Snail. Early Marsh Orchid, Fen Orchid, Marsh Helleborine, Dune Gentian, Petalwort..
Directions: SA3 1DE; SS 430 935 (Llanmadoc car park). Take the A483 at J47 of the M4. After 2.75 miles turn R on to A4216 and R again after 400 yards on to the B4295. The B4295 runs through Gowerton and then W along the S edge of Llanrhidian Marsh to Llanrhidian, passing car parks at the E end of the Marsh at SS 545 959 (toilets) and SS 533 958. At Llanrhidian continue W on minor road and take the R fork at Oldwalls. Continue W through Cheriton to Llanmadoc. Park in farmer's field between Llanmadoc and Cwm Ivy (honesty box).
Public transport: Bus: 116 Swansea-Llanmadoc (infrequent, not Sun), Adventure Travel (02920 442 040).
Visiting: Open all hours, free (honesty box for car park), no facilities but pub in Llanmadoc. Tarmac path from Ll-

anmadoc car park to Cwm Ivy, footpath to dunes, paths through dunes, not all wheelchair/pushchair accessible. Hide in Whiteford Burrows. No paths across marsh, which is flooded by a fast incoming tide. Wales Coast Path runs along S edge of marsh from Llanmadoc to the two car parks (see above) at the E end. *c.* 8.5 miles. Keep dogs on lead near livestock.

Contact: 01792 390 636;

visit.rhosili@nationaltrust.org.uk

There is no road S along the full length of the W coast of the Gower but it is possible to work across the peninsula following minor roads from Llanmadoc to the A4118 at Little Reynoldston. Turn R for **Gower Coast** *and* **Port Eynon** *and then follow the Directions section in the relevant entries or L for* **Oxwich Bay**.

2 GOWER COAST NNR
National Trust/Natural Resources Wales
Habitats: Sea cliffs, beach, Worm's Head tidal island.
Birds: Breeding: Kittiwake, Razorbill, Guillemot. A few Fulmar & Shag, Chough, Dartford Warbler. Puffins used to breed on Worm's Head but decimated by rats. Late summer seawatching: Manx Shearwater, Storm Petrel.
Other:
Directions: SA3 1PR; SS 421 869 Rhosili car park (W end of NNR). Take A4118 from Swansea. At Scurlage turn R on to B4247, follow it to Rhosili. Car park on L.
Public transport: Bus: 118, Swansea-Rhosili, infrequent, Adventure Travel (02920 442 040). Train—Swansea.
Visiting: Rhosili car park charge but NT members free. Car park, coast and accessible toilets open all hours, visitor centre 10am-4pm. Paths from Rhosili surfaced and hard initially, then grass. Paths at E end of NNR more difficult. Dogs on leads. Check tide times at Old Coastguard Station (SS 404 875) if planning to walk to Worm's Head and back. Tidal currents are dangerous.
Contact: NT: 01792 390 707;
visit.rhosili@nationaltrust.org.uk
Either take the B4247 and then the A4118 to **Port Eynon** *or walk the Gower Way along the cliff tops.*

3 PORT EYNON
The Wildlife Trust of South & West Wales
Habitats: Sea cliff, limestone grassland, heath, scrub, woodland, foreshore/beach.
Birds: All year: Common Scoter, Eider, Shag, Peregrine,

5	Crymlyn Bog and Pant y Sais
6	Cwm Clydach
2	Gower Coast
4	Oxwich Bay
3	Port Eynon
1	Whiteford Burrows, Llanrhidian Marsh

Chough, Rock Pipit, Stonechat. *Summer:* Gannet, Manx Shearwater (late-Jul/early Aug). *Passage:* Whimbrel, Common Sandpiper, Wheatear, Ring Ouzel. *Winter:* Red-throated & Great Northern Divers, Purple Sandpiper.
Other: Intertidal spp, Grey Seal, limestone flora.

Directions: W of Swansea on The Gower. Take A4118 to Port Eynon SA3 1NN (SS 467 851 car park). A cluster of Trust sites near Port Eynon: Sedger's Bank (SS 470 844); Port Eynon Point (SS 467 848); Overton Mere (SS 460 850); Overton Cliff (SS 460 848); Long Hole Cliff Overton (SS 455 852).

Public transport: Buses: 118/119 (not Sun) Swansea to Rhossili stops at Port Eynon, Adventure Travel (02920 442 040).

Visiting: Open all hours—accessible from coastal footpaths. Sea watching from Point Eynon Point (esp late-Jul/early Aug). Pay & display car park in Port Eynon, facilities in the village.

Contact: WT of S&W Wales: 01656 724 100; info@welshwildlife.org

Either continue along the Gower Way or head towards Swansea on the A4118.

4 OXWICH BAY NNR

Natural Resources Wales

Habitats: Sand dunes, lakes, woodland, cliffs, salt and freshwater marshes—and there's also a beach.

Birds: Water Rail, Little Egret, Kingfisher, Cetti's, Sedge, Reed & Wood Warblers, Rock Pipit. *Winter:* Wildfowl, divers offshore, Bittern, Woodcock, Snipe, Jack Snipe.

Other: Small Blue butterfly, Beachcomber Beetle, Hairy Dragonfly, Dune Gentian.

Directions: SA3 1LS; SS 503 864. Take A4118 from Swansea. 0.7 mile after Nicholaston church turn L down minor road signposted to Oxwich & Slade. Large car park on L.

Public transport: Bus: 118, Swansea-Perriswood Turn (junction of A4118 and minor road to Oxwich), infrequent, Adventure Travel (02920 442 040). Train—Gowerton or Swansea.

Visiting: Car park, access to NNR and part of beach owned by Penrice Estate. Charge for car park. Toilets, shops, cafe, restaurant. NNR has 2 waymarked circular trails, The longer one, through the woods, steep nattow and with steps. Boardwalk crosses freshwater marsh and reedbeds to hide. Wales Coast Path passes through dunes and edge of wood. Dogs on lead.

Contact: NRW: 0300 065 3000; enquiries@naturalresourceswales.gov.uk

On the other side of Swansea, between the heavily built-up areas of Swansea and Neath lies a large area of fen.

5 CRYMLYN BOG
& PANT Y SAIS NNRs

Natural Resources Wales

Habitats: Crymlyn Bog is the largest lowland fen in Wales. Pant y Sais, another fen, is a nearby NNR that is entered separately. Canals.

Birds: Breeding: Water Rail, Bittern, Marsh Harrier, Red Kite, Cetti's, Reed, Sedge & Grasshopper Warblers, Bearded Tit.

Other: Fen Raft Spider. Marsh Cinquefoil, Greater Spearwort, Royal Fern.

Directions: Crymlyn Bog: SA1 8LN; SS 685 942 (Crymlyn Bog car park). Take the A483 (Fabian Way) for Cardiff and the M4. After 1 mile turn L on to minor road (Wern Terrace) signposted for Ashlands Community Sports Hall. Turn R at T junction on to Tir John North Road. Car park on R 0.75 mile along this road. *Pant y Sais:* SA10 6JZ; SS 712 940. Take the B4290, signposted for Jersey Marine from the A483. Immediately after crossing canal bridge turn L on to School Road/Heol yr Ysgol. Limited parking in this residential road (show consideration for residents. Walk back to B4290 and towards bus stop. Entrance and boardwalk behind railings 250 yards along B4290 from canal bridge.

Public transport: Bus: 53 runs along A483, Adventure Travel (02920 442 040); T6, Swansea-Brecon stops at Jersey Marine, Transport for Wales (0300 200 22 33). Train—Swansea.

Visiting: Free but Crymlyn Bog car park locked overnight. No facilities. Crymlyn Bog has trails (grass and boardwalk sections, some gates) into fen. Pant y Sais has a circular boardwalk. Wheelchair accessible. The Tennant Canal and Wales Coast Path run along S edge of Crymlyn Bog and the Tennant Canal then runs through Pant y Sais. Tennant Canal towpath not suitable for wheelchairs. Dogs on lead.

Contact: NRW: 0300 065 3000; enquiries@naturalresourceswales.gov.uk

Head back to M4 and

6 CWM CLYDACH

RSPB

Habitats: Oak and beech woodland on steep slopes along banks of fast-flowing Lower Clydach River.

Birds: All year: Red Kite, Sparrowhawk, Buzzard, Raven, Green Woodpecker, Dipper and Grey Wagtail. *Summer:* Spotted Flycatcher, Garden Warbler, Wood Warbler, Cuckoo. *Winter:* Woodcock, Siskin, Redpoll.

Other: Fungi, Wood Sorrel, Silver-washed Fritillary and Speckled Wood butterflies.

Directions: SA6 5SU; SN 684 026. N of Swansea. Three miles N of J45 of M4, through village of Clydach on B4291, follow signs for Craig-cefn-Parc. Car park is close to New Inn pub.

Public transport: Bus: 214 & X6C (not Sun) Graig Felen to Craig Cefn Parc stops at reserve entrance. South Wales Transport (01792 799 575).

Visiting: Open all hours, free. Car park (no coaches). Two trails link to network of public footpaths—not suitable for wheelchairs. Dogs on leads.

Contact: RSPB: 02920 353 000; cwm.clydach@rspb.org.uk

Glamorgan

Cardiff Bay is good for passage & wintering waders and has its own wetland reserve on the doorstep of the Senedd. Kenfig Pools have a history of turning up rarities and there are several extensive coastal dune systems that are remnants of what was once a much larger continuous stretch in the west of the county. Inland, a series of valleys drain the Beacons to the north.

Bird Atlas/Avifauna
Birds of Glamorgan
Clive Hurford & Peter Lansdown
(privately published, 1995)

Bird Recorder
East Glamorgan
Phil Bristow, 2 Forest Oak Close, Cyncoed, Cardiff CF23 6QN: phlbrstw@gmail.com

Bird Report
Eastern Glamorgan Bird Report (1985-), from GBC—online only from 2022 report: www.glamorganbirds.org.uk

BTO Regional Representatives
Glamorgan (Mid & South)
Daniel Jenkins-Jones
Wetland Bird Survey (WeBS)
Local Organizer:
East Glamorgan
Daniel Jenkins-Jones
Severn Estuary, North (Gwent/Glamorgan)
See Gwent.

Club
Glamorgan Bird Club (1990; 400)
Alan Rosney (Membership Sec), 10 Parc-y-Nant, Nantgarw, RCT, CF15 7TJ: 07906 558 489; alanrosney@gmail.com; www.glamorganbirds.org.uk
Meetings: 7:30pm, (usually) 1st Tuesday of the month (Oct-Apr). Talks in person or via zoom—contact/see website for details.
Cardiff Naturalists' Society (1867; 80)
Mike Dean (Sec), 36 Rowan Way, Lisvane, Cardiff, CF14 0TD: 07793 265 554;

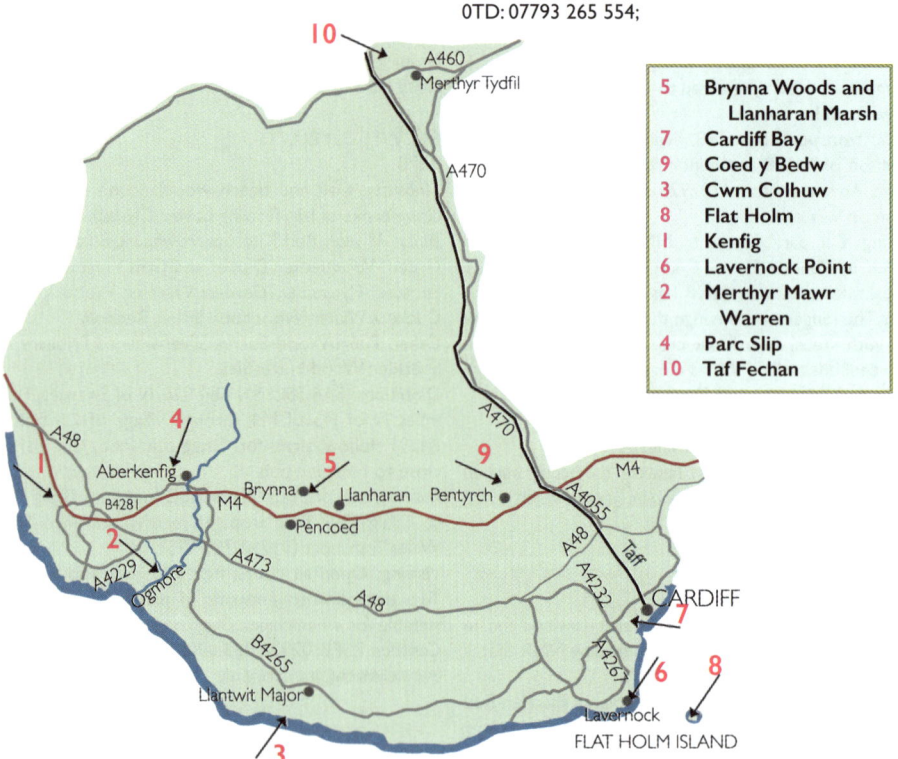

5	Brynna Woods and Llanharan Marsh
7	Cardiff Bay
9	Coed y Bedw
3	Cwm Colhuw
8	Flat Holm
1	Kenfig
6	Lavernock Point
2	Merthyr Mawr Warren
4	Parc Slip
10	Taf Fechan

secretary@cardiffnaturalists.org.uk;
www.cardiffnaturalists.org.uk
Meetings: 7:00pm Mondays (Sep-Apr). Various dates.
Ararat Baptist Church Community Centre, Plas Treoda,
Whitchurch, Cardiff, CF14 1PT. Contact/see website for
details.

Ringing Group/Bird Observatory
Cardiff RG
Flat Holm RG
Fledgemore Nest Recording Group.
Kenfig RG: www.kenfigrg.blogspot.co.uk

RSPB Local Group
None

Wildlife Trust
Wildlife Trust of South and West Wales (2002; 9,000)
The Nature Centre, Fountain Road, Tondu, Bridgend,
Mid-Glamorgan CF32 0EH: 01656 724 100;
info@welshwildlife.org; www.welshwildlife.org

1 KENFIG NNR

Bridgend County Borough Council
Habitats: 1,300 acres, sand dune system, freshwa-
ter lake with reeds, numerous wet dune slacks, sandy
coastline with some rocky outcrops.
Birds: Summer: Warblers inc Cetti's, Sedge, Reed, Grass-
hopper, Willow, Blackcap and Whitethroat. *Winter:*
Wildfowl, Water Rail, Bittern, grebes.
Other: 16 spp. orchid (inc. Fen), Hairy Dragonfly, Red-
veined & Ruddy Darters, Small Blue, Dark Green Fritillary, Grayling and Brown Argus butterflies.
Directions: CF33 4PT; SS 802 811. Seven miles W of
Bridgend. From J37 of M4, take A4229 towards Porthcawl, then R at roundabout on B4283 to North Cornelly, signposted from here.
Public transport: Bus: 63 Bridgend-Porthcawl stops at
North Cornelly (1.5 miles). First South & West Wales.
Visiting: Open all hours. Car park—coach parking available. Toilets (9am-5pm), hides, signposted paths. Unsurfaced sandy paths, not suitable for wheelchairs. Flooding
possible in winter/spring.
Contact: Kenfig NNR warden: 07483 393 944;
warden@kenfignaturecorporation.com
*Return to A4229, head S for Porthcawl, then take A4106,
which connects with the A48.*

2 MERTHYR MAWR WARREN NNR

Merthyr Mawr Estate/Natural Resources Wales
Habitats: 850 acre dune system on calcareous bedrock.
Highest dune, the Big Dipper, in Wales, beach, saltmarsh,
grassland, woods. Ogmore river along SE edge. Dune
system was once continuous with that of **Kenfig NNR**
(q.v.) to W of Porthcawl. SSSI
Birds: Passage and wintering waders inc Purple & Cur-

lew Sandpipers, Avocet. Wintering Hen Harrier.
Other: Specialist dune flora and insects.
Directions: CF32 0LR; SS 838 770 (Newton car park
at W end of dunes, opposite E entrance to Porthcawl
Holiday Park) & SS 872 772 (Candleston car park at NE
tip between woods and dunes). For Candleston leave
M4 at J37 and take A48 for Bridgend, crossing back
over M4 and staying on A48 as it becomes S by-pass
for Bridgend. Take minor road on R for Merthyr Mawr.
Stay on minor road, passing church in R. Car park after
2 miles.
Public transport: Bus: 303 Bridgend-Ogmore by the Sea,
Adventure Travel (02920 442 040) but wrong side of
Ogmore river. Train—Bridgend.
Visiting: Open all hours, 2 pay & display car parks.
Toilets at Candleston. Waymarked walking and horse
riding trails plus numerous paths through dunes and
forest, not suitable for wheelchairs. Welsh Coast Path
runs along edge of dunes.
Contact: 01656 662 413; enquiries@merthyrmawr.com
Continue E on A48, then take B4265.

3 CWM COLHUW

The Wildlife Trust of South & West Wales
Habitats: Unimproved calcareous grassland, woodland,
scrub and Jurassic blue lias cliff. Iron Age promontory
fort on site overlooking Bristol Channel.
Birds: All year: Peregrine Falcon. *Summer:* Cliff-nesting
Fulmar, Whitethroat, Grasshopper Warbler, Linnet, Yellowhammer, House Martin colony. *Autumn:* Large passerine passage. Seawatching vantage point, occasional
passing Chough.
Other: Wild Cabbage. Butterflies (inc. Small Blue).
Directions: CF61 1YX; SS 956 674. SE of Bridgend. From
Bridgend take B4265 S to Llanwit Major (0.6 mile SW
of village). Follow beach road from village to car park.
Public transport: Bus: 303 Bridgend-Barry, alight Llantwit Major and 321 (not Sun) Talbot Green-Llantwit Major. Then walk towards beach. Adventure Travel (02920
442 040). Train—Llantwit Major.
Visiting: Open all year, free. Includes part of Wales
Coast Path. Access from stile at head of valley (SS 968
678) or by steps from car park—unsuitable for wheelchairs. Information boards. Toilets.
Contact: WT of S&W Wales: 01656 724 100;
info@welshwildlife.org
*Return on B4265 to the centres of Bridgend, whence take
the A4061 to J36 of M4..*

4 PARC SLIP NATURE RESERVE

The Wildlife Trust of South & West Wales
Habitats: 300 acres of lakes, grassland, woods.
Birds: Water Rail, Teal, Lapwing, Tawny Owl, Green
Woodpecker, Jay
Other: Grass Snake, Great Crested Newt. Scarce Blue-
tailed Damselfly

Directions: CF32 0EH; SS 882 842. Take A4063 for Maesteg from J36 of M4. After 2 sets of traffic lights, take 2nd exit at roundabout on to B4281 (for Aberkenfig & Pyle), following brown signs for Parc Slip. After 1 mile turn R at Fountain restaurant into Fountain Road. Nature Reserve and Visitor Centre 0.5 mile on L.

Public transport: Bus: 63 from Bridgend bus station stops at bottom of Fountain Road. Train—Tondu & Bridgend.

Visiting: Visitor Centre open 7 days a week, cafe, accessible toilets. Wheelchair accessible paths. Hide overlooking lake. Dogs on lead.

Contact: WT of S&W Wales: 01656 724 100; info@welshwildlife.org

Return to M4.

5 BRYNNA WOODS & LLANHARAN MARSH

The Wildlife Trust of South & West Wales

Habitats: Semi-natural woodland, scrub, marshy and dry grassland. 95 acres.

Birds: Common woodland spp inc Spotted Flycatcher.

Other: Dormouse, Lesser Horseshoe & Barbastelle Bats. Bluebells.

Directions: CF72 9ZR; SS 985 829. Leave M4 at J35, take A473 for Pencoed. Take 2nd exit at each of 3 next roundabouts, taking you to Brynna Road. Follow this road for 1 mile, turn R into woodlands. Reserve signposted henceforward.

Public transport: Bus: 404 Pontypridd-Bridgend, stops in Brynna and Llanharan, Stagecoach South Wales (southwales.enquiries@stagecoachbus.com)/Adventure Travel (02920 442 040); 65 Bridgend-Talbot Green, stops at Llanharan (not Sun), Adventure Travel.

Visiting: Open all hours, free. No facilities. Two circular walks, public footpaths, can get muddy. Dogs on lead.

Contact: WT of S&W Wales: 01656 724 100; info@welshwildlife.org

Return to M4, exit at J33, taking A4232. Exit this just after it cross the Ely River (close to the Cardiff City stadium) and take B4267 (3rd exit) from roundabout

6 LAVERNOCK POINT

The Wildlife Trust of South & West Wales

Habitats: Sea, coastal calcareous grassland and scrub.

Birds: Summer: Chiffchaff, Whitethroat, Lesser Whitethroat, Bullfinch. Important site for migration—*Autumn:* Large flocks of Swallow, thrushes and finches.

Other: Butterflies, wild flowers.

Directions: CF64 5XQ; ST 181 681. Five miles S of Cardiff. Access is from B4267 via Fort Road, signposted Lavernock Point. Limited parking by gate or in public car park at end of Fort Road.

Public Transport: Bus: 94 Cardiff-Barry stops near turn to Fort Road, Cardiff Bus (02920 666 444).

Visiting: Info boards. Access via a stile, unsuitable for wheelchairs.

Contact: WT of S&W Wales: 01656 724 100; info@welshwildlife.org

Return towards Cardiff on B4267. At intersection with A4055 follow this to Cardiff Bay. After crossing the Ely, the A4055 joins the A4232, which passes just the N of

7 CARDIFF BAY WETLAND RESERVE

Cardiff Harbour Auhority

Habitat: The building of the Cardiff Bay Barrage has created a 500 acre freshwater lake fed by the rivers Ely and Taff, together with a small (20 acre) wetland reserve on N shore. Reedbed and enclosed pools, scrub.

Birds: Mallard, Teal, Tufted Duck, Great Crested & Little Grebes, Coot, Moorhen, Grey Heron, Cetti's, Reed & Sedge Warblers. Reed Bunting.

Other:

Directions: CF10 5SD (St David's Hotel); ST 118 741. Immediately S of A4232, exit before underpass. Adjacent to St David's Hotel and Havannah Street car parks (charge).

Public transport: Train—Cardiff Bay station 0.5 mile walk.

Visiting: No access into reserve but public footpath runs all along shore side. Free, no faciltiies. Information panels. Boardwalk out into lake on W side. Boat services from quays to E pass by reserve.

Contact: 029 2087 7921; www.cardiffharbour.com

Immediately to E, exit A4232 before enter underpass, for Mermaid Quay and boats to

8 FLAT HOLM

Cardiff Council.

Habitats: Offshore island, five miles from Welsh mainland. Maritime grassland.

Birds: Summer: Large Lesser Black-backed/Herring Gull colony. Shelduck, Oystercatcher, Rock Pipit.

Spring/autumn: Passage migrants.

Other: Flora (inc Rock Sea-lavender, Wild Leek).

Directions: CF10 4LY (Mermaid Quay, Cardiff); SS 220 648. Bristol Channel, six mile boat trip from Cardiff. Car park at Mermaid Quay currently closed for redevelopment.

Visiting: Access by pre-organized boat trips (subject to tides/weather). Day trips allow 2-3 hours on island. Accomodation for longer stays (contact for further information). Pub! No dogs. Boat fare and landing fee.

Boat trips (Mar-Oct):

Bay Island Voyages: 07393 470476; www.bayislandvoyages.co.uk

Cardiff Cruises: 0845 489 6969; www.cardiffcruises.co.uk

Contact: Cardiff Council: 029 2087 7912; flatholmproject@cardiff.gov.uk; www.cardiffharbour.com/flat-holm-island

On returning to dry land, take A470 N from the centre of Cardiff.

9 COED Y BEDW—PENTYRCH

The Wildlife Trust of South & West Wales

Habitats: Steep N facing slope spanning boundary between calcareous and acidic soils, mix of acidic and lime-rich streams. Alder wood in wet valley bottom, then mixed Oak/Birch and Beech to N and W. Ash on Limestone in S. 42 acres.

Birds: Common woodland spp inc Pied Flycatcher, Redstart, Willow Warbler

Other: Giant Lacewing. Giant Horsetail.

Directions: ST 111 827. 2 miles N of Cardiff. Leave A470 at Taff's Well Junction N of M4. Take the Pentyrch road over the Ynys Bridge. Then turn R at roundabout for Heol Berri Green, Gwaelod-y-Garth on B4262. Wood lies along N side of this road between the road running N for Gwaelod-y-Garth and Pentyrch.

Public transport: Bus: 136, Cardiff-Gwaelod-y-Garth.

Visiting: Open all hours, free, no facilities. Limited parking on road. Footpaths can be muddy, some steps and stiles. Dogs on lead.

Contact: WT of S&W Wales: 01656 724 100; info@welshwildlife.org

Continue N on A470. Turn R on to Vaynor Road just after A470 passes over A465.

10 TAF FECHAN

The Wildlife Trust of South & West Wales

Habitats: 105 acres. Ancient broadleaved woodland (Beech, Birch and Ash; Alder and Grey Willow by river), Hawthorn scrub, grazed calcareous grasslands. 1.5 miles of river gorge and cliffs on both sides of Taff Fechan.

Birds: Common woodland spp inc Pied Flycatcher (summer), Tawny Owl, Dipper, Kingfisher, Grey Wagtail, Peregrine Falcon, Woodcock.

Other: Otter, migrating Salmon. Small Copper, Small Pearl-bordered Fritillary. Bluebells.

Directions: CF48 2HH; SO 033 084, SO 037 076 and SO 045 097 (main entrances). Two miles N of Merthyr Tydfil centre running between two road bridges. A465 in S and minor road (Pont-sarn) to N. Entrances at either end by bridges and footpath just past village of Trefechan.

Public Transport: Bus: 25 (not Sun) Merthyr Tydfil to Trefechan. Stagecoach. Train—Merthyr Tydfil.

Visiting: Open all year, free, no facilities. Information boards. Not accessible to wheelchairs due to steep terrain and steps. Taff Fechan Trail runs length of reserve along river. Do not swim in river, unseen hazards. Small car park at N and closed because of fly tipping. Residential streets nearby, park with consideration.

Contact: WT of S&W Wales: 01656 724 100; info@welshwildlife.org

Gwent

Newport Wetlands Reserve and a cluster of other small reserves on the Gwent Levels and the foreshore have good numbers of wintering wildfowl and waders on the low lying wet meadows and mudflats of the N side of the Severn Estuary. Inland, the Gwent Wildlife Trust is using traditional practices to run several farms and areas of woodland.

Bird Atlas/Avifauna

The Birds of Gwent

WA Venables, AD Baker, RM Clarke, C Jones, JMS Lewis & SJ Tyler

(Christopher Helm, 2008).

Bird Recorder

Chris Jones: countyrecorder@gwentbirds.org.uk

Bird Report

Gwent Bird Report (1973-), from GOS—

Steve Roderick: treasurer@gwentbirds.org.uk

or from

https://www.gwentbirds.org.uk/annual-reports/

BTO Regional Representatives

Richard Clarke

Wetland Bird Survey (WeBS)

Local Organizers: webs@bto.org

Gwent (excl. Severn Estuary)

Richard Clarke

Severn Estuary, North (Gwent/Glamorgan)

Kevin Dupé

Club

Gwent Ornithological Society (1961; 420)

Blair Jones (Sec): secretary@gwentbirds.org.uk; www.gwentbirds.org.uk

Meetings: 7:30pm, Saturdays (Sep-Apr). Goytre Village Hall, Newtown Road, Penperlleni, Pontypool, NP4 0AR. Contact/see website for details.

Ringing Group/Bird Observatory

Goldcliff RG

RSPB Local Group

No Groups

Wildlife Trust

Gwent Wildlife Trust (1963; 8,023)

Chestnut Suite, Mamhilad House, Mamhilad Park Estate, Pontypool, NP4 0HZ: 01600 740 600; info@gwentwildlife.org; www.gwentwildlife.org

Gwent

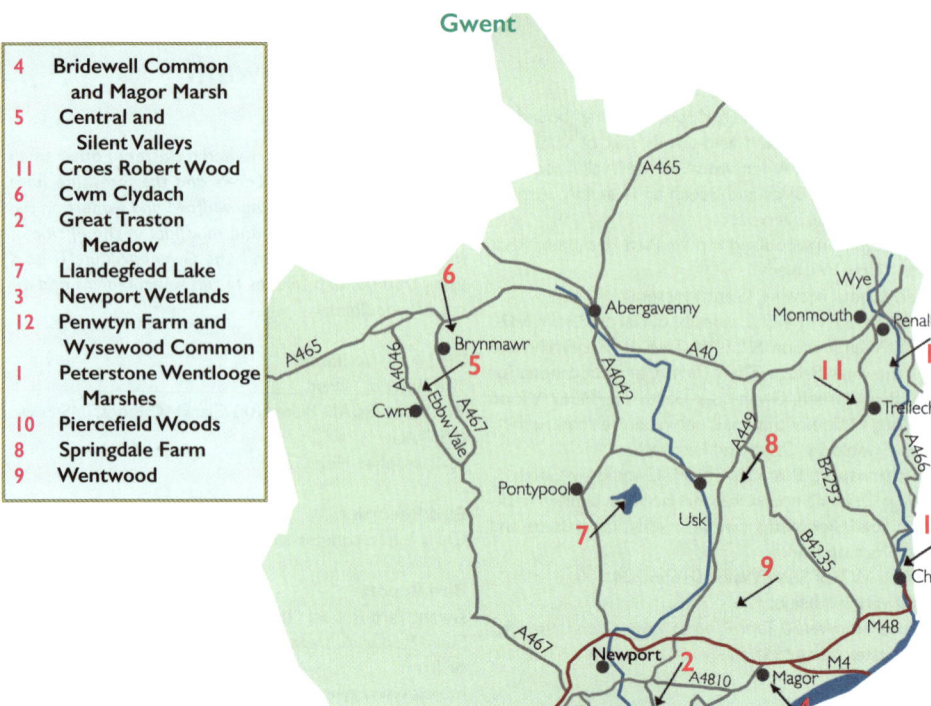

1 PETERSTONE WENTLOOGE MARSHES

Gwent Wildlife Trust

Habitats: Tidal saltmarsh and mudflat on N shore of Severn estuary. Trust owns fishing rights to an area of foreshore. No shoot agreement covering mouth of Peterstone Gout.

Birds: Short-eared Owl, Peregrine Falcon, large numbers of waders on passage and wintering: Dunlin, Turnstone, Redshank, Curlew, Oystercatcher. Also wintering duck inc Teal, Wigeon, Pintail, Shelduck.

Other: Sea Aster, Marshmallow, Sea Milkwort.

Directions: CF3 2TR (St Peter's church); ST 268 802 (lay-by parking opposite church). Leave M4 at J28 and take A48 for Newport. 3rd exit at next roundabout, taking B4239 for St Brides/Duffryn. Stay on the B4239 all the way to St Brides and then on to Peterstone Wentlooge. Park opposite church (worth climbing the tower for the view). Peterstone Wentlooge is close to Cardiff and the B4239 continues on to the Pwll Mawr and Rumney districts.

Public transport: Bus: 31A & 31C, Newport Bus Station-Peterstone Wentlooge, Newport Bus (01633 670 563). Train—Newport, Cardiff.

Visiting: Free, open all hours, no facilities but hotel in village. From church, take path signposted 'Seawall'. Wales Coast Path runs along sea wall to a viewing screen. Do not leave footpath. Foreshore can be dangerous. Cattle and ponies grazing. Keep dogs on lead.

Contact: 01495 307 525; info@gwentwildlife.org

2 GREAT TRASTON MEADOW

Eastman Chemical Ltd (owner)/Gwent Wildlife Trust

Habitats: Marshy grassland traversed by reens (drainage ditches), cut for hay and lightly grazed. 92 acres on the Gwent Levels.

Birds: Snipe, Swift, warblers inc Cetti's, hirundines.

Other: Otter, Water Vole. Shrill Carder Bee. Southern Marsh Orchid (best June/July).

Directions: NP18 2BW; ST 346 863. Take A48 ('City Centre') from J24 of M4. At 5th roundabout (2.5 miles), take 1st exit, Nash Road. At T junction turn R to continue along Nash Road. After 600 yards road curves R, entrance is on R at point pylons cross road.

Public transport: Bus 9A, 9C Newport centre to Retail Park, Newport Bus (01633 670 563), then c.1 mile walk. Train—Newport.

Visiting: Open all hours, free, no facilities. Small car park (2 spaces). Circular trail (uneven, can be muddy) and Welsh Coast Path passes through. Dogs on lead. Sludge beds to W of reserve.

Contact: 01495 307 525; info@gwentwildlife.org

0.5 mile further along Nash Road, take the 1st R, pass through Nash (pub), and on to...

3 NEWPORT WETLANDS NNR

Natural Resources Wales/RSPB/Newport City Council

Habitats: 1,082 acres, wet meadows, saline lagoons, reedbed, scrub & mudflats on Severn estuary.

Birds: Spring/summer: Breeding waders inc Lapwing and Oystercatcher. Bearded Tit, Cetti's Warbler, Cuckoo and regular migrants on passage. *Autumn:* Large numbers of migrating wildfowl and waders—regulars inc Curlew, Dunlin, Ringed Plover, Shoveler. *Winter:* Large Starling roost (up to 50,000 birds). Bittern, nationally important numbers of Black-tailed Godwit, Dunlin and Shoveler.

Other: 16 spp dragonflies, 23 spp butterflies and c.200 spp moths. Badger, Wood Mouse, Otter. Great Crested Newt. Shrill Carder Bee. Orchids in spring.

Directions: NP18 2BZ; ST 334 834. SW of Newport. From J24 or J28 of M4, take A48 to Spytty Retail Park roundabout, exit on to A4810 Queensway Meadows. At first roundabout take 3rd exit onto Meadow Road—follow brown tourist signs to reserve. Close to Uskmouth Power Station.

Public transport: Bus: 45 from Newport city centre to reserve. Newport Bus (01633 670 563).

Visiting: Car park (charge—members free) and Visitor Centre open daily (not 24&25 Dec) 9am-5pm. Cafe (10am-4pm), toilets (inc. disabled). Four trails, hide and viewing screens—wheelchair accessible. Dogs only on perimeter footpath.

Contact: Newport Wetlands Reserve (NRW), RSPB Visitor Centre: 01633 636 363; newport-wetlands@rspb.org.uk

Head E from either Great Traston Meadow or Newport Wetlands along minor roads between the steelworks and the Severn estuary to Redwick and then approach Bridewell Common and Magor Marsh from the S.

4 BRIDEWELL COMMON & MAGOR MARSH

Gwent Wildlife Trust

Two separate but adjacent reserves on the Gwent Levels. Bridewell Common (82 acres) was acquired in 2020 and closed until 2024 for restoration work. Magor Marsh (90 acres).

Habitats: Bridewell is on peat. Magor Marsh is clay fenland. Fields cut for hay and then grazed, with a network of reens (drainage ditches) and willow pollards. Reedbeds and pools.

Birds: Snipe, Barn Owl, Cetti's Warbler, Reed Bunting. Artifical Kingfisher and Sand Martin bank at Magor. *Summer:* Cuckoo. *Winter:* Shoveler, Teal.

Other: Otter, Water Vole. Hairy Dragonfly, Brown-banded Carder Bee. Tubular Dropwort.

Directions: NP26 3DD; ST 428 866 (Magor). Leave M4 at J23A. Then take 1st L off A4810, followed by 3rd exit

at roundabout on to B 4245 for Magor. In Magor turn R for Magor Square (Magor Marsh signposted). Follow road round to R (signposted Llandevenny/Redwick) and past Priory. Turn L immediately after railway bridge. After 400 yards use car park of Trust's Derek Upton Centre on R (the education centre itself is not open to the public but the car park is). No parking or bus at Bridewell, walk from Magor Marsh (entrance to Bridewell 300 yards further along road on L, *caution: cars drive at speed along this road*) or park in Magor or Undy and walk 300 yards S along Whitewall Road.

Public transport: Bus: 74, Newport-Chepstow, Newport Bus (01633 670 563). Get off at Magor-Withy Walk, then 15 minutes walk across railway bridge, following directions as for car.

Visiting: Open all hours, free, no facilities but pubs and restaurants in Magor and Redwick. Magor has surfaced and unsurfaced paths, boardwalks and hide reached by 400 yards of wheelchair accessible surfaced path and boardwalk from car park. Bridewell has no surfaced paths, can be wet. Whitewall entrance to Bridewell has stile. Assistance dogs only (none at Bridewell). Grazing animals.

Contact: 01495 307 525; info@gwentwildlife.org

Head N from Newport

5 CENTRAL VALLEY & SILENT VALLEY

Gwent County Borough Council/Gwent Wildlife Trust

Two separate but nearby reserves. Central Valley is a 50 acre corridor through the heart of the former Ebbw Vale steelworks. Restoration work by GWT began in 2015, ownership returned to GCBC in 2023. Almost due E, Silent Valley is a 125 acre Beech wood on the E slopes of the Vale.

Habitats: Still developing, *Central Valley* comprises recently planted grass and woodland and newly created wetland habitat, whilst *Silent Valley* is an ancient Beech wood, with grassland on the steeper slopes.

Birds: Barn Owl, Kingfisher, Raven, Redstart, plus common woodland spp but remember *Central Valley* is still developing.

Other: Small Pearl-bordered Fritillary, Emerald Damselfly.

Directions: The A4046 runs along the Vale, with Central Valley to the W and Silent Valley to the E. For *Central Valley* (NP23 6AL; SO 174 086), leave A4046 at 1st roundabout N of Cwm/2nd roundabout S of Ebbw Vale. Take the exit signposted Abergavenny/Merthyr Tydfil/ The Works (A4281). At the next roundabout, take 2nd exit, Strand Annealing Lane, pass school on L, then footbridge and Trust's Educational Resource Centre and reserve car park immediately afterwards on L. For *Silent Valley* (NP23 7RX; SO 187 062), leave the A4046 at the N end of the Cwm by-pass. and head S. After c.0.5 mile turn L, following signs for nature reserve into Cendl Terrace. Car park is at top of street on R and entrance is along rough track.

Public transport: Bus: X2 Ebbw Vale-Cwm, stops within walking distance of both reserves, Adventure Travel (02920 442 040). Train—Ebbw Vale Town, Ebbw Vale Parkway.

Visiting: Open all hours, free. Educational Resource Centre at *Central Valley* offering rucksack hire. Entrance to *Central Valley* is by footbridge over railway. Turn R after footbridge. Some paths surfaced but can be uneven and muddy. The paths through *Silent Valley* are steep in places and can become slippery. Dogs permitted, clean up mess.

Contact: 01495 307 525; info@gwentwildlife.org
Head E along the Heads of the Valleys

6 CWM CLYDACH NNR
Natural Resources Wales
Not **Cym Clydach (West Glamorgan)**.

Habitats: Wooded, primarily Beech, steep-sided limestone gorge of River Clydach. 61 acres, SSSI.

Birds: Green Woodpecker, Sparrowhark, Wood Warbler.

Other: Humid atmosphere: good for lichens, mosses, ferns such as Hay-scented Buckler Fern, Powdercap Strangler (don't worry, its a fungus).

Directions: SO 217 124. Take A465 from Abergavenny towards Merthyr Tydfil. After 5 miles take L turn (brown sign on R side of road). Go uphill, pass campsite and picnic area on R, then R into Quarry Road/Heol y Chwarel. Follow road towards quarry, do not turn R into Dan y Coed. Pass Cwm Clydach sign on L and then 2 parking places opposite each other. Park and then follow footpaths into wood.

Public transport: Bus: 76 Abergavenny-Merthyr Tydfil stops at Clydach Bridge, Stagecoach (0345 241 8000).

Visiting: Open all hours, free, no facilities. Some of the paths are steep (it's a gorge!), can be slippery. River fast flowing, waterfalls.

Contact: NRW: 0300 065 3000;
enquiries@naturalresourceswales.gov.uk
S from Abergavenny to Pontypool

7 LLANDEGFEDD LAKE
Welsh Water

Habitats: 434 acre reservoir, meadow, grazed pasture and headgerows, Willow carr, semi-ancient broadleaved woodland. SSSI

Birds: 240 spp recorded. *Passage:* Osprey, waders inc Curlew, Sanderling, Redshank, Grey Phalarope, Common, Little & Black Terns. *Breeding:* Little Ringed Plover, Great Crested Grebe, Little Egret, Kingfisher. *Winter:* Gadwall, Teal, Wigeon et al. Divers, grebes. Wintering wildfowl concentrated at shallower, N end, Divers and grebes in deeper water in middle. Gull roost.

Other: Otter, Daubenton's Common & Soprano Pipistrelles. Green & Brown Hairstreaks, Purple Emperor, Marbled White butterflies. Southern Hawker and Golden-ringed dragonflies. Wasp Spider.

Directions: NP4 0SY. From the A4042, leave at the Pont-y-Felin (New Inn) roundabout, not the crematorium roundabout, In New Inn turn R on to Jerusalem Road, then R into Sluvad Road. Continue over hill, past water treatment works, Do not turn off Sluvad Road whatever satnav says. Follow road across dam to Visitor Centre car park (ST 328 985) by dam at S end. For Fisherman's car park at N end (SO 332 007): stay on Jerusalem Road for c.2.5 miles. Then turn R at crossroads in Glascoed village into 'no through road'. Car park after c.500 yards.

Public transport: Bus: 23 Newport-Pontypool, Stagecoach (0345 241 8000), stops in Llandegfedd Way New Inn. Then a walk of c.2 miles. Train—Pontypool.

Visiting: Visitor centre and main car park (charge) by dam at S end. Open 9am-5:30pm Mar-Oct, 9am-4pm Nov-Feb (gates locked overnight), closed 25, 26 Dec and 1 Jan. Cafe, toilets wheelchair accessible. Disabled parking close to Visitor Centre. Dogs on lead. Waymarked trails, some sections rough. Park by water treatment works for Pettingale Hide in S part of reservoir. Fisherman's car park at N end, open Mar-Sep, 8:30am-5:30pm. Oct-Feb footpath on E side closed. Locked gate. Access during winter by permit only, restricted to Gwent Ornithological Society members. Three hides at N end

Contact: 0330 0413 381;
llandegfeddenquiries@dwrcymru.com
Back down to Newport and then take A449 and the A472 to Usk

8 SPRINGDALE FARM
Gwent Wildlife Trust

Habitats: Working, traditonal farm of 112 acres, with hay meadows, grazing pastures, hedgerows and coppiced woodland.

Birds: Common farmland spp inc Pied Flycatcher.

Other: Bluebells, Ransoms, Blue-eyed Grass, Adder's-tongue Fern.

Directions: NP15 1LL; ST 410 991. Take Priory Street, signposted for Llantrisant, from Usk Square. Veer to R by church, then L on to Maryport Street. Continue S for c.2 miles until road passes under A449. Sharp L immediately after bridge on to Llanllowel Lane. Continue uphill for 1.5 miles until you reach almshouses on R. Reserve entrance opposite on L. Small car park for 5 cars.

Public transport: Bus: 63 Cwmbran-Cheptow goes via Chepstow and Llangwm. Newport Bus (01633 670 563), then 1.25 miles walk.

Visiting: Open all hours, free. Circular walk, steep in parts. Livestock present. Dogs on lead.

Contact: 01495 307 525; info@gwentwildlife.org
Return to Newport and take A48 E.

9 WENTWOOD

Woodland Trust

Habitats: Mixed woodland. Woodland Trust responsible for 873 acres out of a total of 2,500 acres. Most native trees felled in WW2, replanted with conifers in 1956s and 1960s. Native broadleaves now being replanted.

Birds: All year: Buzzard, Goshawk, Sparrowhawk, Siskin, Redpoll, Crossbill, common woodland spp. *Summer:* Woodcock, Nightjar, Turtle Dove, Whinchat, Tree Pipit, Garden & Wood Warblers. *Winter:* Redwing, Fieldfare, Brambling.

Other: Fallow & Muntjac Deer, Hazel Dormouse. Adder, Common Lizard. Flora, fungi, 23 spp butterflies.

Directions: NP15 1NA; ST 422 948. From A48 Newport-Chepstow take road towards Llanfair Discoed and then Usk Road to Foresters' Oaks picnic site/Cadira Beeches car park on L (after 2/2.5 miles).

Public transport: Bus 73 (not Sun) Newport to Chepstow, stops at Parc Seymour (walk one mile N to Wentwood gate), Newport Bus (01633 670 563).

Visiting: Many paths/tracks/bridleways.

Contact: Woodland Trust,: 0330 333 3300; wales@woodlandtrust.org.uk

Return to A48 and head for Chepstow.

10 PIERCEFIELD WOODS NATURE RESERVE

Gwent Wildlife Trust

Habitats: 2 mile stretch of ancient broadleaf wood along banks of River Wye opposite side of river to **Bany-Gor** and **Lancaut** in **Gloucestershire**, 203 acres.

Birds: Peregrine Falcon and Raven on the cliffs, as well as Goshawk, Sparrowhawk and Kestrel. Cormorant, Grey Heron on the Wye.

Other: Very varied range of trees, many ancient. Cosnard's Net Winged Beetle.

Directions: Two free car parks. For the S one at Chepstow Leisure Centre (NP15 5LR; ST 528 947) take the A466 from the W end of the Severn Bridge, then 3rd exit at 2nd roundabout (Crossway Green) on to B4293 (Welsh Street). Take 4th road on L for Leisure Centre car park. For N one, the NRW Lower Wyndcliff car park (NP16 7JB; ST 526 971) continue on A466 for 2 miles, car park immediately off road on R.

Public transport: Bus: 69 Chepstow-Monmouth runs along A466, Newport Bus (01633 670 563).

Visiting: Open all hours, free, facilities in Chepstow. The 136 mile Wye Valley walk starts in Chepstow and its first 2 miles are through Piercefield Woods. This is a permissive right of access that is steep in places and can be muddy. No right of access to other parts of wood because there are dangerous drops from cliff tops into the Wye Valley gorge. Dogs on lead. The Wye Valley Walk then continues N through the adjacent NRW Wyndcliff Wood.

Contact: 01495 307 525; info@gwentwildlife.org

Continue on A466 to Monmouth.

11 CROES ROBERT WOOD

Gwent Wildlife Trust

Habitats: Ancient, now coppiced, working woodland of Hazel and Ash. 37 acres

Birds: Common woodland spp inc Goshawk.

Other: Hazel Dormouse. Bluebells, Golden Saxifrage.

Directions: SO 475 059. Take B4293 from Monmouth to Trellech. In village turn R for Cwmcarvan. After 1.25 miles turn R down steep lane, again for Cwmcarvan. After c.500 yards and immediately after sharp L turn, park in lay-by on R. Entrance is through wooden gate from lay-by.

Public transport: Bus: 65, Monmouth-Chepstow stops in Trellech, Newport Bus (01633 670 563).

Visiting: Open all hours, free, no facilities but pub in Trellech. Steep slopes, paths can be muddy. Dogs permitted.

Contact: 01495 307 525; info@gwentwildlife.org

Also off B4293.

12 PENTWYN FARM & WYSEWOOD COMMON

Gwent Wildlife Trust

Habitats: Pentwyn is a traditionally managed farm: flower-rich, late-cut, lightly grazed hay meadows, hedgerows, 30 acres. Recently purchased, the immediately adjacent *Wysewood Common*, 105 acres, was formerly an intensive dairy farm that is now being returned to a more relaxed regime and the variety of habitats is being increased.

Birds: Yellowhammer, Bullfinch and Skylark are all returning to Wysewood. Red Kite. *Winter:* Fieldfare, Redwing.

Other: Hazel Dormouse. Greater Twayblade, Common Bird's-foot-trefoil, Greater Wild Cherry, Butterfly-orchid.

Directions: NP25 4PE; SO 523 094. Head S from Monmouth on the B4293 towards Trellech. Just over 2 miles after crossing the A40 (and having NOT taken the R fork to Mitchel Troy), take the L fork to Penallt. In Penallt, follow signs for Inn at Penallt, forking R at war memorial. Then take L fork, going past green and then large modern barn rather than to pub. Car park at end of road on either side of medieval stone barn. The entrances to *Pentwyn Farm* and *Wysewood Common* are on either side of this stone barn.

Public transport: Bus: 65, Monmouth-Chepstow stops at Old Baptist Chapel in Penallt, Newport Bus (01633 670 563).

Visiting: Open all hours, free, toilets and pub in Penallt. Waymarked trails gently sloping sites and a number of kissing gates

Contact: 01495 307 525; info@gwentwildlife.org

Take A40 S from Monmouth

Breconshire

The three historic counties of Breconshire, Radnorshire and Montgomeryshire that, with a few chunks taken out here or added there, now make up Powys, are largely rural upland areas of mountains, bogs, coniferous forest plantations and typical Welsh woodlands (home to Redstart, Pied flycatcher and Wood Warbler). Birds of prey are well represented with Hen Harrier, Merlin, Red Kite and Peregrine all well established. Breconshire or Brecknockshire is the southernmost of the three and its southern half is occupied by the eponymous Beacons, now officially renamed the Bannau Brycheiniog.

Bird Atlas/Avifauna
None

Bird Recorder
Andrew King, Heddfan, Pennorth, Brecon, Powys LD3 7EX: 01874 658 351; andy@breconbirds.wales

Bird Report
Breconshire Birds (1962-), from Brecknock Birds —Andrew King (editor): 07967 559 787

BTO Regional Representative
Andrew King:
Wetland Bird Survey (WeBS)
Local Organizer
Andrew King: webs@bto.org

Club
Brecknockbirds: www.brecknockbirds.co.uk
online forum—Andrew King: andy@breconbirds.wales

Ringing Group/Bird Observatory
Llangorse RG
www.llangorseringing.blogspot.com

RSPB Local Group
No Groups

Wildlife Trust
Wildlife Trust of South And West Wales (2002; 9,000).
The Nature Centre, Fountain Road, Tondu, Bridgend, Mid-Glamorgan CF32 0EH: 01656 724 100; info@welshwildlife.org; www.welshwildlife.org

The A4067 running NW from Swansea enters the county at its SW corner.

1 CRAIG-Y-NOS COUNTRY PARK, CRAIG Y RHIWARTH, ALLT RHONGYR, & OGOF FfYNNON DU NNR

Brecon Beacons National Park Authority/Wildlife Trust of South & West Wales/Natural Resources Wales
A country park and 3 adjacent reserves running W to E.
Birds: Common woodland spp in Country Park inc: Cuckoo, Lesser Spotted Woodpecker, Pied Flyctcher and Raven, Redstart, Wheatear on uplands.
Other: Acid and limestone loving flora depending on underlying rock:
Directions: Take the A4067 N from Abercrave
Craig-y-Nos Country Park (BBNPA): SA9 1GL; SN 839 155. Car park immediately off A4067 on R 3.5 miles N of Abercrave. 40 acre Victorian garden. Woods, meadows, ponds, river. Closed 25 Dec. Pay & display car park, cafe, toilets easy trail, all wheelchair accessible.
Craig y Rhiwarth (WTS&WW): SA9 1GL (C-y-N); SN 843 157. Immediately to W of Craig-y-Nos, park in Craig-y-Nos car park (charge). Open all hours, free to enter, no facilities (but adjacent to C-y-N). Paths in C-y-N wheelchair accessible but much of reserve itself scree and cliffs. Small reserve (12 acres) best known for limestone plant communities. Dogs on lead
Allt Rhongyr (WTS&WW): SA9 1GE (Glyntawe); SN 852 156. Turn R off A4607 0.5 mile S of C-y-N on to minor road to Penwyllt. After 1 mile road bends R, goes up hill, reserve on L. Park on lay-by by entrance. Alternatively, walk in from C-y-N and C-y-R. Open all hours, free, no facilities. Limestone grassland, acidic grassland, woodland 75 acres, immediately to E of C-y-R. Open all hours, free, no facilities (though not far from C-y-N). scree slopes and cliffs, not suitable for wheelchairs. Grazed by livestock, dogs on lead.
Ogof Ffynnon Du (NRW): SA9 1GQ; SN 856 155, immediately to E of AR. Continue past entrance to AR and disused quarry. Car park, open all hours, free, at end of road. Extensive area of moorland around abandoned village of Penwyllt and cave system beneath it. Waymarked trails, Beacons Way runs through reserve. Not suitable for wheelchairs. Dogs on lead
Public transport: Bus: T6 Swansea-Brecon runs along A4607 Adventure Travel (02920 442 040).
Visiting: Open all hours, free, no facilities.
Contact: Country Park: 01639 730 395; enquiries@beacons-npa.gov.uk
www.breaconbeacons.org/national-park-visitor-centre.
WT of South & West Wales: 01874 625 708; info@welshwildlife.org
NRW: 0300 065 3000; enquiries@naturalresourceswales.gov.uk
Continue NE on A4067 across W of Beacons. At Defynnog turn R on to A4215, which runs W-E to join A470. Turn L for

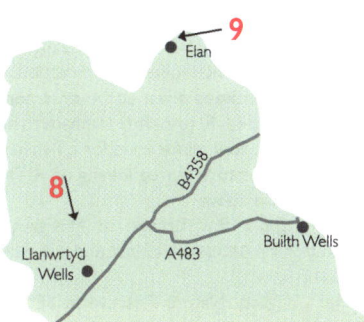

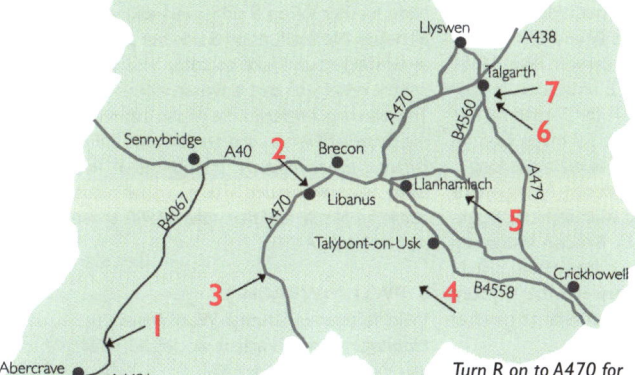

9	**Carngafallt**
3	**Craig Cerrig**
1	**Craig-y-Nos**
5	**Llangorse Lake**
2	**Mynydd Illtud**
	and Daudraeth Illtyd
8	**Nant Irfon and**
	Abergwesyn Commons
7	**Park Wood**
6	**Pwll-y-Wrach**
4	**Talybont Reservoir**

Turn R on to A470 for

2   MYNYDD ILLTUD COMMON & DAUDRAETH ILLTYD NR

Brecon Beacons National Park Authority

Habitats: Upland grazing (sheep, ponies) common, marshy areas formed in glacial depressions. 630 acres includes Illtyd Pools SSSI.

Birds: Traeth Mawr formerly important breeding area for: Lapwing, Water Rail, Spotted Crake, Snipe. Ground nesting birds now largely gone. Short-eared Owl, wintering flock of Teal.

Other: Dragonflies & damselflies, mosses, lichens.

Directions: LD3 8ER; SN 977 262 (Visitor Centre). Take A470 from Brecon to Merthyr Tydfil. After *c.*3 miles turn R in Libanus. Take minor road signed for National Park Visitor Centre. Car park after *c.*1mile.

Public transport: Bus: T4 Brecon-Merthyr Tydfil stops in Libanus (1 mile walk), Stagecoach (0345 241 8000).

Visiting: Pay-and-display car park. Visitor Centre (10am-4pm) has cafe, shop, accessible toilets. Open all year except 25 Dec. Visitor Centre on E edge of Common. All Terrain Mobility Scooter for hire, waymarked trails.

Contact: 01874 623 366;

enquiries@beacons-npa.gov.uk

www.breaconbeacons.org/national-park-visitor-centre

3   CRAIG CERRIG GLEISIAD A FAN FRYNYCH NNR

Natural Resources Wales

Habitats: Crags, moorland, grassland, river. Hawthorn, Rowan, Ash, Whitebeam woods on hillsides.

Birds: Red Grouse, Peregrine Falcon. Raven. *Summer:* Ring Ouzel, Redstart, Whinchat, Tree Pipit

Other: Artic-Alpine flora at UK S limit on the N-facing slopes: Purple & Mossy saxifrages, Serrated Wintergreen, Green Spleenwort.

Directions: LD3 8SU; SN 971 222. Take the A470 from Brecon for Merthyr Tydfil. Youth Hostel on L after *c.*5 miles. After a further 500 yards park in 2nd lay-by on R. Information panel at reserve entrance.

Public transport: Bus: T4 Brecon-Merthyr Tydil, stops at Youth Hostel, Stagecoach (0345 241 8000).

Visiting: Open all hours, free, picnic area at entrance, no other facilities. Two waymarked trails, steep and rough in parts, footpaths up to plateau. Unsuitable for wheelchairs. **Beacons Way** (99 miles) runs along S edge of reserve. Grazed by cattle, sheep and ponies, keep dogs under control

Contact: NRW: 0300 065 3000;

enquiries@naturalresourceswales.gov.uk

Continue on A470 to Merthyr Tydfil. Shortly before you get there, branch L on to A4054 and then take minor road on R for Pontsticil just before crossing the A465 and approach the chain of reservoirs described below from the opposite direction.

4 TALYBONT RESERVOIR
Welsh Water

Habitats: Reservoir (318 acres), wetland, mixed and commercial woodland along shores rising to moorland. *Birds:* Red Grouse, Little & Greated Crested Grebes. Grey Heron, Little Egret. Raven, Dipper, Grey Wagtail. *Summer:* Nightjar, Curlew, Golden Plover, Osprey (now breeding), Wheatear. *Winter:* Goosander, Goldeneye, Pochard, Tufted Duck, Wigeon & Teal. Woodcock, Snipe, Jack Snipe.

Directions: LD3 7YS (Danywenallt Youth Hostel at the dam); hides at SO 100 197, towards N end of W shore; and SO 090 179, hide at head of reservoir. Take B4558 for Talybont-on-Usk from A40 just E of Brecon. In Talybont-on-Usk take minor road on R for Torpantau and Pontsticill. Dam at Danywenallt after 1.7 miles. Continue along W edge of reservoir, which is, c.2 miles long.

Public transport: Bus: 43/X43 Brecon-Abergavenny stops in Talybont-on-Usk (3.7 mile walk to hide), Stagecoach (0345 241 8000). Train—The **Brecon Mountain Railway** runs a steam train service from Pant, just N of Merthyr Tydfil, to Torpantau (between the Talybont and Pentwyn Reservoirs, 4 miles from hide at head of reservoir) via Pontsticill.

Visiting: Open all hours, free. Nearest facilities in T-o-U. Two hides, wheelchair accessible one at S end of reservoir, overlooking wetland area that floods in winter Short path from parking area. There are also car parks on the W shore at SO 100 197 (near 2nd hide) and upstream of the lake at Pont Blaen-y-Glyn (SO 063 170), waterfalls upstream. The road to Torpantau and Pontsticill continues past two further reservoirs: Pentwyn and Pontsticill. The **Beacons Way** runs along the S side of Talybont Reservoir.

Contact: 01495 769 281; talybontcc@gmail.com

Join the A40 from Talybont-on-Usk at Llansantfraed. Llangorse Lake lies behind the steep-sided hill overlooking the village. Head NW on A40 towards Brecon for 1.5 miles, then turn R into minor road at Scethrog. At T junction, after just over 0.5 mile turn R and then, after 1.3 miles L at Treberfydd for Llangasty-Tallylyn. Church another 0.5 mile.

5 LLANGORSE LAKE
Privately owned but access permitted
Habitats: Largest natural lake in South Wales, 340 acres. Reed fringed. SSSI
Birds: Great Crested Grebe, Water Rail, Cetti's, Warbler. *Summer:* Reed, Sedge, Grasshopper & Garden Warblers, Redstart, Pied Flycatcher. *Passage:* Osprey, Common Scoter; Arctic, Common, Sandwich & Black Terns. Various waders. *Winter:* Goldeneye, Gadwall, Pochard, Shoveler, Wigeon, Tufted Duck, Teal, Goosander. Large gull roost

Other: Otter, Water Vole, Scarce Blue-tailed Damselfly. *Directions:* LD3 7UG; SO 133 261 (Llangasty church). Park by church. Either follow the directions from the A40 and Llansantfraed given above or, if coming from Brecon, turn L off A40 just after Llanhamlch and before pub on R and follow minor road for c.1 mile to T junction with road from Scethrog joining on R. Then follow directions given above

Public transport: Bus: Brecon to Abergavenny stops Llanhamlach on A40 (walk of just under 3 miles), Stagecoach.

Visiting: Llangasty Nature Reserve in SE quadrant of lake, water sports excluded. Park by Llangasty church. Hide further W on S side overlooking lake. Free, open all hours. No facilities on S side but path (may be muddy in winter) round lake to camp site and water sports centre on N side by Llangorse village.

The following 2 reserves are on the hills around 1 mile from the centre of Talgarth and are less than a mile apart. Follow different minor roads SE from the town. To reach Talgarth either work way round lake on minor roads to Llangorse village on N side and then take B4580 or return to Brecon and then take A470.

6 PWLL-Y-WRACH
Wildlife Trust of South & West Wales
Habitats: 43 acre ancient woodland, river and spectacular Witches Pool waterfall.
Birds: All year: Dipper, Kingfisher, common woodland spp inc Great Spotted Woodpecker, Mistle & Song Thrushes, Nuthatch. *Spring/summer:* Chiffchaff, Wood Warbler, Pied Flycatcher.
Other: Otter, Dormouse, bats, Common Lizard. Early Purple & Birds' Nest Orchids.
Directions: LD3 0DU; SO 165 326. From Talgarth (on A479) town centre cross over River Enig, then L turn Bell Street. After 50 yards L (opp Bell Hotel) follow minor road one mile, reserve is on R.
Public transport: Bus T14 (not Sun) Hereford to Cardiff stops at Talgarth. Stagecoach (0345 241 8000).
Visiting: Open all year. Information panel in car park. Keep to footpaths. Level, wheelchair-friendly path runs halfway into site—elsewhere paths can be muddy and there are steps. Dogs under close control.
Contact: WT of South & West Wales: 01874 625 708; info@welshwildlife.org

7 PARK WOOD
Woodland Trust
Habitats: 141 acre ancient woodland with some conifer.
Birds: Marsh & Coal Tit, *Summer;* Willow, Wood & Garden Warblers, Redstarts, Spotted & Pied Flycatchers. *Winter:* Redpoll, winter thrushes.
Directions: LD3 0DW; SO 166 346. From the centre of Talgarth take the minor road (The Bank) opposite the

Post Office. Follow this as it becomes Church Street. Just past the church take the R fork and then, after 80 yards, the L fork continue for c.1,000 yards to parking area on L.

Public transport: Bus T14 (not Sun) Hereford to Cardiff stops at Talgarth. Stagecoach (0345 241 8000).

Visiting: Open all hours, free. Nearest facilities in Talgarth. Path through wood, level but rough. Unsuitable for wheelchairs.

Contact: 029 2002 7732; wales@woodlandtrust.org.uk
Take the A479 and then the A470 N from Talgarth to Builth Wells, whence the A483 runs W to Llanwrtyd Wells.

8 NANT IRFON NNR
& ABERGWESYN COMMONS

Natural Resources Wales/National Trust

Habitats: Remnant of ancient Oak woodland in Nant Irfon, whilst the Commons are a high grass moorland ridge, rising to Drygarn Fawr (2,116 ft), running E-W, and sloping down to the **Elan Valley (Radnorshire)** to the N, with steeper river valleys to S on the B4358. c.4,000 acres of the Common was burnt in the spring of 2025. Long-term impact as yet unclear.

Birds: Woodland: Lesser Spotted Woodpecker, Chiffchaff, Wood Warbler, Redstart, Pied Flycatcher, Hawfinch (reported), with Common Sandpiper, Dipper and Grey Wagtail along the river. *Moorland:* Red Grouse, Lapwing, Golden Plover, Merlin, Red Kite, Whinchat, Wheatear.

Other: Globeflower, Bog Asphodel, Wilson's Filmy Fern.

Directions: Abergwesyn Commons (NT) cover 16,500 acres and stretch 12 miles from Nant Irfon (NRW) in W to Llanwrthwl in E. Roads run along the edges of the Common but none cross it or penetrate far into it. A minor road runs from Abergwesyn (LD5 4TW; SN 855 527) at the S edge along the Nant Irfon, the W edge of the reserve, to Tregaron; whilst other minor roads run S from Abergwesyn to Llanwrtyd Wells (on the A483) and E to Beulah (also on A483), whence the B4358 runs to Newbridge-on-Wye (to the SE of the Common), which is also on the A470. Llanwrthwl, near the E edge of the Common, is just off the A470 c.5 miles to the N. The minor roads running along the shores of the S reservoirs in the **Elan Valley** complex skirt the N edge of the Commons, with crossings over the Claerwen and car parks at Rhiwnant (SN 901 615) and the Claerwen dam (SN 872 633), where there are also toilets.

Public transport: Bus: 100 Llandridod Wells-Abergwesyn (infrequent).

Visiting: Open all hours, free, no facilities. Keep dogs on lead near livestock. Not suitable for wheelchairs. For Nant Irfon NNR there is lay-by parking beside the river at SN 834 555. Not only do no roads cross the Commons, there are no established footpaths and nothing beyond roadside parking round the edges.

Contact: NT: 01874 625 515;

brecon@nationaltrust.org.uk
NRW: 0300 065 3000;
enquiries@naturalresourceswales.gov.uk
Continue N from Builth Wells on A470 to Newbridge-on-Wye and then Rhayader.

9 CARNGAFALLT

RSPB

Habitats: Ancient Oak rain forest, wood pasture, moorland rising to 1,530 ft.

Birds: Red Kite. *Summer:* Cuckoo, Curlew, Golden Plover, Dunlin, Wood Warbler, Redstart, Pied Flycatcher, Whinchat, Tree Pipit.

Other: Purple Hairstreak butterfly.

Directions: LD6 5HW; SN 936 652. Nearest car park, **Elan Valley** Visitor Centre (q.v. **Radnorshire**. Welsh Water, charge) LD6 5HP; SN 928 646. Three miles SW of Rhayader (A470), take B4518—don't cross iron bridge, drive over cattle grid to visitor centre.

Public transport: None.

Visiting: Open all hours, reserve free, no facilities at reserve. Trails from car park to W of Elan village through Welsh Water woods. One trail leads to RSPB reserve, which begins E of village and also on other side of River Elan (footbridges). Trails can be muddy and have steep sections. Dogs on lead. Map available at Visitor Centre.

Contact: 01654 700 222; carngafallt@rspb.org.uk

Radnorshire

The middle of the three historic counties of Breconshire, Radnorshire and Montgomeryshire that, with a few chunks taken out here or added there, now make up Powys. Radnorshire lies between England and the Cambrian Mountains, which drain into the chain of Elan Valley reservoirs to the west of Rhayader and thence into the Wye. This river runs down the county's west edge before curving round its southern tip to the English border in the east.

Bird Atlas/Avifauna
The Birds of Radnorshire
Peter Jennings
(Fidedula Books, 2014)

Bird Recorder
Pete Jennings, The Old Farmhouse, Choulton, Lydbury North, Shropshire SY7 8AH: 01588 680 631;
radnorshirebirds@hotmail.com

Bird Report
None

BTO Regional Representative
Gethin Jenkins-Jones
Wetland Bird Survey (WeBS)
Local Organizer: webs@bto.org
Pete Jennings

Club
Radnorshire Bird Group (1988; 75)
Pete Jennings, The Old Farmhouse, Choulton, Lydbury North, Shropshire SY7 8AH: 01588 680 631;
radnorshirebirds@hotmail.com;
Co-ordinates bird recording and surveys in the county through the Bird Recorder.

Ringing Group/Bird Observatory
None

RSPB Local Group
No Groups

Wildlife Trust
Radnorshire Wildlife Trust (1987; 1,000)
Warwick House, High St, Llandrindod Wells, Powys LD1 6AG: 01597 823 298; info@rwtwales.org;
www.rwtwales.org

Just across the county boundary from **Carngafallt** in Breconshire.

1 ELAN VALLEY RESERVOIRS
& CLAERWEN NNR
Elan Valley Trust/Welsh Water/
Natural Resources Wales
Habitats: 45,000 acres of reservoir and rivers with surrounding moorland, bog, woodland.
Birds: 180 spp. *All year:* Red Kite, Buzzard, Sparrowhawk, Peregrine, Tawny & Barn Owls, Raven, Green Woodpecker, Dipper, Grey Wagtail and Marsh Tit. Common woodland spp. *Spring/summer:* Cuckoo, Pied & Spotted Flycatchers, Wood Warbler, Redstart, Tree Pipit. Upland birds inc Curlew, Golden Plover and Dunlin. *Autumn/winter:* Short-eared Owl, Ring Ouzel (autumn), Fieldfare, Redwing.
Other: Internationally important Oak woodlands.
Directions: LD6 5HP; SN 928 646 (Visitor Centre). Three miles SW of Rhayader (A470), take B4518— don't cross iron bridge, drive over cattle grid to Visitor Centre.
Public transport: None.
Visiting: Mostly open access. Pay & display car park with Blue Badge spaces. Coaches, contact in advance for access advice. Visitor Centre, cafe, shop and toilets open daily (not 25 Dec) 9am-5pm. Nature trails. Dogs, keep under close control.
A complex of of 5 reservoirs formed by damming the Elan and Claerwen rivers, with the Visitor Centre standing just below the dam of the southernmost reservoir, *Caban Coch*. This is fed from the W by the Claerwen river and, upstream, the *Claerwen* Reservoir, the largest and most recent of the reservoirs; and from the N by a chain of 3 reservoirs on the Elan. From S to N these are the *Garreg-ddu*, the *Penygarreg* and the *Craig Goch*.
A minor road runs W from the *Caban Coch* dam along the wooded N side of the reservoir to the dam at the foot of the *Garrag-ddu*, where it branches. One road continues W across the dam to a car park at SN 909 639, whence trails run through the wooded slopes above the reservoir. The road itself continues to the head of *Caban Coch*, where there is a car park and bridge across the Claerwen at Rhiwnant (SN 901 615). The road then continues NW alongside the Claerwen to the dam at the foot of the *Claerwen* Reservoir, where there are two car parks, toilets, a picnic area and a bridge across the Claerwen at SN 872 633. These two bridges across the Claerwen offer access on foot to the N slopes of **Abergwesyn Common** (q.v. **Breconshire**). The other road at the *Garreg-ddu* dam runs N along the E shore of the *Garreg-ddu* Reservoir, crossing the Elan at the head of the reservoir at SN 915 673 to a car park and picnic area in the woods by Penbont House. There is a further car park with trails at the W edge of this block of forest at SN 901 672 and the road then

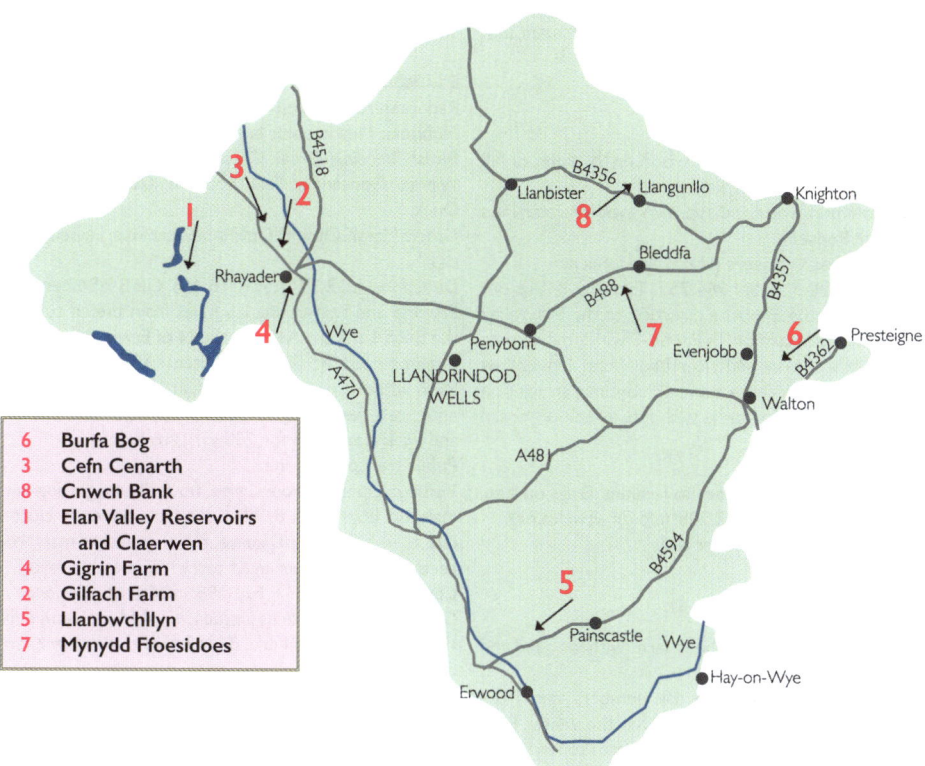

6	**Burfa Bog**
3	**Cefn Cenarth**
8	**Cnwch Bank**
1	**Elan Valley Reservoirs and Claerwen**
4	**Gigrin Farm**
2	**Gilfach Farm**
5	**Llanbwchllyn**
7	**Mynydd Ffoesidoes**

runs N along the W side of the *Penygarreg* Reservoir to the dam at the foot of the *Craig Goch* Reservoir. Across the dam there is a car park with toilets at SN 895 686. This is also served by an even more minor road that runs up the E side of *Penygarreg* from the dam at its foot. The road on the W side now continues N across moorland away from the W side of the *Craig Goch* Reservoir before turning E, crossing the River Elan just before it flows into the reservoir and joining a minor road running NW from the B4518 (the road that leads from Rhayader to Elan, in case you had forgotten) at Llansantffraed Cwmdeuddwr, some 5 miles distant, on the other side of the Wye from Rhayader,

The Claerwen NNR occupies a dome of high moorland between the two arms of the V formed by the reservoirs, with the steep-sided ravine of Nant Hirin running ENE into the Elan and forming the NW edge.

Contact: Visitor Centre: 01597 810 880;
elanvalley@dwrcymru.com;
www.elanvalley.org.uk
NRW: 0300 065 3000;
enquiries@naturalresourceswales.gov.uk
Across the Wye and the N of Rhayader.

2 GILFACH FARM

Radnorshire Wildlife Trust

Habitats: 410 acre former hill farm, Sessile Oak woods, pastures, river, moorland rising to over 1,400 ft.
Birds: Red Kite, Dipper, Linnet, Redpoll, Yellowhammer. *Summer:* Cuckoo, Spotted & Pied Flycatchers, Redstart, Whinchat.
Other: Mountain Bumble Bee, Fox Moth, Small Pear-bordered Fritillary. Green Hairstreak.
Directions: LD6 5LF; SN 962 718. Take the A470 N from Rhayader, after just under 3 miles turn R into minor road at point where Marteg flows into Wye (Pont Marteg). Welcome Gateway car park and picnic area almost immediately on R. Minor road continues E along valley to Old Farmyard at SN 965 717.
Public transport: Bus: X47 Llandrindod Wells-Aberystwyth runs through Rhayader and stops just N of Pont Marteg. Celtic Travel (01686 412 231).
Visiting: Open all hours, donations requested. Welcome Gateway and picnic area is the start and end point for 3 waymarked circular trails, some steep. Accessible toilets at the Old Farmyard, where 2 more trails start, including a wheelchair accessible one. Dogs on lead, clean up mess. Livestock graze farm.

Contact: RWT: 01597 823 298; info@rwtwales.org
Continue along minor road from Gilfach to St Harmon, turn L on to B4518 and then follow directions for...

3 CEFN CENARTH

Radnorshire Wildlife Trust

Habitats: Humid Sessile Oak wood on W slope of hill rising to 1,500 ft, mosses, lichens.

Birds: Common woodland spp. inc Wood Warbler, Pied Flycatcher, Redstart

Other: Witches Whiskers (*Usnea florida*) lichen.

Directions: LD6 5LR; SN 964 759. Take the B4518 out of Rhayader in the opposite direction to the Elan Valley. Pass through St Harmon. In Pant-y-Dwr (5 miles) turn L before bus shelter and after Mid Wales Inn. Follow road for 1.3 miles. Where curves L, continue straight on along forest road. Car park, with interpretation board on R.

Public transport: None.

Visiting: Open all hours, free, no facilities. Dogs on lead.

Contact: RWT: 01597 823 298; info@rwtwales.org
Retrace your steps to Rhayader and

4 GIGRIN FARM

Private

Habitats: 50 acre, upland sheep farm with wooded and wet habitats.

Birds: Red Kites fed once a day, numbers vary from 1-200 during the summer to 4-500 in the winter. Rare leukistic Red Kites regularly visit the farm to feed. Other species inc Buzzard, Raven, Jackdaw, Carrion Crow. Brambling, Yellowhammer and Siskin. A wetland area attracts wild ducks, Grey Heron and wagtails.

Directions: LD6 5BL; SN 978 676. Farm lies 0.5 mile south of Rhayader, Powys off A470.

Public transport: Bus X47 (not Sun) Llandrindod Wells to Aberystwyth stops at Rhayader. Celtic Travel (01686 412 231).

Visiting: Gigrin is a family-owned farm and has been an official Red Kite feeding station for Wales since early 1990's, helping young birds survive in winter. By attracting large numbers of birdwatchers it relieves pressure on nest sites in summer. Open for kite feeding sessions 12:30pm-5pm Sat-Wed (closed Thur/Fri) and daily during school holidays—27 Dec to end-Nov (closed 1-26 Dec). Feeding times: 2pm (winter) & 3pm (summer). Booking ahead via website (see below) strongly recommended. Admission charge applies to all visitors to the farm. Gift and coffee shop, car park, toilets, picnic site, farm walk. Viewing Field plus five hides (three with disabled access), plus specialist photography hides (fees apply). Dogs on leads. Short farm walk across fields and through wooded area—rough terrain.

Contact: Dominique Powell, Gigrin Farm, South Street, Rhayader, Powys LD6 5BL: 01597 810 243; office@gigrin.co.uk; www.gigrin.co.uk

Head S on the A470 along the Wye. Cross it at Erwood bridge and take the B4594 towrds Painscastle.

5 LLANBWCHLLYN

Radnorshire Wildlife Trust/Welsh Water

Habitats: Mesotrophic lake, reedbed, fen, 67 acres.

Birds: Breeding: Great Crested Grebe, Reed Warbler. *Winter:* Goosander, Teal, Pochard, Goldeneye, Tufted Duck.

Other: Marsh Orchid, Devil's-bit Scabious, Lesser Skullcap.

Directions: LD2 3YQ; SO 116 466. Off B4594 between Erwood and Painscastle. 2.5 miles from the junction of the B4594 and the A470 to the N of Erwood, turn L a minor road. At T-junction, after 1,500 yards, turn R. Park, without obstructing road, at Llanbnwchllyn farm, enter reserve through wood on opposite side of road and walk along path for 200 yards to hide.

Public transport: None.

Visiting: Open all hours, free, no facilities, grazing animals, no dogs. Path to hide but hide currently closed due to Ash Dieback Disease. RWT members may proceed beyond hide but must carry membership card.

Contact: RWT: 01597 823 298; info@rwtwales.org
Continue on B4594 to its junction with A44, then turn L for Walton and, at Walton take B4362 towards Presteigne

6 BURFA BOG

Radnorshire Wildlife Trust

Habitats: Grassland, woodland, inc. coppiced Alder, bog, 25 acres.

Birds: Blackcap, Willow Warbler, Chiffchaff, Marsh & Willow Tit.

Other: Butterflies. Heath Spotted and Marsh Orchids, Waxcap fungi.

Directions: LD8 2SH; SO275 613. From the B4362 Walton to Presteigne road turn L at Ditchyeld Bridge (R if coming from Presteigne) on to minor road for Barland/Evenjobb. Reserve entrance on L after 0.25 mile. Park on verge, keep road clear.

Public transport: Bus: 461 Hereford-Llandrindod Wells stops in Evenjobb, Sargeants Bros (01544 230n 481).

Visiting: Open all hours, free, no facilities, no dogs. Circular trail with boardwalk sections.

Contact: RWT: 01597 823 298; info@rwtwales.org
Continue to Presteigne on B4362, whence take B4356 to NW along the Lugg to junction with A488. Then head W.

7 MYNYDD FFOESIDOES

Radnorshire Wildlife Trust

Habitats: Heather moorland with boggy pools, coniferous forest to N. Rising to 2,080 ft, it is one of the high points of the Radnor Forest. 82 acres

Birds: Red Grouse, Peregrine Falcon, Ring Ouzel, Kestrel.

Other: 40 spp beetle inc Ground Beetle and Heather Weevil.

Directions: LD1 5TN; SO 190 649. There are no roads into the Radnor Forest. The A488 between Penybont and Knighton (on the border with Herefordshire) runs across the N of the Forest. Fishpools on the A488 is c.2 miles due N of the reserve. Numerous footpaths run into the Radnor Forest but not all take the direct route to the reserve. There is a shooting range for the testing of weapons in Harley Dingle to the S of the reserve with an extensive Danger Area all around it.

Public transport: Bus: X48 Craven Arms-Builth Wells runs along A488, nearest stop in Llanfihangel Rhydithon (3 miles W of Fishpools on A488, not Sun), Celtic Travel (01686 412 231).

Visiting: Open all hours, free, no facilities, dogs on lead, no grazing animals

Contact: RWT: 01597 823 298; info@rwtwales.org
Continue W on A488 to junction with A44. Turn R for Crossgates, then N on A483 to Llanbister. Turn R on to B4356.

8 CNWCH BANK
Radnorshire Wildlife Trust

Habitats: 200 acres of moorland on S slopes of Beacon Hill massif (rising to 1,640 ft). Heather, Bilberry. Gorge of young River Lugg, along which, further downstream, the Herefordshire Wildlife Trust has established its Lugg Living Landscape project.

Birds: Red Grouse, Peregrine Falcon, Merlin, Raven, Stonechat, Linnet,

Other: Water Purslane, Lesser Twayblade, Pillwort, Orange Foxtail.

Directions: SO 179 746. The B4356 from Llangunllo to Llanbister runs to the S of the massif. The Heart of Wales Line Trail runs N across this road at SO 181 728 and up along flank of Lugg Gorge on Cnwch Bank. Numerous other paths cross the common land but no roads.

Public transport: None.

Visiting: Open all hours, free, no facilities. Heart of Wales Line Trail runs across reserve. Grazed by Sheep and horses. Dogs on lead.

Contact: RWT: 01597 823 298; info@rwtwales.org
Continue N on 483 to Newtown and **Montgomeryshire.**

Montgomeryshire

Northernmost of the three historic counties of Breconshire, Radnorshire and Montgomeryshire that, with a few chunks taken out here or added there, now make up Powys. Its western tip extends to the upper reaches of the the Dyfi/Dovey estuary (also see Ceredigion). Lake Vyrnwy and its associated moorland lie in the Berwyn Mountains to the north, whilst the still young Severn flows north(!) along its south eastern edge.

Bird Atlas/Avifauna
The Birds of Montgomeryshire
B Holt & G Williams
(privately published, 2008)

Bird Recorder
Simon Boyes, Bridge Cottage, Middletown, Welshpool, SY21 8DG. 07708 328 987; montbird@gmail.com

Bird Report
Montgomeryshire Bird Report (1981/82-), from 2013 report, available as a download from montgomerybird-blog.blogspot.co.uk/p/county-reports.html

BTO Regional Representative
Dr Margaret Town
Wetland Bird Survey (WeBS)
Local Organizer: webs@bto.org
Tony Coatsworth
webs@bto.org

Club
Montgomeryshire Bird Group (1996; n/a)
Simon Boyes (Chair): 07708 328 987;
montbird@gmail.com;
www.montwt.co.uk/local-groups/bird-group
Meetings: 7:30pm 3rd Wednesday of the month (Sep-Mar). Usually at Welshpool Methodist Church, 13 High St, Welshpool SY21 7JP—contact/see website for details.

Ringing Group/Bird Observatory
None

RSPB Local Group
No Groups

Wildlife Trust
Montgomeryshire Wildlife Trust (1982; 2,000)
Park Lane House, High Street, Welshpool,
Powys, SY21 7JP.:
01938 555 654;
info@montwt.co.uk;
www.montwt.co.uk

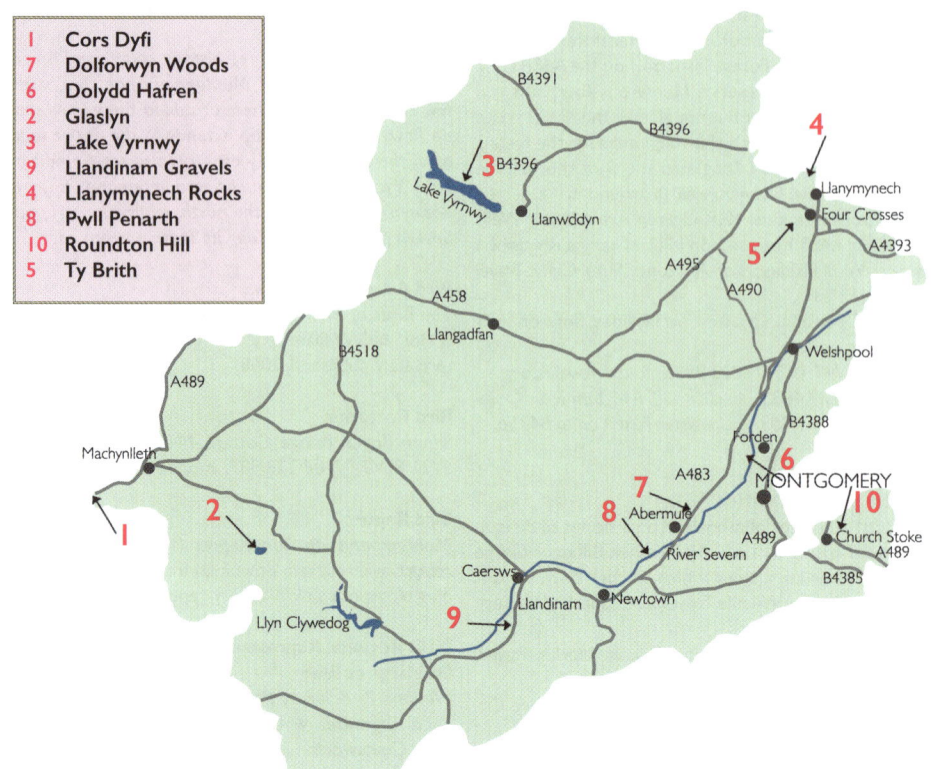

1	Cors Dyfi
7	Dolforwyn Woods
6	Dolydd Hafren
2	Glaslyn
3	Lake Vyrnwy
9	Llandinam Gravels
4	Llanymynech Rocks
8	Pwll Penarth
10	Roundton Hill
5	Ty Brith

If you continue NE for another 2.25 miles along the A487 from Ynis Hir (q.v. Ceredigion) you come to...

1 CORS DYFI NATURE RESERVE
Montgomeryshire Wildlife Trust
Habitats: Bog, wet woodland and scrub. 40 acres.
Birds: Spring/summer: Osprey (first bred 2011), Snipe, Nightjar, Grasshopper, Sedge & Reed Warblers, Stonechat, Reed Bunting. *Winter.* Barnacle Goose, Bittern, Hen Harrier.
Other: Beaver. Common Lizard, Four-spotted Chaser dragonfly.
Directions: SY20 8SR; SN 704 984. Lies 3.5 miles SW of Machynlleth on A487 Abersytwyth road. *c.*2.5 miles S of Derwenlas, turn R after caravan park.
Public transport: Bus X28 Cambrian Coastliner, Machynlleth to Aberystwyth will stop at Osprey Project (not Sun). Lloyds Coaches (01654 702 100).
Visiting: Entry charge, open 10am-5pm Mar-early Sep, last admission 4:30pm 7 days/week inc. Bank Holidays; early Sep-25 Dec & 5 Feb-late Mar open 10am-4pm Wed-Sun. Car park (no large coaches), visitor centre, toilets (inc disabled), small cafe, hides, 360 degree ob-servatory. Extensive boardwalks, all parts of site wheelchair accessible, electric wheelchair lift to observatory. Assistance dogs only.
Contact: Montgomeryshire WT: 01938 555 654;
info@montwt.co.uk;
Osprey Project (Mar-Aug):
enquiries@dyfiospreyproject.com;
www.dyfiospreyproject.com
Continue into Machynlleth on A487 then take

2 GLASLYN
Montgomeryshire Wildlife Trust
Habitats: Upland lake, moorland—part of Cambrian Mountains.
Birds: All year: Red Grouse, Red Kite, Buzzard, Hen Harrier, Skylark, Raven. *Spring/summer:* Golden Plover, Wheatear, Ring Ouzel. *Winter:* Goldeneye, Merlin.
Other: Heathers, quillwort (on lake).
Directions: SY19 7BW; SN 837 952 (locked gate). SE of Machynlleth. Take B4518 off A489 in Machynlleth sign-posted to Llyn Clywedog via narrow mountain road (passes Cadair Viewpoint after seven miles—worth a stop). After 7.5 miles, entrance to reserve marked with

brown sign. Park by locked gate and walk in (one mile to lake edge—lyn means lake). Alternatively take B4518 from A470 at Llanidloes.

Public transport: None.

Visiting: Open all hours. No vehicular access past locked gate so even MWT members must park at gate and walk in. Dogs on lead. Ground can be wet.

Contact: Montgomeryshire WT: 01938 555 654; info@montwt.co.uk

Return to A489, continue along it away from Machynlleth, then on A470 NE towards Dolgellau. At junction with A458 head SE for Welshpool, then take B4395 on L just before Llangadfan. After 6.7 miles turn L on to B4393 and continue on this to dam and car park.

3 LAKE VYRNWY

Severn Trent Water/RSPB

Habitats: 12,500 acres under management. Blanket bog restoration. Heather moorland, woodland (tree nursery), meadows, largest organic farm in England and Wales, conservation grazing. Rocky streams and large reservoir (third largest lake in Wales, 1,120 acres).

Birds: All year: Buzzard, Red & Black Grouse, Raven. *Spring/summer:* Goosander, Cuckoo, Hen Harrier, Peregrine Falcon, Merlin, Hobby, Golden Plover, Curlew, Common Sandpiper, Willow Tit, Wood Warbler, Whinchat, Redstart, Wheatear, Dipper, Kingfisher, Pied Flycatcher.

Other: Otter, Polecat, Brown Hare.

Directions: SY10 0LZ; SJ 016 192. WSW of Oswestry. Nearest village is Llanfyllin on A490. Take B4393 to Llanwddyn and at dam, turn L and L again.

Public transport: None.

Visiting: Open all hours, free (charge for car park, even for RSPB members). Toilets (9am-5pm), cafe (nearby), nine waymarked trails, three hides (one with wheelchair access). There is a circular road around the lake but it was blocked by tree falls in 2024 and work to clear it is only starting as this edition goes to press.

Contact: RSPB: 01691 870 278; vyrnwy@rspb.org.uk

Take B4393 to junction with A490, then A490 E to A495. Turn L on to A495 and follow to Llansantffraid-ym-Mechain, where turn R on to B4393 and cross the Vyrnwy. Take B4398 on L, re-cross Vrynwy and canal and join A483 in Llanymynech. Turn L

Alternatively, continue along the side of Lake Vrynwy and take the minor road through the moorland part of the reserve, to the NW of the lake, over the Berwyns and down into Bala and **Clwyd.**

4 LLANYMYNECH ROCKS

Montgomeryshire Wildlife Trust

Habitats: Disused limestone quarry. Woodland and scrub.

Birds: Peregrine Falcon, Green Woodpecker, common woodland spp.

Other: Dingy & Grizzled Skippers, Pearl-borderd, Dark Green & Silver Washed Fritillaries. Early Purple, Common Spotted Orchids.

Directions: SY22 6HD; SJ 262 216. Straddles Wales/England border. The A483 from Oswestry to Welshpool runs through Llanymynech. A minor road joins the A483 from the W 300 yards N of the town's central crossroads. Follow this road for 650 yards then take entrance track on R.

Public transport: Bus: T12 Wrexham-Machynlleth stops in Llanymynech (not Sun), Lloyds Coaches (01654 702 100)/Tanat Coaches (01691 780 212). Train—Oswestry (6 miles).

Visiting: Open all hours, free, no facilities. Park in Shropshire Wildlife Trust car park off Underhill Lane. Very rough terrain. Grazing sheep, dogs on lead.

Contact: Montgomeryshire WT: 01938 555 654; info@montwt.co.uk

Continue S on A483 towards Welshpool for...

5 TY BRITH

Montgomeryshire Wildlife Trust

Habitats: 4 traditionally managed hay meadows and hedgerows. 12 acres.

Birds: What were once common farmland spp.

Other: 100 spp grasses and flowers.

Directions: SY22 6TE; SJ 244 178. At the roundabout on the A483 in Four Crosses take the B4393 NW for Llansantffraidd-ym-Mechain. Turn L into a Courthouse Lane after 700 yards and follow for just under 1.5 miles. The first of the 4 fields will be on your L after a lane.

Public transport: Bus: T12 Wrexham-Machynlleth stops in Four Crosses (not Sun), Lloyds Coaches (01654 702 100)/Tanat Coaches (01691 780 212). Train—Oswestry (7.5 miles).

Visiting: Park on roadside. Open all hours, free, no facilities. No paths. Grazed by sheep. Dogs on lead.

Contact: Montgomeryshire WT: 01938 555 654; info@montwt.co.uk

Continue S on A483 to Welshpool.

6 DOLYDD HAFREN

Montgomeryshire Wildlife Trust

Habitats: River Severn (Hafren is the Welsh name for the Severn) floodplain—braided river, ox-bow lakes, wet meadows, reedbed, woodland, scrub and willow, arable fields. 100 acres.

Birds: All year: Little Egret, Red Kite, Peregrine Falcon, Kingfisher, Grey Wagtail, Reed Bunting. *Summer:* Goosander, Oystercatcher, Hobby, Little Ringed Plover, Common Sandpiper, Sand Martin, Reed, Sedge & Garden Warblers. *Winter:* Little Grebe, Wigeon, Teal, Pintail, Shoveler, Merlin, Water Rail, Curlew, Snipe, winter thrushes.

Other: 19 spp butterflies, 13 spp dragonflies. Otter,

Brown Hare. Flora (inc. Mudwort, arable weeds).
Directions: SY21 8AH; SJ 201 000. SE of Welshpool. Take A458/A483 S from Welshpool, then A490/B4388 towards Montgomery. After three miles turn R, continue for 1.75 miles, through Forden to Gaer Farm, turn R and follow narrow (rough) track to reserve (0.6 miles). Track not owned by MWT and in a very poor state. Only suitable for 4x4s and should not be attempted in severe weather conditions..
Public transport: None.
Visiting: Open all hours. Parking area, path along S boundary to two hides (with steps). Dogs on leads.
Contact: Montgomeryshire WT: 01938 555 654; info@montwt.co.uk
Return to A483 and continue SW on the other side of the Severn from Abermule... If you had chosen to enter Montgomeryshire from the last reserve featured in Radnorshire, you would meet yourself driving N around here.

7 DOLFORWYN WOODS

Montgomeryshire Wildlife Trust
Habitats: Ancient woodland largely but not completely felled, replanted with a variety of species. 70 acres.
Birds: Woodland spp inc Green Woodpecker, Wood Warbler, Redstart, Pied Flycatcher,
Other: Dormouse. Silver-washed Fritillary. Bluebell, Herb-paris.
Directions: SY15 6JG; SO158 957. Take minor road heading NW from A483 250 yards N of bridge over Severn to Abermule. Small car park on R.
Public transport: Bus: X75 Shewwsbury-Newtown-Rhayader stops in Abermule (bridge over Severn then 300 yard walk) Celtic Travel (01686 412 231). T12 Machynlleth-Newtown-Wrexham stops in Abermule (not Sun), Lloyds Coaches (01654 702 100). Train—Newtown.
Visiting: Open all hours, free, no facilities but adjacent to Dolforwyn Hall Hotel. Numerous paths, some steep. Dogs on lead
Contact: Montgomeryshire WT: 01938 555 654; info@montwt.co.uk
Further along the A483 but on the other side of the Severn, on the outskirts of Newtown....

8 PWLL PENARTH

Montgomeryshire Wildlife Trust
Habitats: Formerly part of the adjacent sewage works. Remodelled in 1996 with pools of varying depths, islands and cliffs. Reedbed, carr. Between River Severn and disused Montgomery Canal. 15 acres.
Birds: 98 spp. Passage waders, Little Grebe, Kingfisher, Reed & Sedge Warblers, Reed Bunting
Other: Otter, Grass Snake. Broad-bodied Chaser.
Directions: SY16 3BA; SO 137 927. In Llanllwchaiarn (E of Newtown) take minor road by church off B4568 for Rock Farm, continue to Montgomery Canal and park

in the small area by the sewage works. Walk along the canal towpath to reach the reserve.
Public transport: Bus: 84 Newtown-Llanfair Caereinion stops in Llanllwchaiarn by church (not Sat or Sun) Owen's Travelmaster (01691 652 126)/Tanat Coaches (01691 780 212). Train—Newtown.
Visiting: Open all hours, free, flat paths, can be muddy. Hide. Dogs on lead.
Contact: Montgomeryshire WT: 01938 555 654; info@montwt.co.uk
Further upstream on the Severn, to the SW of Newtown on the A470...

9 LLANDINAM GRAVELS

Montgomeryshire Wildlife Trust
Habitats: River meadows, river shingle.
Birds: All year: Dipper, Grey Wagtail, Reed Bunting. *Summer:* Little Ringed Plover, Common Sandpiper, Sand Martin, Yellow Wagtail. *Passage:* Green Sandpiper, Wheatear, Whinchat. *Winter:* Goosander, winter thrushes.
Other: Rich in flora. Dragonflies. Otter.
Directions: SY17 5AU; SO 022 876. Beside River Severn at Llandinam. Turn off A470 at Llandinam (over narrow bridge by statue), after c.400 ft turn L on to track and follow for just over 0.5 mile to the car park on L.
Public transport: Bus: X75 Welshpool-Llanidloes stops at Llandinam (not Sun)—c.0.5 mile walk to reserve. Celtic Travel (01686 412 231).
Visiting: Open all hours. Small parking area, waymarked paths across meadows (mainly flat).
Contact: Montgomeryshire WT: 01938 555 654; info@montwt.co.uk
Rather than following the A483 S, leave it at the 1st roundabout S of Welshpool and take the A490 for Churchstoke.

10 ROUNDTON HILL NNR

Montgomeryshire Wildlife Trust
Habitats: Hill rising to 1,200 ft comprising a mixture of grassland, woodland and scrub. 110 acres. SSSI.
Birds: 59 spp. Green Woodpecker, Whitethroat, Skylark, Redstart, Pied Flycatcher, Yellowhammer.
Other: 29 spp butterfly. Rock Stonecrop, Knotted Clover, Carline Thistle, Shepherd's Cress, Upright Chickweed.
Directions: SY15 6EL; SO 293 946. Follow the signs from Churchstoke. Car park is 90 yards after crossing a ford.
Public transport: Bus: 81 Welshpool-Newtown stops in Churchstoke (not Sun) Tanat Coaches (01691 780 212).
Visiting: Open all hours, free, no facilities. Grazed, dogs on lead. terrain steep and uneven
Contact: Montgomeryshire WT: 01938 555 654; info@montwt.co.uk

Gwynedd
(Caernarfonshire, Meirionnydd)

The two historic Welsh counties of Caernarfonshire and Meirionnyd have now been merged into the modern county of Gwynned, which takes its name from that of a Welsh principality. Bardsey Island is a migrant hotspot, the Mawddach Valley area has the typical Welsh woodland species and Gwynedd is the county of Cadair Idris and Yr Wyddfa, Wales's two highest mountain massifs.

Bird Atlas/Avifauna
The Breeding Birds of North Wales
Anne Brenchley, Geoff Gibbs, Rhion Pritchard & Ian M Spence
(Liverpool University Press, 2013).
Scarce and Rare Birds in North Wales: historic records up to and including 2016
Robin Sandham
(privately published, 2018).
Birds of Caernarfonshire
Rhion Pritchard
(Cambrian Ornithological Society, 2017).
The Birds of Meirionnydd
Rhion Pritchard
(Cambrian Ornithological Society, 2012).

Bird Recorder
Caernarfonshire
Rhion Pritchard, Pant Afonig, Hafod Lane, Bangor, Gwynedd LL57 4BU: 01248 671 301;
rhion678pritchard@gmail.com
Meirionnydd
Jim Dustow, Afallon, 7 Glan y Don, Rhiwbryfdir, Blaenau Ffestiniog, Gwynedd LL41 3LW: 01766 830 976;
meinirowen@live.co.uk

Bird Report
Cambrian Bird Report (NW Wales) (1953-),
from Rhion Pritchard, as above.
Bardsey's Wildlife (1953-),
from Bardsey Bird Observatory,
Steve Stansfield (Director of Operations):
warden@bbfo.org.uk
View online at:
www.bbfo.blogspot.com/p/bardseys-wildlife-reports.html

BTO Regional Representative
Caernarfon
Rhion Pritchard:
Meirionnydd
Dave Anning

Wetland Bird Survey (WeBS)
Local Organizers: webs@bto.org
Caernarfonshire
Rhion Pritchard
Foryd bay
Simon Hugheston-Roberts:
Meirionnydd (estuaries), Meirionnydd (other sites)
Jim Dustow:

Club
Cambrian Ornithological Society (1952; 160)
Julian Thompson (Sec), Pensychnant, Sychnant Pass, Conwy, LL32 8BJ: 01492 592 595;
julian.pensychnant@btinternet.com;
www.birdsin.wales/cambrian-ornithological-society
Meetings: 7:30pm, 1st Friday of the month (Sep-May). Pensychnant Centre, Sychnant Pass, Conwy, LL32 8BJ. Some talks are held online—contact/see website for details.
Grwp Adar Bangor Bird Group (1947; 80)
Nigel Brown: bangorbirdgroup@gmail.com;
www.sites.google.com/view/bangorbirdgroup/home
Meetings: 7:30pm, Wednesdays (Oct-Mar). In person venues vary but meetings mainly held on zoom. Contact/see website for details.

Ringing Group/Bird Observatory
Bardsey Bird Observatory
Steve Stansfield (Director of Operations), Cristin, Bardsey Island, Pwllheli, Gwynedd LL53 8DE: 07855 264 151;
warden@bbfo.org.uk; www.bbfo.org.uk

RSPB Local Group
North Wales (1986; n/a)
Jill Wright: Jillian.wright1@btinternet.com;
https://group.rspb.org.uk/northwales/
Meetings: 2:00pm, 3rd Friday of the month (Sep-May). St Davids Church Hall, Penrhyn Bay, Llandudno, Conwy, LL30 3NT. Walks programme on website.
Facebook Groups: RSPB North Wales Local Group

Wildlife Trust
North Wales Wildlife Trust (1963; 10,000)
Llys Garth, Garth Road, Bangor, Gwynedd LL57 2RT.:
01248 351 541; info@northwaleswildlifetrust.org.uk;
www.northwaleswildlifetrust.org.uk

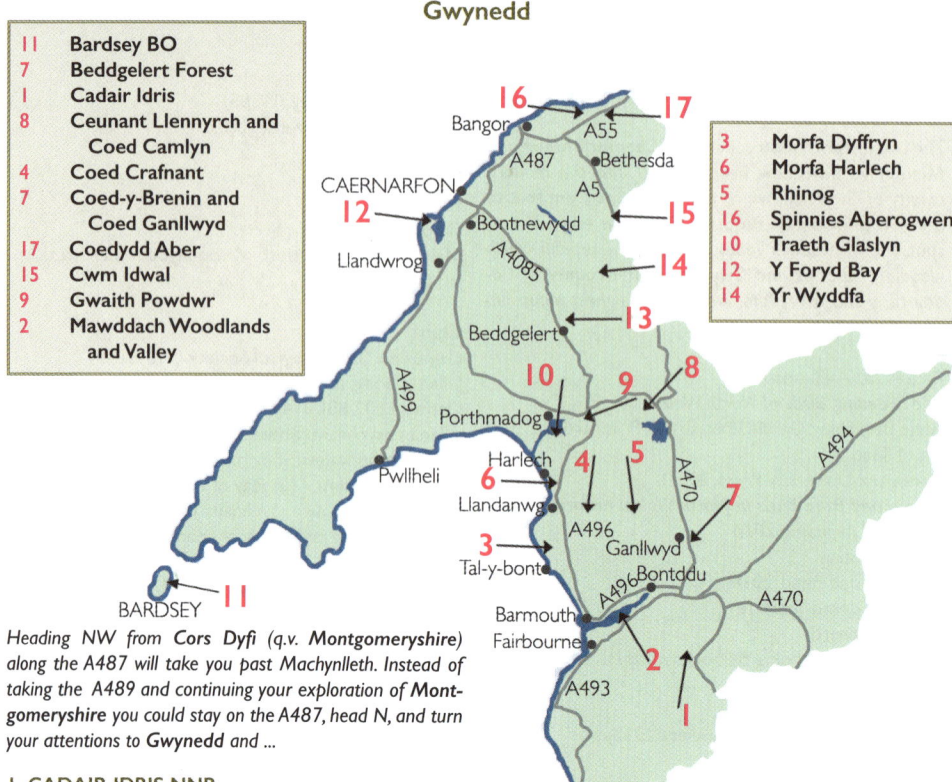

11	Bardsey BO
7	Beddgelert Forest
1	Cadair Idris
8	Ceunant Llennyrch and Coed Camlyn
4	Coed Crafnant
7	Coed-y-Brenin and Coed Ganllwyd
17	Coedydd Aber
15	Cwm Idwal
9	Gwaith Powdwr
2	Mawddach Woodlands and Valley

3	Morfa Dyffryn
6	Morfa Harlech
5	Rhinog
16	Spinnies Aberogwen
10	Traeth Glaslyn
12	Y Foryd Bay
14	Yr Wyddfa

Heading NW from Cors Dyfi (q.v. Montgomeryshire) along the A487 will take you past Machynlleth. Instead of taking the A489 and continuing your exploration of Montgomeryshire you could stay on the A487, head N, and turn your attentions to Gwynedd and ...

1 CADAIR IDRIS NNR

Natural Resources Wales

Habitats: Mountain (2,930 ft), screes, cliffs (up to 1,000 ft high), lakes, grassy slopes, rainforest, bog. 1,500 acres.
Birds: Peregrine Falcon, Chough, Chiffchaff, Wood & Willow Warblers, Ring Ouzel, Dipper, Wheatear, Pied Flycatcher, Redstart, Grey Wagtail
Other: Lesser Horseshoe Bat. Sundews, Hairy Greenweed, Bog Asphodel.
Directions: LL36 9AJ; SH 732 115. The B4405 from Tywyn joins the A487 from Dolgellau at the Minfford hotel, where the Eryri National Park Authority Dol Idris car park is located.
Public transport: Bus: T2 Aberystwyth-Bangor stops at junction of A487 and B4405; 30 Tywyn-Dolgellau, both Lloyds Coaches (01654 702 100). Train—Tywyn.
Visiting: Car park (charge), toilets, open all hours, access to reserve free, 4 waymarked walking trails; 2 easy and 2 strenuous, as well as 1 non-waymarked trail to summit (2,600 ft of ascent).
Contact: NRW: 0300 065 3000;
enquiries@naturalresourceswales.gov.uk
Having climbed Cadair Idris, take the A487 to its junction with the A470. Then follow the A470 past Dolgellau, taking the A493 for Mawddach Woodlands on the S side of the Mawddach or the A496 for the Mawddach Valley on the N side at the following roundabout.

2 MAWDDACH WOODLANDS & VALLEY

RSPB

Two separate but nearby reserves on opposite sides of Mawddach estuary.
Habitats: Oak woodland, bracken and heathland at Coed Garth Gell. Willow and alder scrub and raised bog at Arthog Bog.
Birds:
1: Arthog Bog/Maddach Woodlands. All year: Raven, Buzzard, Sparrowhawk, Peregrine. *Summer:* Migrants inc Cuckoo, Tree Pipit, Grasshopper Warbler. *Winter:* Long-tailed Tit, Redpoll, Siskin. Little Egret and Red-breasted Merganser on nearby estuary.
2: Coed Garth Gell/Mawddach Valley. All year: Buzzard, Peregrine, Sparrowhawk, Lesser Spotted Woodpecker, Grey Wagtail, Dipper, Raven, Hawfinch. *Summer:* Cuckoo, Nightjar, Pied & Spotted Flycatchers, Wood Warbler, Redstart, Tree Pipit.
Other: Coed Garth Gell has Tunbridge Filmy & Beech Ferns. Butterflies. Golden-ringed dragonfly regular.
Directions:
1: Arthog Bog: LL39 1BQ; SH 629 140. Off Dolgellau-Tywyn road (A493), S side of estuary, west of Arthog. Park at Morfa Mawddach station.
2: Coed Garth Gell: LL40 2TT; SH 678 189 (on A496

between Taicynhaeaf and Bontddu), N side of Mawddach estuary, (park in lay-bys/parking spaces).

To travel between the two reserves, the A493 & A496 join the A470 at consecutive roundabouts outside Dolgellau at the hesd of the estuary, further W, close to Coed Garth Gell a toll bridge crossing the Mawddach links them, and there is a foot and rail bridge across the mouth of the Mawddach between Morfa Mawddach and Barmouth.

Public transport: 1: Bus: 28 Dolgellau-Twywn, alight Arthog (0.25 mile from reserve). Lloyds Coaches (01654 702 100). 2: Bus: T3 Dolgellau-Barmouth alight Taicynhaeaf (0.5 mile to reserve). Train—Morfa Mawddach (S side of estuary), Barmouth (N side of estuary)

Visiting: Trails on both sites, open all hours, free. Toilets at Arthog Bog Dogs on leads. Information boards.

Contact: RSPB: 01654 700 222; mawddach@rspb.org.uk

Then, either head E along the A496 to the A470 and then N, in which case jump to 7 Coed-y-Brenin; or head W along the A496, past Barmouth to

3 MORFA DYFFRYN NNR

Natural Resources Wales

Habitats: Active dunes, slacks, saltmarsh, beach. Stretches for 4.5 miles.

Birds: Breeding: Ringed Plover. *Winter:* Wildowl, waders. Hen Harrier, Chough. *Offshore:* Wintering grebes, divers, large rafts of Common Scoter.

Other: Summer: Naked humans. Marsh Helleborine, Northern & Early Marsh-orchids.

Directions: LH44 2HA; SH 572227 (car park). 5 miles N of Barmouth, in the village of Tal y Bont, turn L at the brown and white sign to Dyffryn Seaside Estate and Traeth Benar/Benar Beach. The car park, which is operated by the Eryri National Park Authority, is at the end of the single track Ffordd Benar, past the Dyffryn Seaside Estate.

Public transport: Bus: 39 Dolgellau-Porthmadog stops in Dyffryn Ardudwy (not Sun), Lloyds Coaches (01654 702 100). Train—Dyffryn Ardudwy.

Visiting: Car park (charge). Wheelchair accessible boardwalk from car park. Toilets. Access to dunes free at all hours. Dunes grazed by livestock, keep dogs on lead. Do not touch unexploded munitions.

Contact: NRW: 0300 065 3000; enquiries@naturalresourceswales.gov.uk

Then continue N on A496 and either turn R at Llanbedr on to the minor road signed for Cwm Bychan immediately after crossing the Afon Artro and passing the Victoria Inn for

4 COED CRAFNANT

North Wales Wildlife Trust

Habitats: Atlantic Oak woodland, heathland and moorland. 121 acres

Birds: Cuckoo, Tawny Owl, Wood Warbler, Pied Flycatcher (95 nestboxes installed), Redstart.

Other: Bluebell, Common Cow-wheat.

Directions: LL45 2PF; SH 617 290 (entrance); SH 619 295 (car park). Continue along minor road from Llanbedr, without crossing river, for 1.7 miles to Pen-y-Bont. Park here for S entrance, cross river and follow path to Y Fron. For N entrance continue on road for just under another mile. Park at Pont Cranant. Cross bridge and follow path to reserve entrance. Small car park another 700 yards along road, on opposite side of Artro to reserve.

Public transport: Bus: 39 Dolgellau-Porthmadog stops in Llanbedr (not Sun) Lloyds Coaches (01654 702 100). Train—Llanbedr. Then walk along minor road.

Visiting: Open all hours, free, no facilities. Parking for 2 cars at reserve entrance or in small car park 700 yards along road on other side of river from reserve. Steep NW facing wooded slopes. Paths rough in places. Dogs on lead

Contact: North Wales WT: 01248 351 541; info@northwaleswildlifetrust.org.uk

5 RHINOG NNR

Natural Resources Wales

Habitats: Upland heath, crags, mountain lakes, streams.

Birds: Red & Black Grouse, Hen Harrier, Merlin, Peregrine Falcon, Ring Ouzel, Wheatear.

Other: Lesser Twayblade.

Directions: LL45 2PH; SH 646 315 (Cwm Bychan car park). Continue c.2.5 miles along the minor road from **Coed Crafnant**. Car park immediately after passing Llyn Cwm Bychan. Then enter the reserve from the N.

Public transport: None nearer than Llanbedr.

Visiting: Cwm Bychan car park (private, charge), NNR open all hours, free, portaloos at Cwm Bychan. From Cwm Bychan follow Cambrian Way up the Roman Steps drovers road SE to the saddle between Craig Wion and Rhinog Fawr and then on up to the summit of Rhinog Fawr (an ascent of c.1,900 ft). The Cambrian Way then descends along a ridge to Barmouth 8.7 miles SSW. Paths rocky and steep. There are also routes into the NNR from the S (Cwm Nantcol), also starting from Llanbedr, and the E, starting from the A470 to the N of the **Coed-y-Brenin** and entering through the forest on the E flank.

Contact: NRW: 0300 065 3000; enquiries@naturalresourceswales.gov.uk

or carry straight on N along/return to A496 at Llanbedr to

6 MORFA HARLECH NNR

Natural Resources Wales

Habitats: Active dunes, continuation of same system as Morfa Dyffryn after gap at Llandanwg, slacks, beach, saltmarsh. Area of conifer plantation. 2,600 acres. SAC.

Birds: Ringed Plover. *Winter:* Wildowl, waders. Hen Harrier, Chough. *Offshore:* Wintering grebes, divers, large rafts of Common Scoter.

Other: Small Copper, Dark Green Fritillary, Gatekeeper and Grayling butterflies. Lesser Butterfly Orchid.

Directions: L46 2UG; SH 574 316. By the railway station in Harlech, take Fford Glan Mor for the beach. Min y Don car park 0.5 mile along road.

Public transport: Bus: 39 Dolgellau-Porthmadog stops at Fford Glan Mor in Harlech (not Sun) Lloyds Coaches (01654 702 100). Train—Harlech. Then walk to beach.

Visiting: Car park (Gwynedd Council, charge), toilets, footpath to beach, then turn R for reserve, which continues along S side of Dwyryd estuary, with large areas of saltmarsh here. Dogs on leads.

Contact: NRW: 0300 065 3000; enquiries@naturalresourceswales.gov.uk

If you turned E along the A496 from Mawddach Valley, rejoin the A470 and head N to

7 COED-Y-BRENIN NNR & COED GANLLWYD NNR

Natural Resources Wales/National Trust

Habitats: 9,000 acres of conifer plantation, areas of broadleaf, rivers.

Birds: Common woodland spp inc Goshawk, Sparrowhark, Wood Warbler, Dipper, Spotted & Pied Flycatchers, Redstart, Grey Wagtail.

Other:

Directions: LL40 2TF; SH 727 244 (Dolymelynllyn NT car park, NOT the main NRW visitor centre). Immediately to R of the A470 in village of Ganllwyd.

Public transport: Bus: T2 Bangor-Aberystwyth stops in Ganllwyd, Lloyds Coaches (01654 702 100).

Visiting: Coed-y-Brenin is a large forest that flanks the A470 for some 6 miles as it runs alongside the Mawddach. The forest also extends along the valleys of a number of the Mawddach's tributaries. There are several car parks, a visitor centre (closed) and numerous walking and mountain biking trails.

Enfolded within this forest reserve there is one area, Coed Ganllwyd that is owned by the National Trust. This lies around the village of Ganllwyd at the point where the Gamlan flows into the Mawddach.

Toilets and picnic area at Dolymelynllyn car park (free for NT members). Dogs on lead. Several walking trails through largely deciduous forest taking in torrents, waterfalls and lakes. One suitable for wheelchairs.

Contact: NRW: 0300 065 3000; enquiries@naturalresourceswales.gov.uk NT: 01341 440238 eryri@nationaltrust.org.uk

Continue along the A470, passing the village, lake and disused power station of Trawsfynydd. At Tyddyn dû branch L on to the A487, do not stay on A470. After 500 yards take another L and then fork L almost immediately. You are now on a minor road that runs alongside and above

8 CEUNANT LLENNYRCH NNR & COED CAMLYN NNR

Natural Resources Wales

Habitats: Deep gorge, high cliffs, torrents and waterfall, Oak rainforest. The gorge of the Afon Prysor running from the Trawsfynydd dam to the Dwyryd

Birds: Wood Warbler, Pied Flycatcher, Redstart.

Other: Mosses, 250 spp. lichens.

Directions: LL41 4EU; SH 664 392 (car park). Follow the minor road from Tyddyn dû for 1.7 miles (do not fork L at 0.6 miles but do fork L at 0.9 mile)

Public transport: Bus: closest stop Maentwrog. Train—Penrhyndeudraeth

Visiting: Car park small, not NRW (honesty box). Reserve open all hours, free, no facilities. Walk 100 yards along road to reserve entrance. Marked trail to waterfall. Steep and uneven, can be slippery. Dogs on lead.

Coed Camlyn NNR is not suitable for visitors but is immediately to NE as the Prysor emerges from gorge.

Contact: NRW: 0300 065 3000; enquiries@naturalresourceswales.gov.uk

If wooded Welsh gorges are your thing, further E & N along the Dwyryd there are another three NNRs that are remnants of ancient Oak rainforest: Ceunant Cynfal, Coedydd Maentwrog & Coed Cymerau-isal (the last of these is not suitable for visitors). Stay on the A487 past the turning for Ceunant Llennyrch. Then turn R on to the A496. After crossing the Cynfal at Pont Tal-y-Bont, a path on R leads along the Ceunant Cynfal, the A496 continues towards Coed Cymerau-Isal and minor road branches back towards Coedydd Maentwrog.

0.75 mile beyond Ceunant Llennyrch NNR, the minor road joins the A496 from Morfa Harlech. Turn R, the road is now running along the base of Coed Camlyn NNR, and follow to junction with A487 (from Coed-y-Brenin NNR and the oakwoods upstream along the Dwyryd. Veer L on to the A487 towards Porthmadog. In Penrhyndeudrath.

9 GWAITH POWDWR

North Wales Wildlife Trust

Habitats: 60 acres. Fomer explosives factory now returning to wood and heathland.

Birds: Nightjar, Redstart, Pied Flycatcher, Tree Pipit.

Other: Lesser Horseshoe & Brown Long-eared bats. Adder, Grass Snake, Sow Worm.

Directions: LL48 6LT; SH 621 389. Take road from Penrhyndeudrath for Pont Briwet (bridge to Harlech), then first road into Cooke's Industrial Estate. Reserve gates after 90 yards.

Public transport: Bus: G23 Barmouth-Porthmadog stops in Penrhyndeudraeth, Lloyds Coaches (01654 702 100).

Visiting: Open all hours, free, no facilities. Park at reserve gates (SH 616 388) or along road towards bridge. Contact NWWT in advance for gate code. Most tracks

wheelchair accessible. Grazed by sheep. Dogs on lead.
Contact: North Wales WT: 01248 351 541; info@northwaleswildlifetrust.org.uk
Return to the A487 and at the next roundabout either stay on the A487 and jump to 14 Beddgelert Forest or take the A497 for

10 TRAETH GLASLYN
North Wales Wildlife Trust
Habitats: Flood meadow—saltmarsh, mudflats, wet grassland, wet willow woodland.
Birds: Spring/summer: Sandwich & Common Terns. Osprey (nest at Pont Croesor, visitor centre on B4410 N of Porthmadog). *Winter:* wildfowl and waders inc Teal, Wigeon, Pintail, Goldeneye, Red-breasted Merganser, Redshank, Ruff, Curlew, Dunlin, Black-tailed Godwit.
Other: Flora inc Ragged Robin, Selfheal.
Directions: LL48 6HT; SH 584 379. SE of Porthmadog. At end of Cobb park in lay-by on A497 just past toll cottage. For N part of reserve walk N along road (along estuary, c.1 mile), then turn L at crossroads to reserve boundary (SH 592 389).
Public transport: Bus: 3b from Porthmadog stops at Tollgate & Minffordd (not Sun). Arriva. Train—Porthmadog or Minffordd.
Visiting: Open all year. Hide accessible via small gate near toll cottage. Site is **TIDAL** and can get completely submerged at high tide—check tides before visiting. Paths are muddy—**STAY** on them. No dogs.
Contact: North Wales WT: 01248 351 541; info@northwaleswildlifetrust.org.uk
Ospreys: 07834 575 008; www.glaslynwildlife.co.uk
Continue W on A487 towards the tip of the Lleyn Peninsula.

11 BARDSEY BIRD OBSERVATORY
Bardsey Bird Observatory
Habitats: 440-acre island, sandy beach, rocky coves, mountain, sea-bird cliffs (view from boat). Farm and scrubland, spruce plantation, willow copses and gorse.
Birds: All year: Chough, Peregrine Falcon, Raven. *Spring/summer:* Night walks and talks to see Manx Shearwaters (30,000 pairs), Puffins, seabirds, migrant warblers, chats, thrushes. *Autumn:* Migrants, inc many rarities (Eye-browed Thrush, Lanceolated Warbler, American Robin, Yellowthroat, Cretzschmar's Bunting, Black-and-white Warbler).
Other: Grey Seal, Risso's Dolphin, moths, Autumn Ladies' Tresses. Dark Sky Sanctuary.
Directions: 15 miles SW of Pwllheli. 20 min boat crossing from Porth Meudwy, near Aberdaron. LL53 8DA; SH 163 255.
Public transport: Bus: Pwllheli to Aberdaron.1.6 miles to boat
Visiting: Stay at Bardsey Bird Observatory Lodge Mar-Oct. Comfy rooms: 2 singles, 2 doubles (1 double bed, 1 single), 2 four-bedded rooms, Internet, solar power,

central heating, www.bbfo.org.uk/stay
Day trips: Mar-Nov (4 hours). Bardsey Boat Trips—message Colin Evans (07971 769 895). Observatory Visitor Centre/gift shop, toilets, cafe hides, limited mobile signal. No dogs.
Contact: Steven Stansfield (Director of Operations): 07855 264 151; warden@bbfo.org.uk; www.bbfo.org.uk
Accommodation: stayonbardsey@gmail.com
Return E along the N side of the Lleyn Peninsula on the A499 from Pwllheli. Leave A499 S of Llandwrog (pub). Turn R by church and head N for 1.75 miles to S end of Y Foryd Bay or continue straight on through village. Turn R at T junction after 0.5 mile. Follow this road, to the S boundary of Caernarfon airport. Turn R for Morfa Lodge holiday park, beyond which you come to the sea wall along the W side of

12 Y FORYD BAY LNR
Cyngor Gwynedd (the county council)
Habitats: Partially enclosed tidal bay. 697 acres of sand and mudlfats at low tide. SSSI, SAC
Birds: Summer: Tern roost. *Passage:* Spotted Redshank, Greenshank. *Winter:* Whooper Swan, Brent Goose, Shelduck, Wigeon, Pintail, Curlew, Bar-tailed Godwit, Knot, Oystercatcher, Jack Snipe.
Other: Eelgrass beds, inc 3 areas of Dwarf Eelgrass, with associated invertebrates (Ragworm, Baltic Tellin, Peppery Furrow Shell and Spire Shell), providing food for waterfowl.
Directions: LL54 5TP; SH 440 587 (Morfa Lodge holiday park on W side). For E side of bay take the road from Llandwrog (see above) to S end of bay and then continue N. There is now a new small car park and hide at SH 452 586. Shortly afterwards, the road moves away from the coast in order to crosss the Gwyrfai but then returns and you come to a small car park and picnic area.SH 454 603 on E side of bay.
If travelling out from Caernarfon, take A4871 S from town centre. Immediately after crossing Seiont, turn R. Road will fork immediately. R fork is a minor road that will take you round the coast (views across Menai Strait to **Newborough, Anglesey**), eventually reaching the car park and picnic area from the N. The L fork is a minor road that leads to Llanfaglan. 500 yards beyond Llanfaglan, turn R and follow this road to the car park.
Public transport: Bus: T2 Bangor-Porthmadog stops in Bontnewydd on A4871 (2 mile walk), Lloyds Coaches (01654 702 100).
Visiting: Open all hours, free, no facilities. A path runs N-S along the S part of the W side of the bay from the Morfa Lodge holiday park. Dunes to NW. A new bird hide and small car park on SW corner and a further car park and picnic area further N on E side.
Contact: 01766 771 000; bioamrywiaeth@gwynedd.llyw.cymru
After 12 Y Foryd Bay take A487 (not A4871) and follow it to Bangor. Leave Bangor on the A5 and then, at Llandygái

exit L on to minor road. After crossing the Ogwen, branch L again. Then a sharp L turn after crossing railway. This minor road will cross the railway again and take you to the coast at the mouth of the Ogwen after 0.8 miles and 17 Spinnies Aberogwen.

If you remained on the A487 after 10 Gwaith Powdwr, take the A498, 3rd exit 2 roundabouts later at Porthmadog hospital and follow to Beddgelert. Then turn L on to A4085.

13 BEDDGELERT FOREST

Natural Resources Wales

Habitats: 1,700 acres, mixed conifer and broadleaf forest, 2 separate blocks. Lakes and streams. Set amidst open mountainside.

Birds: Goshawk. Common woodland spp inc Wood Warbler, Redstart, Pied Flycatcher, Siskin, Redpoll, Crossbill. Dipper and Grey Wagtail on streams

Other:

Directions: LL55 4UU; SH 574 503. After 1 mile on the A4085 go past the Forest Holidays entrance and then take an exit in L at 1.4 miles and follow track to car park.

Public transport: Bus: S3 Beddgelert-Bangor, Gwynfor Coaches (01248 722 694).

Visiting: Open all hours, free. Mix of walking and biking trails. Some sections suitable for wheelchairs. The Lôn Gwyrfai trail from Beddgelert to Rhyd Ddu passes through the forest, as does the Welsh Highland Railway. 2 miles further N along the A4085, between the 2 blocks of the Beddgelert Forest, there is a second car park at SH 572 525 at a stop on the WHR and also on the Cambrian Way. Another 1.8 miles N along the A4085, which runs along the SW flank of the Snowdon massif, there is a third car park at SH 565 551, where the Snowdon Ranger path to the summit of Snowdon starts from another WHR station. This car park is on the opposite side of Llyn Cwellyn from the N block of the Beddgelert Forest.

Contact: NRW: 0300 065 3000; enquiries@naturalresourceswales.gov.uk

Or stay on the A498 and turn R in Beddgelert to follow the road up Nant Gwynant along the SE flank of Snowdon/ Yr Wyddfa.

14 YR WYDDFA/SNOWDON NNR

Natural Resources Wales/National Trust

Habitats: 4,100 acres, summit of Snowdon (3,650 ft), lakes.

Birds: Despite the name of the National Park, no eagles. Black & Red Grouse, Merlin, Peregrine Falcon, Chough.

Other: Arctic plants: Snowdon Lily. Slender Green Feather-moss, Floating Water-plantain.

Directions: The A4085 runs between Beddgelert and Caernarfon along the SW flank of the Snowdon massif (see **Beddgelert Forest** for the location of car parks at the start of trails into the NNR).

The A498 runs between Beddgelert and the junction with the A4086 along Nant Gwynant to the SE of the massif. There are car parks car park at SH 605 491; SH 612 493 and Pont Bethania SH 628 507 (toilets), start of the Watkin Path.

The A498 joins the A4086 at Llyn Pen y Gwryd. The A4086 runs along the N side of the massif from Capel Curig to Caenrafon and passes through Llanberis. There is a pay & display car park with toilets at Pen y Pass (LL55 4NY; SH 648 555). This is the start of the Miners' and Pyg Tracks to the summit. There is further car parking down the valley to Llanberis and in Llanberis itself.

Public transport: Snowdon Mountain Railway from Llanberis (LL55 4TU; SH 582 598) to summit. Usually busy. 08444 938 120 or www.snowdonrailway.co.uk Parking charges. Bus: S1, S2, S3 & S4 Sherpa'r Wyddfa run along the A4085, A498 & A4086: www.sherparwyddfa.wales.

Visiting: Charges at some of the car parks. The trails to the summit are mostly rough.

Contact: NRW: 0300 065 3000; enquiries@naturalresourceswales.gov.uk

If, having driven along the A498 to Llyn Pen y Gwryd, you turned R on to the A4086, instead of turning L and heading for Llanberis and, ultimately, Bangor, the A4086 will take you to the junction with the A5 at Capel Curig. Turn L here and the A5 will take you past Llyn Ogwen.

15 CWM IDWAL NNR

Natural Resources Wales/National Trust

Habitats: Mountain, moorland, upland lakes.

Birds: Peregrine Falcon, Merlin, Chough, Raven

Other: Feral Goats. Arctic and Alpine plants, Snowdon Lily, Moss Campion, Alpine Lady's Mantle & Purple saxifrage.

Directions: LL57 3LZ; SH 649 604, Ogwen Centre car park, immediately off A5 between Capel Curig and Bangor. Alternatively, park at Bethesda Football Club (LL57 4AW; SH 625 664, charge) downstream of Llyn Ogwen then take the Bws Ogwen electric shuttle bus to Llyn Ogwen. No roadside parking on many of the roads in the Ogwen valley.

Public transport: Bus: T10 Bangor-Betws y Coed, stops at Ogwen, TrawsCymru (0300 200 22 33).

Visiting: Cwm Idwal Visitor Centre (toilets), adjacent to Ogwen Centre car park (limited capacity, card payments only, no cash). The NNR occupies the massif to the S of Llyn Ogwen. Circular trail around Llyn Idwal.

Contact: NRW: 0300 065 3000; enquiries@naturalresourceswales.gov.uk

Continuing along the A5 past Bethesda will take you to the interchange with the A55. Continue on the A5 past this interchange and then at the 2nd roundabout (Llandygái) take the 2nd exit and follow the instructions as if coming from 13 Y Foryd Bay LNR. Alternatively, head E on A55, leave at J12 and follow directions in following entry.

16 SPINNIES ABEROGWEN
North Wales Wildlife Trust

Habitats: Small but perfectly formed: 7 acres of reed-fringed lagoons beside the estuary of the Ogwen (hence Aberogwen) and the extensive tidal mudlflats and sand of Traeth Lafan offshore stretching towards Anglesey.

Birds: Eider, Water Rail, passage Whimbrel, Greenshank and other waders, Little Egret, Kingfisher.

Other: Marsh Helleborine.

Directions: LL57 3YH; SH 615 723 (car park by beach). Follow brown 'Nature Reserve' sign from J12 of A55 for 1 mile along minor road. Minor road to reserve used by farm traffic, do not block. Large car park at shore

Public transport: Bus: 5/5D Caernarfon-Llandudno passes end of minor road to reserve, Arriva Wales (0344 800 44 11).

Visiting: Open during daylight, free entry, no facilities. Walk back to reserve entrance from shore car park. Stay on paths. Drop-off only for disabled visitors at entrance. 3 hides. Most paths and 2 hides wheelchair accessible. Dogs on lead.

Contact: North Wales WT: 01248 351 541; info@northwaleswildlifetrust.org.uk
Return to A55 and continue E along it for.

17 COEDYDD ABER NNR
Natural Resources Wales

Habitats: Woodland, grassland, moorland, river.

Birds: All year: Goshawk, Merlin, Raven, Chough, Dipper, Grey Wagtail, Siskin, Redpoll, Crossbill. *Summer:* Cuckoo, Ring Ouzel, Redstart, Whinchat, Wheatear, Tree Pipit, Pied Flycatcher, warblers inc Garden & Wood. *Winter:* Woodcock, winter thrushes, Firecrest, Brambling.

Other: Woodland flora (inc Blubells), fungi.

Directions: Parking: LL33 0LP; SH 662 719 (lower), LL33 0EH. SH 675 716 (upper). 7 miles E of Bangor. Take A55 towards Llandudno, turn off at J13 (Abergwyngregyn) and follow brown signs to Aber Falls. Just past lower car park turn R into another car park or continue straight on to upper car park.

Public transport: Bus: 5 Bangor-Llandudno stops at Abergwyngregyn (Aber Falls shelter stop—can walk up to falls via a footpath on R just after village or continue along narrow road to lower car park). Arriva (0344 800 44 11). Train—Llanfairfachan (then bus 5).

Visiting: Open access, Lower (pay & display) and Upper (free) car parks—narrow roads. Network of paths. Dogs on lead. Falls are popular visitor attraction.
Contact: NRW: 0300 065 3000; enquiries@naturalresourceswales.gov.uk

Anglesey/ Ynys Môn

Anglesey, the adopted home of Tunnicliffe, has many highlights including a seabird colony (with Choughs) at South Stack, terns at Cemlyn Bay and waders at Malltraeth. Anglesey has the UK's second largest area of fen, after East Anglia, and has 3 fen NNRs well as the extensive reclaimed grazing marsh of Cors Ddyga and the dunes and forest at Newborough.

Bird Atlas/Avifauna
The Birds of Anglesey
Peter Hope Jones & P Whalley (Menter Mon, 2004).
Also see Gwynned

Bird Recorder
Steve Culley, 22 Cae Derwydd, Cemaes Bay LL67 0LP: 01407 710 542; SteCul10@aol.com

Bird Report
Cambrian Bird Report (NW Wales) (1953-), from Rhion Pritchard, Pant Afonig, Hafod Lane, Bangor, Gwynedd LL57 4BU: 01248 671 301; rhion678pritchard@gmail.com

BTO Regional Representative
Ian Hawkins
Wetland Bird Survey (WeBS)
Local Organizer: webs@bto.org
Ian Sims
webs@bto.org

Club
Cambrian Ornithological Society (1952; 160)
Julian Thompson (Sec), Pensychnant, Sychnant Pass, Conwy, LL32 8BJ: 01492 592 595; julian.pensychnant@btinternet.com; www.birdsin.wales/cambrian-ornithological-society
Meetings: 7:30pm, 1st Friday of the month (Sep-May). Pensychnant Centre, Sychnant Pass, Conwy, LL32 8BJ. Some talks are held online—contact/see website for details.

Ringing Group/Bird Observatory
SCAN RG

RSPB Local Group
North Wales (1986; n/a)
Jill Wright: Jillian.wright1@btinternet.com; https://group.rspb.org.uk/northwales/
Meetings: 2:00pm, 3rd Friday of the month (Sep-May). St Davids Church Hall, Penrhyn Bay, Llandudno, Conwy, LL30 3NT. Walks programme on website.

Facebook Groups: RSPB North Wales Local Group

Wildlife Trust
North Wales Wildlife Trust (1963; 10,000)
Llys Garth, Garth Road, Bangor, Gwynedd LL57 2RT.:
01248 351 541; nwwt@northwaleswildlifetrust.org.uk;
www.northwaleswildlifetrust.org.uk

8	Cemlyn
10	Cors Bodeilio
2	Cors Ddyga
4	Cors Erdreiniog
9	Cors Goch
5	Llyn Alaw
3	Llyn Cefni
1	Newborough
	and Ynys Llanddwyn
11	Puffin Island
7	South Stack Cliffs
	and Valley
6	Valley Wetlands

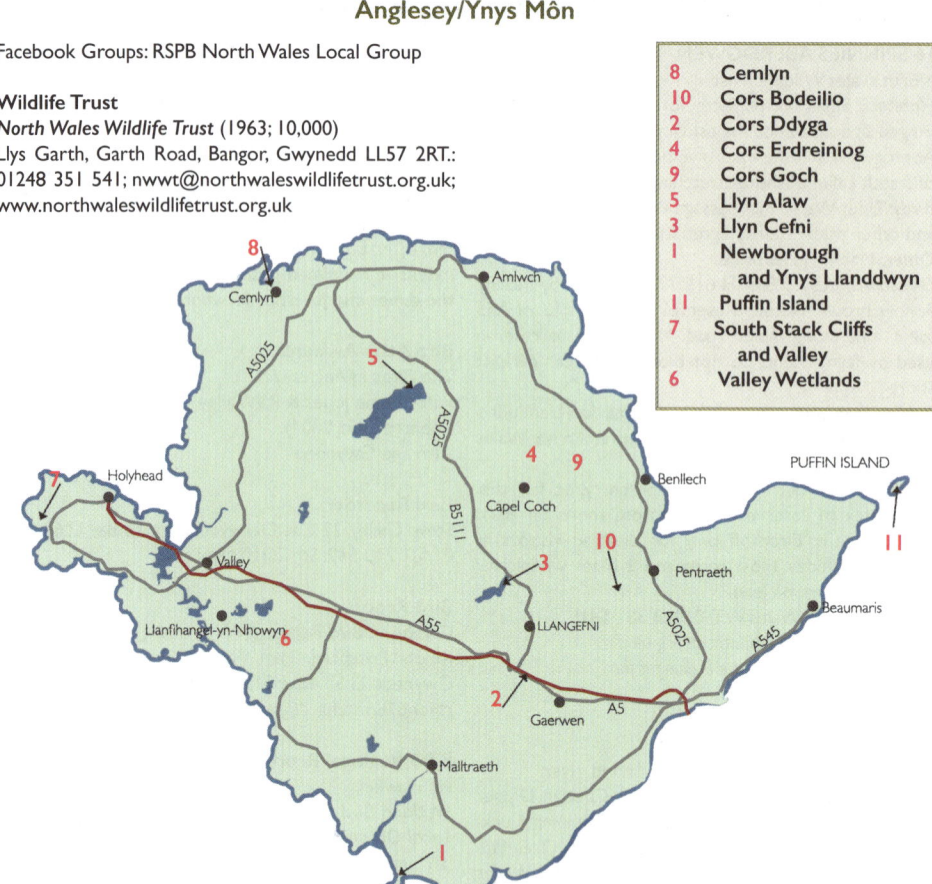

Use the A5 to cross the Menai Strait or, if you cross using the A55, leave the A55 and join the A5 heading W at the first junction.

1 NEWBOROUGH & YNYS LLANDDWYN NNR & NEWBOROUGH FOREST
Natural Resources Wales
Habitats: The NNR consists of an active and fixed dune system, tidal estuary, mudflats and saltmarsh, together with a tidal island, Ynys Llanddwyn. To the W it includes Malltraeth Sands in the Cefni estuary on the seaward side of the Cob, the Cob itself (the dyke built to reclaim **Cors Ddyga/Malltraeth Marsh** q.v.) and Malltraeth Pool, immediately behind the Cob. In the centre, roughly half the original area of dunes was planted with Corsican Pine in the mid 20C. Newborough Forest is not part of the NNR. The main area of dunes in the NNR, the Warren, lies to the E of the Forest. 5,600 acres
Birds: Raven roost, Crossbill. Stonechat, Linnet. Sum-

mer: Ringed Plover, Whitethroat. *Autumn/winter:* Brent Goose, Shelduck, Pintail, Wigeon, Teal. Lapwing, Redshank, Dunlin.
Other: Red Squirrel, Vernal Mining Bee, Petalwort Liverwort.
Directions: LL61 6SG; SH 405 634 Beach (main) car park. Take the A4080 off the A5 after crossing the Menai Strait, follow signs to Newborough village. For the Forest and beach, turn R at the roundabout just before the village, continue on A4080 into village and then turn L on to minor road, follow brown sign for Ynys Llanddwyn. Car park entrance barrier (ANPR) after 0.75 miles, 3 car parks after the entrance barrier. The furthest is the Beach car park, after 1.25 miles.
Other (free) car parks serve other parts of the NNR. Braint & Llyn Rhos Ddu serve the Warren to the E of the Forest. Braint: LL61 6RS; SH 431 643. Turn L on to minor road at roundabout before village, car park after 700 yards on L. Llyn Rhos Ddu: LL61 6RS; SH 426 647.

Go straight across roundabout, follow minor road for 700 yards, car park at end of road.

Llyn Parc Mawr: LL61 6SU; SH413 669. Continue on A4080 through village. Car park after 1 mile on R.

Pen Cob Malltraeth: LL62 5BA; SH 411 671. 250 yards further along A4080 on L. These two car parks serve the Wildlife Pool, the sands on the E side of the Cefni estuary and the N part of the forest. There is a foot/cycle path along the Cob.

Continue on the A4080 across **Cors Ddyga/Malltraeth Marsh** (q.v.) and the Cefni and there is another car park in Malltraeth at SH 407 688 for Malltraeth Pool. Malltraeth is where Charles Tunnicliffe spent the last four decades of his life.

Public transport: Bus: 42/42A (not Sun) Langefni-Bangor stops in Newborough O R Jones (01407 730 204) Train—Bangor or Holyhead (Llanfairpwll... on request).

Visiting: Charges for the Beach and other car parks behind the ANPR entrance gate. Toilets at Beach car park open 8am-6pm (BST); 8:30am-4pm (GMT). Ice cream and catering van at Beach car park: 11am-4pm weekends Apr-Sep and every day during school holidays. Numerous trails from the various car parks, some, including to beach, wheelchair accessible. The Wales Coast Path passes through Newborough. Some seasonal restrictions on dogs to protect ground-nesting birds and beaches.

Contact: 0300 065 3000; enquiries@naturalresourceswales.gov.uk

Instead of leaving the A5 just after crossing the Menai Strait, (if you crossed Menai Strait on A55 take 1st exit for A5) continue through the villages of Gaerwen and Pentre Berw

2 CORS DDYGA [MALLTRAETH MARSH]
RSPB

Habitats: 3,400 acres of reclaimed grazing marsh, pools, reedbed. formed by constructing a dyke (the Cob) in the 19C across the mouth of the Cefni estuary and canalizing the Afon Cefni upstream of the estuary. The 711-acre RSPB reserve ocuppies the NE end of this reclaimed land. SSSI

Birds: Bittern, Great White Egret (regular in winter, bred for first time in 2025), Marsh Harrier includng breeding. *Breeding:* Shoveler, Tufted Duck, Pochard, Great Crested & Little Grebes, Curlew, Lapwing, Cetti's, Grasshopper, Reed & Sedge Warblers, Whitethroat, Skylark, Stonechat, Reed Bunting. *Passage:* Black-tailed Godwit, Ruff. *Winter:* Pintail, Wigeon, Gadwall, Shoveler, Tufted Duck, Pochard, Cetti's Warbler. Black-tailed Godwit.

Other: Otter, Water Vole. Hairy Dragonfly, Variable & Blue-tailed Damselflies. Pillwort, Water Violet, Flowering Rush.

Directions: LL60 6LB; SH 463 725 (RSPB reserve). Turn L off A5 after Pentre Berw, immediately before National speed limit sign. Car park is 350 yards along lane on R at crossroads.

Public transport: Bus: 4/A4/4X Holyhead/Llangefni-Bangor stops in Pentre Berw, Arriva enquiries@arriva.co.uk.

Visiting: Dawn-dusk, free (RSPB reserve). Car park council maintained. No facilities. Dog-free 1.25 mile circular visitor trail starts from it. Various other stone surfaced or tarmac paths (dogs allowed but on lead in presence of livestock or ground-nesting birds). Paths level but can flood in winter, mostly unsuitable for wheel/pushchairs.

Contact: 01248 421 949

Return to the A5 and head W. At the double roundabout over the A55, take the A5114 N into the centre of Llangefni. After a dogleg R continue N out of town along the B5110, forking L on to the B5111.

3 LLYN CEFNI
Welsh Water

Habitats: Reservoir built in 1940s, bisected by causeway of disused railway line. Nature reserve to NE, fishing to SW. Wooded shores.

Birds: Kingfisher, Dipper, Grey Wagtail

Other:

Directions: SH 451 782. Car park and picnic area where Afon Erdreiniog flows into reservoir, 2.2 miles from centre of Llangefni along B5111 from Llangefni to Llanerchymedd.

Public transport: Bus: 32 Llangefni-Amlwch (not Sun) stops on B5111 just before and after LNR, Eifion's Coaches (01407 721 111).

Visiting: Open all hours, free (nature reserve), hide, no facilities. The Lôn Las Cefni cycle path runs around the entire reservoir. The disused railway line that ran across the causeway follows the valley of the Afon Cefni as it flows from the dam to the centre of Llangefni, just over a mile away. Part of this wooded, steep-sided ravine, the **Dingle** or **Nant-y-Pandy**, is also a Local Nature Reserve.

Contact: Welsh Water no longer have a warden at this site.

Continue a further 0.5 mile along the B5111 towards Llanerchymedd turn R at Dolmeinin.

4 CORS ERDREINIOG NNR
Natural Resource Wales

Habitats: Fen, peat bog, wet heath, pools, drainage channels. Drained by Afon Erdreiniog, which flows into **3 Llyn Cefni** (q.v.). 700 acres, SSSI, SAC.

Birds: 150 spp. *Summer:* Snipe, Lapwing, Curlew. Reed, Sedge & Grasshopper Warblers. Stonechat, Reed Buntings. *Winter:* Wildfowl.

Other: 20 spp dragonflies and damselflies, butterflies inc Small Pearl-bordered Fritillary, Marsh Fritillary, Small Copper. Orchids, inc Narrow-leaved Marsh Orchid, Marsh Fragrant Orchid, Lesser Butterfly Orchid, Fly Orchid.

Directions: LL77 7UR; SH 463 819. Turn R off the B5111 at Dolmeinin. After 2 miles, park in Capel Coch (limited roadside parking). Walk down track to reserve entrance.

Public transport: Bus: 32 Llangefni-Amlwch (infrequent, not Sun) stops in Capel Coch, Eifion's Coaches (01407 721 111).

Visiting: No vehicular access to NNR, walk from Capel Coch. Open all hours, free, no facilities. 3.25 miles walking trail from reserve entrance. Path easy but can be muddy. Livestock graze sectons of path. Keep dogs under close control. Wildfowl shooting Sep-Feb.

Contact: NRW: 0300 065 3000; enquiries@naturalresourceswales.gov.uk

Continue along the B5111 to Llanerchymedd

5 LLYN ALAW

Welsh Water

Habitats: Shallow, 900 acre reservoir, islands, scrub around margins, mudflats when water levels low. Created by flooding Cors-y-bol marsh. Remnants of marsh around reservoir; dam at SW end. SSSI.

Birds: Primarily wintering wildfowl: Whooper Swan, Shoveler, Teal, Wigeon, Goldeneye, Pochard, Tufted Duck. Numbers decining recently. Common Tern colony now gone.

Other:

Directions: The lake is c.2 miles NW of Llanerchymedd, whence minor roads go round N and S end of lake. Take B5112 to S and, after 1.23 miles, minor road on R to Llantrisant. At Llantrisant take minor road on R for S end of lake.

Public transport: None

Visiting: Anglesey's largest lake but visitor centre now closed. Visitor trails becoming overgrown and not a complete circuit. Welsh Water no longer have a warden here and the two hides and paths falling into disrepair. Can this reserve be pulled back from the brink?

Contact: Welsh Water no longer have a warden at this site.

Head W on either the A5 or the A55 and take the exit for Llanfihangel yn Nhowyn (J4 of A55).

6 VALLEY WETLANDS

RSPB

Habitats: Marsh, reedbed, lakes, areas of grassland, rocky outcrops.

Birds: Summer: Great Crested Grebe, Bittern (prospect), Reed & Sedge Warblers. *Winter:* Wildfowl.

Other:

Directions: LL65 3NA; SH 311 766. Drive S through the village of Llanfihangel yn Nhowyn with Llyn Penrhyn on R. Past lake, road kinks to R and car park on R.

Public transport: Bus: 4 & X4 Bangor-Holyhead pass reserve entrance, Arriva Wales (enquiries@arriva.co.uk). Train—Valley, 3 miles, then 4/X4 bus.

Visiting: Open dawn-dusk, free. No facilities. Trail from car park, view point. Public footpaths and permissive paths from adjacent villages. Sections of uneven ground, can be muddy, not suitable for wheelchairs or push-chairs. Dogs on leads.

Early '25, access restrictions due to work associated with RAF Valley. Unclear if these have finished.

Contact: 01248 421 949; ian.sims@rspb.org.uk

Return to the A5/A55 and cross the Inland Sea to Holy Island.

7 SOUTH STACK CLIFFS

RSPB

Habitats: Sea cliffs, maritime and lowland heath.

Birds: Spring/early summer: Fulmar, Puffin, Guillemot, Razorbill and passage seabirds. *All year:* Peregrine Falcon, Chough, Shag, Rock Pipit, Stonechat, Linnet, migrant warblers.

Other: Spathulate Fleawort, endemic to South Stack, Adder, lizards, Harbour Porpoise, Risso's, Common & Bottlenose Dolphins, Grey Seals.

Directions: LL65 1YH; SH 211 818 (visitor centre), SH 206 820 (Ellin's Tower info centre). Follow A55 to W end in Holyhead, proceed straight on at roundabout, continue straight on through traffic lights. After another 0.5 mile turn L and follow brown tourist signs for RSPB South Stack.

Public transport: None.

Visiting: RSPB car park (charge, free for RSPB members), Blue Badge parking. Visitor centre, cafe, shop open daily 10am-5pm (not 24/25 Dec). Ellin's Tower Seabird Centre has windows overlooking main auk colony, open daily 10am-4:30pm, Easter to Sep—access via staircase. Reserve covered by extensive network of paths, some accessible to wheelchairs. 'Access for all' track to viewing area overlooking the lighthouse.

Contact: RSPB 01407 762 100; south.stack@rspb.org.uk

Ferries for Northern Ireland depart from Holyhead. Cross back to the main island using the A5, then turn L in Valley on to A5025

8 CEMLYN

North Wales Wildlife Trust

Habitats: Brackish lagoon, shingle ridge, salt marsh, mixed scrub.

Birds: Spring: Wheatear, Whitethroat, Sedge Warbler, Manx Shearwater, Black-tailed Godwit, Whimbrel, Dunlin, Knot, passage migrants. *Summer:* Breeding Arctic, Common & Sandwich Terns, Black-headed Gull, Oystercatcher, Ringed Plover. *Autumn:* Golden Plover, Lapwing, Curlew, Manx Shearwater, Gannet, Kittiwake, Guillemot, passage migrants. *Winter:* Wildfowl inc Shoveler, Shelduck, Red-breasted Merganser. Little & Great Crested Grebes, Purple Sandpiper, Turnstone.

Other: 20 spp butterflies. Sea Kale, Yellow Horned Poppy, Sea Purslane, Sea Beet, Glasswort. Grey Seal, Harbour Porpoise, Bottlenose Dolphin.

Directions: LL67 0DX; SH 336 931. Cemlyn on N coast of Anglesey, signposted from Tregele on A5025 (10.5 miles N of Valley on road to Amlwch). 'Beach' (east) car park: follow road taking sharp R at first fork. 'Bryn Aber' car park: (west/closest to warden's viewpoint, SH 329 935), continue L, taking R turns at next two forks.

Public transport: Bus: 61 (not Sun) Amlwch to Holyhead stops at Tregele (1.5 miles to reserve). Goodsir (01407 764 340) and Lewis Y Llan (01407 832 181).

Visiting: Open all year. In summer walk on seaward side of shingle ridge to minimize disturbance. Dogs on leads.

Contact: North Wales WT: 01248 351 541; info@northwaleswildlifetrust.org.uk

Return to the A5205 and head E around the N side of the island. After passing through Benllech and heading S for Pentraeth taake turning on R for Llanbedrgoch.

9 CORS GOCH NNR
North Wales Wildlife Trust

Habitats: Sandstone and limestone outcrops, fen, open water, reedbeds. heath, Hazel woodland. Peat up to 10 metres thick. 230 acres. Ramsar, SSSI, SAC

Birds: Marsh Harrier, Barn Owl, Grasshopper & Sedge Warblers. Reed Bunting

Other: Water Vole. Adder. Common Darter, Golden-ringed Dragonfly, Small Pearl-bordered Fritillary. Small Copper. Green-winged Orchid, Adder's-tongue Fern.

Directions: LL78 8JZ; SH 504 816. Take A5025 from Pentraeth for 1.5 miles. At junction turn L for Llanbedrgoch. 1 mile beyond Llanbedrgoch signpost for reserve. Park in lay-by (space for 2-3 cars) on L.

Public transport: Bus: 63 (not Sun) Bangor to Llanerchymedd stops in both Pentraeth and Llanbedrgoch. Lewis Y Llan (01407 832 181).

Visiting: Follow track to reserve from lay-by. Open all hours, free, no facilities. Paths and boardwalk, Steep in part, can be slippery. Grazed by cattle and horses. Dogs on lead.

Contact: Chris Wynne: 01248 351 541; info@northwaleswildlifetrust.org.uk

To the SW of Pentraeth

10 CORS BODEILIO NNR
Natural Resources Wales

Habitats: 133 acres. Alkaline fen, reedbed

Birds: 130 spp recorded. Wildfowl. Snipe, Curlew, Lapwing. Reed, Sedge & Grasshopper Warblers. Stonechat, Reed Bunting.

Other: Medicinal Leech, 19 spp butterflies. Fly Orchid plus Narrow-leaved Marsh Orchid, Marsh Fragrant Orchid, Common Twayblade, Marsh Helleborine.

Directions: LL75 7DR; SH 506 773. The A5025 runs between J8 of the A55 just after crossing the Menai Strait and Bellech. In Pentraeth take the B5109 heading W for Llangefni. Take 1st L for school and follow this minor road for 1.25 miles. Car park on R.

Public transport: Bus: 63 (not Sun) Bangor to Llanerchymedd stops in Pentraeth. Lewis Y Lian (01407 832 181).

Visiting: Open all hours, free. 2 marked trails, one wheelchair accessible. Do not leave trails—wet ground and deep pools. Grazed by livestock, keep dogs on lead. Wildfowl shooting Sep-Feb.

Contact: NRW: 0300 065 3000; enquiries@naturalresourceswales.gov.uk

Head across to Beaumaris...

11 PUFFIN ISLAND
aka PRIESTOLM/YNYS SEIRIOL

Habitats: Uninhabited island at NE end of Menai Strait.

Birds: Large Cormorant colony, also Guillemot, Razorbill, Shag, Kittiwake. Eider and Black Guillemot increasing. Eponymous Puffins decimated by rats in 19C. Rats now eradicated, might Puffins return?

Other: Grey Seal, Bottlenose Dolphin, Harbour Porpoise.

Directions: Boat trips depart from Beaumaris Pier (LL58 8BS; SH 606 760). Exit the A55 for Menai Bridge, then take A545 for Beaumaris. In Beaumaris drive to end of High Street, Turn R for sea front car park (charge)

Visiting: Puffin Island is uninhabited and privately owned. There is no landing on the island but boats operating out of Beaumaris offer trips to and around it. Tour operators include:

Anglesey Boat Trips: 01248 716 335; info@angleseyboattrips.com; www.angleseyboattrips.com

Seacoast Safaris: 07854 028 393; hello@seacoastsafaris.co.uk; www.seacoastsafaris.co.uk

Starida: 01248 810 379; book@starida.co.uk; www.starida.co.uk

Clwyd
(Conwy, Denbighshire, Flintshire)

The central Vale of Clwyd with its rich farmland runs roughly N-S with the heather-clad Clwydian hills to the E, and the Denbigh Moors between it and the Conwy Valley to the W, with the Berwyns to the S. The coast is heavily developed but has a series of extensive dune systems between the major roads and the sea. To the E, the Clwydian Hills slope down to the Dee Estaury, with its mix of wetlands and industrial sites.

Bird Atlas/Avifauna
See **Gwynedd**

Bird Recorder
N E Wales (Denbighshire/Flintshire)
Glenn Morris: glennmanc@hotmail.com

Bird Report
North-East Wales Bird Report (2004-), can be downloaded from: www.cofnod.org.uk/CBRG
Wrexham Birdwatchers' Society Annual Report (1981-), from WBWS—Kevin Smith: 07752 618 195; kevjsmith3@hotmail.com

BTO Regional Representative
Clwyd East
Dr Anne Brenchley
Clwyd West
Mel ab Owain
Wetland Bird Survey (WeBS)
Local Organizers: webs@bto.org
Clwyd (Coastal), Clwyd (Inland)
Vacant
Dee Estuary (Clwyd/Merseyside)
Colin Wells:

Club
Clwyd Bird Recording Group (a committee of local birdwatchers who produce the North-East Wales Bird Report). Giles Pepler (Sec), Rosedan, Coleshill Fechan, Bagillt, Flintshire CH6 6DH: 07734 058 138; gilesp64@gmail.com.
Records should be sent to the Report editor: Glenn Morris: glennmanc@hotmail.com
Meetings: No indoor meetings held.
Clwyd Ornithological Society (1956; 45)
Angela Ross: 01745 338 493; angela.ross@talktalk.net
Meetings: 7:30pm, last Tuesday of the month (Sep-Nov & Jan-Apr). Rhuddlan Community Centre, Parliament Street, Rhuddlan, LL18 5AW.
Deeside Naturalists' Society (1973; 620)
Ian M Spence (Secretary): 07943 536 186; secretary@deenats.org.uk; www.deenats.org.uk

Meetings: Currently no indoor meetings are held but contact/see website for further information.
Wrexham Birdwatchers' Society (1981; 55)
Kevin Smith, 6 Penymaes Avenue, Wrexham, LL12 7AP
07752 618 195; kevjsmith3@hotmail.com; (facebook) https://en-gb.facebook.com/groups/103058570152016/
Meetings: 7:30pm, 1st Friday of the month (Sep-Apr). Gresford Memorial Hall, High Street, Gresford, Wrexham, LL12 8PS. Also field trips, usually 1/month in winter and 2/month in summer.

Ringing Group/Bird Observatory
Cheshire Swan Study Group.:
www.cheshireswanstudygroup.wordpress.com
Merseyside RG: www.merseysiderg.org.uk

RSPB Local Group
North Wales (1986; n/a)
Jill Wright: Jillian.wright1@btinternet.com;
https://group.rspb.org.uk/northwales/
Meetings: 2:00pm, 3rd Friday of the month (Sep-May). St Davids Church Hall, Penrhyn Bay, Llandudno, Conwy, LL30 3NT. Walks programme on website.
Facebook Groups: RSPB North Wales Local Group

Wildlife Trust
North Wales Wildlife Trust (1963; 10,000)
Llys Garth, Garth Road, Bangor, Gwynedd LL57 2RT.: 01248 351 541; nwwt@northwaleswildlifetrust.org.uk; www.northwaleswildlifetrust.org.uk

Two reserves to the W of Betws-y-Coed.

1 CWM GLAS CRAFNANT NNR
Natural Resources Wales
Habitats: Upland grassland and woodland, largely Ash, lake nearby.
Birds: Common woodland spp inc Long-tailed Tit, Goldcrest, Siskin, Grey Wagtail.
Other: Rock Stonecrop, Hairy Reck-cress, Green Spleenwort, Mountain Sorrel.
Directions: LL27 0JZ; SH 734 598. Head W out of Betws-y-Coed on the A5, turning R before leaving the town on to the B5106 for Trefriw. In Trefriw turn L up narrow lane opposite Fairy Falls Inn signposted for Llyn Crafnant and follow this road (and the Afon Crafnant) for 2 miles to the lake, at the foot of which there is a NRW car park (charge) and toilets.
Public transport: None.
Visiting: The NNR itself lies beyond the lake, which is flanked by NRW conifer plantations, at the head of the valley. There is a cafe by the lake and a fairly easy track around it but boggy ground between this track and the NNR
Contact: NRW: 0300 065 3000;
enquiries@naturalresourceswales.gov.uk

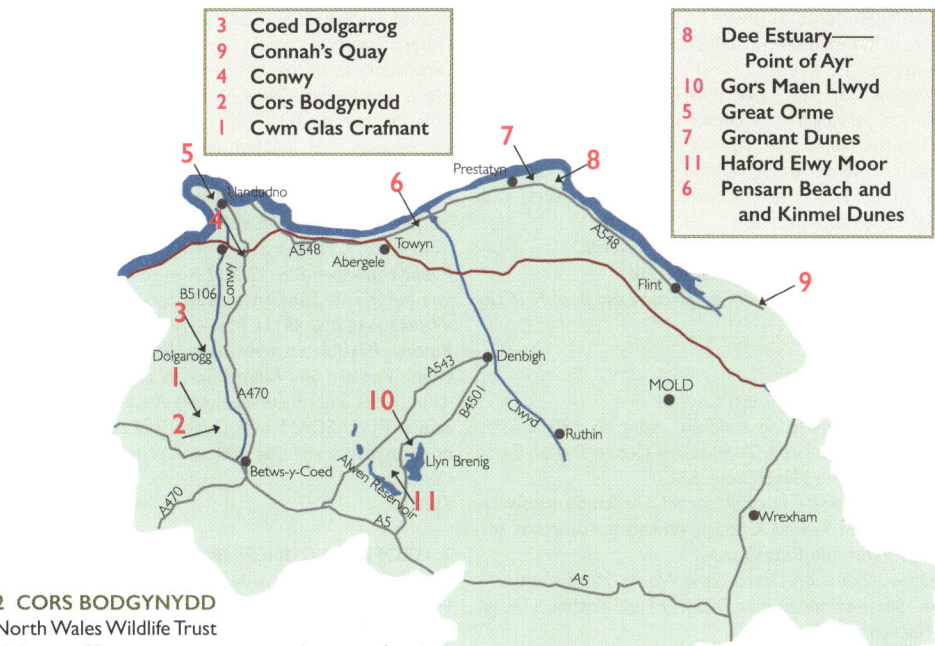

2 CORS BODGYNYDD

North Wales Wildlife Trust

Habitats: 55 acre open water, acidic mire, fen, bog, rocky ridges with heather, bilberry and rowan.

Birds: Nightjar, Cuckoo, Snipe, Woodcock, Kingfisher.

Other: Lesser Horshoe Bat, Small Chocolate-tip Moth, Emperor Dragonfly, Bog Asphodel, Lesser Bladderwort.

Directions: LL27 0YZ; SH 767 597. Head W from Betws-y-Coed on A5. Turn R at Ty Hyll (Ugly House) on to single track road. Take 1st L (not forest track) for Llyn Geirionydd. Parking area on L after 0.6 mile. Entrance to reserve through kissing gate.

Public transport: None

Visiting: Open all hours, free. Stay on footpath (deep water, disused mine shafts). Not suitable for wheelchairs. Grazing livestock. Dogs on lead.

Contact: North Wales WT: 01248 351 541; info@northwaleswildlifetrust.org.uk

Or head N from Betws-y-Code for

3 COED DOLGAROGG NNR

Natural Resources Wales

Habitats: 170 acres of Beech and wet Alder woodland on very steep, E-facing slopes. Base-rich soils.

Birds: Peregrine Falcon. Long-tailed Tit, Wood Warbler, Redstart, Pied Flycatcher, Bullfinch, Redpoll, Siskin.

Other: Yellow-ringed Comb Horn Crane Fly, Beautiful Brocade Moth, Bloomer's Rivulet Moth, Pinion Moth, Brindled Ochre Moth. Bluebells.

Directions: L32 8JX; SH771 662. The village of Dolgarogg is on the B5106 between Conwy and Betws-y-Coed, on the W side of the River Conwy. Park by the bridge over the Afon Porth Llwyd.

Public transport: Bus: 19 Betws-y-Coed to Llandudno stops in Dolgarogg (not Sun), Llew Jones (01492 640 320; sales@llewjones.com). Train—Betws-y-Coed.

Visiting: Open all hours, free. Track from bridge into reserve. Trails inside the reserve have stiles and gates and are rocky and steep in places. Not suitable for wheel/pushchairs. No facilities in reserve but toilets and shops in village.

Contact: NRW: 0300 065 3000; enquiries@naturalresourceswales.gov.uk

Then on up the B1506 to

4 CONWY

RSPB

Habitats: Lagoons, islands, reedbed, scrub, estuary.

Birds: Spring: Passage waders, hirundines and wagtails. *Summer:* Lapwing, waterbirds and warblers. *Autumn:* Black-tailed Godwit and other passage waders (Spotted Redshank on the day I passed this page for press). *Winter:* Kingfisher, Goldeneye, Water Rail, Red-breasted Merganser, wildfowl, major Starling roost.

Other: Common butterflies through summer, esp Common Blue. Display of Cowslips in Mar, Bee Orchids in summer. Otters seen early mornings.

Directions: LL31 9XZ; SH 797 773. On E bank of Conwy Estuary. J18 (Conwy and Deganwy) of A55, reserve on S side of roundabout (signposted).

Public transport: Bus: 27 Conwy to Colwyn Bay and 24 Colwyn Bay to Llandudno Junction both stop at Tesco,

Llandudno Junction (five mins walk from reserve). Arriva in Wales. Train—Llandudno Junction, 0.5 mile from reserve.

Visiting: Car park open daily (not Dec 25) 9am-5pm. Coach parking. Visitor centre (9:30am-5pm), shop, toilets inc disabled, cafe (10am-4:30/ 4pm Nov-Mar). Three trails firm/level, though a little rough in places and wet in winter. Four hides (accessible to wheelchairs) with adjacent viewing screens.

Contact: RSPB: 01492 584 091. For events: 01492 581 025; conwy@rspb.org.uk

Rejoin A55, take A546 at next junction and head N to Llandudno.

5 GREAT ORME
Conwy County Borough Council

Habitats: Limestone headland rising to 680 ft, cliffs, grassland, woodland. Overlooking Conwy Bay on E side of entrance to Menai Strait. SAC

Birds: Breeding: Fulmar, Razorbill, Guillemot, Kittiwake, Cormorant, Kestrel, Chough, Wheatear, Stonechat. *Passage:* Whinchat, Ring Ouzel

Other: Common Lizard, Slow Worm, 20 spp butterfly inc Silver-studdded Blue Fritillary. Feral Kashmiri Goats. 400 spp. wild flowers.

Directions: LL30 2XF; SH 767 834 (summit Visitor Centre and car park). The A546 runs across the neck of land occupied by Llandudno immediately to the SE of the headland between the Conwy Estuary and Llandudno Bay. A minor road (toll), Marine Drive, runs around the headland (c.5 miles), joining the A546 on either side of the neck. Minor roads (steep sections) leave Marine Drive at two points (signed) and ascend to the summit Visitor Centre.

Public transport: A cable car runs between Llandudno Pier and the summit and there is also a tramway/funicular railway from Church Walk to the summit (Mar-Nov). Train—Llandudno, branch line from Llandudno Junction, main line station.

Visiting: Visitor Centre (open Easter-Oct, some weekends out of season) at summit, car park (pay & display), refreshments, toilets. Further car parks, cafe and toilets along length of Marine Drive. Walking trails, steep sections and rough ground. If walking along Marine Drive, stay on pavement, can be busy.

Contact:

The coast of NE Wales is heavily built up but the A548 branches off the A55 at Abergele and runs just behind the coast to Prestatyn and Flint, passing.

6 PENSARN BEACH & KINMEL DUNES LNR
Conwy County Borough Council

Habitats: In W, pebble beach (Pensarn) with shingle bank (Pensarn and in E remnant of once extensive dune system (Kinmel).

Birds: Oystercatcher, Ringed Plover, Common Tern,

Kestrel, Skylark. *Passage:* Lapland & Snow Bunting

Other: Common Lizard.

Directions: To W of the Clwyd Estuary, between Abergele and Towyn. A548 runs parallel to coast. For Pensarn Promenade (LL22 7PP; SH945 787) leave A548 immediately after junction with A55, take bridge over railway to Promenade. Car park (free). Kinmel Dunes: LL18 5EY; SH 987 806 (St Asaph Avenue pay & display car park) In Towyn, take St Asaph Avenue towards coast from A548. Car park at end of road.

Public transport: Bus: 12/X12 Rhyl to Llandudno, stops at Abergele & Pensarn station and in Towyn, Arriva Wales (0344 800 4411). Train—Abergele & Pensarn

Visiting: Possible to walk along Wales Coast Path between Pensarn and Kinmel. Toilets at Pensarn Promenade, kiosk and toilets (summer) at Kinmel, toilets and cafe at Rhyl ASDA. 1 mile Dunes Trail at Kinmel. Keep dogs on lead, some dog exclusion zones.

Contact:

Then

7 GRONANT DUNES NR
Denbighshire Countryside Service

Habitats: Growing dune system. Dune lake. Ramsar, SSSI, SPA, SAC.

Birds: Breeding: Little Tern Tern, Cetti's & Grasshopper Warbler, Lesser Whitethroat. *Passage:* Wheatear, Whinchat. *Winter:* Marsh Harrier, Short-eared Owl. Large Starling roost.

Other: Sand Lizard, Natterjack Toad. Sandhill Rustic & Dark Green Fritillary butterflies. Pyramidal and other orchids.

Directions: LL19 9SS; SH 987 806. Leave the A548 in Gronant and take Shore Road, running N to the railway line and the coast. Free car park 300 yrds on L.

Public transport: Bus: F18 Rhyl-Flint, P & O Lloyd Coaches (01352 710 682; info@polloydcoaches.co.uk) stops in Gronant, then walk along Shore Road. Train—Prestatyn.

Visiting: Open all hours, free (donations welcome). Walk N along Shore Road, over the railway line, where path crosses Wales Coast Path. Pass Prestatyn Gutter and dune lake, then boardwalk to sea viewing platform or turn R for tern shack (no facilities for humans but Prestatyn c.1.25 mile to W). Not accessible for disabled. Colony protected by fencing in place May-Aug. Dogs on lead.

Contact: Denbighshire Countryside Service: 01745 35619; Jim.Kilpatrick@denbighshire.gov.uk For news of the Little Terns: nwlittletern@gmail.com

And then

8 DEE ESTUARY—POINT OF AYR
RSPB

Habitats: Tidal mudflat, saltmarsh, sand dunes.

Birds: Breeding: Oystercatcher, Ringed Plover, Little Tern.

Passage: Wheatear. *Winter:* Pale-bellied Brent Goose, Waders, Peregrine Falcon, Merlin.
Other: Natterjack Toad.
Directions: CH8 9RD; SJ 127 840. From the roundabout in Gwespyr, on the A548 between Prestatyn and Flint, take the Station Road to Talacre (just over 1 mile). Park in public car park (height restrictions, pay & display).
Public transport: Bus: F18 Rhyl-Flint, P & O Lloyd Coaches (01352 710 682; info@polloydcoaches.co.uk), stops on TA548, then walk along Station Road. Train—Prestatyn.
Visiting: Open all hours, free. 0.75 mile walk along sea-wall from car park to hide. No facilities at reserve but toilets and pub in Talacre. Keep dogs under control. Areas of shingle fenced off to protect ground nesters and patrols by wardens to protect high tide roosts from disturbance in autumn and winter.
Alternatively, the **Gronant Dunes Nature Reserve** (q.v.) is a 3 mile walk W along the Wales Coast Path.
Contact: 0151 353 2720; deeestuary@rspb.org.uk
And then to

9 CONNAH'S QUAY NATURE RESERVE

Uniper/Deeside Naturalists' Society
Habitats: Saltmarsh, mudflats, grassland scrub, open water, wetland meadow.
Birds: Summer: Small roosts of non-breeding estuarine birds. *Winter:* High water roosts of waders and wildfowl (inc Oystercatcher, Lapwing, Spotted Redshank, Curlew, Redshank, Black-tailed Godwit, Teal, Pintail, Wigeon).
Other: 17 spp butterflies.
Directions: CH6 5TE; SJ 271 713. Travel W to end of M56 which then becomes A494. Follow signposts for Flint. Take first slip road to L joining large roundabout and turn R on to A548. Continue straight on this road (there are several roundabouts) After crossing the River Dee take first slip road and turn R at 1st roundabout and then straight on at 2nd roundabout. Follow signs for power station: reserve entrance is on L at next roundabout. If approaching from W follow A548, exiting on slip road for Connah's Quay. Turn L at roundabout and follow power station signs.
Public transport: Bus: 10A (10 on Sun, longer walk) Chester to Connah's Quay (Swan Inn). Arriva in Wales.
Visiting: Entry for DNS members only but group bookings possible in advance from DNS. Public welcome on open days—see website for details. Field studies centre, five hides. Wheelchair access.
Contact: Secretary, Deeside Naturalists' Society: secretary@deenats.org.uk
Take the B5129 through Connah's Quay and Shotton to the junction with the A494. Stay on the A494 as it takes you to and round Mold and on to the Clwydian Range AOB and then Ruthin. After passing round the outskirts of Ruthin, leave the A494 at a roundabout and take the B5105, which cuts through the S edge of the Clocaenog Forest, to

Cerrigydrudion, whence take the B4501 N for Denbigh and approach the following two reserves from the S, as opposed to the N.

10 GORS MAEN LLWYD

North Wales Wildlife Trust
Habitats: N end of Llyn Brenig, upland heath, blanket bog. Woodland in wider area.
Birds: All year: Great Crested Grebe, Black & Red Grouse, Hen Harrier, Merlin, Skylark. *Spring/summer:* Osprey, Curlew, Golden Plover, Dunlin, Cuckoo, Sand Martin, Wheatear, Ring Ouzel. *Winter:* Wildfowl inc. Goldeneye, Goosander.
Other: Heathers. Adder.
Directions: LL16 5SW; SH 970 580 (top car park/on B4501). LL16 5RG; SH 983 574 (near bird hide, accessible from B4501)). Seven miles SW of Denbigh (N end of Llyn Brenig)—take B4501 from Denbigh.
Public transport: None.
Visiting: Open all hours. Can also access reserve by parking at Dwr Cymru's Llyn Brenig Visitor Centre and walking around lake in either direction. Dogs on lead.
Contact: North Wales WT: 01248 351 541; info@northwaleswildlifetrust.org.uk
To the W of Llyn Brenig.

11 HAFOD ELWY MOOR NNR

Natural Resources Wales/Welsh Water
Habitats: Heathland, acid bog lying between two reservoirs, Llyn Alwen & Llyn Brenig, with neighbouring commercial conifer plantations.
Birds: Red & Black Grouse, Hen Harrier, Peregrine Falcon, Merlin. Wheatear.
Other:
Directions: LL21 9TT; SH 968 547. Take B4501 from Denbigh to Cerrigydrudion, after 10 miles go past Llyn Brenig Visitor Centre. Llyn Alwen car park (LL21 9TT; SH 956 529), 1 mile further on, track on R to Llyn Alwen car park.
Public transport: None.
Visiting: Llyn Brenig Visitor Centre (cafe, shop, toilets) and car park and Llyn Alwen car park are operated by Dwr Cymru/Welsh Water (charges). Hafod Elwy Moor lies between the two reservoirs, to the N of the car parks, and trails run from the reservoir car parks around and between them, traversing the NNR. Also possible to walk through conifer plantations to NNR from **Gors Maen LLwd** (q.v.) car park Trails shared by cyclists and walkers and the longest is 14 miles long.
Contact: NRW: 0300 065 3000; enquiries@naturalresourceswales.gov.uk
Llyn Brenig Visitor Centre: 01490 389 222; llynbrenig@dwrcymru.com

NORTHERN IRELAND
ORGANIZATIONS

BIRD RECORDER
Northern Ireland no longer has a recorder. Records sent to *NI Birds* (NIbirds@live.co.uk) are passed to the relevant organizations.

BIRD ATLAS/AVIFAUNA
None

BIRD REPORT
Northern Ireland Bird Report is no longer produced. Sightings are searchable on *NI Birds,* which publishes sightings of rare and scarce birds in Northern Ireland. To report news: 07973 403 146 or 07870 863 782; nibirds@live.co.uk; www.nibirds.blogspot.co.uk

The Northern Irish headquarters of a number of organizations focusing on birds or where they live are listed here, in advance of the County Directory. When the organization's UK headquarters is in England, its purpose and activities are presented in the UK/England section and its Northern Irish contact details are listed here.

BRITISH TRUST FOR ORNITHOLOGY (BTO) NORTHERN IRELAND
Undertakes a wide range of monitoring and research in the country and assists the network of voluntary representatives to lead public events and encourage participation of volunteers in core surveys.
BTO Northern Ireland Unit 5, 27, Wallace Studios, Wallace Avenue, Lisburn BT27 4A: 01842 750050; northern.ireland@bto.org; www.bto.org/about-bto/national-offices/bto-northern-ireland

NORTHERN IRELAND ORNITHOLOGISTS' CLUB (1965)
Formed to focus the interests of active birdwatchers in Northern Ireland. There is a programme of lectures (Oct-Apr) and field trips for members and the Club organizes an annual photographic competition.
Contact: Secretary: Jim Wells
NIOC, 7, Bannview Court, Banbridge, County Down BT32 3ZH; 07856 235 144 jimwells6@gmail.com; www.facebook.com/NorthernIrelandOrnithologistsClub.NIOC

NORTHERN IRELAND RARE BIRDS COMMITTEE (1997)
The NIRBC manages the records of rare birds in Northern Ireland and maintains the Northern Ireland Bird List

Contact: NIRCC: NIRBComm@gmail.com
www.nirbc.blogspot.co.uk

ROYAL SOCIETY FOR THE PROTECTION OF BIRDS NORTHERN IRELAND
Northern Ireland Headquarters:
Belvoir Park Forest, Belfast BT8 7QT:
028 9049 1547; rspb.nireland@rspb.org.uk

ULSTER WILDLIFE (1978; 14,000)
Ulster Wildlife is the operating name of the Ulster Wildlife Trust, a registered charity. It manages 18 reserves. For various reasons, some are not open to the public or are only open to Ulster Wildlife members and permission to visit must be secured in advance.
The Ulster Wildlife Trust, McClelland House, 10 Heron Road, Belfast, BT3 9LE:
028 9045 4094; info@ulsterwildlife.org; www.ulsterwildlife.org

WILDFOWL AND WETLANDS TRUST (WWT)
One Wetland Centre in Northern Ireland.
Castle Espie, 78 Ballydrain Road, Comber, Co Down, N Ireland BT23 6EA:
028 9187 4146; info.castleespie@wwt.org.uk

DEPARTMENT OF AGRICULTURE, ENVIRONMENT AND RURAL AFFAIRS (DAERA)
A department of the Northern Ireland government, DAERA has two agencies of particular relevance to birdwatchers.

FOREST SERVICE OF NORTHERN IRELAND
The Forest Service has been responsible for the management of the 153,000 acres of Northern Ireland's nationally owned forests since 1998.
Inishkeen House, Killyhevlin, Enniskllen BT74 4EJ:
028 6634 3165;
customer.forestservice@daera-ni.gov.uk;

NORTHERN IRELAND ENVIRONMENT AGENCY (NIEA)
The NIEA is the executive agency of DAERA responsible for environmental regulation, protection and enforcement; water quality; nature recovery. It manages 7 country parks and 47 nature reserves.
17, Antrim Road, Tonagh, Lisburn, County Antrim BT28 3AL:
0300 200 7856
nieainfo@daera-ni

Irish Grid References

Northern Ireland and the Republic of Ireland share a common grid reference system.

It uses a similar system of metric eastings and northings to Great Britain but it differs in taking its origin from a different, more westerly reference point.

In addition, the 100 km squares (hectads) are prefixed by single letters of the alphabet rather than pairs of letters. Northern Ireland is covered by the letters C, D, H and J.

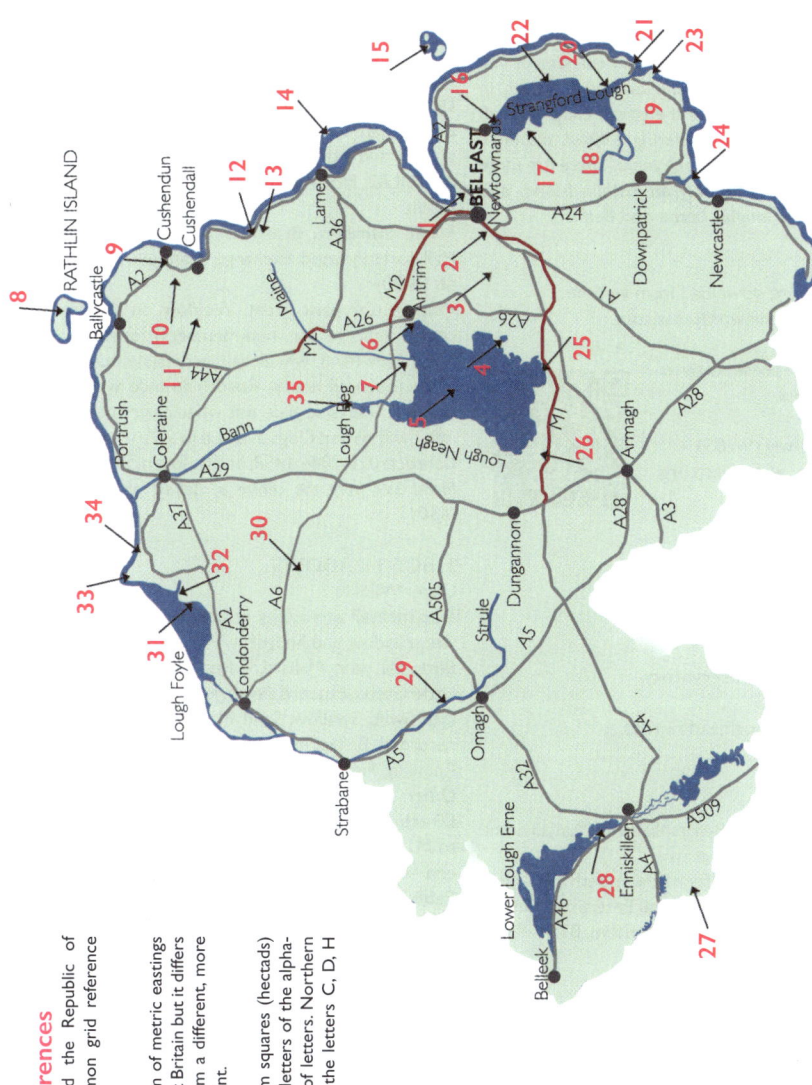

Antrim and Belfast

A range of hills rising to 1,800 ft, the Antrim Hills runs N along the E coast from Belfast in the S to Ballycastle in the N. They are drained by a series of Glens mainly oriented SW to NE. To the W, a broad corridor of low ground connects the large but shallow Lough Neagh, in the centre of the province, to the coast. Lough Neagh attracts large numbers of wintering wilfowl, although numbers have declined in recent years. There are large seabird colonies, most notably on Rathlin Island, and two substantial sea loughs, Larne and Belfast.

Bird Report
Rathlin Bird Report: download from website: www.rathlinstickybeak.wordpress.com

BTO Regional Representatives
Antrim and Belfast
Adam McClure:
Wetland Bird Survey (WeBS)
Local Organizers: webs@bto.org
Antrim (other sites)
Adam McClure
Belfast Lough
Ian Englander
Larne Lough
Doreen Hilditch

Ringing Group/Bird Observatory
Belfast and Down RG
www.facebook.com/BogMeadowsCes

RSPB Local Groups
Antrim (1977; 30)
Michael Ingleston, Rhona Bell: rspbantrim@gmail.com; https://group.rspb.org.uk/antrim/
Meetings: 7:30pm, 2nd Monday of the month (Sep-May). College of Agriculture Food & Rural Enterprise, Greenmount Campus, 45, Tirgracy Road, Antrim, BT41 4PS.
Outings: 2 per month.
Belfast (1972; 40)
Eleanor Brennan: rspbbelfastlg@proton.me; https://group.rspb.org.uk/belfast/
Meetings: 7:30pm, 1st Monday of the month (Sep-Apr). Cooke Centenary Church Hall, Park Road, Belfast, BT7 2FW.
Lisburn (1978; 30)
Ian Raine: rspblisburn@gmail.com; https://group.rspb.org.uk/lisburn/
Meetings: Contact/see website for details.

1 BELFAST'S WINDOW ON WILDLIFE
RSPB
Habitats: Tidal mudflat (Holywood Banks), dry grassland (Harbour Meadows, currently closed), lagoon (Whitehouse Lagoon).
Birds: Breeding: Swift, Common & Arctic Tern. *Passage:* Black-tailed Godwit. *Winter:* Teal, Wigeon, Shelduck
Other:
Directions: BT3 9ED; J37278 77666. Located within Belfast Harbour Estate on Airport Road West between airport and Belfast Lough. 2 main entrances into estate off A2: Holywood Exchange (closed Sun) and Dee Street.
Public transport: Bus: 94/94B (Mon-Fri), Belfast City Hall to Holywood Exchange, Translink Metro (028 90 66 66 30)
Visiting: Car park (free). Window on Wildlife visitor centre (charge for non-members) open 10am-5pm (4pm Nov-Mar), wheelchair accessible, toilets, cafe. 2 hides (open all hours) Roadside hide wheelchair accessible. Trackside hide not wheelchair accessible. Tern raft, Swift tower. Dogs allowed in visitor centre
Contact: 028 9046 1458; belfast.lough@rspb.org.uk
Head SW from the centre of Belfast on the Falls Road (A501).

2 BOG MEADOWS
Ulster Wildlife
Habitats: 47 acres. City centre reserve, pond, reedbed, wet meadow and hedgerow
Birds: All year: Mallard, Tufted Duck, Coot, Moorhen, Little Grebe, Buzzard, Peregrine Falcon, Kingfisher. *Summer:* Swift, Swallow, Sand Martin, Sedge Warbler. Last recorded Belfast breeding site of Corncrake. *Winter:* Redwing, Fieldfare.
Other: 14 spp butterfly
Directions: BT12 6EU; J312 726. Immediately adjacent to M1 on opposite side to River Blackstaff. Car park at end of Milltown Row off Falls Road.
Public transport: 200 yards from Falls Road, numerous regular and tourist bus services.
Visiting: Free car park, open all hours, accessible trails, including circuit of perimeter. Management regime includes grazing by cattle. No facilities. Dogs on lead.
Contact: 028 9045 4094; info@ulsterwildlife.org
Rejoin the A501 and continue on it to Groganstown, where turn R on to Ballycolin Road, and then L again on to Flowbog Road.

3 SLIEVENACLOY NATURE RESERVE
Ulster Wildlife
Habitats: 640 acres. Species-rich grassland, unimproved meadows, purple moor grass, rush pasture. At an altitude of *c.*700 ft.
Birds: Skylark, Meadow Pipit, Stonechat, Linnet, Reed Bunting. *Summer:* Cuckoo, Grasshopper Warbler (rare

in NI). *Passage:* Ring Ouzel.

Other: Ireland's only reptile, Common Lizard. Moths inc Red Carpet, Wood Tiger, Narrow-bordered Bee Hawk-Moth, Marsh Pug. 9 spp orchid.

Directions: BT28 3TE; J 245 712. In Belfast Hills to NE of city between Stoneyford and Divis Mountain. Flow-bog Road runs across it between the A510 and the B10.

Public transport: Bus: 536 Belfast to Stoneyford (school days only) runs along Stoneyford Road lower down hill. Ulsterbus.

Visiting: Open all hours, free, roadside parking. No facilities. Ulster Wildlife's largest reserve.

Contact: 028 9045 4094; info@ulsterwildlife.org

Continue along Flowbog Road to junction with Rock Road (B101) turn L and then R on to Hannahstown Road (N38 for Glenavy. Leave Glenavy on Glen Road (B156). Stay on this road round N side of Portmore Lough and George's island Road will be on L on S side.

4 PORTMORE LOUGH

RSPB

Habitats: Lough, reedbed, fen, wet grassland,

Birds: Lapwing both breed and form flocks in winter. *Breeding:* Snipe, Redshank. Common Tern. Skylark. *Winter:* Whooper Swan, Greylag Goose. Pochard, Tufted Duck. Coot. Golden Plover. Marsh & Hen Harrier.

Other: Irish Hare. Irish Lady's-tresses Orchid.

Directions: BT67 0DW; J105 687. To E of Lough Neagh. Leave M1 motorway at J9 (Moira roundabout). Take A26 for International Airport and Antrim. Pass under railway bridge and Glenavy Road service station on R. Take 2nd L signposted to Aghalee. Follow signposts to reserve from Aghalee, turning R at T-junction by Gawley's Gate pub on to Derryola Bridge road for 1 mile. Reserve signposted off George's Island Road.

Public transport: None.

Visiting: Open 9am-5pm (25 Dec 11am-3pm), free. When car park gates closed, park outside them to access reserve. Accessible toilets. 2 wheelchair-accessible trails. 1 hide overlooking lough and reedbed, accessed by boardwalk from trail, no steps. Tern rafts. Main trail leads to hide overlooking lough. No steps or stiles, wide gates. Keep dogs under control. Clean up mess.

Contact: 028 9265 1936; Laura.Smith@rspb.org.uk

5 LOUGH NEAGH ISLANDS NNR

DAERA/Lough Neagh Partnership

Habitats: Largest freshwater lake in British Isles by area (148 square miles). Relatively shallow; with around 80 islands, which are managed as a nature reserve.

Birds: Populations of breeding birds on islands monitored annually: 500 pairs Mallard, 300 pairs Tufted Duck, 500 pairs Great Crested Grebe (census being carried put in 2025). Historically up to 30,000 pairs Black-headed Gull but now down to c.4,000, 150 pairs Common Tern, 60 pairs Mute Swan. Large flocks of wintering wildfowl but numbers have declined since 1990s.

Other:

Directions: Lough Neagh lies in a depression at the centre of Northern Ireland and is bordered by four of its six counties, with Antrim to the N and E, Londonderry to the N and W, Tyrone to the W and Armagh to the S. The M1 runs a little to the S of it and the M2 to the N. The town of Antrim is in its NE corner.

Visiting: There are seasonal/semi-regular boat trips to two of the larger islands, Rams and Coney.

Rams Island is the largest island in the lough, close to the E shore. Regular but not daily boat trips in summer from Sandy Bay Marina (BT28 2LQ; J 120 716), just off road between Glenavy and Portmore Lough (see above). Booking essential, charge, info@ramsisland.org.

Coney Island is in Armagh. See the **Oxford Island** entry in **Armagh** for details.

Contact site manager before arranging to visit any of the other islands, which offer breeding birds protection from disturbance and predators.

Contact: Site manager: 028 7941 7941.

Return to Glenavy, then take A25 and then A26 for Antrim.

6 REA'S WOOD NR

DAERA

Habitats: Ancient wet woodland: Alder, Willow, Birch stretching for 1 mile along E shore of Lough Neagh. Series of sand bars and alternating peaty hollows resulting from successive lowerings of lough level.

Birds: Lough Neagh waterbirds inc Whooper & Mute Swan, Greylag Goose, Shelduck, Mallard, Tufted Duck Wigeon, Teal, Goldeneye, Red-breasted Merganser, Eider, Lapwing Redshank, Black-headed & Lesser Black-backed Gulls, Coot, Moorhen, Grey Heron, Cormorant, Great Crested & Little Grebes.

Other: Summer Snowflake.

Directions: BT41 4DQ; J 135 867 (Lough Shore Park car park) 1 mile from Antrim on Dublin Road or park in car park of Lough Shore Park and walk S along lough shore

Public transport: Wood is just over 1 mile from Antrim station.

Visiting: Free car park, open 8am-9:30pm. Toilets, cafe. Walk S along lough shore, beside golf course, 0.5 mile from car park to N edge of wood. Viewing platform. Woodland is wet.

Contact: Site manager: 028 3839 9195

Take A8 from Antrim to Randalstown.

7 RANDALSTOWN FOREST NNR

Forest Service of Northern Ireland

Habitats: Deer park with deciduous trees taken over in 1934 by Forest Service. Largely planted with conifers at that time. Replanting with increased proportion of broadleaves. Land along S margin exposed when lough lowered now being colonized naturally by Alder and

Willow and designated NNR. 425 acres. Wildfowl refuge in NE corner of Lough Neagh bordered by this forest.

Birds: Mute & Whooper Swan, Shelduck, Mallard, Gadwall, Tufted Duck, Goldeneye, Scaup, Red-breasted Merganser, Black-headed, Great Black-backed & Herring Gull, Great Crested & Little Grebes, Coot, Moorhen, Grey Heron, Little Egret, Cormorant. Kingfisher. World of Owls conservation centre next to forest.

Other: Fallow Deer viewing enclosure

Directions: BT41 3LE; J 082 887. Take Staffordstown Road S out of Randalstown. After crossing M22 turn L into Shalgus Lane, which leads to car park.

Public transport: Bus: 110 Antrim to Cookstown (Mon-Fri) passes through Randalstown. 110f (infrequent) runs along Staffordstown Road, Ulsterbus (028 90 66 66 30).

Visiting: Open dawn to dusk, free, accessible toilet (RADAR key) Easter-Sep., also toilets at World of Owls. 2.5 mile trail. Large hide overlooking Lough Neagh

Contact: 028 6634 3165;

Return to Antrim and take A26 and then A44 to Ballycastle.

8 RATHLIN ISLAND
RSPB and DAERA

Habitats: 3,400 acre, L-shaped island, 4 miles E-W and 2.5 miles N-S, hosting 3 RSPB reserves and the Rathlin West Light Seabird Centre, as well as one DAERA reserve. Largely unimproved grassland, sea cliffs rising to 350 ft. Some woodland and open water.

Roonivoolin: Near tip of S arm of 'L'.

Craigmacagan: Halfway along S arm of 'L'.

Knockans: On W trail from Church Bay harbour to Seabird Centre

Rathlin West Light Seabird Centre: Housed in lighthouse at W tip of island.

Kebble & Kinramer (DAERA): Felled forestry, swamp, lake, cliffs and stacks at W end of island

Birds: Large seabird colony: Puffin, Gullemot (now largest colony in Britain), Razorbill, Fulmar, Kittiwake. Corncrake, Oystercatcher, Ringed Plover, Snipe, Buzzard, Raven.

Other: Irish Hare.

Directions: BT54 6RT; NR 285 090. Passenger ferry from Ballycastle to Church Bay on the island (6 miles). Cars, apart from disabled badge holders, not permitted on island except by special permit. Park in Ballycastle (seasonal charges in certain areas). Online booking and timetable at www.rathlin-ferry.com. Pre-booking advisable.

Public transport: Shuttle bus service (charge) between Church Bay and Seabird Centre.

Visiting: Seabird Centre 9am-5pm, Apr-Sep, 4 mile walk from Church Bay. Charge for non-members. Large number of steps at Seabird Centre. Cafe and accessible toilets at Seabird Centre. Accessible toilets at Church Bay and Ballycastle. Trails and reserves open all hours,

subject to access to island. No dogs, other than assistance dogs, in Seabird Centre; on lead at all times on reserves.

Contact: 028 2076 0062 (Apr-Sep); 028 9049 1547 (Oct-Mar); rathlin.seabirdcentre@rspb.org.uk

Head E on A2, which runs alongside the coast across the mouths of a series of Glens. As you approach Glendun from the N and descend into it, take B92 on L for Cushenden. Turn R on to Glendun Road. Then as below

9 CREGAGH WOOD LNR
Katy English/Causeway Coast & Glens Borough Council

Habitats: Deciduous wood planted in 19C, originally largely Beech.

Birds: Common woodland spp inc Great Spotted Woodpecker, Chiffchaff, Willow & Wood Warblers, Spotted Flycatcher, Grey Wagtail. Occasional Crossbill.

Winter: Woodcock, Brambling. Historical records for Pied Flycatcher and Redstart but not seen recently.

Other: Red Squirrel, Pine Marten. Bluebells

Directions: B T44 0PZ; D228 322. Leave Cushenden on Glendun Road, park by St Patrick's Church, on L.

Public transport: Bus: 252 Larne to Ballycastle (Mon-Fri) several stops at mouth of glen, Ulsterbus (028 90 66 66 30).

Visiting: Walk to the lower entrance from the church. Trail and Red Squirrel viewing hide. Contact GRSG for access to the hide.

Contact: Glens Red Squirrel Group (GRSG). For access to the hide, text or WhatsApp to 07742 841 273 info@glensredsquirrelgroup.com www.glensredsquirrelgroup.com

Continue up the Glen on Glendun Road.

10 GLENDUN (John McSparran Memorial Farm)
Ulster Wildlife

Habitats: Traditional hill farm managed for wildlife in one of northernmost Glens of Antrim: grassland, scrub, mixed ash woodland, blanket bog, S side of Glendun River. 198 acres

Birds: Red Grouse, Cuckoo, Golden Plover. Willow Warbler, Chiffchaff, Blackcap. Dipper, Stonechat

Other: Otter, Red Squirrel, Emperor Moth

Directions: BT44 0TB; D 201 317. Leave the A2 between Cushendall and Cushendun at the N side of the Glendun Viaduct and take the minor road (Glendun Road) running W along glen. After just under 1 mile farm is S of river. Cross ford to park.

Public transport: Bus: 252 Larne to Ballycastle (Mon-Fri) several stops at mouth of glen, Ulsterbus (028 90 66 66 30). Then walk of c.2 miles up glen.

Visiting: **Only open to members of Ulster Wildlife with prior permission.** Free. No formal paths, steep terrain. No facilities. Grazing livestock. No dogs

Contact: 028 9045 4094; info@ulsterwildlife.org

Continue W along Glendun Road.

11 SLIEVEANORRA NR
DAERA
Habitats: 4 plots of peat bogs in different condition within a much larger expanse of blanket bog. 1 growing raised bog, 2 where the blanket peat has been eroded.
Birds: Red Grouse, Golden Plover, Hen Harrier, Merlin. Watch out for Goshawk as you pass through conifer plantations.
Other: Bog Asphodel, Bog Bean, Sundews. *Hypersia selaga.*
Directions: D 132 265; D135 265; D 147 274; D 155 286. Continue W along Glendun Road for 3.7 miles beyond the UW farm, passing through conifer plantation, then turn R just before the Bryvore Bridge. After a further 0.75 miles the bogs lie in a diagonal line running NE-SW from a plot surrounded by conifer plantation to the NE of the road up to the flanks of the summit of Slieveanorra (1,667 ft) to the SW. Close to long distance path through Antrim.
Public transport: None
Visiting: Open all hours, free. No facilities. Ecosystem fragile; *dangerous swallow holes.* You are now on the watershed of the Antrim Hills. Please contact NIEA site manager in advance to arrange access.
Contact: 07799 867 853; michael.morgan@daera-ni.gov.uk
Return to A2 and head S. On S side of Glencloy, take minor road (Straidkilly Road) on R to reserve, which you approach from the opposite direction to the instructions in the following entry.

12 STRAIDKILLY
Ulster Wildlife
Habitats: Hazel wood with species-rich grass clearings. flanking the steep-sided headland of Straidkilly Point. 22 acres.
Birds: Woodland species mix: Buzzard, Sparrowhawk, Willow Warbler, Chiffchaff, Blackcap, Long-tailed Tit, Bullfinch.
Other: Red Squirrel, Pine Marten. Cryptic Wood White & Silver-washed Fritillary. Bluebells, Lesser Celandine, Wood Vetch, Stone Bramble, Toothwort Birds-nest Orchid.
Directions: BT44 0LQ; D 302 165. Straidkilly Point is the headland between Glencloy (to the N) and Glenarm and the A2 (Bay Road) runs along the coast. For the reserve, leave A2 in Glenarm, bearing L on to Munie Road after the bridge over the Glenarm River. Just before this road bears L take a R on to Straidkilly Road, climb hill and park by quarry.
Public transport: Bus: 252 Larne to Ballycastle (Mon-Fri) stops in Glenarm, Ulsterbus (028 90 66 66 30). Edge of reserve starts on outskirts of Glenarm.
Visiting: Open all hours, free. Park on roadside by old quarry. Do not obstruct gates. Picnic site but no other facilities. No formal paths, some steep inclines. Dogs on lead. Sea views from picnic area.
Contact: 028 9045 4094; info@ulsterwildlife.org
Continue along Straidkilly Road to its junction with Munie Road. Turn R on to Glenarm Road proceed up Glen.

13 GLENARM
Ulster Wildlife
Habitats: Ancient Oak woodland, wet woodland, flanking Glenarm River. 380 acres. ASSI. Adjacent to but separate Forest Service of Northern Ireland Glenarm Forest.
Birds: Woodland species mix: Willow Warbler, Chiffchaff, Blackcap, Treecreeper, Jay. Dipper, Kingfisher. *Winter:* Wooodcock.
Other:
Directions: BT44 0BD; D 304 111. From centre of Glenarm, follow A2 over Glenarm River, then bear L on to Munie Road. Follow it S along the Glen. Car park at entrance to reserve, within Glenarm Estate.
Public transport: Bus: 252 Larne to Ballycastle (Mon-Fri) stops in Glenarm, Ulsterbus (028 90 66 66 30).
Visiting: **Only open to members of Ulster Wildlife with prior permission.** Free. No facilities. Park in angler's car park at entrance. Forest tracks, medium terrain. Grazing animals May to Dec. No dogs.
Contact: 028 9045 4094; info@ulsterwildlife.org
Return to A2 and continue to S end of Larne Lough, leaving at Whitehead

14 ISLE OF MUCK
Ulster Wildlife
Habitats: Island with rocky cliffs, NI's third largest cliff-nesting seabird colony.
Birds: Breeding: Fulmar, Shag, Razorbill, Guillemot, Black Guillemot, Kittiwake. Puffin, non-breeding but occasionally present. Peregrine Falcon, Buzzard. Gannets, Manx Shearwaters, terns, divers feed in the surrounding waters. Skuas on passage.
Directions: BT40 3PG; D 464 024. The Isle of Muck lies off the coast of Islandmagee, the peninsula to the E of Larne Lough. Leave the A2 at Whitehead and take the B150 for Mullaghboy. Drive through Mullaghboy and at the N end take the minor road for Port Muck. Car park after 0.75 miles. Road steep. At the N end of Larne Lough, at the mouth and closer to Port Muck, there is a foot ferry from Larne, which the A2 passed through before reaching Whitehead, to Islandmagee.
Public transport: None.
Visiting: Free parking at Port Muck, toilets, picnic area. No public access but can view island and bird movements from mainland.
Contact: 028 9045 4094; info@ulsterwildlife.org
Return to the A2 and continue in to Belfast.

Down

Strangford Lough is the largest sea lough in the British Isles. Running N-S, it is 20 miles long and up to 5 miles wide with narrow exit to sea at S end. Indented shoreline, numerous islands, especially on W side and extensive mudflats. Large areas of Eelgrass at N end of lough. The Ards peninsula lies to the E of the lough and its E coast, facing the North Channel, is the Outer Ards. Nearly all the Canadian breeding population of Pale-bellied Brent Goose winter in Ireland and in the autumn around 80% of these birds (up to 30,000) are feeding on the eelgrass in Strangford Lough.

BTO Regional Representatives
Kez Armstrong
Wetland Bird Survey (WeBS)
Local Organizers: webs@bto.org
Carlingford Lough
Aoibheann Morrison
Down (other sites)
Kez Armstrong
Dundrum Bay
Vacant
Outer Ards
Vacant
South Down Coast
Kez Armstrong
Strangford Lough
Kerry Mackie

Ringing Group/Bird Observatory
Copeland Bird Observatory
David Galbraith (Booking Secretary): 028 9338 2539 or 07934 416 668; davidgalbraith903@btinternet.com;

From Belfast, Take A2 along S side of Belfast Lough

15 COPELAND BIRD OBSERVATORY
National Trust leased to Copeland Bird Observatory
Habitats: Archipelago of 3 islands at S entrance to Belfast Lough: Copeland, Old Lighthouse & Mew. Observatory on 40 acre Old Lighthouse Island. Cliffs, rocky shore, scrub.
Birds: Manx Shearwater (4-4,500 pairs), Storm Petrel, Fulmar, Puffin, Black Guillemot. Arctic & Common Tern, mixed gull colony. Eider, Shelduck, Red-breasted Merganser, Water Rail. Founded in 1954, the Observatory has many NI firsts to its credit and migrant ringing records going back many decades.
Other: Grey Seal (breeding) and, alas, Otter.
Directions: Boat trips (4 miles) to the island depart from the steps of Donaghadee pier J 595 802. Take the A2 from Belfast, continue on it round Bangor and through Groomsport to Donaghadee.

Public transport: Bus: 7 Belfast Laganside Bus Centre to Donaghadee, Ulsterbus (028 90 66 66 30). Train—Bangor.
Visiting: Observatory not permanently manned and visits only possible when duty officer available. Aim to cover spring & autumn weekends and as many full weeks as possible. Outward trips on Friday, return trips on Sunday. Pre-booking essential. Visit fee includes boat trip to island arranged by Observatory. Bring own food, water and sleeping bag. Allow for delays if weather poor. Landing not permitted other than on trips arranged by Observatory but Island Boat Charters (07815 669 732; info@islandboatchartersdonaghadee.com) also offers tours around the islands.
Contact: David Galbraith (Booking Secretary): 028 9338 2539 or 07934 416 668; davidgalbraith903@btinternet.com; www.thecbo.org.uk

Strangford Lough
Besides the reserves listed below, the National Trust owns or manages some 12,500 acres around Strangford Lough, including almost all the foreshore. In the autumn and winter the mudflats around the lough attract waders such as Curlew, Whimbrel, Black & Bar-tailed Godwit, Greenshank, Redshank, Dunlin and Oystercatcher. Duck include Shelduck, Gadwall, Teal, Pintail, Eider and Red-breasted Merganser. In the summer, there are breeding colonies of Common, Arctic and Sandwich Terns on the islands. Little Egrets and Grey Heron are common all year.

Take the A48 from Donaghadee to Newtownards, at the N end of Strangford Lough. At NW end of Strangford Lough, stretching from Newtownards to the Comber estuary there lies

16 NORTH STRANGFORD LOUGH
National Trust/DAERA
Habitats: 2,400 acres of tidal mud and sandflat, saltmarsh to the N of the Comber estuary.
Birds: Pale-bellied Brent Goose (Sep-Oct). Breeding: Sandwich Tern, Black-headed Gull
Other:
Directions: J 488 687 (Island Hill car park). Take the A20 E from Belfast for Newtonards. Either continue to Newtonards, turn R at roundabout on W edge of town, follow road to roundabout at S edge of town and turn R on to A21 for Comber. After 1.75 miles turn L on to Longland Road and follow this road for 1 mile, bearing L as it becomes Island Hill Road, to the Island Hill car park. Or leave the A20 Dundonald and take the A22 to Comber. Follow it round the town and at the roundabout go straight across, taking the A21 for Newtownards. Turn R after just over 1 mile on to Ringcreevy Road for 1 mile, bearing R until you reach Island Hill car park.
Public transport: Bus: 11 Laganside Bus Centre, Belfast

to Comber, then 5a Comber to Newtownards. Stops on A21 at junctions with Longland and Ringcreevy Roads Ulsterbus (028 90 66 66 30). Then 1 mile walk.
Visiting: Island Hill car park open dawn to dusk, free. Toilets, picnic area. Keep dogs under control.
Contact: The National Trust: 028 4488 1411;
Head back along Ringcreevy Road to the A21 (Newtownards Road). Turn L for Comber and once in Comber, after crossing the Comber River, turn L at roundabout and follow instructions in following entry.

17   WWT CASTLE ESPIE WETLAND CENTRE
WWT
Habitats: Comber estuary, tidal lagoons, eelgrass mats, freshwater ponds and lakes, saltmarsh, reedbed limestone grassland and woodland.
Birds: Spring: Black-tailed Godwit, Common Tern, Little Egret, Sedge Warbler. *Autumn/Winter:* Pale-bellied Brent Goose, Whooper Swan, Shelduck, Eider, Wigeon, Teal, Dunlin, Knot, Grey Plover. Redshnk, Greenshank, Curlew, Long-tailed Tit, Siskin.
Other: Dragonflies: Four Spot Chaser, Common Darter, Emperor. Bee Orchid.
Directions: BT23 6EA; J492671. Take the A22 from Belfast for Comber. At roundabout turn R on to A22 Comber/Killyleagh/Downpatrick road, then 1st L on to Ballydrain Road.
Public transport: Bus: 11 Laganside Bus Centre, Belfast to Comber, Ulsterbus (028 90 66 66 30). Then 2.5 mile/1 hr walk.
Visiting: 12 miles SE of Belfast on NW shore of Strangford Lough. Parking free, entry free for WWT members. Visitor Centre, shop, cafe, toilets. Toilets wheelchair accessible, level access from car park to main entrance. Opening hours: Visitor Centre 10am-5pm, reserve 10am-4:30pm, Kingfisher Cafe 10am-4pm. Closed 24&25 Dec. Aviaries, trails and hides. Assistance dogs welcome.
Contact: 028 9187 4146; info.castleespie@wwt.org.uk
Continue S on A22 to SW quarter of Strangford Lough and estuary of River Quoile

18   QUOILE PONDAGE NNR
DAERA
Habitats: Tidal barrier built across Quoile estuary in 1957 to create a freshwater lake. Reedbeds and marsh developing along former sea shore, woodland on higher shores.
Birds: Common woodland spp, passage waders. Large numbers of Mute Swans. *Breeding:* Gadwall, Coot, Moorhen, Great Crested & Little Grebes, Wintering wildfowl: Teal, Wigeon, Tufted Duck, Great Crested Grebe, Goldeneye.
Other:
Directions: BT30 7JB; J 497 471. Take A22 S from Killyleagh to Quoile Bridge. Cross bridge then turn L Follow

signs for Strangford and Countryside Centre.
Public transport: None
Visiting: Reserve open all hours, free. Car park, toilets, picnic area at Countryside Centre (Centre is not open to public but toilets open during day). Hide. Parts of reserve closed to prevent disturbance.
Contact: Countryside Centre: 028 4461 5520.
Site manager is also responsble for several other DAERA NNRs at the S end of Strangford Lough and its Narrows.
In vicinity of Quoile, upstream of Downpatrick.

Hollymount Forest NNR
Wet Willow and Alder woodland in areas prone to flooding, with Reed Canary-grass and Greater Pondsedge. Principal NI site for Warer Violet, in intermittently filled ditches. Also, a large drumlin covered with woodland dominated by Oak. Scattered understorey of Hazel and Holly. Bluebell and Wold Garlic.
Common woodland bird spp.
Take the A25 from Downpatrick to Strangford and two reserves on either side of mouth of Strangford Lough

19   CLOGHY ROCKS
DAERA
Habitats: Area of rocky and muddy foreshore on W side of mouth of Strangford Lough.
Birds: Brent Goose, Oystercatcher, Redshank. Curlew, Common & Sandwich Terns.
Other: Common (breeding) & Grey Seals.
Directions: BT30 7NW; J 594 478. Take A2 (Shore Road/Lecale Way) S from Strangford to Ardglass for just over a mile and car park is on R.
Public transport: None
Visiting: Open all hours, free. Car park, information point but no facilities.
Contact: Shares site manager with Quoile Pondage: 028 4461 5520
Take the ferry across the narrows from Strangford to Portferry and then take the Shore Road S.

20   GRANAGH BAY
DAERA
Habitats: Bay on E shore of Strangford Narrows. Islands, rocks, intertidal mud and gravel.
Birds: Waders, Wagtails, pipits, wagtails. Winter: Teal.
Other: Common & Grey Seals
Directions: J 606 485. Shore from Portferry runs along coast of Granagh Bay. Park on verges
Public transport: None.
Visiting: Open all hours, free. No facilities.
Contact: Shares site manager with Quoile Pondage: 028 4461 5520
Continue along Shore Road, which becomes Bar Hall Road.

21 BALLYQUINTIN POINT

National Trust/DAERA

Habitats: S tip of Ards Peninsula. Indented rocky coastline. Grassland topped, inland cliffs behind shingle/pebble beach. Pockets of saltmarsh.

Birds: Brent Goose, Oystercatcher, Ringed Plover, Peregrine Falcon, Skylark, Whitethroat, Stonechat, Meadow Pipit, Linnet.

Other: Irish Hare. Common Seal.

Directions: The Point itself is at J 621 458. The main car park is at Port Kelly (BT22 4QE; J 628 466, to N of Point). 3 mile S of Portaferry 1st R off Barr Hall Road.

Public transport: None.

Visiting: Open all hours, free. No facilities. Parking at Ballyquintin Farm (BT22 1RG; J 624 461), no specific disabled parking bays.

Contact: Shares site manager with Quoile Pondage: 028 4461 5520

Instead of heading S from Portaferry, take the A20 N.

22 THE DORN

Crown Estate

Habitats: Cloverleaf of sheltered bays opening to the main lough through a narrow strait, The Dorn; with rocks, shingle, mudflats, saltmarsh stretching to the N along E side of Strangford Lough at its S end.

Birds: Winter: Brent Geese, Shelduck, Teal, Goldeneye. Red-breasted Merganser, Curlew.

Other:

Directions: A20 runs parallel to lough shore N from Portaferry to Kircubbin. Reserve stretches from Bishops Mill (BT22 1HH; J 591 560, on Abbacy Road off A20) in S to Gransha Point in N 584 593)

Public transport: Bus: 10 Belfast Laganside Bus Centre to Portaferry runs alson A20, Ulsterbus (028 90 66 66 30).

Visiting: Open all hours, free. Roadside parking, no facilities.

Contact: Shares site manager with Quoile Pondage: 028 4461 5520

Instead of crossing Strangford Narrows at Strangford, head S along the A2 towards the point at the S tip of the Narrows on their W shore.

23 KILLARD POINT

DAERA

Habitats: Flower-rich grassland topping cliffs formed from glacial debris.

Birds: Nesting Fulmar, Sand Martin, Stonechat. *Winter:* Feeding and roosting birds inc Redshank, Oystercatcher and Turnstone.

Other: Butterflies. Orchids.

Directions: J 610 433. 2.5 miles S of Strangford leave the A2 and take Killard Road, following shore for a further mile to the lay-bay car parking at Mill Quarter Bay (J 599 441), on the N side of the neck of land leading out

to the Point. Walk out along shore. A track from Killard (J 598 433), another 0.5 mile S along the road, leads out to NNR.

Public transport: None

Visiting: Open all hours, free. No facilities. Toilets in Ballyhornan, to S of Point. Coastal path around headland.

Contact: Shares site manager with Quoile Pondage: 028 4461 5520

Rejoin the A2 and continue along the coast through Ardglass. At the junction with the A24 in Clough, turn L for Dundrum.

24 MURLOUGH NNR & DUNDRUM BAY

National Trust

Habitats: Sand dunes, heath, woodland. The area of dunes and heathland is pierced by a narrow channel connecting Dundrum Inner Bay, a tidal estuary fed by several rivers that is largely mudflat at low tide, from Dundrum Outer Bay.

Birds: Inner Bay: wintering duck—Shelduck, Wigeon, Mallard, Teal, Goldeneye, Red-breasted Merganser. Passage and wintering waders—Spotted Redshank, Curlew Sandpiper, Little Stint. *Outer Bay:* Wintering seaduck—large rafts of Scoters, mostly Common, Great Northern & Red-throated Divers, Goldeneye, Scaup, Long-tailed Duck. *Dunes:* Breeding Cuckoo, Blackcap, Grasshopper Warbler, Stonechat

Other: Marsh Fritillary butterfly.

Directions: BT33 0LW (Keel Point office; J 345 338 (main car park). From the centre of Dundrum head S on A2 (Newcastle Road) cross Slidderyford Bridge. Car park a further 400 yards on R

Public transport: Bus: 20 Belfast to Newcastle, alight at Lazy BJ Caravan Park after Dundrum, Ulsterbus (028 90 66 66 30).

Visiting: All-year pay & display car park (NT members free). Reserve 8am-7pm Apr-Sep; 8am-5pm Oct-Mar. Toilets open Sat/Sun Apr & May 10am-4pm; every day Jun-Aug 10am-5pm. Network of trails and boardwalks across dunes. NT coastal footpath runs along inland side of Inner Bay from N tip to near Dundrum. Grazing livestock, dogs on lead.

Contact: 028 4375 1467; murlough@nationaltrust.org.uk

Return to Clough and then take A24m then A49 N to J6 of M1 and head W.

Armagh

Bordering Lough Neagh to the S, Armagh is mainly low lying with higher ground in the S. Largely agricutural with little forest and, other than Lough Neagh, few large expanses of water. No coastline and drained by rivers flowing S to N into Lough Neagh.

BTO Reg ional Representatives
Stephen Hewitt
Wetland Bird Survey (WeBS)
Local Organizers: webs@bto.org
Armagh
(excl. Loughs Neagh and Beg)
Stephen Hewitt
Loughs Neagh and Beg
Vacant

25 OXFORD ISLAND NNR
Armagh City, Banbridge & Craigavon Council
Habitat: Peninsula on SE shore of Lough Neagh with shallow, reed-fringed bays on either side (extensive reedbed to E), managed wet grassland and woodland, dense scrub.
Birds: All year: Gadwall, Tufted Duck, Pochard, Little & Great Crested Grebes, Grey Heron, Little & Great White (occasional) Egrets, Hen Harrier, Kingfisher, Treecreeper, Reed Bunting. *Passage:* Oystercatcher, Ringed Plover, Common Sandpiper, Whimbrel, Black-tailed Godwit. *Summer:* Common Tern, Grasshopper, Sedge & Willow Warblers, Chiffchaff, Blackcap. Hirundines (Sand Martin bank). *Winter:* Whooper & Bewick's (occasional) Swans, Greylag Goose, Wigon, Scaup, Teal, Goldeneye, Golden Plover, Lapwing, Fieldfare, Redwing. Occasional large rafts of Coot. Occasional Long-tailed & Ring-necked Duck, Red-breasted Merganser, Goosander, Smew, Snipe. Attracts seabirds, including rarities, when storms at coast. Large numbers of Great Crested Grebe breed in reedbeds, Common Tern and Black-headed Gull on the islands.
Other: Wildlife garden
Directions: BT66 6NJ; J053 616. Leave M1 at J10 and follow Kinnego Embankment to Oxford Island (peninsula to W of Kinnego Harbour on S shore of Lough Neagh).
Public transport: None
Visiting: Several car parks around site. Reserve and car parks free. Discovery Centre (exhibition space, toilets). Loughside cafe 10am-4pm Wed-Sun (to 5pm weekends and Bank Holidays). 4 miles of Surfaced paths, 5 hides, 2 with disabled access.
Contact: Lough Neagh Discovery Centre:
028 3832 2205
Kinnego Marina immediately to E has car park and toilets. Cafe 10am-4pm Tues-Sun. One starting point for boat trips to:

Coney Island, a 9 acre wooded island in the SW corner of the lough. Owned by the National Trust, it too is managed by Armagh City, Banbridge & Craigavon Council. There are also boat trips to the island from Maghery Country Park (BT71 6NS; H 927 636). Maghery, on the S shore of Lough Neagh, is immediately to the N of Peatlands Park (see below) and is also served by the 75 bus between Dungannon and Portadown.
Rejoin M1 and head W.

26 PEATLANDS PARK
NIEA
Habitats: 657 acres. Lowland raised bog, fen, lough and woodland ASSI.
Birds: Snipe, Woodcock, Cuckoo, Hen Harrier
Other:
Directions: BT71 6NW; H 897 603 (main car park). Immediately to N of and accessed from J13 of M1 and 6.5 miles E of Dungannon.
Public transport: Bus: 75 Dungannon to Portadown skirts the W and N of the park. Translink (Ulsterbus).
Visiting: Includes two reserves established prior to its creations: Annagariff (NNR, ancient woodland, 190 acres) and Mullenakill (NNR, raised bog, 55 acres). Free. Visitor Centre, toilets, network of trails and boardwalks, bog garden, picnic area, and narrow gauge railway (operates in summer, formerly used for turf cutting). Bogs are fragile, stay on trails to avoid causing damage. DAERA recommends visiting Peatland Park and viewing bog from its trails, rather than visiting other reserves with bog habitat but less visitor infrstructure.
Contact: 028 3839 9195;
peatland.park@daera-ni.gov.uk
Rejoin M1, continue W to its end S of Dungannon. Then continue on A4 to Enniskillen.

Fermanagh

In the SW of the province, Fermanagh is dominated by Upper and Lower Lough Erne, two shallow loughs that stretch the length of the county SE to NW. The loughs have numerous wooded islands and are separated by a braided isthmus on which Enniskillen stands. Limestone hills rise to the SW of the loughs. The Ballintempo Forest, together with surrounding forests, forms Northern Ireland's largest continuous area of woodland.

BTO Regional Representatives
Michael Stinson

Wetland Bird Survey (WeBS)
Local Organizers: webs@bto.org
Fermanagh
Michael Stinson
Upper Lough Erne
Vacant

RSPB Local Groups
Fermanagh (1977; 25)
Rozy McConkey: rosalindmcconkey@gmail.com
https://group.rspb.org.uk/fermanagh/
Meetings: 8pm, 4th Tuesday of the month (Sep-Apr). St Macartin's Cathedral Hall, Halls Lane, Enniskillen, BT74 7DR.

27 AGHATIROURKE

RSPB/site managed by Marble Arch Caves Geopark
Habitats: Part of Cuilcagh Lakelands Geopark. Blanket bog, open water, limestone grassland, montane heath rising to 2,182 ft. 1,730 acres.
Birds: Red Grouse, Hen Harrier, Peregrine Falcon, Skylark, Sand Martin, Wheatear.
Other: Irish Hare
Directions: BT92 3BE SA 257 955 (Gortalughany viewpoint). Take A4 Sligo Road W of Enniskillen. Then S on A32. Do not follow Florencecourt and Marble Arch Caves. Turn R for Gortalughany viewpoint, follow road to free car park.
Public transport: Bus: 192 Enniskillin bus station to Swanlinbar (Mon-Fri), Ulsterbus (028 90 66 66 30). Request stop at sign for Gortalughany (c.3 miles to reserve gate).
Visiting: Open all hours, free. No facilities. Waymarked Hiker's Trail to summit. Unsurfaced, steep, often slippery. Only suitable for experienced hillwalkers. **DO NOT** leave trail—underlying limestone cave system with unmarked swallow holes. No dogs other than assistance dogs.
Contact: 028 6632 3991; lower.loughherne@rspb.org.uk
Return to A4, then turn L on to A4 and then B52 for Belleek, with the Bellintempo Forest, watch out for this in the 2027 Yearbook, and the Irish border to your L.

28 LOWER LOUGH ERNE ISLANDS

RSPB
Habitats: 43 islands, many managed as lowland wet grassland or broadleaved woodland. Species-rich hay meadow at Lowery Farm. Forestry at Castle Caldwell.
Birds: Lapwing, Curlew, Snipe. Inland breeding colony of Sandwich Tern.
Other: Irish Whitebeam.
Directions: BT74 7JY; NV 126 271. 5 miles E of Belleek on A47 a wooden sign and stone archway mark entrance of Castle Caldwell forest off A47 Kesh to Belleek road.
Continue round N and E shores of lough to Castle Archdale and seasonal ferry to North Island. Castle Archdale is 11 miles N of Enniskillen on the A47 (or B82, depending upon what OS scale you are viewing it at!).
Public transport: None.
Visiting: Open dawn-dusk, free. No facilities. Only parking at Castle Caldwell. Access by boat (charge, summer only) to 2 of the islands (Lusty More & North Island). 3 circular waymarked trails at Castle Caldwell. 1 trail Lusty More Island. 2 trails suitable for wheel/pushchairs. Dogs on leads on public footpaths.
Contact: 028 6632 3991;
lower.loughherne@rspb.org.uk
Then take B534 for Irvinestown, whence A32 for Omagh.

Tyrone

Stretching from the W side of Lough Neagh to the Irish border. The W end of the Sperrin Mountains occupy the N of Tyrone with what will become the River Foyle flowing round them and N into Londonderry.

BTO Regional Representatives
Steven Fyffe
Wetland Bird Survey (WeBS)
Local Organizers: webs@bto.org
Tyrone
(excl. Loughs Neagh and Beg)
Ciara Laverty:

29 COTTAGE FARM

Ulster Wildlife
Habitats: 20 acres. Ancient woodland, bog, species-rich grassland, hedrows and ponds. Close to River Strule.
Birds: Grey Heron, Kingfisher, Dipper, Treecreeper, Redpoll *Breeding:* Spotted Flycatcher, Bullfinch, Reed Bunting. *Winter:* Woodcock, Blackbird, Mistle & Song Thrush, Fieldfare, Redwing,
Other: Red Squirrel, Otter, Daubenton's & Pipistrelle bats. Large Red and Banded Demoiselle. Ancient woodland flora.
Directions: BT79 7TN; H 437 797. Take A5 N from Omagh. After 3.75 miles turn R on to Gortnagarn Road, cross the Strule and then L on to Carrigan Road. Follow this road to farm.
Public transport: Bus: 273 runs along A5 between Omagh and Strabane and stops at Ulster American Folk Park on opposite side of Strule to reserve, N of Mountjoy Post Office. Goldline Express.
Visiting: **Only open to members of Ulster Wildlife with prior permission.** Free. No facilities. Ulster Wildlife's first reserve. Small but perfectly formed. No dogs.
Contact: 028 9045 4094; info@ulsterwildlife.org
Return to A5 and continue to Strabane, then take B49 E

for Dunnamanagh and then Claudy where you turn R on to B74 for Feeny and on towards Dungiven. Turn R at Rallagh and follow directions in Banagher Glen entry.

Londonderry

The Sperrin Mountains occupy the SE quarter of the county, To the W the River Foyle drains into Lough Foyle, whilst to the E of the Sperrins, the River Bann, which for much of its length forms the border with Antrim, flows N from Lough Neagh to the coast. Mud-flats along the shores of Lough Foyle and extensive dune system at Magilligan Point and Umbra.

BTO Regional Representatives
Claire Hassan
Wetland Bird Survey (WeBS)
Local Organizers: webs@bto.org
Bann Estuary (Londonderry)
Dean Jones
Londonderry (Other Sites)
Claire Hassan

RSPB Local Group
Coleraine (1978; 34)
James McDowell: jdmcdowell12@talktalk.net;
https://group.rspb.org.uk/coleraine/
Meetings: 7:30pm, 3rd Monday of the month (Sep-Nov, Jan-Apr). Ballysally Youth and Community Centre, 25 Ballysally Road, Coleraine, BT52 2QA.

30 BANAGHER GLEN NNR
DAERA
Habitats: Steep-sided glen on N slopes of Sperrin Mountains. Deciduous woods, some ancient oak. 3 torrent streams: Altnaheglish (dammed to form the Altnaheglish Reservoir), Glendra and Cuscapal converge into the Owenrigh River within the reserve. ASSI, SAC.
Birds: Peregrine Falcon. Wood Warbler, Redstart (both rare in NI and possibly no longer present) recorded. Lesser Spotted Woodpecker and good warbler assemblage: Willow Warbler, Chiffchaff, Blackcap.
Other: Red Squirrel, Pine Marten. Silver-washed Fritillary, Chimney Sweep Moth. Fantastic macrophytes and ferns.
Directions: C 672 045. Take B74 S from Dungiven towards Feeny. Turn L at Rallagh. Shortly after a sharp R turn road splits 3-ways. Take central road for another 1.4 miles to car park.
Public transport: None
Visiting: Reserve open all hours, free. Trail Head car park open daily. Marked walking trail to Altnaheglish Reservoir, with unmarked circular path around reservoir. Steep in parts.
Contact: 07799 867 853;
michael.morgan@daera-ni.gov.uk

Return/Continue on to Dungiven.

31 LOUGH FOYLE
RSPB
Habitats: Intertidal mudflat, sandflat, saltmarsh on SE shore of Lough Foyle (a sea lough).
Birds: All year: Lapwing. *Passage and winter:* Pale-bellied Brent Goose, White-fronted Goose, Whooper Swan, Pintail, Wigeon, Teal, Common Scoter, Long-tailed Duck. Slavonian Grebe. Golden & Grey Plover, Whimbrel, Curlew Sandpiper, Little Stint, Spotted Redshank. Hen Harrier, Peregrine Falcon, Merlin. Snow & Lapland Bunting.
Other: Otter, Irish Hare.
Directions: BT56 8AS; C601 566. Access via various minor roads off A2 between Limavady and Londonderry.
Public transport: Bus: 144, Londonderry to Ballykelly, 1 mile walk. Ulsterbus (028 90 66 66 30).
Visiting: Open all hours, free. No designated parking area. Limited access to site, no facilities. Keep dogs under control
Contact: 028 9049 1547;
Gareth.Bareham@rspb.org.uk

32 ROE ESTUARY NR
DAERA
Habitats: The Roe flows into Lough Foyle on its E side, to the N of the RSPB reserve and S of Magilligan Point. Mudflat and saltmarsh
Birds: Passage/wintering waders and wildfowl inc Lapwing, Curlew
Other: Eelgrass persists and mudflats have large populations of lugworm, shrimp ragworm and periwinkle.
Directions: BT49 9EB; C 645 290. 5 miles NW of Limavady. Take the B69 (Seacoast Road) N from A2 roundabout outside Limavady. After 1.6 miles turn L on to B510 for Carrowclare. At T junction turn R and fork R in Carrowclare. Continue to car park at end of road.
Public transport: Bus: 134 Coleraine to Limavady (not Sun) Ulsterbus (028 90 66 66 30) runs along A2. As the duck flies, the A2 comes within c.2 miles of the reserve but the walking route is longer.
Visiting: Open all hours, free. No facilities. No trails. Do not cross railway line or bridge. Take care, soft mud on shore. Grazing livestock, high tide roost—no dogs.
Contact: 07799 867 853;
michael.morgan@daera-ni.gov.uk

33 MAGILLIGAN POINT NR
DAERA
Habitats: Tip of large, constanly changing dune system at mouth of Lough Foyle.
Birds: Good views of seabirds using the narrows.
Winter: Migrating waders and wildfowl.
Other: One of the largest sand dune sytems in the British Isles. Harebell and Bird's-foot Trefoil, Thyme and

Pyramidal Orchids. Butterflies: Common Blue, Cryptic White, Ringlet, Meadow Brown and Six-spot Burnet Moth

Directions: BT49 0LR; C 660 390. Leave the A2 7 miles N of Limavady/11.5 miles W of Coleraine at Magilligan Bridge and take the B202 (Point Road). After *c.*1 mile, the road turns sharp L. Continue 2.7 miles to end of road and car park.

Public transport: Bus: 134 Coleraine to Limavady (not Sun) Ulsterbus (028 90 66 66 30). Walk from A2. Passenger and vehicle ferry across mouth of Lough Foyle between Point and Greencastle in Republic of Ireland.

Visiting: Car park (charge) at end of public road. Open all hours, free (reserve). No facilities in reserve but pub, ferry terminal and museum at Point. No formal trails. To S of Point, on W shore of Lough Foyle and N of **Roe Estuary** (q.v.) *Lough Foyle* Ramsar Site and *Magilligan* SAC. *Ballymaclary NR*, in the same dune system, lies to the E of the Point. Primarily of botanical interest, it lies entirely within an MoD Danger Zone. Not normally accessible.

Contact: 07799 867 853;
michael.morgan@daera-ni.gov.uk

34 UMBRA
Ulster Wildlife

Habitats: Dune grassland, dune slacks, scrub, woodland.
Birds: Sea birds. Peregrine Falcon. *Summer:* Cuckoo, Whitethroat, Goldcrest, Skylark, Meadow Pipit, Linnet, Reed Bunting.

Other: Grey & Common Seals. Northern Mining Bee. Cryptic Wood White, Small Heath, Grayling & Dark Green Fritillary butterflies. Orchids: Marsh Helleborine, Early Purple, Frog, Bee Pyramidal Orchids.

Directions: BT49 0LH; C 726 358. Immediately off Seacoast Road/A2 8 miles W of Coleraine

Public transport: Bus: 134 Coleraine to Limavady (not Sun) Ulsterbus (028 90 66 66 30).

Visiting: **Only open to Ulster Wildlife members**. Prior permission required before visiting. Free. Roadside parking on Seacoast Road. (A2). No facilities or paths. Livestock grazing through winter. No dogs.

Contact: 028 9045 4094; info@ulsterwildlife.org
At Coleraine take A54 S along valley of the River Bann.

35 LOUGH BEG NNR
DAERA

Habitats: The River Bann, flowing out of NW corner of Lough Neagh, widens out to form shallow lough. In winter this floods. This NNR consists of 300 acres of wet grassland on W shore, centred on Church Island.

Birds: Breeding: Lapwing, Redshank, Snipe. *Passage:* Black-tailed Godwit, Green & Wood Sandpipers, Greenshank and Knot *Winter:* Whooper Swan, Wigeon, Teal, Pochard and other ducks in smaller numbers.

Other: Pennyroyal, Irish Ladies' Tresses Orchid.

Directions: BT45 8LF; H 975 960. Take M2 from Belfast, then continue of A6, by-pass Toome, then turn R on to B182 for Ballaghy. Turn R at crossroads after *c.*2 miles. After crossing stream on this road, park opposite Church Island (ruined church and spire). The lough itself is divided between Londonderry and Antrim, but the NNR, on the W side, is in Londonderry.

Public transport: None

Visiting: Open all hours, free. Limited roadside parking. No facilities. In summer, can be dry enough to walk out to Church Island but take care of drainage channels. Livestock grazing, No dogs.

Contact: Site manager: 028 3885 3950

Male [Lesser] Redpoll
Sylvie Soudan
Instagram: Sylvie.Soudan

INTERNATIONAL
ORGANIZATIONS

Since, as the title suggests, this is first and foremost a yearbook for birdwatchers, UK-based wildlife organizations that primarily focus on UK birds or the places where they live are listed in the relevant introductory sections of the county directories. There are, however, a number of other UK-based wildlife organizations that are not specifically focused on birds or that are concerned with birds in places and regions other than the UK. A selection of these organizations are listed in this section. Have a browse.

AFRICAN BIRD CLUB (1994)

Provides a worldwide focus for African Ornithology and raises funds to support conservation projects in Africa and related islands through its Conservation Fund. Liaises and promotes the work of existing regional societies. Provides online resources; develops birding apps; publishes a bulletin twice a year.

Contact: ABC, c/o BirdLife International, The David Attenborough Building, Pembroke Street, Cambridge, CB2 3QZ: contact@africanbirdclub.org; (membership): membership@africanbirdclub.org;
www.africanbirdclub.org

AMPHIBIAN AND REPTILE CONSERVATION TRUST (2009)

Formed out of The Herpetological Conservation Trust (1989) to widen its role, the ARC conserves amphibians and reptiles and their habitats, including managing 80+ reserves.

Contact: ARC, 744 Christchurch Rd, Boscombe, Bournemouth BH7 6BZ. Wildlife enquiries: 01202 091 217;
enquiries@arc-trust.org; www.arc-trust.org

BAT CONSERVATION TRUST (1991)

BCT supports local bat groups across the UK. Their vision includes: learning more about bats and how they use the landscape; taking action to protect bats and to enhance the landscapes they rely on; and inspiring people about bats and their environment.

Contact: Bat Conservation Trust, Studio 15, Cloisters House, Cloisters Business Centre, 8 Battersea Park Road, London SW8 4BG. Bat Helpline: 0345 1300 228 (9:30am-4:30pm Mon-Fri and up to 10:30pm daily May-Sep for emergencies only): enquiries@bats.org.uk; www.bats.org.uk

BIRD STAMP SOCIETY (1986)

Open to anyone interested in collecting bird stamps and bird-related postal history and philatelic material. Quarterly magazine *Flight*.

Contact: Steven Ardron (Mem Sec), Flat 11, Mount St. Michael, Craigs Road, Dumfries, DG1 4UT:

membership@birdstampsociety.org.uk;
www.birdstampsociety.org

BIRDLIFE INTERNATIONAL (1993)

Formerly ICBP—International Committee for Bird Preservation (1922). See p. 499.

BRITISH DECOY AND WILDFOWL CARVERS ASSOCIATION (1990)

Run by carvers to promote all aspects of their art. It keeps members in touch with the art; promotes regional groups; generates local interest; holds competitions and exhibitions; and cares for the interests of bird carvers. Produces *Wingspan* magazine three times a year. Stages the 'Festival of Bird Art' in Bakewell (Peak District) in Sep, which inc. the National Bird Carving Championships.

Contact: via website; www.bdwca.org.uk

BRITISH DRAGONFLY SOCIETY (1983)

The BDS aims to carry out/support research on and the conservation of dragonflies, and to engage the public with dragonflies and their habitats. Members receive two issues of *Dragonfly News* and *BDS Journal* annually and *Hawker*, a monthly e-newsletter.

Dragonfly recorders also receive *Darter*. There are countrywide field trips, an annual members' day, and training is available on aspects of dragonfly ecology and identification.

Contact: Carolyn Cooksey (Sec), British Dragonfly Soc, Ashcroft, Brington Road, Old Weston, Huntingdon, PE28 5LP: secretary@british-dragonflies.org.uk; www.british-dragonflies.org.uk

BRITISH ENTOMOLOGICAL AND NATURAL HISTORY SOCIETY (1872)

The Society promotes and advances research in entomology, holds indoor/outdoor meetings, publishes a journal (4 times year) and offers small grants. Its HQ has a library and reference collections.

Contact: The Secretary, BENHS, c/o The Pelham-Clinton Building, Dinton Pastures Country Park, Davis Street, Hurst, Reading, Berkshire RG10 0TH: enquiries@benhs.org.uk; www.benhs.org.uk

BRITISH FALCONERS' CLUB (1927)

The BFC is the oldest and largest falconry club in Europe with 13 regional groups in the UK. Its aim is to encourage responsible falconers and to conserve birds of prey by breeding, holding educational meetings and providing facilities, guidance and advice to those wishing to take up the sport. Publishes *The Falconer* and a newsletter.
Contact: British Falconers' Club: 07598 516 515; admin@britishfalconersclub.co.uk; www.britishfalconersclub.co.uk

BRITISH LIBRARY SOUND ARCHIVE—
WILDLIFE SOUNDS (1969)

The most comprehensive collection of bird sound recordings in existence: 240,000+ wildlife recordings inc. 10,000+ species (birds, mammals, amphibians, reptiles, fish and insects) from around the world, many accessible for free listening. Copies or sonograms of most recordings can be supplied for private study or research and, subject to copyright clearance, for commercial uses. Contribution of new material and enquiries on all aspects of wildlife sounds and recording techniques are welcome. Publishes a number of magazines and periodicals, CD guides to bird songs and other wildlife, inc. ambience titles.
Catalogue available on-line at: http://cadensa.bl.uk/uht-bin/cgisirsi/x/x/0/49/
Contact: Cheryl Tipp (Curator) Wildlife and Environmental Sounds, The British Library, 96 Euston Road, London NW1 2DB: 020 7412 7403; wildlifesound@bl.uk; www.bl.uk/collection-guides/wildlife-and-environmental-sounds

BRITISH NATURALISTS' ASSOCIATION (1905)

The BNA was founded to promote the interests of nature lovers and bring them together. Encourages and supports schemes and legislation for the protection of the country's natural resources, organizes meetings, field weeks, lectures and exhibitions to help popularize the study of nature. Publishes two magazines, *Country-Side* and *British Naturalist* and has nine local branches.
Contact: General Sec, British Naturalists' Association, 27 Old Gloucester Street, London WC1N 3AX: 0844 892 1817; info@bna-naturalists.org; www.bna-naturalists.org

BUGLIFE (2000)

Devoted to the conservation of all invertebrates; actively engaged in halting the extinction of Britain's rarest slugs, snails, bees, wasps, ants, spiders, beetles and many more. It works to achieve this through practical conservation projects; promoting the environmental importance of invertebrates and raising awareness about the challenges to their survival; assisting in the development of helpful legislation and policy; developing and disseminating knowledge about how to conserve invertebrates; and encouraging and supporting invertebrate conservation initiatives by other organizations in the UK, Europe and worldwide.
Contact: Buglife, G.06, Allia Future Business Centre, London Road, Peterborough PE2 8AN: 0300 102 7375; info@buglife.org.uk; www.buglife.org.uk

BUTTERFLY CONSERVATION (1968)

BC's core aims are to recover threatened butterflies and moths; to increase numbers of widespread species; to promote international conservation actions; and to inspire people to understand and deliver species conservation. Runs over 30 nature reserves in the UK and is involved in landscape-scale projects conserving habitats. There are 40,000 members and 32 volunteer-run branches through the British Isles.
Contact: Head Office, Manor Yard, East Lulworth, Wareham, Dorset, BH20 5QP: 01929 400 209; info@butterfly-conservation.org; www.butterfly-conservation.org
Northern Ireland
northernireland@butterflyconservation.org
Scotland
Balallan House, Allan Park, Stirling, FK8 2QG: 01786 447 753; scotland@butterfly-conservation.org
Wales: c/o National Botanic Garden of Wales (Wallace Room), Llanarthne, Carmarthenshire SA32 8HG: 01792 642 972; wales@butterfly-conservation.org

CENTRE FOR ECOLOGY
AND HYDROLOGY (CEH)

The work of the CEH, a constituent body of the Natural Environment Research Council, includes ornithological research, covering population studies, habitat management and work on the effects of pollution. The CEH has a long-term programme to monitor pesticide and pollutant residues in the corpses of predatory birds sent in by birdwatchers, and carries out detailed studies on affected species. The Biological Records Centre (BRC), part of the CEH, is responsible for the national biological database on plant and animal distributions (excl. birds)—go to www.brc.ac.uk
Contact: UK Centre for Ecology and Hydrology, Maclean Building, Benson Lane, Crowmarsh Gifford, Wallingford, Oxfordshire OX10 8BB: 01491 838 800; via website; www.ceh.ac.uk

(THE) CONSERVATION FOUNDATION (1982)

The CF provides a means for people in public, private and not-for-profit sectors to collaborate on environmental causes. Its programme has included award schemes, conferences, promotions, special events, field studies, school programmes, media work, seminars and workshops. They have created and managed environmental award schemes of all kinds. For information about how to apply for current award schemes visit the website.

Contact: Conservation Foundation, Vicarage House, 58-60 Kensington Church Street, London W8 4DB: 020 7368 3313; info@conservationfoundation.co.uk; www.conservationfoundation.co.uk

EARTHWATCH (1971)

Earthwatch developed the engagement of the general public into the scientific process by bringing together individual volunteers and scientists on field research projects—providing an alternative means of funding, as well as a dedicated labour force for field scientists.

Contact: Earthwatch (Europe), Mayfield House, 102-104 St Aldates, Oxford, OX1 1BT: via website; www.earthwatch.org.uk

EURING (European Union for Bird Ringing) (1963)

EURING co-ordinates bird-ringing schemes throughout Europe. It aims to promote and encourage: scientific and administrative co-operation between national ringing schemes; development and maintenance of high standards in bird ringing; scientific studies of birds, in particular those based on marked individuals; and the use of data from bird ringing for the management and conservation of birds. These objectives are achieved mainly through co-operative projects, the organization of meetings and the collection of data in the EURING Database.

Contact: EURING: enquiries@euring.org; www.euring.org

EUROPEAN COLOUR-RING BIRDING

This platform allows field observers to find out who the project leaders are if they find a colour-ringed bird.

Contact: www.cr-birding.org

FARMING & WILDLIFE ADVISORY GROUP ASSOCIATION (2011)

The FWAG Association has succeeded FWAG as the representative of local groups across the UK. FWAGs provide trusted, independent environmental advice to farmers, helping them to understand the environmental value of their land and to make the most of available agri-environment options.

Contact: FWAG Association. info@fwag.org.uk; www.fwag.org.uk

Local FWAG Groups:

Chris Seabridge & Associates Limited (West Midlands): 07713 333 204; info@chrisseabridge.co.uk; www.chrisseabridge.co.uk

ELM Associates (Cheshire and the North West): info@elmassociates.co.uk/jane@elmassociates.co.uk; https://elmassociates.co.uk

Fraser Hugill (Yorkshire); fjhugill@yahoo.co.uk

FWAG Cymru: 01341 421 456; fwagcymru@btconnect.com

FWAG East (Cambs, Herts, Essex, Beds, Northants): 01223 841 507; hello@fwageast.org.uk; www.fwageast.org.uk

FWAG South East (Kent, Sussex, Surrey, Hants, IoW, Berks, Oxon): 07713 333 182; info@fwagsoutheast.co.uk; www.fwagsoutheast.co.uk

FWAG South West (Gloucs, Somerset, Dorset, Wilts, Devon, Cornwall): 01823 660 684; info@fwagsw.org.uk; www.fwagsw.org.uk

Norfolk FWAG: 01603 814 869; advice@norfolkfwag.co.uk; www.norfolkfwag.co.uk

Nottingham FWAG: info@nottsfwag.co.uk; www.nottsfwag.co.uk

Suffolk FWAG: 01728 748 030; info@suffolkfwag.co.uk; www.suffolkfwag.co.uk

FAUNA AND FLORA INTERNATIONAL (1903)

FFI's mission is to conserve threatened species and ecosystems worldwide by finding sustainable solutions based on sound science and taking human needs into account. They are currently working on more than 120 projects in nearly 50 countries. Members receive a regular newsletter and *Fauna and Flora* magazine. Publishes the journal *Oryx*.

Contact: Flora and Fauna International, The David Attenborough Building, Pembroke Street, Cambridge CB2 3QZ: 01223 571 000; info@fauna-flora.org; www.fauna-flora.org

FIELD STUDIES COUNCIL (1943)

The FSC manages a UK-wide network of centres where students from schools, universities and colleges, as well as individuals of all ages, can stay to study various aspects of the environment under expert guidance. Courses include many bird-related themes. Research workers and naturalists wishing to use the records and resources are welcome. There are centres in England, Scotland and Wales—see website for contacts and courses. Publishes identification charts, guides and handbooks.

Contact: Field Studies Council, Preston Montford, Montford Bridge, Shrewsbury, SY4 1HW: 01743 852 100; enquiries@field-studies-council.org; FSC publications: 01952 208 910; publications@field-studies-council.org; www.field-studies-council.org

FRESHWATER HABITATS TRUST (1988)

FHT aim is to protect freshwater life in ponds, streams, rivers and lakes through research, surveys and practical conservation work. Practical projects are targeted on the places that will bring the greatest benefits for freshwater life at regional and UK scale.

Contact: Freshwater Habitats Trust, Bury Knowle House, North Place, Headington, Oxford, OX3 9HY: 01865 595 505; info@freshwaterhabitats.org.uk; www.freshwaterhabitats.org.uk

FRIENDS OF THE EARTH (1971)

A network of environmental groups represented in 75 countries. In the UK it has a unique network of 200+ campaigning local groups, working in communities in England, Wales, Northern Ireland and Scotland.

It is largely funded by supporters with more than 90% of income coming from individual donations, the rest from special fundraising events, grants and trading.

Contact: Friends of the Earth, The Printworks, 139 Clapham Road, London SW9 0HP: 020 7490 1555; www.foe.co.uk

Friends of the Earth Cymru
Suite 3.01, Floor 3, C12, 12 Cathedral Road, Cardiff, CF11 9LJ: 029 2022 9577; cymru@foe.co.uk; www.foe.cymru

Friends of the Earth Northern Ireland
Gordon House, 22-24 Lombard Street, Belfast, BT1 1RD: 028 9023 3488; foe-ni@foe.co.uk
www.friendsoftheearth.uk/northern-ireland

Friends of the Earth Scotland
Thorn House, 5 Rose Street, Edinburgh EH2 2PR: 0131 243 2700; via website; https://foe.scot

FROGLIFE (1989)

Works to conserve native amphibians and reptiles by: practical conservation, environmental education and communication (advice/information).

Contact: Froglife, Brightfield Business Hub, Bakewell Road, Orton Southgate, Peterborough, PE2 6XU: info@froglife.org; www.froglife.org

INTERNATIONAL WADER STUDY GROUP (1970)

An association of amateur and professional wader enthusiasts, from around the world, the Group aims to maintain contact between them, help organize co-operative studies, and provide a vehicle for the exchange of information. Publishes *Wader Study* three times a year and holds an annual conference.

Contact: IWSG: membership@waderstudygroup.org; www.waderstudygroup.org

JOINT NATURE CONSERVATION COMMITTEE (JNCC) (1990)

Members are from the nature conservation bodies of E,NI, S,W and government appointed independent members. Its role is to provide evidence, information and advice so that decisions are made to protect natural resources and systems, specifically to work on nature conservation issues in the UK as a whole and internationally. JNCC is the UK Government's nature conservation adviser in international fora, taking issues forward from the four home countries to inform policy development and then provide support to ensure that requirements are met.

Contact: JNCC, Quay House, 2 East Station Road, Fletton Quays, Peterborough, PE2 8YY: 01733 562 626; via website; www.jncc.defra.gov.uk

LINNEAN SOCIETY OF LONDON (1788)

Named after Carl Linnaeus, the 18th Century Swedish biologist, who created the modern scientific system of biological nomenclature, the Society promotes all aspects of pure and applied biology. It houses Linnaeus's collection of plants, insects and fishes, library and correspondence. The Society has a major reference library consisting of books, journals and archives.

It publishes a number of titles inc. the *Biological, Botanical, Evolutionary* and *Zoological* Journals and the *Synopsis of the British Fauna* series.

Contact: Linnean Society of London, Burlington House, Piccadilly, London W1J 0BF: 020 7434 4479; info@linnean.org; www.linnean.org

LIPU-UK (1989)

(*Lega italiana protezione uccelli/Italian League for the Protection of Birds*)

A voluntary organisation supporting the work of LIPU in Italy by raising funds to carry out projects there. Members receive *Ali* (Wings) four times a year.

Contact: David Lingard, Fernwood, Doddington Road, Whisby, Lincs LN6 9BX: 01522 689 030; mail@lipu-uk.org; www.lipu-uk.org

MAMMAL SOCIETY (1954)

The Society is dedicated to the study and conservation of all British mammals. It seeks to raise awareness of mammalian ecology and conservation needs, to survey mammals and their habitats, to identify the threats they face, and to promote mammal studies in the UK.

Contact: The Mammal Society, International House, 55 Lomgsmith Street, Gloucester, GL1 2HR: 0238 001 0983; info@themammalsociety.org; www.mammalsociety.org.uk

MARINE CONSERVATION SOCIETY (1983)

MCS is the UK charity that campaigns for clean seas and beaches around the British coastline, sustainable fisheries, and protection for all marine life. MCS is consulted on a wide range of marine issues and provides advice primarily to government, but also to industry, on topics ranging from offshore wind, oil and gas, to marine strategies and fisheries reform. It provides advice to ensure that further action is taken to conserve our seas and reduce the effect of marine activities on marine habitats and species. It has an extensive programme for volunteers, ranging from fund-raising and an annual clean-up of UK beaches, to surveys of species such as basking shark.

Contact: Marine Conservation Society, Overross House, Ross Park, Ross-on-Wye, HR9 7US: 01989 566 017;

info@mcsuk.org; www.mcsuk.org

NATURAL HISTORY MUSEUM AT TRING (1937)
Founded by Lord Rothschild, the museum has 80 million specimens including many rarities and extinct species. Only a tiny fraction ever go on display. The galleries are open daily (Tues-Sun) 10am-5pm excl. Dec 24-26. (booking advisable). *Bird Group:* the Museum at Tring looks after one of the largest ornithological collections in the world—with over a million skins, skeletons, nests, sets of eggs and specimens preserved in spirit, and there is an extensive ornithological library with 80,000+ works. The Bird Group collection and library are not open to the public but can be visited by researchers (enquire by e-mail: via website).

Contact: Natural History Museum at Tring, The Walter Rothschild Building, Akeman Street, Tring, Hertfordshire HP23 6AP: 020 7942 5000; tring-enquiries@nhm.ac.uk www.nhm.ac.uk/visit/tring.html

NEOTROPICAL BIRDING AND CONSERVATION (1994)
(Formerly Neotropical Bird Club)
An international organization for those interested in birds of the Neotropics, the NB&C aims to foster an interest in the region and to increase awareness of the importance of support for conservation there. Publishes *Neotropical Birding* and *Cotinga*.

Contact: Neotropical Birding and Conservation, c/o The Lodge, Sandy, Bedfordshire SG19 2DL: 01255 821 083;

secretary@neotropicalbirdingandconservation.org; www.neotropicalbirdingandconservation.org

ORIENTAL BIRD CLUB (1984)
Membership is open to anyone with an interest in birds of the Oriental region and their conservation. This interest is encouraged; the work of regional bird and nature societies is promoted; and information on Oriental birds is collated and published. Publishes Journal of *Asian Ornithology* and *BirdingASIA*.

Contact: Oriental Bird Club Secretary, 35 Consfield Ave, New Malden, Surrey KT36HD:
mail@orientalbirdclub.org;
www.orientalbirdclub.org

ORNITHOLOGICAL SOCIETY OF THE MIDDLE EAST, THE CAUCASUS AND CENTRAL ASIA (OSME) (1978)
Encourages birdwatchers to visit the region, to partici-

pate in surveys, and to work with others involved there. A conservation and research fund offers small grants. Publishes *Sandgrouse*.

Contact: OSME, c/o The Lodge, Sandy, Bedfordshire SG19 2DL: via website; www.osme.org

PLANTLIFE (1989)
Works nationally and internationally to save threatened wild flowers, plants and fungi. This includes: working with others to protect rare flora and to ensure familiar flowers and plants continue to thrive, managing 24 nature reserves (4,450 acres), and identifying *Important Plant Areas* across the UK.

Contact: Plantlife, Brewery House, 36 Milford Street, Salisbury, Wiltshire SP1 2AP: 01722 342 730;
via website; www.plantlife.org.uk

ROYAL ENTOMOLOGICAL SOCIETY (1833)
The RES promotes and develops entomological science and supports international collaboration, research and publications—demonstrating the importance of studying insects to everyone.

Contact: Royal Entomological Society, The Mansion House, Chiswell Green Lane, St Albans, AL2 3NS: 01727 899 387; info@royensoc.co.uk; www.royensoc.co.uk

ROYAL PIGEON RACING ASSOCIATION (1897)
Promotes the sport of pigeon racing and controls pigeon racing within the Association. Organizes liberation sites, issues rings, calculates distances between liberation sites and home lofts, and assists in the return of strays (may be able to assist in identifying owners of ringed birds found).

Contact: The Royal Pigeon Racing Association, Unit 35-41, Upper Mills Trading Estate, Stonehouse, Gloucestershire GL10 2BJ: 01452 713 529; via website;
www.rpra.org

THE CONSERVATION VOLUNTEERS
(formerly BTCV) (1959)
The Conservation Volunteers helps thousands of people each year to reclaim local green spaces. Through their own environmental projects and through a network of community groups people are enabled to take responsibility for their local environments. TCV has published a series of practical handbooks (digital format/subscribe online).

Contact: TCV, Gresley House, Ten Pound Walk, Doncaster, DN4 5HX: 01302 388 883; information@tcv.org.uk; www.tcv.org.uk

TRAFFIC International (1976)
(the wildlife trade monitoring network)
Works globally on trade in wild animals and plants in the context of biodiversity conservation and sustainable development, ensuring that this trade is not a threat

to the conservation of nature. Publishes The *TRAFFIC Bulletin*.
Contact: Traffic Global Office, The David Attenborough Building, Pembroke Street, Cambridge CB2 3QZ: 01223 331 997; traffic@traffic.org; www.traffic.org

WEST AFRICAN ORNITHOLOGICAL SOCIETY (1964)

Grew out of the Nigerian Ornithologists' Society. The Society's aim is to promote scientific interest in the birds of West Africa (28 countries) and to further the region's ornithology, mainly through *Malimbus* (journal).
Contact: Tim Dodman (Membership Secretary), WAOS, Hundland, Papa Westray, Orkney KW17 2BU: tim@timdodman.co.uk; www.malimbus.org

EAST AFRICA NATURAL HISTORY SOCIETY (1909)

See Kenya/Nature Kenya under BirdLife Africa, pxxx).

WILDLIFE SOUND RECORDING SOCIETY (1968)

Members carry out recording work for scientific purposes as well as for pleasure. A field weekend is held in the spring and an AGM in the autumn. Members organize meetings locally. Four CD sound magazines of members' recordings are produced for members each year and *Wildlife Sound* (magazine) is published twice a year.
Contact: David Mellor (Hon Membership Sec), WSRS, Fuchsia Cottage, Helperthorpe, Nr Malton, North Yorkshire YO17 8TQ: membership@wildlife-sound.org; www.wildlife-sound.org

WORLD OWL TRUST

Works on owl conservation on a national and international scale. The conservation programmes protect populations of endangered owls until their habitat has been restored. A new World Owl Centre is due to open in time for Easter 2026.
Contact: World Owl Trust, Millstones, Bootle, Cumbria LA19 5TJ: 01229 718 080; jen@owls.org; www.owls.org

WORLD PHEASANT ASSOCIATION (1975)

The WPA is committed to the conservation of Galliformes and their habitats by promoting the conservation of those species that are rare or in danger of extinction; advancing the education of the public and the knowledge of such species; and conducting research and studying captive and wild species. Publishes *WPA News* (3x a year).
Contact: Barbara Ingman (administrator), WPA, The Gateway, 85-101 Sankey Street, Warrington, Cheshire, WA1 1SR: 07935 383 992; office@pheasant.org.uk; www.pheasant.org.uk

WWF-UK (1961)

WWF is the world's largest independent conservation organization, working in more than 100 countries. It works to conserve habitats and species, protect endangered spaces, and address global threats to nature by seeking long-term solutions with people in government and industry, education and civil society. Members receive *Action* magazine three times a year.
Contact: WWF-UK, The Living Planet Centre, Rufford House, Brewery Road, Woking, Surrey GU21 4LL: 01483 426 444; supportercare@wwf.org.uk; www.wwf.org.uk & www.panda.org
WWF Cymru, Brunel House, 2 Fitzalan Road, Cardiff, CF24 0EB: 029 2045 4970; wales@wwf.org.uk
WWF Scotland, CodeBase Edinburgh, Argyle House, 3 Lady Lawson Street, Edinburgh, EH3 9DR: 0131 659 9100; scotland@wwf.org.uk

ZOOLOGICAL PHOTOGRAPHIC CLUB (1899)

The Club allows wildlife photographers to view and comment on each others' work on a regular basis and to provide a forum for the discussion of photographic locations, equipment and techniques. Membership is limited to 28, applications can be made to join.
Contact: John Tinning (Hon. Sec), ZPC: john.tinning@btinternet.com; zpc-naturefolio.weebly.com

ZOOLOGICAL SOCIETY OF LONDON (1826)

Carries out research, organizes symposia and holds scientific meetings. Manages London Zoo (opened in 1828) and Whipsnade Zoo near Dunstable, Beds—each with an extensive collection of birds. The ZSL's library holds a large collection of ornithological books and journals. Publications include *Journal of Zoology* and *Animal Conservation*.
Contact: Zoological Society of London, Regent's Park, London NW1 4RY: 0344 225 1826; generalenquiries@zsl.org; www.zsl.org

BIRDLIFE ORGANIZATIONS

BirdLife is a Partnership of non-governmental organizations (NGOs) with a special focus on nature and people. Each NGO Partner represents a unique geographic territory/country.
www.birdlife.org

SECRETARIAT ADDRESSES

Global Office
BirdLife International
birdlife@birdlife.org
The David Attenborough Building, Pembroke Street, Cambridge, CB2 3QZ, UK
+44 (0) 1223 277 318

BirdLife Africa Regional Office
birdlife-africa@birdlife.org
Westcom Point Building 6th Floor, Mahiga Mairu Ave, off Waiyaki Way, Westlands, Nairobi, Kenya
+254 (0) 20 247 3259
+254 (0) 806 8314

West Africa Sub-Regional Office
La Maison de la Conservation
2ème étage, Apt. 82, Capucine Building, Zone B, Rue 111, Dakar, Sénégal
+211 33 865 93 36

BirdLife Americas Regional Office
americas@birdlife.org
Av. Julio Zaldumbide N25-82 y Valladolid. 2do Piso, La Floresta, Zip Code 170109, Ecuador
+593 2 2 2555 361
+593 2 2 233 086

BirdLife Middle East Regional Office
me@birdlife.org
Building 4, Bakr Al-Baw Street, Dahiat Al-Rasheed, P.O. Box 2295, Amman 11953, Jordan
+962 6 515 6015

BirdLife Europe and Central Asia Regional Office
europe@birdlife.org
Stichting BirdLife Europe,
c/o Hive5, Cours Saint-Michel 30
1040 Brussels, Belgium
+32 (0) 2280 08 30

BirdLife Pacific Regional Office
suva.office@birdlife.org
10 MacGregor Road,
GPO Box 18332, Suva, Fuji
+679 331 3492

BirdLife Asia Regional Office— Japan
info@birdlife-asia.org
Unizo Kakigara-cho Kitajima Bldg 1F, 1-13-1 Nihonbashi Kakigara-cho, Chuo-ku, Tokyo 103-0014, Japan
+81 (0) 3 6206 2941

BirdLife Asia Regional Office—Singapore
singapore.office@birdlife.org
354 Tanglin Road, #01-16/17, Tanglin International Centre, Singapore, 247672
+65 6479 3089

AFRICA (26)

Botswana
BirdLife Botswana (BLB), Kgale Siding, Plot K1069, Unit B1, Gaborone.
blb@birdlifebotswana.org.bw;
www.birdlifebotswana.org.bw;
Pub: *Familiar Chat* (newsletter)

Burkina Faso
NATURAMA, 01 B.P. 6133, 01, Ouagadougou.
+226 51 26 64 29 or 54 96 19 23
info@naturama.bf; www.naturama.bf

Burundi
Association Burundaise pour la Protection de la Nature (ABN), Avenue de la Revolution, 2nd Floor No.8, Bujumbura. +257 22 249471; info@abn.bi; www.abn.bi;
Pub: *Inyomvyi* (newsletter)

Cape Verde
Biosfera, Sul do Cemitério, Rua 5, São Vicente.
+238 2317929; geral@biosfera1.com;
www.biosfera1.com; Pub: (newsletter)

Cote d'Ivoire/Ivory Coast
SOS-FORETS (SF), 22 BP 918, Abidjan 22.
+225 27 22 24 35 33; info@sosforets.ci;
www.sosforets.ci

Egypt
Nature Conservation Egypt, 56A Al Mahrousa Street Agouza, Giza +20 233465668 info@natureegypt.org;
www.natureegypt.org; Pub: (newsletter)

Ethiopia
Ethiopian Wildlife and Natural History Society (EWNHS), P.O. Box 13303, Addis Ababa. +251 116-636792;
ewnhs720@gmail.com; www.ewnhs.org.et;
Pub: *Agazen* (school magazine); *Waliya* (semi-scientific journal)

BIRDLIFE ORGANIZATIONS

Ghana
Ghana Wildlife Society (GWS), info@ghanawildlifesociety.org; www.ghanawildlifesociety.org; Pub: *NKO* (magazine); Bongo (newsletter)
Guinea
Guinee-Ecologie, +224 621 277 508; info@guineeecologie.net; www.guineeecologie.net; Pub: (newsletter)
Kenya
NatureKenya, P.O. Box 44486, 00100 GPO, Nairobi. +254 (0) 20 3537568; office@naturekenya.org; www.naturekenya.org; Pub: *Nature Net* (newsletter); *Kenya Birding* (magazine); *Journal of East African Natural History* (scientific); *Scopus* (scientific)
Liberia
The Society for Conservation of Nature in Liberia (SCNL), Oldest Congo Town, Opposite the Nigerian House, Monrovia: scnlliberia@yahoo.com; www.scnlliberia.org; Pub: (newsletter)
Madagascar
Asity Madagascar, Lot IAB 39 Ter C Analamahitsy, Antananarivio: +261(0) 33 15 536 07; contact@asity-madagascar.org; www.asity-madagascar.org
Malawi
Wildlife & Environmental Society of Malawi (WESM), Corner, Churchill Road, Patridge Avenue (Opposite Serendib Heritage hotel), P/Bag 578, Limbe. +265 212 843 502; secretariat@wesm.mw; www.wesm.mw; Pub: (newsletter)
Mauritania
Nature Mauritanie, 6th Arondissement, Ilot 70. BP: 2647, Nouakchott. +222 46 42 10 84; nature.mauritanie@laposte.net; www.natmau.org/en/
Mauritius
The Mauritian Wildlife Foundation, Grannum Road, Vacoas, 73418: +230 697 6097; executive@mauritian-wildlife.org; www.mauritian-wildlife.org; Pub: *Echo News* (newsletter)
Morocco
GREPOM/BirdLife Maroc, Residence Oum Hani IV, Imm 22, Apt 3, 11160 Salé: +212 05378-47663; grepom@grepom.org; www.grepom.org
Nigeria
Nigerian Conservation Foundation (NCF), Km 19, Lekki-Epe Expressway, Lekki. 106104, Lagos. +234 9034 895 750; info@ncfnigeria.org; www.ncfnigeria.org; Pub: (newsletter)
Rwanda
Nature Rwanda, Nova Complex, NM 11 ST, Musanze, Ruhengeri; +250 788 773 177; info@naturerwanda.org;

www.naturerwanda.org
Seychelles
Nature Seychelles, Roche Caiman, Box 1310, Mahe. +248 2519090; nature@seychelles.net; www.natureseychelles.org; www.cousinisland.net; Pub: *Zwazo* (magazine)
Senegal
Nature-Communautes-Developpement, Technopole City, Villa 399, Yaye Djinda Building; +221 33 833 05 78; secretariatncd@gmail.org; www.ncdsenegal.org
Sierra Leone
The Conservation Society of Sierra Leone (CSSL), 86A Main Rd, Congo Town, Freetown: info@cs-sl.org; www.cs-sl.org Pub: (newsletter)
South Africa
BirdLife South Africa (BLSA), Private Bag X16, Pinegowrie, 2123: +27 (0) 11 789 1122; info@birdlife.org.za; www.birdlife.org.za; Pub: *African BirdLife* (magazine); *Ostrich* (scientific); (newsletter)
Tanzania
Nature Tanzania, P.O. Box 683, Arusha; +255 689111313; info@naturetanzania.or.tz; www.naturetanzania.or.tz; Pub: (newsletter)
Tunisia
Association Les Amis des Oiseaux (AAO), Immeubke ERIS, Bureau No 4 au 2eme etage, 14 Rue Ibn El Heni, 2080 Ariana. +255 689111313; secretariat@aao-birdlife.tn; www.aao-birdlife.tn; Pub: (newsletter)
Uganda
Nature Uganda (NU), Bwindi Trust House, Plot 1, Katalima Crescent, Nagurua, Kampala; +256 414 540719; nature@natureuganda.org; www.natureuganda.org; Pub: *The Naturalist* (newsletter)
Zambia
BirdWatch Zambia, 42 Roan Road, Flat 7, Kabulonga, Rhodes Park, Lusaka: +260 211 239 420; bwz.office@gmail.com; www.birdwatchzambia.org; Pub: (newsletter)
Zimbabwe
BirdLife Zimbabwe (BLZ), 35 Clyde Road, Eastlea, Harare; +263 24 2481496; birds@zol.co.zw; www.birdlifezimbabwe.org; Pub: *The Babbler* (newsletter); *Honeyguide* (scientific)

AMERICAS (23)

Argentina
Aves Argentina, Matheu 1246/8, Buenos Aires (C1249AAB): +54 11 4943 - 7216 to 19; info@avesargentinas.org.ar; www.avesargentinas.org.ar; Pub: *Aves Argentinas* (magazine); *Nuestras Aves* (magazine); *El Hornero* (scientific); (newsletter)

BIRDLIFE ORGANIZATIONS

Bahamas
Bahamas National Trust (BNT), P.O. Box 4105, Bay Street Business Centre, Bay St. East, Nassau: +242 393 1317; bnt@bnt.bs; www.bnt.bs; Pub: (newsletter)

Belize
Belize Audubon Society,16 North Park Street, Belize City; +501 223 4988; info@belizeaudubon.org; www.belizeaudubon.org; Pub: *BAS Bulletin* (newsletter)

Bolivia
Asociación Armonía, Av. Lomas de Arena # 400, Zona Palmasola, Santa Cruz de la Sierra: +591 3 3568808; armonia@armonia-bo.org; www.armoniabolivia.org

Brazil
SAVE Brasil, Rua Fernão Dias, 219 cj 2 Pinheiros, São Paulo SP, 05427-010: +11 3815-2862; aves@savebrasil.org.br; www.savebrasil.org.br; Pub: (newsletter)

Canada
Birds Canada, P.O. Box 160, 115 Front Street, Port Rowan, ON N0E 1M0: +1 519 586 3531; hello@birdscanada.org; www.birdscanada.org; Pub: *Birdwatch Canada* (magazine)
Nature Canada, Suite 300, 240 Bank St., Ottawa, ON K2P 1X4: +1 613 562 3447; info@naturecanada.ca; www.naturecanada.ca; Pub: (annual report)

Chile
Comité Nacional Pro Defensa de la Flora y Fauna (CODEFF), Padre Alonso Ovalle 612, Of. 5, Santiago; +56 2 2 777 2534 and +56 2 2 638 3821; comunicadigital@codeff.cl; www.codeff.cl

Colombia
Asociacion Calidris, Cra 24 No. 4-20, B. Miraflores, Cali, calidris@calidris.org.co; www.calidris.org.co
Pub: newsletter

Cuba
Centro Nacional de Areas Protegidas (CNAP), Calle 18a, No 1441e/41 y 47, Playa, Havana 11300; +53 7202 7970; cnap@snap.cu; www.snap.cu

Dominican Republic
Grupo Jaragua (GJI), Calle San Juan Bautista 69, Atala, Santo Domingo; +1 809 472-1036; info@grupojaragua.org.do; www.grupojaragua.org.do; Pub: (newsletter)

Ecuador
Aves y Conservacion, OE6 Martin de Utreras N31-266 y Av. Mariana de Jesús Quito, Pichincha, 170509; direccion@avesconservacion.org; www.avesconservacion.org; Pub: (newsletter)
Jocotoco, Valladolid N24-414 y Luis Cordero, Quito; +593 99 249 9813; info@jocotoco.org.ec; www.jocotoco.org.ec; Pub: (newsletter)

El Salvador
Fundación Ecológica SalvaNATURA (SN), Km 3½ Planes de Renderos, Finca Vista Alegre, 503 San Salvador: info@salvanatura.org.sv; www.salvanatura.org.sv; Pub: (newsletter)

Falkland Islands
Falklands Conservation, Jubilee Villas, Ross Road, Stanley, FIQQ 1ZZ: +500 22247; outreach@conservation.org.fk; www.falklandsconservation.com; Pub: (newsletter); *Wildlife Conservation* (magazine)

Mexico
Pronatura, Calle Franz Bloom 4, Barrio Cuxtitali, San Cristóbal de Las Casas. Chiapas, Mexico. 29230: +52 (967) 67 8 5000 direccion@pronatura-sur.org; www.pronatura-sur.org; Pub: (newsletter)

Panama
Panama Audubon Society (PAS), Apartado 0843-03076, Panama City: +507 232-5977; audubon@audubonpanama.org: www.audubonpanama.org

Paraguay
Guyra Paraguay, Av. Cnel. Carlos Bóveda, Parque Ecológico Capital Verde, Viñas Cué, Asunción, CC 1132: guyra.paraguay@guyra.org.py; www.guyra.org.py

Peru
Asociacion Ecosistemas Andinos,Pasaje Navidad U-10, Urb. Ttio, Wanchaq, Cusco: +51 (84) 227988; info@ecoanperu.org; www.ecoanperu.org

Puerto Rico (to USA)
Sociedad Ornitologica Puertorriquena, Inc. (SOPI), P.O. Box 195166, San Juan, 00919-5166: +1-787-936-7888; info@sopipr.org; www.sopipr.org; Pub: *El Bien Te Veo* (magazine); (newsletter)

Uruguay
Aves Uruguay (GUPECA), Canelones 1198 esquina Z. Michelini, Montevideo. 11100: +598 2902 86 42; secretaria@avesuruguay.org.uy; www.avesuruguay.org.uy; Pub: *Achara* (magazine)

USA
American Bird Conservancy, P.O. Box 249, The Plains, VA 20198: +1 540 253 5780; info@conservationbirding.org; www.abcbirds.org; Pub: *Bird Conservation* (magazine); (newsletter)
Audubon, 225 Varick Street, New York, NY, 10004: +1 212-979-3196; international@audubon.org; www.audubon.org; Pub: *Audubon* (magazine)

ASIA (14)

Bhutan
Royal Society for the Protection of Nature, P.O. Box 325, Building #25, Lhado Lam Kawajangsa, Thimphu-11001: +975 2 326130; rspn@rspnbhutan.org; www.rspnbhutan.org; Pub: *Rangzhin* (newsletter)

Cambodia
NatureLife Cambodia, House #32A, Street 494, Sangkat Phsar Daeum Thkov, Chamkarmon, Phnom Penh: +855 078 732 240; admin@naturelifecambodia.org; www.naturelifecambodia.org

China
BirdLife's China Programme currently operated by HK-BWS. Hong Kong Birdwatching Society (HKBWS) 7C, V Ga Building, 532 Castle Peak Road, Lai Chi Kok, Kowloon: +852 2377 4387; info@hkbws.org.hk; www.hkbws.org.hk;
Pub: *Hong Kong Bird Report*; (newsletter)

India
Bombay Natural History Society (BNHS), Hornbill House, Shaheed Bhagat Singh Road, Mumbai, 400 001, Maharashtra: info@bnhs.org; www.bnhs.org;
Pub: *Hornbill* (magazine); *Journal of BNHS* (scientific)

Indonesia
Burung, Komplek Baranangsiang Indah, Jl. Jatiluhur C8 No. 9B, Bogor, Jawa Barat, 16144: +62 251 835 7222; info@bird.org; www.burung.org

Japan
Wild Bird Society of Japan (WBSJ), Maruw Bldg, 3-9-23, Nishi-Gotanda, Shinagawa-ku, Tokyo 141-0031: fukyu@wbsj.org; www.wbsj.org;
Pub: *Wild Bird* (magazine); *Strix* (scientific); (newsletter)

Malaysia
Malaysian Nature Society (MNS), JKR 641, Jalan Kelantan, Bukit Persekutuan, 50480 Kuala Lumpur: +60 (0)3 2287 9422;
mns@mns.org.my; www.mns.my;
Pub: *Malaysian Naturalist* (magazine); *Malayan Nature Journal* (scientific); (newsletter)

Mongolia
Wildlife Science and Conservation Centre of Mongolia (WSCC), Union Building B-1301, UNESCO Street, Ulaanbataar, 14210; +976 7000 2473; info@wscc.org.mn; www.wscc.org.mn
Pub: *Toodog: Mongolian Journal of Ornithology* (scientific), newsletter

Myanmar
Biodiversity and Nature Conservation Association (BANCA), Building No-F, Room No-102 Parami Condo, Hlaing Township, Yangon: +95 9 42008 0979; admin@bancamm.org; www.banca-env.org;
Pub: (newsletter)

Nepal
Bird Conservation Nepal (BCN), P.O. Box 12465, Lazimpath, Kathmandu-44600: +977 (0)1 4517 805; bcn@birdlifenepal.org; www.birdlifenepal.org;
Pub: (newsletter)

Philippines
Haribon Foundation, Manila Observatory Building, Room 212, Ateneo De Manila University, Katipunan Avenue, Loyola Heights, Quezon City, National Capital Region Philippines 1108: +63 (0)9171744266;

hello@haribon.org.ph; www.haribon.org.ph;
Pub: (newsletter)

Singapore
Nature Society (Singapore) (NSS), 510 Geylang Road, #02-05, The Sunflower, 398466: contact@nss.org.sg; www.nss.org.sg;
Pub: *Nature News* (newsletter); *Nature Watch* (magazine)

Sri Lanka
Field Ornithology Group of Sri Lanka (FOGSL), Dept of Zoology, Univ of Colombo, Colombo 03, 00700: +94 (0)112 592 609; fogsl1976@gmail.com; http://fogsl.cmb.ac.lk; Pub: (newsletter)

Thailand
Bird Conservation Society of Thailand (BCST), FREC Bangkok, 3rd Floor, 77 Lan Luang Rd., Sommanat, Pom Prap Sattru Phai, Bangkok 10100: +66 (0)80 1196 465; bcst@bcst.or.th; www.bcst.or.th;
Pub: *Robin* (magazine); (newsletter)

Vietnam
BirdLife International in Vietnam works closely with Viet Nature Conservation Centre—BirdLife Direct Action Programmes: birdlife@birdlife.org.vn

EUROPE & CENTRAL ASIA (46)

Albania
Protection and Preservation of Natural Environment in Albania (PPNEA), Rr "Janos Hunyadi", Godina 12, Ap. 11-1019, Tirane; +355 4 562 8954; contact@ppnea.org; www.pphea.org

Armenia
Foundation for the Preservation of Wildlife and Cultural Assets (FPWC), 47 Khanjyan Street, Yerevan, 0001; +374 1058 5884; info@fpwc.org; www.fpwc.org

Austria
BirdLife Österreich—Gesellschaft für Vogelkunde Diefenbachgasse 35/1/6, 1150 Vienna: +43 1 523 46 51; office@birdlife.at; www.birdlife.at;
Pub: *VogelSchutz in Osterreich* (magazine); *Egretta* (scientific); (newsletter)

Belgium
Flanders Natuurpunt, Coxiestraat 11, 2800 Mechelen; +32 (0)15 29 72 20; info@natuurpunt.be; www.natuurpunt.be;
Pub: *Natuur.blad* (magazine); (newsletters)

Belgium
Wallonia Natagora, Traverse des Muses, 1, 5000 Namur; +32 (0)81 39 07 20; info@natagora.be; www.natagora.be;
Pub: *Natagora* (magazine); *Aves* (scientific); (newsletter)

Bulgaria
Bulgarian Society for the Protection of Birds (BSPB), P.O. Box 50, Sofia 1111: +359 2 9799500; bspb_hq@bspb.org; www.bspb.org

Croatia
Association BIOM, Cazmanska 2, 10000 Zagreb:

BIRDLIFE ORGANIZATIONS

+385 (0)1 5515 324; info@biom.hr; www.biom.hr;
Pub: *Pogledu Divljinu* (magazine)

Cyprus
BirdLife Cyprus, P.O. Box 12026, 2340 Nicosia:
+357 22 455 072; info@birdlifecyprus.org.cy;
www.birdlifecyprus.org;
Pub: *Annual Bird Report*; *Cyprus Wheatear* (magazine);
(newsletter)

Czech Republic
Czech Society for Ornithology (CSO), Na Belidle 34,
150 00 Prague-Smichov: +420 777 330 355; cso@
birdlife.cz; www.birdlife.cz; Pub: *Ptaci Svet* (magazine);
Sylvia (scientific)

Denmark
Dansk Ornitologisk Forening (DOF), Vesterbrogade
138A, DK-1620 Copenhagen V. +45 3328 3800;
dof@dof.dk; www.dof.dk;
Pub: *Fuglearet* (bird report); *Fugle & Natur* (magazine);
Dansk Ornitologisk Forenings Tidsskrift (scientific)

Estonia
BirdLife Estonia, Veski 4, Tartu, 51005: +372 742 2195;
eoy@eoy.ee; www.eoy.ee;
Pub: *Tiirutaja* (newsletter); *Hirundo* (scientific)

Faroe Islands
Faroese Orginithological Society (FOS), Bøgøta 14, 100
Tórshavn: +298 223 604; info@fuglar.fo; www.fuglar.fo

Finland
BirdLife Suomi, Annankatu 29 A 16, 00100 Helsinki:
+358 90)10 406 6200; toimisto@birdlife.fi;
www.birdlife.fi;
Pub: *Linnut* (magazine); *Ornis Fennica* (scientific)
www.ornisfennica.org; (newsletter)

France
Ligue pour la Protection des Oiseaux (LPO), Fonderies
Royales, 8 rue du Dr Pujos CS 90263, 17305 Rochefort
Cedex: +33 (0)5 46 82 12 34; lpo@lpo.fr; www.lpo.fr;
Pub: *Ornithos* (journal); *L'Oiseau Mag* (magazine); *L'Oiseau
Mag* junior (magazine for juniors), newsletter

Georgia
Society for Nature Conservation (SABUKO), F. Sara-
jishvili St. 3a, Tbilisi. +995 (0)322 90 74 93; office@sabu-
ko.ge; www.sabuko.org

Germany
Nature and Biodiversity Conservation Union (NABU),
Charitestr. 3, 10117 Berlin: +49 (0)30 28 49 84 0;
nabu@nabu.de; www.nabu.de;
Pub: *Naturschutz Heute* (magazine); (newsletter)

Gibraltar
Gibraltar Ornithological & Natural History Society
(GONHS), Field Centre, Jew's Gate, Upper Rock Nature Reserve, P.O. Box 843, Gibraltar: info@gonhs.org;
www.gonhs.org;
Pub: *Gibraltar Bird Report*; *Gibraltar Nature News* (magazine)

Greece
Hellenic Ornithological Society (HOS), 52 Ag. Konstan-
tinou Str, 10437, Athens: +30 210 8227937;
info@ornithologiki.gr; www.ornithologiki.gr;
Pub: (newsletter)

Hungary
Magyar Madartani es Termeszetvedelmi Egyesulet
(MME), Kolto u. 21, Budapest XII: mme@mme.hu;
www.mme.hu;
Pub: *Madartavlat* (magazine); *Ornis Hungarica* (scientific);
Heliaca (yearbook); (newsletter)

Iceland
Fuglavernd—BirdLife Iceland (ISPB), Hverfisgata 105,
101 Reykjavík: +354 562 0477;
fuglavernd@fuglavernd.is; www.fuglavernd.is;
Pub: *Fuglar* (magazine)

Ireland
BirdWatch Ireland, Unit 20, Block D, Bullford Business
Campus, Kilcoole, Co. Wicklow: +353 (0)1 2819878;
info@birdwatchireland.org; www.birdwatchireland.ie;
Pub: *eWings* (newsletter); *Wings* (magazine); *Bird Detec-
tives* (children's magazine); *Irish Birds* (scientific)

Israel
Society for the Protection of Nature in Israel (SPNI), 2
Hanagev St, Tel-Aviv 66186: teva@teva.org.il;
www.teva.org.il. *Clicking on the English version of the He-
brew website redirects away from the actual Birdlife partner
to the sites of US, UK and Canadian supporters of the Israe-
li society:* www.natureisrael.org; www.ukspni.org;
www.natureisrael.ca;
Pub: (newsletter)

Italy
Lega Italiana Protezione Uccelli (LIPU), Via Pasubio 3/B,
43122 Parma: +39 0521 273043; info@lipu.it;
www.lipu.it;
Pub: *Ali & Ali Junior* (magazines); (newsletter)

Kazakhstan
Association for the Conservation of Biodiversity of
Kazakhstan (ACBK), office 406, building 18, Beibitshilik
St, Astana, 010000: +7 (7172) 32 22 65; acbk@acbk.kz;
www.acbk.kz

Latvia
Latvian Ornithological Society (LOB), Skolas Street 3,
4th Floor, 1010 Riga. +371 67 221 580; putni@lob.lv;
www.lob.lv;
Pub: *Putni Daba* (magazine)

Liechtenstein
Botanish-Zoologische Gesellschaft (BZG), Birkenweg 6,
LI-9490 Vaduz: +423 232 48 19 bzg@bzg.li; www.bzg.li

Lithuania
Lithuanian Ornithological Society (LOD), Naugarduko
g. 47-3, LT-03208 Vilnius: +370 (8 5) 213 04 98; lod@
birdlife.lt; www.birdlife.lt; Pub: *Pauksciai* (magazine)

BIRDLIFE ORGANIZATIONS

Luxembourg
Natur&ëmwelt, Kräizhaff, 5 Route de Luxembourg, 1899 Kockelscheuer: +352 29 04 04 1; secretariat@naturemwelt.lu; www.naturemwelt.lu; Pub: *Regulus* (magazine); (newsletter)

Malta
BirdLife Malta, 57/28 Marina Court, Abate Rigord St, Ta'Xbiex, XBX 1120: +356 21347645; info@birdlifemalta.org; www.birdlifemalta.org; Pub: *Malta Bird Report, Bird's Eye View* (magazine); *Il-Huttafa* (children's magazine); *Il-Merill* (scientific)

Montenegro
Center for Protection & Research of Birds of Montenegro (CZIP), Velje brdo 35, 81412 Spuž, Crna Gora: +382 (0)20 272 05; czip@czip.me; www.czip.me

Netherlands
Vogelbescherming Nederland (VBN), P.O. Box 925, 3700 AX Zeist: +31 (0)30 6937700; info@vogelbescherming.nl; www.vogelbescherming.nl; Pub: *Vogels* (magazine); *Vogels Junior* (children's magazine); (newsletter)

North Macedonia
Macedonian Ecological Society (MES), Bul. Boris Trajkovski ul.7 br.9A, 1000 Skopje: +389 (0) 2402 773; contact@mes.org.mk; www.mes.org.mk; Pub: *Macedonian Journal of Ecology and Environment* (scientific), newsletter

Norway
BirdLIfe Norge, Sandgata 30B, 7012 Trondheim: post@birdlife.no; www.birdlife.no; Pub: *Vår Fuglefauna* (magazine); *Fuglevennen* (magazine); *Fugelåret* (yearbook) *Ornis Norvegica* (scientific); (newsletter)

Poland
Polish Society for the Protection of Birds (OTOP), ul. ul. Odrowąża 24 05-270 Marki k. Warszawy; +48 22 761 82 05; biuro@otop.org.pl; www.otop.org.pl; Pub: *Ptaki* (magazine); (newsletter)

Portugal
Portuguese Society for the Study of Birds (SPEA), Av. Almirante Gago Coutinho, 46A, 1700-031, Lisbos: +351 21 322 04 30; spea@spea.pt; www.spea.pt; Pub: *Pardela* (magazine); *AIRO* (scientific); (newsletter)

Romania
Romanian Ornithological Society (SOR)/BirdLife Romania, Calusei entrance no. 12, sector 2, Bucharest, 021357: office@sor.ro; www.sor.ro; Pub: (newsletter)

Serbia
Bird Protection and Study Society of Serbia, Radomira Rase Radujkova 1A/211, 21000 Novi Sad: +381 (0)21 304 49 25; info@pticesrboije.rs; www.pticesrbije.rs; Pub: *Detlic* (magazine); *Ciconia* (scientific)

Slovakia
SOS/BirdLife, Zelinarska 4, 821 08 Bratislava: +421 904 501 437; vtaky@vtaky.sk; www.vtaky.sk; Pub: *Vtáky* (magazine); *Tichodroma* (scientific)

Slovenia
BirdLife Slovenia (DOPPS), Tržaška 2, 1000 Ljubljana: +396 (0)41 712 796; dopps@dopps.si; www.ptice.si; Pub: *Svet Ptic* (magazine); *Acrocephalus* (scientific); newsletter

Spain
SEO/BirdLife, C/Melquiades Biencinto 34, 28053 Madrid: +34 91 43 40 910; seo@seo.org; www.seo.org; Pub: *Aves y Naturaleza* (magazine); *Ardeola* (scientific); newsletter

Sweden
BirdLife Sverige, Stenhusa Gard, Lilla Brunneby 106, Morbylanga, 380 62: +46 (0)485 44 000; info@birdlife.se; www.birdlife.se; Pub: *Var Fagelvarld* (magazine); *Ornis Svecica* (scientific)

Switzerland
BirdLife Switzerland, Wiedingstr. 78, PO Box, CH-8036 Zurich: +41 44 457 70 20; info@birdlife.ch; www.birdlife.ch; Pub: *Ornis/Ornis Junior* (magazines); *Info BirdLife Suisse/ Schweiz* (magazines); newsletters

Turkey
Doga, Orhanlı Mahallesi, 7102 Sokak No:1, Seferihisar/ Izmir: +90 (0)850 840 60 49; doga@dogadernegi.org; www.dogadernegi.org; Pub: *Kuş Sesi* (magazine)

Ukraine
Ukrainian Society for the Protection of Birds (USBP), P.O. Box 143, Kyiv, 03150: +380 44 339 99 81; uspb@birdlife.org.ua; www.birdlife.org.ua; Pub: *Bird* (magazine)

United Kingdom (see *UK organizations*)
Royal Society for the Protection of Birds (RSPB), The Lodge, Sandy, Bedfordshire, SG19 2DL. www.rspb.org.uk

Uzbekistan
Uzbekistan Society for the Protection of Birds (UzSPB), Room 51, Institute of Gene Pool of Plants & Animals of Academy of Science, st. Bogi Shamol, 232 B, Tashkent 100053: +998 71 2890968; roman.kashkarov@iba.uz; www.uzspb.uz; Pub: newsletter

MIDDLE EAST (6)

Iraq
Nature Iraq, P.O. Box 1154-39 Sulaymaniyah: info@natureiraq.org; www.natureiraq.org

Jordan
The Royal Society of the Conservation of Nature (RSCN), Complex No 4 St Baker, Al Baw Street, Dahyet Al-Rasheed, Amman: +962 6 5157656; adminrscn@rscn.org.jo; www.rscn.org.jo; Pub: newsletter

Kuwait

Kuwait Environment Protection Society (KEPS), Farwaniya Governorate, Jleeb Al-Shuyoukh, Block 4, Street 8, Plot; +965 99 537 730; info@keps.org.kw; www.keps.org.kw; Pub: magazine

Lebanon

The Society for the Protection of Nature in Lebanon (SPNL), Horsh Kayfoun, Luc Hoffmann Hima Center, Itani, Kayfoun, Mount Lebanon: +96 15271041; news@spnl.org; www.spnl.org

State of Palestine

Palestine Wildlife Society (PWLS), P.O. Box 89, Beit Sahour: +972 2 2774373; pwls@wildlife-pal.org; www.wildlife-pal.org

Syria

Syrian Society for Conservation of Wildlife (SSCW): info@sscw-syr.org; sscw.syria@gmail.com; www.sscw-syr.org; Pub: newsletter

PACIFIC (7)

Australia

BirdLife Australia, Level 2, Main Building, 54 Wellington Street, Collingwood VIC 3066: +61 (0)3 9347 0757; support@birdlife.org.au; www.birdlife.org.au; Pub: *Australian BirdLife* (magazine); *Australian Field Ornithology* (scientific); *Emu—Austral Ornithology* (scientific)

Cook Islands

Te Ipukarea Society (TIS), P.O. Box 649, Rarotonga; +682 21144; info@tiscookislands.org; www.tiscookislands.org; Pub: newsletter

Fiji

NatureFiji-MareqetiViti, 72 McGregor Road, Suva: +679 310 0598; support@naturefiji.org; www.naturefiji.org; Pub: newsletter

French Polynesia

Société d'Ornithologie de Polynésie (MANU), Residence du plateau Mitirapa, Lot 48, Impasse Des Acacias B.P. 7023, Taravao, 98719, Tahiti: +689 40 52 11 00; sop@manu.pf; www.manu.pf; Pub: *Te Manu* (bulletin)

New Caledonia (to France)

Societe Caledonienne d'Ornithologie (SCO); BP 13641, 98803, Noumea Cedex: +687 838940; via website; www.sco.nc

New Zealand

Forest & Bird, PO Box 631, Wellington 6011; office@forestandbird.org.nz; www.forestandbird.org.nz; Pub: *Forest & Bird* (magazine); newsletters

Palau

Palau Conservation Society (PSC), P.O. Box 1811, Koror, Palau, 96940; +680 488 3993; admin@palauconservation.org; www.palauconservation.org; Pub: newsletter

NOTES

Taking orders for
The **Birdwatcher's Yearbook** *2027*
from 1 July 2026

Reserve yours by going to:
www.thebirdwatchersyearbook.co.uk
or
scan

If you would like to alert the editorial team to an error, information that has changed or to suggest a reserve for inclusion you can scan the QR code, go to the website or e-mail neildstratton@btinternet.com
or
Neil@thebirdwatchersyearbook.co.uk

Visit the **Updates** section of the website to stay abreast of information as it changes.

Male [Common] Redpoll
Sylvie Soudan
Instagram: Sylvie.Soudan